NELSON'S FOUNDATIONAL BIBLE DICTIONARY

Katharine Harris

THOMAS NELSON
Since 1798

NASHVILLE   DALLAS   MEXICO CITY   RIO DE JANEIRO

© 2004 by World Publishing

Published in Nashville, Tennessee by Thomas Nelson. Thomas Nelson is a registered trademark of HarperCollins Christian Publishing, Inc.

Thomas Nelson titles may be purchased in bulk for educational, business, fund-raising, or sales promotional use. For information, please e-mail SpecialMarkets@ThomasNelson.com.

All Scripture quotations are taken from the New King James Version. © 1982 by Thomas Nelson. Used by permission. All rights reserved.

The Open Bible, Expanded Edition, New King James Version® © 1985, 1983 Thomas Nelson.

Dickson's Analytical Study Bible © 1973, 1971, 1966, 1964, 1950, 1947, 1941, 1938, 1931 by John A. Dickson Publishing Company.

Illustrations © 2004 www.clipart.com

ISBN 978-0-7180-1396-7

Previously published as *World's Bible Dictionary*, ISBN 0-529-1-1902-1

Printed in the United States of America
14 15 16 17 18 RRD 5 4 3 2 1

PREFACE

For thousands of years, the Bible has fascinated, puzzled, and inspired the human race. It has sold more copies and been translated into more languages than any other book. It is read by the devout and the skeptical, believers and seekers, those who base their lives on its words and the merely curious. It carries a message so simple that a little child can grasp its meaning, and yet it is so deep and wide and high and long that the most brilliant person can spend a lifetime studying it and never plumb its depths.

The Bible was written for people to read, to ponder, and to understand. The message of God's love for humans transcends time, culture, and language; it comes through loud and clear. Nevertheless, readers of the Bible are often left with questions. The names sound strange to our ears, the geography is often unfamiliar, and we ask, "Who was this person? Is he mentioned somewhere else in the Bible?" "When did this happen?" "Where did it happen?" "Is this a real city?" "Why did this matter enough to write it down?"

Nelson's Foundational Bible Dictionary seeks to answer questions like these, and many more. Included are summaries of each book of the Bible, a biographical sketch of the human author, historical background information concerning the time the book was written, and an outline of the structure of the book. Every person mentioned in the Bible can be found, with a selection of biblical references and pertinent biographical information. The many animals and minerals in the Bible are listed and defined, and the modern equivalents of ancient geographical names are given where possible. Many key theological terms, which may or may not be specifically mentioned in the Bible, are also listed, with discussions of their various meanings and interpretations. Common household items and occupations are included, with cultural and historical information about life in ancient times. The spelling of names and places follows the King James Version.

Nelson's Foundational Bible Dictionary is designed to be a practical, easy-to-use reference tool for ordinary people. Without being exhaustive, or trying to take the place of a concordance, it gives the reader a wide, comprehensive source for answering the "Who?" "When?" "Where?" and "How?" questions that come up when reading God's Word.

KATHARINE HARRIS

ABBREVIATIONS

Old Testament

Ge	Genesis
Ex	Exodus
Le	Leviticus
Nu	Numbers
De	Deuteronomy
Jos	Joshua
Ju	Judges
Ru	Ruth
1 Sa	1 Samuel
2 Sa	2 Samuel
1 Ki	1 Kings
2 Ki	2 Kings
1 Ch	1 Chronicles
2 Ch	2 Chronicles
Ez	Ezra
Ne	Nehemiah
Es	Esther
Job	Job
Ps	Psalms
Pr	Proverbs
Ec	Ecclesiastes
Song	Song of Solomon
Is	Isaiah
Je	Jeremiah
La	Lamentations
Eze	Ezekiel
Da	Daniel
Ho	Hosea
Joel	Joel
Am	Amos
Ob	Obadiah
Jon	Jonah
Mi	Micah
Na	Nahum
Hab	Habakkuk
Zep	Zephaniah
Hag	Haggai
Ze	Zechariah
Mal	Malachi

New Testament

Ma	Matthew
Mk	Mark
Lk	Luke
Jo	John
Ac	Acts
Ro	Romans
1 Co	1 Corinthians
2 Co	2 Corinthians
Ga	Galatians
Ep	Ephesians
Ph	Philippians
Col	Colossians
1 Th	1 Thessalonians
2 Th	2 Thessalonians
1 Ti	1 Timothy
2 Ti	2 Timothy
Tit	Titus
Phile	Philemon
He	Hebrews
Jam	James
1 Pe	1 Peter
2 Pe	2 Peter
1 Jo	1 John
2 Jo	2 John
3 Jo	3 John
Jude	Jude
Re	Revelation

AV	Authorized Version	LXX	Septuagint—ancient Greek OT translation
B.C.	Before Christ		
c.	approximately	NASB	New American Standard Bible
cf.	compare	NEB	New English Bible
ch., chs.	chapter, chapters	NIV	New International Version
A.D.	After the Lord	NKJV	New King James Version
KJV	King James Version	NRSV	New Revised Standard Version
lb., lbs.	pound, pounds	REB	Revised English Bible
		v., vv.	verse, verses

A

A See Alpha.

AA′ RON (enlightened, bright)

1. *Tribe and Family.* Aaron was the oldest son of Amram and Jochebed, of the tribe of Levi (Ex 6:16-27). He was three years older than his brother, Moses (Ex 7:7), and younger than his sister, Miriam. He married Elisheba, a woman of the tribe of Judah, by whom he had four sons—Nadab, Abihu, Eleazar, and Ithamar (Ex 6:23).

2. *Divine Commission.* The Lord appointed Aaron as the spokesman of Moses and instructed him to meet Moses in the wilderness (Ex 4:27). In Israel's first recorded battle with the Amalekites, Aaron and Hur supported the hands of Moses.

3. *At Sinai.* While Moses was on the mount receiving the law, Aaron granted the request of the people that they should have a visible God. The idol was in the form of an Egyptian deity, the Apis-bull.

4. *Aaron the High Priest.* Aaron's family was selected for the priesthood and the office was made hereditary. Thus Aaron, the first high priest, became head of the priestly order (Ex 28). His two sons, Nadab and Abihu, were destroyed for unholy conduct (Le 10:1-3). See PRIEST.

5. *The Period of Wandering.* Aaron and Miriam were jealous of Moses's high position as shown by Miriam's criticism of the marriage of Moses and a Cushite woman. For this offense Miriam was smitten with leprosy (Nu 12). For the story of Korah's rebellion and the Lord's sanction of the Aaronic priestly order, see Numbers 16. Aaron died on Mount Hor. Here, in the sight of all the congregation, his priestly robes were transferred to his son, Eleazar, who succeeded him. Aaron died at the age of 123 (Nu 20:23-29; 33:39). See HOR.

6. *The Aaronic priesthood in the New Testament.* The book of Hebrews explains how the perfect priesthood of Jesus Christ replaces the faulty and human priesthood of Aaron and his descendants (He 5:2-5; 7:11-12). In contrast with the priesthood of Aaron, the priesthood of Christ is compared with the mysterious figure of Melchizedek, King of Salem and priest of God (Ge 15:18-20; Ps 110:4). Melchizedek's priesthood had no beginning and no end; in the same way, the priesthood of Christ is eternal and continuous (He 7:1-3).

AA′ RON·ITES

The priestly descendants of Aaron, part of the tribe of Levi. A large company of Aaronites, under the leadership of Jehoida, came to David's support when he was anointed king at Hebron (1 Ch 12:27).

AA′ RON'S ROD

A staff carried by Aaron. It played a part in the drama of the exodus, acting twice as a sign to Pharaoh, and once to the Israelites. When thrown down in the presence of Pharaoh and his magicians, it became a snake. The magicians imitated the miracle, and Aaron's rod swallowed the rods of the magicians (Ex 7:9-12,15). Later, Aaron struck the water with his rod, bringing about the plague of blood. The Israelites escaped from Egypt, but they became discontented, fearful and rebellious during their sojourn in the desert. During an attempted rebellion, Aaron's rod budded as a sign of divine approval of Moses and Aaron (Nu 17:1-10). It was preserved in the ark (He 9:4).

AB (to be fruitful)

The name of the fifth sacred and eleventh civil month of the Jewish calendar. It is a Chal-

AARON AND HIS SONS

dean name and was not used until after the Babylonian exile. See CALENDAR.

A·BAD′ DON

The transliteration of a Hebrew word usually translated *destruction*.

1. The place of the dead—the place of destruction (Job 26:6; 28:22; 31:12; Ps 88:11). Several times this word is accompanied by the word *Sheol*, which is often translated *hell* or *the grave* (Pr 15:11; 27:20).

2. The angel of the abyss or bottomless pit, called *Apollyon* in Greek (Re 9:11).

A·BAG′ THA

One of the seven eunuchs of King Ahasuerus (Xerxes), the guardians of the royal harem (Es 1:10-11).

AB′ A·NA *(stony)*

A river of Damascus, probably the present Barada. It rises on a high plain on Anti-Lebanon, 23 miles from Damascus, flows through the city, and gives fertility to the surrounding plain. The Abana is one of the rivers mentioned by the Syrian official, Naaman the leper, when he was complaining about being told to bathe in the Jordan River in order to be cleansed from leprosy (2 Ki 5:12). See also PHARPAR.

AB′ A·NAH

A variation of Abana.

AB′ A·RIM *(regions beyond)*

A mountainous area east of the Jordan and the Dead Sea. One of the encampments of the Israelites was in this region (Nu 21:11). The tribe of Reuben was given settlements within it (Nu 32:2-37). Moses viewed the promised land from the heights of Mount Nebo, a part of this mountain range (De 32:49).

ABASE

To make or bring low; to humble (Lk 14:11).

AB′ BA *(father)*

As the everyday language of first century Jews—the language of Christ and the disciples—Aramaic is the first "Christian" language. This Semitic tongue, closely related to Hebrew, was soon to be superseded by the common (*Koine*) Greek of the Roman Empire, especially in the East. As the faith attracted more and more Gentiles, the Jewish and Aramaic flavor became more and more diluted. One of the few early Aramaic expressions to survive in the New Testament was the word *abba,* "father."

In the Old Testament, God was sometimes seen as the Father of the nation Israel, but it was Christ who revealed that all believers are individually children of God by redemption. In a lesser sense, all people are children of God by creation, but in the sense of the model prayer, the "Our Father," only believers can claim that revealed relationship.

Abba, Father is used three times in the New Testament, once in the Gospels and twice by Paul; the Aramaic term being used with a translation. *Abba* is the most intimate term for Father, one of the first words a child would learn. It is akin to our word "Daddy." This word indicates how close the Father wants His children to feel toward Him.

Mark 14:36. In the garden of Gethsemane, His "soul . . . exceedingly sorrowful, even to death," Jesus prayed, "Abba, Father, all things are possible for You. Take this cup away from Me; nevertheless, not what I will, but what You will." At this crisis in His ministry, facing betrayal by Judas and shameful death on the cross, the Lord reverted to the tender word He had first used at Mary and Joseph's knees: *Abba.*

Romans 8:14-16. In one of the most beloved chapters in the Bible, Paul relates a word he no doubt learned as a tiny child to the believer's acceptance as a mature son by adoption, as well as a child by new birth. These blessings come through the third Person of the Trinity: "For as many as are led by the Spirit of God, these are sons of God. For you did not receive the spirit of bondage again to fear, but you received the Spirit of adoption by whom we cry out, 'Abba, Father.' The Spirit Himself bears witness with our spirit that we are children of God."

Galatians 4:6. Paul's other use is similar, only here sonship is contrasted with slavery. We are not merely slaves of God, although we should serve on that level of submission; we are sons. As God's sons and daughters we can boldly say, "Abba, Father!"

AB′ DA *(servant)*

Two Old Testament men:

1. The father of Adoniram (1 Ki 4:6).

2. A Levite, the son of Shammua (Ne 11:17).

He is called Obadiah, the son of Shemaiah in 1 Chronicles 9:16.

AB´DEEL *(servant of God)*

The father of Shelemiah, who was one of the three appointed to arrest Baruch and Jeremiah (Je 36:26).

AB´DI *(servant of Jehovah)*

Two or three Old Testament men bear this name:

1. A Levite of the family of Merari and grandfather of Ethan, the singer (1 Ch 6:44).

2. A Levite and father of Kish, contemporary of Hezekiah, king of Judah. He may be the same person as No. 1 (2 Ch 29:12).

3. A son of Elam who divorced his foreign wife (Ez 10:26).

AB´DI·EL *(servant of God)*

The son of Guni, a Gadite who lived in Gilead (1 Ch 5:15).

AB´DON *(servile)*

The name of four Old Testament men and one city.

1. Son of Hillel of the tribe of Ephraim, a native of Pirathon, and judge of Israel for eight years. He had forty sons and thirty nephews who rode on asses, an indication of affluence (Ju 12:13-15).

2. The son of Shashak, a Benjamite chief (1 Ch 8:23).

3. The firstborn son of Jehiel of Gibeon, a Benjamite and ancestor of Saul (1 Ch 8:30; 9:35-36).

4. The son of Micah who was sent by Josiah to enquire of Huldah concerning the book of the law found in the temple. (2 Ch 34:20). He is also referred to as Achbor (2 Ki 22:12)

5. A town of Asher awarded to the Gershonite Levites, also called Ebron (Jos 21:30).

A·BED´-NE·GO *(a servant of Nego)*

The Chaldean name given to Azariah, one of the three companions of Daniel, when he came into Nebuchadnezzar's service (Da 1:7; 2:49)). He was cast into the fiery furnace, along with Shadrach and Meshach, because they refused to bow down and worship the golden image set up by Nebuchadnezzar. God miraculously preserved them from the flames, and they were restored to their former positions (3:12-30).

A´BEL *(a breath)*

The name of both a man and several geographical locations.

1. One of the sons of Adam, and a shepherd. He was a righteous man whose blood offering was accepted by God. He was slain by his brother, Cain, whose thank offering was rejected because it was not a blood offering like Abel's (Ge 4:2-9). Abel is described by Jesus as a righteous man, and the first martyr (Ma 23:35; Lk 11:51; 1 Jo 3:12). He is listed in the "Hall of Faith," as one who "offered a more excellent sacrifice than Cain" (He 11:4); and it is intimated that righteous Abel's death as a martyr was a foreshadowing of the death of Christ. The blood of Christ, however speaks of better things than the blood of Abel; it speaks of salvation rather than vengeance (He 12:24).

2. A meadow or grassy place. This word is often used as a prefix in place-names.

3. A great stone near Beth-shemesh, in the field of a man named Joshua. When the Philistines returned the ark of the covenant to Israel, the Israelites placed the ark upon this stone, and offered sacrifices to the Lord (1 Sa 6:18).

4. A fortified city (2 Sa 20:14-16). See ABEL BETH MAACHAH.

A´BEL A·CA´CI·A GROVE

Also called Abel Shittim (Nu 33:49; Mi 6:5). Abel Acacia Grove was a site located on the plains of Moab, to the north and east of the Dead Sea, across the Jordan River from the city of Jericho. At the end of the forty years of wandering in the desert, the Israelites made their last camp at Shittim, on the banks of the Jordan. This is where they were staying when the Israelites began to indulge in sexual immorality with the Moabite women, and were enticed into worshipping the Baal of Peor with them. As a result, 24,000 Israelites were killed by a plague (Nu 25:9). Here also, Moses numbered the fighting men of Israel, counting all those who were twenty years of age, or older (Nu 26:2). While Israel was camped at Abel Acacia, God told Moses that he would not be allowed to enter the promised land, but that he would die, leaving Joshua as his successor and the leader of the people (Nu 27:12-23).

After Moses's death, Joshua sent out two spies from Abel Acacia, to discover the state of the people, and the strength of the armies and fortifications they would have to face in the new land they were setting out to conquer (Jos 2:1). These two spies were sheltered by the woman Rahab, in the city of Jericho. After their return, Israel broke camp, and following the ark of the covenant, they at last crossed the Jordan River into the promised land (Jos 3:1).

A'BEL-BETH-MA' A·CHAH *(meadow of the house of Maachah)*

A town in the north of Israel, in the territory of Naphtali (2 Sa 20:15; 1 Ki 15:20; 2 Ki 15:29). When his revolt against David failed, Sheba fled to this place. Joab, David's captain, threatened to assault the town to secure Sheba but spared it when assured that the rebel would be put to death. After the division of the nation, in the days when the godly king Asa ruled Judah, Ben-hadad, king of Amram, seized this town from evil king Baasha of Israel (1 Ki 15:20). Later, Tiglath-pileser, king of Assyria, captured Abel-beth-maachah and several other towns, and mentioned the fact in his annals (2 Ki 15:29).

A·BEL-CHER' A·MIM

A form of ABEL-KERAMIM.

A·BEL-KER' A·MIM *(meadow of vineyards)*

A town near Minnith east of the Jordan to which Jephthah pursued the Ammonites, called *plain of the vineyards* in the Authorized Version (Ju 11:33).

A' BEL-MA' IM

A town in northern Israel (2 Ch 16:4), usually referred to as ABEL-BETH-MAACAH.

A' BEL-ME·HO' LAH *(meadow of dancing)*

The home of Elisha (Ju 7:22; 1 Ki 19:16). It was probably about ten miles south of Bethshan on the west side of the Jordan.

A' BEL-MIZ' RA·IM

See ATAD.

A' BEL-SHIT' TIM *(meadow of acacias)*

It is also called Shittim (Nu 25:1; Jos 2:1; Mi 6:5). It was the final stopping place of the Israelites (Nu 33:49) and where Israel's idolatry was punished by a plague in which 24,000 died. See ABEL ACACIA GROVE.

A' BEZ, E' BEZ *(white)*

A town of Issachar (Jos 19:20), also called EBEZ.

ABHOR (archaic)

Despise; spurn; regard with horror (Job 19:18-19).

A' BI, A·BI' A, A·BI' AH

See ABIJAH.

A' BI-AL' BON *(father of strength)*

One of David's mighty men (2 Sa 23:31), called Abiel in 1 Chronicles 11:32.

A·BI' A·SAPH *(father of gathering)*

A son of Korah, the Levite (Ex 6:16,18,21, 24). He may be the same person as Ebiasaph (1 Ch 6:23; 9:19).

A·BI' A·THAR *(father of abundance)*

The son of Ahimelech, a priest. His father and brothers were slain by Saul because of his father's kindness to David. Abiathar escaped and allied himself with David (1 Sa 22:20-23). When David finally took the throne, the high priesthood was shared by Zadok and Abiathar (2 Sa 15:24; 1 Ch 15:11-12). Under their direction, the ark was brought to Jerusalem (1 Ch 15:11). Abiathar remained loyal to David during Absalom's rebellion but supported Adonijah when the latter attempted to seize the throne in place of Solomon (1 Ki 1:17,19). He was deposed as high priest (1 Ki 2:26,35).

A' BIB *(an ear of corn)*

The first month of the Jewish sacred year (Ex 13:4), after the exile called Nisan (Ne 2:1; Es 3:7). See CALENDAR.

A·BI' DA, A·BI' DAH *(father of knowledge)*

One of the sons of Midian, who was the son of Abraham and Keturah (Ge 25:4; 1 Ch 1:33).

A·BI' DAN *(the father judgeth)*

Son of Gideoni, a prince of the tribe of Benjamin. He was the representative chosen by God to recount the history of his family and tribe when the census of Israel was taken in the wilderness (Nu 1:11; 2:22; 10:24).

A·BI' EL *(father of strength)*

Two Old Testament men.

1. The father of Kish and Ner and grandfather of Saul and Abner according to 1 Sa 9:1; 14:51, but he may have been the grandfather of Kish since Ner is listed as the father of Kish in 1 Chronicles 8:33; 9:39.

2. One of David's mighty men (1 Ch 11:32), called Abialbon, the Arbathite, in 2 Samuel 23:31.

A·BI·E′ZER *(father of help)*

Two men of the Old Testament.

1. Son of Hammoleketh, a descendant of Manasseh. One of his descendants was the famous Gideon who was led by God to defeat the Midianite army with only three hundred men (Jos 17:2; 1 Ch 7:18). The name is sometimes abbreviated to Jeezer or Iezer (Nu 26:30).

2. One of David's mighty men. He is described as an Anathothite, from the tribe of Benjamin. (2 Sa 23:27; 1 Ch 27:12). Much later, the prophet Jeremiah lived in the town of Anathoth (Je 1:1).

A-BI·EZ′RITE

A member of the family of Abiezer (Ju 6:11, 24; 8:32), also called Jeezerite but more properly Iezrite.

AB′I·GAIL *(father of joy)*

Two women of the Old Testament, both associated with David.

1. A beautiful woman who was the wife of both Nabal and David (1 Sa 25:3,14-44; 2 Sa

ABIGAIL MADE CAPTAIN

2:2). She was taken captive by the Amalekites when they seized Ziklag but was rescued by David (1 Sa 30:5,18). Her son by David was Chileab (2 Sa 3:3), called Daniel in 1 Chronicles 3:1.

2. Sister or half sister of David and mother of Amasa, who was made captain of Absalom's army (2 Sa 17:25; 1 Ch 2:16). She was probably the daughter of Jesse, but possibly of Nahash, who may have been a former husband of Jesse's wife. See NAHASH, ZERUIAH.

AB′I·GAL

See ABIGAIL.

AB′I·HA·IL *(father of strength)*

Two women and three men of the Old Testament.

1. The father of Zuriel, a Levite of the family of Merari (Nu 3:35).

2. Wife of Abishur and mother of Ahban and Molid; of the tribe of Judah, descended through Hezron (1 Ch 2:29).

3. A chief of the family of Gad in Bashan, the son of Huri (1 Ch 5:14).

4. The daughter of David's brother Eliab (2 Ch 11:18). It is a little unclear whether she was wife of Rehoboam, or the wife of David's son Jerimoth, and the mother of Rehoboam's wife, Mahalath.

5. Father of Esther and uncle of Mordecai (Es 2:15; 9:29).

A·BI′HU *(God is father)*

One of the four sons of Aaron who were consecrated as the priestly family (Ex 6:23; 24:1; 28:1). He and his brother Nadab used "strange" fire at the altar and were struck dead (Le 10:1-7). Since immediately afterwards a law was pronounced prohibiting priests from using strong drink in the tabernacle (Le 10:9), it is possible that the sin of the two brothers was committed while they were intoxicated.

A·BI′HUD *(father of renown)*

A descendant of Benjamin's son Bela (1 Ch 8:3).

A·BI′JAH, A′BI, A·BI′A, A·BI′AH *(The Lord is my father)*

Nine people in the Old Testament bore this name:

1. A descendant of Eleazar whose family was eighth of the 24 courses into which the priests were divided. He served in David's time (1 Ch 24:1,10).

2. The wife of Hezron of Judah, and mother of Ashur (1 Ch 2:24).

3. The second son of Samuel, and an unworthy judge in Beer–sheba (1 Sa 8:2; 1 Ch 6:28).

4. A descendant of Benjamin through Becher (1 Ch 7:8).

5. A son of King Jeroboam. When the child became ill, Jeroboam sent his wife to Ahijah, the prophet, to inquire as to the outcome. Ahijah spoke the judgment of God upon Jeroboam for his idolatry, declaring the child would die (1 Ki 14:1-18).

6. The son and successor of King Rehoboam and grandson of Solomon (1 Ch 3:10; 2 Ch 12:16; 13:1–14:1), also called Abijam. His mother was Absalom's granddaughter Maachah (2 Ch 11:20-22). During his three-year reign he followed the evil ways of his father and fought against King Jeroboam of Israel (1 Ki 15:6-7), a war in which Israel lost half a million men (2 Ch 13:16-20). He had 14 wives, 22 sons, and 16 daughters (2 Ch 13:21). Also called Abia (Ma 1:7).

7. The mother of Hezekiah, king of Judah. Also called Abi (2 Ki 18:2; 2 Ch 29:1).

8. One of the priests who set his seal upon Nehemiah's covenant (Ne 10:7).

9. A priest who returned to Jerusalem from Babylon with Zerubbabel (Ne 12:4,7). Later, a priestly family bore this name (Ne 12:17) and to this family belonged Zacharias, the father of John the Baptist (Lk 1:5).

A·BI′ JAM

See ABIJAH, No. 6.

AB·I·LE′ NE, ABILA *(meadow)*

A district of Coele-Syria on the eastern side of Anti-Lebanon. Its capital, Abila, was on the Abana (modern Barada) River, about twenty miles northwest of Damascus. Lysanius was the governor at the time John the Baptist began to minister (Lk 3:1).

A·BIM′ A·EL *(father of Mael)*

A descendant of Shem. One of Joktan's thirteen sons, and founder of an Arabian tribe (Ge 10:28; 1 Ch 1:22).

A·BIM′ E·LECH *(royal father)*

Five men of the Old Testament.

1. A Philistine king at Gerar. When Abraham was traveling through the area ruled by Abimelech, he was afraid that someone might kill him because of Sarah's beauty, so he declared Sarah to be his sister. Assuming that she was therefore available, Abimelech took her. After Abimelech had placed her in his harem, God appeared to him in a dream threatening him with death, whereupon he restored Sarah to Abraham. Abraham and Abimelech made a covenant of friendship, and Abraham prayed that God would bless Abimelech with children, for God had closed all the wombs in his household because of Sarah (Ge 20:1-18; 21:22-34).

2. Another Philistine king, perhaps son of the preceding, with whom Isaac had a very similar experience (Ge 26:1-33). Some believe that Abimelech may not be a proper name, but rather a title appertaining to all Philistine kings.

3. A son of Gideon. Assisted by relatives of his mother, Abimelech slew seventy sons of Gideon at Ophrah; Jotham, alone, escaped. Abimelech became king of Shechem, but in less than three years trouble arose among the people. Abimelech was mortally wounded by a woman who dropped a millstone on his head as he was besieging Thebez. Considering it a disgrace to be killed by a woman, Abimelech ordered his armorbearer to slay him (Ju 9:1-57).

4. A priest, the son of Abiathar, whose name should probably read Ahimelech (1 Ch 18:16; 24:6). He served during David's time.

5. In the title of Psalm 34, the name Abimelech is used, apparently as a title for Achish, king of Gash (1 Sa 21:10-15).

A·BIN′ A·DAB *(father of generosity)*

Four men of the Old Testament:

1. A man of Kirjath-jearim in whose house the ark was kept after the Philistines returned it (1 Sa 7:1-2; 2 Sa 6:3; 1 Ch 13:7).

2. A son of Jesse and older brother of David who served in Saul's army when David slew Goliath (1 Sa 16:8; 17:13).

3. A son of Saul who was slain with his father at Gilboa (1 Sa 31:2).

4. The father of Ben-Abinadab who married a daughter of Solomon. Ben-Abinadab was in charge of the district of Dor (1 Ki 4:11). See BEN-ABINADAB.

AB′ INER

See ABNER.

A·BIN′ O·AM *(father of grace)*

The father of Barak, the judge (Ju 4:6; 5:12). He was of the tribe of Naphtali.

A·BI' RAM *(father of elevation)*

Two Old Testament men:

1. A Reubenite, son of Eliab. He and his brother Dathan joined Korah in his rebellion. He and his family were destroyed in an earthquake as punishment for their sin (Nu 16; 26:9-10).

2. The oldest son of Hiel, the Beth-elite. A curse had been pronounced upon the posterity of anyone who should attempt to rebuild Jericho. Hiel undertook to do this, and the curse was fulfilled. When the foundations were laid, his oldest son Abiram died; when the gates were set up, his youngest son Segub died (Jos 6:26; 1 Ki 16:34).

AB' I·SHAG *(father of error)*

A beautiful young woman brought from her home in Shunem to serve David in his old age (1 Ki 1:1-4). Following David's death, his son, Adonijah, desired to marry her and sought the permission of Solomon. Since she had been the wife of David, this request was regarded as leading to a claim for the throne and Adonijah was put to death (1 Ki 2:13-25).

AB' I·SHAI, AB' SHAI *(father of a gift)*

The son of David's sister or half sister, Zeruiah, and brother of Joab and Asahel (2 Sa 2:18; 1 Ch 2:16). He led David to where Saul was sleeping and asked permission to slay him but David refused (1 Sa 26:5-9). When David came to the throne, Abishai entered the army under Joab. He is listed as one of David's mighty men (2 Sa 23:18; 1 Ch 11:20). Among other exploits, he slew 18,000 Edomites in the Valley of Salt and fortified that country (1 Ch 18:12-13). Abishai remained true to David when Absalom rebelled, and wanted to kill Shimei for cursing David (2 Sa 16:9-10; 19:21-22). When Sheba son of Bichri tried to take over the kingdom, Abishai led forces to subdue the rebel (2 Sa 20:2,6). All three of the sons of Zeruiah seem to have had a reputation for being impulsive and hot-headed, but they served David with remarkable loyalty.

A·BI' SHA·LOM

A form of the name Absalom (1 Ki 15:2,10). See ABSALOM.

A·BI' SHU·A *(father of salvation)*

Two Old Testament men:

1. A Benjamite of the family of Bela (1 Ch 8:4). He was the ancestral head of a Benjamite clan.

2. A son of Phinehas, he became the fourth high priest (1 Ch 6:4-5,50; Ez 7:5).

A·BI' SHUR *(father is a wall)*

A son of Shammai of Judah (1 Ch 2:28-29).

A·BI' TAL *(father of the dew)*

A wife of David, the mother of Shephatiah who was the fifth of the six sons born to David at Hebron (2 Sa 3:4; 1 Ch 3:3).

A·BI' TUB *(father of goodness)*

The son of Shaharaim and Hushim, part of the geneology of Saul (1 Ch 8:8-11).

A·BI' UD

Son of Zerubbabel, in the geneology of Christ (Ma 1:13).

AB·LU' TION

Washing, purification. In Scripture, ablutions, washing, and baptism (dipping) are all terms that usually refer to ceremonial washing for spiritual cleansing rather than washing for ordinary physical cleanliness and hygiene.

AB' NER *(father of light)*

The son of Ner and cousin of King Saul. He was commander-in-chief of Saul's army (1 Sa 14:51) and was present when David slew Goliath (1 Sa 17:55-58). After Saul's death, Abner placed Ish-bosheth on the throne (2 Sa 2:8). David's captain, Joab, defeated Abner (2 Sa 2:12-32) and when the latter was retreating from the battle, he killed Asahel, a brother of Joab, in self-defense. Later Abner had a disagreement with his king and switched his allegiance to David. David was willing to accept him, but before Abner could fulfill his promise to rally Israel around David, Joab slew Abner in revenge for his brother's death. David was horrified by Joab's treachery, and mourned for Abner, but left Solomon to deal with the crime (2 Sa 3:6-39; 1 Ki 2:5,28-34).

A' BOM·I·NA' TION OF DES·O·LA' TION

Daniel the prophet foretold an "abomination of desolation" which would be placed in the sanctuary of the Lord, defiling it (Da 11:31; 12:11). This would occur during a time of great trouble in Israel, when one who opposed the covenant of God would make an end of the sacrifices, and blaspheme God (Da 11:28-35). The same term "abomination of desolation" was used by Jesus when He instructed His disciples concerning the last days, quoting Daniel's prophecy as something yet to come (Ma 24:15-16; Mk 13:14). This misuse of the temple was to be a sign of the terrors to come, and those who were in Jerusalem should flee.

The Jews saw the defilement of the temple by Antiochus Epiphanes (168 B.C.) as the fulfillment of Daniel 11:31. Antiochus Epiphanes sacrificed a pig on the altar of the temple, and erected an idolatrous altar to Jupiter Olympius. These certainly were times of great unrest and persecution of God's people. However, since Jesus still referred to Daniel's prophecy as future, nearly two hundred years after Antiochus Epiphanes' deplorable action, many believe that the fulfillment occurred in A.D. 70 when the Romans destroyed the temple (Lk 21:5-7,20-22). Certainly, the sacrifices ceased at that time, and have never been resumed; the temple is desolate. Still others believe that the abomination of desolation is yet to come, when the "man of sin" will sit in the temple, claiming to be God and requiring worship (2 Th 2:3-4). This final act of rebellion and defilement would be the mark of the beginning of the end of the age.

A′ BRA·HAM, A′ BRAM (exalted father)

1. *Lineage and Nativity.* A descendant of Shem's son Arphaxad (Ge 11:10-32). Seven generations after Arphaxad, Terah became the father of Abram, Nahor and Haran. The family lived in Ur of the Chaldees in southern Babylonia. Later, Terah moved his family to Haran on their way to the land of Canaan.

2. *The Call and the Covenant.* Abram (later called Abraham) was divinely called by God to become progenitor of the chosen people. God made a solemn covenant with Abram, promising a land, a posterity, and great blessing to all peoples of the earth. The Messiah, the Savior of the world, would be brought forth from the nation of which Abraham was the founder (Ge 12:1-4). God also commanded Abram to leave Haran, and follow God's leading to a new land. At the age of 75, Abram packed up his family and belongings and set out to obey God's command. By willingly following God, even though he could not know where it would lead, Abra-

ham demonstrated his faith (He 11:8). See also ABRAHAMIC COVENANT.

3. *In Canaan.* Abraham went to Shechem, then to Beth-el (Ge 12). Famine drove him into Egypt where, through his wife, Sarai, whom he introduced as his sister (she was his half sister), he became embroiled with the king and was ordered to leave (Ge 12:10-20). He returned to Beth-el and divided the land with his nephew, Lot; Abraham moved to Hebron (Ge 13). Lot was captured in a war and was rescued by Abraham, who was blessed by Melchizedek as he was returning home (Ge 14:1-24).

4. *The Child of the Promise.* God had promised Abram that He would build his family into a great nation, but Sarai was barren (Ge 12:2; 15:1-6). Even though Abram believed God, his wife Sarai feared that he would never have sons, and offered him her Egyptian maidservant, Hagar. Abram took Hagar, and she bore him a son, Ishmael. Even though God blessed Ishmael, and Hagar, Ishmael was not the son of the promise. Abram would have to wait 14 more years for this child (Ge 16). When Abram was 99 years old, God spoke to him again about the covenant, changing his name to Abraham, and instituting the sign of circumcision. Sarai's name was also changed, to Sarah (Ge 17). A short time later, God once again spoke to Abraham about the son of the promise, this time promising that within a year, Sarah would have a son (Ge 18:9-14). Even though Sarah did not believe that this could happen, when Abraham was one hundred years old and Sarah ninety, their son Isaac was born (Ge 21:1-4). Isaac was the promised son, through whom God's covenant with Abraham would be fulfilled. The great test of Abraham's faith came when he was divinely commanded to sacrifice Isaac. Knowing that Isaac was the son of the promise, and believing that God could raise him up again, he followed God's orders completely and was rewarded when the boy was saved (Ge 22:1-19; He 11:17-19).

5. *Last years and Death.* Sarah died when Abraham was 137 years old (Ge 23). Three years later Abraham sent to Mesopotamia and secured Rebekah as wife for Isaac (Ge 24:67). Another wife of Abraham, Keturah, gave him other sons, Zimran, Jokshan, Medan, Midian, Ishbak, and Shua. Abraham died at the age of 175 years and was buried beside Sarah in the cave of Machpelah (Ge 25:1-9). Abraham's descendants remained the chosen people of God; the subsequent chapters of Genesis and the rest of the Old Testament describe God's working with this people, forging them into a nation, teaching them to obey His commandments, and preparing the way for the coming Messiah.

6. Abraham's Life Indexed:

RECORDED EVENTS	PLACE	REFERENCE
Born in Ur of Chaldees, near the river Euphrates. The son of Terah.	Ur of the Chaldees	Ge 11:27-28
Marries Sarai (afterwards Sarah).		Ge 11:29
Divinely called to leave his native land, not knowing at first the land to which he is to go (He 11:8).	Ur	Ge 12:1
To be the father of a great nation and the ancestor of the Messiah.	Haran	Ge 12:2-3
Leaves Haran at the age of seventy-five, taking with him his nephew, Lot.	Haran	Ge 12:5
Comes to Sichem (Shechem) in the land of Canaan. There he builds an altar.	Sichem	Ge 12:6-7
Pitches his tent near Bethel, and builds an altar to the Lord.	Bethel	Ge 12:8
A famine in the land drives him to Egypt.	Egypt	Ge 12:10-13
Sarai taken into Pharaoh's house supposed to be the sister of Abram. Plagues sent upon Pharaoh.	Egypt	Ge 12:14-17
Abram reproved by Pharaoh and sent out of the country.	Egypt	Ge 12:18-20
Leaves Egypt a rich man and comes to Bethel. Lot is also rich in cattle.	Bethel	Ge 13:1-5
Lot, given his choice, selects the Jordan valley.	Jordan Plain	Ge 13:6-13
The Lord gives to Abram and his seed the whole land. He comes to Hebron and builds an altar to the Lord.	Hebron	Ge 13:14-18
The battle of the kings, Lot taken a prisoner. Abram defeats them, rescues Lot, and restores him and his property to Sodom.	Dan, Hob, Sodom	Ge 14
Meets Melchizedek, king of Salem, and is blessed by him.	The King's Dale	Ge 14:17-20
The Lord renews his promise to Abram, and foretells the sojourn of his seed in Egypt.		Ge 15
The birth of Ishmael, son of Hagar, the maid of Sarai.		Ge 16
The covenant is made with Abram and the seal of the covenant indicated. Abram is 90 years old. His name is changed from Abram to Abraham.	Mamre	Ge 17:1-14
Isaac promised, the heir to the covenant promises.	Mamre	Ge 17:15-22
The visit of the three messengers of God who assure Abraham and Sarah of a son in their old age.	Mamre	Ge 18:1-16

RECORDED EVENTS	PLACE	REFERENCE
Abraham's prayer for Sodom and Gomorrah.		Ge 18:23-33
Destruction of the cities of the plain, the escape of Lot to Zoar.	Sodom, Gomorrah	Ge 19:15-30
Abraham in Gerar. Sarah is represented to Abimelech as Abraham's sister. She actually was his half sister, as well as his wife.	Gerar	Ge 20
Birth of Isaac. Abraham is 100 years old (He 11:11).		Ge 21:1-8
Hagar and Ishmael are cast out.		Ge 21:9-21
Abraham's covenant with Abimelech.	Beer-sheba	Ge 21:22-34
Trial of Abraham's faith in obeying God's command that he offer Isaac as a sacrifice, even though Issac was heir to the promises (He 11:17-19).	Moriah	Ge 22:1-14
God renews His covenant with Abraham, and he returns to Beer-sheba.	Beer-sheba	Ge 22:15-19
Death of Sarah. Abraham purchases Machpelah and there buries Sarah.	Hebron	Ge 23:1-20
Abraham sends his servant to Mesopotamia to secure a wife for Isaac. He secures Rebekah, sister of Laban.	Mesopotamia	Ge 24
Abraham marries Keturah who bears him six children.	Hebron	Ge 25:1-6
Abraham dies at the age of 175, and is buried by Isaac and Ishmael beside Sarah in the cave of Machpelah.	Hebron	Ge 25:7-10

A′ BRA•HAM′ IC COVENANT (Ge 12:1-3)

God's covenant with Abraham is the first of the theocratic covenants (pertaining to the rule of God). It is unconditional, depending solely upon God who obligates Himself in grace, indicated by the unconditional declaration, "I will," to bring to pass the promised blessings. The Abrahamic Covenant is the basis of all the other theocratic covenants and provides for blessings in three areas: (1) national—"I will make you a great nation," (2) personal—"I will bless you and make your name great; and you shall be a blessing," and (3) universal—"in you all families of the earth shall be blessed." This covenant was first given in broad outline and was later confirmed to Abraham in greater detail (Ge 13:14-17; 15:1-7,18-21; 17:1-8). The Abrahamic Covenant constitutes an important link in all that God began to do, has done throughout history, and will continue to do until the consummation of history. It is the one purpose of God for humans into which all of God's programs and works fit. The personal aspects of the Abrahamic Covenant are fourfold: (1) to be the father of a great nation, (2) to receive personal blessing, (3) to receive personal honor and reputation, and (4) to be the source of blessing to others. The universal aspects of the covenant are threefold: (1) blessings for those people and nations which bless Abraham and the nation which comes from him, (2) curses upon those people and nations which curse Abraham and Israel, and (3) blessings upon all the families of the earth through the Messiah, who, according to the flesh, is Abraham's son and provides salvation for the entire world.

A'BRA·HAM'S BO'SOM

The blissful state after death. The Old Testament frequently refers to death in terms of going to join one's ancestors (Ge 15:15; 47:30; De 31:16; Ju 2:10). Since Abraham was the first of the patriarchs, and the one who received the covenant, naturally he was the most important of these ancestors for the Jews. Apparently, the Jews believed they would have fellowship with Abraham in paradise. The only time the term "Abraham's bosom" is used in Scripture is in Jesus's parable of Lazarus and the rich man (Lk 16:22-23). Lazarus was "carried by the angels to Abraham's bosom," while the rich man was separated from Abraham and the other dead by a great chasm, and tormented by the flames of Hades. It is unclear how far the details of this parable can be taken as a foretaste of life after death—some aver that this is not a parable at all, but a true story that Jesus was telling.

A'BRAM

Abraham's name before the covenant of circumcision (Ge 17:5). See ABRAHAM.

AB·RO'NAH, EB·RO'NAH

An encampment of the Israelites in the wilderness (Nu 33:34-35).

AB'SA·LOM *(father of peace)*

David's third son, born in Hebron to Maacah, the daughter of King Talmai of Geshur (2 Sa 3:3). He was physically attractive with beautiful long hair. David's trouble with Absalom began when another of his sons became obsessed with Absalom's full sister, Tamar. Absalom's half brother Amnon raped Tamar, and when David did nothing to punish him, Absa-

lom took matters into his own hands and murdered his brother. David, even though he had not punished the incest according to the law (Le 18:11-29; 20:17), could not ignore a murder and Absalom was exiled for three years. When he was finally allowed to return to Jerusalem, David still refused to see him and he was kept from the court for two additional years. (2 Sa 13–14). Absalom became resentful of his father, and conspired to seize the throne from him (2 Sa 13:1–19:8). He portrayed himself as the friend of the people, and when the time seemed ripe, and enough people followed him, Absalom declared himself king in Hebron (2 Sa 15:7-12). David was obliged to flee from his son, leaving the kingdom in his hands temporarily, but David's mighty men were still with him, and a terrific battle took place between the forces of David and those of Absalom. Twenty thousand men were slain, and David's men pursued Israel through the woods. It was here in the woods that Absalom met his tragic end. As his mount passed beneath a huge terebinth tree in his flight, Absalom was caught in the low hanging branches, and left dangling by his head. David's men came upon him, and in spite of David's strict orders to bring Absalom back alive if possible, Joab and his men brutally murdered him as he hung helpless in the branches of the tree. David's cry when he heard of Absalom's death is a tragedy in itself. In spite of the wrongs that Absalom had done to his father, David's first question of the messenger from the battle lines was to ask, "Is the young man Absalom safe?" When he heard of Absalom's death, David wept, "Oh, my son Absalom—my son, my son Absalom—if only I had died in your place! Oh, Absalom my son, my son!" Absalom was buried by his murderers in a pit in the woods, with a heap of stones cast over him.

AB'SA·LOM'S PILLAR

Also called Absalom's monument. Absalom had this edifice set up as a memorial to himself, since at the time he had no sons (2 Sa 18:18). It was located in the King's Valley, and bears a tragic contrast to his dishonored grave.

ABSTINENCE

The act of deliberately denying oneself certain pleasures. One could choose to abstain from alcohol, certain foods, sexual relations, or other pleasures. In the Old Testament there are various requirements of this nature. Noah was commanded to abstain from blood (Ge 9:4). The sinew that shrank was banned (Ge 32:32). The Jews were not permitted to eat blood, certain animals, and certain parts of animals (Le 3:9-11,17; 11:1-47). They were required to abstain from all things relating to idols (Ex 34:15). God's people were to abstain from sexual relations outside of the strict confines of marriage (Ex 20:14; Le 18). Priests on official duty and Nazirites, during the period of their vow, could not drink wine nor strong drink (Le 10:9; Nu 6:3). To those who still believed that the early Jewish laws of abstinence from unclean meats should hold, Paul said each should follow his conscience (Ro 14:1-3; 1 Co 8). The Council of Jerusalem decided that Gentile Christians should abstain from eating meats offered to idols, blood, and strangled things, and from fornication (Ac 15:29) . Paul also taught that Christians should "abstain from sexual immorality" and "every form of evil" (1 Th 4:3; 5:22).

A·BYSS' *(bottomless)*

The place of the dead—Hades—also called the bottomless pit; especially the place of evil spirits under Apollyon—Satan (Re 9:11; 17:8; 20:1-3). Apparently it is a place that the demons fear, for the demons that Jesus drove out of the Gadarene man begged Him not to send them to the abyss (Lk 8:31). The Septuagint (the Greek version of the Old Testament) uses the word *abyss* to translate the word that English Bibles usually translate *the deep* (Ge 1:2).

A·CA' CI·A

Also called *shittim* and *shittah* (Ex 25:5,10; Is 41:19). The acacia is a large genus of trees and shrubs; many varieties are found around the world. Their round clusters of blossoms are often very sweet smelling, their branches are covered in sharp spines. They produce their seeds in long pods, reminiscent of other members of their botanical family *leguminosae* (the pea family). The acacia is particularly well suited for hot, dry climates. The bark of some varieties of acacia is valued for its high tannin content, and used in processing leather. Some varieties produce attractive, highly figured hard wood. The ark of the covenant and the first tabernacle were constructed of acacia wood (Ex 36:20; 37:1).

A·CA' CI·A GROVE

See ABEL ACACIA GROVE.

A·CA' CI·AS, VALLEY OF

Through the prophet Joel, God described the peace and plenty that would follow the restoration of Israel. The land would flow with wine and milk, all the brooks would be full, and a fountain would come from the temple and water the Valley of Acacias. Apparently this valley was very dry. It may have acquired its name because nothing but acacias would grow there (Joel 3:18).

AC' CAD, AK' KAD

One of the four towns in Shinar which formed the kingdom of Nimrod (Ge 10:10). The name was also applied to the district called the land of Accad. It embraced at one time northern Babylonia and the cities of Babylon and Cutha; the area between the Tigris and Euphrates Rivers. The Accadian language is considered to be one of the earliest written Semitic languages—Babylonian and Assyrian are two of its dialects, as is the Aramaic which was spoken by Jesus and his disciples in New Testament days. The location of ancient Accad is thought to be only a few miles from modern Baghdad.

AC' CARON

See EKRON.

ACCEPT

To agree to receive; to admit with favor or approval; to allow relationship. When Cain and Abel offered their respective offerings, God only accepted Abel's offering, because Abel's offering fulfilled the requirement of blood (Ge 4:3-7). When God gave the law to Moses, He specified exactly how the sacrifices and offerings should be performed in order to be acceptable to Him (Le 1:4; 7:18; 19:7; 22:23-25; 22:27). Sin makes us unacceptable to God—in order to come before Him, blood atonement must be made (Job 42:8-9). However, sacrifices without repentance are not acceptable. When Israel was living in sin and rebellion, God was disgusted by their sacrifices (Je 14:10; Am 5:22; Mal 1:8, 10). However, through the death of Christ as the ultimate sacrifice for sin, we can be accepted into God's intimate family (Ep 1:6). As believers, our goal should be to live out every aspect of our lives with the goal of pleasing God, so that every thought and action is acceptable to Him (Ps 19:14; 2 Co 5:9).

ACCESS

Liberty to approach or communicate with. Through Christ, we have access to God. When Jesus died, the temple curtain between the sanctuary and the holy of holies was torn in two, symbolizing the new relationship that we can have with the Most High (Ma 27:51). Christ's blood has cleansed us from sin; we can come before God without stain or fear (He 10:19-22).

AC′ CHO

See ACCO.

AC′ CO (hot sand)

A city allotted to the tribe of Asher, located south of Tyre, and about eight or nine miles north of Mount Carmel. Even though this city was supposed to be a part of Asher's territory, they never managed to drive out the Canaanite inhabitants. It was taken by Shalmaneser when the Assyrians invaded Israel in the reign of Hoshea. Its name was changed to Ptolemais during the time of the Greek Empire. It came under Roman rule in 65 B.C. It held an important geographical position as a seaport at the entrance to the valley of Jezreel. A Christian community was established in Acco, and on his third missionary journey Paul spent a day there (Ac 21:7). The city is now called Acre.

ACCOMMODATION

God's gracious act of teaching us about Himself in terms that humans can understand. The greatest expression of this is the incarnation of Christ, in which God took on flesh, accommodating Himself to human weakness in order to declare the Father to us (Jo 1:14,18).

ACCOUNTABILITY

The concept that we are responsible for our deeds, and will be held guilty before God for our sins (Ro 3:19; 3:23; 14:12). Until we realize our accountability, and see ourselves as God sees us, we cannot understand the need for a savior, or experience God's grace.

ACCURSED

Under a curse, in the state of having been cursed (Jo 6:17-18; Ga 1:8-9). See also ANATHEMA.

ACCUSER

See SATAN.

A·CEL′ DA·MA

See AKELDAMA.

A·CHAI′ A

Originally the northern part of the Peloponnesus, but the name was applied by the Romans (146 B.C.) to all of Greece and Macedonia. Augustus divided the whole into two provinces. The northern province was Macedonia; it extended westward to the Adriatic. In the south was Achaia, with Corinth as its capital. The latter division is the province referred to in the New Testament (Ac 18:12-17; 19:21; Ro 15:26; 2 Co 1:1; 1 Th 1:7). While Paul was living in Corinth, the Jews brought him before Gallio, the proconsul of Achaia, accusing him of teaching false religion. Gallio refused to pay attention to their charge, and Paul was set free. The region of Achaia was apparently well evangelized, for when Apollos wanted to go there, the Christians in Ephesus were able to send him to other believers in Achaia for hospitality and help (Ac 18:27).

A·CHA′ I·CUS (belonging to Achaia)

A Christian of Corinth. He rendered Paul a service, along with Stephanas and Fortunatus, and is kindly spoken of in the first letter to the Corinthians (1 Co 16:17).

A′ CHAN (trouble)

A son of Carmi of the tribe of Judah who, after the fall of Jericho, stole a wedge of gold and a Babylonian mantle. God had specifically commanded the Israelites not to take any plunder of any kind from the city, but rather to consider everything as belonging to God. Achan's disobedience caused the defeat of Joshua at Ai. After God had showed Joshua through the casting of lots who the culprit was, Achan confessed his sin and was stoned to death (Jos 7:1-26).

A′ CHAR

See ACHAN.

A' CHAZ

See AHAZ.

ACH' BOR *(a mouse)*

Two or possibly three Old Testament men:

1. The father of Baalhanan, king of Edom (Ge 36:38; 1 Ch 1:49).

2. Son of Micaiah and father of Elnathan. In 2 Chronicles 34:20 he is called Abdon. He was an officer of Josiah, and one of the five men sent to inquire of the prophetess Huldah about the book of the Law which had been found in the temple (2 Ki 22:12,14; Je 26:20-23; 36:12).

3. The father of Elnathan, who was one of the men sent by Jehoiakim king of Judah to bring the prophet Urijah back from Egypt in order that he might be put to death (Je 26:20-23; 36:12). Since Jehoiakim was the son of Josiah, it is possible that Elnathan's father was the same person as No. 2.

A' CHIM *(whom God makes firm)*

Born after Israel was taken into captivity in Babylon, son of Zadok and father of Eliud; part of the genealogy of Jesus (Ma 1:14).

A' CHISH *(serpent charmer)*

The king of Gath, a Philistine city, to whom David fled when he was pursued by Saul. David feared for his life when he saw that Achish remembered his reputation as Goliath's killer, and pretended to be insane. Achish was apparently deceived and took no interest in a mad former hero, other than to order that David be taken out of his sight (1 Sa 21:10-15; 27:1-12; 29:1-11). He is called Abimelech in the title of Psalm 34, but it seems likely that this was a title rather than a name, as Pharaoh was for the kings of Egypt.

ACH·ME'THA

The capital of northern Media. It is the same as Ecbatana, a treasure city and the summer residence of the Persian kings. When the Samaritans were hindering the building of the second temple, the Jews declared that Cyrus had issued a decree that the temple should be built. Darius ordered that the claim be investigated, and when nothing could be found in Babylon to establish the veracity of this report, the search was continued in Achmetha. There, in the palace, the decree was found (Ez 5:6–6:2).

The city was conquered in 330 B.C. by Alexander the Great, and destroyed. Today, the site is occupied by the Iranian city of Hamadan.

A' CHOR *(trouble)*

A valley south of Jericho on the northern boundary of Judah. It was here that Achan was stoned to death (Jos 7:24-26; 15:7). The prophets spoke of the Valley of Achor as a place which would be a "door of hope"(Ho 2:15), and a peaceful place for herds to lie down (Is 65:10) when the restoration of Israel came about. See ACHAN.

ACH' SAH, ACH' SA *(anklet)*

Caleb's daughter, who was offered in marriage to the one who should capture Kirjath-sepher (also called Debir). Caleb's near relative, Othniel, the first of the judges, succeeded and won the daughter. She received from her father as her dowry a portion of the Negev, and upon her request he also gave her the valley of springs (Jos 15:16-19; Ju 1:12-15; 1 Ch 2:49).

ACH' SHAPH *(enchantment)*

A city of Canaan (Jos 11:1; 12:7,20; 19:24-25). It was part of the land given to the tribe of Asher, in the north.

ACH' ZIB

Two Israelite towns:

1. A town in the southern section of Palestine included in the territory of Judah, also called Chezib (Ge 38:5; Jos 15:44; Mi 1:14), probably the same as Chozeba (1 Ch 4:22).

2. A seacoast town in Asher, which would be western Galilee (Jos 19:29) from which the Canaanites were not driven (Ju 1:31).

ACQUIT

To hold guiltless (Na 1:3). Also, in the sense of behavior or deportment—ex. *to acquit oneself well* means to behave well, or to carry something off creditably.

AC·RAB' BIM (Jos 15:3)

See MAALEH-ACRABBIM.

ACRE

See ACCO.

ACRE

See WEIGHTS AND MEASURES.

A·CROP′O·LIS

Many important cities of Greece and Asia Minor were protected by strongholds of this name. The Acropolis occupied a lofty position commanding the city and was inaccessible on all sides except one. It contained the most important public buildings and was the last refuge in case of a hostile attack. The Acropolis at Athens contained the Parthenon, or temple of Minerva, the Prophylaea forming an entrance to the Parthenon, and the Erechtheum.

ACROSTIC

A poetic or literary device. A poem or essay may be written in such a way that the first letter of each line, or of each stanza, when taken in order will either spell a word, a phrase, or the alphabet in sequence. Such a literary device may simply be artistic, but it is also frequently employed as a memory aid. The longest psalm in the Bible, Psalm 119, is a good example of an acrostic. Each of the 22 letters of the Hebrew alphabet has a stanza of eight verses, where each verse begins with the same letter. Proverbs 31:10-21 is also an acrostic, celebrating the character qualities of a virtuous woman. Various other examples of acrostics occur in Scripture (Ps 9; 10; 23; 37; 111; 112; 145; and La 1–4 all contain partial acrostics).

AC′SAH

See ACHSAH.

ACTS OF THE A·POS′TLES, BOOK OF

1. The Book of Acts. Jesus's last recorded words have come to be known as the Great Commission: "You shall be witnesses to Me in Jerusalem, and in all Judea and Samaria, and to the end of the earth" (1:8). The book of Acts, written by Luke, is the story of the men and women who took that commission seriously and began to spread the news of a risen Savior to the most remote corners of the known world.

Each section of the book (1–7; 8–12; 13–28) focuses on a particular audience, a key personality, and a significant phase in the expansion of the gospel message. Besides the Gospels, Acts is the only historical book of the New Testament, following the growth of Christianity and the birth of the church after Jesus's resurrection. It is the second volume of a two part work by Luke. Originally, it probably had no separate title, but all available Greek manuscripts use the title *Praxeis,* which is either translated simply "Acts," or by an expanded title like "The Acts of the Apostles." This word was commonly used in Greek literature to summarize the accomplishments of outstanding men. The whole group of apostles is mentioned more than once, and specific stories concerning several of them are included in this book. The bulk of the work, however, is taken up with the acts of Peter (1–12) and Paul (13–28).

The book covers a time span of about 32 years, beginning with the ascension of Christ and finishing with Paul's imprisonment in Rome (about A.D. 30-62).

2. The Author of Acts. While Luke does not actually identify himself as the author of either the Gospel of Luke, or the Book of Acts, it is well accepted that he wrote both accounts. (See LUKE, "The Author of Luke" for the internal and external support for Lucan authorship of Luke.) There are many similarities between the two books. Both are addressed to a man named Theophilus (Lk 1:1-4; Ac 1:1-5), and the similarities of style and vocabulary support the idea that they were written by the same man. The "we" sections of this book (Ac 16:10-17; 20:5–21:18; 27:1–28:16) show that the author of Acts was a close associate of Paul. A careful reading of the "we" sections, comparing the lists of Paul's companions with the other sections of the book, leave one reasonably certain that Luke wrote both Acts and the Gospel bearing his name. The "we" sections were certainly written from his own memories of the time, if not a diary of some sort. He had contact with the principle eyewitnesses for most of the book. Acts 15:23-29 and 23:26-30 hint that Luke may have had access to some written documents as well.

3. The Time of Acts. The book of Acts was written sometime around or after A.D. 62, since the narrative ends at approximately this date, with Paul in prison in Rome. It is generally agreed that Acts was written during the first century, though some have suggested later dates. Because Luke ends so abruptly, leaving Paul awaiting trial in Rome, some believe that Acts was completed right around A.D. 62, just before Paul's trial had occurred. It is reasoned that if the book were written later, Luke would surely have mentioned the outcome of the trial. Also, Acts does not mention any of the important events which followed Paul's trial, such as Nero's persecution of Christians (A.D. 64), Paul's execution (A.D. 68), or the destruction of the temple and the Holy City in A.D. 70.

4. Keys to Acts.

Key Word: The Growth of the Church— While there are four accounts of the life of Jesus, this is the only book that carries on the story from His ascension to the period of the New Testament Epistles. Thus, Acts is the historical link between the Gospels and the Epistles. Because of Luke's strong emphasis on the ministry of the Holy Spirit, this book could be regarded as "the Acts of the Spirit of Christ working in and through the Apostles." As a missionary himself, Luke's interest in the progressive spread of the gospel is obviously reflected in this apostolic history. Luke was personally involved as a participant in this story, so it was not written from a detached point of view.

From a theological standpoint, Acts was written to trace the development of the body of Christ over the one-generation transition from a primarily Jewish to a predominantly Gentile membership. This apologetic work presents Christianity as distinct from Judaism but also as its fulfillment.

Key Verses: Acts 1:8 and 2:42-47—"But you shall receive power when the Holy Spirit has come upon you; and you shall be witnesses to Me in Jerusalem, and in all Judea and Samaria, and to the end of the earth" (1:8).

"And they continued steadfastly in the apostles' doctrine and fellowship, in the breaking of bread, and in prayers. Then fear came upon every soul, and many wonders and signs were done through the apostles. Now all who believed were together, and had all things in common, and sold their possessions and goods, and divided them among all, as anyone had need. So continuing daily with one accord in the temple, and breaking bread from house to house, they ate their food with gladness and simplicity of heart, praising God and having favor with all the people. And the Lord added to the church daily those who were being saved" (2:42-47).

Key Chapter: Acts 2—Chapter 2 records the earth-changing events of the Day of Pentecost when the Holy Spirit came, fulfilling Christ's promise of the Comforter who would both empower and direct the witness. The Spirit transformed a small group of fearful men into a thriving worldwide Church that is ever moving forward and fulfilling the Great Commission.

6. Survey of Acts. The Book of Acts begins where the Gospel of Luke left off, recapping the last events recorded in the Gospel. After Jesus's resurrection, He remained with the disciples for forty days, teaching them and preparing them for His departure. His last words before being taken up into heaven outline the rest of the book: "you shall be witnesses to Me in Jerusalem, and in all Judea and Samaria, and to the end of the earth" (1:8). The three movements of Acts are as follows: The witness in Jerusalem (1:1–8:4); witness in Judea and Samaria (8:5–12:25); and witness to the end of the earth (13–28).

Acts traces important events in the early history of Christianity from the ascension of Christ, to the outpouring of the Holy Spirit, to the rapid progress of the gospel, beginning in Jerusalem and spreading throughout the Roman Empire.

Acts is a pivotal book of transitions: from the Gospels to the Epistles (history), from Judaism to Christianity (religion), from law to grace (divine dealing), from Jews alone to Jews and Gentiles (people of God), and from kingdom to church (program of God).

Witness in Jerusalem (1:1–8:4) After Christ ascended into heaven, the disciples obeyed His instructions to remain in Jerusalem until the promised Holy Spirit should appear. Accordingly, the group of believers (about 300 men and women) continued to gather together to pray. Ten days after the ascension, the disciples were praying in an upper room when the Holy Spirit descended on them with the sound of a rushing mighty wind, and the appearance of tongues of fire. The disciples were transformed from the fearful and uncertain group who had deserted Jesus at the crucifixion, into fearless, empowered preachers of the Word. Three thousand new believers were added to the church that day, after listening to Peter's sermon explaining to the Jews that Jesus was indeed the promised Messiah. Later, after dramatically healing a lame man, Peter delivered another powerful message, resulting in the salvation of thousands more. The religious leaders resented the influence and the disturbance, and arrested Peter and John. After flogging them, they were released under strict orders never to speak of Jesus of Nazareth again. Filled with the new power and courage from the Holy Spirit, Peter and John ignored this injunction, and continued to preach

Christ in the city of Jerusalem. While the early church was full of enthusiasm and joy, they were not without some difficulties as well. The story of Ananias and Sapphira underlines the omniscience of the Holy Spirit, and the serious consequences of trying to deceive God. As a result of their sin, the two died. Besides such internal problems, the believers also suffered persecution at the hands of the unbelieving Jews. Stephen, one of seven men selected to assist the apostles, was brought before the Sanhedrin on fallacious charges of blasphemy. In his defense, Stephen preached a powerful sermon to the religious leaders, encapsulating the Old Testament message of redemption to come, and proving that the same Jesus that they had crucified was the true Messiah. As a result, Stephen was dragged out of the city and stoned to death; the first Christian martyr.

Witness in Judea and Samaria (8:5–12:25) After Stephen's death, the church began to be more heavily persecuted, and was forced to scatter from Jerusalem. Thus, the second part of the Great Commission was put into action. Philip went into the province of Samaria and proclaimed the good news to the Samaritans. It was received with joy, and Peter and John confirmed his work, and prayed for the Samaritans to also receive the Holy Spirit. The acceptance of the Samaritans into the church was the first clear indication that the Messiah was not only for the Jews. Later, Philip also had a unique opportunity to share the gospel with an Ethiopian proselyte of Judaism. Through this man's eager acceptance of the good news, the gospel began to be spread further afield. God sovereignly transformed Saul the persecutor, who held the coats of the men who stoned Stephen. Later, Saul (who became Paul) would be known as the Apostle to the Gentiles, but the first Gentile believers were introduced to the gospel by Peter. God sent a special vision to Peter to make him understand that the old barriers between Jew and Gentile were gone, and that the new message was for all people. After Peter saw Cornelius and his household receive the Holy Spirit, he came back to Jerusalem and convinced the rest of the church that the Gentiles were also a part of the body. In spite of continued persecution, the church continued to grow and spread throughout the Roman Empire.

Witness expands to the rest of the known world (13:1–28:31) At this point, the focus switches from Peter's ministry to the ministry of Paul. After his conversion, Paul went back to his old home in Tarsus for several years. It was not until after a church was established in Antioch that Barnabas went looking for him, and brought him back to Antioch. Since Paul had been a brilliant scholar, trained to study the Scriptures under the foremost teachers of the day, he was well equipped to teach the new believers about God's word. As the number of believers in Antioch grew, it gradually replaced Jerusalem as the headquarters of the church, and it was here that they first began to be called "Christians." All three of Paul's missionary journeys began in Antioch. First, he traveled through Pisidian Antioch, Iconium, Lystra and Derbe. It was after this first journey that the apostles and elders of the Jerusalem church met and decided that it was wrong to expect the new Gentile believers to submit to the law of Moses. On his second journey, Paul again visited the Galatian churches, and then continued into Macedonia and Greece. Most of this journey was spent in Philippi, Thessalonica, and Corinth; he also returned to Jerusalem and Antioch. Paul's third journey included nearly three years in Ephesus, before returning through Macedonia and Greece for the second time. At the end of this journey, Paul was determined to visit Jerusalem, even though he was warned that such a visit would end in his imprisonment. Paul had only been in the city a short time before he was accused by the religious authorities of purposely defiling the temple. Only the intervention of the Romans prevented Paul from being killed by the mob, and any attempts that he made to defend himself produced violent reactions. Finally, Paul was sent as a prisoner to Caesarea, in order to protect his life. Paul was in prison there for two years, and during this time he had many opportunities to present the gospel to Felix, the governor of the area. The Jews continued to press charges against Paul, and during his trial before Festus, Paul finally appealed to Caesar. Because of this appeal, Paul, as a Roman citizen, had to be sent to Rome to stand trial there. After an adventurous journey, including storm and shipwreck, Paul arrived in Rome. He was placed under house arrest, where he remained for at least two years, preaching about the kingdom of God and the Lord Jesus Christ "boldly and without hindrance."

OUTLINE OF ACTS

Part One: The Witness in Jerusalem (1:1–8:4)

I. The Power of the Church (1:1–2:47)

A. Prologue to Acts 1:1-2
B. Appearances of the Resurrected
   Christ 1:3-8
C. Ascension of Christ 1:9-11
D. Anticipation of the Spirit............ 1:12-14
E. Appointment of Matthias 1:15-26
F. Filling with the Holy Spirit............ 2:1-4
G. Speaking with Other Tongues 2:5-13
H. Peter Explains What Has
   Happened 2:14-41
I. Practices of the Early Church ... 2:42-47

II. The Progress of the Church (3:1–8:4)

A. Peter Heals the Lame Man 3:1-11
B. Peter's Second Sermon 3:12-26

C. Peter and John Are Put Into
   Custody 4:1-4
D. Peter Preaches to the
   Sanhedrin 4:5-12
E. Sanhedrin Commands Peter
   and John Not to Preach 4:13-22
F. Apostles Pray for Boldness 4:23-31
G. Early Church Community 4:32-37
H. Ananias and Sapphira's Lie 5:1-11
I. Apostles' Mighty Miracles 5:12-16
J. Persecution of the
   Apostles 5:17-42
K. Deacons Are Appointed 6:1-8
L. Stephen Is Martyred.................. 6:9–7:60
M. Saul Persecutes the
   Church..................................... 8:1-4

Part Two: The Witness in Judea and Samaria (8:5–12:25)

I. The Witness of Philip (8:5-40)

A. Philip Witnesses to the
   Samaritans 8:5-25
B. Philip Witnesses to the Ethiopian
   Treasurer 8:26-40

II. The Conversion of Saul (9:1-31)

A. The Lord Speaks to Saul on the Road
   to Damascus 9:1-9
B. Saul is Filled with the Spirit 9:10-19
C. Saul Preaches in Damascus 9:20-22
D. Saul Witnesses in Jerusalem 9:23-31

III. The Witness of Peter (9:32–11:18)

A. Peter Heals Aenas at Lydda 9:32-35
B. Peter Raises Dorcas at Joppa 9:36-43
C. Peter Witnesses to Cornelius
   at Caesarea 10:1–11:18

IV. The Witness of the Early Church (11:19–12:25)

A. The Witness of the Antioch
   Church.................................. 11:19-30
B. The Persecution by Herod 12:1-25

Part Three: The Witness to the End of the Earth (13:1–28:31)

I. The First Missionary Journey (13:1–14:28)

A. Barnabas and Saul Are Sent From
   Antioch 13:1-3
B. Ministry at Cyprus 13:4-13
C. Ministry at Pisidian Antioch 13:14-50
D. Ministry at Iconium 13:51–14:5
E. Ministry at Lystra.................... 14:6-20
F. Ministry on the Return Trip 14:21-25
G. Report on the First Missionary
   Journey 14:26-28

II. The Jerusalem Council (15:1-35)

A. Debate over Gentiles Keeping the
   Law 15:1-5

B. Peter Preaches Salvation Through
   Grace 15:6-11
C. Paul and Barnabas Testify 15:12
D. James Proves Gentiles Are Free
   from the Law 15:13-21
E. The Council Sends an Official
   Letter 15:22-29
F. Report to Antioch 15:30-35

III. The Second Missionary Journey (15:36–18:22)

A. Contention over John Mark 15:36-41
B. Derbe and Lystra 16:1-5
C. Troas: Macedonian Call 16:6-10
D. Philippi: Extensive Ministry 16:11-40

E. Thessalonica: "Turned the World
Upside Down" 17:1-9
F. Berea: Many Receive the
Word 17:10-15
G. Athens: Paul's Sermon on Mars'
Hill 17:16-34
H. Corinth: One-and-a-half Years of
Ministry 18:1-17
I. Return Trip to Antioch 18:18-22

IV. The Third Missionary Journey
(18:23–21:16)

A. Galatia and Phrygia: Strengthening
the Disciples 18:23
B. Ephesus: Three Years of
Ministry 18:24–19:41

C. Macedonia: Three Months of
Ministry 20:1-5
D. Troas: Eutychus Falls From the
Window 20:6-12
E. Miletus: Paul Bids Farewell to
the Ephesian Elders 20:13-28
F. Tyre: Paul Is Warned About
Jerusalem 21:1-6
G. Caesarea: Agabus's Prediction ... 21:7-16

V. The Trip to Rome (21:17–28:31)

A. Paul witnesses in
Jerusalem 21:17–23:33
B. Paul Witnesses in
Caesarea 23:34–26:32
C. Paul Witnesses in Rome 27:1–28:31

A·DA′ DAH *(festival)*

A town in the southern part of the territory of Judah (Jos 15:22).

A′ DAH *(beauty)*

Two Old Testament women:

1. A wife of Lamech and mother of Jabal and Jubal (Ge 4:19-23).

2. Daughter of Elon, the Hittite, a wife of Esau. Her oldest son was Eliphaz, from whom the Edomites descended (Ge 36:2-4).

A·DAI′ AH *(Jehovah hath adorned)*

Eight Old Testament men:

1. A man of Bozcath, father of Jedidah who was the mother of Josiah, king of Israel (2 Ki 22:1).

2. A Levite descended from Gershom, and an ancestor of Asaph (1 Ch 6:41-42).

3. A Benjamite, son of Shimhi (1 Ch 8:21).

4. Two members of the families of Bani and Binnui who divorced their foreign wives (Ez 10:29,39).

5. The father of Maaseiah who helped to put Joash on the throne of Judah (2 Ch 23:1).

6. Son of Joiarib (Ne 11:5).

7. A Levite of the family of Aaron (1 Ch 9:12).

A·DA′ LI·A

One of Haman's ten sons; he and his brothers were hanged along with their father (Es 9:8).

AD′ AM *(man—human being)*

1. The last work in the creation of the world, man was formed in God's own image (Ge 1:26-

27). Adam, the first man, was made of dust and was brought to life by God's breathing into his nostrils the breath of life (Ge 2:7; 6:17; Job 10:8-12). He was given dominion over all the animals of the earth (Ge 1:26-28) and lived in the garden of Eden (Ge 2:8,15). Through Eve, Adam tasted the forbidden fruit of the tree of knowledge. Because God foresaw that unless he was prevented, Adam would eat of the tree of life also and live forever, He expelled the couple from the garden of Eden (Ge 3:1-24). Only three of Adam's children are mentioned by name: Cain, Abel, and Seth. Adam died at the age of 930. Paul mentions Adam as the first man, a living soul through whom sin and death entered the world, and calls Christ the last Adam, a life-giving spirit in whom all are made alive (Ro 5:12-21; 1 Co 15:22,45).

2. A gender neutral term simply meaning "human" (Ge 5:2).

3. A town on the Jordan River, beside Zaretan, north of the place where the Israelites crossed the Jordan into the promised land (Jos 3:16).

AD′ A·MAH *(soil)*

A fortified city of Naphtali, northwest of the Sea of Galilee (Jos 19: 36).

ADAM AND EVE, BOOK OF

See PSEUDEPIGRAPHA.

AD′ A·MANT *(unbreakable)*

A very hard stone, supposedly impenetrable. The word *adamant* was formerly used in English as a term for diamond. When God instructed the prophet Ezekiel in his ministry, He described the people of Israel as "impudent and hardhearted." Because of this characteristic, God gave Ezekiel a forehead "like adamant stone, harder than flint" (Eze 3:7-9). The Hebrew word used here is elsewhere rendered "diamond" or "flint" (Je 17:1). It is uncertain exactly what is meant, other than a very hard substance, but many believe that this word refers to corundum, which is next to diamond in hardness. Corundum is aluminum oxide, colorless in its purest form, but when "contaminated" with chromium, it forms red rubies; the addition of iron or titanium makes a sapphire. Emery is also a form of corundum.

AD′AM·IC COVENANT (Ge 3:14-21)

The covenant with Adam is the second general or universal covenant. It could be called the Covenant with Mankind, for it sets forth the conditions which will hold sway until the curse of sin is lifted (Is 11:6-10; Ro 8:18-23). According to the covenant, the conditions which will prevail are:

1. The serpent, the tool used by Satan to effect the fall of man, is cursed. The curse affected not only the instrument, the serpent, but also the indwelling energizer, Satan. Great physical changes took place in the serpent. Apparently, it was upright, or at least did not crawl on the ground; now it will go on its belly in the dust (v. 14). It was the most desirable animal of the animal creation; now it is the most loathsome. The sight or thought of a snake should be an effective reminder of the devastating effects of sin.
2. Satan is judged—he will enjoy limited success ("you shall bruise His heel," v. 15), but ultimately he will be overcome ("He shall bruise your head," v. 15).
3. The first prophecy of the coming Messiah is given (v. 15).
4. For the woman, "sorrow and conception" are multiplied, perhaps meaning an increase in conception necessitated by the entrance of death into the world (v. 16)
5. There will be travail (hard, uncomfortable work; struggle; pain) in childbirth (v. 16).

6. The woman is made subject to her husband (v. 16).
7. The ground is cursed and will bring forth weeds among the food which man must eat for his existence (vv. 17-19).
8. The nature of work is changed. Instead of being only good, work will now be hard. Humans must labor for their food until they die (v. 19).
9. Because of sin, man dies spiritually. Ultimately, he will die physically. His flesh will decay until it returns to the dust from which it was originally taken (v. 19).

AD′A·MI NEKEB (man of the pass)

A town of Naphtali, near the lower border (Jos 19:33).

A′DAR

Twelfth month of the Hebrew sacred year (Ez 6:15; Es 3:7,13; 9:15). It extended from the new moon in February to the new moon in March. See CALENDAR.

A′DAR, AD′DAR (height, top)

A place on the southern boundary of Judah (Jos 15:3), also called Hazar–addar in Numbers 34:4.

AD′BEEL (a miracle of God)

One of the twelve sons of Ishmael and head of a tribe (Ge 25:13; 1 Ch 1:29).

AD′DAN, AD′DON

A place in Babylonia (Ez 2:59; Ne 7:61). It was the home of certain persons who returned to Israel from exile but were unable to produce genealogies proving that they were truly Israelites.

AD′DAR (a wide place)

1. A town on the southern boundary of Judah (Nu 34:4; Jos 15:3), also called Adar and Hazar–addar.

2. A Benjamite (Nu 26:49; 1 Ch 8:3). See ARD.

AD′DAX

See ANTELOPE

AD′DER

See SNAKE.

AD′DI

An ancestor of Jesus, the Greek form of IDDO (Lk 3:28).

AD′DON

See ADDAN.

A′DER

See EDER.

AD′I·DA

See ADITHAIM.

AD′I·EL *(ornament of God)*

Three Old Testament men:

1. Head of a family of Simeon (1 Ch 4:36).

2. A priest, son of Jahzerah and father of Maasai (1 Ch 9:12).

3. The father of Azmaveth (1 Ch 27:25).

A′DIN *(effeminate)*

The head of a family, many of which returned from Babylon with Zerubbabel and Ezra (Ez 2:15; 8:6; Ne 7:20). A chief of the family signed the covenant with Nehemiah (Ne 10:16).

AD′I·NA *(delicate)*

One of David's mighty men, the son of Shiza the Reubenite (1 Ch 11:42).

AD′I·NO

Chief of David's mighty men. The name of Adino the Eznite was given to Josheb-Basshebeth, the Tachmonite, when he killed 800 men at one time (2 Sa 23:8).

AD·I·THA′IM *(double prey)*

A town of Judah, sometimes identified with Adida (Jos 15:36).

ADJURE

To earnestly advise or urge, with authority; to solemnly command, as in a courtroom setting. (See 1 Sa 14:24; 1 Ki 22:16; Mk 5:7; Ac 19:13 for examples). When Jesus was being tried before the high priest, the elders and the council, Caiaphas said, "I adjure You by the living God that You tell us if You are the Christ, the Son of God." He was using his authority, both as high priest and as the official of the trial, to command and urge Jesus to tell the truth as one under oath.

AD·LA′I *(God's justice)*

The father of Shaphat. Shaphat was David's servant, one of two men who were in charge of all David's herds (1 Ch 27:29).

AD′MAH *(red earth)*

A city in the vale of Siddim—one of the cities of the plain (Ge 10:19; 14:2,8). It was destroyed with Sodom (Ge 19:25,28-29; De 29:23; Ho 11:8).

AD·MA′THA *(unconquered, God-given)*

A prince of Persia under Ahasuerus at Shushan; one of the seven with privileged access to the king (Es 1:14).

ADMONISH

To instruct; advise; warn (Ac 27:9-10).

AD′NA *(pleasure)*

Two Old Testament men:

1. A priest, the son of Harim, who returned from captivity during the time Joiakim was high priest (Ne 12:15).

2. A son of Pahath–moab who divorced his foreign wife (Ez 10:30).

AD′NAH *(pleasure)*

Two Old Testament men:

1. A man of Judah and high officer in the army of Jehoshaphat (2 Ch 17:14).

2. A man of Manasseh who joined David at Ziklag (1 Ch 12:20).

ADO (archaic)

Fuss; bother; tumult (Mk 5:38-39).

ADONAI *(lord)*

See GOD, NAMES OF.

AD′O·NI-BE′ZEK *(lord of Bezek)*

A king of Bezek. He was captured by soldiers of the tribes of Judah and Simeon, who cut off his thumbs and big toes. Adoni-bezek saw this as a just punishment from God, because he himself had served seventy kings with the same treatment (Ju 1:4-7).

AD-O·NI′JAH *(Jehovah my lord)*

Three Old Testament men:

1. The fourth son of David by his wife Haggith (2 Sa 3:2-4). When David was old, Adonijah attempted to seize the throne just as his brother

Absalom had done earlier. He undoubtedly knew that it was intended that Solomon should succeed David, and apparently did not relish the idea of being ruled by his much younger brother (1 Ki 1:13; 1 Ch 23:1). When Solomon was proclaimed king, Adonijah fled to the altar for protection, and his life was spared. Later however, he made a second attempt to oust Solomon, this time through a seemingly innocent request to Solomon's mother. Adonijah asked Bath-sheba to arrange for him to marry Abishag, the beautiful virgin who had cared for David in his old age. Bath-sheba relayed this request to Solomon, who recognized another attempt to gain control of the kingdom. Solomon and Adonijah both knew that claiming a king's wife or concubine indicated a right to the throne. This time Adonijah's life was not spared; Solomon ordered that he be killed in order to end all attempts to occupy the throne (1 Ki 2:13-25).

2. A Levite appointed by Jehoshaphat to instruct the people (2 Ch 17:8).

3. A leader who sealed the covenant with Nehemiah (Ne 10:16), probably the same person as Adonikam (Ez 2:13).

AD·O·NI′KAM *(the Lord arises)*

The founder of a family, members of which returned from exile with Nehemiah and Ezra (Ez 2:13; 8:13; Ne 7:18), probably the same person as the Adonijah of Nehemiah 10:16.

AD·O·NI′RAM *(the Lord is exalted)*

One who had charge of tribute under David and Solomon, also known as Adoram (2 Sa 20:24) and Hadoram (2 Ch 10:18). He was stoned to death when he attempted to deal with the ten tribes at the time of revolt (1 Ki 4:6; 12:18).

AD′O·NI-ZE′DEK, AD′O·NI-ZE′DEC *(lord of righteousness)*

King of Jerusalem who joined a confederacy of Amorite kings against Joshua. They were defeated (Jos 10:1-27).

ADOPTION

Taking the child of another, and raising it as one's own son or daughter. An example of adoption in the natural sense can be found in the Book of Exodus. Moses was adopted by the daughter of Pharaoh and was as her own son (Ex 2:10). In a theological sense, adoption refers to God's gracious act of mercy in forgiving our sins and allowing us to share in the inheritance of His Son, as His own children. Paul speaks of the adoption of Israel by the Lord (Ro 9:4), and it is Paul, the Apostle to the Gentiles, who explains how anyone who believes in the Son is adopted by the Father to become coheirs of the promise with the Son. God has "predestined us to be adopted as sons" (Ep 1:5). In his letters to Rome and Galatia, Paul speaks of the "Spirit of adoption" which gives us the privilege of calling God "Abba, father," using the familiar term for father that a child uses (Ga 4:6; Ro 8:15-17). Because we are adopted children, heirs of God along with Christ, God has promised to not only redeem the spirit, but the body also. Believers can look forward to one day being bodily raised from the dead (Ro 8:23).

The Hebrew language does not have a specific word for adoption, and it does not appear to have been a common practice in Old Testament days. However, adoption was a fairly common legal, official, arrangement in Roman culture, and it is this adoption that Paul uses as a picture of our relationship with God. In Roman culture, a childless man might adopt a son to carry on his name and inherit his estates. The adopted son was supposed to be of an age to consent to the adoption; once he was legally adopted, it was from then on as though he had been born into the family. He had a new name, a new identity. He was to inherit all his father's goods and responsibilities, he was no different from a son who was born of his father's flesh.

ADOR, ADORA

See ADORAIM.

AD·O·RA′IM *(double honor)*

A lowland city of Judah, fortified and rebuilt by Rehoboam, son of Solomon. It is about five miles southwest of Hebron and is now named Dura (2 Ch 11:9).

AD′O·RAM

See ADONIRAM.

ADORATION

Showing love and devotion to God, a part of worship. While the actual word is not used in most English translations, the concept is implied as all of Scripture teaches that God is worthy of worship, love, devotion, honor, fear and service. (Ps 95:6; 98:1-3; Re 5:11-13).

ADORN

To make more attractive, to decorate, to beautify. Paul urged women to adorn themselves with good works rather than with physical adornments such as expensive clothes or jewelry (1 Ti 2:9-10).

A·DRAM′ ME·LECH *(honor of the king)*

1. An idol of the Sepharvites (2 Ki 17:31).
2. Son of Sennacherib, king of Assyria. Adrammelech and his brother Sharezar killed their father the king (2 Ki 19:37; Is 37:38).

AD·RA·MYT′ TI·UM

A city of Mysia in Asia Minor. Paul sailed in a ship of this city as a prisoner on his way to Rome (Ac 27:2).

A′ DRI·A

See ADRIATIC.

A′ DRI·A′ TIC

The Adriatic Sea is the portion of the Mediterranean Sea east of Italy—so named from the old Etruscan town of Atria (Adria). By New Testament times it included also that portion of the Mediterranean north of a line joining Malta and Crete (Ac 27:27).

A′ DRI·EL *(flock of God)*

A man of the tribe of Issachar. Saul's daughter, Merab, was given him in marriage (1 Sa 18:19).

A·DUL′ LAM *(resting place)*

A town of Judah which was inhabited by Canaanites in the time of Jacob (Ge 38:1-2). It was conquered by Joshua (Jos 12:15) and was fortified by Rehoboam (2 Ch 11:7). After the exile, it was occupied by Jews (Ne 11:30). Near the city was a cave in which David hid for a long time and where he was joined by many of his adherents (1 Sa 22; 2 Sa 23:13; 1 Ch 11:15).

A·DUL′ LAM·ITE

A native or inhabitant of Adullam. Judah's friend Hirah is the only Adullamite mentioned in the Bible (Ge 38:1,12,20).

A·DUL′ TER·Y

Unlawful intercourse of a married person with one who is not that person's wife or husband. It is forbidden by the Seventh Commandment (Ex 20:14) and was punishable by death (Le 20:10). Christ interpreted adultery to be not only the overt act, but also adulterous thoughts and emotions (Ma 5:27-28). He gave it as the only legitimate grounds for divorce (Ma 5:32). The prophets used the term to signify disloyalty to the Lord through the worship of false gods (Je 3:6-10; Eze 23:37,43; Ho 2:2-13).

A·DUM′ MIM *(red things)*

A pass on the boundary between the territories of Benjamin and Judah. In this region was laid the scene of the parable of the good Samaritan (Jos 15:7; 18:17; Lk 10:30).

ADVENT, SECOND

See ESCHATOLOGY; RETURN OF CHRIST.

ADVERSARY

In the original of 1 Samuel 2:10 it signifies *to strive*. The commonly used Hebrew word denotes a *straightener*. Ordinarily an adversary is an enemy or an opponent in a judicial matter (Is 50:8). In particular, the adversary is Satan, the enemy of mankind (Job 1:6-8,12; 1 Pe 5:8).

ADVOCATE

One who acts in behalf of another. Jesus applied the word to the Holy Spirit; in this passage it is often translated *Comforter* (Jo 14:26; 15:26; 16:7). Christ also is called Advocate (1 Jo 2:1).

AE·NE′ AS

A man at Lydda afflicted with palsy eight years. His restoration through Christ resulted in growth of the church (Ac 9:32-35).

AE′ NON *(fountains)*

A locality near Salim which abounded with springs and where many came to be baptized by John the Baptist and to hear him preach (Jo 3:23).

AEON

See AGE.

AFFINITY (archaic)

A marriage alliance (1 Ki 3:1).

AFFLICTION

That which produces pain, trouble, and sorrow. Two kinds of affliction are shown in the

Bible. The most obvious is affliction as God's just punishment for sins (Ro 2:9). Christ bore the affliction for sins that we deserve (Is 53:4). In the last days, great affliction or tribulation will come upon the earth as punishment for millennia of wickedness (Ma 24:29). However, as we learn from the Book of Job, not all affliction is a direct result of sin. Sometimes affliction is used to test the faith; and often it is used to purify, just as a goldsmith uses fire to remove the dross from his metal and make the purest gold (Is 48:10; Ro 5:3-5; 8:18; 2 Th 1:4-7).

AFORE (archaic)

Before (Is 18:5).

AFRESH (archaic)

Again; anew (He 6:4-6).

AG′A-BUS

A prophet of Jerusalem in the time of Paul. He predicted the famine which occurred during the reign of Claudius (Ac 11:28); and warned Paul about what would happen to him in Jerusalem (Ac 21:10-11).

A′GAG (perhaps *flaming*)

1. A king of Amalek mentioned by Balaam (Nu 24:7).

2. The Amalekite king who was spared by Saul and slain by Samuel (1 Sa 15:9-33). The word may be the title of these kings as Pharaoh was the title for the kings of Egypt.

AG′A·GITE

Epithet applied to Haman (Es 3:1,10; 8:3-5).

A-GAPE′

See LOVE.

AG′AR

See HAGAR.

AG′ATE

A variety of quartz, beautifully colored. It is believed to have been named from the river Achates in Sicily where it is found in abundance. In Is 54:12 and Eze 27:16 the Hebrew word means *sparkling*. The word is translated *ruby* by the Revised Version. On the breastplate of the high priest this stone was in middle of the third row of gems (Ex 28:19; 39:12). See also CHALCEDONY.

AGE

The Greek word often translated "age" is *aion,* from which the English word "aeon", or "eon" is derived. An age is a long indefinite period of time. In the New Testament, the word is often used to refer to the present world order, as opposed to end times and the millennial kingdom. In 1 Corinthians 4:4, Paul refers to Satan as "the God of this age," or "the God of this world" (KJV). Hebrews 6:5 speaks of "the age to come." Jesus promised His disciples that He would be with them always, "even to the end of the age" (Ma 28:20). When coupled with the preposition *eis* (into), *aion* takes on the meaning "forever" or "into eternity," as in the Lord's prayer: "For Yours is the kingdom and the power and the glory forever. Amen" (Ma 6:13).

A′GEE *(fugitive)*

A Hararite and father of Shammah, one of David's warriors (2 Sa 23:11).

AG·NOS′TI·CISM

The doctrine which neither asserts nor denies the existence of a personal deity but declares that God is unknowable. It concedes that it is a necessity of thought to believe in the existence of a first cause of the universe, which first cause, having no earlier cause, must have been uncaused. But it goes on to assert that man's intellect, being finite, is incapable of an understanding of the nature and attributes of the infinite. *Agnostic* comes from the Greek word *agnostos* "unknown." The altar which Paul spoke of in Acts was inscribed *Agnosto Theo,* "To an Unknown God."

A·GOR′A

The Greek word for marketplace (Acts 16:19; 17:5).

AG′RA·PHA *(not written)*

A term applied to things reportedly said by Jesus which are not recorded in the Gospels. While John 21:25 distinctly says that Jesus said many things not recorded in Scripture, and Acts 20:35 refers to something that Jesus said which is not in any of the Gospels, outside of the New Testament there are no trustworthy sources of information about Jesus's life and teachings. Many manuscripts exist which claim to report the life of Christ, but none other than the Gospels pass the tests of authenticity.

AG′RI·CUL′TURE

The cultivation of the soil; from the Greek word *agros*, "field." Because farming the land has until recently always gone hand in hand with raising animals either for food or labor, the word "agriculture" can also include animal husbandry. In the Scriptures the farmer is often called a *husbandman*. One might say that agriculture was the first God ordained occupation for humans. Adam was placed in the garden of Eden to care for it (Ge 2:15). The soil was cultivated by Cain (Ge 4:2). Noah planted a vineyard and Isaac sowed (Ge 9:20; 26:12). When the Israelites entered Egypt, they found the people engaged in raising and exporting cereals (Ge 41:49, 57; 43:2). In Israel, such agricultural products as corn, wine, olives, barley, wheat, vines, figs and pomegranates are mentioned (Ge 27:37; Ex 9:31-32; De 6:11). Ezekiel mentions lentils, beans and millet (Eze 4:9). Implements included plows, drawn by oxen, pruning hooks and sickles (De 16:9; 1 Ki 19:19; Is 2:4; 18:5; Joel 3:10; Mi 4:3). The Hebrews were devoted to their soil and flocks and, prior to the time of Solomon, did not engage in commercial activities. The law required that the land be permitted to lay fallow in the Jubilee Year (Ex 23:10-11; Le 25:11).

It is difficult to know exactly what the agricultural calendar of ancient Israel was really like. It seems that the early rains began in October, when people would begin sowing crops to grow throughout the rainy season, which lasted until the latter rains in April. Harvesting would mostly be over by the end of August and September.

A·GRIP′PA

See HEROD.

AGRICULTURE IN ISRAEL

AGUE (archaic)

A fever of the malaria type, with chills, shaking, and sweating (Le 26:16).

A′GUR *(hired* or *gatherer)*

Son of Jakeh who uttered the wisdom in Proverbs 30.

A′HAB *(a father's brother)*

Two Old Testament men:

1. A king of Israel, the son of Omri. His reign began during the closing years of King Asa of Judah (1 Ki 16:29). Idolatry was already established when Ahab came to the throne but it became more widespread, largely because of his wife, Jezebel (1 Ki 16:30-33). Elijah condemned Ahab and Baalism, predicting drought (1 Ki 17:1; Jam 5:17), and at Mt. Carmel called on the Lord to bring down miraculous fire on his sacrifice (1 Ki 18:36). Shalmaneser, king of Assyria invaded Israel, defeating Ahab and his ally, Ben–hadad of Damascus. He was slain in his attempt to recover Ramoth–gilead (1 Ki 16:29–22:40).

2. A prophet, the son of Kolaiah (Je 29:21-23).

A·HAR′AH

Third son of Benjamin (1 Ch 8:1), called Ehi in Genesis 46:21 and Ahiram in Numbers 26:38.

A·HAR′HEL

Son of Harum (1 Ch 4:8).

A·HA′SAI, AH′ZAI

A priest of the family of Immer whose descendants dwelt at Jerusalem after the captivity (Ne 11:13), possibly the same as Jahzerah (1 Ch 9:12).

A·HAS′BAI

A Maachathite, father of Eliphelet, one of David's warriors (2 Sa 23:34).

A·HASH·VE′ROSH

A form of AHASUERUS (Ez 4:6).

A·HAS·U·E′RUS *(mighty man, king)*

Two nobles of the Medo-Persian Empire:

1. Father of Darius the Mede (Da 9:1).

2. A Persian king who deposed his queen and replaced her with Esther, a beautiful Jewess (Es 1:19; 2:17). The events of the Book of Esther are represented as occurring between the first and second expeditions from Babylon, 536-458 B.C. Ahasuerus is almost certainly the Persian king known to the Greeks as Xerxes. He was a grandson of Cyrus and ascended the throne in 486 B.C.

A·HA′VA

A river beside which Ezra gathered the company that returned with him to Jerusalem on the second expedition (Ez 8:15,31). It was probably north of Babylon.

A′HAZ, A′CHAZ

Two Old Testament men:

1. The son of Jotham and twelfth ruler on the throne of Judah. His idolatry was most degrading. He sacrificed his son and established false worship in the high places (2 Ki 16:3-4). When King Rezin of Syria and King Pekah of Israel conspired against him, Isaiah admonished him to place his trust in the Lord and then uttered his great messianic prophecy of the virgin birth of our Lord (Is 7:1-16). Ahaz secured the aid of King Tiglath–pileser of Assyria, for which he gave him the treasures of the temple and palace. Rezin and Pekah were slain, Damascus taken and, when Ahaz visited this city he saw a pagan altar which he later duplicated at Jerusalem. During his reign, Isaiah and Micah prophesied in Judah and Hosea in Israel. His death found the kingdom in a sad state of spiritual decline but Hezekiah, his son, made many corrections.

2. A Benjamite, descendant of Jonathan, son of Saul (1 Ch 8:35-36; 9:42).

A′HAZ, DIAL OF

See DIAL OF AHAZ.

A·HA·ZI′AH *(the Lord has seized)*

Two Old Testament kings:

1. King of Israel, son and successor of Ahab (1 Ki 22:51-53; 2 Ki 1:2-4).

2. King of Judah, grandson of Ahab and Jezebel. He is best known for his violent death at the hands of Jehu who later became king (2 Ki 9:27-28).

AH′BAN

A man of Judah of the family of Hezron (1 Ch 2:29).

A′HER *(another)*

A Benjamite (1 Ch 7:12), probably to be identified with Ahiram.

A′HI *(brother of Jehovah)*

Two Old Testament men:

1. A Gadite chief in Gilead, the son of Abdiel (1 Ch 5:15).

2. A chief of the tribe of Asher, the son of Shamer (1 Ch 7:34).

A·HI′AH

See AHIJAH.

A·HI′AM

A son of Sharar, the Hararite, one of David's warriors (2 Sa 23:33; 1 Ch 11:35).

A·HI′AN *(brotherly)*

One of the four sons of Shemidah who was a member of the tribe of Manasseh (1 Ch 7:19).

A·HI·E′ZER *(brother of help)*

Two Old Testament men:

1. A chief of the tribe of Dan, the son of Ammishaddai (Nu 1:12; 2:25; 7:66).

2. A Benjamite chief who allied himself with David at Ziklag (1 Ch 12:3).

A·HI′HUD *(brother of renown)*

Two Old Testament men:

1. The prince who represented the tribe of Asher when the land was divided (Nu 34:27).

2. A descendant of Bela of Benjamin (1 Ch 8:7).

A·HI′JAH, A·HI′AH *(Jehovah is a brother)*

Nine Old Testament men:

1. A descendant of Jerahmeel (1 Ch 2:25).

2. One who aided in carrying away the people of Geba (1 Ch 8:7).

3. A high priest, the son of Ahitub and grandson of Eli (1 Sa 14:3,18).

4. A mighty man of David, a Pelonite (1 Ch 11:36).

5. A Levite who had charge of the sacred treasures (1 Ch 26:20).

6. A scribe (1 Ki 4:3).

7. The Shilonite prophet who announced to Jeroboam the division of the kingdom (1 Ki 11:29-39). He denounced the sins of Jeroboam and announced that his child would die (1 Ki 14:1-18).

8. Father of Baasha (1 Ki 15:27,33).
9. One who sealed the covenant (Ne 10:26).

A·HI′ KAM *(a brother has appeared)*

An official of Judah (2 Ki 22:12). When Jeremiah's life was threatened by false prophets and priests, he was protected by Ahikam (Je 26:24).

A·HI′ LUD *(brother of one born)*

Father of Jehoshaphat. The latter was David's and Solomon's recorder (2 Sa 8:16; 20:24; 1 Ki 4:3). It is quite likely that this Alihud was also the father of Baana, a purveyor of Solomon (1 Ki 4:12).

A·HI′ MA·AZ *(brother of anger)*

Three Old Testament men:
1. Father of Ahinoam, Saul's wife (1 Sa 14:50).
2. Son of Zadok and supporter of David during Absalom's rebellion, who carried to David the news of Joab's victory (2 Sa 15:27,36; 17:20; 18:19-30).
3. Solomon's purveyor in Naphtali who married Basmath, Solomon's daughter (1 Ki 4:15).

A·HI′ MAN *(brother is a gift)*

Two Old Testament men:
1. Son of Anak (Nu 13:22).
2. A Levite porter of the sanctuary (1 Ch 9:17).

A·HIM′ E·LECH *(brother of a king)*

Two Old Testament men:
1. Son of Ahitub, the chief priest at Nob. He was slain by Saul for befriending David when the latter fled from Saul. David gave him to understand that he was performing a duty for the king, and being in need of food, was given the showbread (1 Sa 21:1-9; Ma 12:4). Doeg, the Edomite, reported the matter, and Saul, assuming that the priests were disloyal, ordered them slain. Abiathar, son of Ahimelech, escaped (1 Sa 21:7; 22:7-23). Many believe that the names Abiathar and Ahimelech have been interchanged in 2 Samuel 8:17 and that Ahimelech is intended in Mark 2:26.
2. A follower of David, a Hittite (1 Sa 26:6).

A·HI′ MOTH *(brother of death)*

Son of Elkanah, a Levite, and descendant of Kohath (1 Ch 6:25).

A·HIN′ A·DAB *(liberal brother)*

A purveyor of Solomon in Mahanaim (1 Ki 4:14).

A·HIN′ O·AM *(pleasant brother)*

Two Old Testament women:
1. Daughter of Ahimaaz (1 Sa 14:50).
2. A wife of David (1 Sa 25:43), captured by the Amalekites at Ziklag (1 Sa 30:5).

A·HI′ O *(brotherly)*

Three Old Testament men:
1. A son of Abinadab who, with his brother, Uzzah, drove the cart that brought the ark to Jerusalem (2 Sa 6:3-4).
2. A Benjamite, son of Jehiel (1 Ch 8:29,31; 9:35,37).
3. A Benjamite, son of Elpaal (1 Ch 8:14).

A·HI′ RA *(brother of evil)*

The head of the tribe of Naphtali in the wilderness (Nu 1:15; 7:78; 10:27).

A·HI′ RAM *(exalted brother)*

A founder of a family of the tribe of Benjamin (Nu 26:38), probably the same as Ehi (Ge 46:21) and Aharah (1 Ch 8:1).

A·HI′ RAM·ITES

Descendants of Ahiram (Nu 26:38).

A·HIS′ A·MACH *(brother of support)*

The father of Aholiab (Ex 31:6).

A·HI′ SHA·HAR *(brother of the dawn—early)*

A son of Bilhan, a Benjamite (1 Ch 7:10).

A·HI′ SHAR *(brother of a singer)*

In a list of "princes" he is named as controller of Solomon's household (1 Ki 4:6), a position of importance.

A·HITH′ O·PHEL *(foolish brother)*

A counselor of David who lived in Giloh (2 Sa 15:12). At the time of Absalom's rebellion he deserted David but when he saw that the rebellion would be crushed, committed suicide, thus winning the title *Judas of the Old Testament* (2 Sa 15:12,31-34; 16:15; 17:23). He may have been the grandfather of Bath-sheba (2 Sa 11:3; 23:34).

A·HI′ TUB *(brother of goodness)*

Three Old Testament men:
1. Son of Phinehas, grandson of Eli, and father of Ahimelech, the priest (1 Sa 14:3; 22:9).
2. Son of Amariah and father of Zadok, the priest (2 Sa 8:17).

3. Grandfather of another Zadok (1 Ch 6:11-12; Ne 11:11).

AH′ LAB *(fertile place)*

A town of the tribe of Asher from which the Canaanites were not expelled (Ju 1:31).

AH′ LA·I

A man and a woman of the Old Testament:
1. Apparently the daughter of Sheahan the Judahite who became the wife of her father's Egyptian slave (1 Ch 2:31,34-35).
2. The father of one of David's warriors (1 Ch 11:41).

A·HO′ AH

The son of Bela, the son of Benjamin (1 Ch 8:4), called Ahiah (1 Ch 8:7).

A·HO′ HI

See AHOHITE.

A·HO′ HITE

A descendant of Ahoah (2 Sa 23:9,28).

A·HO′ LAH *(her tent)*

The harlot who was made a symbol of Samaria (Eze 23:4-5,36,44).

A·HO′ LI·AB *(tent of his father)*

A Danite, son of Ahisamach. He and Bezaleel had the supervision of the construction of the tabernacle (Ex 31:6; 35:34; 38:23).

A·HOL′ I·BAH *(my tent is in her)*

The harlot who was made a symbol of Judah (Eze 23:1-49).

A·HOL·I·BA′ MAH *(tent of the height)*

A man and a woman of the Old Testament:
1. The granddaughter of Zibeon the Hittite and one of the wives of Esau (Ge 36:2). In Genesis 26:34 she is called Judith, the daughter of Beeri the Hittite. Possibly Judith was her original name and Aholibamah one she assumed after marriage to Esau.
2. A duke who descended from Esau (Ge 36:41).

A·HU′ MAI *(brother of water)*

A man of Judah and son of Jahath (1 Ch 4:2).

A·HU′ ZAM, A·HUZ′ ZAM

Son of Ashur of Judah. His mother was Naarah (1 Ch 4:5-6).

A·HUZ′ ZATH *(possession)*

A friend of Abimelech of Gerar (Ge 26:26).

AH′ ZAI, A·HA′ SAI

A priest (Ne 11:13).

A′ I, HA′ I *(heap of ruins)*

1. A town in the territory of Benjamin, east of Beth–el (Jos 7:2; 8:11). Following the destruction of Jericho, Joshua attacked Ai and was defeated. This caused great consternation until the Lord told Joshua that there was sin in the camp—the sin of Achan. Achan was punished and a second attack was successful (Jos 7; 8). At Jericho the Israelites learned the lesson of faith and at Ai the lesson of obedience. Abraham encamped near this city (Ge 12:8; 13:3).
2. A city of the Ammonites (Je 49:3).

AI′ AH, A′ JAH *(vulture)*

Two Old Testament men:
1. Son of Zibeon, a Horite (Ge 36:24; 1 Ch 1:40).
2. The father of Saul's concubine, Rizpah (2 Sa 3:7; 21:8-11).

AI′ ATH

The feminine form of Ai. It is probably the same as Ai, a town near Beth–el (Is 10:28).

AI′ JA

A town mentioned as near Beth–el, hence doubtless Ai (Ne 11:31).

AI′ JA·LON, AJ′ A·LON *(place of harts)*

Three geographical locations in the Old Testament land of Israel:
1. A valley in Dan over which the moon stood still at the command of Joshua in battle with the five kings of the Amorites (Jos 10:12).
2. A Levitical city of the Kohathites near the Valley of Aijalon (Jos 21:20,24; 1 Ch 6:69). When the kingdom was divided, it became part of Benjamin (1 Ch 8:13; 2 Ch 11:10) and was taken by the Philistines in the reign of King Ahaz (2 Ch 28:18).
3. A place in Zebulun where Elon, the judge, was buried (Ju 12:12).

AI′ JE·LETH SHA′ HAR,
 AI′ JE·LETH-HASH·SHA′ HAR
 (hind of the morning)

An expression in the title of Psalm 22, indicating probably the tune to which the psalm was set.

A′ IN *(eye or spring)*

Two geographical locations in the Old Testament land of Israel:

1. A place west of Riblah, perhaps near the source of the Orontes (Nu 34:11).

2. A town near Rimmon in Judah (Jos 15:32), transferred to Simeon and made a priestly city (Jos 19:7; 21:16).

AIR

The region of the atmosphere (Ac 22:23). Satan is called the ruler of the powers of the air (Ep 2:2), for, according to Jewish tradition, the air is inhabited by demons. The air which surrounds the earth is often called *heaven* (2 Sa 21:10).

A′ JAH

See AIAH.

AJ′ A·LON

See AIJALON.

A′ KAN

See JAAKAN.

A·KEL′ DA·MA, A·CEL′ DA·MA *(field of blood)*

A small field near Jerusalem purchased by the priests with the thirty pieces of silver thrown away by Judas. It is called the potter's field and the field of blood because it was here that Judas hanged himself. Traditionally, it is located on the southern side of the Valley of Hinnom (Ma 27:7-8; Ac 1:18-19).

AK′ KAD

See ACCAD.

AK′ KUB *(cunning)*

Four Old Testament men:

1. Son of Elioenai of the family of David (1 Ch 3:23-24).

2. A Levite who founded a family of temple porters (Ez 2:42; Ne 12:25).

3. The head of a family of Nethinim (Ez 2:45).

4. A Levite, appointed by Ezra to instruct the people (Ne 8:7).

AK·RAB′ BIM

An ascent near the southern point of the Dead Sea, east of Beer–sheba, north of the desert of Zin; also called Maaleh–acrabbim (Nu 34:4; Jos 15:3).

AL′ A·BAS′ TER

A name possibly derived from a place in Egypt called Alabastrum or Alabastron where small vessels for perfumes were made. Modern alabaster is a form of gypsum or sulphate of lime, but Oriental alabaster was carbonate of lime. This white stone was much used in antiquity in the ornamentation of buildings, and was the expensive material out of which vases and bottles for the holding of precious ointments were made. The box that contained the perfume used in the anointing of Jesus at Bethany was of alabaster (Ma 26:7; Mk 14:3).

AL′ A·METH

See ALEMETH.

A·LAM′ MME·LECH

See ALLAMELECH.

AL′ A·MOTH *(maidens)*

A musical term (1 Ch 15:20; Ps 46, title). It may refer to soprano voices.

ALARM

(Nu 10:1-10; Je 4:19)

AL′ E·METH, AL′ A·METH *(covering)*

Two men and a town of Old Testament Israel:

1. A Benjamite, descendant of Becher (1 Ch 7:8).

2. The grandson of Ahaz, a descendant of Saul (1 Ch 8:36; 9:42).

3. A town (1 Ch 6:60). See ALMON.

A′ LEPH

The first letter of the Hebrew alphabet. It is the heading of verses 1-8 of Psalm 119; in Hebrew each of these eight verses began with the letter aleph. See also ACROSTIC.

AL·EX·AN′ DER *(defending men)*

1. Alexander the Great, who followed his father, Philip, as king of Macedonia in 336 B.C. In his youth he was a pupil of Aristotle. He conquered all of the eastern world in thirteen years. According to Josephus, though questioned by many scholars, Alexander entered Jerusalem but was generous toward the Jews and extended many privileges to them in his newly founded city of Alexandria in Egypt. At the age of 33 Alexander died in Babylon (323 B.C.) and his vast empire was divided between his four generals, each taking the title of king—Ptolemy in Egypt, Seleucus in Syria, Antipater in Macedonia, and Philetaerus in Asia Minor. Palestine was annexed to Egypt and thus came under the rule of the Ptolemies and afterwards under the Syrian kings. Daniel 8 prophesies the story of Alexander in a vision.

2. A son of Simon of Cyrene. His father was compelled to carry the cross of Jesus (Mk 15:21).

3. A prominent person in Jerusalem at the time that John and Peter were brought before the authorities (Ac 4:6).

4. A man who was with Paul during the disturbance at Ephesus (Ac 19:33).

5. A convert to Christianity who renounced his faith and became a blasphemer. He was excommunicated by Paul (1 Ti 1:19-20).

AL·EX·AN′DRI·A

A city named after Alexander the Great who founded it in 332 B.C. Situated on the northern coast of Egypt west of the Nile, an advantageous site for commercial purposes, it was considered the second city of the Roman Empire and had a population of over half a million—Egyptians, Greeks, Jews and Romans. With its famous library of several hundred thousand volumes, founded by the Ptolemies, it was regarded as one of the greatest intellectual centers of the world. It was here that the Hebrew Scriptures were translated into Greek. Called the Septuagint (Version of the Seventy), it was begun in the reign of Ptolemy Lagos and finished in the reign of Ptolemy Philadelphus, about 285 B.C. Through close contact with the Greeks in this Hellenistic center, Judaism became affected by Greek philosophy. The Alexandrian Jews had a synagogue in Jerusalem which participated in the persecution of Stephen (Ac 2:10; 6:9) and Apollos, who labored at Corinth, was an Alexandrian Jew (Ac 18:24-25).

AL·EX·AN′DRI·ANS

Residents of the city of Alexandria (Ac 6:9).

AL′GUM, AL′MUG

Probably red sandalwood, a leguminous tree (belonging to the same botanical family as the pea and the acacia), with pea-like blossoms and hard, heavy, fine grained reddish wood. It grows in India, but it is different from the fragrant white sandalwood which is used in China and India to perfume houses. It was brought from Ophir by King Hiram of Tyre for making the pillars and musical instruments of Solomon's temple (1 Ki 10:11-12; 2 Ch 9:10-11).

A·LI′AH

See ALVAH.

AL′I·AN

See ALVAN.

ALIEN

A foreigner, a non-Hebrew. A sojourner of this sort did not have the same rights and privileges as the Israelites, but they were required to keep certain parts of the law (Ex 20:10; De 14:21; Job 19:15; Ps 69:8). See FOREIGNER.

AL·LAM′ME·LECH, A·LAM′ME·LECH
(perhaps *king's oak*)

A town of Asher (Jos 19:26).

AL′LE·GO′RY

A metaphor in which certain actions are described in terms of others. The Song of Solomon is regarded by many as an allegory where the love of the two lovers is designed to express the mutual love of Christ and his church. A true story may also be used in an allegorical sense, as Paul used the history of Abraham, Sarah, and the son of the promise (Ga 4:21-31). The events recorded really happened, but they are also a picture of the difference between a child of bondage (works) and the child of freedom (grace).

AL·LE·LU′IA, HAL·LE·LU′JAH *(praise ye the Lord)*

The Greek transliteration of the Hebrew *hallelujah*. See HALLELUJAH.

AL·LI′ANCE

In Scripture there are several accounts of alliances, treaties, covenants, and leagues between nations. Such an alliance was made by Abraham with some of the Canaanite princes (Ge 14:13) and there were alliances with the Philistines (Ge 21:22-24,32; 26:27). The Israelites were expressly forbidden to ally themselves with pagan nations (Le 18:3-4; 20:22-23). From the time of David through the period of the divided kingdom, alliances with other nations were frequent (2 Sa 5:11; 1 Ki 5:1-18; 2 Ki 16:5-7). The prophets denounced alliances with idolatrous people (Eze 16:23-34).

AL′LON (an oak)

A man and a place of the Old Testament:

1. A Simeonite, the son of Jedaiah (1 Ch 4:37).

2. A place listed among the cities of Naphtali (Jos 19:33).

AL′LON-BA•CHUTH,
AL′LON-BA•CUTH (oak of weeping)

The oak under which Deborah, the nurse of Rebekah, was buried (Ge 35:8).

ALMIGHTY

See GOD, NAMES OF.

AL•MO′DAD

The son of Joktan of the line of Shem and progenitor of an Arabian tribe (Ge 10:26; 1 Ch 1:20).

AL′MON (hidden)

A town of Benjamin (Jos 21:18), called Alemeth in 1 Chronicles 6:60. It is between Geba and Anathoth.

AL′MOND

A tree from the same botanical family as the peach, and resembling it in both form and fruit. It is found on Lebanon and Hermon and is the first to blossom in the spring. Jacob and his sons took almonds into Egypt (Ge 43:11). Aaron's rod budded, blossomed, and yielded almonds (Nu 17:8). Almond blossoms were the models for the cups on the stems of the golden candlestick (Ex 25:33-34). Jeremiah had a vision of the rod of an almond tree (Je 1:11) and in Ecclesiastes 12:5 almond is used to denote age. Genesis 30:37 mentions a hazel tree which many believe is actually the almond.

AL′MON-DIB•LA•THA′IM

One of the stations or encampments of the Israelites between Shittim and the Arnon (Nu 33:46).

ALMS

Money given to the poor and destitute, as a religious observance. God commanded His peo-

ALMONDS

ple to be generous to the needy (De 15:11). (See also Le 19:9-10; 23:22; De 24:19; 26:2-13; Ru 2:2; Job 31:17; Pr 10:2; 11:4; Es 9:22; Ps 112:9; Ac 9:36; 10:2; Ma 6:1-4; Lk 14:13; Ac 20:35; Ga 2:10; Ac 11:30; Ro 15:25-27; 1 Co 16:1-4.)

AL′MUG

See ALGUM.

AL′OES

Two very different plants of this name are mentioned in the Bible.

1. In the Old Testament, the word most probably refers to eaglewood, a large tree native to China and India with a fragrant oily wood, used for making perfume and incense. Its fragrance gives significance to Psalm 45:8; Proverbs 7:17; Song of Solomon 4:14. The lign aloe mentioned in Numbers 24:6 is thought to be the same tree.

2. Nicodemus brought aloes to anoint the body of Jesus (Jo 19:39). These were probably true aloes, a plant native to parts of Africa, but cultivated in various warm parts of the world. Aloes are members of the lily family, their flowers are yellow or red, the leaves are fleshy. The pulp of these fleshy, juicy leaves was used for medicinal purposes and also in embalming.

ALOOF (archaic)

At a distance, but within view (Ps 38:9-11).

A′LOTH, BE•A′LOTH (ascents)

Part of a district in northern Israel from which Solomon received supplies (1 Ki 4:16).

AL′PHA

The first letter of the Greek alphabet. It is derived from the Phoenician and corresponds to Aleph, the first letter of the Hebrew alphabet. The last letter of the Greek alphabet is Omega, hence the statement "I am Alpha and Omega," signifies that Christ is the beginning and the end of all things (Re 1:8,11; 21:6; 22:13).

AL′PHA·BET

The word is derived from the first two letters of the Greek alphabet—*Alpha, Beta.* Latin, the source of the English alphabet, was developed from the Greek alphabet, which came from the Phoenician. As early as the eighth century B.C. a common alphabet was used by the Phoenicians, Aramaeans, Moabites, and Hebrews. The divisions of Psalm 119 are marked by the 22 letters of the Hebrew alphabet.

AL·PHAE′US *(successor)*

Two New Testament men:

1. Husband of the Mary that stood by the cross of Jesus and father of James the Less and Joses (Ma 10:3; Mk 15:40). Through the comparison of the Gospels (Ma 27:56, Mk 3:18, and Lk 6:15), it has been ascertained that Mary, the wife of Cleophas and Mary, the mother of James the Less, were the same. Some have said that Mary, the wife of Cleophas, and the sister of Mary, the mother of Jesus, were the same person, but it is improbable that two sisters should have the same name. Hence it is assumed that Alphaeus was also called Cleophas.

2. Father of Levi who was later called Matthew, one of the apostles (Ma 9:9; Mk 2:14).

AL′TAR

An altar was a platform or elevated place on which a priest placed a sacrifice as an offering to God. The Hebrew word for altar means "a place of slaughter or sacrifice," but the altars of the Old Testament were not limited to sacrificial purposes. Sometimes an altar was built as a testimony of one's faith for future generations (Jos 22:26-29).

Altars of the Old Testament: The first altars were probably built of earth, or piles of stone, on which burnt offerings were placed. When Noah left the ark, he built an altar (Ge 8:20) and in the time of the patriarchs altars were made wherever the tents were pitched (Ge 12:7; 35:1,7).

When God spoke with Moses on the mountain and gave him the design of the tabernacle, everything pertaining to the altar was divinely specified. He was directed to make two altars: **1.** *The altar of burnt offering.* Ordinarily called simply *the altar,* it was square, small, and portable—five cubits long, five cubits wide, and three cubits high. Its acacia wood frame was overlaid with brass and a horn projected from each corner (Ex 27:1-8). This altar stood in the outer court directly in front of the tabernacle. **2.** *The altar of incense.* This stood within the tabernacle in the holy place before the veil which separated the holy place from the holy of holies. It was a cubit square and two cubits high, was made of acacia wood and overlaid with gold (Ex 30:1-10,34-37; Le 16:18-19). These were the permanent altars on which sacrifices and incense could be offered according to the divine will (De 12:2-7). But in other places where God manifested himself altars could be raised and sacrifices offered, as in the case of Gideon and Manoah (Ju 6:20-25; 13:15-23).

As the first king of Israel, Saul built an altar during his conquest of the Philistines (1 Sa 14:35). King David of Judah erected an altar on the threshing floor (2 Sa 24:15-25). This site became the central place of sacrifice in Solomon's temple. After building the temple in Jerusalem, Solomon constructed an altar larger than the one David had built, probably adapting it to the size of the temple (2 Ch 4:1).

The Bible speaks frequently of pagan altars, particularly those associated with the false worship of the Canaanites. God gave specific instructions that pagan altars should be destroyed before altars dedicated to His worship were built (De 12:2-3). The New Testament also refers to the pagan altars in Athens, one of which was erected to an unknown god (Ac 17:23).

Altars of the New Testament: Worship in the early Christian church did not include an altar for sacrifices. The statement "We have an altar" (He 13:10) refers to the sacrifice of Christ. Christians have no need for an altar of burnt offerings because atonement for our sins is complete through the sacrificial death of Christ on the cross. We remember our personal acceptance of His sacrifice through participation in the Lord's Supper (also known as Communion, the Lord's table, and the Eucharist).

AL-TAS' CHITH, AL-TASH' HETH *(do not destroy)*

A word in the titles of Psalms 57, 58, 59, and 75, probably signifying the tune to which the psalms were to be sung.

A' LUSH

A place between Egypt and Sinai where Israel encamped during the wanderings in the wilderness (Nu 33:13-14).

AL' VAH, AL' I·AH

A chieftain of Edom, a descendant of Esau (Ge 36:40; 1 Ch 1:51).

AL' VAN, AL' I·AN *(high, tall)*

A son of Shobal (Ge 36:23; 1 Ch 1:40).

A' MAD *(station)*

A town near the border of Asher (Jos 19:26).

A' MAL *(sorrow)*

One of the four sons of Helem of the tribe of Asher (1 Ch 7:35).

AM' A·LEK

Son of Eliphaz by his concubine Timna and the grandson of Esau (Ge 36:12; Ex 17:8; 1 Ch 1:36).

A·MAL' EK·ITES

Descendants of Esau, a nomadic people, inhabiting the peninsula of Sinai and the wilderness between the southern portion of Palestine and Egypt (Ge 36:12; Nu 13:29; 1 Sa 15:7). About the time of the exodus they occupied the region near Kadesh-barnea. Israel's first battle was fought with these people at Rephidim on their way to Sinai. The Amalekites were defeated but in the next encounter, when the Israelites were at Kadesh, the Amalekites were victorious (Ex 17:8; Nu 14:45). In the time of the judges they were the ally of the Midianites when the latter invaded and oppressed Israel (Ju 3:13; 6:3,33). They suffered a crushing defeat by Saul (1 Sa 15), and were completely suppressed by David (1 Sa 27:8; 30:1-20).

A' MAM *(gathering-spot)*

A town in the southern section of Judah (Jos 15:26).

A·MA' NA *(fixed, established)*

A mountain where the Abana River has its source (2 Ki 5:12; Song 4:8). See also ABANA.

AM' A·RANTH

The name comes from the Greek word *amarantos* which means "unwithering," and is applied to various garden plants and weeds. The amaranth was associated with immortality. Peter uses this same word to describe the believer's inheritance in heaven (1 Pe 1:4; 5:4), as "unfading," something which will never wear out or grow old.

AM·A·RI' AH *(Jehovah hath said)*

Nine Old Testament men:

1. Son of Meraioth in the line of the high priests (1 Ch 6:7,52).

2. A priest, son of Azariah (1 Ch 6:11; Ez 7:3).

3. A Levite, a descendant of Kohath (1 Ch 23:19; 24:23).

4. A Levite appointed to distribute the freewill offerings (2 Ch 31:14-15).

5. A priest who accompanied Zerubbabel to Jerusalem (Ne 12:2,7).

6. A priest who sealed the covenant with Nehemiah (Ne 10:3).

7. A man who divorced his foreign wife (Ez 10:42).

8. A descendant of Judah through Pharez (Ne 11:4).

9. An ancestor of the prophet, Zephaniah (Zep 1:1).

A·MAR' NA

A city in Egypt, where important archeological discoveries have been made of large quantities of clay tablets containing letters from various kings of Canaan to the kings of Egypt, during the time of the Israelite invasion under Joshua. These documents provide insight into the culture of the Canaanites, as well as corroboration for the Old Testament stories.

A·MA' SA *(burden-bearer)*

Two Old Testament men:

1. A cousin of Joab and the son of Abigail, the half sister of David. He joined Absalom in his rebellion and was captain of his army (2 Sa 17:25). Later he served David as a captain (2 Sa 19:13). He was slain by Joab (2 Sa 20:1-13).

2. A prince of Ephraim and son of Hadlai. He opposed bringing into Samaria the prisoners whom Pekah of Israel had taken in his campaign against Ahaz (2 Ch 28:12).

A·MA′ SAI *(burdensome)*

1. A Kohathite ancestor of Heman, the singer (1 Ch 6:35).

2. A captain who joined David at Ziklag (1 Ch 12:18).

3. A priest who blew the trumpet when David brought the ark from the home of Obed-edom (1 Ch 15:24).

4. A Kohathite (2 Ch 29:12).

A·MA′ SHAI

The son of Azareel and a priest who lived in Jerusalem (Ne 11:13).

A·MA′ SHSAI

See AMASHAI.

AM·A·SI′ AH *(Jehovah hath borne)*

Son of Zichri, a military officer of high rank under Jehoshaphat of Judah (2 Ch 17:16).

AM·A·ZI′ AH *(Jehovah is strong)*

Four Old Testament men:

1. King of Judah, son of Joash, who took the reins of government when his father, on account of sickness, was unable to rule (2 Ki 14:1). After defeating the Edomites in the Valley of Salt, he brought back the idols of Edom and worshipped them. He was defeated by King Jehoash of Israel. A conspiracy was formed against him which caused him to flee but his life was ended by assassins (2 Ki 14:1-20; 2 Ch 25:1-27).

2. A Levite of the family of Merari (1 Ch 6:45).

3. A priest of Beth-el who brought charges against Amos (Am 7:10-17).

4. A Simeonite (1 Ch 4:34).

AMBASSADOR

The Hebrew words signify an *interpreter,* a *messenger.* When Hanun became king of the Amorites, David sent ambassadors to voice his congratulations (2 Sa 10:2). Similarly, Hiram, king of Tyre, sent ambassadors to Solomon when he succeeded David (1 Ki 5:1).

AM·BAS′ SAGE (archaic)

Delegation, embassy (Lk 14:32).

AM′ BER

True amber is fossilized resin from an extinct variety of pine tree which grew in the southeastern part of what is now the bed of the Baltic Sea. It ranges in color from pale yellow to deep brownish orange-gold. It can be highly polished, and was prized in ancient times as a gemstone. The prophet Ezekiel mentioned a brilliant substance which is translated as "amber" or "gleaming amber" in some versions, others translate the word as brass, metal or sapphire (Eze 1:4, 27; 8:2). Ezekiel was comparing this substance to the glory of God.

AMBITION, SELFISH

A spirit of self-service and strife which is incompatible with Christianity (2 Co 12:20; Ga 5:20).

A′ MEN *(steadfast, firm)*

The word *amen* comes from the ancient verb *aman* ("confirm," "support," "be established," "believe"). Many people are only familiar with *amen* as the last word of a prayer or choral anthem. It is also used as a way of expressing agreement with something that has been said, especially in church.

In one form of the Hebrew verb, used in a very important text, we read that Abraham "believed [a form of *aman*] in the LORD, and He accounted it to him for righteousness" (Ge 15:6). Someone has paraphrased this, "Abraham said *amen* to God, and He justified him." While not a literal rendering, it does express the truth of justification by faith. The New Testament uses Abraham as a figure representing salvation by grace through faith. He is the father of the faithful, not only of the Jews who believed God's word, but also of the Christians.

This also fits in with Hebrews 11, the great faith chapter, where faith is seen basically as a certainty, an established belief.

The popular word *amen* is derived from the verb *aman.* It means "verily," "truly," or "assuredly." Sometimes it is just transliterated from the Hebrew as *amen.* Our Christian usage of *amen* at the end of prayers and hymns has good Old Testament precedent to say the least. The five books of Psalms all end in *amens,* and the last psalm is itself an "amen" to the whole book.

After David's great psalm in 1 Chronicles 16:8-36 was delivered, "all the people said, 'Amen!'

and praised the LORD." A similar response is seen in Ezra's blessing of the Lord in Nehemiah 8:6.

Surprisingly, *amen* is used over twice as often in the New Testament as in the Old. In His letter to the lukewarm Laodiceans, Jesus called Himself "the Amen, the faithful and true witness" (Re 3:14). He meant, "You can count on Me to be firm and true!"

A usage of *amen* that is unique to our Lord shows up in the Greek text, the Latin Vulgate, and the old Douay-Rheims Version. Wherever Jesus prefaced His remarks with *verily* (KJV), *truly* (NASB), or *assuredly* (NKJV), the original reads *amen*. Twenty-five times in John it is a double *amen*. Jesus was saying that His following words were very important. The NKJV translates the double *amen* by "most assuredly," since repeating such a long word ("assuredly, assuredly") would sound odd.

A literal rendering of John 5:24 would read, "*Amen, amen,* I say to you, he who hears My word and believes in Him who sent Me has everlasting life, and shall not come into judgment, but has passed from death into life."

Those who believe this gracious promise can well respond: "Hallelujah! Amen!"

AM′ E·THYST

A glassy, clear quartz, violet-blue, nearly purple in color, a precious stone having a place in the high priest's breastplate as the third stone in the third row (Ex 28:19). In the New Jerusalem of Revelation 21:20 the twelfth foundation is adorned by this stone.

A′ MI

See AMON.

AMIABLE (archaic)

Dear; lovely; beloved (Ps 84:1-2).

A·MIN′ A·DAB

See AMMINADAB.

A·MIT′ TAI (true)

The father of Jonah, the prophet (2 Ki 14:25; Jon 1:1).

AM′ MAH (beginning)

A hill to which Joab and Abishai came (2 Sa 2:24).

AM′ MI (my people)

The name to be applied to Israel at the time of the restoration (Ho 2:1).

AM′ MI·EL (people of God)

Four Old Testament men:

1. The one who represented the tribe of Dan when the twelve spies were sent to Canaan from Kadesh-barnea (Nu 13:12).

2. The father of Machir (2 Sa 9:4-5; 17:27).

3. A son of Obed–edom (1 Ch 26:5).

4. The father of Bath–sheba, a wife of David and mother of Solomon (1 Ch 3:5).

AM′ MI·HUD (kinsman of praiseworthiness)

Five Old Testament men:

1. An Ephraimite, father of Elishama (Nu 1:10).

2. A Simeonite, father of Shemuel (Nu 34:20).

3. A man of Naphtali, father of Pedahel (Nu 34:28).

4. Father of Talmai, king of Geshur. To him Absalom fled after slaying his brother (2 Sa 13:37).

5. A man of Judah, a descendant of Pharez (1 Ch 9:4).

AM·MIN′ A·DAB, A·MIN′ A·DAB

Three Old Testament men:

1. Father of Nahshon (Nu 1:7; 2:3; Ma 1:4), an ancestor of David (Ru 4:19-20; 1 Ch 2:10). He was probably the Amminadab whose daughter was the wife of Aaron (Ex 6:23).

2. A Levite, the son of Kohath (1 Ch 6:22).

3. A Levite who was one of those appointed by David to bring the ark to Jerusalem (1 Ch 15:10-11).

AM·MI′ NA·DIB (the people are generous)

An expression which is not to be regarded as a proper name, but is translated literally *the chariots of my willing and noble people* (Song 6:12).

AM·MI·SHAD′ DAI (the Almighty, an ally)

The father of Ahiezer, a Danite (Nu 1:12; 2:25).

AM·MI′ ZA·BAD (people of endowment)

A son of Benaiah and one of David's warriors (1 Ch 27:6).

AM′MON

Another form of Ben-ammi. He was Lot's younger son and became the ancestor of the Ammonites (Ge 19:38).

AM′MON·ITES

A Semitic people located east of the Jordan between the land of Moab and the river Jabbok, represented as descendants of Ben-ammi, a son of Lot (Ge 19:38). It appears that they had not been long in this land when Israel captured Jericho. Through the following centuries they had many clashes with the Hebrews, notably in the time of Jephthah (Ju 11:4-33) and David (2 Sa 10:6-14; 12:26-31). After the exile they became an object of hatred for their alleged participation in the destruction of the kingdom (Eze 25:1-7). They obstructed the rebuilding of the walls of Jerusalem (Ne 4:3,7).

AM′MON·IT·ESS

An Ammonite woman. Solomon's wife Naamah, the mother of Rehoboam was an Ammonitess (1 Ki 14:21), as was Shimeath, the mother of Zabad (2 Ch 24:26).

AM′NON (faithful)

Two Old Testament men:

1. Son of David and Ahinoam, born while David was ruling over Judah at the beginning of his reign. He was murdered by Absalom because of his disgraceful treatment of Tamar, Absalom's half sister (2 Sa 13).

2. Son of Shimon of the family of Caleb (1 Ch 4:20).

A′MOK (deep)

One of the priests who came with Zerubbabel from Babylon (Ne 12:7).

A′MON (workman)

1. Son of Manasseh and a king of Judah whose reign was characterized by idolatry. He was murdered by his servants (2 Ki 21:19-26).

2. Governor of the city of Samaria (1 Ki 22:26).

3. A descendant of one of Solomon's servants (Ne 7:59), called Ami in Ez 2:7.

AM′O·RITES (mountaineers)

A powerful Semitic people who inhabited Canaan prior to the conquest of Joshua (Ge 15:21; Ex 3:8). In the time of Abraham they held a strong position in the hill country and the name was applied to the inhabitants of that region (Ge 15:16) but, later, to the inhabitants of all Canaan in general (Jos 7:7; Ju 6:10). Prior to the exodus they conquered districts east of the Jordan (Nu 21:26-30). They seized the land from the Arnon to Hermon (Jos 2:10; 9:10; Ju 11:22) and were settled between Jerusalem and Hebron and westward to the Shephelah and to the territory of Ephraim in the north (Jos 10:5-6; 11:3; Ju 1:35). They were not completely expelled by Joshua (Ju 1:35; 3:5) and became a test of the loyalty of Israel to the Lord.

A′MOS (burden-bearer)

Two men bear this name:

1. One of the twelve Minor Prophets. In the reign of Jeroboam II he appeared at Beth–el where Jeroboam I had set up the golden calves. His zeal in denouncing the sins of Israel led Amaziah, the priest at Beth–el, to declare to the king that Amos was guilty of conspiracy and a menace to the kingdom. See "The Author of Amos" under AMOS, BOOK OF.

2. An ancestor of Jesus (Lk 3:25).

A′MOS, BOOK OF

1. The Book of Amos. Amos prophesied during a period of national optimism in Israel. Business was booming and boundaries were bulging. But below the surface, greed and injustice were festering. Hypocritical religious motions replaced true worship, creating a false sense of security and a growing callousness to God's disciplining hand. Famine, drought, plagues, death, destruction—nothing could force the people to their knees.

Amos, the farmer-turned-prophet, lashed out unflinchingly at sin, trying to visualize the nearness of God's judgment and mobilize the nation to repentance. The nation, like a basket of rotting fruit, stood ripe for judgment because of its hypocrisy and spiritual indifference.

The name Amos is derived from the Hebrew root amas, "to lift a burden, to carry." Thus, his name means "Burden" or "Burden-Bearer." Amos lived up to the meaning of his name by bearing up under his divinely given burden of declaring judgment to rebellious Israel. The Greek and Latin titles are both transliterated in English as Amos.

2. The Author of Amos. The only Old Testament appearance of the name Amos is in this book. (He should not be confused with Amoz, the father of Isaiah). Concerning his background, Amos said, "I was no prophet, nor was I a son of a prophet, but I was a herdsman and tender of sycamore fruit" (7:14). Nevertheless, he was gripped by God and divinely commissioned to bring his prophetic burden to Israel (3:8; 7:15). He came from the rural area of Tekoa in Judah, twelve miles south of Jerusalem, where he tended a special breed of small sheep that produced wool of the best quality. As a grower of sycamore figs, he had to puncture the fruit before it ripened to allow the insects inside to escape. Amos lived a disciplined life, and his knowledge of the wilderness often surfaces in his messages (3:4-5,12; 5:8,19; 9:9). Amos was from the country, but he was well-educated in the Scriptures. His keen sense of morality and justice is obvious and his objective appraisal of Israel's spiritual condition was not well received, especially since he was from Judah. He delivered his message in Beth-el because it was the residence of the king of Israel and a center of idolatry. His frontal attack on the greed, injustice, and self-righteousness of the people of the northern kingdom made his words unpopular.

3. The Time of Amos. Amos prophesied "in the days of Uzziah king of Judah, and in the days of Jeroboam the son of Joash, king of Israel, two years before the earthquake" (1:1). Uzziah reigned from 767-739 B.C. and Jeroboam II reigned from 782-753 B.C., leaving an overlap from 767 to 753 B.C. The earthquake of Uzziah's reign was mentioned over two-hundred years later by Zechariah (Ze 14:5). Amos 7:11 anticipates the 722 B.C. Assyrian captivity of Israel, and indicates that at the time of writing Jeroboam II was not yet dead. Thus Amos prophesied in Beth-el about 755 B.C. Astronomical calculations indicate that a solar eclipse took place in Israel on June 15, 763 B.C. This event was probably fresh in the minds of Amos's hearers (8:9).

Amos ministered after the time of Obadiah, Joel, and Jonah, and just before Hosea, Micah, and Isaiah. During Amos's ministry, Uzziah reigned over a prosperous and militarily successful Judah. He fortified Jerusalem and subdued the Philistines, the Ammonites and the Edomites. In the north, Israel was ruled by the capable King Jeroboam II. Economic and military circumstances were almost ideal, but prosperity only increased the materialism, immorality

and injustice of the people (2:6-8; 3:10; 4:1; 5:10-12; 8:4-6). During these years, Assyria, Babylon, Syria and Egypt were relatively weak. Thus the people found it difficult to imagine the coming disaster predicted by Amos. However, it was only three decades until the downfall of Israel.

4. The Christ of Amos. The clearest anticipation of Christ in Amos is found at the end of the book. He has all authority to judge (1:1–9:10), but He will also restore His people (9:11-15).

5. Keys to Amos.

Key Word: The Judgment of Israel—The basic theme of Amos is the coming judgment of Israel because of the holiness of Yahweh and the sinfulness of His covenant people. Amos unflinchingly and relentlessly visualized the causes and course of Israel's quickly approaching doom. God is gracious and patient, but His justice and righteousness will not allow sin to go unpunished indefinitely. The sins of Israel were heaped as high as heaven: empty ritualism, oppression of the poor, idolatry, deceit, self-righteousness, arrogance, greed, materialism, and callousness. The people had repeatedly broken every aspect of their covenant relationship with God. Nevertheless, God's mercy and love are evident in His offer of deliverance if the people will only turn back to Him. God graciously sends Amos as a reformer to warn the people of Israel of their fate if they refuse to repent. But they reject his plea, and the course of judgment cannot be altered.

Key Verses: Amos 3:1-2; 8:11-12—"Hear this word that the LORD has spoken against you, O children of Israel, against the whole family which I brought up from the land of Egypt, saying: You only have I known of all the families of the earth; therefore I will punish you for all your iniquities" (3:1-2).

"'Behold, the days are coming,' says the Lord God, 'that I will send a famine on the land, not a famine of bread, nor a thirst for water, but of hearing the words of the LORD; they shall wander from sea to sea, and from north to east; they shall run to and fro, seeking the word of the LORD, but shall not find it'" (8:11-12).

Key Chapter: Amos 9—Set in the midst of the harsh judgments of Amos are some splendid prophecies of the restoration of Israel. Within the scope of just five verses the future of Israel becomes clear, and the Abrahamic, Davidic, and

Land covenants are focused on their climactic fulfillment in the return of the Messiah.

6. Survey of Amos. The basic theme of Amos is the coming judgment of Israel because of the holiness of God and the sinfulness of His covenant people. Unsurprisingly, Amos's earnest and forceful message against Israel's sins and abuses was not well received. The prophet of Israel's Indian summer presented a painfully clear message: "prepare to meet your God, O Israel" (4:12). The four divisions of Amos are: the eight prophecies (1:1–2:16), the three sermons (3:1–6:14), the five visions (7:1–9:10), and the five promises (9:11-15).

The Eight Prophecies (1:1–2:16): Amos is called by God to the unenviable task of leaving his homeland in Judah to preach a harsh message of judgment to Israel. Each of his eight oracles in chapters 1 and 2 begins with the statement "For three transgressions of . . . and for four." The fourth transgression is equivalent to the last straw; the iniquity of each of the eight countries is full. Amos begins with the nations that surround Israel as his catalog of catastrophes gradually spirals in on Israel herself. Seven times God declares, "I will send a fire" (1:4,7,10,12,14; 2:2,5), a symbol of judgment.

The Three Sermons (3:1–6:14): In these chapters, Amos delivers three sermons, each beginning with the phrase "Hear this word" (3:1; 4:1; 5:1). The first sermon (3) is a general pronouncement of judgment because of Israel's iniquities. The second sermon (4) exposes the crimes of the people and describes the ways God has chastened them in order to draw them back to Himself. Five times He says, "Yet you have not returned to Me" (4:6,8-11). The third sermon (5; 6) lists the sins of the house of Israel and calls the people to repent. But they hate integrity, justice and compassion, and their refusal to turn to God will lead to their exile. Although they arrogantly wallow in luxury, their time of prosperity will suddenly come to an end.

The Five Visions (7:1–9:10): Amos's three sermons are followed by five visions of coming judgment upon the Northern Kingdom. The first two judgments of locusts and fire do not come to pass because of Amos's intercession. The third vision of the plumb line is followed by the only narrative section of the book (7:10-17). Amaziah, the priest of Beth-el, wanted Amos to go back to Judah. The fourth vision pictures Israel as a basket of rotten fruit, overripe for judgment. The fifth vision is a relentless portrayal of Israel's unavoidable judgment.

The Five Promises (9:11-15): Amos has hammered upon the theme of divine retribution with oracles, sermons, and visions. Nevertheless, he ends his book on a note of consolation, not condemnation. God promises to reinstate the Davidic line, to renew the land and to restore the people.

OUTLINE OF AMOS

I. Introduction to Amos (1:1-2)

II. The Eight Judgments (1:3–2:16)

A. Judgments on Damascus 1:3-5
B. Judgment on Gaza 1:6-8
C. Judgment on Tyre....................... 1:9-10
D. Judgment on Edom 1:11-12
E. Judgment on Ammon 1:13-15
F. Judgment on Moab 2:1-3
G. Judgment on Judah 2:4-5
H. Judgment on Israel 2:6-16

III. The Three Sermons of Judgment (3:1–6:14)

A. The First Sermon: Israel's
   Present.................................... 3:1-15

B. The Second Sermon: Israel's Past ... 4:1-13
C. The Third Sermon: Israel's
   Future 5:1–6:14

IV. The Five Visions of Judgment (7:1–9:10)

A. Vision of the Locusts 7:1-3
B. Vision of the Fire 7:4-6
C. Vision of the Plumb Line.............. 7:7-9
D. Opposition of Amaziah (Historical
   Parenthesis) 7:10-17
E. Vision of the Summer Fruit 8:1-14
F. Vision of the Stricken Doorposts ... 9:1-10

V. The Five Promises of the Restoration of Israel (9:11-15)

A'MOZ (strong)

Father of Isaiah (Is 1:1; 13:1; 38:1). Jewish tradition says that Amoz was also a prophet, and the brother of Amaziah, king of Judah.

AM·PHIP'O·LIS (about the city)

An important city of Macedonia. Deriving its name from the fact that it was almost surrounded by the Strymon River, it was founded in the fifth century B.C. Paul and Silas passed through it as they were traveling from Philippi to Thessalonica. It was about thirty miles southwest of Philippi (Ac 17:1).

AM'PLI·AS (enlarged)

A Christian of the church at Rome (Ro 16:8).

AMP·LI·A'TUS

A form of AMPLIUS.

AM'RAM (exalted people)

Three Old Testament men:

1. Son of Kohath of the tribe of Levi, the husband of Jochebed and father of Moses, Aaron and Miriam. He died at the age of 137 years (Ex 6:20). The Amramites were strong in number in the time of Moses (Nu 3:17,19,27).

2. A son of Bani, who put away his foreign wife (Ez 10:34).

3. Another spelling for the name Hamran, one of the descendants of Esau (1 Ch 1:41). In Genesis 36:26, he appears as Hemdan.

AM'RAM·ITES

Descendants of Amram (Nu 3:27; 1 Ch 26:23), a branch of the Kohathite family of priests.

AM·RA'PHEL

King of Shinar and ally of Chedorlaomer in the invasion of Palestine when Lot was taken prisoner (Ge 14:1,5,9). The name has often been identified with that of Ammurabi or Hammurabi, lawgiver, king, and founder of the old Babylonian Empire. Hammurabi conquered the Elamites, seized Larsa and brought all Babylon under his rule. He greatly improved and strengthened his country, built temples, and so contributed to the welfare of his people that he was called father to his people. His code of laws, known as the "Hammurabi Code," discovered in 1902, is the oldest code of laws that has come to light. It has attracted special attention because of its close resemblance to the Mosaic Code (Ex 20:23–23:33). Since Hammurabi was king of Babel about 1955 B.C., he must have antedated Moses by several centuries. The remarkable thing in this resemblance of the two codes is that the less fortunate members of society were regarded by both Babylonians and Israelites as possessing rights that could be recognized by the state. See HAMMURABI.

AM'U·LET

Anything worn that was believed to be a protection against accident, sickness, or other misfortunes. It might be a precious stone, gold, or a parchment bearing some inscription. Emblems of various deities were used by the Egyptians. The word amulet does not appear in the Authorized Version but "earring" is rendered amulet by the Revised Version in Is 3:20.

AM'ZI (strong)

Two Old Testament men:

1. A descendant of Merari of the tribe of Levi (1 Ch 6:46).

2. A priest of the course of Malchijah (Ne 11:12).

A'NAB (place of grapes)

A mountain town of Judah from which the Anakim were driven by Joshua (Jos 11:21; 15:50).

A'NAH (answering)

Two men and one woman in the Old Testament:

1. Daughter of Zibeon and mother of Esau's wife, Aholibamah (Ge 36:2,14).

2. Son of Zibeon who discovered the hot springs ("mules" in Authorized Version) in the wilderness (Ge 36:24; 1 Ch 1:40).

3. A Horite chief, the son of Seir (Ge 36:20; 1 Ch 1:38).

A·NA'HA·RATH (pass)

A town of Issachar (Jos 19:19).

A·NAI'AH (Jehovah hath answered)

Two Old Testament men:

1. One, perhaps a priest, who stood beside Ezra as he read the law to the people (Ne 8:4).

2. A Jew who signed the covenant (Ne 10:22).

A′ NAK *(long-necked)*

In Numbers 13:22,28 he appears to have been the founder of Kirjath-arba (Hebron) and ancestor of the race of giants called Anakim. The name usually denotes the Anakim collectively.

AN′ A·KIM

A race of giants, the descendants of Arba (Jos 15:13; 21:11). They are called the sons of Anak (Nu 13:22). The Israelites were terrified by them (Nu 13:28; De 9:2) but, under the leadership of Joshua, drove them out (Jos 10:36,39) and they settled in the country of the Philistines (Jos 11:21-22). Caleb expelled three families of them from Hebron (Jos 15:14).

AN′ A·MIM

Descendants of Mizraim (Ge 10:13; 1 Ch 1:11).

A·NAM′ ME·LECH *(Anu is king)*

One of the gods worshipped by the people who were brought into Samaria after the fall of Israel (2 Ki 17:31).

A′ NAN *(a cloud)*

One who sealed the covenant with Nehemiah (Ne 10:26).

A·NA′ NI

The seventh son of Elioenai, a descendant of Zerubbabel (1 Ch 3:24).

AN·A·NI′ AH *(Jehovah hath covered)*

Two Old Testament men:

1. An ancestor of Azariah who assisted Nehemiah in rebuilding the walls of Jerusalem (Ne 3:23).

2. A town of Benjamin between Nob and Hazer, believed to be the Old Testament name for Bethany (Ne 11:32).

AN·A·NI′ AS *(Jehovah is gracious)*

Three New Testament men:

1. The husband of Sapphira. He and his wife, Christian Jews of Jerusalem, held back from the common fund part of the price they received from the sale of property, while trying to give the impression that they had sacrificially given it all. Peter denounced the fraud and they were divinely smitten with death (Ac 5:1-11).

2. A high priest, appointed to office by Herod about A.D. 48. A few years later he was sent to Rome charged with mistreatment of the Samaritans but was cleared and returned to Jerusalem. Paul was tried before him and he was one of the Apostle's accusers before Felix (Ac 23:2; 24:1). Ananias was deposed and assassinated in A.D. 67.

3. A Jewish disciple at Damascus who aided in the conversion of Paul (Ac 9:10-18).

A′ NATH *(answer)*

Father of Shamgar, third judge of Israel; or possibly the town from which Shamgar came (Ju 3:31; 5:6).

A·NATH′ E·MA

The Greek equivalent of the Hebrew word signifying a person or thing devoted to destruction. The word in Paul's writings is usually translated *accursed*, which is explained as excommunication (Ro 9:3; 1 Co 12:3; Ga 1:8-9). *Anathema Maran-atha* apparently signified one accursed until the coming of the Lord (1 Co 16:22).

AN′ A·THOTH *(answers)*

A city and two men of the Old Testament:

1. A city of priests in the territory of Benjamin (Jos 21:18; 1 Ch 6:60). It is two and one-half miles northeast of Jerusalem and is now called Anata. Abiathar lived here (1 Ki 2:26) and it was the native city of Jeremiah (Je 1:1; 11:21).

2. A son of Becher (1 Ch 7:8).

3. A chief who signed the covenant with Nehemiah (Ne 10:19).

AN′ A·THOTH·ITE

One who lives in or comes from Anathoth (2 Sa 23:27; 1 Ch 27:12).

ANCESTOR WORSHIP

The deification of one's dead progenitors. In various cultures around the world, people pray to their ancestors, offer sacrifices to them, and try to enhance their experience in the afterlife. The Hebrews were forbidden to do such things (Le 19:28; De 14:1; 26:14).

AN′ CHOR

A heavy object on a rope or chain, thrown overboard to keep a boat from drifting in deep water. The Greeks used large stones for anchors and the Romans used iron anchors. The passage in Acts 27:29-40 indicates that two anchors were used, one at the bow and the other at the stern. In a spiritual sense, an anchor is symbolic of the power of hope in Christ, as something which will keep a person steady and even keeled in spite of the many insecurities of life (He 6:19).

ANCIENT OF DAYS

One of the names of God, used by Daniel to describe God sitting on His throne to judge the world (Da 7:9,13,22). The name emphasizes the fact that God has been here since before time began; He has seen all that has ever happened on this earth. See GOD, NAMES OF.

ANCIENTS

See ELDER.

AN′DREW (manliness)

One of the twelve apostles (Ma 4:18; Jo 1:40) and brother of Simon Peter. Both he and Peter were fishermen and lived at Bethsaida beside the Sea of Galilee (Mk 1:16-18). He brought Peter to Jesus (Jo 1:35-42) and was made an apostle (Ma 10:2; Mk 3:18). According to tradition he preached the Gospel in Greece and died a martyr in Achaia.

AN·DRO·NI′CUS (man conquering)

A Christian at Rome (Ro 16:7).

A′NEM (two fountains)

A town of Issachar assigned to the sons of Gershom (1 Ch 6:73).

A′NER

Two Old Testament men:
1. A town of Manasseh west of the Jordan (1 Ch 6:70).
2. An Amorite ally of Abraham in his conflict with Chedorlaomer (Ge 14:13-14).

AN·E·THO′THITE, AN·E·TO′THITE

An inhabitant of Anathoth (2 Sa 23:27; 1 Ch 27:12).

AN′GEL (messenger)

An order of created beings, superior to man, employed in the service of God (Ps 8:5; He 1:14; 2:7). Angels have or at least can take on some sort of body. We are told "Do not forget to entertain strangers, for by so doing some have unwittingly entertained angels unawares" (He 13:2). Scripture records different orders of angels as indicated by the expressions archangel and chief angel (Da 8:16; 9:21; 10:13,21; 12:1; Lk 1:19,26), as well as different kinds of angelic beings such as cherubim and seraphim, and the four living creatures of Revelation 4:7-8. Angels appear to be organized—Jesus said that he could call on twelve legions of angels to rescue him.

Most people would be amazed to learn that some church fathers believed that the last book of the Old Testament was written by an angel. This idea was started partly because Malachi names no father or grandfather, as most prophets do. But no doubt it was mostly due to his name. *Malachi* means "my messenger," the Hebrew word for "messenger" being *mal'ak*. But this is also the standard word for an angel, a messenger of God. The double meaning also exists in the Greek word *angelos*, "messenger," from which our English word "angel" is derived.

Angel, Messenger (mal'âk): Mal'ak is used of both humans and angels, and suggests an envoy with a commission; not only carrying a message, though this is the primary function (Ze 1:9; 5:5).

The effect of traditional art on most people's concept of angels is most unfortunate. They are usually portrayed as pale delicate young men or women, with golden curls, snowy robes, and feathered wings like a dove's. The picture that Scripture paints of angels is far different. The messengers from God who were sent to speak to humans are usually described as looking like men (Ge 18:16; 19:1-2). They are not described as having wings, as are the cherubim. Furthermore, when an angel appears in Scripture, it's first words are usually, "Do not be afraid" (Lk 1:13,30; 2:10). From this fact we may deduce that angels present an unexpected and terrifying appearance, except for the times when they appear as completely ordinary human beings. There seems to be no room for the winged and gentle creatures of popular Christian art.

The tradition of "guardian angels" is biblical (see Matthew 18:10 and Hebrews 1:14), and protection is one of their great ministries. Angels protected Israel in the wilderness (Ex 23:20). The devil quoted Psalm 91:11 to our Lord in the temptation: "For He shall give His angels charge over you, to keep you in all your ways." Satan's angelology was accurate, but his aim was evil. Angels wrought deliverance, like Lot's rescue from Sodom (Ge 19:12-17) or Peter's release from prison (Ac 12:7), and executed judgment (2 Sa 24:17). Angels are also active in praising the Lord (Ps 148:2; Re 5:11).

Cherub (kerûb): Actually angels are powerful spirit beings. The concept of a "cherub" as a rosy-faced little child on a pink cloud is even worse than the popular picture of angels in general. The origin of the word cherub is unknown, but the meaning of a cognate word in Akkadian, a language related to Hebrew, fits what we know about cherubim from the Bible: they praise, bless, and adore.

We first read of cherubim (plural) in Genesis 3:24, as they guarded the way to the tree of life after the fall. Golden images of these mighty angelic beings were placed over the mercy seat on top of the ark of the covenant. Representations of cherubim were widely used in the decoration of the tabernacle and temple.

The description in Ezekiel 10 of the cherubim with their several wings, four faces, and "throne" with wheels, is awesome, as befits worshipful guardians of God's glory.

Seraphim. Seraphim are mentioned only in Isaiah 6, when Isaiah received his commission from God. The word *seraphim* comes from the verb *sâraph* ("to burn") and appears in the context of holiness. Isaiah sensed his own lack of holiness in the light of the seraphim's ascription of praise to God: "Holy, holy, holy!" Seraphim are seen as burning with holiness. They have six wings, and fly. Their specific function seems to be to declare the holiness of God. Some scholars believe cherubim and seraphim are not really that different. In fact, the living creatures in Revelation seem to have some characteristics of both.

It should be underscored that the study of angels is not theoretical; it should be practical and encouraging. Hebrews 1:14 gives believers a wonderful assurance: "Are they not all ministering spirits sent forth to minister for those who will inherit salvation?" Eventually, we will understand first hand more about the nature of angelic beings, for Jesus declared that humans will be like angels after the resurrection (Lk 20:36).

Angels in the New Testament. Angels are active throughout the New Testament as special messengers of God (He 1:14). The news that she would give birth to the Messiah, the Savior of the world, was brought to Mary by the angel Gabriel (Lk 1:26-38). The New Testament also reveals that angels guide, instruct, and protect God's people. Angels are still active today even though we are usually unaware of their work as they continue to fulfill their role as messengers of God and ministers to God's people.

Following are other New Testament events in which angels played a significant role:

Personality	Angel's Action	Reference
Zacharias	Revealed the forthcoming birth of John the Baptist	Lk 1:11-20
Joseph	Assured Joseph of Mary's purity; warned him of Herod's plot; told Joseph about Herod's death	Ma 1:20-25; 2:13,19-20
Shepherds	Announced the birth of Christ	Lk 2:8-15
Jesus	Ministered to Jesus during His temptations; strengthened Him in the garden of Gethsemane; rolled away the stone from the tomb and announced His resurrection	Ma 4:11; Lk 22:43; Ma 28:2-6
Apostles	Predicted the second coming of Jesus; released the apostles from prison	Ac 1:10-11; 5:17-20
Philip	Sent Philip into the desert to meet the eunuch	Ac 8:26
Cornelius	Instructed Cornelius to send for Peter	Ac 10:3-8
Peter	Released Peter from prison	Ac 12:7
Herod	Judged Herod because of his blasphemy	Ac 12:23
Paul	Reassured Paul in a storm at sea	Ac 27:23-24

ANGEL OF THE LORD, ANGEL OF GOD

The Angel of the Lord in the Old Testament is a mysterious being, whose precise nature is unknown. He appears to be an audible and sometimes visible manifestation of God to man. In some way, the God whom no man can see in all His glory and still live (Ex 33:20), arranged a way to show Himself to humans. The Angel of the Lord is frequently referred to as one who appeared to be a man (Ge 18:1-2; Jos 5:13-15). Unlike the angel that showed John the revelation of the end times (Re 19:10; 22:8), the Angel of the Lord accepted worship (Jos 5:14). When the Angel of the Lord is speaking to humans, the text uses the term "LORD" and "Angel of the LORD" interchangeably (Ex 3:1-8). At the same time, there are times when the Angel of the Lord seems to be distinct from God, as when He interceded with God for men (Ze 1:12;

3:1-5). Many believe that the Angel of the Lord was a pre-incarnate appearance of Christ, although Scripture does not specifically say so. The description of the "one like the Son of God" who was with Daniel's three friends in the fiery furnace is assumed to be the Angel of the Lord, and the title "Son of God," of course, belongs to Christ. Following is a list of some of the prominent appearances of the Angel of the Lord:

Personality	Action	Reference
Hagar	Instructed Hagar to return to Sarah and told her she would bear many descendants	Ge 16:7-10
Abraham	Promised Isaac's birth, and warned of the destruction of Sodom and Gomorrah; prevented Abraham from sacrificing his son Isaac	Ge 18:1–19:2; 22:11-13
Jacob	Wrestled with Jacob through the night and blessed him at daybreak	Ge 32:24-30
Moses	Spoke to Moses from the burning bush, promising to deliver Israelites from enslavement	Ex 3:1-8
Israelites	Protected the children of Israel from the pursuing Egyptians	Ex 14:19-20
Israelites	Prepared the children of Israel to enter the promised land	Ex 23:20-23
Balaam	Blocked Balaam's path, then sent him to deliver a message to the prince Balak	Nu 22:22-35
Joshua	Reassured Joshua in his role as commander of the army of the Lord	Jos 5:13-15
Israelites	Announced judgment against Israelites for their sinful alliance with the Canaanites	Ju 2:1-3
Gideon	Commissioned Gideon to fight against the Midianites	Ju 6:11-24
Elijah	Provided food for Elijah in the wilderness	1 Ki 19:4-8
David	Appeared to David on the threshing floor of Ornan, where David built an altar	1 Ch 21:16-22
Jerusalem	Delivered the citizens of this city from the Assyrian army	Is 37:36

ANGELOLOGY

The study of angels. See ANGEL, and ANGLES, FALLEN.

ANGELS, FALLEN

There were fallen angels who had left their first estate (Ma 25:41; Re 12:7,9). When Satan rebelled against God, he fell from heaven and with him one third of the angels who had joined his rebellion (Is 14; Eze 28). See SATAN.

ANGLE (archaic)

Fishing hook (Is 19:8; Hab 1:15).

A·NI′AM *(sighing of the people)*

A son of Shemida of the tribe of Manasseh (1 Ch 7:19).

A′NIM *(fountains)*

A town in the hill country of Judah probably about eleven miles west of Hebron (Jos 15:50).

ANIMALS OF THE BIBLE

Many animals are mentioned in our English Bible by their specific names. The problem is that many of these names are only the best guesses of the translators, because accurate information about the exact meaning of the Hebrew words has been lost. In some cases, the word is well-known, or the context makes it easy to figure out what animal is meant. In other cases, it is not so simple. The animal life of the land of Israel has changed over the thousands of years that it has been inhabited. Some of the animals mentioned in Scripture may now be extinct, or no longer naturally occur in that area, like wolves in England, or the passenger pigeons of North America.

The Bible classifies animals in broad categories: fish, fowl and living things (Ge 1:28). The word "beast" is often used to refer to any animal; the word "flesh" to any animal used for meat. "Cattle" refers to domesticated animals of all kinds. The most important division of animal life was the division between clean and unclean animals. Detailed information about which animals fell into which category does not appear until Leviticus 11, but it is clear that this knowledge dated back much further than the law of Moses. When Noah entered the ark, he took with him one pair of every unclean animal, and seven pairs of every clean animal. As far back as Cain and Abel, people seem to have had a very good idea of which animals made an acceptable sacrifice and which animals were not appropriate. The picture of the perfect lamb as a sin offering can be found consistently in Scripture from Genesis through Revelation.

Following is a list of the animals mentioned in the Bible. More information about each creature may be found under its name in the appropriate section of the dictionary: *Ant, Antelope, Ass, Baboon, Badger, Bat, Bear, Bee, Beetle,*

Behemoth, Bittern, Boar, Buck, Bull, Bustard, Calf, Camel, Cankerworm, Cat, Caterpillar, Cattle, Chameleon, Chamois, Chicken, Cobra, Cock, Cockatrice, Colt, Coney, Cormorant, Cow, Crane, Cricket, Cuckoo, Deer, Doe, Dog, Dove, Dragon, Dromedary, Eagle, Eagle Owl, Elephant, Ewe, Falcon, Fallow Deer, Fawn, Ferret, Fish, Flea, Fly, Fowl, Fox, Frog, Gazelle, Gier Eagle, Glede, Gnat, Goat, Goose, Greyhound, Griffon, Hare, Hart, Hawk, Heifer, Hen, Heron, Hind, Hoopoe, Horned Owl, Hornet, Horse, Hound, Hyena, Ibex, Jackal, Jackdaw, Jerboa, Kid, Kine, Kite, Lamb, Lapwing, Leech, Leopard, Leviathan, Lice, Lion, Lizard, Locust, Maggot, Mare, Mole, Monkey, Moth, Mouse, Mule, Night Creature, Nighthawk, Osprey, Ossifrage, Ostrich, Owl, Ox, Palmerworm, Panther, Partridge, Peacock, Pelican, Pig, Porcupine, Porpoise, Pygarg, Quail, Rabbit, Ram, Rat, Raven, Rock Badger, Rock Goat, Roe Buck, Satyr, Scorpion, Sea Mew, Sea Monster, Sheep, Snail, Snake, Sow, Sparrow, Spider, Sponge, Stag, Stork, Swallow, Swan, Swift, Swine, Thrush, Tortoise, Turtle, Unicorn, Viper, Vulture, Weasel, Whale, Wolf, and Worm.

ANIMAL WORSHIP

ANIMALS, UNCLEAN

See UNCLEAN ANIMALS.

ANIMALS, WORSHIP OF

Many pagan peoples held certain animals to be sacred to certain gods, or even to be manifestations of these gods. Even the Hebrews, with their sure knowledge of the true God, fell into this sin. Twice in Israel's history the people made a golden calf to represent God, and they bowed down to this image and worshipped it (Ex 20:2-5; De 5:6-9; 1 Ki 12:25-33). Also see GODS, PAGAN.

AN′ISE

An herb used for seasoning. Anise flowers are yellow, and its seeds have a flavor reminiscent of licorice. Aniseed oil is not uncommon as a flavoring in certain ethnic dishes today. The word occurs only once in Scripture (Ma 23:23). Many scholars believe that this word should be translated *dill* rather than *anise*. See DILL.

ANKLE CHAIN

A silver or gold chain which linked the ankle bracelets together, forcing the wearer to take small mincing steps (Is 3:16). Perhaps this kind of ornament was what let the blind prophet Ahijah know that Jeroboam's wife was approaching (1 Ki 14:6).

ANK′LET

An ornament of metal or glass for the ankles (Is 3:18). Anklets were fashionable, and came in many shapes and designs. They may have had bells attached, or a woman may have worn several on each ankle to enhance the jingling when she walked.

AN′NA (grace)

A prophetess in Jerusalem. She was of the tribe of Asher, a widow, and daughter of Phanuel. When the child Jesus was brought to the temple to be presented before the Lord, she immediately recognized Him as the Messiah, and praised God (Lk 2:36-38).

AN' NAS *(grace of Jehovah)*

The father-in-law of Caiaphas. In Acts 4:6 Annas is called the high priest. In Luke 3:2 both are called high priests. Jesus appeared before Annas as one accused (Jo 18:13). Annas was made high priest in A.D. 7 by Quirinius and held great influence (Lk 3:2). Some believe that Caiaphas was the actual high priest and that Annas was president of the Sanhedrin.

ANNUNCIATION

Announcement. Specifically, the news the angel Gabriel brought to Mary, telling her that she would have the privilege of being the mother of the Messiah (Lk 1:26-38).

A·NOINT' ING

Anointing, the pouring or rubbing of oil or ointment on the head, hair, beard, or other part of the body, was a common practice in Bible times. A guest in a home was anointed, partly as a token of honor and esteem, and partly to moisten the skin after the visitor had been exposed to the hot, dry climate of Israel (Lk 7:46). During an anointing, the person customarily knelt while the oil was poured over his head. The substance used was olive oil, myrrh, or sweet cinnamon.

Anointing was also a distinct religious rite among the Jewish people. A person was sometimes anointed to set him apart for a particular work or service. Many times in Scripture, anointing is a ceremonial "setting apart." Aaron and the priests were ordained by anointing (Ex 28:41; 30:30). The altar and tabernacle were anointed (Ex 29:36; 30:26). Saul was anointed when the Israelites demanded a king (1 Sa 8:4-22; 10:1). Samuel anointed David as king of Israel (1 Sa 16:1-13), and Solomon was also anointed as David's successor (1 Ki 1:39).

These kings, called "anointed ones," were anointed by prophets acting on God's behalf. They ruled as God's representatives to the people and were to rely on God's wisdom as leaders and rulers.

Jesus was God's "anointed one" or the Messiah, who had been foretold by the prophets of the Old Testament (Ps 45:7; Is 61:1). A woman poured perfume on Jesus's head as an anointing before His death (Mk 14:3-9). This showed that Jesus had fulfilled His purpose as God's special messenger.

Anointing also refers to a spiritual process in which the Holy Spirit empowers a person's heart and mind with God's truth and love (2 Co 1:21; 1 Jo 2:20,27). On the Day of Pentecost, after Jesus's ascension, the disciples of Jesus were anointed for special service in a great outpouring of His Holy Spirit on believers (Ac 2:1-4). The apostle Paul declared that all followers of Christ are anointed as God's very own and set apart to His service.

In the New Testament, anointing was also frequently used in connection with healing. Jesus's disciples anointed the sick (Mk 6:13), and James instructed the elders of the church to anoint the sick with oil (Jam 5:14). This anointing was for the purpose of healing.

ANON (archaic)

Immediately (Ma 13:20).

ANT

A wise and diligent insect (Pr 6:6; 30:25).

AN' TE·DI·LU' VI·ANS *(before the deluge)*

The people who lived before the flood. The first people, Adam and Eve, and their descendants had obeyed the command to multiply and fill the earth, but the offspring of the first couple were tainted with the sin they had brought into the world. Beginning with Cain murdering Abel, their descendants grew more and more wicked. In spite of their wickedness, the antediluvians were clever and made advances in technology. We cannot know how advanced they were, but we know that they built cities, raised flocks and herds, played musical instruments, and worked with bronze and iron (Ge 4:16-22). Therefore, they must have had mines and smelters, and sharp tools for carving the harps and flutes. They must have had some engineering skills in order to build cities, or for Noah to have constructed something so large as the ark. The antediluvian people also lived for a very long time, most of them for hundreds of years. The oldest man of all was Methuselah, who lived to be 969 years old.

Not all the people were entirely wicked. Both Noah and Enoch were righteous men (Ge 5:24; 6:9), who preached of God to the corrupt and disobedient people around them (2 Pe 2:5; Jude 14-15). However, their preaching was not well received, and Noah made ready to escape God's wrath on the ark, as he had been commanded; only his wife and his sons and their wives accompanied him. Noah was the only righteous man that God could find on the entire earth at that time.

The antediluvians did not believe Noah's warning, and they were eating and drinking and making merry right up until the last moment. People today react in the same way to the message of the gospel. Jesus warned His followers that when the last day comes, people will be like the antediluvians, wrapped up in their everyday affairs and ignoring the coming wrath of God which will punish their corruption (Ma 24:37-41; Lk 17:26). Believers need to have a different attitude, to be watchful and ready (1 Th 5:5-11).

AN'TE·LOPE

One of the ceremonially clean animals, also called *addax, gazelle, oryx* and *wild ox.* Antelope are mentioned in the list of clean wild animals, and in the list of food for Solomon's table (De 14:5; 1 Ki 4:23). Antelope run in herds, and are very fleet of foot. Joab's brother Asahel was compared to a gazelle because of his speed and endurance (2 Sa 2:18). Sometimes hunters used nets to snare them (Is 51:20). Antelope have a keen sense of smell, which helps them to find water, and are good at sensing the presence of an enemy, even at a distance. Dorcas (Tabitha), the name of the woman Peter raised from the dead, means "gazelle" (Ac 9:36).

AN·THO·THI' JAH, AN·TO·THI' JAH
(answers of Jehovah)

A Benjamite descended through Shashak (1 Ch 8:24).

AN' THRO·PO·MORPH' ISM

Describing God in terms of human form, such as talking about God's hands (Jo 10:26), His eyes (De 32:10), His arms (De 33:27), His

ANTELOPE OR GAZELLE

face (Nu 6:25). The Scripture clearly teaches that God is not like His creatures (Job 9:32; Jo 4:24), but it also teaches that humans are made "in the image of God" (Ge 1:27). It is unclear exactly how far this "image" carries, but it is very clear that God is spirit, and entirely different from humans (Jo 4:24). In any case, the Bible frequently uses human terminology to describe God's actions, and it is clear that this is done for our better comprehension of Him. The final, complete "anthropomorphism" is Jesus Christ, who is God in human flesh—not just looking human, but a real human (Jo 1:14). He was "in the form of God," and took "the form of a servant" (Ph 2:6-8). God expressed Himself in the most human of terms, in order to reach us, to die for us, to save us, "to give the light of the knowledge of the glory of God in the face of Jesus Christ" (2 Co 4:6).

AN' THRO·PO·PATH' ISM

Describing God in terms of human emotion. Since God is personal, He responds to what His creatures think and feel and do. Some downplay the references to God's emotions as simply describing Him in terms that humans can understand; His ways are beyond anything we can really understand (Is 40:18; 1 Co 2:14; 1 Ti

6:16). However, we cannot say that God does not truly have and show the emotions Scripture credits Him with. God created human emotion because He is a personal God who was making personal creatures that He would relate to. He is shown as having anger (Ps 77:9), mercy (Ps 103:8), jealousy (Ex 20:5), love (Ro 8:38), grief and sorrow (Ge 6:6). Whatever view a person may hold, it is clear that the references to God's emotion are meant to show us that He cares about us, and that what we do matters to Him.

AN' TI·CHRIST

The word signifies *against Christ,* an *enemy of Christ, in the place of Christ* (1 Jo 2:18,22; 4:3; 2 Jo 7). The coming of Antichrist, according to John's statement, will mark "the last days" before the second coming of Christ. The Antichrist is apparently a specific person and John emphasizes the spirit of Antichrist as it manifests itself in the denial of Jesus's incarnation and messiahship. While the term is used by John alone, he is not the only one who teaches this doctrine. Christ uttered a warning regarding "false Christs" (Ma 24:23-24; Mk 13:21-22). Paul clearly describes the Antichrist and his satanic claims and operations (2 Th 2:3-12), stating that the lawless one, the masterpiece of Satan, will appear before the second coming of Christ. John describes the same person as the "beast" (Re 13) and both Paul and John declare he will be destroyed by Christ at his second coming. According to these teachings Christ will return to the world when apostasy and iniquity come to full expression in the Antichrist.

ANTIMONY

A metal with a hard crystalline structure and a fairly low melting point, often used in lead alloys to lend hardness. In ancient times, antimony was pulverized into a black powder which was used as eye make-up, to give the eyes the appearance of being large and dark (Je 4:30; Eze 23:40). Jerome's translation of the Bible says that the wicked queen Jezebel painted her eyes with "stibium," which is a name for antimony (2 Ki 9:30). According to some versions, antimony was included in the materials David assembled for the temple (1 Ch 29:2).

AN' TI·OCH

Two cities of the same name figure prominently in the Book of Acts.

1. The Syrian Antioch, the capital of Syria in the time of the Greek dynasty. Situated on the most important trade routes of the day, Antioch was an ideal city for a flourishing missions-minded church that was destined to play a key role in the expansion of early Christianity. It was founded by Seleucus Nicator about 300 B.C., who named it after his father Antiochus. Situated at a bend of the river Orontes on its southern side, Antioch was about 16 miles from the Mediterranean Sea and about 300 miles north of Jerusalem. With a population of more than half a million, it was the third largest city of the Roman Empire, ranking behind only Rome and Alexandria.

Under the Roman rulers, Antioch became one of the most beautiful cities of the Roman Empire. Its main street, about two miles long, was paved with marble and flanked on both sides by hundreds of columns, which supported ornamented porches and balconies. Its cultural splendor and beautiful buildings, including the temple of Artemis, the amphitheater, and royal palaces, contributed to its reputation as the "Paris of the Ancient World" among scholars and researchers.

Antioch was also a city of many philosophies and cults. It prided itself on its tolerance. When persecution of Christians at Jerusalem arose upon the martyrdom of Stephen, many fled to Antioch. But in spite of the tolerant atmosphere, and an abundance of religion, many citizens sought a more significant spiritual experience than the old Greek and Roman gods offered. The Christians who had immigrated to the city began to preach the gospel, first to the Jews, but also among interested Gentiles. Many accepted the gospel and committed themselves to Christ. Barnabas came from Jerusalem to engage in this work and was the means of bringing Paul to the city. Because this church was made up of both Gentiles and Jews, city officials sought a name that would distinguish them from other religious groups. They nicknamed them "Christians," meaning "Christ Followers" or "People of Christ," and the name stuck. According to the Book of Acts, "the disciples were first called Christians in Antioch" (Ac 11:26).

Except for Jerusalem, Antioch played a larger part in the early life of the Christian church than any other city of the Roman Empire. It became the birthplace of foreign missions as Paul used the Antioch church as a base of operations for his missionary tours into Asia Minor. Antioch flourished under the Seleucid kings and contained magnificent buildings. It was made a free city by Pompey.

2. Pisidian Antioch. In Asia Minor Seleucus Nicator founded another town which he also named in honor of his father, Antiochus. It was in Phrygia near the borders of Pisidia, and was called the Pisidian Antioch to distinguish it from the Syrian Antioch. It was a military center and was called Caesarea by the Romans. It had a Jewish synagogue (Ac 13:14) and was visited by Paul and Barnabas on their first missionary journey (Ac 13:14-52; 14:19-21).

AN·TI' O·CHUS *(endurer)*

Thirteen Syrian rulers of the Seleucid dynasty were named Antiochus. Two of them were particularly associated with Israel:

1. *Antiochus the Great.* He came to the throne of Syria in 223 B.C. and was the sixth ruler of the Seleucidan dynasty. After the death of Ptolemy IV he seized Palestine in 198 B.C. He invaded Europe but was defeated in the battle of Magnesia (190 B.C.) and forced to pay Rome an excessive tribute. While plundering a temple in 187 B.C., he was murdered by a mob.

2. *Antiochus Epiphanes.* The youngest son of Antiochus the Great. A hostage at Rome for fifteen years, he was released shortly after his father's death and came to the throne in 175 B.C., obtaining his kingdom by flatteries (Da 11:21). He enraged the Jews by looting the temple, setting up in it a statue of Jupiter, sacrificing swine on the altar, and destroying the walls of Jerusalem. These insults he followed with a frightful massacre of the Jews and this action precipitated the revolt of the Maccabees. See INTERTESTAMENTAL PERIOD.

AN' TI·PAS

Two men of the New Testament era:

1. A Christian martyr of Pergamos (Re 2:12-13). According to tradition he was the bishop of that place.

2. Son of Herod the Great. See HEROD.

AN·TIP' A·TRIS *(city of Antipater)*

The town to which Paul was taken by night (Ac 23:31). Its Old Testament name was Aphek (Jos 12:18; 1 Sa 4:1; 29:1).

AN·TO' NI·A, TOWER OF

A castle at the northwestern corner of the temple area. It rose forty cubits above the rock. Here Paul was brought after his rescue from the mob (Ac 21:30).

AN·TO·THI' JAH

See ANTHOTHIJAH.

AN' TO·THITE

An inhabitant of Anathoth (1 Ch 11:28).

A' NUB *(confederate)*

Son of Coz (Hakkoz) (1 Ch 4:8).

ANVIL

The large iron block used by a blacksmith or other metalsmith as a foundation for hammering and shaping hot metal. The word is only found once in Scripture, in Isaiah 41:7.

APACE *(archaic)*

Swiftly, at a quick pace (2 Sa 18:25; Ps 68:12; Je 46:5).

APE

There is no genuine ape either in Malabar or any other part of India. If the animals which were brought to Palestine by the vessels that went to Ophir for gold (1 Ki 10:22) came from India, they were tailed monkeys. This animal is common in that country and was an object of worship.

A·PEL' LES

A Christian in Rome to whom Paul sent a salutation (Ro 16:10). According to tradition he was bishop of Smyrna.

A·PHAR·SA' CHITES, A·PHAR·SATH' ·CHITES

Probably Assyrian tribes from which came certain of those who settled in Samaria after the fall of the Northern Kingdom of Israel (Ez 4:9; 5:6).

A' PHEK *(fortress)*

Four Old Testament cities:

1. A city of the Canaanites (Jos 12:18), probably the same as Aphekah in Joshua 15:53.

2. A city of Asher near Sidon (Jos 19:30; Ju 1:31), also called Aphik.

3. A place near Shiloh where the Philistines gathered before the battle in which ark was captured (1 Sa 4:1).

4. A town near Jezreel (1 Sa 29:1).

5. A city six miles east of the Sea of Galilee (1 Ki 20:26).

A·PHE' KAH *(fortress)*

A city in the hill country of Judah (Jos 15:53).

A·PHI' AH

An ancestor of Saul, a Benjamite (1 Sa 9:1).

A' PHIK

See APHEK.

APH' RAH, BETH·LE·APH' RAH

A town mentioned in Micah 1:10.

APH' SES

The priests were divided into 24 families. Aphses was the head of the eighteenth (1 Ch 24:15). A form of HAPPIZZEZ.

APIS

One of the gods worshipped by the ancient Egyptians, the sacred bull-god of Noph (Memphis). It has been supposed that the golden calf that the Israelites made in the wilderness (Ex 32) was modeled after the Apis-bull.

A·POC' A·LYPSE *(revelation)*

See REVELATION, BOOK OF.

A·POC' A·LYP·TIC LITERATURE

The Greek word *apocalypses* means "revelation." Apocalyptic literature is writing which reveals hidden things. The Books of Daniel and Ezekiel are good examples of Old Testament apocalyptic literature, while the Book of Revelation follows the same pattern in the New Testament. After the last prophet, Malachi, pseudo-apocryphal writing became popular, probably modeled after the Old Testament prophets. A number of books in the pseudepigrapha are apocalyptic. Apocalyptic literature is characterized by the following: Visions, ethics, powerful symbolism, warning messages, imminent end times, angels and demons, the involvement of the whole created universe, the kingdom of God, a coming Messiah, the passing away of the present order, and the coming of a new order when the promises will be fulfilled to God's people. See PSEUDEPIGRAPHA.

A·POC' RY·PHA *(hidden)*

The apocryphal books can be divided into two groups: **1.** The Old Testament apocrypha, about fifteen books written between 190 B.C. and 70 A.D. (when the temple was destroyed). These books were written by the Jewish people during years of oppression under ungodly rulers, and include several books of history. **2.** The New Testament apocrypha was written mainly in the second and third centuries A.D., long after the apostles and eyewitnesses of the early church were dead. The Old Testament apocrypha was not accepted by all Jews; it was included in some versions and not in others. None of the New Testament apocrypha was accepted by the early church, because its content does not match the rest of Scripture. Some people over the centuries have accepted the Old Testament books which were accepted by some Jews. This is why Catholic Bibles contain the Old Testament apocrypha while Protestant Bibles do not.

Old Testament Apocrypha: The Old Testament apocryphal books are generally arranged in the following order:

First Esdras
Second Esdras
Tobit
Judith
The Additions to Esther
The Wisdom of Solomon
Ecclesiasticus, or the Wisdom of Jesus, the Son of Sirach
Baruch
The Letter of Jeremiah
The Prayer of Azariah and Song of the Three Young Men
Susanna
Bel and the Dragon
The Prayer of Manasseh
First Maccabees
Second Maccabees

In alphabetical order, a brief summary of each book:

Baruch. This book is set in the time of the prophet Jeremiah, and his scribe, Baruch (c. 585 B.C.), but it is believed to have actually been written much later (c. 142-63 B.C.). Its theme is the encouragement that God will not forget His people.

Bel and the Dragon. Additions to the Book of Daniel, written around 50 B.C. This book is written to demonstrate the falsity of pagan religions, emphasizing the trickery of their priests, and the nonexistence of their gods. In this story, Daniel is in the lion's den (again), and Habakkuk is miraculously brought from Israel to give Daniel his lunch.

Ecclesiasticus, or the Wisdom of Jesus the Son of Sirach. Written in the second century B.C., this book is a "wisdom" book, similar to the Book of Proverbs. It provides advice for successful living.

Esdras, Books of. The Book of 1 Esdras is a historical narrative beginning in the days of King Josiah of Judah, and extending through the time of Nehemiah. It was probably written about 150 B.C., and its theme is to promote the proper worship of God. It also provides interesting historical background for the conflict between the Samaritans and the Jews.

The Book of 2 Esdras was written much later, about the same time that John was writing the Book of Revelation. It is also an apocalyptic book, dealing with the problem of evil in the world, the destruction of Jerusalem and the end of the age. This book has a rather dark aspect, but also carries the theme that God will one day redeem His people, and is still in control.

Esther, Additions to. These additions to the Book of Esther, while not considered to be accurate history, or written at the same time as the rest of the book, are nevertheless interesting to read. The additions dramatize the story, and also add the references to God that are singularly lacking in that book. It is generally believed that the additions were written for this purpose, to explicitly acknowledge God's hand in the story.

Jeremiah, Letter of. A sermon attacking idolatry. Its date is very uncertain, some fragments of this letter were found in the Dead Sea Scrolls.

Judith. A fictional account of a brave Jewish woman named Judith, who was a devout follower of God and remained faithful to the law of Moses. She courageously slew an Assyrian general, thereby saving her town from disaster. The book was probably written sometime between 142 and 63 B.C., and contains many geographical and historical errors, as well as a strong emphasis on salvation by works.

Maccabees, Books of. The books of Maccabees contain the history of the intertestamental period. They deal with the period when the Hasmonean family was in leadership over the Jews in Judea. The most famous of this family was Judas Maccabaeus, for whom these books are named. They deal with the Jews' struggle against the corrupt ruler Antiochus Epiphanes, and the Maccabean revolt. They also detail the proper celebration of Chanukah, the Festival of lights, and the story behind this new feast. **1 Maccabees** was written by a Sadducee, and does not focus on spiritual matters. Josephus consulted this book as accurate history. **2 Maccabees** is a Pharisaic account of the same events, with more emphasis upon religious values and resurrection. Some of its verses are used to support the idea of purgatory.

Prayer of Azariah and the Song of the Three Young Men. Another addition to the Book of Daniel, detailing the experience of the three in the fiery furnace. In the furnace, Azariah (Abednego) is supposed to have prayed this prayer, and then the three sang a hymn of praise together.

Prayer of Manasseh. Manasseh, son of the righteous king Hezekiah, was one of Judah's most wicked kings (2 Ch 33:6). However, at the end of his life he repented of his wickedness and turned to God (2 Ch 33:10-13). This apocryphal writing is a prayer of repentance, supposed to come from the lips of Manasseh. It was probably written long after the actual event, and is not considered to be accurate (in the sense that it was not actually written by Manasseh). Nevertheless, it is a beautiful expression of contrition, following the typical form of praise, confession, request for forgiveness, and thanksgiving.

Song of the Three Young Men.

Susanna. Another story loosely connected with the Book of Daniel. Susanna, a young woman living in Babylon at the time of Daniel, was the victim of an attempted assault by two respected elders. In order to cover their own tracks, the elders accused the innocent Susanna of adultery; she was tried and nearly condemned to death when Daniel (as a young man) stepped in and proved her innocence by demanding that the "two or three witnesses" required by Old Testament law be examined separately. The results of these two private examinations did not match, and the two elders were proven to be liars. As punishment for their sin, they were taken out and stoned. This book provides an interesting look at the Jewish courts and law of the day. It was probably written sometime between 110 and 60 B.C.

Tobit. The fictional account of a Jewish captive in Nineveh, a devout follower of God who experienced various trials, and eventually learned that God responds to prayer. In one part of the story, his son Tobias is engaged to a beautiful girl named Sarah. Unfortunately, a demon is also in love with this girl, and this demon makes a practice of destroying her lovers. Several times she has married a young man, only to have him slain on their wedding night. Some believe that the Sadducees may have been thinking of this story when they asked Jesus their trick questions about marriage at the resurrection (Lk 20:27-33). The Book of Tobit ends happily, as God listens to the prayers of Tobit and Sarah, and sends an angel to help them. Tobias defeats the demon, marries Sarah, and lives happily ever after.

Wisdom of Solomon. Composed sometime in the first century B.C., this book was probably named as a tribute to Solomon the Wise. It is also, rather like the Book of Proverbs, containing practical advice and an exhortation to wisdom.

New Testament Apocrypha: The apocryphal writings of the New Testament are not accepted in any canon. They are largely imaginative narratives of things which are supposed to have happened in the life of Christ or to the apostles; or else writings designed to promote a certain doctrine. Some are heretical, some are nonsensical. The group of writings and fragments can be divided into four categories:

1) **Gospels:**
Arabic Gospel of the Infancy
Armenian Gospel of the Infancy
Assumption of the Virgin
Gospel of Bartholomew
Book of the Resurrection of Christ by Bartholomew
Gospel of Basiliades
Gospel of the Ebionites
Gospel according to the Egyptians
Gospel according to the Hebrews
Protoevangelium of James
History of Joseph the Carpenter
Gospel of Marchio
Gospel of the Birth of Mary
Gospel of Matthias
Gospel of the Nazarenes
Gospel of Peter
Gospel of Philip
Gospel of Pseudo-Matthew
Gospel of Thomas

2) **Acts:**
Apostolic history of Adbias
Acts of Andrew
Fragmentary Story of Andrew
Acts of Andrew and Matthew
Acts of Andrew and Paul
Acts of Barnabas
Ascents of James
Acts of James the Great
Acts of John
Acts of John by Procurus
Martyrdom of Matthew
Acts of Paul
Passion of Paul
Acts of Peter
Passion of Peter
Preaching of Peter
Slavonic Acts of Peter
Acts of Peter and Andrew
Acts of Peter and Paul
Passion of Peter and Paul
Acts of Philip
Acts of Pilate
Acts of Thaddeus
Acts of Thomas

3) **Epistles:**
Epistles of Christ and Abgarus
Epistles of the Apostles
Third Epistle to the Corinthians
Epistle to the Laodiceans
Epistle to the Lentulus
Epistles of Paul and Seneca
Apocryphal Epistle of Titus

4) **Apocalypses:**
Apocalypses of James
Apocalypses of Paul
Apocalypses of Peter

Apocalypses of Thomas
Apocalypses of the Virgin
Revelation of Stephen

These books have been rejected as inspired Scripture for various reasons. Simply put, they do not match the rest of the New Testament either in theology, style or content. An example of this can be found in the Gospel of Thomas. This narrative describes a supposed event in the childhood of Jesus, where another child mistreats Him in some way. In this story, Jesus turns around and retaliates by striking the child dead. This is clearly incompatible with the character and teachings of Jesus which are shown in the four canonical Gospels, the prophecies of the Old Testament, and the rest of the New Testament. For this reason, the Gospel of Thomas is rejected as unsound. In spite of the heretical and nonsensical content of much of the New Testament apocrypha, they provide an interesting glimpse into the thinking and ideas of some of the early church.

AP·OL·LO′ NI·A *(pertaining to Apollo)*

A city of Macedonia about forty miles from Thessalonica (Ac 17:1).

A·POL′ LOS

A learned and eloquent Jew of Alexandrian birth, a disciple of John the Baptist (Ac 18:24-25). His preaching that Jesus was the Christ was attended with great success in Corinth and throughout Achaia (Ac 18:24-28). He was involved in the division of the church at Corinth (1 Co 1:12; 3:4-6; 4:6), and was a friend of Paul (1 Co 16:12; Tit 3:13). Some believe that he was the author of the Epistle to the Hebrews.

A·POL′ LY·ON *(destroyer)*

The Greek form of the Hebrew word *Abaddon,* the angel of the bottomless pit (Re 9:11).

APOSTASY

Departing from the truth, falling away. King Saul fell into apostasy, rejecting God's rule in his life (1 Sa 15:11). The nation of Israel became apostate over and over again; each of the Old Testament prophets had to deal with the faithlessness of God's people. In the New Testament era, the Christians were accused of apostasy, they were considered by the unbelieving Jews to have abandoned the faith, and turned to a false religion (Ac 21:21). Apostasy is not just error, or ignorance, but a deliberate turning away from the truth, willfully rejecting Christ as Savior and God's rule over a person's life (He 10:26-29).

A·POS′ TLE *(one who is sent, a messenger)*

The name applied to the twelve selected by Jesus to be with him, receive his training, be witnesses of the events of his life, and to preach the gospel (Ma 4:18-22; 10:2-4; Lk 6:13-16). The original twelve were plain men of humble occupations and without specialized training except that given by Jesus (Ac 1:21-22). Paul was Apostle to the Gentiles.

APOSTOLIC AGE

The age in which the apostles were still alive.

APOSTLES' CREED

This creed was written after all the books of the New Testament were completed; even though it bears their name, it was not actually written by the apostles. However, it was based upon their writings, and has been used over the centuries as a statement of true faith.

I believe in God the Father Almighty, Maker of heaven and earth, and in Jesus Christ His only Son our Lord; who was conceived by the Holy Ghost, born of the Virgin Mary, suffered under Pontius Pilate, was crucified, died, and was buried. He descended into hell. The third day He rose again from the dead. He ascended into heaven, and sitteth on the right hand of God the Father Almighty; from thence He shall come to judge the quick and the dead. I believe in the Holy Ghost, the holy catholic church, the communion of saints, the forgiveness of sins, the resurrection of the body, and the life everlasting.

APOSTOLICAL COUNCIL

The council held at Jerusalem about A.D. 50. It was an assembly of apostles and elders of the church (Ac 15).

A·POTH′ E·CA-RY

One engaged in making perfumes and ointments (Ex 30:25; 2 Ch 16:14; Ec 10:1).

AP′ PA·IM *(nostrils)*

A son of Nadab and the father of Ishi (1 Ch 2:30-31).

APPAREL

Clothing (1 Ti 2:9).

APPEAL

A legal term, the request to take a case into a higher court for a rehearing. God set up a system of appeals, arranging legal matters in such a way that a person could appeal to a higher court if the case was too difficult for the district judge to decide (De 17:8-9; 2 Ch 19:8; Ez 7:25). When Paul was arrested in Jerusalem under false charges, he never received an adequate trial. Festus, wanting to please the Jews, was ready to bring Paul to trial for the crimes he was accused of, even though he knew that Paul was innocent. Paul appealed to Caesar, requesting that his case be taken into the highest Roman court (Ac 25:11). Because of this appeal, Paul was sent to Rome, where he was imprisoned for at least two years awaiting trial.

APPH'I·A

A Christian woman addressed by Paul in his letter to Philemon, probably the wife of Philemon (Phile 2).

AP'PI·AN WAY

One of the Roman highways, from Brundisium on the Adriatic Sea to Rome. It was built by and named for Appius Claudius. Paul traveled on this road from Puteoli to Rome, on his journey to be tried before Caesar (Ac 28:13-16).

AP'PI·I FOR'UM (market of Appius)

A station on the Appian Way about 43 miles from Rome. When the Christians in Rome heard that Paul was coming, they traveled as far as this place to meet him and encourage him as he was being brought into Rome as a prisoner (Ac 28:15).

AP'PLE

The identity of the particular tree intended by the Hebrew word *tappuach is* not certain. It is held by many to denote the quince or citron. Some regard it as the orange and some the modern apple, though there are grave objections to these views. Others are of the opinion that the word should be translated apricot. The apple of the Bible is described as being sweet and fragrant (Song 2:3; 7:8), while its tree provided comfortable shade (8:5). It was considered precious (Pr 25:11) and used as a symbol of joy and prosperity (Joel 1:12). The Israelites are frequently described as being "the apple of God's eye," to express how precious God's people are to Him (De 32:10; Ps 17:8; Ze 2:8).

APPLE OF THE EYE

A symbolic term for the pupil of the eye, used to denote something which is cherished and valuable to the owner, something which is worth protecting carefully (De 32:10; Ps 17:8).

APRICOT

See APPLE.

A'PRON

The first aprons were those made by Adam and Eve after their fall (Ge 3:7). The word probably means a loin cloth of some sort, such as continued to be worn by working people (Ac 19:12).

AQ'A·BA, GULF OF

See RED SEA.

AQUEDUCT

A man-made conduit or duct for moving large quantities of water by gravitation. The Romans particularly were famous for their aqueducts, many of which remain today as evidence of their superb engineering skills and sense of beautiful design. Long before the days of the Romans, however, humans had been grappling with the problem of how to move and store water to provide irrigation and drinking water during the dry parts of the year, or to bring water to a more convenient location inside a city or town. King Hezekiah of Judah constructed a well-known aqueduct to carry water into the city of Jerusalem; it is still in existence today (2 Ki 20:20; 2 Ch 32:30). See also HEZEKIAH'S WATER TUNNEL.

A·QUIL'A (eagle)

A Christian Jew and tentmaker who, with his wife, Priscilla, entertained Paul in Corinth. He was born in Pontus, had come to Italy, but was driven from Rome by an edict of Claudius (Ac 18:1-3). Aquila and Priscilla accompanied Paul to Ephesus where they helped in the Christian training of Apollos (Ac 18:18-19,26).

AR *(city)*

A chief city of Moab situated in the valley of the Arnon (Nu 21:15; De 2:18). It was later called Areopolis.

AR′A

A man of Asher (1 Ch 7:38), one of the three sons of Jether.

AR′AB *(ambush)*

A town of Judah in the hill country (Jos 15:52).

AR′A·BAH *(desert)*

The deep gorge which extends from Hermon through the Jordan Valley and Dead Sea apparently to the Red Sea (Jos 18:18), usually rendered *plain* or *wilderness* in the Authorized Version.

A·RA′BI·A

A vast peninsula lying between the mainlands of Asia and Africa. In the Scriptures only that portion is usually meant which is known as Arabia Petraea, the region comprising the Sinaitic Peninsula and the territory south and east of Palestine. Paul, after his conversion, went to Arabia (Ga 1:17).

AR′AD *(wild ass)*

A man and a town in the Old Testament:

1. A Benjamite, son of Beriah who helped expel the inhabitants of Gath (1 Ch 8:15).

2. A town in the south of Judah belonging to the Canaanites (Nu 21:1; Jos 12:14; Ju 1:16).

AR′A·DUS

See ARVAD.

AR′AH *(wayfarer)*

Two Old Testament men:

1. A son of Ulla of the tribe of Asher (1 Ch 7:39).

2. The founder of a family, members of which came to Jerusalem from Babylon in the first expedition (Ez 2:5; Ne 7:10).

AR′AM *(exalted)*

Four Old Testament men, and an area:

1. One of the sons of Shem (Ge 10:22-23).

2. The country lying to the northeast of Palestine. It embraced both Syria and northern Mesopotamia. That portion of Aram in which Abraham had lived before coming to Canaan and in which Nahor remained is biblically known as Mesopotamia and Padan-aram (Ge 24:10; 28:2,5). It lay east of the Euphrates. It is rendered Padan in Genesis 48:7.

3. Son of Shamer of the tribe of Asher (1 Ch 7:34).

4. Son of Kemuel (Ge 22:21).

5. Son of Hezron, the same as Ram, the father of Aminadab (Ma 1:3-4; Lk 3:33).

AR·A·MA′IC LAN′GUAGE

A group of Semitic languages and dialects including biblical and Palestinian Aramaic. Documents in Aramaic have been discovered dating from about the tenth century B.C. It spread throughout the Euphrates Valley and Palestine, becoming the common language of most Semitic peoples. During and after the exile it supplanted the Hebrew language among the Jews. Considerable portions of the books of Ezra and Daniel are in Aramaic. The language of Jesus was Aramaic. See also ABBA, HALLELUJAH, and MARANATHA.

AR′AM DAM′ME·SEK

Another name for Syria of Damascus (2 Sa 8:5-6).

AR′A·ME·ANS

The people of Aram (see ARAM No. 2). Israel and the Arameans sometimes lived peacefully, and sometimes at war. As judgment for their sins, God allowed the Aramean Chushanrishathaim, king of Mesopotamia, to invade and conquer Israel in the days of the judges (Ju 3:8-10). Hadadezer of Zobah and Toi of Hamath, whom David subdued, were Aramean rulers (2 Sa 8:1-13). Rezon the Aramean official, founded the city-state of Damascus, and Israel and Damascus were foes for many years (1 Ki 11:23-24; 15:18-20; 2 Ki 16:5,7-18).

AR·AM·I′TESS

A woman of Aram. One of Manasseh's concubines is referred to as an Aramitess (1 Ch 7:14, KJV).

AR′AM-MA′A·CAH

See MAACAH.

AR′AM-NA·HA·RA′IM *(Aram of the two rivers)*

The part of Aram which lay east of the great bend of the northern Euphrates, the probable location of Padan–aram (Ge 28:5); the Aram of the patriarchs before entering Canaan. Here stood the city of Haran and at a later date Edessa, the center of Syrian culture. David's war with this district of Syria is mentioned in the title of Psalm 60.

AR'AM-ZO'BAH

That part of Aram which lay between Hamath and Damascus (Ps 60, title).

AR'AN *(wild goat)*

One of the sons of Dishan and grandson of Seir, the Horite (Ge 36:28; 1 Ch 1:42).

AR'A·RAT

A district of Armenia, a lofty plateau overlooking the plain of the river Araxes on the north and Mesopotamia on the south. Opinions differ as to the peak on which the ark of Noah rested (Ge 8:4). It is probably to be identified with the lofty snowclad summit of Massis, called by the Persians *Kuh-i-Nuh* (mountain of Noah). It is nearly 17,000 feet above sea level. About seven miles distant is a lesser peak— little Ararat—some 13,000 feet in height.

A·RAU'NAH, OR'NAN

A Jebusite from whom David purchased a threshing floor on Mount Moriah as a site for an altar (2 Sa 24:18-25; 2 Ch 3:1).

AR'BA

Father or leading man of Anak and founder of Kirjath-arba, later called Hebron (Jos 14:15; 15:13; Ju 1:10). See HEBRON.

AR'BAH

The city of Hebron (Ge 35:27).

AR'BA·THITE

A native of Arabah or Betharabah (2 Sa 23:31; 1 Ch 11:32).

AR'BITE

A native of Arab in Judah (2 Sa 23:35).

ARCHANGEL

Chief angel (1 Th 4:16).

AR·CHE·LA'US *(a chief)*

Ethnarch of Judea at the time of the return from Egypt of Joseph, Mary, and the child Jesus

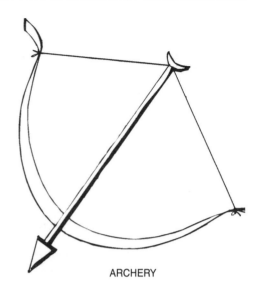
ARCHERY

(Ma 2:22). He was the elder son of Herod the Great by his fourth wife, Malthace. In A.D. 6 he was charged with tyranny and was banished to Vienne in Gaul where he died. See also HEROD.

AR'CHER·Y

The shooting of arrows or bolts with a bow. A bow for shooting arrows is a machine which stores and transfers energy. A long supple piece of wood (sometimes backed with horn or sinew for greater strength, flexibility, and power) is drawn into a "C" shape by means of a string, shorter than the length of the bow, tied to the two ends. When this string is drawn, energy is transferred to the bow. When the string is released, the wood wants to return as near to its natural straight position as possible. When an arrow is fitted to the string, drawn back, and released, the stored energy of the bow is transferred to the arrow, causing it to fly far and fast. A war bow, with a draw of 100 pounds or more, could shoot an arrow which would pierce the heaviest armor. A practiced archer can shoot with deadly accuracy, and archers were particularly valued (or feared) in ancient warfare because they could shoot and kill from a safe distance (1 Sa 31:13; 2 Sa 11:24; 1 Ch 10:3). Ishmael became an archer (Ge 21:20).

AR'CHE·VITES

The inhabitants of Erech, some of whom were placed in Samaria by Asnapper following the overthrow of Israel (Ez 4:9).

AR' CHI
A city on the border of Ephraim (Jos 16:2).

AR·CHIP' PUS *(master of the horse)*
A Christian and officer of the church at Colosse (Col 4:17; Phile 2).

AR' CHITE
The Archites were a Canaanite tribe who settled on the boundary between Ephraim and Benjamin (2 Sa 15:32; 17:5,14).

ARCHWAY
A part of the temple, apparently a roofed and partially enclosed porch-like area. Also described as a portico, arch, or vestibule (1 Ki 6:3; 1 Ch 28:11; Eze 40:16-36).

ARC·TU' RUS
A bright red star of the northern sky known as the guard or keeper of the Great Bear (Ursa Major, "The Big Dipper," or "The Plough"). The biblical word *Arcturus* is probably not the guard but the Great Bear itself (Job 9:9; 38:32).

ARD
Son of Bela and grandson of Benjamin (Ge 46:21; Nu 26:38,40). In 1 Chronicles 8:3 he is called Addar.

ARD' ITES
Descendants of Ard (Nu 26:40).

AR' DON
A man of the family of Hezron, of the house of Caleb, of the tribe of Judah (1 Ch 2:18).

A·RE' LI
One of the seven sons of Gad, founder of the family of Arelites (Ge 46:16; Nu 26:17).

A·RE' LITES
A family descended from Areli (Nu 26:17).

AR·E·OP' A·GITE
A judge of the court of Areopagus (Ac 17:34).

AR·E·OP' A·GUS *(hill of Area)*
A rocky height in Athens opposite the western end of the Acropolis. It was called Mars' Hill from the supposed fact that Mars, or Area, was here tried for murder by Neptune. Here met the Council of the Areopagus, a tribunal composed of ex-archons. Sixteen steps still lead up to the top of the hill where extends the bench on which the judges sat. Here Paul delivered a notable address (Ac 17:18-34).

AR' E·TAS
King of Arabia Petraea and father-in-law of Herod Antipas. When Herod desired to divorce his wife and marry Herodias, Aretas made war on him and defeated him. Rome supported Herod and sent Vitellius to punish Aretas but the order was never executed. For a short time Aretas was in possession of Damascus (2 Co 11:32).

AR' GOB *(stony)*
A man and a region of the Old Testament:
1. A man slain by Pekah (2 Ki 15:25).
2. A region of Bashan within or near Trachonitis (De 3:4,13–14; Jos 13:30; 1 Ki 4:13).

AR' I·DAI
Son of Haman who was hanged with his father (Es 9:9).

AR·I·DA' THA
Son of Haman (Es 9:8).

AR' I·EH
Companion of Argob (2 Ki 15:25).

AR' I·EL *(lion of God)*
Two men and a city bear this name:
1. A leading man who, with certain others, was directed by Ezra to visit Iddo, the chief at Casiphia (Ez 8:16–17).
2. A designation of Jerusalem by Isaiah (Is 29:1,2,7). The significance of the word is obscure, but probably denotes *lion of God* or *altar* or *hearth of God*.
3. A Moabite (2 Sa 23:20) in the Revised Version.

AR·IM·A·THAE' A *(heights)*
The native town of Joseph of Arimathaea (Ma 27:57). It may have been the Ramah of 1 Samuel 1:19.

AR' I·OCH *(servant of the moon god)*
Two men of the Old Testament:
1. A captain of Nebuchadnezzar's guard (Da 2:14-15).
2. King of Ellasar (Ge 14:1,9).

AR′I·SAI

One of the ten sons of Haman. He was slain by the Jews (Es 9:9).

AR·IS·TAR′CHUS *(best ruler)*

A Macedonian who was with Paul on his third missionary journey. He was of Thessalonica and was with Paul at Ephesus (Ac 19:29). He came with Paul into Asia (Ac 20:4-6), accompanied him to Rome (Ac 27:2), and was afterwards his fellow-prisoner (Col 4:10; Phile 24).

A·RIS·TO·BU′LUS *(best counsellor)*

A Christian at Rome (Ro 16:10).

ARK

A box or basket made of bulrushes, slime, and pitch, within which the infant Moses was hidden in the Nile (Ex 2:3-6). (Simply speaking, an archaic word for box or chest.) Two important *arks* figure in Scripture.

1. *Noah's Ark.* Constructed by divine order and specification, it was made to preserve Noah and his family during the flood (Ge 6:14–8:19). Assuming that the cubit was the ordinary cubit of eighteen inches, the length of the ark was 450 feet, the breadth 75 feet, and the height 45 feet. Within its three stories the animals were placed. Although it has been questioned whether two of each species of animals could be accommodated within the dimensions given, computations have shown that there was not only sufficient room, but room to spare. Scholars have calculated that a vessel of this size would hold more than 43,000 tons.

After almost a year on the water, the ark came to rest on Mount Ararat in what is now Turkey. Numerous attempts across the centuries to find the remains of the vessel have been futile. Shifting glaciers, avalanches, hidden crevices, and sudden storms make mountain climbing in the area extremely dangerous.

The ark reveals both the judgment and mercy of God. His righteous judgment is seen in the destruction of the wicked, but His mercy and care are demonstrated in His preservation of Noah, and, through him, of the human race. The ark is a striking illustration of Christ, who preserves us from the flood of divine judgment through His grace.

From the ancient world there are several other

ARK OF THE COVENANT

flood stories that are remarkably similar to the biblical account in many details. In the most famous of these, Utnapishti, the Babylonian "Noah," constructed a boat, which was about 180 feet long, 180 feet wide, and 180 feet high—hardly a seaworthy design. In stark contrast to these stories, the Book of Genesis presents a holy and righteous God who sent the flood of judgment against sin and yet mercifully saved Noah and his family because of their righteousness.

In the New Testament, Jesus spoke of the flood and of Noah and the ark, comparing "the days of Noah" with the time of "the coming of the Son of Man" (Ma 24:37-38; Lk 17:26-27). Other New Testament references to the flood include Hebrews 11:7; 1 Peter 3:20; and 2 Peter 2:5.

2. *Ark of the Covenant, Ark of the Testimony.* An oblong chest two and a half cubits long and one and a half in breadth and depth. It was made of shittim, or acacia wood, overlaid within and without with pure gold. It was covered by a lid of solid gold. It was carried by means of staves that passed through two golden rings on each side (Nu 7:9; 10:21). The lid on the ark, called the mercy seat, was made of gold. The Hebrew word traditionally translated "mercy seat" could be rendered "place of atonement," because this was where the high priest sprinkled blood once a year on the Day of Atonement as the atonement for sin (Le 16:15). Mounted on this lid were two winged creatures (cherubim), which faced each other with outstretched wings. The cherubim were symbolic of Jehovah's presence dwelling between the cherubim (Ex 25:10-22; Nu 7:89). The ark contained the two stone tablets inscribed with the Ten Commandments, which Moses had received from God at Mount Sinai (Ex 25:21; De 10:3,5); a pot of manna; Aaron's rod that blossomed; and the

Book of the Law (Ex 16:34; De 31:26; He 9:4). The Kohathites, a family of the Levites to which Moses and Aaron belonged, had charge of the ark (Nu 3:29-31; 4:4-15). The ark, borne by the priests, preceded the Israelites in their desert wanderings and in the crossing of the Jordan (Nu 10:33; Jos 4:9-11). It was carried around Jericho (Jos 6:1-20) and was placed in Shiloh (1 Sa 3:3). In the time of Eli the Israelites took the ark into the battlefield, thinking its presence would give them the victory, but it was captured by the Philistines (1 Sa 4:1-22). The Philistines returned the ark to the Hebrews (1 Sa 5:1–6:11) and it was next brought by David to Jerusalem and placed in a tent (2 Sa 6:17). Finally, Solomon had it placed within the holy of holies of the temple (1 Ki 8:1-9). Nothing has been known of it since the destruction of Jerusalem by Nebuchadnezzar, 586 B.C.

AR′ KITE

A family of the Canaanites descended from Ham (Ge 10:17; 1 Ch 1:15). They were located in the north of Phoenicia and founded the city of Arks, which is about twelve miles north of Tripolis.

ARM

A symbol of God's power and strength. Scripture often speaks of God's "mighty hand and outstretched arm" (De 26:8), or similar phrases (Ps 77:15; 89:13; Is 53:1; 63:12).

AR·MA·GED′ DON, HAR·MA·GED′ ON
(mountain of Megiddo)

A gathering place or battleground where the final battle of this world order will be fought (Re 16:16). It is apparently the great plain of Megiddo lying between the Galilaean hills and the mountains of Israel, a notable battleground in Old Testament history. Here Barak defeated the Canaanites and Gideon the Midianites (Ju 5:19; 7:9). Two national tragedies were enacted at or near the place: the slaying of Saul (1 Sa 31:8); and the slaying of Josiah (2 Ki 23:29).

AR·ME′ NI·A *(land of Aram, mountains of Minni)*

A region north of Lake Van between the Black and Caspian Seas. It included the district which had earlier been known as Ararat. It is mentioned as the land to which the sons of

Sennacherib fled after having slain their father (2 Ki 19:37; Is 37:38). See ARARAT.

ARM′ LET

This ornament was worn on the arm between the wrist and elbow (Ex 35:22). It was worn by kings in the East, embellished with jewels, signifying their regal authority (2 Sa 1:10).

AR·MO′ NI *(belonging to the palace)*

A son of Saul and Rizpah. He was hanged by the Gibeonites (2 Sa 21:8-11).

ARMORER

One who makes armor. This trade is not mentioned in the Bible, but it is clear that the Hebrews had armor, so it follows that they must have had armorers.

ARMOR BEARER

An assistant to a military officer of high rank who bore the latter's armor, delivered orders, and performed other duties (Ju 9:54; 1 Sa 14:6; 16:21; 31:4).

ARMS AND ARMOR OF THE BIBLE

1. *For Defense.*

The **helmet,** made of leather and later of iron and brass, was used by various nations (1 Sa 17:5,38; Je 46:4; Eze 27:10).

The **shield** was used by all nations. The large shield covered the whole person while a smaller one, the buckler, was used by archers (1 Ch 5:18). They were oblong, round, or oval and were made of layers of leather or of leather-covered wood (Eze 39:9); also of brass (1 Ki 14:27); and even of gold (1 Ki 10:17).

The **breastplate** (cuirass), also called harness, was a coat of mail which protected the breast, shoulders, and back, and was made of leather, iron, or brass (1 Sa 17:5; Re 9:9).

Greaves which protected the legs below the knees were made of thin plates of metal (1 Sa 17:6).

2. *For Offense.* Offensive armor consisted of the sword, spear, dart, mace, javelin, sling, bow, and arrow. Paul set forth, in his Epistle to the Ephesians, a detailed description of the Christian's armor (Ep 6:13-17), for defending oneself from spiritual attacks.

Following is a list of the arms and armor mentioned in the Bible. More information about each item may be found under its name in the appropriate section of the dictionary:

Arrow, Battering Ram, Battle Ax, Belt, Body Armor, Bow, Breastplate, Brigandine, Chariot, Coat of Mail, Dagger, Dart, Girdle, Greaves, Helmet, Javelin/Spear, Lancet, Mace, Maul, Quiver, Shield, Sling, Spear, and Sword.

AR'MY

From the time the Israelites left Egypt, they had a military organization. It consisted of infantrymen who used the spear, the sling and bow (Nu 11:21; 1 Sa 15:4). Every man over twenty years of age was a soldier (Nu 1:3). Even the Levites, who were not numbered with the other tribes, might be enrolled if conditions required it (Nu 1:48-50). Each tribe had its own regiment, its officer, and banner (Nu 2:2; 10:14). When war threatened, men were dispatched throughout the land to muster the forces by trumpet blast, by proclamation, or other means. These forces were divided into thousands and hundreds under their officers (Nu 31:14; Ju 6:34-35). A standing army dates from the time of Saul. He had a band of 3,000 men (1 Sa 13:2). Under David the army was greatly increased. It consisted of twelve divisions of 24,000 footmen each (1 Ch 27). Chariots also came into use, and Solomon greatly increased the number of chariots in the Israelite army (1 Ki 9:19). The army was supported by public funds but it is doubtful if the soldiers were paid.

AR'NAN *(agile)*

A descendant of Zerubbabel (1 Ch 3:21).

AR'NI

The father of Amminadab, also called Ram (Ru 4:19; Lk 3:33).

AR'NON *(noisy, or rushing stream)*

This river was the boundary between Moab and the Amorites (Nu 21:13-14,26; Ju 11:22). After the conquests of Joshua, it separated Moab from the tribe of Reuben (Jos 12:1-2; 13:9,16). It empties into the Dead Sea.

AR'OD, A·RO'DI

A son of Gad (Ge 46:16; Nu 26:17), ancestor of the Arodites.

AR'O·DITES

See AROD.

A·RO'ER *(naked)*

Three towns of Old Testament Israel:

1. A town in the south of Judah to which David sent booty taken from the Amalekites (1 Sa 30:28).

2. A city on the northern bank of the Arnon. It was in the southern part of the kingdom of Sihon afterwards inhabited by the tribe of Reuben (De 2:36; 3:12; Jos 12:2). It was captured by King Mesha of Moab and later by King Hazael of Syria (2 Ki 10:33). In the time of Jeremiah Moab possessed it (Je 48:19).

3. A town of Gilead belonging to Gad (Nu 32:34; Jos 13:25).

A·RO'ER·ITE

A native or inhabitant of Aroer (1 Ch 11:44).

AR·PACH'SHAD

See ARPHAXAD.

AR'PAD AR'PHAD

A city in Syria near Damascus and Hamath (2 Ki 18:34; 19:13; Is 10:9; Je 49:23). It was besieged and captured by Tiglath-pileser II in 742-740 B.C. An uprising in 720 B.C. was crushed by Sargon.

AR·PHAX'AD, AR·PACH'SHAD

A son of Shem (Ge 10:22,24; 1 Ch 1:17-18) and an ancestor of Abraham.

ARRAY (archaic)

To put on; to clothe (Ma 6:27-29).

AR'ROW

A straight slender shaft of wood, with a stone or metal tip, made to be shot from a bow. Arrows were used both in hunting and in war (Ge 27:3). They were carried in a quiver (Is 22:6) and it would appear from Job 6:4 that they were sometimes poisoned. Figuratively, they denote danger, injury, bitterness, falsity.

AR·TA·XERX'ES *(exalted king)*

Any one of several Persian kings, as Artaxerxes I, the third son of Xerxes (Ahasuerus). He reigned 464-424 B.C. and was called Artaxerxes

ARROW

Longimanus which according to some, denoted the long length of his hands, but others regard it as a figurative expression indicating the extent of his kingdom. It was probably he who listened to the enemies of the Jews and stopped the work on the second temple (Ez 4:7); but when the edict of Cyrus was found, the building operations were renewed (Ez 6:1-4). In his twentieth year (445 B.C.), he commissioned Nehemiah to go to Jerusalem and rebuild the walls (Ne 2:1). After an absence of twelve years Nehemiah returned to Persia but in a short time was permitted to return to Jerusalem. During his entire stay in Jerusalem, Nehemiah acted in the capacity of governor (Ne 13:6). Longimanus did more for the Jews than any other Persian king except Cyrus.

AR'TE·MAS

A companion of Paul and, according to tradition, a prominent bishop of Lystra (Tit 3:12).

AR'TE·MIS

Greek goddess of hunting, corresponding to the Roman goddess, Diana (Ac 19:24).

AR'TI·FI·CERS

Workmen especially skilled in working in metals, wood carving, gold plating, setting precious stones, and designing embroideries (Ge 4:22; 1 Ch 29:5; 2 Ch 34:11; Is 3:3). See also METALSMITH.

AR'TIS·AN

See ARTIFICER and METALSMITH.

A·RU'BOTH *(the lattices)*

A city or district of which the son of Hesed was purveyor (1 Ki 4:10).

A·RU'MAH *(a height)*

A town near Shechem. At one time it was the residence of Abimelech (Ju 9:41) and was possibly the same as Rumah (2 Ki 23:3b).

AR'VAD *(wandering)*

The most northerly of the Phoenician cities, a sort of second Tyre, built on the rocky island of Aradus. In the time of Ezekiel men of this city defended Tyre (Eze 27:8,11).

AR'VA·DITE

An inhabitant of the island of Aradus or Arvad. They were descendants of the sons of Canaan (Ge 10:18). See ARVAD.

AR'ZA *(delight)*

A steward over the house of Elah (1 Ki 16:9).

A'SA *(physician)*

Two Old Testament men:

1. Third king of Judah, the son of Abijam and grandson of Rehoboam. He had a peaceful reign for his first ten years (2 Ch 14:1). He punished his mother for idolatry (1 Ki 15:9-13). He defeated Zerah, the Ethiopian, when the latter invaded Judah (2 Ch 14:9-15) and, aided by Azariah, reformed the people (2 Ch 15:1-15). He made an alliance with Damascus for which he was reproved by Hanani (1 Ki 15:16-22; 2 Ch 16:1-10). In his old age Asa was diseased in his feet and was less loyal to the Lord than he had been earlier (1 Ki 15:23; 2 Ch 16:12).

2. A Levite, son of Elkanah. He lived in one of the Netophathite villages (1 Ch 9:16).

AS'A·HEL *(God hath made)*

Four Old Testament men:

1. The brother of Joab, son of David's sister Zeruiah (1 Ch 2:16). He is described as being "fleet of foot as a wild gazelle." Abner killed him in self-defense (2 Sa 2:12-23).

2. One employed by Hezekiah to have charge of offerings and tithes (2 Ch 31:13).

3. A Levite appointed by Jehoshaphat to instruct the people (2 Ch 17:8).

4. Father of a certain Jonathan, who opposed Ezra (Ez 10:15).

A·SAHI'AH

See ASAIAH.

A·SAI'AH *(the Lord hath made)*

Four Old Testament men:

1. A chief of the family of Merari (1 Ch 6:30; 15:6,11).

2. A descendant of Simeon (1 Ch 4:36).

3. An officer sent by Josiah to consult Huldah (2 Ki 22:12,14).

4. A man of Judah, son of Baruch and head of the family of Shelah (1 Ch 9:5; Ne 11:5), also called Maaseiah.

A′ SAPH *(gatherer)*

Three Old Testament men:

1. A Levite, son of Berachiah, and a leader of David's choir (1 Ch 6:32,39). He was appointed to sound the cymbals (1 Ch 16:4-7), and his family was one of the three families responsible for temple music (1 Chr 25:1-9). Some of this family were apparently also appointed as gatekeepers (1 Ch 26:1). The family of Asaph, consisting of 128 or more persons, returned from Babylon (1 Ch 9:15; Ez 2:41; Ne 7:44), and had charge of the music when the foundations of the second temple were laid (Ez 3:10). Psalm 50 and Psalms 73-83 were written by members of the family of Asaph.

2. The father of the chronicler Joah, in the reign of Hezekiah (2 Ki 18:18,37).

3. One who had charge of the royal forests in Israel, appointed to the office by the king of Persia (Ne 2:8).

A′ SAPH, SONS OF

See ASAPH #1.

A′ SAPH•ITE

Descendant of Asaph.

AS′ A•REEL *(God hath bound)*

One of the four sons of Jehaleleel (1 Ch 4:16) of the tribe of Judah.

AS•A•RE′ LAH, ASH•A•RE′ LAH *(right toward God)*

A son of Asaph the Levite. Under David he had duties in connection with the temple music (1 Ch 25:2). In 1 Chronicles 25:14 he is called Jesharelah.

AS′ CA•LON

See ASHKELON.

AS•CEN′ SION

To *ascend* means simply "to go up." In Scripture, the word has a more specific meaning, describing what happens when a person is taken straight to heaven, body and all, without dying.

1. Enoch, one of the descendants of Seth and the ancestor of Noah, was in some manner taken to heaven without dying. The Bible simply says "he was not, for God took him," in contrast to all his ancestors and descendants

whose ends are described thus: "and he died." Enoch was 365 years old when God took him. (Ge 5:18-23; He 11:5).

2. Elijah ascended in a chariot of fire at Jericho (2 Ki 2:9-13). This was clearly a bodily ascension. At first the other prophets did not believe Elisha's account of what had happened, and wasted some time in a fruitless search for Elijah's body. They never found it, for God had taken it away. Centuries afterwards Elijah appeared with Moses in the scene of Christ's transfiguration (Ma 17:1-9).

3. The ascension of Jesus from the Mount of Olives is a dramatic end to His bodily presence on earth. After His resurrection, he remained with the disciples for forty days, teaching them and preparing them for what they would have to face next. At the end of this time, He gathered them together on the Mount of Olives and after commanding them to wait in Jerusalem for the promised Holy Spirit, He rose up into the air and was hidden from their sight by a cloud (Ps 68:18; Lk 24:51; Ac 1:4-11; Ep 4:8-10). As they stood staring up at the now empty skies, an angel appeared to them, and told them that Jesus would one day return in the same way and to the same place.

4. Translation of the Church. Paul states this will occur at the time of the resurrection of the dead in Christ at the first stage of Christ's second coming. Believers will be "caught up," and together with the resurrected believers, they will meet Christ in the air (1 Co 15:51-52; 1 Th 4:13-18).

ASCENT OF AK•RAB′ BIM

See AKRABIM.

ASCENTS, SONG OF

Fifteen of the Psalms have this phrase in their title lines (Ps 120–134). This group of psalms was sung by the pilgrims returning to Jerusalem to worship in the temple. Jerusalem is on a hill (Mount Zion), thus the common phrase "going up to Jerusalem" no matter what direction the traveler is coming from. The temple was also on a hill (Mount Moriah), so a traveler returning to worship would be climbing up to Jerusalem, and then up to the temple. For this reason, the songs sung by the travelers are referred to as songs of ascent.

AS′E·NATH

Daughter of Poti-phera, priest of On. She was the wife of Joseph and mother of Manasseh and Ephraim (Ge 41:45,50-52; 46:20).

AS′ER

See ASHER.

ASH

A tree out of which idols were carved (Is 44:14), probably a species of pine.

ASH′AN (smoke)

This town was allotted to Judah. Later it was assigned to Simeon and then to the Levites (Jos 15:42; 19:7; 1 Ch 4:32). The various renderings, Bor–ashan, Chor–ashan, Cor–ashan, as in 1 Samuel 30:30, may be variants of Ashan.

ASH·A·RE′LAH

See ASARELAH.

ASH·BE′A (adjuration)

A descendant of Shelah of the tribe of Judah. The members of this family wrought fine linen (1 Ch 4:21).

ASH′BEL

The second son of Benjamin and founder of a tribal family (Ge 46:21; 1 Ch 8:1). His descendants were called Ashbelites (Nu 26:38).

ASH′BEL·ITES

Descendants of Ashbel.

ASH′CHE·NAZ

See ASHKENAZ.

ASH′DOD (fortress)

One of five Philistine cities, some twenty miles from Gaza (Jos 13:3; 1 Sa 5:1). It was held by the Anakim and was never taken by the Israelites (Jos 15:46-47). When the ark was captured by the Philistines, it was placed here in the temple of Dagon (1 Sa 5:1-8). Psammeticus, king of Egypt, besieged Ashdod for 29 years. In New Testament times it was called Azotus and Philip the Evangelist labored from this point to Caesarea (Ac 8:40).

ASH′DOD·ITES, ASH′DO·THITES

Inhabitants of Ashdod (Jos 13:3; Ne 4:7).

ASH′DOTH-PIS′GAH

The slopes, spurs, and ravines of Pisgah, the summit of which is Mount Nebo, east of the Dead Sea (De 3:17; 4:49; Jos 12:3; 13:20).

ASH′ER (happy)

The eighth son of Jacob and second by Zilpah, the handmaid of Leah (Ge 30:13). The tribe of Asher was assigned the district that ran north from Carmel along the sea shore. To the east of it lay the tribes of Zebulun and Naphtali (Jos 19:24-31).

A·SHE′RAH

Name of a Canaanite goddess, frequently associated with Baal. It appears that she was symbolized by sacred poles or trees and that frequently the word does not signify the goddess, but only these symbols. In the Authorized Version Asherahs are called *groves*.

ASH′ER·ITE

A member of the tribe of Asher (Ju 1:32).

ASH′ES

A priest was required each morning to remove the ashes from the altar of burnt offering and put them in a clean place (Le 6:10-11). The ashes of the red heifer were invested with a purifying power (He 9:13). Sitting in ashes or sprinkling them upon one's person was a symbol of grief (Job 2:8; 42:6; Je 6:26; Ma 11:21). Eating ashes was an expression of humiliation and misery (Ps 102:9; Is 44:20). "Dust and ashes" was a proverbial expression for human fraility (Ge 18:27).

ASH′HUR

See ASHUR.

A·SHI′MA

The name of a divinity worshipped by the people of Hamath (2 Ki 17:30).

ASH′KE·LON, AS′KE·LON

One of the five chief cities of the Philistines (Jos 13:3; 1 Sa 6:17). It was on the Mediterranean about twelve miles north of Gaza. In the time of the judges it was taken by Judah (Ju 1:18) but was soon under its old rulers (Ju 14:19; 1 Sa 6:17). It was the birthplace of Herod the Great and residence of Salome, his sister.

Its inhabitants are called Eshkalonites in Joshua 13:3.

ASH·KE′NAZ

The eldest son of Gomer (Ge 10:3). In 1 Chronicles 1:6 and Jeremiah 51:27 the name is spelled Ashchenaz.

ASH′NAH (strong)

Two towns of Judah:
1. A town in Judah near Zorah (Jos 15:33).
2. A town farther south in Judah (Jos 15:43).

ASH′PE·NAZ

Chief of the eunuchs of Nebuchadnezzar who was kind to Daniel and his associates (Da 1:3,7,11-16).

ASH′RI·EL

See ASRIEL.

ASH′TA·ROTH

1. A city in Bashan (De 1:4; Jos 9:10). Named after the goddess Astarte, it was the capital of Og, king of the remnant of the giants (Jos 12:4; 13:12). Ashtaroth was allotted to Machir, son of Manasseh, but later, having become a Levitical city, it became the residence of the children of Gershom (1 Ch 6:71).
2. Plural form of the Canaanitish goddess of fertility. See ASHTORETH.

ASH·TE′RA·THITE

Inhabitant of Ashtaroth (1 Ch 11:44).

ASH′TE·ROTH KAR·NA′IM (Ashtaroth of the two horns)

It may be the full name of Ashtaroth or it may have been the place known as Carnaim. In his invasion against the cities of the plain this city was smitten by Chedorlaomer (Ge 14:5).

ASH′TO·RETH (a wife)

The principal female divinity of the Phoenicians, called Astarte by the Greeks and Romans and Ishtar by the Assyrians. The worship of this goddess was established at Sidon (1 Ki 11:3,5; 2 Ki 23:13) and was practiced by the Hebrews in the time of the judges (Ju 2:13; 10:6). Solomon gave it his support (1 Ki 11:5; 2 Ki 23:13).

ASH′UR, ASH′HUR (blackness)

Son of Hezron by his wife, Abiah. He had two wives, Helah and Naarah, and seven children through whom he became ancestor of the inhabitants of Tekoah (1 Ch 2:24; 4:5-7).

ASH·UR·BAN′I·PAL

The son of the Assyrian king Esarhaddon. He is probably the Osnapper mentioned in Ezra 4:10. See ASNAPPER

ASH′U·RITES

Subjects of Ish-bosheth (2 Sa 2:9), probably the Asherites (Ju 1:32).

ASH·UR·NAS′IR·PAL

The king of Assyria during the reigns of Ahab of Israel and Jehoshaphat of Judah.

ASH′VATH

A son of Japhlet and great-grandson of Asher (1 Ch 7:33).

A′SIA

The word in modern usage denotes the largest of the continents, but as used biblically it refers only to the western portion of Asia Minor. It was the richest, and except for Africa, the most important of the Roman provinces. Its capital was the large and ancient city of Ephesus. To the east lay Bithynia, Galatia, Pisidia, and Lycia. Across the strait, now known as the Dardanelles, lay Macedonia. When Paul went on his second missionary journey, he was forbidden by the Holy Spirit to go into Asia (Ac 16:6-10), but later this area, especially the section around Ephesus, was the scene of many of Paul's activities (Ac 19:10,22,26; 20:4,6,18; 1 Co 16:19; 2 Ti 1:15). In this rich province were located the seven churches of Asia (Re 1–3).

A′SIA MINOR

The peninsula which is modern Turkey, the westernmost bit of the continent of Asia. It is bound by the Black Sea on the north, the Aegean Sea on the west, and the Mediterranean Sea on the south.

A′SI·ARCHS (chiefs of Asia)

A college of ten superintendents of public games and religious rites of proconsular Asia.

Among Paul's friends and supporters were the asiarchs of Ephesus (Ac 19:31).

AS′ I·EL *(God hath made)*

A Simeonite, ancestor of Jehu (1 Ch 4:35).

AS′ KE·LON

See ASHKELON.

AS′ NAH *(a bramble)*

The head of a family of Nethinims (Ez 2:50).

AS·NAP′ PER, OS·NAP′ PER

An Assyrian official, a ruler, Esar–haddon or his general or, more probably, Assurbanipal, son of Esar–haddon. He settled foreign tribes, the Cuthaeans, in the cities of Samaria after the fall of Israel (Ez 4:10).

ASP

See SNAKE.

AS·PA′ THA

A son of Haman slain by the Jews (Es 9:7).

ASPEN

See MULBERRY TREE.

ASPHALT

A sticky black or dark brown substance, ranging in consistency from a thick liquid to a solid resembling coal. Natural asphalt is thought to be the same organic materials which form petroleum, in an earlier stage of break-down. Asphalt can also be made from petroleum, but natural asphalt is somewhat different, usu-ally being mixed with mineral materials such as sand and dust. The chemical composition of natural asphalt varies, but generally speaking, it is hydrocarbon combined with nitrogen, sul-fur and oxygen. Natural deposits of asphalt are found in various parts of the world, the area around Sodom was home to a quantity of as-phalt pits (Ge 14:10). The post-flood people who built the Tower of Babel used asphalt for mortar (Ge 11:3), and Moses's mother water-proofed her child's basket-boat with asphalt (Ex 2:3). In some translations, this word is ren-dered *bitumen, slime, tar,* or *clay.*

ASPHODEL

See ROSE.

AS′ RI·EL, ASH′ RI·EL *(vow of God)*

A son of Gilead and great-grandson of Ma-nasseh (Nu 26:31; Jos 17:2).

AS′ RI·E·LITES

Descendants of Asriel (Nu 26:31).

ASS

A donkey. Donkeys technically belong to the horse family, and can be bred with horses, but they will produce sterile offspring. Donkeys are much smaller than horses. Standing only about four feet high, they are closer in size and pro-portion to ponies. They are typically red-brown, grey, or occasionally white. Particular interest is attached to the white ass (Ju 5:10). Donkeys were considered unclean animals, in that it was not permitted to eat them, but they were widely used as beasts of burden, to turn a millstone, to trample grain, or to carry a traveler on a journey. Donkeys are very strong, have a great deal of endurance, and eat much less than horses do, which makes them economical and reliable servants.

In Scripture, there are five Hebrew words translated *ass* or *donkey.* (1) *Chamor* indicates the male domestic donkey (jack), although the word can also sometimes include the female (jenny). In eastern countries the domestic don-key was not only a beast of burden, but was ridden by rich and poor alike. (2) *Athon,* the domestic female donkey was used by Baalam and Saul (2 Ki 4:22,24; 1 Ch 27:30). (3) *Pere,* the wild ass of Syria which is found in northern Arabia, Mesopotamia and Syria (Job 24:5; 39:5;

ASS

Is 32:14; Je 14:6). (4) *Arold* (Job 39:5) an animal of great speed. (5) *Avir,* a young ass or colt (Ge 32:15; Ju 10:4; Ze 9:9). Jesus made his triumphal entry into Jerusalem (Ma 21:2) on a donkey colt.

Donkeys and oxen appear to have been the most popular working animals in Bible times. The Jews were not permitted to yoke an ass and ox together (De 22:10); nor to breed mules, which are the offspring of a jack donkey and a mare horse (Le 19:19). Even though they were not permitted to breed them, the Israelites imported mules from other nations from the time of David (2 Sa 18:9; 1 Ki 1:33; 18:5), and they brought 245 mules with them from Babylon when they returned from captivity (Ez 2:66).

ASSASINS

A terrorist group of the first century, made up of zealots who were trying to overthrow Rome and re-establish the nation of Israel. The Roman commander assumed Paul was a part of this group (Ac 21:38).

ASSEMBLY

Those who are gathered together. This is one translation of the Greek word *ecclesia* which is usually translated *church,* and sometimes *assembly* or *congregation.* The words "assembly" and "congregation" are more literal translations. Most of the time when it is used in the New Testament, the word *ecclesia* refers to the church, the body of Christ. Occasionally, however, it is used in other senses. Stephen used this word to refer to the Hebrews in the wilderness (Ac 7:38), and Luke describes the mob at Ephesus with the same word (Ac 19:32).

ASSENT

To agree upon (Ac 24:5-9).

ASSH'UR

A son of Shem (Ge 10:22; 1 Ch 1:17). His descendants inhabited the land of Assyria. See ASSYRIA.

ASSH·U'RIM

A people that sprang from Dedan and more remotely from Abraham by Keturah (Ge 25:3). According to one theory, they are the same as the Ashurites mentioned in 2 Samuel 2:9.

AS·SI·DE'ANS

See HASIDAEANS.

AS'SIR *(captive)*

Three Old Testament men:

1. Son of Korah (Ex 6:24). He was born in Egypt.

2. A descendant of the preceding (1 Ch 6:23-27).

3. Son of Jeconiah, the son of Jehoiakim (1 Ch 3:17).

AS'SOS

A seaport of Mysia, a few miles from Troas (Ac 20:13-14).

AS'SUR

See ASSYRIA.

ASSURANCE OF NEW LIFE

The believer's sure knowledge that God has changed his or her heart and will, without fail, bring that person into eternal life. Christians not only can possess salvation, they can know for certain that they possess it, and live without fear or doubt of what their final end will be. This knowledge comes in three ways:

The Promise of God: Often the Christian will doubt his salvation because he doesn't feel saved, not understanding that the basis for that salvation is the promise of God and not emotional feelings. All three persons of the Trinity are involved in this:

A. The promise and work of the Father in our salvation. He has promised to graciously accept in Christ all repenting sinners (Ep 1:6; Col 3:3). This means a Christian has the right to be in heaven someday for he is in Christ. God guarantees to us that He will work out all things for our good (Ro 8:28).

B. The promise and work of the Son. He has promised us eternal life (Jo 5:24) and abundant life (Jo 10:10). This covers not only our final destiny in heaven, but also our present Christian service here on earth. He is, in fact, right now praying for us and ministering to us at His Father's right hand (He 8:1; 9:24).

C. The promise and work of the Holy Spirit. The Holy Spirit is said to indwell the believer (Jo 14:16). In addition, He places all believing sinners into the body of Christ, thus assuring us of union with God Himself (1 Co 12:13).

The Witness of the Spirit: While it is true that one need not always feel spiritual to have new life in Christ, nevertheless, feelings and emotions do play a vital role in our salvation. Both Paul (Ro 8:16) and John (1 Jo 3:24) inform us that we can experience an inner witness of the Holy Spirit to our spirit. What does this mean? It means we can enjoy the quiet confidence given by the Spirit that we have indeed passed from death unto life. It means we can now approach the mighty Creator of the vast universe and refer to Him as Abba, Father (Ro 8:15). *Abba* is a very personal and intimate term for one's father. Prior to Pentecost, only Christ had used this title for God (Mk 14:36). It is almost akin to our modern title *daddy* or *papa*. It not only means we can approach the throne of grace with a holy boldness (He 4:16), but we can also experience the blessing of knowing that the Father will hear and answer our prayers (1 Jo 3:22).

The apostle Paul experienced this witness during a crisis in his life, while preaching in Corinth (Ac 18:9-10).

The Changed Life: The first stanza of a famous Christian song begins: "What a wonderful change in my life has been wrought since Jesus came into my heart." Without doubt, the greatest proof of the new birth is a changed life. The child of God now suddenly loves the following:

  A. He loves Jesus. Before conversion, the sinner might hold Christ in high esteem, but after conversion he loves the Savior (1 Jo 5:1-2).

  B. He loves the Bible. We should love God's Word as the psalmist did in Psalm 119. He expresses his great love for God's Word no less than 17 times. See verses 24,40,47-48,72,97,103,111,113,127,129, 140,143,159,162,165,168.

  C. He loves other Christians. "We know that we have passed from death to life, because we love the brethren" (1 Jo 3:14).

  D. He loves his enemies (Ma 5:43-45).

  E. He loves the souls of all people. Like Paul, he too can cry out for the conversion of loved ones. "Brethren, my heart's desire and prayer to God for Israel is that they may be saved" (Ro 10:1; 2 Co 5:14).

  F. He loves the pure life. John says if one loves the world, the love of the Father is not in him (1 Jo 2:15-17; 5:4).

  G. He loves to talk to God and about the things of God. "Speaking to one another in psalms and hymns and spiritual songs, singing and making melody in your heart to the Lord" (Ep 5:19).

AS·SYR′I·A, ASSH′UR, AS′SUR

The land lying on the Tigris between Padan-aram, Babylon, Armenia, and Media. The name is derived from Asshur, the son of Shem (Ge 10:22) who was later worshipped by the Assyrians as a deity. While Moses appears to have known about Assyria (Ge 2:14; 25:18; Nu 24:22), it did not become important to Jewish history until the reign of Menahem. The Assyrians were a Semitic people who originated in Babylon (Ge 10:11). They conquered Babylonia about 1300 B.C. and under Tiglath–pileser I became the strongest power in the East. They are mentioned in the Bible chiefly for their warlike aggressions. During the days of David and Solomon, Assyria had declined under the successors of Tiglath-pileser I, and it was not a serious threat to the expansion of the kingdom of Israel. However, when Tiglath-pileser III came into power, Assyria began to stretch its power and influence. In Scripture, this Assyrian king is also called Pul (2 Ki 15:19). When under pressure from Pekah, king of Israel, and Rezin of Syria, Ahaz, king of Judah gave Tiglath-pileser gifts of treasure in exchange for protection. In consequence of his association with Assyria, Ahaz made the mistake of rearranging the altars and furnishings of the temple; replacing the altar with a copy of one he had seen in Damascus, and offering sacrifices on it himself.

Tiglath-pileser was succeeded by his son Shalmanesar, and Shalmanesar began to put pressure on Israel, demanding tribute. One year, Hoshea refused to pay, and Shalmanesar took swift action. In the year 722 B.C., the nation of Israel was invaded, conquered, and carried captive into Assyria. The nation never recovered from this depredation, and the ten northern tribes were scattered and mixed and forgot their ancestry. Most of the exiles never returned to the land.

Some years later, another Assyrian king, Sennacharib, came up against Jerusalem when Hezekiah was king. This time, however, Judah had a righteous ruler, and God rescued His people from the hands of the Assyrians (2 Ki 18:17–19:37). See SENNACHERIB'S PRISM.

The Assyrians were a pagan people, whose idol worship was strongly condemned by several Old Testament prophets (Is 10:5; Eze 16:28; Ho 8:9). They emphasized the worship of nature, believing that the natural elements were possessed by a spirit. Along with the national deity, Assur, the Assyrian people worshipped Shemach, the sun god; Sin, the moon god; and Hadad, the god of thunder.

The Assyrians were notorious for their savagery in warfare. They burned and looted cities and showed little mercy to their captives. In stone carvings discovered by archeologists, Assyrian soldiers are shown torturing children, blinding warriors, chopping off hands, impaling victims on stakes, and beheading their enemies.

Because of the cruelty and paganism of the Assyrians, the Hebrew people harbored deep-seated resentment and hostility toward this nation. This attitude is revealed clearly in the Book of Jonah. The reluctant prophet Jonah, like the rest of the Israelites, hated and despised the Assyrians. When God told him to go and preach repentance to the Assyrian capital city of Nineveh, Jonah refused. When he finally obeyed God, and the city actually repented, Jonah was angry with God for forgiving such a wicked people, instead of destroying them as he had prophesied (See JONAH, BOOK OF).

The entire Book of Nahum is a prediction of God's judgment against the Assyrians. Nahum informed the nation that its days as a world power were drawing to a close. In an oracle of woe, the prophet described Nineveh as a "bloody city . . . full of lies and robbery" (Na 3:1). But soon the city of Nineveh would be laid waste, and Assyria would crumble before the judgment of God. This happened as Nahum prophesied when the Babylonians and Medians formed a coalition to defeat the Assyrians about 612 B.C.

The Assyrians were a wicked people, guilty of much cruelty and evil, but nevertheless God used them to scourge the disobedient nations of Judah and Israel.

ASTAROTH

See ASHTORETH.

AS·TAR′TE

See ASHTORETH and GODS, PAGAN.

ASTONIED (archaic)

Astonished, taken by surprise (Is 52:13-14).

AS·TROL′O·GERS

Those who study astrology.

ASTROLOGY

The study of the heavenly bodies (sun, moon, stars and planets), not in the scientific sense of astronomy, but rather in a religious sense. Astrologists believe that human affairs are affected by the planets, and by means of them future events can be predicted. The ancient astrologers' observations contributed much to the science of astronomy. In Scripture, astrology is generally linked with the practice of sorcery or divination (Is 47:13). Apparently the Babylonians were particularly interested in such things; astrologists are mentioned numerous times in the Book of Daniel, along with "wise men," "sorcerers," "Chaldeans," and "soothsayers" (Da 1:20; 2:2,10,27; 4:7; 5:7,11,15).

Scripture links astrology with the practice of magic. Any attempt to know the future that does not come directly from God, is bound to lead to deception. To believe that the stars affect or control human events is to deny or belittle God's control over all the universe, and the practice of astrology is clearly not compatible with faith. As in the stories of Moses and Daniel, anytime a magician or astrologer is really put to the test, they will fail. Only one who has communication with the one true God can give accurate prophecy or interpretations of dreams, or real wisdom for the living of daily life.

The practice of watching the stars and using the changes in the heavens to predict the future is very, very old. When God created the sun, moon and stars, He said that they were "to divide the day from the night . . . for signs and seasons, for days and years" (Ge 1:14). Clearly, the "dance of the heavens" is something which was designed by God to be useful to humans. Some even speculate that the constellations (some of which are given remarkably similar names in many different cultures and times) were set up as signs and reminders of God's purpose with humans. Certainly the beauty and majesty of the heavens "declare the glory of God" (Ps 19:1). After sin and rebellion entered the world, it was not long before people were worshipping the beauties of creation rather than the Creator, and the sun, moon, stars, and particularly the planets, became associated with various pagan gods (2 Ki 23:5). Because of the association with these gods, and the way the stars give us both a calendar and a clock, people began to look to the stars to predict other things in the future. Such frightening events as eclipses and comets, as well as the normal movement of the planets were interpreted as signs from the gods.

It has been suggested that the Magi who came from the East to worship the infant Christ were astrologers (Ma 2:1-12). If this were so, it would account for their intense interest in the strange star which eventually led them to the Lord.

ASTRONOMY

Scientific study of the heavenly bodies: the sun, moon, stars, planets, solar system and galaxies. Unlike astrology, astronomy does not attempt to assign spiritual meanings to the movement of the stars and planets. Instead, astronomy relies on observation and calculation to understand characteristics, movement, size and purpose of the different heavenly bodies.

God created the sun, moon, stars, and planets "to divide the day from the night . . . for signs and seasons, for days and years" (Ge 1:14). The fixed positions of the stars, combined with the orbit of the earth around the sun, provides humans with the most accurate calendar possible. The constant orientation of the earth's axis with the pole star, combined with the daily rotation of the earth, makes the night sky an accurate timepiece, while the position of the "rising and setting" sun in the sky does the same for the day. The moon's regular orbit of the earth divides the year into easily differentiated months. In the fall, due to the specific conditions, the full moon appears extra large and bright for several days longer than usual, providing extra light for the harvest. Such details show God's love and care for His creatures.

The precise nature of the astronomical calendar, combined with the writings of the earliest astronomers, enable scholars to come up with accurate dates for some of the biblical events.

A·SUP′ PIM *(stores)*

A building near the southern gate of the outer court of the temple used as a storehouse (1 Ch 26:15).

ASYLUM

See CITIES OF REFUGE.

A·SYN′ CRI·TUS *(unlike)*

A Christian at Rome to whom Paul sent a salutation (Ro 16:14).

A′ TAD *(thornbush)*

A threshingfloor of unknown site between Egypt and Hebron where the funeral party bearing Jacob's body halted seven days (Ge 50:10-11). It is also called Abel–mizraim.

AT′ A·RAH *(a crown)*

The second wife of Jerahmeel and mother of Onam (1 Ch 2:26).

AT′ A·ROTH *(crowns)*

Three towns and an unknown geographical location:

1. A town in Gilead built by the tribe of Gad and captured by King Mesha of Moab (Nu 32:3,34).

2. A town of Ephraim near Jericho (Jos 16:2), possibly the same as Ataroth–addar (Jos 16:5).

3. A place name, listed among the descendants of Judah (1 Ch 2:54).

4. A town on the northeast border of Ephraim (Jos 16:7).

AT′ A·ROTH-AD′ DAR

See ATAROTH.

A′ TER *(shut)*

Two men of the Old Testament:

1. A man, probably a descendant of Hezekiah. Ninety-eight of his descendants returned from Babylon (Ez 2:16; Ne 7:21; 10:17).

2. A porter of the temple (Ez 2:42; Ne 7:45).

A′ THACH *(lodging)*

To this city of Judah, David gave the spoils taken from the Amalekites (1 Sa 30:30).

A·THAI′ AH

A son of Uzziah of Judah of the family of Perez (Ne 11:4).

ATH·A·LI′ AH *(whom Jehovah afflicts)*

One woman and two men of the Old Testament:

1. The daughter of Ahab and Jezebel and the wife of King Jehoram of Judah (2 Ki 8:18,26; 2 Ch 21:6). Her marriage was the result of an alliance between Ahab and Jehoshaphat, the father of Jehoram. Athaliah inherited the character of her mother. When her son, King Ahaziah, was slain by Jehu, she put to death all her grandsons except Joash, who was saved by an aunt. She then seized the throne and reigned six years. An insurrection brought about her death and put Joash on the throne (2 Ki 11:1-21).

2. A Benjamite of the house of Jeroham (1 Ch 8:26).

3. Father of Jeshaiah (Ez 8:7).

ATHANASIAN CREED

This creed was originally thought to be written by St. Athanasius, but most scholars now believe that it was written by some unknown believer in the fourth century. It mainly affirms the doctrine of the hypostatic union (that Jesus Christ is fully God and fully man) and the concept of reward or punishment after death for the deeds done in the flesh.

We believe and confess that our Lord Jesus Christ, the Son of God is at once both God and Man. He is God of the substance of the Father, begotten before the worlds, and He is man, of the substance of His mother, born in the world; perfect God; perfect man; of reasoning soul and human flesh consisting; equal to the Father as touching His Godhead; less than the Father as touching His manhood, who, although He be God and man, yet He is not two, but is one Christ; one, however, not by change of Godhead into flesh but by taking of manhood into God; one altogether, not by confusion of substance but by unity of person. For as reasoning soul and flesh is one man, so God and man is one Christ; who suffered for our salvation, descended to the world below, rose again from the dead, ascended into heaven, and sat down at the right hand of the Father to come from thence to judge the quick and the dead, at whose coming all men shall rise again with their bodies, and shall give account for their own deeds. And they that have done good will go into life eternal; they that have done evil into eternal fire.

ATH′A·RIM

Designation in the Revised Version of a caravan road (Nu 21:1).

ATHEISM

A term signifying the denial of God. It is derived from the Greek word *atheos*—without God. The Bible describes the one who denies the being of God as a "fool" (Ps 53:1). Paul describes those who are without Christ as *atheoi*, "godless ones," this is the only time the actual word occurs in the Bible (Ep 2:12). The natural attitude of the human mind is theistic and not atheistic. We are created with the need, desire, and capacity to worship God; those who reject God, or deny His existence, will end up putting something else in God's place, creating their own gods to try and fulfill that basic need.

A·THE′NI·ANS

The people of the city of Athens (Ac 17:21).

ATH′ENS

The capital city of the ancient Greek state of Attica, celebrated for the distinction it attained in learning and civilization. It dates to before 3000 B.C., and has a long history of famous and successful military campaigns. Athens was the center of art, architecture, literature, and politics during the "golden age" of the Greeks (fifth century B.C.). Many famous philosophers, playwrights, and other artists lived in Athens during this time. In fact, philosophy, properly considered, began in Athens with the pre-Socratic thinkers and came to its greatest expression in Socrates, Plato, Aristotle. It was destined to leave a deep impression on the Jewish and Christian schools of Alexandria.

The city is recognized even today as the birthplace of western civilization and culture. Modern visitors to Athens are impressed by the city's ancient glory, with the ruins of the Parthenon and several other massive buildings that were devoted to pagan worship. In ancient days, the city was adorned by the great statue of the Virgin Goddess of the Parthenon and the colossal bronze figure of Athena on the Acropolis, executed by Phidias. In religious interests, Pausanias says that in the attention paid to the gods, the Athenians surpassed all other states, and the city was filled with sacred buildings, temples and altars. Paul observed this fact when he visited Athens during his second missionary journey (Ac 17:15–18:1). While waiting in the city for Silas and Timothy to catch up to him, he spent some time sightseeing (Ac 17:23). He noticed the Athenians erected statues to all the gods, and even to "unknown" gods. Paul described Athens as a city "given over to idols" (Ac 17:16).

During his visit, Paul met "certain Epicurean and Stoic philosophers" (Ac 17:18) and preached to them about Jesus. This led them to bring him before the court of Areopagus—an institution revered from the city's earliest times. This court met upon the hill called Areopagus (Mars' Hill). Its purpose was to decide religious matters. Members of the court were curious about Paul's proclamation of the god they worshipped without knowing (Ac 17:23).

Paul's speech to the court (Ac 17:22-31) provides a model for communicating the gospel to a group that has no Bible background. He drew from his surroundings by mentioning the Athenians' love for religion, demonstrated by their many idols. He then made his plea for Christianity by declaring that God does not dwell in man-made temples.

In spite of this approach, most of the Athenians were not responsive to Paul's preaching. They could not accept Paul's statement about the resurrection of Jesus (Ac 17:32).

Following apostolic times a Christian Church was in Athens. Although not mentioned in the New Testament, it doubtless arose from the labors of the great apostle. Dionysius was converted through that sermon on Mars' Hill. He was a member of the supreme court of Areopagus and is called the Areopagite. According to tradition he was the first bishop of Athens (Ac 17:15–18:1; 1 Th 3:1).

ATH·LA′ I

An Israelite, son of Bebai, who divorced his foreign wife (Ez 10:28).

A·TONE′ MENT

In the scriptural sense, atonement is the expiation of sin by the sacrificial work of Jesus Christ. It is the means by which reconciliation between God and the sinner is effected. A true study of Scriptures leads to the rejection of the view that the essential truth of the atonement is expressed by what is signified by *at-one-ment,* that is reconciliation. This is an entirely non-etymological dissection of the word, a creative attempt to define the word by what appears to be its parts. The words *atonement* and *reconciliation* in Scripture have an entirely different application. The death of Christ looks toward God rather than toward man. In other words, it is not the moral effect it will have upon the heart of man to induce or influence him to be reconciled to God, but the position the divine Sufferer takes in relation to the law which car-

ries the death sentence of the guilty. Atonement is not synonymous with reconciliation, atonement is necessary to bring about reconciliation; The scriptural significance of atonement is expressed by the following:

1. Redemption, restored by ransom (Ma 20:28).

2. The purchase price (1 Co 6:20).

3. Covering. The Hebrew *cover* as used in sacrificial and propitiatory relations (Ro 4:7).

4. Responsibility assumed (He 7:22).

5. Bearing of penalty (Le 24:15; Is 53:4-6; He 9:28).

6. Propitiation by sacrifice required by God, that is, the securing of the pardon of an offended God (Ro 5:10; 1 Jo 2:2-3).

7. Escaping the death sentence of the law through one upon whom the sentence fell (Ga 3:13).

A·TONE′ MENT, DAY OF

The tenth day of the seventh month was divinely appointed for the expiation of the sins of the nation. On this day the high priest offered sacrifices for the priests, the people and also the sanctuary (Le 16; 23:26-32; Nu 29:7-11). This was the only fast required by the law. Clothed in white linen, the high priest offered a sacrifice for himself and the priests, by which was indicated the imperfection of the Levitical priests, contrasted with which is the perfection of Christ our High Priest. The priest then took the blood of the offering into the holy of holies and sprinkled it on the mercy seat. This was the only day of the year when he entered this inner sanctuary. He then took the two goats which the nation provided. One was slain as a sin offering for the people and the blood was sprinkled within the holy of holies, making atonement for the inner sanctuary and then for the holy place and altar of burnt offering. On the head of the other goat he placed his hands and confessed the sins of the people and then sent it into the wilderness. The goat thus symbolized the sin-bearer, Christ. (He 9). See AZAZEL.

AT′ ROTH

See ATROTH-SHOPHAN.

AT′ ROTH-BETH-JO′ AB *(crowns of the house of Joab)*

A family or village of Judah (1 Ch 2:54).

AT' ROTH-SHO' PHAN (*crowns of Shopan*)

A Gadite town of unknown site, improperly regarded in the Authorized Version as two towns (Nu 32:35).

AT' TA·I

Three Old Testament men:

1. A man of Judah whose father was an Egyptian slave but his mother was a descendant of Jerahmeel and Hezron (1 Ch 2:34-36).

2. A warrior of David, a Gadite, who came to him at Ziklag (1 Ch 12:11).

3. A son of Rehoboam and Maacah (2 Ch 11:20).

AT·TA' LI·A

A city of Pamphylia. It was built by Attalus Philadelphus, king of Pergamos, and named after him (Ac 14:25).

ATTENDANT

See SLAVE.

ATTIRE

Clothing, apparel.

AUGERY

Divination, the foretelling of the future.

AUGUSTAN REGIMENT

A regiment, also called a cohort, was made up of about 600 men, commanded by a tribune; under the tribune were the centurions who were each in command of 100 foot soldiers. When Paul was sent to Rome as a prisoner, a centurion named Julius was put in charge of him (Ac 27:1). This Julius was part of the Augustan Regiment, which was one of five cohorts stationed in the area of Caesarea.

AU·GUS' TUS

The title of Octavius who succeeded Julius Caesar, his great-uncle. Following the death of Caesar he, Antony and Lepidus formed a triumvirate. Augustus afterwards shared the empire with Antony but by his victory in the battle of Actium (31 B.C.), he was made sole emperor by the Senate and had conferred on him the title Augustus (27 B.C.). It was in the reign of Augustus that Jesus was born (Lk 2:1). It was he who issued the decree for the enrollment that brought Joseph and Mary to Bethlehem (Mi 5:2).

AU·GUS' TUS BAND

See AUGUSTAN REGIMENT.

AUNT

Either the wife of an uncle, or the sister of a father or mother (Le 18:14; 20:20; Ex 6:20).

AUTHORIZED VERSION

Better known as the King James Version, for many years the definitive English language Bible. First published in 1611, major revisions were published in 1629, 1638, 1762 and 1769. The 1769 version is the "KJV" that most are familiar with today.

A' VA

See AVVA.

A' VEN (*nothingness, vanity*)

A geographical and city name:

1. An abbreviation of Beth-aven applied by Hosea to Beth-el. It is no longer the "house of God," as spoken by Jacob, but of idolatry, as here Jeroboam set up his idol (Ho 10:8).

2. The "plain of Aven" in the kingdom of Damascus, so called doubtless because of the prevalence of idol worship there (Am 1:5).

3. The city of On in Egypt which the Greeks called Heliopolis (Eze 30:17).

A·VEN' GER OF BLOOD

When one was slain, either by accident or intent, the nearest relative of the one slain was allowed to avenge his death, hence the expression, *avenger of blood* or *revenger of blood*. One who had slain another might flee to one of the six cities of refuge. Here he was given a trial, and if it was established that the act was accidental and not intentional, he was not put to death (Nu 35:19,21,27; De 24:16; 2 Sa 14:11; 2 Ki 14:6; 2 Chr 25:4; Je 31:29-30; Eze 18:20). See CITIES OF REFUGE.

AVERSE (archaic)

Turned backward or away from (Mi 2:8-9).

A' VIM

See AVVIM.

A' VITES

People of Avvim. Members of a tribe, and the inhabitants of a town:

1. A Canaanite tribe; the early inhabitants of Philistia (De 2:23; Jos 13:3), also called AVVIM.

2. The inhabitants of a town of the tribe of Benjamin (Jos 18:23), possibly the same as Ai.

A′VITH *(ruins)*

A city of the Edomites, the native city of Hadad, king of Edom (Ge 36:35; 1 Ch 1:46).

AV′VA, A′VA

An Assyrian city in the northwestern portion of Babylonia. After the fall of Israel, people were brought from Ava to colonize Samaria. (2 Ki 17:24).

AV′VIM, A′VIM

A tribe and a town:

1. A Canaanite tribe; the early inhabitants of Philistia (De 2:23; Jos 13:3), also called AVITES.

2. A town of the tribe of Benjamin (Jos 18:23), possibly the same as Ai.

AWL

A tool with a sharp point for boring holes. A slave who wished to remain with his master instead of being freed when his time of service ended could elect to do so, and would then be marked by having an awl thrust through his ear into his master's door (Ex 21:6; De 15:17).

AXLETREE (archaic)

Axle (1 Ki 7:30,32). Solomon had ten bronze carts with bronze axles built for the temple.

AY′IN

The sixteenth letter of the Hebrew alphabet. It is the heading of verses 121-128 of Psalm 119. In Hebrew each of these eight verses began with the letter ayin. See also ACROSTIC.

AY′YAH

A town belonging to Ephraim (1 Ch 7:28). Possibly Aija (Ne 11:31), another name for AI.

A′ZAL

See AZEL.

AZ·A·LI′AH *(Jehovah hath reserved)*

Son of Meshullam and father of Shaphan, the scribe (2 Ki 22:3).

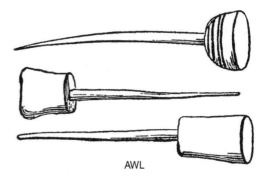

AWL

AZ·A·NI′AH *(Jehovah hath heard)*

The father of Jeshua (Ne 10:9).

AZ′A·RAEL

See AZAREEL.

AZ′A·REEL, AZ′A·REL *(God has helped)*

Six Old Testament men:

1. A Korhite who joined David at Ziklag (1 Ch 12:6).

2. A musician of the family of Heman in the time of David, also called Uzziel (1 Ch 25:18).

3. Prince of the tribe of Dan when David numbered the people (1 Ch 27:22).

4. A son of Bani who was induced by Ezra to renounce his foreign wife (Ez 10:41).

5. A priest of the family of Immer who returned from Babylon (Ne 11:13).

6. A musician of priestly descent, possibly the same as the preceding (Ne 12:36).

AZ′A·REL

See AZAREEL.

AZ·A·RI′AH *(Jehovah has helped)*

At least twenty-four Old Testament men:

1. One of Solomon's officials, son of Zadok (1 Ki 4:2).

2. Son of Nathan and a chief officer of Solomon (1 Ki 4:5).

3. The tenth king of Judah (2 Ki 14:21; 15:1-7,32), frequently called Uzziah.

4. A man of Judah, the son of Ethan (1 Ch 2:8).

5. Son of Jehu and father of Helez; a descendent of Judah (1 Ch 2:38-39).

6. A high priest, son of Ahimaaz and grandson of Zadok (1 Ch 6:9).

7. Son of Johanan and grandson of Azariah #6. This Azariah ministered in Solomon's temple (1 Ch 6:10).

8. A high priest, the son of Hilkiah (1 Ch 6:13-14; 9:11; Ez 7:1). He served during the time of King Josiah of Judah.

9. An ancestor of Samuel (1 Ch 6:36).

10. The son of Oded, a prophet who exhorted Asa, king of Judah to follow the Lord (2 Ch 15:1-8).

11. Two sons of King Jehoshaphat (2 Ch 21:2), probably of different mothers. The second is also called Azaryahu or Azariahu.

12. The son of Jehoram, king of Judah (2 Ch 22:6). In the next verse he is called Ahaziah, calling him Azariah appears to be a copyist's error.

13. A captain who was allied with Jehoiada, the priest who was keeping Joash hidden. He assisted in dethroning Athaliah (2 Ch 23:1,14). His father was also named Jehoram.

14. The son of Obed, another officer engaged in the same conspiracy (2 Ch 23:1).

15. A high priest who rebuked King Uzziah (2 Ch 26:17-20).

16. A prince of Ephraim (2 Ch 28:12).

17. A Kohathite, the father of Joel who assisted in the religious reforms of King Hezekiah (2 Ch 29:12).

18. A Merarite, son of Jehalelel, who assisted in the religious reforms of King Hezekiah (2 Ch 29:12).

19. Chief priest in the reign of Hezekiah (2 Ch 31:10-13).

20. Son of Meraioth, ancestor of Ezra (Ez 7:3). Compare this geneology with 1 Chronicles 6:1-15. Some names appear to be missing from Ezra's list, but this is certainly either Azariah #6 or #7.

21. The son of Maaseiah, who worked on the walls of Jerusalem in the days of Nehemiah (Ne 3:23-24).

22. One who returned to Jerusalem with Zerubbabel (Ne 7:7).

23. A Levite who instructed the people in the law (Ne 8:7).

24. A priest who sealed the covenant with Nehemiah (Ne 10:2), and who participated in the dedication of the wall (Ne 12:33). Azariah #23 may be the same person.

25. One who declared that Jeremiah was a false prophet (Je 43:2).

26. The Hebrew name of Abed–nego, the contemporary of Daniel (Da 1:6-7,11,19; 2:17). Abed-nego and his friends were thrown into the fiery furnace by Nebuchadnezzar, but God rescued them.

AZARIAH, PRAYER OF

See APOCRYPHA.

A′ZAZ *(strong)*

A Reubenite, the son of Shema and father of Bela (1 Ch 5:8).

A·ZA′ZEL

A Hebrew word rendered in the Authorized Version *the scapegoat* (Le 16:8,10,26). The word occurs in this one passage only, but there are several translations of it. According to one it signifies a solitary desert. By another interpretation it means dismissal. Still other interpretations are: a demon of the wilderness, a fallen angel who causes men to sin, and a being. The literal meaning is "going away" (*azel*) "goat" (*az*). Of the two goats, one became a sin offering and the other symbolized the removal of sin. The going away goat was dismissed and sent away into the wilderness. See ATONEMENT, DAY OF.

AZ·A·ZI′AH *(Jehovah is strong)*

Three Old Testament men:

1. A Levite who served as harpist when the ark was brought to Jerusalem (1 Ch 15:21).

2. Father of a prince of Ephraim (1 Ch 27:20).

3. An overseer of the temple offerings (2 Ch 31:13).

AZ′BUK

The father of a certain Nehemiah who labored on the wall (Ne 3:16).

A·ZE′KAH *(tilled)*

A town to which the kings that were besieging Gibeon were driven. It was near Socoh (Jos 10:10-11). Near it the Philistines encamped when David slew Goliath (1 Sa 17:1). It was fortified by Rehoboam, the first king of Judah (2 Ch 11:9). Nebuchadnezzar besieged it (Je 34:7).

A′ZEL, A′ZAL

1. A descendant of Jonathan (1 Ch 8:37-38; 9:43-44). **2.** An unidentified place near Jerusalem (Ze 14:5).

A′ZEM

See EZEM.

AZ′GAD *(Gad is strong)*

An Israelite whose descendants returned with Zerubbabel and with Ezra from Babylon (Ez 2:12; 8:12; Ne 7:17).

A′ZI·EL

See JAAZIEL.

A·ZI′ZA (robust)

A descendant of Zattu who, under the influence of Ezra, divorced his foreign wife (Ez 10:27).

AZ·MA′VETH (death is strong)

Four men and a town of the Old Testament:
1. A Benjamite whose sons came to David at Ziklag (1 Ch 12:3).
2. A descendant of Jonathan, son of Saul (1 Ch 8:36).
3. One of David's treasury officers (1 Ch 27:25).
4. One of David's mighty men (2 Sa 23:31).
5. A town near Jerusalem (Ez 2:24), also called Beth-azmaveth (Ne 7:28).

AZ′MON (robust)

A place on the southern boundary of Palestine near "the river of Egypt" (Nu 34:4-5; Jos 15:4).

AZ′NOTH-TA′BOR (peaks of Tabor)

A place near mount Tabor on the boundary of Naphtali (Jos 19:34).

A′ZOR

Son of Eliakim, descendant of Zerubbabel and ancestor of Christ (Ma 1:13-14).

A·ZO′TUS

See ASHDOD.

AZ′RI·EL (God is help)

Three Old Testament men:
1. A chief of Manasseh (1 Ch 5:24).
2. A chief of Naphtali (1 Ch 27:19).
3. Father of Seraiah (Je 36:26).

AZ·RI′KAM (help hath arisen)

Four Old Testament men:
1. A Merarite (1 Ch 9:14).
2. Son of Neariah, a descendant of David and of the royal messianic line (1 Ch 3:23).
3. Son of Azel, a descendant of Jonathan, son of Saul (1 Ch 8:38; 9:44).
4. Governor of the palace of King Ahaz of Judah. He was slain by Zichri when Pekah, king of Israel, invaded Judah (2 Ch 28:7).

A·ZU′BAH (forsaken)

Two Old Testament women:
1. A wife of Caleb (1 Ch 2:18-19).
2. The mother of Jehoshaphat, king of Judah (1 Ki 22:42).

A′ZUR

See AZZUR.

AZ′ZAH

See GAZA.

AZ′ZAN (strong)

Father of Paltiel, prince of the tribe of Issachar under Moses (Nu 34:26).

AZ′ZUR, A′ZUR (helper)

Three Old Testament men:
1. Father of the false prophet Hananiah (Je 28:1).
2. Father of Jaazaniah, a prince whom Ezekiel denounced (Eze 11:1).
3. One who sealed the covenant with Nehemiah (Ne 10:17).

B

BA′AL (lord, master)

A god, two men and a town:
1. The principal male deity of the Canaanites and Phoenicians. He was adopted by other

BAAL

nations and, as early as the time of Moses, was worshipped by the Moabites (Nu 22:41). In the time of the judges altars were built to him by the Israelites (Ju 2:13; 6:28-32). Jezebel, the wife of King Ahab and a Phoenician by birth, thoroughly established Baalism in Israel. Through Athaliah, the daughter of Jezebel who married King Jehoram of Judah, this false worship took root in that kingdom also (2 Ch 17:3; 21:6). On Mount Carmel Elijah proposed a great test which completely discredited Baal and vindicated Jehovah (1 Ki 16:31-32; 18:17-40). Jehu and Hezekiah both checked Baalism during their reigns, but after their deaths it was revived (2 Ki 21:3). The prophets denounced it (Je 19:4-5). The worship of Baal was attended by lascivious ceremonies and human sacrifice (1 Ki 14:24; Je 19:5).

2. A town of Simeon (1 Ch 4:33).

3. A Benjamite, son of Jehiel and brother of Kish (1 Ch 8:30; 9:35-39).

4. A Reubenite (1 Ch 5:5).

BA′A·LAH *(mistress)*

Two towns and a hill:

1. A town in the northern section of Judah (Jos 15:9-10). It is the same as Kirjath-jearim.

2. A town in the south of Judah (Jos 15:29), probably the same as Balah (Jos 19:3), also Bilhah (1 Ch 4:29).

3. A hill on the northern boundary of Judah (Jos 15:11).

BA′A·LATH *(mistress)*

A town in the territory of Dan (Jos 19:44), possibly the place of that name fortified by Solomon (1 Ki 9:18; 2 Ch 8:6).

BA′A·LATH-BEER *(mistress of the well)*

A city of Simeon, probably the same as Baal (1 Ch 4:33) and Ramoth of the South (Jos 19:8).

BA′AL-BE′RITH *(covenant of a lord)*

A god worshipped in Shechem (Ju 8:33; 9:4), also called El-berith (Ju 9:46).

BA′A·LE

A town of Judah, also called Baalah and Kirjath-jearim (Jos 15:9-10), from which David brought the ark to Jerusalem (2 Sa 6:2).

BA′AL-GAD *(lord of fortune)*

A place in the valley of Lebanon (Jos 11:17; 12:7; 13:5).

BA′AL-HA′MON *(lord of a multitude)*

The site of Solomon's vineyard (Song 8:11), perhaps the same as Baal-hermon.

BA′AL-HA′NAN *(the lord is gracious)*

1. A king of Edom (Ge 36:38; 1 Ch 1:49).

2. A Gederite who had charge of the olive and sycamore trees of David (1 Ch 27:28).

BA′AL-HA′ZOR *(lord of a village)*

A place in Ephraim where Absalom slew Amnon (2 Sa 13:23). It was four and a half miles northeast of Beth-el.

BA′AL-HER′MON *(lord of Hermon)*

A place east of Jordan in the northwestern part of the territory of the tribe of Manasseh (Ju 3:3; 1 Ch 5:23). It was on or near Mount Hermon.

BA′A·LI *(my master)*

A word signifying *master* and used of the Lord (Ho 2:16).

BA′A·LIM

The plural of Baal.

BA′A·LIS *(son of delight)*

A king of the Ammonites about the time of the fall of Judah in 586 B.C. Johanan sent word to Gedaliah, appointed as governor of the remnant left in the land, that Baalis sent Ishmael to slay him (Je 40:13-14).

BA′AL-ME′ON *(lord of dwelling)*

An old city of the Amorites on the border of Moab (Nu 32:38). It was rebuilt by the Reubenites. In Jeremiah 48:23 it is called Beth-meon, and in Joshua 13:17 it is Beth-baal-meon.

BA′AL-PE′OR *(lord of Peor)*

A deity worshipped by the Moabites with impure rites on Mount Peor. Through the counsel of Balaam, the Israelites were led to worship this god. For this they were punished by a plague (Nu 25:1-9; Ho 9:10).

BA′AL-PER·A′ZIM *(lord of breaches)*

At this place near the valley of Rephaim, David had a signal victory over the Philistines (2 Sa 5:18-20; 1 Ch 14:9-11).

BA′AL-SHAL′I·SHAH (*lord of Shalisha*)

It was from this village that bread and corn were brought to Elisha when he was at Gilgal (2 Ki 4:42-44).

BA′AL-TA′MAR (*lord of the palm*)

At this point in Benjamin the army of the Israelites gathered when about to attack Gibeah (Ju 20:33).

BA′AL-ZE′BUB (*lord of the fly*)

The god of Ekron (2 Ki 1:6,16). See BEEL-ZEBUB.

BA′AL-ZE′PHON (*lord of the watchtower*)

A place near Pi-hahiroth between Migdol and the sea where the Israelites encamped just before passing through the sea (Ex 14:2,9; Nu 33:7).

BA′A·NA

1. Two of Solomon's officials (1 Ki 4:12,16, Revised Version).

2. Father of a certain Zadok (Ne 3:4).

BA′A·NAH

1. A Benjamite, the son of Rimmon. He and his brother, Rechab, slew Ishbosheth, successor of Saul. They carried his head to David at Hebron, thinking they would be rewarded for their deed, but David had them executed as criminals (2 Sa 4:1-12).

2. Father of Heled, one of David's warriors, a Netophathite (1 Ch 11:30).

3. The son of Hushai and one of Solomon's purveyors in Asher (1 Ki 4:16).

4. A Babylonian captive who returned with Zerubbabel (Ez 2:2; Ne 7:7).

BA′A·RA

A wife of Shaharaim of the tribe of Benjamin (1 Ch 8:8).

BA·A·SEI′AH (*work of Jehovah*)

A descendant of Gershom, a Levite, and ancestor of Asaph, the singer (1 Ch 6:40).

BA·ASH′A

Founder of the second dynasty of Israel, son of Ahijah. He came to the throne by murdering Nadab, son of Jeroboam, and all of that house (1 Ki 16:7). His capital was at Tirzah (1 Ki 15:27).

TOWEL OF BABEL

While fortifying Ramah in his conflict with Asa, his operations were stopped by Ben-hadad of Damascus (1 Ki 15:16-21). He reigned 24 years.

BABBLER

When Paul spoke to the Epicurean and Stoic philosophers in Athens, some of them derisively called him a "babbler," literally a "seed-picker," because he spoke to them of Jesus and the resurrection (Ac 17:18). To call someone a "seed-picker" was to indicate that he collected bits and pieces of philosophies the way a bird pecks for seeds. They were saying that Paul's preaching didn't make sense to them.

BA′BEL, TOW′ER OF

The Tower of Babel was built on the plain of Shinar, a site probably in ancient Babylonia in southern Mesopotamia, some time after the great flood of Noah's time. A symbol of man's sinful pride and rebellion, the structure was built to satisfy the people's vanity: "Let us make a name" (Ge 11:4). The pyramid-like tower was expected to reach heaven. These people were trying to approach God on their own self-serving terms, but they learned that the gates of heaven cannot be stormed. Men and women must approach the holy God in reverence and humility.

This tower was built of bricks and mortar, since no stones were available in the flat plains of southern Mesopotamia. The Babel tower appears to be similar to the ziggurats the ancient inhabitants of southern Mesopotamia built as places for the worship of their gods. Both Assyrian and Babylonian kings prided themselves on the height of these pagan temples, boasting of building them as high as heaven.

One such tower, built in Ur, Abraham's ancestral city in southern Mesopotamia, about 2100 B.C., was a pyramid consisting of three terraces of diminishing size. The temple was climbed by converging stairways. The uppermost part of the tower was an altar devoted to pagan worship.

God intervened to prevent the builders of Babel from partaking of the power and glory that belongs only to Him. The language of the builders was confused so they could no longer communicate with one another. In their frustration, they abandoned the project. Then the prideful builders were scattered abroad (Ge 11:7-8). In comparison with God's power, their "great tower" was small and insignificant. Humankind's misguided efforts at self-glorification brought on confusion and frustration and their dispersion throughout the world.

BABOON

King Solomon, the wealthiest and wisest of Israel's kings, took pleasure in demonstrating his wealth by importing exotic creatures and valuables from the far corners of the world. First Kings 10:22 and 2 Chronicles 9:21 describe some of these items, including a variety of primates. The NKJV says "apes and monkeys," the NIV translates the second word as "baboons," while KJV, NRSV, and NASB render it "peacocks." It is not unlikely that baboons may have been among the "apes and monkeys" Solomon imported for his zoo.

Some have suggested that the KJV "satyrs" of Isaiah 13:21 and 34:14 may be a species of baboon.

BAB′Y·LON (Babel, confusion)

Babylon, the ancient walled capital of the Babylonian Empire, was located between the Tigris and Euphrates rivers in southern Mesopotamia. The city was part of the empire of Nimrod referred to in Genesis 10:10. Babylon was an old city even when Abraham left southern Mesopotamia about 2000 B.C. (Ge 11:27-31), but it was comparatively unimportant until about 1900 B.C. when it became the capital of a dynasty of kings. It reached the height of its splendor under King Nebuchadnezzar II (he ruled 605-562

B.C.). He enlarged the city into an area of about six square miles and beautified it with magnificent buildings.

According to Herodotus and other ancient writers, the city was laid out in the form of a huge square with the Euphrates flowing diagonally through it. The walls were fourteen miles in extent on each side and were approximately 85 feet thick. It was said to have possessed one hundred gates of brass and 250 towers.

In Nebuchadnezzar's time, eight major gates led into the city. The main gate, known as the Ishtar Gate, opened to a sacred processional way, which led to the temple of the pagan Babylonian god Marduk. The gate and the city walls were decorated with colored bricks, which featured drawings of lions, dragons, and bulls.

The city also contained a palace complex, or residence for the king. The famous hanging gardens of Babylon, one of the seven wonders of the ancient world, were located near these buildings. According to tradition, Nebuchadnezzar built these gardens for one of his foreign wives to remind her of the scenery of her homeland.

Babylon is the city to which the citizens of Judah were carried as captives after the Babylonians overran their nation in 586 B.C. One of these captives, the prophet Daniel, interpreted a dream for King Nebuchadnezzar, making it clear that God would judge the Babylonians because of their mistreatment of God's people, as well as because of their paganism and idolatry (Da 4).

This happened as Daniel predicted in 539 B.C., when Babylonia fell to the Persians. After the Persian conquest (538 B.C.) the city gradually declined and gave place to other cities on the Tigris, of which Baghdad continues to our day. The ruins of this ancient city are an eloquent testimony to the passing of mighty empires and the hand of God in human history.

BAB·Y·LO′NI·A

Babylonia was an ancient pagan empire between the Tigris and Euphrates rivers in southern Mesopotamia. A long narrow country, it was about forty miles wide at its widest point, covering an area of about eight thousand square miles. It was bordered on the North by Assyria, on the South and West by the Arabian Desert, and on the Southeast by the Persian Gulf. The region was also called Shinar (Ge

10:10; 11:2) and the land of the Chaldeans (Je 24:5; 25:12; Eze 12:13). Some of its ancient cities were Ur (Ge 11:28,31; 15:7; Ne 9:7), Erech, Babel, Accad (Ge 10:10), and Nippur.

The fortunes of the Babylonians rose and fell during the long sweep of Old Testament history. In its early history Hammurabi (who probably reigned 1792-1750 B.C.) emerged as ruler of the group of city states on the plains of Shinar. He expanded the borders of the empire and organized its laws into a written system. This was about the time that Abraham's family left Ur, one of the ancient states of lower Babylonia (Ge 11:27-32).

During its long history, Babylonia was constantly at war with Assyria, its neighbor to the North. About 1270 B.C. the Assyrians overpowered Babylonia, reducing its power and influence so effectively that it remained a second-rate nation for the next six or seven centuries. But this began to change dramatically when Nebuchadnezzar became ruler of Babylonia about 605 B.C. During his reign of forty-four years, the Babylonians built an empire, which stretched from north of the Mediterranean Sea to south through Israel along the Red Sea to the Persian Gulf in the East.

Because of his long reign and many military conquests, Nebuchadnezzar is mentioned several times in the Old Testament (2 Ki 24:10-17; Da 1:1-3). In 586 B.C. the Babylonian army under Nebuchadnezzar's leadership destroyed Jerusalem and carried Israel's leading citizens to Babylon as captives (2 Ch 36:6-13). This was a fulfillment of the warning of the prophets Jeremiah and Ezekiel that God would punish His people unless they turned from their idolatry to worship the one true God (Je 27; Eze 23:17-21).

The Babylonians had a system of gods, each with a main temple in a particular city. The system included gods of heaven, air, the ocean, sun, moon, storms, love, and war. Their worship included elaborate festivals and many different types of priests, especially the exorcist and the diviner, whose function was to drive away evil spirits.

Babylonian literature was dominated by mythology and legends. Among them was a creation legend written to glorify a god known as Marduk, who created heaven and earth on a whim from the corpse of the goddess Tiamat. This is a dramatic contrast to the account of God's creation of the world in the Book of Genesis. The biblical writer declares that God created the world from nothing, and He did it with purpose and order in a cycle of six days, resting on the seventh (Ge 1:1-2:3).

Babylonian dominance of the ancient world came to an end with the fall of their capital city, Babylon, to the Persians about 539 B.C. This was a clear fulfillment of the prophecies of Isaiah and Jeremiah. They predicted God would punish the Babylonians because of their destruction of Jerusalem and their deportation of the citizens of Judah into captivity (Is 14:22; 21:9; 43:14; Je 50:9; 51:37).

BABYLONIAN GARMENT

The piece of clothing imported from Babylon which tempted Achan to sin against the Lord by taking spoils from Jericho (Jos 7:21).

BA′ CA *(weeping)*

In Psalm 84:6 mention is made of the valley of Baca. If an actual valley is intended, it may be so named from the presence there of balsam trees which, because of their exudations of tearlike drops of resin, suggest weeping.

BACH′ RITES

Descendants of Becher, son of Ephraim (Nu 26:35).

BACKBITINGS

Evil speaking; slander (Ps 15:3; Ro 1:30; 2 Co 12:20).

BADG′ ER

The skin of this animal was used for the outer covering of the tabernacle (Ex 26:14; 35:7; Eze 16:10). It was also used for sandals. While the common badger is found in Palestine, this may not be the creature referred to in the Bible. The Hebrew word *tahash,* which NKJV and KJV translate "badger skins" is rendered "hides of sea cows" in the NIV, and "porpoise skins" in the NASB.

BAG

A sack, pouch, purse, or satchel. Naaman placed money in a bag (2 Ki 5:23). David placed his sling stones in his shepherd's bag (1 Sa 17:40,49). The sons of Jacob carried grain in bags (Ge 42:25). The bag carried by Judas may have been a small box (Jo 12:6; 13:29) or a purse (Lk 10:4).

BAGPIPE

This instrument is only mentioned in one passage of Scripture, Daniel chapter 3 (NASB). The sound of the bagpipe and other instruments was the signal for the people to bow down and worship Nebuchadnezzar's image. As with all the instruments mentioned in the Bible, it is difficult to know for certain what is meant by this word. The KJV translates it "dulcimer," the NIV and NRSV use "pipes." See DULCIMER.

BA·HA·RU′MITE

A native of Bahurim (2 Sa 23:31; 1 Ch 11:33).

BA·HU′RIM

A village on the road from Jerusalem to the Jordan not far from the Mount of Olives (2 Sa 16:5). It figures in the life of David. Shimei, who cursed him, came from this town and here two of David's men concealed themselves (2 Sa 3:16; 16:5; 17:18; 1 Ki 2:8).

BA′JITH *(house)*

A slighting reference to the temple of Moabitish gods (Is 15:2).

BAK·BAK′KAR

A Levite (1 Ch 9:15).

BAK′BUK *(a bottle)*

One of the Nethinim, head of one of the families that returned from Babylon under Zerubbabel (Ez 2:51; Ne 7:53).

BAK·BU·KI′AH *(wasting of Jehovah)*

Two Old Testament men:

1. A Levite who occupied a high position in Jerusalem after the exile (Ne 11:17).

2. A Levite, perhaps a representative of the family of the preceding. He was employed as a porter of the gates of the temple in the time of Nehemiah (Ne 12:25).

BAK′ER

Among the ancient Hebrews, baking for the family may have been done by the women of the household, but in the towns of Eastern countries there were also public ovens (1 Sa 8:13; Ho 7:6). These shops may have been lo-cated on particular streets (Je 37:21). Pharaoh had his chief baker (Ge 40:1,22; 41:10).

BA′LAAM

A soothsayer, the son of Beor of Pethor, a city of Mesopotamia (Nu 22:5; 24:1). King Balak of Moab attempted to have Balaam curse the Israelites who were invading the land but, receiving the word of God, Balaam had to bless the invaders rather than curse them (Nu 24:1-9). He was slain in battle (Nu 31:8).

BA′LAC

Variant of BALAK (Re 2:14).

BAL′A·DAN *(a son has been given)*

The father (or possibly a more remote ancestor) of Merodach-baladan, also called Berodach-baladan (2 Ki 20:12; Is 39:1). The name appears to be an abbreviation of Merodach-baladan.

BA′LAH

A town whose location is unknown, in the territory of Simeon (Jos 19:3), perhaps the Baalah of Joshua 15:29.

BA′LAK *(empty)*

King of the Moabites when the Israelites invaded the plains of Moab. He attempted to influence Balsam to curse the invaders (Nu 22-24).

BAL′ANCES *(scales)*

There are frequent references to balances in the Old Testament, indicating that they were in common use among the Hebrews (Le 19:36; Job 6:2; 31:6; Ho 12:7). Similar to those now used, they consisted of a crossbeam that turned upon a pin at the top of an upright piece of wood. Supported from each end of the crossbeam was a hook or pan that held the objects as they were being weighed. The Scriptures employ the balance figuratively to convey the idea of equity, fairness (Job 31:6; Ps 62:9; Pr 11:1). The handwriting on the wall in the palace of Babylon declared that Belshazzar was weighed in the balances and found wanting (Da 5:27).

BALD LOCUST

An edible species of locust or grasshopper (Le 11:22, KJV). The Hebrew word *solam* is also translated "devouring locust" (NKJV) or "devastating locust" (NASB).

BALDNESS

The loss of the hair of the head. The Book of Leviticus gives instructions for discerning the difference between natural baldness and baldness caused by leprosy (Le 13:40-44). When a group of youths mocked Elisha for his baldness, they were punished by being mauled by bears (2 Ki 2:23). The prophets often used baldness as a symbol of judgment and mourning (Is 15:2; Je 7:29; 47:5).

BALM

A product of Gilead, celebrated as a healing agent and article of commerce (Ge 37:25; 43:11; Je 8:22; 46:11; 51:8; Eze 27:17); apparently an aromatic gum or resin, though its exact nature and appearance are now unknown.

BALSAM

The balsam fir *(Abies balsamea)* is also called Balm of the Gilead tree; its aromatic sap may be the balm that is referred to in Scripture.

BA′MAH *(high place)*

Hebrew word for high place (Eze 20:29).

BA′MOTH *(high places)*

One of the encampments of the Israelites north of the river Arnon, probably the same as Bamoth-baal (Nu 21:19).

BA′MOTH-BA′AL *(high places of Baal)*

A city of the Reubenites (Jos 13:17). It is probably to be identified with Bamoth, a camping place of the Israelites north of the Arnon (Nu 21:19-20). It may be the "high places of Baal" from which Balaam viewed Moab (Nu 22:41).

BAND

Cohort, tenth of legion, 400-600 men (Ma 27:27).

BA′NI *(built)*

1. One of David's mighty men of the tribe of Gad (2 Sa 23:36).

2. A man of Judah of the line of Perez (1 Ch 9:4).

3. A family that returned with Zerubbabel (Ez 2:10; Ne 10:14).

4. A Levite, a Merarite (1 Ch 6:46).

5. A Levite, the father of Rehum (Ne 3:17; 10:13).

6. Founder of a family (Ez 10:34).

7. A Levite of the sons of Asaph, a Gershonite (Ne 11:22).

BANISH

(Is 16:3-4; 2 Sa 13:37-38; 14:13-14; Re 1:9).

BANK

1. The table of a banker or moneychanger (Lk 19:23). In New Testament times money was placed on deposit and interest on it was paid (Ma 25:27). The banker loaned money and was given security. Money changing was a phase of this business. For a small commission a Hebrew coin would be changed for a foreign coin or vice versa (Ma 21:12; Jo 2:15), and money of one denomination, such as a shekel, would be exchanged for that of another, such as a half shekel. See MONEY CHANGER.

2. A mound of earth in siegecraft (2 Sa 20:15; 2 Ki 19:32; Is 37:33).

3. The edge of a river (Ge 41:17; Jos 12:2; 13:9,16; 2 Ki 2:13).

BANKER

In the law of Moses, God forbade the Israelites to charge interest from one another (De 23:19-20); and also commanded that every seven years they forgive all debts (De 15:2). Even though charging interest was forbidden among the Jews, apparently banking was well-known by New Testament times. It is thought that the Hebrews learned banking from the Babylonians during the years of captivity, and apparently they considered that the ban against charging interest only extended to their fellow Jews. In Jesus's parable of the talents, the master was angry with his servant for burying his money rather than depositing it with the bankers to earn interest and, therefore, increase (Ma 25:27). It had also become the practice for bankers to set up tables in the temple courts, along with those who sold animals for sacrifice. The bankers (moneychangers) exchanged foreign currency, for a fee (Ma 21:12).

BANNER

See STANDARD.

BAN′QUET

A means of social enjoyment, the frequent accompaniment of religious festivities. It might be in commemoration of a birthday (Ge 40:20), the weaning of a son (Ge 21:8), a marriage (Ju 14:10; Es 2:18; Ma 22:2-4), or something like a sheep shearing (1 Sa 25:2,8,11; 2 Sa 13:23-29). It usually began in the evening and often extended over a period of days. Invitations were sometimes sent out, the disregarding of which was considered a grave insult.

BAP' TISM

The subject of baptism is of vital interest to all Christians. However, views and interpretations differ, especially in regard to the *meaning* of baptism, the *modes* of baptism, and the *subjects* of baptism. This article states necessarily, briefly, and without interpretation, some of the main points of view and doctrines.

1. *The Baptism of John.* Some regard John's baptism as Jewish, rather than Christian, because it preceded by some three years the baptism that was instituted by Jesus. Among the Jews, at that time, baptisms or ceremonial purifications were common and there were frequent ceremonial washings, signifying purification and consecration. This was true especially of priestly purifications (Ex 29:4; 40:12; Le 8:6; Mk 7:24). John preached "the baptism of repentance for the remission of sins" (Mk 1:4). Those who were obedient to John's call to "prepare ye the way of the Lord" (Mk 1:3) and repented, "confessing their sins," were "all baptized of him" (Mk 1:5). Lutherans and others hold, on the basis of Mark 1:4, that John's baptism was a means of grace for the engendering of faith unto the remission of sins.

2. *The Baptism of Jesus.* Jesus "was baptized of John" (Mk 1:9), not "unto repentance" nor for "remission of sins" because he had no sins to repent of nor to confess. His baptism, as declared by himself, was "to fulfil all righteousness" (Ma 3:15). The voice, "This is my beloved Son, in whom I am well pleased" (Ma 3:17) set the heavenly seal of approval upon his act of righteousness. It was an appropriate and solemn induction into his public ministry.

3. *Christian Baptism.* Whether Christ personally baptized or delegated this work to his disciples is not definitely known (Jo 3:22; 4:1-2). The difference between the baptism of John and Jesus is recorded in Matthew 3:11; Mark 1:8; Luke 3:16; John 1:33; Acts 1:5. Jesus referred to the baptism of John in Mark 11:30 and John referred to the baptism of Jesus in John 1:32-33. Some hold that there was no essential difference between the baptism of Christ and that of his way-preparer so far as the object and efficacy are concerned. It was just prior to his ascension that Jesus ordained baptism "in the name of the Father, and of the Son, and of the Holy Ghost" as a permanent institution among "all nations" and "unto the end of the world" (Ma 28:18-20). When Paul found that "certain disciples" at Ephesus had been baptized "unto John's baptism," he (Paul) explained it as "the baptism of repentance" and said, "they should believe . . . on Christ Jesus. When they heard this, they were baptized in the name of the Lord Jesus" (Ac 19:1-5). Belief in the Lord Jesus Christ, repentance, and baptism in his name for the remission of sins go hand-in-hand in the New Testament. The apostles administered Christian baptism on the Day of Pentecost (Ac 2:38,41).

4. *The Meaning of Baptism.* The meaning of baptism has been the subject of much controversy. Passages such as, "Repent and be baptized . . . for the remission of sins" (Ac 2:38), "arise and be baptized and wash away thy sins" (Ac 22:16), "by the washing of regeneration" (Tit 3:5), "the baptism of repentance for the remission of sins" (Mk 1:4), are taken to support the view that baptism is for the remission of sins, as is held by numerous denominations. The Lutheran church teaches: "The sacred act which constitutes sacramental baptism comprises more than a mere application of water; it is a 'washing of water by the word' (Ep 5:26)—a literal translation. By divine institution, this water is constituted a sacrament, a means whereby men are made disciples of Christ, sanctified and cleansed by him who has redeemed them, giving himself as a ransom for all (Ma 28:19; Ep 5:26). By it we are sanctified, entering into a holy relation to, and union with, that God who has revealed himself as the triune God, the God of our salvation." Some oppose the view that baptism is essential to salvation. To support this they quote the reply to the jailer's question (Ac 16:30-31) and Paul's statement, "I thank God that I baptized none of you but Crispus and Gaius—for Christ sent me not to baptize, but to preach the gospel" (1 Co 1:14-17). Others point out that baptism is a seal of the work of grace already performed in the soul before baptism is administered, and that the subjects of baptism have already experienced regeneration and because of this are proper subjects for baptism. The Society of Friends (Quakers) for example, who believe in the spiritual character of Christianity, hold that the baptism of the Holy Spirit alone is requisite. The Socinian view regards baptism as merely a mode of professing faith in Christ, a ceremony of initiation into the Christian church. Calvinistic churches hold to the doctrine stated in the Westminster Confession: "Baptism is a sacrament of the New Testament, ordained by Jesus Christ, not only for the solemn admission of the party baptized into the visible church; but also to be unto him a sign and seal of the covenant of grace, of his engrafting into Christ, of regeneration, of remission of sins, and of his giving up unto God through Jesus Christ to walk in newness of life."

5. *Modes of Baptism.* (1) *The Immersionist View.* Immersionists hold to the belief that baptism is one of the ordinances of the church setting forth the central truths of Christianity in sacred symbolism (Ro 6:3-4; Col 2:12). Authority for its practice is based upon the command of Christ as stated in the great commission (Ma 28:19; Mk 16:15-16). The verb used in the New Testament to describe the act of baptizing is *baptizo.* The Greek-English Lexicon by Liddell and Scott gives the meaning of *baptizo* as *dip, dip under.* In agreement with this, Thayer's Lexicon gives the meaning of *baptizo* as being *to dip, to immerse, submerge.* Thayer goes on to say that "it was an immersion in water, performed as a sign of removal of sin." The late Dr. A. T. Robertson, one of the greatest of modern Greek scholars, said: "As is well-known not only in Greece but all over Russia, wherever the Greek church prevails, immersion is the unbroken and universal practice." (These words were written during the days of religious freedom in Russia.) The Greek word, from which the word baptism comes, is transliterated *baptisma.* Of this word, Liddell and Scott give the meaning as *that which is dipped.* With this Thayer also agrees, saying that *baptisma* is a word peculiar to ecclesiastical writers, meaning *immersion* or *submersion.* The fact that *baptizo* means *to dip,* and that the river of Jordan was the place of baptizing, and that "much water" (Jo 3:23) was needed for baptism, all argue for baptism by immersion. The Greek prepositions used in describing the ceremony also are given as evidence that the baptism, spoken of in the New Testament, was by

immersion. In Mark 1:9-10 it is stated that Jesus "was baptized of John in (or *into*) the Jordan. And straightway coming up *out of* the water." In Acts 8:38 the same prepositions are found: "They both went down *into* the water, and he baptized him, and when they came up *out of* the water." That baptism should be by immersion is also argued from the symbolism used by Paul in Romans 6:3-5. "Know ye not, that so many of us as were baptized into Jesus Christ were baptized into his death? Therefore we are buried with him by baptism into death: that like as Christ was raised up from the dead by the glory of the Father, even so we also should walk in newness of life. For if we have been planted together in the likeness of his death, we shall be also in the likeness of his resurrection." The same symbolism is referred to in Colossians 2:12: "Buried with him in baptism, wherein also ye are risen with him through the faith of the operation of God, who hath raised him from the dead."

(2) *The Non-immersionist View.* A number of Christian churches hold to the view that what is essential to baptism is not the mode but the application of water "in the name of the Father, of the Son, and of the Holy Spirit." This view admits any mode of baptism—pouring, sprinkling or immersion. The *Didache* (The Teaching of the Twelve Apostles, c. A.D. 120) says, "But concerning baptism, baptize in this way; having said these things in advance, baptize in the name of the Father and the Son and the Holy Spirit in living (running) water. But if you do not have living water, baptize into other water; but if you are not able [to baptize] in cold, [then baptize] in warm. But if you should not have either, pour water onto the head thrice, in the name of the father and the son and the Holy Spirit." It is held by historians that immersion wholly in water was the prevailing type of baptism in the first century, but apparently the Christians did not consider it a matter to be strict about. Immersion was preferable, but they used what was available. Cyprian said in his Epistle concerning the baptism of the sick: "Baptism by sprinkling is pure—is of the Lord's faithfulness made sufficient." The method of administering the water of separation was sprinkling (Nu 19:17-18; He 9:19). Lutheran doctrine holds: "In apostolic days, there are instances of Christian baptism recorded where immersion was excluded by the

circumstances. When the three thousand were baptized in one day, the Day of Pentecost, at Jerusalem, where was the river or pool in the city or its environments in which three thousand men, women, and children might have been immersed? The eunuch (Ac 8:26-39) was on his way through a desert country, where water was and is to this day scarce, the water courses being few and low in their bed. That Philip and the eunuch 'went down into the water' and 'came up out of the water' is far from establishing an instance of baptism by immersion; it rather describes the simplest way in which the two might get into position to permit Philip to lift water with his hand even from a low and shallow brook or pool and pour it upon the eunuch's head." It is thus believed that immersion is not the only mode signified by the Greek word; that it is not sufficient to show that in classic Greek the word always means to immerse, even if true; it must be shown that such is the only use of the word in the New Testament. In Luke 11:38, the word signifies "wash." It does not require that Jesus would be expected to immerse himself before eating. The same is true of Mark 7:4, which refers to the purification of the Jews in coming from public places in case they had become ceremonially unclean. In Hebrews 9:10, "which stood only in meats and drinks, and divers washings," the Greek noun *baptismo,* derived from the verb, is used. It would not be true to fact relative to the Levitical washings to translate this, "and divers immersions." The argument is that the language used in certain instances does not prove immersion; that "It is contrary to the whole spirit of Christ's teaching to attach great importance to details of ceremony"; also, that baptism, which is a universal rite, may properly and must, of necessity, be varied in mode according to climate and other circumstances.

6. *The Subjects of Baptism.* (1) *Believers.* The immersionists usually contend that baptism should be administered only to believers. They reject making infants the subjects of baptism on the ground that the Scriptures require that repentance and faith are essential to baptism (Ac 2:38; 8:36-37; 19:4-5). Since infants are incapable of meeting those requirements, they are not proper subjects of baptism. The following passages support this view: At the conclusion of Peter's great sermon on the Day

of Pentecost, anxious inquirers asked, "Men and brethren what shall we do?" In answer Peter said, "*Repent* and be *baptized*" (Ac 2:38) and in the verses that follow it is stated, "Then they that *gladly received his word* were *baptized*" (Ac 2:41). Acts 8:5-8 tells that Philip went into Samaria to preach the gospel, and states further (v. 12) "when they *believed* . . . they were *baptized,* both men and women." The record of Paul's conversion says, "he arose and was *baptized*" (Ac 9:18). Other passages could be quoted, but these are sufficient to show faith in Christ was required by the early gospel preachers of those who were to be baptized.

(2) *Infants.* With the exception of the immersionists, most Protestant denominations, as also the Roman Catholic Church, practice infant baptism. Baptists and others contend that baptism should be administered only to believers. Many churches, however, from the earliest time have administered it also to children who have sponsors to care for their Christian nurture. The Lutheran doctrine is stated thus: "There is universal sin, universal need of salvation, under the Old Testament and under the New. Accordingly, when God would make a covenant with his people through Abraham, 'the father of the faithful,' he caused Abraham to receive the seal of that covenant—circumcision. The rule was that people were to be brought into the covenant in infancy, at the age of eight days (Ge 17:12; Le 12:3). If adults and infants in the Old Testament needed to be brought into the covenant, they need the same relationship with God now. In Colossians 2:11 Paul speaks of a circumcision made without hands and in the next verse we learn that he is speaking of baptism. The law of heredity set forth by Christ states: 'That which is born of flesh is flesh' (Jo 3:6). The offspring of sinners can be nothing but sinners. Being by nature sinners, infants as well as adults, need to be baptized. Every child that is baptized is begotten anew of water and of the Spirit, is placed in covenant relation with God, and is made a child of God and an heir of his heavenly kingdom."

7. *The Importance of Baptism.* The importance of baptism is shown by the fact that the Lord Jesus Christ himself submitted to it "to fulfil all righteousness" (Ma 3:15) and that he included it as a part of his great commission (Ma 28:19; Mk 16:15-16). By observing this sacred ordinance, as instituted by Christ, we honor his name and show our love for him.

BAPTISM FOR THE DEAD

It is not known exactly what this practice was. Paul mentions it in his argument concerning the reality of Christ's resurrection and the resurrection of believers in the last day (1 Co 15:29). Some speculate that early Christians may have practiced baptism by proxy for people who died believing but unbaptized. It is hard to imagine Paul sanctioning such a practice, but he speaks quite casually of "baptism for the dead" as though it was common, even if it was unnecessary.

BAPTISM OF FIRE

When John was baptizing in the Jordan, he described the coming Messiah, who would baptize "with the Holy Spirit and fire" (Ma 3:11; Lk 3:16). True to this prophecy, when the Holy Spirit came upon the waiting believers in the upper room at Pentecost, it was accompanied with tongues of fire (Ac 2:3-4).

BAPTIZE

To immerse; to dip or dye a thing (Ac 2:38-40). See BAPTISM.

BAR

An Aramaic prefix meaning "son of," just as the Hebrew prefix *ben* is used in the Old Testament. Peter is referred to as "Simon Bar-Jona," in other words, "Simon, son of Jonah" (Ma 16:17).

BAR·AB′BAS *(son of a father)*

A prisoner, a robber, who raised an insurrection and committed murder. At the Passover season it was the custom for the procurator to release a prisoner selected by the people. Pilate, anxious to save Jesus, offered the Jews the choice of releasing him or Barabbas. They were induced by the priests to choose Barabbas, and to demand that Jesus be crucified (Ma 27:16-26).

BA·RA′CHEL *(God has blessed)*

The father of Elihu, the Buzite (Job 32:2,6).

BAR·A·CHI′AH, BAR·A·CHI′AS
(Jehovah hath blessed)
See BERECHIAH.

BAR′AK *(lightning)*

A man of Kadesh. Israel was oppressed by the Canaanites when Barak, encouraged by Deborah the prophetess, enlisted 10,000 men of Naphtali and Zebulun. They completely routed the enemy and broke the yoke of Jabin and his general, Sisera (Ju 4:1–5:12; He 11:32).

BAR·BA′RI·AN

A term which arose in the days of Greek independence and was applied to all who did not speak the Greek language. When Greece became subject to Rome, the Romans were included with the Greeks as the people differentiated from all others. The word was used, not offensively, but in the sense of foreigner (Ac 28:2,4; Ro 1:14; 1 Co 14:11; Col 3:11).

BAR′BER

On account of the attention paid to the hair and beard by the ancients, barbering must have been a well-known vocation (Eze 5:1). See HAIR.

BARE′FOOT

In the East to go barefoot denoted distress (2 Sa 15:30; Is 20:2-4). The shoes were taken off at any place regarded as holy (Ex 3:5).

BAR·HU′MITE

Another form or perhaps misreading of Baharumite (2 Sa 23:31). See BAHURIM.

BA·RI′AH *(fugitive)*

A son of Shemaiah, descendant of David (1 Ch 3:22).

BAR-JE′SUS

See ELYMAS.

BAR-JO′NA

The surname of Peter (Ma 16:17), meaning son of Jonah (Jo 1:42; 21:15-17).

BAR′KOS *(painter)*

The head of a family of the Nethinim (Ez 2:53; Ne 7:55).

BAR′LEY

A cereal of Palestine (Le 27:16; De 8:8; Ru 2:17). The Hebrews, especially the poorer class, made it into bread. It was mixed with wheat, millet and other ingredients (Ju 7:13; 2 Ki 4:42;

Eze 4:9). It was used as fodder for horses and oxen (1 Ki 4:28). The barley harvest occurred in some regions as early as March and in others as late as May, but it preceded the wheat harvest (Ru 1:22; 2 Sa 21:9-10).

BARN

Several words concerning the gathering or storing of crops are translated rather indiscriminately: *storehouse* (De 28:8); *barnfloor* (2 Ki 6:27); and *garner* and *barn* (Joel 1:17).

BAR′NA•BAS *(son of exhortation)*

The surname of Joses, a Levite of the island of Cyprus. He was one of the disciples who sold his holdings and brought the money to the apostles after the Day of Pentecost (Ac 4:36-37). It was Barnabas who satisfied the doubting Jewish Christians of the genuineness of Paul's conversion and commended him to the brethren (Ac 9:27). He was sent by the church at Jerusalem to aid in preaching the gospel at Antioch (Ac 11:19-24). He brought Paul (Saul) from Tarsus (Ac 11:22-26) and later they were sent to Jerusalem to distribute alms (Ac 11:27-30). The church at Antioch then commissioned Paul and Barnabas to preach the gospel to the Gentiles, which resulted in the first missionary journey with John Mark accompanying them as far as Pamphylia (Ac 13:1-14). Returning to Antioch, they were sent by that church as commissioners to the council at Jerusalem (Ac 15:1-2,12). The council commissioned them to report to the churches in Syria and Asia Minor the decree of the council. A second missionary journey was proposed by Paul, but when Barnabas insisted upon taking Mark, who had left them on the first journey, Paul objected and chose Silas as his companion instead (Ac 15).

BARRACKS

The building or group of buildings set aside for soldiers to live in. When Paul was set upon by the mob in Jerusalem and was arrested, the commander took Paul back to the barracks for questioning and safekeeping (Ac 21:34; 22:24; 23:10).

BARREL

A translation (KJV) of the Hebrew *kad,* also translated "bin" (1 Ki 17:12,14,16) and "waterpot" (18:33). A *kad* was probably a large earthenware pot or jar, rather than a wooden tub or barrel.

BARREN

A person thus afflicted was believed to be under some divine punishment (1 Sa 1:6-7; Is 47:9; Lk 1:25). Among the Hebrews this state was deplored, since every woman cherished the hope she might be the mother of the Messiah. It frequently happened that to escape this reproach women had their husbands bear children by a handmaiden, and the wife regarded such children as her own (Ge 16:2; 30:3).

BARREN FIG TREE, PARABLE OF

(Luke 13:6-9).

BAR′SA•BAS *(son of Saba)*

Two New Testament men:

1. Joseph Barsabas was one of two disciples nominated to fill the place of Judas Iscariot, but when the lots were cast, Matthias was chosen (Ac 1:23).

2. Judas Barsabas, with Paul, Barnabas, and Silas, was sent with letters to Antioch (Ac 15:22).

BAR′SAB•BAS

See BARSABAS.

BAR•THOL′O•MEW *(son of Tolmai)*

One of the twelve apostles (Ma 10:3; Mk 3:18; Lk 6:14; Ac 1:13). Bartholomew is probably the surname of Nathanael (Jo 1:45-46).

BARTHOLOMEW, GOSPEL OF

See APOCRYPHA.

BAR•TI•MAE′US *(son of Timaeus)*

At Jericho this blind beggar, hearing that Jesus was passing, appealed to Jesus to have mercy upon him and was healed (Mk 10:46).

BAR•TI•ME′US

See BARTIMAEUS.

BAR′UCH *(blessed)*

Three Old Testament men:

1. Son of Neriah, the amanuensis and faithful friend of Jeremiah (Je 32:12; 36:4-32). At Jeremiah's request he wrote from dictation many of Jeremiah's prophecies (Je 36:1-8). He read these in public and gave them into the hands of the princes, but the king burned the roll and ordered the arrest of Baruch and Jeremiah. They escaped (Je 36:14-26) and a new copy was made. The enemies of Baruch accused him of influencing Jeremiah in favor of the Chaldeans (Je 43:3). After the fall of the city, the remnant at Jerusalem took him and Jeremiah to Egypt (Je 43:1-7).

2. Son of Zabbai, one who aided Nehemiah in building the wall (Ne 3:20).

3. A Shilonite of Judah (Ne 11:5).

BAR·ZIL·LA′I *(made of iron)*

Three Old Testament men:

1. A wealthy friend of David, a man of Gilead. When David was at Mahanaim, a fugitive at the time of Absalom's rebellion, he provided David and his people with food (2 Sa 17:27-29). When David left Mahanaim, Barzillai conducted him across the Jordan. David urged him to become a member of his household, but because of his advanced age he declined and the honor was given to his son, Chimham (2 Sa 19:31-40).

2. A Meholathite whose son, Adriel, married Michal, Saul's daughter (2 Sa 21:8).

3. A priest, a son-in-law of Barzillai, the Gileadite, who took the name of his father-in-law (Ez 2:61; Ne 7:63).

BASE (archaic)

Lowly, meek (2 Co 10:1).

BAS′E·MATH *(fragrance)*

Two or perhaps three Old Testament women:

1. A wife of Esau, the daughter of Elon the Hittite (Ge 26:34), called Adah in Genesis 36:2.

2. A wife of Esau, daughter of Ishmael (Ge 36:3-4,13,17). Many believe that Esau had but one wife of this name and that the accounts giving her relationships are at variance. She is called Mahalath in Genesis 28:9.

3. A daughter of Solomon. She married the king's tax-gatherer for the district of Naphtali (1 Ki 4:15).

BA′SHAN *(open, smooth, or fertile land)*

A district east of the Jordan extending from Gilead to Hermon on the North (De 3:10,14; Jos 12:5). Following the defeat of Sihon, it was taken by the Israelites before they crossed the Jordan. Its last king was Og, defeated at Edrei (Nu 21:33-35). This district was assigned to the half tribe of Manasseh (De 3:13). It is a fertile pastureland and was famous for its cattle (De 32:14; Ps 22:12; Eze 39:18), also for its oak trees (Is 2:13; Eze 27:6).

BA′SHAN-HA′VOTH-JA′IR

The name Jair gave to the places he conquered in Bashan. The rendering in the Revised Version is "and called them, even Bashan, after his own name, Havothjair" (De 3:14). This district contained sixty cities, strongly protected (Jos 13:30; 1 Ki 4:13).

BA′SHAN, MOUNTAIN OF

Mount Hermon (Ps 68:15).

BASH′E·MATH

See BASEMATH.

BAS′I·LISK

A translation which appears only in the English, not in the American Revised Version. In the Authorized Version, the word used is *cockatrice* (Is 11:8; 14:29; 59:5; Je 8:17). The species of serpent intended is unknown.

BA′SIN

Translation for several Hebrew words denoting certain vessels or containers.

1. *Aggan,* a small vessel (Ex 24:6), is rendered *cup* in Isaiah 22:24 and *goblet* in Song of Solomon 7:2.

2. *Mizrak,* was a large bowl for tabernacle use (Nu 4:14). In Numbers 7:13 it is rendered *bowl* and was used for the meal offering; in Zechariah 9:15 for holding the blood of sacrifices. Gold, brass or silver were used in its construction (Ex 27:3; Nu 7:84; 1 Ki 7:45,50).

3. *Saph* indicated a shallow vessel for domestic use (2 Sa 17:28), also for holding the blood of sacrifices (Ex 12:22) and for use in the temple (Je 52:19).

BAS′KET

Ancient peoples made baskets out of a variety of materials such as cane, reeds, rope, twigs, or even straw and mud, and they were used for a variety of purposes. Food was carried and stored in baskets (Ge 40:17; Ju 6:19; Je 24:1; Ps 81:6) and baskets were used to carry offerings to the Lord (Ex 29:3; De 26:2). The disciples used baskets to pick up the leftovers after Jesus fed the four thousand and the five thousand (Mk 8:19-20). Baskets were made in many sizes, including one large enough to hold a man

(Ac 9:25; 2 Co 11:33). Occasionally, baskets were used for more gruesome purposes, as when the elders of Samaria slaughtered Ahab's sons and sent their heads to Jehu in baskets (2 Ki 10:7).

BASKETMAKER

One who makes baskets. No basketmaker is specifically mentioned in Scripture, but many baskets are mentioned so it is safe to assume that this was a not untypical trade or occupation during Bible times.

BAS'MATH

See BASEMATH.

BAS'TARD

The word denotes one to whose birth a reproach is attached (De 23:2; Ze 9:6). As used in the Old Testament, it also signifies one born of a "mixed" marriage, as between an Israelite and an alien, as well as one born out of wedlock. The author of Hebrews says that if anyone has not experienced the Lord's discipline, he is illegitimate, not a true son (He 12:8).

BAT

A small flying mammal. In Palestine some seventeen varieties have been identified. Bats conceal themselves by day in dark recesses such as caves (Is 2:20-21). They are classed as unclean (Le 11:13,19; De 14:11,18).

BATH

A unit of liquid measure (2 Ki 7:26,38; Ez 7:22). It was one-tenth of a kor or about six gallons. See WEIGHTS AND MEASURES.

BATH'ING

In hot countries of the East bathing was frequent, as in the case of Pharaoh's daughter (Ex 2:5). Upon entering a house, persons washed the dust from their feet (Ge 18:4; 43:24; Jo 13:10). It was a part of the Jewish system of ceremonial purification (Le 14:8; 17:15; Nu 19:7-8). Before entering the temple, or offering a sacrifice on the altar, the priests washed their hands and feet (Ex 30:19-21). On coming from the market, in case they had touched something that rendered them ceremonially unclean, they washed themselves. In the time of Christ the Jews scrupulously washed their hands before eating (Mk 7:3-4).

BATH-RAB'BIM *(daughter of many)*

A gate of Heshbon (Song 7:4).

BATH'-SHE•BA *(daughter of an oath)*

The wife of Uriah the Hittite. The black page of David's history was his adulterous relationship with this woman. Uriah, who had been placed on the most dangerous position of the battlefront by the king's command, was slain, and David married Bath-sheba. She became the mother of Solomon (2 Sa 11:3-4; 12:24; 1 Ki 1:11).

BATH'-SHU•A *(daughter of riches)*

Two Old Testament women:
1. Daughter of Shua and wife of Judah (1 Ch 2:3).
2. Variant of Bath-sheba (1 Ch 3:5).

BATTERING ENGINE

See BATTERING RAM.

BATTERING RAM

An ancient weapon of offensive warfare (Eze 4:2; 21:22; 26:9). It was a formidable weapon in siegecraft. It was designed to demolish walls and gates by continuous battering with a heavy blunt beam, possibly metal headed. A simple battering ram might have been nothing more than a tree trunk carried by a couple of dozen men and rammed repeatedly into a gate or wall to break it down.

BAT'TLE

In the course of ages the Hebrews varied in their mode of warfare, being influenced by the practices of more military nations, but they frequently seemed to exhibit more valor than discipline. The first battle mentioned in Scripture is in Genesis 14:8, where the kings of the cities of the plains joined in battle against one another. It is safe to assume that this is not the first battle to have occurred, however; God destroyed the earth in the flood because of the evil actions of its people, and it is unlikely that these evil actions did not include warfare. The last battle of Scripture is the battle of Armageddon, where Christ will once and for all defeat the wicked (Re 16:14; 20:8). See WARFARE IN BIBLE TIMES.

BATTLE AX

A battle ax is simply an ax used in battle. Because of its metal or stone head, a battle ax is a more effective weapon than a mere club (Je 51:20 KJV, NKJV, REB). This term is also sometimes translated "war club" (NIV, NASB). It could also be translated "mace," which is a club with a metal head—not a sharpened blade like an ax, but sometimes filled with spikes.

BATTLE BOW

See BOW.

BAT′TLE·MENT (ledge)

A structure surrounding the flat roofs of Eastern houses to prevent accidents. Sometimes it denotes the parapet of a city wall (De 22:8; Je 5:10).

BA·VA′I, BAV·VA′I

A son of Henadad (Ne 3:18).

BAY TREE

Rendering in the Authorized Version of the Hebrew word ezrach (Ps 37:35). It is also translated "a native green tree" (NKJV), or something similar.

BAZ′LITH (nakedness)

The head of one of the families of the Nethinim, some of whom returned from the exile (Ez 2:52; Ne 7:54).

BDEL′LI·UM

A precious substance listed with gold and onyx as products of the land of Havilah (Ge 2:12). The exact identity of bdellium is not known, but it was probably a resinous gum. It was the same color as manna (Nu 11:7), and since manna is also described as "frost" (Ex 16:14) many people assume that it was whitish in color.

BEACON

A signal, usually fire on a hilltop, or a light on a pole or tower (Is 30:17). The NKJV translates this as "pole" rather than beacon, but a beacon might have been set on a pole.

BE·A·LI′AH (Jehovah is Lord)

A warrior of the tribe of Benjamin who joined David at Ziklag (1 Ch 12:5).

BE·A′LOTH (mistresses)

1. A village in the south of Judah. It may be the same as Baalath-beer (Jos 15:24; 19:8).

2. A place near the territory of Asher (1 Ki 4:16).

BEAM

A plank or log, a piece of lumber used in building (Ma 7:3). The contrast between a mote (speck of dust) and a beam is exaggeratedly obvious.

BEANS

A common item in Middle Eastern cooking. Beans were sometimes mixed with grain and made into a bread of a coarse type (2 Sa 17:28; Eze 4:9). Beans are nitrogen fixing legumes, which means they make good rotation crops with various grains. They are also high in protein, which makes them a particularly desirable vegetable food source, especially among poor people who cannot afford to eat much meat.

BEAR

The Syrian bear was common in Palestine. One, near Bethlehem, was killed by David (1 Sa 17:34) and two she-bears came out of the woods near Beth-el to maul the youths who mocked Elisha (2 Ki 2:24). In Daniel's vision the second beast, which looked like a bear, probably represented the Medo-Persian Empire (Da 7:5).

BEARD

The Jews gave much attention to the beard as expressing the dignity of manhood and regarded the neglect of it as indicative of weakness or infirmity (1 Sa 21:13; 2 Sa 19:24). In times of mourning it was customary to cut it off (Ez 9:3; Is 15:2). The Egyptians shaved the face and the head, but allowed the hair to grow as a mark of mourning. Before appearing before Pharaoh, Joseph shaved his beard (Ge 41:14).

BEAST

A large four-footed animal (Ge 1:29-30). In the Bible the word includes both wild and domesticated animals (Le 26:22; Je 50:39; Mk 1:13) and also denotes the lower orders of animals that fly and creep (Ps 147:9; Ac 28:5). Beast is frequently used in the Scriptures in a symbolic way to designate that which is brutal, sensual, and ferocious (Ps 73:22). Men are represented as wild beasts (1 Co 15:32). In Daniel's prophecy the four beasts are representative of the four great kingdoms (Da 7:3,17,23). In Revelation, antichrist and the false prophet are represented as beasts (Re 13:1; 15:2; 17:8).

BEATING

According to the law, a wicked man should be beaten for his crimes, but the beating must not exceed forty blows so that the one administering the punishment would not be carried away and so that the sinner would not be too humiliated (De 25:2-3). For this reason, Paul received "forty stripes, less one" (2 Co 11:24). By New Testament times, the Jews had made a practice of administering 39 blows in order to be certain that they did not break the law. See SCOURGE.

BEATITUDES, THE

"Beatitude" is a state of blessedness or happiness, or a special instruction for attaining that quality of bliss. The "Beatitudes" of Jesus, found in Matthew 5:3-12, are so called because each verse begins with the word "Blessed" (or "happy"). Many Psalms contain beatitude statements (Ps 1:1; 34:8; 65:4; 128:1), and there are several more in the New Testament as well (Jo 20:29; Ro 14:22; Ja 1:12; Re 14:13). See SERMON ON THE MOUNT.

BEAUTIFUL GATE

One of the gates into the temple area where a lame beggar routinely sat begging. When he asked Peter and John for alms, they healed him instead (Ac 3:10). See GATES OF JERUSALEM AND THE TEMPLE.

BE·BA' I

Two Old Testament men:
1. The head of a family, members of which returned from exile with Zerubbabel and Ezra (Ez 2:11; 8:11; Ne 7:16).
2. One who signed the covenant (Ne 10:15).

BE' CHER (young camel)

Two Old Testament men:
1. A son of Benjamin (Ge 46:21; 1 Ch 7:6).
2. A son of Ephraim (Nu 26:35), called Bered in 1 Chronicles 7:20.

BECHERITES

See BACHRITES.

BECOME (archaic)

To exactly suit, to be fitting (He 7:24-26).

BE·CO' RATH, BE·CHO' RATH (first-born)

An ancestor of King Saul (1 Sa 9:1), possibly the same as Becher (1 Ch 7:6,8).

BED

Travelers and the poor frequently slept on the ground (Ge 28:11). Rugs or mats, which could be rolled up or carried, were used as beds. Beds that were elevated from the floor were common (2 Ki 1:4-6). Bedsteads were made of wood or iron (De 3:11). Bedsteads, inlaid with ivory (Am 6:4) and having costly coverings (Pr 7:16), belonged to the rich.

BE' DAD (separation)

The father of Hadad, king of Edom (Ge 36:35; 1 Ch 1:46).

BE' DAN

A leader mentioned in 1 Samuel 12:11 as being between Jerubbaal (that is Gideon) and Jephthah, hence probably a Hebrew judge. Some have identified him with Jair and some with Abdon (Ju 10:3; 12:13).

BE·DEI' AH (servant of Jehovah)

A son of Bani who divorced his foreign wife (Ez 10:35).

BEE

Canaan, a land flowing with milk and honey, was evidently a land where bees were abundant (Ex 3:8; Eze 27:17). They lived in rocks and woods (1 Sa 14:25; Ps 81:16; Eze 27:17). Their activities and habits are described in the Scripture (De 1:44; Ps 118:12; Is 7:18).

BEE·LI' A·DA (whom the Lord knows)

A son of David (1 Ch 14:7). He is also called Eliada (2 Sa 5:16; 1 Ch 3:8).

BE·EL' ZE·BUB

The title of a heathen deity. A slight change in spelling is Baal-zebub, the god of Ekron. To the Jews Beelzebub was the prince of evil spirits (Ma 10:25; 12:24; Mk 3:22; Lk 11:15-19). Jesus identifies him with Satan (Ma 12:26; Mk 3:23; Lk 11:18).

BE·EL' ZE·BUL

A form of BEELZEBUB.

BEER *(a well)*
1. An encampment of the Israelites on the border of Moab (Nu 21:16-18).
2. A place to which Jotham fled (Ju 9:21).

BEER′ A *(a well)*
A son of Zophah (1 Ch 7:37)

BEER′ AH *(a well)*
The son of Baal, a prince of Reuben (1 Ch 5:6).

BEER-E′ LIM *(well of heroes)*
A village of Moab (Is 15:8).

BEER′ I *(man of a well)*
Two Old Testament men:
1. A Hittite, father of Judith who was a wife of Esau (Ge 26:34).
2. The father of Hosea, the prophet (Ho 1:1).

BEER-LA′ HAI-ROI, LA′ HAI-ROI *(the well of him that liveth and seeth me)*
A well where Hagar came to realize that she was under the care of the Lord (Ge 16:7,14).

BEER′ OTH *(wells)*
Two locations in the Old Testament:
1. A city of the Gibeonites assigned to the tribe of Benjamin (Jos 9:17;18:25). This city was one of four which formed a league with Joshua, and it was the native city of Nahari, Joab's armourbearer (2 Sa 23:37). Following the exile, persons of this city returned with Zerubbabel (Ez 2:25).
2. A halting place of the Israelites (De 10:6).

BEER′ OTH-BEN′ E-JA′ A·KAN
See BEEROTH No. 2.

BEER′ O·THITE
An inhabitant of Beeroth (2 Sa 4:2; 23:37).

BEER-SHE′ BA *(well of seven or well of the oath)*
A well dug by Abraham near the Philistine border (Ge 21:22-32). Abraham lived here for several years before moving to Hebron. The wells were filled up, but were later opened by Isaac who made a covenant with the king of Gerar here (Ge 26:1-33). On his way to Egypt Jacob sacrificed at this well (Ge 46:1-5) and near it a town arose (Jos 15:28) which was as-

signed to Simeon (Jos 19:1-2). It was at the southern limit of Palestine, hence the famous expression "from Dan to Beersheba." Samuel's sons were judges here (1 Sa 8:2).

BE·ESH′ -TE′ RAH *(temple of Astarte)*
A Levitical city assigned to the Gerahonites (Jos 21:27; 1 Ch 6:71), probably the same as Ashtaroth.

BEE′ TLE
Leviticus 11:22 (KJV) is the only mention of a beetle in the Bible, and considering the information in verse 21, it seems likely that this word should really have been translated "cricket" or even "katydid." Beetles do not jump and fly, while crickets are related to locusts and have legs for jumping.

BEEVES (archaic)
Horned cattle fit to plough (Le 22:19).

BEGAT (archaic)
To become the father of (Ma 1:1-16).

BEGGAR
One who lives by begging for food or money. To be reduced to begging was considered a shame, and a result of wickedness (Ps 109:10; Lk 16:3). Sometimes people became beggars because physical deformities or blindness made them unable to work (Mk 10:46; Lk 18:35; Jo 9:8; Ac 3:10). Begging could be the result of laziness (Pr 20:4). God commanded his people to be generous to the poor, and to give or lend them all that they needed (De 15:1-11).

BEGINNING
In the beginning, God created the heavens and the earth (Ge 1:1). In the beginning, Jesus was with God and participated in the creation (Jo 1:2). Paul describes Jesus as "the beginning," and the firstborn from the dead (Col 1:18). Jesus described Himself as "the Beginning and the End"(Re 1:8; 21:6; 22:13) and the "Beginning of the creation of God" (Re 3:14).

BEGOTTEN, ONLY
Only, unique, one of a kind. John several times describes Jesus Christ as the "only begotten Son of God (John 1:14,18; 3:16-18; 1 Jo 4:9). The Greek word he uses is *monogenes.* The KJV translates *monogenes* as "only begot-

ten," following the probable root of *mono* (alone, only) plus *genao* (to generate, beget). The word seems to be used in this sense in the Septuagint to refer to Abraham's son Isaac. This word is also used in the Luke's Gospel to describe three "only children" (Lk 7:12; 8:42; 9:38). Many scholars think, however, that the word has a deeper meaning, and should more properly be translated "only, unique." This rendering would adequately fit all the other instances of this word, and in many ways is preferable to "only begotten" because it emphasizes the "one of a kind" rather than the begetting. The word is used definitively in this sense in other Greek literature, for instance to describe the mysterious and unique bird, the Phoenix.

BE′ HE·MOTH

Behemoth (Behçmôt) is the plural of the common Hebrew word for cattle or animal (*behçmah,* it occurs 137 times). *Behçmôt,* however, occurs only once, in Job 40:15. The ASV of 1901 and the French Louis Segond Version translate the word "hippopotamus." The NASB, and updating of the ASV, changes the text to "Behemoth," probably because there are a number of details in the passage's description of the beast that do not fit a hippopotamus. For example, a hippo's tail is small, short, and insignificant; it could not be called impressive "like a cedar" (v. 17). Second, verse 19's observation that the behemoth "is first in the ways of God" is a bit too grandiose for a hippopotamus, no matter how "poetic" one may become.

It has been suggested that perhaps the Hebrew word for "tail" (*zanab*) really means a "trunk," which is somewhat tail-like in shape. This would suggest an elephant or mammoth, a much more majestic creature than a hippopotamus.

Those who believe that the Bible contains mythology have no problem with these creatures; to them, they simply never existed. Aside from putting the Bible on a purely human level, this view also destroys the whole argument of the passage. God is contending with Job and using Behemoth as a proof of His own creativity. How can Job consider a nonexistent species to be proof of God's majesty?

Some creationists are convinced that God is describing His most impressive of all land animals: a dinosaur. One of the mighty lizards, such as the brontosaurus or brachiosaurus,

which dragged behind them enormous tails the size of cedar trees, seems like a possibility. Of course, most people believe that dinosaurs were long extinct when Job lived and this idea is ruled out. But there are extrabiblical records of sightings of creatures that sound very much like Job 40:15-24.

The "tail like a cedar" (v. 17) fits perfectly. It is believed that some dinosaurs ate "grass like an ox" (v. 15) and were at home in marshy reeds and overflowing rivers (vv. 21-23). Other dinosaur-like traits mentioned in the passage are strong hips and powerful stomach muscles (v. 16, tightly knit sinews (v. 17), bones like bronze beams and ribs like iron bars (v. 18).

The only final answer that can be given about the behemoth is "identity unknown." It is not like any animal living today and it is only mentioned once in the Bible. But the fact that we do not recognize this creature does not mean that Job 40:15-24 is not a careful and accurate description of a real animal. When European explorers first brought back reports from Africa of a spotted animal with legs like stilts and neck so tall that it reached the treetops, many people scoffed and said no such creature existed or could exist. Today, every major zoo has at least one or two giraffes. We still do not know everything about the ancient animal kingdom.

BE′ KA

Half a shekel, the weight of about 0.2 ounces (5.7 g). A beka was equal to 10 gerahs. (Ge 24:22; Ex 38:26). See MONEY OF THE BIBLE and WEIGHTS AND MEASURES.

BE′ KAH

See BEKA.

BEK′ ER

See BECHER.

BEL (*lord*)

The patron or chief god of Babylon (Is 46:1; Je 50:2; 51:44).

BEL AND THE DRAGON

See APOCRYPHA.

BE′ LA (*destruction*)

Three Old Testament men and a city:

1. A king of Edom and son of Beor (Ge 36:32).

2. A son of Benjamin, founder of a family (Ge 46:21; Nu 26:38).

3. A chief of the Reubenites (1 Ch 5:8).

4. One of the cities of the plain—Zoar (Ge 14:2,8).

BE′LAH

See BELA.

BE′LA·ITES

Descendants of Bela (Nu 26:38).

BE′LI·AL *(wickedness)*

Wickedness or ungodliness (De 15:9; Ps 41:8; Pr 19:28). Paul applied the term to Satan (2 Co 6:15).

BELIED (archaic)

To lie against; to speak falsely (Jer 5:11-12).

BELIEVE

See FAITH.

BELL

Small bells of gold were attached to the robe of the high priest. It was part of his official dress and they were designed to herald his approach (Ex 28:33-34). Little bells were worn by women on their wrists and ankles as ornaments (Is 3:16,18). In Zechariah 14:20 "bells of the horses" are mentioned. These were flat pieces of brass strung together and placed upon the necks of horses.

BEL′LOWS

A tool for pumping air. Bellows were probably made of wood or pottery and leather. They were worked by either the hands or the feet, and used to feed extra air into a furnace to make the fire burn hotter (Je 6:29).

BELLY

The human abdomen. Sometimes this is a simple anatomical term (Ju 3:21-22; Ps 17:14). It is also used to indicate the seat of emotion, the same way we use the word "heart" (Jo 7:38; Ro 16:18; Ph 3:19). See HEART.

BELOVED DISCIPLE

In John's Gospel, there are numerous mentions of "the beloved disciple" (Jo 13:23; 19:26; 20:2; 21:7,20). By comparing the texts of the different Gospels, most have come to the con-clusion that John himself is the "beloved disciple."

BEL·SHAZ′ZAR *(Bel protect the king)*

The leader in command of the Babylonian forces at the time Babylon was captured by the Persians (Da 5:28,30). He was the son of Nabonidus (last king of the New Babylonian Empire) and coregent with the king in the latter years of the reign. His relationship to Nebuchadnezzar was possibly that of grandson—son of the king's daughter (Da 5:11).

BELT

A belt was important to both everyday clothing and to battle armor. A belt, sash, or girdle was used as we use our pockets today, to tuck away money or small valuables. In terms of armor, the word "belt" may refer to the piece of armor designed to protect the lower abdomen, or possibly simply a belt to hold the separate pieces of armor together (1 Sa 18:4). Ephesians 6:14 tells us to "gird our waists with truth," other translations speak of a "belt of truth."

BEL·TE·SHAZ′ZAR

When Daniel was taken to Babylon, this was the name given him by the prince of the eunuchs (Da 1:7).

BEN *(son)*

1. A Levite, a porter appointed by David in the service of the ark (1 Ch 15:18).

2. Hebrew prefix meaning "son of" (Ge 19:38; 35:18; 1 Sa 3:6,16).

BEN-A·BIN′A·DAB *(son of Abinadab)*

Solomon's son-in-law (1 Ki 4:11).

BE·NAI′AH (Jehovah hath built)

Eleven Old Testament men:

1. Son of Jehoiada (2 Sa 23:20-21) and chief priest (1 Ch 27:5). He commanded David's bodyguard (2 Sa 8:18) and held a high position in the army under Solomon (1 Ki 2:35; 4:4).

2. A Levite who played the psaltery when the ark was brought to Jerusalem (1 Ch 15:18, 20).

3. A Levite of the sons of Asaph (2 Ch 20:14).

4. An overseer of offerings (2 Ch 31:13).

5. The father of Pelatiah (Eze 11:1,13).

6. One of David's mighty men (2 Sa 23:30; 1 Ch 11:31; 27:14).

7. A prince of Simeon who helped slay the shepherds of Gedor (1 Ch 4:36-41).

8. Four men who married and divorced foreign wives (Ez 10:25,30,35,43).

BEN-AM' MI *(son of my people)*

A son of Lot by his younger daughter, ancestor of the Ammonites (Ge 19:38).

BEN-DE' KER *(son of Deker)*

Solomon's purveyor in Beth-shemesh and other places (1 Ki 4:9).

BEN' E-BE' RAK *(sons of Berak)*

A town of the tribe of Dan, east of Joppa (Jos 19:45).

BEN' E-JA' A·KAN

See JAAKAN.

BEN' E-KE' DEM *(sons of the east)*

A people group mentioned in connection with the Amalekites and Midianites (Ge 29:1; Ju 6:3,33; 7:12; 8:10; Job 1:3). They harassed the Israelites during the days of the judges.

BEN-GE' BER *(son of Geber)*

A purveyor of Solomon in Ramoth-gilead (1 Ki 4:13).

BEN-HA' DAD *(son of Hadad)*

The name of three kings who ruled at Damascus:

1. The grandson of Hezion. He made an alliance with King Asa of Judah against King Baasha of Israel when the latter was building Ramah. Ben-hadad invaded Israel and captured much territory (1 Ki 15:18-21; 2 Ch 16:1-6).

2. Son of the preceding who, in the time of Ahab, besieged Samaria but was defeated. The following year the war was renewed, but he was again defeated and peace was made (1 Ki 20:1-34). He was later joined by Ahab and ten other allies in his conflict with the Assyrians whom they met at Karkar on the Orontes in 854 B.C. Though the Assyrian king claimed a great victory, in reality he suffered a severe reverse. At a later time Ben-hadad besieged Samaria, but a panic in the Syrian camp brought the siege to an end (2 Ki 6:8–7:20). He was murdered and was succeeded by Hazael (2 Ki 8:15).

3. Son of Hazael under whom Damascus lost her conquests in Palestine (2 Ki 13:24).

BEN-HA' IL *(son of strength)*

A prince commissioned by Jehoshaphat to teach in the cities of Judah (2 Ch 17:7).

BEN-HA' NAN *(son of a gracious one)*

One of the four sons of Shimon of the tribe of Judah (1 Ch 4:20).

BEN-HAY' IL

See BEN-HAIL.

BEN-HE' SED *(son of Hesed)*

The purveyor of Solomon in Aruboth (1 Ki 4:10).

BEN' -HUR *(son of Hur)*

Solomon's purveyor in Mount Ephraim (1 Ki 4:8).

BE·NI' NU *(our son)*

A Levite who sealed the covenant with Nehemiah (Ne 10:13).

BEN' JA·MIN *(son of the right hand)*

Three Old Testament men:

1. The youngest son of Jacob. His mother was Rachel and Joseph was his full brother. His mother died at his birth (Ge 35:16-20). The strong paternal affection of Jacob for Benjamin is seen in his hesitancy in allowing him to go to Egypt with his other sons (Ge 43:1-17). Benjamin was also greatly loved by Joseph (Ge 43:29-34). Benjamin had five sons (Ge 46:21; Nu 26:38-41).

2. A warrior, son of Bilhan (1 Ch 7:10).

3. One who took a foreign wife (Ez 10:32), probably the same as in Nehemiah 3:23; 12:34.

BEN' JA·MIN, TRIBE OF

When the land was divided, the section allotted to Benjamin was between Judah and Ephraim; its eastern limit was the Jordan (Jos 18:11-20). Its chief towns were Jerusalem, Jericho, Bethel, Gibeon, Gibeath, and Mizpeh (Jos 18:21-28). It was one of the smaller tribes, numbering at the time of the exodus only 35,400. For protecting the guilty inhabitants of Gibeah (Ju 19-21) the tribe was nearly annihilated, only 600 escaping. Saul was a Benjamite. When the ten tribes revolted under Jeroboam, a large part of this tribe remained with Judah. Paul, the Great Apostle to the Gentiles, was a descendant of this tribe (Ph 3:5).

BEN' JA·MIN, GATE OF

A gate in the north wall of Jerusalem, called also the high gate (2 Ch 23:20; Je 20:2; 37:13; 38:7; Ze 14:10). See GATES OF JERUSALEM AND THE TEMPLE.

BEN' JA·MITE

A member of the tribe of Benjamin (Ju 3:15; 19:16; 1 Sa 9:1,4,21).

BE' NO *(his son)*

One of the sons of Jaaziah, a Levite of the family of Merari (1 Ch 24:26-27).

BEN-O' NI *(son of my sorrow)*

The name Rachel gave her child whose birth caused her death. Jacob changed the name to Benjamin (Ge 35:18).

BEN-ZO' HETH *(son of Zoheth)*

A son or grandson of Ishi (1 Ch 4:20).

BE' ON

A locality east of Jordan (Nu 32:3), probably a contraction of Baal-meon.

BE' OR *(a torch)*

Two Old Testament men:

1. Father of King Bela of Edom (Ge 36:32; 1 Ch 1:43).

2. Father of Balaam (Nu 22:5) called Bosor in 2 Pe 2:15.

BE' RA

A king of Sodom. He was defeated by Chedorlaomer and his allies when they invaded the country (Ge 14:2).

BE·RA' CAH *(blessing)*

A man and a valley of the Old Testament.

1. A man of Benjamin who joined David at Ziklag (1 Ch 12:3).

2. A valley southwest of Tekoa in Judah. It was here that Jehoshaphat gave thanks after defeating the Moabites, Edomites, and Ammonites (2 Ch 20:26). Some regard it as the valley of Jehoshaphat (Joel 3:2,12).

BE·RA' CHAH

See BERACAH.

BER·A·CHI' AH

See BERECHIAH.

BE·RAI' AH *(Jehovah has created)*

A son of Shimei, a Benjamite of Jerusalem (1 Ch 8:21).

BE·RE' A

A Macedonian city with a large Jewish population. On his second journey, Paul came to this city and the Bereans searched the Scriptures to confirm the things Paul declared (Ac 17:10-13).

BER·E·CHI' AH *(Jehovah hath blessed)*

Seven Old Testament men:

1. The father of Asaph, a Gershonite, also called Berachiah (1 Ch 6:39; 15:17).

2. A Levite in David's reign, a doorkeeper for the ark (1 Ch 15:23-24).

3. An Ephraimite in the reign of Pekah. He befriended the captives from Judah (2 Ch 28:12).

4. Son of Zerubbabel (1 Ch 3:20).

5. A descendant of Elkanah of Netophah, a Levite (1 Ch 9:16).

6. Father of Zechariah (Ze 1:1,7; Ma 23:35). He is also called Barachias or Barachiah. See also JEBERECHIAH (Is 8:2).

7. Father of Meshullum (one who repaired the wall of Jerusalem), and son of Meshezabeel (Ne 3:4,30; 6:18).

BE' RED *(hail)*

1. A place in the wilderness of Shur near Kadesh (Ge 16:7,14).

2. A son of Shuthelah and grandson of Ephraim (1 Ch 7:20). Some have identified him with Becher (Nu 26:35).

BERENI' CE

See BERNICE.

BE' RI

A son of Zophah (1 Ch 7:36).

BE·RI' AH

Four Old Testament men:

1. Son of Asher and head of a family (Ge 46:17; Nu 26:44).

2. Son of Ephraim (1 Ch 7:23).

3. A Benjamite. He and his brother Shema were ancestors of the people of Aijalon (1 Ch 8:13).

4. A son of Shimei (1 Ch 23:10).

BE′RI·ITES

Descendants of Beriah, the son of Asher (Nu 26:44).

BE′RITES

Rendering in 2 Samuel 20:14 for a people visited by Joab in his pursuit of Sheba. They are believed to have been descendants of Bichri.

BE′RITH

A god or idol (Ju 9:46), called Elberith in the Revised Version.

BER·NI′ CE, BERENI′ CE *(victorious)*

The eldest daughter of Herod Agrippa I. She was the wife of her uncle, Herod, king of Chalcis. After his death, her relations with her brother, Agrippa II, gave rise to scandal. She married Polemo, king of Cilicia, but soon left him and returned to her brother. She was with Agrippa II when he visited Festus (Ac 25:23; 26:30). Later she became the mistress of both Vespasian and Titus.

BER·O′ DACH-BAL′ A·DAN

See MERODACH-BALADAN.

BE·ROE′ A

See BEREA.

BE·RO′ THAH *(wells)*

A town between Hamath and Damascus (2 Sa 8:8; Eze 47:16). In 1 Chronicles 18:8 the Authorized Version calls it *Chun* and the Revised Version *Cun*.

BE·RO′ THAI

See BEROTHAH.

BE·RO′ THITE

An inhabitant of Beeroth (1 Ch 11:39).

BE·RU′ THA

See BEROTHAH.

BER′ YL

This is the rendering of the Hebrew *tarshish,* a word derived probably from the place of that name. It was the first stone of the fourth row on the breastplate of the high priest (Ex 28:20; 39:13; Eze 1:16; Da 10:6). In Revelation 21:20 the eighth foundation of the wall of the New

Jerusalem is called beryl (Greek *berullos*). In Ezekiel's vision, the wheels are described as "like the color of beryl." Other translations translate this word as "tarshish stone" (NASB), "topaz" (REB), or "chrysolite" (NIV). Beryl is essentially made up of beryllium, aluminum, silicon, and oxygen, but trace amounts of other minerals give it different colors. Beryl is harder than quartz, and has been used as a gemstone since ancient times. In its most common pale-green state, it is known as aquamarine. Emeralds are dark green beryl. It can also be pink, golden yellow, or colorless.

BE′ SAI

One of the Nethinim whose descendants returned from the Babylonian exile (Ez 2:49; Ne 7:52).

BESEECH (archaic)

To appeal; to call upon; to beg (Ro 12:1).

BES·O·DEI′ AH *(in the intimacy of Jehovah)*

The father of Meshullam who aided in repairing the gate of Jerusalem (Ne 3:6).

BE′ SOM

A broom, the besom of destruction (Is 14:23). A metaphor in the East for utter ruin is that of sweeping away as with a broom.

BE′ SOR *(cool)*

A brook that flows into the Mediterranean about five miles south of Gaza. Here a large number of David's men encamped while the remainder of his troops pursued the Amalekites (1 Sa 30:9-10).

BESOUGHT (archaic)

Entreated; asked; called; pleaded (2 Co 12:8-9).

BESTIALITY

Humans having sexual relations with animals. This was strictly forbidden by God, and the penalty for both the human and the beast was death (Ex 22:19; Le 18:23; De 27:21).

BESTOW (archaic)

To put or place (Lk 12:16-18).

BE′ TAH *(trust)*

A city of Aram-zobah (2 Sa 8:8), called Tibhath in 1 Chronicles 18:8.

BE′TEN *(valley)*

A city on the border of Asher (Jos 19:25).

BETH

The second letter of the Hebrew alphabet. It is the heading of verses 9-16 of Psalm 119; in Hebrew each of these eight verses began with the letter beth. See ACROSTIC.

BETH·AB′A·RA *(house of the ford)*

A place where John the Baptist baptized (Jo 1:28). Apparently, it was a ford on the Jordan. It corresponds with Bethany No 2.

BETH-A·CA′CIA

See BETH-SHITTAH.

BETH-A′NATH *(house of Anath)*

A fortified city of Naphtali (Jos 19:35,38) from which the Israelites did not drive the Canaanites (Ju 1:33).

BETH-A′NOTH *(house of Anath)*

A town in the mountains of Judah (Jos 15:59).

BETH′A·NY *(house of dates)*

Two Israelite towns:

1. A small town on the eastern slope of the Mount of Olives (Mk 11:1; Lk 19:29) near the road from Jericho to Jerusalem. Jesus found retirement and rest in Bethany. It was the town of Lazarus and his sisters, Mary and Martha (Jo 11:1; 12:1). The closing scenes of Jesus's life are more intimately associated with this place, than any other. Simon the Leper, at whose house Jesus was anointed, lived in Bethany (Ma 26:6-13; Mk 14:3).

2. A place east of the Jordan where John was baptizing at the beginning of Christ's public ministry (Jo 1:28). See BETH-ABARA.

BETH-APH′RAH

A city of the Philistines (Mi 1:10). Also called Beth-le-aphrah, Aphrah, and Beth Ophrah.

BETH-AR′A·BAH *(house of the desert)*

A village of Judah on the boundary line between Judah and Benjamin (Jos 15:6,61; 18:22). In Joshua 18:18 it is called Arabah.

BETH-A′RAM

See BETH-HARAN.

BETH-AR′BEL *(house of God's ambush)*

A place of uncertain site (Ho 10:14).

BETH-A′VEN *(house of vanity, that is, idols)*

1. A town of Benjamin near Ai (Jos 7:2) and west of Michmash (1 Sa 13:5; 14:23).

2. This name was applied by Hosea to Beth-el after Jeroboam made it a center of idolatry (Ho 4:15; 5:8; 10:5).

BETH-AZ·MA′VETH

See AZMAVETH.

BETH-AZ′MOTH

See AZMAVETH.

BETH-BA′AL-ME′ON

See BAAL-MEON.

BETH-BAR′AH

A ford of the Jordan near the scene of Gideon's great victory (Ju 7:24), possibly the same as Beth-abara, the scene of John's baptizings.

BETH-BIR′E·I

A town of Simeon populated by the descendants of Shimei (1 Ch 4:31). This is probably the Beth-lebaoth of Joshua 19:6. Also called Beth-biri.

BETH′-CAR *(house of a lamb)*

The place to which the Philistines were driven by the Israelites after their defeat at Ebenezer (1 Sa 7:11).

BETH-DA′GON *(house of Dagon)*

Two Old Testament towns:

1. A town in the lowlands of Judah about halfway between Joppa and Lydda (Jos 15:33, 41).

2. A town of Asher near the border of Zebulun (Jos 19:27).

BETH-DIB·LA-THA′IM *(house of fig cakes)*

A city of Moab denounced by Jeremiah (Je 48:21-22). It may be the Almon-diblathaim of Numbers 33:46.

BETH EDEN

A city of Syria. Amos the prophet foretold the exile of the people of this town as a part of the judgment on Damascus (Am 1:5).

BETH′-EL *(house of God)*

Two Old Testament towns:

1. An ancient town west of Ai and southwest of Shiloh (Ge 12:8; Ju 21:19). When he arrived in Palestine, Abraham pitched his tent here (Ge 13:3). The Canaanites called it Luz, but Jacob named it Beth-el because here he had his vision (Ge 28:19; 31:13), and it was the site of an altar he erected (Ge 35:1-15). Beth-el was assigned to Benjamin and was on the border between that tribe and Ephraim (Jos 16:2). It became a center of idolatry under Jeroboam (1 Ki 12:29-33; 13:1-32). Because of this, it was denounced by the prophets (Je 48:13; Ho 10:15; Am 3:14; 4:4). Hosea gave it the contemptuous name of Beth-aven (Ho 4:15). Amos preached here (Am 7:10-13), and Josiah destroyed its pagan altars (2 Ki 23:4; 15-20).

2. A town of Simeon (Jos 19:4; 1 Sa 30:27). See BETHUEL.

BETH′-EL•ITE

A person from Beth-el (1 Ki 16:34).

BETH-E′ MEK *(house of the valley)*

A town of Asher northwest of the Sea of Galilee (Jos 19:27).

BE′ THER *(division)*

Probably a common noun denoting a rugged country (Song 2:17).

BETH•ES′ DA *(house of mercy)*

A pool or reservoir with five porches at Jerusalem (Jo 5:2,4). A stone ledge at the pool was large enough to accommodate many sick people. The ill and diseased came hopefully to this pool because it was said that an angel came to stir the waters, and whenever this happened, someone could be healed by dipping into the pool.

BETH-E′ ZEL

A town, probably southwest of Hebron (Mi 1:11), though some identify it with Azal near Jerusalem (Ze 14:5).

BETH-GA′ DER *(house of a wall)*

A town of Judah (1 Ch 2:51), probably the same as Gedor (Jos 15:58).

BETH-GAM′ UL *(camel house)*

A town of Moab between Medeba and the river Arnon (Je 48:23).

POOL OF BETHESDA

BETH-GIL′ GAL

A proper name used in the Revised Version for the house of Gilgal (Ne 12:29), perhaps the same as Gilgal.

BETH-HAC′ CHE•REM,
   BETH-HAC′ CE•REM *(house of the vineyard)*

A town of Judah (Ne 3:14; Je 6:1). It is west of Jerusalem.

BETH-HAGG′ UN *(garden house)*

(2 Ki 9:27).

BETH-HAK′ KEREM

See BETH-HACCHERIM.

BETH-HAR′ AM

See BETH-HARAN.

BETH-HAR′ AN *(mountain house)*

A town in the valley of the Jordan (Nu 32:36; Jos 13:27).

BETH-HOG′ LAH *(house of the partridge)*

A village of Benjamin on the border between Benjamin and Judah (Jos 15:6; 18:19,21).

BETH-HOR′ ON *(house of the hollow)*

Two towns on the road between Gibeon and Azekah. They are about two miles apart and are known as the upper and nether Beth-horon (Jos 16:3,5; 18:13-14). One of them was assigned to the Kohathite Levites (Jos 21:22; 1 Ch 6:68). They controlled the pass down which the Amorites fled before Joshua (Jos 10:10). Solomon fortified them (2 Ch 8:5).

BETH-JESH´I·MOTH (house of the wastes)

A town near Pisgah east of the Jordan (Jos 12:3; 13:20). It was the southern limit of the camp of the Israelites at Shittim (Nu 33:49). It was in the territory of the tribe of Reuben (Jos 13:20) but in the last period of Judah was held by the Moabites (Eze 25:9).

BETH-JES´I·MOTH

See BETH-JESHIMOTH.

BETH-LE-APH´RAH

See APHRAH.

BETH-LE·BA´OTH (house of lionesses)

A town assigned to the Simeonites in the south of Judah (Jos 19:6). In Joshua 15:32 it is called Lebaoth. See also BETH-BEREI.

BETH´-LE·HEM (house of bread)

1. Located in the hill country of Judah in southern Palestine, the humble village of Bethlehem is famous as the home of David and the birthplace of Jesus Christ. Bethlehem is situated five miles south of Jerusalem. It was formerly called Ephrath, or Ephratha (Ge 35:16,19; 48:7; Mi 5:2). Rachel died and was buried near this town (Ge 35:16,19).

The region around Bethlehem today is known for its fertile hills and valleys. Its busy marketplaces and religious shrines continue to attract tourists. Bethlehem's main attraction is the Church of Nativity, which is supposedly built over the birthplace of the Savior. Most scholars agree this is one of the best authenticated sites in the Holy Land. The present building, erected over the cave area which served as a stable for the crowded inn, was built by the Roman emperor Justinian I in the sixth century A.D. The city and the church are especially popular as destinations for pilgrims during Christmas celebrations.

Bethlehem is also closely associated with King David, Israel's favorite king. Known as the city of David, Bethlehem is his ancestral home and the site where Samuel anointed David as Saul's successor. The Prophet Micah foresaw the com-

ing of a Ruler in the line of David who would be born in Bethlehem (Mi 5:2). The city was the original home of Naomi, and it served as the setting for much of the Book of Ruth.

Other popular attractions at Bethlehem for Holy Land tourists are the fields of Boaz, where Ruth gleaned grain after the fields had been harvested (Ru 2:3), and Shepherd's Field, where the angels announced the birth of Jesus to the shepherds (Lk 2:8-18).

The name *Bethlehem* means "House of Bread," probably commemorating the reputation of the entire region as a grain-producing center in Old Testament times. It is appropriate that Jesus Christ, who is the Bread of Life, was born in a town with such a name.

2. A town in the territory of Zebulun (Jos 19:15).

BETH´-LE·HEM·ITE

One from Bethlehem (1 Sa 16:1,18).

BETH´-LE·HEM-JU´DAH

Another name for Bethlehem.

BETH-MA´A·CHAH (house of Maacah)

A town near Mount Hermon to which Joab went in search of Sheba, son of Bichri (2 Sa 20:14-15). See ABEL-BETH-MAACAH.

BETH-MAR´CA·BOTH (house of the chariots)

A town of Simeon (Jos 19:5; 1 Ch 4:31).

BETH-ME´ON

See BAAL-MEON.

BETH-NIM´RAH (house of the leopard)

This town in the Jordan Valley, east of Jordan, was assigned to Gad (Nu 32:36; Jos 13:27). It was once called Nimrah (Nu 32:3).

BETH-OPH´RAH

See BETH-APHRAH.

BETH-PA´LET

See BETH-PELET.

BETH-PAZ´ZEZ (house of dispersion)

A town of Issachar (Jos 19:21).

BETH-PE´LET (house of escape)

A town in the extreme south of Judah (Jos 15:27). It was assigned to Simeon and mention is made of its inhabitants after the exile (Ne 11:26).

BETH-PE′OR *(house of Peor)*

A town on the east side of Jordan near Pisgah. It was in the tribe of Reuben (De 3:29; Jos 13:20). It was near here that Moses was buried (De 34:6).

BETH′PHA·GE *(house of figs)*

A village on the Mount of Olives, on the road that runs from Jericho to Jerusalem (Mk 11:1; Lk 19:29).

BETH-PHE′LET

See BETH-PELET.

BETH-RA′PHA *(house of the giants)*

A name appearing in the genealogy of Judah (1 Ch 4:12).

BETH-RE′HOB *(house of a street)*

A town in the north of Palestine, also called Rehob (Nu 13:21; Ju 18:28). Syrians who were allied with the Ammonites against David inhabited this town (2 Sa 10:6).

BETH·SA′I·DA *(house of fish or fishing)*

A town on the lake of Gennesaret near the Jordan, the native place of Peter, Andrew, and Philip (Jo 1:44; 12:21). Jesus retired to this town after the death of John the Baptist (Mk 6:31; Lk 9:10). Jesus healed a blind man there (Mk 8:22-23) and once denounced the town (Ma 11:21).

BETH-SHE′AN, BETH′-SHAN *(house of quiet)*

A town west of the Jordan about fourteen miles south of the Sea of Galilee. This formidable town, though within the territory of Issachar (Jos 17:16), was assigned to Manasseh (Jos 17:11,16) but this tribe, instead of expelling the Canaanites, made them pay tribute (Jos 17:12,16; Ju 1:27-28). It was here the Philistines fastened the bodies of Saul and his sons to a wall (1 Sa 31:10-13; 2 Sa 21:12-14).

BETH-SHE′MESH, IR-SHE′MESH *(house of the sun)*

Four towns mentioned in the Old Testament:
1. A town in the vale of the Sorek, on the boundary line of Judah but assigned to Dan

(Jos 15:10; 19:41) and made a city of the Levites (Jos 21:16; 1 Ch 6:59). It was to this town the ark was brought when the Philistines wanted to get rid of it. Here many men were struck dead for profanely looking into the ark (1 Sa 6:19).
2. A city of Naphtali (Jos 19:38; Ju 1:33).
3. An unidentified town in Issachar (Jos 19:22).
4. An Egyptian city, thought to be On or Heliopolis, where the sun was worshipped (Je 43:13).

BETH-SHE′MITE

An inhabitant of Beth-shemesh (1 Sa 6:14).

BETH-SHIT′TAH *(house of the acacia)*

A town near Abel-meholah in the Jordan Valley (Ju 7:22).

BETH-TAP′PU·AH *(house of apples)*

A town in the hill country of Judah (Jos 15:53) about three miles northwest of Hebron. It is now called Tuffuh.

BE·THU′EL

A man and a town of the Old Testament:
1. Son of Nahor, the father of Rebekah and Laban, and the nephew of Abraham (Ge 22:20-23; 24:15,29; 28:2,5).
2. A town of Simeon (Jos 19:4; 1 Ch 4:30), called Chesil in Joshua 15:30.

BETH′UL

See BETHUEL.

BETH′-ZUR

A town in the hill country of Judah fortified by Rehoboam (Jos 15:58; 2 Ch 11:7). The people of this city responded to the call of Nehemiah and aided in rebuilding the wall of Jerusalem (Ne 3:16).

BETIMES (archaic)

Early; quickly (Pr 13:24).

BET′O·NIM *(pistachio nuts)*

A town in the territory of Gad (Jos 13:26).

BETROTHAL

Betrothal is the promise of marriage, a contract or engagement to marry. Biblical betrothal cannot be exactly equated with modern engagement. It was usually arranged by intermediates, and involved a serious contract, sometimes written. The betrothal and its accompanying ceremony and feast was an important part of a marriage. One of the most interesting examples of betrothal in the Bible is found in the story of Mary and Joseph. Mary was already betrothed to Joseph when the angel informed her that she would be the mother of the Messiah (Lk 1:27). Joseph's reaction when he heard the news of Mary's pregnancy gives us insight into the importance of the betrothal contract. In order to end their engagement, he would have to divorce Mary, even though their marriage had not been consummated (Ma 1:18-19). When they traveled to Bethlehem, Mary was referred to as Joseph's "betrothed wife" (Lk 2:5). In the law, a betrothed man was to be released from military service, in order to stay home and marry the girl (De 20:7). See MARRIAGE.

BETWIXT (archaic)

Between; in an intermediate position (Song 1:13).

BEU′ LAH *(married)*

The name to be given Palestine in its future greatness and when restored to divine favor. It is used figuratively of Israel (Is 62:4).

BEWITCH

To cast a spell on, hypnotize, charm. Paul asked the Galatians who had "bewitched" them, inferring that their ideas were nonsensical and out of character (Ga 3:1).

BEWRAY (archaic)

To make manifest, clear, evident; make obvious, betray (Ma 26:72-74).

BE·ZA·A·NAN′ NIM

See ZAANANNIM.

BE·ZA′ I

The founder of a family, members of which returned from the Babylonion exile (Ez 2:17; Ne 7:23; 10:18).

BEZ′ A·LEEL, BEZ′ A·LEL *(in the protection of God)*

Two Old Testament men:

1. A grandson of Hur of the family of Caleb of Judah (1 Ch 2:20) and a skillful worker in metals and precious stones, Bezaleel was appointed chief architect for the construction of

tabernacle furniture, preparation of the priestly garments, and procurement of oils and incense.

2. A son of Pahath-moab who put away his foreign wife (Ez 10:30).

BE′ ZEK *(lighting)*

A town and a place in the Old Testament:

1. A town in the mountains near Jerusalem and the residence of Adoni-bezek (Ju 1:4-5).

2. A place where Saul numbered his forces before going to the relief of Jabesh-gilead (1 Sa 11:8).

BE′ ZER *(fortress)*

A man and a place in the Old Testament:

1. Son of Zophah (1 Ch 7:37).

2. A city of Reuben east of the Jordan which was given to the Levites and was designated a city of refuge (De 4:43; Jos 20:8; 21:36).

BI′ BLE

Chrysostom, patriarch of Constantinople (A.D. 398-404) is believed to have been the first to apply the Greek word *Biblia* to the Scriptures. *Biblia* simply means "book." In the library of the world, this book alone deserves the title of *"The* Book." It is the word of God, the operating manual for life on this earth. The Bible is made up of sixty-six shorter books, written by some forty different human authors, in three different languages, over a period of about fifteen hundred years. It stands alone in its message and impact on world history.

1. *The Two Testaments:* The Bible is divided into two major sections, called the Old Testament and the New Testament. The Old Testament begins with creation and traces God's relationship with mankind. His covenant with Abraham and His dealings with the covenant people, the Israelites, are the main subject matter, as well as the source of the term "Old Testament," or "Old Covenant." The New Testament is concerned with the coming of the Messiah, Jesus, and the formation of the Christian church. It is called the "New Testament" or "New Covenant" referring to the prophecy of Jeremiah 31:31-34. Because of Christ, a new relationship with God is available, based not upon the law but upon the grace and mercy of God.

2. *Basic divisions:*

The Old Testament: The first five books of the Bible are called the **Pentateuch,** or the **Law of Moses.** Genesis, Exodus, Leviticus,

Numbers and Deuteronomy are considered to have all been written by Moses. Next come the books of **History:** Joshua, Judges, Ruth, 1 and 2 Samuel, 1 and 2 Kings, 1 and 2 Chronicles, Ezra, Nehemiah, and Esther. The books of **Wisdom** include Job, Psalms, Proverbs, Ecclesiastes, and Song of Solomon. Isaiah, Jeremiah, Lamentations, Ezekiel, and Daniel are called the **"Major Prophets,"** not because they are more important, but because their books are the longest. Hosea, Joel, Amos, Obadiah, Jonah, Micah, Nahum, Habakkuk, Zephaniah, Haggai, Zechariah, and Malachi are called the **"Minor Prophets"**. The order of the books in our English Bibles is derived from the order used in the Septuagint.

The Hebrew Old Testament arranges the books in a slightly different order. The Law (Torah) consists of Genesis, Exodus, Leviticus, Numbers, and Deuteronomy. Next come the Prophets, divided into two sections. The Former Prophets include Joshua, Judges, Samuel, and Kings. The Latter Prophets are Isaiah, Jeremiah, Ezekiel, and The Twelve. After the Prophets come the Writings. The Poetical Books are Psalms, Proverbs, and Job. The Five Rolls contain Song of Solomon, Ruth, Lamentations, Ecclesiastes, and Esther. The list ends with the Historical Books: Daniel, Ezra, Nehemiah, and Chronicles.

The New Testament: The first four books, Matthew, Mark, Luke, and John, are known as the Gospels (Good News), because they tell the story of Christ's life on earth and His sacrificial death. They are followed by Acts, the only other New Testament history book. The Epistles of Paul (Letters from Paul) are Romans, 1 and 2 Corinthians, Galatians, Ephesians, Philippians, Colossians, 1 and 2 Thessalonians, 1 and 2 Timothy, Titus, and Philemon. The General Epistles, so called because they are addressed generally rather than to a specific church or person, include Hebrews, James, 1 and 2 Peter, 1, 2, and 3 John, Jude, and Revelation.

3. *The canon of Scripture.* For information concerning the acceptance of each book into the canon of Scripture, see the article concerning the book in question.

4. *Language of the Bible.* With the exception of a few sections written in Aramaic, the Old Testament was written in Hebrew and the New Testament in Greek.

5. *Division into chapters and verses.* The division into chapters did not occur until the thir-

teenth century and is generally ascribed to Cardinal Hugo of St. Cher. The New Testament was divided into verses by Robert Stephens in his Greek and Latin New Testament published at Geneva in 1551. It was in the Latin Bible of Sanctus Pagninus in 1528 that division of the entire Bible into chapters and verses first appeared. The first English Bible so divided was the Geneva Bible of 1560.

6. *Apocryphal books of the Old Testament.* See APOCRYPHA.

7. *Inspiration of the Bible.* See INSPIRATION.

8. *Progress of doctrine.* See DOCTRINE, PROGRESS OF.

9. *Importance.* The Bible is the most widely published and circulated of any book. In full or in part it has been translated into more than 1,200 languages and dialects. The Bible stands alone in its greatness.

BIBLIOLOGY

The formal study of the Bible as God's word (a part of Systematic Theology). See INSPIRATION; ILLUMINATION; HERMENEUTICS.

BICH′ RI *(youthful)*

A Benjamite whose son Sheba instigated a rebellion (2 Sa 20:1).

BID′ KAR

The captain of Jehu who threw the body of Jehoram into the field of Naboth (2 Ki 9:25).

BIER *(archaic)*

A stretcher, litter, or handbarrow; particularly that used for carrying a coffin (2 Sa 3:31; 2 Ch 16:14; Lk 7:14).

BIG′ THA

A chamberlain in charge of the harem of Ahasuerus (Es 1:10).

BIG′ THAN, BIG·THA′ NA

A keeper of the palace door of Xerxes (Ahasuerus). He and Teresh conspired against the king and were frustrated by Mordecai. They were hanged (Es 2:21; 6:2).

BIG·VA′ I

Two Old Testament men:

1. The head of a family, a leader of the exiles who returned from Babylon under Zerubbabel (Ez 2:2).

2. A chief of the people, two thousand of whose family returned from Babylon (Ez 2:14; Ne 7:19). A large number returned with Ezra about eighty years later (Ez 8:14).

BIL′ DAD

One of Job's three friends with whom he debated the question of suffering and affliction. He is called "the Shuhite," hence was perhaps a descendant of Shuah, Abraham's son by Keturah (Job 2:11; 8:1; 18:1; 25:1).

BI′ LE•AM

A town in the territory of Manasseh west of the Jordan. It was allotted to the Levitical family of Kohath (1 Ch 6:70).

BIL′ GAH *(cheerfulness)*

Two Old Testament men:
1. A descendant of Aaron, head of the fifteenth course of the priests (1 Ch 24:1,6,14).
2. A priest who returned from Babylon with Zerubbabel (Ne 12:5,7). At a later time this was the name of a priestly house (Ne 12:18).

BIL•GA′ I *(cheerfulness)*

A priest who sealed the covenant with Nehemiah (Ne 10:8), probably the same as Bilgah.

BIL′ HAH *(bashfulness)*

A woman and a town in the Old Testament:
1. Maidservant of Rachel, Jacob's wife. She was the mother of Dan and Naphtali (Ge 30:1-8; 1 Ch 7:13).
2. A town of Simeon (1 Ch 4:29).

BIL′ HAN *(bashful)*

Two Old Testament men:
1. A son of Ezer, a Horite (Ge 36:27; 1 Ch 1:42).
2. A member of the family of Jediael (1 Ch 7:10).

BILLOW (archaic)

A swelling or heap of water (Ps 42:7).

BIL′ SHAN

One of the twelve princes of the Jews who returned from Babylon under Zerubbabel (Ez 2:2; Ne 7:7).

BIM′ HAL

A great-great-grandson of Asher and son of Japhlet (1 Ch 7:33).

BINDING AND LOOSING

A reference to Jesus's authority over the spiritual realm (Ma 16:19; 18:18).

BI′ NE•A

A son of Moza (1 Ch 8:37; 9:43).

BIN′ NU•I *(building)*

Four Old Testament men:
1. Father of Noadiah, a Levite. The son helped to weigh the gold and silver brought from Babylon (Ez 8:33).
2. A son of Pahath-moab. He relinquished his foreign wife after the return from Babylon (Ez 10:30).
3. An Israelite, a son of Bani, who put away his foreign wife (Ez 10:30,38).
4. The son of Henadad, a Levite (Ne 10:9). He returned from Babylon with Zerubbabel (Ne 12:8). Some of his family assisted in building the wall (Ne 3:24) and one of them sealed the covenant (Ne 10:9).

BIRDS

Thirty species are native to Palestine but as many as 348 species have been found in the country. In the Mosaic law they were distinguished as clean and unclean (Le 11:13-19; De 14:11-20). Doves and pigeons were sacrificed (Le 1:14; Lk 2:24). "Fatted fowl" was used as food (1 Ki 4:23), as were quails and partridges.

BIR′ SHA

A king of Gomorrah, defeated by Chedorlaomer (Ge 14:2,8,10).

BIRTH

The passage of offspring from the womb to the world. As a result of the curse, birth and labor are difficult and painful (Ge 3:16; Ps 48:6), but the birth of a child is still joy (Jo 16:21).

BIRTHDAY

The birth of a child was a joyful occasion, often attended with a feast (Je 20:15) and the observance of birthdays was an ancient custom (Ge 40:20; Job 1:4). In Persia and Egypt they were celebrated with banquets. On the occasion of his birthday (though some interpret it as the anniversary of his accession) Herod Antipas celebrated with a banquet. During the festivities John the Baptist was beheaded (Ma 14:6-12; Mk 6:21-28).

BIRTH, NEW
See-REGENERATION.

BIRTHRIGHT
The term *birthright* appears several times in the Bible. The word refers to the inheritance rights of the firstborn son in a Hebrew family in Old Testament times. The property of a father was normally divided among his sons at his death. But a larger amount, usually a double portion, went to the oldest son (De 21:17), who assumed the care of his mother and unmarried sisters.

The birthright, with its privileges and responsibilities, could be forfeited by behavior that was offensive to the father or opposed God's will. For example, Reuben apparently lost his birthright by committing incest with his father's concubine (Ge 35:22; 49:3-4; 1 Ch 5:1). Esau foolishly squandered his birthright by trading it to his brother Jacob for a bowl of stew made from lentils (Ge 25:29-34).

In New Testament times, inheritance practices were influenced by Greek and Roman regulations which focused less on the elder son. The Greeks relied on wills to pass on their property. However, if no will existed, property was divided equally among sons in good standing. Under Roman law, the property of a man who died without a will went to his wife and children.

Paul described Jesus as the "firstborn over all creation" (Col 1:15), and emphasized the spiritual birthright of all Christians as "heirs of God and joint heirs with Christ, if indeed we suffer with Him" (Ro 8:17). A willingness to share in the sufferings of Christ is the condition for the blessings we receive as His spiritual heirs.

BIRTHSTOOL
In some times and places it has been customary to give birth in a squatting position, or sitting on a specially designed stool. The Hebrew word in Exodus 1:16 means "two stones." The same word is used in Jeremiah 18:3 for a potter's wheel.

BIRTH, VIRGIN
See VIRGIN BIRTH.

BIR-ZA′ ITH, BIR-ZA′ VITH *(olive well)*
A name in the genealogies of Asher (1 Ch 7:31).

BISH′ LAM *(son of peace)*
A Persian officer of Artaxerxes (Ez 4:7).

BISHOP
The word "bishop" (*episkopos*) was originally a secular word meaning "over-" (*epi*) "seer" (*skopos*), or "superintendent," or "one who watches over (to protect)." The noun itself occurs only five times in the New Testament. The first time it is used, it is a synonym for elder (compare v. 17 and v. 28 of Ac 20). Here the KJV translated it "overseer," though everywhere else as "bishop." The epistle to the church in Philippi (1:1) is addressed to three groups: "the saints" together with "the bishops and the deacons." The office was obviously plural, at least at that time and place.

The fifth New Testament occurrence of *bishop* is unique; Jesus Christ is described as the "*episkpos*" of our souls (1 Pe 2:25). It seems apparent that at this time the term did not have an exclusive definition as a particular church office. However, in the organization of Christian churches it was necessary to establish a particular order for the superintendence of pastoral work. Hence Peter's exhortation that the elders tend the flock of God, "taking the oversight" (1 Pe 5:2). The elders were the shepherds to care for, direct, support, and encourage the church (1 Th 5:14; He 13:17). Paul specified their qualifications (1 Ti 3:1-7; Tit 1:7-9). The words elder, presbyter, and bishop, all carry the same meaning; in several places, both titles are applied to the same persons (1 Ti 5:17; 1 Pe 5:1-2). See ELDER.

BISHOPRIC (archaic)
Guardianship; office of overseeing (Ac 1:18-20).

BISHOP'S BIBLE
So called because all the translators either were bishops at the time of the translation, or became so later. It was published in 1568, and sponsored by church leaders in England as a rival to the Geneva Bible.

BIT
See BRIDLE.

BITH′ I•AH *(daughter, that is, worshipper of Jehovah)*

The wife of Mered and daughter of Pharaoh (1 Ch 4:18).

BITH′ RON *(division, a cut)*

A region north of the Jabbok near Mahanaim (2 Sa 2:29).

BI•THYN′ IA

A province in northwestern Asia Minor (Ac 16:7; 1 Pe 1:1). When Paul purposed to labor in this region, he was divinely directed not to do so. Its chief town, Nicaea, was the scene of the Council of Nicaea (A.D. 325).

BIT′ TER HERBS

A part of the Passover meal. God commanded the Hebrews to eat bitter herbs, along with unleavened bread and roast lamb (Ex 1:14; 12:8; Nu 9:11). They were to be a reminder of the bitterness of slavery from which God had rescued them. Today, most Jewish celebrations of the Passover Seder use horseradish for the bitter herbs.

BIT′ TERN

A species of water bird, similar to the heron. Its cry is an eerie, hollow booming sound. This word is one translation of the Hebrew *kippod,* a creature which inhabited places of desolation and ruin (Is 14:23; 34:11; Zep 2:14). It may have been a species of owl or a wading bird, but was more probably a quadruped. The NRSV and the NKJV, following the Septuagint and Vulgate, translate *kippod* "porcupine," and "hedgehog." NIV uses "owl."

BITTERWEED

See WORMWOOD.

BI•TU′ MEN, SLIME

Mineral pitch. Bitumen can be one of several hydrocarbons, such as asphalt, crude petroleum, or tar. It is found at the Dead Sea, on the Euphrates, and elsewhere. It was used as mortar in the building of the Tower of Babel (Ge 11:3).

BIZ′ I•O•THI•AH

See BIZJOTHJAH.

BIZ•JOTH′ JAH *(contempt of Jehovah)*

A term denoting a place in Judah (Jos 15:28).

BIZ′ THA

A chamberlain in the court of Xerxes (Ahasuerus) in the time of Esther. He was ordered to bring Vashti to the king's banquet (Es 1:10).

BLACK VULTURE

See OSPREY.

BLAIN

A serum-filled blister on the skin. The sixth plague on the Egyptians (Ex 9:8-11). See BOIL.

BLAS′ PHE•MY

Christians use the word blasphemy primarily to mean "harsh speech against God or sacred persons or things" (Ps 74:18; Is 52:5; Ro 2:24). The Mosaic law made this a capital offense punishable by stoning (Le 24:16). In secular Greek the word was originally used more widely, including the slander of other people. Most, but not all, New Testament usages refer to defaming sacred things. The adjective *blasphemous* occurs four times, once used by Paul in describing his pre-conversion days as a blasphemer and a persecutor (1 Ti 1:13). The Pharisees accused Jesus (Ma 9:3; 26:65-66; Jo 10:36) and Stephen, the first Christian martyr, of blaspheming God (Ac 6:11,13).

Blasphemy against the Holy Spirit (Ma 12:22-32; Mk 3:22-30) has been variously explained. The strict context and the special occasion which elicited Christ's teaching concerning this form of blasphemy make it appear to consist of ascribing to satanic power the performance of the mighty works which Christ wrought under the direction of the Holy Spirit. Some sensitive Christians fear they have committed this, the "unpardonable sin," but their very concern shows that they need not be afraid. One who desires to please God, and who has been born again, has been changed into a "new creation" (2 Co 5:17). It is not possible to commit the "unforgivable sin" by accident, nor is it possible for one who has once been born again into God's family to be unborn.

BLAST

To blight or wither (Am 4:9; Ge 41:6).

BLAS′ TUS *(sprout)*

The chamberlain of Herod Agrippa (Ac 12:20).

BLEACHER
See FULLER.

BLEMISH
Imperfection, deformity. An animal with a blemish was unfit for a sacrifice or offering (Ex 12:5; 1 Pe 1:19).

BLESS, BLESSING
The bestowal of divine favor and benefits (Ge 1:22; 9:1-7; 39:5). It includes recognition of God's goodness in a thankful and adoring manner (Ps 103:1; Ma 26:26; 1 Co 11:24) and invoking God's favor upon another (Ge 27:4,12, 27-29; Ps 129:8).

BLESSED (archaic)
Happy (Ps 1:1-2). See BEATITUDES.

BLESSING, CUP OF
The cup of wine used for communion (1 Co 10:16). See CUP.

BLIGHT
To wither with intense dry heat; to destroy with mildew or disease (Ge 41:6,23,27; Am 4:9).

BLIND'NESS
A common affliction in the East, frequently met with in the ministry of Jesus (Ma 9:27; 12:22; 20:30). The law required that the blind be treated with sympathy (Le 19:14; De 27:18). In certain instances persons were smitten with temporary blindness (2 Ki 6:18-20; Ac 9:9; 13:11).

BLOOD
The blood represented life—the life is in the blood (Le 17:11,14; De 12:23), and the life God regarded as sacred. After the flood it was forbidden that the blood of animals be eaten (Ge 9:3-4; Ac 15:20,29). The law was announced that the shedding of man's blood would be punishable by death (Ge 9:6). The penalty of sin was the loss of life (He 9:22), as denoted by the death of animals used in the offerings for sin under the Mosaic law: the shedding of blood signified atonement (Le 17:10-14; De 12:15-16), hence the expressions "the blood of Jesus Christ," or, "the blood of the Lamb" denote the atoning death of our Lord (1 Co 10:16; He 9:14; 1 Pe 1:2,19; 1 Jo 1:7; Re 12:11).

BLOOD, AVENGER OF
See AVENGER OF BLOOD.

BLOOD, FLOW OF
A woman's menstrual cycle. According to the law, a woman was ceremonially unclean during this time each month (Le 15:25).

BLOODY FLUX
See DYSENTERY.

BLOOD'Y SWEAT
See SWEAT.

BO·AN·ER'GES (sons of thunder)
A name Jesus gave to John and James, sons of Zebedee, because of their zeal and impetuosity (Mk 3:17; Lk 9:54).

BOAR
A wild male pig. Wild swine were to be found all over Israel. They can be very destructive to agriculture; being possessed with sharp tusks and teeth, they are also dangerous when angered (Ps 80:13).

BOAT
See SHIP.

BO'AZ, BO'OZ (fleetness)
1. A resident of Bethlehem, a man of wealth, a kinsman to Naomi's husband Elimelech. He married Ruth, the daughter-in-law of Naomi, and redeemed the estate of her deceased husband. Their son, Obed, became the grandfather of David, hence Boaz became an ancestor of Christ in the line of David (Ru 2–4; Ma 1:5).

2. The name of a pillar, eighteen cubits high, set in the porch of Solomon's temple (1 Ki 7:15, 21).

BO'CHE·RU (firstborn)
A son of Azel (1 Ch 8:38).

BOAR

BO' CHIM *(weepers)*

At this place near Gilgal Israelites expressed their sorrow when reproved (Ju 2:1-5).

BODY

See SPIRIT AND SOUL.

BODY ARMOR

Garments designed to protect the body during warfare. Body armor may have been made of thick leather, metal plates, or chain mail. As early as 3000 B.C. some sorts of primitive body armor were being used. In the Bible, several pieces of body armor are mentioned: a breastplate, belt, and greaves. Saul tried to lend David a suit of armor to fight the heavily armored giant Goliath (1 Sa 17:5-6; 38).

BODY, GLORIFIED

The body which we will have after resurrection. It is no longer subject to decay or sin (1 Co 15:42-44), but it apparently functions in some ways like our present bodies. The glorified body can eat and digest food (Lk 24:42). In other ways, the glorified body is obviously quite different from our present bodies. Jesus, in His post-resurrection glorified body was able to enter a locked room without any difficulty (Jo 20:19). Of course, we don't know whether this is a quality of the post-resurrection body, or something special that only Jesus can do.

BODY OF CHRIST

1. A term for the church, the company of all believers in Christ, past, present, and future (Ro 12:4-6; 1 Co 12:12-27; Ep 4:4-12; Col 1:18-24).

2. The earthly, physical body of the incarnate Christ (1 Jo 4:3).

3. The resurrected, glorious body of Christ now, which we will one day share (Ph 3:31).

4. The bread of communion, which Jesus described as His body (1 Co 10:16).

BO' HAN *(thumb)*

A son of Reuben. A stone which indicated the boundary line between Judah and Benjamin was given his name (Jos 15:6; 18:17).

BOIL

A sore swelling of the skin or an itching skin ulcer which, with blains, produced the sixth Egyptian plague (Ex 9:9-11). Job was afflicted with boils (Job 2:7). Isaiah prescribed a poultice of figs for Hezekiah's boil (Is 38:21).

BO' KE•RU

See BOCHERU.

BO' KIM

See BOCHIM.

BOLLED (archaic)

Blossomed; in the seed or pod (Ex 9:31-32).

BOL' STER

The rendering for a Hebrew word meaning *head place*. It is rendered *head* in the Revised Version (1 Sa 19:13,16; 26:7,11-12,16). It is not a pillow in the sense of a soft headrest.

BOLT

See LOCK.

BOND

(Ju 15:14; Is 58:6; Eze 20:37; Ep 4:3)

BONDAGE

Slavery.

BONDMAN, BOND SERVANT

See SLAVE.

BONES

(Ex 13:19; Eze 37:1-14)

BON' NET (archaic)

A headdress (Ex 28:40; 29:9; Is 3:20; Eze 44:18).

BOOK

At an early time inscriptions were made on clay or cut into stone. Skin and papyrus were also used at an early age. Skin as a writing material was rolled up and was called a scroll (Ps 40:7; Je 36:2; Eze 2:9). Among the Hebrews books were not mentioned until after leaving Egypt (Ex 17:14). In that country they saw writings in many forms. The Hebrew writings are not limited to the Scriptures. Many other books were written such as the Book of Jasher (Nu 21:14; Jos 10:13); the History of Nathan the Prophet (1 Ch 29:29); the Chronicles of David, perhaps the beginning of royal annals (1 Ch 27:24). When the books of Chronicles were written, it is evident from the many citations that many other books were consulted (2 Ch 13:22; 20:34; 26:22; 33:18-19; 35:25).

BOOK OF THE COVENANT
See COVENANT, BOOK OF.

BOOK OF LIFE
Also called the Lamb's book of life. At the end of all time, when all the dead are gathered before the Great White Throne of Judgment, each person will be judged according to the record which God has kept in His book of life. All our deeds, both good and evil, are recorded here (Re 20:11-14). Anyone whose name is not in the book will be cast into the eternal fire (Re 20:15; 21:27). When Moses was pleading with God for the Israelites, God told him that those who sin against God will have their names blotted from the book of life (Ex 32:32-33).

BOOTH
A structure made of branches. Jacob made booths for his cattle, hence the name of his place of residence, Succoth (Ge 33:17). In commemoration of their sojourn in the wilderness the Israelites were required to live in booths made of palm and willow branches during the Feast of Tabernacles (Le 23:39-43; Ne 8:14).

BOOTHS, FEAST OF
See TABERNACLES, FEAST OF and FEAST.

BOOTY
The things of value taken from a captured town. This included goods of every kind, money, cattle, and the people who were made slaves (Ge 14:11-12,16; Nu 31:9,26-52; Jos 7:21). When the Israelites entered Canaan to possess the land, they were commanded to destroy the idolatrous inhabitants and all their possessions. There was to be no chance for the Israelites to collect the idols and shrines of the Canaanites, or learn their idolatrous ways from them. In their conquests outside of the land of Canaan, women and children were spared and possessions were taken (Nu 33:52; De 20:14-16). There were instances when the spoils were devoted to the sanctuary or dedicated to the Lord (Nu 31:26-47; Jos 6:19; 1 Sa 15:2-3).

BOOZ
Greek. See BOAZ.

BOR-ASH' AN
See ASHAN.

BORN AGAIN
See REGENERATION.

BORROW
Borrowing necessarily carries the intention of returning the items borrowed. God encouraged the Israelites to lend to one another in a neighborly fashion (De 15:1-11); if a pledge was taken, they were to be generous and not cause hardship to the borrower (Ex 22:26-27). Jesus commanded his people to lend to those who asked, and not to demand repayment (Lk 6:30). The guiding rule for borrowing and lending must be Luke 6:31, which says, "And just as you want men to do to you, you also do to them likewise."

BOS' CATH
See BOZKATH.

BOSOM
The chest area of the human body. In Scripture, the bosom is often associated with comfort and security (Is 40:11; Ps 35:13; Jo 1:18).

BOSOM, ABRAHAM'S
See ABRAHAM'S BOSOM.

BO' SOR
1. A town of Gilead. It may have been Bezer in the tribe of Reuben (Jos 20:8).
2. The Grecian form of Beor (2 Pe 2:15).

BOTCH (archaic)
Boil (De 28:27,35, KJV). See BOIL.

BOT' TLE
Various materials were used in making bottles. At first the skins of animals were sewn into the form of a bottle or bag, the neck of the animal in many cases being the neck of the bottle. The Arabs used goatskin which was drawn from the body of the dead goat. The effect of heat and fermentation upon the skin is indicated by Psalm 119:83; Matthew 9:17. Metal and earthenware were also used by Assyrians, Greeks, Egyptians, and later by the Jews. That they had something of this nature is clear from Judges 4:19; 5:25 and Jeremiah 19:1,10-11.

BOTTOMLESS PIT
See ABYSS.

BOUNDARY STONES

Stones used to mark the borders of fields (Ge 31:51-52). Removing boundary stones was a serious offense (De 19:14; Pr 23:10).

BOW

An offensive weapon used for both hunting and military applications. It was made of strong elastic timber which might be mounted with iron or bronze (Job 20:24; Ps 18:34). Oxgut usually formed the string while reedlike shafts tipped with flint served as arrows. See ARCHERY.

BOWELS (archaic)

Inward parts, intestines. This word is a literal translation of the Greek *splagna,* which is a term used to speak symbolically of the affections, or inward feelings. Modern translations typically translate this word as ''heart'' (Col 3:12).

BOWING

Prostrating oneself, particularly to show honor and reverence to another (Ge 33:3).

BOWL

Bowls or basins of gold were made for use in the tabernacle services (Ex 25:29-34; Nu 7:13-85). In the Book of Revelation, symbolic bowls of wrath are poured out on the earth. See BASIN; CUP; VESSEL.

BOWSHOT

The distance an arrow traveled from the bow (Ge 21:16).

BOX

A covered vessel for holding ointment and other things (2 Ki 9:1; Ma 26:7).

BOX TREE

Box trees have very hard wood, and glossy dark green leaves. They can grow to be quite tall, but because of their shrubby nature, they generally do not produce large logs. Isaiah mentioned box trees among the woods which would be used to beautify God's temple (Is 60:13); it is also used to illustrate God's greatness (Is 41:19). As with many botanical terms in the Bible, it is uncertain exactly what plant is meant. The Hebrew word denotes a straight tree. Mount Lebanon was noted for fir, pine, and box.

BOZEZ (shining)

The name of the rock on one side of the pass through which Jonathan tried to reach the Philistines (1 Sa 14:4-5).

BOZKATH, BOSCATH (elevated, stony ground)

A city at the most southern point of Judah (Jos 15:39); also mentioned as the birthplace of Adaiah, King Josiah's mother (2 Kings 22:1).

BOZRAH (sheepfold)

Two cities of Old Testament times:

1. An important city of Edom (Ge 36:33; 1 Ch 1:44). It is mentioned by Isaiah (Is 34:6; 63:1). The judgment that will fall on it is predicted by Amos (Am 1:12) and its complete destruction by Jeremiah (Je 49:13,22). It is located 22 miles southeast of the Dead Sea.

2. A city of Moab denounced by Jeremiah, perhaps the same as Bezer (Je 48:24).

BRACELET

Bracelets were worn as ornaments on the wrist or arm by both sexes (Eze 16:11). The KJV uses the word bracelet to translate several Hebrew words. Chains (Is 3:19) were worn on the arms. In 2 Samuel 1:10, it probably refers to an armband. In Song of Solomon 5:14 gold rings, apparently bracelets, are mentioned as being worn by men.

BRAMBLE

This is the translation of the Hebrew word *atad* (Ju 9:14-15). In Psalm 58:9 the rendering is thorn. In the region of the Dead Sea the thorn is common, also in the Jordan Valley and about the Sea of Galilee.

BRANCH

A limb or shoot of a tree. It is a symbol of prosperity (Ge 49:22; Pr 11:28; Eze 17:6) and is also used to signify uselessness (Is 14:19). Jeremiah and Zechariah apply the word as a title of Christ, the offspring of David (Je 23:5; 33:15; Ze 3:8; 6:12). The term was similarly used by Isaiah (Is 11:1). In like manner believers are related to Christ as branches to the vine (Jo 15:5-6).

BRASS

The Hebrew word *nehosheth* is inaccurately translated brass. The correct translation is copper, but in some instances it possibly means bronze. Bronze is an alloy of copper and tin, while brass is a compound of copper and zinc. Copper was known at an early time. It was taken from the ground and smelted (De 8:9; Job 28:2). It was found in the peninsula of Sinai, in Cyprus and Lebanon. Such articles as basins, pots, pans, spoons, and shovels were made from copper (Ex 38:3; Le 6:28; Nu 16:39). Pieces of armor, such as helmets, mirrors, musical instruments, and later coins were formed from copper (2 Sa 8:10; 21:16; 2 Ki 25:7,13; Ma 10:9); also things pertaining to the temple (1 Ki 7:41-46; 2 Ch 4:1-17).

BRAWLER (archaic)

One who is inclined to fight (1 Ti 3:2-3).

BRAYED (archaic)

To groan, wail; to make a foul noise (Job 30:7).

BRA'ZEN SEA

An enormous bronze bowl which Solomon had made for the new temple. It was approximately fifteen feet in diameter, and seven and a half feet deep. It rested on a base made of twelve cast bronze bulls (1 Ki 7:23-26; 1 Ki 7:13-14; 2 Ch 4:6; 2 Ki 25:13).

BRA'ZEN SER'PENT

In the wilderness when the Israelites were bitten by fiery serpents, Moses was commanded to form a serpent of metal and place it upon a pole. When they looked upon this with faith in the promise of God, the Israelites were healed (Nu 21:8-9). The lifting up of the brazen serpent on a pole in the wilderness was likened by Jesus to his death on the cross (Jo 3:14-15). At a later time, when the Israelites used the brazen serpent as an object of worship, Hezekiah had it destroyed (2 Ki 18:4).

BREAD

The use of bread as an article of food dates back to an early time (Ge 18:6). Among the Hebrews the best bread was made of wheat. It was ground in a mill and sifted (Ju 6:19; 1 Sa 28:24; 1 Ki 4:22). It was made in the form of round flat cakes about an inch thick and nine inches in diameter, as will be found in Palestine today. In the sacred offerings "fine flour" was used (Ex 29:40; Le 2:1; Eze 46:14). The bread of poor people was made of barley (Jo 6:9,13).

BRAZEN SERPENT

The oven consisted of a metal jar about three feet high with fire kindled inside and the cakes of dough placed against the sides (1 Ki 17:12; Is 44:15).

BREAD, FEAST OF UNLEAVENED

See PASSOVER and FEAST.

BREAST

The chest area of the human body (Jo 13:23, 25). In some cultures, beating the breast is a way of expressing great grief or distress (Lk 23:48). See BOSOM.

BREAST'PLATE

1. The breastplate of the Jewish high priest was a piece of embroidered cloth about ten inches square. Attached to it were twelve precious stones, each bearing the name of one of the twelve tribes (Ex 28:15-30).

2. A piece of armor to protect the breast of the warrior. The term is also used figuratively, as in the "breastplate of righteousness" (Is 59:17; Ep 6:14; 1 Th 5:8).

BREATH

This word is used in several different senses: When God created man out of the dust of the ground, He "breathed into his nostrils the breath of life" (Ge 2:7). Some see this as a reference to the human soul; others see it as simply "life," since other creatures also seem to have it (Ge 6:17; Job 12:10). The word breath is also used as a simile, describing the transitory nature of man's sojourn on earth (Ps 144:4). Job speaks of God doing things by His "breath" as he describes His power (Job 37:10). Jesus breathed on His disciples, as He blessed them (Jo 20:22).

BREECHES (archaic)

Trousers (Eze 44:18).

BRETHREN OF THE LORD

The four brothers of Jesus as given by the Gospels are James, Joses, Simon, and Judas (Ma 13:55; Mk 6:3). These are mentioned in connection with Mary (Ma 12:47-50; Mk 3:31-35; Lk 8:19-21). They appeared at Capernaum shortly after Jesus began his ministry (Jo 2:12). None of them were apostles, as they did not believe in Jesus's messiahship until after the resurrection (Jo 7:5) when they joined the company of believers (Ac 1:14). James became the acknowledged leader of the church at Jerusalem (Ac 21:18; Ga 1:19). See JAMES, BOOK OF, "The Author of James" for more information about James, the brother of the Lord.

BREWER

One who makes beer, wine, or other fermented drinks. While no brewers are mentioned in the Bible, "strong drink" is mentioned many times, all the way back to the days of Noah. Fermented drinks were made both from grain and from fruit juices.

BRIBE

To offer money, privilege, security, or material goods in exchange for an illegal act. The taking of a bribe was forbidden because it perverted justice (1 Sa 8:3; 12:3; Eze 22:12). Samuel's sons took bribes (1 Sa 8:3).

BRICK

Herodotus states that in building the walls of Babylon the clay was formed into bricks and burned in kilns. In Egypt and Assyria bricks were sun-dried. The Egyptians mixed straw with the clay, which kept the bricks from cracking. After Moses's first attempt to interfere for the benefit of his countrymen, the Hebrew slaves were compelled to gather their own straw for brickmaking, without reducing the quota they were required to produce each day (Ex 1:13-14; 5:7). The Hebrews may have followed the Egyptian method of brickmaking, but by the time of David, kiln fired bricks were in use (2 Sa 12:31).

BRICKMAKER, BRICKWORKER

One who makes bricks. The first mention of brickmaking in Scripture is in Genesis 11:3, when the people of the earth began to build the Tower of Babel.

BRIDE

A woman who is either about to be married or is just married. In ancient times (and even recently in many cultures) it was customary for the parents to arrange marriages for their children (Ge 34:4,8-9; 38:6; Ex 2:21; Ju 14:2). In the Old Testament, the nation of Israel was described as an unfaithful bride, likening her relationship to God as the relationship between husband and wife (Is 54:6; Je 3:1-20). The relationship between Christ and the church is described in the same way (Re 21:9; Ep 5:22-23).

BRIDE'GROOM

Christ is represented as the Bridegroom and the church as his bride (Ma 9:15; Jo 3:29; Re 21:9).

BRIDEGROOM, FRIEND OF THE

The friend of the bridegroom, the "best man," was the one who helped the bridegroom prepare for the wedding. When John's disciples perceived Jesus as a rival teacher, John explained to them that he was only the friend of the Bridegroom, the one who prepared the way for the Bridegroom's coming (Jo 3:29).

BRI'DLE, BIT

The words represent three objects: the bridle including the bit (Ps 32:9; Pr 26:3; Jam 1:26; Re 14:20); the halter (Job 30:11; 41:13; Is 30:28); and the muzzle which was used to prevent the animal from biting (Ps 39:1). Bridles were sometimes highly ornamented.

BRI'ER

The English rendering for one Greek and six Hebrew words. The *sirpad,* in the place of which shall come up the myrtle tree, was probably a nettle (Is 55:13). The Greek *tribolos* was probably a thistle (He 6:8) and is so rendered in Matthew 7:16. See THORNS and BRAMBLE.

BRIG'AN·DINE

A coat of mail (Je 46:4; 51:3 KJV).

BRIM'STONE

The substance known as roll sulphur. It was plentiful in the region of the Dead Sea. Sodom and other cities of the plain were destroyed by brimstone and fire (Ge 19:24; De 29:23; Re 9:17-18; 14:10).

BROIDERED (archaic)

Embroidered.

BRONZE

An alloy of copper and tin. See BRASS.

BRONZE SEA

See BRAZEN SEA.

BRONZE SERPENT

See BRAZEN SERPENT.

BRONZE WORKER

See METALSMITH.

BROOD (archaic)

The group of chicks hatched from a single clutch of eggs (Lk 13:34).

BROOK

The word is sometimes used in the sense of a small perennial stream such as the Jabbok (Ge 32:23) or the Kishon (1 Ki 18:40), but it more usually refers to a stream that forms in the time of rain and dries up in the hot season, such as the Kidron (2 Sa 15:23; Jo 18:1) or the Zered (De 2:13).

BROOM

A bush having many branches, with few, small leaves and pink and white flowers (Job 30:4). The prophet Elijah rested under its shade (1 Ki 19:4-5). Broom was apparently burned for charcoal (Ps 120:4).

BROTH'ER

The Hebrew word is used in various senses.

1. A male person having the same parental relationship as another or others; also a half brother (Ge 27:6; 28:2; Ju 8:19).

2. A near relation, such as a nephew (Ge 14:16).

3. A countryman of a kindred nation (De 23:7; Ne 5:7).

4. A political ally (Am 1:9) or coreligionist (Ac 9:17; Ro 1:13; 2 Co 2:13).

5. One affectionately or familiarly addressed (2 Sa 1:26; 1 Ki 20:32).

6. A member of the human race (Ma 5:22; 18:35).

BROTHERLY LOVE

Believers are commanded to be "kindly affectionate to one another with brotherly love, in honor giving preference to one another" (Ro 12:10). As part of the body of Christ, all believers are bound together as one family with the ties of affection and kinship. Jesus calls the poor and needy His brothers, and said that when we minister to these, we are ministering to Him (Ma 25:40). The ultimate expression of brotherly love is Paul's longing for the Jews, his kinsmen, to be saved (Ro 9:3). In the Old Testament Law, God commanded His people to love their neighbors as themselves (Le 19:17-18), and Jesus reinforced this by calling this one of the most important commandments. Jesus said that the love they would bear for one another would be the identifying mark of His disciples (Jo 13:35). Over and over again, believers are instructed to love one another with this type of familial affection (He 13:1; 1 Pe 2:17; 1 Pe 3:8).

BROTHERS, LORD'S

See BRETHREN OF THE LORD.

BROTHER'S WIFE

Sister-in-law (De 25:7). See LEVIRATE MARRIAGE.

BRUISE

A wound which does not break the skin. Bruised animals were considered unfit for sacrifice (Le 22:24), but Jesus, the ultimate sacrifice, was bruised for our sins (Is 53:10).

BRUTISH (archaic)

Stupid; lacking in intelligence or refinement of character. Used to liken a human to an animal (Pr 12:1).

BUCK

Male deer. See DEER.

BUCK'LER

See SHIELD.

BUFFALO

See CATTLE (2 Sa 6:13, NEB).

BUFFET (archaic)

To strike with a clenched fist (Ma 26:66-68).

BUGLE

See TRUMPET.

BUILDER

One who constructs buildings, walls, or other structures. Mankind has been building since their earliest days. Cain built a city for himself and his sons (Ge 4:17); the post-flood descendants of Noah planned to build a tower reaching heaven (Ge 11). God is the master builder, building the church of Christ on the foundation of the prophets, with Christ Himself as the chief cornerstone (1 Co 3; Ep 2:20).

BUK′KI

1. The chief of the tribe of Dan, the son of Jogli, one of the commission appointed by Moses for the division of the land (Nu 34:22).

2. The son of Abishua and descendant of Aaron (1 Ch 6:5, 51; Ez 7:4).

BUK·KI′AH (tested by Jehovah)

The son of Heman (1 Ch 25:4,13).

BUL (rain month)

Canaanite name for the eighth month of the sacred and second of the civil year, corresponding to a part of October and November (1 Ki 6:38). See CALENDAR.

BULL

The male of any large quadruped, especially of domestic cattle. Bashan was famous for its bulls (Ps 22:12). In De 14:5; Is 51:20 the Hebrew word is rendered wild ox and wild bull in the Authorized Version but antelope by the Revised Version. A bullock was a young bull (Je 31:18). It was one of the animals offered in sacrifice (Ex 29:1; 1 Ch 29:21).

BULLOCK

See BULL.

BUL′RUSH

The Hebrew word *agmon* is variously rendered *reed, rope, rush,* and *bulrush.* It was a plant that grew in swamps, and which could be twisted into ropes (Job 41:2; Is 9:14; 58:5). Another Hebrew word *gome* is rendered *rush* in Is 35:7. This was used for making the ark in which the baby Moses was preserved (Ex 2:3). It was also used in the construction of larger boats and in the manufacture of writing material. *Gome* was the famous papyrus plant.

BULRUSHES, ARK OF

See ARK.

BUL′WARK

Several Hebrew words are so rendered; also a turret (2 Ch 26:15); a mound used by those besieging a city (De 20:20); a rampart (Is 26:1).

BU′NAH (discretion)

A descendant of Judah through Jerahmeel (1 Ch 2:25).

BUN′NI (built)

1. A Levite. Shemaiah, one of his descendants, was made an overseer of the second temple (Ne 11:15).

2. A Levite who returned from Babylon and sealed the covenant with Nehemiah (Ne 9:4; 10:15).

BUR′DEN

It is used in the familiar sense of a load to be carried. It is also a solemn prophetic utterance or oracle denoting a divine judgment (Is 14:28; Eze 12:10; Ho 8:10; Na 1:1).

BURGLARY

See CRIME.

BUR′I·AL

When a person died, friends came to the home and lamented the death of the deceased (Mk 5:38). This act was performed even by hired mourners (Je 9:17). After the body was washed and bound with cloth (Ma 27:59; Jo 11:44), those who could afford it anointed the body with perfumes and spices (Jo 12:7; 19:39). The usual type of sepulchre was a cave (Ge 25:9-10; Ma 27:60). See SEPULCHRE.

BURN

This word is used literally, as in the case of the burning bush (Ex 3:2), or the fiery furnace (Da 3:20-25). It is also used figuratively in the sense of burning with anger (Ex 32:10-11; Ps 79:5), or with emotion (Lk 24:32).

BURNING BUSH

The burning bush that Moses saw is believed to have been a kind of acacia, a thorny tree that grows in the peninsula of Sinai and in Palestine near the Dead Sea (Ex 3:2-4; Mk 12:26).

BURNT OF'FER·ING

See OFFERINGS.

BUSH'EL

The rendering of the Greek *modios*, an ancient measure of about a peck (Ma 5:15; Mk 4:21). See WEIGHTS AND MEASURES.

BUSTARD

Any of a family of large terrestrial game birds found in Europe and Asia. They are slow on the ground (the name is thought to come from the Latin *avis tarde* "slow bird"), but they are capable of flight and can be swift when occasion demands. It is uncertain whether this is a fair translation of the Hebrew or not. The word has also been translated PORCUPINE and VULTURE.

BUSYBODY

One who minds the business of everyone other than themselves. Christians are supposed to be a hardworking people in order to prevent this type of behavior (2 Th 3:11).

BUT'LER

See CUPBEARER.

BUT'TER

Butterfat is separated from cream by churning. Probably, as in more modern times in Palestine, milk was placed in a skin-bottle suspended from three poles, then swung from side to side by women. Butter is only mentioned a few times in Scripture. Abraham served butter to his heavenly visitors, along with bread and meat (Ge 18:8, KJV). Other translations render this word "curds." It is uncertain whether butter (butterfat separated from the milk) is meant, or whether it refers to some kind of cheese (curdled milk, usually cooked to harden the curds).

BUYING

Exchanging valuable items for goods or services. Humans have been buying and selling probably since the beginning of history. Abraham bought the cave at Machpelah (Ge 23) to bury Sarah, his wife. Joseph's brothers sold him to the Midianites (Ge 37:28). Jesus Christ bought us with His blood (Ac 20:28).

BUZ *(contempt)*

Two men and a place in the Old Testament:
1. A tribe descended from a son of Nahor, brother of Abraham (Ge 22:20-21).
2. A man of the tribe of Gad (1 Ch 5:14).
3. A place probably in northern Arabia, exact location unknown (Je 25:23). Elihu's father came from this area, or possibly was descended from Buz No.1 (Job 32:2,6).

BU'ZI

Father of Ezekiel, the prophet (Eze 1:3).

BU'ZITE

See BUZ No. 3.

BUZZARD

See VULTURE.

BYBLOS

See GEBAL.

BY AND BY (archaic)

While today this phrase is often used to signify "in a little while," here it should be understood as "immediately," or "right away" (Mk 6:24-25).

C

CAB

A unit of measure. Its capacity was about 1.16 quarts as a dry measure (2 Ki 6:25), or two quarts as a liquid measure. See WEIGHTS AND MEASURES.

CAB'BON *(a bond)*

A place in the lowland of Judah (Jos 15:40). It may be the same as Machbenah (1 Ch 2:49).

CAB'IN

A cell within a dungeon for the separate confinement of prisoners (Je 37:16). This word is rendered *cell* in the Revised Version.

CA'BUL *(sterile)*

1. A town near the southeastern border of Asher, a few miles southeast of Acre (Jos 19:27).

2. A district of Galilee. It contained twenty towns. These Solomon gave to Hiram, king of Tyre, for service rendered by him in the construction of the temple. Hiram was so displeased with them that he called the region Cabul and returned them to Solomon who fortified there (1 Ki 9:13; 2 Ch 8:2).

CAE' SAR

The surname borne by the Julian family. After the death of the illustrious Gaius Julius Caesar, Augustus adopted the name as an official title, as did practically every other Roman emperor thereafter for some two hundred years. While eleven Caesars (emperors) fall within the scope of New Testament times, only four are mentioned. Caesar Augustus (31 B.C.-A.D. 14) issued the decree that the world should be taxed (Lk 2:1). It was in the fifteenth year of Tiberius Caesar (A.D. 14-37) that John the Baptist began his ministry (Lk 3:1). In the days of Claudius Caesar (A.D. 41-54) the famine predicted by Agabus came to pass. Claudius also commanded all Jews, including Aquila and Priscilla, to leave Rome (Ac 11:28; 18:2). Nero Caesar (A.D. 54-68) is called merely Caesar in Philippians 4:22. It was to Nero that Paul made his famous appeal (Ac 25:10-12).

CAE·SA·RE' A

Caesarea, a city in central Palestine on the Mediterranean Sea, served as the commercial port for the Roman-dominated Jewish territories during New Testament times. Built by the master Roman builder Herod the Great between 25 and 13 B.C., Caesarea was named for the Roman emperor Caesar Augustus. The city was known throughout the Roman world for its beauty, as well as its spacious, well-protected harbor.

In addition to its commercial importance, Caesarea also served as Rome's administrative capital for the Jewish territories during the New Testament era. This is why Caesarea is mentioned so prominently in connection with the ministry of the apostle Paul and other New Testament personalities. Philip preached at Caesarea (Ac 8:40), and Peter was sent to this administrative capital to minister to Cornelius, the Roman centurion (Ac 10:24). Herod Agrippa died here (Ac 12:19,23). Paul made Caesarea his port of call after his second and third missionary journeys. A Roman official sent Paul to the Roman governor Felix for trial after he was charged with disturbing the peace in Jerusalem (Ac 23:23-24,30). The apostle spent two years in prison at Caesarea before making his celebrated defense before Festus and Agrippa (Ac 25). After his long Caesarean imprisonment, he finally sailed from the harbor in chains to appeal his case before the emperor in Rome (Ac 27:1).

Herod's seaport city was built on the site of an ancient Phoenician seaport city known as Strato's Tower. He constructed an impressive breakwater system, using massive stones 50 feet long. Even after more than two thousand years, some of those stones are still visible today.

Other ruins on the site that demonstrate the splendor of ancient Caesarea are a large amphitheater and sections of an aqueduct, which was used to pipe water from the mountains to the coastal city.

Caesarea attained ecclesiastical importance by becoming the seat of a bishop in the second century.

CAE·SA·RE' A PHI·LIP' PI

A city in the extreme northern part of Palestine at the foot of Mount Hermon, the scene of Christ's famous charge to Peter and of the transfiguration (Ma 16:13-20; 17:1-13).

CAESAR'S HOUSEHOLD

While Paul was in prison in Rome, he had the opportunity to evangelize a remarkable variety of people, including some who were a part of Caesar's household (Ph 4:22). In New Testament times, a man's "household" included not only his family, but also his slaves and servants. The "saints" in Caesar's household were undoubtedly either slaves or freemen who worked for the emperor. Some think that the term includes servants who worked in other parts of the empire, as well as his immediate household.

CAGE

A box in which birds were kept, or a trap for catching them (Je 5:27).

CAI' A·PHAS (depression)

A Sadducee, the son-in-law of Annas (Jo 18:13) and high priest between A.D. 18 and 36. He demanded the death of Jesus (Ma 26:3-5; Jo 11:49-53; 18:14). Caiaphas participated in the trial of Peter and John (Ac 4:5-7).

CAIAPHAS AND CHRIST

CAIN *(lance)*

1. Eldest son of Adam and Eve, brother of Abel, whom he slew. An agriculturist, Cain presented to God an offering from the fruit of the ground, while his brother Abel made a blood sacrifice. Since sin requires death, the vegetable offering was inadequate as a sin offering, and God rejected it. Envious of his brother, whose offering was acceptable to God, Cain murdered Abel. When confronted by God, Cain at first denied his sin, and expressed no repentance. Exiled, he went to Nod where he married; his wife being one of the descendants of Adam. He built a city which he named after his son, Enoch, and became the progenitor of a race distinctive along mechanical lines. (Ge 4:1-25; 1 Jo 3:12; Jude 11).

2. A city of Judah a few miles southeast of Hebron (Jos 15:57).

CA·I′NAN

1. Son of Enos (Ge 5:9-14; Lk 3:37-38). He died at the age of 940 and was of the line of Seth.

2. Son of Arphaxad in the line of the Messiah (Lk 3:36), also called Kenan.

CAKE

See BREAD.

CA′LAH

One of the four cities of Assyria and one of the most ancient of that country (Ge 10:11-12). It was rebuilt and adorned by Shalmaneser I

(1276-1257 B.C.), and having fallen into decay, was restored by Assurnazipal who made it the king's residence. The ruins, about twenty miles south of Nineveh, are now called Nimrud.

CAL′A·MUS *(reed)*

This plant has a sweet smelling odor (Song 4:14) and was an ingredient of the anointing oil (Ex 30:23). It was used for sacrificial purposes (Is 43:24). Also called sweet cane, it was brought from Greece and western Asia Minor to Tyre (Eze 27:19).

CAL′COL *(sustenance)*

A son of Mahol (1 Ki 4:31; 1 Ch 2:6).

CAL′DRON

See POT.

CA′LEB *(dog, or bold)*

1. Son of Jephunneh, called the Kenezite (Nu 32:12; Jos 14:6,14). He was one of the twelve spies sent from Kadesh to Canaan and strongly advised that the Israelites go forward and take the land. For this demonstration of faith in the Lord, he and Joshua alone, of all the Israelites who were over twenty years of age at the time, were permitted to enter the promised land (Nu 13:2,6,30; 14:6,24,38; Jos 14:6,14). He represented the tribe of Judah in the division of the land (Nu 34:19). He received the city of Hebron as an inheritance (Jos 14). His daughter, Achsah, became the wife of his near relative, Othniel.

2. Son of Hezron and father of Hur (1 Sa 25:3; 1 Ch 2:18-20).

CA′LEB-EPH′RA-TAH

See CALEB-EPHRATHAH.

CA′LEB-EPH′RA·THAH

The place where Hezron died (1 Ch 2:19,24). Ephrathah is not infrequently a designation for the district about Bethlehem. The name apparently means that part of Ephrathah which belonged to the clan of Caleb.

CA′LEB·ITE

A descendant of Caleb.

CALENDAR

The Jews used two kinds of calendars: the *Civil Calendar,* the official calendar of kings, childbirth, and contracts; and the *Sacred Calendar,* from which festivals were computed.

Names of Months	Corresponds With	Number of Days	Month of Civil Year	Month of Sacred Year
Tishri	Sept-Oct	30	1st	7th
Heshvan	Oct-Nov	29 or 30	2nd	8th
Chislev	Nov-Dec	29 or 30	3rd	9th
Tebeth	Dec-Jan	29	4th	10th
Shebat	Jan-Feb	30	5th	11th
Adar	Feb-Mar	29 or 30	6th	12th
Nisan	Mar-Apr	30	7th	1st
Iyar	Apr-May	29	8th	2nd
Sivan	May-June	30	9th	3rd
Tammuz	June-July	29	10th	4th
Ab	July-Aug	30	11th	5th
Elul	Aug-Sept	29	12th	6th

Hebrew months were alternately 30 and 29 days long. Their year, shorter than ours, had 354 days. Therefore, about every 3 years (7 times in 19 years) an extra 29-day month, Veadar, was added between Adar and Nisan.

The Jewish day was from sunset to sunset, in 8 equal parts:

First Watch	Sunset to 9 P.M.
Second Watch	9 P.M. to Midnight
Third Watch	Midnight to 3 A.M
Fourth Watch	3 A.M. to Sunrise

* * * * * * * * * * * * *

First Hour	Sunrise to 9 A.M.
Third Hour	9 A.M. to Noon
Sixth Hour	Noon to 3 P.M.
Ninth Hour	3 P.M. to Sunset

CALF

A young cow or bullock, used for food (Ge 18:7) and for sacrificial purposes (He 9:12,19). It was one of the animals worshipped by the Egyptians which, no doubt, suggested to the Israelites at Sinai the making of a golden calf (Ex 32:4; Ps 106:19-20). When Jeroboam founded the Northern Kingdom, he set up two golden calves, one at Beth-el and one at Dan (1 Ki 12:29). He probably had seen Apis, the sacred bull worshipped in Egypt, where he had fled from Solomon (1 Ki 11:40).

CALF WORSHIP

See GOLDEN CALF.

CALK' ER

One who seals the seams in a ship (Eze 27:9, 27).

CALL

To give a name to (Ge 2:19; 17:5; Lk 1:13), or to address by name (Ps 55:16-17).

CALLING

Occupation, life purpose (Ro 8:28-30; 1 Th 2:12; 1 Co 7:20).

CAL' NEH *(fortress)*

1. A Babylonian city of the kingdom of Nimrod (Ge 10:10).

2. A city of Syria (Am 6:2), probably the same as Calno (Is 10:9).

CAL' NO

A city, apparently in Syria, which unsuccessfully resisted Assyria (Is 10:9). See CALNEH.

CAL' VA•RY *(skull)*

The name is derived from the Latin *calvaria,* a skull (Lk 23:33). It corresponds to the Aramaic word *Golgotha* (Ma 27:33; Mk 15:22; Jo 19:17). Jerome offered as a possible explanation of the name applied to the little hill the fact that unburied skulls may have been there. Others suggest that it was so called because it was a place of execution. Still others suppose that the skull-shape of the hill gave rise to the name. It was outside the city wall, and here the crucifixion of Christ occurred (Ma 27:33; Jo 19:17,20; He 13:11-13). It was perhaps close to a highway (Ma 27:39). There are different views relative to the location of Calvary. One is that the site is marked by the Church of the Holy Sepulchre which is within the walls of the present city. To establish this claim it would be necessary to prove that this site was outside the walls of Jerusalem in the time of Christ—a task which apparently is impossible. The site that better meets the conditions is the little hill on the north side of the city about 250 yards outside of the wall.

CAM' EL

This animal was early known to the Egyptians (Ge 12:16). Called the ship of the desert, it has great powers of endurance, and while generally obedient, does not possess a sweet disposition. The camel was used by Abraham and Jacob (Ge 12:16; 30:43), and a camel carried Joseph into Egypt (Ge 37:25). The camel is peculiarly adapted for desert travel (Ex 9:3; Ju 6:5; 1 Ki 10:2).

CAMEL'S HAIR

In Bible times, the hair of the camel was woven into a coarse cloth, used for utilitarian purposes. Camel's hair makes a sturdy, insulating fabric which was used for tents and outer robes. John the Baptist wore a robe of camel's hair (Ma 3:4; Mk 1:6)—a "coarse robe" as befitted a prophet, rather than the "soft clothes" of kings and princes (Ma 11:8; Lk 7:25).

CAMEL-THORN

See CYPRESS.

CA'MON

See KAMON.

CAMP

An encampment or stopping-place of a moving body of people or an army (Ex 14:19; 1 Sa 4:5; 2 Ki 7:7). In their journeying through the wilderness the Hebrew camp was well planned, with the tabernacle in the center (Nu 1:47–2:34; 3:14-39).

CAM'PHIRE

The old spelling of camphor. It is the rendering of the Hebrew word for henna in Song of Solomon 1:14; 4:13. See HENNA.

CA'NA *(place of reeds)*

A village of upper Galilee, about midway from the Mediterranean to the Sea of Galilee. It was the scene of the first miracle performed by Jesus and his later miracle of healing the nobleman's son (Jo 2:1-11; 4:46-54). It was the native village of the apostle, Nathanael (Jo 21:2).

CA'NA·AN *(low)*

1. The son of Ham and grandson of Noah (Ge 10:6; 1 Ch 1:8). His oldest son, Zidon, founded the city of his name (Sidon) in Phoenicia, and thus he became the progenitor of that nation. Canaan's other sons were fathers of tribes in Syria and Palestine (Ge 10:15-19; 1 Ch 1:13-16).

2. By this name the country itself is sometimes understood. It was probably first employed to denote the coastline of Palestine (Nu 13:29; Jos 11:3). It was then applied to the Jordan district and later to the whole country. It is called the promised land because it was promised to Abraham; the holy land because it was holy unto the Lord; and Palestine, or Philistia because it was, in part at least, the land of the Philistines.

CANAAN

CA'NAAN·ITE

The Canaanites, an ancient tribe, highly developed in their culture, occupied Palestine long before the Hebrews arrived to drive them out under the leadership of Joshua about 1405 B.C.

Archeological evidence indicates the Canaanites must have settled the land of Canaan at least six hundred years before Joshua's time. They had a well-developed system of walled cities, including Jericho, Ai, Lachish, Hebron, Debir, and Hazor. Under God's leadership, Joshua was successful in taking these cities from the Canaanites (Jos 6–12).

The Canaanites also had their own written language, based upon a unique alphabet, which they apparently developed. Discovery of a number of Canaanite documents at Ras Shamra in northern Palestine has given scholars many insights into Canaanite culture and daily life.

The religion of the Canaanite people posed a peculiar threat to the new inhabitants of Canaan. The Canaanites worshiped many pagan gods that appealed to their animal instincts. Baal, the god who controlled rain and fertility, was their main god.

Baal religion was basically a fertility cult. At temples scattered throughout their land, Canaanite worshippers participated in lewd, immoral acts with sacred prostitutes. Bestiality and child-sacrifice were other evils associated with this depraved form of religion.

The threat of Baal worship explains why Moses issued a stern warning to the people of Israel about the Canaanites several years before they actually occupied the land of promise. "You shall conquer them and utterly destroy them," Moses commanded. "You shall make no covenant with them nor show mercy to them" (De 7:2).

Canaanite religion continued to exert its influence throughout the land for many years after Joshua's conquest. The Hebrew people had to be called back again and again to worship the one true God, who demanded holy and ethical living from His people.

CA'NAAN·IT·ESS

A Canaanite woman (1 Ch 2:3).

CA-NA·NAE'AN, CA'NAAN·ITE

A member of a Jewish patriotic party; equivalent to the Greek word "Zealot" (Ma 10:4).

CAN'DA·CE

A queen of Ethiopia. For some time Ethiopia was governed by female rulers who took the name of Candace. The kingdom of this queen was probably in southern Nubia. A eunuch of prominence belonging to her court was returning from Jerusalem when, in the desert of Gaza, he met Philip the evangelist who interpreted to him Isaiah 53. He was converted to Christianity and was baptized (Ac 8:26-39).

CAN'DLE

A hardened fat, such as tallow or wax, i.e. beeswax or bayberry, with a braided cotton or linen wick imbedded into the wax or fat. As far as we know, ancient peoples did not use candles as we know them. Instead, they used lamps which burned a liquid such as olive oil. See LAMP.

CAN'DLE·STICK

Lampstand. The candlestick, or lampstand, of the tabernacle had a base and shaft supporting six branches. It was one of the articles of the holy place (Ex 25:31-40; Le 24:2-4). Pure olive oil was used and the light burned from evening until morning (Ex 27:20-21; 1 Sa 3:3).

CANE

The Hebrew *ganeh,* rendered sweet cane in Isaiah 43:24 and Jeremiah 6:20. It was an aromatic plant. See CALAMUS.

CANKER (archaic)

A spreading infection or sore which destroys body tissue; gangrene (2 Ti 2:17).

CAN'KER·WORM

Probably insect larvae which damage or destroy plants by eating the buds and foliage (Na 3:16). The word is rendered *caterpillar* in some versions (Je 51:27), and some translate it as some kind of locust (Joel 2:25).

CAN'NEH

A place probably in Mesopotamia (Eze 27:23), perhaps the same as Calneh.

CAN'ON OF SCRIPTURE

The word *canon* signifies a straight rod or a rule, such as a carpenter's rule. Hence a canon is whatever is qualified to determine or regulate other things. The Scriptures are considered as a rule of faith and practice. If a book has a right to a place in the Bible, it is called canonical; if not, it is declared to be uncanonical. When, for example, the apocryphal books are said to be uncanonical, it means that for certain reasons they are not to be considered as divinely inspired and are not entitled to a place in the Scriptures, and are not a rule of faith or of biblical doctrine.

The Old Testament was formed during an extended period. First was the Pentateuch, the books of Moses (De 31:24-26). This was added to by Joshua (Jos 24:26), and Samuel (1 Sa 10:25). The book of the Law was found in the time of Josiah (2 Ki 22:8-20). The prophets wrote the books bearing their names, and quoted the writings of each other (Is 2:2-4; Mi 4:1-3). The New Testament refers to the Scriptures of the Old Testament as the Word of God (Ma 21:42; 26:56; Mk 14:49; Jo 10:35; Ro 3:2; 2 Ti 3:15; He 5:12; 1 Pe 4:11). In no instance does the New Testament recognize the apocryphal books, and the fact that they are excluded from the Hebrew collection is sufficient to establish their non-canonicity. From the time of Ezra the

Old Testament appears as a whole. The Canon of the New Testament as we have it was ratified in the fourth century A.D. For more information about the acceptance of each book into the Scriptural canon, see the article about that individual book. Also see APOCRYPHA.

CANOPY

A roof with no walls. A canopy could be portable, like a tent, or it could be a form of porch (1 Ki 7:6; Eze 41:25). The heavens are described as a canopy (Job 36:29).

CAN'TI·CLES

See SONG OF SOLOMON.

CAPERBERRY

A shrubby plant which grows in such inhospitable locations as cracks in walls or clefts in the rocks. It produces berries and flowers. Today it is cultivated for its buds, called "capers" which are pickled and used in condiments and sauces. This word is also translated "desire" (Ec 12:5).

CA·PER'NA·UM *(village of Nahum)*

A town on the northwestern coast of the Sea of Galilee (Ma 4:13-16; Lk 4:31; Jo 6:17-24). It was a city of importance, had its own synagogue, and was probably a military post (Ma 8:5-13; Lk 7:1-10). When Jesus was rejected at Nazareth, he made Capernaum his headquarters (Ma 9:1; Mk 2:1). It was the scene of many of his miracles and teachings. The Centurion's servant, Peter's mother-in-law, a man sick of the palsy, a nobleman's son, and others were healed here (Ma 8:5-13; Mk 1:29-31; 2:1-13; Lk 7:1-10; Jo 4:46-54). In the synagogue and other places in the city Jesus taught (Mk 9:33-50; Jo 6:24-71). A custom station was located here; and here Matthew, the tax-gatherer, was called as one of the apostles (Ma 9:9-13; Mk 2:14-17). Jesus was deeply concerned about the lack of belief demonstrated by the citizens of Capernaum. He pronounced a curse upon the city (Ma 11:23-24) and predicted its destruction (Lk 10:15). So strikingly did His prophecy come true that only recently has the site of Capernaum been positively identified.

CAPH'TOR

An island or seacoast from which the Philistines came (Je 47:4; Am 9:7). Originally the Philistines were apparently Cretans, as were possibly the Cherethites (1 Sa 30:14; Eze 25:16); hence Caphtor was quite probably Crete.

CAPH'TO·RIM, CAPH'THO·RIM

The land of Caphtor (Ge 10:14; 1 Ch 1:12); also its people who drove out the Avvim and settled on their land (De 2:23). From them were descended the Philistines (Je 47:4; Am 9:7).

CAPITAL

The ornate top of a pillar or column (1 Ki 7:16).

CAPITAL CITIES

Important Capital Cities of the Old Testament:

Achmetha: Also known as Ecbatana, Achmetha was capital of the Median Empire (Ez 6:2); and served as the summer residence of Persian kings.

Babylon: Capital city of the Babylonian Empire in the land of the Chaldeans (Je 24:5); city to which citizens of Judah were carried after the fall of Jerusalem (2 Ch 36; 18-20).

Damascus: Capital of Syria and important trade center; oldest continually inhabited city in the world (Ge 14:15).

Hebron: David's capital as he ruled Judah (2 Sa 2:1-4). Abraham's home after his return from Egypt (Ge 13:18).

Jerusalem: Made capital of the united kingdom of Israel by David (2 Sa 5:6-7); location of Solomon's temple, known as the holy city and Zion by the Jewish people.

Nineveh: Capital of Assyria; this ancient walled city was scene of the prophet Jonah's reluctant preaching mission (Jon 3:1-3).

No: Also known as Thebes, No was capital of Egypt and the center of pagan worship on the banks of the Nile River (Eze 30:13-16).

Samaria: Permanent capital of the Northern Kingdom; built by Omri, sixth king of Israel, in 880 B.C. (1 Ki 16:23-24).

Shechem: First capital city of the Northern Kingdom following Solomon's reign, located in the hill country of Ephraim (Ge 12:6).

Shushan: Also known as Susa, Shushan was capital of ancient Elam and later capital of the Persian Empire; most events in the Book of Esther occurred in this city (Es 1:2-5).

Ur: Capital of ancient Sumer on the Euphrates River; Abraham lived here before moving to Haran (Ge 11:31).

Important Capital Cities of the New Testament:

Alexandria: Capital of Egypt during the Greek and Roman periods; established by Alexander the Great; home of Apollos (Ac 18:24).

Antioch: Capital province of Syria during the Roman period; missionary base for Paul and Barnabas (Ac 13:1-3).

Athens: Capital of ancient Greece; center of culture and politics during Greece's golden age; visited by Paul on his second missionary journey (Ac 17:16-34).

Caesarea: Important seaport built by Herod the Great and named for Caesar Augustus; it became the Roman provincial capital of the Jewish nation for 600 years.

Corinth: Capital of the Roman province of Achaia in ancient Greece; a thriving trade and shipping center when Paul arrived here to establish a church (Ac 18:1).

Jerusalem: Religious capital of the Jewish people during the Roman occupation.

Pergamos: Capital of the Roman province of Asia; location of the "compromising" church addressed by John (Re 2:12-17).

Rome: Capital of the Roman Empire and present capital of Italy; the apostle Paul was imprisoned and probably executed at Rome (Ac 28:16).

Thessalonica: Capital of the Roman province of Macedonia; Paul founded a church here (Ac 17:1-4).

CAP·PA·DO′CI·A

A province of Asia Minor, having on its north Pontus, Cilicia on the south, Syria on the east and Lycaonia and Galatia on the west (Ac 2:9; 1 Pe 1:1).

CAPSTONE

The final stone on the top of a wall, a coping stone. The capstone holds the previous stones in place, and may tie two walls together. Figuratively, the capstone refers to the most important position, the highest place, the one who finishes and holds everything together (Ze 4:7).

CAPTAIN

In the Old Testament the Hebrew word *sar* is rendered captain (Ju 4:2; 1 Sa 14:50; 2 Sa 10:16), as the commander of a division (2 Sa 18:2), or an officer over a certain number (Nu 31:14,48; 2 Ki 1:9). In the New Testament the word was used broadly denoting the commander of a gar-

rison, or an officer of a legion (Ac 21:31-32). In Acts 28:16 the captain was the head officer of the Praetorian Guard.

CAP′TIVE

One who is held against his will. When one nation conquered another, it was not uncommon for the conquered people to be taken as captives. They might be simply relocated, as the Jews were relocated to Assyria and Babylon (2 Ki 25:7), or they might be made slaves (2 Sa 8:2).

CAP·TIV′I·TY

Using the term in the sense of holding in bondage in a foreign land, the Egyptian bondage is the first of the captivities of the chosen people. But the two instances to which the word usually applies are the captivity of Israel and the captivity of Judah. In the case of the former, Assyria overthrew the kingdom in 722 B.C. After the besieging of Samaria by Shalmaneser, Sargon, in his first year, took it and carried away a great number of the people to Mesopotamia and Media (2 Ki 17:5-6). The captivity of Judah was in three stages. The first was in the reign of Jehoiakim in 606 B.C. (2 Ch 36:2-7; Da 1:1-3) by Nebuchadnezzar, who carried off Daniel and others. The second stage or deportation was eight years later (597 B.C.) in the reign of Jehoiachin, when the king and about 11,000 of the people were taken to Babylon (2 Ki 24:14-16). The third stage was the fall of Jerusalem in 586 B.C. when Nebuchadnezzar destroyed the city and carried away the people, leaving a remnant (2 Ki 25:2-21). The captivity of Judah was predicted 150 years before it happened. The date should be reckoned from the first deportation, 606. It was declared that the captivity would last seventy years, and true to the promise of God, the Jews were released by Cyrus in 536 B.C.

CARAVAN

A group of travelers, generally merchants, traveling from city to city in order to buy, sell and trade (Job 6:19). Joseph's brothers sold him as a slave to a caravan of Midianite traders (Ge 37:25).

CARAWAY

See CUMMIN.

CAR′BUN·CLE

An archaic word for any red gemstone, such as ruby or garnet. The Hebrew word in Isaiah 54:12 denotes a bright or shining gem of any kind. Another word thus rendered—but probably an emerald—appears among the gems of the breastplate of the high priest (Ex 28:17; Eze 28:13). See EMERALD.

CAR′CAS

One of the seven chamberlains who served King Ahasuerus (Es 1:10).

CAR′CASS

A dead body. By Mosaic law the presence of a dead body made a tent or house ceremonially unclean. Anyone touching the carcass of an animal was unclean until the evening of that day (Le 11:39).

CAR·CHE′MISH

On the western bank of the upper Euphrates this city occupied a position of great commercial advantage. It was captured by Sargon in 717 B.C. (Is 10:9). It was here that Nebuchadnezzar defeated Pharaoh-necho in 605 B.C. (Je 46:2).

CA·RE′AH

See KAREAH.

CARGO

The load carried by a ship. When the great storm came up and battered the boat Jonah was traveling in, the sailors sought to lighten the load by throwing the cargo overboard (Jon 1:5).

CAR′ITES

Probably mercenary soldiers from Caria, as Cherethites were probably from Crete (2 Ki 11:4), called captains in Authorized Version.

CARKAS

See CARCAS.

CAR′MEL (park)

1. A high promontory which juts into the Mediterranean some 25 miles west of the Sea of Galilee; also, the short mountain range which begins with the promontory. Running southeastwardly, it joins the central ranges near Samaria. It was the scene of the great test to which Elijah put Baal (1 Ki 18:17-40). It was

CARMEL

here the cloud as big as a man's hand was seen that was to terminate the drought. It was visited by Elisha (2 Ki 2:25; 4:25).

2. A town in the hill country of Judah (Jos 15:55). It was here that Nabal had his possessions (1 Sa 25:2-40).

CARMELITE

A native of the town of Carmel. Nabal, the first husband of David's wife Abigail, was described as a Carmelite (1 Sa 30:5; 2 Sa 2:2; 3:3). One of David's mighty men, Hezrai, was also a Carmelite (2 Sa 23:35). He is called Hezro in 1 Chronicles 11:37.

CARMELITESS

A woman from the town of Carmel. Abigail, David's wife was a Carmelitess (1 Sa 27:3; 1 Ch 3:1).

CAR′MI (vinedresser)

1. Son of Reuben, the head of a tribal family (Ge 46:9; Nu 26:6).

2. The father of Achan (Jos 7:1).

CAR′MITES

A Reubenite family descended from Carmi (Nu 26:6).

CAR·NA′IM

See ASHTEROTH-KARNAIM.

CARNAL

Of the flesh. Used in Scripture to refer to fallen human nature (1 Co 3:3).

CAR′PEN·TER

Carpentry as a distinct occupation is first mentioned in the Scriptures when carpenters of Tyre came to Jerusalem to build David's house (2 Sa 5:11). Various tools are mentioned, such as the hammer, nail, saw, and ax (Je 10:4; Is 10:15); plane, and compass line (Is 44:13). Jesus worked as carpenter in Nazareth (Mk 6:3).

CAR′PUS

A man of Troas (2 Ti 4:13).

CARRIAGE (archaic)

That which is carried (1 Sa 17:22; Is 10:28; Ju 18:21; Is 46:1).

CARRION VULTURE

See VULTURE.

CAR·SHE′NA *(spoiler)*

A Persian prince in the court of Ahasuerus (Es 1:14).

CART

A two-wheeled or four-wheeled cattle-drawn vehicle used for the transportation of various goods (Nu 7:3). Joseph sent carts to help transport his father's household to Egypt (Ge 45:19, 21,27; 46:5). They were generally made of wood (1 Sa 6:14).

CARV′ING

In making images, letters, and designs various materials were used—stone, wood, ivory. The carving for the tabernacle was done by Bezaleel of Judah and Aholiab of Dan (Ex 31:1-7; 35:30-35). Flowers and trees were carved in the temple (1 Ki 6:18,29,35).

CASE′MENT

A part of a window operated by a hinge allowing that part to be opened (Pr 7:6). In Judges 5:28 the Hebrew word is rendered *lattice.*

CAS·I·PHI′A

A place in the Persian Empire. During the exile Levites resided here (Ez 8:17).

CAS·LU′HIM

A people of Mizraim. In the list of the sons of Mizraim they stand between the Pathrusim and the Caphtorim. It is probable they were settled in upper Egypt (Ge 10:14; 1 Ch 1:12).

CAS′SI·A

In the rendering of the Hebrew word in Ezekiel 27:19 an aromatic wood is designated. It was one of the ingredients of the anointing oil (Ex 30:24).

CAS′TA·NET′

A musical instrument used by David. The word signifies *chestnut,* being derived from the word *castanea.* An ancient custom was to attach two chestnuts to the fingers and beat them together. In 2 Samuel 6:5, Revised Version, they were probably miniature cymbals.

CAST ANGLE (archaic)

To fish with a hook (Is 19:7-8).

CASTAWAY

Cast off, rejected (1 Co 9:27).

CASTING OF LOTS

The casting of lots was a custom or rite used in ancient times to make decisions. It is not dissimilar to the way we practice drawing straws or flipping a coin today, except that for the Hebrews at least, they were not looking at it as a matter of blind chance. They believed that God would direct the casting of the lots, and regarded it as a way of discovering His will. Several examples of this ancient practice occur in both the Old and New Testaments.

Lots were cast by the high priest to select the scapegoat on the Day of Atonement (Le 16:8-10). This method was also used to divide the land of Canaan after its conquest under Joshua (Nu 26:55-56; Jos 14:2). Lots were cast to select warriors to fight against the men of Gibeah (Ju 20:9-10) and apparently to choose Saul as the first king of Israel (1 Sa 10:19-21). Sailors on the ship bound for Tarshish with Jonah on board used lots to determine who had caused the stormy seas (Jon 1:7).

In the New Testament, Roman soldiers cast lots for Jesus's garments (Ma 27:35). After prayer, the apostles used lots to choose Matthias as successor to Judas (Ac 1:24-26).

We can only speculate about what materials were used in the casting of lots. Some scholars believe several stones, or perhaps precious gems, were cast from a clay jug. Others connect the practice with the Urim and Thummim, precious stones that were on, by, or in the breastplate of the high priest of Israel. The high priest used these stones in making important decisions, but it is not known exactly how this was done (Ex 28:30).

Proverbs 16:33 demonstrates that casting lots was not considered magic, because the decision was from the Lord. Despite this, there seems to be little justification for this practice today. Since the coming of God's Holy Spirit at Pentecost, we have this ever-present resource to guide us in our decision making. As enlightened believers, we are urged to bring our needs to the Father in prayer and rely on the direction of the Holy Spirit (Jo 14:13; 15:16).

CAS′ TLE

A fortified building to be used as a stronghold. The castle of the Jebusites within the site of modern Jerusalem was captured by David (1 Ch 11:5,7). This became his residence and was called the city of David. Castles were built in the cities and forests of Judah (2 Ch 17:12; 27:4). Certain habitations, rendered *castles* in the Authorized Version, are called *encampments* in the Revised Version (Ge 25:16; Nu 31:10; 1 Ch 6:54).

CAS′ TOR AND POL′ LUX

The twin sons of Jupiter and Leda, Greek and Roman divinities. They appeared in the heavens as the constellation Gemini—Twin Brothers— the protectors of mariners (Ac 28:11).

CAT

Cats are mentioned nowhere in the Bible, even though they were well-known in the ancient world. Egyptian cat-worship is well-known, and perhaps the Hebrews avoided the animals for this reason. It is equally possible that they were used as they are all over the world to keep down the rats and mice in the granaries and barns.

CATACOMBS

Underground tunnels and chambers designed for the burial of the dead. The famous catacombs under Rome are not mentioned in the Bible, but they are nevertheless important to Christianity. Hundreds of miles of these subterranean passages exist outside the city; the early Christians took refuge here when persecution became unbearable.

CAT′ ER·PIL′ LAR

The rendering of the Hebrew word signifying *devourer.* It is associated with the locust. It is destructive of vegetation, an unusual instance of which occurred in the time of Joel (1 Ki 8:37; Ps 78:46; Is 33:4; Joel 1:4; 2:25). This term may refer simply to the plant-devouring larvae of various insects.

CATHOLIC EPISTLES

The word *catholic* simply means "general." James, 1 and 2 Peter, 3 John and Jude are referred to as the General Epistles because they are not addressed to an individual person or church.

CAT′ TLE

In the Old Testament the term applies to domestic animals, sheep, goats, horses, camels, oxen (Ge 26:13-14; 30:32; 47:16-18). In one place the word is actually translated "buffalo" (2 Sa 6:13, NEB), though the actual definition of the Hebrew word is uncertain.

CAU′ DA

See CLAUDA.

CAUL

1. The fatty envelope above the liver. Together with the kidneys and certain specified fats, it was burned as an offering (Ex 29:13,22; Le 3:4).
2. The pericardium (Ho 13:8).
3. Probably a small head veil (Is 3:18).

CAVALRY

The mounted portion of an organized army, from the Latin word for horse. Solomon's army included cavalry units (1 Ki 9:19,22; 2 Ch 8:6,9). The Syrians and the Chaldeans also had cavalries (1 Ki 20:20; Hab 1:8), as did the Egyptians and Canaanites (Ex 14:9; 15:19; Ju 4:15). The term probably also includes the chariots.

CAVE

The largest number of caves are to be found in limestone countries, such as Palestine, where the people often dwelt in them (1 Ki 19:9). After the destruction of Sodom, Lot and his family found protection in a cave (Ge 19:30); the same was true of David and of Elijah (1 Sa 22:1; 1 Ki 19:9). Caves were used for burial purposes (Ge 23:1-20; Jo 11:38), and many believe that the inn stable in Bethlehem was actually a cave.

CEDAR

CE′DAR

The Hebrew *erez* which, with the possible exception of Numbers 24:6, always designates the famous tall and stately tree of Lebanon (1 Ki 5:6; Is 2:13). It was used in the building of palaces and temples, notably the temple of Solomon. Greatly prized, durable and attractively scented, cedar wood was also used for other purposes (1 Ki 6:9-10,18; Is 44:14; Eze 27:5).

CE′DRON

See KIDRON.

CEILED

Paneled or plastered. Today the word "ceiling" specifically means the paneling or plaster which covers the top facet of a room, concealing the beams or joists of the upper floor or roof, but in the older sense it can apply to walls as well (1 Ki 6:9,15; 7:3; 2 Chr 3:5,9; Je 22:14; Eze 41:116; Hag 1:4).

CELEBRATE

See WORSHIP.

CELLAR

A man-made cave or pit dug into the ground or into rock, generally used for food storage. Because it is underground, a cellar is ideal for keeping foods such as oil or wine which need to be stored in a cool dark place (1 Ch 27:27-28).

CEN·CHRE′A *(millet)*

The eastern harbor of Corinth, about nine miles from the city. It had a Christian church, the deaconess of which was Phebe (Ro 16:1). It was visited by Paul (Ac 18:18).

CEN·CHREA′A

See CENCHREA.

CEN′SER

A vessel used for the burning of incense (Le 16:12-13). Those of the tabernacle were made of brass (Nu 16:39), while those of the temple were of gold (1 Ki 7:50).

CEN′SUS

The Hebrews had a system of registering by tribe, family and house (Nu 1:18). There was also the numbering of classes, as of the firstborn (Nu 3:43). There were three specific numberings of Israel; the first at Sinai after leaving Egypt (Nu 1). The number of males over twenty years of age was 603,550. The tribe of Levi, counted separately, numbered 22,000 (Nu 3:39). The second census was taken at the close of the wandering and was almost the same as the first—601,730 (Nu 26:1-51), while the Levites numbered 23,000 (Nu 26:62). The third census was taken by David and showed 1,300,000 fighting men (2 Sa 24:1-9; 1 Ch 21:1-6). Shortly before the birth of Christ, Augustus ordered an enrollment of the people which brought Joseph and Mary to Bethlehem, the city of David (Lk 2:1).

CEN·TU′RI·ON

This word is derived from the Latin *centum,* one hundred. It was the title of a Roman army officer who had command of one hundred soldiers (Ac 21:32; 22:26). Cornelius of Caesarea was a Centurion. He was brought into the church by Peter (Ac 10). Julius, who had charge of Paul and other prisoners, was a Centurion (Ac 27:1,3,43). Two others, whose names are not given, one at Capernaum (Ma 8:5-13), the other at the cross (Ma 27:54), were also Centurions.

CE′PHAS *(stone)*

Simon Peter. Jesus gave Simon, son of Jonah, the nickname "rock," early on. In Greek, this is Peter; in Aramaic it is Cephas (1 Co 1:12; 3:22; 15:5; Ga 2:9).

CEREMONIAL LAWS

The concept of ceremonial holiness in Leviticus springs from the truth that God is holy, and only persons who are clean can approach Him in worship: "For I am the LORD your God. You shall therefore sanctify yourselves, and you shall be holy; for I am holy" (Le 11:44). Chapters 17–26 of Leviticus are known as the "Holiness Code," but the Books of Numbers and Deuteronomy also contain many related regulations.

Some actions that were not sinful were considered ceremonially defiling. These included eating unclean foods, such as the vulture or buzzard because of their scavenger habits; and contact with unclean objects or people, such as with a leper or a dead body (Le 11:24-47).

Persons guilty of minor offenses could be cleansed simply by ceremonial washing. However, penalties for uncleanness could range from prohibition from the priesthood (Le 21:16-24) to expulsion from the camp and social isolation (Le 13:44-46).

Priests were especially restricted—in their personal lives, as well as in their conduct at the altar (Le 21). Even a descendant of Aaron could not officiate at the altar if he had a physical defect (Le 21:17).

Israel was warned that sexual immorality was defiling to them, just as it was to their heathen neighbors (Le 18:24). Lust was prohibited, along with all types of unnatural sexual relations, such as incest, homosexuality, and bestiality (Le 18; 20).

While this ceremonial system served a valuable purpose for God's people in Old Testament times, the sacrifice of Christ, the great High Priest, has removed the need for ceremonial regulations while stressing the moral law.

CHAFF

The leaves, husks, and bits of straw which are left mixed with the grain after threshing. After grain was threshed (either by being trodden by animals or by beating with sticks) the straw was lifted with a fork, leaving the grain and chaff on the threshing floor. Then the grain had to be winnowed to remove the chaff. This was done by tossing the grain into the air and allowing the breeze to blow away chaff while the heavier grain fell back to the floor (Job 21:18; Ps 1:4; Is 17:13; 41:15; Zep 2:2). The Hebrew word rendered *chaff* in Jeremiah 23:28 is in Exodus 5:7,10 rendered *straw*. This useless portion of the grain stalk is used figuratively to denote false doctrine (Ps 1:4; Is 33:11; Ma 3:12).

CHAIN

Several Hebrew and Greek words are thus rendered. To indicate his official position a chain

of gold was placed upon Joseph (Ge 41:42). Golden chains were similarly used in Persia, and Hebrew men and women also used chains simply for ornamental purposes. Such chains often took the form of necklaces embellished with pearls or corals. Heavy chains, also called fetters (2 Sa 3:34), were used to secure prisoners or to fasten a prisoner to a soldier (Ac 28:20; Ep 6:20; 2 Ti 1:16).

CHAL·CED′O·NY

This word is used in Revelation 21:19 as one of the precious stones in the wall of the New Jerusalem. It is a species of quartz found in the mines of Chalcedon near Constantinople. It was probably a greenish stone, silicate of copper. Agate, carnelian, flint, onyx, jasper, bloodstone, and chrysprase are varieties of chalcedony.

CHAL′COL

See CALCOL.

CHAL·DE′A

Originally the southern portion of Babylonia, but the name came to be applied to the entire alluvial plain from the northward to above Babylon. The term is used for the Hebrew *Kasdim*. In the South were the cities of Ur and Erech and in the North Babylon, Cutha, Sippara.

CHAL-DE′AN

A native of Chaldea. At an early day Chaldeans were settled on the shores of the Persian Gulf. They conquered Babylonia but their leader, Merodach-baladan, was defeated by Sennacherib, king of Assyria. Nabo-polassar, a Chaldean, founded the New Babylonian Empire in 625 B.C. and in 605 B.C. was followed on the throne by his illustrious son, Nebuchadnezzar. The magicians, astrologers, and priests—the learned class, were called Chaldeans. It was from Ur of the Chaldees that God called Abraham, the head of the messianic nation (Ge 11:31; 12:1).

CHALDEES

See CHALDEAN.

CHALK′STONE

A very fine, soft variety of limestone. Chalk is often white, though it can be grayish or yellowish as well. It is easily ground into powder (Is 27:9).

CHAM′BER

A room, often a bedroom or private room. Both Joseph and David retreated to such a room to weep when overcome by emotion (Ge 43:30; 2 Sa 18:33). Daniel customarily prayed in his upper room, or chamber (Da 6:10).

CHAM′BER·LAIN

One appointed to have charge of the royal chambers, wardrobe, etc., such as Blastus, the chamberlain of Herod (Ac 12:20). Erastus, the chamberlain of the city of Corinth, was the city treasurer (Ro 16:23).

CHA·ME′LE·ON

An unclean, lizardlike animal characterized by its ability to change its color to match surrounding objects (Le 11:30). This word is rendered *mole* in the Authorized Version. Another animal (*koach*) of the same verse is rendered *chameleon* in the Authorized Version but *land-crocodile* in the Revised Version. See LIZARD.

CHAM′OIS

This is the translation of the Hebrew word *Zemer* which signifies *leaper* (De 14:5). The chamois of the European mountains is not found in Palestine; since it is listed among the clean animals suitable for food it seems that it must have been a familiar animal, and most believe that the word would be better translated "wild goat."

CHAM·PAIGN′ *(open country)*

A plain, rendered *Arabah* in the Revised Version (De 11:30).

CHAMPION

Goliath was the champion of the Philistine army (1 Sa 17:4,23,51). It was not uncommon for two warring nations to choose a champion, a strong man, and set up a two-man combat. It was sometimes used as a way to victory with less loss of life than a full-scale battle.

CHA′NA·AN

Form of Canaan (Ac 7:11; 13:19). See CANAAN.

CHANCELLOR

See GOVERNMENT OFFICIAL.

CHANGED LIFE

The first stanza of a famous Christian song begins: "What a wonderful change in my life has been wrought, since Jesus came into my heart."

Without doubt, the greatest proof of the new birth is a changed life. The child of God now suddenly loves the following:

a. He loves Jesus. Before conversion the sinner might hold Christ in high esteem, but after conversion he loves the Savior (1 Jo 5:1-2).

b. He loves the Bible. We should love God's Word as the psalmist did in Psalm 119. He expresses his great love for God's Word no less than 17 times. See verses 24,40,47,72, 97,103,111,113,127,129,140,143,159,162, 165,168.

c. He loves other Christians. "We know that we have passed from death to life because we love the brethren" (1 Jo 3:14).

d. He loves his enemies. (Ma 5:43-45).

e. He loves the souls of all people. Like Paul, he too can cry out for the conversion of loved ones. "Brethren, my hearts desire and prayer to God for Israel is that they may be saved" (Ro 10:1; 2 Co 5:14).

f. He loves the pure life. John says if one loves the world, the love of the Father is not in him (1 Jo 2:15-17; 5:4).

g. He loves to talk to God. "Speaking to one another in psalms and hymns and spiritual songs, singing and making melody in your heart to the Lord" (Ep 5:19).

CHANGERS, MONEY

See MONEY CHANGER.

CHANT

To sing.

CHAP′I·TER

See CAPITAL.

CHAP′MAN

A merchant or peddler (2 Ch 9:14).

CHA·RA′SHIM *(craftsman)*

A valley in Judah (1 Ch 4:14). After the exile it was occupied by Benjamites (Ne 11:35). In Nehemiah it is called valley of craftsmen.

CHAR·CHE′MISH
See CARCHEMISH.

CHARCOAL
A black carbon substance used as fuel. It is made by charring wood in a kiln from which air has been excluded (so that the wood does not burn up). Charcoal burns hot and clean and was used for cooking, heating, and blacksmithing (Pr 26:21; Is 47:14; Jo 18:18; Is 44:19; Jo 21:9; Is 44:12; 54:16).

CHARGED (archaic)
Burdened; weighed down (1 Ti 5:16).

CHAR′GER (archaic)
Platter or large dish, such as the dish or platter on which the head of John the Baptist was brought to Salome, the daughter of Herodias (Ma 14:8). The silver dishes presented at the dedication of the altar are also called chargers in the KJV (Nu 7:13).

CHAR′I·OT
A two-wheeled vehicle used for both hostile and peaceful purposes. The body of the chariot rested on the axle and was open behind. The first mention of a chariot in the Bible is in connection with Joseph who was honored by being placed in the chariot of Pharaoh (Ge 41:43) and later rode in his own chariot (Ge 46:29). When used for military purposes, the strength of a nation was considered in terms of the number of its chariots. Pharaoh pursued the Israelites with 600, Jabin had 900 (Ju 4:3), the Philistines had 30,000 (1 Sa 13:5). They were poorly adapted to the hills of Palestine, hence were not much

CHARIOT

used by Hebrews. The chariot-borne warrior had a driver and sometimes a shieldbearer (2 Ki 9:24).

CHARIOTEER
A soldier who fought from a chariot (1 Ki 22:34; 2 Ch 18:33).

CHARIOTS OF THE SUN
Some sort of idolatrous images which Josiah had removed from the temple of the LORD (2 Ki 23:11). The Israelites were forbidden to worship the sun (De 17:3), but it was apparently a recurring sin, nevertheless (Eze 8:16).

CHARITY (archaic)
Love (1 Co 13).

CHARM
An object used for some kind of magic practice. See MAGIC, SORCERY, AND DIVINATION.

CHAR′RAN
A form of Haran (Ac 7:2,4). See HARAN.

CHASTE (archaic)
Pure; untouched; undefiled (2 Co 11:1-2; Tit 2:5; 1 Pe 3:2).

CHASTEN
To punish or discipline for the purpose of purifying. The Scripture tells us that the Lord chastens those He loves (He 12:5-6). Even though we do not enjoy the process, we can rejoice in the product and be grateful that the Lord takes the trouble to purify us rather than leaving us to wallow in our sins and filth.

CHASTISEMENT
Punishment, discipline. The purpose of any godly discipline is to teach, to train, to make better (Job 4:3; 2 Ti 2:25; Pr 22:15). This word chastisement generally has the connotation of physical beating or scourging. Jesus bore the chastisement we deserve when He died for our sins on the cross (Is 53:5). See CHASTEN and DISCIPLINE.

CHE′BAR
A stream of Chaldea where some of the Hebrew captives were settled (Eze 1:3) and where Ezekiel received some of his visions (Eze 3:15,

23; 10:15,20). It was a great canal southeast of Babylon.

CHECKER WORK (archaic)

Lattice, network.

CHED·OR·LA·O′MER

A king of Elam with wide dominion in western Asia. In the time of Abraham, he invaded the region about the Dead Sea with three other kings and subjugated it. Chedorlaomer carried off Lot from Sodom and Abraham rescued him (Ge 14:1-16). He apparently ruled in or about the time of Hammurabi, Babylonian king and lawgiver.

CHEEK

The side of the human face. Because this portion of the anatomy is both sensitive and highly personal, it is very insulting to be struck on the cheek (Job 16:10; Mi 5:1). In many cultures over history, to strike one on the cheek was considered an open and insulting attempt to force a fight. As a part of His revolutionary teaching, Jesus commanded His followers to not strike back when they were thus insulted, but rather to bear it with humility (Ma 5:39).

CHEESE

It is mentioned only three times in the Bible (1 Sa 17:18; 2 Sa 17:29; Job 10:10). How the Hebrew terms translated "cheese" correspond with what is known as cheese today is not certain. Since milk does naturally curdle when it is left in a warm place for several days, there is every reason to suppose that people have been making cheese of some kind as long as they have been drinking milk. As cheese is now made in the East, it is in the form of white round cakes. The Tyropean valley of Jerusalem, literally translated, is the Cheesemaking valley, it seems that cheesemaking was a fairly significant industry.

CHE′LAL (perfection)

A son of Pahath-moab. He divorced his Gentile wife after the return from Babylon (Ez 10:30).

CHEL′LUH

See CHELUH.

CHE′LUB (cage or bird trap)

1. A brother of Shush and father of Mehir of the tribe of Judah (1 Ch 4:11).

2. The father of Ezri, the officer David placed over his gardeners (1 Ch 27:26).

CHE·LU′BAI

A son of Hezron (1 Ch 2:9). In verses 18 and 42 of this chapter he is called Caleb.

CHE′LUH

A son of Bani who divorced his foreign wife in the time of Ezra (Ez 10:35).

CHE·LU′HI

See CHELUH.

CHEM′A·RIM

Idolatrous priests who officiated at Beth-el (2 Ki 23:5; Ho 10:5) and in the high places of Judah (Zep 1:4).

CHE′MOSH (fire)

The god worshipped by the Moabites (Nu 21:29; Je 48:46). According to Judges 11:24 he seems also to have been the national god of the Ammonites, but Milcom may be intended here, since the latter was the special deity of the Ammonites. Human sacrifices were sometimes offered to Chemosh (2 Ki 3:27). In the days of his apostasy Solomon built a high place for this god which Josiah destroyed (1 Ki 11:7; 2 Ki 23:13).

CHE·NA′A·NAH

1. A Benjamite, the fourth son of Bilhan, a warrior in the time of David (1 Ch 7:10).

2. The father of the false prophet Zedekiah (1 Ki 22:11; 2 Ch 18:10).

CHE·NA′NI

A Levite who exercised a beneficent influence on the exiles who returned from Babylon (Ne 9:4).

CHEN·A·NI′AH (Jehovah is firm)

A chief of the Levites of the house of Izhar. When the ark was removed from the house of Obed-edom (1 Ch 15:27), he had charge of the musical services. He and his sons were officers of the sanctuary (1 Ch 26:29).

CHE′PHAR-AM′MO·NI (village of the Ammonites)

A town of Benjamin (Jos 18:24).

CHE′PHAR-HA·AM′MO·NAI

See CHEPHAR-AMMONI.

CHE·PHI′ RAH *(village)*

A city of the Gibeonites assigned to the Benjamites (Jos 9:17; 18:26). After the captivity it was an inhabited city (Ez 2:25; Ne 7:29). Its site is identified with the ruin Kefireh about eight miles northwest of Jerusalem.

CHE′ RAN

A son of Dishon, a Horite (Ge 36:26; 1 Ch 1:41).

CHER′ E·THITES

Tribesmen of Philistia, originally probably from Crete (1 Sa 30:14; Eze 25:16; Zep 2:5-6). Some served in David's bodyguard (2 Sa 8:18; 15:18; 1 Ki 1:38,44). See CAPHTOR and CARITES.

CHE′ RITH *(gorge)*

The brook where Elijah concealed himself during the time of the drought (1 Ki 17:3,5). It was "before Jordan," hence doubtless east of Jordan in Gilead.

CHER′ UB

1. An angelic being. See ANGEL.

2. A place in Babylonia. From it came persons whose descent as Israelites could not be established (Ez 2:59; Ne 7:61).

CHER′ U·BIM

Plural of CHERUB.

CHES′ A·LON *(trust)*

This town was on the northern boundary of Judah (Jos 15:10), about ten miles west of Jerusalem on Mount Jearim.

CHES′ ED

A son of Nahor and Milcah (Ge 22:22).

CHES′ IL *(a fool)*

A village in the southern section of Judah (Jos 15:30).

CHEST

1. A box. The word could apply to several different sorts of boxes, from a coffin (Ge 50:26) to collection boxes (2 Ki 12:9-10; 2 Chr 24:8-11) to chests for carrying merchandise (Eze 27:24).

2. The upper trunk of the human body (Da 2:32). See also BOSOM and BREAST.

CHEST′ NUT

See PLANE TREE.

CHE·SUL′ LOTH *(loins)*

A town of Issachar on the boundary line (Jos 19:18).

CHETH.

See HITTITES.

CHE′ ZIB

See ACHZIB.

CHICKEN

Chickens are one of the oldest domesticated fowls. People have been keeping flocks of chickens for thousands of years, and there is archeological evidence that roosters were bred for cockfighting in ancient times. Even so, chickens are only mentioned a few times in the Bible. Jesus spoke longingly of Jerusalem, saying that He longed to protect and care for her in the same way that a hen gathers her brood under her wings (Ma 23:37; Lk 13:34). He also predicted that Peter would deny Him three times before the rooster crowed in the wee hours of the morning (Ma 26:34; Mk 14:30; Lk 22:34; Jo 13:38). There are numerous mentions of unidentified "fowls," particularly for food. These could have included chickens along with pigeons, geese, ducks or quail.

CHIDE (archaic)

Contend; strive (Ps 103:9-10).

CHI′ DON *(javelin)*

At this threshing floor Uzzah was smitten with death for placing his hand upon the ark to steady it (1 Ch 13:9). It was near Jerusalem but the exact site is unknown. In 2 Samuel 6:6 it is called Nachon.

CHIEF

The head of a tribal family (Ge 36:15-43); or the head of a division of servants, such as Pharaoh's chief baker and butler (Ge 40:2–41:10).

CHILDREN OF GOD

See SONS OF GOD.

CHI′ LE·AB

Son of David by Abigail, born at Hebron (2 Sa 3:3). In 1 Chronicles 3:1 he is called Daniel.

CHI′ LI·ON *(pining)*

The younger of the two sons of Elimelech and Naomi. He was the husband of Orpah and brother-in-law of Ruth. He died in Moab (Ru 1:2,5).

CHIL' MAD

A place spoken of in connection with Sheba and Asshur (Eze 27:23).

CHIM' HAM *(longing)*

The son of Barzillai, the Gileadite. He was sent to Jerusalem in the place of his father (2 Sa 19:37-38). He probably resided at Bethlehem where, at a later time, an inn was named for him.

CHIMNEY

A hole in the roof or wall of a house through which the smoke of a fire is meant to pass (Ho 13:3).

CHIN' NE·RETH

1. A city of Naphtali (Jos 19:35).
2. An inland sea better known as Lake Gennesaret (Jos 13:27; Lk 5:1) and Sea of Galilee (Jo 6:1). Chinnereth was perhaps an ancient Canaanite name (Nu 34:11; Jos 13:27).

CHI' OS

An island in the Greek Archipelago, north of Samos. It lies five miles from the mainland and claims to be the birthplace of Homer. It is named by Paul in his account of his voyage from Troas to Caesarea (Ac 20:15).

CHISEL

A tool with a sharp metal blade, used for cutting and shaping stone or wood. It is typically operated by setting the sharp end on the wood or stone and then tapping the other end with a mallet to make the cut. This gives the most control possible while carving something very resistant (1 Ki 6:7; Is 44:13).

CHIS' LEU

See CHISLEV.

CHIS' LEV

The third month of the civil and ninth of the sacred year, corresponding to a part of November and December (Ne 1:1; Ze 7:1).

CHIS' LON *(hope)*

The father of Elidad (Nu 34:21).

CHIS' LOTH-TA' BOR *(flanks of Tabor)*

A place near Mount Tabor on the boundary line of Zebulun (Jos 19:12). It is probably the same as Chesuloth (Jos 19:18).

CHITH' LISH

A village in the lowland of Judah (Jos 15:40).

CHIT' TIM

Descendants of Javan, son of Japheth (Ge 10:4; 1 Ch 1:7). They inhabited Cyprus and other Mediterranean islands and coasts. Balaam predicted that the Assyrians would be afflicted by ships that would proceed from Chittim (Nu 24:24). In Isaiah 23:1,12 it is spoken of as the resort of the ships of Tyre. Cyprus (Chittim) was the first outport for Phoenician maritime trade. Chittim is frequently mentioned in the Scriptures (Je 2:10; Eze 27:6; Da 11:30).

CHI' UN

Properly Kaiwan, the Babylonian name of the planet Saturn (Am 5:26).

CHLO' E *(green grass)*

A Christian woman, possibly residing in Corinth (1 Co 1:11).

CHOENIX

A dry measure of about one quart. See WEIGHTS AND MEASURES.

CHOR·ASH' AN

See ASHAN.

CHO·RA' ZIN

A town about one mile north of the Sea of Galilee, mentioned in connection with its denunciation by Jesus (Ma 11:21; Lk 10:13).

CHOSEN

See ELECTION.

CHOSEN PEOPLE

The family of Abraham, specifically the nation which began with Israel (Jacob) and his twelve sons. God chose this family and nation to be His special people, to be given the privilege of knowing the true God, and the responsibility of showing forth His glory to the other nations (Ex 19:4-6; De 7:6-8; Ps 105:43). God has not forgotten His chosen people, but when the Jews rejected their Messiah, God's plan for them was put on hold. Today, anyone, Jew or Gentile, who has accepted Jesus Christ is considered a part of God's chosen people (1 Pe 2:9).

CHO·ZE′ BA

See COZEBA.

CHRIST *(anointed)*

The Anointed One, the title of the One God promised to send to crush Satan's head (Ge 3:15), and to restore Israel (Ma 16:16,20; Mk 8:29). The word "Christ" is the translation of the Hebrew word, Messiah. The Messiah, or Anointed One, is so called in the New Testament only twice—once by the early disciples (Jo 1:41) and once by the woman of Samaria (Jo 4:25). We begin to feel the impact of the title "Christ" on the original audience if we sometimes substitute the word "Messiah" for "Christ" when we read passages with Jewish connotations. Saying "Jesus Christ" is the same as saying, "Yeshua of Nazareth is the Messiah," anointed by God to be the Savior of the world. See also JESUS and MESSIAH.

CHRIST, ASCENSION OF

See ASCENSION.

CHRIST, CRUCIFIXION OF

See CRUCIFIXION.

CHRIST, DEATH OF

See ATONEMENT; CRUCIFIXION.

CHRIST, DIVINITY OF

See INCARNATION; JESUS CHRIST.

CHRIST, HUMANITY OF

See INCARNATION; JESUS CHRIST.

CHRIST, PERSON OF

See INCARNATION; JESUS CHRIST.

CHRIST, TEMPTATION OF

See TEMPTATION.

CHRIST, TITLES OF

The two most popular titles or names Christians use in speaking of our Lord are *Jesus,* a transliteration of the Hebrew word *Joshua,* which means "Yahweh is Salvation," and *Christ,* a transliteration of the Greek term

Christos, meaning "Anointed One" or Messiah." Following are some other significant names or titles for Christ used in the New Testament. Each title expresses a distinct truth about Jesus and His relationship to believers.

Name or Title	Significance	Reference
Adam, Last Adam	First of the new race of the redeemed	1 Co 15:45
Alpha and Omega	The beginning and ending of all things	Re 21:6
Bread of Life	The one essential food	Jo 6:35
Chief Cornerstone	A sure foundation for life	Ep 2:20
Chief Shepherd	Protector, sustainer, and guide	1 Pe 5:4
Firstborn from the Dead	Leads us into resurrection and eternal life	Col 1:18
Good Shepherd	Provider and caretaker	Jo 10:11
Great Shepherd of the Sheep	Trustworthy guide and protector	He 13:20
High Priest	A perfect sacrifice for our sins	He 3:1
Holy One of God	Sinless in His nature	Mk 1:24
Immanuel (God With Us)	Stands with us in all of life's circumstances	Ma 1:23
King of kings, Lord of lords	The Almighty, before whom every knee will bow	Re 19:16
Lamb of God	Gave His life as a sacrifice on our behalf	Jo 1:29
Light of the World	Brings hope in the midst of darkness	Jo 9:5
Lord of Glory	The power and presence of the living God	1 Co 2:8
Mediator between God and Men	Brings us into God's presence redeemed and forgiven	1 Ti 2:5
Only Begotten of the Father	The unique, one-of-a-kind Son of God	Jo 1:14
Prophet	Faithful proclaimer of the truths of God	Ac 3:22
Savior	Delivers from sin and death	Lk 1:47
Seed of Abraham	Mediator of God's covenant	Ga 3:16
Son of Man	Identifies with us in our humanity	Ma 18:11
The Word	Present with God at the creation	Jo 1:1

CHRIS′ TIAN

The word signifies a follower of Christ. In the original Greek and in precise translations, "Christian" occurs only three times.

We do not often have an authoritative history of the origin of a word. However, in Acts 11:26, we have the inspired record of the people of

Antioch coining the term *Christian*. Antiochians were witty, worldly, and rather wicked. There is no reason to believe that they were being complimentary when they used the term *Christian* to describe followers of Jesus. It was no doubt like *Quaker* or *Methodist*—a term of reproach which became a badge of honor. Before Antioch, the disciples were called *brethren* (1 Co 7:12), *disciples* (Ac 9:26; 11:29), or *believers* (Ac 5:14).

The word "Christian" is also used in an evangelistic context, when Paul witnessed to the Jewish ruler Agrippa (Ac 26:28). Whether "almost persuaded" to be a Christian is a sincere remark (or as many think) a cynical one is not certain. At any rate, *Christian* was by then becoming the standard word to describe those who follow Jesus as their Messiah.

Third, suffering and Christianity were closely related in the early church and still are in many countries. Hence, Peter tells believers that there is no shame in suffering as a Christian, but it is a shame to suffer for wrongdoing (1 Pe 4:16).

CHRISTIANITY

The religion based on the person and work of Jesus Christ, the finish and consummation of the Judaism of the Old Testament. The basic teaching of Christianity is this: Humans are sinful and separated from God. Nothing that they can do on their own is adequate to bring them back into relationship with God. In fact, all humans deserve death, because the wages of sin is death, and not one is without sin. But because God loved the world, He sent His only Son into the world so that the world might be saved. Jesus Christ lived a sinless and perfect life, and He was unjustly condemned to a cruel death. By submitting to this death, He paid the price for our sins, and made a way for humans to once again have a relationship with God. Through the work of the Holy Spirit in the lives of those who believe this message, Christians are changed in their hearts and actions, and spend the rest of their lives trying to be more like Jesus.

CHRIST′ MAS (*Christ's Mass or Festival*)

The annual festival in memory of the birth of Christ which begins the evening of December 24 and continues until Epiphany (January 6). Ancient authorities are not agreed as to the date of our Lord's birth. Epiphanius says that in Egypt it was held he was born January 6, while according to Clement of Alexandria some hold the

time to be April 20, and others May 20. The Western Church adopted December 25, and the Eastern Church did the same.

CHRON′ I·CLES, BOOKS OF

1. The Books of Chronicles. The Books of 1 and 2 Chronicles cover the same period of Jewish history described in 2 Samuel through 2 Kings, but the perspective is different. These books are no mere repetition of the same material, but rather form a divine editorial on the history of God's people. While 2 Samuel and 1 and 2 Kings give a political history of Israel and Judah, 1 and 2 Chronicles present a religious history of the Davidic dynasty of Judah. The former are written from a prophetic and moral viewpoint, the latter from a priestly and spiritual perspective. The Book of First Chronicles begins with the royal line of David and then traces the spiritual significance of David's righteous reign.

The Books of 1 and 2 Chronicles were originally one continuous work in the Hebrew. The title . . . *Dibere Hayyamim,* meaning "The words [accounts, events] of the Days." The equivalent meaning today would be "The Events of the Times." Chronicles was divided into two parts in the third-century B.C. Greek translation of the Hebrew Bible (the Septuagint). At that time it was given the name *Paraleipomenon,* "Of Things Omitted," referring to the things omitted from Samuel and Kings. Some copies add the phrase, *Basileon Iouda,* "Concerning the Kings of Judah." The first book of Chronicles was called *Paraleipomenon Primus,* "The First Book of Things Omitted." The name "Chronicles" comes from Jerome in his Latin Vulgate Bible (A.D. 385-405): *Chronicorum Liber.* He meant his title in the sense of "The Chronicles of the Whole of Sacred History."

2. The Author of Chronicles. Although the text does not identify the author, several facts seem to support the tradition in the Jewish Talmud that Ezra the priest was the author. The content points to the priestly authorship because of the emphasis on the temple, the priesthood, and the theocratic line of David in the Southern Kingdom of Judah. The narrative also indicates that Chronicles was at least written by a contemporary of Ezra. Chronicles is quite similar in style to the Book of Ezra, and both share a priestly perspective: genealogies, temple worship, ministry of the priesthood, and obedience to the law of God. In addition, the closing verses of 2 Chronicles (36:22-23) are repeated with minor changes as the opening verses of Ezra (1:1-3). Thus, Chronicles and Ezra may have been one consecutive history as were Luke and Acts.

Ezra was an educated scribe (Ez 7:6), and according to the apocryphal book of 2 Maccabees 2:13-15, Nehemiah collected an extensive library which was available to Ezra for his use in compiling Chronicles. Many of these documents and sources are listed in the book. Scholars of Israel accumulated and compared historical material, and the author of Chronicles was actually a compiler who drew from many sources under the guidance and inspiration of the Holy Spirit.

3. The Time of Chronicles. Ezra probably completed Chronicles between 450 and 430 B.C. and addressed it to the returned remnant. Ezra led some of the exiles to Jerusalem in 457 B.C. and ministered to the people as their spiritual leader. During Ezra's time, Nehemiah was the political leader and Malachi was the moral leader. Chronicles spends a disproportionate time on the reigns of David and Solomon because they bring the nation to its pinnacle. The book is written to the people of Israel's "Second Commonwealth" to encourage them and to remind them that they must remain the covenant people of God. This reminds the Jews of their spiritual heritage and identity during the difficult times they are facing.

The genealogies in chapters 1–9 of 1 Chronicles cover the time from Adam to David, and chapters 10–29 focus on the thirty-three years of David's rule over the united kingdoms of Israel and Judah (1004-971 B.C.). However, the genealogies extend to about 500 B.C., as seen in the mention of Zerubbabel, grandson of King Jeconiah, who led the first return of the Jews from exile in 538 B.C.; and also Zerubbabel's two grandsons Pelatiah and Jeshaiah (3:21).

Chapters 1–9 of 2 Chronicles cover the forty years from 971 B.C. to 931 B.C.; and chapters 10–36 cover the 393 years from 931 B.C. to 538 B.C. Jeremiah's prediction of a seventy year captivity in Babylon (36:21; Je 29:10) is fulfilled in two ways: (1) a political captivity in which Jerusalem is overcome from 605 B.C. to 536 B.C., and (2) a religious captivity involving the destruction of the temple in 586 B.C. and the completion of the new temple in 516 or 515 B.C.

4. The Christ of Chronicles. See SAMUEL, BOOKS OF; "The Christ of Samuel" for descriptions of David as a type of Christ. The Davidic Covenant of 2 Samuel 7 is found again in 1 Chronicles 7:11-14. Solomon fulfilled part, but the promise of the eternality of David's throne can only point to the coming of the Messiah.

The tribe of Judah is placed first in the national genealogy in 1 Chronicles because the monarchy, temple, and Messiah (Ge 49:10) will come from this tribe. Since the books of Chronicles are the last books of the Hebrew Bible, the genealogies in chapters 1–9 are a preamble to the genealogy of Christ in the first book of the New Testament.

In 2 Chronicles, the throne of David has been destroyed, but the line of David remains. Murders, treachery, battles, and captivity all threaten the messianic line; but it remains clear and unbroken from Adam to Zerubbabel. The fulfillment in Christ can be seen in the genealogies of Matthew 1 and Luke 3.

The temple also prefigures Christ. Jesus says, "in this place there is One greater than the temple" (Ma 12:6). He also likens His body to the temple: "Destroy this temple, and in three days I will raise it up" (Jo 2:19). In Revelation 21:22 He replaces the temple: "But I saw no temple in it, for the Lord God Almighty and the Lamb are its temple."

5. Keys to 1 Chronicles.
Key Verses: 1 Chronicles 17:11-14; 29:11— "And it shall be, when your days are fulfilled, when you must go to be with your fathers, that I will set up your seed after you, who will be of your sons; and I will establish his kingdom. He shall build Me a house, and I will establish his throne forever. I will be his Father, and he shall be My son: and I will not take My mercy away from him, as I took it from him who was before you. And I will establish him in My house and in My kingdom forever: and his throne shall be established forever" (17:11-14).

"Yours, O LORD, is the greatness, the power and the glory, the victory and the majesty; for all that is in heaven and in earth is Yours: Yours is the kingdom, O LORD, and You are exalted as head over all" (29:11).

Key Chapter: 1 Chronicles 17—Pivotal for the Book of 1 Chronicles as well as for the rest of the Scriptures is the Davidic Covenant recorded in 2 Samuel 7 and 1 Chronicles 17. God promises David that He will "establish him [David's ultimate offspring, Jesus Christ] in My house and in My kingdom forever; and his throne shall be established forever" (1 Ch 17:14).

6. Survey of 1 Chronicles. Chronicles retraces the whole story of Israel's history up to the return from captivity in order to give the returned remnant a divine perspective on the developments of their past. The whole book of 1 Chronicles, like 2 Samuel, is dedicated to the life of David. It begins with the royal line of David (1–9) before surveying key events in the reign of David. (10–29).

Royal line of David (1–9). These nine chapters are the most comprehensive genealogical tables in the Bible. They trace the family tree of David and Israel as a whole, but in a highly selective manner. The genealogies place a strong emphasis on the tribes of Judah and Benjamin, because Chronicles is not concerned with the Northern Kingdom but with the Southern Kingdom and the Davidic dynasty. They show God at work in selecting and preserving a people for Himself from the beginning of human history to the period after the Babylonian exile. The genealogies move from the patriarchal period (Adam to Jacob; 1:1–2:2) to the national period (Judah, Levi, and the other tribes of Israel; 2:3–9:44). They demonstrate God's keeping of His covenant promises in maintaining the Davidic line through the centuries. The priestly perspective of Chronicles is evident in the special attention given to the tribe of Levi.

Reign of David (10–29). Compared with 2 Samuel, David's life in 1 Chronicles is seen in an entirely different light. This is clear from both the omissions and the additions. Chroni-

cles completely omits David's struggles with Saul, his seven-year reign in Hebron, his various wives, and Absalom's rebellion. It also omits the event in 2 Samuel that hurt the rest of his life—his sin with Bath-sheba. Chronicles is written from a more positive perspective, emphasizing God's grace and forgiveness, in order to encourage the Jews who had just returned from captivity. Chronicles adds events not found in 2 Samuel, such as David's preparations for the temple and its worship services.

Only one chapter is given to Saul's reign (10), because his heart was not right with God. David's story begins with his coronation over all Israel after he has already reigned for seven years as king over Judah. Chronicles stresses his deep spiritual commitment, courage and integrity. It emphasizes his concern for the things of the Lord, including his return of the ark and his desire to build a temple for God. God establishes His crucial covenant with David (17), and the kingdom is strengthened and expanded under his reign (18–20). David's sin in numbering the people is recorded to teach the consequences of disobeying God's law. Most of the rest of the book (22–29) is concerned with David's preparation for the building of the temple and the worship associated with it. The priestly perspective of Chronicles can be seen in the amount of space given to the temple and the priests. David was not allowed to build the temple (28:3), but he designed the plans, gathered the materials, prepared the site, and arranged for the Levites, priests, choirs, porters, soldiers and stewards. The book closes with his beautiful public prayer of praise and the accession of Solomon.

OUTLINE OF FIRST CHRONICLES

Part One: The Royal Line of David (1:1–9:44)

I. The Genealogy from Adam to Abraham (1:1-27)

A. The Genealogy from Adam to Noah... 1:1-4
B. The Genealogy from Noah to Abraham 1:5-27

II. The Genealogy from Abraham to Jacob (1:28-54)

A. The Genealogy from Abraham to Isaac 1:28-34
B. The Genealogy from Isaac to Jacob 1:35-54

III. The Genealogy from Jacob to David (2:1-55)

A. The Genealogy of the Sons of Jacob 2:1-2
B. The Genealogy of the Sons of Judah 2:3-55

IV. The Genealogy from David to the Captivity (3:1-24)

A. The Genealogy of the Sons of David 3:1-9

B. The Genealogy of the Sons of
Solomon 3:10-24

V. The Genealogies of the Twelve Tribes (4:1–8:40)

A. The Genealogy of Judah 4:1-23
B. The Genealogy of Simeon 4:24-43
C. The Genealogy of Reuben 5:1-10
D. The Genealogy of Gad 5:11-22
E. The Genealogy of Manasseh 5:23-26
F. The Genealogy of Levi 6:1-81
G. The Genealogy of Issachar 7:1-5
H. The Genealogy of Benjamin 7:6-12
I. The Genealogy of Naphtali 7:13

J. The Genealogy of Manasseh 7:14-19
K. The Genealogy of Ephraim 7:20-29
L. The Genealogy of Asher 7:30-40
M. The Genealogy of Benjamin 8:1-40

VI. The Genealogy of the Remnant (9:1-34)

A. The Genealogy of the Twelve Tribes
who Returned............................. 9:1-9
B. The Genealogy of the Priests who
Returned 9:10-13
C. The Genealogy of the Levites who
Returned 9:14-34

VII. The Genealogy of Saul (9:35-44)

Part Two: The Reign of David (10:1–29:30)

I. The Accession of David (10:1–12:40)

A. Death of Saul 10:1-14
B. Anointing of David as King............ 11:1-3
C. Conquest of Jerusalem.................. 11:4-9
D. The Account of David's
Mighty Men 11:10–12:40

II. The Acquisition of the Ark of the Covenant (13:1–17:27)

A. Improper Transportation of the
Ark 13:1-14
B. Prosperity of David's
Reign 14:1-17
C. Proper Transportation of the Ark... 15:1-29
D. Celebration at the Ark in
Jerusalem 16:1-43
E. Institution of the Davidic
Covenant 17:1-27

III. The Military Victories of King David (18:1–20:8)

A. David's Early Victories
Summarized 18:1-17

B. David's Later Victories
Summarized 19:1–20:8

IV. The Preparation and Organization of Israel for the Temple (21:1–27:34)

A. Sinful Census of David.............. 21:1-30
B. Material Provision for the
Temple's Construction 22:1-5
C. Leaders are Charged to Construct
the Temple 22:6-19
D. Organization of the Temple
Leaders 23:1–26:32
E. Organization of the Leaders of the
Nation of Israel 27:1-34

V. The Last Days of David (28:1–29:30)

A. Final Exhortations of David 28:1-10
B. Final Provisions for the
Temple 28:11–29:9
C. David's Final Prayer of
Thanksgiving 29:10-19
D. Coronation of Solomon.............. 29:20-25
E. Death of King David.................. 29:26-30

---

7. Keys to 2 Chronicles.

Key Word: Priestly View of Judah—The Book of 2 Chronicles provides topical histories of the end of the united kingdom of Israel (Solomon) and the kingdom of Judah. More than historical annals, Chronicles is a divine editorial on the spiritual characteristics of the Davidic dynasty. This is why it focuses on the Southern rather than the Northern Kingdom. Most of the kings fail to realize that apart from the true mission as a covenant nation called to bring others to Yahweh, Judah has no calling, no destiny, and no hope of becoming great on her own. Only what is done in accordance with God's will has any lasting value. Chronicles concentrates on the kings who are concerned with maintaining proper service to God and the times of spiritual reform. However, growing apostasy inevitably leads to judgment.

The temple in Jerusalem is the major unifying theme of 1 and 2 Chronicles. Much of the material found in 2 Samuel to 2 Kings is omitted from Chronicles because it does not develop this theme. In 1 Chronicles 11–29, the central message is David's preparation for the construction and service of the temple. Most of 2 Chronicles 1–9 is devoted to the building and consecration of the temple. Chapters 10–36 omit the kings of Israel in the north because they have no ties with the temple. Prominence is given to the reigns of Judah's temple restorers (Asa, Jehoshaphat, Joash, Hezekiah, and Josiah). The temple symbolizes God's presence among His people and reminds them of their high calling. It provides the spiritual link between their past and future. Thus, Ezra wrote this book to encourage the people to accept the new temple raised on the site of the old and to remind them of their true calling and God's faithfulness despite their low circumstances. The Davidic line, temple, and priesthood are still theirs.

Key Verses: 2 Chronicles 7:14; 16:9—"If My people who are called by My name will humble themselves, and pray and seek My face, and turn from their wicked ways, then I will hear from heaven, and will forgive their sin and heal their land" (7:14).

"For the eyes of the LORD run to and fro throughout the whole earth, to show Himself strong on their behalf of those whose heart is loyal to Him. In this you have done foolishly; therefore from now on you shall have wars" (16:9).

Key Chapter: 2 Chronicles 34—2 Chronicles records the reforms and revivals under such kings as Asa, Jehoshaphat, Joash, Hezekiah, and Josiah. Chapter 34 traces the dramatic revival that takes place under Josiah when the "Book of the Law" is found, read, and obeyed.

8. Survey of Second Chronicles. This book repeatedly teaches that whenever God's people forsake Him, He withdraws His blessings, but trust in and obedience to the Lord bring victory. Since everything in Chronicles is related to the temple, it is not surprising that the book concludes with Cyrus's edict to rebuild it. Solomon's glory is seen in chapters 1–9, and Judah's decline and deportation in chapters 10–36.

Solomon's Reign (1–9). The reign of Solomon brings in Israel's golden age of peace, prosperity, and temple worship. The kingdom was united and its boundaries extend to their greatest point. Solomon's wealth, wisdom, palace, and temple became legendary. His mighty spiritual, political and architectural feats raised Israel to her zenith. However, it is in keeping with the purpose of Chronicles that six of these nine chapters concern the construction and dedication of the temple.

The Reign of Judah's Kings (10–36). Unfortunately, Israel's glory was short lived. Soon after Solomon's death the nation is divided, and both kingdoms begin a downward spiral that can only be delayed by the religious reforms. The nation generally forsakes the temple and the worship of Yahweh, and is soon torn by warfare and unrest. The reformation efforts on the part of some of Judah's kings are valiant, but never last beyond one generation. Nevertheless, about seventy percent of chapters 10–36 deals with the eight good kings, leaving only thirty percent to cover the twelve evil rulers. Each king is shown in his relationship to the temple as the center of worship and spiritual strength. When the king serves Yahweh, Judah is blessed with political and economic prosperity.

Here is a brief survey of Judah's twenty rulers: (1) *Rehoboam*—Although he was not a righteous king, he humbled himself before God and averted His wrath (12:12). (2) *Abijah*—He enjoyed a short and evil reign, but he conquered Israel because "the children of Judah . . . relied on the LORD God" (13:18). (3) *Asa*—Although he destroyed foreign altars and idols, conquered Ethiopia against great odds through his trust in God, and restored the altar of the Lord, yet he failed to trust God when threatened by Israel. (4) *Jehoshaphat*—He brought in a great revival; "his heart took delight in the ways of the LORD" (17:6). Jehoshaphat overthrew idols, taught God's Word to the people and trusted in God before battle. (5) *Jehoram*—A wicked king, he followed the ways of Ahab and married his daughter. He led Judah into idolatry and when he died in pain, departed "to no one's sorrow" (21:20). (6 and 7) *Ahaziah* and *Athaliah*—Ahaziah is as wicked as his father, as is also his mother Athaliah. Both are murdered. (8) *Joash*—Although he repaired the temple and restored the worship of God, when Jehoida the priest died, Joash allowed the people to abandon the temple and return to idolatry. (9) *Amaziah*—Mixed in his relationship to God, he later forsook the Lord for the gods of Edom. He was defeated by Israel and later murdered. (10) *Uzziah*—He began well with the Lord, and was blessed with military victories. However, when he became strong, he proudly and presumptuously played the role of priest by offering incense in the temple. Because of this sin, God struck him with leprosy. (11) *Jotham*—Because he rebuilt the gate of the temple, and revered God, the Lord blessed him with prosperity and victory. (12) *Ahaz*—A wicked king and an idolater, he was oppressed by his enemies and forced to give tribute to the Assyrians from the temple treasures. (13) *Hezekiah*—He repaired and reopened the temple and put away the altars and idols set up by his father, Ahaz. Judah was spared destruction by Assyria because of his righteousness. His reforms are only given a few verses in Kings, but fill three chapters of Chronicles. (14 and 15) *Manasseh* and *Amon*—Manasseh was Judah's most wicked king. He set up idols and altars all over the land. In the end, when he was carried away to Assyria,

Manasseh repented. God brought him back to Judah, and he made a halfway reform, but it came too late. Amon, his son, followed in his father's wickedness. Both kings are murdered. (16) *Josiah*—A leader in reforms and spiritual revival, he centered worship around the temple, found the law and obeyed it, and reinstituted the Passover. (17, 18, and 19) *Jehoahaz, Jehoiakim, Jehoiachin*—Their relentless evil finally brought the downfall of Judah. The temple was ravaged in each of their reigns. (20) *Zedekiah*—Judah's last king was also wicked. Jerusalem and the temple were destroyed and captivity began.

In spite of the wickedness of many of Judah's kings, and the sorrow of the captivity, 2 Chronicles ends on a note of hope, when Cyrus issues a decree for the restoration of Judah: "Who is there among you of all His people? May the LORD his God be with him, and let him go up" (36:23).

OUTLINE OF SECOND CHRONICLES

Part One: The Reign of Solomon (1:1–9:31)

I. The Inauguration of Solomon as King (1:1-17)

A. The Worship of Solomon 1:1-6
B. The Petition for Wisdom 1:7-10
C. The Provision of Wisdom........... 1:11-12
D. The Wealth of Solomon 1:13-17

II. The Completion of the Temple (2:1–7:22)

A. The Preparation to Build the Temple 2:1-18
B. Construction of the Temple 3:1–5:1
C. Dedication of the Temple........... 5:2–7:22

III. The Glory of the Reign of Solomon (8:1–9:28)

A. Enlargement of Solomon's Territory 8:1-6
B. Subjugation of the Enemies of Solomon 8:7-10
C. Religious Practices of Solomon ... 8:11-16
D. Economic Operations of Solomon 8:17-18
E. The Queen of Sheba Visits 9:1-12
F. Solomon's Wealth 9:13-28

IV. The Death of Solomon (9:29-31)

Part Two: The Reigns of the Kings of Judah (10:1–36:23)

I. The Reign of Rehoboam (10:1–12:16)

A. Division of the Kingdom 10:1-19
B. Kingdom of Judah is Strengthened 11:1-23
C. Kingdom of Judah is Weakened... 12:1-12
D. Death of Rehoboam 12:13-16

II. The Reign of Abijah (13:1-22)

A. War of Abijah and Jeroboam 13:1-20
B. Death of Abijah 13:21-22

III. The Reign of Asa (14:1–16:14)

A. Evaluation of Asa 14:1-8
B. Victory over the Ethiopians 14:9-15
C. Exhortation of Azariah 15:1-7
D. Reforms of Asa 15:8-19
E. Victory over the Syrians................................... 16:1-6
F. Rebuke of Hanani 16:7-10
G. Death of Asa 16:11-14

IV. The Reign of Jehoshaphat (17:1–20:37)

A. Evaluation of Jehoshaphat 17:1-6
B. Instruction by the Priests and Levites 17:7-9
C. Expansion of the Kingdom 17:10-19
D. Alliance with Ahab 18:1–19:4
E. Organization of the Kingdom...... 19:5-11
F. Victory over Moab and Ammon 20:1-30
G. Summary of the Reign of Jehoshaphat 20:31-34
H. The Sin and Death of Jehoshaphat 2:35-37

V. The Reign of Jehoram (21:1-20)

A. Evaluation of Jehoram................. 21:1-7
B. Revolt by Edom and Libnah 21:8-11
C. Warning of Elijah 21:12-15
D. Invasion by Philistia and Arabia 21:16-17
E. Death of Jehoram 21:18-20

VI. The Reign of Ahaziah (22:1-9)

VII. The Reign of Athaliah (22:10–23:15)

VIII. The Reign of Joash (23:16–24:27)

A. Revival of Jehoida..................... 23:16-21
B. Evaluation of Joash 24:1-3
C. Repair of the Temple 24:4-14
D. Death of Jehoida 24:15-16
E. Murder of Jehoida's son 24:17-22
F. Destruction of Judah by Syria...................................... 24:23-24
G. Death of Joash 24:25-27

IX. The Reign of Amaziah (25:1-28)

A. Evaluation of Amaziah................. 25:1-4
B. Victory over Edom..................... 25:5-13
C. Idolatry of Amaziah 25:14-16
D. Defeat of Judah by Israel 25:17-24
E. Death of Amaziah 25:25-28

X. The Reign of Uzziah (26:1-23)

A. Evaluation of Uzziah 26:1-5
B. Victories of Uzziah 26:6-15
C. Sinful Offering of Uzziah 26:16-21
D. Death of Uzziah........................ 26:22-23

XI. The Reign of Jotham (27:1-9)

XII. The Reign of Ahaz (28:1-27)

A. Evaluation of Ahaz 28:1-4
B. Defeat of Judah 28:5-21
C. Idolatry of Ahaz........................ 28:22-25
D. Death of Ahaz 28:26-27

XIII. The Reign of Hezekiah (29:1–32:33)

A. Evaluation of Hezekiah 29:1-2
B. Reformation under Hezekiah ... 29:3–31:21
C. Invasion by Assyria 32:1-22
D. Restoration of Hezekiah 32:23-26
E. Wealth of Hezekiah 32:27-30
F. Sin of Hezekiah 32:31
G. Death of Hezekiah...................... 32:32-33

XIV. The Reign of Manasseh (33:1-20)

XV. The Reign of Amon (33:21-25)

XVI. The Reign of Josiah (34:1–35:27)

A. Evaluation of Josiah 34:1-2
B. Early Reforms of Josiah 34:3-7
C. Repair of the Temple 34:8-13
D. Discovery of the Law 34:14-33
E. Celebration of the Passover 35:1-19
F. Death of Josiah 35:20-27

XVII. The Reign of Jehoahaz (36:1-3)

XVIII. The Reign of Jehoiakim (36:4-8)

XIX. The Reign of Jehoiachin (36:9-10)

XX. The Reign of Zedekiah (36:11-21)

A. Evaluation of Zedekiah 36:11-12
B. Destruction of Jerusalem 36:13-21

XXI. The Proclamation by Cyrus to Return to Jerusalem (36:22-23)

CHRONOLOGY

See GOSPELS HARMONIZED.

CHRYS′O·LITE *(gold stone)*

Some golden-colored stone, as yellow as quartz or jacinth, one of the stones of the foundation of the New Jerusalem (Re 21:20).

CHRYS′O·PRASE, CHRYS′O·PRAS·US
(golden-green stone)

A chalcedony of golden tinted, leek-green color, a color produced by the oxide of nickel. This gem was a variety of semiopaque silica. In John's vision of the New Jerusalem the tenth foundation of the city consists of this stone (Re 21:20).

CHUB

See CUB.

CHUN

See BEROTHAH (1 Ch 18:8).

CHURCH

Opinions differ as to the derivation of the word. In the English New Testament, the word "church" is the chosen translation of the Greek word *Ekklesia,* which simply means "assembly" (See ASSEMBLY). The Greek word is employed by the New Testament to denote the body of Christian people, a Christian community, the followers of Christ, and the place of assembly for purposes of worship. This use of the word occurs in the New Testament (Ma 16:18; 18:17). In different cities believers formed themselves into an assembly, or church, and the Scripture speaks of "churches" in the plural (Ro 16:4; 1 Co 7:17). The term "church" is also used of the universal invisible church, the Body of Christ, which includes all believers, past, present, and future. Those truly united to Christ by saving faith in him are of the invisible Church and may come into fellowship with an external body (1 Co 1:2; 12:12; Col 1:24; 1 Pe 2:9-10). The officers of local churches were elders or bishops, and deacons (Ac 6:3; 14:23; 1 Ti 3:1,8; Tit 1:5-9), and had the direction and government of the church (Ac 15:2,4,22; 1 Ti 4:14; 5:17; 1 Pe 5:1). The apostles sustained a special relation in matters of authority (Ac 5:2; 6:6; 1 Co 12:28; 2 Pe 3:2).

The ultimate purpose of the church is to bring honor and glory to its head, Jesus Christ. It does this as it fulfills its two purposes related to God's program for the world. The one purpose of the church, as it relates to the world, is evangelism. This program is spelled out in the Great Commission (Ma 28:19-20), which has never been rescinded. The program is to "make disciples of all the nations." The way this is to be done is twofold: by "baptizing them in the name of the Father and of the Son and of the Holy Spirit," and by "teaching them to observe all things that I have commanded you." Baptism is not an optional afterthought. It is a vital part of evangelism and making disciples. By baptism, one indicates that he has been identified with Christ in His death, burial, and resurrection (i.e., he is a member of the universal church, the Body of Christ) and wishes to be identified with the local church. A responsible parent not only brings a child into the world, but also provides what is necessary for the child's growth. So in the church, teaching must accompany evangelism so that the child of God can learn all that God expects of him and has provided for him.

Another purpose of the church, as it relates to the world, is edification. According to Ephesians 4:12 the saints need to be edified (built up) for one goal, "for the equipping of the saints for the work of ministry." The believers who compose the church's membership need to be built up so that they may realize all that God has provided for Christian living and that they may come to spiritual maturity. They also need to be equipped to perform that work in the body of Christ that God wants them to perform. In a real sense, each member of the church is to be a Christian worker so that God's purposes may be accomplished through the local church.

CHURL (archaic)

A rude, fraudulent person (Is 32:7).

CHU' SHAN-RISH·A·THA' IM

See CUSHANRISH-ATHAIM.

CHU' ZA

The steward of Herod Antipas. His wife, Joanna, rendered Jesus service (Lk 8:3).

CI·LIC' I·A

A province in the southeast of Asia Minor, having on the west Pamphylia, Syria on the east, on the north Lycaonia and Cappadocia, and on the south the Mediterranean. Its chief town was Tarsus, the native city of St. Paul (Ac 21:39; 23:34). This province formed part of the kingdom of Syria. Paul labored in this province (Ac 9:30; Ga 1:21).

CIN' NA·MON

An ingredient used by the Jews in the sacred anointing oil (Ex 30:23). One of the uses of this fragrant substance was to perfume beds (Pr 7:17). It is the bark of a tree of the laurel order. Oil is extracted from the bark.

CIN' NE·ROTH

See CHINNERETH.

CIR·CUM·CIS' ION

Circumcision was a ritualistic operation that removed all or part of the foreskin from the male sex organ. The practice is of ancient origin, depicted on Egyptian tombs, and also practiced by African, Australian, Aztec, and American Indian tribes. It functioned in most cultures as a "rite of passage" or an initiation ceremony into manhood.

Circumcision of the Jewish male, however, was required as a visible, physical sign of the covenant between the Lord and His people. Any male not circumcised was to be "cut off from his people" (Ge 17:14) and regarded as a covenant breaker (Ex 12:48). In most cultures of the ancient world the ceremony was performed when the youth was about twelve, but among the Hebrews it occurred on the eighth day after birth (Ge 17:12).

Although circumcision was required by the Mosaic law, the rite was neglected during the days when the people of Israel wandered in the wilderness. Perhaps this was a sign that the nation had broken their covenant with God through their disobedience. The rite was resumed when they entered the land of Canaan, with Joshua performing the ritual on the generation born in the wilderness (Jos 5:1-8).

Moses and the prophets used the term *circumcision* as a symbol for purity of heart and readiness to hear and obey. Through Moses the Lord challenged the Israelites to submit to "circumcision of the heart," a reference to their need for repentance. "If their uncircumcised hearts are humbled, and they accept their guilt," God declared, "then I will remember My covenant" (Le 26:41-42; De 10:16). The prophet Jeremiah characterized rebellious Israel as having "uncircumcised" ears (6:10) and being "uncircumcised in the heart" (9:26).

The Hebrew people came to take great pride in their circumcision, and it became a badge of their spiritual and national superiority. Other peoples, such as the Philistines, were disdainfully called "the uncircumcised" (2 Sa 1:20), and male converts to Judaism were required to be circumcised.

During New Testament times, a crisis erupted in the church at Antioch when the Judaizers taught, "Unless you are circumcised according to the custom of Moses, you cannot be saved" (Ac 15:1-2). A council was convened at Jerusalem to resolve the issue (Ac 15:6-29).

The apostle Peter argued during this meeting that to insist on circumcision for the Gentiles would impose a burdensome yoke (Ac 15:10). Years later Paul reinforced this decision when he wrote that Abraham, "the father of circumcision" (Ro 4:12), was saved by faith, long before the physical act of circumcision was required of Jewish males (Ro 4:9-13).

Paul also spoke of the "circumcision of Christ" (Col 2:11), referring to His atoning death which "condemned sin in the flesh" (Ro 8:3) and nailed our sins "to the cross" (Col 2:14). All that ultimately matters for both Jew and Gentile, Paul declared, is a changed nature, which comes only through faith and repentance as a person commits himself to Christ (Ep 2:14-18).

CIRCUMSPECT

Careful, cautious (Ex 23:13).

CIS

See KISH.

CIS'TERN

The dry summer months in Palestine and the scarcity of springs made it necessary to dig cisterns to collect the rain water (2 Ki 18:31; Je 2:13). They were out in the open, on top of the towers of the wall, and in courtyards (2 Sa 17:18; Je 38:6). Empty cisterns were sometimes used as dungeons. It was probably in one of these that Joseph was put (Ge 37:22). See WELL.

CITADEL

Fortified keep of a city (2 Ki 15:25).

CITIES OF REFUGE

Six Levitical cities were appointed as cities of refuge for the protection of those who had unintentionally caused the death of another. (See AVENGER OF BLOOD). Three of these cities were west and three east of the Jordan. On the east were Bezer in the tribe of Reuben, Ramothgilead in the tribe of Gad and Golan in Manasseh. On the west of the Jordan were Kedesh in Naphtali, Shechem in Ephraim and Hebron in Judah. It would not be a difficult thing for any one to reach the city nearest to him. Here he received a fair trial. If guilty of willful murder, he paid the death penalty. If innocent, he was protected, but if he left the city while the high priest lived, he did so at his peril (Nu 35; De 19; Jos 20).

CITIES OF THE PLAIN

Five cities were so called: Sodom, Gomorrah, Admah, Zeboiim, and Bela or Zoar (Ge 13:12; 19:29). All of these cities except Zoar were destroyed for their sin (Ge 19:21-22,28-29). See DEAD SEA.

CITIZENSHIP, ROMAN

The apostle Paul was born at Tarsus, the chief city of the Roman province of Cilicia in southeast Asia Minor. While he was thoroughly Jewish by nationality, he was also born a Roman citizen (Ac 22:28), a privilege which worked to his advantage on several occasions during his ministry.

As the ruling world power of Paul's time, the Romans consolidated their empire by granting Roman citizenship to certain non-Romans. Paul's parents must have enjoyed this right before him, and he automatically became a Roman citizen at birth.

A Roman citizen could not be bound or imprisoned without a trial. Neither could he be beaten or scourged—the common form of torture used by the Romans to extract a confession from a prisoner. Finally, if a Roman citizen felt he was not receiving a fair trial under local authorities, he could appeal his case to Rome.

Paul and his partner Silas were bound, beaten, and imprisoned by Roman authorities at Philippi. When Paul made it clear they were Roman citizens, the authorities quickly released them and begged them to leave town (Ac 16:12-40).

Later, in Jerusalem, Paul was taken into protective custody by Roman soldiers as a group of Jewish zealots threatened his life. He was spared a scourging by the soldiers and granted a hearing before their commander when he revealed his Roman citizenship (Ac 22:24-29). The soldiers also gave him safe passage out of Jerusalem when the zealots persisted in their threats against Paul (Ac 23:23-24).

Imprisoned by Roman officials at Caesarea for two years, Paul finally appealed to Rome (Ac 25:11-12). He was sent on a merchant ship to Rome (Ac 27), where he spent two years under house arrest. Here he was allowed to preach and make converts (Ac 28:30-31).

Even the tradition that Paul was beheaded in Rome shows the influence of his Roman citizenship; non-Roman criminals were generally crucified. Beheading was a more honorable and merciful form of capital punishment reserved for Roman citizens.

CITRON

The exact nature of this plant is unknown. See APPLE.

CITY

According to the Hebrew use of the word a city consisted of a permanent community of people in a definitely established place of habitation, particularly if protected by a wall (Ge 18:26; Nu 13:19; Jos 10:39; Lk 23:51). Cities could be more easily defended when built upon hills (Jos 11:3; 1 Ki 16:24; Ma 5:14). Walls for the protection of a city were often twenty or more feet in thickness and the gate was very strong. In a tower over the gateway a watchman was stationed (2 Sa 18:24,33; 2 Ki 7:10; Ne 13:19). At the gate people gathered for business and legal purposes (Ru 4:1,11; 1 Ki 22:10; Ne 8:1).

CITY CLERK

An important government official; the clerk of a city would be in charge of many aspects of the political life of the city, including handling important communications, archives, minutes of meetings, and at least in Ephesus, presiding over the public assemblies (Ac 19:35).

CITY, HOLY

Jerusalem, the city where the temple was located. Because worship was centered around the temple, which was the dwelling place of God's presence, the whole city became associated with it. Jerusalem was the center of the religious life of the people (Ne 11:1; Da 9:24).

CITY OF DA'VID

See DAVID, CITY OF.

CITY OF MO'AB

See AR.

CITY OF SALT

A city belonging to the territory of Judah (Jos 15:62).

CITY OF WATERS

Also translated "the city's water supply" (2 Sa 12:27).

CLAMOUR (archaic)

An outcry or protest (Ep 4:31-32).

CLAU'DA

A small island southwest of Crete (Ac 27:16).

CLAU'DI·A

A Christian woman at Rome (2 Ti 4:21).

CLAU'DI·US

Fourth roman emperor; 41-54 A.D. during which time there were many famines (Ac 11:28-30; 18:2); he was poisoned by his fourth wife, Nero's mother. See CAESAR.

CLAU'DI·US LYS'I·AS

A Roman officer in Jerusalem, the commander of a thousand men. He protected Paul from the Jewish mob and, when he learned of Paul's Roman citizenship, he unbound him and by night sent him under guard to Caesarea (Ac 22:24–23:35).

CLAW

The talon of a bird or the sharp curved nail of a beast. When Nebuchadnezzar sinned against the Lord by glorifying himself, he was punished by losing his mind. He lived like an animal, and his untended fingernails grew like the claws of a bird (Da 4:33).

CLAY

The Hebrew word *teet* is usually rendered *mire* (Ps 69:14) and *dirt* (Is 57:20). Clay for bricks or pottery is the rendering of *khomer* (Is 45:9; Je 18:4). *Potter's clay* and *miry clay* are the renderings of other words (Da 2:33-35,43,45). Clay was used for sealing jars and sepulchres (Je 32:14; Ma 27:66). From an early time clay was used in the East for tablets and cylinders to be used as records (Eze 4:1).

CLAY TABLETS

Probably the oldest of the world's "disposable" writing surfaces. Clay tablets were smoothed and written on with a stylus while wet, and then allowed to dry. If the writing was to be permanent, the tablet could be baked and turned into a fairly durable item. If the writing was temporary, a fresh layer of wet clay could be spread on the tablet and it could be written on again. The remaining clay tablets of the early civilizations of the world give us most of the information we have about their cultures and customs.

CLEAN

Pure, uncontaminated. God divided the animal kingdom into two categories, the clean animals, which were suitable for sacrifice and for food, and the unclean animals, which were to be avoided. The full list appears in Leviticus 11–15. (See UNCLEAN ANIMALS). People in certain conditions of health were also considered unclean, especially lepers, or those with contagious diseases (Le 13:1-14,57; 2 Ki 5; Ma 8:2-3).

Clean hands and heart are used as symbols of spiritual and moral purity (Ps 23:3; 51:10). God is more interested in internal cleanness than external rules (Je 33:8; Eze 36:33; 37:23). Spiritual cleansing comes from Him, and is freely given when we confess our uncleanness (1 Jo 1:7-9).

CLEANNESS OF TEETH (archaic)

Famine (Am 4:6).

CLEFT (archaic)

An opening; break; split (Ob 1:3).

CLEM'ENT *(kind)*

A Christian (Ph 4:3).

CLE'O·PAS

To him and another disciple on their way to Emmaus Jesus appeared on the day of the resurrection (Lk 24:18).

CLE'O·PHAS

See CLOPAS.

CLERK, CITY

See CITY CLERK.

CLOAK

Cloke (archaic); outer garment; clothing (Ma 5:40).

CLO'PAS

The husband of Mary who stood at the foot of the Cross with Mary the mother of Jesus and Mary Magdalene (Jo 19:25). This Mary is also described as the mother of James the Less (Ma 10:3) and this James is called the son of Alphaeus (Mk 15:40), so it is supposed that Alphaeus and Clopus are the same person, or possibly that James's father had died and his mother remarried. See ALPHAEUS. This Clopas should not be confused with Cleopas (Lk 24:18).

CLOSET

A small inner room, a secret place (Joel 2:16; Ma 6:6; Lk 12:3).

CLOTH

A fabric woven from various plant and animal substances, used for making clothing. Cloth was made from the hair of goats, sheep and camels, and woven from the fibers of flax plants (linen), hemp, and silk (the cocoons of silk worms).

CLOTH' ING

Leaves and skins were first used (Ge 3:7,21), later clothes were made from wool (Le 13:47), linen (Ex 9:31), camel's hair (Ma 3:4), and byssus, a fine fabric woven from flax (Lk 16:19). One garment, usually called a coat, reached nearly to the knees. It ordinarily had short sleeves, though it might have sleeves of full length. Other clothing included: a cloth in a single piece caught at the waist by a girdle (Jo 19:23-24); a mantle, a square piece of cloth thrown over the shoulders (1 Ki 11:30; Ac 9:39); and a long garment, fastened by a girdle and worn by the high priest (Le 8:7; 1 Sa 2:19) and people of distinction. Sandals, with soles of wood or leather, were fastened to the feet by straps (Is 5:27; Ac 12:8). When strangers were present women wore a veil (Ge 24:65). The Mosaic law forbade the wearing by one sex of garments of the opposite sex (De 22:5; 1 Co 11:6,14). Priests were not allowed to wear wool, all the priestly garments were of fine linen.

CLOUD, PIL' LAR OF

A miraculous cloud in the form of a pillar, the symbol of the Lord's presence. It preceded the Israelites in the wilderness to guide them by day. At night it assumed the form of, or yielded its place to, a pillar of fire (Ex 13:21-22; Ne 9:19). It was the means by which God revealed his presence to Israel during the marching of the exodus (Nu 12:5; De 31:15).

CLOUTED (archaic)

Patched (Jos 9:5; Je 38:11-12).

CLOVEN (archaic)

Divided, such as an animal with a divided hoof; separated (Ac 2:1-3).

CLUB

A blunt weapon used in warfare, probably the simplest of all weapons: a big stick which could be used to beat or whack (2 Sa 23:21; 1 Ch 11:23).

CNI' DUS

A city of Caria on the southwest coast of Asia Minor. Paul passed it on his way to Rome (Ac 27:7).

COAL

As used in the Bible, this word does not denote coal as a mineral, but charcoal, or coal made by burning wood. There is no evidence that coal was known to the Jews (Is 47:14; Jo 18:18; 21:9).

COAST

In the KJV this word usually refers to a boundary rather than the seacoast (Nu 34:6; Ju 5:17).

COAT

See CLOTHING.

COAT OF MAIL

A shirt made of fine loops of metal chained closely together. It was more flexible than a solid breastplate, but provided some protection against swords and arrows. See BODY ARMOR.

COBRA

Over 20 different words for snake or serpent appear in the Bible, and we can only guess which word should apply to which variety. There are snakes of the cobra family in Palestine. See SNAKE.

COCK

The male of the domestic fowl. Time was indicated by cock-crowing, the third watch of the night being so designated (Mk 13:35). See CHICKEN.

COCK' A·TRICE

In English, a cockatrice is a creation of the imagination; a vile creature with a deadly glance, hatched by a serpent from the egg of a cock on a dunghill. It is used in the KJV to translate two different Hebrew words (Is 11:8; 14:29; Je 8:17). In Proverbs 23:32, one of these words is translated *adder*. As usual, it is a matter of guesswork to determine what species of snake is meant here. See SNAKE.

COCK CROWING

The third watch of the night, the wee hours of the morning. Jesus predicted that on the night of His betrayal and trial, Peter would deny Him three times before the cock crowed, and it happened just as He said (Mk 13:35; Ma 26:34; Mk 14:30; Lk 22:34; Jo 13:38).

COCK′ LE

An offensive wild plant found among grain and in the borders of fields. It was some sort of stinkweed (Job 31:40). An alternate rendering considered by the revisers of the text was "noisome weeds."

CODEX

An early form of book, much more like modern books than the scrolls. It consisted of several sheets of paper (papyrus) folded together and sewed along the fold, like a single signature of a modern book.

COFFER

A box or chest. See CHEST.

COHORT

A division of the Roman army, consisting of 400 to 600 men commanded by a tribune. Under the tribune were the Centurions, each in charge of one hundred men. See ITALIAN REGIMENT.

COINS

See MONEY OF THE BIBLE.

COL·HO′ ZEH (all-seeing one)

The son of Hazaiah and father of Baruch (Ne 11:5). He is perhaps the same as the father of Shallun who, under Nehemiah, repaired part of the wall of Jerusalem (Ne 3:15).

COLLECTION

The required tithe of the law (2 Ch 24:6,9; Ex 30:12; Ex 30:16); and the voluntary generous giving that is expected of Christians (Ro 15:25-27; 1 Co 16:1-4; 2 Co 8:1-15; 2 Co 9:15). Both were collected and used for God's work.

COL′ LEGE

This is a wrong translation of *mishneh* in 2 Kings 22:14. It denotes a suburb or quarter of the city and is rendered *second quarter* in the Revised Version. In Zephaniah 1:10 it is also rendered *second quarter* in the Revised Version, and *the second* in the Authorized Version.

COLLOP (archaic)

A piece of flesh (Job 31:39-40).

COL′ O·NY

When Roman citizens formed a settlement in a conquered place, it became a colony by the ruling of the senate. Thus Philippi became a colony under Augustus (Ac 16:12). Antioch in Pisidia, Alexandria, and Troas became colonies.

COL′ ORS

Skins were dyed in various colors by the Hebrews (Ex 25:5). Vestments were woven of various colored threads. Reddish purple and blue dyes were extracted from different kinds of shellfish (Ex 27:16; Ac 16:14; Eze 23:6). Scarlet was obtained from an insect (Is 1:18). In the Bible white signifies purity (Mk 16:5; Re 3:4). In Revelation 6:2-8 the white horse denotes victory, the black, famine; the red, war and bloodshed; and the pale, death. Purple was the color of princes and the wealthy (Ju 8:26; Es 8:15; Lk 16:19).

CO·LOS′ SAE, CO·LOS′ SE

Colosse was a city in the Roman province of Asia about a hundred miles east of Ephesus. During the fifth century B.C., Colosse was an important trading center on the Lycus River. Under the Romans it remained a free city and was celebrated for its manufacture of wool. By New Testament times, however, it had declined to the status of a small town, as its two neighbor cities, Laodicea and Hieropolis—about ten and twenty miles away, respectively—grew to the status of regional trading centers.

In A.D. 61 the city of Colosse suffered a devastating earthquake. It was rebuilt, only to be abandoned again in the eighth century when the residents moved to a more suitable location at modern Honaz about three miles south. Only a mound of dirt and rubble remains today to mark the site of ancient Colosse.

The establishment of a church there was probably due to the labors of Epaphras, a disciple of Paul, and to the work of Archippus (Col 1:2,7; 4:17; Phile 2). Paul's reference to the Colossian Christians as among those who "have not seen my face in the flesh" (Col 2:10) seems to indicate that he never visited the church. Philemon and Onesimus were members of the church in Colosse (Col 4:9).

Paul's letter to the Colossian Christians focuses on the person and work of Jesus Christ. It contains a majestic hymn to Christ, emphasizing His role in creation and redemption (Col 1:9-23). Paul also warned the Colossians about false teachers who were apparently trying to add useless rules and regulations to the simple faith in Christ required by the gospel (Col 2:11-23).

In this brief letter, Paul also mentioned ten of his friends, some of whom had connections in the city of Colosse. This indicates that Paul had numerous coworkers who helped him preach the gospel and nurture churches.

Paul's friends in Colosse: Epaphras (1:7; 4:12), Tychicus (4:7), Onesimus (4:9), Aristarchus (4:10), Mark (4:10), Jesus Justus (4:11), Demas (4:14), Luke (4:14), Nymphas (4:15), and Archippus (4:17).

CO·LOS′SI′ANS, E·PIS′TLE TO THE

1. The Book of Colossians. If Ephesians can be labeled as the epistle portraying the "Church of Christ," then Colossians must surely be "the Christ of the Church." Ephesians focuses on the Body; Colossians focuses on the Head. Like Ephesians, the little Book of Colossians divides neatly in half with the first portion doctrinal (1 and 2) and the second practical (3 and 4). Paul's purpose is to show that Christ is preeminent—first and foremost in everything—and the Christian's life should reflect that priority. Because believers are rooting in Him, alive in Him, hidden in Him and complete in Him, it is utterly inconsistent for them to live life without Him. Clothed in His love, with His peace ruling in their hearts, they are equipped to make Christ first in every area of life.

This epistle became known as *Pros Kolossaeis,* "To the Colossians," because of 1:2. Paul also wanted it to be read in the neighboring church at Laodicea (4:16).

2. The Author of Colossians. The external testimony to the Pauline authorship of Colossians is ancient and consistent, and the internal evidence is also very good. It not only claims to be written by Paul (1:1,23; 4:18), but the personal details and close parallels with Ephesians and Philemon make the case even stronger. Nevertheless, the authenticity of this letter has been challenged on the internal grounds of vocabulary and thought. In its four chapters,

Colossians uses fifty-five Greek words that do not appear in Paul's other epistles. However, Paul commanded a wide vocabulary, and the circumstances and subject of this epistle, especially the references to the Colossian heresy, account for these additional words. The high Christology of Colossians has been compared to John's later concept that Christ is the Logos (cf. 1:15-23 and John 1:1-18), with the conclusion that these concepts were too late for Paul's time. However, there is no reason to assume that Paul was unaware of Christ's work as Creator, especially in view of Philippians 2:5-11. It is also wrong to assume that the heresy refuted in Colossians 2 refers to the fully developed form of Gnosticism that did not appear until the second century. The parallels only indicate that Paul was dealing with an early form of Gnosticism.

3. The Time of Colossians. Colosse was a minor city about one hundred miles east of Ephesus in the region of the seven Asian churches of Revelation 1–3. Located in the fertile Lycus Valley by a mountain pass on the road from Ephesus to the East, Colosse once was a populous center of commerce, famous for its glossy black wool. By the time of Paul, it had been eclipsed by its neighboring cities, Laodicea and Hieropolis (4:13), and was on the decline. Apart from this letter, Colosse exerted almost no influence on early church history. It is evident from 1:4-8 and 2:1 that Paul had never visited the church at Colosse. The Colossian church was apparently founded by Epaphras. On his third missionary journey, Paul devoted almost three years to an Asian ministry centered in Ephesus (Acts 19:10; 20:31), and Epaphras probably came to Christ during this time. He carried the gospel to the cities in the Lycus Valley and years later came to visit Paul in his imprisonment (4:12-13; Phile 23).

Colossians, Philemon, and Ephesians were evidently written about the same time and under the same circumstances, judging by the overlapping themes and personal names (compare Col 4:9-17 and Phile 2,19,23-24). Although Caesarea and Ephesus have been suggested as the location of authorship, the bulk of the evidence indicates that Paul wrote Colossians, along with Philemon, Ephesians and Philippians (often called the Prison Epistles), during his first Roman imprisonment. If so, Colossians was written in A.D. 60 or 61 and sent with Tychicus and the converted slave Onesimus to Colosse (4:7-9, see Ep 6:21; Phile 10-12).

Epaphras' visit and report about the conditions in Colosse prompted this letter. Although the Colossians had not yet succumbed (2:1-5), an encroaching heresy was threatening the predominantly gentle Colossian church (1:21,27; 2:13). The nature of this heresy can only be deduced from Paul's incidental references to it in his refutation in 2:8-23. It was apparently a religious system that combined elements from Greek speculation (2:4,8-10), Jewish legalism (2:11-17), and Oriental mysticism (2:18-23). It involved a low view of the body (2:20-23), and probably nature as a whole. Circumcision, dietary regulations, and ritual observances were included in this system, which utilized asceticism, worship of angels and intermediaries, and mystical experiences as an approach to the spiritual realm. Any attempt to fit Christ into such a system would undermine His person and redemptive work.

4. The Christ of Colossians. This singularly Christological book is centered on the cosmic Christ—"the head of all principality and power" (2:10), the Lord of creation (1:16-17), and the Author of reconciliation (1:20-22; 2:13-15). He is the basis for the believer's hope (1:5, 23,27), the source of the believer's power for a new life (1:11,29), the believer's Redeemer and Reconciler (1:14,20-22; 2:11-15), the embodiment of full deity (1:15,19; 2:9), the Creator and Sustainer of all things (1:16-17), the Head of the church (1:18), the resurrected God-Man (1:18; 3:1), and the all-sufficient Savior (1:26; 2:3,10; 3:1-4).

5. Keys to Colossians.

Key Word: The Preeminence of Christ— The resounding theme in Colossians is the preeminence and sufficiency of Christ in all things. The believer is complete in Him alone and lacks nothing because "in Him dwells all the fullness of the Godhead bodily" (2:9); He has "all the treasures of wisdom and knowledge" (2:3). There is no need for speculation, mystical visions, or ritualistic regulations as though faith in Christ were insufficient. Paul's predominant purpose, then, is to refute a threatening heresy that is devaluing Christ. This false teaching is countered by a positive presentation of His true attributes and accomplishments. A proper view of Christ is the antidote for heresy. Paul also writes this epistle to encourage the Colossians

to "continue in the faith, grounded and steadfast" (1:23), so that they will grow and bear fruit in the knowledge of Christ (1:10). A firm adherence to the true gospel will give them stability and resistance to opposing influences.

Key Verses: Colossians 2:9-10 and 3:1-2— "For in Him dwells all the fullness of the Godhead bodily; and you are complete in Him, who is the head of all principality and power" (2:9-10).

"If then you were raised with Christ, seek those things which are above, where Christ is, sitting at the right hand of God. Set your mind on things above, not on things on the earth" (3:1-2).

Key Chapter: Colossians 3—Chapter 3 links the themes of Colossians (see "Key Word") together, showing their cause and effect relationships. Because the believer is risen with Christ (3:1-4), he is to put off the old man and put on the new (3:5-17), which will result in holiness in all relationships (3:18-25).

6. Survey of Colossians. Colossians is perhaps the most Christ-centered book in the Bible. In it Paul stresses the preeminence of the person of Christ and the completeness of the salvation He provides, in order to combat a growing heresy that is threatening the church at Colosse. This heresy seeks to devaluate Christ by elevating speculation, ritualism, mysticism, and asceticism. But Christ, the Lord of creation and Head of the Body, is completely sufficient for every spiritual and practical need of the believer. The last half of this epistle explores the application of these principles to daily life, because doctrinal truth (1 and 2) must bear fruit in practical conduct (3 and 4). The two major topics are: supremacy of Christ (1 and 2) and submission to Christ (3 and 4).

Supremacy of Christ (1 and 2). Paul's greeting (1:1-2) is followed by an unusually extended thanksgiving (1:3-8) and prayer (1:9-14) on behalf of the believers at Colosse. Paul expresses his concern that the Colossians come to a deeper understanding of the person and power of Christ. Even here Paul begins to develop his major theme of the preeminence of Christ, but the most potent statement of this theme is in 1:15-23. He is supreme both in creation (1:15-18) and in redemption (1:19-23), and this majestic passage builds a positive case for Christ as the most effective refutation of the heresy that will be exposed in chapter 2. Paul describes his own ministry of proclaiming the mystery of "Christ in you, the hope of glory" (1:27) to the Gentiles and assures his readers that although he has not personally met them, he strongly desires that they become deeply rooted in Christ alone, who is preeminent in the Church (1:24–2:3). This is especially important in view of false teachers who would defraud them through enticing rationalism (2:4-7), vain philosophy (2:8-10), and useless asceticism (2:20-23). In each case, Paul contrasts the error with the corresponding truth about Christ.

Submission to Christ (3 and 4). The believer's union with Christ in His death, resurrection, and exaltation is the foundation upon which his earthly life must be built (3:1-4). Because of his death with Christ, the Christian must regard himself as dead to the old sins and put them aside (3:5-11); because of his resurrection with Christ, the believer must regard himself as alive to Him in righteousness and put on the new qualities that are prompted by Christian love (3:12-17). Turning from the inward life (3:1-17) to the outward life (3:18–4:6), Paul outlines the transformation that faith in Christ should make in relationships inside and outside the home. This epistle concludes with a statement concerning its bearers (Tychicus and Onesimus), greetings and instructions, and a farewell note (4:7-18).

OUTLINE OF COLOSSIANS

Part One: The Supremacy of Christ in the Church (1:1–2:23)

I. Introduction (1:1-14)

A. Paul's greeting to the Colossians ... 1:1-2
B. Paul's Thanksgiving for the
   Colossians 1:3-8
C. Paul's Prayer for the Colossians ... 1:9-14

II. The Preeminence of Christ (1:15–2:3)

A. Christ is Preeminent in
   Creation 1:15-18
B. Christ is Preeminent in
   Redemption............................. 1:19-23

C. Christ is Preeminent in the
   Church 1:24–2:3

III. The Freedom in Christ (2:4-23)

A. Freedom from Enticing Words 2:4-7
B. Freedom from Vain Philosophy 2:8-10
C. Freedom from the Judgment of
   Men 2:11-17
D. Freedom from Improper
   Worship 2:18-19
E. Freedom from the Doctrines of
   Men 2:20-23

Part Two: The Submission to Christ in the Church (3:1–4:18)

I. The Position of the Believer (3:1-4)

II. The Practice of the Believer (3:5–4:6)

A. Put off the Old Man 3:5-11
B. Put on the New Man 3:12-17
C. Personal Commands for
   Holiness 3:18–4:6

III. Conclusion (4:7-18)

A. Commendation of Tychicus............ 4:7-9
B. Greetings from Paul's
   Friends.................................. 4:10-14
C. Introductions Regarding This
   Letter 4:15-18

COLT

The young of a donkey or horse. The word usually refers to a male offspring, but terms are not always strict. In fulfillment of the prophecy of Zechariah (Ze 9:9), Jesus rode into Jerusalem on a colt, the foal of a donkey (Ma 21:1-10).

COM′FORT·ER, THE

See HOLY SPIRIT.

COM·MAND′MENT

An order, more than a request. God gave His chosen people a number of commands, promising that if they kept them they would be blessed (Ex 20:3-17; De 5:7-21).

COMMANDMENT, NEW

Jesus gave His disciples a new commandment: that they love one another (Jo 13:34). Love is to be the distinguishing characteristic of all believers.

COMMANDMENTS, TEN
See TEN COMMANDMENTS.

COM'MERCE
From early times Egypt carried on extensive commercial relations with other nations. "Caravans," says Maspero, "plied between Egypt and the lands of Chaldean civilization, crossing Syria and Mesopotamia, perhaps even by the shortest route, as far as Ur and Babylon." Such a caravan bearing spices carried Joseph into Egypt (Ge 39:1). Sidon was a shipbuilding and exporting center of Phoenicia. Tyre, another city of Phoenicia, later surpassed Sidon and about 600 B.C., reached her climax commercially (Eze 27). Israel's prominence commercially dates from the time of Solomon when trading by sea and land with foreign countries was extensively developed. Yarn, linen, horses, and chariots were imported (1 Ki 10:22-29). Small cities were built for the storing of goods (1 Ki 9:18-19; 2 Ch 8:4,6). Following the reign of Solomon, commerce declined but Judea furnished Phoenicia oil, wheat, and honey (1 Ki 5:11; Eze 27:17) and oil was also exported to Egypt (Ho 12:1).

COMMON LANDS
Every town given to the Levites was provided with an area of common pastureland where the people dwelling in the town could graze their animals. It belonged to the town in common, and was not to be sold (Le 25:34). The Levites were not provided with a tribal area of their own, to be divided up into farms for each family. Instead, the whole tribe was consecrated to serve the Lord. They were provided with towns to live in, and by providing pastureland as well, they were then able to raise animals for meat, or keep a horse or a donkey (Nu 35:2-7; Jos 21:2-42; 1 Ch 6:55-81).

COMMON LIFE
See COMMUNION.

COMMUNICATE (archaic)
To share with or have things in common (1 Ti 6:17-18).

COMMUNION
The cluster of Greek words based on the root *koin-* ("common") is so rich that English needs to use several different vocabulary entries to cover the concepts. Such words as *common, share, fellowship, communion,* and *partner* are used to translate the Greek text.

Common (koinos): Common occurs fourteen times in the Greek New Testament. This adjective can mean "common" in the sense of defiled or unclean, for example, "unwashed hands" (Mk 7:2) or nonkosher food (Ac 10:14).

A more positive meaning of *koinos* is "common" in the sense of widely shared. The very name of the language in which the New Testament was originally written is called "the common dialect" (*he koine dialectos*). The earliest Christians shared "all things in common" (Ac 2:44; 4:32). This was not communism, but a voluntary sharing as needs arose. Paul called Titus "a true son in our common faith" (Tit 1:4), and Jude wrote to the saints about "our common salvation" (Jude 3).

Partake, Share (koinoneo): Partake, share, a verb built on this rood, is used eight times. Twice it has a negative context of sharing in other people's "sins" (1 Ti 5:22) or "evil deeds" (2 Jo 11). Paul used this verb for "distributing to the needs of the saints" (Ro 12:13), the Gentiles being "partakers of their [the Jews'] spiritual things" (Ro 15:27), and to command Christians who are taught the Scriptures to "share in all good things with him who teaches" (Ga 6:6).

Partaker, Partner (koinonos): Partaker, partner occurs ten times. It is used twice in the Gospels: the scribes and Pharisees denied that they would have "been partakers" with their ancestors in murdering the prophets (Ma 23:30). Luke used the word in a business sense by telling us that James and John "were partners" with Simon Peter in the fishing trade (Lk 5:10).

Paul used *koinonos* five times, twice translated "partner"—once in reference to Titus (2 Co 8:23) and once to himself as Philemon's partner (Phile 17). The original recipients of the Epistle to the Hebrews were companions of those who were suffering for Christ (10:33).

Peter used the word twice, calling himself "a partaker of the glory that will be revealed" (1 Pe 5:1), and prayed that his readers "may be partakers of the divine nature" (2 Pe 1:4).

The compound form of this noun (*synkoinonos*) occurs four times with the same general meanings. The compound verb *synkoinoneo* occurs three times and is translated about the same. The prefix *syn* slightly strengthens the "sharing" motif. Paul used the noun in Philippians 1:7 regarding his original readers' partaking of grace with him; in 4:14 he used the verb to commend them for sharing in his distress.

Fellowship, Sharing, Communion (koinonia): Fellowship, sharing, communion occurs nineteen times. This beautiful Greek word has become almost as popular in English-speaking congregations as the well-known *agape.* Fellowship groups and Bible classes are sometimes called "koinonias." Fellowship is one of the four staples of the New Testament church, along with the apostles' doctrine, prayer, and the breaking of bread (Ac 2:42). The breaking of bread is *koinonia* ("communion") of the body and blood of Christ. We can have *koinonia* with God "the Father and with His son Jesus Christ" and with the apostles (1 Jo 1:7), with the Spirit (Ph 2:1), and with Christ's sufferings.

Even such mundane things as money and goods become *koinonia* when shared for Christ's sake, making the contribution itself "fellowship" (Ro 15:26; 2 Co 9:13; Ph 1:5).

Paul ends 2 Corinthians on this widely quoted note of fellowship: "The grace of the Lord Jesus Christ, and the love of God, and the communion of the Holy Spirit be with you all. Amen" (2 Co 13:14).

COMMUNITY OF GOODS (Ac 2:44-47; 4:32–5:11)

See COMMUNION.

COMPASS

A tool used for drawing circles. It is only mentioned once in the Bible, in Isaiah 44:13. A simple compass can be made by fastening a string to a tack in the center, and to a writing utensil on the other end. If the string is held taut, a fair circle can be drawn in this way.

COMPASSION

See MERCY.

COMPLAINING *(gongysmos)*

The words in the Greek New Testament that mean "murmur," "complain," "grumble," "gripe," and so on, sound like what they represent. Say the word *gongysmos,* and it suggests the grumbling undertones of complaint. (The English word *murmur* does the same.) The verb occurs eight times, the abstract noun occurs four times, and the word for "grumbler" once (Jude 16, of the apostates).

It is easy for us to sneer at the Pharisees for murmuring against the Lord Jesus (Lk 5:30). But even the disciples complained. It is easy to put down the ancient Hebrews in the wilderness for grumbling against Moses, but Paul warns us not to do the same (1 Co 10:10).

Paul commands Christians to "do all things without murmuring and disputing" (Ph 2:14) and Peter tells us to "be hospitable to one another without grumbling" (1 Pe 4:9). Apparently these two apostles knew human nature only too well.

COMPTROLLER

One who controls financial matters. See GOVERNMENT OFFICIAL.

CO·NA·NI′ AH *(Jehovah hath sustained)*

1. A Levite in the time of Hezekiah who had charge of the offerings and tithes (2 Ch 31:12-13).

2. A Levite in the reign of Josiah who held a prominent position and contributed generously to the offerings (2 Ch 35:9).

CON·CI′ SION

A term used by Paul contemptuously of those who zealously insisted upon circumcision (Ph 3:2).

CONCORD (archaic)

Agreement; unison (2 Co 6:14-15).

CON′ CU·BINE

A concubine was a wife of lower rank and was ordinarily selected from slaves or captives. They were not wedded in the usual manner, and did not have the same status as a wife. Some examples of concubines include Hagar (Ge 16:2-3; 21:10) and Bilhah (Ge 29:29). A concubine could be discarded in a way that a wife could not, most likely because there was no dowry issue, and no offended father to deal with (Ge 21:10-14), and yet they had rights according to Mosaic law (Ex 21:7-11; De 21:10-14). Solomon had three hundred concubines (1 Ki 11:3).

CONCUPISCENCE (archaic)

Strong desire, passion; often used in the sense of lust (Col 3:5-6).

CONDEMN

To declare a person guilty and sentence him to punishment. Because of sin, humans are condemned. Nevertheless, Jesus came into the world not to condemn it but to save it (Jo 3:17-18). Because of Him, we are no longer under condemnation (Ro 8:1,3). Jesus also taught us that we are not to try and be in the position of judge to others. That is God's job (Lk 6:37).

CONDUIT

An aqueduct or water channel (2 Ki 18:17; 20:20; Is 7:3; 36:2). See AQUEDUCT; HEZEKIAH'S WATER TUNNEL.

CO′ NEY

This doubtless denotes the rockbadger, a rabbit sized animal that lived among the rocks (Le 11:5). See ROCK BADGER.

CON·FEC′ TION

Perfume made by the apothecary of the temple (Ex 30:35,37). A confectionary was a female perfumer (1 Sa 8:13).

CONFECTIONER

One who made perfume and incense.

CONFESSION

As unpleasant as we find it, the only way to restoration after sin is through repentance and confession. (Jos 7:19; 2 Ch 30:22; Ez 10:11; Ro 10:9-10). We often think that we would like to skip the confession step; it is hard to admit out loud what we have done wrong, but this is an irreplaceable part of restoration. The good news is that God has promised to freely forgive when we confess (1 Jo 1:9).

CONFIRM

To make firm, as an oath (Nu 30:13-14). To agree with and ratify, as a covenant. (Da 9:27; Ga 3:15,17).

CON′ GRE·GA′ TION

A community or assembly of likeminded people. Every circumcised Jew was a member of the congregation. The English word also signifies the whole body, male and female (Le 4:13, 15; Nu 1:2; 20:11); an assembly for religious worship (1 Ki 8:14,65; Nu 10:7; Jos 8:35); and the tabernacle of the congregation or the tent of meeting, the place where God met with his people (Ex 25:22; 27:21).

CO-NI′ AH

See JEHOIACHIN.

CO·NO·NI′ AH

See CONANIAH.

CON′ SCIENCE

Not to be confused with the judgment that discerns the right and wrong thing, but what Kant calls the "categorical imperative." Our best judgment of right may not be a right judgment, but it is not corrected by conscience. Conscience, the moral sense, follows the judgment with the command that we act in conformity with judgment. The Scriptures speak of a *good* conscience (Ac 23:1; 1 Ti 1:5,19), a *pure* conscience (1 Ti 3:9; 2 Ti 1:3), a conscience *defiled* or *seared* (1 Co 8:7; 1 Ti 4:2). The relation of conscience to judgment is expressed by Paul when he said to Agrippa, "I verily thought with myself that I ought to do many things contrary to the name of Jesus" (Ac 26:9)—that is he ought to execute the dictates of judgment.

CON′ SE·CRA′ TION

The dedication to the service of God of one's person or possessions (Ex 29:9; Le 8:33; Jos 6:19; 2 Ch 29:31).

CONSOLATION

The Consolation of Israel was a name for the coming Messiah (Lk 2:25).

CONSTELLATIONS

See ASTRONOMY.

CONSUMMATION

Completing, bringing to a finish. See ESCHATOLOGY.

CONSUMPTION

Tuberculosis. God warned the Israelites that if they disobeyed, they would be struck with this disease (De 28:22). It is also translated "wasting disease."

CONTEMN (archaic)

To despise with mockery (Ps 10:13).

CONTENTIOUS

Loving a quarrel; fond of strife (Ro 2:7-8).

CONTENTMENT

Being at rest with one's state, even if it is not ideal (1 Ti 6:6). Contentment does not come with comfortable circumstances, or lack of trials, but rather with a knowledge of who God is, and a glimpse of His bigger picture.

CONTRITE

Repentant, humble (Ps 34:18; Ps 51:17; Ma 5:4; Lk 6:21; 2 Co 7:10).

CONVENIENT (archaic)

Proper; appropriate (Ro 1:28).

CON′ VER·SA′ TION

An archaic rendering in the Authorized Version of various Greek and Hebrew words. In Philippians 3:20 it should be read *citizenship*. It also means behavior or conduct (Ep 4:22; He 13:5; 1 Pe 1:15).

CON·VER′ SION

Convert (strepho, epistrepho) means "to turn," and to Christians it generally means the turning from sin to God (Lk 1:16; Ac 26:18; Jam 5:19-20). People raised in Christian homes often find it hard to conceive of being "converted" to Christ since they learned to know Him gradually. However, whether one knows the time or not, there must be a point when one turns from self and sin to accept the Lord Jesus. "Unless you are converted (*strepho*) and become as little children, you will by no means enter the kingdom of heaven" (Ma 18:3). Children don't have to become like adults to come to Christ—just the opposite.

Epistrepho is translated "convert" more frequently, although it often means simply "turn" (Re 1:12).

In his defense before Agrippa, Paul spoke of both repentance and conversion. "They [Paul's

CONVERSION OF SAUL

hearers] should repent [*metanoeo*], turn to [*epistrepho*] God, and do works befitting repentance" (Ac 26:20). What Paul told his hearers to do, all should do by coming to faith in the lord Jesus Christ.

Conversion properly defined in terms of the sinner's action is not to be confused with regeneration and justification. The latter have to do with the divine action in which we have no part. It is God who justifies on the grounds of the faith exercised by the one who comes by divine action to the state of justification (Ro 5:1). See also REPENT.

CONVINCETH (archaic)

Convict (Jo 8:45-47).

CONVICTION

Strong belief, also the prodding of the Holy Spirit to bring one to a sense of one's own sinfulness (Ps 32:51; Ac 2:37; Ro 7:7-25).

CON′ VO·CA′ TION

An occasion when the Hebrews were required to come together and refrain from all forms of work. Such times included the Sabbath (Le 23:1-3), Pentecost (Le 23:15-21), Day of Atonement (Le 23:24-28).

COOK′ ING

Preparation of food with heat. Roasting over an open fire is an obvious simple method of cooking (Ge 25:29; Ex 12:9,46). We do not know at what time people began using pots and ovens, but in the days of Eli some of the offerings were boiled in water (1 Sa 2:13), and bread was baked in some way (Ho 7:4). Cooking on the Sabbath was forbidden (Ex 35:3).

CO′ OS (Ac 21:1)

See COS.

COPPER

Copper is a brown-red soft metal and has been known to and used by humans for thousands of years. Copper alloyed with tin forms bronze. People have been making bronze for between five and six thousand years, at least. Copper was used to make many articles (Ez 8:27; Je 15:12; Ex 38:8; 1 Sa 17:5-6; 38:2; 2 Sa 21:16). See BRASS.

COPPERSMITH

One who works with copper, forming it into various objects. See METALSMITH.

COR

A homer (Eze 45:14). See WEIGHTS AND MEASURES.

COR'AL

A bony material formed in the ocean by certain sea creatures. Coral comes in various shades of red, and was used in ancient times for jewelry (Job 28:18; Eze 27:16).

COR ASHAN

See ASHAN.

COR'BAN

A gift or an offering made to God (Le 1:2-3; Nu 7:12-17). Jesus censured the practice of escaping obligations by declaring that the means of caring for such obligations were *corban*, that is dedicated to God (Ma 15:5; Mk 7:11).

CORD

Rope, strands of fiber twisted together (Is 19:9; Jo 2:15; Ac 27:32).

COR'E

See KORAH.

CO'RI·AN'DER

A plant which produces grayish white seeds used as herbs in cooking and also in medicine (Ex 16:31; Nu 11:7).

CORINTH

Corinth was a busy commercial city in ancient Greece, strategically located on the narrow strip of land connecting the peninsula to the mainland. The city had two excellent harbors, Cenchrea and Lechaeum. A cosmpopolitan center of about 500,000 people when Paul arrived, this metropolis has dwindled to only a small city in modern times.

In Paul's view, Corinth was an ideal city for a church. The constant movement of travelers, merchants, and pilgrims through the city would make it possible for the gospel to influence people from every part of the Roman world.

In addition to its commercial importance, Corinth was a center of idolatry, with numerous pagan temples dedicated to worship of the Greek and Roman gods. The infamous temple of Aphrodite, a fertility goddess, had a poisonous effect on the city's culture and morals. Paul

ANCIENT CORINTH

must have been moved by the godless masses that were consumed with the pursuit of profit and pleasure.

With the Corinthian church made up of people from these backgrounds, learning to live together in harmony was most difficult. Paul's two letters to the young church at Corinth (1 and 2 Corinthians) contain instruction on Christian living in a pagan environment.

Along with their struggles, the Corinthian church also experienced significant Christian victories (Ac 18:8). One noted convert may have been the city treasurer, Erastus, mentioned in Romans 16:23. A bronze plaque, known as the Erastus Inscription, found near the ruins of a large amphitheater, mentions a generous patron by this name.

Paul labored with the church at Corinth for about eighteen months. After he left the city, a Christian community apparently was established at Corinth's eastern port of Cenchrea (Ro 16:1).

CO·RIN'THI·ANS, E·PIS'TLES TO THE

1. The Book of First Corinthians. Corinth, the most important city in Greece during Paul's day, was a bustling hub of worldwide commerce, degraded culture and idolatrous religion. There Paul founded a church (Acts 18:1-17), and two of his letters are addressed "To the church of God which is at Corinth."

First Corinthians reveals the problems, pressures, and struggles of a church called out of a pagan society. Paul addresses a variety of problems in the lifestyle of the Corinthian church: factions, lawsuits, immorality, questionable practices, abuse of the Lord's Supper, and spiritual gifts. In addition to words of discipline, Paul shares words of counsel in answer to questions raised by the Corinthian believers.

The oldest recorded title of this epistle is *Pros Korinthious A,* in effect, the "First to the Corinthians." The *A* was no doubt a later addition to distinguish the book from 2 Corinthians.

2. The Author of First Corinthians. Pauline authorship of 1 Corinthians is almost universally accepted. Instances of this widely held belief can be found as early as A.D. 95, when Clement of Rome wrote to the Corinthian church and cited this epistle in regard to their continuing problem of factions among themselves.

3. The Time of First Corinthians. Corinth was a key city in ancient Greece until it was destroyed by the Romans 146 B.C. Julius Caesar rebuilt it as a Roman colony in 46 B.C. and it grew and prospered, becoming the capital of the province of Achaia. Its official language was Latin, but the common language remained Greek. In Paul's day, Corinth was the metropolis of the Peloponnesus, since it was strategically located on a narrow isthmus between the Agean Sea and the Adriatic Sea that connects the Peloponnesus with northern Greece. Because of its two seaports it became a commercial center, and many small ships were rolled or dragged across the Corinthian isthmus to avoid the dangerous 200-mile voyage around southern Greece. Nero and others attempted to build a canal at the narrowest point, but this was not achieved until 1893. The city was filled with shrines and temples, but the most prominent was the temple of Aphrodite on top of an 1,800-foot promontory called the Acrocorinthus. Worshippers of the "goddess of love" made free use of the 1,000 Hieroduli (consecrated prostitutes). This cosmopolitan center thrived on commerce, entertainment, vice, and corruption; pleasure-seekers came there to spend money on a holiday from morality. Corinth became so notorious for its evils that the term *Korinthiazomai* ("to act like a Corinthian") became a synonym for debauchery and prostitution.

In Paul's day the population of Corinth was approximately 700,000, about two-thirds of whom were slaves. The diverse population produced no philosophers, but Greek philosophy influenced any speculative thought that was there. In spite of these obstacles to the gospel, Paul was able to establish a church in Corinth on his second missionary journey (3:6,10; 4:15; Ac 18:1-7). Persecution in Macedonia drove him south to Athens, and from there he proceeded to Corinth. He made tents with Aquila and Priscilla and reasoned with the Jews in the synagogue. Slias and Timothy joined him (they evidently brought a gift from Philippi; 2 Co 11:8-9; Ph 4:15), and Paul began to devote all his time to spreading the gospel. Paul wrote 1 and 2 Thessalonians, moved his ministry from the synagogue to the house of Titius Justus because of the opposition, and converted Crispus, the leader of the synagogue. Paul taught the Word of God in Corinth for eighteen months in A.D. 51 and 52. After Paul's departure, Apollos came from Ephesus to minister in the Corinthian church (3:6; Ac 18:24-28).

When Paul was teaching and preaching in Ephesus during his third missionary journey, he was disturbed by reports from the household of Chloe concerning the quarrels in the church at Corinth (1:11). The church sent a delegation of three men (16:17), who apparently brought a letter that requested Paul's judgment on certain issues (7:1). Paul wrote this epistle as his response to the problems and questions of the Corinthians (he had already written a previous letter; 5:9). It may be that the men who came from Corinth took this letter back with them. Paul was planning to leave Ephesus (16:5-8), indicating that 1 Corinthians was written in A.D. 56.

4. The Christ of 1 Corinthians. This book proclaims the relevance of Christ Jesus to every area of the believer's life. He "became for us wisdom from God—and righteousness and sanctification and redemption—(1:30), and these are the themes Paul addresses in this epistle.

5. Keys to 1 Corinthians.

Key Word: Correction of Carnal Living— The basic theme of this epistle is the application of Christian principles to carnality in the individual as well as in the church. The cross of Christ is a message that is designed to transform the lives of believers and make them different as people and as a corporate body from the surrounding world. However, the Corinthians were destroying their Christian testimony because of immorality and disunity. Paul wrote this letter as his corrective response to the news of problems and disorders among the Corinthians. It was designed to refute improper attitudes and conduct and to promote a spirit of unity among the brethren in their relationships and worship. Paul's concern as their spiritual father (4:14-15) is tempered with love, and he wants to avoid visiting them "with a rod" (4:21).

6. Survey of First Corinthians. Through the missionary efforts of Paul and others, the church was established in Corinth, but Paul found it very difficult to keep Corinth out of the church. The pagan lifestyle of Corinth exerts a profound influence upon the Christians in that corrupt city—problems of every kind plague them. In this disciplinary letter, Paul was forced to exercise his apostolic authority as he deals firmly with problems of divisiveness, immorality, lawsuits, selfishness, abuses of the Lord's Supper and spiritual gifts, and denials of the resurrection. This epistle is quite orderly in its approach as it sequentially addresses a group of problems that have come to Paul's attention. Paul also gives a series of perspectives on various questions and issues raised by the Corinthians in a letter. He uses the introductory words "Now concerning" or "Now" to delineate those topics (7:1, 25; 8:1; 11:2; 12:1; 15:1; 16:1). The three divisions of 1 Corinthians are: answer to Chloe's report of divisions (1-4); answer to report of sexual sin (5-6); and answer to letter of questions (7-16).

Answer to Chloe's Report of Divisions (1-4). Personality cults centering around Paul, Apollos, and Peter had led to divisions and false pride among the Corinthians (1). Their wisdom or cleverness did not bring them to Christ; divine wisdom is contrary to human wisdom. The truth of the gospel is spiritually apprehended (2). Factions that existed among the saints at Corinth were indications of their spiritual immaturity (3). They should pride themselves in Christ, not in human leaders who are merely His servants (4).

Answer to Report of Sexual Sin (5-6).

The next problem Paul addressed was that of incest between a member of the church and his stepmother (5). The Corinthians had exercised no church discipline in this matter, and Paul ordered them to remove the offender from their fellowship until he repented. Another source of poor testimony was the legal action of believer against believer in civil courts (6:1-8). Christians must learn to arbitrate their differences within the Christian community. Paul concluded this section with a warning against immorality in general (6:9-20).

Answer to Letter of Questions (7-16). In these chapters the apostle Paul gives authoritative answers to thorny questions raised by the Corinthians. His first counsel concerns the issues of marriage, celibacy, divorce and remarriage (7). The next three chapters are related to the problem of meat offered to idols (8:1-11:1). Paul illustrated from his own life the twin principles of Christian liberty and the law of love, and he concluded that believers must sometimes limit their liberty for the sake of weaker brothers (Ro 14). The apostle then turned to matters concerning public worship, including improper observances of the Lord's Supper and the selfish use of spiritual gifts (11:2-14:40). Gifts are to be exercised in love for the edification of the whole body. The Corinthians also had problems with the resurrection, which Paul sought to correct (15). His historical and theological defense of the resurrection includes teaching on the nature of the resurrected body. The Corinthians probably had been struggling over this issue because the idea of a resurrected body was disdained in Greek thought. The epistle closes with Paul's instructions for the collection he will make for the saints in Jerusalem (16:1-4), followed by miscellaneous exhortations and greetings (16:5-24).

OUTLINE OF FIRST CORINTHIANS

Part One: In Answer to Chloe's Report of Divisions (1:1–4:21)

I. Introduction (1:1-9)

A. Greetings of
   Grace 1:1-3
B. Prayer of
   Thanksgiving 1:4-9

II. Report of Divisions (1:10-17)

III. Reasons for Divisions (1:18–4:21)

A. Misunderstanding of the Gospel
   Message 1:18–3:4
B. Misunderstanding of the Gospel
   Messenger 3:5–4:5
C. Misunderstanding of Paul's
   Ministry 4:6-21

Part Two: In Answer to Reports of Sexual Sin (5:1–6:20)

I. On Incest (5:1-13)

A. Deliver the Sinner to Discipline...... 5:1-8
B. Separate Yourselves from
   Immoral Believers........................ 5:9-13

II. Concerning Litigation Between Believers (6:1-11)

III. Warnings Against Sexual Immorality (6:12-20)

Part Three: In Answer to the Letter of Questions (7:1–16:24)

I. Counsel Concerning Marriage (7:1-40)

A. Principles for Married Life 7:1-9
B. Principles for the Married
   Believer 7:10-16
C. Principles of Abiding in God's
   Call 7:17-24
D. Principles for the
   Unmarried 7:25-38
E. Principles for Remarriage 7:39-40

II. Counsel Concerning Things Offered to Idols (8:1–11:1)

A. Principles of Liberty and the Weaker
   Brother 8:1-13
B. Illustration of Paul and His
   Liberty 9:1-27
C. Warning against Forfeiting
   Liberty 10:1-13
D. Exhortation to Use Liberty to
   Glorify God 10:14–11:1

III. Counsel Concerning Public Worship (11:2–14:40)

A. Principles of Propriety in Prayer ... 11:2-16
B. Rebuke of Disorders at the Lord's
   Supper 11:17-34
C. Principles of Exercising Spiritual
   Gifts 12:1–14:40

IV. Counsel Concerning the Resurrection (15:1-58)

A. Fact of Christ's Resurrection 15:1-11
B. Importance of Christ's
   Resurrection 5:12-19
C. Order of the Resurrection 5:20-28
D. Moral Implications of Christ's
   Resurrection 5:29-34
E. Bodies of the Resurrected Dead... 5:35-50
F. Bodies of the Translated Living... 5:51-58

V. Counsel Concerning the Collection for Jerusalem (16:1-4)

VI. Conclusion (16:5-24)

---

7. The Book of Second Corinthians. Since Paul's first letter, the Corinthian church had been swayed by false teachers who stirred the people against Paul. They claimed he was fickle, proud, unimpressive in appearance and speech, dishonest, and unqualified as an apostle of Jesus Christ. Paul sent Titus to Corinth to deal with these difficulties, and upon his return, rejoiced to hear of the Corinthian's change of heart. Paul wrote this letter to express his thanksgiving for the repentant majority and to appeal to the rebellious minority to accept his authority. Throughout the book he defends his conduct, character, and calling as an apostle of Jesus Christ.

To distinguish this epistle from 1 Corinthians, it was given the title *Pros Korinthious B,* the "Second to the Corinthians." The *A* and *B* were probably later additions to *Pros Korinthious.*

8. The Author of 2 Corinthians. External and internal evidence amply support the Pau-

line authorship of this letter. As with Romans, the problem of 2 Corinthians is with its lack of unity, not with its authorship. Many critics theorize that chapters 10–13 were not part of this letter in its original form because their tone contrasts with that of chapters 1–9. It is held that the sudden change from a spirit of joy and comfort to a spirit of concern and self-defense points to a "seam" between two different letters. Many hypotheses have been advanced to explain the problem, but the most popular is that chapters 10–13 belong to a lost letter referred to in 2:4. Several problems arise with these attempts to dissect 2 Corinthians. Chapters 10–13 do not fit Paul's description of the "lost" letter of 2:4 because they are firm but not sorrowful and because they do not refer to the offender about whom that letter was written (2:5-11). Also, this earlier material would have been appended at the beginning of 2 Corinthians, not at the end.

There is simply no external (manuscript, church fathers or tradition) or internal basis for challenging the unity of this epistle. The difference in tone between 1–9 and 10–13 is easily explained by the change of focus from the repentant majority to the rebellious minority.

9. The Time of 2 Corinthians. (See also "The Time of 1 Corinthians.") Paul was in Ephesus when he wrote 1 Corinthians and expected Timothy to visit Corinth and return to him (1 Co 16:10-11). Timothy apparently brought Paul a report of the opposition that had developed against him in Corinth, and Paul made a brief and painful visit to the Corinthians (this visit is not mentioned in Acts, but it can be inferred from 2 Co 2:1; 12:14; 13:1-2). Upon returning to Ephesus, Paul regretfully wrote his sorrowful letter to urge the church to discipline the leader of the opposition (2:1-11; 7:8). Titus carried this letter. Paul, anxious to learn the results, went to Troas and then to Macedonia to meet Titus on his return trip (2:12-13; 7:5-16). Paul was greatly relieved by Titus's report that the majority of the Corinthians had repented of their rebelliousness against Paul's apostolic authority. However, a minority opposition still persisted, evidently led by a group of Judaizers (10–13). There in Macedonia Paul wrote 2 Corinthians and sent it with Titus and another brother (8:16-24). This took place late in A.D. 56, and the Macedonian city from which it was written may have been Philippi. Paul then made his third trip to Corinth (12:14; 13:1-2; Ac 20:1-3) where he wrote his letter to the Romans.

There is an alternative view that the anguished letter of 2:4 and 7:8 is, in fact, 1 Corinthians and not a lost letter. This would require that the offender of 2 Corinthians 2:5-11 and 7:12 be identified with the offender of 1 Corinthians 5.

10. The Christ of 2 Corinthians. Christ is presented as the believer's comfort (1:5), triumph (2:14), Lord (4:5), light (4:6), judge (5:10), reconciliation (5:19), substitute (5:21), gift (9:15), owner (10:7), and power (12:9).

11. Keys to 2 Corinthians.

Key Word: Paul's Defense of His ministry—The major theme of 2 Corinthians is Paul's defense of his apostolic credentials and authority. This is especially evident in the portion directed to the still rebellious minority (10–13), but the theme of vindication is also clear in chapters 1–9. Certain false apostles had mounted an effective campaign against Paul in the church at Corinth, and Paul was forced to take a number of steps to overcome the opposition. This epistle expresses the apostle's joy over the triumph of the true gospel in Corinth (1–7), and it acknowledges the godly sorrow and repentance of the bulk of the believers. It also urges the Corinthians to fulfill their promise of making a liberal contribution for the poor among the Christians in Judea (8–9). This collection would not only assist the poor, but it would also demonstrate the concern of the Gentile Christians in Macedonia and Achaia for Jewish Christians in Judea, thus displaying the unity of Jews and Gentiles in the body of Christ.

The opposition addressed in chapters 10–13 apparently consists of Jews (Palestinians or Hellenistic; 11:22) who claim to be apostles (11:5, 13; 12:11) but who preach a false gospel (11:4) and are enslaving in their leadership (11:20). Chapters 10–13 are intended to expose these "false apostles" (11:13), and defend Paul's God-given authority and ministry as an apostle of Jesus Christ.

Key Verses: 2 Chronicles 4:5-6 and 5:17-19—"For we do not preach ourselves, but Christ Jesus the Lord, and ourselves your servants for Jesus's sake. For it is the God who commanded light to shine out of darkness who has shone in our hearts to give the light of the knowledge of the glory of God in the face of Jesus Christ" (4:5-6).

"Therefore, if anyone is in Christ, he is a new creation; old things have passed away; behold, all things have become new. Now all things are of God, who has reconciled us to Himself through Jesus Christ, and has given us the ministry of reconciliation, that is, that God was in Christ reconciling the world to Himself, not imputing their trespasses to them, and has committed to us the word of reconciliation" (5:17-19).

Key Chapters: 2 Corinthians 8 and 9—Chapters 8 and 9 are really one unit and comprise the most complete revelation of God's plan for giving found anywhere in the Scriptures. Contained therein are the principles for giving (8:1-6), the purposes for giving (8:7-15), the policies to be followed in giving (8:16–9:5), and the promises to be realized in giving (9:6-15).

12. Survey of 2 Corinthians. Second Corinthians describes the anatomy of an apostle. The Corinthian church has been swayed by the false teachers who have stirred the people against Paul, especially in response to 1 Corinthians,

Paul's disciplinary letter. Throughout this letter (2 Co) Paul defends his apostolic conduct, character, and call. The three major sections are: Paul's explanation of his ministry (1–7); Paul's collection for the saints (8–9); and Paul's vindication of his apostleship (10–13).

Paul's Explanation of his Ministry (1–7). After his salutation and thanksgiving for God's comfort in his afflictions and perils (1:1-11), Paul explains why he has delayed his planned visit to Corinth. It is not a matter of vacillation: the apostle wants them to have enough time to repent (1:12–2:4). Paul graciously asks them to restore the repentant offender to fellowship (2:5-13). At this point, Paul embarks on an extended defense of his ministry in terms of his message, circumstances, motives and conduct (2:14–6:10). He then admonishes the believers to separate themselves from defilement (6:11–7:1), and expresses his comfort at Titus's news of their change of heart (7:2-16).

Paul's Collection for the Saints (8–9). This is the longest discussion of the principles and practice of giving in the New Testament. The example of the Macedonians' liberal giving for the needy brethren in Jerusalem (8:1-6) is followed by an appeal to the Corinthians to keep their promise by doing the same (8:7–9:15). In this connection, Paul commends the messengers for the large gift they have promised. Their generosity will be more than amply rewarded by God.

Paul's Vindication of his Apostleship (10–13). Paul concludes this epistle with a defense of his apostolic authority and credentials that is directed to the still rebellious minority in the Corinthian Church. His meekness in their presence in no way diminishes his authority as an apostle (10). To demonstrate his apostolic credentials, Paul is forced to boast about his knowledge, integrity, accomplishments, sufferings, visions, and miracles (11:1–12:13). He reveals his plans to visit them for the third time and urges them to repent so that he will not have to use severity when he comes (12:14–13:10). The letter ends with an exhortation, greetings, and a benediction (13:11-14).

OUTLINE OF SECOND CORINTHIANS

Part One: Paul's Explanation of His Ministry (1:1–7:16)

I. Introduction (1:1-11)

A. Paul's Thanksgiving to God 1:1-7
B. Paul's Trouble in Asia 1:8-11

II. Paul's Explanation of His Change of Plans (1:12–2:13)

A. Paul's Original Plan 1:12-22
B. Paul's Change of Plans 1:23–2:4
C. Paul's Appeal to Forgive 2:5-13

III. Paul's Philosophy of Ministry (2:14–6:10)

A. Christ Causes Us to Triumph...... 2:14-17
B. Changed Lives Prove Ministry 3:1-5

C. New Covenant Is the Basis of Ministry 3:6-18
D. Christ Is the Theme of Ministry ... 4:1-7
E. Trials Abound in the Ministry 4:8-15
F. Motivation in the ministry 4:16–5:21
G. Giving No Offense in the Ministry 6:1-10

IV. Paul's Exhortations to the Corinthians (6:11–7:16)

A. Paul's Appeal for Reconciliation 6:11-13
B. Paul's Appeal for Separation from Unbelievers.............................. 6:14–7:1
C. Paul's Meeting with Titus 7:2-7
D. Corinthian's Response to Paul's Letter 7:8-16

Part Two: Paul's Collection for the Saints (8:1–9:15)

I. Example of the Macedonians (8:1-6)

II. Exhortation to the Corinthians (8:7–9:15)

A. Example of Christ 8:7-9

B. Purpose of Giving 8:10-15
C. Explanation of the Delegation 8:16–9:5
D. Exhortation to Giving 9:6-15

Part Three: Paul's Vindication of His Apostleship (10:1–13:14)

I. Paul Answers His Accusers (10:1-18)

A. The Charge of Cowardice Is Answered.................................. 10:1-2
B. The Charge of Walking in the Flesh Is Answered 10:3-9
C. The Charge of Personal Weakness Is Answered 10:10-18

II. Paul Defends His Apostleship (11:1–12:13)

A. Paul's Declaration of His Apostleship 11:1-15
B. Paul's Sufferings Support His Apostleship 11:16-33

C. Paul's Revelations Support His Apostleship 12:1-10
D. Paul's Signs Support His Apostleship 12:11-13

III. Paul Announces His Upcoming Visit (12:14–13:10)

A. Paul's Concern Not To Be a Financial Burden 12:14-18
B. Paul's Concern Not to Find Them Carnal 12:19-21
C. Paul's Warning to Examine Yourselves 13:1-10

IV. Conclusion (13:11-14)

COR′ MO·RANT

Two Hebrew words are thus rendered. One denotes a pelican, a ceremonially unclean bird (Le 11:17; De 14:17). The other is some kind of plunging bird, probably the common cormorant. The latter is a great eater, a proverbial trait (Is 34:11; Zep 2:14).

CORN

Grain of all kinds. In America, the word *corn* has come to be almost exclusively applied to maize, rather than retaining its older meaning as a general term for grains such as wheat, barley, spelt, millet, etc. (Ge 27:28; De 7:13; 8:8).

COR·NE′ LI·US

A Roman centurion stationed at Caesarea and a devout Gentile follower of Israel's God. Cornelius and those of his household are generally regarded as the first Gentile converts to Christ (Ac 10:1-48).

COR′ NER·STONE′

The stone that binds together the sides of a building (Ps 118:22; Is 28:16; Ze 4:7). It was a term often applied to Christ (Ro 9:33; Ep 2:20; 1 Pe 2:6) who was also called the head of the corner (Ma 21:42; 1 Pe 2:7).

COR′ NET

A wind instrument made of a ram's horn, the Hebrew *shaphar* (1 Ch 15:28; Ps 98:6; Ho 5:8). The word is also translated *trumpet* (Le 25:9). The *peren,* originally made from the horn

of an animal, was later made of metal (Da 3:5, 7,10,15). A third word is rendered *castanets* in the Revised Version (2 Sa 6:5).

CORRECTION

Reproof or chastisement, making right (Pr 3:11-12; 13:18; 15:10; Hab 1:12; 2 Ti 3:16).

CORRUPTION

Decay, either physically in terms of the rotting of the physical dead body, or spiritual, in terms of the decay and rot of sin in the soul (Ac 2:27,31; 2 Pe 1:4; 1 Co 15:42,50-54).

COR·RUP′ TION, MOUNT OF

Designation of the southern side of the hill east of Jerusalem where Solomon built altars to the gods worshipped by his pagan wives. It is also called the Mount of Offense (2 Ki 23:13).

CORNELIUS

CO·RUN′DUM
See ADAMANT.

COS
An island between Miletus and Rhodes (Ac 21:1).

CO′SAM
The son of Elmodam, a descendant of David through Nathan and ancestor of Zerubbabel and Christ (Lk 3:28).

COSMETICS
Unknown lotions, perfumes, or paints used to enhance beauty (Es 2:3; Song 1:12). Women painted around their eyes with black to make them appear larger; apparently this was somewhat disreputable (Je 4:30; Eze 23:40). Some kinds of ointments were used to anoint a body for burial (Lk 7:37; Jo 19:39-40).

COSTLY PEARL, PARABLE OF
(Ma 13:45-46).

COTES (archaic)
Enclosures for flocks (2 Ch 32:28).

COTTON
Incorrect translation of the word for linen. As far as we know, cotton was not grown or used in the Bible lands, although it seems to have been known in India at that time.

COUCH
See BED.

COUL′TER (archaic)
Plow or knife (1 Sa 13:20-21; Is 2:4; Joel 3:10; Mi 4:3). The English word (spelled *colter*) now refers to the sharp knife or rotary blade which cuts through the sod ahead of the plowshare and moldboard.

COUN′CIL
This word usually refers to the Sanhedrin, the highest legislative body of the Jews. It was composed of 71 members including the high priest, who was its president. It had the power of life and death (Ma 26:3,57; Ac 4:5-6,15; 6:12, 15) but because Israel was an occupied country, they could not execute the sentence of death. This kind of sentencing was the prerogative of Rome. Jesus was tried before this body (Ma 26:59; Mk 14:55; Jo 11:47), as were the apostles (Ac 4:5-6, 15; 5:21,27), Stephen (Ac 6:12), and Paul (Ac 22:30; 23:15; 24:20).

COUNCIL OF JERUSALEM
See JERUSALEM COUNCIL, THE.

COUN′SEL·OR
One who serves as adviser, especially to kings (2 Sa 15:12; 1 Ch 27:32; Ez 7:28; Job 3:14); also a member of the Sanhedrin, as Joseph of Arimathaea (Mk 15:43; Lk 23:50).

COUNTERVAIL (archaic)
To be made equal; to offset; to compensate (Es 7:3-4).

COUPLINGS
Joints, beams joining walls together (Ex 26:3-24; 2 Ch 34:11).

COURAGE
That which enables one to bear fear and to do what is right in the face of opposition (Jo 1:6-7,9,18; 23:6; 2 Ch 19:11). Real courage comes from trust in God.

COURS′ES OF PRIESTS AND LE′VITES
David divided the priests and Levites into 24 orders or courses, each of which served one week, the order being determined by lot (1 Ch 24:1-18; 27:1-15; 2 Ch 23:8).

COURT
An uncovered enclosure connected with a house or palace (2 Sa 17:18; 1 Ki 7:8-9; Es 4:11; 5:1). There were courts about the temple (1 Ki 6:36; 2 Ki 21:5).

COURT OF THE GENTILES
The outermost court of Herod's temple. Gentiles were allowed to enter this court, but could penetrate no further into the temple (Ma 27:51; Ep 2:14).

COURT, SANCTUARY
See TABERNACLE; TEMPLE.

COURTIER
One who serves in the court of a king. His exact duties are not specified. See GOVERNMENT OFFICIAL.

COUSIN

The child of the sibling of your parent. As with many family relationships mentioned in Scripture, sometimes cousinship is a little unclear. Sometimes the words translated "cousin" might be better understood as "kinsman" (Col 4:10; Lk 1:36; Je 32:7-9,12). Mordecai was actually Esther's first cousin (Es 2:15; 2:7).

COV'E·NANT

An agreement or compact (Ge 21:27,32; 1 Sa 18:3; 23:18; 1 Ki 20:34). God made a covenant with Adam and Eve, promising divine favor in return for obedience (Ge 2:16-17). God covenanted with Noah that he would survive the deluge (Ge 6:18) and that there would never again be such a flood (Ge 9:12-16). One of the most mysterious and yet theologically significant events is recorded in Genesis 15. In a vision, God told Abram to take a heifer, a goat, a ram, a turtledove, and a young pigeon, and cut all except the birds in half. Then he was told to place each piece opposite the other.

"Now when the sun was going down, a deep sleep fell upon Abram; and behold, horror and great darkness fell upon him" (v. 12). Then God predicted the 400 year bondage of Abram's descendants in a foreign land and their return to Canaan at the end of four generations.

"And it came to pass, when the sun went down and it was dark, that behold, there was a smoking oven and a burning torch that passed between those pieces. On the same day the LORD made [literally, "cut"] a covenant with Abram" (vv. 17-18). Then followed the prediction of the extent of the land to be given to Abram's descendants.

The Hebrew idiom *to cut a covenant* was based on the custom of cutting up an animal and those who were making the covenant walking between the pieces. In this case, only God (visualized as "a smoking oven and a burning torch") went through. This suggests to many that it was an unconditional covenant on God's part, no matter what Abram did or did not do. *Covenant* is a word with many shades of meaning, being used for all sorts of formal agreements between people, or between God and men.

Covenants Between Men: Between friends, such as David and Jonathan, a covenant is an alliance of brotherly love and loyalty (1 Sa 18:3; 20:8; 23:18). In Proverbs 2:16-17, the "seductress" is described who deserts her husband

"and forgets the covenant [marriage contract] of her God." A covenant can also be an agreement or pledge, as between Jehoida and his captains (2 Ki 11:4). Between countries it is a treaty or alliance, as between Israel and the Gibeonites (Jos 9), Solomon and Hiram (1 Ki 5:2-6), and Judah and Tyre (Amos 1:9). Between a king and his people, as between Saul and Israel, it was not unlike a simpler form of a constitutional monarchy.

Between God and Man: Most important of all, between God and man, a covenant was "cut" with animal sacrifices, an oath and promised blessings for obedience and curses for disobedience. The whole Book of Deuteronomy can be seen as a written covenant, with the requirements of God and the consequences of disobedience clearly defined and ratified by both parties.

Covenants of the Bible:

The Edenic Covenant(Ge 2:15-17). See EDENIC COVENANT.

The Adamic Covenant (Ge 3:14-31). See ADAMIC COVENANT.

The Noahic Covenant(Ge 9:1-19). See NOAHIC COVENANT.

The Abrahamic Covenant (Ge 12:1-3). See ABRAHAMIC COVENANT.

The Mosaic Covenant (Ex 19:5-8). See MOSAIC COVENANT.

The Land Covenant (De 29:10-15; 30:11-20).

The Davidic Covenant (2 Sa 7:4-17). See DAVIDIC COVENANT.

The New Covenant (Je 31:31-34). See NEW COVENANT.

The Covenants and Bible Doctrine: All Bible believing Christians believe in the covenants, but some make them central to their theology and some see them as an important part of a larger framework.

Those who fit the whole Bible into a covenantal framework are known as "covenant theologians." Those who see the covenants as within larger administrations (dispensations) are known as "dispensationalists." Recently, conservative Christians from both groups have found out that they have much more in common than they previously thought. Whether one favors covenants or dispensations, or both, the main program is neither the one nor the other, but the Person of Christ, who is all in all, and in all.

COVENANT, BOOK OF THE

The Laws of Exodus 20:22–23:33; 24:7. Josiah found the Book of the Covenant when he began the restoration of the temple (2 Ki 23:2-3, 21; 2 Ch 34:3-31). This may have included more of the Pentateuch than just these chapters.

COVENANT OF SALT

An expression of permanence, a covenant which would not be broken (Nu 18:19). The covenant was symbolized by both parties taking a little salt and mixing it together. Just as the salt could never be separated, the covenant would never be set aside.

COVENANT PEOPLE

The nation Israel, descendants of Abraham and heirs of the covenant (Ge 12:1-3; Lk 22:20; 2 Co 3:6). See CHOSEN PEOPLE.

COVERING THE HEAD

The practice of the early church for women to cover their heads when praying or prophesying. Paul addresses the issue as he is teaching the Corinthian church (1 Co 11:1-16). Christians today disagree about how literally this passage should be taken. Some view it as a command related to certain cultural customs of the day, and feel that it has no application for today. Others believe that the passage is teaching that women must have long hair, and men must have short hair. In some groups, the women wear some kind of covering during certain meetings of the church. In a very few conservative groups, women wear a head covering all the time. The influence of this passage can be seen in our culture today in the still strong custom for men to remove their hats inside a building and particularly inside a church or during a religious service.

COVERT (archaic)

A hiding place (Is 4:6).

COVETOUSNESS

The sin of wanting what is not available for you to have. God commanded His people not to covet (Ex 20:17; De 5:21), for covetousness leads to further sin (Jos 7:21).

COW

Cows were known to have been in Palestine and Egypt at an early date (Ge 41:2; De 7:13).

Abraham had cows (Ge 12:16; 32:15). Milk was a favorite food (2 Sa 17:29). It was unlawful to kill a cow and her calf the same day (Le 22:28). See CATTLE.

COZ

See HAKKOZ.

COZ′BI (false)

A Midianitess slain by Phinehas (Nu 25:6-8, 14-18).

CO·ZE′BA, CHO·ZE′BA

A village of Judah (1 Ch 4:22), often identified with Chezib.

CRACKNEL (archaic)

A small dry cake; cracker (1 Ki 14:3).

CRAFTINESS

Cleverness with guile, slyness, sneakiness. The serpent, Satan, is described as being "crafty" as he sought to bring Eve down into sin (Ge 3:1), and he is still marked by this trait (2 Co 11:3).

CRAFTSMAN

See METALSMITH.

CRANE

A large bird that migrates to the south when winter is near (Is 38:14; Je 8:7).

CREATE

In a cosmic sense, to make something out of nothing as opposed to building something out of previously existing materials.

CREATION

The Bible opens with the doctrine that God is the author of creation, that he caused to be that which did not previously exist (Ge 1; Ps 51:10; 148:5; Is 40:26; Am 4:13). God created the world and all that is in it in six days. Then He declared it all to be "very good" (Ge 1:31). The Creator rested on the seventh day (Ge 2:1-3).

While there were other "creation stories" among the pagan nations of the ancient world, the biblical account is unique in that God existed before creation and called the physical world into being from nothing (Ge 1:1-2; Jo 1:2-3). These pagan nations, particularly the Babylonians, believed the material universe was eternal and that it brought their gods into being. But Genesis describes a God who is clearly superior to the physical world.

The general account is given in Genesis 1:1–2:3. God began organizing a shapeless and barren earth (Ge 1:2), providing light (1:3-5), and separating land from water (1:6-10). The creation of plant and animal life followed, including creatures of the sea, air, and land (1:11-25). Man and woman were created on the sixth day (1:26-28), before the Creator's Sabbath rest (2:1-3). The second chapter of Genesis gives a more detailed account of the creation of Adam and Eve on the sixth day.

Scholars have disagreed about the length of the six days of creation. In order to reconcile Scripture with the modern theory of evolution, it has been proposed that the "days" actually represent indefinite but very long periods of time—perhaps millions of years. This would give time for macro-evolution to have occurred, and still acknowledge God's hand in some fashion. This idea is generally called "theistic evolution;" in other words, the world did evolve, but not on its own or by accident. God directed its evolution. Aside from the fact that it is setting aside a clear, straightforward explanation of a clear, straightforward passage in favor of a meaning which is not obvious to any ordinary reading of the text, the theory that the "days" were in fact ages does not fit at all comfortably with the theory of evolution. For the "days" to represent long periods of time would have to mean that all the trees, herbs, and plants of the earth (day three) evolved millions of years *before* the sun, moon, and stars (day four).

The "gap" theory was also advanced as a theory to support theistic evolution. The obvious problems of the "day/age" theory make it hard to accept as a reasonable explanation. The "gap" theory holds that creation in Genesis 1:1 was followed by catastrophe (1:2; possibly when Satan rebelled), then succeeded by God's re-creation or reshaping of the physical world (1:3-31), after a gap of millions of years when evolution was in progress. This theory seems very attractive to some, in spite of the fact that there is no mention of such a gap in Genesis. It seems extraordinary that millions of years of death, struggle, and amazing evolutionary changes should go unmentioned between verses one and two.

Still another group of Christian scholars be-lieve that the creation account in Genesis is both true and precise. This group believes the "days" of Genesis one are literal, twenty-four hour days. They hold that the geologic record does not support evolution at all, but rather is evidence of the worldwide flood of Noah's day. They point to the well-known lack of transitional forms, and the ease with which science can be fit in with the biblical record as soon as the theory of evolution is not assumed to be proven fact.

The doctrine that all things were created by the mighty power of God is clearly taught in the Old Testament (Ps 33:6-9; 90:2; 104:1-14, 30; Is 40:26-28; 42:5; 44:24; 45:7-13,18; Je 51:15; Am 4:13). The New Testament further unfolds this teaching by revealing the creative work of Christ, the Word (Jo 1:1-3; Col 1:15-18; He 1:1-3,10).

CREATURE

Created beings, living things (Ge 1:3-24; Ps 33:6; He 11:3). Jesus Christ is not a "creature" as man is, because He was not created, but rather participated in creation (Jo 1:1-3).

CREDITOR

See LOAN.

CREED

Statement of belief. The English word "creed" comes from the Latin *credo,* "I believe." A formal creed is a carefully worded, succinct statement affirming a certain doctrine. Three of the most famous and continually used creeds of the church are the NICENE CREED, the APOSTLE'S CREED, and the ATHANASIAN CREED.

CRES' CENS *(increasing)*

A companion of Paul mentioned in 2 Timothy 4:10. He had apparently been with Paul while he was in prison, and then for reasons which are not stated he left Paul and went into Galatia.

CRETANS

Inhabitants of the island of Crete. Some Cretans were present in Jerusalem on the Day of Pentecost when the Holy Spirit came upon the believers (Ac 2:11). Later Paul wrote to Titus, who was going to Crete to strengthen the church there (Tit 1:5), quoting from Epimenides of Knossus (c. 600 B.C.), "Cretans are always liars, evil beasts, lazy gluttons" (Tit 1:12).

In the words of one of their own, the Cretans had some societal problems.

CRETE

A large island in the Mediterranean between Syria and Malta, also known as Candia. It is about 160 miles long and 35 miles broad at its widest point. In 66 B.C. it was captured by the Romans and Jews settled there (Ac 2:11). Christianity was established there at an early date by those Cretans who were in Jerusalem at Pentecost. Titus was placed there by Paul (Tit 1:5,10,14).

CRETES

See CRETANS (Ac 2:11).

CRIB

See MANGER.

CRICK′ET

Rendering in the Revised Version for the Hebrew *chargol* which was listed among insects permitted as food (Le 11:22). As some crickets are edible, this translation is preferable to *beetle* as in the Authorized Version, particularly considering the fact that beetles do not have jumping legs, as the law specified, and crickets do.

CRIME

Breaking the law (Ju 9:24; Eze 7:23; Ac 18:14; Jo 7:21-25; Is 28:15; Ga 5:19; Ex 20:14).

CRIMINALS, THE TWO

When Jesus was crucified, two men were crucified with Him, one on His right and the other on His left. The men were law-breakers, although exactly what crimes they had committed to bring about their execution is not mentioned (Lk 23:32-33,39).

CRISPING PINS

It is not known exactly why the KJV uses this word to translate Isaiah 3:22. It seems to be more accurate to translate this as a heavily decorated purse or handbag.

CRIS′PUS

Ruler of the Jewish synagogue at Corinth. He and his household were brought to faith in Christ through the preaching of Paul (Ac 18:8; 1 Co 1:14).

CROCUS

See ROSE.

CROP

1. The gizzard of a bird. Birds, instead of having teeth for chewing their food, have a habit of eating small stones. These lodge in the gizzard, the food passes through the gizzard first and is ground up by the stones before it reaches the bird's stomach (Le 1:16).

2. An old fashioned word for "cut off" (Eze 17:4,22).

3. The harvest (Ex 9:32; Ma 13:8,26).

CROSS

Crucifixion was common among some nations of antiquity. The cross consisted of two pieces of wood, fastened together at right angles, upon which the victim was placed. To the upper part of the cross, above the head of the victim, a sign bearing his name or crime was placed (Ma 27:37; Mk 15:26; Jo 19:19). Crucifixion was regarded with the same feeling of horror that is associated with *gallows* today (Jo 19:31; 1 Co 1:23; Ga 3:13; He 12:2). Paul gloried in the cross of Christ because it signified the atoning work of the Saviour (Ga 6:14; Ep 2:16; Col 1:20). See CRUCIFIXION.

CROW

See RAVEN.

CROWN

A headdress for ornamentation or denoting high position worn by high priests (Ex 29:6; 39:30; Eze 21:26). On it was inscribed, "Holiness to the Lord." It was a gold plate attached with blue lace. The royal crown was of gold (Ps 21:3) and was often studded with gems (2 Sa 12:30; Ze 9:16). At his crucifixion a crown of thorns was placed on Jesus's head in derision of his alleged claims (Ma 27:29). Paul wrote to Timothy of the crown of righteousness (2 Ti 4:8), and Christ is described as being crowned with glory and honor (He 2:9).

CROWN OF THORNS

When the Roman soldiers were mocking and beating Jesus before His execution, they formed a crown of sharp thorns and beat it derisively down upon His head, mocking the title "King of the Jews" (Ma 27:29).

CRU′CI·FIX′ION

A method of capital punishment in which the victim was affixed alive to a cross. This method of torture and execution was used many centuries before the time of Jesus by several nations of the ancient world, including the Assyrians, the Medes, and the Persians. Alexander the Great crucified one thousand Tyrians and Antiochus Epiphanes used crucifixion as punishment for Jews who refused to renounce their religion. Adopted by the Romans as their most severe form of capital punishment, it was reserved for criminals and slaves. No Roman citizen could be crucified.

Crucifixion involved attaching the victim with nails through the wrists or with leather thongs to a crossbeam attached to a vertical stake. At times the feet were also nailed to the vertical stake. As the victim hung dangling by the arms, blood could not circulate to his vital organs. He died of suffocation or exhaustion, normally after a long period of agonizing pain.

Usually the victim was beaten before His crucifixion. Jesus's flogging must have been severe, since He could not carry His cross afterward (Ma 27:26; Mk 15:21). This also may explain His relatively quick death on the cross. By the ninth hour, probably 3:00 P.M., and only six hours after He was placed on the cross, Jesus was dead. There was no need for the soldiers to break His legs to hasten His death (Mk 15:33-37; Jo 19:31-33).

Jesus's body was not left to decompose in disgrace as was the case with most crucifixion victims. The followers of Jesus were able to secure Pilate's permission to give Him a proper burial (Ma 27:57-60). The cross has been a major stumbling block for many people, preventing the Jewish nation from accepting Jesus as the Messiah. According to Jewish teaching, a person who had been killed "by hanging on a tree"—or crucifixion—was "accursed of God" (De 21:23; Ac 5:30; Ga 3:13). This form of death was so repulsive to the Jewish people that they refused to discuss it in polite society. It is therefore worth noting that instead of stoning Jesus according to their customs, they insisted that the Roman's crucify Him.

For Christians, the apostle Paul best summarized the importance of the crucifixion: "We preach Christ crucified, to the Jews a stumbling block and to the Greeks foolishness, but to those who are called, both Jews and Greeks, Christ the power of God and the wisdom of God" (1 Co 1:23-24). Other New Testament references to His crucifixion include Romans 6:6; 1 Corinthians 2:2; and Hebrews 6:6. See also CROSS.

CRUSE

A small vessel, jug, or flask for holding water (1 Sa 26:11), oil (1 Ki 17:12), or ointment (Ma 26:7).

CRYS′TAL

This is the rendering of a Hebrew word in the Authorized Version of Job 28:17. In the Revised Version it is *glass*. Another Hebrew word, rendered *crystal* in Eze 1:22, is elsewhere often translated *ice* (Job 6:16; 38:29; Ps 147:17). The substance generally denoted by the word "crystal" is rock crystal—a transparent, colorless quartz (Re 4:6; 22:1).

CUB

A nation allied with Egypt (Eze 30:5).

CU′BIT

This word is derived from the Latin *cubitum*, an elbow, signifying the length of the arm to the elbow. The royal cubit of Egypt was a little more than twenty and a half inches and the Babylonian a little longer. The common Hebrew cubit was about eighteen inches (De 3:11; 2 Ch 3:3), while another cubit measure was a handbreadth longer (Eze 40:5; 43:13). See WEIGHTS AND MEASURES.

CUCKOO

An unclean bird (Le 11:16; De 14:15), rendered *sea-mew* in the Revised Version. It was probably a variety of gull or petrel.

CUCKOW

See CUCKOO.

CU′CUM·BER

A vegetable familiar to the Israelites in Egypt and longed for by them in the wilderness (Nu 11:5).

CUD

The partially digested grass and hay that a cow is constantly chewing. Cows and other cud-chewing animals have a system of several stomachs. The hard fibers of the grass are regurgitated for further mastication as part of the digestive process. One of the rules for distinguishing clean animals from unclean animals was the cud. All animals that both chewed the cud and had cloven hooves were suitable for food (Le 11:3; De 14:6).

CUDGEL

See CLUB.

CUMBERED (archaic)

To be distracted with cares (Lk 10:40).

CUMI

See TALITHA CUMI.

CUM'MIN

A plant, cultivated in Palestine, the seeds of which were used as a seasoning. Jesus criticized the Pharisees for the exactitude with which they tithed cummin (Ma 23:23). Black cummin is also translated "dill," "fitches," "caraway," and "holm tree."

CUN

See BEROTHAH.

CUNEIFORM

An ancient form of writing. It is not mentioned in Scripture, but it is noteworthy because existing samples of ancient cuneiform writing give us insight into the cultures and times of Bible days.

CUP

The drinking cup of the Bible was made of earthenware, metal, or horn (2 Sa 12:3; Je 51:7; Mk 9:41). The expression *contents of the* cup was used figuratively for what befalls one (Is 51:17; Je 16:7; Ma 26:39).

CUP'BEAR'ER

A butler in the Egyptian, Persian, and Assyrian courts. This official poured the drink into the cup of the king and gave it to him. To insure the safety of the king against poisoning, the cupbearer was required to be absolutely trustworthy. It was his responsibility to taste the wine before the king to ensure against this danger. In the Persian court Nehemiah, the Hebrew, was the cupbearer of Artaxerxes (Ne 1:11; 2:1).

CURSE

To invoke or pray for harm to someone. The whole creation is under a curse because of the sin of Adam and Eve (Ge 3; Ro 8:22). God warned the Israelites that if they did not obey they would be cursed (De 28:15-68). Balak tried to hire Balaam to curse the Israelites as they prepared to enter the land, but the curse backfired and Balaam could do nothing but bless them (Nu 22-24). Goliath called down curses on David, but they did not come to pass (1 Sa 17:43). Jesus taught that we should return curses with blessing, rather than responding in kind (Lk 6:28). In the end, when Christ returns again and the new heaven and earth are put into place, the curse on the creation will be lifted forever (Re 22:3).

CURTAIN

The holy of holies in the tabernacle was made of curtains (Ex 26:1-13; 36:8-17), and later the temple also had a curtain, or veil between the Most Holy place and the outer part. When Jesus died, this curtain was torn in two from top to bottom, emphasizing and illustrating the fact that humans can once more have direct access to God (Ma 27:51; Mk 15:38; Lk 23:45; He 6:19; 9:3; 10:20).

CUSH

1. Land bordering the Gihon river, named after the son of Ham (Ge 2:10-14).

2. A son of Ham and his descendants (Ge 10:6-8; 1 Ch 1:8-10).

3. The country of the Cushites (Is 11:11). Generally speaking, it refers to the upper Nile region, also called Ethiopia (2 Ki 19:9; Es 1:1; Eze 29:10). Some think there was a second land of Cush in southwestern Arabia.

4. A Benjamite, an enemy of David (Ps 7, title).

CU'SHAN (pertaining to Cush)

Probably that part of Arabia occupied by Cushites (Hab 3:7).

CU'SHAN-RISH·A·THA'IM, CHU'SHAN-RISH·A·THA'IM

A king of Mesopotamia who oppressed the Israelites (Ju 3:5-11).

CU'SHI (an Ethiopian)

Three Old Testament men:

1. Father of Zephaniah (Zep 1:1).

2. One of the men who informed David of the defeat of his son, Absalom (2 Sa 18:21-23,31-32).

3. An ancestor of Jehudi (Je 36:14).

CUSHION

See PILLOW.

CUSH′ITE

A descendant of Cush.

CUSTODIAN

See SCHOOLMASTER.

CUTH, CU′THAH

One of the cities (probably northeast of Babylon) from which Shalmanezer brought colonists to Samaria (2 Ki 17:24,30).

CUTTINGS IN THE FLESH

The detestable practice of cutting and disfiguring one's body as a part of worship (1 Ki 18:28). It was apparently also a symbol of mourning. This practice was strictly forbidden (Le 19:28; 21:5; De 14:1), but it appears to have been well-known, nevertheless (Je 16:6).

CUZA

See CHUZA.

CYM′BAL

A musical instrument consisting of two concave plates of brass which give a clanging sound (2 Sa 6:5; 1 Ch 15:19; 1 Co 13:1).

CY′PRESS

The Hebrew *tirzah* is an evergreen tree of which about ten species are known. One variety attains a height of sixty feet. In the Revised Version it is rendered *holm-tree* (Is 44:14).

CY′PRUS

An island of the Mediterranean about forty miles from the coast of Cilicia, having about 3,584 square miles. It is first mentioned in the New Testament as the native place of Barnabas (Ac 4:36). During the persecution, following the martyrdom of Stephen, Christians went to Cyprus, though it appears that the gospel had already been carried to the island. Paul and Barnabas, on the first missionary journey, visited it (Ac 13:4) and afterwards it was visited by Barnabas and Mark (Ac 15:39).

CY·RE′NE

A city of Libya in northern Africa, in the district now known as Tripoli. Simon, who was forced

to carry the cross of Jesus, was a native of Cyrene (Ma 27:32; Mk 15:21; Lk 23:26). Cyrenians had a synagogue in Jerusalem (Ac 6:9). Lucius, prominent member of the church at Antioch, was a Cyrenian (Ac 13:1).

CY·RE′NI·AN

A native of Cyrene (Mk 15:21; Lk 23:26; Ac 6:9).

CY·RE′NI·US

See QUIRINIUS.

CY′RUS

The founder of the Persian Empire. Isaiah names him as the divine instrument for the release of the Jews from the Babylonian exile (Is 44:28; 45:1-14). In 536 B.C., a few years after the fall of Babylon, Cyrus issued a proclamation which permitted the Jews to return to their own land. He restored the sacred vessels of the temple which had been carried to Babylon by Nebuchadnezzar (Ez 1:1-11; 5:13-14; 6:3).

D

DAB′A·REH

See DABERATH.

DAB′BA·SHETH *(hump of a camel)*

A town of Zebulun (Jos 19:11).

DAB′BE·SHETH

See DABBASHETH.

DAB′E·RATH *(pasture)*

A town of the Levites in Issachar, probably just to the northwest of Mount Tabor (Jos 19:12; 21:28; 1 Ch 6:72), also called Dabareh.

DAGGER

A short sword. Ehud, the left-handed judge of Israel, made use of the convenience and concealable nature of a dagger when he slew the enormously fat king, Eglon (Ju 3:16-22).

DA′GON

The national god of the Philistines. Its head, arms and body had the appearance of a human form, while the lower portion was like the tail of a fish (1 Sa 5:3-4).

DAILY OFFERING

See SACRIFICIAL OFFERINGS.

DA-LAI′AH

See DELAIAH.

DALETH

Fourth letter of the Hebrew alphabet. It is the heading of verses 25-32 of Psalm 119, in which each of the eight verses begins with the letter daleth in the original Hebrew.

DALE, THE KING'S

The valley of Shaveh or King's Vale near Jerusalem. Here Absalom built a monument, often erroneously called the tomb of Absalom (Ge 14:17; 2 Sa 18:18). See ABSALOM'S PILLAR.

DAL·MA·NU′THA

A town near the Sea of Galilee, apparently near Magdala (Ma 15:39; Mk 8:10).

DAL·MA′TIA

The province of Illyricum on the eastern shore of the Adriatic Sea or, as sometimes regarded, its southern half. The province was formed after the tribes were conquered by Augustus Caesar and Tiberius in A.D. 9. In this neighborhood Paul preached (Ro 15:19) and to this district he sent Titus (2 Ti 4:10).

DAL′PHON

One of the ten sons of Haman slain by the Jews (Es 9:7).

DAM (archaic)

A mother, particularly referring to livestock (Ex 22:29-30).

DAM′A·RIS

A woman at Athens who heard Paul preach and was converted to Christianity (Ac 17:34).

DAM′AS·CENE

An inhabitant of Damascus (2 Co 11:32).

DA·MAS′CUS

Damasus is the oldest continually inhabited city in the world. As the current capital of Syria, the city is located on the border of some of the most important highways in the ancient Near Eastern world. Because of its ideal location, the

DAMASCUS

city has always been an important trade center. Its name may be derived from a patterned cloth known as damask, its most important export item in Old Testament times (Eze 27:18).

According to Josephus, the founder of Damasus was Uz, grandson of Shem (Ge 5:32; 10:21, 23). It lay in a fertile plain, about thirty miles in diameter, which was watered by the Pharpar and Abana Rivers (2 Ki 5:12). Eliezer, servant of Abraham, was a native of Damascus (Ge 14:15; 15:2). Rezin, a subject of King Hadadezer of Zobah, captured Damascus and founded the kingdom of Syria. From this time onward the state was often in conflict with Israel. Ahab held Damascus for a time but, after his death, Israel was overrun by the Syrians (1 Ki 20,22; 2 Ki 6:24; 7:6-7). In the reign of King Ahaz of Judah, Rezin of Damascus and his ally, Pekah of Israel, captured Jerusalem. Ahaz, in league with King Tiglath-pileser of Assyria, captured Damascus and carried off its people (2 Ki 16:5-9; Is 7:1–8:6; 10:9).

After periods of dominance by the Assyrians and the Persians, Damascus was conquered by Alexander the Great in 333 B.C. In 63 B.C. the city became part of the Roman Empire, the capital of the Roman province of Syria. In the early years of Roman influence in Syria, many Jews from Judea moved to Damascus. The city had a large Jewish community during New Testament times.

All references to Damascus in the New Testament are associated with the apostle Paul's conversion and early ministry. He was blinded in a vision while traveling to Damascus to persecute early Christians (Ac 9:1-8). After his conversion, Paul went to the house of Judas on "Straight Street" in Damascus. There he met Ananias, a Christian citizen of the city who healed Paul's blindness (Ac 9:10-22). After regaining his sight, Paul preached in the Jewish synagogue in Damascus, astonishing those who remembered him as a persecutor of the Christian faith. Eventually Paul was forced to flee Damascus because of threats on his life.

Damascus is still a trading center filled with open-air markets and crowded streets, some of which are very similar to those which Paul might have visited.

DAMNED

Condemned; judged against (Mk 16:15-16). See CONDEMN.

DAN *(a judge)*

A man, a tribe, and a town.

1. Fifth son of Jacob by Bilhah, Rachel's maid (Ge 30:5-6). Jacob foretold the future of the tribe which would descend from him (Ge 49:16-17).

2. The tribe which descended from the above. In the wilderness census the number of Danites was 62,700; second in size to the tribe of Judah. Its territory was in Palestine between Ephraim on the north and east and Judah on the south. Among its towns were Zorah, Ajalon, and Ekron (Jos 19:40-43; 21:5,23). Samson was a Danite (Ju 13:2,24).

3. A town in the northern part of Palestine, hence the expression "from Dan to Beer-sheba," denoting the extent of the land (Ju 20:1). It was originally called Laish.

DANCE

Among the Hebrews dancing was often an expression of rejoicing (Ju 11:34; 1 Sa 18:6-7; 29:5). It was practiced by both men and women (Ps 30:11; Ec 3:4; La 5:15; Lk 15:25) and was accompanied by tambourines. Dancing sometimes formed a part of a religious ceremony or act of worship (Ex 15:20; Ju 21:21,23; 2 Sa 6:14-23).

DAN' IEL *(God is my judge)*

Three Old Testament men:

1. Second son of David whose mother was Abigail (1 Ch 3:1), called Chileab in 2 Samuel 3:3.

2. A priest who signed the covenant with Nehemiah (Ez 8:2; Ne 10:6).

3. The prophet of the captivity. He belonged to a prominent family of Judah (Da 1:3-7).

DANIEL, APOCRYPHAL ADDITIONS TO

See APOCRYPHA (Bel and the Dragon; the Prayer of Azariah and the Song of the Three Young Men; Susanna).

DAN' IEL, BOOK OF

1. The Book of Daniel. Daniel's life and ministry bridge the entire seventy-year period of Babylonian captivity. Deported to Babylon at the age of sixteen, and handpicked for government service, Daniel became God's prophetic mouthpiece to the Gentile and Jewish world declaring God's present and eternal purpose. Nine of the twelve chapters in his book revolve around dreams, including God-given visions involving trees, animals, beasts and images. In both his personal adventures and prophetic visions, Daniel showed God's guidance, intervention, and power in the affairs of men.

The name *Daniye'l* or *Dani'el* means "God is my judge," and the book is, of course, named after the author and principal character. The Greek form *Daniel* in the Septuagint is the basis for the Latin and English titles.

2. The Author of Daniel. Daniel and his three friends were evidently born into noble Judean families and were "young men in whom there was no blemish, but good-looking, gifted in all wisdom, possessing knowledge and quick to understand" (1:4). He was given three years of training in the best of Babylon's schools (1:5). As part of the re-identification process, he was given a new name that honored one of the Babylonian deities: *Belteshazzar* meant "Bel Protect His Life" (1:7; 4:8; Je 51:44). Daniel's wisdom and divinely given interpretive qualities brought him into a position of prominence, especially in the courts of Nebuchadnezzar and Darius. He is one of the few well-known Bible characters about whom nothing negative is ever written. His life was characterized by faith, prayer, courage, consistency, and lack of compromise. This "greatly beloved" man (9:23; 10:11,19) was mentioned three times by his sixth-century contemporary Ezekiel as an example of righteousness. Daniel claimed to write this book (12:4), and he used the autobiographical first person from 7:2 onward. The Jewish Talmud agrees with this testimony, and Jesus attributed a quote from 9:27 to "Daniel the prophet" (Ma 24:15).

3. The Time of Daniel. Babylon rebelled against the Assyrian Empire in 626 B.C. and overthrew the Assyrian capital of Nineveh in 612 B.C. Babylon became the master of the Middle East when it defeated the Egyptian armies in 605 B.C. Daniel was among those taken captive to Babylon that year when Nebuchadnezzar subdued Jerusalem. He ministered for the full duration of the Babylonian captivity as a prophet and a government official and continued on after Babylon was overcome by the Medes and Persians in 539 B.C. His prophetic ministry was directed to the Gentile courts of Babylon (Nebuchadnezzar and Belshazzar) and Persia (Darius and Cyrus), as well as to his Jewish countrymen. Zerubbabel led a return of the Jews to Jerusalem in the first year of Cyrus, and Daniel lived and ministered at least until the third year of Cyrus (536 B.C.). As he predicted, the Persian Empire continued until Alexander the Great (11:2-3), who extended the boundaries of the Greek Empire as far east as India. The Romans later displaced the Greeks as the rulers of the Middle East.

For various reasons, many critics have argued that Daniel is a fraudulent book that was written in the time of the Maccabees in the second century B.C., not the sixth century B.C. as it claims. However, the arguments of these critics are not compelling:

(1) The prophetic argument holds that Daniel could not have made such accurate predictions; it must be a "prophecy after the events." Daniel 11 alone contains over one hundred specific prophecies of historical events that literally came true. The author, the critics say, must have lived at the time of Antiochus Epiphanes (175-163 B.C.) and probably wrote this to strengthen the faith of the Jews. But this argument was developed out of a theological bias that assumes true prophecy cannot take place. It also implies that the work was intentionally deceptive.

(2) The linguistic argument claims that the book uses a late Aramaic in 2-7 and that the Persian and Greek words also point to a late date. But recent discoveries show that Daniel's Aramaic is actually a form of early Imperial Aramaic. Daniel's use of some Persian words is no argument for a late date since he continued living in the Persian period under Cyrus. The only Greek words are names of musical instru-

ments in chapter 3, and this comes as no surprise since there were Greek mercenaries in the Assyrian and Babylonian armies. Far more Greek words would be expected if the book were written in the second century B.C.

(3) The historical argument asserts that Daniel's historical blunders argue for a late date. But recent evidence has demonstrated the historical accuracy of Daniel. Inscriptions found at Haran show that Belshazzar reigned in Babylon while his father was fighting the invading Persians. Darius the Mede (5:31; 6:1) has been identified as Gubaru, a governor appointed by Cyrus.

4. The Christ of Daniel. Christ is the Great Stone who will crush the kingdoms of this world (2:34-35,44), the Son of Man who is given dominion by the Ancient of Days (7:13-14), and the coming Messiah who will be cut off (9:25-26). It is likely that Daniel's vision in 10:5-9 was an appearance of Christ (Re 1:12-16).

The vision of the sixty-nine weeks in 9:25-26 pinpoints the coming of the Messiah. The decree of 9:25 took place on March 4, 444 B.C. (Ne 2:1-8). The sixty-nine weeks of seven years equals 483 years, or 173,880 days (using 360-day prophetic years). This leads to March 29, A.D. 33, the date of the Triumphal Entry. This is checked by noting that 444 B.C. to A.D. 33 is 476 years, and 476 times 365.24219 days per year equals 173,855 days. Adding twenty-five days for the difference between March 4 and March 29 gives 173,880 days.

5. Keys to Daniel.

Key Word: God's Program for Israel—Daniel was written to encourage the exiled Jews by revealing God's sovereign program for Israel during and after the period of gentile domination. The "Times of the Gentiles" began with the Babylonian captivity, and Israel would suffer under Gentile powers for many years. But this period is not permanent, and a time will come when God will establish the messianic kingdom which will last forever. Daniel repeatedly emphasizes the sovereignty and power of God over human affairs. "The Most High rules in the kingdom of men, and gives it to whomever He chooses" (4:25). The God who directs the forces of history has not deserted His people. They must continue to trust in Him, because His promises of preservation and ultimate restoration are as sure as the coming of the Messiah.

Key Verses: Daniel 2:20-22 and Daniel 2:44—"Daniel answered and said, 'Blessed be the name of God forever and ever, for wisdom and might are His. And He changes the times and the seasons; He removes kings and raises up kings; He gives wisdom to the wise and knowledge to those who have understanding. He reveals deep and secret things; He knows what is in the darkness, and light dwells with Him'" (2:20-22).

"And in the days of these kings the God of heaven will set up a kingdom which shall never be destroyed: and the kingdom shall not be left to other people; it shall break in pieces and consume all these kingdoms, and it shall stand forever" (2:44).

Key Chapter: Daniel 9—Daniel's prophecy of the seventy weeks (9:24-27) provides the chronological frame for messianic prediction from the time of Daniel to the establishment of the kingdom on earth. It is clear that the first sixty-nine weeks were fulfilled at Christ's first coming. Some scholars affirm that the last week has not yet been fulfilled because Christ relates its main events to His second coming (Ma 24:6,15). Others perceive these words of Christ as applying to the Roman desecration of the temple in A.D. 70.

6. Survey of Daniel. Daniel, the "Apocalypse of the Old Testament," presents a surprisingly detailed and comprehensive sweep of prophetic history. After an introductory chapter in Hebrew, Daniel switches to Aramaic in chapters 2–7 to describe the future course of the Gentile world powers. Then in 8–12, Daniel reverts back to his native language to survey the future of the Jewish nation under Gentile domination. The theme of God's sovereign control in the affairs of world history clearly emerges and provides comfort to the future church, as well as to the Jews whose nation was destroyed by the Babylonians. The Babylonians, Persians, Greeks and Romans will come and go, but God will establish His kingdom through His redeemed people forever. Daniel's three divisions are: the personal history of Daniel (1), the prophetic plan for the Gentiles (2–7), and the prophetic plan for Israel (8–12).

The Personal History of Daniel (1). This chapter introduces the book by giving the background and preparation of the prophet. Daniel is deported along with other promising youths and placed in an intensive training program in Nebuchadnezzar's court. Their names and diets are changed so that they will lose their Jewish identification, but Daniel's resolve to remain faithful to the Lord is rewarded. He and his friends are granted wisdom and knowledge.

The Prophetic Plan for the Gentiles (2–7). Only Daniel can relate and interpret Nebuchadnezzar's disturbing dream of the great statue (2). God empowers Daniel to foretell the way in which He will sovereignly raise and depose four Gentile empires. The Messiah's kingdom will end the times of the Gentiles. Because of his position revealed in the dream, Nebuchadnezzar erects a golden image and demands that all bow to it (3). The persecution and preservation of Daniel's friends in the fiery furnace again illustrates the power of God. After Nebuchadnezzar refuses to respond to the warning of his vision of the tree (4), he is humbled until he acknowledges the supremacy of God and the foolishness of his pride. The feast of Belshazzar marks the end of the Babylonian kingdom (5). Belshazzar is judged because of his arrogant defiance of God. In the reign of Darius, a plot against Daniel backfires when he is divinely delivered in the den of lions (6). Daniel's courageous faith is rewarded, and Darius learns a lesson about the might of the God of Israel. The vision of the four beasts (7) supplements the four-part statue vision of chapter 2 in its portrayal of the four Gentile empires. But once again, "the saints of the Most High shall receive the kingdom, and possess the kingdom forever" (7:18).

The Prophetic Plan for Israel (8–12). The focus in chapter 8 narrows to a vision of the ram and goat that shows Israel under the Medo-Persian and Grecian Empires. Alexander the Great is the large horn of 8:21 and Antiochus Epiphanes is the little horn of 8:9. After Daniel's prayer of confession for his people, he is privileged to receive the revelation of the seventy weeks, including the Messiah's atoning death (9). This gives the chronology of God's perfect plan for the redemption and deliverance of His people. Following is a great vision that gives amazing details of Israel's future history (10 and 11). Chapter 11 chronicles the coming kings of Persia and Greece, the wars between the Ptolemies of Egypt and the Seleucids of Syria, and the persecution led by Antiochus. God's people will be saved out of tribulation and resurrected (12).

OUTLINE OF DANIEL

Part One: The Personal History of Daniel (1:1-21)

I. The Deportation of Daniel to Babylon (1:1-7)

II. The Faithfulness of Daniel in Babylon (1:8-16)

III. The Reputation of Daniel in Babylon (1:17-21)

Part Two: The Prophetic Plan for the Gentiles (2:1–7:28)

I. Nebuchadnezzar's Dream of the Great Image (2:1-49)

A. Nebuchadnezzar Conceals His Dream 2:1-13
B. God Reveals the Dream to Daniel 2:14-23
C. Daniel Interprets the Dream 2:24-45
D. Nebuchadnezzar Promotes Daniel 2:46-49

II. Nebuchadnezzar's Image of Gold (3:1-30)

A. Nebuchadnezzar's Image Is Erected...................................... 3:1-7
B. Daniel's Friends Refuse to Worship 3:8-12
C. Daniel's Friends Trust God 3:13-18
D. Daniel's Friends Are Protected in the Furnace 3:19-25
E. Daniel's Friends Are Promoted ... 3:26-30

III. Nebuchadnezzar's Vision of the Great Tree (4:1-37)

A. Nebuchadnezzar's Proclamation ... 4:1-3
B. Nebuchadnezzar's Vision.............. 4:4-18
C. Daniel's Interpretation of the Vision 4:19-27

D. Nebuchadnezzar's Humiliation ... 4:28-33
E. Nebuchadnezzar's Restoration ... 4:34-37

IV. Belshazzar and the Handwriting on the Wall (5:1-31)

A. Belshazzar Defiles the Temple Vessels 5:1-4
B. Belshazzar Sees the Handwriting 5:5-9
C. Daniel Interprets the Handwriting 5:10-29
D. Belshazzar Is Killed 5:30-31

V. Darius' Foolish Decree (6:1-28)

A. Daniel Is Promoted 6:1-3
B. Darius Signs the Foolish Decree ... 6:4-9
C. Daniel Prays Faithfully 6:10-15
D. Daniel Is Saved in the Lion's Den 6:16-24
E. Darius' Wise Decree 6:25-28

VI. Daniel's Vision of the Four Beasts (7:1-28)

A. The Revelation of the Vision 7:1-14
B. The Interpretation of the Vision 7:15-28

Part Three: The Prophetic Plan for Israel (8:1–12:13)

I. Daniel's Vision of the Ram and Male Goat (8:1-27)

A. The Revelation of the Vision 8:1-12
B. The Length of the Vision............ 8:13-14
C. The Interpretation of the Vision 8:15-27

II. Daniel's Vision of the Seventy Weeks (9:1-27)

A. The Understanding of Daniel......... 9:1-2
B. The Intercession of Daniel 9:3-19
C. The Intervention of Daniel 9:20-23

D. The Revelation of the Seventy Weeks 9:24-27

III. Daniel's Vision of Israel's Future (10:1–12:13)

A. The Preparation of Daniel 10:1-21
B. The Revelation of the Sixty-nine Weeks 11:1-35
C. The Revelation of the Seventieth Week....................................11:36–12:3
D. The Conclusion of the Visions of Daniel 12:4-13

DANIEL'S LIFE, INDEXED		
Recorded Events	**Place**	**Reference**
In the third year of Jehoiakim, Nebuchadnezzar besieges Jerusalem, and carries away many people to Babylon, among whom is Daniel. His name is changed to Belteshazzar.	Babylon	Da 1:1-7
Daniel proposes that, instead of eating the king's meat and drinking his wine, that he and his three friends be given pulse and water for a ten days' test. At the end of that time they show a better condition than the others, and are released from eating and drinking what the king had commanded. They are greatly favored by the king.	Babylon	Da 1:8-21
Nebuchadnezzar has a dream which he does not understand. He calls upon the magicians and astrologers and asks them to prove their powers by telling him what his dream was, and then to interpret it for him. All the wise men fail this test, and the king orders them to be slain.	Babylon	Da 2:1-13
Daniel intercedes for them and promises to satisfy the king. He and his three friends invoke Divine assistance and that night in a vision the secret is revealed to Daniel, for which Daniel thanks God.	Babylon	Da 2:14-23
He relates to the king the dream of the historical image, and then interprets it as related to the Universal Empires. For this the king makes him chief ruler of the nation, and overseer of the wise men of Babylon.	Babylon	Da 2:24-49
Nebuchadnezzar builds a golden image and requires that all the people worship it. The penalty for not doing so is to be cast into a fiery furnace. Daniel's three friends refuse to worship the king's god, are cast into the furnace, but are miraculously preserved by Jehovah.	Babylon	Da 3
The king has another dream, that of a great tree, which Daniel interprets, and according to which the king is to be driven into the field for a time to live with the beasts. At the end of that experience he acknowledges and honors the Most High.	Babylon	Da 4
The next great scene in which Daniel figures is at the end of the kingdom in the reign of Belshazzar, the last king of Babylon. In the midst of revelry handwriting appears on the wall. The wise men are unable to interpret it. The queen tells the king of Daniel. He is brought in and he interprets the writing, which spells the doom of the empire, which occurs that night.	Babylon	Da 5
Upon the fall of Babylon new honors await Daniel in the Medo-Persian State. He is placed above the presidents of the provinces and set over the whole realm.	Persia	Da 6:1-3
Those persons jealous of Daniel induce the king to sign a decree that anyone offering a petition to God or man, excepting the king, for thirty days, should be cast		

Recorded Events	**Place**	**Reference**
into a den of lions, knowing that Daniel would not cease his praying to God.	Persia	Da 6:4-9
The decree could not be altered and Daniel is placed among the lions. He is divinely preserved, as were his three friends in Babylon, while those who had arranged the plot are cast to the lions.	Persia	Da 6:10-28
Daniel is prospered during the reigns of Darius and Cyrus and he utters his great prophecies relating especially to the Times of the Gentiles.	Persia	Da 7–12

DAN'ITE

A descendant of Dan or a member of his tribe (Ju 13:2; 18:1,11; 1 Ch 12:35).

DAN-JA'AN

A place to which Joab and his officers came when taking the census (2 Sa 24:6).

DAN'NAH

A town in the hill country of Judah (Jos 15:49), a few miles southwest of Hebron.

DAR'A

See DARDA.

DAR'DA *(pearl of wisdom)*

One who was noted for wisdom, a son of Mahol of the tribe of Judah (1 Ki 4:31; 1 Ch 2:6).

DAR'IC

A gold coin of Persia worth about five dollars (1 Ch 29:7; Ez 2:69; 8:27; Ne 7:70-71), called *dram* in the Authorized Version. See MONEY OF THE BIBLE.

DA·RI'US

The name of several kings of Media and Persia.

1. *Darius the Mede,* son of Ahasuerus (Da 5:31; 6:1; 9:1; 11:1). When Babylon was taken by the army of Cyrus in 538 B.C., he is said to have been made king over Chaldea.

2. *Darius Hystapsis,* called *the Great.* When the rebuilding of the temple at Jerusalem was interrupted by foes of the Jews, Darius had a search instituted for an edict previously issued by Cyrus which permitted the work (Ez 6:1-12). He extended his kingdom from India to the Grecian archipelago. He was defeated at Marathon in 490 B.C. and died in 484 B.C.

3. *Darius the Persian* (Ne 12:22), probably Darius Codomannus, king of Persia (336-330 B.C.).

DARK' NESS

On three occasions darkness is especially noted in the Scriptures.

1. At creation (Ge 1:2-4).
2. As one of the plagues of Egypt (Ex 10:21).
3. At the crucifixion of Jesus (Ma 27:45).

DAR' KON

The founder of a family, descendants of whom returned from Babylon under Zerubbabel (Ez 2:56; Ne 7:58).

DARLING

Only one; beloved; sole (Ps 22:19-20).

DART

An arrow or spear (Ps 7:13; 120:4; Ep 6:16).

DA' THAN

A Reubenite, the son of Eliab. He and his brother, Abiram, were leaders in the rebellion of Korah (Nu 16:1-35; 26:9; Ps 106:17).

DAUB

To cover or plaster (Eze 13:10-11).

DAUGH' TER

A term which includes daughter in the usual sense, granddaughter, and other female descendants. By extension it designates a female of some particular race, country, or town (Ge 27:46; Ju 21:21; Lk 23:28). Daughters of music (Ec 12:4) means women musicians.

DA' VID (beloved)

The son of Jesse and one of the greatest men of the Bible. His life can be roughly divided into five periods:

1. *His youth in Bethlehem.* He was the youngest of eight brothers (1 Sa 16:10-11; 17:12-14) and is described as ruddy and beautiful in appearance (1 Sa 16:12). He was a shepherd over his father's sheep (1 Sa 16:11; 17:34-36) and was a talented harpist.

2. *His relations with Saul.* David became armorbearer and musician to Saul and a valiant warrior, as was shown by his single-handed defeat of the giant, Goliath (1 Sa 16:14-18,21; 17:32-58). David and Jonathan, a son of Saul, became devoted friends and David married a daughter of Saul. David's deeds in war won him such great renown that Saul became jealous and an enemy of David (1 Sa 15:17-29; 19:4-9).

YOUNG DAVID

3. *His life as fugitive and outlaw.* Fleeing from Saul, David was given food by the high priest at Nob (1 Sa 21:1-9). He took refuge in the cave of Adullam (1 Sa 22:1) and, gathering a band of six hundred men, he defeated the Philistines at Keilah (1 Sa 23:1-5). Twice he refused opportunities to take Saul's life (1 Sa 24,26). King Achish permitted him to occupy Ziklag for which kindness he protected the Philistines against the raids of desert tribes (1 Sa 27). Saul was finally slain in battle at Gilboa (1 Sa 31).

4. *On the throne of Judah.* The tribe of Judah elected David king and he set up his court at Hebron (2 Sa 2:1-10). David reigned over Judah for about seven years when the death of Ishbosheth, who reigned over the other tribes, occurred (2 Sa 2:12–4:12).

5. *King of all Israel.* Israel proposed that both kingdoms be reunited under David (2 Sa 5:1-5). This was done and Jerusalem was taken from the Jebusites and made capital. The nation was thus centralized (2 Sa 5:6-10). David subjugated the Philistines and captured Gath. The ark was brought to Jerusalem (2 Sa 6:1-23). Worship of the Lord was organized (1 Ch 15-16). David sinned greatly in making Bathsheba his wife but repented deeply (2 Sa 11:1-12,24; Ps 51). David died after having reigned forty years, turning over the kingdom to his son, Solomon (1 Ki 2:10-11).

DA' VID, CI' TY OF

1. Jerusalem, the stronghold of Zion which David took from the Jebusites (2 Sa 5:6-9; 1 Ch 11:5,7). It was on a ridge south of Mount Moriah. David and Solomon were buried here (1 Ki

2:10; 11:43) as were many later kings of Judah (1 Ki 14:31; 15:8,24; 2 Ki 8:24).

2. Bethlehem, the birthplace of David (Lk 2:4,11).

DAVIDIC COVENANT

The covenant with David is the fourth of the theocratic covenants (pertaining to the rule of God). In this covenant David is promised three things: (1) a land forever (v. 10); (2) an unending dynasty (vv. 11,16); and (3) an everlasting kingdom (vv. 13,16). The birth of Solomon, David's son who was to succeed him, is predicted (v. 12). His particular role is to establish the throne of the Davidic Kingdom forever (v. 13). His throne continues, though his seed is cursed in the person of Jeconiah (Coniah), who was the king under whom the nation was carried captive to Babylon. Jeremiah prophesied that no one whose genealogical descent could be traced back to David through Jeconiah and Solomon would ever sit on David's throne (Je 22:24-30). Joseph, the legal, but not physical, father of Jesus traces his lineage to David through Jeconiah (Ma 1:1-17). David, however, had another son, Nathan. His line was not cursed. Mary, the physical mother of Jesus, traces her lineage back to David through Nathan (Lk 3:23-38). Notice the care and the extent to which God goes to keep His word and to preserve its truthfulness. The virgin birth was absolutely essential not only to assure the sinless character of Jesus, but also to fulfill the Davidic Covenant. Jesus receives His "blood right" to David's throne through His earthly mother, Mary, and His "legal right" to David's throne through his adoptive earthly father, Joseph. The virgin birth guarantees that one of David's line will sit on David's throne and rule forever, while at the same time preserving intact the curse and restriction on the line of descent through Jeconiah.

DAVID'S LIFE, INDEXED		
Recorded Events	Place	Reference
David, the youngest son of Jesse, the grandson of Obed who was the son of Ruth and Boaz, was born in Bethlehem. While a lad, during the reign of Saul, Samuel is sent to Bethlehem to anoint David king.	Bethlehem	1 Sa 16:1-13
Saul, when mentally disturbed, needs someone who can play the harp to pacify him. David is a harpist and is brought to the court of Saul.	Gibeah	1 Sa 16:14-23

Recorded Events	Place	Reference
Israel is at war with the Philistines, and Goliath defies any Israelite to meet him in single combat. David accepts the challenge and slays him with his sling.	Shochoh	1 Sa 17
A deep love springs up between David and Jonathan, Saul's son. Saul becomes insanely jealous of David's popularity. David marries Saul's daughter.	Gibeah	1 Sa 18
Saul commands that David be slain. Jonathan remains loyal to David, who is made an outlaw and is compelled to flee from place to place.	Nob Adullam En-gedi	1 Sa 19–23
With 3,000 men Saul pursues David and his band. David twice spares Saul's life. He defeats the Amalekites.	Gath	1 Sa 24–27
In his last battle with the Philistines at Mt. Gilboa, Saul is defeated. He dies by his own hand. David again defeats the Amalekites.	Gilboa Ziklag	1 Sa 28–31
After the death of Saul, David is made king of Judah. The balance of the tribes maintain the house of Saul and remain a separate kingdom. David's capital is at Hebron.	Hebron	2 Sa 1–4
After reigning over Judah for seven years the tribes of Israel accept David as king, and he becomes king of all the tribes. He defeats the Jebusites and takes Jerusalem, which becomes the capital. He defeats the Philistines.	Jerusalem	2 Sa 5
David brings the ark and sets it up in Jerusalem. God speaks His promises to him. David subdues his enemies and establishes the kingdom.	Jerusalem	2 Sa 6–10
He commits his great sin with Bathsheba, and arranges the death of her husband, Uriah. He confesses his sin, and judgment is pronounced upon him. The child conceived by adultery dies, but later Solomon is born to Bathsheba.	Jerusalem	2 Sa 11–12
Absalom, David's son, kills Amnon and flees to Geshur, where he remains three years. He returns home and raises an insurrection against David. He is defeated and slain by Joab. David mourns for Absalom.	Jerusalem	2 Sa 13–18
Sheba revolts and is slain. David numbers the people, which is punished by a pestilence sent upon Israel. David purchases the threshing floor of Araunah to build an altar. It becomes the site of the future temple.	Jerusalem	2 Sa 19–24
In his old age David's son Adonijah attempts, by the help of Joab, to usurp the throne. This is defeated and Solomon is anointed king. His last act is the charge he gives to Solomon. He reigned forty years.	Jerusalem	1 Ki 1:1–2:11

DAVID, TOWER OF

A fortified tower built by David for an armory or arsenal (Song 4:4, Ne 3:19).

DAWN

The first light of the new day (Job 7:4; Ma 28:1; 4:16; Ac 27:33). The word is also used figuratively to describe the entrance of God's goodness into a sin darkened world (Is 58:10).

DAY

The Hebrews reckoned it from evening to evening (Ge 1:5,8; Ex 12:18; Le 23:32). The days of the week, excepting the Sabbath, were numbered rather than named. In symbolic sense Job 20:28; Is 2:12; 13:6,9; Am 5:18-20; 1 Th 5:2; 2 Pe 3:10; 1 Co 5:5; 2 Pe 3:8

DAY OF ATONEMENT

See ATONEMENT, DAY OF.

DAY OF CHRIST, THE

The day of Christ's return. All believers are looking forward to this time, eagerly awaiting Jesus's coming. The New Testament is full of injunctions to live our lives in the light of that expectation, desiring to be found worthy when Christ returns (1 Co 1:8; 2 Co 1:14; Ph 1:10; 1 Co 5:5).

DAY OF JUDGMENT

At the end of time, after the millennium and the final rebellion of sinful man, all the dead will be gathered before God to be judged. Their deeds will be weighed, and the book of life will be consulted. All whose names are written in the book of life will be saved, but those whose names are not written there will be damned (Re 20:11-15). Also called the Great White Throne Judgement.

DAY OF THE LORD

The day of the Lord is a period at the end of human history when God's purpose for humankind will be fulfilled. The period will begin with the return of Christ and will end with the cleansing of the heavens and the earth with fire (2 Pe 3:10-13; Re 21).

Some scholars believe the day of the Lord will be a long period of time. Others feel it will be an instantaneous event when Christ returns to earth to claim His own faithful believers and to consign unbelievers to eternal judgment (Re 20:14-15).

The prophets of the Old Testament were the first to speak of the coming day of the Lord. This day "will be darkness, and not light," Amos warned the unsuspecting residents of Judah (Am 5:18). Isaiah declared that the day of the Lord will come as "destruction from the Almighty" (Is 13:6), and Jeremiah referred to it as "a day of vengeance" (Je 46:10). Along with judgment, the prophets emphasized the restorative and redemptive elements connected with the day of the Lord.

The prophet Joel envisioned God's Spirit being poured out "on all flesh" (2:28) just before the coming of the "great and terrible day of the LORD" (2:31). The occasion for Joel's prophecy was the invasion of Judah by a swarm of locusts, followed by a severe drought (Joel 1:1-4). As tragic as this destruction was, Joel declared, it would be as nothing compared with the coming day of the Lord.

The New Testament emphasizes the suddenness of the Lord's coming (Lk 12:40; Re 3:3), the certainty of His judgment on unbelief (Ma 25:32), and the restoration of heaven and earth by fire (2 Pe 3:10). Christ will fulfill these prophecies on the day of the Lord as He judges all nations from the "throne of His glory" (Ma 25:31).

Rather than speculating about the exact time of God's judgment, our pressing task is to proclaim His message of redemption to a lost world until the day of the Lord is fulfilled.

DAY'S JOURNEY

About twenty miles. See WEIGHTS AND MEASURES.

DAYS' MAN

One who acted as arbitrator (Job 9:33).

DAYSPRING

Sunrise (Lk 1:76-79).

DAY-STAR

See LUCIFER.

DEA'CON

Deacon is another word for servant. *Diakonos* is used in a general sense for ministry and in a technical sense for the office of deacon. In this latter sense, it occurs with *episkopos* in Philippians 1:1 and 1 Timothy 3:8,12. Acts 6 is believed by many to be the origin of the office.

The twelve apostles appointed seven men to administer the charitable funds of the church (Ac 6:1-6). While the seven chosen there are not called *diakonoi* as such, the verb form *diakoneo* is used (v. 2). The standards for deacons are nearly as strict as for elders, but nothing is said about their being able to teach (1 Ti 3:8-13). They did have to have a grasp of the Christian faith and doctrine however. Deacons generally have done practical service, under the leadership of elder-overseers. Eventually the deacon came to be regarded as a church official alongside the bishop (Ph 1:1).

DEA'CONESS

A woman who serves in the church. The word occurs only once in the Bible, in Romans 16:1 where Paul commends "Phebe our sister" who is described as a *diakonon* of the church in Cenchrea. Many versions simply translate this as "servant." It is impossible to tell whether Phebe held a more formal office like the deacons mentioned in 1 Timothy 3, or whether Paul was simply describing her as a "servant of the church," in other words, a woman who was active in working with the local body. We know from contemporary sources that the Christian church ordained women as deaconesses by the second century A.D. These women most likely ministered primarily to other women, particularly in situations where it would not have been suitable for a man to do the work. Since the role of a deacon is to serve the body, it is clear that both men and women are needed to fulfill the requirements of a church which has both male and female members.

DEAD, THE

Those whose physical bodies are not alive. When a person dies, the physical body decays and returns to the earth. The soul however, does not cease to exist. In the beginning, God created people to live forever. When Adam and Eve sinned, they introduced death into the world, both physical death for the body, and spiritual death (Ge 2:17; 3:24; Ro 5:12). Those who are not born again into new life in Christ are "dead in trespasses and sins" (Ep 2:1). If unbelief persists, physical death will be followed by everlasting death, separation from God for eternity (Re 2:11; 21:8). See SHEOL and HELL.

DEAD, ABODE OF THE
See HELL.

DEAD, BAPTISM FOR THE
See BAPTISM FOR THE DEAD.

DEAD SEA

The Dead Sea is a lake about 50 miles long and 10 miles wide in southern Palestine. The Jordan River and other smaller streams flow into it, but because it lies at the lowest point on the earth (about 1,300 feet below the Mediterranean), no water flows out of it. The deepest point of the sea is another 1,300 feet lower yet. Because of its rapid water loss through evaporation, salts and other minerals have become highly concentrated and its saltiness is about four times that of the ocean. This has made the lake unfit for marine life; thus its name "the Dead Sea."

In Abraham's time five cities known as the "cities of the plain" were situated at the south end of the Dead Sea (Ge 14:2,8). Because of their great wickedness, four of these cities—Sodom, Gomorrah, Admah, and Zebolim—were destroyed by earthquakes and fire (Ge 19:28-29; De 29:23). Many scholars believe the remains of these cities were covered in later years by the Dead Sea as the waters shifted when other earthquakes struck the area.

In addition to the destruction of Sodom and Gomorrah, many other biblical events occurred along the shores of the Dead Sea. The springs of En Gedi provided a refuge for David in his flight from King Saul (1 Sa 24:1). In the Valley of Salt south of the Dead Sea, David was victorious over the Edomites (2 Sa 8:13; 1 Ch 18:12-13).

The Dead Sea is also famous because of the discovery of ancient biblical manuscripts in the caves on its northwest coast. Known as the Dead Sea Scrolls, these manuscripts include a complete copy of the Book of Isaiah and portions of several other books of the Bible, as well as many nonbiblical manuscripts. They are dated to the period between 250 B.C. and A.C. 135.

These manuscripts, some of the earliest copies of biblical texts yet discovered, helped scholars establish dates for several important biblical events and gave helpful information on the development of the Hebrew language.

Other names for the Dead Sea used in the Bible are the Salt Sea (Jos 3:16), the Sea of Arabah (De 3:17), and the eastern sea (Joel 2:20).

DEAD SEA SCROLLS

These scrolls and fragments, about 800 in all, were discovered in a series of caves near Qumran (on the northeast shore of the Dead Sea) in 1947. This tremendous archeological find has helped scholars to understand much more about both Judaism and early Christianity, and has provided some of the oldest manuscripts available for portions of the Scripture. Most of the scrolls were written between 250 B.C. and A.D. 68.

Qumran was a religious community near Jericho, probably of the Essene sect of Jews. Some believe that some of John's early disciples may have come from this community. They carefully preserved many religious manuscripts, storing them in clay jars in caves near the community. Seven of these scrolls were in fairly good shape: 1) The book of Isaiah in Hebrew, a complete manuscript. 2) The book of Isaiah in Hebrew, a partial manuscript (these are the oldest copies of Isaiah that are known at this time). 3) *The Manual of Discipline,* a book of the laws and customs of the Qumran community. 4) *The Thanksgiving Psalms,* not a part of the canonical Book of Psalms, but much in the same style. 5) *The War Scroll,* a battle plan for war against the forces of evil. 6) *Peshur on Habakkuk,* a commentary on that prophet. 7) *The Genesis Apocryphon,* a commentary on the Book of Genesis, written in Aramaic, probably about 50 B.C.

Besides these seven scrolls, there are numerous fragments of parchment or papyrus with portions of other Old Testament and apocryphal books. At least a part of every Old Testament book except Esther was found.

DEAF

Unable to hear. Jesus healed a deaf man (Mk 7:33-35).

DEALER

See MERCHANT.

DEARTH

See FAMINE.

DEATH

Physical death happens when the "breath of life" departs from the body. The heart stops beating, the lungs stop taking in air, and the vital organs shut down. In spite of great advances in medical science, there is no way to stop death.

Ultimately, every one of us will die. Spiritual death is separation from God. Because of the sin which entered the world in the time of Adam, we are all dead spiritually. Unless we are born again into a new spiritual life in Christ, we must remain dead. We cannot raise ourselves.

DEATH, SECOND

See HELL.

DE´BIR

1. A king of Eglon who was conquered and slain by Joshua (Jos 10:3,27).

2. A city in the hill country of Judah, also known as Kirjath-sepher and Kirjath-sannah (Jos 15:15,49; Ju 1:11). Joshua took it from the Anakim (Jos 10:38-39; 11:21; 12:13). Caleb offered Achsah, his daughter, to the man who would capture the city. Othniel, Caleb's younger brother, did so and won his niece to wife (Ju 1:13; 3:9).

3. Town in Gad, probably the same as Lodebar (Jos 13:26; 2 Sa 17:27).

4. A place in Judah between Jerusalem and Jericho (Joel 15:7).

DEB´O•RAH *(a bee)*

1. The nurse of Rebekah (Ge 24:59; 35:8).

2. A prophetess, the wife of Lappidoth. She lived in Mount Ephraim where she served as a judge. At his request, she accompanied Barak who defeated Sisera's army (Ju 4:4-14), a victory celebrated in her triumphant song (Ju 5:1-31).

DEBT

There is no mention of commercial debt in the Old Testament. Private debts were frequently contracted, particularly by the poor. Thriftlessness, sickness, and crop failures were perennial causes of debt. Providing surety for friends and

DEBORAH

neighbors was another. The charging of interest on loans to fellow Jews was forbidden (Ex 22:25; Le 25:36; De 23:19). All loans (except to foreigners) were cancelled every seven years (De 15:1-3). In the New Testament debts and loans were regarded as normal factors of social life. Roman law permitted imprisonment for debt (Ma 5:25; 18:30; Lk 12:58).

DEC′A·LOGUE

This word was adopted by the Greeks to designate the Ten Commandments, the laws delivered to Moses in Mount Sinai (Ex 20:1-17; De 5:6-21). See TEN COMMANDMENTS.

DE·CAP′O·LIS *(ten cities)*

A district, containing ten cities, located southeast of Galilee (Ma 4:25; Mk 5:20; 7:31). These were built by the followers of Alexander the Great and consisted of Scythopolis, Damascus, Hippos, Philadelphia, Gadara, Pella, Dion, Gerasa, Kanatha, Raphana.

DE·CIS′ION, VALLEY OF

See JEHOSHAPHAT, VALLEY OF.

DE·CREE′

Sometimes the words thus rendered in English were translated *edict* or *law.* Decrees of the kings of the East were sometimes publicly announced by heralds or criers (1 Sa 11:7; Je 34:8-9; Da 3:4; 5:29; Am 4:5).

DE′DAN

1. A son of Raamah, the son of Cush (Ge 10:7).
2. Son of Jokshan, the son of Abraham and Keturah (Ge 25:3).
3. A territory on the southern border of Edom.

DE′DA·NIM

See DEDANITES.

DE′DAN·ITES

A nomadic Arabian tribe (Is 21:13) descended from Abraham and Keturah through Jokshan (Ge 25:1,3). They are described as merchants (Eze 25:13; 27:15).

DED′I·CA′TION, FEAST OF *(Chanukah, or the Feast of Lights)*

This festival was instituted in 165 B.C. by Judas Maccabaeus to commemorate the purification of the temple and the restoration of worship after the desecration of the temple by Antiochus Epiphanes. It was somewhat of the nature of the feast of tabernacles and continued for eight days. Jesus was present at one of these feasts and spoke to the people (Jo 10:22).

DEEP, THE

The first time this term occurs is in Genesis 1:2, "The earth was without form, and void; and darkness was on the face of the deep. And the Spirit of God was hovering over the waters." People speculate as to the exact meaning of "the deep" in this passage. The simplest explanation is that it refers to the oceans which covered the unformed world. Elsewhere in Scripture, "the deep" is a term for the ocean (Pr 8:28; Jon 2:3; 2 Co 11:25). When God covered the earth with a flood, "the fountains of the great deep were broken up" (Ge 7:11; 8:2; Ps 104:6). Occasionally, in some translations, "the deep" can refer to the abyss, or the "bottomless pit" (Ro 10:7; Lk 8:31; Re 9:1-2,11; 20:1). The word is also used as a simile of the depth of God's judgment, wisdom, and understanding (Ps 36:6; 92:5; Ro 11:33; 1 Co 2:10).

DEER

A clean game animal. Deer were served at the kings table in the days of Solomon (1 Ki 4:23). Many references to deer in the Bible describe these animals as being graceful, agile, and fleet of foot (Is 35:6). As with many Bible animals, it is uncertain exactly which species of deer is meant by the several Hebrew words. Some translations speak of the fallow deer (De 14:5, KJV), others use "roe deer" ("roe buck" NRSV). The words for other deer-like creatures, such as "antelope" and "gazelle" are also used.

DEFER

To delay; postpone (Is 48:8-10).

DEFILE

To make unclean, to foul (Song 5:3; Je 3:1; Eze 37:23; Mk 7:1-23).

DEGREES, SONGS OF

See ASCENTS, SONG OF.

DE·HA′ITES, DE·HA′VITES

After the fall of the Northern Kingdom (722 B.C.) these and other peoples were brought from the East by the Assyrians to resettle Samaria (Ez 4:9).

DE′KER, DE′KAR *(piercing)*

The father of Ben-deker, Solomon's purveyor (1 Ki 4:9).

DEL·AI′AH, DAL·AI′AH *(delivered by Jehovah)*

1. A descendant of Aaron and ancestral head of a course of priests (1 Ch 24:18).

2. One who advised King Jehoiakim not to destroy the roll prepared by Jeremiah (Je 36:12,25).

3. Ancestor of a family of servants (Ez 2:60; Ne 7:62).

4. A son of Elioenai (1 Ch 3:24).

DE·LI′LAH *(languishing, lustful)*

The Philistine woman who lived in the valley of Sorek (Ju 16:4-18). She was paid a large sum of money by Philistine chiefs to induce Samson to disclose to her the secret of his strength.

DELIVERANCES, MIRACULOUS

One of the clearest messages of the Old Testament is that God is a compassionate deliverer who will use His power to help His people. Sennacherib, king of Assyria, discovered this truth about 701 B.C. when he attacked the city of Jerusalem. With his large army and instruments of siege warfare, he felt certain he could prevail over the weaker Judean forces under King Hezekiah. But the Lord intervened on behalf of His people: "The angel of the LORD went out, and killed in the camp of the Assyrians one hundred and eighty-five thousand; and when people arose early in the morning, there were the corpses—all dead" (2 Ki 19:35).

God has the power to deliver, even today, if we will give Him control and let Him work His will in our lives. Here are several other specific cases of God's miraculous deliverance of His people in Old Testament times:

Name	God's Action	Reference
Noah and his family	Delivered from the flood by the ark	Ge 6-8
Lot and his family	Saved from the fiery destruction of Sodom and Gomorrah	Ge 19:29
Nation of Israel	Delivered from Egyptian slavery through the exodus; preserved by miraculous feedings in the wilderness	Ex 12-17

Name	God's Action	Reference
Israelites	Saved from fiery serpents by looking at a bronze serpent on a pole	Nu 21:6-9
David and his army	Saved from capture by Saul's army on numerous occasions	1 Sa 23
Elijah	Fed by the ravens in the wilderness	1 Ki 17:2-6
Three young Hebrew men	Delivered from Nebuchadnezzar's fiery furnace	Da 3:19-30
Daniel	Preserved, unharmed, among the lions	Da 6:1-24

In New Testament times Christian believers were often delivered from grim circumstances through a miraculous display of God's power. Paul and Silas, for example, were beaten and imprisoned as troublemakers because of their preaching in Philippi. While they prayed and sang during the night, the prison was shaken by an earthquake and they were released to continue their work (Ac 16:16-40). God's power to deliver is still available today for those who will exercise faith and seek His will in their lives.

Here are several other specific insurances of God's miraculous deliverance of people of faith in New Testament times:

Name	God's Action	Reference
Gadarene with unclean spirit	Delivered from demon possession by Jesus	Mk 5:1-15
Lazarus	Raised from the dead by Jesus	Jo 11:38-44
Apostles	Freed from prison by an angel	Ac 5:17-20
Dorcas	Raised from the dead by Peter	Ac 9:36-41
Peter	Released from prison by an angel	Ac 12:1-11
Eutychus	Revived by Paul after his fall from a window	Ac 20:1-12
Paul	Delivered from a pressing burden (unnamed) in Asia	2 Co 1:8-11
Paul	Delivered unharmed to the island of Malta after a shipwreck	Ac 28:1

DEL′UGE

See FLOOD, THE.

DE′MAS

A fellow-laborer of Paul (Col 4:14; Phile 24). Unwilling to endure privation, he deserted Paul and went to Thessalonica (2 Ti 4:10).

DE·ME′TRI·US

1. A silversmith at Ephesus whose business of making silver shrines of the goddess, Diana, was threatened by Paul's teachings. Demetrius stirred up a riot, whereupon Paul left Ephesus (Ac 19:24-41).

2. A Christian whom John commends (3 Jo 12).

DE′MON

One of the lower order of spiritual beings who left their "first estate," called *devils* in the Authorized Version (Ma 25:41). Satan is the prince of demons (Ma 9:34; Lk 11:15). There are many demons but one devil. Persons possessed by demons suffered from diseases and were tortured (Lk 4:33; 8:30; Jo 7:20). They are represented as speaking (Mk 1:23-24; 5:7), and as being distinct from those whom they possessed (Ma 8:31). They exhibited unusual knowledge (Mk 1:24). Some Jews believed that demons were the spirits of the sinful dead. See DEVIL.

DEMONIACS

People who are possessed (or oppressed) by demons. The Greek word is literally "demonized" (Ma 4:24). We don't really know exactly what this means, or how it can happen, but apparently a demon can enter a person's body and control and torment that person, at least to some extent. One example of this is the man of the Gadarenes who lived among the tombs. The demons apparently gave him superhuman strength, for he tore apart the chains and shackles with which people attempted to bind him (Mk 5:4). He was tormented by the evil spirits who possessed him, but when he saw Jesus, he ran to worship Him. It is clear that the demons recognized Jesus as the Son of God, and feared him as such (Lk 4:41). They knew that they had to obey Jesus, but they begged Him not to send them to the abyss, a place which they evidently feared greatly. Instead, Jesus allowed them to enter a herd of pigs, and the maddened pigs rushed over the cliff and died (Ma 8:28-34; Mk 5:1-20). Why they wanted to enter the pigs is unknown. Jesus healed many who were afflicted by demons (Lk 6:17-19). More than once Jesus cast out demons that caused muteness, in a clearly illogical argument the Pharisees said He did it by the power of Satan (Ma 9:32-34; 12:22). There is a curious connection mentioned between epilepsy and demonization (Ma 17:15; 9:17-27). Apparently, some demons tormented their hosts by causing convulsions, frothing at the mouth, and attempting to kill the person. When Jesus cast out the demon in the synagogue, it caused a convulsion in the man as it left (Mk 1:24,32).

There is much about demonization that is impossible to explain. The unseen spiritual world is something that we cannot observe and test scientifically, nor should we spend much time trying to learn how the malignant spirits function. In turning our eyes and hearts to Christ there is both safety and power so that we need not fear the dark side of the spiritual realm. Jesus said that after He returned to the Father, the disciples would cast out demons (Mk 16:17-18), and this was fulfilled in the early church. Paul cast the demon out of the girl who told fortunes in Philippi, thus ending her usefulness to her masters (Acts 16:16-18). Enraged at their loss of income, they had Paul and Silas beaten and thrown into prison. As a result of this encounter, the jailer and his entire family were born again.

DEMONIZED

See DEMONIACS.

DEMON POSSESSION

See DEMONIACS.

DEN

The dwelling (either natural or manmade) of lions (Job 37:8; Da 6:7-24; Na 2:12).

DE·NAR′I·US

A Roman silver coin in the time of Christ. A typical denarius of Christ's day bore the image of Emperor Tiberius. It was a popular coin among the Jews and in the KJV it is called "a penny." It was the ordinary pay for a day's labor (Ma 20:2; Mk 12:15; Re 6:6). See MONEY OF THE BIBLE.

DEPRAVITY

Perversion, corruption. The state of unregenerate man.

DEP′U·TY

This is the rendering of several words. An officer appointed by the king (Es 9:1-3) or ruling in the place of a king (1 Ki 22:47). In the Revised Version of the New Testament deputy is more accurately rendered proconsul (Ac 13:7; 18:12; 19:38).

DER′BE

A small town about 35 miles southeast of Lystra in Lycaonia in Asia Minor. After being stoned at Lystra, the home of Timothy, Paul went to Derbe. This was on the first missionary journey (Ac 14:6,20). He passed through it again on the second journey.

DERISION
Ridicule (Ps 2:2-4).

DESCENT INTO HADES
It is unclear exactly what this "descent into Hades" is precisely, but apparently Jesus, before His resurrection, went down into this place. In Peter's sermon at Pentecost, he quotes Psalm 16, saying, "Because you will not leave my soul in Hades, nor will you allow your Holy One to see corruption (Ac 2:27). It could therefore be inferred (since God would not *leave* him in Hades, that He was actually there). Paul says that Jesus descended "into the lower parts of the earth" (Ep 4:9), though exactly what this means is not clear either. First Peter 3:18-20 tells us that Jesus "went and preached to the spirits in prison," apparently speaking of "the dead." We don't really know anything much about the intermediate state, but it seems clear that the popular view of a fiery hell with Satan in charge is far from accurate, and whatever Hades, Sheol or the grave indicate, it is not the lake of fire mentioned in Revelation. See ABRAHAM'S BOSOM, HELL, SHEOL.

DESERT
The rendering of several Hebrew words usually meaning an uncultivated plain or wilderness (Ex 3:1; De 32:10; Lk 15:4). Another word means the plain about the Jordan and Dead Sea (2 Sa 2:29; Eze 47:8), called *Arabah* in the Revised Version. Other Hebrew words denote a waste, desolate place (Ps 78:40; Is 43:19-20; 48:21; Eze 13:4).

DESIRE OF ALL NATIONS
A title of the Messiah (Hag 2:7; Mal 3:1).

DESOLATION, ABOMINATION OF
See ABOMINATION OF DESOLATION.

DESPITE (archaic)
Contempt (Eze 25:6-7).

DESTROYER
God's agent for destroying sinners. By placing the blood of the Passover lamb on their doors, the Israelites could be passed over by the destroyer (Ex 12:23). "The destroyer" brought punishment to the Hebrew people when they complained in the desert as well (1 Co 10:10). The enemies of Israel, who were usually sent from God to chastise His disobedient people, are also referred to as destroyers (Is 49:17; Je 22:7; 50:11).

DESTRUCTION
See ABADDON.

DEU′ EL (known of God)
The father of Eliasaph, of the tribe of Gad (Nu 1:14; 7:42). In Numbers 2:14 he is called Reuel (friend of God).

DEU·TER·ON′ O·MY, BOOK OF
(repetition of the law)

1. The Book of Deuteronomy. Deuteronomy, Moses's "Upper Desert Discourse," consists of a series of farewell messages by Israel's 120 year-old leader. It is addressed to the new generation destined to possess the land of promise—those who survived the forty years of wilderness wandering.

Like Leviticus, Deuteronomy contains a vast amount of legal detail, but its emphasis is on the laymen rather than the priests. Moses reminds the new generation of the importance of obedience if they are to learn from the sad example of their parents.

The Hebrew title of Deuteronomy is *Haddebharim,* "The Words," taken from the opening phrase in 1:1, "These are the words." The parting words of Moses to the new generation are given in oral and written so that they will endure to all generations. Deuteronomy has been called "five-fifths of the Law" since it completes the five books of Moses. The Jewish people have also called it *Mishneh Hattoreh,* "repetition of the Law," which is translated in the Septuagint as *To Deuteronomion Touto,* "this Second Law." Deuteronomy, however, is not a second law but a repetition and expansion of much of the original law given on Mount Sinai. The English title comes from the Greek title *Deuteronomion,* "Second Law." Deuteronomy has also been appropriately called the "Book of Remembrance."

2. The Author of Deuteronomy. The Mosaic authorship of Deuteronomy has been vigorously attacked by critics who claim that

Moses is only the originator of the tradition on which these laws are based. Some critics grant that part of Deuteronomy may have come from Mosaic times through oral tradition. The usual argument is that it was anonymously written not long before 621 B.C. and used by King Josiah to bring about his reform in that year (2 Ki 22-23). There are several reasons why these arguments are not valid.

External Evidence: (1) The Old Testament attributes Deuteronomy and the rest of the Pentateuch to Moses (see Jos 1:7; Ju 3:4; 1 Ki 2:3; 2 Ki 14:6; Ez 3:2; Ne 1:7; Ps 103:7; Da 9:11; Ma 4:4). (2) Evidence from Joshua and 1 Samuel indicates that these laws existed in the form of codified written statutes and exerted an influence on the Israelites in Canaan. (3) Christ quotes it as God's Word in turning back Satan's three temptations (Ma 4:4,7,10), and attributes it directly to Moses (Ma 19:7-9; Mk 7:10; Lk 20:28; Jo 5:45-47). (4) Deuteronomy is cited more than eighty times in seventeen of the twenty-seven New Testament books. These citations support the Mosaic authorship (see Ac 3:22; Ro 10:19). (5) Jewish and Samaritan tradition point to Moses.

Internal Evidences. (1) Deuteronomy includes about forty claims that Moses wrote it. Read Deuteronomy 31:24-26 (see also 1:1-5; 4:44-46; 29:1; 31:9). (2) Deuteronomy fits the time of Moses, not Josiah: Canaan is viewed from the outside; the Canaanite religion is seen as a future menace; it assumes the hearers remember Egypt and the wilderness; Israel is described as living in tents; and there is no evidence of a divided kingdom. (3) A serious problem of misrepresentation and literary forgery would arise if this book were written in the seventh century B.C. (4) Geographical and historical details indicate a firsthand knowledge. (5) Deuteronomy follows the treaty form used in the fifteenth and fourteenth centuries B.C. (6) Moses's obituary in chapter 34 was probably written by Joshua.

3. The Time of Deuteronomy. Like Leviticus, Deuteronomy does not progress historically. It takes place entirely on the plains of Moab due east of Jericho and the Jordan River (1:1; 29:1; Jos 1:2). It covers about one month: combine Deuteronomy 1:3 and 34:8 with Joshua 5:6-12. The book was written at the end of the forty-year period in the wilderness (c. 1405 B.C.) when the new generation was on the verge of entering Canaan. Moses wrote it to encourage the people to believe and obey God in order to receive God's blessings.

4. The Christ of Deuteronomy. The most obvious portrait of Christ is found in 18:15: "The LORD your God will raise up for you a Prophet like me from your midst, from your brethren, Him you shall hear" (see also 18:16-19; Ac 7:37). Moses is a type of Christ in many ways as he is the only biblical figure other than Christ to fill the three offices of prophet (34:10-12), priest (Ex 32:31-35), and king (although Moses was not king, he functioned as ruler of Israel; 33:4-5). Both are in danger of death during childhood; both are saviors, intercessors, and believers; and both are rejected by their brethren. Moses is one of the greatest men who ever lived, combining not just one or two memorable virtues, but many.

5. Keys to Deuteronomy.

Key Word: Covenant—The primary theme of the entire Book of Deuteronomy is the renewal of the covenant. Originally established at Mount Sinai, the covenant is enlarged and renewed on the plains of Moab.

Key Verses: Deuteronomy 10:12-13; 30:19-20—"And now, Israel, what does the LORD your God require of you, but to fear the LORD your God, to walk in all His ways and to love Him, to serve the LORD your God with all your heart and with all your soul, and to keep the commandments of the LORD and His statutes which I command you today for your good?" (10:12-13).

"I call heaven and earth as witnesses today against you, that I have set before you life and death, blessing and cursing, therefore choose life, that both you and your descendants may live; that you may love the LORD your God, that you may obey His voice, and that you may cling to Him, for He is your life and the length of your days; and that you may dwell in the land which the LORD swore to your fathers, to Abraham, Isaac, and Jacob, to give them" (30:19-20).

Key Chapter: Deuteronomy 27—The formal ratification of the covenant occurs in Deuteronomy 27 as Moses, the priests, the Levites, and all of Israel "take heed and listen, O Israel: This day you have become the people of the LORD your God" (27:9).

6. Survey of Deuteronomy. Deuteronomy, in its broadest outline, is the record of the renewal of the Old Covenant given at Mount Sinai. This covenant was reviewed, expanded, and finally ratified in the plains of Moab. Moses accomplishes this primarily through three sermons that move from a retrospective, to an introspective, and finally a prospective look at God's dealings with Israel.

Moses's First Sermon (1:1–4:43). Moses reached into the past to remind the people of two undeniable facts in their history: (1) the moral judgment of God upon Israel's unbelief, and (2) the deliverance and provision of God during times of obedience. The simple lesson is that obedience brings blessing and disobedience brings punishment.

Moses's Second Sermon (4:44–26:19). This moral and legal section is the longest in the book because Israel's future as a nation in Canaan will depend upon a right relationship with God. These chapters review the three categories of the law: (1) *The testimonies (5–11).* These are the moral duties—a restatement and expansion of the Ten Commandments plus an exhortation not to forget God's gracious deliv-

erance. (2) *The statutes (12:1–16:17).* These are the ceremonial duties—sacrifices, tithes, and feasts. (3) *The ordinances (16:18–26:19).* These are the civil (16:18–20:20) and social (21–26) duties—the system of justice, criminal laws, laws of warfare, rules of property, personal and family morality, and social justice.

Moses's Third Sermon (27–34). In these chapters Moses wrote history in advance. He predicted what would befall Israel in the near future (blessings and cursings) and in the distant future (dispersion among the nations and eventual return). Moses listed the terms of the covenant soon to be ratified by the people. Because Moses would not be allowed to enter the land, he appointed Joshua as his successor and delivered a farewell address to the multitude. God Himself buried Moses in an unknown place, perhaps to prevent idolatry. Moses finally entered the promised land when he appeared with Christ on the Mount of Transfiguration (Ma 17:3). The last three verses of the Pentateuch (34:10-12) are an appropriate epitaph for this great man of God.

OUTLINE OF DEUTERONOMY

Part One: Moses' First Sermon: "What God Has Done for Israel" (1:1–4:43)

I. The Preamble of the Covenant (1:1-5)

II. The Review of God's Acts for Israel (1:6–4:43)

A. From Mount Sinai to Kadesh 1:6-18

B. At Kadesh 1:19-46

C. From Kadesh to Moab 2:1-23

D. Conquest of East Jordan 2:24–3:29

E. Transition of Leadership 3:21-29

F. Summary of the Covenant 4:1-43

Part Two: Moses's Second Sermon: "What God Expects of Israel" (4:44–26:19)

I. The Introduction to the Law of God (4:44-49)

II. The Exposition of the Decalogue (5:1–11:32)

A. The Covenant of the Great King 5:1-33

B. The Command to Teach the Law 6:1-25

C. The Command to Conquer Canaan..................................... 7:1-26

D. The Command to Remember the Lord 8:1-20

E. The Commands about Self-Righteousness 9:1–10:11

F. The Commands Regarding Blessings and Cursings 10:12–11:32

III. The Exposition of the Additional Laws (12:1–26:19)

A. The Exposition of the Ceremonial Laws 12:1–16:17

B. The Exposition of the Civil Laws.............................. 16:18–20:20

C. The Exposition of the Social Laws....................................21:1–26:19

Part Three: Moses's Third Sermon: "What God Will Do for Israel" (27:1–34:12)

I. The Ratification of the Covenant in Canaan (27:1–28:68)

A. Erection of the Altar 27:1-8
B. Admonition to Obey the Law 27:9-10
C. Proclamation of the Curses 27:11-26
D. Warnings of the Covenant 28:1-68

II. The Institution of the Palestinian Covenant (29:1–30:20)

A. The Covenant is Based on the Power of God 29:1-9
B. Parties of the Covenant 29:10-15

C. Warnings of the Covenant ... 29:16–30:10
D. Ratification of the Palestinian Covenant 30:11-20

III. The Transition of the Covenant Mediator (31:1–34:12)

A. Moses Charges Joshua and Israel 31:1-13
B. God Charges Israel 31:14-21
C. The Book of the Law is Deposited 31:22-30
D. The Song of Moses 32:1-47
E. The Death of Moses 32:48–34:12

DEVIL

The KJV translation of the Greek *daimon,* and also *diabolos* (slanderer, accuser). The word is used frequently to refer to Satan, the chief of the fallen spirits (Lk 10:18; 2 Pe 2:4; Re 12:7-9). It is generally believed that the sin of pride was what caused him to fall from his former state (1 Ti 3:6). He is the enemy of God and of the divine order (Ma 13:38-39; Re 12:17). He was the tempter of Adam and Eve (Ge 3:1-15; 2 Co 11:3), Jesus (Ma 4:1-11), and man (Jo 13:2; Ac 13:9-10). He is a murderer and liar (Jo 8:44; Re 20:10). Peter represents him as a devouring lion (1 Pe 5:8). He is subtle but can be resisted and put to flight (Ep 4:27; 6:11-16; Jam 4:7). Jesus came to destroy his works (Ge 3:15; 1 Jo 3:8). At Christ's coming he will be bound for 1,000 years (Re 20:2-3). See SATAN, DEMON, also see WORLD, FLESH, DEVIL.

DEW

The dews of Palestine are very heavy, often having the appearance of recent rain. It is very important to the growth of crops because there is little or no rain in the summer. It is used figuratively in the Bible for refreshing heavenly blessings which are silently and invisibly bestowed (De 32:2; 33:13; Ps 110:3; Pr 19:12; Mi 5:7). When dew failed, it was regarded as a judgment (2 Sa 1:21; 1 Ki 17:1; Hag 1:10).

DI′A·DEM

A headdress for both sexes (Job 29:14). In Isaiah 3:23 the rendering in the Authorized Version is *hoods,* in the Revised Version *tur-*

bans. A diadem was worn by kings (Is 62:3). In Zechariah 3:5 it is translated *miter,* a headdress of the high priest. In Isaiah 28:5 a crown is denoted.

DI′AL OF AHAZ

An instrument, set up by Ahaz for the indication of time and called the dial or sundial of Ahaz (2 Ki 20:11; Is 38:8). It was some sort of sun-clock, probably a flight of stairs near an obelisk. The shadow of the obelisk falling upon the steps would indicate the hours or half-hours. God set the shadow back ten steps on the sundial as a sign to Hezekiah that he would indeed be healed and that Jerusalem would be delivered from the hand of Assyria.

DIAMOND

An unusually hard, transparent mineral. "Diamond" is the KJV rendering of a Hebrew word for a precious stone—a treasure of the king of Tyre (Eze 28:13). It was one of the stones in the breastplate of the high priest (Ex 28:18). The precious stone intended was probably an onyx, a variety of silica. A word elsewhere translated *adamant* is rendered *diamond* in Jeremiah 17:1. See ADAMANT, ONYX.

DI·AN′A

The Roman goddess of the moon. According to ancient authorities the image of Diana of the Ephesians was of wood (Ac 19:35). Silver models of it were made by Demetrius and others (Ac 19:24).

DIANA

DI·AS'PO·RA
See DISPERSION.

DIB'LAH, DIB'LATH
A name occurring only in Ezekiel 6:14. The place intended is generally believed to be Riblah, a town in the far north, on Ezekiel's prophetic border of Palestine.

DIB·LA'IM
The father of Gomer, the wife of Hosea (Ho 1:3).

DIB'LATH
See DIBLAH.

DI'BON (wasting away, pining)
Two Old Testament towns:

1. A town east of the Jordan, north of the Arnon. It was taken by the Gadites (Nu 32:3,34) and was rebuilt by them and called Dibon-gad (Nu 33:45-46). It came into the territory of Reuben (Jos 13:9,17). In the time of Isaiah and Jeremiah it was held by Moab (Is 15:2; Je 48:18,22).

2. A town of Judah, the residence of members of that tribe after returning from Babylon, probably the same as Dimonah (Ne 11:25).

DI'BON-GAD
See DIBON.

DIB'RI
Father of Shelomith, a woman whose son was stoned for blasphemy (Le 24:11-14).

DID'A·CHE
A document discussing church practice and doctrine, written between A.D. 50 and 225. It is written in Greek, and while it is not part of the Scriptures, nor does it claim to be, it contains much interesting information and provides insight into the way the early Christians viewed various matters. Many of the teachings of Jesus are recapped, and instructions are given regarding things such as baptism (see BAPTISM) and the proper treatment of traveling teachers: "Therefore, receive anyone who comes and teaches you all these things we have already said. But if the teacher turns and teaches another doctrine, so as to destroy, do not hear him. If he teaches so as to increase righteousness and knowledge of the Lord, receive him as the Lord. But concerning the apostles and prophets, according to the law of the gospel do thus: let every apostle who comes to you be received as the Lord, [if he is a true prophet] he will not stay longer than one day, or two if there is a need. But if he should remain three days, then he is a false prophet. The traveling apostle should take nothing but bread, unless he spends the night; but if he should demand silver [then you know] that he is a false prophet."

DI·DRACH'MA
Two drachmas. A drachma was a Greek coin worth about a day's wage. See MONEY OF THE BIBLE.

DID'Y·MUS (a twin)
See THOMAS.

DIGNITARIES
Literally, "glorious ones" (2 Pe 2:10; Jude 8). Rulers, those who deserve respect (Ex 22:28).

DIGNITIES (archaic)
See DIGNITARIES.

DIK'LAH (palm tree)
A son of Joktan (Ge 10:27; 1 Ch 1:21).

DI'LE·AN
A town of Judah (Jos 15:38).

DILL (Ma 23:23)
An herb used in cooking. Both its aromatic foliage and its seeds are used. Many think that

the word translated "anise" should rather be translated dill.

DIM' NAH

Variant of Rimmon.

DI' MON

A place east of the Dead Sea, probably the same as Dibon (Is 15:9).

DI·MO' NAH

A town near Edom in the south of Judah, perhaps the same as Dibon (Jos 15:22; Ne 11:25).

DI' NAH *(judged, avenged)*

Daughter of Jacob and Leah (Ge 30:21). She was ravished by Shechem. Her brothers, Simeon and Levi, avenged her by slaying all the men of Shechem's city (Ge 34:1-29).

DI' NA·ITES

Assyrian colonists who were settled in Samaria (Ez 4:9).

DIN' HA·BAH

A city of Bela, king of Edom (Ge 36:32; 1 Ch 1:43).

DIN' NER

First main meal of the day (Ma 22:4). See MEALS.

DI·O·NYS' I·US *(of Dionysos)*

An Areopagite, a member of the supreme court of Areopagus of Athens. He was converted to Christianity through Paul's sermon on Mars' Hill (Ac 17:34).

DI·OT' RE·PHES *(Jove-nourished)*

A person in 3 John 9-10 who is represented as being inhospitable, resentful of the writer's authority, and as "loving the preeminence." He is supposed by some to have been a presbyter or deacon.

DI' PHATH

See RIPHATH.

DISCERN

To examine, prove or test; scrutinize (Lk 12:54-56).

DISCERNING OF SPIRITS

A spiritual gift which allows one to recognize whether something comes from God, or is the work of some other spirit (1 Co 12:10; 14:12,26).

DIS·CI' PLE

A pupil or learner. The word is used once in the Old Testament in this sense (Is 8:16) and occurs frequently in the New Testament, meaning followers of a teacher, such as the disciples of Paul or of Christ (Ma 10:24; Lk 14:26-27; Jo 4:1; 6:66), the term is used of the apostles (Ma 5:1; 10:1; 12:1). See TWELVE, THE.

DISCIPLINE

Teaching or training which is designed to strengthen and perfect the character (1 Co 9:27). Systematic training in a certain subject.

DISDAIN

To reject; to despise (Job 30:1).

DIS·EAS' ES

For definitions of specific maladies consult the various entries. The violation of certain physical laws which tend to disease are sins (Pr 2:17-22; 23:29-32). In certain instances persons were struck with disease as divine judgment (Nu 11:33; 12:9-11; De 28:21-22,35; 2 Ki 5:27). At other times, disease is used by God to refine the Christian character and teach reliance on Him (2 Co 12:9). The diseases mentioned in the Bible include: *ague, blains, blindness, bloody flux, boils, botch, canker, consumption, diseased feet, dropsy, dumbness, dysentery, eczema, emerod, epilepsy, fever, gangrene, hemorrhage, insanity, itch, leprosy, lunacy, madness, muteness, palsy, paralysis, scabs, scall, scurf, scurvy, sores, tumors, ulcers, wasting disease, worms.*

DI' SHAN

The youngest son of Seir (Ge 36:21,28; 1 Ch 1:38,42).

DI' SHON *(antelope)*

Two Old Testament men:
1. The fifth son of Seir (Ge 36:21,26; 1 Ch 1:38).
2. The grandson of Seir (Ge 36:25; 1 Ch 1:41).

DISPENSATION

A segment of time and its attendant revelations from God. During a given dispensation, humans are responsible only to live according to the light they have been given (Ep 1:10; Ep 3:2; Col 1:25). Dispensationalist theologians label seven dispensations: Innocence (in the garden of Eden), Conscience (from the expulsion from the garden to the flood), Human Government (from the Noahic covenant to Abraham's day), Promise (from Abraham to Moses), Law (from Moses to Christ), Grace (the church age, from Christ's death and resurrection until His return), Kingdom (after Christ's return and the millennial kingdom is set up on earth). At present, we are in the age of Grace.

DIS·PER'SION

A general term applied to the scattering of the Jews after the exile. Only a remnant of the Jews of the Dispersion returned to Jerusalem (Ez 1:1–3:1). Most of them remained settled in foreign lands and did not return to Palestine. With their synagogues scattered throughout the Roman world, they constituted a most valuable preparation for the coming of Christianity. It was among them that the missionaries did their first work of evangelization. The term, which appears in the Revised Version, is clearly implied in the Authorized Version (Jo 7:35; Ac 2:6-11; Jam 1:1; 1 Pe 1:1).

DISPERSION OF THE NATIONS

After the flood, God instructed the people to disperse themselves, and fill the earth. The people disobeyed, however, and decided instead to try and make themselves into a mighty nation. As they were engaged in building a huge tower, God confused their languages, thereby stopping construction and later forcing the dispersion He had ordered (Ge 10:32; 11:9).

DISSEMBLE (archaic)

To use deceit; to feign (Je 42:19-21)

DISSENSION

Quarreling, discord, disorder (Ac 24:5).

DISSIPATION

Wasteful, dissolute, intemperate living (Ep 5:18; Tit 1:6).

DISTAFF

The staff used for holding a mass of carded wool or heckled flax, ready for spinning (Pr

DISTAFF

31:19). The distaff may be attached to the spinning wheel, or used with a hand spindle.

DIVERS (archaic)

Various, different, unequal, diverse (Pr 20:10).

DIV'I·NA'TION

The art that claims that things of the future may be ascertained by certain signs or be communicated by a form of inspiration. Such signs were seen in the entrails of animals (Eze 21:21) and in the flight of birds. The stars were declared to exercise an influence in the destiny of persons (Is 47:13) and it was believed that the future could be disclosed by summoning the spirits of the dead (1 Sa 28:8). Diviners were found in great numbers among heathen nations (De 18:9-12; 1 Sa 6:2; Eze 21:21; Da 2:2; Ac 16:16). The Israelites were forbidden to consult such soothsayers (Le 20:6,27; De 18:10; Is 2:6; Ze 10:2). Diviners were paid (Nu 22:7, 17-18; Ac 16:16).

DIVINER

One who practices divination, a witch. Divination was forbidden to the Israelites, but occasionally they still resorted to it (2 Ki 17:17; 21:6).

DIVINER'S TEREBINTH TREE

A particular terebinth tree, probably very large, which could be seen from the gates of Shechem (Ju 9:37). Some think that it is the same tree mentioned in Genesis 12:6 and 35:4. The reference to "diviners" probably means that the tree was considered sacred by those who practiced magic, probably in very much the same way that the English oak was considered sacred to the druids.

DIVORCE

Divorce was permitted under Mosaic law when the wife was guilty of some unseemly thing. She was permitted to remarry, but if divorced by the second husband, might not again marry the first (De 24:1-4; Je 3:8). In the New Testament divorce appears to be completely forbidden (Mk 10:11-12; Lk 16:18; 1 Co 7:10,39). In only two passages (Ma 5:32; 19:9) is an allowable exception mentioned. Jesus taught that under God's law a man and his wife were joined together by a permanent compact and that fornication was the only possible grounds for divorce. Furthermore, that if a man abandoned his wife on other grounds and married another, he was guilty of adultery, and the same was true if one married a divorced woman (Ma 5:31-32; 19:3-9; Lk 16:18).

DI′ZA•HAB *(abounding in gold)*

A place associated with the last addresses of Moses (De 1:1).

DOCTOR

In some cases used in the sense of teacher or instructor, rather than in the sense of a medical practitioner (Lk 2:46). See RABBI.

DOCTRINE, PROGRESS OF

One of the remarkable things about the Bible is its vast scope and the varied conditions under which its truths are expressed. History, biography, adventure, poetry, statesmanship, domestic life and its problems, the rise and fall of nations, heroes and heroines, crises both national and individual, good and evil in conflict are all here, giving this marvelous book a range unequaled by anything else. In it all and through it all stands one great design, one central truth.

There is a progressive development in the unfolding of the great doctrines of the Bible. There are truths that were not communicated to Abraham, Jacob, and Moses. We do not find in Genesis or throughout the Pentateuch what we find in the Psalms and the Prophets. This great system was unfolded step-by-step as Israel developed as a nation, and as the time became propitious for each new disclosure. There is a regular, definite procedure as to the time and manner of these revelations. Therefore, we do not find them just anywhere throughout the Scriptures.

1. UNFOLDING THE MESSIANIC IDEA

The Bible is Christo-centric. Take Christ out of the Old Testament, and the whole structure falls apart. One of the most interesting and profitable studies in the Old Testament is to trace the progressive development of the messianic idea. This great doctrine begins with a promise. It is the fall in Eden that necessitates a Saviour by whom the fallen race will be restored to God. In that moment God announces His gracious purpose to redeem the Adamic race. It is this promise of the "seed of the woman" (Ge 3:15), that became the germ of the whole biblical system, which we see unfolding from stage to stage.

(1) *The first period extends from the fall to the flood.* In Seth the historical messianic line is chosen, and it proceeds for centuries through the individuals of that line—Seth, Enos, Cainan, Mahalaleel, Jared, Enoch, Methuselah, Lamech, Noah—to the second great crisis in the history of the race, the flood.

(2) *The second period extends from Noah and the flood to Abraham in the Shemitic line.* The great races of the world take their rise in the family of Noah. The line is to proceed through one of the great divisions of the human race, and it must be narrowed down to one branch of that division. There were several Shemitic races; but at this point the Bible fastens our attention upon one branch of Shem, that of Arphaxad, for the purpose of indicating the national stage in messianic unfolding. It leads to Abraham, who was in the ninth generation after Shem.

(3) *The third period is the Patriarchal, from Abraham to Jacob.* It is a family history. The calling of Abraham is a remarkable exemplification of faith. In him we are to have the great example of justification by faith. It is by faith that the saving work of Christ is to be received by a lost world. A messianic nation means a messianic seed, and this is promised to Abraham. It means a national home, and this is a promise of the covenant. The significance of it all is given in the statement that it is for the spiritual blessing of the world. It is the second definite announcement of the coming Redeemer: the first in Eden, the second at the genesis of the nation that is to bring Him forth.

(4) *The fourth period is the Tribal.* The line must run through one branch of the nation. The nation is to consist of twelve tribes, of which Judah is chosen. This is a new unfolding, for the line is thus narrowed down to the tribe which is to bring forth the Messiah, the promised seed of the woman. There will be no more disclosures of this historical development for several

centuries. It was for Jacob to declare, by divine direction, which of the tribes should be selected; this he did, in his dying words. At the proper historical moment the next great stage will be given.

(5) *The fifth period is the Institutional Unfolding.* The messianic nation must live under messianic institutions, divinely communicated at the beginning of their national career. Of these institutions, two in particular typify the office work of the coming Messiah—priesthood and sacrifice. In these institutions the nation is grounded and by their faith as it was expressed in the fulfillment of the divine prototype.

(6) *The sixth period is that of the royal messianic family.* The line, narrowed to the tribe, must be narrowed again to the family. This is announced in the Book of Ruth, in the time of the judges, thus introducing the family of Jesse and David, the Lord's anointed. Here is the final stage in this historical development. We now know the family of the Messiah. It will be a thousand years before it will bring forth Him who is called the Son of David; and, during that time, the chosen nation will pass through the periods of the Monarchy, the Dual Kingdom, the Captivity, and the postexilic days after the return to Jerusalem.

(7) *The Prophetical Announcements.* These were made during the time of the divided kingdom and the 100 years after the exile, and at a still earlier period that brought forth the messianic Psalms. In these Scriptures we have a marvelous unfolding of the person and work of the coming Messiah. They tell us definitely of His coming—born of a virgin, in the city of Bethlehem—and actually give the time of His coming. They tell us of His residence in Palestine, of His ministrations, His betrayal, crucifixion, His words on the cross, and other circumstances of His death. They inform us of His resurrection and ascension, His second coming, and His gracious sovereignty over the whole world.

We see from these seven points how the great messianic doctrines have been unfolded from stage to stage in their progressive revelation, becoming clearer, fuller, and more specific at every step. They began with a promise back in the dim age of Eden and developed from age to age until every vital fact of the Messiah and His office work was made known centuries before His actual appearance.

2. THE DOCTRINE OF IMMORTALITY

In this brief statement it is impossible to take up all the doctrines and show their progressive development. A few of these will set forth sufficiently the progress of doctrine in the Bible. One of the most interesting examples is that of the Doctrine of Immortality.

The student of the Bible soon discovers that *the Old Testament has very little to say about this doctrine,* and that fact may have caused some perplexity. Such importance is attached to this doctrine that the question arises, "Why is it not more explicitly set forth in the Old Testament?" There are a few intimations and a few direct statements of this doctrine. One of the latter is David's statement after the death of his son: "I shall go to him, but he shall not return to me" (2 Sa 12:23).

The ancient religions, especially that of Egypt, have much to say about the future life. In their conception it is a very well-defined doctrine. It is surprising to many people that other systems should contain so much along this line, and that the Old Testament should be so silent in regard to life after death. They think it should be the other way around. This leads us to a very important conclusion.

We have the right to believe that, *if the Bible were a man-made book, the Old Testament would set forth this doctrine as distinctly as do these other religions.* Because this is peculiar to such religions, there is no reason for supposing that the Jewish religion would be an exception to the rule. The Jews' acquaintance with the other religions would lead them to formulate their own theory of immortality, and their religious interests would be an added inducement to do so.

The Pharisees, one of the leading religious parties of the Jews, had a doctrine of immortality. It was an important point of distinction between them and the Sadducees, who did not believe in a future life. Why, then, do we not find this doctrine in the Jewish Scriptures? If the Bible were a human production, speculations on immortality would have abounded as truly as they do in the other religions; the Bible is given added significance by the fact that they do not. This shows the difference between the Bible and other systems in all other points. If the Doctrine of Immortality were stated comprehensively, we could account for it on the ground that this doctrine is found in most religions. Because this is true, it becomes necessary to explain why it does not appear in any completeness in the Old Testament. We would be at a loss to explain satisfactorily its absence as a human product; but, as a divinely inspired book, the reason is obvious. Only God is immortal and humanity is shown in all its weaknesses, including mortality. There is no attempt to glorify the human authors.

In the progress of doctrine, the Old Testament was not the place for unfolding this great truth. The conditions were not present to make possible a statement of this doctrine in its fullness and in connection with other doctrines that belong to New Testament teachings.

We may go still further and say that *even Christ did not formulate the doctrine as completely as it was done later.* It was not His design to do so. He said much about eternal life and life after death, as well as some things about the resurrection and the believer's heavenly home. He also discussed the destiny of the unrepentant sinner. But He said less about the time and nature of the resurrection. Therefore, it would be impossible to gather from the four Gospels anything that would enable us to formulate completely a doctrine on these points; Paul's statements are much more comprehensive.

It is no more strange that our Lord should not formulate this doctrine in detail than that He should leave for others the formulation of other doctrines in the Christian system, after the advent of the Holy Spirit. He knew that the time had not come for these divine revelations. The Apostle Paul could set forth in greater fullness the doctrine of the resurrection, because his teaching could have as its foundation the resurrection of Jesus. Paul can and does show that man's resurrected body will partake of the glory of Christ's resurrected body. His statement in 1 Corinthians 15 treats the subject so thoroughly that it stands as a well-defined doctrine, systematically presented.

In addition, Paul also presents clearly the doctrine of the translation of the living church and the resurrection of the saints at the second coming of Christ (1 Th 4:14-17). John, in the Book of the Revelation, goes further in setting forth the two resurrections and the significance of each. Thus we see that, at the very close of the Bible, this doctrine in its relation to that of

the future life is made clear and distinctive and more specific than in any other portion of the Scriptures. *It was left to these two apostles, Paul and John, to systematically formulate this doctrine.*

3. THE HOLY SPIRIT AND HIS WORK

Not until we come to the Prophets do we have clear intimations of the personality and operations of the third person of the Trinity, the Holy Spirit. Prior to that time, God is represented under various names. His natural and moral attributes are shown. The Messiah appears everywhere in the Old Testament, as its central fact. But not until we come to the more particular unfolding of the Messiah's mission in the Prophets does the Holy Spirit definitely appear in the Old Testament—that, too, in connection with Messiah's work. The advent and effusion of the Spirit is declared by Joel (2:28-32). It was this, and not Pentecost, that Joel predicted; but it was at Pentecost that the Spirit came. Any outpouring of the Holy Spirit would be in fulfillment of Joel's prophecy.

We can now understand why the New Testament, with its full announcement of the Holy Spirit and His work, should unfold so fully the doctrines of Regeneration, Justification, Adoption, and Sanctification. These are the work of the Spirit. It is in the dispensation of the Spirit that these can be made known and become a part of the Christian system. The same is true of those other functions of the third person of the Godhead in which He teaches, directs, illumines, quickens, and performs other functions in His divine operations.

DO'DAI

See DODO.

DO'DA·NIM, RO'DA·NIM

A tribe descended from Javan (Ge 10:4; 1 Ch 1:7).

DO'DA·VAH

A man of Mareshah, the father of Eliezer (2 Ch 20:37).

DO'DO *(beloved)*

Three Old Testament men:

1. The father of Puah and grandfather of Tola (Ju 10:1).

2. An Ahohite, father of Eleazar (2 Sa 23:9), probably the same as Dodai (1 Ch 27:4).

3. Father of Elhanan (2 Sa 23:24; 1 Ch 11:26).

DOE

A female deer (Pr 5:19, RV). See DEER.

DO'EG *(timid)*

An Edomite, the chief of Saul's herdsmen. He was at Nob when David fled there from Saul (1 Sa 21:7; Ps 52, title). He reported to Saul that Ahimelech, the priest, had befriended David. On orders from King Saul, Doeg slew Ahimelech, the other priests associated with him, and all the inhabitants of Nob (1 Sa 22:7-23).

DOG

The dog of Palestine prowled about the streets, feeding upon whatever it could find (Ex 22:31; Ps 59:6,14). Sometimes they ate dead bodies (1 Ki 14:11; 16:4; 2 Ki 9:35-36), and packs of dogs were known to attack people (Ps 22:16,20). Dogs were used to protect flocks (Job 30:1) and were sometimes domesticated (Mk 7:28; Lk 16:21). To call a person a dog was an insult (De 23:18; 1 Sa 17:43; 2 Ki 8:13; Pr 26:11; 2 Pe 2:22).

DOLEFUL

Gloomy, mournful, depressing (Is 13:21 KJV). Elsewhere these "doleful creatures" are translated as "wild beasts of the desert" (NKJV).

DONKEY

See ASS.

DOOR

The entrance to a tent or building (Ge 18:1; Eze 47:1). Jesus described Himself as the Door, the only opening through which one can reach God (Jo 10:9).

DOORKEEPER

One who watches over a door or gate, opening and shutting it for people, deciding who may or may not come into a house. See PORTER.

DOORPOSTS

The frame of a door, particularly the side pieces. The Israelites spread the blood of their Passover lambs on their doorposts and lintels as a sign that they belonged to God (Ex 12:7). Later, God instructed them to write on their doorposts the law of God, so that they would see it every day and never forget it (De 6:9; 11:20).

DOPH'KAH

One of the stations of the Israelites on their way to Sinai (Nu 33:12-13).

DOR *(dwelling)*

A town of the Canaanites on the Mediterranean a few miles north of Caesarea (Jos 11:2). Joshua defeated its king (Jos 12:23).

DOR'CAS *(gazelle)*

A charitable Christian woman of Joppa, also called Tabitha, who gave much of her time making garments for the needy. Through the prayer of Peter, she was raised from the dead, a fact which caused many to accept Christianity (Ac 9:36-43).

DOT

The smallest mark with the pen. See TITTLE.

DOTH (archaic)

Third person singular of "to do" (Ma 6:19-20).

DO'THA·IM

See DOTHAN.

DO'THAN *(wells)*

An ancient town ten miles north of Samaria on the highway which led through Palestine from Babylonia (Ge 37:17; 2 Ki 6:13). It was here that Joseph was cast into a pit (Ge 37:17-28).

DOUBT

Doubt may be defined as an uncertainty of belief or lack of confidence in something. Applied to the Christian life, doubt refers to the unbelief in God and His word that Christians occasionally exhibit. It is possible that in a moment of infirmity a Christian may doubt the existence of God in spite of the fact that it is not reasonable for a person to disbelieve this obvious truth (Ps 14:1). A Christian is more likely to doubt his salvation after sinning or after a spiritual defeat. A misunderstanding of such verses as 1 John 3:9 contributes to this doubt: "Whoever has been born of God does not sin." It is crucial to note that this verse speaks of a lifestyle of sin, not instances of sin.

A Christian may also doubt God's sovereignty or His goodness. In such circumstances as sickness, suffering, injustice, opposition, economic problems, family problems, national calamity, or apparently unanswered prayer, a Christian may be tempted to doubt the goodness of God. One must remember that it is not always possible to discern God's good hand in the affairs of life. The person of faith believes God even when circumstances appear to the contrary.

All doubt may be traced ultimately to unbelief in the Word of God, which affirms beyond question the existence and character of God. To regard doubt as the sin of unbelief and then confess it to God as sin is therefore the first step toward conquering it.

One of the most potent sources of doubt is introduced in the early chapters of Genesis. It is Satan himself who causes Eve to doubt God by questioning His Word: "Has God indeed said, 'You shall not eat of every tree of the garden'?" (Ge 3:1). Satan even tries to get the long-suffering Job to curse God (Job 1:11). Satan is said to be seeking to devour Christians (1 Pe 5:8). This statement must not be taken literally, but means that Satan wants to devour the Christian's commitment to God and testimony before others. One way he does this is by introducing doubt into the mind.

The world system is another source of doubt. Since it has its own set of values and objectives that are opposed to God, it also has its own worldly wisdom (1 Co 2:6). This wisdom stands in direct opposition to the wisdom of God taught by the Holy Spirit (1 Co 2:13). It is clearly revealed, for example, in the opposition of the evolutionary theory to the truth of the creation of man (1 Ti 6:20).

Probably the greatest source of doubt Christians face is simply their own spiritual immaturity. James traces doubting in prayer to double-mindedness and instability (Jam 1:8). Paul explains that when Christians doubt sound doctrine, it is because they are children in the faith and thus are easily deceived (Ep 4:14). Conquering this kind of doubt demands a growing obedient relationship with God.

The cure for doubt depends to some extent on the thing doubted. However, the real problem is not in the object doubted but in the subject who doubts. Therefore, the following steps should be taken by the doubting Christian:

a. Confess the doubt to God as sin. Doubt is basically unbelief in God and His Word and is therefore sin (Ro 14:23; He 11:6). God has promised to hear our confessions of even the darkest unbelief.

b. Study the evidence for the Christian faith. Christians have nothing to fear by looking into the facts from any source of knowledge. The greatest evidence for the validity of Christianity, the resurrection of Christ, is attested by many proofs. Among these are the empty tomb, post-resurrection appearances, and transformed disciples. Since the resurrection is fact, it verifies everything the Bible says.

c. Make certain of your salvation. Paul exhorts Christians to examine themselves to make sure they are Christians (2 Co 13:5). So did the author of Hebrews (He 6:1-9). Salvation from sin is by simple trust in Jesus Christ. Until you are assured of your salvation you will be troubled by enormous doubts.

d. Faithfully study the Word of God. "Faith comes by hearing, and hearing by the word of God" (Ro 10:17). Through study and application of the Bible, our faith is strengthened and matured. Most especially, we must master the doctrines or basic teachings of the Bible if we are to be stable, mature Christians (1 Ti 4:13; 2 Ti 3:16; Tit 2:1,10).

e. Pray. The surest way to face doubts when they come is to have an extensive past history of answered prayer. The more a Christian prays with faith, the more that Christian sees God answer prayer; the more a person sees God answer prayer, the stronger that person's faith becomes while the doubt becomes less.

DOUGH

See BREAD.

DOVE

A bird frequently mentioned in the Scriptures, many varieties of which (including the turtledove) were native to Palestine. Turtledoves and pigeons might be offered in sacrifice (Le 1:14; Lk 2:24). Rocks and valleys served them as nesting places (Je 48:28). The plumage of doves was strikingly beautiful (Ps 68:13). Their eyes were like those of lovers (Song 1:15; 4:1). Other characteristics include their swift flight, their mournful cooing, their gentleness, harmlessness, and innocence. The dove is a symbol of the Holy Spirit (Lk 3:22).

DOVE'S DUNG

When the people of Samaria were under siege and experiencing famine, 2 Kings 6:25 says that "one-fourth of a kab of dove droppings [sold] for five shekels of silver." No one knows for sure whether this was literally the manure of doves or pigeons, or some kind of plant or seed. NIV translates it "seed pods," REB says "locust beans." The term "dove's dung" may have been a "slang" term for some kind of bean or seed, a heap of which could be seen as looking rather like bird droppings.

DOW'RY

It was the custom among the Hebrews for the bridegroom or his father to pay a sum of money as a dowry to the father of the bride (Ge 29:15-20; Ex 22:17; 1 Sa 18:25). The average amount of dowry was apparently fifty shekels (De 22:29). The bride's father might also give the bride a gift (Jos 15:19; 1 Ki 9:16).

DOXOLOGY

Literally, "words of praise." The angel's praise of God on the night Christ was born is a good example of a doxology: "Glory to God in the Highest, and on earth peace, good will toward men!" (Lk 2:14). David's prayer of thanksgiving at the end of his life is another beautiful doxology (1 Ch 29:11), and the Book of Psalms contains many more (Ps 8:1; 41:14; 72:18-19; 89:52; 106:48; 150).

DRACH'MA

A Greek coin worth one day's wage (Lk 15:8-9). See MONEY OF THE BIBLE.

DRAGNET

A fishing net. It is dragged along the bottom of a stream or lake to gather up fish and trap them (Hab 1:15-16; Ma 13:47).

DRAGNET, PARABLE OF

(Ma 13:47-50).

DRAG'ON

Rendering in Authorized Version of different Greek and Hebrew words for various land and water animals. It frequently refers to a howling desert animal such as the wolf and is translated *jackal* in the Revised Version (Job 30:29; Ps 44:19; Is 13:22; 34:13, 35:7; Je 10:22; 49:33). Pharaoh (Eze 29:3) and Nebuchadnezzar (Je 51:34) are both called "dragons" or "monsters" to illustrate their characters and actions. In the New Testament the Greek *drakon* is applied to Satan (Re 12:3-4,7,9,13,16-17; 20:2).

DRAGON, BEL AND THE

See APOCRYPHA.

DRAG'ON'S WELL

A well near Jerusalem, possibly the same as En-rogel southeast of the city (Ne 2:13).

DRAM

See DARIC.

DRAUGHT (archaic)

A catch of fish (Lk 5:4,9) or a container or place of elimination (2 Ki 10:27; Ma 15:17; Mk 7:19).

DREAM

A series of images, thoughts, or emotions occurring during sleep. Throughout the Bible significance is attached to dreams (Ge 37:6,9; Ju 7:13; Da 2:28; 7:1; Ma 1:20; 2:12-13,19). They were not infrequently regarded as genuine communications from God (Job 33:14-17; Je 23:28). There are warnings against deception by false dreamers and their lying dreams (Je 23:25,32; Ze 10:2). The interpretation of dreams belongs to God (Ge 40:8).

In New Testament times, God often used dreams (when a person was asleep) and visions (when a person was awake) to make His will known. The apostle John, exiled on the Isle of Patmos, received a series of seven visions from God, which he faithfully recorded for future generations in the Book of Revelation. Dreams and visions were also prominently associated with the birth of Jesus and the conversion and ministry of the apostle Paul.

Does God still speak today through visions and dreams? Some scholars believe He does; while others insist there is no need for such revelation today, since God communicates with all believers directly through His Holy Spirit.

Other significant dreams and visions in the New Testament include the following:

DREAMS		
Personality	Message of Dream	Reference
Joseph	Three separate dreams: a. Assured of Mary's purity b. Warned to flee to Egypt c. Told to return to Nazareth	Ma 1:20 Ma 2:13 Ma 2:19-23
Wise Men	Warned of Herod's plot against the baby Jesus	Ma 2:12

VISIONS		
Personality	Message of Vision	Reference
Paul	Converted to Christianity in a blinding vision of Christ on the Damascus road	Ac 9:3-9
Ananias	Instructed to minister to Saul in Damascus	Ac 9:10-13
Cornelius	Instructed to ask Peter to come to Joppa	Ac 10:3-6
Peter	Told to eat unclean animals—a message to accept the Gentiles	Ac 10:9-18, 28
Paul	Beckoned to do missionary work in the province of Macedonia	Ac 16:9
Paul	Assured of God's presence in Corinth	Ac 18:9-10
Paul	Promised God's presence during his trip to Rome	Ac 23:11
Paul	Viewed the glories of the third heaven	2 Co 12:1-4

DREGS

Sediment (Is 51:17).

DRESS

See CLOTHING.

DRINK

The chief drinks of the Hebrews were wine and water. Milk was commonly served with meals (Ge 18:8; De 32:14; Ju 4:19; 5:25). Light beverages were probably made from barley and water and fig cakes and water. Diluted vinegar and sour wine was much used by the poorer classes.

DRINK OF′FER·ING

An oblation (Le 23:13). See OFFERINGS.

DRINK, STRONG

Grain or fruit that has been fermented to produce alcohol. The priests were forbidden from drinking intoxicating beverages before they entered the tent of meeting (Le 10:9). Proverbs warns us to be careful of strong drink lest it make us forget the law (Pr 31:4). Abstaining from strong drink is often a sign of being set apart for the Lord. The Lord kept the Israelites in the wilderness, not allowing their clothing to wear out, or their shoes. During the whole forty years they had no bread or wine, so that they would know that the Lord is God. (De 29:6). The Nazirite vow included abstaining from alcohol (Nu 6:3; Ju 13:4,7,14). John the Baptist was also ordered not to drink strong drink (Lk 1:15). Eli thought Hannah was drunk as she poured out her heart to God, and urged her to give up alcohol (1 Sa 1:15). Isaiah pronounced woe to drunkards (Is 5:11), and he gives a nauseating description of people who have erred through wine; they err in vision and stumble in judgment, vomiting over everything (Is 28:7). At the same time, drinking wine or strong drink is not completely forbidden. We must be aware of the pitfalls and dangers that it presents, particularly the sin of allowing it to become a comfort for life, rather than relying upon God. Using alcohol to forget is what leads to drunkenness and sin. See DRUNKENNESS.

DRIVER

Slave driver, overseer.

DROM′E·DAR′Y

The one-hump camel. The word in Is 60:6; Je 2:23 indicates a swift camel but in 1 Kings 4:28; Esther 8:10 is probably a horse.

DROP′SY

A disease occasioned by an abnormal accumulation of watery substance in some cavity of the body (Lk 14:2).

DROSS

The impurities which are skimmed off the top of molten precious metal, such as gold or silver (Is 1:22-25).

DROUGHT

A lack of moisture, especially such as is needed for growing crops and watering cattle.

Between May and October there is practically no rain in Palestine, hence the great value of the excessively heavy dews. Mention is made of the drought by day and of summer (Ge 31:40; Ps 32:4). It makes the heavens like brass and the earth like iron (De 28:23). See FAMINE.

DROVE (archaic)

Flock; company (Ge 32:15-16).

DRUNK′ EN·NESS

The state characterized by being drunk or intoxicated. Its earliest biblical mention is in connection with Noah (Ge 9:21). Warnings against strong drink are frequent in the Bible (Le 10:9; Pr 23:29-32). Drunkenness is a reproach (Ro 13:13; Ga 5:21; Ep 5:18; 1 Th 5:7). It is represented as a vice to which the wealthy were particularly addicted (Da 5:1-4). Drunkards are to be excluded from Christian fellowship and from the kingdom of heaven (1 Co 5:11; 6:10).

DRU·SIL′ LA

The youngest daughter of Herod Agrippa I, and Cypros his wife. She was to become the wife of a certain Epiphanes on the condition that he embraced Judaism. He finally rejected the proposal and the marriage did not occur. When Azizus, king of Emesa, accepted the condition, she became his wife. When Felix, procurator of Judea, became passionately fond of her, Drusilla left her husband and, in defiance of Jewish law, married the foreigner and idolater. It was before Felix and Drusilla that Paul spoke (Ac 24:24-25).

DUKE (archaic)

The head of a family or tribe (Ge 36:15).

DUL′ CI·MER

A musical instrument, generally believed to have been a form of bagpipe (Da 3:5,10,15).

DU′ MAH *(silence)*

1. A son of Ishmael (Ge 25:14; 1 Ch 1:30).

2. A town in Judah about eight miles southwest of Hebron (Jos 15:52).

3. A figurative designation of Edom (Is 21:11).

DUMBNESS

The inability to speak, muteness.

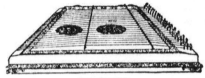

DULCIMER

DUMB SPIRIT

An evil spirit which prevents the person it is oppressing from speaking. See DEMONIACS.

DUNG

Manure, the excrement of animals (Is 25:10; 5:25). It is valuable in agricultural applications as a fertilizer.

DUNGEON

See PRISON.

DUNG GATE

A gate southwest of the temple (Ne 3:13).

DUNG HILL

Manure pile, refuse heap (Is 25:10).

DUNG PORT

See DUNG GATE.

DU′ RA

A plain in Babylon where the image of Nebuchadnezzar was set up (Da 3:1).

DURST (archaic)

Past tense of "to dare" (Lk 20:37-40).

DUST

In countries having extended periods of drought the soil works into the form of dust which is carried by the winds as heavy dust storms. The Israelites were told that if they forsook Jehovah, a storm of dust and ashes should descend upon them (De 28:24). Covering the head with dust was an expression of deep grief (Jos 7:6) and sitting in the dust denoted degradation (Is 47:1). To "lick the dust" expressed humiliating submission (Ps 72:9).

DUTY

Proper behavior, obligatory conduct. The whole duty of man is to fear God and keep His commandments (Ec 12:13), these commandments are listed in Exodus 20:1-17. Jesus listed the two greatest commandments as "love the Lord your God with all your heart, with all your soul, and with all your mind," and "love your neighbor as yourself" (Ma 22:37,39).

DWELLING

Living, abiding (Ge 25:27; 2 Sa 7:1; 1 Ki 8:30; Ps 90:1).

DYS′EN·TER·Y

An inflammation and ulceration of the lower part of the intestines attended by fever (Ac 28:7-8).

E

EA′GLE

One of the unclean birds (Le 11:13). Eagles were admired for their beauty and majestic flight. They can fly swiftly (2 Sa 1:23), but are also remarkable for their ability to glide for hours on the air currents without apparently moving their wings at all (Is 40:31). Eagles build nests on high inaccessible crags, or in tall trees, returning every year to the same nest to lay from one to four eggs. Typically, both parents care for the young. It taught its young to fly by forcing them out of the nest. Scripture speaks of the eagle carrying its young on its wings (Ex 19:4-5; De 32:11). People dispute the accuracy of this statement; ornithology has not observed this happening. However, not everything is known about the habits of the animal kingdom. The reference may simply be to the strength of an eagle's flight, saying that God bears us up as easily and powerfully as an eagle. There was an ancient belief that after molting, the eagle renews its youth and strength (Ps 103:5). Eagles do, in fact, live an unusually long time—20 to 30 years in the wild. The word "eagle" has historically been loosely applied to any large raptor, and specifically to a number of birds of the same family as hawks and old world vultures. The most famous is the golden eagle, once prized as a hunting bird for kings.

EAGLE OWL

One of the largest birds, also called the great owl. The term "eagle owl" probably comes from the practice of loosely applying the name "eagle" to any large raptor.

EAR

At consecration blood was put on the right ear of the priest (Le 8:23) and also on the right ear of a leper who was to be cleansed (Le 14:14). As a mark of perpetual servitude, holes were bored in the ears (Ex 21:6; De 15:17).

EARING (archaic)

Plowing; tilling the ground (Ge 45:6).

EARNEST

A down payment, a pledge or guarantee that the buyer is in earnest, and will return with the full amount. The Holy Spirit has been given to us as the guarantee of Christ's return (2 Co 1:22; 5:5; Ep 1:14)

EAR′RING

Earrings were worn by women, men, and children (Ex 32:2; Eze 16:12). Aaron used earrings for making the molten calf (Ex 32:2-4).

EARTH

The world in which we live as distinguished from the heavens (Ge 1:1); dry land (Ge 1:10); and the inhabitants of the world (Ge 11:1). Mention is made of the foundations of the earth (Ps 102:25; 104:5-9; Is 48:13). The earth is represented as supported by pillars erected by God (1 Sa 2:8; Job 9:6; Ps 75:3).

EARTH, ENDS OF THE

The extent of the known world; the whole earth omitting no place. The term is used to describe the extent of God's judgment (1 Sa 2:10), His knowledge (Job 28:24), ruling authority (Ps 59:13), and creative power (Is 40:28). God has promised to gather His people Israel from the ends of the earth (Je 31:8). Jesus has commissioned believers to spread the gospel to the ends of the earth (Ac 1:8), in order to fulfill God's promise to Abraham that through him all the nations of the earth would be blessed (Ge 12:3; Ga 3:8).

EARTH′EN·WARE

See POTTERY.

EARTH, FOUR CORNERS OF THE

The four compass points. A figurative way of speaking of the farthest portions of the world (Is 11:12; Re 7:1).

EARTH, NEW

Because of sin, the whole creation is cursed (Ge 3:17-19) and is groaning, waiting for the day of redemption (Ro 8:22). After Christ returns, and the final judgment has occurred, God will create a new heaven and a new earth (Re 21–22). John said, "And I saw a new heaven and a new earth, for the first heaven and the first earth had passed away . . . And there shall be no more curse, but the throne of God and of the Lamb shall be in it, and His servants shall serve Him" (Re 21:1; 22:3).

EARTH, PILLARS OF THE

A figurative description of the world, portraying it as setting upon strong pillars. The term is used as a description of God's power (1 Sa 2:8), also translated "foundations of the earth" (Ps 18:15; Je 31:37; Mi 6:2). God Himself is the true foundation of the whole creation.

EARTH′ QUAKE

A shaking of the earth caused by subterraneous forces. A remarkable instance in Palestine occurred in the time of Uzziah (Am 1:1; Ze 14:5) which Josephus interpreted as an expression of divine judgment upon Uzziah (2 Ch 26:16). During severe earthquakes mountains may appear to rock to and fro and their very foundations be shaken (Ps 18:7; Je 4:24). In the seventh year of Herod the Great an earthquake destroyed much cattle and about 10,000 people. At the time of the crucifixion of Jesus there was an earthquake accompanied with darkness (Ma 27:45, 51-54). Another earthquake occurred at the time of the resurrection (Ma 28:2). Philippi was shaken by an earthquake (Ac 16:26).

EARTH, VAULTED

A description of the sky, perhaps indicating that the ancient Hebrews thought of it as a solid "vault" over the earth (Am 9:6, NRSV, NASB).

EAST, CHIL′ DREN OF THE

Tribes of the east country on the border of Ammon and Moab (Eze 25:4,10), the region extending north to Haran, and south into Arabia.

EAST COUN′ TRY

The region east of Palestine (Ze 8:7), in particular the Syrian and Arabian deserts (Ge 25:6).

EAST′ ER

The Christian festival in celebration of the resurrection of Jesus. Its annual date corresponds roughly to the Jewish Passover. The only appearance of the name in the Authorized Version (Ac 12:4) is more correctly rendered *Passover* in the Revised Version. Easter is a movable feast, falling on the Sunday after the first full moon following the vernal equinox.

EASTERN SEA

The Dead Sea (Eze 47:18).

EAST GATE

See GATES OF JERUSALEM AND THE TEMPLE.

EAST WIND

A hot and sultry wind, coming over the Arabian Desert (Ho 13:15), which affected vines and vegetation in Palestine (Eze 17:6-10; 19:10-12) and withered corn in Egypt (Ge 41:23,27).

E′ BAL

1. A son of Shobal and descendant of Seir (Ge 36:23; 1 Ch 1:40).

2. The same as Obal (Ge 10:28; 1 Ch 1:22).

3. A mountain on the north side of the valley that separates it from Gerizim (De 27:12-14). Under Joshua some of the Israelites pronounced curses while standing upon Ebal, while the others pronounced blessings as they stood upon Gerizim (De 11:29; 27:9-26; Jos 8:30-35).

E′ BED *(servant)*

1. Father of Gaal (Ju 9:28,30).

2. Son of Jonathan and head of the descendants of Adin who returned from Babylon with the expedition of Ezra (Ez 8:6).

E′ BED-MEL′ ECH *(servant of the king)*

An Ethiopian eunuch of King Zedekiah who drew Jeremiah out of the dungeon (Je 38:7-13; 39:15-18).

EB′ EN•E′ ZER *(stone of help)*

A stone set up by Samuel to commemorate the Lord's deliverance of the Israelites from the Philistines. This was near Mizpah (1 Sa 7:10,12). At this point, twenty years before, the Israelites had been defeated by the Philistines (1 Sa 4:1).

E′ BER, HE′ BER *(the region beyond)*

1. A descendant of Arphaxad, son of Shem (Ge 10:22,24) and progenitor of the Hebrews (Ge 11:16-26), the Joktanide Arabs (Ge 10:25-30), and the Aramaean tribes descended from Nahor (Ge 11:29; 22:20-24).

2. A priest in the days of Joiakim (Ne 12:20).

3. A Gadite chief (1 Ch 5:13).

4. Son of Elpaal (1 Ch 8:12).

E′ BEZ

See ABEZ.

E·BI′ A·SAPH

See ABIASAPH.

EB′ ON·Y

A hard, heavy, black wood. An article of commerce in the markets of Tyre, it was brought there for trade purposes, probably from India or Ceylon (Eze 27:15).

E′ BRON

A town on the border of Asher (Jos 19:28), perhaps the same as Abdon. See HEBRON.

EBRO′ NAH

See ABRONAH.

EC·BAT′ A·NA

See ACHMETHA.

ECCE HOMO *(Latin)*

Pilate's words in John 19:5, "Behold the man!"

EC·CLE′ SI·AS′ TES, BOOK OF

1. The Book of Ecclesiastes. The key word in Ecclesiastes is *vanity*, the futile emptiness of trying to be happy apart from God. The Preacher (traditionally taken to be Solomon—1:1,12—the wisest, richest, most influential king in Israel's history) looks at life "under the sun" (1:9) and, from the human perspective, declares it all to be empty. Power, popularity, prestige, pleasure—nothing can fill the God-shaped void in man's life but God Himself. But once seen from God's perspective, life takes on meaning and purpose, causing Solomon to exclaim, "Eat . . . drink . . . rejoice . . . do good . . . live joyfully . . . fear God . . . keep His commandments!" Skepticism and despair melt away when life is viewed as a daily gift from God.

The Hebrew title *Qoheleth* is a rare term; found only in Ecclesiastes (1:1,2,12; 7:27; 12:8-10). It comes from the word *qahal*, "to convoke an assembly, to assemble." Thus, it means "one who addresses an assembly, a preacher." The Septuagint used the Greek word *Ekklesiastes* as its title. Derived from the word *ekklesia*, "assembly, congregation," it simply means "preacher." The Latin *Ecclesiastes* means "speaker before an assembly."

2. The Author of Ecclesiastes. There are powerful arguments that the author of Ecclesiastes was Solomon.

External Evidence: Jewish Talmudic tradition attributes the book to Solomon but suggests that Hezekiah's scribes may have edited the text (see Pr 25:1). Solomonic authorship of Ecclesiastes is the standard Christian position, although some scholars, along with the Talmud, believe the work was later edited during the time of Hezekiah or possibly Ezra.

Internal Evidence: The author calls himself "the son of David, king in Jerusalem" in 1:1,12. Solomon was the best-qualified Davidic descendant for the quest in this book. He was the wisest man who ever taught in Jerusalem (see 1:16; 1 Ki 4:29-30). The descriptions of Qoheleth's (The Preacher) exploration of pleasure (2:1-3), impressive accomplishments (2:4-6), and unparalleled wealth (2:7-10) were fulfilled only by King Solomon. The proverbs in this book are similar to those in the Book of Proverbs (Ec 7; 10). According to 12:9 The Preacher collected and arranged many proverbs, perhaps referring to the two Solomonic collections in Proverbs. The unity of authorship of Ecclesiastes is supported by the seven references to Qoheleth.

3. The Time of Ecclesiastes. Some scholars argue that the literary forms in Ecclesiastes are postexilic, but they are in fact, unique, and cannot be used in dating this book. The phrase "all who were before me in Jerusalem" in 1:16 has been used to suggest a date after Solomon's time, but there were many kings and wise men in Jerusalem before the time of Solomon. However, Solomon was the only son of David who reigned over Israel from Jerusalem (1:12).

Ecclesiastes was probably written late in Solomon's life, about 935 B.C. If this is so, the great glory that Solomon ushered in early in his reign was already beginning to fade; and the disruption of Israel into two kingdoms would soon take place. Jewish tradition asserts that Solomon wrote Song of Solomon in his youthful years, Proverbs in his middle years, and Ecclesiastes in his latter years. This book may be expressing his regret for his folly and wasted time due to carnality and idolatry (1 Ki 11).

There are no references to historical events other than to personal aspects of the Preacher's life. The location was Jerusalem (1:1,12,16), the seat of Israel's rule and authority.

4. The Christ of Ecclesiastes. Ecclesiastes convincingly portrays the emptiness and perplexity of life without a relationship with the Lord. Each person has eternity in his heart (3:11), and only Christ can provide ultimate satisfaction, joy, and wisdom. Man's highest good is found in the "one Shepherd" (12:11) who offers abundant life (Jo 10:9-10).

5. Keys to Ecclesiastes.

Key Word: Vanity—Ecclesiastes reports the results of a diligent quest for purpose, meaning, and satisfaction in human life. The Preacher poignantly sees the emptiness and futility of power, popularity, prestige, and pleasure apart from God. The word *vanity* appears thirty-seven times to express the many things that cannot be understood about life. All earthly goods and ambitions, when pursued as ends in themselves, lead to dissatisfaction and frustration. Life "under the sun" (used twenty-nine times) seems to be filled with inequities, uncertainties, changes in fortune, and violation of justice. But Ecclesiastes does not give an answer of atheism or skepticism; God is referred to throughout. In fact, it claims that the search for man's *summum bonum* must end in God. Satisfaction in life can be found only by looking beyond this world. Ecclesiastes gives an analysis of negative themes but it also develops the positive theme of overcoming the vanities of life by fearing a God who is good, just, and sovereign (12:13-14). Wisdom involves seeing life from a divine perspective and trusting God in the face of apparent futility and lack of purpose. Life is a daily gift from God and it should be enjoyed as much as possible (see 2:24-26; 3:12-13,22; 5:18-20; 8:15; 9:7-10; 11:8-9). Our comprehension is indeed limited, but there are many things we can understand. Qoheleth recognized that ultimately God will judge all people. Therefore he exhorted: "Fear God and keep His commandments" (12:13).

Key Verses: Ecclesiastes 2:24 and 12:13-14—"There is nothing better for a man than that he should eat and drink, and that his soul should enjoy good in his labor. This also, I saw, was from the hand of God" (2:24).

"Let us hear the conclusion of the whole matter; Fear God and keep His commandments, for this is the whole duty of man. For God will bring every work into judgment, including every secret thing, whether it is good or whether it is evil" (12:13-14).

Key Chapter: Ecclesiastes 12—At the end of the Book of Ecclesiastes, the Preacher looks at life through "binoculars." On the other hand, from the perspective of the natural man who only sees life "under the sun," the conclusion is, "All is vanity." Life's every activity, even though pleasant for the moment, becomes purposeless and futile when viewed as an end in itself.

The Preacher carefully documents the latter view with a long list of his own personal pursuits in life. No amount of activities or possessions has satisfied the craving of his heart. Every earthly prescription for happiness has left the same bitter aftertaste. Only when the Preacher views his life from God's perspective "above the sun" does it take on meaning as a precious gift "from the hand of God" (2:24).

Chapter 12 resolves the book's extensive inquiry into the meaning of life with the single conclusion, "Fear God and keep His commandments, for this is the whole duty of man" (12:13).

6. Survey of Ecclesiastes. Ecclesiastes is a profound and problematic book. It is a record of an intense search for meaning and satisfaction in life on this earth, especially in view of all the iniquities and apparent absurdities that surround us. It takes the perspective of the greatest answers that wisdom under the sun can produce. If the Preacher is identified as Solomon, Ecclesiastes was written from a unique vantage point. Possessing the greatest mental, material and political resources ever combined in one man, he was qualified beyond all others to write this book. Ecclesiastes is extremely difficult to synthesize, and several alternate approaches have been used. The one used here follows this general outline: The thesis that "all is vanity" (1:1-11), the proof that "all is vanity" (1:12–6:12), the counsel for living with vanity (7:1–12:14).

The Thesis that "All is Vanity" (1:1–11) After a one-verse introduction, the Preacher states his theme: "Vanity of vanities, all is vanity" (1:2). Life under the sun appears to be futile and perplexing. Verses 3-11 illustrate this theme in the endless and apparently meaningless cycles found in nature and history.

The Proof that "All is Vanity" (1:12–6:12):

The Preacher describes his multiple quest for meaning and satisfaction as he explores his vast personal resources. He begins with wisdom (1:12-18) but finds that "he who increases knowledge increases sorrow." Due to his intense perception of reality he experiences just the reverse of "ignorance is bliss." The Preacher moves from wisdom to laughter, hedonism, and wind (2:1-3) and then turns to works, women, and wealth (2:4-11); but all lead to emptiness. He realizes that wisdom is far greater than foolishness, but both seem to lead to futility in view of the brevity of life and universality of death (2:12-17). He concludes by acknowledging that contentment and joy are found only in God.

At this point, Ecclesiastes turns from the Preacher's situation in life to a philosophical quest; but the conclusion remains the same. The Preacher considers the unchanging order of events and the fixed laws of God. Time is short, and there is no eternity on earth (3:1-15). The futility of death seems to cancel the difference between righteousness and wickedness (3:16-22). Chapters 4 and 5 explore the futility in social relationships (oppression, rivalry, covetousness, power) and in religious relationships (formalism, empty prayer, vows). In addition, the world's offerings produce disappointment, not satisfaction. Ultimate meaning can be found only in God.

The Counsel for Living with Vanity (7:1–12:14): A series of lessons on practical wisdom is given in 7:1–9:12. Levity and pleasure seeking are seen as superficial and foolish; it is better to have sober depth of thought. Wisdom and self-control provide perspective and strength in coping with life. One should enjoy prosperity and consider in adversity that God made both. Avoid the twin extremes of self-righteousness and immorality. Sin invades all men, and wisdom is cut short by evil and death. The human mind cannot grasp ultimate meaning. Submission to authority helps one avoid unnecessary hardship, but real justice is often lacking on earth. The uncertainties of life and certainty of the grave show that God's purposes and ways often cannot be grasped. One should, therefore, magnify opportunities while they last, because fortune can change suddenly. Observations on wisdom and folly are found in 9:13–11:6. Wisdom, the most powerful human resource, is contrasted with the meaningless talk and effort of fools. In view of the unpredictability of circumstances, wisdom is the best course to follow in order to minimize grief and misfortune. Wisdom involves discipline and diligence. In 11:7–12:7 the Preacher offers exhortations on using life well. Youth is too brief and precious to be squandered in foolishness or evil. A person should live well in the fullness of each day before God and acknowledge Him early in life. This section closes with an exquisite allegory of old age (12:1-7).

The Preacher concludes that the "good life" is only attained by revering God. Those who fail to take God and His will seriously into account are doomed to lives of foolishness and futility. Life will not wait upon the solution of all its problems; nevertheless, real meaning can be found by looking not "under the sun" but beyond the sun to the "one Shepherd" (12:11). (See also VANITY OF VANITIES).

OUTLINE OF ECCLESIASTES

Part One: The Thesis That "All is Vanity" (1:1-11)

I. Introduction of Vanity (1:1-3)

II. Illustrations of Vanity (1:4-11)

Part Two: The Proof That "All is Vanity" (1:12–6:12)

I. Proof of "All is Vanity" from Experience (1:12–2:26)

A. Vanity of Striving After Wisdom 1:12-18
B. Vanity of Striving After Pleasure ... 2:1-3
C. Vanity of Great Accomplishments ... 2:4-17
D. Vanity of Hard Labor 2:18-23
E. Conclusion: Be Content 2:24-26

II. Proof of "All is Vanity" from Observation (3:1–6:12)

A. Immutability of God's Program 3:1-22
B. Inequalities of Life 4:1-16
C. Insufficiencies of Human Religion 5:1-7
D. Insufficiencies of Wealth 5:8-20
E. Inescapable Vanity of Life 6:1-12

Part Three: The Counsel for Living with Vanity (7:1–12:14)

I. Coping in a Wicked World (7:1–9:18)

A. Wisdom and Folly Contrasted......... 7:1-14
B. Wisdom and Moderation 7:15-18
C. Strength of Wisdom 7:19-29
D. Submit to Authority 8:1-9
E. Inability to Understand All God's
    Doing 8:10-17
F. Judgment Comes to All Men 9:1-6
G. Enjoy Life While You Have It......... 9:7-12
H. Value of Wisdom 9:13-18

II. Counsel for the Uncertainies of Life (10:1–12:8)

A. Wisdom's Characteristics............ 10:1-15
B. Wisdom Related to the King 10:16-20
C. Wisdom Related to Business 11:1-6
D. Wisdom Related to the
    Youth 11:7–12:8

III. Conclusion: "Fear God and Keep His Commandments" (12:9–14)

ECCLESIASTICUS

See APOCRYPHA.

ECLIPSE

Several times the prophets speak of the sun and moon being darkened or "turned to blood" (Is 13:10; Joel 2:31). Many assume that this is speaking of an eclipse of the sun or moon. An eclipse of the sun occurs when the moon moves between the sun and the earth, temporarily blocking the sun from view. An eclipse of the moon occurs when the shadow of the earth comes between the sun and the full moon, causing the moon to appear a dark bloody copper color.

ECZEMA

A skin disease which includes itching, oozing scaly lesions, redness and inflammation (Le 21:20; 22:22). Also translated "scurvy" (KJV), "itching disease" (NRSV), and "festering sores" (NIV).

ED *(witness)*

An altar erected by the two and one-half tribes east of the Jordan as a witness to the fact that they were a part of Israel even though they were on the other side of the river (Jos 22:10,34).

E´ DAR

See EDER.

E´ DAR, TOWER OF

See EDER.

E´ DEN

1. See EDEN, GARDEN OF (Ge 3:4-6).
2. A Levite, son of Joah, a Gershonite. He lived during the reign of Hezekiah (2 Ch 29:12).

3. A region that was associated with Damascus (Am 1:5).
4. 2 Ki 19:12; Is 37:12.

EDEN, GARDEN OF

The garden of Eden was the first home of Adam and Eve, the first man and woman (Ge 2:4–3:24). Eden is a translation of a Hebrew word which means "Delight," suggesting a "Garden of Delight." The garden contained many beautiful and fruit bearing trees, including the "tree of life" and "the tree of the knowledge of good and evil" (Ge 2:9).

Pinpointing the exact location of the garden of Eden is difficult, although the best theory places it near the source of the Tigris and Euphrates rivers in the Armenian highlands. A major catastrophe, such as the flood of Noah's time, may have wiped out all traces of the other two rivers mentioned—the Pishon and the Havilah (Ge 2:11). But modern space photography has produced evidence that two rivers, now dry beds, could have flowed through the area centuries ago.

God commanded Adam and Eve not to eat of the tree of the knowledge of good and evil (Ge 2:17). They fell from their original state of innocence when Satan approached Eve through the serpent and tempted her to eat of the forbidden fruit (Ge 3:1-5). She ate the fruit and also gave it to her husband to eat (Ge 3:6-7). Their disobedience plunged them and the entire human race into a state of sin and corruption.

Because of their unbelief and rebellion, they were driven from the garden. Other consequences of their sin were loss of their innocence (Ge 3:7), pain in childbearing and subjection of the wife to her husband (Ge 3:16), the cursing of the ground and the resultant hard labor for man (Ge 3:17-19), and separation from God (Ge 3:23-24).

The apostle Paul thought of Christ as the Second Adam who would save the old sinful Adam through His plan of redemption and salvation. "As in Adam all die, even so in Christ all shall be made alive" (1 Co 15:22).

EDENIC COVENANT

The covenant in Eden is the first of the general or universal covenants. In it, Adam is charged to: (1) populate the earth (Ge 1:28); (2) subdue the earth (Ge 1:28); (3) exercise dominion over the animal creation (Ge 1:28); (4) care for the garden of Eden and enjoy its fruit (Ge 1:29; 2:15); and (5) refrain from eating the fruit of the tree of the knowledge of good and evil, under penalty of death (Ge 2:16-17). The Edenic Covenant was terminated by man's disobedience when Adam and Eve ate of the fruit of the tree of the knowledge of good and evil, resulting in their spiritual and physical deaths. This failure necessitated the establishment of the covenant with Adam (Ge 3:14-21).

E´DER, E´DAR, A´DER

1. A tower near which Jacob camped (Ge 35:21).

2. A town in the south of Judah (Jos 15:21).

3. A Benjamite, son of Elpaal (1 Ch 8:15).

4. A Levite, son of Mushi of the family of Merari (1 Ch 23:23; 24:30).

E´DOM

1. A name of Esau (Ge 25:30; 36:1,8,19).

2. Another name for the Edomites (Nu 20:18, 20; Am 1:6,11; Mal 1:4).

3. The territory of the descendants of Edom, also called Idumaea.

E´DOM·ITES

The descendants of Edom (Ge 36:1-19). Their early rulers were called dukes (Ge 36:15-19,40-43) and kings (Ge 36:31-43; 1 Ch 1:43-51). Because they were descendants of Abraham, the Israelites were not permitted to war against them (Nu 20:14-21). They were the subjects of direful prophecies (Eze 35:5-6).

ED´RE·I (mighty)

1. A fortified city of Naphtali (Jos 19:37).

2. Chief city of Bashan (De 3:10; Jos 12:4; 13:12,31). It was here that the Israelites defeated Og (Nu 21:33-35; De 1:4; 3:1,10).

EG´LAH (heifer)

A wife of David and mother of Ithream (2 Sa 3:5; 1 Ch 3:3).

EG´LA·IM (two ponds)

A town of Moab (Is 15:8).

EG´LATH-SHEL´I·SHI´YAH (third Eglath)

A place in Moab (Is 15:5; Je 48:34).

EG´LON

1. A king of Moab who captured Jericho and exacted tribute from Israel for eighteen years. He was slain by Ehud (Ju 3:12-30).

2. A town assigned to Judah whose king was overthrown by Joshua (Jos 10:3-23,34-37; 12:12; 15:39).

E´GYPT

The history of Egypt stretches back to about 3000 B.C., at least a thousand years before the time of Abraham. During their formative years as a nation, the Hebrew people spent 430 years as slaves in Egypt (Ex 12:40) before they were released miraculously through God's power under the leadership of Moses.

According to the table of nations in the Book of Genesis, Egypt was founded by Mizraim, one of the sons of Ham (Ge 10:6,13-14). In the Old Testament, Egypt is referred to in a symbolic way as Mizraim (1 Ch 1:8,11).

Soon after arriving in the land of Canaan about 2000 B.C., Abraham migrated into Egypt for a time to escape a famine (Ge 12:10). Still after, Joseph was sold into Egyptian slavery by his brothers (Ge 37:12-36). Joseph rose to a position of prominence in the cabinet of the Egyptian Pharaoh (Ge 41:37-46). This led Joseph's family to move to Egypt, and the Hebrew people were eventually enslaved when a new line of Pharaohs rose to power (Ex 1:6-14).

After the exodus of the Hebrews from Egypt, the once powerful Egyptian Empire declined in strength and influence, becoming a second-rate political power. During the time of David and Solomon (about 1000 B.C.), Egypt's weakness and fragmentation contributed to the establishment of Israel as a strong nation. During Isaiah's time, about 730 B.C., the prophet warned the king of Judah about forming an alliance with Egypt against the Assyrians, predicting that "trust in the shadow of Egypt shall be your humiliation" (Is 30:3).

The Egyptians worshipped many gods. Many of these were the personification of nature, including the earth, sun, and sky. Even the Nile River was thought to be divine, because its periodic flooding enriched the soil of the Nile delta for a premium agricultural harvest. Several of the plagues God sent upon the Egyptians (Ex 7–12) affected the Nile, proving the weakness of the entire Egyptian religious system.

EGYPT, BROOK OF

The Wadi el-Arish, a dry streambed which formed the boundary between Egypt and Canaan (Jos 15:4; Is 27:12).

EGYPTIAN

A native of the land of Egypt.

E′HI

Son of Benjamin (Ge 46:21); also called Ahiram (Nu 26:38) and Aharah (1 Ch 8:1).

E′HUD *(union)*

Two Old Testament men:
1. The deliverer of the Israelites from King Eglon of Moab. He went to the king on the pretext that he had a present for him from the children of Israel. When Ehud was left alone with the king, he stabbed him and fled to the hill-country of Ephraim. Ehud was left-handed (Ju 3:12-30).
2. A Benjamite, son of Bilhan (1 Ch 7:10).

E′KER

A son of Ram and the grandson of Jerahmeel (1 Ch 2:27).

EK′RON *(eradication)*

One of the five chief cities of the Philistines (Jos 13:3; 1 Sa 6:16-17). It was assigned to Judah (Jos 15:45-46); later to Dan (Jos 19:43). It was recaptured by the Philistines. When the ark was taken from the Israelites in the time of Eli, it was sent to Ekron and then returned to Israel (1 Sa 5:10).

EK′RON·ITE

An inhabitant of Ekron (Jos 13:3; 1 Sa 5:10).

EL *(God)*

See GOD, NAMES OF.

EL′A·DAH, EL′E·A·DAH *(God has adorned)*

A descendant of Ephraim (1 Ch 7:20).

E′LAH

Six Old Testament men:
1. The father of Shimei (1 Ki 4:18).
2. A duke of Edom (Ge 36:41; 1 Ch 1:52).
3. A son of Caleb (1 Ch 4:15).
4. A Benjamite, son of Uzzi (1 Ch 9:8).
5. Son and successor of Baasha, king of Israel. He reigned less than two years. He was slain by Zimri (1 Ki 16:6,8-10).
6. The father of Hoshea (2 Ki 15:30; 17:1; 18:1).

ELAH, THE VALLEY OF

The valley in which the Israelites were fighting the Philistines when the shepherd boy, David, was pitted against the Philistine champion, Goliath (1 Sa 17:2,19).

E′LAM

Six Old Testament men and a country:
1. A son of Shem (Ge 10:22; 1 Ch 1:17) and ancestor of the Elamites (Ez 4:9).
2. An important country of western Asia. Its southern boundary was the Persian Gulf; its territory was in the area that is now part of Iran, including a part of the Karun River. It was bounded on the east and southeast by Persia (Iran), and on the north by Assyria and Media (now parts of Iraq and Syria). "Chedorlaomer, king of Elam" held dominion over three other kings in the time of Abraham (Ge 14:1-9). Elam was one of the places to which God's people were exiled (Is 1:11), they were a warlike people (Is 22:6), who would one day experience the wrath of God (Je 25:15,25; Eze 32:24-25). After the Assyrians had taken over the Northern Kingdom of Israel, they relocated several foreign peoples, including the Elamites, to Samaria (Ez 4:9). Daniel and Esther refer to Shushan, the capital of Elam (Es 1:2; 8:14-15; Da 8:2), during the time that this area was under Babylonian domination. Centuries later, Elamites were among those present in Jerusalem when the Holy Spirit came upon the believers at Pentecost (Ac 2:9).
3. A Benjamite, son of Shashak (1 Ch 8:24).
4. A Korhite, fifth son of Meshelemiah who was a porter of the tabernacle in the time of David (1 Ch 26:3).

5. The head of a family which returned from Babylon (Ez 2:1,2,7; Ne 7:12)

6. The head of another family which returned from Babylon with Zerubbabel (Ez 2:31; Ne 7:34).

7. The ancestor of Jeshaiah son of Athaliah, who returned to Israel with Ezra (Ez 8:7).

8. The grandfather (or more distant ancestor) of Shecaniah, who confessed to having taken a pagan wife, and suggested that he and all who had done so should "put them away" (Ez 10:3)

9. One of the leaders of the people who signed the covenant to follow the God of Israel (Ne 10:14).

10. A priest who participated in the dedication of the walls (Ne 12:42).

Several of these entries may actually be the same person, such as Nos. 5,6,7 or 8,and 9 and 10.

E′ LAM·ITES

Inhabitants of Elam (Ez 4:9). See ELAM No. 2.

EL·A′ SAH *(God has made)*

1. A son of Shaphan. He and another were sent by Zedekiah on a mission to Nebuchadnezzar, and at the same time they carried a letter from Jeremiah to the captives in Babylon (Je 29:3).

2. A son of Pashur. He was led by Ezra to renounce his pagan wife (Ez 10:22).

E′ LATH, E′ LOTH

An Edomite town on the northeast arm of the Red Sea. The Israelites passed it in their wanderings (De 2:8). It appears that Elath was destroyed, for in 2 Kings 14:22 it is spoken of as being rebuilt by Judah.

EL-BE′ RITH

See BAAL-BERITH.

EL-BETH′ -EL *(God of Beth-el)*

Jacob gave this name to an altar he set up at Beth-el when he returned from Padan-aram. It commemorated God's previous appearance to him there in a dream (Ge 35:7).

EL·DA′ AH *(God hath called)*

One of the sons of Midian, the son of Abraham and Keturah (Ge 25:4; 1 Ch 1:33).

EL′ DAD *(God has loved)*

One of the seventy whom Moses selected to aid him in the government of the people. For some reason Eldad and Medad remained in the camp when Moses gathered the elders of the people together to hear from the Lord, but nevertheless, the divine Spirit rested on them as upon the others and they prophesied in the camp. A young man ran to tell Moses what was happening; when Joshua asked Moses to forbid this, Moses rebuked him, declaring he wished the Lord would endow all the people with his spirit (Nu 11:26-29).

EL′ DER

An officer who was head of a family or tribe (Ju 8:14,16; 1 Ki 8:1-3). The name signified that he was a man of mature age. The elder exercised authority over the people (De 27:1; Ez 10:8) and in matters of state, elders represented the people (Ex 3:18; Ju 11:5-11; 1 Sa 8:4). A body of seventy elders aided Moses when he was overburdened with the responsibility of supplying the people with food (Nu 11:16,24). The elders of a town had charge of civil and religious affairs. In the early Christian church such designations as elder, presbyter and bishop, if not strictly synonymous, were interchangeable (Ac 20:17; Tit 1:5,7). Elders were in the church at Jerusalem in A.D. 44 (Ac 11:30). On his first journey, Paul appointed elders in every church (Ac 14:23). They cooperated with the apostles in the government of the church (Ac 15:2,4,6, 22; 16:4). They had spiritual care of the congregation (1 Ti 3:5; 5:17; Tit 1:9; 1 Pe 5:1-4). See BISHOP and PRESBYTER.

EL′ E·AD

A descendant of Ephraim. In attempting to drive away the cattle from Gath, a city of the Philistines, he and his brother were killed by the people (1 Ch 7:20-22).

EL′ E·A′ DAH

See ELADAH.

EL·E·A′ LEH

A town near Heshbon in Moab rebuilt by the Reubenites (Nu 32:3,37). It was later retaken by the Moabites (Is 15:4; 16:9; Je 48:34).

EL·E·A′ SAH *(God hath made)*

1. A Judahite (1 Ch 2:39).

2. Son of Rapha (1 Ch 8:37).

EL·E·A′ ZAR *(God hath helped)*

1. The third son of Aaron and the father of Phinehas (Ex 6:23,25; Nu 3:2). With Nadab,

Abihu, and Ithamar, his brothers, he was consecrated priest and was chief over the Levites (Ex 6:23; 28:1; Nu 3:2,32). After his brothers died, he succeeded his father as chief priest (Le 10:6-20; Nu 20:25-28). Eleazar took an active part in the division of Canaan (Jos 14:1). Upon their return from Babylon, the Zadokite priests traced their descent from Aaron through Eleazar, ignoring the house of Eli (1 Ch 6:3-8).

2. A son of Abinadab in whose house the ark was kept after it was returned to the Israelites by the Philistines. He was appointed by the men of Kirjath-jearim to attend the ark (1 Sa 7:1-2).

3. A Levite (1 Ch 23:21; 24:28).

4. One of David's three mightiest men, a son of Dodo the Ahohite (2 Sa 23:9; 1 Ch 11:12).

5. A son of Phinehas who was associated with the Levites in taking care of the sacred vessels (Ez 8:33).

6. A son of Parosh who divorced his foreign wife (Ez 10:25).

7. A priest, one of the musicians when the wall was dedicated (Ne 12:42).

8. Son of Eliud and an ancestor of the family of Jesus (Ma 1:15).

E·LEC'TION

Used in the Scriptures in three ways. (1) Of elect nations, such as Israel (Ex 19:5-6; Ps 135:4; Is 41:8; Is 45:4). (2) Of individuals, such as the apostles, divinely elected to a certain service (Lk 6:13). (3) Of certain individuals elected to salvation in Christ. This last usage has been the cause of many bitter theological controversies, two views resulting. The *Calvinistic View* is stated well in the Westminster Confession: "God from all eternity did by the most wise and holy counsel of His own will freely and unchangeably ordain whatsoever comes to pass; yet so as thereby neither is God the author of sin, nor is violence offered to the will of the creatures, nor is the liberty or contingency of second causes taken away, but rather established. Although God knows whatsoever may or can come to pass upon all supposed conditions, yet hath He not decreed anything because He foresaw its future, or as that which would come to pass upon such conditions. By the decree of God, for the manifestation of His glory some men and angels are predestinated unto everlasting life and others foreordained to everlasting death. These angels and men thus predestinated and foreordained are particularly and

unchangeably designed, and their number is so certain and definite that it cannot be either increased or diminished." (Ac 2:23; Ro 8:29-30; Ep 1:4-11; 1 Pe 1:2-20). The *Arminian View* states that election is not absolute but conditioned "contingent upon the proper acceptance of such gifts of grace as God by His Spirit and providence puts within the reach of men." To this view the Scriptures teach that man's eternal destiny is settled by his own choice and that though God desires the salvation of all men, only those will perish who wickedly resist his will (Jo 5:40; Ac 7:51; 1 Ti 2:4; 4:10). Also, this view states that certain passages of Scripture by their various exhortations and warnings teach that the number of the elect can be increased or diminished. (Ma 24:4,13; 2 Pe 1:10-11).

ELECT LADY

The unknown recipient of John's second epistle (2 Jo 1). Some believe that she was an actual woman, others think that this is a euphemism for the church in general.

EL-EL'O·HE-IS'RA·EL *(God, the God of Israel)*

The name Jacob gave an altar which he erected not far from Shechem (Ge 33:20).

ELEMENTS

The building blocks of the physical world. At the end of time, the earth will be consumed with fire, and the elements melted (2 Pe 3:10,12). Paul uses this word in a different sense, talking about being "in bondage under the elements of the world" (Ga 4:3, NKJV). This is also translated "basic principles" (NIV), or "elemental things." Considering the context, it seems to be a reference to the law.

EL'EPH

A town belonging to Benjamin (Jos 18:28).

EL'E·PHANT

The elephant was used both in battles and on hunts. Assyrian reliefs show they were taken in tribute by conquerors. Ivory was extensively used for art objects (1 Ki 10:22).

EL·HA'NAN, EL·THA'NAN *(God is gracious)*

1. A son of Dodo, a Beth-lehemite, one of David's thirty heroes (2 Sa 23:24; 1 Ch 11:26).

2. A son of Jair, a Beth-lehemite. In the original of 2 Samuel 21:19 it says that he killed Goliath, the Gittite. But the Authorized Version says that he killed the brother of Goliath, thus bringing the passage into agreement with 1 Chronicles 20:5.

E′LI

High priest at the temple of Shiloh during the eleventh century B.C. He helped to train Samuel (1 Sa 1:9,24-28). Although a man of great piety, he was unable to control his sons, Hophni and Phinehas, whose conduct was disgraceful (1 Sa 2:23-25; 3:13). God's denunciation of Eli and his house was spoken through the boy Samuel and through an unnamed prophet (1 Sa 2:27-36; 3:11-18).

E′LI, E′LI, LAMA SABACHTHANI

As Jesus hung on the cross, he cried these words, quoting from the first words of Psalm 22: *"My God, my God, why have you forsaken me?"*

E·LI′AB *(God is father)*

Six Old Testament men:

1. Son of Pallu, a Reubenite and father of Dathan and Abiram (Nu 16:1,12; 26:8-9).

2. An ancestor of Samuel, a Levite (1 Ch 6:27-28).

3. Chief of the family of Zebulun in the wilderness, the son of Helon (Nu 1:9; 2:7; 7:24,29; 10:16).

4. The oldest son of Jesse and brother of David. From his fine appearance Samuel was sure he was the one to be king of Israel but the

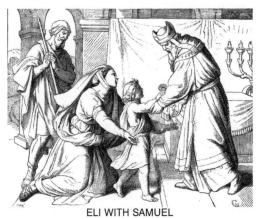
ELI WITH SAMUEL

Lord showed Samuel that he was deceived by appearances (1 Sa 16:6-7; 17:13).

5. A Gadite who allied himself with David at Ziklag (1 Ch 12:9).

6. A Levite, one of David's musicians, who accompanied the ark to Jerusalem (1 Ch 15:20).

E·LI′A·DA

Three Old Testament men:

1. Father of Rezon of Zobah (1 Ki 11:23).

2. A son of David, also called Beeliada, born after David captured Jerusalem (2 Sa 5:16; 1 Ch 3:8).

3. A chief captain of Jehoshaphat, a Benjamite (2 Ch 17:17).

E·LI′A·DAH

See ELIADA.

E·LI′AH

See ELIJAH.

E·LI·AH′BA *(God will hide)*

A Shaalbonite (2 Sa 23:32; 1 Ch 11:33).

E·LI′A·KIM *(God will establish)*

Five Old Testament men:

1. A son of Hilkiah who was one of three sent by King Hezekiah to confer with the commander of Sennacherib when the Assyrians threatened Jerusalem (2 Ki 18:18,26,37; Is 36:3,11,22). Eliakim was commended by Isaiah (Is 22:20-25).

2. A son of Josiah who was placed on the throne by Pharaoh Necho and whose name was changed to Jehoiakim (2 Ki 23:34; 2 Ch 36:4).

3. A priest who participated in the dedication of the wall (Ne 12:41).

4. An ancestor of the family of Christ (Lk 3:30-31).

5. An ancestor of the family of Christ (Ma 1:13).

E·LI′AM *(people's God)*

Two Old Testament men:

1. Father of Bath-sheba whose first husband was Uriah and whose second husband was David (2 Sa 11:3). In 1 Chronicles 3:5 Eliam's name is changed to Ammiel and Bath-sheba's to Bath-shua.

2. The son of Ahithophel (2 Sa 23:34).

E·LI′A·S

Greek for Elijah (Mk 9:5). See ELIJAH.

E·LI′ A·SAPH *(God has added)*

Two Old Testament men:

1. The son of Lael, a Levite. During the wilderness period he was the prince of the Gerahonites (Nu 3:24).

2. The head of the Gadites in the wilderness (Nu 1:14; 2:14; 7:42).

E·LI·ASH′ IB *(God restores)*. Six Old Testament men:

1. A son of Elioenai, a descendant of the royal family of Judah (1 Ch 3:24).

2. A priest in the time of David (1 Ch 24:12).

3. Father of Jehohanan (Johanan), the head of a house of Levi (Ez 10:6; Ne 12:22-23).

4. A Levite, a singer who renounced his foreign wife (Ez 10:24).

5. A son of Zattu who renounced his foreign wife (Ez 10:27).

6. A son of Bani who renounced his foreign wife (Ez 10:36).

7. The high priest in the time of Nehemiah. He and the priests built the sheep gate in Jerusalem (Ne 3:1,20-21). Possibly No. 3.

E·LI′ A·THAH *(God has come)*

A musician, son of Heman (1 Ch 25:4,27).

E·LI′ DAD

A Benjamite, the son of Chislon, who was assigned to help divide up the land (Nu 34:21).

EL·IEH·O·E′ NAI

See ELIOENAI.

E·LI′ EL *(my God is God)*

Nine Old Testament men:

1. A Levite of the Kohath family. He was an ancestor of Samuel (1 Ch 6:34). See ELIHU.

2. A Gadite who joined David at Ziklag (1 Ch 12:11).

3. A Mahavite who was one of David's warriors (1 Ch 11:46).

4. One of David's heroes (1 Ch 11:47).

5. Son of Shimhi, a Benjamite (1 Ch 8:20).

6. Son of Shashak, a Benjamite (1 Ch 8:22).

7. Son of Hebron, a Levite living at the time of David (1 Ch 15:9,11). He helped move the ark to Jerusalem.

8. A leader in eastern Manasseh; also a warrior (1 Ch 5:24).

9. A Levite appointed by Hezekiah to take charge of the offerings of the temple (2 Ch 31:13).

E·LIE′ NA·I

A Benjamite, son of Shimei (1 Ch 8:20).

EL·I·E′ ZER *(God is help)*

Eleven Old Testament men:

1. The servant of Abraham, a man of Damascus. He was sent to Mesopotamia to secure a wife for Isaac (Ge 15:2).

2. A son of Moses and Zipporah (Ex 18:4; 1 Ch 23:15,17).

3. Son of Becher, grandson of Benjamin (1 Ch 7:8).

4. One of the priests who blew the trumpet before the ark (1 Ch 15:24).

5. A son of Zichri. In David's reign he was captain of the Reubenites (1 Ch 27:16).

6. Son of Dodavah of Mareshah. He was the prophet who predicted that the vessels of Jehoshaphat would be wrecked because of his league with the family of Ahab (2 Ch 20:37).

7. One of those sent by Ezra to Casiphia to get Levites for the temples (Ez 8:16-17).

8, 9, 10. Three men of this name—a priest, a Levite, and a son of Harim—renounced their foreign wives (Ez 10:18,23,31).

11. An ancestor of the family of Christ (Lk 3:29).

ELI·HOE′ NAI

Son of Zerahiah and descendant of Pahath-Moab (Ez 8:4).

E·LI·HOR′ EPH

Son of Shisha. He and his brother, Ahijah, were appointed royal scribes by Solomon (1 Ki 4:3).

E·LI′ HU *(he is my God)*

Five Old Testament men:

1. Son of Tohu and an ancestor of Samuel (1 Sa 1:1). He was also known as Eliab or Eliel (1 Ch 6:27,34).

2. David's eldest brother, also called Eliab (1 Sa 16:6; 1 Ch 27:18).

3. A captain of Manasseh who joined David at Ziklag (1 Ch 12:20).

4. A member of the family of Obed-edom who was a porter of the temple (1 Ch 26:7).

5. The son of Barachel the Buzite who reproved Job (Job 32–37).

E·LI′ JAH

Four Old Testament men:

1. One of the greatest of the prophets, a Tishbite who lived in Gilead (1 Ki 17:1). Little

ELIJAH

else is known of his origin. He appeared suddenly during the reign of Ahab (about 876-854 B.C.) to denounce the king and his wife, Jezebel, for their idolatry and crimes. His purpose was to save Israel from the worship of Baal. On Mount Carmel he succeeded in discrediting the 400 prophets of Baal by calling fire from heaven to consume a water-soaked altar (1 Ki 18:19-46). Following the scene on Mount Carmel, Elijah fled from the furious Jezebel to Mount Horeb, where, like Moses, he was divinely sustained for forty days (Ex 24:18; 34:28; De 9:9,18; 1 Ki 19:8). The Lord rebuked him for leaving Israel and commanded him to return. When Naboth was murdered at the instigation of Jezebel, Elijah met Ahab and declared the judgments of God upon him (1 Ki 21:1-29). Like Enoch, Elijah was translated to heaven without dying. This was on the east of the Jordan. Elisha was with him when he was carried away by a whirlwind into heaven (2 Ki 2:1-12). Elijah appeared with our Lord in the transfiguration (Ma 17:4; Lk 9:30). He was one of the most rugged and colorful characters of the Scriptures. The last two verses of the Old Testament predict that Elijah will appear on earth before the dreadful day of the Lord (Mal 4:5-6). While the New Testament explains this in terms of John the Baptist, who, in some respects, was like Elijah (Ma 3:4; Mk 1:6; Lk 1:17), it is believed by some, that while John appeared in

the spirit and power of Elijah, the prophet is yet to come in person before the second advent of Christ.

2. A son of Jeroham, a Benjamite, who resided at Jerusalem (1 Ch 8:27).

3. A son of Harim, a priest, who married a Gentile (Ez 10:21).

4. An Israelite in the time of Ezra who renounced his foreign wife (Ez 10:26).

EL´IKA

A Harodite, one of David's mighty men (2 Sa 23:25).

E´LIM

Oasis of seventy palm trees and twelve springs of water (Ex 15:27; 16:1; Nu 33:9-10).

E·LIM´E·LECH

Husband of Naomi (Ru 1).

EL·I·O·E´NAI

Seven Old Testament men:

1. A Benjamite of the Becher family (1 Ch 7:8).

2. A Simeonite (1 Ch 4:36).

3. Son of Neariah, a descendant of Zerubbabel (1 Ch 3:23-24).

4. A son of Meshelemiah, a Korhite porter of the temple (1 Ch 26:3).

5. A priest, son of Pashur, who divorced his foreign wife (Ez 10:22).

6. A priest at the dedication of the wall of Jerusalem (Ne 12:41).

7. A son of Zattu who renounced his foreign wife (Ez 10:27).

E·LI´PHAL *(God has judged)*

A son of Ur and one of David's warriors (1 Ch 11:35).

E·LIPH´ALET (2 Sa 5:15; 1 Ch 14:7).

See ELIPHELET.

E·LI´PHAZ *(God is strong)*

Two Old Testament men:

1. Son of Esau and Adah (Ge 36:4).

2. One of the friends of Job, a Temanite (Job 2:11; 4:1; 15:1; 22:1; 42:7,9).

E·LIPH´E·LEH

One of the gatekeepers who played the harp when the ark was brought from the home of Obed-edom (1 Ch 15:18,21).

E·LI·PHE·LE′ HU

See ELIPHELEH.

E·LIPH′ E·LET

Six Old Testament men:

1. Son of Eshek and a descendant of Jonathan (1 Ch 8:39).

2. A son of David, born in Jerusalem (1 Ch 3:6; 14:5).

3. Another son of David, probably born after the death of the first son of that name (1 Ch 3:6,8).

4. One of David's warriors, son of Ahasbai (2 Sa 23:34). He was also called Eliphal (1 Ch 11:35).

5. Son of Hashum. He renounced his foreign wife (Ez 10:33).

6. One of those who accompanied Ezra to Jerusalem, son of Adonikam (Ez 8:13).

E·LIS′ A·BETH *(God is an oath)*

A descendant of Aaron, wife of Zacharias and mother of John the Baptist. An angel revealed to her husband the fact that she was to be the mother of the forerunner of Christ. She was a kinswoman of Mary, mother of Jesus (Lk 1:5-45).

E·LI′ SHA *(God his salvation)*

The son of Shaphat who lived in Abel-meholah in the Jordan Valley. He was plowing his father's field when Elijah found him and appointed him his successor (1 Ki 19:16,19). Leaving his home, Elisha joined Elijah and was with him when Elijah was transported to heaven (2 Ki 2:1-18). His miracles were designed to establish the being and truth of Jehovah at a time when the kingdom of Israel was committed to Baal. Included among his miracles: causing water to spring from barren land (2 Ki 2:19-22); the death of the children who mocked his bald head (2 Ki 2:23-25); the increase in the oil to pay the widow's debts (2 Ki 4:1,7); the son restored to life (2 Ki 4:8-37); the feeding of the hundred men (2 Ki 4:42-44); the healing of Naaman (2 Ki 5:1-19); and blinding of the Syrian soldiers who pursued him (2 Ki 6:17-23); and the prediction of the death of Ben-hahad (2 Ki 8:7-15). The body of a dead man, who was placed in the same sepulchre as Elisha, touched the prophet's bones and was restored to life (2 Ki 13:20-21).

E·LI′ SHAH

Eldest son of Javan (Ge 10:4; 1 Ch 1:7). He seems to have given the name to the "isles of Elishah." (Eze 27:7).

E·LI′ SHA·MA *(God has heard)*

Six Old Testament men:

1. Son of Jekamiah. a descendant of Judah (1 Ch 2:41).

2. The son of Ammihud, chief of the Ephraimites at the time of the sojourn in the wilderness (Nu 1:10; 2:18). He was an ancestor of Joshua (1 Ch 7:26).

3. A son of David (2 Sa 5:16). Elishua (2 Sa 5:15; 1 Ch 14:5) is probably the more exact name.

4. Another son of David (1 Ch 3:8; 14:7).

5. The father of Nethaniah and grandfather of Ishmael (2 Ki 25:25; Je 41:1).

6. A priest commissioned by Jehoshaphat to teach the law to the people of Judah (2 Ch 17:8).

7. A scribe to Jehoiakim (Je 36:12,20-21).

E·LI·SHA′ PHAT *(God has judged)*

A captain who led a revolt against Athaliah (2 Ch 23:1).

E·LI′ SHE·BA *(God is an oath)*

Daughter of Amminadab and sister of Naashon. She became the wife of Aaron. Their four sons were Nadab, Abihu, Eleazar, and Ithamar (Ex 6:23).

E·LI′ SHU·A *(God is salvation)*

A son of David (2 Sa 5:15; 1 Ch 14:5). In 1 Chronicles 3:6, David's son Elishua is called Elishama.

E·LI′ UD

The son of Achim and father of Eleazar in Christ's genealogy (Ma 1:14-15).

ELIZABETH

See ELISABETH.

E·LI·ZA′ PHAN

Two Old Testament men:

1. The son of Uzziel. He was the chief of the Kohathites in the wilderness (Ex 6:18,22; Nu 3:30). He and his brother, Mishael, removed the bodies of Nadab and Abihu when they were burned to death for their sacrilegious offering to the Lord. In the reign of David his family helped bring the ark to Jerusalem (1 Ch 15:8).

2. Son of Parnach and chief of the tribe of Zebulun. He assisted in dividing the land (Nu 34:25).

E•LI′ZUR

Son of Shedeur and prince of the tribe of Reuben (Nu 1:5; 2:10; 7:30; 10:18).

EL•KA′NAH *(God has possessed)*

Eight Old Testament men:

1. A son of Korah and brother of Assir and Abiasaph (Ex 6:24).

2. The husband of Hannah and father of Samuel (1 Sa 1:1; 2:11,20; 1 Ch 6:27,34).

3. The father of Zophai and a descendant of Assir (1 Ch 6:23).

4. Son of Joel and father of Amasai (1 Ch 6:25-26).

5. The head of a Levite family who lived in the village of the Netophathites (1 Ch 9:16). **6.** A Korite who lived in Benjamin. He joined David at Ziklag (1 Ch 12:6).

7. A doorkeeper for the ark during the reign of David (1 Ch 15:23).

8. A chief officer in the court of Ahaz of Judah. He was slain by Zichri when Pekah of Israel invaded Judah (2 Ch 28:7).

EL′KOSH

The residence and probably birthplace of the prophet, Nahum (Na 1:1).

ELLASAR

A Mesopotamian nation, whose king was Arioch (Ge 14:1). Together with the kings of Elam and Shinar, he made war on the kings of Sodom and Gommorah, Admah, Zeboiim, and Bela.

ELM

One translation of the Hebrew word *Elah* in Hosea 4:13. In Genesis 35:4 and Judges 6:11, 19, the word is translated *oak* in the KJV. It should probably be properly translated *terebinth,* rather than either oak or elm. See TEREBINTH.

EL•MO′DAM

Son of Er and father of Cosam, an ancestor of Christ (Lk 3:28).

EL•NA′AM *(God is delight)*

Father of two of David's warriors (1 Ch 11:46).

EL•NA′THAN *(God has given)*

Three Old Testament men:

1. The father of Nehushta, mother of Jehoiachin, king of Judah (2 Ki 24:8).

2. The son of Achbor who was among those sent by King Jehoiakim to bring Urijah, the prophet, from Egypt (Je 26:22). The prophet failed to persuade Jehoiakim not to destroy the written prophesy of Jeremiah (Je 36:12,25).

3. Three men sent by Ezra to secure Levites for the temple (Ez 8:16).

EL•O′HIM

The plural of **EL•O′AH** *(mighty),* sometimes used in the sense of gods, true or false (Ex 12:12; 35:2,4). On the use of Elohim and Jehovah in the O.T. Dr. W. H. Green says: "Jehovah (Yahweh) represents God in His special relation to the chosen people, as revealing Himself to them, their guardian and object of their worship; Elohim represents God in His relation to the world at large, as Creator, providential ruler in the affairs of men, and controlling the operations of nature. Elohim is used when Gentiles speak or are spoken to or spoken about, unless there is a specific reference to Jehovah, the God of the chosen people. Elohim is used when God is contrasted with men or things, or when the sense requires a common rather than a proper noun." See GOD, NAMES OF.

EL′O•I

See ELI, ELI, LAMA SABACTHANI.

E′LON *(an oak)*

Three Old Testament men and a town:

1. A Hittite and father of Adah who was the wife of Esau (Ge 36:2). Adah is also called Bashemath (Ge 26:34).

2. A son of Zebulun, the head of the family of Elonites (Nu 26:26).

3. A member of the Zebulunite family who was a judge of Israel for ten years (Ju 12:11-12).

4. A town on the border of Dan (Jos 19:43).

E′LON-BETH-HA′NAN

Probably the same as Elon, a town in Dan (1 Ki 4:9).

E′LON·ITES

Descendants of Elon, a son of Zebulun (Ge 46:14; Nu 26:26).

EL′OTH

See ELATH.

EL·PA′AL

A Benjamite, son of Shaharaim and his wife Hushim (1 Ch 8:11).

EL·PA′LET

See ELPELET.

EL·PAR′AN (Ge 14:6)

See PARAN.

EL·PE′LET

A son of David born in Jerusalem (1 Ch 14:5).

EL′TE·KEH (God is its fear)

A town of Dan (Jos 19:44; 21:23). It was the scene of the defeat of the Egyptians by Sennacherib in 701 B.C.

EL′TE·KON

A town of Judah (Jos 15:59).

EL·TO′LAD

A town in the southern part of Judah (Jos 15:30) which was allotted to Simeon (Jos 19:4). It is probably the Tolad of 1 Chronicles 4:29.

E′LUL

Sixth month of the sacred, and twelfth of the civil year (Ne 6:15), corresponding roughly with the end of August/beginning of September. See CALENDAR.

EL·U′ZAI (God is my strength)

A warrior of Benjamin who joined David (1 Ch 12:5).

EL′Y·MAS

A Jew, Bar-jesus (Son of Joshua), an imposter, who claimed to be able to tell future events. Paul met him at Paphos where he attempted to prevent the conversion of Sergius Paulus, the Roman deputy. Paul denounced him and he was smitten with blindness for a time. The deputy immediately accepted Christianity (Ac 13:6-12).

EL·ZA′BAD (God has given)

1. A Gadite warrior who allied himself with David at Ziklag (1 Ch 12:12).

2. A Levite, son of Shemaiah, of the family of Obed-edom (1 Ch 26:7).

EL′ZA·PHAN

A Levite, son of Uzziel (Ex 6:22).

EMBALM

From early time the Egyptians embalmed their dead. Their idea was that the preservation of the body was essential to the life of the soul—that its future depended upon the preserved state of the body to receive the soul. It was not often practiced by the Hebrews, but Joseph had his father's body embalmed, and he himself was also embalmed (Ge 50:2,26). This was probably in order to make it possible for their bodies to be carried back to Canaan for burial in the cave at Machpelah, as Jacob had made his sons promise they would do (Ge 50:5). When the Hebrews left Egypt, they took with them the four hundred year old bones of Joseph (Ge 50:25; Ex 13:19). The Jews did not embalm because their regulations about touching dead bodies (Nu 19:11-19) would have made such extended work with corpses impractical—an embalmer would have been perpetually unclean. They anointed the body with oil (Jo 12:7) and wrapped it in spiced linen (Jo 19:39).

EMBALMER

One who does the work of embalming. While the word "embalmer" does not appear, the "physicians" mentioned in Genesis 50:2 are clearly embalmers.

EMBROIDERER

This word is often used interchangeably with "weaver" when talking about persons skilled in producing beautifully decorated textile products. An embroiderer is skilled in applying ornamental needlework designs to finished cloth. Embroiderers and weavers worked on the hangings for the tabernacle (Ex 27:1,16; 28:4,15).

EMBROIDERY

Ornamental needlework as distinct from plain sewing. The materials used were colored silk, silver or gold thread (Ex 35:35; 38:23). Parts of the tabernacle and girdle of the high priest were embroidered (Ex 26:36; 27:16; 28:39; 39:29). Embroidered garments were worn by the wealthy (Ju 5:30; Ps 45:14).

E'MEK-KE'ZIZ

A town of Benjamin, apparently near Jericho and Beth-hoglah. It is referred to as the valley of Keziz in the Authorized Version (Jos 18:21).

EM'ER·ALD

A type of precious stone imported into Tyre by the Syrians (Eze 27:16). They were used in the second row of the breastplate of the high priest (Ex 28:18; 39:11). In the New Jerusalem the fourth foundation of the wall of the city will be garnished with emeralds (Re 21:19). Emerald is a variety of beryl.

EM'ER·ODS

A disease of the anal region in the form of tumors (De 28:27). It was sent as a judgment upon the Philistines of Ashdod and Ekron for holding the ark (1 Sa 5:6; 6:11).

EMERY

See ADAMANT.

E'MIM

The early inhabitants of Moab. They were a powerful people (De 2:9-11).

EMMANUEL

See IMMANUEL.

EM·MA'US

The real site of this town is a matter of dispute. It was about seven miles from Jerusalem (sixty furlongs). Near this town Christ revealed himself to two of his disciples after the resurrection (Lk 24:13).

EMMOR (Ac 7:16)

See HAMOR.

EMPEROR

See AUGUSTUS and CAESAR.

EMPEROR WORSHIP

In some times and nations, the emperor was considered to be a god, and it was customary (and obligatory) to worship him accordingly. Daniel and his friends experienced this twice, once when Nebuchadnezzar demanded that all wor-

ship his image (Da 3), and once when Darius demanded that all prayers be offered up to him, and no other (Da 9).

While the New Testament never mentions emperor worship, we know from history that several of the Roman emperors had such a high opinion of themselves that they demanded this tribute. In societies which already boasted numerous gods, the addition of the mighty Roman conquerors to the list seemed easy. The emperor Caligula proclaimed himself a god, and tried to force the Jews to worship him. Later, the emperor Trajan heavily persecuted Christians who would not renounce Christ in favor of emperor worship. Emperor worship was an important part of official Roman religion until the time of Constantine.

EMULATION (archaic)

Jealousy, envy, contentious rivalry (Ga 5:19-21).

EN (spring, fountain)

Prefixed to geographical names to show where springs of water were located.

E'NAIM

See ENAM.

E'NAM (fountains)

A town in the lowland of Judah (Jos 15:34).

E'NAN

Father of Ahira (Nu 1:15; 2:29).

EN·CHANT'ER

A conjurer who employed incantations to obtain the aid of evil spirits or to liberate those tormented by such spirits. Enchantment includes magic (Ex 7:11), exorcism (Da 2:2), sorcery (Ac 8:9,11; 13:8,10). Such practices were condemned by Mosaic law (Le 19:26; De 18:10). The wicked Queen Jezebel was involved in witchcraft (2 Ki 9:22).

EN'DOR

A town in Manasseh about four miles from Mount Tabor (Jos 17:11). It was here the witch lived whom Saul consulted the night before his death (1 Sa 28:7).

EN-EG'LA·IM (fountain of two calves)

This place is mentioned by Ezekiel (Eze 47:10) in the vision of holy waters.

EN-GAN′ NIM *(fountain of gardens)*

1. A town of Issachar (Jos 19:21) allotted to the Levites (Jos 21:29).

2. A town in Judah (Jos 15:34).

EN-GE′ DI

A town, also called Hazazon-tamar, located on the edge of the wilderness on the west shore of the Dead Sea (Jos 15:62). Its inhabitants, the Amorites, were attacked by Chedorlaomer (Ge 14:7). In one of its many caves David found refuge after fleeing from Saul (1 Sa 23:29). Here he cut off a piece of Saul's robe instead of killing him (1 Sa 24:1-22).

ENGINE (archaic)

Machine (2 Ch 26:15; Eze 26:9; Eze 4:2; 21:22).

ENGRAVER

One who carves stone or metal in delicate designs, particularly writing (Ex 28:11,21,36).

EN-HAD′ DAH

A border town of Issachar (Jos 19:21).

EN-HAK·KOR′ E

The name of a fountain at Lehi (Ju 15:15, 18,19).

EN-HA′ ZOR *(fountain of the village)*

A fenced city of Naphtali (Jos 19:37).

ENJOIN (archaic)

To command; charge (He 9:19-20).

EN-MISH′ PAT *(fountain of judgment)*

The earlier name of Kadesh-barnea (Ge 14:7).

E′ NOCH

Two Old Testament men:

1. The eldest son of Cain (Ge 4:17-18).

2. Son of Jared and father of Methuselah; he belonged to the Seth line, "the antediluvian line of the Messiah" (Ge 5:18-24). Enoch was a righteous man. He did not die, but instead "he was not for the Lord took him." A prophecy of Enoch is found in the Epistle of Jude (Jude 14-15).

ENOCH, BOOK OF

See PSEUDEPIGRAPHA.

E′ NOS

See ENOSH.

E′ NOSH *(man)*

Son of Seth, the grandson of Adam (Ge 5:6-11; Lk 3:38).

ENQUIRE OF THE LORD

See INQUIRE OF THE LORD.

EN-RIM′ MON *(fountain of the pomegranate)*

A town in southern Judah (Ne 11:29), called Ain in Joshua 15:32, and Remmon in Joshua 19:7.

EN-RO′ GEL *(fountain of the fuller)*

A fountain near Jerusalem (Jos 15:7; 18:16; 2 Sa 17:17).

ENROLLMENT

Registration, census taking (Lk 2:1-5).

ENSAMPLE (archaic)

Example (1 Th 1:7-8).

EN-SHE′ MESH *(fountain of the sun)*

A fountain and town on the road from Jerusalem to Jericho (Jos 15:7; 18:17).

ENSIGN (archaic)

Standard or banner (Song 2:4; Is 13:2; 18:3). See STANDARD.

ENSUE (archaic)

To follow after (1 Pe 3:10-11).

ENTAPPUAH (Jos 17:7)

See TAPPUAH.

ENVIRON

To surround; compass (Jos 7:9). Root of the word environment.

ENVOY

Messenger. See AMBASSADOR.

ENVY

Jealousy. Christians must not allow envy to take hold of their lives; it is a sin which causes more destruction than we are at first aware of (Ro 13:13; 1 Pe 2:1). James tells us that envy springs from selfishness (James 3:14,16).

EP-AE′ NE·TUS, EP-E′ NE·TUS
(praiseworthy)

A convert to Christianity in Achaia (Ro 16:5).

EP′ A·PHRAS

A member of the Colossian church and possibly the founder of it. He came to Paul at Rome during his first imprisonment. In Paul's epistle to that church he joined the apostle in sending salutations (Col 1:7-8; 4:12). Paul speaks of him as "my fellow prisoner" (Phile 23).

EP·APH·RO·DI′ TUS

A Christian sent with gifts from the church at Philippi to Paul, then a prisoner at Rome. Epaphroditus became ill while there but, upon recovery, he returned to Philippi taking with him Paul's epistle to that church (Ph 2:15-30; 4:18).

EP-E′ NE·TUS

See EPAENETUS.

E′ PHAH (gloom)

A unit of measure, two men and a woman:

1. A unit of dry measure equal to one tenth of an omer or about 0.65 bushels (Ex 16:36), used for measuring commodities such as grain (Ru 2:17). See WEIGHTS AND MEASURES.

2. One of the five sons of Midian (Ge 25:4; 1 Ch 1:33). His descendants formed a branch of the Midianites and lived in the northeastern part of Arabia (Is 60:6).

3. A concubine of Caleb of the tribe of Judah (1 Ch 2:46).

4. The son of Jahdai of Judah (1 Ch 2:47).

E′ PHAI

A Netophathite. When Jerusalem fell in 586 B.C., his sons came to Gedaliah, the governor placed over the remnant left in the city, and were assured of protection. They were slain with Gedaliah by Ishmael (Je 40:8; 41:3).

E′ PHER (gazelle)

Three Old Testament men:

1. A son of Midian who was the son of Abraham and Keturah (Ge 25:4; 1 Ch 1:33).

2. A son of Ezra (1 Ch 4:17).

3. A leader of a family of Manasseh (1 Ch 5:24).

E′ PHES-DAM′ MIM

A place in Judah between Shochoh and Azekah where the Philistines were encamped when David killed Goliath (1 Sa 17:1). In 1 Chronicles 11:13 it is called Pas-dammim.

E·PHE′ SIAN

The inhabitants of the city of Ephesus. Paul's friend Trophimus was an Ephesian (Ac 21:29).

E·PHE′ SIANS, E·PIS′ TLE TO THE

1. The Book of Ephesians. Ephesians is addressed to a group of believers who are rich beyond measure in Jesus Christ, yet living as beggars because they are ignorant of their wealth. They have relegated themselves to living as spiritual paupers. Paul begins by describing in chapters 1–3 the contents of the Christian's heavenly "bank account": adoption, acceptance, redemption, forgiveness, wisdom, inheritance, the seal of the Holy Spirit, life, grace, citizenship—in short, every spiritual blessing. Drawing upon that huge spiritual endowment, the Christian has all the resources needed for living "to the praise of the glory of His grace" (1:6). Chapters 4–6 resemble an orthopedic clinic, where the Christian learns a spiritual walk rooted in his spiritual wealth. "For we are His workmanship, created in Christ Jesus (1–3) for good works, . . . that we should walk in them (4–6)" (2:10)

The traditional title of this epistle is *Pros Ephesious,* "To the Ephesians." Many ancient manuscripts, however, omit the words *en Epheso,* "in Ephesus," from the introduction in 1:1. This has led a number of scholars to challenge the traditional view that this message was directed specifically to the Ephesians. The encyclical theory proposes that it was a circular letter sent by Paul to the churches of Asia. It is argued that Ephesians is really a Christian treatise designed for general use: it involves no controversy and deals with no specific problems in any particular church. This is also supported by the phraseology ("after I heard of your faith," 1:15; if they "have heard" of his message, 3:2). These things seem inconsistent with the relationship Paul must have had with the Ephesians after a ministry of almost three years among them. On the other hand, the absence of personal greetings is not a support for the encyclical theory because Paul might have done this to avoid favoritism. The only letters that greet specific people are Romans and Colossians, and they were addressed to churches Paul had not visited. Some scholars accept an ancient tradition that Ephesians is Paul's letter to the Laodiceans (Col 4:16), but there is no way to be sure. If Ephesians began as a circular letter, it eventually became associated with Ephesus, the foremost of the Asian churches. Another plausible option is that this epistle was directly addressed to the Ephesians, but written in such a way as to make it helpful for all the churches in Asia.

2. The Author of Ephesians. All internal (1:1) and external evidence strongly supports the Pauline authorship of Ephesians. In recent years, however, critics have turned to internal grounds to challenge the unanimous ancient tradition. It has been argued that the vocabulary and style are different from other Pauline epistles, but this overlooks Paul's flexibility under different circumstances (for instance, compare Romans and 2 Corinthians). The theology of Ephesians in some ways reflects a later development, but this must be attributed to Paul's own growth and meditation on the church as the body of Christ. Since the epistle clearly names the author in the opening verse, it is not necessary to theorize that Ephesians was written by one of Paul's pupils or admirers, such as Timothy, Luke, Tychicus, or Onesimus.

3. The Time of Ephesians. At the end of his second missionary journey, Paul visited Ephesus where he left Priscilla and Aquila (Ac 18:18-21). This city, strategically located on the Mediterranean coast, was the commercial center of Asia Minor, but heavy silting required that a special canal be maintained so that ships could reach the harbor. Ephesus was a religious center as well, famous especially for its magnificent temple of Diana, or Artemis as she was called in Greek. This temple was considered to be one of the seven wonders of the ancient world (Ac 19:35). The practice of magic and the local economy were clearly related to this temple. Paul remained in Ephesus for nearly three years on his third missionary journey (Ac 18:23–19:41); the Word of God was spread throughout the province of Asia. Paul's effective ministry began to seriously hurt the traffic in magic and images, leading to an uproar in the huge Ephesian theater. Paul then left for Macedonia, but afterward he met with the Ephesian elders while on his way to Jerusalem (Ac 20:17-38).

Paul wrote the "Prison Epistles" (Ephesians, Philippians, Colossians, and Philemon) during his first Roman imprisonment in A.D. 60-62. These epistles all refer to his imprisonment (Ep 3:1; 4:1; 6:20; Ph 1:7,13-14; Col 4:3,10,18; Phile 9-10,13,23), and fit well against the background in Acts 28:16-31. This is especially true of Paul's references to the palace guard (governor's official residential guard, Ph 1:13) and "Caesar's household" (Ph 4:22). Some commentators believe that the imprisonment in one or more of these epistles refers to Paul's Caesarean imprisonment or to a hypothetical Ephesian imprisonment, but the weight of evidence favors the traditional view that they were written in Rome. Ephesians, Colossians, and Philemon were evidently written about the same time (Ep 6:21-22; Col 4:7-9) in A.D. 60-61. Philippians was written in A.D. 62, not long before Paul's release.

4. The Christ of Ephesians. Paul's important phrase "in Christ" (or its equivalent) appears about thirty-five times, more than in any other New Testament book. The believer is in Christ (1:1), in the heavenly places in Christ (1:3), chosen in Him (1:4), adopted through Christ (1:5), in the Beloved (1:6), redeemed in Him (1:7), given an inheritance in Him (1:11), given hope in Him (1:12), sealed in Him (1:13), made alive together with Christ (2:5), raised and seated with Him (2:6), created in Christ (2:10), brought near by His blood (2:13), growing in Christ (2:21), a partaker of the promise in Christ (3:6), and given access through faith in Him (3:12).

5. Keys to Ephesians.
Key Word: Building the Body of Christ— Ephesians focuses on the believer's responsibility to walk in accordance with his heavenly calling in Christ Jesus (4:1). Ephesians was not written to correct specific errors in a local church, but to prevent problems in the church as a whole by encouraging the body of Christ to maturity in Him. It was also written to make believers more aware of their position in Christ because this is the basis for their practice on every level of life.

Key Verses: Ephesians 2:8-10 and 4:1-3— "For by grace you have been saved through faith, and that not of yourselves; it is the gift of God, not of works, lest anyone should boast. For we are His workmanship, created in Christ Jesus for good works, which God prepared beforehand that we should walk in them" (2:8-10).

"I, therefore, the prisoner of the Lord, beseech you to have a walk worthy of the calling with which you were called, with all lowliness and gentleness, with longsuffering, bearing with one another in love, endeavoring to keep the unity of the Spirit in the bond of peace" (4:1-3).

Key Chapter: Ephesians 6—Even though

the Christian is blessed "with every spiritual blessing in the heavenly places in Christ" (1:3), spiritual warfare is still the daily experience of the Christian while in the world. Chapter 6 is the clearest advice for how to "be strong in the Lord and in the power of His might" (6:10).

6. Survey of Ephesians. Paul wrote this epistle to make Christians more aware of their position in Christ and to motivate them to draw upon their spiritual source in daily living: "walk worthy of the calling with which you were called" (4:1; see 2:10). The first half of Ephesians lists the believer's heavenly possessions: adoption, redemption, inheritance, power, life, grace, citizenship, and the love of Christ. There are no imperatives in chapters 1–3, which focus only on divine gifts. But chapters 4–6 include thirty-five directives in the last half of Ephesians that speak of the believer's responsibility to conduct himself according to his individual calling. So Ephesians begins in heaven, but concludes in the home and in all other relationships of daily life. The two divisions are: the position of the Christian (1:1–3:21) and the practice of the Christian (4:1–6:20).

The Position of the Christian (1:1–3:21). After a two-verse prologue, in one long Greek sentence Paul extols the triune God for the riches of redemption (1:3-14). This hymn to God's grace praises the Father for choosing us (1:3-6), the Son for redeeming us (1:7-12), and the Spirit for sealing us (1:13-14). The saving work of each divine person is to the praise of the glory of His grace (1:6,12,14). Before continuing, Paul offers the first of two very significant prayers (1:15-23; 3:14-21). Here he asks that the readers receive spiritual illuminations so that they may come to perceive what is, in fact, true. Next, Paul describes their former condition with their present spiritual life in

Christ, as salvation attained not by human works but by divine grace (2:1-10). This redemption includes Jews, yet also extends to those Gentiles who previously were "strangers from the covenants of promise" (2:12). In Christ, the two for the first time have become members of one body (2:11-22). The truth that Gentiles would become "fellow heirs, of the same body" (3:6) was formerly a mystery that has now been revealed (3:1-13). Paul's second prayer (3:14-21) expresses his desire that the readers be strengthened with the power of the Spirit and fully apprehend the love of Christ.

The Practice of the Christian (4:1–6:20). The pivotal verse of Ephesians is 4:1, because it draws a sharp line between the doctrinal and the practical divisions of this book. There is a cause and effect relationship between chapters 1–3 and 4–6 because the spiritual walk of a Christian must be rooted in his spiritual wealth. As Paul emphasized in Romans, behavior does not determine blessing; instead, blessing should determine behavior.

Because of the unity of all believers in the body of Christ, growth and maturity come from "the effective working by which every part does its share" (4:16). This involves the exercise of spiritual gifts in love. Paul exhorts the readers to "put off, concerning your former conduct, the old man" (4:22) and "put on the new man" (4:24) that will be manifested by a walk of integrity in the midst of all people. They are also to maintain a walk of holiness as children of light (5:1-21). Every relationship (wives, husbands, children, parents, slaves, and masters) must be transformed by their new life in Christ (5:22–6:9). Paul's colorful description of the spiritual warfare and the armor of God (6:10-20) is followed by a word about Tychicus and then a benediction (6:21-24).

OUTLINE OF EPHESIANS

Part One: The Position of the Christian (1:1–3:21)

I. Praise for Redemption (1:1-14)

A. Salutation from Paul 1:1-2
B. Chosen by the Father 1:3-6
C. Redeemed by the Son 1:7-12
D. Sealed by the Spirit 1:13-14

II. Prayer for Revelation (1:15-23)

III. Position of the Christian (2:1–3:13)

IV. The Christian's Position Individually (2:1-10)

A. The Christians' Position Corporately 2:11–3:13

V. Prayer for Realization (3:14-21)

Part Two: The Practice of the Christian (4:1–6:24)

I. Unity in the Church (4:1-16)

A. Exhortation to Unity 4:1-3
B. Explanation of Unity 4:4-6
C. Means for Unity: The Gifts............ 4:7-11
D. Purpose of the Gifts 4:12-16

II. Holiness in Life (4:17–5:21)

A. Put Off the Old Man 4:17-22
B. Put On the New Man 4:23-29
C. Grieve Not the Holy Spirit 4:30–5:12
D. Walk as Children of Light 5:13-17
E. Be Filled with the Spirit 5:18-21

III. Responsibilities in the Home and at Work (5:22–6:9)

A. Wives: Submit to Your
Husbands 5:22-24
B. Husbands: Love Your Wives 5:25-33
C. Children: Obey Your Parents 6:1-4
D. Service on the Job....................... 6:5-9

IV. Conduct in the Conflict (6:10-24)

A. Put On the Armor of God 6:10-17
B. Pray for Boldness 6:18-20
C. Conclusion 6:21-24

EPH'ES·US

Ephesus was an important city on the western coast of Asia Minor where the apostle Paul founded a church. As the most favorable seaport in the Roman province of Asia, this city was the most important trade center west of Tarsus. Today the city lies in swampy ruins about six miles from the sea, because of centuries of silting from the Cayster River.

During Paul's years in Ephesus, the city was a cultural center with a population of about 300,000 people. Ephesus boasted a great amphitheater, which seated about 25,000 people. The city also had a number of gymnasiums, baths, and impressive public buildings.

Religion was a prominent feature of life in Ephesus. The temple of Artemis (or Diana, as the Romans called her) ranked as one of the Seven Wonders of the Ancient World. As the daughter of Zeus, Artemis was variously known as the moon goddess, the goddess of hunting, and the patroness of young girls. The Ephesians took pride in the beautiful temple, which was supported by scores of stone columns.

The church at Ephesus may have been established by Priscilla and Aquila (Ac 18:18). It was about two years old when Paul settled in the city. Timothy was also involved in ministry at Ephesus (1 Ti 1:3). Paul taught daily in the lecture hall of Tyrannus (Ac 19:9). Influence from Paul's three-year ministry likely resulted in the planting of churches in the Lycus River Valley at Laodicea, Hieropolis, and Colosse. The apostle wrote 1 Corinthians during his stay in Ephesus.

Some time after Paul's ministry, the apostle John settled and ministered at Ephesus. Exiled

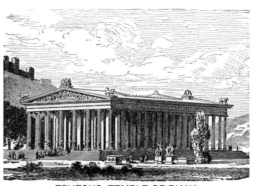

EPHESUS, TEMPLE OF DIANA

on the Isle of Patmos off the coast of Ephesus, he addressed the Book of Revelation to the seven churches of Asia Minor, which included the congregation at Ephesus (Re 1:11; 2:1-7). The traditional tomb of John is located at the Church of St. John in Ephesus.

EPHLAL

Son of Zabad and father of Obed, in the genealogy of the sons of Judah (1 Ch 2:37).

E'PHOD *(a covering)*

1. Father of Hanniel, a leader of the tribe of Manasseh in the wilderness (Nu 34:23).

2. An official garment of the Jewish high priest which he was required to wear when engaged in religious duties (Ex 28:4). Suspended from the shoulders it covered both back and front. On the shoulders were two onyx stones on which the names of the tribes were engraved (Ex 28:9; 39:6-7). Attached to the ephod was the breastplate (Ex 28:25-28; 9:19-21).

EPH′PHA·THA

An Aramaic word which carries a command "be opened" (Mk 7:34).

E′PHRA·IM *(fruitful)*

Joseph's younger son. His mother, Asenath, was the daughter of Potipherah, priest of On. He was born after Joseph became prime minister of Egypt (Ge 41:45-52). When Jacob placed his right hand on the head of Ephraim, the younger son, he explained to Joseph that Ephraim would be the greater and would be the ancestor of a multitude of peoples. The descendants of the two sons were to be regarded as two tribes (Ge 48:8-20).

E′PHRA·IM, CITY OF

A city of Judea to which Jesus fled after restoring Lazarus (Jo 11:54).

E′PHRA·IM, FOREST OF

The Forest or Wood of Ephraim was the scene of the decisive battle between the armies of David and his rebellious son, Absalom (2 Sa 18:6-17). The area was given to Ephraim because the sons of Joseph were so numerous (Jos 17:14-18).

E′PHRA·IM, GATE OF

A gate of Jerusalem, probably in the northeast portion of the wall (2 Ki 14:13; 2 Ch 25:23; Ne 8:16; 12:39). See GATES OF JERUSALEM AND THE TEMPLE.

E′PHRA·IMITE

See EPHRATHITE.

E′PHRA·IM, MOUNTAINS OF

A mountain ridge in central Palestine within the territories of Ephraim and the western half-tribe of Manasseh. Samuel's parents were from Mount Ephraim (1 Sa 1:1). Joshua's inheritance was in the mountains of Ephraim (Jos 19:50).

E′PHRA·IM, TRIBE OF

The descendants of Joseph's younger son (Jos 16:4,10; Ju 5:14). A year after the exodus, when the census was taken, the tribe numbered 40,500. At the close of the wandering, in the second census, they numbered 32,500 (Nu 26:37). Joshua was an Ephraimite (Jos 19:50; 24:30). In the division of the land, on the south of Ephraim was Benjamin, on the north Manasseh, and on the

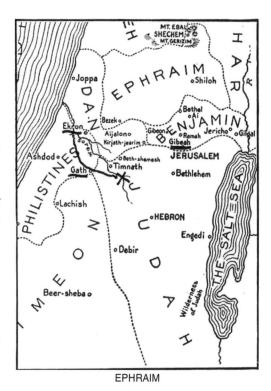

EPHRAIM

west Dan. Strongest of the northern tribes, Ephraim was resentful of Judean supremacy and was critical of the undertakings of other tribes, such as those led by Gideon and Jephthah (Ju 8:1-33; 12:1-6).

E′PHRA·IN

A town of Israel, taken in battle by Abijah, king of Israel, in the days of Jeroboam king of Israel (2 Ch 13:19).

EPH′RA·TAH

A town and a woman:

1. The name by which Bethlehem was originally known; the place where Rachel was buried (Ge 35:19; 48:7; Ru 4:11). The city was also called Beth-lehem Ephratah (Mi 5:2). See BETHLEHEM.

2. The wife of Caleb and mother of Hur (1 Ch 2:19,50; 4:4).

E′PHRATH

See EPHRATAH.

EPH′RA·THAH

See EPHRATAH.

EPH′ RA·THITE

1. A native of Ephrath, that is, Bethlehem (1 Sa 17:12; Ru 1:2).

2. One belonging to the tribe of Ephraim (1 Sa 1:1; 1 Ki 11:26).

E′ PHRON

A town, a man, and a mountain:

1. The son of Zohar, a Hittite, who lived at Hebron. He owned the cave of Machpelah and sold it to Abraham (Ge 23:8; 25:9).

2. A city captured by Abijah from Jeroboam (2 Ch 13:19). In the KJV the city is called Ephrain.

3. A mountain on the border between Benjamin and Judah (Jos 15:9).

EP·I·CU·RE′ ANS

A philosophical sect of Greece and Rome. The name is derived from the philosopher Epicurus, born about 341 B.C. on the island of Samos. He was the founder of a school in Athens in which he taught until his death in 270 B.C. According to his ethical ideas, pleasure should be sought and pain avoided. The Epicureans were present when Paul preached Christianity in Athens (Ac 17:18-20).

EPILEPSY

A disorder of the central nervous system which produces seizures, or convulsions. These can range from mere involuntary twitching to grand mal seizures in which the victim is unconscious, froths at the mouth, the muscles stiffen, and the body is thrown into a severe convulsion. In scripture, epilepsy is connected with demonic activity. See DEMONIACS.

EPIPHANES

See ANTIOCHUS.

E·PIS′ TLE

A letter, particularly one with a formal style and containing a specific teaching or doctrine. Twenty-one of the twenty-seven books of the New Testament are in the form of formal letters, or epistles. Usually they were addressed to individuals, groups, or churches. With two exceptions they open with a statement as to authorship or destination. About a dozen such letters are attributed to Paul. Four others claim as their authors James, Peter, and Jude. Three are ascribed to John. The author of the Epistle

to the Hebrews is not named. These letters were written to meet definite needs, such as correcting the conditions of the churches, teaching Christian doctrine, or refuting heretical ideas.

ER *(watchful)*

Three Old Testament men:

1. The eldest son of Judah. His mother was Shua, a Canaanite. His wickedness caused the Lord to kill him (Ge 38:1-7; 46:12; 1 Ch 2:3).

2. Son of Shelah of Judah (1 Ch 4:21).

3. Son of Jose, an ancestor of Joseph, husband of Mary (Lk 3:28-29).

ERAN

Son of Shuthelah, a descendant of Ephraim (Nu 26:36).

ERANITES

The clan or family descended from Eran, the Ephraimite (Nu 26:36).

E·RAS′ TUS *(beloved)*

A Christian whom Paul sent with Timothy from Ephesus (Ac 19:22). He is probably the same as the chamberlain of Corinth (Ro 16:23).

ERE (archaic)

Before (Job 18:2).

ERECH

A city of the kingdom of Nimrod, the mighty hunter descended from Ham (Ge 10:10).

E′ RI *(watching)*

The fifth son of Gad and founder of a tribal family (Ge 46:16; Nu 26:16).

E·SA′ IAS

Greek form of Isaiah. See ISAIAH.

E·SAR·HAD′ DON

Son of Sennacherib, king of Assyria. His being favored by his father so angered two of his brothers that they assassinated their father and fled into Armenia (2 Ki 19:36-37; 2 Ch 32:21; Is 37:37-38). At that time, Esarhaddon was conducting a campaign in Armenia. When he heard of this foul deed, he returned with his army to Nineveh but on the way encountered the rebel forces and defeated them. In 680 B.C., he succeeded to the throne.

E' SAU *(hairy)*

The oldest son of Isaac and Rebekah; a hunter. He sold his birthright to his brother, Jacob, for a mess of red pottage. For this he was given the name Edom which means red (Ge 25:27-34; He 12:16-17). He married Judith and Adah, both Hittites (Ge 26:34-35; 36:1-2), and a daughter of Ishmael (Ge 28:9; 36:3). Esau was cheated from receiving the blessing of his father by the deception of Jacob and Rebekah. Esau's fury at this caused Jacob to flee to Mesopotamia (Ge 27:1–31:55). However, Esau treated Jacob kindly when he returned from Mesopotamia (Ge 32:3–33:15). His descendants were called Edomites (De 2:4,12,22).

E' SAU'S WIVES

Esau was married to two Hittite women, Judith and Adah (also called Basemath). This greatly displeased his parents (Ge 26:34,46). When Esau realized that they were unhappy with his foreign wives, he took another wife, one of Ishmael's daughters (Ge 28:8-9). Seeing Isaac send Jacob back to Rebekah's relatives to find a wife probably gave him the idea that one of Abraham's family would be more acceptable to his parents.

ESCHATOLOGY

From the Greek *eschatos* ("last"); the study of End Times. The Scripture abounds with prophecy concerning the last days, particularly in the Books of Daniel, Ezekiel, and Revelation. However, since most of this prophecy is given in highly colored, symbolic language, opinions differ on exactly how it should be interpreted. It is clear that there will be a time of great tribulation before the return of Christ, and that in the end, after Christ's return, the earth will be consumed with fire, and replaced with a new heaven and earth in which the effects of the curse are no longer applied (2 Pe 3:10-12; Re 20–21). See EARTH, NEW. There is much disagreement concerning how literally to take the prophecies. Some believe that nearly all the prophecies are symbolic, while others take them as literally as possible.

There are three main systems of eschatology: *post-millennialism* holds that Christ will return after the 1000 year reign discussed in Revelation 20. The "millennial kingdom" is thought to be the present age, where the church is spreading and influencing the world. According to this system, this age is characterized by the spread of Christianity and increased righteousness. God's kingdom is increasing gradually, and through the influence of the church, Christ reigns on earth. There will be a period of apostasy before Christ returns; when He returns (in the body), the dead will be raised and all men will be judged. Part of the reasoning behind this system is the teaching of Christ in the Gospels concerning the kingdom of heaven. The Jews were clearly expecting the Messiah to usher in an earthly political kingdom, and Jesus was offering a spiritual kingdom. The post-millennial view is expecting to see God's kingdom on earth before Christ returns.

Amillennialism (literally "no millennium"), teaches that the 1000 year reign of Christ is not a literal reign, but rather the reign of Christ in the hearts of believers, or the reign of Christ over believers who have already died. References to the future kingdom of God are seen to refer to the new heaven and earth. Amillennialism differs from post-millennialism in that it has a less optimistic view of the present age. The "millennial kingdom" only applies to believers; the rest of the world is growing in apostasy. The amillennial view is expecting the return of Christ at any time. When He comes, the dead will be raised and all men will be judged.

Pre-millennialism holds that the millennial kingdom is a literal earthly kingdom that is still in the future. Instead of the gradual introduction taught by the post-millennial system, the end times will begin suddenly, without any warning, when Christ returns to rapture the church. The word "rapture" means "caught up" and comes from the Latin word for birds of prey snatching their food in their talons. The biblical concept is found in 1 Thessalonians 4:16-17, and Revelation 3:3, where Jesus says that He will come "as a thief in the night." After the church is gone, the Great Tribulation will occur, and the terrible events detailed in Revelation will come to pass. Finally, Christ will return and reign on earth for a thousand years (Re 19:11–20:6). When this time is over, the last great rebellion occurs (Re 20:7-10), the final judgment of man is carried out (Re 20:11-15) and the earth is destroyed. Last of all, a new heaven and earth are created, the curse is lifted, and all believers will live in the presence of God forever. The pre-millennial view is unique in that it expects the millennial kingdom to be the literal fulfillment of the promises to the nation Israel, rather than assuming that the prophecies concerning Israel have been transferred to the church.

Many people feel passionately about their own eschatological views, believing that what one believes about the end times will affect how one behaves in the present age. While this can certainly be true, one's eschatology is not considered to affect one's orthodoxy.

ESCHEW (archaic)

To avoid; turn aside from (1 Pe 3:10-11).

ES′ DRA-E′ LON, PLAIN OF

See MEGIDDO.

ES′ DRAS

The Greek form of Ezra. See APOCRYPHA.

E′ SEK *(contention)*

A well dug by Isaac and claimed by the Philistines (Ge 26:20).

E′ SHAN, ESH′ E·AN *(support)*

A town in the mountains of Judah (Jos 15:52).

ESH·BA′ AL

See ISH-BOSHETH.

ESH′ BAN

A son of Dishon, the Horite (Ge 36:26; 1 Ch 1:41).

ESH′ COL *(a cluster)*

A man and a valley:

1. A valley near Hebron (Nu 13:22-23; De 1:24) which is renowned for its great clusters of grapes. From here the scouts sent out by Moses brought back to the Israelites at Kadesh-barnea a cluster of grapes so large that it took two men to carry it (Nu 13:24).

2. The Amorite brother of Mamre (Ge 14:13,24).

ESH′ E·AN

See ESHAN.

E′ SHEK *(oppression)*

A descendant of Saul (1 Ch 8:39).

ESH′ KA·LON·ITE

See ASHKELON.

ESH′ TA·OL

A town between Judah and Dan which was eventually assigned to Dan (Jos 15:33; 19:41). Samson was born near here (Ju 13:24-25).

ESH·TA·U′ LITE

An inhabitant of Eshtaol (1 Ch 2:53).

ESH·TE·MO′ A

A man and a town:

1. A son of Hodiah (1 Ch 4:19).

2. A town of Judah assigned to the priests (Jos 15:50; 21:14). When David captured Ziklag, he sent to this town some of the spoils (1 Sa 30:28).

ESH·TE·MO′ AH

See ESHTEMOA.

ESH′ TON

A Judahite (1 Ch 4:11-12).

ES′ LI

An ancestor of Jesus (Lk 3:25).

ESPOUSAL

See BETROTHAL.

ESPY (archaic)

To see; behold (Ge 42:27-28).

ES′ ROM

See HEZRON.

ESSENES

A sect of Judaism noted for their separatism and strict religious discipline. They practiced communal living, and strove for simplicity in dress and lifestyle. They were flourishing at the time of Christ, and one community of them lived at Qumran, near the Dead Sea, a few miles from Jericho. It was this community which stored copies of the Scriptures and other religious manuscripts in clay jars in the nearby caves. These were rediscovered in the 1940's and proved to be of great interest. (See DEAD SEA SCROLLS). While it is speculated that some of John's early disciples were from the Essene communities, as a whole the Essenes rejected Jesus and continued to wait for the Messiah.

ES'THER *(star)*

The beautiful daughter of Abihail, a Benjamite (Es 2:15). Her Hebrew name was Hadassah (myrtle). After being brought up by her first cousin, Mordecai, she became the favorite wife (or concubine) of King Ahasuerus.

ES'THER, ADDITIONS TO

See APOCRYPHA.

ES'THER, BOOK OF

1. The Book of Esther. God's hand of providence and protection on behalf of His people is evident throughout the Book of Esther, even though His name does not appear once. Haman's plot brings grave danger to the Jews and is countered by the courage of beautiful Esther and the counsel of her wise cousin Mordecai, resulting in a great deliverance. The Feast of Purim became an annual reminder of God's faithfulness on behalf of His people.

Esther's Hebrew name was *Hadassah,* "Myrtle" (2:7), but her Persian name *Ester* was derived from the Persian word for "star." The Greek title for this book is *Esther,* and in Latin the title is *Hester.*

2. The Author of Esther. While the author's identity is not indicated in the text, the evident knowledge of Persian etiquette and customs, the palace in Susa, and details of the events in the reign of Ahasuerus indicate that the author lived in Persia during this period. The obvious Jewish nationalism and knowledge of Jewish customs further suggests that the author was Jewish. If this Persian Jew was not an eyewitness, he probably knew people who were. The book must have been written soon after the death of King Ahasuerus (464 B.C.), because 10:2-3 speaks of his reign in the past tense. Some writers suggest that Mordecai himself wrote the book; this seems unlikely, for although Mordecai did keep records (9:20), 10:2-3 implies that his career was already over. Nevertheless, the author certainly made use of Mordecai's records and may have had access to the Book of the Chronicles of the Kings of Media and Persia (2:23; 10:2). Ezra and Nehemiah have also been suggested for authorship, but the vocabulary and style of Esther is dissimilar to that found in their books. It seems likely that a younger contemporary of Mordecai composed the book.

3. The Time of Esther. Ahasuerus is the Hebrew name and Xerxes the Greek name of Khshayarsh, king of Persia in 486-464 B.C. According to 1:3, the feast of Xerxes took place in his third year, or 483 B.C. The historian Herodotus refers to this banquet as the occasion of Xerxes' planning for a military campaign against Greece. But in 479 B.C. he was defeated by the Greeks at Salamis, and Herodotus tells us that he sought consolation in his harem. This corresponds to the time when he held a "contest" and crowned Esther queen of Persia (2:16-17). Since the events of the rest of the book took place in 473 B.C. (3:7-12), the chronological span is ten years (483-473 B.C.). The probable time of authorship was between about 464 B.C. (the end of Xerxes' reign; see 10:2-3) and about 435 B.C. (the palace at Susa was destroyed by fire during that period, and such an event would probably have been mentioned). The historical and linguistic features of Esther do not support a date later than 400 B.C., as there is no trace of Greek influence in the book.

Xerxes was a boisterous man of emotional extremes, whose actions were often strange and contradictory. This fact sheds light on his ability to sign a decree for the annihilation of the Jews, and two months later to sign a second decree allowing them to overthrow their enemies.

Esther was addressed to the many Jews who did not return to their homeland. Not all the godly people left—some stayed in Persia for legitimate reasons. Even though some stayed in Persia through disobedience, God continued to care for His people in exile.

4. The Christ of Esther. Esther, like Christ, put herself in the place of death for her people, but received the approval of the king. She also portrays Christ's work as an advocate on our behalf. This book reveals another satanic attempt to destroy the Jewish people and thus, the messianic line. God continued to preserve His people in spite of opposition and danger, and nothing could prevent the coming of the Messiah.

5. Keys to Esther.

Key Words: Providence—The Book of Esther was written to show how the Jewish people were protected and preserved by the gracious hand of God from the threat of annihilation. Although God disciplines His covenant people, He never abandons them. The God of Israel is the sovereign controller of history, and

His providential care can be seen throughout this book: He raises a Jewish girl out of obscurity to become the queen of the most powerful empire in the world; He ensures that Mordecai's loyal deed is recorded in the palace records; He guides Esther's admission to the king's court; He superintends the timing of Esther's two feasts; He is involved in Ahasuerus's insomnia and the cure he uses for it; He sees that Haman's gallows will be utilized in an unexpected way; He gives Esther great favor in the sight of the king; and He brings about the new decree and the eventual victory of the Jews.

Key Verses: Esther 4:14; 8:17—"For if you remain completely silent at this time, relief and deliverance will arise for the Jews from another place, but you and your father's house will perish. Yet who knows whether you have come to the kingdom for such a time as this?" (4:14)

"And in every province and city, wherever the king's command and decree came, the Jews had joy and gladness, a feast and a holiday. Then many of the people of the land became Jews, because the fear of the Jews fell upon them" (8:17).

Key Chapter: Esther 8—According to the Book of Esther, the salvation of the Jews is accomplished through the second decree of King Ahasuerus, allowing the Jews to defend themselves against their enemies. Chapter 8 records this pivotal event with the accompanying result that "many of the people of the land became Jews" (8:17).

6. Survey of Esther. The story of Esther fits between chapters 6 and 7 of Ezra, between the first return led by Zerubbabel and the second return led by Ezra. It provides the only biblical portrait of the vast majority of Jews who choose to remain in Persia rather than return to Palestine. God's guiding and protective hand on behalf of His people is evident throughout this book, even though His name does not appear in it. The clearly emerging message is that God uses ordinary men and women to overcome impossible circumstances to accomplish His gracious purposes. Chapters 1–4 describe the threat to the Jews, and chapters 5–10 describe the triumph of the Jews

The Threat to the Jews (1–4). The story begins in Ahasuerus's winter palace at Susa. The king provided a lavish banquet and display of royal glory for the people of Susa, and proudly sought to make Queen Vashti's beauty

a part of the program. When she refused to appear, the king was counseled to depose her and seek another queen, because it was feared that the other women of the kingdom would become insolent to their husbands if Vashti were left unpunished. The king agreed, and collected a large number of beautiful girls to enter a "beauty contest" for the position of queen. One of these was the Jewish girl, Hadassah, also called Esther. Esther found favor in the eyes of Ahasuerus, and was made queen. At her cousin Mordecai's instruction, she kept her nationality a secret. With her help, Mordecai was able to warn the king of an assassination plot, and his deed was recorded in the palace records. Meanwhile, Haman became captain of the princes, and was infuriated by Mordecai's refusal to bow down to him. When Haman learned that Mordecai was Jewish, he plotted for a year to eliminate all Jews, as his rage and hatred grew. He cast lots (purim) daily during this period, until he determined the best day to have them massacred. Through bribery and lies he convinced Ahasuerus to issue an edict that all Jews in the empire would be slain eleven months hence in a single day. Haman conceived his plot in envy and a vengeful spirit, and he executed it with malicious craft. The decree created a state of confusion, and Mordecai asked Esther to appeal to the king, convincing her that she had been called to her high position for that very purpose.

The Triumph of the Jews (5–10). After fasting, Esther appeared before the king and wisely invited him to a banquet along with Haman. At the banquet she requested that they attend a second banquet, as she seeks the right moment to divulge her request. Haman was flattered, but his large self-consequence was still impaired by Mordecai's presence on earth. At his wife's suggestion, Haman built a large gallows for Mordecai (he could not wait eleven months to see him slain). That night Ahasuerus decided to treat his insomnia by reading the palace records. Reading about Mordecai's deed, he wanted to honor him. Mistakenly thinking that the king wanted to honor him, Haman advised the king on how to best bestow this honor, only to find out that the reward was for Mordecai. The king ordered Haman to carry out the honor he suggested, and Haman was infuriated and mortified to be forced to bring recognition to the man he loathes. At Esther's second banquet, Ahasuerus offered her as much as half of his kingdom for the third time. She then made her plea for her people and accused Haman of his treachery. The king had Haman hanged on the gallows he had prepared for Mordecai. The gallows, seventy-five feet high, was originally designed to make Mordecai's downfall a city-wide spectacle. Ironically, Haman died receiving the public attention he desired so much.

Persian law sealed with the king's ring (3:12) could not be revoked, but at Esther's request the king issued a new decree to all the provinces that the Jews might assemble and defend themselves on the day when they would be at-

tacked by their enemies. This decree changed the outcome intended by the first order and produced great joy. Mordecai was also elevated and set over the house of Haman. When the fateful day of the two decrees arrived, the Jews defeated their enemies in their cities throughout the Persian provinces, but did not take the plunder. The next day became a day of celebration and an annual Jewish holiday called the Feast of Purim. The word is derived from the Assyrian *puru,* meaning "lot," referring to the lots cast by Haman to determine the day decreed for the Jewish annihilation. The narrative closes with the advancement of Mordecai to a position second only to the king.

OUTLINE OF ESTHER

Part One: The Threat to the Jews (1:1–4:17)

I. The Selection of Esther as Queen (1:1–2:20)

A. The Divorce of Vashti 1:1-22
B. The Marriage to Esther 2:1-20

II. The Formulation of the Plot by Haman (2:21–4:17)

A. Mordecai Reveals the Plot to Murder the King 2:21-23
B. Haman Plots to Murder the Jews 3:1–4:17

Part Two: The Triumph of the Jews (5:1–10:3)

I. The Triumph of Mordecai over Haman (5:1–8:3)

A. Setting for the Triumph 5:1–6:3
B. Mordecai is Honored..................... 6:4-14
C. Haman Dies on Gallows Prepared for Mordecai 7:1-10
D. Mordecai is Given Haman's House ... 8:1-3

II. The Triumph of Israel over Her Enemies (8:4–10:3)

A. Preparation for the Victory of Israel 8:4-17
B. Israel's Victory over Her Enemies 9:1-16
C. Israel's Celebration 9:17–10:3

E′ TAM *(hawk ground)*

1. A place in the lowland of Judah, later transferred to the territory of Simeon (1 Ch 4:32). For a time Samson dwelt in a rock near here (Ju 15:8,11).

2. A town near Bethlehem (1 Ch 4:3; 2 Ch 11:6).

ETERNAL LIFE

The destiny of those who believe God and accept the salvation of Jesus Christ (Jo 3:36; 5:24). Daniel prophesied that in the end, the dead will be raised up, "some to everlasting life, some to shame and everlasting contempt

(Da 12:2). Jesus defines eternal life thus "And this is eternal life, that they may know You, the only true God, and Jesus Christ whom You have sent" (Jo 17:3). Paul tells us that "he who sows to his flesh will of the flesh reap corruption, but he who sows to the Spirit will of the Spirit reap everlasting life" (Ga 6:8). John's first epistle was written "that you may know that you have eternal life, and that you may continue to believe in the name of the Son of God (1 Jo 5:13). See EVERLASTING LIFE.

ETERNITY

We are accustomed to thinking of eternity as "time without end," but it is harder for us to grasp the idea of "time without beginning." Our world had a beginning (Ge 1:1), each person has a beginning, but God has no beginning and no end. He is the one "who is and who was and who is to come" (Re 1:4). God "inhabits eternity" (Is 57:15). He is God "from everlasting to everlasting" (Ps 90:2).

E′ THAM

The location of the first encampment of the Israelites (Ex 13:20; Nu 33:6).

E′ THAN *(perpetuity)*

Three Old Testament men:

1. A Levite of the family of Gershom (1 Ch 6:42-43).

2. A Levite of the family of Merari, a singer in the time of David (1 Ch 6:44,47; 15:17,19).

3. A descendant of Judah, of the family of Zerah (1 Ch 2:6), probably the one who was renowned for his wisdom (1 Ki 4:31; Ps 89, title).

ETH′ A·NIM

The seventh month of the sacred and first month of the civil year, also called Tishri. See CALENDAR.

ETH·BA′ AL *(with Baal)*

King of Tyre and Sidon and father of Jezebel (1 Ki 16:31).

E′ THER *(abundance)*

A village in the lowland of Judah assigned to Simeon (Jos 15:42; 19:7).

E·THI·O′ PI·A

A country in the upper Nile Valley called Cush by the Hebrews (2 Ch 16:8; Ps 68:31; Is 20:3-5; Eze 30:4-5; Da 11:43; Na 3:9). The people were tall and dark skinned. Its topaz was celebrated (Job 28:19). The inhabitants traded with other countries (Is 45:14) and prospered (Is 43:3). They were defeated by Asa of Judah (2 Ch 14:9-15; 16:8). The twenty-fifth dynasty of Egypt was Ethiopian. The modern nation of Ethiopia is far from the biblical land of Cush, separated from upper Egypt by the country of Sudan.

E·THI·O′ PI·AN

A native of Ethiopia, a Cushite (Je 13:23; 2 Ch 14:9; Je 38:7,10,12; 39:16).

E·THI·O′ PI·AN EUNUCH

The treasurer of Candace, Queen of Ethiopia. He was apparently a proselyte to Judaism, because he traveled all the way to Jerusalem to worship at the temple. He was traveling back to his home when the Lord sent Philip to talk to him and explain the meaning of the prophecies of Isaiah concerning the Messiah. The eunuch believed and was baptized, and returned to his own country rejoicing (Ac 8:26-39).

ETH-KA′ ZIN

A place on the boundary of Zebulun (Jos 19:13).

ETH′ NAN *(gift)*

A son of Helah (1 Ch 4:7).

ETH′ NARCH

Governor or ruler of a province or people.

ETH′ NI *(munificent)*

A Levite of the family of Gerahom (1 Ch 6:41). In 1 Chronicles 6:21 he is called Jeaterai.

EU·BU′ LUS *(prudent)*

A Christian in Rome (2 Ti 4:21).

EU′ CHAR·IST

The Lord's Supper. It is based on the Greek word *eucharistesas,* "to give thanks." At his last supper Jesus gave thanks for the bread and wine. He told his disciples to eat and drink for the bread would symbolize his body, the wine his blood (Ma 26:26-28; Lk 22:15-20).

EU·NI′ CE *(good victory)*

The mother of Timothy (Ac 16:1; 2 Ti 1:5).

EU′ NUCH *(bed-keeper)*

A chamberlain, one who had charge of beds and bedchambers. Those chosen for the office were men who were either born sterile or castrated (Ma 19:12). This class frequently rose to high position and considerable authority. Three of Pharaoh's officers were eunuchs (Ge 37:36; 40:2,7). Eunuchs served in Babylon (Da 1:3) and in the palace of the Persian king (Es 1:10; 2:21). The officer in charge of a king's harem was typically a eunuch, for obvious reasons. Queens such as Jezebel (1 Ki 22:9; 2 Ki 8:6; 9:32), and Mariamne, the wife of Herod the Great, were served by eunuchs. The treasurer of Candace, Queen of Ethiopia, was a eunuch and was converted to Christianity (Ac 8:27-38). (See ETHIOPIAN EUNUCH). A eunuch was not allowed to serve before the Lord (Le 21:20), but God assured them that they were not forgotten and would give them a place in His house "better than sons and daughters" (Is 56:3-5).

EU·O′DI·AS

A member of the church of Philippi, whose quarrel with Syntyche, another member of the church, Paul tried to end (Ph 4:2-3).

EU·PHRA′TES

One of the great rivers of Asia, the Euphrates rises in northeast Turkey, flows through Syria and Iraq, and empties into the Persian Gulf. It is 1,780 miles long. About 90 miles above its mouth it is joined by the Tigris. In ancient times, the greatest city along its banks was Babylon. It was the eastern boundary of the land of Israel (Ge 15:18; 1 Ki 4:21,24).

EU·RAQ′UI·LO

See EUROCLYDON.

EU·ROC′LY·DON

A violent wind from the northeast. This wind caught Paul's ship as it sailed along the coast of Crete, blew it to the open sea, then wrecked it on the island of Melita (Ac 27:14-44).

EU′TY·CHUS (good fortune)

A young man of Troas who, while sleeping, fell from a window. Paul restored him to life (Ac 20:9-10).

E·VAN′GEL·IST (messenger of good tidings)

In the early church a class of men who went from place to place preaching the gospel. They were distinct from apostles, pastors, and teachers (Ep 4:11). Philip, who was instrumental in the conversion of the Ethiopian eunuch, was an evangelist (Ac 6:5; 8:5; 26; 21:8) and should not be confused with Philip the apostle. Paul enjoined Timothy to do the work of an evangelist (2 Ti 4:5).

EVE (life)

The mother of all living (Ge 3:20), fashioned from a rib taken from the side of Adam (Ge 2:18-22). She and Adam were forbidden to eat the fruit of a particular tree, as a test of their obedience. Under the influence of Satan, the serpent persuaded Eve to violate the command, and she induced Adam to do likewise (Ge 3:1-24; 2 Co 11:3; 1 Ti 2:13).

EVENINGTIDE (archaic)

Evening time (Is 17:14).

EVERLASTING

Without end, forever and ever, eternal. One of God's names is Our Redeemer from Everlasting (63:16); and His kindness is everlasting (Is 54:8).

EVERLASTING LIFE

One benefit of finding new life in Christ is called in the Bible "everlasting (eternal) life." The character of this great reality may be summarized by carefully looking at each word. The word *life* stresses the quality of this new relationship to God (Jo 10:10). It does not mean, of course, that we are not physically alive before salvation; it simply stresses the fact that we enter a new, personal relationship with God that gives us a fullness of spiritual vitality that we lacked before (Jo 17:3).

The word *everlasting* emphasizes life without end. Though it will not be completely fulfilled until our future bodily redemption (Ro 8:23), it is still a present possession that can never perish (Jo 10:28).

Everlasting life must not be conceived of as an exclusively future possession. Rather, its possession is clearly seen in our actions. Thus, "no murderer has eternal life abiding in him" (1 Jo 3:15). Indeed, love is the confirming evidence that we do, in fact, have eternal life (1 Jo 3:14).

The greatness of this spiritual reality constitutes a wonderful incentive to vigorously proclaim the gospel to those who are still "dead in trespasses and sins" (Ep 2:1). See ETERNAL LIFE.

EVERY, SEVERAL (archaic)

Each individual; each one separately (Re 21:19-21).

E′VI

A king of Midian (Nu 31:8; Jos 13:21).

E′VIL

The Bible alone has given us the origin of evil in the story of the fall in Eden. Our first parents were created innocent, having moral capacity, the power to act morally, but, in the nature of the case, could not be created *holy* in the moral sense of that term. They were placed under law which they had the power to maintain or violate. God is not, and could not be the author of sin, but under the conditions of our moral constitution, he permitted it. The fall afforded God the opportunity of manifesting his grace and infinite love in Jesus Christ, the Savior of mankind, the rejection of whom lays upon the sinner the consequences of sin under the law.

EVIL EYE

Evil intents of the heart, the selfish, sinful motivation of the wicked (De 15:9; Ma 6:23; 20:15).

E′ VIL-MER′ O·DACH

A Babylonian king, son of Nebuchadnezzar (2 Ki 25:27-30; Je 52:31-34).

EVIL ONE

See DEVIL; SATAN.

EVIL-SPEAKING

James warns us sharply of the sins of the tongue in his very practical (and convicting) epistle: "And the tongue is a fire, a world of iniquity. The tongue is so set among our members that it defiles the whole body, and sets on fire the course of nature; and it is set on fire by hell" (3:6). The Greek language has a vocabulary rich in words that express the sins of the tongue.

Evil speaking (katalalia) occurs twice in this noun form, five times as a verb, and once as an adjective used as a noun. It is easy to see how *kata* ("down") *lalia* ("speech") was formed and it closely parallels the modern expression to "put someone down." Three times in one verse James uses this word: "Do not speak evil of one another, brethren. He who speaks evil of a brother and judges his brother, speaks evil of the law and judges the law. But if you judge the law, you are not a doer of the law but a judge" (4:11). Other translations of these words include "backbite," "revile," "defame," "slander" (2 Co 12:20). See BLASPHEMY; SLANDER.

EVIL SPIRIT

See DEMON.

EWE

A female sheep. Since sheep were clean animals, specified as suitable for sacrifice, and good for producing wool, milk, and meat, sheep were among the most common domesticated animals. See SHEEP.

EXACTOR (archaic)

Overseer (Is 60:16-18).

EXCOMMUNICATE

To cut off, to expel from fellowship. Jesus told His disciples that they were blessed when the world cut them off for His sake (Lk 6:22). The New Testament teaches that a believer who is deliberately sinning and refuses to repent, must be put out of fellowship. The Corinthian church was tolerating a particularly noxious sin, as one of their members was openly living in sexual sin. Paul commanded them to cut this person off if he would not repent, and not to allow such behavior to go unchecked (1 Co 5). Blasphemy was apparently cause for such action (1 Ti 1:20); a divisive man who will not listen to reproof is also to be rejected (Tit 3:10). However, this rejection is not for the purpose of simply being cruel to the sinner, nor is it to be done in a self-righteous manner. The goal of discipline is always restoration and improvement (2 Ti 3:17), and Paul urged the Corinthian church to quickly and freely forgive and restore the repentant sinner he had addressed in his first letter (2 Co 2).

EXECUTIONER

One who kills criminals or political offenders by the authority invested in them by the government. Benaiah, the son of Jehoiada, acted as Solomon's executioner, and put Adonijah to death (1 Ki 2:25,34). According to Old Testament law, there were certain crimes which carried the death sentence, including murder and certain sexual perversions (Ge 9:6; De 13:10; 21:22).

EXEGESIS *(drawing out)*

Explanation or exposition of Scripture, wherein one reads the words and seeks to draw out the meaning and personal application. See HERMENEUTICS.

EXERCISE, BODILY

Paul compares the spiritual life to athletics, pointing out the fact that only a seasoned athlete can hope to win the crown. In the same way, we are to run our spiritual "race" with the kind of determination and discipline that makes a winning Olympic track star (1 Co 9:24-27; 2 Ti 2:5; 4:7). The intense effort that an athlete puts into bodily exercise will only profit him temporally, but that same level of effort put into spiritual growth will be of eternal value (1 Ti 4:8).

EXHORTATION

Encouragement (1 Co 14:2-3).

EX' ILE

See CAPTIVITY.

EX' O·DUS *(a way out)*

The departure of the Israelites from their life of bondage in Egypt, under the leadership of Moses. This spectacular event marks the beginning of the history of the Israelites as a nation. They left Rameses in Goshen and traveled to Succoth (Ex 12:37). The shortest route to Canaan would have been through the land of the Philistines, but they were led instead through the wilderness by the Red Sea (Ex 13:17-18). God was not interested in the fastest trip possible. He knew that the Israelites were in no way ready to conquer the promised land, or to stay true to His commandments, so He led them into the desert to make His covenant with them and mold them into a mighty nation. At Pi-hahiroth they passed through the Red Sea, which had been made dry for them (Ex 14:1-31). They then entered the wilderness of Shur (Ex 15:22; Nu 33:8) and traveled along the coast of the Red Sea toward Mount Sinai. They reached the land of Canaan 40 years after they left Egypt.

EX' O·DUS, BOOK OF

1. The Book of Exodus. Exodus is the record of Israel's birth as a nation. Within the protective "womb" of Egypt, the Hebrew family of seventy rapidly multiplied. At the right time, accompanied with severe "birth pains," an infant nation, numbering between two and three million people, is brought into the world where it is divinely protected, fed, and nurtured.

The Hebrew Title, *We'elleh Shemoth,* "Now These Are the Names," comes from the first phrase in 1:1. Exodus begins with "Now" to show it as a continuation of Genesis. The Greek title is *Exodus,* a word meaning "exit, depar-

ture, or going out." The Septuagint uses this word to describe the book by its key event (19:1, "gone out"). In Luke 9:31 and in 2 Peter 1:15, the word *exodus* speaks of physical death (Jesus and Peter). This embodies Exodus's theme of redemption, because redemption is accomplished only through death. The Latin title is *Liber Exodus,* "Book of Departure," taken from the Greek title.

2. The Author of Exodus. Critics have challenged the Mosaic authorship of Exodus in favor of a series of oral and written documents that were woven together by editors late in Israel's history. Their arguments are generally weak and far from conclusive, especially in view of the strong external and internal evidence that points to Moses as the author.

External Evidence. Exodus has been attributed to Moses since the time of Joshua (compare Ex 20:25 with Jos 8:30-32). Other biblical writers attribute Exodus to Moses: Malachi (Mal 4:4), the disciples (Jo 5:46), and Paul (Ro 10:5). This is also the testimony of Jesus (Mk 7:10; 12:26; Lk 20:37; Jo 5:46-47; 7:19,22-23). Jewish and Samaritan traditions consistently hold to the Mosaic authorship of Exodus.

Internal Evidence. Portions of Exodus are directly attributed to Moses (15; 17:8-14; 20:1-17; 24:4,7,12; 31:18; 34:1-2). Moses's usual procedure was to record events soon after they occurred in the form of historical annals. It is clear from Exodus that the author must have been an eyewitness of the Exodus and an educated man. He was acquainted with details about the customs and climate of Egypt and the plants, animals and terrain of the wilderness. A consistency of style and development also points to a single author. Its antiquity is supported by the frequent use of ancient literary constructions, words, and expressions.

3. The Time of Exodus. If the early date for the Exodus (c. 1445 B.C.) is assumed, this book was composed during the forty-year wilderness journey, between 1445 B.C. and 1405 B.C. Moses probably kept an account of God's work, which he then edited in the plains of Moab shortly before his death. Exodus covers the period from the arrival of Jacob in Egypt (c. 1875 B.C.) to the erection of the tabernacle 431 years later in the wilderness (c. 1445 B.C.).

4. The Christ of Exodus. Exodus contains no direct messianic prophecies, but it is full of types and portraits of Christ. Here are seven:

(1) *Moses:* In dozens of ways Moses is a type of Christ (De 18:15). Both Moses and Christ are prophet, priest, and king (although Moses was never crowned king, he served as the ruler of his people); both are kinsman-redeemers; both were endangered in infancy; both voluntarily renounce power and wealth; both are deliverers, lawgivers, and mediators. (2) *The Passover:* John 1:29,36 and 1 Corinthians 5:7 make it clear that Christ is the Passover Lamb, through whose blood we escape death. (3) *The seven feasts:* Each of these feasts portrays some aspect of the ministry of Christ. (4) *The Exodus:* Paul relates baptism to the exodus event because baptism symbolizes death to the old and identification with the new (Ro 6:2-3; 1 Co 10:1-2). (5) *The manna and water:* The New Testament applies both to Christ (Jo 6:31-35, 48-63; 1 Co 10:3-4). (6) *The tabernacle:* In its materials, colors, furniture, and arrangement, the tabernacle clearly speaks of the person of Christ and the way of redemption. The development is progressive from suffering, blood, and death, to beauty, holiness, and the glory of God. The tabernacle is theology in a physical form. (7) *The High Priest:* In several ways the high priest foreshadows the ministry of Christ, our great High Priest (He 4:14-16; 9:11-12,24-28).

5. Keys to Exodus.

Key Word: Redemption—Central to the Book of Exodus is the concept of redemption. Israel was redeemed from bondage in Egypt and into a covenant relationship with God. From the redemption of Moses in the Nile to the redeeming presence of God in the tabernacle, Exodus records God's overwhelming acts of deliverance, by which He demonstrates His right to be Israel's king.

Key Verses: Exodus 6:6; 19:5-6—"Therefore say to the children of Israel: 'I am the LORD; I will bring you out from under the burdens of the Egyptians, I will rescue you from their bondage and I will redeem you with an outstretched arm and with great judgments' (6:6).

" 'Now therefore, if you will indeed obey My voice and keep My covenant, then you shall be a special treasure to Me above all people, for all the earth is Mine. And you shall be to Me a kingdom of priests and a holy nation' " (19:5-6).

Key Chapters: Exodus 12–14—The climax of the entire Old Testament is recorded in chapters 12–14: the salvation of Israel through

blood (the Passover) and through power (the Red Sea). The exodus is the central event of the Old Testament as the cross is of the New Testament.

5. Survey of Exodus. Exodus abounds with God's powerful redemptive acts on behalf of His oppressed people. It begins in pain and ends in liberation; it moves from the groaning of the people to the glory of God. It is the continuation of the story that begins in Genesis with the seventy descendents of Jacob who move from Canaan to Egypt. They have multiplied under adverse conditions to a multitude of over two million people. When the Israelites finally turned to God for deliverance from their bondage, God quickly responded by redeeming them "with an outstretched arm and with great judgments" (6:6). God faithfully fulfills His promise made to Abraham centuries before (Ge 15:13-14).

This book falls into two parts: (1) redemption from Egypt (1–18); and (2) revelation from God (19–40).

Redemption from Egypt (1–18). After four centuries of slavery, the people of Israel cry to the God of Abraham, Isaac and Jacob for deliverance. God has already prepared Moses for this purpose, and has commissioned him at the burning bush to stand before Pharaoh as the advocate for Israel. However, Pharaoh hardens his heart: "Who is the LORD, that I should obey His voice to let Israel go?" (5:2).

God soon reveals Himself to Pharaoh through a series of object lessons, the ten plagues. These plagues grow in severity until the tenth brings death to the firstborn of every household of Egypt. Israel is redeemed through this plague by means of the Passover lamb. The Israelites' faith in God at this point becomes the basis for their national redemption. As they leave Egypt, God guides them by a pillar of fire and smoke, and saves them from Egypt's pursuing army through the miraculous crossing of the Red Sea. In the wilderness He protects and sustains them throughout their journeys.

Revelation from God (19–40). Now that the people have experienced God's deliverance, guidance, and protection, they are ready to be taught what God expects of them. The redeemed people must now be set apart to walk with God. This is why the emphasis moves from narration in chapters 1–18 to legislation in chapters 19–40. On Mount Sinai, Moses received God's moral, civil and ceremonial laws, as well as the pattern for the tabernacle to be built in the wilderness. After God judged the people for their worship of the golden calf, the tabernacle was constructed and consecrated. It was a building of beauty in a barren land and revealed much about the person of God and the way of redemption.

OUTLINE OF EXODUS

Part One: Redemption from Egypt (1:1–18:27)

I. The Need for Redemption from Egypt (1:1-22)

A. Israel's Rapid Multiplication 1:1-7
B. Israel's Severe Affliction 1:8-14
C. Israel's Planned Extinction 1:15-22

II. The Preparation of the Leaders of the Redemption (2:1–4:31)

A. Moses is Redeemed from Murder 2:1-10
B. Moses Tries to Redeem by Murder 2:11-22
C. Israel Calls upon God 2:23-25
D. God Calls upon Moses 3:1–4:17
E. Moses Accepts the Call.............. 4:18-26
F. Israel Accepts the Call of Moses as Deliverer............................ 4:27-31

III. God's Redemption of Israel from Egypt (5:1–15:21)

A. Moses Confronts Pharaoh by Word 5:1–6:9
B. Moses Confronts Pharaoh with Miracles 6:10–7:13
C. Moses Confronts Pharaoh Through Plagues 7:14–11:10
D. Israel Redeemed by Blood Through the Passover 12:1–13:16
E. Israel Redeemed by Power from Egypt 13:17–15:21

IV. The Preservation of Israel in the Wilderness (15:22–18:27)

A. Preserved from Thirst 15:22-27
B. Preserved from Hunger 16:1-36
C. Preserved from Thirst Again 17:1-7
D. Preserved from Defeat............... 17:8-16
E. Preserved from Chaos 18:1-27

Part Two: Revelation from God (19:1–40:38)

I. The Revelation of the Old Covenant (19:1–31:38)

A. The Preparation of the People 19:1-25
B. The Revelation of the Covenant 20:1-26
C. The Judgments 21:1–23:33
D. The Formal Ratification of the Covenant 24:1-11
E. The Tabernacle 24:12–27:21
F. The Priests 28:1–29:46
G. Institution of the Covenant 30:1–31:18

II. The Response of Israel to the Covenant (32:1–40:38)

A. Israel Willfully Breaks the Covenant 31:1-6
B. Moses Intercedes for Israel's Salvation 32:7-33
C. Moses Convinces God Not to Abandon Israel 32:34–33:23
D. God Renews the Covenant with Israel 34:1-35
E. Israel Willingly Obeys the Covenant 35:1–40:33
F. God Fills the Tabernacle with His Glory...............................40:34-38

EXORCISM

The older meaning of the word is to conjure up or call upon an evil spirit. In the more modern sense it refers to the casting out of evil spirits, usually by calling on a higher power, or reciting a charm or spell which is supposed to effect the cure. Jesus's power over evil spirits was obviously quite different than the sometimes complicated rituals which usually accompanied attempted exorcisms. He simply commanded, and the evil spirits were immediately expelled (Ma 12:24-28; Mk 1:23-27).

EX′OR·CIST

A person who claimed to have the power to expel evil spirits (Ac 19:13-19).

EXPEDIENT

Efficient, suitable, practical, proper (Jo 11:50; 18:14).

EXPIATION

To atone for or appease. See ATONEMENT.

EXTOL

To lift up; esteem; praise (Ps 145:1-2).

EXTORTION

To compel unjust payment from someone by force, intimidation, or the abuse of authority. Extortion was named as a sin in the law, and restitution was required as well as a trespass offering (Le 6:2-7; Is 16:4). Extortioners will not be in heaven, and Christians are not to even eat with those who claim to be Christians and yet live such a lifestyle (1 Co 5:10-11; 6:10).

EYE OF A NEEDLE

Jesus illustrated the difficulty that the wealthy have with spiritual concepts by comparing them to a camel trying to go through the eye of a needle (Ma 19:24; Mk 10:25; Lk 18:25). Some have attempted to explain this by saying that Jesus was talking about a small gate in the city walls, called the Needle's Eye. When the gates of the city were closed for the night, a late arriving foot traveler could still enter the city by this small gate. It was too small, however for a loaded camel to pass through, so if a merchant wanted to enter the city with his goods, he would have to unload the camels, and lead them through the narrow aperture. While this makes an attractive story, there is far more reason to think that Jesus was really talking about a genuine needle and camel. There is no historical evidence that such a gate existed in Jesus's day. The disciples' response further confirms that Jesus figure of speech should be understood just as it sounds. They asked, "Who then can be saved?" clearly thinking that Jesus was saying that salvation is impossible (threading a camel through the eye of

a needle certainly is!). Jesus answered, "With men this is impossible, but with God all things are possible" (Ma 19:26).

EYESALVE (archaic)

Medicine for the eyes (Re 3:18).

EYES, COVERING OF THE

A figure of speech indicating a vindication, a payment to atone for wrongs committed (Ge 20:16, KJV). The idea is obvious—by paying Abraham a large sum of money, Abimelech trusted that they would "forget" the wrong he had done them.

EYESERVICE

Service rendered only when the servant is being watched. Paul adjured Christian slaves to serve their masters not only when they were under the master's eye, and not only to gain favor with their masters, but as though they were serving Christ (Ep 6:6; Col 3:22).

EYES, PAINTING OF

Some women painted dark rims around their eyes to make them appear larger and darker (Je 4:30). Apparently, at least some of the time, this was associated with women of ill repute (Eze 23:40). Jezebel, the wicked queen, painted her eyes when she heard that Jehu was coming, apparently believing that she could beguile him with her feminine charms (2 Ki 9:30). See ANTIMONY.

EYEWITNESS

One who has seen a certain event with his own eyes. Luke wrote his Gospel after consulting eyewitnesses to the events he recorded (Lk 1:2). Peter wrote in his second epistle, "For we did not follow cunningly devised fables when we made known to you the power and coming of our Lord Jesus Christ, but were eyewitnesses of His majesty" (2 Pe 1:16).

EZAR

See EZER.

EZ′BAI

Father of Naarai (1 Ch 11:37).

EZ′BON

Two Old Testament men:
1. A Benjamite, head of a house of the family of Bela (1 Ch 7:7).

2. A son of Gad (Ge 46:16), also called Ozni (Nu 26:16).

E·ZEK′ IAS

(Ma 1:9-10). See HEZEKIAH.

E·ZEK′ IEL *(God strengthens)*

One of the Major Prophets, a Zadokite priest and the son of Buzi (Eze 1:3). He was among the captives taken by Nebuchadnezzar to Babylonia in about 597 B.C. (2 Ki 24:10-16). During the captivity, he was consulted by the elders on important matters (Eze 8:1; 14:1; 20:1). See EZEKIEL, BOOK OF; The Author of Ezekiel.

E·ZEK′ IEL, BOOK OF

1. The Book of Ezekiel. Ezekiel, a priest and a prophet, ministered during the darkest days of Judah's history, the seventy-year period of Babylonian captivity. Carried to Babylon before the final assault on Jerusalem, Ezekiel used prophecies, parables, signs, and symbols to dramatize God's message to His exiled people. Though they are like dry bones in the sun, God will reassemble them and breathe life into the nation once again. Present judgment will be followed by future glory so that "you shall know that I am the LORD" (6:7).

The Hebrew name *Yehezke'l* means "God Strengthens" or "Strengthened by God." Ezekiel is indeed strengthened by God for the prophetic ministry to which he is called (3:8-9). The name occurs twice in this book and nowhere else in the Old Testament. The Greek form in the Septuagint is *Iezekiel* and the Latin form in the Vulgate is *Ezechiel.*

2. The Author of Ezekiel. Ezekiel, the son of Buzi (1:3), had a wife who died as a sign to Judah when Nebuchadnezzar began his final siege on Jerusalem (24:16-24). Like Jeremiah, he was a priest who was called to be a prophet of the Lord. His prophetic ministry shows a priestly emphasis in his concern with the temple, priesthood, sacrifices, and Shekinah (the glory of the Lord). Ezekiel was privileged to receive a number of visions of the power and plan of God, and he was careful and artistic in his written presentation. Some objections have been raised, but there is not a good reason to overthrow the strong evidence in favor of Ezekiel's authorship. The first person singular is used throughout the book, indicating that it is the work of a single personality. This person is iden-

tified as Ezekiel in 1:3 and 24:24, and internal evidence supports the unity and integrity of Ezekiel's prophetic record. The style, language, and thematic development are consistent throughout the book; and several distinctive phrases are repeated throughout, such as, "they shall know that I am the LORD," "Son of man," "the word of the LORD came to me," and "glory of the LORD."

3. The Time of Ezekiel. Nebuchadnezzar destroyed Jerusalem in three stages. First, in 605 B.C., he overcame Jehoiakim and carried off key hostages, including Daniel and his friends. Second, in 597 B.C., the rebellion of Jehoiakim and Jehoiachin brought further punishment; and Nebuchadnezzar made Jerusalem submit a second time. He carried off ten thousand hostages, including Jehoiachin and Ezekiel. Third, in 586 B.C., Nebuchadnezzar destroyed the city after a long siege and disrupted all of Judah. If "thirtieth year" in 1:1 refers to Ezekiel's age, he was twenty-five years old when he was taken to Babylon and thirty years old when he received his prophetic commission (1:2-3). This means he was about seventeen when Daniel was deported in 605 B.C., so that Ezekiel and Daniel were about the same age. Both men were about twenty years younger than Jeremiah who was ministering in Jerusalem. According to this chronology, Ezekiel was born in 622 B.C., deported to Babylon in 597 B.C., prophesied from 592 B.C. to at least 570 B.C., and died about 560 B.C. Thus, he overlapped the end of Jeremiah's ministry and the beginning of Daniel's ministry. By the time Ezekiel arrived in Babylon, Daniel was already well-known; and he was mentioned three times in Ezekiel's prophecy (14:14,20; 28:3). Ezekiel's Babylonian home was at Tel Abib, the principal colony of Jewish exiles along the River Chebar, Nebuchadnezzar's "Grand Canal" (1:1; 3:15,23).

From 592 to 586 B.C., Ezekiel found it necessary to convince the disbelieving Jewish exiles that there was no hope of immediate deliverance. But it was not until they heard that Jerusalem was destroyed that their false hopes of returning were abandoned.

Ezekiel no doubt wrote this book shortly after the incidents recorded in it occurred. His active ministry lasted for at least twenty-two years (1:2; 29:17), and his book was probably completed by 565 B.C.

4. The Christ of Ezekiel. Ezekiel 17:22-24 depicts the Messiah as a tender twig that becomes a stately cedar on a lofty mountain, as He is similarly called the Branch in Isaiah (11:1), Jeremiah (23:5; 33:15), and Zechariah (3:8; 6:12). The Messiah is the King who has the right to rule (21:26-27), and He is the true Shepherd who will deliver and feed His flock (34:11-31).

5. Keys to Ezekiel.

Key Word: The Future Restoration of Israel—The broad purpose of Ezekiel is to remind the generation born during the Babylonian exile of the cause of Israel's current destruction, of the coming judgment on the gentile nations, and of the coming national restoration of Israel. Central to that hope is the departure of the glory of God from Israel and the prediction of its ultimate return (43:2).

Key Verses: Ezekiel 36:24-26 and 36:33-35—"For I will take you from among the nations, gather you out of all countries, and bring you into your own land. Then I will sprinkle clean water on you, and you shall be clean; I will cleanse you from all your filthiness and from all your idols. I will give you a new heart and put a new spirit within you. I will take the heart of stone out of your flesh and give you a heart of flesh" (36:24-26).

"Thus says the Lord GOD: 'On the day that I cleanse you from all your iniquities, I will also enable you to dwell in the cities, and the ruins shall be rebuilt. The desolate land shall be tilled instead of lying desolate in the sight of all who pass by. So they will say, "This land that was desolate has become like the garden of Eden; and the wasted, desolate, and ruined cities are now fortified and inhabited"'" (36:33-35).

Key Chapter: Ezekiel 37—Central to the hope of the restoration of Israel is the vision of the valley of the dry bones. Ezekiel 37 outlines with clear steps Israel's future.

5. Survey of Ezekiel.
Ezekiel prophesied among the Jewish exiles in Babylon during the last days of Judah's decline and downfall. His message of judgment is similar to that of his older contemporary Jeremiah, who remained in Jerusalem. Judah would be judged because of her unfaithfulness, but God promised her future restoration and blessing. Like Isaiah and Jeremiah, Ezekiel proclaimed a message of horror and hope, of condemnation and consolation. But Ezekiel placed special emphasis on the glory of Israel's sovereign God who says, "They shall know that I am the LORD." The book breaks into four sections: the commission of Ezekiel (1–3), the judgment on Judah (4–24), the judgment on the Gentiles (25–32), and the restoration of Israel (33–48).

The Commission of Ezekiel (1–3). God gave Ezekiel an overwhelming vision of His divine glory and commissioned him to be His prophet (compare the experiences of Moses (Ex 3:1-10), Isaiah (Is 6:1-10), Daniel (10:5-14), and John (Re 1:12-19). Ezekiel was given instructions, enablement, and responsibility.

The Judgment on Judah (4–24). Ezekiel directs his prophecies against the nation God chose for Himself. The prophet's signs and sermons (4–7) point to the certainty of Judah's judgment. In 8–11, Judah's past sins and coming doom are seen in a series of visions of the abominations in the temple, the slaying of the wicked, and the departing glory of God. The priests and princes are condemned as the glory leaves the temple, moves to the Mount of Olives, and disappears in the east. Chapters 12–24 speak of the cases and extent of Judah's coming judgment through dramatic signs, powerful sermons, and parables. Judah's prophets are counterfeits and her elders are idolators. They have become a fruitless vine and an adulterous wife. Babylon will swoop down like an eagle and pluck them up, and they will not be aided by Egypt. The people are responsible for their own sins, and they are not being unjustly judged for the sins of their ancestors. Judah was unfaithful, but God promised that her judgment ultimately would be followed by restoration.

The Judgment on the Gentiles (25–32). Judah's nearest neighbors may gloat over her destruction, but they will be next in line. They too will suffer the fate of siege and destruction by Babylon. Ezekiel shows the full circle of judgment on the nations that surround Judah by following them in a clockwise circuit: Ammon, Moab, Edom, Philistia, Tyre, and many scholars believe that the "king of Tyre" in 28:11-19 may be Satan, the real power behind the nation. Chapters 29–32 contain a series of oracles against Egypt. Unlike the nations in chapters 25–28 that were destroyed by Nebuchadnezzar, Egypt would continue to exist, but as the "lowliest of kingdoms" (29:15). Since that time it has never recovered its former glory or influence.

The Restoration of Israel (33–48). The prophecies in these chapters were given after the overthrow of Jerusalem. Now that the promised judgment has come, Ezekiel's message no longer centers on coming judgment but on the positive theme of comfort and consolation. Just as surely as judgment has come, blessing will also come; God's people will be regathered and restored. The mouth of Ezekiel, God's watchman, is opened when he is told that Jerusalem has been taken. Judah has had false shepherds (rulers), but the true Shepherd will lead them in the future. The vision of the valley of dry bones pictures the reanimation of the nation by the Spirit of God. Israel and Judah will be purified and reunited. There will be an invasion by the northern armies of Gog, but Israel will be saved because the Lord will destroy the invading forces.

In 572 B.C., fourteen years after the destruction of Jerusalem, Ezekiel returned in a vision to the fallen city and was given detailed specifications for the reconstruction of the temple, the city, and the land (40–48). After an intricate description of the new outer court, inner court, and temple (40–42), Ezekiel viewed the return of the glory of the Lord to the temple from the east. Regulations concerning worship in the coming temple (43–46) are followed by revelations concerning the new land and city (47–48).

OUTLINE OF EZEKIEL

Part One: The Commission of Ezekiel (1:1–3:27)

I. Ezekiel Sees the Glory of God (1:1-28)

A. Time of the Vision 1:1-3
B. The Four Living Creatures 1:4-14
C. The Four Wheels 1:15-21
D. The Firmament 1:22-25

E. The Appearance of a Man 1:26-28

II. Ezekiel is Commissioned to the Word of God (2:1–3:27)

A. Ezekiel Is Sent to Israel 2:1–3:3
B. Ezekiel Is Instructed About His Ministry 3:4-27

Part Two: Judgment on Judah (4:1–24:27)

I. Four Signs of Coming Judgment (4:1–5:17)

A. Sign of the Clay Tablet 4:1-3
B. Sign of Ezekiel's Lying on His Side 4:4-8
C. Sign of the Defiled Bread 4:9-17
D. Sign of the Razor and Hair............ 5:1-4
E. Explanation of the Signs 5:5-17

II. Two Messages of Coming Judgment (6:1–7:27)

A. Destruction Because of Idolatry...... 6:1-14
B. Description of the Babylonian Conquest 7:1-27

III. Four-Part Vision of Coming Judgment (8:1–11:25)

A. Vision of the Glory of God 8:1-4
B. Vision of the Abominations in the Temple 8:5-18
C. Vision of the Slaying in Jerusalem 9:1-11

D. Departure of the Glory of God to the Threshold.............................. 10:1-8
E. Vision of the Wheels and Cherubim 10:9-22
F. Vision of the Twenty-five Wicked Rulers 11:1-12
G. Promise of the Restoration of the Remnant 11:13-21
H. Departure of the Glory of God from the Mount of Olives 11:22-25

IV. Signs, Parables, and Messages of Judgment (12:1–24:27)

A. Sign of Belongings for Removing 12:1-16
B. Sign of Trembling 12:17-28
C. Message Against the False Prophets 13:1-23
D. Message Against the Elders 14:1-23
E. Parable of the Vine 15:1-8
F. Parable of Israel's Marriage 16:1-63
G. Parable of the Two Eagles 17:1-24

H. Message of Personal Judgment
for Personal Sin 18:1-32
I. Lament for the Princes of Israel ... 19:1-9

J. Parable of the Withered Vine 19:10-14
K. Message of Judgment on
Jerusalem 20:1–24:27

Part Three: Judgment on Gentiles (25:1–32:32)

I. Judgment on Ammon (25:1-7)

II. Judgment on Moab (25:8-11)

III. Judgment on Edom (25:12-14)

IV. Judgment on Philistia (25:15-17)

V. Judgment on Tyre (26:1–28:19)

A. Destruction of Tyre 26:1-21
B. Lament over Tyre 27:1-36
C. Fall of the Prince of Tyre 28:1-19

VI. Judgment on Sidon (28:20-26)

VII. Judgment on Egypt (29:1–32:32)

A. Egypt to Be Desolate 29:1-16
B. Egypt to Be Taken by Babylon ...29:17-21
C. Egypt to Be Destroyed 30:1-26
D. Egypt Is Cut Down Like
Assyria 31:1-18
E. Egypt Is Lamented 32:1-16
F. Egypt in Sheol 32:17-32

Part Four: Restoration of Israel (33:1–48:35)

**I. The Return of Israel to the Land
(33:1–39:29)**

A. The Appointment of Ezekiel as
Watchman 33:1-33
B. The Message to the Shepherds ... 34:1-31
C. The Judgment of Edom 35:1-15
D. The Prophecies Concerning
Israel 36:1–37:28

E. Prophecies Concerning Gog
and Magog 38:1–39:29

**II. The Restoration of Israel in the
Kingdom (40:1–48:35)**

A. The New Temple 40:1–43:27
B. The New Worship 44:1–46:24
C. The New Land 47:1–48:35

E´ ZEL

The hiding place of David where he received Jonathan's report (1 Sa 20:19).

E´ ZEM, A´ ZEM (*a bone*)

A village allotted to the tribe of Judah near the border of Edom. It was afterwards assigned to Simeon (Jos 15:29;19:3; 1 Ch 4:29).

E´ ZER, E´ ZAR

Six Old Testament men:

1. A Horite tribe (Ge 36:21,30; 1 Ch 1:38).

2. The father of Hushah of Judah, a descendant of Hur (1 Ch 4:4).

3. A son of Ephraim who was killed by the men of Gath (1 Ch 7:21).

4. A Gadite who allied himself with David at Ziklag (1 Ch 12:9).

5. A priest who participated in the dedication of Nehemiah's wall (Ne 12:42).

6. Son of Jeshua (Ne 3:19).

E´ ZI·ON-GA´ BER

See EZION GEBER.

E´ ZI·ON-GE´ BER

A town on the coast of the Gulf of Akaba (De 2:8) used as a port by Solomon (1 Ki 9:26). It was one of the camps of Israelites during their wanderings (Nu 33:35).

EZNITE

Josheb-Basshebeth the Tachmonite, the "chief of the captains" and one of David's mighty men, was given the nickname "Adino the Eznite," "because he had killed 800 men at one time" (2 Sa 23:8). The definition of this nickname is not known. He is also called Jashobeam, the son of a Hachmonite (1 Ch 11:11).

EZ´ RA (*help*)

Two Old Testament men:

1. A famous priest, reformer, scribe, and student of law, who lived during the time of the Babylonian captivity. Artaxerxes, the Persian king, permitted Ezra and a group of his followers to return to Jerusalem. When he arrived there, he found religious affairs at a low ebb. He thereupon initiated reforms, among them the decree that foreign wives be divorced (Ez 10:9-17). Ezra disappears from the biblical narrative here although as Ezra, the scribe, he reappears later to read the law of Moses (Ne 8:1-13). See EZRA, BOOK OF; The Author of Ezra.

2. A priest who accompanied Zerubbabel from exile in Babylon to Jerusalem (Ne 12:1,13,33).

EZ′RA, BOOK OF

1. The Book of Ezra. Ezra continues the Old Testament narrative of 2 Chronicles by showing how God fulfills His promise to return His people to the land of promise after seventy years of exile. Israel's "second exodus," this time from Babylon, is less impressive than the return from Egypt because only a remnant chose to leave Babylon.

Ezra relates the story of two returns from Babylon—the first led by Zerubbabel to rebuild the temple (1–6), and the second under the leadership of Ezra to rebuild the spiritual condition of the people (7–10). Sandwiched between these two accounts is a gap of nearly six decades, during which Esther lived as queen of Persia.

Ezra is the Aramaic form of the Hebrew word *ezer*, "help," and perhaps means "Yahweh helps." Ezra and Nehemiah were originally bound together as one book because Chronicles, Ezra, and Nehemiah were viewed as one continuous history. The Septuagint, a Greek-language version of the Old Testament translated in the third century B.C., calls Ezra-Nehemiah, *Esdras Deuteron,* "Second Esdras." First Esdras is the name of the apocryphal Book of Esdras. The Latin title is *Liber Primus Esdrae,* "First Book of Ezra." In the Latin Bible, Ezra is called 1 Ezra and Nehemiah is called 2 Ezra.

2. The Author of Ezra. Although Ezra is not specifically mentioned as the author, he is certainly the best candidate. Jewish tradition (the Talmud) attributes the book to Ezra, and portions of the book (7:28–9:15) are written in the first person from Ezra's point of view. The vividness of the details and descriptions favors an author who was an eyewitness of the later events of the book. As in Chronicles, there is a strong priestly descendant of Aaron through Eleazar, Phineas and Zadok (7:1-5). He studied, practiced, and taught the law of the Lord as an educated scribe (7:1-12). Also according to 2 Maccabees 2:13-15, he had access to the library of written documents gathered by Nehemiah. Ezra no doubt used this material in writing Ezra 1–6 as he

did in writing Chronicles. Some think that Ezra composed Nehemiah as well by making use of Nehemiah's personal diary.

Ezra was a godly man marked by strong trust in the Lord, moral integrity, and grief over sin. He was a contemporary of Nehemiah (Ne 8:1-9; 12:36) who arrived in Jerusalem in 444 B.C. Tradition holds that Ezra was the founder of the Great Synagogue where the canon of Old Testament Scripture was settled. Another tradition says that he collected the biblical books into a unit and that he originated the synagogue form of worship.

Ezra wrote this book probably between 457 B.C. (the events of Ezra 7–10) and 444 B.C. (Nehemiah's arrival in Jerusalem). During the period covered by the Book of Ezra, Gautama Buddha (c. 560-480 B.C.) was in India, Confucius (551-479 B.C.) was in China, and Socrates (470-399 B.C.) was in Greece.

3. The Time of Ezra. The following table shows the chronological relationship of the books of Ezra, Nehemiah, and Esther:

538-515 B.C.	483-473 B.C.
Zerubbabel	Esther
Ezra 1–6	Book of Esther
First Return	

457 B.C.	444-c. 425 B.C.
Ezra	Nehemiah
Ezra 7–10	Book of Nehemiah
Second Return	Third Return

These books fit against the background of these Persian kings:

Cyrus	(559-530 B.C.)
Cambyses	(530-522 B.C.)
Smerdis	(522 B.C.)
Darius I	(521-486 B.C.)
Ahasuerus	(486-464 B.C.)
Artaxerxes I	(464-423 B.C.)
Darius II	(423-404 B.C.)

Cyrus the Persian overthrew Babylon in October 539 B.C. and issued his decree allowing the Jews to return in 538 B.C. The temple is begun in 536 B.C. The exile lasted only fifty years after 586 B.C., but the seventy-year figure for the captivity is taken from a beginning date of 606 B.C. when the first deportation to Babylon takes place. The rebuilding of the temple is discontinued in 534 B.C., is resumed in 520 B.C., and completed in 515 B.C. It is begun under Cyrus and finished under Darius I. The two intervening kings, Cambyses and Smerdis, are not mentioned in any of these books. The prophets Haggai and Zechariah ministered during Zerubbabel's time, about 520 B.C. and following years. Esther's story fits entirely in the reign of Xerxes, and Ezra ministered during the reign of Artaxerxes I, as did Nehemiah. There were three waves of deportation to Babylon (606, 597, and 586 B.C.) and three returns from Babylon: 538 B.C. (Zerubbabel), 457 B.C. (Ezra), and 444 B.C. (Nehemiah).

4. The Christ of Ezra. Ezra reveals God's continued fulfillment of His promise to keep David's descendants alive. Zerubbabel himself is part of the line of Joseph as the grandson of Jeconiah (Jehoiachin, 1 Ch 3:17-19; see Ma 1:12-13). There is a positive note of hope in Ezra and Nehemiah because the remnant has returned to the land of promise. In this land the messianic promises will be fulfilled, because they are connected with such places as Bethlehem, Jerusalem, and Zion. Christ would be born in Bethlehem (Mi 5:2), not in Babylon.

The Book of Ezra as a whole also typifies Christ's work of forgiveness and restoration.

5. Keys to Ezra.

Key Word: Temple—The basic theme of Ezra is the restoration of the temple and the spiritual, moral, and social restoration of the returned remnant in Jerusalem under the leadership of Zerubbabel and Ezra. Israel's worship is revitalized and the people are purified. God's faithfulness is seen in the way He sovereignly protects His people through a powerful empire while they are in captivity. They prosper in their exile, and God raises up pagan kings who are sympathetic to their cause and encourage them to rebuild their homeland. God also provides zealous and capable spiritual leaders who direct the return and the rebuilding. He keeps His promise: "I will be found by you, says the LORD, and I will bring you back from your captivity; I will gather you from all the nations and from all the places where I have driven you, says the LORD, and I will bring you to the place from which I cause you to be carried away captive" (Je 29:14).

Key Verses: Ezra 1:3; 7:10—"Who is there among you of all His people? May his God be with him! Now let him go up to Jerusalem, which is in Judah, and build the house of the LORD God of Israel (He is God), which is in Jerusalem" (1:3).

"For Ezra had prepared his heart to seek the Law of the LORD, and to do it, and to teach statutes and ordinances to Israel" (7:10).

Key Chapter: Ezra 6—Ezra 6 records the completion and dedication of the temple which stimulates the obedience of the remnant to keep the Passover and separate themselves from the "filth of the nations of the land" (6:21).

6. Survey of Ezra. Ezra continues the story exactly where 2 Chronicles ends, and shows how God's promise to bring His people back to their land is fulfilled (Je 29:10-14). God is with these people; and although their days of glory seem over, their spiritual heritage still remains and God's rich promises will be fulfilled. Ezra relates the story of the first two returns from Babylon, the first led by Zerubbabel and the second led decades later by Ezra. Its two divisions are the restoration of the temple (1–6) and the reformation of the people (7–10), and they are separated by a fifty-eight year gap during which the story of Esther takes place.

The Restoration of the Temple (1–6). King Cyrus of Persia overthrew Babylon in 539 B.C. and issued a decree in 538 B.C. that allowed the exiled Jews to return to their homeland. Isaiah prophesied two centuries before that the temple would be rebuilt and actually named Cyrus as the one who would bring it about (Is 44:28–45:4). Cyrus may have read and responded to this passage. Out of a total Jewish population of perhaps 2 or 3 million, only 49,897 chose to take advantage of this offer. Only the most committed were willing to leave a life of relative comfort in Babylon, endure a trek of nine hundred miles, and face further hardship by rebuilding a destroyed temple and city. Zerubbabel, a "prince" of Judah (a direct descendant of David), led the faithful remnant back to Jerusalem. Those who returned were from the tribes of Judah, Benjamin, and Levi; but it is evident that representatives from the other ten tribes eventually return as well. The ten "lost tribes" are not entirely lost.

Zerubbabel's priorities were in the right place; he first restored the altar and the religious feasts before beginning work on the temple itself. The foundation of the temple is laid in 536 B.C., but opposition arises and the work ceases from 534 to 520 B.C. while Ezra 4:1-5,24 concerns Zerubbabel, 4:6-23 concerns opposition to the building of the wall of Jerusalem some time between 464 and 444 B.C. These verses may have been placed here to illustrate the antagonism to the work of rebuilding. The prophets Haggai and Zechariah exhorted the people to get back to building the temple (5:1-2), and work began again under Zerubbabel and Joshua the high priest. Tattenai, a Persian governor, protests to King Darius I about the temple building and challenges their authority to continue. King Darius found the decree of Cyrus and confirmed it, even forcing Tattenai to provide whatever was needed to complete the work. It was finished in 515 B.C.

The Reformation of the People (7–10). A smaller return under Ezra took place in 457 B.C., eighty-one years after the first return under Zerubbabel. Ezra the priest was given authority by King Artaxerxes I to bring people and contributions for the temple in Jerusalem with their valu-able gifts from Persia. Many priests but few Levites returned with Zerubbabel and Ezra (2:36-42; 8:15-19). God used Ezra to rebuild the people spiritually and morally. When Ezra discovered that the people and the priests had intermarried with foreign women, he identified with the sin of his people, and offered a great intercessory prayer on their behalf. During the gap of fifty-eight years between Ezra 6 and 7, the people fell into a confused spiritual state and Ezra was alarmed. They quickly responded to Ezra's confession and weeping by making a covenant to put away their foreign wives and to live in accordance with God's law. This confession and response to the Word of God brought about a great revival and changed lives.

OUTLINE OF EZRA

Part One: The Restoration of the Temple of God (1:1–6:22)

I. The First Return to Jerusalem Under Zerubbabel (1:1–2:70)

A. Decree of Cyrus 1:1-4
B. Gifts from Israel and
   Cyrus 1:5-11
C. Census of the Returning
   People 2:1-63
D. The Return Completed 2:64-70

II. The Construction of the Temple (3:1–6:22)

A. Construction of the Temple
   Foundation 3:1-13
B. Interruption of the Temple
   Construction 4:1-24
C. Completion of the Temple 5:1–6:18
D. Celebration of the Passover 6:19-22

Part Two: The Reformation of the People of God (7:1–10:44)

I. The Second Return to Jerusalem Under Ezra (7:1–8:36)

A. The Decree of Artaxerxes 7:1-28
B. Census of the Returning
   Israelites 8:1-14
C. Spiritual Preparation for the
   Return 8:15-23
D. The Return Is Completed 8:24-36

II. The Restoration of the People (9:1–10:44)

A. Israel
   Intermarries 9:1-2
B. Ezra Intercedes with
   God 9:3-15
C. Reformation of
   Israel 10:1-44

EZ′ RAH

See EZRA.

EZ′ RA·HITE, EZ′ RA·RITE

The family name of Ethan and Heman (1 Ki 4:31; Ps 88, title; Ps 89, title).

EZ′ RI *(my help)*

Son of Chelub (1 Ch 27:26)

F

FA′ BLE

A fictitious story that draws its moral through the use of plants or animals endowed with human characteristics. Only two fables appear in the Bible: Jotham's fable of the tree choosing a king (Ju 9:8-15) and Jehoash's fable of the thistle and the cedar (2 Ki 14:9). In the New Testament, the word is used to mean falsehood or invention of the imagination (1 Ti 1:4; 4:7; 2 Ti 4:4; Tit 1:14).

FACE

The front of the human head, that part of the anatomy which most particularly identifies a person and sets a person apart from others. Also a symbolic term for God's presence. When Adam and Eve sinned, they were afraid for the first time, and hid from God's presence, or *face* (Ge 3:8). This fear persists because we are sinners and unworthy to see God. Jacob was awed and frightened to have met the Angel of the Lord face to face (Ge 32:30). However, because of His great love for us, God has shown us Himself in the face of Jesus Christ (2 Co 4:6). When we are finally in heaven with Him, we will see Him face-to-face, we will physically be in His presence, and we will understand all that has been dark to us here (1 Co 13:12).

FACES, BREAD OF (Ex 25:30)

See SHOWBREAD.

FAIN (archaic)

To desire earnestly; to long for (Lk 15:13-16).

FAIR

This word has multiple meanings in English. In the Bible it is used in three senses: Lovely, beautiful (Song 1:15); equitable (Pr 1:3, NIV); good weather (Ma 16:2).

FAIR HA'VENS

This harbor in the island of Crete is near the city of Lasea (Ac 27:8).

FAIRS

This word occurs seven times in Ezekiel 27:12-33, probably signifying "wares," or "merchandise."

FAITH

There are three main words in the Greek New Testament about faith and believing: *pistis,* a noun, *pisteuo,* a verb, and *pistos,* an adjective.

Faith (pistis). *Faith* is defined in a practical way in Hebrews 11:1: "Now faith is the substance [or substantiation] of things hoped for, the evidence of things not seen." The writer

of Hebrews goes on for thirty-nine additional verses to illustrate these who took God at His word and had faith in what He said. They were not all outstanding believers. Jacob, Gideon, and Samson were all too human in their failure, and even father Abraham slipped up a few times. But they were believers.

What is faith? It is confidence that someone or something is reliable. Our whole life is based on faith. Without it, banks and post offices would not be possible. Paper money and credit cards (the very word *credit* is from the Latin verb "to believe") would never be accepted.

We must have some content to our Christianity. Paul puts the facts of the faith in a nutshell: "That Christ died for our sins according to the Scriptures, and that He was buried, and that He rose again the third day according to the Scriptures" (1 Co 15:3-4).

Faith can also refer to the body of beliefs, as in "the Christian faith." Paul uses it this way in 1 Timothy 5:8: "But if anyone does not provide for his own, and especially for those of his household, he has denied the faith and is worse than an unbeliever."

Believe (pisteuo). *Believe* is a prominent verb in the New Testament. Many people think Acts 16:31 is too easy and simple a method of salvation: "Believe on the Lord Jesus Christ, and you will be saved." Actually, simply believing is very hard for most people. If salvation consisted of faith, plus giving $100 dollars to the church, most people would prefer it. But God does not want human boasting, so salvation is "by grace," and "through faith," "not of works" (Ep 2:8-9).

Believing is intellectual in the sense that faith has to have some facts to rest upon. We must believe what God says in His Word. But believing also involves deciding either for or against Christ and His offer of salvation (Ro 6:23).

The verb *pisteuo* can be used with different prepositions. It is often used with *en* (in). The most beloved Gospel verse in the New Testament uses this expression (Jo 3:16). It means "to confide in someone or something."

Pisteuo is also used with *epi* (on), as in Acts 16:31. This stresses laying hold of the object of faith.

Sometimes this verb is followed not by a preposition, but by a clause or clauses: "If you confess with your mouth the Lord Jesus and believe in your heart that God has raised Him from the dead, you will be saved" (Ro 10:9).

To make belief in Christ clearer, since it is the most important step in one's spiritual life, the New Testament uses several terms that are practically synonymous with "believe" when used in the context of faith: "Receive" (Jo 1:12), "ask" (Jo 4:10), "confess" (Ro 10:9), and "call upon" (Ro 10:13).

Faithful, Believing (pistos). The usual translation of *pistos* is "faithful" but it can mean "believing" (a believer, whether faithful or not). In Titus 1:6, a qualification for an elder is that his children be *pistos*. Another translation of *pistos* is "reliable" or "trustworthy," especially when talking about words or sayings (Tit 3:8; Re 21:5).

The importance of having faith to believe can hardly be overstated: "But without faith it is impossible to please Him, for he who comes to God must believe that He is, and that He is a rewarder of those who diligently seek Him" (He 11:6). See FAITHFULNESS.

FAITHFULNESS

The condition of being full of faith, believing (Ga 5:22). The word also bears the connotation of trustworthiness, dependability, and steadfast loyalty (He 10:23). See FAITH.

FAL'CON

A bird of prey, designated as a vulture or kite in the Authorized Version (Job 28:7). All the birds of prey were classed as unclean (Le 11:14; De 14:13).

FALL, THE

When Adam and Eve sinned in the garden and ate of the tree which God had forbidden, they were cast out of the garden and placed under a curse (Ge 3). This episode is referred to as "the fall," because man fell from his state of innocence and fellowship with God into a state of sin and rebellion, cut off from God.

FAL'LOW DEER

One of the animals listed as clean and therefore edible (De 14:5). See DEER.

FAL'LOW GROUND

This is farmland which has been plowed but not planted during the crop season (Je 4:3; Ho 10:12).

FALLOW DEER (3 ft. high at the shoulders)

FALSE CHRISTS

Evildoers who pretend to be anointed by God but really design to lead people astray (Ma 24:24; Mk 13:22). See ANTICHRIST.

FALSE PROPHET, THE

In the last days, a "beast" and a false prophet will arise, who will rule the earth, persecuting believers and demanding worship for the beast (Re 13:1-12). They will prophesy falsely and perform miraculous signs by the aid of demons (Re 16:13), but when Christ returns, they will be thrown alive into a lake of fire where Satan will later be also thrown (Re 19:20; 20:10).

FALSE PROPHETS

A prophet who claims to speak for God, but whose prophecies do not come to pass. The law commanded that such a deceiver be put to death (De 13:1-18). The false prophet Bar-jesus was struck with blindness for trying to turn an enquirer away from the faith (Ac 13:6-12).

FA·MIL'IAR SPIR'IT

The word is applied to those who have the ability to contact the dead or who have other such unearthly powers. Those who had such powers were said to have familiar spirits (Le 20:27; De 18:11; Is 29:4).

FAM'ILY

In the Scriptures the family is represented as of divine origin. In biblical times a man's house or family included his wife or wives and concubines, their children, the families of the children, and the servants or slaves. Parents were obligated to maintain and educate their children (Ex 12:26-27; De 6:6-7; Ep 6:4; 1 Ti 5:8). The child owed obedience to the parents as well as reverence and respect (Ex 20:12; Lk 2:51; Ep 6:1; Col 3:20).

FAM´INE

Crop failure was the chief cause of famines in biblical times, although they also occurred in cities under siege. Notable famines in the Scriptures took place in the time of Abraham (Ge 12:10), Isaac (Ge 26:1), Joseph in Egypt (Ge 41:27-57), Jacob (Ge 42:1-3; 47:1-13), Judges (Ru 1:1), David (2 Sa 21:1), Elijah (1 Ki 17:1–18:46), Elisha (2 Ki 4:38; 8:1), in the reign of Claudius, A.D. 41-54 (Ac 11:28), at the siege of Samaria (2 Ki 6:24–7:20), and at the siege of Jerusalem (2 Ki 25:1-3).

FAMISHED (archaic)

Suffering from hunger; starving (Is 5:13).

FAN

A winnowing fork. Threshed grain was scooped up with such a tool, and tossed into the air to allow the wind to blow the chaff away while the heavier grain fell to the floor (Is 30:24; Je 15:7).

FARE

1) To consume food, to eat or dine. 2) to get along (as in "he fared well" versus "he fared ill"). The rich man in Jesus parable "fared sumptuously" every day. This is also translated "lived in luxury." It seems fair to assume both senses of the word, but particularly the sense of eating well (Lk 16:19-21).

FARM, FARMING

See AGRICULTURE.

FARMER

One who practices agriculture, raising crops or animals. The Bible uses several different terms to describe various types of farming. Abel was "a keeper of sheep" and Cain was "a tiller of the ground" (Ge 4:2). Isaiah speaks of "the plowman" and "vinedresser" (Is 28:24; 61:5). Jesus described Himself as the true vine, and the Father as the vinedresser. Just as a farmer cares for and prunes his vineyard to pro-

FAN OR WINNOWING FORK

duce the best fruit, God cares for and "prunes" us to produce spiritual fruit (Jo 15:1-8). A farmer might also lease the land he owned to tenant farmers, who would tend the crops and then divide the produce with the landlord (Ma 21:33).

FAR´THING (archaic)

One fourth of a penny. The KJV uses this word to translate the *assarius,* which was worth $\frac{1}{16}$ of a denarius (Ma 10:29; Lk 12:6), and also the *kodrantes,* worth $\frac{1}{4}$ of an assarius (Ma 5:26). See MONEY OF THE BIBLE.

FAST

The words *to fast* and *fasting* are not found in the Pentateuch, and injunctions to fast do not appear in the Mosaic law. The first instance of voluntary fasting is that of David when he refused to eat during the sickness of his child (2 Sa 12:22). In the later books many instances of fasting are recorded (Ez 8:21; Ne 9:1; Es 4:3; Ps 69:10; Da 6:18; 9:3). In times of calamity fasts were sometimes proclaimed to create a serious attitude of mind (Je 36:9; Joel 1:14). It signified a state of humility before God because of sin (1 Sa 7:6; 1 Ki 21:9,12). In the postexilic period there were fasts in the fourth, fifth, seventh, and tenth months (Ze 8:19). These commemorated the siege and capture of Jerusalem, the destruction of the temple, and slaying of Gedaliah, the governor. The Pharisees fasted twice a week (Lk 18:12), a formalism criticized by Jesus (Ma 6:16-17).

FAT

Prior to the Mosaic law, Abel offered Jehovah the fat of the firstling of his flock (Ge 4:4). In Leviticus 3:16; 7:23,25, the law was that the fat of animals sacrificed belonged to the Lord. The fat and blood should not be eaten but burned (Ex 29:13,22; Le 3:3-5; 4:31).

FAT (archaic)

Vat. (Joel 2:24; 3:13).

FA′THER

A word with various meanings in the Scriptures, including the begetter of children, a forefather, the founder of a tribe or nation, originator of an art, and a protector or benefactor. The father held unquestioned authority in a family. Some of his iniquities could be visited upon his children. Much importance was attached to receiving his blessing (Ge 27:27-40; 48:15-20,49). Jesus often referred to God as Father (Jo 17:1).

FATHER, GOD THE

See GOD, NAMES OF.

FATHERLESS

See ORPHAN.

FATH′OM

A unit of measure used to ascertain the depth of water. A fathom is six feet (Ac 27:28-29).

FATLING (archaic)

Fat cattle (Is 11:6).

FATTED

An animal that has been grain fed, to fatten quickly and produce tender, juicy meat. Animals that feed exclusively on grass do not get fat as quickly and produce a tougher meat. Fattened animals were used for sacrifices, and for special feasts (2 Sa 6:13; 1 Ki 4:23). When the prodigal son returned home, his father prepared a celebration with a fattened calf (Lk 15:23-24).

FAWN

A young deer (Song 4:5; 7:3). See DEER.

FEAR OF GOD

"The fear of the LORD is the beginning of knowledge, but fools despise wisdom and instruction" (Pr 1:7; 9:10). While we like to emphasize God's love, or His fatherly care for us, the Old Testament also emphasizes a less comfortable but important concept: the fear of God. God is holy and just, He cannot tolerate any sin. When Adam and Eve sinned, their first response was fear of God. Guilt produces fear; they knew that they were guilty before a holy God, and they were afraid of His judgment (Ge 3:8). God will not tolerate sin, and His wrath will be revealed at the ungodliness of men (Ro 1:18-28). Only a fool will deny the existence of God and His right and power to judge sin. That is why the beginning of wisdom is the fear of God. Until we realize that God is holy and mankind is sinful and deserving of judgment, we have no tools for understanding the problems of this world. At the same time, no believer needs to live in terror of God's judgment. For someone who is in right standing with God, fear of God is a healthy respect mingled with the honor and love that we bear for him. To fear God is to recognize His holiness and His prerogative to judge.

FEAST

Many religious feasts and festivals were observed by the Jewish people during Old and New Testament times. During these events, the people stopped all manual labor and devoted themselves totally to these celebrations. The accounts of these festivals in the Bible suggest they included a potluck type of meal, with some parts of the feast reserved for the priests and the rest given to those who gathered at the temple or the altar for worship. Observed with thanksgiving, worship, and joyous feasting, these feasts commemorated significant events in Israel's history as God's covenant people.

Three of these feasts were required by Mosaic law. The first was Passover, on the fourteenth day of the first month, which was followed the next day by the Feast of Unleavened Bread (Le 23:5-6). The second annual festival was the Feast of Weeks, later called Pentecost, occurring fifty days after the Firstfruits were offered (Le 23:15-16; Ac 2:1). The third festival was the Feast of Tabernacles, on the fifteenth day of the seventh month. Lasting for seven days, it commemorated the period in the wilderness (Le 23:34-44). All adult males were required to appear on these three occasions (Ex 23:17; De 16:16).

Following is a list of the feasts and festivals of the Bible times. A fuller description of each one may be found in the appropriate section of the dictionary.

Day of Atonement
Feast of Tabernacles (Feast of Booths)
Feast of Dedication (Hanukkah, Chanukah, Feast of Lights)

Firstfruits
Year of Jubilee
New Moon
*Passover and the Feast of Unleavened
Bread*
Pentecost (Feast of Weeks, Feast of Harvest)
Feast of Purim
Sabbath
Sabbatical Year
Feast of Trumpets (Seventh Month Festival)

A CALENDAR OF JEWISH FEASTS				
Feast of	Month on Jewish Calendar	Day	Corresponding Month	Reference
Passover	Nisan	14	March-April	Ex 12:1-14
Unleavened Bread	Nisan	15-21	March-April	Ex 12:15-20
Firstfruits	Nisan or Sivan	16 or 6	March-April May-June	Le 23:9-14 Nu 28:26
Pentecost	Sivan	6 (50 days after barley harvest)	May-June	De 16:9-12; Ac 2:1
Trumpets	Tishri	1,21	September-October	Nu 29:1-6
Day of Atonement	Tishri	10	September-October	Le 23: 26-32; He 9:7
Tabernacles	Tishri	15-22	September-October	Ne 8:13-18; Jo 7:2
Dedication	Chislev	25 (8 days)	November-December	Jo 10:22
Purim	Adar	14,15	February-March	Es 9:18-32

FEEBLE KNEES
Exhaustion (Job 4:4).

FEEBLEMINDED (archaic)
Fainthearted, discouraged (1 Th 5:14).

FEET, DISEASED
Probably gout, a disease which causes periodic painful inflammation of the joints and ligaments and is particularly prone to attack the feet. It is marked by excessive uric acid in the blood, and deposits of urates in the inflamed areas (2 Ch 16:12).

FEET, WASHING OF
See FOOT WASHING.

FEIGNED (archaic)
Deceitful, false, "put on" (Ps 17:1).

FE´LIX (happy)
A Roman official, procurator of Judea. He was liberated from slavery by Claudius, who appointed him to his high position. Felix had a reputation for being very corrupt. When Paul was arrested in Jerusalem, he was sent to Caesarea to be tried before Felix (Ac 23:24,34). When Paul spoke before Felix and his wife, Drusilla, who was a Jewess, Felix was deeply affected by the story of Paul's conversion. He continued to call Paul back again, hoping to be bribed into letting him go. However, failing to receive a bribe from Paul and to placate the Jews, he left Paul in prison (Ac 24:24-27).

FELLOES
The semicircular pieces which make up a wheel's outer rim, and to which the spokes are attached (1 Ki 7:33, KJV).

FELLOW
A slightly derisive, or at least disrespectful way of speaking about someone; "this fellow" (Ma 26:61). Also in a positive sense, as "companion," "the one alongside" as Paul speaks of his "fellow workers" (Ph 4:3).

FELLOWSHIP
See COMMUNION.

FEN (archaic)
Marsh; swamp (Job 40:15-21).

FENCED CIT´IES
Towns fortified by means of walls and towers (2 Ch 8:5; Ne 3:1-32). The cities of the Amorites and Canaanites were fortified (Nu 13:28; Jos 14:12). Many of the cities taken by the Israelites were similarly protected (2 Sa 20:6; 2 Ki 14:13; Je 5:17; Zep 1:16).

FER´RET
An unclean creeping animal (Le 11:30) which is called *gecko* in the Revised Version. The ferret is not found in Palestine. The animal intended is probably a variety of lizard. See LIZARD.

FERRYBOAT
A boat which exclusively runs back and forth across the current of a river, from the mainland shore to an island, or across any similar stretch

of water, for the purpose of carrying goods and passengers to the other side in the absence of a bridge (2 Sa 19:18).

FESTIVALS
See FEAST.

FES'TUS, POR'CI·US
The successor of Felix as procurator of Judea (Ac 24:10,27) about A.D. 60. He listened to Paul's defense in the presence of Agrippa II. Festus was satisfied as to Paul's innocence but proposed that he be tried in Jerusalem. This was unwise and Paul asserted his right to appeal to Caesar (Ac 25:1–26:32).

FETCHED A COMPASS (archaic)
Made a circuit (Ac 28:12-13).

FETTERS
Shackles, chains; used to restrain a prisoner. Fetters were made of bronze (Ju 16:21) and iron (Ps 149:8).

FE'VER
A disease characterized by abnormally high body temperature (De 28:22), also called the burning ague (Le 26:16).

FIDELITY
See FAITHFULNESS; FAITH.

FIELD
A section of land, cleared of trees and stones to make it suitable for agriculture, or an open pasture or grazing land.

FIELD OF SHARP SWORDS
The site of a universally fatal hand-to-hand combat between David's men and Ishbosheth's men, and the ensuing battle in which Abner (Ishbosheth's general) and his men were beaten (2 Sa 2:16).

FIFE
An instrument of the flute family. See FLUTE.

FIG
A tree of Palestine and its edible fruit. Some of these trees grow to a height of fifteen feet. Looking like a small green knob, the young fruit appears in the early spring before the leaf buds. This fact is alluded to by Jesus in the parable about the barren fig tree (Mk 11:13-14). Figs were a staple article of food in Palestine and a crop failure caused great distress. Occasionally figs were used medicinally (2 Ki 20:7; Is 38:21).

FIG TREE, BARREN; PARABLE OF
(Lk 13:6-9).

FILLETS
Bands, possibly curtain rods (Ex 27:10).

FILLY
A young female horse (Song 1:9)

FILTH
Dirt, especially that which is corrupt, rotten, and polluting. Because of our moral failure, our attempts at righteousness are like trying to cover oneself with filthy rags (Is 64:6). However, if we humbly confess our sins, God will make us truly clean (1 Jo 1:7-9).

FINER
Refiner. See METALSMITH.

FINGER
This word is often used as a way to express God's interventive power on behalf of humans. The Egyptian magicians recognized "the finger of God" in the plagues (Ex 8:19). The Psalmist described creation as "the work of His fingers" (Ps 8:3). The Lord wrote the Ten Commandments on the stone tablets with His finger (De 9:10). Jesus cast out demons by "the finger of God" (Lk 11:20).

FINING POT
Refining pot, used to melt down metal so that the dross could be removed.

FINS
The regulations concerning clean seafood include only those creatures which have fins and scales (Le 11:9; De 14:9-10). Thus, the sea mammals were unclean, as were sharks (they have no scales) and all shellfish.

FIR TREE
A tree of Lebanon (1 Ki 5:8,10), used to make ships (Eze 27:5), musical instruments (2 Sa 6:5), and in the construction of Solomon's tem-

ple (1 Ki 6:34; 2 Ch 3:5). Some think this may be a variety of pine, cypress, or juniper.

FIRE

Among the Hebrews, it symbolized the Lord's presence and was used also to consume the sacrifice (Ge 4:4; 8:20). It was also used for cooking and heating (Je 36:22; Mk 14:54; Jo 18:18).

FIRE BAPTISM

See BAPTISM OF FIRE.

FIREBRAND (archaic)

Firewood; torch (Is 7:4).

FIRE, LAKE OF

See HINNOM, VALLEY OF.

FIRE PAN

A container used to remove charcoal and ashes from the temple altar and burnt lamp wax from the golden candlesticks. It was made of silver, brass, or gold (Ex 27:3; Le 16:12; 1 Ki 7:50; 2 Ki 25:15).

FIR'KIN

Translation of the Greek *metretes* ("measure") a unit of liquid measure equal to about 10 gallons (Jo 2:6). See WEIGHTS AND MEASURES

FIR'MA·MENT

The expanse of space surrounding the earth, which includes everything between the earth and the stars. This expanse is compared to a tent spread out above the earth (Ps 104:2; Is 40:22) and also to a mirror (Job 37:18). It was spoken of as having doors and windows (Ge 7:11; 2 Ki 7:2; Ps 78:23).

FIRST BEGOTTEN

See FIRSTBORN.

FIRST'BORN

God claimed the firstborn, both of men and animals. In the tenth plague of Egypt, the firstborn of the Egyptians were slain and by the sprinkling of blood the firstborn of the Hebrews were preserved, hence they were dedicated to Jehovah (Ex 12:12-13,23,29). Every firstborn male was presented to the Lord at the sanctuary (Nu 18:15; Lk 2:22). In place of each

firstborn the tribe of Levi was chosen (Nu 3:12,41,46; 8:13-19) for the service of the sanctuary. In this way, the firstborn were redeemed by substitution, but a redemption price, not exceeding five shekels, was still paid by the parents (Nu 18:16).

FIRST'FRUITS

The first ripe fruits of the season which many ancient peoples, including the Hebrews, presented as divine offerings. The offering of firstfruits was required by Mosaic law (Ex 23:19).

FIRST GATE

A gate of Jerusalem (Ze 14:10).

FIRSTLING

The firstborn lambs of a flock (Ge 4:4). The firstborn were to be dedicated to God (Ex 13:11-16).

FISH

Only fish with fins and scales were considered clean and suitable for food (Le 11:9). Since Israel has a long coastline as well as inland lakes and streams, fish was an important part of the Jewish diet. No specific varieties of fish are mentioned in the Bible.

FISHERMAN

A number of Jesus's disciples were fishermen (Mk 1:16-20). Fishing was done with nets, hooks, and sometimes spears (Is 19:8; Job 41:7).

FISHER OWL

See CORMORANT.

FISH GATE

One of the gates of Jerusalem (2 Ch 33:14; Ne 3:3; 12:39).

FISHHOOK

Used as a symbol of God's judgment (Am 4:2; Hab 1:14-15).

FISH'ING

An important occupation of both Egypt and Palestine where it was carried on chiefly in the Nile and Sea of Galilee. Four of Christ's disciples were fishermen (Ma 4:18-22).

FITCH′ES

1. The black cummin whose aromatic seeds were used in cooking (Is 28:25,27).

2. Spelt, an inferior variety of wheat (Eze 4:9). It is also translated *rie* or *rye* (Ex 9:32; Is 28:25).

FLAG

A kind of reed, sedge, bulrush, or other coarse herbage along marshy riverbanks (Ex 2:3,5; Job 8:11; Is 19:6). It is called *weed* in Jonah 2:5.

FLAG′ON

A container for holding liquids, probably made of skins or earthenware (Is 22:24). The flagon of wine (2 Sa 6:19; 1 Ch 16:3; Ho 3:1, KJV), called simply flagons (Song 2:5, KJV), should properly be translated as a pressed raisin cake.

FLANGE

A projecting edge (1 Ki 7:35-36).

FLANK

The side of an animal, between the ribs and hip (Le 3:4; Job 15:27; Ps 38:7).

FLASK

A bottle or container, often used for carrying anointing oil (1 Sa 10:1; 2 Ki 9:1,3); a pottery jar or pitcher (Je 19:1,10); a box or jar for perfumed oil or ointment (Mk 14:3).

FLAX

This plant was raised in Egypt and other countries (Ex 9:31). It furnished the fiber for linen and the seed was valuable for its oil.

FLAY (archaic)

To strip (Mi 3:1-3).

FLAGON

FLEA

An insect pest, common in warm climates such as Palestine. In his flight from Saul, David compares his own importance with that of a flea (1 Sa 24:14; 26:20).

FLEECE

The wool shorn from a sheep (Ju 6:37-40).

FLESH

1. In the ordinary sense, the word *flesh* denotes the human body as distinct from the human spirit (Job 14:22; Is 10:18; Col 2:5). It is also used to contrast mortal men with God who is the spirit (Ps 56:4; Is 31:3; Joel 2:28-29; Ma 16:17). The term *having mind for the flesh* means having carnal desires (Ro 8:5-8). See WORLD, FLESH, DEVIL.

2. The term *flesh* is also used to denote meat of any kind, in the modern sense of the word *meat* (the flesh of an animal), as opposed to *meat* meaning food in general. See MEAT.

FLESH HOOK

A fork for lifting meat out of its cooking pot (Ex 27:3; Nu 4:14; 1 Sa 2:13-14).

FLESH POT

A cooking pot used for preparing meat (Ex 16:3).

FLINT

A very hard, dark grey quartz. It has been used since ancient times for a variety of purposes. It breaks in sharp-edged flakes, which are useful for making knives, arrowheads and ax heads. Moses's wife circumcised her children with a sharp stone (Ex 4:25). Apparently there was flint in the wilderness (De 8:15; 32:13); the word is also used to describe determination (Is 50:7; Eze 3:9).

FLOCK

A group of domesticated animals, particularly sheep or goats (1 Sa 25:2; Job 1:3).

FLOOD, THE

The deluge at the time of Noah which, according to the Scriptures, was divine judgment for the wickedness of man (Ge 6:5–7:24). Only the righteous Noah, his family, and a large number of animals were permitted to escape by riding out the flood in an ark. The rain began on the seventeenth day of the second month, and on the seventeenth day of the seventh month the ark rested on the mountains of Ararat (Ge 8:1-4). Three months later the tops of the mountains appeared. Noah left the ark on the twenty-seventh day of the second month of the New Year. The flood had lasted about a year (Ge 8:14-19).

FLOOR, THRESHING

A clean floor, of stone or possibly hardened clay, used for beating or treading the harvested grain to separate the straw from the grain (2 Sa 24:18).

FLOUR

The chief ingredient in bread made from grain which has been pulverized by pounding or grinding (Ju 6:19; 1 Sa 28:24). Fine flour, obtained by sifting the coarse flour or meal through a fine sieve, was used for sacrificial offerings (Le 2:1,4-5,7; 5:11).

FLUTE

A Babylonian wind instrument, used with other instruments to remind the people to worship Nebuchadnezzar's golden image (Da 3:5,7, 10,15). Flutes are also mentioned in connection with temple worship in Psalm 150:4. Other translations for this word are "organ" (KJV), "fife," or "reed-pipe" (REB), "pipe" (NRSV).

FLUX, BLOODY (archaic)

An intestinal disease; dysentery (Ac 28:8).

FLY, FLIES

An insect, occasionally used by the Lord to frighten enemies. A plague of flies was sent to the land of the Egyptians in order to frighten them into allowing the Israelites to leave their country (Ex 8:21; Ps 105:31). The "devouring flies" of Psalm 78:45 were probably biting flies.

FOAL

A baby horse.

FODDER

Animal feed, particularly hay (Job 6:5).

FOLD

See SHEEPFOLD.

FOLLY

See FOOL, FOOLISHNESS.

FOOD

While the Hebrews were wandering in the wilderness, God fed them with manna and occasionally quail. Mosaic law stated that only animals which chewed the cud and had cloven hoofs were edible. Serpents, creeping things, and fish without scales were forbidden (Le 7:26; 11:10; 17:10-14; De 12:16). After they arrived in the promised land, the "land flowing with milk and honey," their diet changed. The manna stopped, and they ate the fruit of their own labors, both from their flocks and herds and from tilling the ground. Bread was the staple of the table. Lentils were also important. Onions, leeks, cucumbers, and garlic were used as relishes. Preferred condiments were cummin, fitches, dill, mint, and mustard. Edible fruits were figs, olives, grapes, pomegranates, almonds, and melons. Foods derived from the animal kingdom were honey, locusts, milk, curds, meat, and fish. The vineyards provided wine and the olives provided oil for cooking and for light.

FOOL

The word is used for two purposes—to indicate one who is stupid and unwise (1 Sa 26:21) and to indicate one who disregards God or does not believe in him (Ps 14:1; 92:6; Pr 14:9; Je 17:11).

FOOLISHNESS

Acting like a fool.

FOOT' MAN

One who acted as the king's bodyguard or courier (1 Sa 22:17). A footsoldier, or infantryman, as distinguished from cavalry (2 Ki 13:7; 1 Ch 18:4).

FOOT WASHING

It was customary to offer guests the opportunity to wash their feet when they entered the house. Foot washing was a simple act of courtesy and hospitality (Lk 7:44). At the last supper, Jesus showed His disciples how to serve one another when He washed their feet (Jo 13). He was their leader, and not only that, He was God. Nevertheless, Jesus "took the form of a servant" (Ph 2:7), and commanded His disciples to do likewise for one another.

FORBEARANCE

Bearing with patience, refusing to be provoked (Ro 2:3-4).

FORBORNE (archaic)

Ceased (Je 51:30).

FORD

A shallow place in a river or other body of water that may be crossed on foot (Jos 2:7; Ju 3:28; 12:5-6). The Old Testament mentions the fords of three rivers: the Jabbok, Jordan, and Arnon (Ge 32:22; Jos 2:7; Ju 3:28; Is 16:2).

FOR′EIGN·ER

In the Authorized Version the translation is often *stranger*, identifying one who was not of Israel and had no allegiance to the God of Israel, such as an Egyptian (Ex 2:22) or a Philistine (2 Sa 15:19). A proselyte to Judaism would not be considered a foreigner (Is 56:6-8; Ac 2:10). Intermarriage with foreigners was forbidden (Ex 34:16; De 7:3; Ez 10:2; Ne 13:26-27). Foreigners among the Israelites were required to abstain from idolatrous worship (Le 20:2), to honor the Sabbath (Ex 20:10), and not to eat leavened bread during the Passover season (Ex 12:19). They were accorded civil rights and enjoyed protection under Israel's laws (Le 25:47). In order to have the full rights of citizenship a foreigner had to receive the rite of circumcision (Ex 12:48; Ro 9:4).

FOREKNOWLEDGE

An aspect of God's omnipotence; His knowledge of all things in the future, both real and possible. God knows exactly how long each person's life will be (Job 14:5). Jesus is the Beginning and the End (Re 1:8,17; 21:6). Paul says that those whose belief God foreknew, He predestined to become like Jesus (Ro 8:29) and that the Israelites, whom He also foreknew, He has not forgotten (Ro 11:2). God foreknew all that would happen to Jesus (Ac 2:23; 1 Pe 1:20). Believers are "elect according to the foreknowledge of God" (1 Pe 1:2).

FOREMAN

See OVERSEER.

FORE·RUN′NER

A runner who preceded a distinguished official, kept the way open, or proclaimed his approach (1 Sa 8:11; 1 Ki 1:5; Es 6:9). John the Baptist was the forerunner of Christ (Ma 11:10).

FORESKIN

See CIRCUMCISION.

FORESWEAR (archaic)

To swear falsely (Ma 5:33).

FORGE

The furnace used by a metalsmith to heat metal for shaping (Is 44:12, NIV).

FORGER

See METALSMITH.

FORGIVENESS

The state of being absolved or pardoned for sin. When David had sinned with Bath-sheba, he repentantly wrote, "Have mercy upon me, O God, according to Your lovingkindness; according to the multitude of your tender mercies. Blot out my transgressions ... Hide Your face from my sins, and blot out all my iniquities" (Ps 51:1, 9). God is a holy, righteous God, but He is also compassionate and merciful. When people realize their sin and humbly repent before God, He is willing to forgive (Is 38:17). He is like the father in the parable of the prodigal son: instead of giving the son what he deserved and not receiving him, or even just keeping him as a slave, the father lovingly restores his son to the bosom of the family (Lk 15:11-32). He does not even remember the wrongs committed (He 10:17).

FORK

Probably a pitchfork or similar farm implement (1 Sa 13:21); also a fork used for handling the sacrifices (Ex 27:3; 1 Ch 28:17).

FORMER GATE

A gate of Jerusalem, also called the First Gate (Ze 14:10).

FORNICATION

Premarital sexual relations. This is strictly forbidden for followers of Christ (Ro 13:13; 1 Co 5:11; Ga 5:19; Ep 5:3; Col 3:5; Re 14:8; 17:4).

FORTIFICATIONS

See FENCED CITIES.

FOR·TU·NA′TUS *(fortunate)*

A Roman and a member of the church at Corinth. With two others he came to Paul at Ephesus (1 Co 16:17).

FORTUNE TELLING

Foretelling the future by the aid of divination. The Philippian slave girl told fortunes by the aid of the demon which oppressed her (Ac 16:16).

FOUNDATION GATE

A gate of Jerusalem (Ne 3:15; 12:37).

FOUNDER

See METALSMITH.

FOUN′TAIN

Literally, the word is used to denote a spring of running water (De 8:7; 33:28; 1 Sa 29:1). Figuratively, it is used in regard to the spiritual blessings of God and Christ (Ps 36:9; 87:7; Je 17:13; Ze 13:1).

FOWL

Bird (1 Ki 4:23; Lk 12:24).

FOWL′ER

One who catches birds. Usually a net and snare were used (Ps 124:7; Pr 6:5). The word is used figuratively to denote one who ensnares the innocent to lead them into sin (Ps 91:3; 124:7; Ho 9:8).

FOX

A sly animal which lived in holes (Ma 8:20) and inhabited parts of Palestine. However, certain references in the Old Testament may refer to the jackal instead of the true fox. For example, the 300 foxes caught by Samson were probably jackals (Ju 15:4).

FRANK′IN·CENSE

A fragrant white gum or vegetable resin obtained from various kinds of trees (Ex 30:34-36; Le 2:1; Ma 2:11).

FREEDMAN

One who is freed from slavery (Ac 6:9). Paul taught that a slave who becomes a believer is spiritually a freeman (1 Co 7:22).

FREEDOM

The opposite of bondage. Slaves were freed in the Year of Jubilee (Le 25:27). As unbelievers, humans are slaves to sin, but when they put their trust in Christ, they enter a different world of freedom, where they are free and empowered to choose righteousness (Ro 6:22). Jesus explained that truth leads to freedom (Jo 8:32), and He Himself *is* Truth (Jo 14:6). Christ is the only one who can bring true freedom.

FRET

To be grieved; troubled; displeased (Ps 37:8-9).

FRIEND

Friendship is a beautiful gift from God, a special connection between two people that is not based on blood ties or necessity, but on a deeper heart connection. God greatly honored Abraham by calling him His friend, rather than merely His servant (Ex 33:11). Jesus said, "No longer do I call you servants, for a servant does not know what his master is doing; but I have called you friends, for all things that I heard from My Father I have made known to you" (Jo 15:15). One of the most moving examples of friendship in Scripture is the friendship between David and Jonathan (1 Sa 18:1-4). They loved one another deeply, their "souls were knit." Even after Jonathan was dead, David was loyal to Jonathan, and cared for his crippled son.

FRIEND OF THE BRIDEGROOM

See BRIDEGROOM, FRIEND OF THE.

FRINGE

See TASSEL.

FROG

An amphibian, mentioned biblically in two connections: with one of the plagues of Egypt (Ex 8:2-14; Ps 78:45) and as a form assumed by unclean spirits (Re 16:13-14).

FRONT′LET

A band with a leather case attached, worn on the forehead by Jewish men. Inside the case were pieces of parchment on which were inscribed scriptural quotations (Ex 13:1-16; De 6:4-9; 11:13-21). Wearing it was symbolical of obedience to the commands of God. See PHYLACTERY. (Ma 23:5; Mk 7:3-4; Lk 5:33).

FRUIT

In a physical sense, fruit referred to the produce of agricultural endeavors, from figs to grain (see FIRSTFRUITS). In a slightly more narrow sense, fruit usually includes only such foods as figs, raisins, grapes, pomegranates, etc. Spiritually speaking, "fruit" is the power of God working in our lives. Jesus said that if we abide (rest) in Him, we will bear spiritual fruit (Jo 15:5,7). Galatians 5:22-23 lists seven "fruits of the spirit": love, joy, peace, patience, longsuffering, kindness, goodness, faithfulness, gentleness and self-control. "Against such there is no law." In other words, you can't overdo on these fruits, no moderation is necessary.

FUEL

Oil was used as fuel for lamps (Eze 4:15). Wood and charcoal were burned for cooking and heating. Dried manure was also used for fuel (Eze 4:15).

FULFILL

See PLEROMA.

FULL′ER

One who cleans or fulls garments or cloth. The process of fulling consisted of applying to the cloth an alkaline solution which served as a crude soap or bleaching agent. Then the cloth was allowed to dry in a field, hence the name Fuller's Field (2 Ki 18:17). The whiteness of the garments of Jesus at the transfiguration was contrasted with the whiteness obtainable by fulling (Mk 9:3).

FULL′ER'S FIELD

A field mentioned several times, apparently quite near Jerusalem, where fullers spread their cloth to bleach in the sun (2 Ki 18:17,26; Is 7:3; 36:2).

FULLER'S SOAP

A soap made from a naturally occurring alkaline salt derived from certain Asiatic plants (Mal 3:2).

FULLNESS

See PLEROMA.

FUNERAL

See BURIAL.

FUR′LONG

A unit of linear measure which is the equivalent of the Greek *stadium*. It was about 606 feet long; shorter than the English furlong (Jo 6:19; 11:18; Re 14:20).

FUR′NACE

1. A furnace for refining gold, silver, brass, etc. (Pr 17:3; 27:21; Eze 22:18,20). The term is probably also used to indicate ovens for baking.
2. A word used figuratively to denote the bondage in Egypt (De 4:20).

(Also seeGe 19:28; Ex 9:8,10; 19:18; Is 33:12; Am 2:1; Da 3:22-23; Je 29:22).

FURNACES, TOWER OF THE

See OVENS, TOWER OF THE.

FURNITURE

Articles used to furnish the tabernacle (Ex 31:7-9). Today we think of furniture in terms of only the large furnishings of a home, but this word includes everything: tables, lamps, altars, forks and fire shovels, etc.

FURROW

The marks left by a plow in a cultivated field. God's judgment against Israel sprang up "like hemlock in the furrows of the field" (Ho 10:4).

FURY

The wrath of God. In His mercy, God did not require Israel to drink the cup of His fury to the dregs (Is 51:22).

FUTURE

That which is yet to come. The future seems uncertain to us, but God knows all that will come to pass, and none of it is out of His hand. He has given us some information about end times (Da 8:17-26); and also information about what will affect our destiny. The future of the upright will be peace, while the wicked will be cut off (Ps 37:37-38).

G

GA′AL (loathing)

The son of Ebed. He helped the Shechemites in their revolt against Abimelech but was unsuccessful (Ju 9:26-41).

GA′ASH (quaking)

A hill in the district of Mount Ephraim whose brooks and streams are occasionally mentioned (Jos 24:30; Ju 2:9; 2 Sa 23:30; 1 Ch 11:32).

GA′BA

See GEBA.

GAB·BA′I (tax gatherer)

A Benjamite who dwelt at Jerusalem (Ne 11:8).

GAB′ BA·THA *(an elevation)*

The equivalent of the Hebrew *pavement*. Pilate sat in judgment of Jesus in this place (Jo 19:13).

GA′ BRI·EL *(man of God)*

A heavenly messenger high in rank among the angels. He was sent to Daniel to interpret a vision received by the prophet (Da 8:16-27). The same occurred in connection with the prophecy of the seventy weeks (Da 9:21-27). Centuries afterwards he appeared to Zacharias to announce the birth of John the Baptist (Lk 1:11-22), and at Nazareth he declared to Mary her great distinction and honor (Lk 1:26-31). Gabriel's special job seems to have been the announcing of things concerning the Messiah.

GAD *(good fortune)*

1. The son of Jacob and Zilpah, Leah's handmaid (Ge 30:10-11). The tribe was commended by Moses (De 33:20-21). Gad had seven sons (Nu 26:15-18).

2. The tribe of Gad (Nu 1:14; De 27:13). In the first numbering it had 45,650 men (Nu 1:25), but in the second census the number was 40,500 (Nu 26:15-18). The tribe was assigned territory east of the Jordan. It was required to assist the other tribes in the conquest of the country (Nu 32:6-34). The territory of Reuben was south of that of Gad and the half tribe of Manasseh was on the north. It was rich pastureland (Nu 32:1-4). Ramoth, a city of refuge, was in this territory (Jos 20:8).

3. A prophet in the time of David. It was he who advised David to leave Adullam (1 Sa 22:5).

GAD, RAVINE OF

One of the places Joab and his men camped when they went out to take a census of the fighting men at David's command (2 Sa 24:5). Also called "river of Gad," it probably refers to the River Arnon, east of the Dead Sea.

GAD′ A·RA

A city of the Decapolis. It is not mentioned in the Bible, but the "country of the Gadarenes" which is "opposite Galilee" is mentioned. Some versions say "Gerasenes" (Lk 8:26-37). See GADARENES.

GAD′ A·RENES

Residents of Gadara and the surrounding area. The "country of the Gadarenes" was an area south and east of the Sea of Galilee, related to the area of the Decapolis. It was near here that Jesus cured a demoniac by permitting the outcast demons to enter a herd of swine which in turn plunged into the sea (Lk 8:26-37). The word *Gergesenes* is used in Matthew 8:28 and the word *Geresenes* is used in the Authorized Version (Mk 5:1; Lk 8:26).

GADDEST *(archaic)*

Second person singular; to roam; to go away (Je 2:36-37).

GAD′ DI *(fortunate)*

One of the spies, or scouts, representing the tribe of Manasseh (Nu 13:11).

GAD′ DI·EL *(fortune of God)*

One of the twelve spies, or scouts, sent to Canaan (Nu 13:10).

GA′ DI *(a Gadite)*

Father of Menahem, king of Israel (2 Ki 15:14).

GADITES

The people of the tribe of Gad (De 3:12; Jos 1:12).

GA′ HAM

A son of Nahor (Ge 22:24).

GA′ HAR

The head of the family of Nethinim (Ez 2:47; Ne 7:49).

GA′ I

A name used in the Revised Version for valley (1 Sa 17:52). It may be Gath.

GAI′ US

A Roman name sometimes written, Caius. Four men of the New Testament:

1. Gaius of Macedonia was a traveling companion of Paul. In the riot in Ephesus he was seized by the Ephesians (Ac 19:29).

2. Gaius of Derbe accompanied Paul on his last journey to Asia (Ac 20:4).

3. Gaius of Corinth, Paul's host, was baptized by Paul (Ro 16:23; 1 Co 1:14). He was probably the same as Gaius of Derbe.

4. The Gaius to whom John addressed his third epistle (3 Jo 1).

GAL' A·AD (Greek form)

See GILEAD.

GA' LAL

Two Old Testament men:

1. A Levite, the son of Jeduthun, and father of Shemaiah (1 Ch 9:16; Ne 11:17).

2. Another Levite (1 Ch 9:15).

GA·LA' TIA

A district of central Asia Minor named for the Gallic tribes from Macedonia and Greece who lived there. They were given the territory by Nicomedes, king of Bithynia, in return for military service (Ac 16:6; 18:23; Ga 1:2).

GA·LA' TIANS, E·PIS' TLE TO THE

1. The Book of Galatians. The Galatians, having launched their Christian experience by faith, seemed content to leave their voyage of faith and chart a new course based on works— a course Paul found disturbing. His letter to the Galatians is a vigorous attack against the gospel of works and a defense of the gospel of faith.

Paul begins by setting forth his credentials as an apostle with a message from God: blessing comes from God on the basis of faith, not law. The law declares men guilty and imprisons them; faith sets men free to enjoy liberty in Christ. But liberty is not license. Freedom in Christ means freedom to produce the fruits of righteousness through a Spirit-led lifestyle.

The book is called *Pros Galatas,* "To the Galatians," and it is the only letter of Paul that is specifically addressed to a number of churches ("To the churches of Galatia," 1:2). The name *Galatians* was given to this Celtic people because they originally lived in Gaul before their migration to Asia Minor.

2. The Author of Galatians. The Pauline authorship and the unity of this epistle are virtually unchallenged. The first verse clearly identifies the author as "Paul, an apostle." Also in 5:2, we read, "Indeed I, Paul, say to you." In fact, Paul actually wrote Galatians (6:11) instead of dictating it to a secretary, as was his usual practice.

3. The Time of Galatians. The term *Galatia* was used in an ethnographic sense (that is, cultural and geographic origin) and in a political sense. The original ethnographic sense refers to the central part of Asia Minor where these Celtic tribes eventually settled after their conflicts with the Romans and Macedonians. Later, in 189 B.C. Galatia came under Roman domination, and in 25 B.C. Augustus declared it a Roman province. The political or provincial Galatia included territory to the south that was not originally considered part of Galatia (for example, the cities of Pisidian Antioch, Iconium, Lystra, and Derbe). There are two theories regarding the date and setting of Galatians.

The *North Galatian Theory* holds that Paul was speaking of Galatia in its earlier, more restricted sense. According to this theory, the churches of Galatia were north of the cities Paul visited on his first missionary journey. Paul visited the ethnographic Galatia (the smaller region to the North) for the first time on his second missionary journey, probably while he was on his way to Troas (Ac 16:6). On his third missionary journey, Paul revisited the Galatian churches he had established (Ac 18:23) and wrote this epistle either in Ephesus (A.D. 53-56) or in Macedonia (A.D. 56).

According to the *South Galatian Theory,* Paul was referring to Galatia in its wider political sense as a province of Rome. This means that the churches he had in mind in this epistle were in the cities he evangelized during his first missionary journey with Barnabas (Ac 13:13–14:25). This was just prior to the Jerusalem Council (Ac 15), so the Jerusalem visit in Galatians 2:1-10 must have been the Acts 11:27-30 famine relief visit. Galatians was probably written in Syrian Antioch in A.D. 49 just before Paul went to the Council in Jerusalem.

Paul wrote this epistle in response to a report that the Galatian churches were suddenly taken over by the false teaching of certain Judaizers who professed Jesus yet sought to place Gentile converts under the requirements of the Mosaic law (1:7; 4:17,21; 5:2-12; 6:12-13).

4. The Christ of Galatians. Christ has freed the believer from bondage to the law (legalism) and to sin (license) and has placed him in a position of liberty. The transforming cross provides for the believers deliverance from the curse of sin, law, and self (1:4; 2:20; 3:13; 4:5; 5:24; 6:14).

5. Keys to Galatians.

Key Word: Freedom from the Law—This epistle shows that the believer is no longer under the law but is saved by faith alone. It has been said that Judaism was the cradle of Christianity, but also that it was very nearly its grave as well. God raised up Paul as the Moses of the Christian church to deliver them from this bondage. Galatians is the Christian's Declaration of Independence. The power of the Holy Spirit enables the Christian to enjoy freedom within the law of love.

Key Verses: Galatians 2:20-21 and 5:1—"I have been crucified with Christ; it is no longer I who live, but Christ lives in me; and the life which I now live in the flesh I live by faith in the Son of God, who loved me and gave Himself for me. I do not set aside the grace of God; for if righteousness comes through the law, then Christ died in vain" (2:20-21).

"Stand fast therefore in the liberty by which Christ has made us free, and do not be entangled again with a yoke of bondage" (5:1).

Key Chapter: Galatians 5—The impact of the truth concerning freedom is staggering: freedom must not be used "as an opportunity" for the flesh, but through love serve one another" (5:13). This chapter records the power, "Walk in the Spirit" (5:16), and the results, "the fruit of the Spirit" (5:22), of that freedom.

6. Survey of Galatians.

The Epistle to the Galatians has been called "the Magna Carta of the Christian liberty." It is Paul's manifesto of justification by faith, and the resulting liberty. Paul directs this great charter of Christian freedom to a people who are willing to give up the priceless liberty they possess in Christ. The oppressive theology of certain Jewish legalizers has been causing the believers in Galatia to trade their freedom in Christ for bondage to the law. Paul writes this forceful epistle to do away with the false gospel of works and demonstrate the superiority of justification by faith. This carefully written polemic approaches the problem from three directions: the gospel of grace defended (1 and 2), the gospel of grace explained (3 and 4), and the gospel of grace applied (5 and 6).

The Gospel of Grace Defended (1 and 2). Paul affirms his divinely given apostleship and presents the gospel (1:1-5) because it has been distorted by false teachers among the Galatians (1:6-10). Paul launches into his biological argument for the true gospel of justification by faith in showing that he received his message not from men but directly from God (1:11-24). When he submits his teaching of Christian liberty to the apostles in Jerusalem, they all acknowledge the validity and authority of his message (2:1-10). Paul also must correct Peter on the matter of freedom from the law (2:11-21).

The Gospel of Grace Explained (3 and 4). In this section Paul uses eight lines of reasoning to develop his theological defense of justification by faith: (1) The Galatians began by faith, and their growth in Christ must continue to be by faith (3:1-5). (2) Abraham was justified by faith, and the same principle applies today (3:6-9). (3) Christ has redeemed all who trust in Him from the curse of the law (3:10-14). (4) The promise made to Abraham was not nullified by the law (3:15-18). (5) The law was given to drive men to faith, not to save them (3:19-22). (6) Believers in Christ are adopted sons of God and are no longer bound by the law (3:23–4:7). (7) The Galatians must recognize their inconsistency and regain their original freedom in Christ (4:8-20). (8) Abraham's two sons allegorically reveal the superiority of the Abrahamic promise to the Mosaic law (4:21-31).

The Gospel of Grace Applied (5 and 6). The Judaizers seek to place the Galatians under bondage to their perverted gospel of justification by law, but Paul warns them that law and grace are two contrary principles (5:1-12). So far, Paul has been contrasting the liberty of faith with the legalism of law, but at this point he warns the Galatians of the opposite extreme of license or antinomianism (5:13–6:10). The Christian is not only set free from bondage of law, but he is also free of the bondage of sin because of the power of the indwelling Spirit. Liberty is not an excuse to indulge in the deeds of the flesh; rather, it provides the privilege of bearing the fruit of the Spirit by walking in dependence upon Him. This letter closes with a contrast between the Judaizers—who are motivated by pride and a desire to avoid persecution—and Paul, who has suffered for the true gospel, but boasts only in Christ (6:11-18).

OUTLINE OF GALATIANS

I. The Gospel of Grace Defended (1:1–2:21)

A. Introduction 1:1-9
B. Gospel of Grace is Given by
Divine Revelation 1:10-24
C. Gospel of Grace is Approved by
Jerusalem Leadership 2:1-10
D. Gospel of Grace is Vindicated by
Rebuking Peter 2:11-21

II. The Gospel of Grace Explained (3:1–4:31)

A. Holy Spirit is Given by Faith, Not
by Works 3:1-5
B. Abraham was Justified by Faith Not
by Works 3:6-9

C. Justification is by Faith, Not
by the Law 3:10–4:11
D. Galatians Receive Blessings by
Faith, Not by the Law 4:12-20
E. Law and Grace Cannot Coexist ... 4:21-31

III. The Gospel of Grace Applied (5:1–6:18)

A. Position of Liberty: "Stand
Fast" 5:1-12
B. Practice of Liberty: Love One
Another 5:13-15
C. Power for Liberty: Walk in the
Spirit 5:16-26
D. Performance in Liberty: Do Good
to All Men 6:1-10
E. Conclusion 6:11-18

GAL'BA·NUM

A gum with a fragrant odor, one of the ingredients in incense (frankincense) (Ex 30:34).

GA'LEED (heap of witness)

This was the name given by Jacob to a pile of stones in Gilead, north of the river Jabbok. It was a memorial of the covenant between Laban and Jacob, under which each agreed not to pass the pillar (Ge 31:45-54). See MIZPAH.

GAL·I·LAE'AN, GAL·I·LE'AN

A native or inhabitant of Galilee (Ma 26:69; Mk 14:70; Lk 13:1; Jo 4:45).

GAL'I·LEE (circle, district)

In New Testament times Galilee was one of the three provinces of Palestine. It was located in the northern part. In the Old Testament it was considered to be roughly the territories of Asher, Naphtali, Zebulun, and Issachar. Many Canaanites lived in this district (Ju 1:30-33; 4:2). Many Gentiles continued to live here after the conquest of the land, as was indicated by the expression "Galilee of the nations" (Is 9:1; Ma 4:15). Jesus was raised in Galilee and performed several miracles there.

GAL'I·LEE, SEA OF

The beautiful Sea of Galilee, also referred to in the Bible as the Sea of Tiberias (Jo 6:1), the Lake of Gennesaret (Lk 5:1), and the Sea of

Chinnereth (Nu 34:11), was the geographical center of much of the ministry of Jesus. Almost thirteen miles long and about eight miles wide, the fresh-water lake is surrounded by high mountains. It is fed by the river Jordan from the North, and the Jordan flows out of it again on the South. Interestingly, the Sea of Galilee is one of the lowest points on earth, standing 680 feet below sea level.

The region around the Sea of Galilee in the upper Jordan River Valley in northern Palestine is a lush garden, with an abundance of fertile soil, water, fish, and a hot climate. About 200,000 people, mostly Gentiles, were scattered in the many towns along the shores of the lake and throughout the upper Jordan Valley when Jesus taught and healed in Palestine.

Because of their openness to new ideas, Jesus appealed to the common people of Galilee, and many of them "heard Him gladly" (Mk 12:37). Jesus recruited eleven of His disciples from this area. Many of them, including brothers Peter and Andrew and brothers James and John, were fishermen who earned their livelihood from the waters of this lake. Settlements along the shores of Lake Galilee in the time of Jesus included Tiberias, Magdala, Capernaum, and Bethsaida. In this region Jesus taught the multitudes and healed the sick (Mk 7:31-37).

Powerful winds sometimes sweep down from the mountains along the shores of the lake,

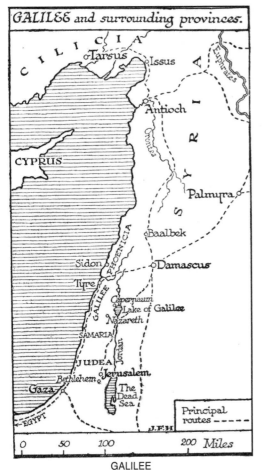

GALILEE and surrounding provinces.

GALILEE

clashing with heat waves rising from the water's surface. The resulting turbulence creates sudden, violent storms. This is probably the type of storm that Jesus calmed on the lake in response to the pleas of His disciples. "Who can this be," the people marveled, "that even the winds and the sea obey Him?" (Ma 8:27).

GALL

1. Bile, the bitter secretion of the liver. The ancients believed that the poison of asps was their bile (Job 20:14). The "gall of bitterness" signified a venomous attitude toward that which is good (Ac 8:23).

2. A bitter, poisonous herb called rosh in Hebrew (De 29:18; 32:32; Ps 69:21). Wine mixed with gall was a stupefying drink given to those about to be crucified to deaden the pain. Such a drink was offered to Jesus at the crucifixion (Ma 27:34).

GAL'LER·Y

A translation of a Hebrew word of uncertain meaning. It is used to describe a section of Ezekiel's temple (Eze 41:15; 42:3,5); in Song of Solomon 7:5 (KJV) it should probably be translated "tresses" (of hair).

GAL'LEY

A flat, low ship, having one or more rows of oars (Is 33:21).

GAL'LIM (heaps)

A village south of Jerusalem. Here lived Phalti (Phaltiel) to whom Saul gave Michal, the wife of David (1 Sa 25:44; 2 Sa 3:15).

GAL'LI·O

The proconsul of Achaia under Claudius. He was the brother of Seneca, the Roman philosopher, to whom he probably owed much of his political advancement. When the labors of Paul at Corinth aroused opposition, the Jews brought him before Gallio to be tried for breaking the Mosaic law. Gallio refused to hear the case, declaring that matters involving religious laws or customs were not in his jurisdiction. Likewise when the Greeks beat Sosthenes, the ruler of the synagogue, he again refused the case (Ac 18:12-17).

GALLON

Four quarts. See WEIGHTS AND MEASURES.

GAL'LOWS

The frame or tree on which persons were hanged. However, the more customary method of execution used by the Jews was stoning (Ex 17:4; Ac 14:5). Occasionally a person was hanged after being killed, for it was felt that anyone

GALLEY

who was hanged was then "accursed of God" (De 21:22-23). Persons hanged had to be buried the same day (De 21:23). The gallows built by Haman on which to hang Mordecai was fifty cubits (75 feet) high (Es 5:14).

GA·MA′LI·EL *(reward of God)*

Two Old Testament men:

1. Son of Pedahzur, head of the tribe of Manasseh in the wilderness (Nu 1:10; 2:20; 7:54, 59).

2. A doctor of the law, a Pharisee, and a member of the Sanhedrin. He was held in high regard by the Jews. Paul received his training in the law under this man (Ac 22:3). Gamaliel opposed the persecution of the apostles (Ac 5:34-39). He died about A.D. 50.

GAMES

The four important Grecian games were the Olympic at Olympia, the Nemean at Argos, the Pythian at Delphi, the Isthmian on the Isthmus of Corinth. In the games they indulged in racing, wrestling, boxing, and spearthrowing. There are various references in the epistles to the training, the running, the laying aside of impeding garments, and the prize (Ga 2:2; 5:7; Ph 2:16; 3:14; 2 Ti 2:5).

GAM′MAD

A group of people who defended Tyre (Eze 27:11).

GAM′MA·DIM

See GAMMAD.

GAM′UL *(weaned)*

An Aaronite. In the reign of David his family was appointed as the twenty-second course of priests (1 Ch 24:17). See COURSES OF PRIESTS AND LEVITES.

GANGRENE

The death of the soft tissues of the body, because of wound or infection. Blood stops flowing to the area, and the flesh then rots on the person's body. Once gangrene sets in it will continue to spread unless the affected part is amputated.

GAPE

To open wide the mouth (Ps 22:11-13).

GAR′DEN

The first garden mentioned in the Scriptures was the garden of Eden occupied by Adam and Eve (Ge 2:8-17; 3:4-6,23). In Egypt, water stored up from the overflow of the Nile was released by a foot-operated contrivance to water the gardens (De 11:10). There were gardens at Jerusalem (2 Ki 25:4) and in Shushan (Es 1:5). Gardens were usually protected by walls or hedges (Song 4:12; Is 5:2,5). Some used them for idolatrous purposes (Is 1:29; 65:3; 66:17) and some for burial purposes (Jo 19:41).

GARDENER

One who cares for a garden. When Jesus appeared to Mary near the garden tomb on the morning of the resurrection, she at first assumed that He was the gardener (Jo 20:15).

GARDEN HOUSE (2 Ki 9:27)

GARDEN OF EDEN

See EDEN, GARDEN OF.

GAR′EB *(scabby)*

1. One of David's warriors (2 Sa 23:38).

2. The name of a hill near Jerusalem (Je 31:39).

GAR′LIC

A plant resembling the onion. It has a pungently flavored bulb which has been prized for cooking for thousands of years (Nu 11:5).

GAR′MENT

See CLOTHING.

GAR′MITE

An epithet of obscure meaning apparently denoting the family or the residents of Keilah (1 Ch 4:19).

GAR′NER (archaic)

A granary for storing grain (Ps 144:13; Joel 1:17; Ma 3:12).

GAR′NISH

To decorate, to adorn (2 Ch 3:6; Ma 12:44; Re 21:19). The heavens are so described (Job 26:13).

GAR′RI·SON

A fortified post (1 Sa 13:23; 14:1,15). The word is also used to mean pillar (Eze 26:11).

GASH′MU

See GESHEM.

GA′TAM *(puny)*

A son of Eliphaz and grandson of Esau (Ge 36:11).

GATE

In walled cities gates were often fortified by towers (2 Ch 26:9). To protect them against an attack bars were fixed across them (1 Ki 4:13; 2 Ch 8:5).

GATEKEEPER

See PORTER.

GATES OF JERUSALEM AND THE TEMPLE

Many different gates for the City of Jerusalem and for the temple are mentioned in Scripture. It is difficult to identify all of these exactly—there are so many that probably some of the names overlap one another.

Listed in alphabetical order with references, gates named in the NKJV:

Beautiful Gate (Ac 3:10), Benjamin's Gate (Je 38:7; Ze 14:10), Corner Gate (2 Ki 14:13; 2 Ch 25:23; 26:9; Je 31:38; Ze 14:10), East Gate (1 Ch 26:14; 2 Ch 31:14), Ephraim, Gate of (2 Ki 14:13; 2 Ch 25:23; Ne 8:16; 12:39), First Gate (Ze 14:10) also called *Former Gate, Fish Gate (2 Ch 33:14; Ne 3:3; 12:39; Ze 1:10), Foundation Gate (Ne 3:15; 12:37), Horse Gate (2 Ch 23:15; Ne 3:28; Je 31:40), Joshua, Gate of (2 Ki 23:8), King's Gate (1 Ch 9:18), Middle Gate (Je 39:3), Miphkad Gate (Ne 3:31)* also called *Inspection Gate* or *Muster Gate, New Gate (Je 36:10), North Gate (1 Ch 26:14), Old Gate (Ne 3:6; 12:39)* also called *Jeshanah Gate, Potsherd Gate (Je 19:2), Prison, Gate of the (Ne 12:39)* also called *Guard Gate, Gate of the Guardhouse, Refuse Gate (Ne 2:13; 3:13-14; 12:31)* also called *Dung Gate,* or *Dung Port, Shallecheth Gate (1 Ch 26:16), Sheep Gate (Ne 3:1,32; 12:39; Jo 5:2)* also called *Sheep Market, South Gate (1 Ch 26:15), Upper Gate (2 Ki 15:35; 2 Ch 23:20; 27:3)* also called *Upper Gate, Valley Gate (2 Ch 26:9; Ne 2:13, 15; 3:13), Water Gate (Ne 3:26; 8:1,3,16; 12:37), and West Gate (1 Ch 26:16).*

GATH *(wine press)*

A city of the Philistines (Jos 13:3; 1 Sa 6:17; 7:14). The Anakim, men of strong build and of great stature, lived here (Jos 11:22). One of these men was Goliath (1 Sa 17:4; 2 Sa 21:15-22). The town was taken by David (1 Ch 18:1), and was later fortified by Rehoboam (2 Ch 11:8). Hazael captured it (2 Ki 12:17).

GATH-HE′PHER *(wine press of the well)*

A town of Zebulun near Nazareth, the native city of Jonah (2 Ki 14:25). It is once called Gittah-hepher (Jos 19:13).

GATH-RIM′MON *(wine press of the pomegranate)*

The name of two towns, one of Dan (Jos 19:45), the other of Manasseh, west of the Jordan (Jos 21:25).

GAUL·AN·IT′US

An area east of the Sea of Galilee, named after the city of Golon (De 4:43).

GA′ZA

One of the five main cities of the Philistines, the scene of many struggles between the Israelites and the Philistines (Jos 13:3; Ju 1:18; 1 Sa 6:17). It is located on the Mediterranean Sea not far from the desert. It was the scene of many exploits in Samson's career, including the destruction of the temple of Dagon (Ju 16:23-31). Dire predictions were made about the city by the prophets (Je 47:1,5; Am 1:6-7; Zep 2:4; Ze 9:5). It is referred to as Azzah three times in the Authorized Version.

GAZA

GA´ZA·THITE

See GAZITE.

GA·ZELLE´

A small antelope, which is called roe or roebuck in the Authorized Version (2 Sa 2:18; 1 Ch 12:8; Song 2:9,17; 8:14).

GA´ZER

A variant form of Gezer. See GEZER.

GA´ZEZ *(shearer)*

Two Old Testament men:

1. A son of Caleb of Judah. His mother, Ephah, was Caleb's concubine (1 Ch 2:46).

2. A grandson of Caleb (1 Ch 2:46).

GA´ZITE

An inhabitant of Gaza (Ju 16:2).

GAZ´ZAM *(devouring)*

Progenitor of a family of Nethinim (Ez 2:48).

GE´BA, GA´BA *(a hill)*

A frontier city of Benjamin near the border of Judah, assigned to the Levites (Jos 18:24; 21:17). David drove the Philistines from Geba to Gezer (2 Sa 5:25). Asa rebuilt the city (1 Ki 15:22).

GE´BAL

1. A mountainous region south of the Dead Sea whose inhabitants were part of a league against Israel (Ps 83:7).

2. A Phoenician town (Eze 27:9).

GEBALITES

Inhabitants of Gebal (Jo 13:5; 1 Ki 5:18; Eze 27:9).

GE´BER *(man)*

Two Old Testament men:

1. The father of one of Solomon's twelve food officers in Ramoth-gilead. Each of these twelve officers was responsible for providing food for the king's household for one month of the year (1 Ki 4:7,13).

2. Son of Uri and purveyor of food for Solomon in Gilead (1 Ki 4:19).

GE´BIM *(trenches)*

A town of Benjamin north of Jerusalem (Is 10:31).

GECK´O

See FERRET.

GED·A·LI´AH *(Jehovah is great)*

1. Son of Jeduthun, member of the Levitical choir and of the second course, or order, of priests appointed by David for the sanctuary (1 Ch 25:3,9).

2. A Jewish prince who sought to have Jeremiah imprisoned (Je 38:1).

3. An ancestor of Zephaniah, the prophet (Zep 1:1).

4. A priest who divorced his foreign wife (Ez 10:18).

5. The son of Ahikam, a man of Judah appointed by Nebuchadnezzar as governor of the remnant left in the land at the fall of Jerusalem (2 Ki 25:22-26; Je 39:14; 40:5–41:18).

GED´E·ON

A variant form of Gideon. See GIDEON.

GE´DER *(a wall)*

A town in the south of Judah taken by Joshua (Jos 12:13).

GE·DE´RAH *(sheepfold)*

A town of Judah (Jos 15:36).

GE´DER·A·THITE

A man of Gederah. Jozabad, one of David's mighty men, was a Gederathite (1 Ch 12:4).

GE·DE´RITE

A man of Geder or Gederah (1 Ch 27:28).

GE·DE´ROTH *(enclosures)*

A town of Judah (Jos 15:41).

GE·DE·RO·THA´IM *(two enclosures)*

A place listed as one of the cities of Judah (Jos 15:36).

GE´DOR *(wall)*

1. A hill town of Judah near Hebron (Jos 15:58), probably the place from which a number of warriors joined David at Ziklag (1 Ch 12:7).

2. A district from which the Simeonites drove out the Hamite settlers (1 Ch 4:39-40).

3. An ancestor of Saul (1 Ch 8:31; 9:37).

4. Ancestors of two Judahite families (1 Ch 4:4,18).

GE·HA·RA′ SHIM

See CHARASHIM.

GE·HA′ ZI (valley of vision)

The servant of Elisha (2 Ki 4:8-37; 5:20-27).

GE·HEN′ NA (Valley of Hinnom)

The valley of Hinnom south of Jerusalem became notorious as a place of child sacrifice to Molech (2 Ch 28:3; 33:6). King Josiah wiped out this dreadful practice (2 Ki 23:10), and the place later became a garbage dump with its continually burning fires.

The place name was already beginning to take on the New Testament meaning of the place of judgment for sinners in Jeremiah 7:32 and 19:6. Three terms are combined in both verses: "the valley of the son of Hinnom," "Tophet," and "the valley of slaughter."

In the New Testament, James uses *Gehenna* once for "hell" (3:6), and Christ Himself uses it eleven times in the Synoptic Gospels with the same meaning.

Since hell is a fearful place, it is a comfort to know that the One who talked the most about it also made a way to escape its torments. See HELL.

GE·LI′ LOTH (circles)

A place in Benjamin, probably Gilgal (Jos 18:17).

GE·MAL′ LI (camel driver)

The father of Ammiel (Nu 13:12).

GEMARA

A part of the Jewish Talmud. It is written in Aramaic, and is essentially a commentary on the Mishnah, the first part of the Talmud. See TALMUD.

GEM·A·RI′ AH (Jehovah has perfected)

1. Son of Shaphan, the scribe. From Gemariah's chamber in the temple Baruch read to the people the prophecies of Jeremiah. Gemariah was among those who vainly sought to deter Jehoiakim from burning the written record of the prophecy (Je 36:10-12,25).

2. Son of Hilkiah (Je 29:3).

GEMS

See JEWELS AND PRECIOUS STONES OF THE BIBLE.

GEN′ E·AL′ O·GY

Even as many families do today, the Jewish people of Bible times kept detailed family histories. These were important records that helped determine inheritances and provided identification and continuity with the past. These lists of descendants also helped identify the people who were qualified to serve as priests—descendants of Levi and the house of Aaron.

During the Hebrews' years of wilderness wandering, the military organization of the tribes was established by these family records, or genealogies (Nu 1:2-4). These lists were also used to allocate taxes and offerings for the sanctuary (Nu 7:11-89). The first genealogies of the Hebrews were probably memorized and passed down by word of mouth to succeeding generations, as well as being written down.

The Book of Genesis contains several important genealogical tables, including the descendants of Adam (ch. 5), Noah (ch. 10), Jacob (46:8-25), and the ancestors of Abraham (11:10-32).

In the New Testament, both Matthew (1:2-17) and Luke (3:23-38) listed the earthly ancestors of Jesus to show that Jesus the Messiah was descended from the line of David.

Scholars who have studied these genealogical tables in the Bible have noted that not all the ancestors of descendants are included. Apparently, the purpose of the biblical writers who compiled genealogies was to establish the broad line of descent without including all the details.

The apostle Paul cautioned his young minister colleague Timothy to avoid "fables and endless genealogies, which cause disputes rather than godly edification" (1 Ti 1:4). This should serve as a warning to all persons not to place undue emphasis on their family history. What really matters is not our line of descent but our commitment as individuals to Jesus Christ and His will for our lives.

GEN′ E·AL′ O·GY OF JESUS CHRIST

The Gospels list two separate genealogies of Jesus Christ, one in Matthew 1:1-17, and the other in Luke 3:28-38. From the time of David to the Christ, these two genealogies differ considerably: the account in Matthew traces the line through David's son Solomon and his descendants, while the account in Luke traces the line through David's son Nathan and his descendants. Matthew's genealogy starts with Abraham, while Luke begins with Jesus and traces the line all the way back to Adam. The lists are essentially the same between Abraham and David (Luke's list has two more names). Many have attempted to reconcile these differences by suggesting that Luke's genealogy is actually Mary's family line, but the fact that Mary is not even mentioned in Luke's list makes this a bit of a problem. The discrepancies in the number of generations listed may be because genealogies were not necessarily expected to contain every detail (see GENEALOGY). The point of the genealogies is clearly to show that Jesus was qualified to be the Messiah, as a descendant of David. Except for the fact that neither list says so, it is reasonable to suppose that one of them must be Mary's family tree—she was doubtless a daughter of the Davidic line herself.

GEN′ ER·A′ TION

Biblical usage of this term varies according to different periods through which the Hebrews lived. In the patriarchal age, a generation was reckoned at a century—the 400 years of the sojourn in Egypt were referred to as four generations (Ge 15:13-16). In other passages the word refers to a period of about thirty-five to forty years (Job 42:16). It also implies the group of ancestors one joins at death (Ps 49:19), or the posterity which comes after one (Le 3:17), or in the present-day sense, one's children and grandchildren, etc. (Ex 20:5).

GENEROSITY (2 Co 9:5)

See ALMS, GIVING.

GEN′ E·SIS, BOOK OF

1. The Book of Genesis. The first part of Genesis focuses on the beginning and spread of sin in the world and culminates in the devastating flood in the days of Noah. The second part of the book focuses on God's dealings with one man, Abraham, through whom God promised to bring salvation and blessing to the world. Abraham and his descendants learned first hand that it is always safe to trust the Lord in times of famine and feasting, blessing and bondage. From Abraham to Isaac to Jacob to Joseph, God's promises began to come to fruition in a great nation possessing a great land.

Genesis is a Greek word meaning "origin," "source," "generation," or "beginning." The original Hebrew title *Bereshith* means "In the Beginning."

The literary structure of Genesis is clear and is built around eleven separate units, each headed with the word *generations* in the phrase "These are the generations" or "The book of the generations": (1) Introduction to the Generations (1:1–2:3); (2) Heaven and Earth (2:4–4:26); (3) Adam (5:1–6:8); (4) Noah (6:9–9:29); (5) Sons of Noah (10:1–11:9); (6) Shem (11:10-26); (7) Terah (11:27–25:11); (8) Ishmael (25:12-18); (9) Isaac (25:19–35:29); (10) Esau (36:1–37:1); (11) Jacob (37:2–50:26).

2. The Author of Genesis. Although Genesis does not directly name its author, and although Genesis ends some three centuries before Moses was born, the whole of Scripture and church history are unified in their adherence to the Mosaic authorship of Genesis.

The Old Testament is replete with both direct and indirect testimonies to the Mosaic authorship of the entire Pentateuch (Ex 17:14; Le 1:1-2; Nu 33:2; De 1:1; Jos 1:7; 1 Ki 2:3; 2 Ki 14:6; Ez 6:18; Ne 13:1; Da 9:11-13; Ma 4:4). The New Testament also contains numerous testimonies (Ma 8:4; Mk 12:26; Lk 16:29; Jo 7:19; Ac 26:22; Ro 10:19; 1 Co 9:9; 2 Co 3:15).

The Early Church openly held to the Mosaic authorship, as does the first-century Jewish historian Josephus. As would be expected, the Jerusalem Talmud supported Moses as author.

It would be difficult to find a man in all the range of Israel's history who was better prepared or qualified to write this history. Trained in the "wisdom of the Egyptians" (Ac 7:22), Moses had been providentially prepared to understand and integrate, under the inspiration of God, all the available records, manuscripts, and oral narratives.

3. The Time of Genesis. Genesis divides neatly into three geographical settings: (1) the Fertile Crescent (1–11); (2) Israel (12–36); (3) Egypt (37–50).

The setting of the first eleven chapters changes rapidly as it spans more than two thousand years and fifteen hundred miles, and they paint the majestic acts of the creation, the garden of Eden, the Noahic flood, and the towering citadel of Babel.

The middle section of Genesis rapidly funnels down from the broad brim of the two millennia spent in the Fertile Crescent to less than two hundred years in the little country of Canaan. Surrounded by the rampant immorality and idolatry of the Canaanites, the godliness of

Abraham rapidly degenerated into gross immorality in some of his descendants.

In the last fourteen chapters, God dramatically saves the small Israelite nation from extinction by transferring the "seventy souls" to Egypt so that they may grow and multiply. Egypt is an unexpected womb for the growth of God's chosen nation Israel, to be sure, but one in which they are isolated from the maiming influence of Canaan.

Genesis spans more time than any other book in the Bible; in fact, it covers more than all sixty-five other books of the Bible put together.

Utilizing the same threefold division noted above, the following dates can be assigned:

A. 2,000 or more years, 4000-2090 B.C. (Ge 1–11).
   1. Creation, 4000 B.C. or earlier (Ge 1:1)
   2. Death of Terah, 2090 B.C. (Ge 11:32)
B. 193 years, 2090-1897 B.C. (Ge 12–36)
   1. Death of Terah, 2090 B.C. (Ge 11:32)
   2. Joseph to Egypt, c. 1897 B.C. (Ge 37:2)
C. 93 years 1897-1804 B.C. (Ge 37–50)
   1. Joseph to Egypt, c. 1897 B.C. (Ge 37:2)
   2. Death of Joseph, 1804 B.C. (Ge 50:26)

4. The Christ of Genesis. Genesis moves from the general to the specific in its messianic predictions: Christ is the seed of the woman (3:15), from the line of Seth (4:25), the son of Shem (9:27), the descendant of Abraham (12:3), of Isaac (21:12), of Jacob (25:23), and of the tribe of Judah (49:10).

Christ is also seen in people and events that serve as types. (A "type" is a historical fact that illustrates a spiritual truth.) Adam is "a type of Him who was to come" (Ro 5:14). Both entered the world through a special act of God as sinless men. Adam is the head of the old creation; Christ is the head of the new creation. Abel's acceptable offering of a blood sacrifice points to Christ, and there is a parallel in his murder by Cain. Melchizedek ("righteous king") is "made like the Son of God" (He 7:3). He is the king of Salem ("peace") who brings forth bread and wind and is the priest of the Most High God. Joseph is also a type of Christ. Joseph and Christ are both objects of special love by their fathers, both are hated by their brothers, both are conspired against and sold for silver, both are condemned though innocent, and both are raised from humiliation to glory by the power of God.

5. Keys to Genesis.

Key Word: Beginnings—Genesis gives the beginning of almost everything, including the beginning of the universe, life, man, Sabbath, death, marriage, sin, redemption, family, literature, cities, art, language, and sacrifice.

Key Verses: Genesis 3:15; 12:3—"And I will put enmity between you and the woman, and between your seed and her Seed; He shall bruise your head, and you shall bruise His heel" (3:15).

"I will bless those who bless you, and I will curse him who curses you; and in you all the families of the earth shall be blessed" (12:3).

Key Chapter: Genesis 15—Central to all of Scripture is the Abrahamic Covenant, which is given in 12:1-3 and ratified in 15:1-21. Israel receives three specific promises: (1) the promise of a great land—"from the river of Egypt to the great river, the River Euphrates" (15:18); (2) the promise of a great nation—"and I will make your descendants as the dust of the earth" (13:16); and (3) the promise of a great blessing—"I will bless you and make your name great; and you shall be a blessing" (12:2).

6. Survey of Genesis. Genesis is not so much a history of man as it is the first chapter in the history of the *redemption* of man. As such, Genesis is a highly selective spiritual interpretation of history. Genesis is divided into four great events (1–11) and four great people (12–50).

The Four Great Events. Chapters 1–11 lay the foundation upon which the whole Bible is built and center on four key events. (1) *Creation.* God is the sovereign Creator of matter, energy, space, and time. Man is the pinnacle of the creation. (2) *Fall:* Creation is followed by corruption. Because of the first sin, man is separated from God (Adam from God), and in the second sin, man is separated from man (Cain from Abel). In spite of the devastating curse of the fall, God promised hope of redemption through the seed of the woman (3:15). (3) *Flood:* As man multiplied, sin also multiplied until God was compelled to destroy humanity, with the exception of Noah and his family. (4) *Nations:* Genesis teaches the unity of the human race: we are all children of Adam through Noah, but because of rebellion at the Tower of Babel, God fragmented the single culture and language of the post-flood world and scattered people over the face of the earth.

The Four Great People. Once the nations were scattered, God focused on one man and his descendants (12–50). (1) *Abraham:* The calling of Abraham (12) is the pivotal point of the book. The three covenant promises God made to Abraham (land, descendants, and blessing) are foundational to His program of bringing salvation upon the earth. (2) *Isaac:* God established His covenant with Isaac as the spiritual link with Abraham. (3) *Jacob:* God transformed this man from selfishness to ser-vanthood, and changed his name to Israel, the father of the twelve tribes. (4) *Joseph:* Jacob's favorite son suffers at the hands of his brothers and becomes a slave in Egypt. After his dramatic rise to the rulership of Egypt, Joseph delivered his family from famine and brought them out of Canaan to Goshen.

Genesis ends on a note of impending bondage with the death of Joseph. There is great need for the redemption that is to follow in the Book of Exodus.

OUTLINE OF GENESIS

Part One: Primeval History (1:1–11:9)

I. The Creation (1:1–2:25)

A. Creation of the World 1:1–2:3
B. Creation of Man........................... 2:4-25

II. The Fall (3:1–5:32)

A. The Fall of Man 3:1-24
B. After the Fall: Conflicting Family Lines..................................... 4:1–5:32

III. The Judgment of the Flood (6:1–9:29)

A. Causes of the Flood 6:1-5
B. Judgment of the Flood.................. 6:6-22

C. The Flood 7:1–8:19
D. Results of the Flood................................... 8:20–9:17
E. After the Flood 9:18-29

IV. The Judgment on the Tower of Babel (10:1–11:9)

A. Family Lines After the Flood..................................... 10:1-32
B. Judgment on All the Family Lines.. 11:1-9

Part Two: Patriarchal History (11:10–50:26)

I. The Life of Abraham (11:10–25:18)

A. Introduction of Abram............... 11:10-32
B. The Covenant of God with Abram 12:1–25:18

II. The Life of Isaac (25:19–26:35)

A. The Family of Isaac 25:19-34
B. The Failure of Isaac 26:1-33
C. The Failure of Esau 26:34-35

III. The Life of Jacob (27:1–36:43)

A. Jacob Gains Esau's Blessing ... 27:1–28:9
B. Jacob's Life at Haran 28:10–31:55

C. Jacob's Return 32:1–33:20
D. Jacob's Residence in Canaan............................... 34:1–35:29
E. The History of Esau 36:1-43

IV. The Life of Joseph (37:1–50:26)

A. The Corruption of Joseph's Family 37:1–38:30
B. The Exaltation of Joseph......... 39:1–41:57
C. The Salvation of Jacob's Family 42:1–50:26

GEN·NES'A·RET

The land of Gennesaret is mentioned in connection with the crossing of the Sea of Galilee by Jesus and his disciples (Ma 14:34; Mk 6:53). See GALILEE, SEA OF.

GEN'TILES

All non-Jews. In the Old Testament, the word *goy* ("nation," "people," "heathen," "Gentile") has several usages and is hard to define. Basically, it refers to a defined group of people or a large subdivision of people.

Genesis 10's "table of nations" uses *goy* without labeling the mentioned nations as "heathen" or by other pejorative terms.

Unsurprisingly, *goy* is used for Egypt and Syria, but in view of the tendency to associate the word with Gentiles, it is interesting to note how the Hebrew Old Testament used *goy* for Israel. God promised to make Abraham "a great nation [*goy*]" (Ge 17:20). Moses reminded God to "consider that this nation [*goy*] is Your people" (Ex 33:13). While the plural form is used for ethnic groups that would be descendants of Abraham (Ge 17:16), as time passed the term more and more came to be used for the Gentiles. Even the concept of their being pagan or heathen is evident in some texts (Ju 4:2,13,16). The "uncircumcised" were idolaters, usually wicked, and often enemies of Israel.

Nevertheless, the Old Testament does predict a bright future for the Gentiles when they come to know the Messiah (Is 11:10; 42:6). The shortest chapter in the Bible, Psalm 117 (perhaps made short to draw attention to a truth that was unpopular in Israel), calls on all the Gentiles (*goyim*) and all the peoples to praise the Lord. In the New Testament the term is used for the word *nations* (Ma 24:7; Ac 2:5) and for the word *Greek* (Ro 2:9; 1 Co 12:13).

GENTILES, COURT OF
See COURT OF THE GENTILES.

GE·NU' BATH *(robbery)*
Son of Hadad (1 Ki 11:20).

GE' RA *(a grain)*
Son of Bela (1 Ch 8:3) and grandson of Benjamin (Ge 46:21).

GERAH
A unit for measuring weight, ¹⁄₂₀ of a shekel (about 0.02 oz.). See WEIGHTS AND MEASURES.

GE' RAR
An ancient city south of Gaza (Ge 10:19; 20:1; 26:26). At an early time it was held by the Philistines (Ge 26:1). Abimelech was its ruler (Ge 20:2; 26:16-17).

GERASA
One of the ten cities of the Decapolis. It is not mentioned in the Bible, but the Gospels record Jesus healing a man from "the country of the (Gerasenes)" (Mk 5:1; Lk 8:26,37). Many versions say "Gadarenes." Gadara was also a city of the Decapolis, exactly which one is meant is unclear. The Decapolis was south and east of the Sea of Galilee. See GADARENES.

GER' A·SENES
See GADARENES.

GER' GE·SENES
See GADARENES.

GE·RI' ZIM
The mountain of the Gerizites across the valley from Mount Ebal. It was on Mount Gerizim that Abraham was directed to sacrifice Isaac, according to the Samaritans. At the base of the mountain is the well of Jacob (Jo 4:6) and a little to the North is the tomb of Joseph (Jos 24:32). After entering the valley, Moses directed that the law be read from Mount Gerizim and Mount Ebal (De 11:29; Jos 8:33).

GERIZITES (1 Sa 27:8)
See GERZITES.

GER' SHOM *(expulsion)*
1. The firstborn of Moses by his wife, Zipporah, daughter of Jethro (Ex 2:22; 18:3). He was circumcised by his mother. Gershom's descendants through his son, Jonathan, worshipped graven images (Ju 18:30-31).

2. The eldest son of Levi, the name being spelled Gershon in several passages (1 Ch 6:16-17,20,43; 15:7).

3. The head of the family of Phinehas (Ez 8:2).

GER' SHOM·ITES
Family descended from Gershom (1 Ch 6:62,71, NRSV). Other versions say Gershon.

GER' SHON *(expulsion)*
The eldest son of Levi who went into Egypt with Jacob (Ge 46:11; Ex 6:16). The sons of Gershon had charge of the coverings, curtains, and hangings of the tabernacle (Nu 3:21-26; 4:22-28).

GER' SHON·ITES
The descendants of Gershon, son of Levi. See GERSHON.

GER′ UTH KIMHAM
See CHIMHAM.

GERZITES
A Canaanite nation which had inhabited the land "from of old" (1 Sa 27:8). David and his men raided this group during the time he was running from Saul.

GE′ SHAM
See GESHAN.

GE′ SHAN
A son of Jahdai of the family of Caleb of Judah (1 Ch 2:47).

GE′ SHEM
An Arabian, and probably the chief of an Arabian tribe (Ne 2:19; 6:1,2,6).

GE′ SHUR
A district in Bashan. It joined Argob (De 3:14) and Aram (2 Sa 15:8). It was an Aramaean kingdom. One of David's wives was of this district and to it Absalom fled after slaying Amnon (2 Sa 3:3; 13:37).

GE·SHU′ RITES
1. Inhabitants of Geshur (De 3:14; Jos 12:5; 13:11).
2. A tribe between Arabia and Philistia (Jos 13:2; 1 Sa 27:8).

GE′ THER
A son of Aram (Ge 10:23).

GETH·SEM′ A·NE *(an oil press)*
A garden traditionally located near the foot of Mount Olivet (Lk 22:39). At the time of Christ, it contained many olive trees but these were probably cut down in the first Christian century by Titus. This garden was often visited by Jesus and his disciples (Jo 18:2). It was here that Jesus was betrayed by Judas and taken prisoner by soldiers and priests.

GEU′ EL *(majesty of God)*
The son of Machi (Nu 13:15).

GE′ ZER
An ancient city of Canaan. It was taken by Joshua and its inhabitants were slain (Jos 10:33; 12:12). It was on the southern boundary of Ephraim (Jos 16:3) and was allotted to the Levites (Jos 21:21; 1 Ch 6:67).

GEZ′ RITE
See GIRZITE.

GHI′ MEL
See GIMEL.

GHOST (archaic)
Spirit. The KJV uses the phrase "gave up the ghost" to indicate death, since the spirit departs from the body at this time (Ge 25:8; Job 3:11; Je 15:9; Jo 19:30).

GHOST, HOLY
See HOLY SPIRIT.

GI′ AH *(fountain)*
A place indicating the position of the hill Ammah (2 Sa 2:24).

GI′ ANT
The Hebrew word *nephilim* is used to describe demigods, or men of great renown, who were the offspring of the sons of God and the daughters of men (Ge 6:4). The word *rephaim* was used to denote true giants as far as stature was concerned. They were found by the Israelites among the Canaanite inhabitants of Palestine. Among them were the Anakims of Philistia and the Emims of Moab (De 2:10-11). The word *giant,* is also used for the four mighty Philistines—Ishbi-benob, Saph, Goliath the Gittite, and a giant with 12 fingers and 12 toes (2 Sa 21:15-22).

GIANTS, VALLEY OF
See REPHAIM.

GIB′ BAR *(hero)*
Ninety-five children of Gibbar returned with Zerubbabel (Ez 2:20).

GIB′ BE·THON *(a height)*
A town of Dan (Jos 19:44), later given to the Kohathite branch of the Levites (Jos 21:23).

GIB′ E·A
One of the grandsons of Caleb (1 Ch 2:49).

GIB′ E·AH *(a hill)*
This name was given to several towns on or near hills.

1. A city in the mountain district of Judah (Jos 15:57). It was probably south of Hebron.

2. One of a group of towns of Benjamin near Jerusalem (Jos 18:28). It was also called Gibeath. Located between Jerusalem and Ramah (Ju 19:13), it was Saul's place of residence and capital of his kingdom. The same town was probably the place where the ark of the covenant was kept (2 Sa 6:3-4).

GIB′E·ATH

See GIBEAH.

GIB′E·ATH EL·OHIM′ *(hill of God)*

The hill where Samuel told Saul that the Spirit of the Lord would come upon him as a sign that his anointing was really from God (1 Sa 10:5).

GIB′E·A·THITE

A native of Gibeah (1 Ch 12:3).

GIB′E·ON *(hill city)*

A city of the Hivites about six miles northwest of Jerusalem. Its people made a league with Joshua to escape being destroyed (Jos 9:3-15). It was in the territory of Benjamin (Jos 18:25) but was assigned to the priests (Jos 21:17).

GIB′E·ON, POOL OF

A battle between David's forces and Saul's son, Ishbosheth, began with a meeting "by the pool of Gibeon" (2 Sa 2:13). The book of the prophet Jeremiah, written hundreds of years after David's time, also referred to as "the great pool that is in Gibeon" (Je 41:12). This "great pool" was obviously an impressive feature of the city.

Archeologists have discovered a huge well dug through solid limestone at the site of the Old Testament city of Gibeon, located about seven miles north of Jerusalem. About 40 feet in diameter and 80 feet deep, this giant well apparently provided water for the Canaanite city of Gibeon as early as Joshua's time about 1400 B.C. (Jos 9). It must have still been in use about eight centuries later during the ministry of the prophet Jeremiah, when the citizens of Judah occupied the site.

Digging a well like this with hand tools was a massive undertaking. But a dependable water supply was essential for ancient cities of Bible times. Access to the precious water was provided by a spiraling stairway cut into the rock around the edge of the shaft. The women of Gibeon made the long climb every day to bring up fresh water for their households.

In addition to this well at Gibeon, the wells dug by Isaac (Ge 26:18-22) and Uzziah (2 Ch 26:10) are also mentioned in the Bible. David longed for water from the well in his hometown of Bethlehem (2 Sa 23:15-16), and Jesus spoke about His free gift of unfailing water to the woman at the well in Samaria (Jo 4:1-26).

GIBEONITES

A Canaanite tribe which deceived Israel into making a contract with them, promising to protect them and not wipe them out (Jos 9:17, 23,27; 2 Sa 21:1-2,5-6,9).

GIB′LITE

An inhabitant of Gebal, a town in Phoenicia. Mention is made of their work on Solomon's temple. In the Revised Version the word Gebalite is used (Jos 13:5; 1 Ki 5:18).

GID·DAL′TI *(I have magnified)*

A son of Heman, the king's seer (1 Ch 25:4, 29).

GID′DEL *(gigantic)*

The children of Giddel returned with Zerubbabel from Babylon and were included both among the Nethinim (Ez 2:47; Ne 7:49) and among the children of Solomon's servants (Ez 2:56; Ne 7:58).

GID′E·ON *(feller of trees)*

A Manassite, son of Joash. He lived in Ophrah (Ju 6:11-15). By clever strategy, he managed to defeat the Midianites with only a very small army (Ju 7:19-24). He was probably the greatest of the judges.

GID·E·O′NI *(cutting down)*

Father of Abidan (Nu 1:11; 2:22; 7:60,65).

GI′DOM

A place near Gibeah to which the Benjamites fled (Ju 20:45).

GIER EAGLE

An unclean bird (Le 11:18; De 14:17), probably the carrion-eating Egyptian vulture. It has white body plumage, grayish black quills, yellow forehead and upper throat feathers.

GIFT OF HEALING

See SPIRITUAL GIFTS.

GIFT OF TONGUES

See TONGUES, GIFT OF.

GIFTS

The giving and receiving of presents was a custom of the East and was a formal proceeding. There was nothing of an offhand nature about the presentation. It was distinctive, ostentatious. The refusal of a present was an insult and the same was true if a present was not given when the circumstances so prescribed (1 Sa 10:27). They were bestowed by rulers for service rendered (Da 2:48). The expense of religious worship was defrayed by gifts (Ma 5:23,34; 8:4; Lk 21:5).

GIFTS, SPIRITUAL

See SPIRITUAL GIFTS.

GI' HON (a stream)

1. One of the rivers of Eden (Ge 2:13).

2. A spring in the valley of the Kidron beside which Solomon was anointed king (1 Ki 1:33, 38,45). Located near Jerusalem, it provided the city with some of its water (2 Ch 32:30; 33:14).

GIL' A·LAL

The son of a priest who was present when the wall was dedicated (Ne 12:36).

GIL·BO' A (bubbling fountain)

A mountain near the city of Jezreel on the eastern side of the plain of Esdraelon (1 Sa 28:4). Here the forces of Israel under Saul were defeated by the Philistines. The sons of Saul were killed in the battle and Saul committed suicide by falling on his sword (1 Sa 31:1; 2 Sa 1:6; 21:12).

GIL' E·AD

1. A picturesque mountainous region east of the Jordan (Ge 31:21). It is sometimes called Mount Gilead (Ge 31:25) and sometimes the land of Gilead (Nu 32:1). The southern half of the area was assigned to Gad and the northern half to the half-tribe of Manasseh (Jos 13:24-31).

2. A mountain of unknown location mentioned in connection with Gideon (Ju 7:3).

3. Son of Machir, grandson of Manasseh (Nu 26:29-30), the head of a tribal family.

4. Father of Jephthah (Ju 11:1-2).

GILEAD, BALM OF

See BALM.

GILEADITES

Descendants of Gilead, grandson of Manasseh (Nu 26:29).

GIL' GAL (circle, rolling)

Four geographical locations in the Old Testament.

1. The first camp of the Israelites after they crossed the Jordan. It was in the plain of Jericho. Here twelve stones were set up as a memorial (Jos 4:19-20) and here the first Passover was celebrated in Canaan (Jos 5:9-10).

2. A place, probably near Beth-el, mentioned in connection with Elijah's last days (2 Ki 2:1).

3. A place whose location is not known. Its king was defeated by Joshua (Jos 12:23).

4. A place on the northern border of Judah (Jos 15:7).

GI' LOH (exile)

A mountain town of Judah (Jos 15:51). It was the native place of David's counselor, Ahithophel (2 Sa 15:12; 17:23).

GI' LO·NITE

A native of Giloh, specifically Ahithophel (2 Sa 15:12; 23:34).

GIMEL

Third letter of the Hebrew alphabet, heading for verses 17-24 of Psalm 119. Each line begins with the letter gimel in Hebrew. See ACROSTIC.

GIM' ZO (full of sycomores)

A town of Judah (2 Ch 28:18).

GIN

A trap, consisting of a net with a spring or trigger, used to catch animals and birds (Job 18:9; Am 3:5).

GI' NATH

Father of Tibni (1 Ki 16:21-22).

GIN′ NE·THO *(gardener)*

A priest who returned with Zerubbabel from Babylon (Ne 12:4).

GIN′ NE·THOI

See GINNETHON.

GIN′ NE·THON *(gardener)*

A priest who sealed the covenant with Nehemiah (Ne 10:6), probably the same as Ginnetho.

GIR′ DLE

An important article of dress in the East. It was used by both sexes. Made of leather (2 Ki 1:8; Ma 3:4), this belt was sometimes embroidered with silver and gold thread (Da 10:5; Re 1:13; 15:6). It was adorned at times with precious stones. Men wore the girdle about the loins (Is 5:27; 11:5). The military girdle worn about the waist was used to carry the sword (Ju 3:16; 2 Sa 20:8).

GIR′ GA·SHITES

One of the tribes living in Canaan before the land was taken by Joshua and the Israelites (Ge 10:16; De 7:1; Jos 24:11; Ne 9:8). They probably lived west of the Jordan.

GIR′ ZITE

A people who occupied a district south of the Philistines (1 Sa 27:8).

GISH′ PA

An overseer of the Nethinim after the return from Babylon (Ne 11:21).

GIS′ PA

See GISHPA.

GIT′ TAH-HE′ PHER

See GATH-HEPHER.

GIT·TA′ IM *(two wine presses)*

A village of Benjamin (Ne 11:31,33). To escape the cruelty of Saul the people of Beeroth fled to this city (2 Sa 4:3).

GIT′ TITE

A native of the city of Gath (Jos 13:3). The six hundred members of the "bodyguard" of David, under the command of Ittai, were called Gittites (2 Sa 15:18-19).

GIRDLE

GIT′ TITH

A word appearing in the titles of three psalms (Ps 8,81,84). It probably denotes that these psalms were to be played on a Gittite instrument or sung to a Gittite tune.

GIVING

There is no better indicator of growth in the new life than in the area of giving. Second Corinthians 9:6-8 deals with the attitude one should have in his giving—it should be cheerful. When giving is cheerful, it will also be generous. The important rule of thumb is not how much is given, but how much is left after the giving. God is not primarily occupied with the amount of the gift, but with the motive that lies behind it. All the money in the world belongs to God. Our gifts to Him do not make Him any richer; they make us richer spiritually because of the realization that everything we have is His and that we give because we love Him and want to give.

The formula for giving is found in 1 Corinthians 16:2 where three principles can be seen: (1) giving should be regular, "on the first day of the week"; (2) giving should be systematic, "let each one of you lay something aside"; and (3) and giving is to be proportionate, "as he may prosper."

Failure to give of the money which God has given is a serious matter. The person who fails to honor God with his money actually robs God (Mal 3:8), not because it impoverishes God but because it denies the God-ordained means for the support of His work and His ministers. For the child of God who honors God with his money, God promises abundant blessing (Mal 3:1; Lk 6:38) and the provision of his every need (Ph 4:19). Giving is an important key to growth in the new life.

GI'ZON·ITE

The designation of Hashem, the Gizonite, the ancestor of two members of David's warrior band (1 Ch 11:34).

GIZ'RITES

See GIRZITE.

GLASS

The Hebrew word which occurs only in Job 28:17 is rendered *crystal* in the Authorized Version. While there is no specific allusion to glass in the Old Testament, paintings have been found in tombs and at other places showing glass-blowing, and we know that the invention goes back to the time of Joseph, 3500 or 3700 years ago. Parts of wine vessels have been found in Egypt that belonged to the time of the exodus. Hence the Hebrews must have known of glass. It is mentioned in Revelation 4:6; 15:2; 21:18.

GLASS, SEA OF

See SEA OF GLASS.

GLEANERS

The poor who supplemented their income by gleaning in the fields and vineyards of the well to do (Ru 2:7,9,16).

GLEAN'ING

Following the harvesters to pick up any cut grain that was dropped, or to strip the last fruit from the vines or trees. The *poor law* of the Hebrews required that the gleaning of the fields, fruit trees, and vineyards be left to the poor. What produce was not removed by the reapers was taken by the gleaners (Ju 8:2; Ru 2:7,9,16; Is 17:6). The law required that no field or vineyard be gleaned by its owner (Le 19:9-10; 23:22; De 24:19).

GLEDE

The old name for the kite, vulture, which occurs only in De 14:13. It is a bird of prey and was classified as unclean.

GLORIFY

To bring glory to, especially to God (Ps 86:12; Jo 17:1).

GLORY OF GOD

God has revealed Himself to people in remarkable and unusual ways. Sometimes He has made His will known through dreams (Ge 37:5-10; Ma 1:20-21). He has also shown Himself through nature (Ro 1:20). But His greatest and most meaningful revelation to the Christian believer is through the second and third persons of the Trinity, Jesus Christ and the Holy Spirit (Jo 3:16; 14:16).

The Bible speaks often of the "glory of God"—the visible appearance of His moral beauty and perfection. In the Old Testament, He used several different dramatic appearances of His glory to get the attention of His people. He disclosed Himself to Moses in a burning bush in Midian (Ex 3:1-6), and in a cloud on Mount Sinai (Ex 24:9-17). The cloud of His glory also covered the tabernacle in the wilderness (Ex 40:34) and filled the temple in Jerusalem (1 Ki 8:10-11).

When Aaron made his first sacrifice in the wilderness as a priest, God's glory "appeared to all the people" (Le 9:23). In these manifestations, He revealed His righteousness, holiness, truth, wisdom, and love. These are all aspects of God's distinctiveness, which may be spoken of as His glory.

Nowhere has God's glory been more fully expressed than through His Son, Jesus Christ (Jo 1:14). This is a glory in which all believers share (Jo 17:5-6,22). At the end of this age, Christians will be glorified in the heavenly presence of God (Ro 5:2; Col 3:4), whose glory will be seen everywhere. The believer's response is one of praise and adoration (Ps 115:1).

GLUTTON

One who does not control the natural appetites, particularly one who eats greedily and excessively. Gluttony and drunkenness often go hand in hand; the result of gluttony will be poverty (Pr 23:21; De 21:20). The Pharisees accused Jesus of being a glutton because He did not fast religiously as they did (Ma 11:19).

GNASHING OF TEETH

Grinding the teeth together, a sign of extreme distress and anguish. (Job 16:9; Ma 13:42,50)

GNAT

A small insect. Its bite was annoying and this caused people to sleep under mats for protection. These insects also fell into food and had to be strained out (or else ignored). The word occurs in Matthew 23:24 where Christ criticized those who strain out "a gnat but swallow a camel."

GNOS' TI·CISM

A heresy which crept into the early church, teaching that knowledge (Greek *gnosis*) was the true way to salvation. All matter is evil and in order to awaken the spirit (the only non-material and therefore good part of a human) one must pursue knowledge. Eventually, the awakened spirit would be able to join God. The knowledge the Gnostics sought for was mystical in nature, and found only by the elite few. Some Gnostics carried the view of the evil of matter so far that they declared that since the body is evil, it doesn't matter what one does with it, and therefore they participated in all kinds of sin.

GOAD

A rod about eight feet long sharpened to a point which was sometimes covered with iron. It is still used in parts of southern Europe and western Asia (Ju 3:31; 1 Sa 13:21). It was used in driving cattle. The words of the wise are compared to goads (Ec 12:11). An animal injuring itself by coming against the sharp point of the goad is the metaphor used by Christ to Saul (Ac 9:5).

GO' AH

See GOATH.

GOAT

In Palestine and Syria there are two or three varieties of the ordinary goat. Goats and sheep were under the care of the same shepherd (Ge 27:9; 30:32), but were kept apart (Ma 25:32). Cloth was made from the hair (Ex 25:4; 35:26). It provided milk and its flesh was eaten (Le 7:23; De 14:4). It was used as a burnt and sin offering (Ex 12:5; Le 1:10; Ps 66:15; He 9:12).

GO' ATH *(lowing)*

A place near Jerusalem (Je 31:39).

GOATHERD

See SHEPHERD.

GOAT, SCAPE

See ATONEMENT, DAY OF.

GOAT'S HAIR

Along with wool, flax, and camel's hair, goat's hair was used to make cloth in Bible times. Many of the curtains of the tabernacle were made of goat's hair (Ex 25–36).

GOB *(a pit)*

The place where the brother of Goliath was killed by El-hanan (2 Sa 21:18-19).

GOBLET

A cup or bowl for wine or other drinks (Song 7:2; Is 22:24; Ex 24:6).

GOD

The Bible opens with the fact of God—"In the beginning God." The Bible is the record of the revelation of God. It is because man "by searching" cannot "find out the Almighty unto perfection," cannot know God as he has revealed himself, that such a revelation of God is necessary—the fact grounded in the need.

The Greek philosopher worked from the world and its phenomena up to God, but the Bible works in exactly the opposite direction. The writers did not reason from the world to God; they began with God as the source, and the world and all things followed.

    I. *Unity of God.* There is but one self-existing being. The Bible reveals God to us as the one, and the only God. There cannot be more than one God for eternity; infinity, omnipresence, etc., cannot apply to more than one such being. Two such beings would limit and exclude each other and thus render impossible the being of God. God makes Himself known in the Scriptures as Father, Son and Holy Spirit, three separate personalities: three persons in one Godhead, but not three Gods. It is the Trinity and not tri-theism (De 6:4; 1 Ki 8:60; Is 44:6; Mk 12:29; Jo 10:30; 1 Co 8:4; Ep 4:6).

    II. *God the Creator.* God is the creator of the heavens and the earth (Ge 1:1; Ex 20:11; Ps 8:3; 19:1; Jo 1:3; Ac 14:15; Ro 11:36; He 1:2), and the creator of man (Ge 1:26; 5:1; Ex 4:11; Job 10:8-12; Ps 33:15; Ec 12:1; Is 43:1; Ac 17:25-29; 1 Co 15:38). See CREATION.

    III. *Natural Attributes.* Properties or qualities of the Divine Being. The true representations of God as revealed by Himself in His Word. They are inseparable from His nature. Being God He must be what He is in these essential attributes or perfections.

1. *Infinity.* His infinitude expressed in all things. In no manner limited. He is unconditioned (1 Ki 8:27; Ps 139:8; Ac 15:18; He 4:13).

2. *Eternity.* He is infinite, not finite in the duration of His being. He is not only without beginning, always was, but in the nature of that perfection is timeless. Time has no place in His eternal nature. There can be no progression, advancing from point to point, in His being (Ge 21:23; Ex 3:14-15; Ps 90:2; 2 Pe 3:8).

3. *Omnipotence.* Unlimited in might and power. It is sometimes superficially asked, "If He can do all things can He make two hills without a valley between?" This is not a *thing* but an absurdity. He is not less than omnipotent because He does not do what involves an absurdity or contradiction (Ge 1:1,3; 18:14; De 32:39; Ps 66:3; Is 40:12; Da 4:35; Ma 19:26; Ro 1:20).

4. *Omniscience.* All-knowing. God is infinite in understanding just as He is in power. There can be no advance or progression in knowledge. He already knows everything that has happened, that will happen, and every possible combination of "what ifs"(Job 37:16; Ps 33:13; 119:168; Je 23:24; Ma 10:29; Ac 1:24; 15:18).

5. *Omnipresence.* Simultaneously present everywhere, always. His presence as His power extends over all His works. There is no place we can go where we are out of His reach (Job 34:21-22; Ps 139:7-12; Is 66:1; Ac 17:27).

6. *Immutability.* Unchangeable. God is no more subject to change than to any other limitation (Ps 33:11; Is 46:10; Mal 3:6; He 1:12; 6:17-18; Jam 1:17).

7. *Wisdom.* God's wisdom is perfect, and beyond our understanding (Job 36:5; Ps 104:24; Is 28:29; Ro 16:27; 1 Ti 1:17).

IV. *Moral Perfections of God.* As the natural attributes appear in the statements relative to His own nature, and in rela-

tion to His acts of power, His relations to the universe and His creatures, so the Scriptures reveal His moral attributes in His dealings with man in His moral constitution and conduct, and His relation to the moral order. In a marvelous manner the Bible sets forth the ethical God.

1. *Holiness.* God is as essentially and infinitely holy as He is essentially omnipotent, and requires holiness of the beings made in his image (Le 19:2; Jos 24:19; 1 Sa 2:2; Job 36:2-3; Ps 89:35; Is 5:16; 6:3; Ho 11:9; 1 Pe 1:15).

2. *Justice.* In the Scriptures justice and righteousness are used synonymously. In the being of God, it is a necessary outflow from His holiness, the manifestation of that holiness in the moral government of the world. He is perfectly just as the righteous governor of the world, and His perfect righteousness appears in the penalties pronounced and rewards bestowed (Ge 18:25; De 10:17; Job 8:3,20; Ps 9:8; 119:142; Je 11:20; Da 9:7; Ro 2:11; Re 15:3).

3. *Mercy.* The divine goodness and compassion exercised toward the guilty and wretched in harmony with truth and justice, the ministry of love for the relief of those unworthy of it (Ex 34:7; De 4:31; Ps 51:1; 117:2; Is 55:7; Je 3:12; Lk 1:50; 6:36; Ep 2:4; Tit 3:5; He 4:16).

4. *Faithfulness.* This divine attribute is noted especially in the Psalms. By it we are assured that God will fulfill His promises regarding temporal necessities (Ps 84:11; Is 33:16; 1 Ti 4:8); support in temptation and persecution (Is 41:10; 1 Co 10:13; 1 Pe 4:12-13); comfort in afflictions (He 12:4-12); guidance in trouble (2 Ch 32:22; Ps 32:8), power to persevere (Je 32:40); and spiritual blessings and final glory (1 Co 1:9; 1 Jo 2:25).

5. *Love.* Our conceptions of God must be derived from the revelation of Himself in his Word, and in that revelation He declares this attribute of love. Not only so, but it is the only attribute by which His being as such is defined—"God is love." In no instance is another attribute so employed, as "God is power," or "God is omniscience." Love is the distinctive characteristic of God in which all others harmoniously blend. In both the Old and New Testaments God's gracious love to men is so strongly and frequently declared it would take considerable space to set down the passages (Ex 34:6; Is 63:9; Je 31:3; Jo 3:16; 1 Jo 4:10). The highest expression of divine love is in redemption—God in Christ reconciling the world to Himself (Ro 5:8; 8:32-39; 1 Jo 4:9-10).

V. *The Triune God—Father, Son, Holy Spirit.* The Scriptures set forth the Godhead in this distinction of persons with absolute unity of essence. At the beginning of our Lord's ministry, the three persons are exhibited at His baptism; the Holy Spirit rested on Him as a dove, and the Father spoke acknowledging the Son. In the formula of baptism the doctrine of Trinity is established by the resurrected Lord (Ma 28:19).

1. *The Father is God* (Ma 11:25; Jo 6:27; 8:41; Ro 15:6; 1 Co 8:6; Ep 4:6; Jam 1:27).

2. *The Son is God* (Jo 1:1,18; 20:28; Ro 9:5; Ph 2:6; Col 2:9; He 1:8; 2 Pe 1:1).

3. *The Spirit is God* (Ac 5:3-4; 1 Co 2:10-11; Ep 2:22).

4. *The distinctness of the three from one another* (Jo 15:26; 16:13-14; 17:1-8, 18-23).

GOD, CHILDREN OF
See SONS OF GOD.

GODDESS
A female deity. See GODS, PAGAN.

GODHEAD
A term which emphasizes the supremacy of God; deity (Ro 1:20; Col 2:9).

GOD, IMAGE OF
See IMAGE OF GOD.

GODLINESS
The condition of living and acting in a way that is pleasing and acceptable to God; conforming to His Son (1 Ti 2:2).

GOD, NAMES OF
The One True God is addressed by numerous names in the Old and New Testaments. Each of these names emphasizes one aspect of God's nature and character.

Adonai—This name means "my Lord," or "master." When reading the Scriptures aloud, it became customary to replace the name Yahweh with Adonai, as a precaution against possible disrespect. Moses addressed God as "Adonai" when he talked with Him at the burning bush (Ex 4:10,13).

YHWH (Jehovah, Yahweh, I AM). When Moses spoke with God at the burning bush, asking Him what to say when the Israelites inquired who sent him, God replied, "I AM WHO I AM." The name Yahweh or Jehovah comes from the Hebrew state of being verb. This name emphasizes God's exclusive and unique nature: He is defined only by Himself.

In Hebrew, the name is written YHWH. Because of the custom of reading "Adonai" when reading aloud, the original pronunciation has been lost. Jehovah and Yahweh are the most used forms, though most Bible translations follow the tradition and translate it LORD (all capital letters). This name could reasonably be called the most important name of God. It is used some 6,800 times in Scripture.

Several compound names of God are based on this name.

Jehovah-Jireh The LORD who Provides. When Abraham was about to sacrifice Isaac, God provided a substitute (Ge 22:14).

Jehovah-Nissi The LORD Is My Banner. This name celebrated the victory God gave the Israelites over the Amalekites (Ex 17:15).

Jehovah-Shalom The LORD Is My Peace. Gideon gave this name to the altar he built after the Lord told him that he would defeat the Midianites (Ju 6:24).

Jehovah-Shammah The LORD Is There. (Eze 48:35).

Jehovah-Saboath (Jehovah-tsebaoth) The LORD of Hosts, signifying that God is surrounded by hosts of angels who obey Him (1 Sa 1:3).

Jehovah Elohe Yisrael The LORD God of Israel; this name appears many times throughout the Old Testament.

El Simply, God (De 5:9).

El Elohe Israel God, the God of Israel (Ge 32:28-30).

El Olam The Everlasting God (Ge 21:33).

El Shaddai God Almighty (Ex 6:3).

Elohim Plural form of El. This is the name used in the creation story (Ge 1:1-3).

God-Who-Forgives A title that shows God's great mercy (Ps 99:8). See FORGIVENESS.

Branch of Righteousness A title used to describe the coming Messiah, Jesus (Je 23:5-6).

Shepherd The most popular and well-known psalm begins with the words "The Lord is my shepherd" (Ps 23:1). The image of God as a shepherd is one that is repeated over and over in Scripture (Is 40:11; Je 31:10; Eze 34:11-16; Lk 15:4-7; Jo 10:11-16).

Servant The coming Messiah is described as a servant (Is 42:1-4; 49:1-7; 53:1-12) Jesus fulfilled this as He "put on the form of a servant and came in the likeness of men" (Ph 2:7).

See CHRIST, TITLES OF.

GOD, SONS OF

See SONS OF GOD.

GODS, PAGAN

Numerous pagan gods and goddesses are mentioned in the pages of Scripture. God strictly forbade His people from worshipping or bowing down to any of these and commanded them to destroy the idolatrous pagan Canaanites so that they would not be ensnared in their evil practices. The worship of pagan deities was often accompanied by gross sexual immorality, self-disfigurement, and in some cases, human sacrifice.

Following is a list of the false deities mentioned in the Bible:

Adrammelech (2 Ki 17:31, also called Annamelech), Asherah (1 Ki 18:19), Ashima (2 Ki 17:30), Ashtoreth (2 Ki 23:13), Baal (Nu 22:41), Baal-Berith (Ju 9:4), Baal of Peor (Ps 106:28), Baal-Zebub (2 Ki 1:2-3; Mk 3:22), Bel (Is 46:1), Chemosh (Je 48:7, 13), Chiun (Am 5:26), Dagon (1 Sa 5:2-7), Diana (Ac 19:24,27-28), Gad (Is 65:11), Golden Calf (Ex 32), Hermes (Ac 14:12), Mammon (Lk 16:13), Meni (Is 65:11, also called Fate), Merodach (Je 50:2), Molech (Le 18:21; Zep 1:5; Ac 7:43, also called Milcom and Moloch), Nebo (Is 46:1), Nehushtan (2 Ki 18:4), Nergai (2 Ki 17:30), Nisroch (Is 37:38), Remphan (Ac 7:43), Rimmon (2 Ki 5:18), Sikkuth (Am 5:26), Succoth Benoth (2 Ki 17:30), Tammuz (Eze 8:14), Tartak (2 Ki 17:31), Twin Brothers, Castor and Pollux (Ac 28:11), Zeus (Ac 14:12-13), also called Jupiter.

GOD, UNKNOWN

Along with all the pagan deities the Greeks worshipped, they had gone so far as to set up an altar to an unknown god. In this way, they could feel safe that they were not offending any god by ignoring it (Ac 17:23).

GOG

1. Son of Shemaiah, a Reubenite (1 Ch 5:4).

2. The prince of Meshech and Tubal. It was prophesied that he would be defeated in his expedition against Israel (Eze 38–39).

3. Figuratively, the terms Gog and Magog are used to represent the nations Satan will gather about him to attack the forces of the Messiah (Re 20:8-15). See MAGOG.

GOIIM *(nations, Gentiles)*

The word is used to describe the "nations" who battled the kings of Sodom and Gomorrah (Ge 14:1,9) as well as a tribe Joshua conquered (Jos 12:23). See GENTILES.

GO′LAN

A city of Bashan (Jos 20:8).

GOLD

It has been used from earliest times (Ge 2:11). At first it was used for ornaments (Ge 24:22) and not until much later was it coined as money. In ancient times it was abundant (1 Ch 22:14; 2 Ch 1:15; Da 3:1). It was found in Arabia, Sheba and Ophir (1 Ki 9:28; 10:1; Job 28:16), also in Uphaz (Je 10:9; Da 10:5), and Parvaim (2 Ch 3:6). Working with gold is mentioned in Psalms 66:10; Proverbs 17:3; 27:21; Isaiah 46:6. The sacred articles of the tabernacle and temple were overlaid with gold (Ex 25:18; 1 Ki 6:22,28).

GOLD, PIECE OF

See MONEY OF THE BIBLE.

GOLDEN CALF

The idol the Hebrews made at Sinai after they had grown tired of waiting for Moses to descend from the mountain. While this was ostensibly a representation of the "God who led them out of Egypt," they probably modeled it after the Egyptian worship of the Apis Bull (Ex 32; 1 Ki 12:26-33). When God saw what they had done, He had Moses grind the idol into powder and make them drink it.

GOLDSMITH

One who makes objects of gold. See METAL-SMITH.

GOL′ GO•THA

See CALVARY.

GO•LI′ ATH *(exile)*

A Philistine giant of the city of Gath. For forty days he defied the army of Israel (1 Sa 17). Estimating a cubit as eighteen inches he was over nine feet tall, and over ten feet if the cubit is reckoned as twenty-one inches. He was challenged by David, and in the valley of Terebinth he was slain by a stone from David's sling.

GO′ MER

1. The oldest son of Japheth (Ge 10:2-3). He was included by Ezekiel in the army of Gog (Eze 38:3,6). He represents the people known as Cimmerians whose original home was north of the Black Sea and who later migrated to Asia Minor.

2. The daughter of Diblaim, and wife of Hosea (Ho 1:3).

GO•MOR′ RAH

One of the five cities of the plain. With the exception of Zoar (formerly Bela), these cities were destroyed by fire from heaven (Ge 19:23-29). It was in Zoar that Lot, a resident of Gomorrah, took refuge and was spared.

GONG

Probably some kind of bell. KJV and NKJV translate this as "sounding brass" (1 Co 13:1).

GOODMAN (archaic)

Head of household, master (Lk 12:39).

GOOD SAMARITAN, PARABLE OF.

(Lk 10:25-37).

GOOSE

A large domesticated bird, raised for meat and feathers. Geese can be both fierce and territorial, making them into good "watch-dogs."

The "fatted fowl" that King Solomon ate (1 Ki 4:23) may have been geese.

GO′ PHER WOOD

The timber from which Noah's ark was constructed (Ge 6:14). See CYPRESS.

GO′ SHEN

Three geographical areas of the Old Testament:

1. The district in Egypt in which the Israelites lived between the time of Jacob's entry and the exodus. It was near the frontier of Canaan and was rich in pastureland (Ge 46:34).

2. A district in the south of Judah taken by Joshua (Jos 10:41; 11:16).

3. An unidentified town of Judah (Jos 15:51).

GOS′ PEL *(from god and spell, Anglo-Saxon, good message or news)*

This is applied to the four inspired histories of the life and teaching of Christ. They were not written until the latter half of the first century—Matthew and Mark prior to the destruction of Jerusalem, Luke about A.D. 64, and John towards the close of the century, or not earlier than about 90 A.D. Thus ten of Paul's Epistles were written before any of the Gospels, and John's Gospel about twenty-two years after the death of Paul. "As a matter of literary history," says Dr. William Smith, "nothing can be better established than the genuineness of the Gospels."

GOS′ PELS, THE FOUR

Many readers of the New Testament wonder why it contains four different Gospels (accounts) of the one authentic gospel (the good news of salvation in Jesus Christ). Perhaps the main reason is that any one of these Gospels alone would not do justice to Jesus's life and ministry. Each Gospel writer wrote about Jesus to a different audience for a different purpose to give a unique perspective on His life. Together, the four Gospels give us a complete picture of who Jesus was and what He accomplished during His ministry.

Different symbols for the Gospels are often used to communicate the distinctives of each account. A lion, symbolizing Matthew, represents strength and royal authority; a bull, representing Mark, portrays service and power; the figure of a man, for Luke, stands for wisdom and character; and an eagle, John's symbol, represents deity. The following capsule summaries of the Gospels should help to make clear the distinct characteristics of each book.

Matthew—Written to a Jewish audience to show that Jesus was the promised Messiah of Old Testament prophecy; key expression is "that it might be fulfilled"; quotes more from the Old Testament than any other Gospel. Matthew uses alternating sections of didactic and narrative material to emphasize Jesus as a teacher. A major theme is the kingdom of heaven or the kingdom of God—God's rule in the world and in human hearts. Other dominant themes are the church (16:18; 18:19), the second coming of Jesus (ch. 25), and the ethical teachings of Jesus (chs. 5–7).

Mark—Probably the first Gospel written; Matthew and Luke may have used Mark as a source. Mark focuses on Jesus as a servant who ministers to the physical and spiritual needs of others. It is the shortest Gospel, written to a Gentile audience, particularly Roman citizens. It is characterized by brevity in accounts, with rapid movement, to give a sense of urgency to the gospel message; the key expression is "immediately." Mark's purpose was to show that Jesus was the Son of God; a Roman soldier's words at Jesus death were, "Truly this Man was the Son of God!" (15:39).

Luke—Written by a Gentile writer for Gentiles, to give the full story of Jesus's life, from His birth to the birth of the church. It records many of Jesus's parables not found in the other Gospels. It is universal in outlook, portraying Jesus as the compassionate Savior of the world, with love for all people, whether rich or poor, Jew or Gentile; He reaches out especially to women and the poor and outcast of society. Mark emphasizes the work of the Holy Spirit and the central place of prayer in Jesus's life and ministry. The key expression is "it happened" or "it came to pass."

John—Focuses on the theological meaning of Jesus's actions, rather than on the actions themselves: John emphasizes who Jesus is, rather than what He did. It includes many lengthy discourses of Jesus around which narrative is woven. It uses many key words, such as *life, light, believe, love, witness, glory, water,* and *truth,* to portray Jesus as God's eternal Son. John presents Jesus as God incarnate through seven miraculous signs; the key expression is "believe." His clear purpose in writing is "that you may believe that Jesus is the Christ, the Son of God, and that believing you may have life in His name (20:31).

See MATTHEW, MARK, LUKE, JOHN.

GOSPELS HARMONIZED

A Harmony of the Gospels, or the Gospels Harmonized, signifies a chronological arrangement of the four Gospels. By this system of harmonizing, the periods of our Lord's life are readily grasped and the four records appear distinctly as contributing to this history. The discourses, parables, and miracles are placed where they belong chronologically.

	Ma	Mk	Lk	Jo
THE THIRTY YEARS				
Introductory				
Prologue of John's Gospel				1:1-18
Preface to Luke's Gospel			1:1-4	
Genealogies	1:1-17		3:23-38	
Announcements				
1. John the Baptist promised			1:5-25	
2. To Mary			1:26-38	
3. To Joseph	1:18-25			
4. Mary's visit to Elisabeth			1:39-56	
Birth of John and of Jesus				
1. John the Baptist			1:57-80	
2. Birth of Jesus	1:18-25		2:1-7	
3. Announcement to the shepherds			2:8-20	

	Ma	Mk	Lk	Jo
THE THIRTY YEARS—*Cont'd*				
Infancy of Jesus				
1. Circumcision			2:21	
2. Presented at the temple			2:22-39	
3. The Magi—Wise men	2:1-12			
4. In Egypt. Return to Nazareth	2:13-23			
The Years in Nazareth				
1. Childhood	2:23		2:39-40	
2. In Jerusalem at the age of twelve			2:41-50	
3. Remaining years in Nazareth			2:51-52	
BEGINNING OF HIS MINISTRY				
1. Labors of John the Baptist	3:1-12	1:1-8	3:1-20	
2. Baptism of Jesus	3:13-17	1:9-11	3:21-23	
3. Temptation of Jesus	4:1-11	1:12-13	4:1-13	
4. John's statement to priests and Levites				1:19-28
5. The Lamb of God				1:29-34
6. First disciples				1:35-42
7. Philip and Nathanael				1:43-51
8. The first miracle—at Cana				2:1-11
9. In Capernaum				2:12
EARLY JUDEAN MINISTRY				
In Jerusalem				
1. First cleansing of the temple				2:13-22
2. The First Discourse—Nicodemus				3:1-21
In Judea				
1. Christ baptizing				3:22-24
2. John at Aenon—his testimony				3:25-36
In Samaria				
1. Leaving Judea	4:12	1:14		4:1-3
2. The woman of Samaria				4:4-26
3. In Sychar. The people believe				4:27-42
THE GALILEAN MINISTRY				
First Period				
I. To the First Circuit				
1. Beginning of the ministry	4:12-17	1:14-15	4:14-15	4:43-45
2. Healing the Nobleman's Son				4:46-54
3. First rejection at Nazareth			4:16-30	
4. Settles in Capernaum	4:13-16		4:31	
II. The First Circuit				
1. Call of the Four	4:18-22	1:16-20	5:1-11	
2. Miracles in Capernaum	8:14-17	1:21-34	4:31-41	
3. Preaching in Galilee	4:23; 8:1-4	1:35-45	4:42-44; 5:12-16	
III. Enmity of Scribes and Pharisees				
1. Healing the Paralytic	9:1-8	2:1-12	5:17-26	
2. The call of Matthew	9:9-13	2:13-17	5:27-32	

	Ma	Mk	Lk	Jo
3. Concerning fasting	9:14-17	2:18-22	5:33-39	
4. The Impotent Man				5:1-16
5. Christ and the Father				5:17-47
6. Plucking grain on the Sabbath	12:1-8	2:23-28	6:1-5	
7. Healing the Withered Hand	12:9-14	3:1-6	6:6-11	
Second Period				
I. Organizing the Kingdom				
1. Teaching and increasing fame	4:23-25; 12:15-21	3:7-12	6:17-19	
2. Selection of the Twelve	10:2-4	3:13-19	6:12-19	
3. Sermon on the Mount	5–7		6:20-49	
II. The Second Circuit				
1. Healing the Centurion's Servant	8:5-13		7:1-10	
2. Raising the Widow's Son—at Nain			7:11-17	
3. Messengers from John the Baptist	11:2-30		7:18-35	
4. Anointing of Jesus in Simon's house			7:36-50	
5. The companions of Jesus			8:1-3	
III. Teaching by the Sea of Galilee				
1. Scribes and Pharisees warned	12:22-45	3:19-30		
2. True kinship with Christ	12:46-50	3:31-35	8:19-21	
3. Parables by the Sea	13:1-53	4:1-34	8:4-18	
IV. Miracles by the Sea				
1. Stilling the Storm	8:18, 23-27	4:35-41	8:22-25	
2. The Gadarene Demoniac	8:28-34	5:1-20	8:26-39	
3. Raising Jairus' Daughter	9:18-26	5:21-43	8:40-56	
4. Two Blind Men and Demoniac	9:27-34			
V. The Third Circuit				
1. The second rejection at Nazareth	13:54-58	6:1-6		
2. The Twelve commissioned	9:35–11:1	6:7-13	9:1-6	
3. Death of John the Baptist	14:1-12	6:14-29	9:7-9	
VI. At Capernaum				
1. Feeding the Five Thousand	14:13-23	6:30-46	9:10-17	6:1-15
2. Jesus Walking on the Sea	14:24-36	6:47-56		6:16-21
3. The Bread of Life				6:22-71
4. Hypocrisy of Scribes and Pharisees	15:1-20	7:1-23		
Third Period				
I. Withdrawal to the North				
1. Toward Tyre and Sidon	15:21-28	7:24-30		
2. Returning through Decapolis	15:29-31	7:31-37		
II. Returning to the Sea of Galilee				
1. Feeding Four Thousand	15:32-38	8:1-9		
2. Pharisees demand a sign from heaven	15:39–16:12	8:10-21		
3. The Blind Man Near Bethsaida		8:22-26		

	Ma	Mk	Lk	Jo
THE GALILEAN MINISTRY—*Cont'd*				
III. Second Northern Withdrawal				
1. Peter's great confession	16:13-20	8:27-30	9:18-21	
2. First announcement of coming death	16:21-28	8:31–9:1	9:22-27	
3. The Transfiguration	17:1-13	9:2-13	9:28-36	
4. The Demoniac Boy	17:14-20	9:14-29	9:37-43	
5. Second announcement of coming death	17:22-23	9:30-32	9:43-45	
IV. In Capernaum				
1. The Temple-tax—Tribute Money	17:24-27	9:33		
2. Humility and Forgiveness	18	9:33-50	9:46-50	
V. The Visit to Jerusalem				
1. At the Feast of Tabernacles				7:1-52
2. The woman taken in adultery				7:53–8:11
3. Christ the Light of the World				8:12-30
4. Spiritual Freedom				8:31-59
THE PEREAN MINISTRY				
To the Feast of Dedication				
1. Departure from Galilee	19:1-2	10:1	9:51-62	
2. The Seventy commissioned			10:1-24	
3. The Good Samaritan			10:25-37	
4. Visits Bethany—Martha and Mary			10:38-42	
5. The Man Born Blind				9:1-42
6. The Good Shepherd				10:1-21
7. At the Feast of Dedication				10:22-42
From the Feast to the Withdrawal				
1. Discourse on Prayer			11:1-13	
2. Healing the Demoniac			11:14	
3. Discourse Against the Pharisees			11:15-54	
4. Trust in God; the Coming Christ			12:1-59	
5. The Galileans slain by Pilate			13:1-9	
6. The Crippled Woman			13:10-21	
7. Those that shall be saved			13:22-30	
8. Warned against Herod. Christ's reply			13:31-35	
9. Dining with a Pharisee			14:1-24	
10. Counting the Cost			14:25-35	
11. Receiving sinners defended by 3 parables			15	
12. Parables of Warning			16	
13. The Nature of True Service			17:1-10	
14. The Raising of Lazarus				11:1-46
15. Withdrawal to Ephraim				11:47-54
To the Return to Jerusalem				
1. Healing of Ten Lepers			17:11-19	
2. The Coming of the Kingdom			17:20–18:8	

	Ma	Mk	Lk	Jo
3. The Pharisee and Publican			18:9-14	
4. Concerning divorce	19:3-12	10:2-12		
5. The children blessed	19:13-15	10:13-16	18:15-17	
6. The rich young ruler	19:16-30	10:17-31	18:18-30	
7. Labourers in the vineyard	20:1-16			
8. Third announcement of His coming death	20:17-19	10:32-34	18:31-34	
9. Ambition of James and John	20:20-28	10:34-45		
10. The Blind Men near Jericho	20:29-34	10:46-52	18:35-43	
11. Zacchaeus, chief publican at Jericho			19:1-10	
12. Parable of the Pounds			19:11-28	
13. Jesus anointed by Mary of Bethany	26:6-13	14:13-9		12:1-8
THE PASSION WEEK				
Sunday				
The triumphal entry into Jerusalem	21:1-11	11:1-11	19:29-44	12:12-19
Monday				
1. The fig tree cursed	21:18-19	11:12-14		
2. Second cleansing of the temple	21:12-17	11:15-19	19:45-48	
Tuesday				
1. The Withered Fig Tree	21:20-22	11:20-25		
2. Christ's authority challenged	21:23-27	11:27-33	20:1-8	
3. Parables of Warning	21:28–22:14	12:1-12	20:9-19	
4. Questions by Jewish rulers	22:15-40	12:13-34	20:20-40	
5. Christ's unanswerable question	22:41-46	12:35-37	20:41-44	
6. Arraignment of the Pharisees	23:1-39	12:38-40	20:45-47	
7. The widow's mites		12:41-44	21:1-4	
8. Jesus sought by the Gentiles				12:20-36
9. Christ rejected by the Jews				12:37-50
10. The Olivet Discourse	24–25	13	21:5-38	
11. The plot. Chief priests and Judas	26:1-5, 14-16	14:1-2, 10-11	22:1-6	
Wednesday				
No record of this day				
Thursday				
1. The Passover and the Lord's Supper	26:17-30	14:12-26	22:7-30	13:1-30
2. Last Discourses	26:31-35	14:27-31	22:31-38	13:31–16:33
3. The Intercessory Prayer				17
Friday				
1. In Gethsemane	26:30, 36-46	14:26, 32-42	22:39-46	18:1
2. Betrayal and arrest	26:47-56	14:43-52	22:47-53	18:1-11
3. The trial. Before Jewish authorities	26:57–27:10	14:53-72	22:54-71	18:12-27
4. Christ before Pilate	27:2, 11-31	15:1-20	23:1-25	18:28–19:16

	Ma	Mk	Lk	Jo
THE PASSION WEEK—*Cont'd*				
5. The crucifixion	27:32-56	15:21-41	23:26-49	19:16-37
6. In the tomb	27:57-61	15:42-47	23:50-56	19:38-42
Saturday				
The tomb under guard	27:62-66			
FROM THE RESURRECTION TO THE ASCENSION				
1. The Empty Tomb	28:1-10	16:1-11	23:56–24:12	20:1-18
2. The report of the guard	28:11-15			
3. The walk to Emmaus		16:12-13	24:13-35	
4. Appearances				
To the disciples in Jerusalem, Thomas not present		16:14	24:36-43	20:19-25
To Thomas with the others				20:26-29
To seven disciples by the sea of Galilee				21:1-24
To the Eleven in Galilee	28:16-20	16:15-18		
Final appearance and ascension		16:19-20	24:44-53	

GOSSIP

Rumors and indiscreet talk about other people; one who engages in spreading such. Paul warns believers not to be idle or gossips (1 Ti 5:13). Gossips are also called "tattlers," and "busybodies." It will serve us well to heed Paul's warning, for Jesus said that we will one day have to answer for every careless word we utter (Ma 12:36).

GOURD

A plant or vine which God prepared to shelter Jonah from the heat (Jon 4:6-10). It was probably the bottle gourd, a kind of squash-like vine. In Palestine a wild gourd will survive a drought when all other vegetation has died from the lack of moisture (2 Ki 4:39). When a poisonous gourd was eaten, it was miraculously rendered harmless by Elisha (2 Ki 4:38-41).

GOVERNMENT OFFICIAL

Many government officials are mentioned in the Bible, but all of their titles are not easily translatable. Different scholars have chosen different words to convey the meaning of the original Hebrew, but the exact definitions of all these positions is not really known. Government positions mentioned in various Bible translations include: *Chancellor, commissioner, comptroller, courtier, deputy, magistrate, officer, pre-*

GOURD

fect, president, procurer, recorder, treasurer, trustee, and viceroy. Some of these officials were part of civil government, others were probably connected with the military.

GOVERNMENT OF ISRAEL

The government of Israel may be considered under two important headings: the laws, and the leaders.

The Laws:
- a) The "commandments," especially the Ten Commandments, revealed God's holiness and set up a divine standard of righteousness for the people to follow (Ex 20:1-17).
- b) The judgments governed the social life of the people and concerned masters and servants (Ex 21:1-11), physical injuries (Ex 21:12-36), protection of property rights (Ex 22:1-15), etc.

c) The ordinances included the sacrifices that showed that blood must be shed for sinners to be forgiven (Le 1-17).

The Leaders: At first Moses was the sole leader; then he was replaced by Joshua. After Joshua's death the nation was governed for many years by judges, who were usually raised up by God to oppose a specific enemy. Finally, at the people's request, God granted them a king, thus establishing the monarchy (1 Sa 8:5,22). Under the monarchy there were four key leaders:

a) The king was the Lord's representative who ruled the people, but only as the Lord's servant. He led in war (1 Sa 8:20) and made judicial decisions (2 Sa 15:2); but he could not make law, since he himself was under the law (De 17:19). His relationship was so close to the Lord that he was adopted by the Lord (2 Sa 7:14; Ps 2:7).

b) The priest taught the Lord's laws and officiated at the offering of the sacrifices (Le 1:5; Je 18:18).

c) The prophet was the man of God who spoke for God and gave divine pronouncements for the present (forthtelling) or for the future (foretelling).

d) The wise man produced literary works stressing practical wisdom (Pr 1:1), taught discipline of character to the young (Pr 22:17), and gave counsel to the king (2 Sa 16:20). The choice of these men indicates an important biblical principle: God uses people to reach other people, a principle that is also evident in the Great Commission given to Christians (Ma 28:19-20).

GOV'ER·NOR

The subordinate of a ruler appointed to govern a particular area. This was the position Joseph held when Pharaoh made him the prime minister of Egypt (Ge 43:6; 45:26). The Jews following the exile were ruled by Persian governors. Zerubbabel and Nehemiah were also appointed to this office (Ne 2:9; 7:7). In Matthew 28:14, Pilate is called governor of Judea, although his Roman title was *procurator.*

GO'ZAN

A district in Mesopotamia on the river Habor (2 Ki 17:6; 18:11; 19:12; 1 Ch 5:26; Is 37:12).

Captives were transported to it from Israel after the fall of Samaria (722-721 B.C.).

GRACE

Since *grace* is the most characteristic of all Christian words, it is well worth our while to trace briefly its move from classical to Christian usage.

Grace (charis) is derived from the verb *rejoice (chairo).* Luke apparently makes a little play on this word in Acts 11:23: "When he [Barnabas] came and had seen the grace of God, he was glad [*echare*]." To a Greek, anything of beauty, favor, or delight in which a person could rejoice spoke of *charis.* This usage, with no religious connotations, still exists today in our ideas of graceful beauty and gracious entertaining.

Those who are familiar with the rich and lovely Hebrew word *hesed* (see LOVING-KINDNESS) might expect that the translators of the Septuagint (LXX) would have chosen *charis* to translate it into Greek. In Esther 2:17, where *hesed* ("mercy," "lovingkindness") occurs, along with the somewhat similar word *hen,* they are translated by *charis.* Generally, *charis* in the LXX renders *hen* not *hesed,* but a good argument could be made for translating *hesed* by "grace" in modern translations. This is because the concept that we associate with *charis*—divine favor that is completely undeserved by man—is not far from the meaning of *hesed* in many contexts.

In the New Testament itself (and those books, sermons, and hymns deeply rooted in that book), the message of *charis* comes to full flower. Every New Testament book, except Matthew, Mark, and 1 John, uses *charis.* Common expressions include "the grace of God," "grace of the Lord," "the grace of Christ," and "the word [message] of grace."

It is fitting that the first New Testament use of "grace" is by the angel announcing the coming of the Messiah: "Do not be afraid, Mary, for you have found favor [*charis*] with God" (Lk 1:30). Then he goes on to predict the grace that the incarnation of God the Son would bring to the world. This is not to say that the Old Testament is without grace. God is always gracious. But only in the New Testament do we see the complete exposition of God's favor in the salvation freely offered by grace through faith to all who will believe. The Bible ends also on a "grace note." The last verse of God's Word reads: "The grace of our Lord Jesus be with you all" (Re 22:21).

Between Luke and Revelation, grace abounds (2 Co 9:14) and "super abounds" (1 Ti 1:14).

GRAFT

To splice a branch onto a rootstock; a method of engineering improvements and specializing fruits. An orchardist or vinedresser will take a hardy root stock and cut a small slit in the trunk. A live branch (scion) from another plant with certain desired characteristics is inserted into the slit, and the joint is covered with wax to prevent infection. If the graft is successful, the new branch will become part of the old tree, flourish, and bear fruit. Scripture says that the Gentiles have been "grafted in" to God's plan (Ro 11:17-24).

GRAIN

Plants in the grass family, raised for the sake of their seed heads, which are eaten as food. These include wheat, barley, spelt, oats, and many more.

GRANARY

A storehouse for grain.

GRAPE

See VINE.

GRASSHOPPER

See LOCUST.

GRATE, GRATING

A "network of bronze" for the altar of sacrifice (Ex 27:4-7). A grate is a basket or flat metal network for holding a fire and allowing air to reach it from underneath to create a better draft.

GRATITUDE

See THANKSGIVING.

GRAVE

See BURIAL.

GRAVECLOTHES

The linen clothes that bodies were wrapped in for burial. When Lazarus came out of the grave, he was still wrapped in these strips of cloth (Jo 11:44).

GRAV' EN IM' AGE

A carved image, specifically an idol or something meant to represent God. Stone, wood, and metal were used (Is 30:22; 44:15,17; 45:20). They were made by the Canaanites before the land was taken by the Israelites (De 7:5; 12:3) and in other countries (Je 50:38; 51:47). The sin of making them was constantly impressed upon the Jews (Ex 20:4; De 5:8; 27:15; Is 44:9; Je 51:17).

The second commandment, "You shall not make for yourselves any graven image" has been often been misinterpreted. Some view it as a mere repetition of the First Commandment, to have no other gods than God. Actually, this is much more than a repetition. It is wrong to worship other gods, but it is just as wrong to make an image of the One True God. Any picture or representation that we make will be skewed, inadequate, and present a false idea of who God is. If we worship these images, we will be worshipping our own false ideas rather than the true God.

Others view this commandment as a ban of any form of representational art. However, this is clearly not the case, because God's design for the tabernacle included many examples of representational art. Making images of created things is not the issue; the sin lies in making images that are supposed to represent God, and/or worshipping such images. The golden calf that Aaron and the Israelites made is an excellent example of this.

GREAT BANQUET (or SUPPER), PARABLE OF

(Lk 14:15-24).

GREAT LIZARD

See LIZARD.

GREAT OWL

See OWL.

GREAVES

Shin guards, made of leather or metal, to protect the lower legs during battle.

GRE' CIANS

This word is used to describe not only the people who lived in Greece (Joel 3:6), but Greek speaking Jews as distinguished from those who spoke Aramaic (Ac 6:1; 9:29). See GREECE.

GREECE

The Anglicized Roman term for lands called Hellas by the inhabitants. The name is derived from a small tribe, the Graeci, who lived along the Adriatic coast. The Old Testament word for Greece is Javan (Ge 10:4-5; Is 66:19).

Greece was a nation of the ancient world, which rose to the status of a world power near the end of the Old Testament era. The Greeks exerted great influence on the Jewish people, particularly during the period between the Old and New Testaments. Greek culture also paved the way for the expansion of Christianity in the first century A.D.

Under the leadership of the great military conqueror Alexander the Great (ruled 336-323 B.C.), the Greek Empire was extended through Asia Minor to Egypt and the borders of India. The rule of Greece was foretold by the prophet Daniel (Da 11:3-35).

Alexander's conquests and his passion to spread Greek culture contributed to the advancement of Greek ideas throughout the ancient world. This adoption of Greek ideas by the rest of the world was known as Hellenism. So thoroughly did Greek ideas penetrate the other nations that the Greek language became the dominant language of the ancient world.

The Greece of New Testament times consisted of two Roman provinces: Macedonia and Achaia, with Corinth as the chief city and seat of the pro-consul. Athens was the great center of learning.

Since Greek was the universal language, the apostle Paul could communicate easily with the various nations and provinces he visited during his missionary journeys to spread the gospel. Paul visited such major cities as Philippi, Thessalonica, Athens, and Corinth, all of which retained distinct Greek cultural ideas, although they were ruled by the Romans. He showed a deep understanding of Greek thought and was able to communicate the gospel so the Greek mind could understand (Ac 17).

In the New Testament, the word "Greeks" refers to all people who have been influenced by Greek culture and who are not Jews (Mk 7:26). But the term "Hellenists" refers to Greek-speaking Jews (Ac 9:29) who lived in areas outside Palestine. Converts to Christianity included people from both these groups.

GREEK

After the East was conquered by the Macedonians, the name *Greek* was applied to all those who spoke Greek or who settled in the lands conquered by Alexander. In the New Testament Greek commonly means a foreigner or stranger (Ro 1:14,16; 10:12). The New Testament was written in Greek.

GREEKS

People born in Greece, or with Greek ancestors; also in the New Testament this word is used as a general term for Gentiles (non-Jews). In Mark 7:26, the Syro-Phoenician woman is called a "Greek."

GREEN FELDSPAR

Probably emerald.

GREEN JASPER

See JASPER.

GREY'HOUND

This is a rendering of a Hebrew word signifying *slender* or *girt in the loins* (Pr 30:31). This animal was probably not a dog and may have been a horse.

GRIEF

Sorrow, emotional pain. Jesus Christ has "borne our griefs" (Is 53:4).

GRIFFON

A variety of vulture.

GRIND

To pulverize, to crush into a powder. Grain was ground between two stones to make fine flour or coarse meal. See MILL.

GRINDERS (archaic)

Teeth (Ec 12:3).

GRISLED, GRIZZLED

Spotted; speckled (Ze 6:3)

GRIFFON

GROVE

In the Authorized Version *grove* is a mistaken translation of the Hebrew *Asherah* (Ju 6:25-26,28,30; 1 Ki 14:15,23). The asherah were wooden poles used as a symbol of the Canaanite goddess, Asherah (Ge 21:33).

GRUB

See WORM.

GUARANTEE

A down payment, earnest. God has given the Holy Spirit to us as a sure promise that He will follow through and bring us to eternal life (2 Co 5:5). See EARNEST.

GUARD

A bodyguard for the protection of the king. Potiphar was the captain of Pharaoh's guard (Ge 37:36). Nebuzar-adan was the captain of Nebuchadnezzar's guard (2 Ki 25:8; Je 39:9-10).

GUARD, GATE OF THE

One of the gates of Jerusalem, in the new wall built by Nehemiah and the Israelites (Ne 12:39).

GUARDHOUSE, GATE OF THE

See GUARD, GATE OF THE.

GUDGODAH (De 10:7)

See HOR-HAGGIDGAD.

GUEST

Strangers were regarded as guests and treated kindly (Ge 18:1-8; 19:3; Ju 3:15; Job 31:32). In the best homes there was a guest chamber (2 Ki 4:10; Mk 14:14; Lk 22:11). A visitor's stay in the home of another might have been for only a few hours, but he was regarded a guest and given the hospitality of the home (1 Ki 1:41; Zep 1:7; Ma 22:10-11; He 13:2). See HOSPITALITY.

GUILE

Deceit; craftiness (Jo 1:46-48).

GUILT OFFERING

See OFFERINGS.

GULF

A deep gap or ravine separating two places. Jesus's parable (or true story) of the rich man and Lazarus tells of the great uncrossable gulf that lies between Abraham's bosom and hell (Lk 16:26).

GUM RESIN

See BDELLIUM.

GU′ NI (colored)

1. A Gadite, father of Abdiel, and grandfather of the chief of the Gadites (1 Ch 5:15).

2. A son of Naphtali. He founded a tribal family. His descendants were called Gunites (Ge 46:24; Nu 26:48; 1 Ch 7:13).

GUR, ASCENT TO (a lion's whelp)

A place near Ibleam (2 Ki 9:27).

GUR-BA′ AL (sojourn of Baal)

A place of undetermined site mentioned as a residence of Arabians (2 Ch 26:7).

GUTTER

A trench or trough; watering trough (Ge 30:38), also the water shaft connecting Jerusalem to it's water supply outside the city walls (2 Sa 5:8, KJV).

GYMNASIUM

From the Greek *gymnos,* "naked." An ancient Greek training institution which taught philosophy and athletics to young men. It derived its name from the fact that the athletes practiced naked.

H

HA′ A·HASH′ TA·RI

A Judahite and son of Ashur and Naarah (1 Ch 4:6).

HA·BAI′ AH (Jehovah hath hidden)

A priest whose descendants returned from Babylon (Ez 2:61; Ne 7:63).

HA·BAK′ KUK (embrace)

A prophet of God to the nation of Judah. From one or two references it is inferred that he was of the tribe of Levi, but apart from this and the fact that he was a prophet of Judah, we know nothing about him. See "The Author of Habakkuk."

HA·BAK′KUK, BOOK OF

1. The Book of Habakkuk. Habakkuk ministered during the "death throes" of the nation of Judah. Although repeatedly called to repentance, the nation stubbornly refused to change her sinful ways. Habakkuk, knowing the hardheartedness of his countrymen, asked God how long this intolerable condition could continue. God replied that the Babylonians would be His chastening rod upon the nation—an announcement that sent the prophet to his knees. He acknowledged that the just in any generation shall live by faith (2:4), not by sight. Habakkuk concluded by praising God's wisdom even though He didn't fully understand God's ways.

Habaqqaq is an unusual Hebrew name derived from the verb *habaq,* "embrace." Thus his name probably means "one who embraces" or "one who clings." At the end of his book this name becomes appropriate because Habakkuk chooses to cling firmly to God regardless of what happens to his nation (3:16-19). The Greek title in the Septuagint is *Ambakouk,* and the Latin title in Jerome's Vulgate is *Habacuc.*

2. The Author of Habakkuk. In the introduction to the book (1:1) and in the closing psalm (3:1), the author identifies himself as Habakkuk the prophet. This special designation seems to indicate that Habakkuk was a professional prophet. The closing statement at the end of the psalm, "To the Chief Musician. With my stringed instruments," suggests that Habakkuk may have been a priest connected with the temple worship in Jerusalem. He mentions nothing of his genealogy or location, but speculative attempts have been made to identify him with certain unnamed Old Testament characters. In the apocryphal book of Bel and the Dragon, Daniel is rescued a second time by the prophet Habakkuk.

3. The Time of Habakkuk. The only explicit time reference in Habakkuk is to the Babylonian invasion as an imminent event (1:6; 2:1; 3:16). Some scholars suggest Habakkuk was written during the reign of Manasseh (686-642 B.C.) or Amon (642-640 B.C.) because of the list of Judah's sins in 1:2-4. However, the descriptions of the Chaldeans indicated that Babylon had become a world power; and this was not true in the time of Manasseh when Babylon was under the thumb of Assyria. It is also unlikely that this prophecy took place in the time of King Josiah (640-609 B.C.), because

the moral and spiritual reforms of Josiah do not fit the situation in 1:2-4. The most likely date for the book is in the early part of Jehoiakim's reign (609-597 B.C.). Jehoiakim was a godless king who led the nation down the path of destruction (cf. 2 Ki 23:34–24:5; Je 22:17).

The Babylonians began to rise in power during the reign of Nabopolassar (626-605 B.C.), and in 612 B.C. they destroyed the Assyrian capital of Nineveh. By the time of Jehoiakim, Babylon was the uncontested world power. Nabopolassar's successor, Nebuchadnezzar, came to power in 605 B.C. and carried out successful military expeditions in the west, advancing into Palestine and Egypt. Nebuchadnezzar's first invasion of Judah occurred in his first year, when he deported ten thousand of Jerusalem's leaders to Babylon. The nobles who oppressed and extorted from the poor were the first to be carried away. Since Habakkuk prophesied prior to the Babylonian invasion, the probable date for this book is about 607 B.C.

4. The Christ of Habakkuk. The word *salvation* appears three times in 3:13,18 and is the root word from which the name *Jesus* is derived (Ma 1:21). When He comes again, "the earth will be filled with the knowledge of the glory of the LORD, as the waters cover the sea" (2:14).

5. Keys to Habakkuk.

Key Word: "The Just Shall Live by His Faith"—The circumstances of life sometimes appear to contradict God's revelation concerning His power and purposes. Habakkuk struggles in his faith when he sees men flagrantly violate God's law and distort justice on every level, without fear of divine intervention. He wants to know why God allows this growing iniquity to go unpunished. When God reveals His intention to use Babylon as His rod of judgment, Habakkuk is even more troubled, because the nation is more corrupt than Judah. God's answer satisfies Habbakuk that he can trust Him even in the worst of circumstances because of His matchless wisdom, goodness and power. God's plan is perfect, and nothing is big enough to stand in the way of its ultimate fulfillment. In spite of appearances to the contrary, God is still on the throne as the Lord of history and the Ruler of the nations. God may be slow to wrath, but all iniquity will be punished eventually. He is the worthiest object of faith, and the righteous man will trust in Him at all times.

Key Verses: Habakkuk 2:4; 3:17-19—"Behold the proud, his soul is not upright in him; but the just shall live by his faith" (2:4).

"Though the fig tree may not blossom, nor fruit be on the vines; though the labor of the olive may fail, and the fields yield no food, though the flock be cut off from the fold, and there be no herd in the stalls—yet I will rejoice in the LORD, I will joy in the God of my salvation. The LORD God is my strength; He will make my feet like deer's feet, and He will make me walk on my high hills. To the Chief Musician. With my stringed instruments" (3:17-19).

Key Chapter: Habakkuk 3—The Book of Habakkuk builds to a triumphant climax reached in the last three verses (3:17-19). The beginning of the book and the ending stand in stark contrast: mystery to certainty, questioning to affirming, and complaint to confidence. Chapter 3 is one of the most majestic of all Scripture and records the glory of God in past history and in future history (prophecy).

6. Survey of Habakkuk. Habakkuk was a freethinking prophet who was not afraid to wrestle with issues that would test his faith. He openly and honestly directed his problems to God and waited to see how He would respond to his probing questions. After two rounds of dialogue with the Lord, Habakkuk's increased understanding of the person, power, and plan of God caused him to conclude with a psalm of unqualified praise. The more he knew about the Planner, the more He could trust His plans. No matter what God brings to pass, "the just shall live by his faith" (2:4). The two divisions of this book are: the problems of Habakkuk (1–2) and the praise of Habakkuk (3).

The Problems of Habakkuk (1–2): Habakkuk's first dialogue with God takes place in 1:1-11. In 1:1-4, the prophet asks God how long He will allow the wickedness of Judah to go unpunished. The people of Judah sin with impunity, and justice is perverted. God's startling answer is given in 1:5-11: He is raising up the fierce Babylonians as His rod of judgment upon sinful Judah. The Chaldeans will come against Judah swiftly, violently, and completely. The coming storm from the East will be God's answer to Judah's crimes.

This answer leads to Habakkuk's second dialogue with God (1:12–2:20). The prophet is more perplexed than ever and asks how the righteous God can punish Judah with a nation that is even more wicked (1:12–2:1). Will the God whose eyes are too pure to approve evil reward the Babylonians for their cruelty and idolatry? Habakkuk stands upon a watchtower to wait for God's reply. The Lord answered with a series of five woes—of greed and aggression (2:5-8), exploitation and extortion (2:9-11), violence (2:12-14), immorality (2:15-17), and idolatry (2:18-20). God is aware of the sins of the Babylonians, and they will not escape His terrible judgment. But Judah is guilty of the same offenses and stands under the same condemnation. Yahweh concludes His answer with a statement of His sovereign majesty: "But the LORD is in His holy temple. Let all the earth keep silence before Him" (2:20).

The Praise of Habakkuk (3). Habakkuk begins by questioning God, but he concludes his book with a psalm of praise for the person (3:1-3), power (3:4-12), and plans (3:13-19) of God. He now acknowledges God's wisdom in the coming invasion of Judah, and although it terrifies him, he will trust the Lord. God's creative and redemptive work in the past gives the prophet confidence in the divine purposes, and hope at a time when he would otherwise despair. "Yet I will rejoice in the LORD, I will joy in the God of my salvation (3:18).

OUTLINE OF HABAKKUK

I. The Problems of Habakkuk (1:1–2:20)

A. The First Problem of Habakkuk ... 1:1-4
B. God's First Reply 1:5-11
C. The Second Problem of
    Habakkuk 1:12–2:1
D. God's Second Reply 2:2-20

II. The Praise of Habakkuk (3:1-19)

A. Habakkuk Prays for God's
    Mercy 3:1-2
B. Habakkuk Remembers God's
    Mercy 3:3-15
C. Habakkuk Trusts in God's
    Salvation 3:16-19

HA·BAZ·I·NI′ AH

Variant spelling of HABAZZINIAH.

HA·BAZ·ZI·NI′ AH

The father of one Jeremiah (not the prophet) and grandfather of Jaazaniah, a Rechabite (Je 35:3).

HAB′ ER·GEON

A breastplate, a coat of mail (Ex 28:32; 2 Ch 26:14; Ne 4:16).

HABITATION

Dwelling place. Solomon built a beautiful temple to be God's earthly habitation (2 Ch 6:2); now His habitation is the body of believers (Ep 2:22).

HA′ BOR *(joining together)*

A river of Mesopotamia (2 Ki 17:6; 18:11; 1 Ch 5:26).

HAC·A·LI′ AH

See HACHALIAH.

HACH·A·LI′ AH *(darkness of Jehovah)*

Father of Nehemiah (Ne 1:1).

HA·CHI′ LAH *(dark)*

A hill not far from Maon in the wilderness of Ziph (1 Sa 26:1-3).

HACH·MO′ NI *(wise)*

The father of Jehiel, and founder of the family of Hachmonites (1 Ch 11:11; 27:32).

HAC·MO′ NI

See HACHMONI.

HA′ DAD

Four Old Testament men:

1. Son of Ishmael (1 Ch 1:30).

2. An Edomite king, son of Bedad (Ge 36:35-36).

3. An Edomite king of the city of Pai (1 Ch 1:50) who is called Hadar in Genesis 36:39.

4. A prince of Edom who as a child escaped to Egypt when Joab and the Israelites began to slay the males of Edom (1 Ki 11:14-22).

HAD·A·DE′ ZER *(Hadad is helper)*

Son of Rehob and king of Zobah in Syria (2 Sa 8:3). He is also called Hadarezer. He was

king in the time of David and fought many battles against David and the Israelites before he was finally beaten decisively (2 Sa 10:6-19; 1 Ch 19:16-19).

HA·DAD·RIM′ MON

A city in the valley of Megiddo in the plain of Jezreel (Ze 12:11). It was near here that Josiah was slain in his conflict with Pharaoh-necho (2 Ch 35:22-25).

HA′ DAR

See HADAD.

HAD·A·RE′ ZER

See HADADEZER.

HA·DASH′ AH *(new)*

A village of Judah in the lowland (Jos 15:37).

HA·DAS′ SAH *(a myrtle)*

The Jewish name of Esther (Es 2:7). See ESTHER.

HA′ DES

See HELL.

HA′ DID *(sharp)*

A town inhabited by Benjamites (Ez 2:33; Ne 11:34).

HAD·LA′ I

The father of Amasa (2 Ch 28:12).

HA·DOR′ AM

Three Old Testament men:

1. One of the sons of Joktan from whom an Arabian tribe was descended (Ge 10:27; 1 Ch 1:21).

2. A son of Tou, king of Hamath (1 Ch 18:10). He was sent by his father to congratulate David on his victory over Hadadezer.

3. An officer of the tribute appointed by Rehoboam of Judah (2 Ch 10:18), probably the same as Adoniram of 1 Kings 4:6; 5:14.

HA′ DRACH

A country or region of Syria mentioned in Zechariah 9:1.

HAFT (archaic)

A handle (Ju 3:21-22).

HA' GAB *(a locust)*

Head of a family of Nethinim (Ez 2:46).

HAG' A·BA *(locust)*

Head of a family of Nethinim (Ez 2:45; Ne 7:48).

HAG' A·BAH

See HAGABA.

HA' GAR

Sarah's Egyptian bondwoman (Ge 16:1). She bore Abraham a son, Ishmael, after the patriarch decided to wait no longer for God's promise of an heir to be fulfilled through his 76-year old wife, Sarah. When Sarah bore Isaac, Ishmael mocked the boy with the result that Hagar and Ishmael were expelled from Abraham's house into the wilderness. When Hagar's water supply was exhausted the Lord directed her to a well (Ge 21:19).

HAG' A·RENE

See HAGARITE.

HAG' A·RITE

A people inhabiting the region east of Gilead. They were defeated by the Reubenites in the time of Saul (1 Ch 5:10), and are listed as enemies of Israel in Psalm 83:6.

HAG' E·RITE

See HAGARITE.

HAG' GAI *(festive)*

The tenth of the Minor Prophets and the first to prophesy after the exile. He accompanied Zerubbabel from Babylon. His prophesies were made in the second year of Darius Hystaspis in 520 B.C. (Hag 1:1,15; 2:1,10,20). See "Author of Haggai."

HAG' GAI, BOOK OF

1. The Book of Haggai. With the Babylonian exile in the past, and a newly returned group of Jews back in the land, the work of rebuilding the temple could begin. However, sixteen years after the process was begun, the people had yet to finish the project because their personal affairs were interfering with God's business. Haggai preached a fiery series of sermons designed to stir up the nation to finish the temple. He called the builders to renewed courage in the Lord, renewed holiness of life, and renewed faith in God who controls the future.

The etymology and meaning of *haggay* is uncertain, but it is probably derived from the Hebrew word *hag,* "festival." It may also be an abbreviated form of *haggiah,* "festival of Yahweh." Thus, Haggai's name means "festal" or "festive," possibly because he was born on the day of a major feast, such as the Feast of Tabernacles (Haggai's second message took place during that feast, 2:1). The title in the Septuagint is *Aggaios* and in the Vulgate it is *Aggaeus.*

2. The Author of Haggai. Haggai's name is mentioned nine times (1:1,3,12-13; 2:1,10,13-14,20); the authorship and date of the book are virtually uncontested. The unity of theme, style, and dating is obvious. Haggai is known only from this book and from two references to him in Ezra 5:1 and 6:14. There he is seen working alongside the younger prophet Zechariah in the ministry of encouraging the rebuilding of the temple. Haggai returned from Babylon with the remnant under Zerubbabel and evidently lived in Jerusalem. Some think 2:3 may mean that he was born in Judah before the 586 B.C. Captivity and was one of the small company who could remember the former temple before its destruction. This would mean Haggai was about seventy-five when he prophesied in 520 B.C. It is equally likely, however, that he was born in Babylon during the captivity.

3. The Time of Haggai. In 538 B.C. Cyrus of Persia issued a decree allowing the Jews to return to their land and rebuild their temple. The first return was led by Zerubbabel, and in 536 B.C. work on the temple began. Ezra 4–6 gives the background to the Book of Haggai and describes how the Samaritans hindered the building of the temple and wrote a letter to the Persian king. This opposition only added to the growing discouragement of the Jewish remnant. Their initial optimism upon returning to their homeland was dampened by the desolation of the land, crop failure, hard work, hostility, and other hardships. They gave up the relative comfort of Babylonian culture to pioneer in a land that seemed unproductive and full of enemies. Finding it easier to stop building than to fight their neighbors, the work on the temple ceased in 534 B.C. The pessimism of the people led to spiritual lethargy, and they became preoccupied with their own building projects. They used political opposition and a theory that the temple was not to be rebuilt until some later time (perhaps after Jerusalem was rebuilt) as excuses for neglecting the house of the Lord.

It was in this context that God called His prophets Haggai and Zechariah to the same task of urging the people to complete the temple. Both books are precisely dated: Haggai 1:1, September 1, 520 B.C.; Haggai 1:15, September 24, 520 B.C.; Haggai 2:1, October 21, 520 B.C.; Zechariah 1:1, November, 520 B.C.; Haggai 2:10,20, December 24, 520 B.C.; Zechariah 1:7, February 24, 519 B.C.; Zechariah 7:1, December 4, 518 B.C. Zechariah's prophecy commenced between Haggai's second and third messages. Thus, after fourteen years of neglect, work on the temple was resumed in 520 B.C. and was completed in 516 B.C. (Ezra 6:15). The Talmud indicates that the ark of the covenant, the Shekinah glory, and the Urim and Thummim were not in the rebuilt temple.

Darius I (521-486 B.C.) was king of Persia during the ministries of Haggai and Zechariah. He was a strong ruler who consolidated his kingdom by defeating a number of revolting nations.

4. The Christ of Haggai. The promise of Haggai 2:9 points ahead to the crucial role the second temple is to have in God's redemptive plan. Herod the Great later spent a fortune on the project of enlarging and enriching this temple, and it was filled with the glory of God incarnate every time Christ came to Jerusalem.

The Messiah is also portrayed in the person of Zerubbabel: "'I will take you, Zerubbabel . . . and I will make you as a signet ring; for I have chosen you'" (2:23). Zerubbabel became the center of the messianic line and is like a signet ring, sealing both branches together.

5. Keys to Haggai.

Key Word: The Reconstruction of the Temple—Haggai's basic theme is clear: the remnant must reorder its priorities and complete the temple before it can expect the blessing of God upon its efforts. Because of spiritual indifference the people fail to respond to God's attempts to get their attention. In their despondency they do not realize that their hardships are divinely given symptoms of their spiritual disease. Hag-

gai brings them to an understanding that circumstances become difficult when people place their own selfish interests before God's. When they put God first and seek to do His will, He will bring His people joy and prosperity.

Key Verses: Haggai 1:7-8; 2:7-9—"Thus says the LORD of hosts: 'Consider your ways! Go up to the mountains, and bring wood and build the temple, that I may take pleasure in it and be glorified, says the LORD'" (1:7-8).

"'And I will shake all nations, and they shall come to the Desire of All Nations, and I will fill this temple with glory,' says the LORD of hosts. 'The silver is Mine, and the gold is Mine,' says the LORD of hosts. 'The glory of this latter temple shall be greater than the former,' says the LORD of hosts. 'And in this place I will give peace,' says the LORD of hosts" (2:7-9).

Key Chapter: Haggai 2—Verses 6-9 record some of the most startling prophecies in Scripture: "I will shake heaven and earth, the sea and dry land" (the tribulation) and "they shall come to the Desire of All Nations" and "in this place I will give peace" (the second coming of the Messiah.)

6. Survey of Haggai. Haggai is second only to Obadiah in brevity among Old Testament books, but this strong and frank series of four terse sermons accomplishes its intended effect. The work on the temple had ceased, and the people had become more concerned with the beautification of their own houses than with the building of the central sanctuary of God. Because of their misplaced priorities, their labor was no longer blessed by God. Only when the people put the Lord first by completing the task He had set before them would His hand of blessing once again be upon them. Haggai acted as God's man in God's hour, and his four messages are: the completion of the latter temple (1:1-15), the glory of the latter temple (2:1-9), the present blessings of obedience (2:10-19), and the future blessings of promise (2:20-23).

The Completion of the Latter Temple (1:1-15). When the remnant returned from Babylon under Zerubbabel, they began to rebuild the temple of the Lord. However, the work soon stopped and the people found excuses to ignore it as the years passed. They had no problems in building rich dwellings for themselves ("paneled houses," 1:4) while they claimed that the time for building the temple had not yet come (1:2). God withdrew His blessing and they sank into an economic depression. However, they did not recognize what was happening because of their indifference to God and indulgence of self; so God communicated directly to the remnant through His prophet Haggai. Zerubbabel the governor, Joshua the high priest, and all the people responded; twenty-three days later they again began to work on the temple.

The Glory of the Latter Temple (2:1-9). In a few short weeks, the enthusiasm of the people soured into discouragement; the elders remembered the glory of Solomon's temple, and bemoaned the puniness of the present temple (see Ezra 3:8-13). Haggai's prophetic word of encouragement reminds the people of God's covenant promises in the past (2:4-5), and of His confident plans for the future (2:6-9): "The glory of this latter temple shall be greater than the former" (2:9).

The Present Blessings of Obedience (2:10-19). Haggai's message to the priests illustrates the concept of contamination (2:11-13) and applies it to the nation (2:14-19). The Lord requires holiness and obedience, and the contamination of sin blocks the blessing of God. Because the people have obeyed God in building the temple, they will be blessed from that day forward.

The Future Blessings of Promise (2:20-23). On the same day that Haggai addressed the priests, he gave a second message to Zerubbabel. God would move in judgment, and in His power He would overthrow the nations of the earth (2:21-22). At that time, Zerubbabel, a symbol of the Messiah to come, would be honored.

OUTLINE OF HAGGAI

I. The Completion of the Latter Temple (1:1-15)

A. The Temple Is Not Complete 1:1-6
B. The Temple Must Be
Completed 1:7-15

II. The Glory of the Latter Temple (2:1-9)

A. The Latter Temple Is Not as
Glorious as the First..................... 2:1-3
B. The Latter Temple Will Be More
Glorious than the First 2:4-9

III. The Present Blessings of Obedience (2:10-19)

A. The Disobedience of the
Remnant 2:10-14
B. The Solution: The Obedience of
the Remnant 2:15-19

IV. The Future Blessings Through Promise (2:20-23)

A. The Future Destruction of the
Nations 2:20-22
B. The Future Recognition of
Zerubbabel 2:23

HAG′ GE·DO·LIM

The father of Zabdiel who was chief officer of the priests who returned to live in Jerusalem (Ne 11:14). In some translations, Zabdiel is called "the son of one of the great men" (NKJV).

HAG·GE′ RI

The father of Mibhar, one of David's warriors (1 Ch 11:38).

HAG′ GI *(festive)*

One of the sons of Gad and the founder of the family of Haggites (Ge 46:16; Nu 26:15).

HAG·GI′ AH *(festival of Jehovah)*

A Levite of the family of Merari (1 Ch 6:30).

HAG′ GITES

The tribal family descended from Haggi the son of Gad (Nu 26:15).

HAG′ GITH *(festal)*

A wife of David and mother of Adonijah (2 Sa 3:4; 1 Ki 1:5).

HAG′ I·O′ GRA·PHA *(Holy Writings)*

Following the Law and the Prophets, the Hagiographa is the third section of the Hebrew Scriptures. It is also called simply the Writings. It includes Psalms, Proverbs, Job, Song of Solomon, Ruth, Lamentations, Ecclesiastes, Esther, Daniel, Ezra-Nehemiah, 1&2 Chronicles.

HAG′RI

See HAGGERI.

HA′GRITE

See HAGARITE.

HA·HIR′OTH

See PI-HAHIROTH.

HA′I

See AI.

HAIL

Frozen rain. In the Scriptures rain is sometimes considered an instrument of judgment. The seventh Egyptian plague was a hailstorm (Ex 9:18-35). It was used by God to defeat the Amorites (Jos 10:11).

HA′INES

An Egyptian city, probably in middle Egypt (Is 30:4).

HAIR

The Hebrews regarded long hair on the chin and head as a mark of manliness. Long hair was sometimes used as a mark of separation, as when a person chose to take a Nazirite vow (Nu 6:5). Samson's long hair was a symbol of his separation to God, and the power of God working through him. When Delilah cut his hair, the vow was broken, and Samson's supernatural strength was gone (Ju 13-16). David's son Absalom was renowned for his manly beauty, including an extraordinary head of hair (2 Sa 14:26).

The law forbade the Hebrews from cutting the hair at the temples (some translations say "shaving"). This injunction is listed along with such practices as cutting oneself for the dead, or tattooing the body, and it is speculated that such hair cutting was associated with pagan religious practices (Le 19:27).

Hair was worn long by the Assyrians, while the Egyptians cut theirs short except for times of mourning. Hebrew women wore their hair longer than the men. Both sexes used hair oil (Ps 23:5; Ma 6:17).

HAKILAH

See HACHILAH.

HAK′KA·TAN (*little, junior*)

Father of Johanan (Ez 8:12).

HAK′KOZ

Two Old Testament men:

1. A descendant of Aaron. In the time of David his family was made the seventh course, or order, of priests (1 Ch 24:10). When members of this family first returned from Babylon they were unable to establish their genealogy and thus lost their place in the priesthood (Ez 2:61-62; Ne 7:63-64).

2. A man of Judah (1 Ch 4:8).

HA·KU′PHA (*crooked*)

The ancestor of certain Nethinim (Ez 2:51; Ne 7:5,53).

HA′LAH

A place in Assyria to which Israelite captives were deported after the fall of Samaria (2 Ki 17:6; 18:11; 1 Ch 5:26).

HA′LAK (*bare*)

A mountain mentioned in connection with Joshua's conquests (Jos 11:17; 12:7). It was in the south of Palestine.

HALE

To draw; drag; force; to compel (Lk 12:58).

HALF-SHEKEL

Exodus 30:13. See SHEKEL and MONEY OF THE BIBLE.

HALF-TRIBE

When the Israelites began to settle the promised land, the tribe of Manasseh was divided in two. Half of Manasseh, along with Gad and Reuben, wanted to settle on the east side of the Jordan while the other half chose to enter the land with the rest of the tribes (Nu 32:33-42; De 3:12-13; Jos 1:12-18).

HAL′HUL

A village in the hill country of Judah (Jos 15:58) about three miles north of Hebron.

HA′LI (*necklace*)

A town of the tribe of Asher (Jos 19:25).

HAL·LEL′ (*praise the Lord*)

A song of praise to God, sung at Passover time, and at other feasts to commemorate God's mighty works on the behalf of His people. This song is made up of Psalms 113–118.

HAL′LE·LU′JAH

A Hebrew word of adoration which appears at the beginning and end of many psalms and sometimes at both the beginning and end. In the Authorized Version of the Old Testament the Hebrew word is translated "Praise ye the Lord."

Hallelujah is a command (imperative) from the Hebrew verb *halal, praise.* Sometimes *halal* is used to praise merely human qualities: Sarah's beauty (Ge 12:14-15), Absalom's good looks (2 Sa 14:25), an outstanding wife and mother (Pr 31:28,31).

By far the most common use of the verb is to praise the Lord. The *hallelu-* part of the word is not only a command, but the form is plural in Hebrew. This suggests congregational praise. Hence, we are not surprised that the Book of Psalms contains about a third of these uses, because Psalms constitutes the praises of Israel— and now of the church as well.

The praise of God is very important. It should be a delight to His people, not a chore. All of creation should join in His praise (Ps 148:1-2).

Ancient Israel praised the Lord with music, choirs, congregational singing, dance, and even speaking (Je 31:7). The modern church does much the same.

HAL·LO′HESH, HA·LO′HESH

The father of Shallum (Ne 3:12; 10:24).

HALLOWED

Set apart as holy; considered sacred (Ma 6:9).

HA·LO′HESH

See HALLOHESH.

HALT (archaic)

Lame; crippled in the feet (Ma 18:8).

HAM

1. The youngest son of Noah, born when Noah was five hundred years old (Ge 5:32; 6:10; 9:18). He and his two brothers survived the flood with Noah. After Ham mocked his father's nakedness, Noah cursed Ham's son, Canaan, to a life of continual servitude to his brothers (Ge 9:22-27). Ham was founder of one of the three great families that repeopled the earth after the flood (Ge 10:1; 6-20).

2. A term for Egypt used only in biblical poetry (Ps 78:51; 105:23,27; 106:22).

3. A place east of the Jordan where the Zuzim were defeated by Chedorlaomer (Ge 14:5).

4. Some of the inhabitants of Gedor were men of Ham (1 Ch 4:40).

HA′MAN

Son of Hammedatha (Es 3:1). He was called an Agagite (Es 3:1; 9:24), based on his real or alleged descent from Agag whom Samuel cut to pieces (1 Sa 15:33). He was a high official in the court of King Ahasuerus. His intrigue against the Jews was exposed by Esther (Es 7–9). See ESTHER, BOOK OF.

HAMARTIOLOGY

The study of sin as a part of Systematic Theology.

HA′MATH, HE′MATH

1. A city on the Orontes north of Damascus where the Canaanites settled (Ge 10:18). Its King Toi sent his son to congratulate David on his victory over Hadadezer (2 Sa 8:9-10). It was taken by Solomon (2 Ch 8:3-4), but shortly afterwards came again into the hands of the former inhabitants. It was captured by Jeroboam II of Israel (2 Ki 14:28) and later was taken by the Assyrians (2 Ki 18:34; 19:13).

2. The district under the government of the city. One of its towns was Riblah (2 Ki 23:33). It was regarded as the northern border of Israel (Nu 13:21; 34:8; 1 Ki 8:65).

HA′MATH·ITES

The people of Hamath (Ge 10:18).

HA′MATH-ZO′BAH

A city mentioned in 2 Chronicles 8:3, possibly Hamath on the Orontes.

HAMITES

Descendants of Ham.

HAM′MATH (warm springs)

1. The founder of the house of Rechab, a Kenite family (1 Ch 2:55).

2. A fenced city of Naphtali (Jos 19:35). It was probably the same as Hammoth-dor and Hammon (Jos 21:32; 1 Ch 6:76).

HAM·ME·DA′THA

Father of Haman, an Agagite (Es 3:1).

HAM′ME·LECH *(the king)*

Father of Jerahmeel (Je 36:26).

HAM′MER

An ancient tool for smoothing metals, crushing stone, driving tent pins, etc. (Ju 4:21; Is 41:7; Je 23:29).

HAM·MO′LE·CHETH

See HAMMOLEKETH.

HAM·MO′LE·KETH *(the queen)*

The daughter of Machir and the sister of Gilead (1 Ch 7:17-18). Through her son, Abiezer, Gideon was descended (Ju 6:11).

HAM′MON *(warm)*

1. A town of Naphtali. See HAMMATH.

2. A town of Asher (Jos 19:28), a few miles south of Tyre.

HAM′MOTH-DOR *(hot springs of Dor)*

See HAMMATH.

HAM·MU′EL *(warmth of God)*

A son of Mishma of Simeon (1 Ch 4:26).

HAMMURABI

An ancient king of Babylon, who ruled between approximately 1792 and 1750, about 300 years after Abraham. While he is not mentioned in the Bible, he is interesting to Bible students because of his famous law code, called the Code of Hammurabi. This code, which Hammurabi claimed to have received from Shamash, the god of justice, bears striking resemblance to many of the laws of Moses, providing regulations for dealing with crimes, marriage, selling property, the rights of the firstborn, and many other social issues. The seven foot stone pillar containing Hammurabi's code was discovered in 1901-02 at Susa.

HA·MO′NAH *(multitude)*

A city to be built in commemoration of the anticipated defeat of Gog (Eze 39:16).

HA′MON-GOG *(multitude of Gog)*

The name Ezekiel gives to the valley where Gog and his forces were to be destroyed (Eze 39:11,15).

HA′MOR

Prince of the Shechemites (Ge 34:20; Jos 24:32). After his son, Shechem, defiled Dinah,

CODE OF HAMMURABI

daughter of Jacob, he and his son were killed by Dinah's brothers, Simeon and Levi (Ge 34:1-31).

HAM′RAN

See HEMDAN.

HAMSTRING

On a human, the group of tendons reaching from the back of the knee to the muscles of the upper leg; on an animal, the tendon directly above the hock. To "hamstring" means to cripple by cutting this tendon. After a battle, the conquerors would sometimes hamstring the enemies' horses in order to make it impossible for the army to recover or to escape (Jo 11:6,9; 2 Sa 8:4; 1 Ch 18:4).

HAM·U′EL

See HAMMUEL.

HAM′UL *(pitied, spared)*

The younger of the two sons of Pharez and founder of a tribal family of Judah (Ge 46:12; Nu 26:21; 1 Ch 2:5).

HAM′UL·ITES (Nu 26:21)

HAMURAPI

See HAMMURABI.

HA·MU′TAL *(kin to the dew)*

Daughter of Jeremiah of Libnah, wife of Josiah, king of Judah, and mother of Jehoahaz and Zedekiah (2 Ki 23:31; 24:18; Je 52:1).

HAN′A·MEEL

Son of Shallum and cousin of Jeremiah (Je 32:6-12).

HAN′A·MEL

See HANAMEEL.

HA′NAN *(merciful)*

Nine Old Testament men:

1. Son of Shashak, a Benjamite (1 Ch 8:23).

2. Son of Azel, a descendant of Jonathan (1 Ch 8:38; 9:44).

3. One of David's mighty men and son of Maachah (1 Ch 11:43).

4. Chief of a family of Nethinim, some of which came with Zerubbabel from Babylon (Ez 2:46; Ne 7:49).

5. One who assisted Ezra in reading and teaching the law (Ne 8:7)

6. A Levite who sealed the covenant with Nehemiah (Ne 10:10).

7. Two chiefs of the people. They sealed the covenant (Ne 10:22,26).

8. A Levite who was appointed as treasurer over the storehouse of tithes. He was the son of Zaccur (Ne 13:13).

9. Son of Igdaliah, a prophet (Je 35:4). His sons occupied a chamber in the temple.

HAN′A·NEEL *(God has favored)*

A tower near the sheep-gate at Jerusalem and possibly another name for the tower of Meah (Ne 3:1; 12:39; Je 31:38; Ze 14:10).

HAN′A·NEL

See HANANEEL.

HA·NA′NI *(gracious)*

Five Old Testament men:

1. Father of Jehu, the prophet (1 Ki 16:1). He denounced Asa, king of Judah, and was imprisoned (2 Ch 16:7).

2. Son of Heman. He was the head of the eighteenth course of musicians appointed by David for the sanctuary (1 Ch 25:4,25).

3. Son of Immer, a priest. He rejected his foreign wife (Ez 10:20).

4. Nehemiah's brother (Ne 1:2; 7:2).

5. A Levite musician who officiated at the dedication of the wall of Jerusalem (Ne 12:36).

HAN·A·NI′AH *(Jehovah has been gracious)*

1. Son of Zerubbabel and father of Pelatiah and Jeshaiah (1 Ch 3:19,21).

2. Son of Shashak, a Benjamite (1 Ch 8:24).

3. A son of Heman and head of the sixteenth course of musicians appointed by David for the sanctuary (1 Ch 25:4,23).

4. A captain of Uzziah, king of Judah (2 Ch 26:11).

5. One of the family of Bebai who divorced his foreign wife (Ez 10:28).

6. A perfumer who labored on the wall of Jerusalem (Ne 3:8).

7. Son of Shelemiah and a laborer on the wall of Jerusalem (Ne 3:30).

8. One associated with the brother of Nehemiah as governor of the castle at Jerusalem (Ne 7:2).

9. One of the leaders of the people who, with Nehemiah, sealed the covenant (Ne 10:23).

10. A priest of the house of the father of Jeremiah after the exile (Ne 12:12).

11. A priest who participated in the dedication of the wall of Jerusalem (Ne 12:41).

12. Son of Azur, a prophet of Gibeon. He prophesied that the captives would return after two years' captivity. His false prophecy brought upon him the penalty of death (Je 28:1-17).

13. The father of Zedekiah (Je 36:12).

14. The grandfather of Irijah (Je 37:13-15).

15. The original name of Shadrach, one of Daniel's three companions (Da 1:6-7,11; 2:17).

HAND'BREADTH

The breadth of the palm of the hand, with the fingers together (Ex 25:25); used figuratively of the span of life (Ps 39:5). See WEIGHTS AND MEASURES.

HAND'KER·CHIEF

A square of cloth used for various different purposes. It was used in burial to bind the head of the corpse (Jo 11:44; 20:7). Apparently a handkerchief or napkin was a common, useful article, for Acts records that God's power was so strong in Paul that even his handkerchief healed people when they touched it (Ac 19:12). In a parable told by Jesus a man used a napkin as a wrapping for his master's money (Lk 19:20).

HANDS, LAYING ON OF

See LAYING ON OF HANDS.

HANDSPIKE

See JAVELIN, SPEAR.

HANDSTAFF

See JAVELIN, SPEAR.

HANES

See HAINES.

HANG'ING

The usual form of capital punishment among the Jews was stoning, but to emphasize the disgrace the dead body was sometimes hung (Ge 40:19,22; De 21:22; Jos 10:26; 2 Sa 4:12). The hanging body was designed to proclaim the fact that the penalty had been paid. At nightfall it was buried (De 21:23; Jos 8:29). Sometimes one took his life by this means, such as Ahithophel (Absalom's advisor) and Judas (2 Sa 17:23; Ma 27:5). See GALLOWS.

HAN'I·EL *(grace of God)*

Two Old Testament men:

1. Son of Ulla, of Asher (1 Ch 7:39).

2. Son of Ephod, prince of Manasseh (Nu 34:23).

HAN'NAH *(grace)*

One of the two wives of Elkanah; the mother of Samuel. She was especially favored by her husband which aroused the hostility of the other wife who subjected her to annoyances. Hannah was childless, but vowed that if she became the mother of a son, she would dedicate him to the Lord's service. Samuel was born and Hannah kept her vow (1 Sa 1:1-28). Her triumphant song (1 Sa 2:1-10) may have been in the mind of Mary (Lk 1:26-55).

HAN'NA·THON *(favored)*

A town of Zebulun near the border of Asher (Jos 19:14).

HAN'NI·EL

See HANIEL.

HANNUKAH *(Feast of Dedication)*

See Feast.

HA'NOCH *(dedicated)*

Two Old Testament men:

1. A son of Midian and grandson of Abraham and Keturah (Ge 25:4; 1 Ch 1:33).

2. Son of Reuben (Ge 46:9; Ex 6:14; Nu 26:5; 1 Ch 5:3).

HA'NOCH·ITES

Descendants of Hanoch, son of Reuben (Nu 26:5).

HA'NUN *(favored)*

1. Two Jews of that name labored on the wall of Jerusalem under Nehemiah (Ne 3:13,30).

2. A king of the Ammonites. When Hanun's father, Nahash, died, David sent his condolence. His motives were misjudged and it was believed that David's messengers were spies to gather facts that would aid David to capture the capital. They were ill-treated and humiliated. Knowing David would resent this, Hanun secured an alliance with the Syrians but was defeated (2 Sa 10:1–11:1; 1 Ch 19:1–20:3).

HAPH'A·RA·IM

See HAPHRAIM.

HAPH'RA·IM *(two pits)*

A border town of Issachar (Jos 19:19).

HAP′ PIZ·ZEZ

An Aaronite (1 Ch 24:15).

HA′ RA *(mountainous)*

Captives of Israel were taken to this place in Assyria (1 Ch 5:26).

HA·RA′ DAH *(terror)*

An encampment of the Israelites (Nu 33:24).

HAR′ AN

A city and three men of the Old Testament:

1. A city of Mesopotamia in which Abraham settled after leaving Ur. He remained there until after the death of his father, Terah, and then he started for Canaan. The city was a commercial center. Jacob lived in Haran for a time (Ge 28:10; 29:4). It was near this city that Crassus was defeated by the Parthians in 55 B.C.

2. A son of Terah and brother of Abraham who died in Ur. Lot was his son and Milcah and Iscah, his daughters (Ge 11:29).

3. A son of Caleb and Ephah (1 Ch 2:46).

4. A Gershonite Levite of the family of Shimei (1 Ch 23:9).

HAR′ A·RITE

Probably the inhabitant of a place called Harar (2 Sa 23:11,33).

HAR·BO′ NA

A chamberlain in the court of Ahasuerus (Es 1:10; 7:9).

HAR·BO′ NAH

See HARBONA.

HARD BY (archaic)

Beside; close by; next to (1 Ki 21:1).

HARD SAYING

A concept that is difficult to understand, such as Jesus's teaching that He was the Bread of Life (Jo 6:60).

HARE

An unclean animal related to the rabbit (Le 11:6; De 14:7). They appear to chew the cud because of their constant nibbling and gnawing habits, but they do not regurgitate their food for continued chewing as true cud-chewing animals do. Also, they certainly do not have cloven hooves.

HAREM

See HOUSE.

HAR′ EPH

Son of Caleb (1 Ch 2:51).

HARETH, THE FOREST OF

A forest in the land of Judah where David hid from Saul (1 Sa 22:5).

HAR·HAI′ AH

Father of Uzziel, the goldsmith (Ne 3:8).

HAR′ HAS

An ancestor of Shallum, husband of the prophetess Huldah (2 Ki 22:14). In 2 Chronicles 34:22 he is called Hasrah.

HAR′ HUR *(fever)*

Ancestor of certain Nethinim (Ez 2:51; Ne 7:53).

HAR′ IM *(flat-nosed)*

Several Old Testament men:

1. A name connected with certain priestly families. Of the children of Harim, 1,017 returned from Babylon with Zerubbabel (Ez 2:39; Ne 7:42). Certain of the sons of Harim took foreign wives (Ez 10:21). One bearing the name sealed the covenant (Ne 10:5). Another was head of the third order of priests (1 Ch 24:8). Adna represented the family as a priest in the time of Joiakim (Ne 12:12,15). Malchijah, son of Harim, labored on the wall of Jerusalem (Ne 3:11). Once the name appears as Rehum (Ne 12:3).

2. A lay family, representatives of which returned from Babylon with the same caravan as the priests of this name (Ez 2:32; Ne 7:35), married foreign women (Ez 10:31), and signed the covenant (Ne 10:27).

HAR′ IPH *(autumnal)*

Founder of a family, many members of which came to Jerusalem from Babylon with Zerubbabel (Ne 7:24). A prince of this name sealed the covenant (Ne 10:19). It is rendered Jorah in Ez 2:18.

HAR′LOT

A prostitute (Ge 38:15; Le 21:7; De 23:18; Ju 16:1). The Hebrew word most generally used in the Old Testament denotes licentiousness on the part of either sex, married or single, or the wrong conduct of a concubine (Ju 19:2). It is used figuratively to indicate the renouncing of Jehovah for other gods (Je 2:20; 3:1; Eze 23:5). Prostitution was forbidden by the Mosaic law (Le 19:29; 21:9).

HAR MAGEDON

See ARMAGEDDON.

HARMON

The location of this place is not known, but God warned the people of Samaria that they would be cast into Harmon because of their disobedience (Am 4:3).

HAR′NE·PHER

A son of Zophah, a chief of Asher (1 Ch 7:36).

HAR′OD (fear)

It was at the well of Harod that the Israelites under Gideon gathered, preparing to fight the Midianites who were in the nearby valley by the hill of Moreh. Here Gideon carried out his famous test which reduced his army to the 300 men required by the Lord (Ju 7:1-7).

HAR′OD′ITE

A native or resident of the town of Harod (2 Sa 23:25).

HAR·O′EH

A descendant of Shobal, one of the tribe of Judah (1 Ch 2:52).

HAR′O·RITE

Shammoth, one of David's mighty men, is described as a Harorite (1 Ch 11:27).

HA·RO′SHETH HA·GOY′IM

A city called Harosheth of the Gentiles. It is now identified with a village on the northern bank of the Kishon. Here Sisera lived (Ju 4:2,13,16).

HARP

A popular musical instrument among the Hebrews. Its invention antedated the flood (Ge

HARROW

4:21). According to Josephus it had ten strings and was played with a plectrum. However, David played it with his hand (1 Sa 16:23). The harp was a portable instrument which could be hung up (Ps 137:2).

HARPOON

A barbed spear, used to kill large sea animals (Job 41:7).

HAR′ROW

A tool or instrument used by David to torture the Ammonites (2 Sa 12:31; 1 Ch 20:3). It was probably a sledge or pick.

HAR′SHA (enchanter)

The ancestor of certain Nethinim (Ez 2:52; Ne 7:54).

HART

A deer; considered a clean animal (De 12:15; 14:5; 1 Ki 4:23). Its thirst was proverbial (Ps 42:1). See DEER.

HAR′UM (exalted)

The father of Aharhel of Judah (1 Ch 4:8).

HA·RU′MAPH (flat-nose)

Father of Jedaiah (Ne 3:10).

HA·RU′PHITE

A member of the family of Hariph (1 Ch 12:5).

HAR′UZ (active)

The father-in-law of Manasseh, king of Judah (2 Ki 21:19).

HAR′VEST

In the southern portion of Palestine and in the plains the crops ripened about the middle of April, but in the northern sections about the first week of May. Barley preceded wheat by about two weeks (Ru 2:23). In the Jordan Valley, where the heat was more intense, barley was harvested in April (Jos 3:15; 1 Sa 12:17-18). Great rejoicings attended the harvesting (Is 9:3).

HAR′ VEST, FEAST OF

See WEEKS, FEAST OF.

HARVESTER

A daily laborer who hired himself out to different farmers at harvest time. See LABORER.

HAS·A·DI′ AH *(kindness of Jehovah)*

Son of Zerubbabel (1 Ch 3:20).

HAS·E·NU′ AH

See HASSENUAH.

HASH·A·BI′ AH *(Jehovah regards)*

Nine Old Testament men:

1. A Levite of the family of Merari (1 Ch 6:45).

2. Son of Jeduthun, a Merarite Levite. He was appointed by David to be head of a company of musicians for the sanctuary (1 Ch 25:3,19).

3. A Levite of the family of Hebron (1 Ch 26:30).

4. Son of Kemuel, a Levite. He was a captain during the reign of David (1 Ch 27:17).

5. A chief of the Levites during the reign of Josiah (2 Ch 35:9).

6. A Levite of the family of Merari who came with Ezra from Babylon and who, with others, had charge of the treasure and the temple music (Ez 8:19,24; Ne 10:11; 12:24).

7. A ruler of Keilah in the time of Nehemiah. He worked on the wall of Jerusalem (Ne 3:17).

8. Grandfather of Uzzi, the overseer of the Levites (Ne 11:22).

9. A priest of the house of Hilkiah (Ne 12:21).

HA·SHAB′ NAH

One who sealed the covenant with Nehemiah (Ne 10:25).

HASH·AB·NE·I′ AH

See HASHABNIAH.

HASH·AB·NI′ AH

1. A Levite who, with others, exhorted the people regarding the sealing of the covenant (Ne 9:5).

2. Father of Hattush. The son labored on the wall of Jerusalem (Ne 3:10).

HASH·BA·DA′ NA

One who stood at Ezra's left as the law was read (Ne 8:4).

HASH·BAD·DA′ NA

Variant of HASHBADANA.

HASH′ EM

One of those listed among David's warriors; a Gizonite (1 Ch 11:34). See JASHEN.

HASH·MO′ NAH *(fertility)*

A place where the Israelites encamped (Nu 33:29-30).

HASH′ UB

See HASSHUB.

HA·SHU′ BAH *(esteemed)*

A son of Zerubbabel (1 Ch 3:20).

HASH′ UM *(wealthy)*

The head of a family, members of which came with Zerubbabel from Babylonia (Ez 2:19; 10:33; Ne 7:22).

HA·SHU′ PHA

See HASUPHA.

HAS·MO·NE′ AN

The family dynasty which ruled Israel during the years from 135 to 63 B.C. When Antiochus Epiphanes defiled the temple in an attempt to subdue the Jews, Judas Maccabeus led the revolt which brought independence to the nation. Judas Maccabeus's brother was appointed as High Priest, and this brother's son, John, was the first Hasmonean ruler. The Hasmoneans ruled Israel until 63 B.C. when Rome took over. See INTERTESTAMENTAL PERIOD.

HAS′ RAH

The grandfather of the husband of Huldah the prophetess. He is also described as "the keeper of the wardrobe" (2 Ch 34:22; in 2 Ki 22:14 he is called Harhas).

HAS·SE·NA′ AH *(thorny)*

Father of the men who built the fish-gate of Jerusalem (Ne 3:3). Without the article the name is *Senaah*. About 3,000 of his descendants returned from Babylon with Zerubbabel (Ez 2:35; Ne 3:3; 7:38).

HAS·SE·NU′AH, HAS·E·NU′AH *(thorny)*

1. Father of Hodaviah, a Benjamite (1 Ch 9:7).

2. Father of Judah, a Benjamite overseer of Jerusalem (Ne 11:9). The name is rendered *Senuah* in the KJV.

HAS′SHUB, HASH′UB

1. A Levite; father of Shemaiah (1 Ch 9:14; Ne 11:15).

2. Laborers on the wall of Jerusalem (Ne 3:11, 23).

3. A signer of the covenant (Ne 10:23).

HAS·SO′PHE·RETH

See SOPHERETH.

HA·SU′PHA, HA·SHU′PHA

Head of a family of Nethinim, some of the members of which returned from Babylon (Ez 2:43; Ne 7:46).

HAT

An article of clothing worn by Shadrach, Meshach, and Abed-nego when they were thrown into the fiery furnace (Da 3:21, KJV). It is translated *turban* in the NKJV.

HA′TACH

A chamberlain in the court of Ahasuerus. He served Esther (Es 4:5,10).

HA′THACH

See HATACH.

HA′THATH *(terror)*

A son of Othniel of Judah (1 Ch 4:13).

HA·TI′PHA

Founder of a family of Nethinim, some of the members of which returned with Zerubbabel from Babylon (Ez 2:54; Ne 7:56).

HA·TI′TA *(dug)*

Ancestor of a family of porters, or gatekeepers. Some of this family returned from Babylon with Zerubbabel (Ez 2:42; Ne 7:45).

HAT′TIL *(vacillating)*

A servant of Solomon. Members of his family were of the company of Zerubbabel (Ez 2:57; Ne 7:59).

HAT′TUSH

Five Old Testament men:

1. A descendant of David who came with Ezra to Jerusalem (Ez 8:2).

2. Son of Shemaiah of Judah (1 Ch 3:22).

3. A priest who came with Zerubbabel to Jerusalem (Ne 12:2,7).

4. A son of Hashabniah. He helped to build the wall of Jerusalem (Ne 3:10).

5. A priest who sealed the covenant with Nehemiah (Ne 10:4).

HAUGHTY

Proud; arrogant; lifted up (Ps 131:1).

HAU′RAN *(cave land)*

This district, south of Damascus, was known to the Greeks and Romans as Auranitis. On the north and northwest were Trachonitis and Batanea (Eze 47:16,18). This district was given to Herod the Great by Augustus but later, in the division of his kingdom, these sections fell to the tetrarchy of Philip (Lk 3:1).

HAVEN

A calm harbor or port for ships to land; figuratively a safe place, a refuge (Ps 107:30).

HAVENS, FAIR

See FAIR HAVENS.

HAV′I·LAH

1. A son of Cush or of Joktan (Ge 10:7,29).

2. A district probably in central or southwestern Arabia, famous for its gold and precious stones (Ge 2:11). It bordered the territory of the Ishmaelites and was bounded by the Pison River (Ge 2:10-12).

HA′VOTH-JA′IR *(hamlets of Jair)*

A group of towns east of the Jordan in Gilead (Nu 32:40-41; Ju 10:3-4) or in Bashan (De 3:13-14; Jos 13:30).

HAV′VOTH-JA′IR

See HAVOTH-JAIR.

HAWK

One of the unclean birds (Le 11:16; De 14:15). In Lebanon, and in the hilly regions of Galilee, the sparrow hawk is numerous.

HAY

Grass which has been cut and dried for use as fodder for animals (Pr 27:25; Is 15:6; 33:1; 5:24).

HA·ZA′ EL *(God has seen)*

A Syrian whom Jehovah directed Elijah to anoint king over Syria (1 Ki 19:15,17). Ben-hadad was then king; his capital being at Damascus. Elisha came to the city. The king was seriously ill and he sent Hazael to Israel's prophet to inquire the issue of his sickness. When Hazael was informed that the king would die and that he would take the throne, he returned to Ben-hadad and falsely stated that the king would recover, and the following day assassinated him (2 Ki 8:7-15). Shortly after he ascended the throne, Shalmaneser, king of Assyria, came into conflict with him and demanded that he pay tribute. In the reign of Jehu, king of Israel, Hazael attacked the tribes east of the Jordan (2 Ki 10:32). In the reign of Jehoahaz he severely oppressed the Israelites (2 Ki 13:4-7), captured Gath, the city of the Philistines, and would have attacked Jerusalem had not the treasures of the temple been given to him (2 Ki 12:17-18).

HA·ZAI′ AH *(Jehovah has seen)*

Son of Adaiah, a descendant of Perez (Ne 11:5).

HA′ ZAR-AD′ DAR

See ADDAR.

HA′ ZAR-E′ NAN *(village of fountains)*

A village of Palestine near Damascus (Nu 34:9; Eze 47:17; 48:1).

HA′ ZAR-E′ NON

See HAZAR-ENAN.

HA′ ZAR-GAD′ DAH *(village of fortune)*

A town in Judah (Jos 15:27).

HA′ ZAR-HAT′ TI·CON

See HAZER-HATTICON.

HA·ZAR·MA′ VETH *(village of death)*

The son of Joktan (Ge 10:26; 1 Ch 1:20).

HA′ ZAR-SHU′ AL *(fox village)*

Town in the south of Judah (Jos 15:28; 19:3; 1 Ch 4:28).

HA′ ZAR-SU′ SAH *(village of horses)*

A village of Simeon in southern Judah (Jos 19:5; 1 Ch 4:31).

HA′ ZAR-SU′ SIM

See HAZAR SUSAH.

HAZ′ A·ZON-TA′ MAR

See EN-GEDI.

HA′ ZEL

A tree mentioned as being found in the region in which Laban lived (Ge 30:37, KJV). Many believe that a more correct translation would be *almond*.

HAZ·EL·EL-PO′ NI

A woman of Judah, daughter of Etam (1 Ch 4:3).

HA′ ZER-HAT′ TI·CON

A border town of the Hauran (Eze 47:16).

HA·ZE′ RIM *(villages)*

The towns peopled by the Avvim (De 2:23).

HA·ZE′ ROTH

A place in the wilderness where the Israelites camped after leaving Sinai (Nu 11:35; 12:16; 33:17; De 1:1); the scene of the sedition of Miriam and Aaron (Nu 11:35–12:16).

HA·ZE′ ZON-TA′ MAR

See EN-GEDI.

HA′ ZI·EL *(vision of God)*

Son of Shimei, a Levite of the family of Gershon (1 Ch 23:9).

HA′ ZO *(vision)*

The son of Nahor (Ge 22:22).

HA′ ZOR

Four towns and a district:

1. The capital of the Canaanites in the northern part of Palestine. In the time of Joshua the king was Jabin. It was destroyed by Joshua (Jos 11:1-13; 12:19) and afterwards assigned to Naphtali (Jos 19:36). In the time of the judges another Jabin ruled. His general, Sisera, was defeated by Deborah and Barak (Ju 4:1-24; 1 Sa 12:9).

2. A village of Benjamin (Ne 11:33). After the exile it was inhabited by Benjamites.

3. A town in the extreme south of Judah. It was also called Kerioth-hezron (Jos 15:25). See HEZRON.

4. An unidentified town of southern Judah (Jos 15:23).

5. A district in the Arabian desert (Je 49:28-33).

HA' ZOR-HA·DAT' TAH

A town of Judah (Jos 15:25). The KJV translates this as two towns, Hazor and Hadattah.

HAZ·ZEL·EL·PO' NI

See HAZELELPONI.

HEAD' BAND

An article of female dress, some think the word probably ought to read "sash" or "girdle" (Is 3:20). It is translated *attire* in Jeremiah 2:32.

HEADDRESSES

An article of female attire; a veil or shawl worn as a head covering (Is 3:20). Various different sorts of headdresses were worn in different parts of the country, and by different classes of women.

HEADY (archaic)

Reckless; hasty; headstrong (2 Ti 3:1-4).

HEALING, GIFT OF

See SPIRITUAL GIFTS.

HEART

The word in the Scriptures has a wide range of meanings:

First, the physical heart, the center of bodily life (Ps 40:8,10,12), and the things that contribute to its health and strength (Ju 19:5; Ac 14:17).

Second, the higher rational, spiritual activities. The set purpose to do a thing (Es 7:5; Ro 6:17); holding firmly and steadfastly to a purpose (1 Co 7:37); rational activities in thought, perception, understanding (De 29:4; Pr 8:5; 14:10; Is 44:18), reflecting (Lk 2:19) and judging (Pr 16:9). The seat of the affections and emotions as joy (Is 65:14); fear (De 28:28; Ps 143:4); hatred (Le 19:17); love (1 Ti 1:5).

Third, as an expressive of moral characteristics and conditions. The hardening of the heart (Is 6:10; 63:17; Je 16:12; 2 Co 3:15); the keeping

of the heart because it determines the issues of life (Pr 4:23), as true of thoughts, words and deeds (Ma 12:34; Mk 7:21); the seat of passions (Mk 4:15; Ro 1:24); for the moral government of life God's law is written in the heart (Is 51:7; Je 31:33; Ro 2:15; He 10:22).

Fourth, the deeper spiritual life. The dwelling place of Christ (Ep 3:17) and of the Holy Spirit (2 Co 1:22); where the love of God is felt (Ro 5:5), and his peace is realized (Col 3:15); where we enjoy the deeper communion with God (Ep 5:19).

See also BOWELS.

HEARTH

Fireplace or firepit. (Ge 18:6; Je 36:23).

HEATH

A shrub or small tree; possibly a variety of juniper (Je 17:6; 48:6-7).

HEA' THEN

Worshipers of false gods, or those who do not worship the God of the Bible. The Greek *Ethnos,* which is frequently translated *heathen,* is literally "nation" or "people." Their hostility to the true religion brought them under divine judgment (Ps 79:1,6,10; Je 10:25; Eze 36:6,7,15). The Jew, under strict legal requirements, did not eat food that came from the heathen, and did not sit down for a meal at a Gentile table (Ac 11:3; Gal 2:12). See GENTILES.

HEAV' EN, THE HEAV' ENS

1. The region about the earth—the heavens and the earth (Ge 1:1), comprising the universe (Ge 14:19; Je 23:24). The mass beyond the visible firmament (Ge 1:7; Ps 108:4). To the Jews the highest, or seventh heaven, was God's dwelling place. Paul relates a personal experience in which he was carried into the third heaven, but whether he was bodily transported to it, or it was a vision, he did not know (2 Co 12:1-4).

2. The place of God's presence from whence Christ came and to which he returned (Ps 80:14; Is 66:1; Ma 5:16,45,48; Jo 3:13; Ac 1:11). It is from here he will come in his return to the earth (Ma 24:30; Ro 8:33-34; 1 Th 4:16; He 6:20). Heaven is the dwelling place of angels (Ma 28:2; Lk 22:43) and the future home of the redeemed (Ep 3:15; 1 Pe 1:4; Re 19:1-4).

HEAVENLY CITY

The city which will be the dwelling place of God and His saints after the end of the world; also called the New Jerusalem (He 11:10,16; 12:22; 13:14; Re 21–22).

HEAVENS, NEW (Is 66:22)

See EARTH, NEW.

HEAVE OFFERING

See OFFERINGS.

HE′BER

Seven Old Testament men:

1. A Benjamite, son of Elpaal, a descendant from Shaharaim (1 Ch 8:17).

2. Son of Beriah and grandson of Asher (Ge 46:17). His descendants were called Heberites (Nu 26:45).

3. A descendant of Hobab, a Kenite. It was his wife, Jael, who slew Sisera (Ju 4:11-24).

4. A Judahite descendant of Ezra and ancestor of the men of Socoh (1 Ch 4:18).

5. One of the chiefs of the Gadites in Bashan (1 Ch 5:13).

6. A Benjamite, son of Shashak (1 Ch 8:22).

7. The son of Sala and father of Phalec (Lk 3:35).

HE′BER·ITES

Descendants of Heber, the grandson of Asher (Nu 26:45; Ge 46:17).

HE′BREW (pertaining to Eber)

A designation first applied to Abraham, a descendant of Eber (Ge 14:13). It was applied by foreigners to the Israelites (Ge 39:14,17; 41:12; Ex 1:16; 1 Sa 4:6,9), and the Israelites used the word in regard to themselves (Ge 40:15; Ex 1:19). In the New Testament it is used to describe those whose speech was Aramaic to distinguish them from Greek-speaking Jews (Ac 6:1). Paul called himself a Hebrew of the Hebrews, indicating that his parents were of Hebrew stock (Ph 3:5).

HE′BREW LANGUAGE

Hebrew was the language of the Israelites. It is a Semitic language consisting of twenty-two consonants and reads from right to left. The Old Testament, with the exception of a few portions written during the exile and the restoration, was written in Hebrew. To the time of the Captivity the language was quite pure, but following the exile it was mixed with Aramaic until it ceased to be used. By the time of Christ, Aramaic prevailed and was called Hebrew (Jo 19:13, 17,20; Ac 21:40; 22:2; 26:14).

HE′BREWS, EPIS′TLE TO THE

1. The Book of Hebrews. Many Jewish believers, having stepped out of Judaism into Christianity, wanted to reverse their course in order to escape persecution by their countrymen. The writer of Hebrews exhorts them to "go on to perfection" (6:1). His appeal is based on the superiority of Christ over the Judaic system. Christ is better than the angels, for they worship Him. He is better than Moses, for He created him. He is better than the Aaronic priesthood, for His sacrifice was once for all time. He is better than the law, for He mediates a better covenant. In short, there is more to be gained in Christ than to be lost in Judaism. Pressing on in Christ produces tested faith, self-discipline, and a visible love seen in good works.

Although the King James Version uses the title "The Epistle of Paul the Apostle to the Hebrews," there is no early manuscript evidence to support it. The oldest and most reliable title is simply *Pros Ebraious,* "To Hebrews."

2. The Author of Hebrews. Like the ancestry of Melchizedek, the origin of Hebrews is unknown. Uncertainty plagues not only its authorship, but also where it was written, its date, and its readership. The question of authorship delayed its recognition in the West as part of the New Testament canon in spite of early support by Clement of Rome. Not until the fourth century was it generally accepted as authoritative in the Western church, when the testimonies of Jerome and Augustine settled the issue. In the Eastern church, there was no problem of canonical acceptance because it was regarded as one of the "fourteen" epistles of Paul. The issue of its canonicity was again raised during the Reformation, but the spiritual depth and quality of Hebrews bore witness to its inspiration, despite its anonymity.

Hebrews 13:18-24 tells us that this book was not anonymous to the original readers; they evidently knew the author. For some reason, however, early church tradition is divided over the identity of the author. Part of the church attributed it to Paul; others preferred Barnabas,

Luke, or Clement; and some chose anonymity. External evidence does not provide much to help determine the author.

Internal evidence must be the final court of appeal, but here, too, the results are ambiguous. Some aspects of the language, style, and theology of Hebrews are very similar to Paul's epistles, and the author also refers to Timothy (13:23). However, significant differences have led the majority of biblical scholars to reject Pauline authorship of this book: (1) The Greek style of Hebrews is far more polished and refined than that found in any of Paul's recognized epistles. (2) In view of Paul's consistent claims to be an apostle and an eyewitness of Christ, it is very doubtful that he would have used the phraseology found in 2:3: "which at first began to be spoken by the Lord, and was confirmed to us by those who heard Him." (3) The lack of Paul's customary salutation, which includes his name, goes against the firm pattern found in all his other epistles. (4) While Paul used both the Hebrew text and the Septuagint to quote from the Old Testament, the writer of Hebrews apparently did not know Hebrew and quoted exclusively from the Septuagint. (5) Paul's common use of compound titles to refer to the Son of God is not followed in Hebrews, which usually refers to Him as simply Christ, Jesus, or Lord. (6) Hebrews concentrates on Christ's present priestly ministry, but Paul's writings have very little to say about the present work of Christ. Thus, Hebrews appears not to have been written by Paul although the writer shows a Pauline influence. The authority of Hebrews in no way depends upon Pauline authorship, especially since it does not claim to have been written by Paul.

Tertullian referred to Barnabas as the author of Hebrews, but it is unlikely that this resident of Jerusalem (Ac 4:36-37) would include himself as one of those who relied on others for eyewitness testimony about Jesus (2:3). Other suggestions have included Luke, Clement of Rome, Apollos, Silvanus (Silas), Philip, and even Priscilla. Some of these may be reasonable possibilities, but we must agree with the third-century theologian Origen who wrote: "Who it was that really wrote the Epistle, God only knows."

3. The Time of Hebrews. Because of the exclusive use of the Septuagint (Greek translation of the Hebrew Old Testament) and the elegant Greek style found in Hebrews, some recent scholars have argued that this book was written to a gentile readership. However, the bulk of the evidence favors the traditional view that the original recipients of this letter were Jewish Christians. In addition to the ancient title "To Hebrews," there is also the frequent use of the Old Testament as an unquestioned authority, the assumed knowledge of the sacrificial ritual, and the many contrasts between Christianity and Judaism, which are designed to prevent the readers from lapsing into Judaism.

Many places have been suggested for the locality of the readers, but this letter's destination cannot be determined with any certainty. In the past, Jerusalem was most frequently suggested, but this view is hindered by four problems: (1) It is unlikely that a book addressed to Hebrews in Israel would quote exclusively from the Septuagint rather than the Hebrew Old Testament. (2) Jewish believers in Palestine were poor (Ro 15:26), but these readers were able to financially assist other Christians (6:10). (3) Residents of Jerusalem would not be characterized by the description in 2:3 because some would have been eyewitnesses of the ministry of Christ. (4) "You have not yet resisted to bloodshed" (12:4) does not fit the situation in Jerusalem. The majority view today is that the recipients of Hebrews probably lived in Rome. The statement "Those from Italy greet you" in 13:24 seems to suggest that Italians away from Italy are sending their greetings home.

The recipients of this letter were believers (3:1) who had come to faith through the testimony of eyewitnesses of Christ (2:3). They were not novices (5:12), and they had successfully endured hardships because of their stand for the gospel (10:32-34). Unfortunately, they had become "dull of hearing" (5:11) and were in danger of drifting away (2:1; 3:12). This made them particularly susceptible to the renewed persecutions that were coming upon them (12:4-12), and the author found it necessary to check the downward spiral with "the word of exhortation" (13:22). While there is disagreement over the specific danger involved, the classic position that the readers were on the verge of lapsing into Judaism to avoid persecution directed at Christians seems to be supported by the whole tenor of the book. Hebrews' repeated emphasis on the superiority of Christianity over Judaism would have been pointless if the readers were about to return to Gnosticism or heathenism.

The place of writing is unknown, but a reasonable estimate of the date can be made. Hebrews was quoted in A.D. 95 by Clement of Rome, but its failure to mention the ending of the Old Testament sacrificial system with the destruction of Jerusalem in A.D. 70 indicates that it was written prior to that date. Timothy was still alive (13:23), persecution was mounting, and the old Jewish system was about to be removed (12:26-27). All this suggests a date between A.D. 64 and 68.

4. The Christ of Hebrews. Christ is our eternal High Priest according to the order of Melchizedek. He identified with man in His incarnation and offered no less a sacrifice than Himself on our behalf.

Hebrews presents Christ as the divine-human Prophet, Priest, and King. His deity (1:1-3,8) and humanity 2:9,14,17-18) are asserted with equal force, and over twenty titles are used to describe His attributes and accomplishments (e.g., Heir of all things, Apostle and High Priest, Mediator, Author and Perfecter of faith). He is superior to all who went before and offers the supreme sacrifice, priesthood, and covenant.

5. Keys to Hebrews.

Key Word: The Superiority of Christ— the basic theme of Hebrews is found in the word *better,* describing the superiority of Christ in His person and work (1:4; 6:9; 7:7,19,22; 8:6; 9:23; 10:34; 11:16,35,40; 12:24). The words *perfect* and *heavenly* are also prominent. He offers a better revelation, position, priesthood, covenant, sacrifice, and power. The writer develops this theme to prevent the readers from giving up the substance for the shadow by abandoning Christianity and retreating into the old Judaic system. This epistle is also written to exhort them to become mature in Christ and to put away their spiritual dullness and degeneration. Thus, it places heavy stress on doctrine, concentrating on Christology and soteriology (the study of salvation).

Key Verses: Hebrews 4:14-16 and 12:1-2— "Seeing then that we have a great High Priest who has passed through the heavens, Jesus the Son of God, let us hold fast our confession. For we do not have a High Priest who cannot sympathize with our weaknesses, but was in all points tempted as we are, yet without sin. Let us therefore come boldly to the throne of grace,

that we may obtain mercy and find grace to help in time of need" (4:14-16).

"Therefore we also, since we are surrounded by so great a cloud of witnesses, let us lay aside every weight, and the sin which so easily ensnares us, and let us run with endurance the race that is set before us, looking unto Jesus, the author and finisher of our faith, who for the joy that was set before Him endured the cross, despising the shame, and has sat down at the right hand of the throne of God" (12:1-2).

Key Chapter: Hebrews 11—The hall of fame in the Scriptures is located in Hebrews 11 and records those who willingly took God at His word even when there was nothing to cling to but His promise. Inherent to all those listed is the recognition that "without faith it is impossible to please Him, for he who comes to God must believe that He is, and that He is a rewarder of those who diligently seek Him" (He 11:6).

6. Survey of Hebrews. Hebrews stands alone among the New Testament Epistles in its style and approach, and it is the only New Testament book whose authorship remains a real mystery. This profound work builds a case for the superiority of Christ through a cumulative argument in which Christ is presented as "better" in every respect. In His person He is better than the angels, Moses, and Joshua; and in His performance He provides a better priesthood, covenant, sanctuary, and sacrifice. Evidently, the readers are in danger of reverting to Judaism because of the suffering they are beginning to experience for their faith in Christ. However, by doing so, they would be retreating from the substance back into the shadow. In addition to his positive presentation of the supremacy of Christ, the writer intersperses five solemn warnings about the peril of turning away from Christ (2:1-4; 3:7–4:13; 5:11–6:20; 10:19-39; 12:25-29). These parenthetical warnings include cautions against neglect (2:1-4) and refusal (12:25-29). After using the Old Testament to demonstrate the superiority of Christ's person (1:1–4:13) and the superiority of Christ's work (4:14–10:18), the writer applies these truths in a practical way to show the superiority of the Christian's walk of faith (10:19–13:25).

The Superiority of Christ's Person (1:1–4:13). Instead of the usual salutation, this epistle immediately launches into its theme—the supremacy of Christ even over the Old Testament prophets (1:1-3). Christianity is built upon the highest form of divine disclosure: the personal revelation of God through His incarnate Son. Christ is therefore greater than the prophets, and He is also greater than the angels, the mediators of the Mosaic law (1:4–2:18; see 2:2; Ac 7:53). This is seen in His name, and His incarnation. The Son of God partook of flesh and blood and was "made like His brethren" in all things (2:17) in order to bring "many sons to glory" (2:10). Christ is also superior to Moses (3:1-6), for Moses was a servant in the house of God, but Christ is the Son over God's household. Because of these truths, the readers are exhorted to avoid the divine judgment that is visited upon unbelief (3:7–4:13). Their disbelief had prevented the generation of the exodus from becoming the generation of the conquest, and the rest that Christ offers is so much greater than what was provided by Joshua. The readers are therefore urged to enter the eternal rest that is possessed by faith in Christ.

The Superiority of Christ's Work (4:14–10:18). The high priesthood of Christ is superior to the Aaronic priesthood (4:14–7:28). Because of His incarnation, Christ can "sympathize with our weaknesses," having been "in all points tempted as we are, yet without sin" (4:15). Christ was not a Levite, but He qualified for a higher priesthood according to the order of Melchizedek. The superiority of Melchizedek to Levi is seen in the fact that Levi, in effect, paid tithes through Abraham to Melchizedek (7:9-10). Abraham was blessed by Melchizedek, and the "lesser is blessed by the better" (7:7). The par-

enthetical warning in 5:11–6:20 exhorts the readers to "go on to perfection" by moving beyond the basics of salvation and repentance.

By divine oath (7:21), Christ has become a permanent and perfect high priest and the "Mediator of a better covenant" (8:6). The new covenant has made the old covenant obsolete (8:6-13). Our great high priest similarly ministers in "the greater and more perfect tabernacle not made with hands, that is, not of this creation" (9:11). And unlike the former priests, He offers Himself as a sinless and voluntary sacrifice once and for all (9:1–10:18).

The Superiority of the Christian's Walk of Faith (10:19–13:25). The author applies what he has been saying about the superiority of Christ by warning his readers of the danger of discarding their faith in Christ (10:19-39). The faith that the readers must maintain is defined in 11:1-3 and illustrated in 11:4-40. The triumphs and accomplishments of faith in the lives of Old Testament believers should encourage the recipients of "something better" (11:40) in Christ to look "unto Jesus, the author and finisher of our faith" (12:2). Just as Jesus endured great hostility, those who believe in Him will sometimes have to endure divine discipline for the sake of holiness (12:1-29). The readers are warned not to turn away from Christ during such times, but to place their hope in Him. The character of their lives must be shared by their dedication to Christ (13:1-19), and this will be manifested in their love of each other through their hospitality, concern, purity, contentment, and obedience. The author concludes this epistle with one of the finest benedictions in Scripture (13:20-21) and some personal words (13:22-25).

OUTLINE OF HEBREWS

Part One: The Superiority of Christ's Person (1:1–4:13)

I. The Superiority of Christ over the Prophets (1:1-3)

II. The Superiority of Christ over the Angels (1:4–2:18)

A. Christ is Superior Because of His Deity 1:4-14

B. First Warning: Danger of Neglect 2:1-4

C. Christ is Superior Because of His Humanity 2:5-18

III. The Superiority of Christ over Moses (3:1–4:13)

A. Christ is Superior to Moses in His Work 3:1-4

B. Christ is Superior to Moses in His Person 3:5-6

C. Second Warning: Danger of Unbelief 3:7–4:13

Part Two: The Superiority of Christ's Work (4:14–10:18)

I. The Superiority of Christ's Priesthood (4:14–7:28)

A. Christ is Superior in His Position 4:14-16

B. Christ is Superior in His Qualifications 5:1-10

C. Third Warning: Danger of Not Maturing 5:11–6:20

D. Christ is Superior in His Priestly Order 7:1-28

II. The Superiority of Christ's Covenant (8:1-13)

A. A Better Covenant 8:1-6

B. A New Covenant 8:7-13

III. The Superiority of Christ's Sanctuary and Sacrifice (9:1–10:18)

A. Old Covenant's Sanctuary and Sacrifice 9:1-10

B. New Covenant's Sanctuary and Sacrifice 9:11–10:18

Part Three: The Superiority of the Christian's Walk of Faith (10:19–13:25)

I. Exhortation to Full Assurance of Faith (10:19–11:40)

A. Hold Fast the Confession of Faith 10:19-25

B. Fourth Warning: Danger of Drawing Back 10:26-39

C. Definition of Faith 11:1-3

D. Examples of Faith 11:4-40

II. Endurance of Faith (12:1-29)

A. Example of Christ's Endurance 12:1-4

B. Exhortation to Endure God's Chastening 12:5-24

C. Fifth Warning: Danger of Refusing God 12:25-29

III. Exhortation to Love (13:1-17)

A. Love in the Social Realm 13:1-6

B. Love in the Religious Realm 13:7-17

IV. Conclusion (13:18-25)

HE´BRON *(alliance)*

Two men and two towns of the Old Testament:

1. A son of Kohath and grandson of Levi, the founder of a tribal family (Ex 6:18; Nu 3:19; 1 Ch 6:2,18). His descendants are called Hebronites (Nu 3:27).

2. The son of Mareshah, a descendant of Judah (1 Ch 2:42-43).

3. A town in the hill country of Judah, the oldest town of Palestine and one of the oldest in the world. It is about twenty miles from Beersheba and the same distance from Jerusalem. The original name was Kirjath-arba (Ge 23:2; Jos 14:15; 20:7). Included in it were the plains of Mamre (Ge 13:18; 35:27). It antedated Zoan in Egypt by seven years (Nu 13:22). For a long time it was the residence of Abraham (Ge 13:18) and here Sarah was buried (Ge 23:17-20). Isaac and Jacob also lived here (Ge 35:27) and David made it his capital until the taking of Jerusa-

lem (2 Sa 2:1-4; 5:5; 1 Ki 2:11). It was also one of the Levitical cities of refuge. See CITIES OF REFUGE.

4. A town of Asher (Jos 19:28). See EBRON.

HE´BRON·ITES

Descendants of Hebron, the Kohathite (Nu 3:27).

HEDGEHOG

See PORCUPINE.

HE´GAI

A chamberlain of Ahasuerus (Es 2:3,8,15).

HE´GE

See HEGAI.

HEIF´ER

A young female cow (Ge 15:9; 1 Sa 6:7-12; Job 21:10; Is 7:21).

HEIR

Hebrew law relative to inheritance was simple. The property was divided between the sons of a legitimate wife. The sons of a concubine did not inherit. Ishmael, the son of Hagar, the bondwoman, could not inherit because of Abraham's other son, Isaac, the son of Sarah, the free woman (Ge 21:10). The birthright falling to the eldest son secured for him a double portion of the property (De 21:15-17). When the children consisted wholly of daughters, they received the property (Nu 27:1-8), but they were required to marry in their tribal family (Nu 36:1-12). If a man died childless the brothers inherited and if he had no brethren, the property went to his father's brethren (Nu 27:9-11). In the case of a widow being childless the law required the nearest of kin on her husband's side to marry her, and if he refused, the next of kin (Ru 3:12-13).

HE′LAH (rust)

One of the two wives of Ashur (1 Ch 4:5,7).

HE′LAM

A place east of the Jordan where David defeated Hadarezer (2 Sa 10:16-19).

HEL′BAH (fatness)

A town of Asher in which the Canaanites were allowed to remain (Ju 1:31).

HEL′BON (fertile)

This town of Syria, north of Damascus (Eze 27:18), was famous for its wines.

HEL′DAI

Two Old Testament men:
1. A descendant of Othniel. He was a captain in David's army and commanded 24,000 men (1 Ch 27:15).
2. One who returned from Babylon. With the gold and silver he carried with him, Zechariah made crowns for Joshua (Ze 6:10-14).

HE′LEB (fatness)

One of David's mighty men (2 Sa 23:29), elsewhere called Heled.

HELECH

The NIV and NRSV translate Ezekiel 27:11 as "men of Arvad and Helech," while the NKJV and KJV say, "men of Arvad with your army."

HE′LED (endurance)

Son of Baanah, one of David's warriors (1 Ch 11:30).

HE′LEK (a portion)

Son of Gilead of Manasseh (Nu 26:30; Jos 17:2).

HE′LEK·ITES

Descendants of Helek, grandson of Manasseh (Nu 26:30).

HE′LEM (strength)

Two Old Testament men:
1. Brother of Shomer and Japhlet, one of the leaders of the Asher family (1 Ch 7:32,35), probably the same as Hotham.
2. One of those who assisted Zechariah in crowning Joshua, the high priest. He was probably the same as Heldai (Ze 6:10,14).

HE′LEPH

A town of Naphtali (Jos 19:33).

HE′LEZ

Two Old Testament men:
1. An Ephraimite, one of David's warriors (2 Sa 23:26; 1 Ch 11:27).
2. Son of Azariah of Judah, descended from Hezron (1 Ch 2:39).

HE′LI (Greek form of Eli)

Father of Joseph who was the husband of Mary, the mother of Jesus (Lk 3:23).

HELIOPOLIS

See ON.

HEL·KA′I

A priest in the time of Joiakim (Ne 12:15).

HEL′KATH (field)

A town on the eastern border of Asher (Jos 19:25), assigned to the Levites (Jos 21:31). In 1 Chronicles 6:75 it is called Hukok.

HEL′KATH-HAZ·ZU′RIM (full of sharp edges)

The name given to the place near the pool of Gibeon (2 Sa 2:16). See FIELD OF SHARP SWORDS.

HELL

A word meaning the place of the dead. It is a frequent translation of the Hebrew word *sheol* and the Greek words *hades* and *gehenna*. The early Hebrews regarded it merely as the place to which the dead go but later the word came to mean a place of punishment.

1. *Sheol* in Hebrew meant the realm of the dead. But the Semitic conception of it was vague. They thought of it as beneath the earth (Eze 31:17; Am 9:2), entered by gates (Is 38:10). In Sheol the sinful and the righteous were either punished or rewarded. See SHEOL.

2. *Hades,* a Greek term used in the New Testament. According to a parable told by Jesus it was a place where good and evil people lived close together, but were separated by a chasm. Those who had led a good life on earth were comforted; those who had not were punished. See ABRAHAM'S BOSOM.

3. *Gehenna,* the place of eternal punishment, the antithesis of heaven, to which the wicked were cast after the last judgment. It is depicted as a fiery furnace (Ma 13:42), and as a lake of fire (Re 19:20; 20:10,14-15; 21:8). See GEHENNA.

HEL'LEN·IST *(Grecian)*

A Greek-speaking Jew (Ac 6:1; 9:29).

HEL'MET

Armor designed to protect the head (1 Sa 17:5; Je 46:4). Metal is the most effective material for a helmet, but such materials as thick leather may also have been used.

HELMSMAN

The one who sets the course and steers the boat (Ac 27:11). Also referred to as the pilot, master, or captain.

HE'LON *(strong)*

Father of Eliab, prince of Zebulun (Nu 1:9; 2:7; 7:24,29; 10:16).

HELPER

When Jesus was preparing His disciples for His departure, He promised them that He would send them a Helper, the Holy Spirit (Jo 14:16,26; 15:26; 16:7). See HOLY SPIRIT.

HELPMEET

God saw that it was not good for Adam to be alone and designed Eve as a helpmeet for him (Ge 2:18). Because of God's unique creative de-

sign, men and women have quite different, but complimentary characteristics.

HEM

The border of an outer garment (Ex 28:33; Nu 15:38-39; Ma 9:20; 14:36; 23:5).

HE'MAM

See HOMAM.

HE'MAN *(faithful)*

Three Old Testament men:

1. Son of Joel and grandson of Samuel, the Kohathite prophet (1 Ch 6:33; 15:17), a singer in the time of David.

2. One who was distinguished for his wisdom in the time of Solomon (1 Ki 4:31).

3. A son (or clan) of the Judahite Zerah (1 Ch 2:6), probably alluded to in the title of Psalm 88 as Heman the Ezrahite.

HE'MATH

See HAMATH.

HEM'DAN *(pleasant)*

Son of Dishon (Ge 36:26). He is called Amram (Hamran in the Revised Version) in 1 Chronicles 1:41.

HEM'LOCK

A poisonous herb (Ho 10:4), translated *gall* in Amos 6:12 and *wormwood* in Amos 5:7.

HEMORRHAGE

Uncontrolled flow of blood. The woman whom Jesus healed in Luke 8:43-44 apparently had some kind of menstrual complication which resulted in a continual bleeding, and hence, continual uncleanness.

HEN

1. A female fowl (Ma 23:37; Lk 13:34).
2. Son of Zephaniah (Ze 6:14).

HEMLOCK

HE' NA

A town which fell to the Assyrians (2 Ki 18:34; 19:13; Is 37:13).

HEN·A' DAD *(favor of Hadad)*

A Levite (Ez 3:9; Ne 3:18).

HEN' NA

A fragrant plant having clusters of white flowers (Song 1:14; 4:13). It was found in the region of En-gedi and Jericho. The leaves were used to dye the fingernails and feet. It is called camphire in the KJV.

HE' NOCH

See ENOCH and HANOCH.

HE' PHER *(pit, well)*

Three men and a town of the Old Testament:
1. Son of Gilead and great-grandson of Manasseh (Nu 27:1; Jos 17:2). His descendants were called Hepherites (Nu 26:32).
2. Son of Ashur of Tekoa, a Judahite (1 Ch 4:6).
3. One of David's heroes, a Mecherathite (1 Ch 11:36).
4. A town west of the Jordan taken by Joshua (Jos 12:17).

HE' PHER·ITES

Descendants of Hepher, the grandson of Manasseh (Nu 26:32).

HEPH' ZI·BAH *(my delight is in her)*

1. Wife of Hezekiah of Judah and mother of Manasseh (2 Ki 21:1).
2. A symbolic name given Zion by Isaiah. Once Zion had been called "Forsaken," but this name was changed to Hephzi-bah when it found favor with the Lord (Is 62:4).

HERALD

One who makes announcements or carries a message, especially for a king (Da 3:4). A herald often had the job of going before a king to prepare the way for him. One might say that John the Baptist was a herald, and also that those who preach the gospel are heralds.

HERB

In the creation account of Genesis, this word is used to indicate green plants of all kinds (Ge 1:12).

HERBS, BITTER

See BITTER HERBS.

HERD

A group or flock of domestic animals which feed together and are cared for together. Herds of cattle, sheep, camels, donkeys and horses were kept by ancient peoples (Job 1:3; Ge 13:5; 32:7; 45:10).

HERDSMAN

One who cares for a herd of domestic animals. Amos the prophet was a herdsman (Am 1:1; 7:14).

HE' RES *(sun)*

A mountain in Aijalon to which the children of Dan were forced by the Amorites (Ju 1:34-35).

HE' RESH *(artificer)*

A Levite (1 Ch 9:15).

HER' E·SY

A New Testament expression used to denote a sect or party with perceived false or incorrect beliefs (or its beliefs) within a Christian group (Ac 24:14; 1 Co 11:19). See HERETIC.

HER' ETH

See HARETH, THE FOREST OF.

HERETIC

One who promotes heresy (Tit 3:10-11).

During the Middle Ages and after the Reformation, untold thousands were burned at the stake as heretics. The word simply meant they held views different from the ones taught by the established church. Sometimes this meant they were people who denied a major doctrine of the orthodox Christian Faith (such as the Trinity). Often it meant they went back to the Bible and believed doctrines that were no longer taught by the church. One example would be salvation by grace through faith, and not of works (Ep 2:8-9).

Titus 3:10 is the only place in the New Testament where *hairetikos* occurs; the KJV translates it as "a man that is an heretick." However, this is a later meaning of the word. The word comes from the verb "to choose," which occurs three times in the Greek New Testament. It means to choose one's own opinion, and it came to mean "to cause a faction or split around that view." Hence, nearly all modern versions translate this verse much like the NKJV: "Reject a divisive man after the first and second admonition, knowing that such a person is warped and sinning, being self-condemned" (Tit 3:10-11). It is not necessary to teach a major heresy to split a church, school, or denomination. A divisive person can gather followers around any kind of minor detail of religion.

While we must maintain freedom of religion, we must also be submissive to the standard doctrine of God's Word. Otherwise, we can become guilty of starting a sect (Gr. *hairesis,* from which word we get *heresy,* although we have added the thought of false doctrine to the word).

HERITAGE

See HEIR.

HER′MAS

A Christian who lived in Rome; one of those to whom Paul sent greetings in his Epistle to the Romans (Ro 16:14).

HERMENEUTICS *(interpretation)*

Proper interpretation of the Bible. This can be seen as both a science and an art, because proper interpretation is carried out by following scientific principles, but it also requires skill and discernment. The whole goal of hermeneutics, or Bible interpretation, is to discover the intended meaning of the author, both the human instrument and the divine author. It is not a method for discovering personal or special meanings for Scripture passages.

Good hermeneutics must begin with three presuppositions: First, we must understand that we are working with a divinely inspired book, not just any ancient writing. We do not have to sort truth from error. Second, each passage has only one right interpretation. The meaning will not change with the times, or according to who is reading it. Each passage may have many, many applications, and even a multifaceted interpretation, but it will not have several contradictory interpretations. Third, we must look at Scripture realizing that most of it is very straightforward and easy to interpret. It has been said, "If the plain sense makes good sense, seek no other sense, lest you produce nonsense." Because the Bible is a spiritual book, it can be tempt-

ing to "spiritualize" some otherwise simple and clear passages. We must carefully avoid this. Only when there is overwhelming reason (such as the rest of Scripture) for not taking a passage in its plain, natural, obvious meaning, can we begin to look for a nonobvious interpretation.

The study and interpretation of the Bible should be accompanied by prayer, humility, and openness. One of the first ways we get into trouble with Bible interpretation is when we struggle to "interpret" it according to our preconceived notions. In order to be good interpreters, we need to be open to the Bible changing our views on some things.

It would be hard to put too much stress on the importance of taking Scripture in context. There are many humorous and painful examples of out of context phrases and sentences being used to "prove" a certain doctrine or point. If we are really serious about understanding God's Word, we must look at each verse in the context in which God placed it. In the same way, it is important to check out the historical and cultural background. Understanding the culture of the times will often give us insight into the full significance of a passage. It can also be very helpful to look at how other Christians over the centuries have interpreted certain passages, and why they did so.

Whenever a difficult passage is reached, in which the plain sense does not seem to make good sense, the difficult passage must always be interpreted with other Scripture. In this way we can avoid saying, "I don't like what this says, I think that it really must mean this instead," with no real basis for our opinions. If, on the other hand, we examine the rest of Scripture for any verses bearing on the subject of the difficult passage, we can be pretty sure of coming to the right conclusion.

When the Bible is read carefully, with an open heart, and the mind is used to examine the text with both wisdom and common sense, God's Holy Spirit will open the Scriptures to us and give us insight and understanding.

HER′MES

1. The messenger of the gods. The Greek Hermes corresponds to the Roman Mercury with his swift winged feet (Ac 14:12).

2. A Christian at Rome, to whom Paul sent greetings (Ro 16:14).

HER·MOG′ E·NES *(sprung from Hermes)*

One of those who abandoned Paul. He lived in the Roman province of Asia (2 Ti 1:15).

HER′ MON *(peak or sacred)*

A mountain on the northern boundary of the territory taken by the Israelites from the Amorites (De 3:8; Jos 11:3,17; 12:1,5). It rises 10,000 feet above the sea and is visible from most parts of Palestine. Snow can be seen at the summit during the entire year. The Jordan River rises here. Hermon was doubtless the high mountain on which Christ was transfigured (Mk 9:2).

HER′ MO·NITES

Natives of Mount Hermon (Ps 42:6).

HER′ OD

Herod was the family name of several Roman rulers who served as provincial governors of Palestine and surrounding regions during New Testament times.

The first Herod, known as Herod the Great, was the Roman ruler of Palestine during the days of the Roman Emperor Caesar Augustus when Jesus was born in Bethlehem (Ma 2:1; Lk 3:1). All the other different Herods mentioned in the New Testaments were the sons or grandsons of this Herod.

Herod the Great (ruled 37-4 B.C), was known as a master builder, organizer, and developer, although his policies were considered cruel and ruthless by the Jewish people. His most notable achievement was the rebuilding of the temple in Jerusalem—a project that required almost fifty years. He also rebuilt and enlarged the city of Caesarea into a port city on the Mediterranean Sea. Caesarea served as the Roman provincial capital for Palestine during the New Testament era. The magnificent aqueducts that he built at this city are still visible today.

Herod's son Antipas succeeded him as Roman governor of Galilee and Perea (Ma 14:1). Antipas was responsible for the imprisonment and death of John the Baptist (Lk 3:19-20; Ma 14:1-12).

Herod the Great's grandson Agrippa was named ruler over all of Palestine by the Roman emperor Caligula. Agrippa is known as a persecutor of early Christians. He had James put to death and had Peter arrested. Because of his cruelty and blasphemy, Agrippa was slain by an angel of the Lord (Ac 12).

In A.D. 50, Agrippa's son, known as Agrippa II, was made ruler of the king of Chalcis's territory. Later he was given Abilene, Trachonitis, Acra, and important parts of Galilee and Perea. The only reference to this Herod in the New Testament occurs in Acts 25:13–26:32, which deals with Paul's imprisonment in Caesarea. Agrippa II listened to Paul's defense, but the apostle appealed to Rome. Agrippa II had no power to set him free.

The other two Herods mentioned in the New Testament are Herod Archelaus (Ma 2:22) and Herod Philip (Lk 3:1). Both of these rulers were sons of Herod the Great; they ruled parts of the territory administered by their father.

THE HERODIAN FAMILY
HEROD THE GREAT
1. Son of Antipater an Idumean, born 62 B.C., died 4 B.C. (Ma 2; Lk 1).
2. His titles: Herod the King; King of Judea; Herod the Great.
3. Herod given Galilee by his father in 47 B.C.
4. Won the favor of Antony, and Herod and his brother Phasael were appointed tetrarchs of Judea.
5. By the aid of Antony he was made King of Judea.
6. Under Augustus, nearly all of Palestine was added to his territory.
7. His satanic sister, Salome, encouraged him in his crimes.
8. Sought to destroy Jesus, massacred the infants.
9. He had nine wives. The principal ones are given below.
PRINCIPAL WIVES AND POSTERITY OF HEROD
I. Doris. Mother of Antipater. The son executed by his father a few days before his own death.
II. Mariamne, daughter of Alexander and Alexandra, of the Maccabees (Hasmoneans). Put to death by Herod B.C. 29. Her two sons:
1. Alexander. Executed B.C. 5.
2. Aristobulus. Executed B.C. 5.
a. Herod Agrippa I. Son of Aristobulus.
(1) Made tetrarch of Abilene and of the districts formerly pertaining to the tetrarchy of Philip.
(2) Winning favor in Rome he obtained Galilee and Perea, and later Judea and Samaria —the whole of Palestine.
(3) To please the Jews he killed James, the brother of John, and proceeded to take Peter (Ac 12:1-3).
(4) His awful death (Ac 12).
b. Herod Agrippa II. Son of Herod Agrippa I.
(1) Given the small principality of Chalcis by Claudius.
(2) Shortly afterwards made sovereign of the tetrarchies formerly belonging to Philip and Lysanias.
(3) He, Bernice and Festus, addressed by Paul (Ac 25–26).
(4) His wife (niece), Bernice.
c. Drusilla. Daughter of Herod Agrippa I, and sister of Herod Agrippa II (Ac 12:1,9).
(1) Betrothed to Antiochus Epiphanes, prince of Commagene, but married Azizas, king of Emesa. Celebrated for her beauty.
(2) Felix, procurator of Judea, brought about her seduction by means of the Cyprian sorcerer, Simon, and took her as his wife.
(3) She was with Felix in Caesarea when Paul addressed them, and Felix trembled. (Ac 24:24).

PRINCIPAL WIVES AND POSTERITY OF HEROD—*Cont'd*

(4) They had a son named Agrippa who, with his mother, perished in the eruption of Vesuvius, 79 A.D.
(5) Felix had three wives, each named Drusilla, and one of them the granddaughter of Antony and Cleopatra, the latter the last of the Ptolemies.

III. Mariamne, second, daughter of Simon, the high priest. Mother of Herod Philip.
   1. Philip was disinherited.
   2. In private life only (Ma 14; Mk 6; Lk 3:19).
   3. His wife, Herodias, deserted him for Herod Antipas, son of Malthace.
   4. Salome, the dancer, his daughter by Herodias (Ma 14:6).

IV. Malthace, of Samaria. Her two sons:
   1. Archelaus.
      a. Brought up in Rome.
      b. He received Judea, Samaria, Idumea.
      c. Married Glaphyra, widow of Alexander, son of Mariamne.
      d. The worst of the sons of Herod.
      e. After he had ruled nine years Judah and Samaria could no longer endure his tyranny and complained to Augustus.
      f. Banished to Vienne by Augustus. From this time to 41 A.D., Palestine was under Roman procurators.
      g. Mentioned once in the New Testament (Ma 2:22).
   2. Herod Antipas.
      a. Brought up in Rome with Archelaus his brother.
      b. Received Galilee and Perea of his father's estate.
      c. His wife, daughter of King Aretas of Arabia.
      d. Formed an unholy attachment for Herodias, wife of his half-brother Philip.
      e. Aretas, to avenge his daughter, sent an army against Herod, who appealed to Rome, and Aretas was ordered to desist.
      f. Rebuked by John the Baptist for taking his brother, Philip's wife, he imprisoned John. Made a foolish vow when pleased with the dancing of Salome, daughter of Herodias. She requested the head of John, whom Herod then beheaded. References: Ma 14:1-12; Mk 6:14-28; Lk 3:19-20; 9:.9; Ac 12:20-23.
      g. Went to Rome to obtain the title of King, was accused of hostility to Rome. Caligula banished him and Herodias to Spain, where he died in misery.

V. Cleopatra of Jerusalem. Mother of Herod Philip, the Tetrarch.
   1. Received of his father's estate, Auranitis, Trachonitis, Paneas, Batanea. Luke speaks of Iturea and Trachonitis (Lk 3:1. See also Ac 13:1).
   2. Characterized by justice and moderation.
   3. Married his niece, Salome, the dancer, daughter of Herodias and Philip.
   4. Ruled for 38 years and maintained peace in his country.

HE·RO′DI·ANS

An influential group, probably a Jewish political party which is thrice mentioned in the New Testament (Ma 22:16; Mk 3:6; 12:13).

HE·RO′DI·AS

Granddaughter of Herod the Great and sister of King Herod Agrippa. Herodias deserted her first husband, Herod Philip, and married Herod Antipas, Philip's half-brother. Antipas divorced his first wife, the daughter of the king of Arabia, and when John the Baptist denounced this, he was imprisoned. Herodias was the mother of the dancer, Salome, who asked for and received the head of John the Baptist (Ma 14:3-12; Mk 6:17-29; Lk 3:19-20).

HE·RO′DI·ON

A Christian at Rome to whom Paul sent his greeting (Ro 16:11).

HER′ON

An unclean bird having a long bill, long legs, and large wings (Le 11:19; De 14:18). Herons are marsh and lake birds which eat fish and frogs.

HE′SED

Father of one of Solomon's officers of provisions (1 Ki 4:10).

HESH′BON

An ancient city of Moab about 20 miles east of the Dead Sea, taken by Sihon, king of the Amorites, who made it his capital. It and the surrounding cities were allotted by Moses to Gad and Reuben (Nu 32:1-3; 31-37; Jos 13:10). Eventually it became a Levitical city (Jos 13:26; 21:39). The pools of Heshbon are mentioned in Song of Solomon 7:4.

HESH′MON *(fatness)*

A town in the south of Judah (Jos 15:27).

HESRON

See HEZRON.

HETH

See HITTITES.

HETH′LON *(hiding place)*

A city on the ideal boundary of Palestine (Eze 47:15; 48:1).

HEW

To cut and shape wood with an ax or adze (2 Ch 2:10; Am 5:11). In the days before circular saws and such machinery, large beams were hewed out of logs with a sharp tool.

HEXETEUCH

Sometimes the first six books of the Bible are grouped together as the Hexeteuch, including Joshua with the five books of Moses rather than with the Former Prophets (Judges, 1 and 2 Samuel, 1 and 2 Kings).

HEZ′E·KI

See HIZKI.

HEZ·E·KI′AH

Four Old Testament men:

1. King of Judah, son of Ahaz. Unlike his godless father, he was a man of outstanding piety in his service of Jehovah. He reorganized the temple service and celebrated the Passover to which he invited the tribes of Israel (2 Ch 29:1–30:13). He brought about a revival of religion and worked earnestly to drive out idolatry. He was greatly assisted by the prophet, Isaiah.

2. A son of Neariah of Judah (1 Ch 3:23).

3. Head of a family which returned from exile (Ez 2:16; Ne 7:21).

4. Ancestor of the prophet Zephaniah (Zep 1:1).

HEZ·E·KI′AH'S WATER TUNNEL

The long underground shaft known as Hezekiah's water tunnel, or the Siloam tunnel was dug through solid rock under the city wall of Jerusalem by King Hezekiah of Judah in the eighth century B.C. (2 Ki 20:20). The tunnel linked the Gihon Springs outside the city walls to the water reservoir known as the Pool of Siloam inside the city walls. It was dug to provide water to the city in case of a prolonged siege by Assyrian forces.

Built around 700 B.C., the crooked shaft is 1,750 feet long, often running 60 feet below the surface of the earth. It was rediscovered in 1838, but little scientific exploration and excavation work was done on the channel until 1866. Not until 1910 was it cleared of debris left by the destruction of Jerusalem in 586 B.C. A walk through Hezekiah's tunnel is a popular activity for modern tourists while visiting Jerusalem.

An inscription in Hebrew found in the tunnel near the Pool of Siloam describes the construction project. Two separate crews worked from opposite ends and eventually met in the middle of the shaft. Digging far below the earth's surface in bedrock, they labored for months in semidarkness with crude hand tools under difficult breathing conditions. But their hard work was rewarded when the Pool of Siloam began to fill with precious water that would spell the difference between life and death for Jerusalem if the Assyrians should attack the city.

A tactic used by besieging armies against walled cities was to cut off food and water supplies to the people inside (2 Ki 6:26-29). Hezekiah's tunnel and pool was more than a marvel of ancient engineering; it was a brilliant survival strategy. Hezekiah's tunnel may not have been the first water shaft dug at Jerusalem. There is some evidence that when David captured the city from the Jebusites, about three hundred years before Hezekiah's time, his men gained entrance to the walled city through some sort of water shaft.

HE′ZI·ON *(vision)*

Father of Tabrimmon and grandfather of Ben-hadad (1 Ki 15:18).

HE′ZIR *(swine)*

Two Old Testament men:

1. A descendant of Aaron. In the time of David his family became the seventeenth course of the priests (1 Ch 24:15).

2. One of the chief men with Nehemiah (Ne 10:20).

HEZ′RA·I *(walled in)*

One of David's mighty men, a Carmelite (2 Sa 23:35).

HEZ′RO

See HEZRAI.

HEZ′RON

1. A son of Reuben. His descendants were called Hezronites (Ge 46:9; Ex 6:14; Nu 26:6; 1 Ch 5:3).

2. A Judahite whose descendants were also called Hezronites (Ge 46:12; Nu 26:21; Ru 4:18).

3. A place on the southern boundary of Judah (Jos 15:3). It is identified with Hazor in Jos 15:25.

HID·DA′I

One of David's mighty men (2 Sa 23:30).

HID′DE·KEL

One of the four rivers of Eden (Ge 2:14), usually identified with the Tigris.

HIDDEN TREASURE, PARABLE OF (Ma 13:44)

HI′ EL *(God liveth)*

A native of Beth-el. In the reign of Ahab he rebuilt Jericho (1 Ki 16:34), thus bringing upon himself the curse pronounced by Joshua (Jos 6:26).

HI·ER·A′ PO·LIS *(sacred city)*

A town of Asia Minor in the valley of the Lycos (Col 4:13).

HIG·GAI′ ON

A Hebrew word found in three psalms. In Psalm 9:16 it is transliterated as a technical musical term, the meaning of which is lost.

HIGH GATE

A gate of Jerusalem (2 Ch 23:20; 27:3), also called the Upper Gate.

HIGH PLACE

The Hebrew *bamah,* originally a height or elevation; specifically a place of worship (Nu 22:41). In the course of time the term was extended to include sanctuaries regardless of elevation—some were even in valleys. It was a center of worship often used by Israelites as well as by their heathen neighbors. Usually it consisted of a small plot of comparatively level ground containing a rude altar and religious symbols, especially stone pillars and asherahs, or wooden poles. Before the building of Solomon's temple, Israel often worshipped Jehovah in a high place (1 Sa 9:12-14,19). But because of the heathenism pervading these centers, the worship of Jehovah became increasingly corrupted. They were condemned by law (Nu 33:52; De 33:29) and by the prophets (Is 16:12; Je 7:31; Eze 6:13).

HIGH PRIEST

When the priesthood was instituted in the wilderness, Moses consecrated his brother Aaron as the first high priest of Israel (Ex 28:29; Le 8–9). The priesthood was set within the tribe of Levi, from which Aaron was descended, and Aaron's sons inherited the position of high priest from their father.

The high priest's dress (see illustration) represented his function as mediator between God and people. Over his regular priestly garments the high priest wore an ephod, a two-piece apron. He also wore a breastplate of judgment with twelve precious stones. These were engraved with the names of the twelve tribes of Israel (Ex 28:15-30). In the pocket of the breastplate, directly over the high priest's heart, were the Urim and Thummim (Ex 28:30), the medium through which God communicated His will to the people.

The high priest was responsible for seeing that the duties of all the priests were carried out (2 Ch 19:11). His most important responsibility occurred annually on the Day of Atonement. On this day he entered the holy of holies, or the Most Holy Place, in the tabernacle and made sacrifice first for his own sins, then for the sins committed by all the people during the year just ended (Ex 30:10).

David organized twenty-four groups of priests to serve at the tabernacle during his reign as king of Judah. Kings Hezekiah and Josiah assisted the high priest in reform and restoration of the temple. In the New Testament, the high priest was referred to as ruler of the people (Ac 23:4-5) and presided over the Sanhedrin, the highest ruling body of the Jews (Ma 26:57-59).

The New Testament speaks of Jesus in figurative terms as a "high priest." He was not of the order of Aaron but of Melchizedek, an eternal priesthood (He 5:10). He had no need to offer sacrifices for His own sin, for He had no sin (He 7:27-28). He offered His own blood, once for all (He 9:12,26; 10:10,12). Therefore, we may come boldly into the presence of God through the "one Mediator between God and men, the Man Christ Jesus" (1 Ti 2:5).

HIGHWAY

See ROADS, PALESTINIAN and ROADS, ROMAN.

HI′ LEN

See HOLON.

HIL·KI′ AH *(Jehovah is my portion)*

Eight Old Testament men:

1. Father of Eliakim in the reign of Hezekiah (2 Ki 18:18,26; Is 22:20; 36:3).

2. The high priest who found the Book of the Law in the reign of Josiah and assisted the reform work of the king (2 Ki 22:4-14; 23:4; 1 Ch 6:13; 2 Ch 34:9-22).

3. Son of Amzi, a Levite, of the Merari family (1 Ch 6:45-46).

4. Son of Hosah, a Levite of the Merari branch (1 Ch 26:11).

5. The father of Jeremiah, priest of Anathoth (Je 1:1).

6. Father of Gemariah in the time of Jeremiah (Je 29:3).

7. One who was associated with Ezra (Ne 8:4).

8. A priest who returned with Zerubbabel from Babylon (Ne 12:7).

HIL′ LEL *(he has praised)*

1. Father of Abdon, the judge; a Pirathonite (Ju 12:13,15).

2. A famous Jewish rabbi who flourished from about 30 B.C. to A.D. 9.

HILL OF FORESKINS *(Gibeath-haaroloth)*

The place where Joshua circumcised all the Israelites who had been born during the forty years in the wilderness (Jo 5:3,9).

HILL OF GOD

A hill where a high place was set up for worshipping God. Saul was filled with the Spirit here, and prophesied (1 Sa 10:5).

HILT

The handle of a sword or dagger. Eglon, slain by the left-handed Israelite hero Ehud, was so fat that the hilt of the dagger disappeared in his flesh (Ju 3:12-30).

HIN

A liquid measure equal to about one gallon (Ex 29:40). See WEIGHTS AND MEASURES.

HIND

The female hart or fallow deer (Ge 49:21; Ps 18:33; Song 2:7). See DEER.

HINDER. (archaic)

Latter; rear; behind (Ze 14:8)

HINGE

In the East doors turned on pivot pins, the weight of the door resting on the lower pin. The pivots fitted into sockets. The hinges of the doors to the temple were solid gold (1 Ki 7:50; Pr 26:14).

HIN′ NOM, VAL′ LEY OF

A rocky ravine stretching west and south of Jerusalem (Jos 15:8, 18:16). It was here that parents sacrificed their children to Moloch by making them walk through fire. Hezekiah's father, Ahaz, and his son, Manasseh, were guilty of this practice (2 Ch 28:3; 33:6). The high place, or point of worship, was broken down by Josiah (2 Ki 23:8,10). See GEHENNA and HELL.

HI′ RAH (nobility)

An Adullamite who became a friend of Judah (Ge 38:1,12).

HIRAM, HURAM

1. A king of Tyre who greatly enlarged his city. When David captured Jerusalem, Hiram sent to him an embassy and later furnished the timber and workmen for David's house (2 Sa 5:11). He was also a friend of Solomon and contracted with him to furnish timber and workmen for the building of the temple (1 Ki 5:1-12; 2 Ch 2:3-16). He assisted Solomon in securing from Ophir precious metals (1 Ki 9:26-28). Solomon offered him twenty towns in Galilee which he did not accept (1 Ki 9:10-12; 2 Ch 8:1-2).

2. One whose mother was a widow of either the tribe of Naphtali or of Dan. His father was from Tyre (1 Ki 7:13-14). Hiram was a workman on Solomon's temple (1 Ki 7:13-46; 2 Ch 2:13-14).

HIRELING (archaic)

A laborer employed on hire (Is 16:14).

HISS

An expression of scorn and contempt (Job 27:23; La 2:15-16).

HIT′ TITES

The Hittites were a people of the ancient world who flourished in Asia Minor and surrounding regions between about 1900 B.C. and 1200 B.C. While the Hittites are mentioned prominently in the Bible, some scholars questioned the existence of these people for many years because there was little physical evidence of their empire. But recent discoveries of Hittite culture by archeologists have confirmed the accuracy of the biblical accounts.

The Hittite nation, with Hattusa as capital (see photo), eventually spread into northern Syria, then into the land of Canaan. Hittites are mentioned in the Bible during the earliest time of Israel's history.

When Sarah died, Abraham bought a burial cave from Ephron the Hittite (Ge 23:10-20). Isaac's son Esau took two Hittite women as wives (Ge 26:34). Several centuries later, the Hittites were included among the groups that would have to be driven out of Canaan before Israel could possess the land (Ex 3:8; De 7:1).

In David's time, Ahimelech the Hittite was a trusted companion of David during his flight from Saul (1 Sa 26:6). Uriah the Hittite, Bath-sheba's husband, was sent to his death by David to cover up his adultery with Bath-sheba (2 Sa 11:14-15). Since Uriah was a brave soldier in David's army, this shows that at least some of the Hittites had been assimilated into Israelite culture by this time in their history.

In Solomon's time, Solomon disobeyed God's instructions and married a Hittite woman to seal an alliance with these ancient people (1 Ki 11:1-2). This shows how objectionable the Hittite religious system was in God's eyes. The Hittites worshipped many different pagan gods, including several adopted from the Egyptians and the Babylonians. Solomon's marriages became a corrupting influence that pulled the nation of Israel away from worship of the one true God (1 Ki 11:9-13).

HITTITE, URIAH THE

See URIAH

HI′VITES

One of the nations of Canaan prior to the conquest of the land by Joshua (Ge 10:17; Ex 3:17; Jos 9:1). Some Hivites were in Shechem when Jacob returned from Padan-aram (Ge 34:2). Later, fearing that Joshua's army would destroy them, a number of them disguised themselves as distant tribesmen and by this ruse succeeded in forming a treaty with Joshua (Jos 9). One section of them was settled in the extreme north even as late as David's time (Jos 11:3). Some became bond-servants of Solomon (1 Ki 9:20-22).

HIZ′KI

Son of Elpaal, a Beniamite (1 Ch 8:17).

HIZ·KI′AH

See HEZEKIAH.

HIZ·KI′JAH

A signer of the covenant (Ne 10:17).

HOARY (archaic)

White, as with frost (Job 38:28-29).

HO′BAB *(beloved)*

The son of Reuel and a relative of Moses. He joined Moses and the Israelites at Rephidim (Ex 18:1,5,27), at which time the Scripture refers to him as Jethro, the father-in-law of Moses (Nu 10:29,32).

HO′BAH

A town north of Damascus (Ge 14:15).

HO·BAI′AH

See HABAIAH.

HOD

Son of Zophah, a descendant of Asher (1 Ch 7:37).

HO·DAI′AH

See HODAVIAH.

HO·DA·VI′AH

Four Old Testament men:
1. A Benjamite (1 Ch 9:7).
2. A leader of the half-tribe of Manasseh east of the Jordan (1 Ch 5:24).
3. A son of Elioenai, descended from David through Shechaniah (1 Ch 3:24).
4. Head of a Levitical family (Ez 2:40).

HO′DESH *(new moon)*

A wife of Shaharaim of Benjamin (1 Ch 8:9).

HO′DE·VAH

See HODAVIAH.

HO·DI′AH

The husband of the sister of Naham (1 Ch 4:19).

HO·DI′JAH

1. A Levite who assisted Ezra (Ne 8:7; 9:5).
2. One who ratified the covenant along with Nehemiah (Ne 10:18).

HOE

An agricultural tool, a long handle with a thin blade, used for chopping weeds and loosening soil (Is 7:25). The KJV translates this *mattock.*

HOG′ LAH *(a partridge)*

A daughter of Zelophehad (Nu 26:33).

HO′ HAM

A king of Hebron (Jos 10:1-27).

HOLDEN (archaic)

Held (Is 42:14-15).

HOLIDAYS

See FEAST.

HOLINESS OF GOD

Our greatest failing is in not realizing who God is and what His character is like. God is NOT human. He is God, and as such there is an infinite gap between the highest in us and the lowest in God. The gap between God and us is unbridgeable from our side. If the gap is to be bridged, it must be from God's side—for God is holy. To be holy means "to be set apart." God is set apart from the power, practice, and presence of sin, and is set apart to absolute righteousness and goodness. There is no sin in God and God can have nothing to do with sin. If we are to approach God, we must do so on God's terms. Somehow, we must be made holy—just as holy as God is. Any holiness which falls short of God's holiness will not be able to stand in the presence of God. Therefore, because of the holiness of God, we must have a new life in which our sins have been forgiven and done away with so that we actually can be as separated from sin as God is. This is the good news of the gospel—that Christ died for our sins, having taken them upon Himself, and has set us apart from them. This is our position before God which will never change. Because of what Jesus has done, we can enter boldly into the presence of God.

HOLM TREE

The Hebrew word *tirzah,* rendered *cypress* in the Authorized Version (Is 44:14).

HO′ LON

1. A town of Moab (Je 48:21), perhaps Horon.
2. A town of Judah (Jos 15:51). It was assigned to the priests (Jos 21:15). In 1 Chronicles 6:58 it is called Hilen.

HOLPEN (archaic)

Helped (Ps 86:16-17).

HO′ LY

Separated, or that which is set apart for holy purposes. Things which in themselves were ordinary, such as utensils, became sacred, or holy when devoted to the service of the sanctuary. The same was true of those separated from the body of the people for the sacred office of the priesthood. Certain seasons and days were also holy (Ex 20:8; 31:10; Le 21:7; Ne 8:9). Holiness is ascribed to God, since he is apart from and above every being in his infinite perfections and attributes. (1 Sa 2:2; Is 6:3; Re 4:8).

HOLY CITY

See CITY, HOLY.

HOLY DAY (Ex 35:2; Is 58:13; Ne 8:9-11; 10:31)

See FEAST.

HOLY GHOST

See HOLY SPIRIT.

HO′ LY OF HO′ LIES

See HOLY PLACE.

HO′ LY PLACE

The innermost sanctuary of the tabernacle, where the ark of God rested, with His presence between the wings of the cherubim. The holy of holies could only be entered by the High Priest, after sacrifices had been made to atone for his sin (Ex 25:10-22; Le 16). See also TABERNACLE and ATONEMENT, DAY OF.

HO′ LY SPIR′ IT

The third person of the Trinity, frequently "the Spirit" or "the Spirit of the Lord" or "the Holy Spirit." He is designated in the Old Testament only three times as "Holy Spirit" (Ps 51:11; Is 63:10-11), though His work is frequently mentioned.

The Person of the Holy Spirit: One of the most serious errors in the minds of many people concerning the Holy Spirit is that He is simply a principle or an influence. On the contrary, the Holy Spirit is as much a person (individual existence of a conscious being) as the Father and the Son. He is the third person of the Trinity, thus not simply a divine energy or influence proceeding from God. As a person, He possesses intelligence, self-consciousness and self-determination. His personality is explicitly described (Ma 3:16-

17; 28:19; Jo 14:16-17; 15:26). Personal pronouns are used of Him (Jo 16:13-14; Ac 13:2). The Bible speaks of the mind (Ro 8:27) and will (1 Co 12:11) of the Holy Spirit. He is often described as speaking directly to men in the Book of Acts. During Paul's second missionary journey the apostle was forbidden by the Spirit to visit a certain mission field (Ac 16:6-7) and then was instructed to proceed toward another field of service (Ac 16:10). It was God's Spirit who spoke directly to Christian leaders in the Antioch church, commanding them to send Paul and Barnabas on their first missionary journey (Ac 13:2).

Divinity: When the personality of the Holy Spirit is admitted there is little disputation as to his divinity. He is distinctly addressed as God and designations are used that belong only to God (Ac 5:3-4; 2 Co 3:17-18; He 10:15). Having the divine attributes of eternity, knowledge, sovereignty (1 Co 2:11; 12:11; He 9:14). Operations ascribed to Him are of a divine nature, as creation (Ge 1:2; Job 26:13), and regeneration (Jo 3:5-8). The unpardonable sin is the sin against the Holy Spirit (Ma 12:31-32), and sin is not committed against an influence or an energy. It is committed against God alone.

In His relation to Father and Son, He is the same as they in divine substance, in power and glory. He proceeds from the Father and Son and in this relation is subordinate (not inferior) to them as they operate through Him (Jo 15:26; 16:13; Ph 1:19). As is God the Father, the Holy Spirit is everywhere at once (Ps 139:7). As the Son is eternal, the Holy Spirit has also existed forever (He 9:14). He is often referred to as God in the Bible (Ma 3:16-17; Ac 5:3-4) and is mentioned by Jesus Himself just prior to His ascension from the Mount of Olives (Ma 28:19-20).

O.T. Teaching. The Holy Spirit is described as brooding over the surface of the deep during the creation (Ge 1:2; Ps 139:7). The Holy Spirit is the giver of life; physical, mental, and moral (Ge 6:3; Job 32:8; 33:4; 34:14; Ps 104:30). The prophets were inspired by the Holy Spirit (1 Sa 10:6; Ho 9:7; Mi 3:8; Ze 7:12), and they predicted the effusion of the Spirit in messianic times (Is 44:3; Eze 36:26; Joel 2:28; Ze 12:10).

Beginning of the Christian Age: The Holy Spirit was directly involved in the conception of Jesus (Ma 1:18-20). At Jesus's baptism, the Holy Spirit came down in the form of a dove and rested on Him while the Father voiced His approval (Ma 3:16; Mk 1:10; Jo 1:32). The effu-

sion of the Spirit which the prophets had foretold occurred at Pentecost (Ac 2:4), when the disciples were waiting in the upper room in Jerusalem. A sound came like a mighty rushing wind and tongues of fire appeared resting on each believer. They were filled with the Spirit, and spoke boldly for Christ in different languages.

HOLY SPIRIT, SIN AGAINST
See BLASPHEMY.

HOLY WEEK

The Gospel writers devoted many pages to the events leading up to the crucifixion of Jesus. The final week of His earthly ministry began with the triumphal entry into Jerusalem and the "Hosannas" from the crowd that changed to cries of "Crucify Him!" before the week was over. Jesus apparently spent most of the week teaching in the temple area during the day. His evenings were spent in the home of Mary, Martha, and Lazarus in Bethany. Significant events during this week included the plot of the Sanhedrin, Jesus's betrayal and the arrest, the trials of Jesus, His journey to Golgotha down the Jerusalem street known as the Via Dolorosa, and the resurrection. Jesus ministered another forty days before His ascension.

Day	Event	Reference
Sunday	The triumphal entry into Jerusalem	Mk 11:1-11
Monday	Jesus cleanses the temple in Jerusalem	Mk 11:15-19
Tuesday	The Sanhedrin challenges Jesus authority	Lk 20:1-8
	Jesus foretells the destruction of Jerusalem and His second coming	Ma 24–25
	Mary anoints Jesus at Bethany	Jo 12:2-8
	Judas bargains with the Jewish rulers to betray Jesus	Lk 22:3-6
Thursday	Jesus eats the Passover meal with His disciples and institutes the Memorial Supper	Jo 13:1-30 / Mk 14:22-26
	Jesus prays in Gethsemane for His disciples	Jo 17
Friday	His betrayal and arrest in the garden of Gethsemane	Mk 14:43-50
	Jesus questioned by Annas, the former high priest	Jo 18:12-24
	Condemned by Caiaphas and the Sanhedrin	Mk 14:53-65
	Peter denies Jesus three times	Jo 18:15-27
	Jesus is formally condemned by the Sanhedrin	Lk 22:66-71
	Judas commits suicide	Ma 27:3-10
	The trial of Jesus before Pilate	Lk 23:1-5
	Jesus appears before Herod Antipas	Lk 23:6-12
	Formally sentenced to death by Pilate	Lk 23:13-25

Day	Event	Reference
	Jesus is mocked and crucified between two thieves	Mk 15:16-27
	The veil of the temple is torn as Jesus dies	Ma 27:51-56
	His burial in the tomb of Joseph of Arimathea	Jo 19:31-42
Sunday	Jesus is raised from the dead	Lk 24:1-9

See GOSPELS HARMONIZED.

HOMAGE

Honor, reverence, allegiance (1 Ki 1:16,31).

HO' MAM *(destruction)*

A son of Lotan (1 Ch 1:39). In Genesis 36:22 it is Hemam.

HO' MER

A measure that was equivalent to ten ephahs; about six and a half bushels. See WEIGHTS AND MEASURES.

HOMOSEXUAL

One who has sexual relations with a member of his or her own gender. The Scriptures have harsh words about homosexual activity. God called this an abomination and commanded that such offenders be put to death (Le 20:13). The cities of Sodom and Gomorrah were destroyed because of this particular sin (Ge 19:4-5,12-13). Paul taught the early church that unrepentant homosexuals will not be a part of the kingdom of God (1 Co 6:9). Scripture also says that those who commit this sin will "receive in themselves the penalty of their error which is due" (Ro 1:26-27).

HON' EY

A sweet syrupy food manufactured by bees, and deposited in the cells of their comb (Ju 14:8; Ps 19:10). Bees nests were found in trees, rocks, and other places (De 32:13; Ju 14:8; 1 Sa 14:25; Ma 3:4) and honey was prized as food (Ge 43:11; 1 Sa 14:26; 2 Sa 17:29).

HONOR

Respect, deference, consideration. Christians are to honor God above all others, because He is holy (1 Ch 16:27; Re 4:9-11). Christians are supposed to treat one another with honor, giving others preferential treatment ahead of themselves (Ph 2:4; 1 Ti 5:17).

HOOF

The horny covering on the feet of certain animals. Hoofs may be cloven, or cleft, as with cows, or uncloven as with horses (Ex 10:26; Is 5:28; Je 47:3). In distinguishing between animals clean and unclean for the purposes of food the law stated that the Israelites might eat any animals which both chewed the cud and had a completely divided cloven hoof (Le 11:3-8.)

HOOK

Hooks were used for various purposes. They were sometimes used for fishing (Job 41:1; Hab 1:15). Slain animals were hung up by hooks (Eze 40:43). The tabernacle curtains were caught by hooks (Ex 26:32,37; 27:10). Pruning hooks were employed by vinedressers (Is 2:4; 18:5).

HOOPOE

An unclean bird (Le 11:19; De 14:18), also called the lapwing (KJV). They have beautiful plumage, with a notable crest on the head, and a long slender beak used for collecting insects from decaying organic matter.

HOPE

A desire that is cherished with expectation that it will one day be fulfilled. The believer's hope is in the Lord (Ps 39:7). This hope is not vague wishing, or wistful dreaming. Hope is very much wrapped up in faith, and looks forward with assurance to the fulfillment of a promise (He 11:1,7). The object of the believer's hope includes salvation and eternal life (1 Th 5:8; Tit 1:2; 3:7).

HOPH' NI

A son of Eli and a brother of Phinehas. In Eli's old age the two brothers officiated in the priestly office and were notorious for their lust and greed. The two were killed while bringing the ark of the covenant onto the battlefield while the Israelites were fighting against the Philistines (1 Sa 2:22–4:22).

HOOPOE

HOPH′RA

One of the Egyptian Pharaohs, whose overthrow was prophesied by Jeremiah (Je 44:30).

HOR *(mountain)*

1. The mountain on the border of the land of Edom; the place where Aaron died and was buried (Nu 20:22-29; 33:37-39; De 32:50).
2. A mountain on the northern border of Palestine, probably Hermon (Nu 34:7-8).

HOR′AM *(lofty)*

A king of Gezer. He was defeated and slain by Joshua (Jos 10:33).

HOR′EB *(desert)*

See SINAI.

HOR′EM *(sacred)*

A city of Naphtali (Jos 19:38).

HOR′ESH *(forest)*

A place where David hid from the pursuing Saul (1 Sa 23:15).

HOR-HAG·GID′GAD

One of the encampments of the Israelites in the wilderness (Nu 33:32), probably the same as Gudgodah (De 10:6-7).

HOR-HA·GID′GAD

See HOR HAGGIDGAD.

HOR′I *(cave dweller)*

Two Old Testament men:
1. The son of Lotan and grandson of Seir (Ge 36:22; 1 Ch 1:39).
2. The father of the Simeonite spy, Shaphat (Nu 13:5).

HOR′IMS

See HORITES.

HOR′ITES

The original inhabitants of Seir (Ge 36:20,29-30).

HOR′MAH *(devoted to destruction)*

A city of uncertain site in southern Palestine where the Israelites were defeated by the Amalekites and the Canaanites (Nu 14:45). Later, however, the Israelites defeated the Canaanites here and thereupon named the place Hormah (Nu 21:1-3).

HORN

The Israelites had many uses for the horns of animals. They made them into trumpets (Jos 6:13), and they used them as containers for oil (1 Sa 16:1,13). The horn was also a symbol of power (Ps 132:17; Je 48:25) and of the monarchy (Da 7:8,11,21; Ze 1:18-19). The corners of the altar for burnt offerings resembled horns (Ex 29:12; Le 4:7). When one's horn was exalted by God, it signified divine favor (1 Sa 2:10; Ps 89:24). The expression, to lift up one's horn, denoted arrogance and pride (Ps 75:4-5).

HORNED OWL (Le 11:16, NIV)

An unclean animal. See OWL.

HOR′NET

A large species of wasp with a very painful sting (Ex 23:28; De 7:20; Jos 24:12).

HOR·O·NA′IM *(two caverns)*

A city of the Moabites (Is 15:5; Je 48:3,5,34).

HOR′ON·ITE

A native of Horonaim, or more probably of Beth-horon (Ne 2:10,19).

HORSE

Horses were widely used by the Egyptians (Ge 47:17; Ex 9:3). Chariots and horses pursued the Israelites at the time of the exodus (Ex 14:9; 15:19). They were brought in great numbers from Egypt by Solomon. In the period of the divided kingdom they became common (2 Ki 9:18) and were employed in warfare (1 Ki 22:4; 2 Ki 3:7; 9:33). Lowliness on the part of a monarch was expressed by riding upon an ass instead of a stately war horse (Ze 9:9).

HORSE GATE

A gate of Jerusalem, apparently leading into the royal palace (2 Ch 23:15; Ne 3:28; Je 31:40).

HORSE′LEECH

A kind of leech mentioned in Proverbs 30:15, so-called because of its habit of attacking the nose and throat of horses which were drinking.

HORSEMEN

Mounted soldiers. Solomon's cavalry was probably the first in Israel (1 Ki 10:26).

HO'SAH

1. A town on the border of Asher near Tyre (Jos 19:29).

2. A Levite of the family of Merari (1 Ch 16:38; 26:10).

HO·SAN'NA *(save now)*

Hosanna is the Aramaic form of the Hebrew cry for help. It occurs six times in the gospel narratives of Christ's triumphal entry into Jerusalem. By the time of our Lord, the expression was more a shout of praise, but perhaps some of the more thoughtful remembered the words, "Save now, I pray, O LORD" (Ps 118:25) as they waved their palm fronds and cried out: "Hosanna! 'Blessed is He who comes in the name of the LORD!' The King of Israel!" (Jo 12:13).

HO·SE'A *(salvation)*

One of the Minor Prophets; son of Beeri, a native of the Northern Kingdom. His labors extended over a long period, probably to the overthrow of Israel in 722 B.C.

HO·SE'A, BOOK OF

1. The Book of Hosea. Hosea, whose name means "Salvation," ministered to the Northern Kingdom of Israel. Outwardly, the nation was enjoying a time of prosperity and growth; but inwardly, moral corruption and spiritual adultery permeated the people. Hosea, instructed by God to marry a woman named Gomer, found his domestic life to be an accurate and tragic dramatization of the unfaithfulness of God's people. During his half century of prophetic ministry, Hosea repeatedly echoed his threefold message: God abhors the sins of His people; judgment is certain, but God's loyal love stands firm.

The names Hosea, Joshua, and Jesus are all derived from the same Hebrew root word. The word *hoshea* means "salvation," but "Joshua" and "Jesus" include an additional idea: "Yahweh is Salvation" (see JOSHUA, BOOK OF). As God's messenger, Hosea offered the possibility of salvation if only the nation would turn from idolatry back to God.

The English Bible spells them differently, but Hosea the prophet, and Hoshea the last king of Israel actually bore the same Hebrew name. The Septuagint writes the name *Hosea,* while the Latin translation is *Osee.*

2. The Author of Hosea. Few critics refute the claim in 1:1 that Hosea is the author of this book. His place of birth is not given, but his familiarity and obvious concern with the Northern Kingdom indicate that he lived in Israel, not Judah. This is also seen when he calls the king of Samaria "our king" (7:5). Hosea was the son of Beeri (1:1), husband of Gomer (1:3), and father of two sons and a daughter (1:4,6,9). Nothing more is known of him since he is not mentioned elsewhere in the Bible.

Hosea had a real compassion for his people, and his personal suffering because of Gomer gave him some understanding of God's grief over their sin. Thus, his words of coming judgment are passionately delivered but tempered with a heart of tenderness. He upbraids his people for their lying, murder, insincerity, ingratitude, idolatry, and covetousness with cutting metaphors and images; but his messages are punctuated with consolation and future hope.

3. The Time of Hosea. Hosea addressed the Northern Kingdom of Israel (5:1), often called Ephraim after the largest tribe (5:3,5,11,13). According to 1:1, he ministered during the reigns of Uzziah (767-739 B.C.), Jotham (739-731 B.C.), Ahaz (731-715 B.C.), and Hezekiah (715-686 B.C.), kings of Judah. When Hosea began his ministry, Jeroboam II (782-753 B.C.) was still reigning in Israel. This makes Hosea a younger contemporary of Amos, another prophet to the Northern Kingdom. Hosea was also a contemporary of Isaiah and Micah who ministered to the Southern Kingdom. Hosea's long career continued after the time of Jeroboam II and spanned the reigns of the last six kings of Israel from Zechariah (753-752 B.C.) to Hoshea (732-722 B.C.). Hosea evidently compiled the book during the early years of Hezekiah, and his ministry stretched from about 755 B.C. to about 710 B.C. The Book of Hosea represents approximately forty years of the prophetic ministry.

When Hosea began his ministry, Israel was enjoying a temporary period of political and economic prosperity under Jeroboam II. However, the nation began to crumble after Tiglath-pileser III (745-727 B.C.) strengthened Assyria. The reigns of Israel's last six kings were relatively brief since four were murdered and a fifth was carried captive to Assyria. Confusion and decline characterized the last years of the

Northern Kingdom, and her people refused to heed Hosea's warning of imminent judgment. The people were in a spiritual stupor, riddled with sin and idolatry.

4. The Christ of Hosea. Matthew 2:15 applies Hosea 11:1 to Christ in Egypt: "When Israel was a child, I loved him, and out of Egypt I called My son." Matthew quotes the second half of the verse to show that the exodus of Israel from Egypt as a new nation was a prophetic type of Israel's Messiah who was also called out of Egypt in His childhood. Both Israel and Christ left the land of Israel to take refuge in Egypt.

Christ's identification with our plight and His loving work of redemption can be seen in Hosea's redemption of Gomer from the slave market.

5. Keys to Hosea.

Key Word: The Loyal Love of God for Israel—The themes of chapters 1–3 echo throughout the rest of the book. The adultery of Gomer (1) illustrates the sin of Israel (4–7); the degradation of Gomer (2) represents the judgment of Israel (8–10); and Hosea's redemption of Gomer (3) pictures the restoration of Israel (11–14). More than any other Old Testament prophet, Hosea's personal experiences illustrate his prophetic message. In his relationship to Gomer, Hosea portrays God's faithfulness, justice, love, and forgiveness toward His people. The theme of God's holiness is developed in contrast to Israel's corruption and apostasy. Hosea utters about 150 statements concerning the sins of Israel, and more than half deal specifically with idolatry. The theme of God's justice is contrasted with Israel's lack of justice. There has never been a good king in Israel, and judgment is long overdue. The theme of God's love is seen in contrast to Israel's hardness and empty ritual. God's loyal love is unconditional and ceaseless; in spite of Israel's manifold sins, God tries every means to bring His people back to Himself. He pleads with the people to return to Him, but they will not. "O Israel, return to the LORD your God, for you have stumbled because of your iniquity" (14:1).

Key Verses: Hosea 4:1; 11:7-9—"Hear the word of the LORD, you children of Israel, for the LORD brings a charge against the inhabitants of the land: there is no truth or mercy or knowledge of God in the land" (4:1).

"My people are bent on backsliding from Me. Though they call to the Most High, none at all exalt Him. How can I give you up, Ephraim? How can I hand you over, Israel? How can I make you like Admah? How can I set you like Zeboiim? My heart churns within Me; My sympathy is stirred. I will not execute the fierceness of My anger; I will not again destroy Ephraim. For I am God, and not man, the Holy One in your midst; and I will not come with terror" (11:7-9).

Key Chapter: Hosea 4—The nation of Israel has left the knowledge of the truth and followed the idolatrous ways of their pagan neighbors. Central to the book is Hosea 4:6—"My people are destroyed for lack of knowledge. Because you have rejected knowledge, I also will reject you from being priest for Me; because you have forgotten the law of your God, I also will forget your children."

6. Survey of Hosea. Hosea is called by God to prophesy during Israel's last hours, just as Jeremiah will prophesy years later to the crumbling kingdom of Judah. As one commentator has noted, "What we see in the prophecy of Hosea are the last few swirls as the Kingdom of Israel goes down the drain." This book represents God's last gracious effort to plug the drain. Hosea's personal tragedy is an intense illustration of Israel's national tragedy. It is a story of one-sided love and faithfulness that represents the relationship between Israel and God. As Gomer is married to Hosea, so Israel is betrothed to God. Both relationships gradually disintegrate—Gomer runs after other men, and Israel runs after other gods. Israel's spiritual adultery is illustrated in Gomer's physical adultery. The development of the book can be traced in two parts: the adulterous wife and faithful husband (1–3) and the adulterous Israel and faithful Lord (4–14).

The Adulterous Wife and Faithful Husband (1–3). Hosea married a woman named Gomer who bore him three children appropriately named by God as signs to Israel. Jezreel, Lo-Ruhamah, and Lo-Ammi mean "God Scatters," "Not Pitied," and "Not My People." Similarly, God would judge and scatter Israel because of her sin.

Gomer sought other lovers and deserted Hosea. In spite of the depth to which her sin carried her, Hosea redeemed her from the slave market and restored her.

The Adulterous Israel and Faithful Lord (4–14). Because of his own painful experience, Hosea could feel some of the sorrow of God over the sinfulness of His people. His loyal love for Gomer was a reflection of God's concern for Israel. However, Israel had fallen into the dregs of sin and was hardened against God's gracious last appeal to return. The people had flagrantly violated all of God's commandments, and they were indicted by the holy God for their crimes. Even at that point, God wanted to heal and redeem them (7:1,13), but in their arrogance and idolatry they continued to rebel.

Chapters 9–10 give the verdict of the case God has just presented. Israel's disobedience would lead to her dispersion. "They sow the wind" (4–7), "and reap the whirlwind" (8–10). Israel spurned repentance, and the judgment of God could no longer be delayed.

God is holy (4–7) and just (8–10), but He is also loving and gracious (11–14). God must discipline, but because of His endless love, He will ultimately save and restore His wayward people. "How can I give you up, Ephraim? . . . I will heal their backsliding, I will love them freely for My anger has turned away from him" (11:8; 14:4).

OUTLINE OF HOSEA

I. The Adulterous Wife and Faithful Husband (1:1–3:5)

A. The Introduction to the Book of Hosea 1:1

B. The Prophetic Marriage of Hosea to Gomer 1:2–2:1

C. The Application of the Adultery of Gomer 2:2-23

D. The Restoration of Gomer to Hosea 3:1-5

II. The Adulterous Israel and Faithful Lord (4:1–14:9)

A. The Spiritual Adultery of Israel 4:1–6:3

B. The Refusal of Israel to Repent of Her Adultery 6:4–8:14

C. The Judgment of Israel by God 9:1–10:15

D. The Restoration of Israel to the Lord 11:1–14:9

HOSEN (archaic)

Leggings, stockings, trousers (Da 3:21).

HO·SHAI′AH *(Jehovah has saved)*

Two Old Testament men:

1. Father of Jezaniah (Je 42:1) or Azariah (Je 43:2). The son accused Jeremiah of prophesying falsely.

2. A man who participated in the dedication of the wall of Jerusalem (Ne 12:32).

HO′SHA·MA *(Jehovah has heard)*

A son of Jehoiachin (1 Ch 3:18).
HO·SHE′A.

1. The former name of Joshua, changed to Joshua by Moses (Nu 13:8,16). In the Authorized Version of this passage it is Oshea *(save).*

2. Son of Azaziah. He was the prince of the tribe of Ephraim in the reign of David (1 Ch 27:20).

3. Israel's last king, son of Elah. He slew Pekah and seized the throne (2 Ki 15:30; 17:3).

4. One who sealed the covenant (Ne 10:23).

HOSPITALITY

Welcoming friends and strangers into one's home to feed, lodge or entertain them. Abraham was hospitable to the strangers who stopped at his home, washing their feet and bringing choice food (Ge 18:1-15), and it turned out that they were angels. The writer of the Hebrews enjoined his readers to "not forget to entertain strangers, for by so doing some have unwittingly entertained angels."

God has commanded His people to be hospitable (Le 19:33-45; Lk 14:13-14; 1 Pe 4:9) in both the Old and New Testaments. The leaders of the church are particularly required to show hospitality (Tit 1:7-8; 1 Ti 3:2). Godly hospitality is loving, gracious, and service oriented.

HOST

A large body of things or people, such as an army. The stars are described as the "host of heaven" (De 4:19; 2 Ki 23:5). The word also denotes all the beings of heaven; hence the angels are a heavenly host (1 Ki 22:19; Ps 148:2;

Lk 2:13). The word also refers to the owner of a house at which one might stay (Ro 16:23).

HOSTAGE

Prisoners of war (2 Ki 14:14; 2 Ch 25:24).

HOST OF HEAVEN

Sometimes this is a poetic term for the stars (De 4:9; 2 Ki 23:5; Is 45:12). At the end of the world host of heaven shall be destroyed, and the sky rolled up as a scroll (Is 34:4). The host of heaven were designed to "declare the glory of God" (Ps 19:1-6), and therefore they are very beautiful. It is a measure of man's sinfulness that he ignores the proclamation of nature (Ro 1:20-21) and worships the created thing rather than the creator (Ac 7:42).

The "host of heaven" can also be a description of the angelic hosts (Is 24:21).

HOSTS, LORD OF

See GOD, NAMES OF.

HO′THAM (a seal, a ring)

Two Old Testament men:

1. An Aroerite. Two of his sons were warriors of David (1 Ch 11:44).

2. Son of Heber (1 Ch 7:32).

HO′THAN

See HOTHAM.

HO′THIR

A son of Heman (1 Ch 25:4).

HOUGH (archaic)

Hamstring.

HOUND

See DOG.

HOUSE

It was not until the Israelites were dwellers in Egypt and in Palestine after taking the country that they lived in houses. The houses of the common people consisted ordinarily of one story and often of a single room. The materials were furnished by the locality. In Egypt mud or sunburnt brick were used. In Palestine brick, lime, and sandstone were used, while only the houses of the rich were made of hewn stone (1 Ki 7:9; Is 9:10). Houses of the more prosperous classes were built around a court-

yard having a well (2 Sa 17:18). The second story contained the upper room or chamber (1 Ki 17:19; 2 Ki 4:10; Mk 14:15; Ac 1:13; 9:37). The roof surrounded by a low wall was useful for storing things (Jos 2:6), for social intercourse (1 Sa 9:25-26) and for religious purposes (2 Ki 23:12; Ac 10:9). The roof could be reached by an outside stairway (Ma 24:17).

HOUSEHOLD

The family (probably including several generations) and the slaves and servants who live together in one house (1 Sa 27:3; 2 Sa 15:16). Abraham was commanded to circumcise any males of his household, including slaves and those born into the family (Ge 17:23,27). When the Philippian jailer turned to Christ and was baptized, the rest of his household followed suit (Ac 16:15); because of the close family relationships, such a decision may well have been a group decision, to be a Christ following family (1 Co 1:16; Ac 10:41,48). This is not to downplay the necessity of an individual relationship with Christ, but to emphasize the strong unit a household is. Believers in Christ now all belong to one household, the household of faith with God as its head (Ga 6:10; Ep 2:19).

HOUSEHOLDER

The head of a household, the master; also the owner of a field or vineyard (Ma 13:27; 13:52; Ma 20:1; Mk 14:14).

HO′ZA·I

Probably the proper name for the one who wrote a history about Manasseh, king of Judah. The expression "history of Hozai" is rendered "sayings of the seers" in 2 Ch 33:19, KJV.

HUB

The center of a wheel, to which the spokes are attached, and which is fastened to the axle. The hubs of Solomon's chariot wheels were cast bronze (1 Ki 7:33).

HUK′KOK (decreed)

A town a few miles west of Capernaum (Jos 19:34).

HU′KOK

See HELKATH.

HUL (circle)

Second son of Aram (Ge 10:23; 1 Ch 1:17).

HUL′DAH *(weasel)*

A prophetess, the wife of Shallum, in the time of King Josiah. She assured this godly king that the judgment against Jerusalem would not be fulfilled in his day (2 Ki 22:12-20; 2 Ch 34:20-28).

HUMAN SACRIFICE

Under God's law, the penalty for human sacrifice was death (Le 20:2-5; De 18:10). Because of the clear teaching of the law that God considers human sacrifice to be detestable, it is difficult to understand His command to Abraham that he sacrifice his only son (Ge 22:1-19). However, it is clear that God did not allow this to actually occur, and that the whole incident was designed as a way to test Abraham's faith. Abraham passed the test with flying colors, and God restored his son to him. The Book of Hebrews tells us that Abraham prepared to sacrifice Isaac, believing that God would raise him to life again, since it was through Isaac that the seed of the promise was to pass on (He 11:17-19). Jephthah's foolish vow, and subsequent sacrifice of his daughter are also hard to explain, but it must be noted that the Book of Judges offers no comment on this story—it simply recounts the events (Ju 11:29-40). In the Book of Judges, almost the only comment from "God's perspective" is that "everyone did what was right in his own eyes"(Ju 21:25). There is more reason to assume that God approved of Jephthah's action than that He approved of the gruesome events of chapter 19. In later years, the Israelites were horrified by the king of Moab who sacrificed his son when the battle began to go against him (2 Ki 3:26-27). Both Ahaz and Manasseh, wicked kings of Judah, sacrificed their children to pagan gods (2 Ki 16:3; 21:6), and Jeremiah prophesied against Judah because of such foul deeds (Je 19:5-6; 32:35).

HUMILITY

The absence of selfishness and arrogance. One who is humble does not "think of himself more highly than he ought to think" (Ro 12:3). Humility includes "in honor giving preference to one another" (Ro 12:10). The ultimate example of humility is Christ who left His glory to come down as a servant, even though He is king of all. It is His example that we are commanded to imitate (Ph 2:1-15).

HUMPS

The hump of a camel is where fat and fluid are stored, perfectly suiting camels for desert journeys where there is very little food or water. The KJV translates this word "bunches" (Is 30:6).

HUM′TAH

A town of Judah (Jos 15:54).

HUNDRED, TOWER OF THE

A part of the wall of Jerusalem (Ne 3:1; 12:39).

HUNGER

Lack of adequate food. Hunger is the penalty for slothfulness (Pr 19:15). Hunger can also be thought of in a spiritual sense, as the longing for God and His rightness in our confusing and sin-marred lives. Jesus said that He is the Bread of Life, and that whoever feeds on Him will not be hungry in this way ever again (Jo 6:35).

HUN′TER, HUNTING

Monarchs of Babylonia and Assyria indulged in the sport of hunting and recorded their achievements by means of sculpture and inscriptions. Game inhabited various sections of Palestine. Undesirable beasts were hunted to rid the countryside of them (Ex 23:29; 1 Ki 13:24). Hunting was also indulged in for sport and to secure food (Ge 27:3). The Israelites were forbidden to eat the blood of slain animals (De 12:15-16,22). The principal weapons and snares were the bow (Is 7:24), nets and traps (Job 18:10), and pits (2 Sa 23:20; Eze 19:4,8).

HU′PHAM

A son or more remote descendant of Benjamin and founder of a tribal family (Nu 26:39); called Huppim in Genesis 46:21. In 1 Chronicles 7:12 he is called son of Ir, also a Benjamite.

HU′PHA·MITES

The descendants of Benjamin's offspring Hupham (Nu 26:39).

HUP′PAH *(a covering)*

A priest, a descendant of Aaron (1 Ch 24:13).

HUP′PIM

See HUPHAM.

HUR

Four Old Testament men:

1. A king of Midian whom Moses killed when the Israelites were in the plain of Moab (Nu 31:8; Jos 13:21).

2. The grandfather of Bezaleel of the family of Hezron and house of Caleb (Ex 31:1-2; 1 Ch 2:18-20).

3. One who, with Aaron, during the battle with the Amalekites supported the arms of Moses while he prayed (Ex 17:10-12). While Moses was in Mount Sinai, Hur aided Aaron in the management of things (Ex 24:14).

4. Father of Benhur (1 Ki 4:8).

5. Father of Rephaiah (Ne 3:9).

HU·RA′I

One of David's warriors (1 Ch 11:32). He is called Hiddai in 2 Samuel 23:30.

HU′RAM *(noble)*

1. A Benjamite, son of Bela (1 Ch 8:5).

2. A king of Tyre who assisted in the building of Solomon's temple (2 Ch 2:3). See HIRAM.

3. An artificer of Tyre (2 Ch 4:11,16). See HIRAM.

HU′RI *(linen worker)*

Father of Abihail of the tribe of Gad (1 Ch 5:14).

HUR′RI·ANS

See HORITES.

HUSBAND

The Role of the Husband: Paul tells the husband to love his wife (Ep 5:25), while Peter tells the husband to live with his wife "with understanding" (1 Pe 3:7). The husband cannot live with his wife as Peter says unless he loves in the way that Paul says. The love that the husband is commanded to have for the wife is not primarily sexual or emotional (though both of these concepts are involved); it is a love that loves in spite of the response (or lack of it) in the one loved. It is the kind of love that God has for the world (Jo 3:16) and is the fruit of the Spirit (Ga 5:22). A husband can only love his wife properly if he is a Christian and under the control of the Holy Spirit.

The two responsibilities the husband has in the family are to dwell with his wife in an understanding manner, and to render to his wife the honor which is due her because she is his wife. See MARRIAGE.

HUSBANDMEN (archaic)

A farmer; one who tills the ground and cares for animals (Joel 1:10-11).

HU′SHAH *(haste)*

The son of Ezer, a descendant of Hur (1 Ch 4:4).

HU′SHAI *(hasty)*

An Archite, one of the two chief counselors of David (2 Sa 15:32-37; 17:5-16).

HU′SHAM *(haste)*

A Temanite king of Edom (Ge 36:34-35; 1 Ch 1:45-46).

HU′SHA·THITE

An inhabitant of Hushah (2 Sa 21:18; 23:27).

HU′SHIM

1. The sons of Aher, a Benjamite family (1 Ch 7:12).

2. One of the wives of Shaharaim, a Benjamite in the land of Moab (1 Ch 8:8,11).

3. Son of Dan (Ge 46:23). In Numbers 26:42 he is called Shuham, possibly the same as in 1 Chronicles 7:12.

HUSK

The pod of the carob tree, also called locust bean and St. John's bread (Lk 15:16).

HUZ (Ge 22:21)

See UZ.

HUZ′ZAB *(to decree)*

A word of uncertain meaning appearing in Nahum 2:7. It may be a verb or noun. If the former it may refer to the Assyrian queen or to Nineveh. If the latter, it may be rendered as in the Revised Version, *it is decreed.*

HY′A·CINTH

A precious stone; one of the twelve stones in the breastplate of the high priest (Ex 28:19). See JACINTH.

HY·E′NA

A hated animal of Palestine. A cowardly, carnivorous mammal, it lives in caves by day and prowls by night (1 Sa 13:18).

HY·ME·NAE′ US *(pertaining to Hymen, the god of marriage)*

A man of Ephesus (1 Ti 1:20).

HYMN

The Hebrews were a music-loving people. Several musical instruments, including the tambourine or timbrel are mentioned in the Bible (Ps 81:2). Merrymaking and music were part of their feasts and festivals.

The earliest recorded song in the Bible is referred to as the Song of Moses (Ex 15). This hymn was sung by the people to celebrate God's miraculous deliverance of the Hebrews from the Egyptian army at the Red Sea (Ex 14:3-30). Other significant hymns and songs of the Bible include the following:

Personality	Description	Reference
Israelites	Sung by the people as they dug life-saving wells in the wilderness	Nu 21:14-18
Moses	A song of praise to God by Moses just before his death	De 32:1-44
Deborah and Barak	A victory Song after Israel's defeat of the Canaanites	Ju 5:1-31
Israelite Women	A song to celebrate David's defeat of Goliath	1 Sa 18:6-7
Levite Singers	A song of praise at the dedication of the temple in Jerusalem	2 Ch 5:12-14
Levite Singers	A song of praise, presented as a marching song as the army of Israel prepared for battle	2 Ch 20:20-23
Levite Singers	A song at the temple restoration ceremony during Hezekiah's Reign	2 Ch 29:25-30
Mary	The Song of Mary, upon learning that she as a virgin would give birth to the Messiah	Lk 1:46-55
Zacharias	A song of joy at the circumcision of his son, who would serve as the Messiah's forerunner	Lk 1:68-79
Jesus and Disciples	A song in the Upper Room as they celebrated the Passover together just before the arrest of Jesus	Ma 26:30
Paul and Silas	A song of praise to God at midnight from their prison cell in Philippi	Ac 16:25
All Believers	The spiritual songs of thanksgiving and joy, which God wants all believers to sing	Ep 5:19 Col 3:16
144,000 believers	A new song of the redeemed in heaven, sung to glorify God	Re 14:1-3

HYPOCRITE

One who behaves falsely, claiming to be one thing, when all the time in reality he is something quite different.

"I could never join the church: It's full of hypocrites!" We have all heard this line, and unfortunately there are too many—but also in the club, the school, the political party, the lodge, the government, and even the home. Hypocrisy *(hypokrisis)* does not mean we don't measure up to our beliefs—we would all be hypocrites by that standard. *Hypocrisy* is pretending to be something we know we are not. The word comes from the Greek theater; literally used of an actor, it means "to answer *(krinomai)* from under *(hypo)* [a mask]." Someone has well said, "Hypocrisy is the compliment that vice pays to virtue." That means that the person recognizes a certain good category—such as that of a Christian gentleman, for example—and pretends to be one, knowing all the while that he is playacting. This is exactly what our Lord accused the Pharisees of: religious hypocrisy (Lk 20:20). Pretending to be righteous by keeping punctilious little traditions of hand washings and tithing mint, meanwhile they cheated widows out of their houses and violently opposed the only completely righteous Person who ever lived! Fourteen times in the Gospels *hypocrite* occurs, nearly always used by Jesus to describe the Pharisees.

Can a *real* Christian ever be guilty of hypocrisy? Unless we are prepared to read Peter and Barnabas out of the faith, the answer must be "yes." Six times in the New Testament *hypocrisy* occurs (seven if we accept the interesting textual variant in James 5:12). Paul accused Peter of hypocrisy in Galatians 2 for eating with Gentile believers, but then ceasing to do so when strict legalists showed up from Jerusalem who might criticize his (to them) too free lifestyle. Paul was shocked, not so much that impulsive Peter erred here, but "that even Barnabas was carried away with their hypocrisy" (v.13). Sincerity was Barnabas's hallmark. So we all have to watch out for hypocrisy in our own lives.

James was strongly against a religion of all talk and no reality. As he ends his letter he pleads for sincerity: "But lest you fall into judgment" (5:12). Actually, a majority of manuscripts read "into hypocrisy" here, and since this also fits the context so well it may be what James originally wrote.

HYPOSTATIC UNION

The doctrine of the union of two natures (divine and human) forming one person in Christ.

Jesus Christ was not a divine/human schizophrenic, or simply God in a human body. He was both fully God and completely human, the two natures united forever in one person. His deity is undiminished, and His humanity is perfect.

HYS′SOP

A small plant of Egypt and Palestine, probably a species of marjoram (Ex 12:22; 1 Ki 4:33). It was used by the Hebrews for ritualistic sprinkling of blood and water (Le 14:4,6,51-52; Nu 19:6,18; Ps 51:7).

I

I AM; I AM THAT I AM

The name by which God revealed Himself to Moses at the bush (Ex 3:14). It represents God as the self-existent one. He is defined by Himself, not by comparison with something higher, or something that we know. Jesus electrified His Jewish audience by claiming this title for Himself, thereby clearly identifying Himself as God (Jo 8:58-59). See GOD, NAMES OF.

IB′EX

A type of wild goat of the land of Canaan, also referred to as mountain goat or pygarg (De 14:5). See GOAT.

IB′HAR (chosen of God)

A son of David born in Jerusalem (2 Sa 5:15; 1 Ch 14:5).

I′BIS

A bird in the stork and heron class, held sacred by the Egyptians. See HERON.

IB′LE·AM

A city belonging to the territory of Issachar. It was given to the half-tribe of Manasseh, on the west side of the Jordan River, about ten miles southeast of Megiddo (Jos 17:11-12). The tribe of Manasseh failed to drive out the inhabitants and the Canaanites living there were allowed to remain (Ju 1:27). The town of Bileam, mentioned in 1 Chronicles 6:70, is probably the same as Ibleam.

IB·NEI′AH (built of Jehovah)

Son of Jeroham, a Benjamite; the head of one of the families returning from captivity (1 Ch 9:8).

IBEX

IB·NI′JAH (built by Jehovah)

Father of Reuel, a Benjamite (1 Ch 9:8).

IB′RI (Hebrew)

A Levite, he lived during the reign of King David (1 Ch 24:27).

IB′SAM, JIB′SAM

A man of Issachar of the family of Tola (1 Ch 7:2).

IB′ZAN (active)

A judge over Israel for seven years; Ibzan was the father of thirty sons and thirty daughters (Ju 12:8-10).

ICE

The climate of Israel is mild, so snow and ice are rarely seen, except on the highest mountains. The Book of Job uses ice and snow to describe God's power, specifically His power over weather and the elements (Job 37:10; 38:29-30).

I′CHA·BOD (inglorious)

Son of Phinehas and grandson of Eli, the high priest who mentored the young Samuel. His mother, dying after a difficult premature labor brought on by the news of her husband's death, her father-in-law's death, and the Philistine capture of the ark of the Lord, gave Ichabod this name as a symbol of what she believed was happening to Israel (1 Sa 4:19-22).

I·CO′NI′UM

An important city of Asia Minor, in the fertile plain of Lycaonia. On his first missionary journey with Barnabas Paul visited the city (Ac

13:51-52; 14:1-6,19-22; 16:1-2; 2 Ti 3:11). Today, Iconium is known as Konya or Konia.

I'DA·LAH

A city of Zebulun (Jos 19:15). Located near Nazareth, it is called Khirbet el-Hawarah today.

ID'BASH *(honeyed)*

A man of the tribe of Judah, one of the sons of Etam (1 Ch 4:3).

ID'DO

The name of at least six men in the Old Testament:

1. Father of Ahinadab, purveyor of food for Solomon at Mahanaim (1 Ki 4:14).

2. A descendant of Gershom, son of Levi (1 Ch 6:21); also called Adaiah (1 Ch 6:41).

3. Son of Zechariah, ruler of the half-tribe of Manasseh east of the Jordan in the time of King David (1 Ch 27:21).

4. A seer who wrote a book about events in the reign of Solomon (2 Ch 9:29), a book of genealogies recording deeds of Rehoboam (2 Ch 12:15), and a history concerning Abijah (2 Ch 13:22). These books are lost, but they may have formed a part of the foundation of the Books of Chronicles.

5. Grandfather of Zechariah the prophet (Ze 1:1,7), probably a chief of the priests who was of the company of Zerubbabel (Ne 12:4,16).

6. A chief of the Jews, living in Casiphia in Babylon (Ez 8:17-20).

IDLE

Inactive; doing nothing, with a connotation of laziness and uselessness. The Book of Proverbs highlights the virtues and rewards of hard work as opposed to idleness (Pr 14:23; 19:15).

IDOL, IMAGE

A picture or statue made to represent a god, and used as an object of worship. In ancient times, idols were made of wood, stone, gold, silver, or other valuable materials (Ex 20:4-5; Ju 17:3; Ps 115:4; 135:15; Is 44:13-17; Ro 1:23). Perhaps one of the best known idols in the Old Testament is the infamous golden calf which the Israelites made as God spoke to Moses on the mountain (Ex 32:2-6). When God gave the Ten Commandments to Israel, two of those Commandments dealt with the problem of idols and images. The first command prohibits the worship of other gods, while the second command prohibits the use of images. Many times, we see the second command as merely a repeat of the first, but in fact it has an added dimension. Not only is the worship of idols representing false gods a sin, it is also a sin to make a material representation of the true God (Ex 20:1-6). God is spirit, and is to be worshipped "in spirit and in truth" (Jo 4:23-24). He is also much more than anything we can imagine. God does not want us to produce for ourselves pictures or statues or even truncated ideas of who He is, and bow down to these smaller versions. We humans long for a tangible God, that we can see and touch and understand, but we have to realize that a God small enough to see and touch and understand that way would be too small to be worthy of worship.

IDOLATRY

The worship of a god assumed to live within an idol, or the worship of the idol itself. This practice goes back to an early period in human history. In Babylon, prior to Abraham's time, idols were worshipped (Jos 24:2). The first reference to idolatry among the Hebrews is in the account of Rachel's theft of the images of Laban's "household gods" (Ge 31:30,32-35). After they arrived in Canaan the Israelites were divinely commanded to destroy the idols of the Canaanites (Nu 33:52; De 7:5; 29:17). With the exception of the Persians, all the nations with which the Israelites had dealings worshipped idols. When the ten tribes revolted and formed the kingdom of Israel, Jeroboam set up images by which to worship Jehovah. Soon the idols came to represent other divinities and Jehovah was forsaken. This was especially true during the era of Baalism in the fourth dynasty. Idolatry was encouraged by such kings as Ahab and Manasseh (1 Ki 16:31-33; 2 Ki 21:2-7). In New Testament times, Paul denounced the idolatry he encountered outside of Palestine (Ac 15:29; 17:24-30; 1 Co 8:1-8).

The prophet Isaiah most effectively describes the futility and inadequacy of idol worship, as well as the self-deception involved. The craftsman worships one part of a tree, and cooks his food over the other part (Is 44:13-20).

I·DU·MAE'A

The name the Greeks and Romans gave to Edom (Is 34:5-6; Eze 35:15; 36:5; Mk 3:8). Herod the Great was an Edomite, or Idumean.

I·DU·ME′A

See IDUMAEA.

I-E′ZER

See ABIEZER.

I′GAL *(the Lord redeems)*

Three Old Testament men:

1. The Issacharite spy sent by Moses with other scouts to Canaan (Nu 13:7).

2. Son of Nathan of Zobah; one of David's mighty men (2 Sa 23:36).

3. Son of Shemaiah; a descendant of Jehoiachin, also called Igeal or Igar (1 Ch 3:22).

IG·DA·LI′AH *(great is the Lord)*

Father of Hanan (Je 35:4).

I′GE·AL

See IGAL.

IGNOMINY

Disgrace; shame; dishonor (Pr 18:3).

I′IM *(ruins)*

1. A town in the extreme south of Judah (Jos 15:28-29).

2. A town east of the Jordan (Nu 33:45). See IYE-ABARIM.

I′JE-AB′A·RIM

See IYE-ABARIM.

I′JIM

See IJON.

I′JON *(ruin)*

A town of Naphtali. At the suggestion of Asa, king of Judah, it was captured from King Baasha of Israel by Ben-hadad of Syria (1 Ki 15:20; 2 Ch 16:4). Later, the inhabitants of this town were carried into captivity in Assyria (2 Ki 15:29).

IK′KESH *(perverse)*

Father of Ira, a Tekoite and a captain of David's troops (2 Sa 23:26; 1 Ch 11:28; 27:9).

I′LA·I *(supreme)*

One of David's mighty men (1 Ch 11:29). He is also called Zalmon (2 Sa 23:28).

I′LEX

See CYPRESS.

ILLUMINATION

To give light to, to enlighten, to make clear. Illumination is the last of three important steps taken by God in communicating His Word to us. The first step was revelation, which occurred when God spoke to the Bible authors. The second step was inspiration, that process whereby God guided them in correctly writing or uttering His message. But now a third step is needed to provide understanding for men and women as they hear God's revealed and inspired message. This vital step is illumination, that divine process whereby God causes the written revelation to be understood by the human heart.

This third step is needed because unsaved man is blinded both by his fallen, fleshly nature (1 Co 2:14) and by Satan himself (2 Co 4:3-4). The person behind this illumination is the Holy Spirit. Just prior to His crucifixion, Christ promised to send the Holy Spirit, who would illuminate both unsaved people (Jo 16:8-11) and Christians (Jo 14:26; 16:13-14).

An important example of the Holy Spirit's using God's Word to illuminate sinners is seen at Pentecost, where three thousand people are saved after hearing Simon Peter preach about Christ and the Cross (Ac 2:36-41).

Christians also need this illumination to help them fully grasp the marvelous message in God's Word. Paul tells us that the Holy Spirit will show these tremendous truths to us as we read the Scriptures (1 Co 2:10; 2 Co 4:6).

IL·LYR′I·CUM

A district lying along the eastern coast of the Adriatic Sea. It is mentioned only once in the New Testament, as the territorial limit to Paul's preaching (Ro 15:19). Its people were wild mountaineers whose acts of piracy brought them into conflict with the Romans. By Paul's time, the area had become a Roman province. The northern half was called Liburnia, the southern half, Dalmatia (2 Ti 4:10). Later, the whole district was called Dalmatia. Today, this area includes Albania and former Yugoslavia. See DALMATIA.

IMAGE

See IDOL.

IMAGE, NEBUCHADNEZZAR'S

Nebuchadnezzar's Image can refer to two things:

1. The story of Nebuchadnezzar's image is told in Daniel chapter two. Nebuchadnezzar had a frightening dream, in which he saw an enormous statue or image, apparently of a human form. The head of the statue was made of gold; the chest and arms were silver, the body of bronze, the legs of iron, and the feet of iron and clay. As he watched, a rock was cut out, not by human hands, and smashed the statue, leaving it in fragments which were blown away by the wind. As he looked, Nebuchadnezzar saw the rock become a huge mountain, and he was left feeling greatly disturbed, because he did not understand the dream.

Daniel, an exiled Jew in Babylon, was given the interpretation by God and he went to the king to explain the dream and its meaning. The statue, and the different metals it was made of, represented the ruling kingdoms of the earth. The golden head represented Nebuchadnezzar himself, the king of Babylon. The silver and bronze symbolized the two kingdoms which would arise after Babylon, each a little less great than the last. The iron legs were a fourth kingdom, strong enough to break to pieces the kingdoms which came before it or opposed it, and finally, the iron mixed with clay represented the time when the iron kingdom would be divided, partly strong and partly brittle. In those days, when the kingdom of iron was weakened by division, a different sort of kingdom would arise, one which would never be destroyed itself, but which would bring to an end all that had come before it (Da 2:31-35).

Scripture specifically states that the golden head stood for Babylon. The examination of world history produces the widely held view that the silver chest and arms represent Medo-Persia (including Darius and Belshazzar); the bronze body is Greece, under Alexander the Great; and the iron symbolizes Rome. The iron and clay could therefore be representative of the declining Roman Empire, maybe specifically when Theodosius I divided the kingdom between his two sons in 395, beginning the permanent breakup of the empire. The rock, cut out "not by human hands" seems to clearly represent the coming of Christ, but it is somewhat problematic to decide whether the first or the second coming is meant. If the four kingdoms end with Rome, then it might be supposed that the huge mountain that grew from the rock is representative of the spread of Christianity, and the spiritual

NEBUCHADNEZZAR'S IMAGE

sense of "the kingdom of heaven." Of course, part of the difficulty here is that Christ came well before the Roman Empire became "iron and clay mixed;" Theodosius I was actually the one who declared Christianity to be the official religion of Rome. On the other hand, when Nebuchadnezzar's image is compared with Daniel's vision of the four beasts in chapter 7, it seems clear that the fourth kingdom is yet to come. In that case, the second coming of Christ will bring about the fulfillment of these prophecies, when "all peoples, nations and men of every language" will worship Him (Da 7:14), earthly empires will be finally done away with, and God's kingdom will fill the whole earth.

2. King Nebuchadnezzar caused a ninety foot golden statue to be made and set up on the plain of Dura, commanding that all of Babylon bow down to worship it (Da 3:1-6). The three friends of Daniel—Shadrach, Meshach, and Abednego—were tossed into the fiery furnace as punishment for refusing to bow down to the image (Da 3:19-23). When Nebuchadnezzar saw how God miraculously preserved them, not allowing even their clothes to be singed, he acknowledged the superiority of the Hebrews' God over the gods of Babylon (Da 3:28-29).

IMAGE OF GOD

According to the Genesis account, God created humans in His own image (Ge 1:26-27). While we do not know precisely in what ways we are in the image of God, we know that this is what specifically distinguishes us from all the rest of His creation. We can assume that the special ability to communicate and to have a personal relationship with God, which is not shared by other creatures, is part of what is meant here. The term "image of God" is used several times in Scripture. Genesis 9:6 gives this as a reason for the severe death penalty for murder. First Corinthians 11:7 adds a certain complexity to the discussion of men and women together being created in God's image (Ge 1:27). In the New Testament, we are shown another dimension of being made in God's image. Because of the introduction of sin to this world, our portrayal of God's image has become distorted and scarred. In the Christian life, the process of sanctification is designed to mold us into the likeness of Christ (Ro 8:29; 1 Co 15:49; 2 Co 3:18; Ep 4:24; Col 3:10), thus fulfilling God's original plan for us. Furthermore, we see that Christ Himself is called "the image of God" (Col 1:15; He 1:3).

The human position of being created "in the image of God," made "a little lower than the angels" (Ps 8:5), ought to make us respect and value one another more highly. Each human life is "fearfully and wonderfully made" (Ps 139:14) by God, and therefore should be treated with care and consideration.

IMAGERY

That which is produced by the human imagination, either mental images or physical images. The reference to imagery in Ezekiel 8:12 probably means idols or carved images of false gods.

IMAGINATION (archaic)

This word is used in the sense of evil purposes or plans devised by the human mind (Ge 8:21; Je 7:24; Lk 1:51), rather than in the sense of the ability of the human intellect to produce fiction.

IM′LA (full)

Father of the prophet Micaiah (1 Ki 22:8-9; 2 Ch 18:7-8). Micaiah was a prophet during the reign of Ahab, the king of Israel and husband of Jezebel.

IM′LAH

See IMLA.

IM•MAN′U•EL, EM•MAN′U•EL (God is with us)

The symbolic name of the child whose birth Isaiah promised as a sign of deliverance and safety to King Ahaz (Is 7:14). The name is repeated in Isaiah 8:8. This prophecy was made at a time of national crisis (735 B.C.) when the kingdom of Ahaz was threatened with defeat by the combined armies of Syria and Ephraim. In addition to its immediate significance as a sign to Ahaz, this prophecy has always been regarded as a forewarning of the Messiah. Matthew specifically tells us that it was fulfilled in the birth of Christ (Ma 1:23). The ultimate fulfillment of "God with us" will be found in the New Jerusalem, where we will be finally in God's presence forever (Re 21:2-4).

IM′MER

This is both the name of a town, and the name of several men in the Old Testament.

1. A descendant of Aaron, Immer was a priest in the time of David. His family was made the sixteenth course of priests of the twenty-four divisions who served in the tabernacle (1 Ch 24:1,6,14).

2. Apparently the name of a town in Babylon, Immer was the exile home of certain priestly families who could not establish their descent from Israel (Ez 2:59; Ne 7:61).

3. Father of Pashur. Pashur was the priest who had Jeremiah beaten and put in the stocks (Je 20:1-2).

4. A priest and the father of Meshillemith (1 Ch 9:12; Ne 11:13). Over one thousand of Immer's descendants accompanied Zerubbabel to Jerusalem (Ez 2:37; Ne 7:40).

5. Father of Zadok, who labored on the wall of Jerusalem under Nehemiah (Ne 3:29).

IMMORALITY

Behavior or a heart attitude that is contrary to the moral laws that God has set up. Often this term is applied specifically to sexual sin (Pr 2:16; 1 Co 5:1; Ga 5:19), and also to Israel's deplorable habit of worshipping pagan gods (Eze 23:8,17).

IMMORTALITY

The doctrine of continued existence after the death of the body. The question, "If a man die, shall he live again?" (Jo 14:14) is answered in the affirmative by Hebrews who regarded man as a body inhabited by a soul (Ge 2:7). At death the body returns to the ground (Ge 3:19; Ec 12:7), but the soul lives on (Job 19:25-27; Ps 49:15; Da 12:2-3). One distinguishing difference between the Pharisees and Sadducees was that the former believed in a resurrection and immortality while the latter denied both (Lk 20:27-38). The New Testament teaches that the righteous will be rewarded and the wicked punished after death (Ma 13:37-43; Jo 6:47-58; 14:1-2; 1 Co 15:19-58; Ga 6:7-8; 1 Th 4:13-18; Re 14:13; 20:12-15).

IMMUTABILITY

One of the attributes of God, which states that His nature does not, has not, and will never change (Mal 3:6). James 1:17 states that God has "no variation or shadow of turning." Our earth is constantly moving in relation to our light source, and therefore we are accustomed to the "variations and shadow of turning." In contrast, God's position in relation to us never changes, He is always the same (He 13:8). Because God is always the same, we can trust in His steadfast love (De 5:10; Ps 103:4; Is 63:7), knowing that He is the one who holds all things together (He 1:3).

IM' NA *(he will restrain)*

A son of Helem, a descendant of Asher (1 Ch 7:35).

IM' NAH

Two Old Testament men:

1. A son of Asher, founder of a tribal family (Ge 46:17; Nu 26:44; 1 Ch 7:30).

2. The father of Kore, a Levite (2 Ch 31:14). Kore lived during the reign of Hezekiah, king of Judah.

IMPEDIMENT

Something that obstructs or hinders. In Mark 7:31-37, this word is used to indicate the speech problem of a deaf man whom Jesus healed.

IMPENITENT

Without remorse (Ro 2:5-6).

IMPERIOUS

Haughty, arrogant, overbearing; other versions have translated the word describing the harlot in Ezekiel 16:30 as "brazen."

IMPLACABLE

Unyielding, obstinate (Ro 1:28-31).

IMPLEAD

A legal term: to sue at law, prosecute, bring charges against (Ac 19:38).

IMPORTUNATE WIDOW, PARABLE OF

(Lk 18:1-8)

IMPORTUNITY

Persistence; annoying urgency; pressing, incessant requesting (Lk 11:7-8). One who asks for something with importunity will not give up until the request is granted. While we may have a negative view of this kind of pestering, Jesus taught His disciples that this is how we should pray: without giving up, asking, seeking and knocking until we are answered (Lk 11:9-10).

IMPOTENCE

Lack of power, inability. Specifically, the inability of a man to father children. A man who was a eunuch, either by design or because of an accident, was not allowed to serve as a priest before the Lord (Le 21:20).

IMPRECATORY PSALMS

To *imprecate* is to pray that evil will befall someone, to curse or invoke harm. The imprecatory Psalms are psalms in which the writers are asking God to bring His wrath upon their ungodly foes, to subject the evil to His righteous judgment and thus vindicate and rescue His followers. These Psalms address the age-old struggle of why God so often allows evil people to go their way unchecked, even when it is His children who are suffering at their hands. (See Ps 5; 11; 17; 35; 55; 59; 69; 109; 137; 140 for examples.)

IMPURITY

See UNCLEANNESS.

IMPUTE

To reckon or charge something to someone's account (Ro 4:8; Phile 18). We see the concept of imputation at work in our lives in four distinct ways:

1. Adam's sin is imputed to the entire human race (Ro 5:12-19). Through Adam, sin entered into the world, and from Adam we have all inherited a fallen, sinful human nature (1 Co 15:21-22).

2. Besides Adam's sin, each of us deserves to have our own personal sins charged to our accounts (2 Co 5:19).

3. Instead of having to bear the consequences of the sins imputed to us, God has chosen to impute our sins, rather, onto Christ.

Jesus, the Perfect Man, was born free from the taint of Adam's sin, and committed no sins Himself, living a sinless life. When He died in our place, He died bearing our sins, taking the punishment as though He deserved it. Our sins were *imputed* to His account, and He paid the debt (Is 53:6; 2 Co 5:21; 1 Pe 2:24).

4. Not only were our sins charged to Christ, leaving us free; God has also imputed Christ's righteousness to all believers (Ro 4; 1 Co 1:30; 2 Co 5:21; Ph 3:9; Jude 24). Because of this, we can stand before God, *considered righteous,* and therefore be allowed into His presence.

IM′ RAH *(stubborn)*

A son of Zophah of the tribe of Asher (1 Ch 7:36).

IM′ RI *(eloquent)*

1. Son of Bani and descendant of Perez (1 Ch 9:4). This Imri may possibly be the same person as Amariah (Ne 11:4).

2. Father of Zaccur, who labored on the wall (Ne 3:2).

INCANTATION

The casting of a magic spell. See MAGIC, SORCERY, AND DIVINATION.

INCARNATION

The word simply means *becoming flesh* or *enfleshment.* This word is not actually used in the Bible; it is a theological term for the coming of Jesus Christ as God in flesh (Ro 8:3; Ep 2:15; Col 1:22). As the second person of the Trinity, the Son of God is fully and completely God. In the incarnation, God became man, putting on human flesh and coming as a helpless infant, born of a woman just like any other human child. Jesus Christ, the man, was fully and completely human, without ceasing to be fully and completely God.

God dwells "in inapproachable light, whom no man has seen or can see;" we are taught that no one may see God and live (1 Ti 6:16; Ex 33:20). Nevertheless, God has arranged a way for finite humans to know Him, by coming Himself in a form like ours, and experiencing life as a human (Jo 1:1,14,18). Because of this, we now have an advocate who is able to have compassion on our weakness, fully understanding all that it means to be human (He 2:17-18; 4:14-16; 5:2,7-8).

It is impossible for us to grasp what it means for Jesus to be both fully man and fully God, but we must not fail to realize that both are true. Only a perfect man could offer Himself for our sins; only God can be perfect. We will be out of balance if we emphasize Christ's humanity and downplay His divinity; we will be equally wrong if in honoring Him as God, we become uncomfortable with the idea that He came as a real man.

INCENSE

A fragrant substance burned in the religious services of the Israelites (Ex 25:6; 35:8,28). When God gave Moses the plans for the tabernacle, and the instructions for sacrifice and worship, one of the things that He set up was an altar for incense. The high priest was to burn incense each morning and evening, as a pleasant aroma to God (Ex 30:1-9). The Israelites were given a special formula for the incense that was to be burned in the tabernacle, a compound of stacte, onycha, galbanum and pure frankincense. Only this recipe was to be used, and it was to be considered holy to the Lord (Ex 30:34-36). Apparently, incense was something that people used in their homes as well as in worship, for the Israelites were strictly charged to never take this special incense recipe and produce it for their own personal use (Ex 30:37-38).

Around the world, incense seems to be associated with worship; even now many religions ceremonially burn incense before their idols or icons, in their worship services or before the spirits of their ancestors. Burning incense before false gods was one of the things that Israel did when the people were straying from God's ways (2 Ki 22:17; Je 11:12,17; 48:35).

The sweet smell of burning incense is compared in Scripture to the prayers of the saints, which are offered up to God as a pleasing aroma (Ps 141:2; Re 8:3-4).

INCENSE

INCEST

Sexual relations with a close relative. This sin is strictly forbidden in the law (Le 20:10-21). God's people were warned against committing adultery with the wife of any other man, against homosexual relations, and also forbidden to have relations with the following: one's mother, stepmother, daughter-in-law, mother-in-law, sister, sister-in-law, aunt, or the wife of an uncle. The penalty for ignoring these injunctions was death.

INCH

See WEIGHTS AND MEASURES.

INCONTINENT

Unbridled, uncontrollable (2 Ti 3:1-3).

IN'DI·A

The India mentioned in the Old Testament probably included approximately the same area which today makes up the nations of India and Pakistan. India is part of the continent of Asia, south of the Himalaya Mountains. Its name comes from the Indus River, which rises in Tibet, and flows southward to the Arabian Sea. India is named in Scripture as the easternmost boundary of the Persian Empire under Ahasuerus, who reigned over 127 provinces from India to Ethiopia (Es 1:1; 8:9). Solomon's fleets may have gone as far as India on their voyages in search of treasures for Solomon's court (1 Ki 10:22).

INDITING (archaic)

Prompting or dictating the composition of something in literary form (Ps 45:1).

INERRANT

Incapable of error, trustworthy, true in every sense. See INSPIRATION.

INFALLIBLE

Not subject to failure, always accomplishing its purpose. See INSPIRATION.

INFANT BAPTISM

See BAPTISM.

INFIDEL

One who is unfaithful: an unbeliever (1 Ti 5:8).

INFINITY

Without end or boundary. A theological term used to describe God's quality of having no end or beginning, not being constrained by time or space. The human mind is finite; it has limitations. Therefore the concept of infinity is difficult to grasp, but we can take great comfort in knowing that God is so much more than His creation—that nothing that happens is outside of His control or knowledge. God's infinity is part of several of His other attributes, such as omniscience (Ma 10:30; Ps 147:4-5), eternity (Ex 3:14), omnipresence (Ps 139), and omnipotence (He 1:3).

INFIRMITY

Weakness, illness. The prophet Isaiah prophesied that the coming Messiah would relieve us of the burden of our infirmities (Is 53:4). Jesus Christ fulfilled that promise more than literally, not only healing the physical sickness of the people who came to Him (Ma 8:17), but also doing the greater thing by providing a way for us to be healed and cleansed from the spiritual sickness of sin (1 Pe 2:24).

INGATHERING, FEAST OF

See TABERNACLES, FEAST OF.

INHERITANCE

See HEIR.

INIQUITY

Sin, unrighteousness, disobedience, wickedness, depravity (Ge 15:16; Ps 51:5,9; 2 Pe 2:16; Re 18:5).

INK

A writing fluid, probably a solution of charcoal or soot and diluted gum (Je 36:18; 2 Co 3:3; 2 Jo 12; 3 Jo 13).

INKHORN

A receptacle made of wood, horn, or metal for holding ink. Sometimes, a writer would carry his inkhorn attached to his belt (Eze 9:2-3,11).

INLET

A cove or small bay along the coastline of a body of water, where the water is quiet and moderately shallow. The tribe of Asher, which was given territory along the sea, was described as staying by its inlets, rather than supporting Deborah and Barak in their struggle against the Caananites under Sisera (Ju 5:17).

INN

A place to pass the night. The characteristic hospitality of the people of ancient Palestine to travelers made the inn less necessary than it is in modern society (Ju 19:15-21; 2 Ki 4:8; Ac 28:7; He 13:2). Some Old Testament references to inns may simply mean a place with a well or stream where travelers could camp for the night, rather than a house or other permanent dwelling open for lodging (Ge 42:27, KJV).

By New Testament times, inns in a more modern sense seemed to have become common-place. Luke mentions one such place (Ac 28:15), and Jesus, in His parable about the Good Samaritan, mentioned an inn as the natural place for the Samaritan to bring the wounded traveler (Lk 10:33-37). Of course, the most significant and interesting inn of all is the inn which refused room to Mary and Joseph when they traveled to Bethlehem. The young couple had no choice but to spend the night in the stable with the animals, and in this humble setting the King of kings was born. God sent His Son to earth as a man, not in pomp and dignity, but in poverty and humiliation. His birth was heralded by angels, but they did not sing the glad tidings to the wealthy or powerful, they came to some poor shepherds, looking after their flocks in the fields at night (Lk 2).

INNOCENCE

Guiltlessness, freedom from blame (Ge 20:5; Ps 26:6). The first people God created lived in the garden of Eden in a state of innocence. They had no sin. Then the serpent tempted Eve to eat the forbidden fruit, and Eve, in her turn, led Adam into sin (Ge 3:1-24). Because of the disobedience of Adam and Eve, sin entered the world, and the whole human race has been tainted. Only Jesus Christ was able to live a completely innocent life, blameless and guilt-less (Ro 3:9-18; 2 Co 5:21). Because of His death, those who believe can be declared inno-cent before God and receive eternal life (Ro 10:9).

INNOCENTS, SLAUGHTER OF

The mass murder of all the male children under the age of two in Bethlehem and the surrounding area. Herod the king was disturbed by the Magi who came to Jerusalem to look for the "King of the Jews." Fearing a possible rival or trouble with Rome, Herod sought to eliminate the possibility of such a child surviving to adulthood (Ma 2:2,13-18). The tragic events of this time were foretold by the prophet Jeremiah (Je 31:15). A similar slaughter of inno-cent children was planned by Pharoah in the days of Israel's slavery in Egypt, but his plans were foiled by the Hebrew midwives (Ex 1:15-22).

IN NO WISE (archaic)

By no means, assuredly not (Ma 5:17-18).

INORDINATE

Without restraint; immoderate (Eze 23:10-11).

INQUIRE OF THE LORD

To ask for God's guidance and direction before taking action, or simply to answer a question (Ge 25:22; Ju 20:27; 2 Sa 2:1). Besides inquir-ing, people sometimes used other methods for determining God's direction. See URIM AND THUMMIM, and CASTING OF LOTS.

INSANITY

Insanity in the Bible is a complex subject. Even then as now, the division between body and spirit was not easy to define. It is impossible to tell when a disorder of the intellect is a physical problem with the organ of the brain, or a spiritual problem. Many times, insanity in Scripture was linked to demonic activity, or to other spiritual problems. Saul exhibited symptoms of a mental disorder which sounds similar to manic depression, and the Bible clearly links this with his spiritual state, specifically with his disobedience to God (1 Sa 15:24-26; 16:14-23). Nebuchadnezzar also experi-enced madness as a result of sin. When he began to take upon himself the glory that belongs only to God, he became insane as a punishment (Da 4:33). In fact, when the law was given to Israel, they were warned that mental disorder would be one of the punishments for disobedience (De 28:28).

When David fled from Saul, he at first went to the Philistines, but became afraid of what they would do to him as the one who killed Goliath. In order to protect himself, he pretended to be insane. The Philistine king left him alone, apparently feeling that an insane man was not to be interfered with (1 Sa 21:10-15). It was a widespread ancient belief that insanity had a spiritual source, indicating anything from great sin to the capriciousness of the gods. While modern psychology and medicine have developed physical explanations and drugs for treating mental and emotional instability, it is still unclear how much of this kind of illness is related more to spiritual problems than to physical abnormality.

INSCRIPTION

A carved, engraved or printed notice, such as the indictment which Pilate caused to be hung on Jesus's cross for all to see (Mk 15:26; Lk 23:38).

INSPECTION GATE

See GATES OF JERUSALEM.

INSPIRATION

The work of the Holy Spirit in producing the written word of God. The Bible is a book compiled over a period of many hundreds of years, written down by over forty different authors. It might seem that such a document would be a patchy affair, full of confusing contradictions; however, the Bible displays no such difficulties. Instead, it works together as a beautiful whole to show us both God's love and His judgment in His gracious dealings with humankind.

The word *inspiration* is found but once in the New Testament; in 2 Timothy 3:16-17 where Paul says that "All Scripture is given by inspiration of God, and is profitable for doctrine, for reproof, for correction, for instruction in righteousness, that the man of God may be complete, thoroughly equipped for every good work." A very literal translation would read, "All Scripture is God-breathed." Divine inspiration logically follows divine revelation. In revelation God speaks to man's ear, while by inspiration He guides the pen to ensure that the imparted message is correctly written down.

There are several ideas about the process of inspiration. One is called the natural theory. This says that the Bible authors were inspired only in a natural sense, as one might say that William Shakespeare was inspired. Another theory, called the content theory, suggests that God merely gave the writer the main content or idea, allowing him to choose his own words to express that concept. In contrast, Jesus Him-

self said that the very letters of the words were also chosen by God (Ma 5:18). This position is referred to as the plenary-verbal view. The word *plenary* means "full," plenary inspiration refers to the fact that every part of the Bible is inspired by God. It is not a compilation, with some parts from God and some from man, or some parts more fully from divine inspiration than others. The entire book, every paragraph, every page, is equally from God. The concept of verbal inspiration is an extension of plenary inspiration. Not only is the gist of the Bible inspired, not only the message, but the very words used to convey the message. Every word in every sentence was the exact term chosen by God to convey His truth. Scripture does not just "contain God's word," Scripture actually is His word. The Bible authors understood that their writings were being guided by the Spirit of God, even as they wrote them. Peter said this was true of the Old Testament authors (2 Pe 1:20-21). He then stated that his own letters (1 and 2 Peter) were inspired by God (2 Pe 3:1-2). Finally, he pointed out that this was also true concerning Paul's writings (2 Pe 3:15-16).

Because it is inspired by God, the Bible is both *inerrant* and *infallible*. To be inerrant is to be incapable of error, to be wholly true. We can be certain that God's word is trustworthy and reliable. It does not contain mistakes; it will not lead us astray with false ideas or half-truths. The Bible is not only wholly true, it is infallible; that is, it cannot fail. God's message to us must always accomplish its purpose. He chose words that would be sure to adequately convey to us what He wants us to know, and the ideas and commands that are thus conveyed are guaranteed to be effective in our lives (Is 55:11). Because God is holy and true, we can trust that His words will also be holy and true, faultless and faithful (Re 3:7; 21:5).

Because God was sending His message to a fallen human race, He chose a unique and particularly effective way to arrange this. Rather than sending down a finished book from heaven, He used a variety of human authors to preserve His words, working through and using the unique personality and writing style of each person. A relatively small proportion of the Bible was written down by human scribes as God audibly dictated the words (Ex 19:3-6; Re 21:5-8). The Books of the Prophets were certainly written by men who knew that they were under the influence of the Holy Spirit, and were receiving a message directly from God (Is 1:1; 2 Pe 1:20-21; Re 1:10-11), but the majority of Scripture was written down with a more subtle, and probably many times unrealized, influence of the Holy Spirit upon the human author (Lk 1:1-4). A good example of this is Psalm 22. David wrote this psalm describing the innocent suffering at the hands of evil men, apparently abandoned by God, but there is no indication that David himself realized that this was more than an outpouring of his own troubled soul. Looking at the greater picture, with the perspective of finished history, we can clearly see that this psalm was more than it appeared, and in fact was a specific and detailed prophecy of the cross (Ps 22:16-18). David could not have made up such a prophecy on his own, nor would it have been either humanly possible or reasonable for Jesus to have arranged all the details of fulfilling an obscure psalm in order to deceive the disciples. Only words inspired by God could have been written, preserved, and fulfilled in such a way.

When doubt is cast upon the viability of certain portions of Scripture, it is interesting to note that the New Testament records some key statements of Jesus Christ which validate some of the more controversial stories of the Old Testament (Ma 19:4; 22:29; 24:37-39; Lk 11:51; 17:28-30; 24:25,44; Jo 5:46). Clearly, Jesus believed in the accuracy and historical truth of the Old Testament.

When the whole of Scripture and the redemption story are considered together, we must see that to accept one is to accept the other. Considering the claims that Scripture makes for itself, and the fact that our Savior endorsed it as truth, the only consistent response we can make is to believe it as the inspired word of God. If the basic claims of inerrancy and divine inspiration are lies, then the rest of the book cannot be classified as a "good book." Good books are not based on deception. If the Bible's claims of truth and inspiration are false, then we could have no reason for believing that the gospel that it teaches is true either. A person cannot believe in Christ for salvation, and call God's book a lie without at least a very serious mental dichotomy.

One final thing should be said about inspiration. Plenary-verbal inspiration does not guarantee the inspiration of any translation, but only of the original Hebrew and Greek manuscripts.

INSTANT (archaic)

Insistent; steadfast; urgent; fervent (Lk 7:4; 23:22-23; Ac 26:7; Ro 12:12).

INSURRECTION

Rebellion against the governing authorities. The rebuilding of the city of Jerusalem after the Babylonian captivity was thwarted because of alleged former insurrection (Ez 4:15,19). The prisoner Barabbas, who was released to the Jews instead of Jesus, was an outlaw involved in an attempted rebellion against the Romans (Mk 15:7). Because of such insurrectionists, anyone who caused a great stir was bound to be regarded with suspicion by the authorities. Paul was once mistaken for an insurrectionist, after he was involved in a near riot in Jerusalem (Ac 21:34-39).

INTEGRITY

Sincerity; honor; acting without deceit or hollowness; not two-faced; uprightness; consistency; blamelessness. This word comes from the same root as the mathematical term *integer*, meaning *whole*. Integrity could be seen as wholeness of spirit. A person of integrity is one whose principles, motives, and actions work together as a whole; someone who functions uprightly. Noah (Ge 6:9), Abraham (Ge 17:1; 25:27), David (1 Ki 9:4), and Job (Job 1:1,8; 2:3,9; 4:6; 27:5; 31:6) are all described as people of integrity. Jesus taught that purity of heart and motive, and singleness of mind are godly characteristics that we should strive for (Ma 5:8; 6:1-6,22).

INTERCESSION

Petitioning, entreating, or praying on behalf of another; seeking as a third party to reconcile opponents. Because of the fallen nature of humanity, people are continually in a state of conflict, both with one another and with God. The first example we see in Scripture of a righteous man interceding with God for his fellow man is in Genesis 18. Abraham knew that God planned to destroy Sodom and Gomorrah because of their wickedness, and he entreated God to spare the righteous from the impending disaster. Later, when Pharaoh was detaining the Israelites in Egypt, and God smote him with plagues, he asked Moses to intercede for him with God, entreating the removal of the plagues (Ex 8:28). Moses also interceded for the whole nation of Israel when they sinned against God by making and worshipping the golden calf. They deserved to be destroyed, but Moses entreated God to show mercy to them (Ex 32:11-14; 30-33). While God is a merciful God—longsuffering and willing to listen to entreaty, ongoing willful sin is not something that He will tolerate; as in the case of Eli's wicked sons (1 Sa 2:25; Je 7:16).

Because we are ongoing sinners, and cannot make ourselves righteous, we stand in continual need of an intercessor. Jesus Christ is that intercessor for us: "He is also able to save to the uttermost those who come to God through Him, since He ever lives to make intercession for them (He 7:25). While Jesus was here on earth, He interceded for His disciples (Lk 22:32; Jo 17), and even for those who were wrongfully killing Him (Lk 23:34). When we are praying, and do not know what to say or what to ask for, the Holy Spirit works as our intercessor, translating our inarticulate groaning into petition for exactly what He knows we need (Ro 8:26-27). God has also commanded us to intercede in prayer on behalf of others (1 Ti 2:1).

INTEREST
See USURY.

INTERMEDIATE STATE

The time between death and the final resurrection which will happen at the second coming of Christ. Typically, we think of heaven and hell as the immediate destination after death, but this view does not quite fit in with all that Scripture has to say on the subject. The information we do have is scanty, and leaves some gaps in our understanding. In several passages, death is referred to in terms of sleep (Ma 9:24; 1 Co 15:20,51; 2 Pe 3:4). Paul called the believers who have already died "those who are asleep," and taught that when Christ returns the second time, these "dead in Christ" would be raised up first, and then those who are still alive will join them in the air (1 Th 4:13-17). This fits in with the Great White Throne Judgment described in Revelation 20:11-15, where all the dead are gathered together and judged according to their deeds. At this point, the

wicked are condemned to the lake of fire, and the redeemed righteous enter paradise. All this sounds as though there is some kind of waiting period between death and judgment, but evidence can be shown which lets us know that this is not a passive state. Paul, in his discussion of death and the earthly body, says that to be absent from the body is to be present with the Lord (2 Co 5:1-8). Jesus assured the penitent thief on the cross that "this day" he would be with Christ in paradise (Lk 23:43). Paul talks about a man who was caught up into paradise (2 Co 12:4), and Revelation 2:7 describes paradise as the final reward of those who overcome.

Jesus told the story of the rich man and Lazarus, which describes the rich man being tormented in Hades while Lazarus was far off "in Abraham's bosom" (Lk 16:19-31). It is a matter of dispute, whether this story is a parable whose details should not be too closely followed, or an accurate picture of life after death. We do not know what "Abraham's bosom" is, but Hades is mentioned again when John describes the judgment at the Great White Throne. He says that "the sea gave up the dead who were in it, and Death and Hades delivered up the dead who were in them." *Death and Hades* may be the same as the Hebrew *sheol* or *grave,* which is often mentioned in the Psalms. Death and Hades are obviously not the same as the lake of fire, which is the final destination of Satan and his angels, and of the wicked.

Whatever the intermediate state may or may not be, it is clear that after death the unrighteous and unbelieving will be condemned to punishment while the redeemed of the Lord will be with Him forever.

INTERPRETATION
See HERMENEUTICS.

INTERPRETATION OF TONGUES
See TONGUES, GIFT OF.

INTERTESTAMENTAL PERIOD

Approximately four hundred years of silence between the last of the prophets and the coming of Christ. During this time, no more prophecies were given to Israel. When they returned to the land after the Babylonian captivity, they were able to rebuild Jerusalem, and reinstate the priesthood and proper observance of the law, but they were still dominated by the Persian Empire. When the Persian Empire fell to the Greeks under Alexander the Great, the entire ancient world was profoundly affected by Greek culture and religion. It was during this time that the additional laws of the Talmud were added onto Judaism in an attempt to protect their religion from the corrupting influence of Greek culture and religion. The different sects of the Pharisees and Sadducees, so familiar to the New Testament writings, were developed in this period.

In an attempt to force Hellenization on the stubborn Israelites, the ruler Antiochus Epiphanes purposely defiled the temple by sacrificing a pig on its holy altar in 168 B.C. After this outrage, a rebellion occurred, led by the family of Maccabeus. Under Judas Maccabeus, the Jews finally won concessions from the government to worship as they chose, and the temple was cleansed and worship begun again. Chanukah, the Jewish festival of lights, was started at this time to celebrate the miracle that kept the temple's lampstand burning until enough of the proper oil could be procured.

The waning Greek Empire was taken over by Rome, and in 64 B.C. the land of Israel was under Roman rule. After hundreds of years of domination by pagan empires, the faithful remnant of Israel was eager for their Messiah to come and set them free.

INTESTINES

The lower part of the gastrointestinal tract, after the stomach. As part of the digestive process, the small intestines take the food which has been broken down by the gastric juices in the stomach, and distribute the nutrients to the bloodstream. Waste products pass into the large intestine, where they are processed for removal from the body. Jehoram, king of Judah, was struck down by a horrible intestinal illness because of his wickedness (2 Ch 21:15-19).

INTESTINES, DISEASE OF

See DYSENTERY.

I'OB

A form of JASHUB.

IPH·DEI'AH (Jehovah delivers)

A son of Shashak (1 Ch 8:25).

IPH·E·DEI'AH

See IPHDEIAH.

IPH'TAH

A town of Judah (Jos 15:43).

IPH'TAH-EL

A valley that lies between Zebulun and Asher (Jos 19:14,27).

IR

The father of Shuppim and Huppim, a descendant of Benjamin (1 Ch 7:12). Maybe the same person as Iri.

I'RA (watchful)

Two or three of David's entourage.

1. Son of Ikkesh, a Tekoite, one of David's mighty men (2 Sa 23:26; 1 Ch 11:28).

2. An Ithrite, one of David's mighty men, and possibly the same as Ira I (2 Sa 23:38; 1 Ch 11:40).

3. A Jairite, "chief minister" under David (2 Sa 20:26).

I'RAD

Son of Enoch (Ge 4:18).

I'RAM

A chief of Edom (Ge 36:43; 1 Ch 1:54).

IR HA-HERES (city of destruction)

Some versions translate this as City of the Sun, that is, Heliopolis (Is 19:18). See also ON.

I'RI

A son of Bela (1 Ch 7:7), possibly the same as Ir .

I·RI'JAH

A captain of the guard at the time the Chaldeans besieged Jerusalem (Je 37:13).

IR-NA'HASH (city of a serpent)

A town of Judah (1 Ch 4:12).

I'RON

1. A metal first mentioned in the Scriptures in the statement that Tubal-cain worked in brass and iron (Ge 4:22). The bed of Og was fashioned of iron (De 3:11), as were chariots in the time of Joshua (Jos 17:16; Ju 1:19; 4:3,13).

Iron was also used in making weapons (1 Sa 17:7), tools (1 Ki 6:7; Job 19:24; Je 17:1), and harrows and threshing instruments (2 Sa 12:31; Am 1:3). Iron ore in Egypt and Palestine was smelted in furnaces (De 4:20; 1 Ki 8:51). In this process a bellows was used (Eze 22:20). At the time of David's battle with the giant Goliath, the Israelites were at an extreme disadvantage in their struggle with the Philistines, because they lacked iron and blacksmiths. Thus, the Philistines were able to prevent them from making effective weapons, besides forcing the Israelites to apply to them even to have tools or farm implements mended or made (1 Sa 13:19-22).

2. A fortified city of Naphtali, (Jos 19:38); probably the present day Galilean town of Yarun.

IR′ PEEL *(God heals)*

A town of Benjamin, not far from Jerusalem (Jos 18:27).

IRRIGATION

The process of artificially watering crops when rain is lacking. The land of Israel was described as "flowing with milk and honey" partly because it did not require extensive irrigation, being well watered at that time by the early and latter rains (De 11:9-12). Water was sometimes stored in cisterns, but this seems to be more for convenience, or for drinking water (2 Ki 18:31).

IR-SHE′ MESH *(city of the sun)*

A town in the territory of Dan (Jos 19:41); it appears to be the same as Beth-shemesh (Jos 15:10; 21:16; Ju 1:33).

I′ RU *(citizen)*

A son of Caleb. His father was sent with Joshua to spy in the land of Canaan (1 Ch 4:15).

I′ SAAC *(laughter)*

The son and heir of Abraham and Sarah was born in Beer-sheba when his father was about one hundred years old and his mother about ninety (Ge 17:17; 21:2-3; 22:1-2). When God made His covenant with Abraham, He promised that a great nation would be descended from Abraham and Sarah (Ge 13:16; 15:4-6). Abraham believed that God would one day send him children to fulfill the promise, but Sarah

was anxious about her barrenness, and arranged for Abraham to have children with her Egyptian servant, Hagar. While God promised that Ishmael would also be the father of many descendants, he was not the son of the promise. It was thirteen more years before God again addressed the problem of Abraham and Sarah's childlessness. The parents were amazed and incredulous when they were told that a son would be born to them in their advanced age, but nothing is too hard for God (Ge 18:9-15).

Isaac, the son of promise, had reached young manhood (Ge 22:6) when his father was commanded to offer him as a burnt offering. When the Lord was convinced that Abraham passed this test of faith, He spared Isaac's life (Ge 22:12). Isaac was in a special position in terms of his birthright. While Abraham provided materially for his other sons (Ishmael, and the sons of his second wife, Keturah, and of his concubines), Isaac received not only the birthright of an oldest son, but he also inherited the blessings and responsibility of the covenant with God.

When forty years old, Abraham arranged a marriage for Isaac with Rebekah, sister of Laban, and granddaughter of Abraham's brother Nahor (Ge 24). After Abraham's death, they settled in Gerar because of famine (Ge 26:1,6). Two sons were born to them, Esau and Jacob (Ge 27-28). Later Isaac moved to Hebron where he died at the age of one hundred and eighty years. There he was buried beside his parents and his wife in the cave of Machpelah (Ge 35:28; 49:30-31).

I•SA′ IAH THE PROPHET *(Jehovah has saved)*

Also Esaius (Greek form). Isaiah is called the "messianic prophet," because so much of the prophecy concerning Christ is in his book. He began prophesying in the year that King Uzziah of Judah died (Is 6:1,8), and continued through the reigns of Jotham, Ahaz and Hezekiah in Jerusalem (Is 1:1). Besides the Book of Isaiah, he also wrote biographies of Uzziah and Hezekiah, which have been lost (2 Ch 26:22; 32:32). Not much is known about Isaiah's personal life. He was the son of a man named Amoz. He was married to a woman who is described as "the prophetess," but never named (Is 8:3). They had two sons, each of whom was given a special symbolic name which was in

ISAIAH

itself a message to Israel of how God was going to deal with them (Is 7:3; 8:3).

When God called Isaiah to prophesy for Him, He warned Isaiah that the people would not listen to him (Is 6:9-10). For forty years, Isaiah faithfully prophesied the doom and destruction which would fall upon an unrepentant nation, as well as the future deliverance of Israel and the glorious future that would be theirs when they turned again to their God. In Isaiah's lifetime, Israel did not listen, just as God had said. When the Messiah came, God's words to Isaiah were further fulfilled (Ma 13:14-15).

Jewish tradition says that Isaiah was martyred, being sawn in two by the order of the evil king Manasseh, son of Hezekiah. While Scripture does not specifically say that this is so, the writer of Hebrews mentions an unnamed hero of the faith who met just such a death (He 11:37). Because of the strong tradition, it is generally assumed that this verse refers to the prophet Isaiah.

ISAIAH, BOOK OF

1. The Book of Isaiah. Isaiah is the longest of the prophetic books of the Old Testament. Isaiah prophesied to Israel approximately between 740 and 701 B.C., a span of time covering the reign of five kings of Judah, from Uzziah to Manasseh (2 Ch 26–33).

The 66 chapters of the Book of Isaiah can be divided into three main sections. The first section (chapters 1–35) deals mainly with prophecies of condemnation for rebellious Israel and the pagan nations, and prophecies concerning the day of the Lord. These chapters are interspersed with many references of the coming Messiah, praising and thanking God for the promised restoration. Chapters 36–39 are an interlude of historical material, closely paralleling 2 Kings 18–20 and 2 Chronicles 29–32. These chapters deal with Hezekiah, one of the

few righteous kings of Judah; the deliverance from Assyria, Hezekiah's illness and recovery, and Hezekiah's sin. The final chapters of the book (40–66) are prophecies of comfort, detailing Israel's deliverance and glorious future. This section contains the Servant Songs, which beautifully describe our Savior (Is 42:1-9; 49:1-7; 50:1-11; 52:13–53:15).

Some have compared the organization of the Book of Isaiah to a miniature version of the Bible itself. Its 66 chapters correspond to the 66 books of the Bible. The first 39 chapters (corresponding to the 39 books of the Old Testament) deal with judgment and history; the last 27 chapters (corresponding to the 27 books of the New Testament) detail the Messiah and redemption. While we must be aware that the chapter divisions are not a part of the original inspired text, this is a very useful way to remember the basic divisions of the book.

The Book of Isaiah is particularly valuable to us, as it makes known to us the nature and character of God. First, God is holy. Isaiah describes Him as "the Holy One of Israel" 26 times, and when confronted by a vision of God's glory, Isaiah's immediate response was a realization of his own unworthiness in the face of God's holiness (6:1-8). God's righteous judgment is the theme of much of the first portion of the book, but the primary focus is redemption. The word *salvation* occurs more times in Isaiah than in all the other books of the Prophets combined. Isaiah's own name "Jehovah has saved" is a fitting title for this message from God.

Yesha'yahu and its shortened form *yeshaiah* mean "Yahweh is Salvation." This name is an excellent summary of the contents of the book. The Greek form in the Septuagint is *Hesaias,* and the Latin form is *Esaias* or *Isaias.*

2. The Author of Isaiah. Isaiah, the "St. Paul of the Old Testament," was apparently from a distinguished Jewish family. His education is evident in his impressive vocabulary and style. His work is comprehensive in scope and beautifully communicated. Isaiah maintained close contact with the royal court, but his exhortations against alliances with foreign powers were not always well received. This great poet and prophet was uncompromising, sincere, and compassionate. (See ISAIAH THE PROPHET.)

The unity of this book has been challenged

by critics who hold that half of the book was written long after Isaiah's death. It is generally well accepted that he wrote the first part of the book, and the historical portions that occurred during his lifetime (ch. 1–39); but some believe that chapters 40–66 were written by a "second Isaiah," sometime during or after the Babylonian captivity. They argue that 1–39 has an Assyrian background, while 40–66 is set against a Babylonian background. But Babylon is mentioned more than twice as often in chapters 1–39 as in 40–66. The only shift is one of perspective from present time to future time. Critics also argue that there are radical differences in the language, style, and theology of the two sections. Actually, the resemblances between 1–39 and 40–66 are greater than the differences. These include similarities in thoughts, images, rhetorical ornaments, characteristic expressions, and local coloring. It is true that the first section is more terse and rational, while the second section is more flowing and emotional, but much of this is caused by the different subject matter; condemnation versus consolation. Critics often forget that content, time, and circumstances typically affect any author's style. In addition, there is no theological contradiction between the emphasis on the Messiah as King in 1–39 and as Suffering Servant in 40–66. While the thrust is different, the Messiah is seen in both sections as King and Servant. Another critical argument is that Isaiah could not have predicted the Babylonian captivity and the return under Cyrus (mentioned by name in 44 and 45) 150 years in advance. But this is not the only time a prophet mentioned a future ruler by name. During the reign of Jeroboam of Israel, a prophecy came from the Lord concerning Josiah, king of Judah. This was about three hundred years prior to the time of Josiah (1 Ki 13:2). If we admit that predictions were uttered through the inspiring Spirit, then it is inconsistent to deny that Isaiah could by inspiration mention Cyrus by name. This critical view is based on the mere assumption that divine prophecy is impossible, rejecting the predictive claims of the book (see 42:9). The theory cannot explain the amazing messianic prophecies of Isaiah that were literally fulfilled in the life of Christ.

The unity of Isaiah is supported by the apocryphal Book of Ecclesiasticus, the Septuagint, and the Talmud. The discovery of the Dead Sea Scrolls further supports the one author view. The Isaiah scroll is one of the best preserved in this collection, containing the entire Book of Isaiah. No differentiation at all is made between the first and second portions of the book, where the division in authorship is supposed to have occurred. Early tradition does not support the two author view, and in the more than 50 times that the Book of Isaiah is quoted in the New Testament, no intimation is given that any such division should be seen. The New Testament writers clearly believed that Isaiah wrote both sections. John 12:37-41 quotes from Isaiah 6:9-10 and 53:1 and attributes it all to Isaiah. In Romans 9:27 and 10:16-21, Paul quotes from Isaiah 10, 53, and 65 and gives the credit to Isaiah. The same is true of Matthew 3:3 and 12:17-21, Luke 3:4-6, and Ac 8:28.

If 40–66 was written by another prophet after the events took place, then the book would have to be considered a misleading and deceptive work.

3. The Time of Isaiah. Isaiah's long ministry ranged from about 740-680 B.C. (1:1). He began his ministry near the end of Uzziah's reign (790-739 B.C.) and continued through the reigns of Jotham (739-731 B.C.), Ahaz (731-715 B.C.), and Hezekiah (715-686 B.C.). Assyria was growing in power under Tiglath-pileser who turned toward the West after his conquests in the East. He plucked up the small nations that dotted the Mediterranean coast, including Israel and much of Judah. Isaiah lived during this time of military threat to Judah, and warned its kings against trusting in alliances with other countries rather than the power of Yahweh. As a contemporary of Hosea and Micah, he prophesied during the last years of the Northern Kingdom but ministered to the Southern Kingdom of Judah who was following the sins of her sister Israel. After Israel's demise in 722 B.C., he warned Judah of judgment not by Assyria but by Babylon, even though Babylon had not yet risen to power.

Isaiah ministered from the time of Tiglath-pileser (745-727 B.C.) to the time of Sennacherib (705-681 B.C.) of Assyria. We know that Isaiah outdated Hezekiah by a few years because 37:38 records the death of Sennacherib in 681 B.C. Hezekiah was succeeded by his wicked son Manasseh who overthrew the worship of Yahweh and no doubt opposed the work of Isaiah. Tradition teaches that Manasseh was responsible for Isaiah's death.

4. The Christ of Isaiah. When he speaks about Christ, Isaiah sounds more like a New Testament writer than an Old Testament prophet. His messianic prophecies are clearer and more explicit than those in any other Old Testament book. They describe many aspects of the person and work of Christ in His first and second advents, and often blend the two together. Here are a few of the Christological prophecies with their New Testament fulfillments: 7:14 (Ma 1:22-23); 9:1-2 (Ma 4:12-16); 9:6 (Lk 2:11; Ep 2:14-18); 11:1 (Lk 3:23,32; Ac 13:22-23); 11:2 (Lk 3:22); 28:16 (1 Pe 2:4-6); 40:3-5 (Ma 3:1-3); 42:1-4 (Ma 12:15-21); 42:6 (Lk 2:29-32); 50:6 (Ma 26:67; 27:26,30); 52:14 (Ph 2:7-11); 53:3 (Lk 23:18; Jo 1:11; 7:5); 53:4-5 (Ro 5:6,8); 53:7 (Ma 27:12-14; Jo 1:29; 1 Pe 1:18-19); 53:9 (Ma 27:57-60); 53:12 (Mk 15:28); 61:1-2 (Lk 4:17-19,21). The Old Testament has over three hundred prophecies about the first advent of Christ, and Isaiah contributes a number of them. The odds that even ten of them could be fulfilled by one person is a statistical marvel. Isaiah's messianic prophecies that await fulfillment in the Lord's second advent include: 4:2; 11:2-6,10; 32:1-8; 49:7; 52:13,15; 59:20-21; 60:1-3; 61:2-3.

Isaiah 52:13–53:12 is the central passage of the consolation section (40–66). Its five stanzas present five different aspects of the saving work of Christ: (1) 52:13-15—His wholehearted sacrifice (burnt offering); (2) 53:1-3—His perfect character (meal offering); (3) 53:4-6—He brought atonement that ushers in peace with God (peace offering); (4) 53:7-9—He paid for the transgression of the people (sin offering); (5) 53:10-12—He died for the effects of sin (trespass offering).

5. Keys to Isaiah.

Key word: Salvation is of the Lord—The basic theme of this book is found in Isaiah's name: "Salvation is of the Lord." The word *salvation* appears twenty-six times in Isaiah, but only seven times in all the other prophets combined. Chapters 1–39 portray man's great need for salvation, and chapters 40–66 reveal God's great provision of salvation. Salvation is of God, not man; and He is seen as the supreme Ruler, the sovereign Lord of history, and the only Savior. Isaiah solemnly warns Judah of approaching judgment because of moral depravity, political corruption, social injustice, and especially spiritual idolatry. Because the nation does not turn

away from its sinful practice, Isaiah announces the ultimate overthrow of Judah. Nevertheless, God will remain faithful to His covenant by preserving a godly remnant and promises salvation and deliverance through the coming Messiah. The Savior will come out of Judah and accomplish the dual work of redemption and restoration. The Gentiles will come to His light and universal blessing will finally take place.

Key Verses: Isaiah 9:6-7 and 53:6—"For unto us a Child is born, unto us a Son is given; and the government will be upon His shoulder. And His name will be called Wonderful, Counselor, Mighty God, Everlasting Father, Prince of Peace. Of the increase of His government and peace there will be no end, upon the throne of David and over His kingdom, to order it and establish it with judgment and justice from that time forward, even forever. The zeal of the LORD of hosts will perform this (9:6-7).

"All we like sheep have gone astray; we have turned, every one, to his own way; and the LORD has laid on Him the iniquity of us all" (53:6).

Key Chapter: Isaiah 53—Along with Psalm 22, Isaiah 53 lists the most remarkable and specific prophecies of the atonement of the Messiah. As Jesus fulfilled each clear prophecy, He was shown without doubt to be the Messiah.

6. Survey of Isaiah. Isaiah, the "Shakespeare of the prophets," has often been called the "evangelical prophet" because of his incredibly clear and detailed messianic prophecies. The "gospel according to Isaiah" has three major sections: prophecies of condemnation (1–35), historical parenthesis (36–39), and prophecies of comfort (40–66).

Prophecies of Condemnation (1–35). Isaiah's first message of condemnation is aimed at his own countrymen in Judah (1–12). Chapter 1 is a capsulized message of the entire book. Judah is riddled with moral and spiritual disease. The people are neglecting God as they bow to ritualism and selfishness. But Yahweh graciously invites them to repent and return to Him because this is their only hope of avoiding judgment. Isaiah's call to proclaim God's message is found in chapter 6, and this is followed by the book of Immanuel (7–12). These chapters repeatedly refer to the Messiah (see 7:14; 8:14; 9:2,6,7; 11:1-2) and anticipate the blessing of His future reign.

The prophet moves from local to regional judgment as he proclaims a series of oracles against the surrounding nations (13–23). The eleven nations are Babylon, Assyria, Philistia, Moab, Damascus (Syria), Ethiopia, Egypt, Babylon (again), Edom, Arabia, Jerusalem (Judah), and Tyre. Isaiah's little apocalypse (24–27) depicts universal tribulation followed by the blessings of the kingdom. Chapters 28–33 pronounce the woes on Israel and Judah for specific sins. Isaiah's prophetic condemnation closes with a general picture of international devastation that will precede universal blessing (34 and 35).

Historical Parenthesis (36–39). This historical parenthesis looks back to the Assyrian invasion of Judah in 701 B.C. and anticipates the coming Babylonian invasion of Judah. Judah escaped captivity by Assyria (36; 37; 2 Ki 18; 19) but they would not escape from the hands of Babylon (38; 39; 2 Ki 20). God answered King Hezekiah's prayers and delivered Judah from Assyrian destruction by Sennacherib. Hezekiah also turned to the Lord in his illness and was granted a fifteen-year extension of his life. But he foolishly showed all his treasures to the Babylonian messengers, and Isaiah told him that the Babylonians would one day carry his treasure and descendants into captivity.

Prophecies of Comfort (40–66). Having pronounced Judah's divine condemnation, Isaiah comforted them with God's promises of hope and restoration. The basis for this hope is the sovereignty and majesty of God (40–48). Of the 216 verses in these nine chapters, 115 speak of God's greatness and power. The Creator is contrasted with idols, the creations of men. His sovereign character is Judah's assurance of future restoration. Babylon will indeed carry them off; but Babylon will finally be judged and destroyed, and God's people will be released from captivity.

Chapters 49–57 concentrate on the coming Messiah who will be their Savior and Suffering Servant. This rejected but exalted One will pay for their iniquities and usher in a kingdom of peace and righteousness throughout the earth. All who acknowledge their sins and trust in Him will be delivered (58–66). In that day, Jerusalem will be rebuilt, Israel's borders will be enlarged, and the Messiah will reign in Zion. God's people will confess their sins and His enemies will be judged. Peace, prosperity, and justice will prevail, and God will make all things new.

OUTLINE OF ISAIAH

Part One: Prophecies of Condemnation (1:1–35:10)

I. Prophecies Against Judah (1:1–12:6)

A. The Judgment of Judah 1:1-31
B. The Day of the Lord 2:1–4:6
C. The Parable of the Vineyard 5:1-30
D. The Commission of Isaiah 6:1-13
E. The Destruction of Israel by
    Assyria 7:1–10:4
F. The Destruction of Assyria
    by God 10:5–12:6

II. The Prophecies Against Other Nations (13:1–23:18)

A. Prophecies Against Babylon ... 13:1–14:23
B. Prophecies Against Assyria 14:24-27
C. Prophecies Against Philistia 14:28-32
D. Prophecies Against Moab 15:1–16:14
E. Prophecies Against Damascus
    and Samaria 17:1-14
F. Prophecies Against Ethiopia 18:1-7
G. Prophecies Against Egypt 19:1–20:6
H. Prophecies Against Babylon 21:1-10

I. Prophecies Against Dumah
    (Edom) 21:11-12
J. Prophecies Against Arabia 21:13-17
K. Prophecies Against Jerusalem ... 22:1-25
L. Prophecies Against Tyre 23:1-18

III. The Prophecies of the Day of the Lord (24:1–27:13)

A. Judgments of the Tribulation...... 24:1-23
B. Triumphs of the Kingdom 25:1–27:13

IV. The Prophecies of Judgment and Blessing (28:1–35:10)

A. Woe to Ephraim........................ 28:1-29
B. Woe to Ariel (Jerusalem) 29:1-24
C. Woe to Egyptian Alliance......... 30:1–31:9
D. Behold the Coming King 32:1-20
E. Woe to the Spoiler of Jerusalem
    (Assyria) 33:1-24
F. Woe to the Nations 34:1-17
G. Behold the Coming Kingdom 35:1-10

Part Two: The Historical Parenthesis (36:1–39:8)

I. Hezekiah's Salvation from Assyria (36:1–37:38)

A. Assyria Challenges God 36:1-22
B. God Destroys Assyria 37:1-38

II. Hezekiah's Salvation from Sickness (38:1-22)

III. Hezekiah's Sin (39:1-8)

Part Three: The Prophecies of Comfort (40:1–66:24)

I. The Prophecies of Israel's Deliverance (40:1–48:22)

A. Comfort Because of Israel's Deliverance 40:1-11
B. Comfort Because of God's Character 40:12-31
C. Comfort Because of God's Greatness 41:1-29
D. Comfort Because of God's Servant 42:1-25
E. Comfort Because of Israel's Restoration 43:1–44:28
F. Comfort Because of God's Use of Cyrus 45:1-25
G. Comfort Because of Babylon's Destruction 46:1–48:22

II. The Prophecy of Israel's Deliverer (49:1–57:21)

A. The Messiah's Mission 49:1-26
B. The Messiah's Obedience 50:1-11

C. The Messiah's Encouragement to Israel 51:1–52:12
D. The Messiah's Atonement ... 52:13–53:12
E. The Messiah's Promise of Israel's Restoration 54:1-17
F. The Messiah's Invitation to the World............................. 55:1–56:8
G. The Messiah's Rebuke of the Wicked 56:9–57:21

III. The Prophecies of Israel's Glorious Future (58:1–66:24)

A. Blessings of True Worship 58:1-14
B. Sins of Israel 59:1-21
C. Glory of Israel in the Kingdom ... 60:1-22
D. Advents of the Messiah 61:1-11
E. Future of Jerusalem 62:1-12
F. Vengeance of God 63:1-6
G. Prayer of the Remnant 63:7–64:12
H. The Lord's Answer to the Remnant 65:1-16
I. Glorious Consummation of History............................. 65:17–66:24

IS′ CAH (watchful)

A daughter of Abraham's brother Haran, and sister of Milcah who married Abraham's other brother Nahor (Ge 11:27,29).

IS·CAR′ I·OT (man of Kerioth)

Judas, the apostle who betrayed his Lord. (Ma 10:4; Lk 6:16). Judas is called Iscariot to differentiate him from the other apostle named Judas, and also from the Lord's brother (Mk 6:3; Lk 6:16; Ac 1:13,16). It probably denotes that he was a native of Kerioth (Jos 15:25).

ISH′ BAH (he praises)

A descendant of Judah; son of Mered and father of Eshtemoa (1 Ch 4:17).

ISH′ BAK (relinquish)

Son of Abraham and his second wife, Keturah (Ge 25:2).

ISH′ BI-BE′ NOB (my seat is at Nob)

A Philistine giant slain by Abishai, son of Zeruiah, in the days of David the king (2 Sa 21:16-17).

ISH-BO′ SHETH (man of shame)

A son of Saul (2 Sa 2:8). He escaped being slain in Saul's last battle, where both Saul and Jonathan died. Possibly he was elsewhere. After Saul died, David became king of Judah, but the other tribes did not join him. Abner, Saul's captain, placed Ishbosheth on the throne over

ISCARIOT

the rest of Israel, succeeding his father Saul. During his brief reign of two years he came into conflict with David (2 Sa 2:12–3:1). After he insulted Abner by falsely accusing him of misbehaving with one of Saul's former concubines, Abner offered his services to David. Joab, David's captain, murdered Abner as vengeance for the death of Joab's brother, and without his strong leadership Ishbosheth's rule was short lived. Ishbosheth was assassinated by two of his own followers, the captains of his troops. The assassins apparently thought that this action would bring them favor with the new ruler, but David had them put to death for their lawless and cold-blooded murder (2 Sa 4:5-12). This brought the house of Saul to an end.

ISH' HOD, I' SHOD *(man of renown)*

A man of the tribe of Manasseh, son of Gilead's sister Hammoloketh (1 Ch 7:18).

ISH' I *(salutary)*

1. Son of Appaim of the house of Jerahmeel (1 Ch 2:31).

2. Father of Zoheth of Judah, a descendant of Caleb (1 Ch 4:20).

3. A Simeonite whose sons led a force to mount Seir, overcame the Amalekites and seized their territory (1 Ch 4:42).

4. A chief of the half-tribe of Manasseh (1 Ch 5:24).

5. A special name which Israel will use after the restoration, as a symbol of the close relationship that will come about between God and His people (Ho 2:16-17).

ISH·I' AH

See ISSHIAH.

ISH·I' JAH

A son of Harim, one of those who had taken a foreign wife (Ez 10:31).

ISH' MA *(desolate)*

A man of Judah. He is a son of the father (founder) of Etam (1 Ch 4:3).

ISH' MA·EL *(God hears)*

Six Old Testament men bear this name:

1. The son of Abraham by Hagar, Sarah's Egyptian maid. At his birth Abraham was eighty-six years old (Ge 16:3,15). Ishmael was about fourteen years of age when Isaac was born, the child of promise and heir to the covenant promises (Ge 21:5). Paul makes use of the allegory relative to the mocking of Isaac by Ishmael (Ga 4:22-31). For this Ishmael and his mother were expelled from the home of Abraham, and in their distress in the wilderness were divinely provided for. He married an Egyptian (Ge 21:3-21) and became the ancestor of princes (Ge 17:20; 25:12-16). His daughter became the wife of Esau (Ge 28:9; 36:10). He died at the age of 137 (Ge 25:17).

2. Son of Azel, a descendant of Saul (1 Ch 8:38; 9:44).

3. The father of Zebadiah, a leader of Judah in the time of Jehoshaphat (2 Ch 19:11).

4. Son of Jehohanan; the captain of a company. He aided Jehoiada in the uprising against Athaliah and placed Joash on the throne of Judah (2 Ch 23:1–24:2).

5. Son of Pashur who abandoned his foreign wife (Ez 10:22).

6. Son of Nethaniah who played a leading role in the murder of Gedaliah (2 Ki 25:22-26; Je 40:7; 41:15).

ISH' MAE·LITE

A descendant of Ishmael. There were twelve Ishmaelite princes (Ge 17:20; 25:12-16) who settled in northern Arabia. Modern day Arabs consider themselves to be descendants of Ishmael.

ISH·MAI' AH

1. A Gibeonite. During David's outlawry he allied himself with David at Ziklag (1 Ch 12:4).

2. Son of Obadiah, ruler of the tribe of Zebulun (1 Ch 27:19).

ISH′MEE·LITE
See variant of ISHMAELITE.

ISH′ME·RAI
Son of Elpaal, a descendant of Benjamin (1 Ch 8:18).

I′SHOD
See ISHHOD.

ISH′PAH
Son of Beriah, a descendant of Benjamin (1 Ch 8:16).

ISH·PAN
Son of Shashak, a descendant of Benjamin (1 Ch 8:22).

ISHTAR
See GODS, PAGAN.

ISH′TOB *(man of Tob)*
See TOB (2 Sa 10:6,8).

ISH′U·AH
See ISHVAH.

ISH′U·AI
See ISHVI.

ISH′U·I
See ISHVI.

ISH′VAH
A son of Asher (Ge 46:17; 1 Ch 7:30).

ISH′VI
Two Old Testament men:
1. A son of Asher and head of a tribal family (Ge 46:17; Nu 26:44; 1 Ch 7:30).
2. A son of Saul (1 Sa 14:49).

ISHYO
A form of ISHVI.

IS′LAND, ISLE
In the New Testament, this word is used in the conventional sense of a portion of dry land, completely surrounded by water. Several islands are mentioned in the accounts of Paul's missionary journeys in Acts: Cyprus (Ac 13:4,6; 15:39); Samothrace (16:11); Chios (20:15); Samos (20:15); Crete (27:7,12-13,21); Cauda (27:16); and Malta (28:1-11). John was imprisoned on the island of Patmos when he received the vision of Revelation.

In some versions of the Old Testament, the word *island* is used somewhat ambiguously. In some instances it may be the conventional meaning of the word; in other places it may be better understood as coastlands, lands across the water from Palestine, or simply habitable dry land (Is 11:11; 20:6; 42:15; Je 25:22; Eze 26:18).

IS·MA·CHI′AH *(Jehovah sustains)*
A Levite who was a temple overseer in the days of Hezekiah, king of Judah (2 Ch 31:12-13).

IS·MAI′AH
See ISHMAIAH.

IS′PAH
See ISHPAH.

IS′RA·EL *(having power with God)*
1. The name God gave to Jacob after the night he spent at Peniel on his way to Canaan from Mesopotamia. This night, where he wrestled with the angel and saw the ladder up to heaven, was a turning point in his life (Ge 32:22-30).

2. The covenant people, descendants of Jacob. Dating from the change of his name, Jacob's descendants were called "the children of Israel" (Ge 32:32). The name was often used during the period in the wilderness (Ex 32:4; De 4:1; 27:9). While the name referred to the Hebrew people as a whole, a separation began to exist between Judah and the other tribes prior to the actual disruption of the kingdom (1 Sa 11:8; 17:52; 18:16).

3. The designation of the Northern Kingdom after the disruption of the united kingdom. Division took place when the already rebellious northern tribes were confronted with the fact that Rehoboam, Solomon's son and successor, would not reduce the taxes and other burdens imposed by Solomon (1 Ki 12:9-17). When the northern tribes broke away from Judah, their king, Jeroboam feared that loyalty to the temple in Jerusalem would undermine the solidarity of his new kingdom. To combat this possibility, he set up new worship centers, including two golden calves for the people to worship (1 Ki 12:26-33). While he initially presented these as means for worshipping the true God, eventually they became centers of pagan worship, particularly of Baal. Idolatry was especially strong during the reign of Ahab because of the encouragement given it by Ahab's wife, Jezebel (1 Ki 16:30-33). Elijah labored in vain to destroy the idolatry. The Kingdom of Israel ended with the fall of Samaria (721 B.C.), at which time many of the people were carried away to Assyria (2 Ki 17:3-6).

Israel, God's Covenant People

Selection of Israel: The selection of Israel as a special nation to God was part of God's plan (Ro 11:2). Historically, the selection of Israel began with the Lord's promise to Abraham, "I will make you a great nation" (Ge 12:2). The name *Israel* actually is from the new name which God gave to Abraham's grandson, Jacob. It was occasioned by Jacob's spiritual victory at the ford of Jabbock (Ge 32:28). This fact explains why his descendants are often called the children of Israel.

The motivation for the Lord's choice of Israel as His select nation did not lie in any special attraction it possessed. Its people were, in fact, the least in number among all the nations (De 7:6-8). Rather, the Lord chose them because of His love for them and because of His covenant with Abraham. This fact does not mean that God did not love other nations, because it was through Israel that He intended to bring forth the Savior and to bless the entire world (Ge 12:8).

History of Israel. The biblical history of Israel covers 1,800 years and represents a marvelous panorama of God's gracious working through promise, miracle, blessing, and judgment. Israel began as only a promise to Abraham (Ge 12:2). For over four hundred years the people of Israel relied on that promise, especially during the period of bondage to Egypt. Finally, in God's perfect timing, He brought the nation out of Egypt with the greatest series of miracles known in the entire Old Testament (Ex 7–15). This event is called the exodus, meaning *a going out.* Since it constitutes the miraculous birth of the nation, it is to this great act of redemption that the nation always looks back as the foremost example of God's care for His people (Ps 77:14-20; 78:12-55; Ho 11:1).

Once God had redeemed Israel He established His covenant with them at Mount Sinai (Ex 19:5-8). From that point forward the nation was truly the Lord's possession, and He was their God. The covenant foretold gracious blessings for obedience and severe judgments for disobedience. The rest of Israel's history demonstrates the certainty of that prophecy. Through the periods of conquest, judges, monarchy, exile, restoration, and Gentile domination, Israel was blessed when she obeyed and judged when she disobeyed. The nation was finally destroyed in A.D. 70, although this event is not described in the New Testament. Many prophecies, however, promise a future redemption for Israel (Ro 11:26).

The practical value of studying Israel's history is threefold:

a. It sets forth examples to be followed or avoided (1 Co 10:6).
b. It shows God's control of all historical events, in that He was able to deal with Israel as He chose (Ps 78).
c. It serves as a model for all ages of God's kindness and mercy toward His people (Ps 103:14).

Purpose of Israel. The modern day student of the Bible may well ask why so much of Scripture is taken up with the history of a single nation. Certainly many Christians wonder why one nation should be called "God's chosen people." The answer to this question is bound up in God's purpose for Israel. When God promised Abraham that he would become the father of a great nation, He also promised that He would bless all peoples through that nation (Ge 12:1-3). Therefore Israel was to be a channel of blessing as well as a recipient. Even their deliverance from Egypt was partially designed to show other nations that Israel's God was the only true God (Ex 7:5; 14:18; Jos 2:9-11). It was further prophesied by Isaiah that the Messiah would bring salvation to the Gentiles (Is 49:6). Also in the Psalms there are many invitations to other nations to come and worship the Lord in Israel (Ps 2:10-12; 117:1). Ruth the Moabitess is an example of a foreigner who believed in Israel's God.

It is clear that God's promise to Abraham to bless the whole world through him is still being fulfilled. The life, ministry, and death of Jesus

Christ, and the existence and influence of the church today, all came about through God's choice of Israel. All whom the church wins to Christ, whether Jew or Gentile, enter into those great blessings channeled through Israel.

The Government of Israel. The government of Israel may be considered under two important headings: the laws, and the leaders.

The Laws:

a. The "Commandments," especially the Ten Commandments, revealed God's holiness and set up a divine standard of righteousness for the people to follow (Ex 20:1-17).
b. The judgments governed the social life of the people and concerned masters and servants (Ex 21:1-11), physical injuries (Ex 21:12-36), protection of property rights (Ex 22:1-15), among others.
c. The ordinances included the sacrifices that showed that blood must be shed for sinners to be forgiven (Le 1-17).

The Leaders: At first Moses was the sole leader; then he was replaced by Joshua. After Joshua's death the nation was governed for many years by judges, who were usually raised up by God to oppose a specific enemy. Finally, at the people's request, God granted them a king, thus establishing the monarchy (1 Sa 8:5,22). Under the monarchy there were four key leaders:

a. The *king* was the Lord's representative who ruled the people, but only as the Lord's servant. He led in war (1 Sa 8:20) and made judicial decisions (2 Sa 15:2), but he could not make law, since he himself was under the law (De 17:19). His relationship was so close to the Lord that he was adopted by the Lord (2 Sa 7:14; Ps 2:7).
b. The *priest* taught the Lord's laws and officiated at the offering of the sacrifices (Le 1:5; Je 18:18).
c. The *prophet* was the man of God who spoke for God and gave divine pronouncements for the present (forthtelling) or for the future (foretelling).
d. The *wise man* produced literary works stressing practical wisdom (Pr 1:1), taught discipline of character to the young (Pr 22:17), and gave counsel to the king (2 Sa 16:20). The choice of these men indicates an important biblical principle: God uses

people to reach other people, a principle that is also evident in the Great Commission given to Christians (Ma 28:19-20).

Worship by Israel: The central aspect of Israel's worship was the object of their worship, the Lord. While other nations paid homage to many gods (De 29:18), only Israel worshipped the one true God (Ex 20:3). This worship could be private (Ex 34:8), as a family (Ge 22:5), or corporate (1 Ch 29:20).

The first place of worship for the people of Israel was the tabernacle constructed by Moses (Ex 25–27; 30–31; 35–40) and later the magnificent temple constructed by Solomon (1 Ch 22:5). The structures served to localize the worship of the entire nation. This geographic limitation stands in bold contrast to the privilege of immediate and direct access to God now available to the new Testament believer who himself is the temple of God (He 4:16; 1 Co 6:19).

IS'RAEL•ITE

A descendant of Israel, who was previously called Jacob (Le 23:42-43).

IS'SA•CHAR *(he will bring reward)*

1. The ninth son of Jacob by his first wife, Leah (Ge 30:17-18; 35:23). He and his four sons went to Egypt with Jacob (Ge 46:13; Ex 1:3).

2. A son of Obed-edom, a Korhite Levite (1 Ch 26:5).

IS'SA•CHAR, TRIBE OF

The descendants of Jacob and Leah's son Issachar. It consisted of four tribal families, the descendants of Issachar's four sons (Nu 26:23-24). When the land was divided, the territory of Issachar was south of Zebulun and Naphtali; north of Manasseh and bound on the east by the Jordan.

IS•SHI'AH

1. A great-grandson of Moses and head of the house of Rehabiah (1 Ch 24:21).

2. A man of Issachar, of the posterity of Tola (1 Ch 7:3).

3. Son of Uzziel; a descendant of Levi's son, Kohath (1 Ch 23:20; 24:25).

4. One who allied himself with David at Ziklag (1 Ch 12:6).

ISSHIJAH

A form of Ishijah.

IS′U·AH

See ISHVAH.

IS′U·I

See ISHVI.

ITALIAN BAND

See ITALIAN REGIMENT.

ITALIAN REGIMENT

The military division posted at Caesarea; a Roman cohort which would have consisted of 600 men under the command of a tribune. Cornelius, the first Gentile convert, was a Centurion of this regiment (Ac 10:1).

IT′A·LY

The long, boot-shaped peninsula extending from the European continent into the Mediterranean Sea. It is bound on three sides by the sea, and on the North by the Alps. Its most important city is Rome, the New Testament era capital of the Roman Empire (Ac 18:2; 27:1,6; He 13:24).

ITCH, ITCHING DISEASE (De 28:27)

See ECZEMA.

I′THAI

See ITTAI.

ITH′A·MAR *(palm-coast)*

The youngest son of Aaron (Ex 6:23; 1 Ch 6:3; 24:1). Along with his brothers, he was consecrated to the priesthood (Ex 28:1; 1 Ch 24:2).

I′THI·EL *(God with me)*

1. Son of Jesaiah, a Benjamite. One of his descendants returned from Babylon (Ne 11:7).

2. One of the two persons to whom Agur, writer of a portion of the Book of Proverbs, addressed his confession and instructions (Pr 30:1).

ITH′LAH

A town of Dan (Jos 19:42).

ITH′MAH *(bereavement)*

A Moabite, part of David's bodyguard (1 Ch 11:46).

ITH′NAN

A town in Judah (Jos 15:23).

ITH′RA *(excellence)*

An Israelite, but more correctly an Ishmaelite, who married David's sister, Abigail. His son was Amass (2 Sa 17:25; 1 Ki 2:5,32). He is also called Jether.

ITH′RAN *(abundance)*

1. Son of Dishon, a Horite, grandson of Seir (Ge 36:26; 1 Ch 1:41).

2. Son of Zophah of Asher (1 Ch 7:37).

ITH′RE·AM *(abundance of people)*

A son of David and his sixth wife, Eglah (2 Sa 3:5; 1 Ch 3:3).

ITH′RITE

A family who lived at Kirjath-jearim, the descendants of Ithra (1 Ch 2:53).

IT′TAH-KA′ZIN

See ETH-KAZIN.

IT·TA′I

1. A Gittite, and native of Gath. When David fled from Absalom's rebellion, Ittai and six hundred men joined David's entourage. Ittai became one of the commanders of David's army during the struggle with Absalom (2 Sa 15:18-22; 18:2,5).

2. Son of Ribai of Gibeah, one of David's warriors (2 Sa 23:29), called Ithai in 1 Chronicles 11:31.

I·TU·RAE′A

A province on the northeastern border of Palestine (Ge 25:15; 1 Ch 1:31).

I′VAH

See IVVAH.

IVORY

Ivory comes from the tusks of elephants or mastodons; it was used to make various kinds of ornaments and decorations. The first mention of ivory in the Bible occurs when it was imported into Palestine by Solomon (1 Ki 10:22; 2 Ch 9:21). During Old Testament times, ivory was a rare and expensive item found only in the palaces of kings and the homes of the very wealthy (Ps 45:8; Eze 27:6-7). Ornate ivory carvings were inlaid in furniture and the wooden paneling used in elegant homes. A mark of the wealth of King Solomon (reigned 971-931 B.C.) was his royal throne made of ivory (2 Ch 9:17).

After Solomon's reign, and the division of his kingdom into two separate nations, the upper classes of the Northern Kingdom continued the lavish display of their wealth by using ivory in their homes and palaces. The prophet Amos condemned these people for their excesses and for exploiting the poor, predicting that those who rested upon "beds of ivory" would be judged by God (Am 6:4).

King Ahab of Israel (reigned 874-853 B.C.) was an avid builder who loved to display his wealth with ornate buildings and elegant furnishings. He completed and adorned the capital city of Samaria, which his father Omri (reigned 880-874 B.C.) had begun several years before. Excavations of the royal palace in Samaria have yielded evidence of the extravagant practices Amos condemned. The outside of Ahab's "ivory house" (1 Ki 22:39; Am 3:15) was faced with white stone, which gave the appearance of ivory. It was also decorated throughout with numerous ivory carvings and inlaid ivory panels.

The two-story palace was constructed on a high hill, surrounded by numerous courtyards. One of these courtyards featured a large pool. Excavators believe this may have been the pool where the blood of Ahab was washed from his chariot after he was killed in battle (1 Ki 22:38). Discovered nearby was a large storeroom, which contained five hundred pieces of ivory, ready to be inlaid in walls and furniture throughout the royal palace.

Ahab's ivory palace is a symbol of the fleeting nature of power and riches. He is remembered as a cruel and idolatrous king whose wealth passed to others after his violent and inglorious death.

IV′ VAH

A city of Samaria, captured by the Assyrians. Sennacherib attempted to intimidate Hezekiah by boasting of the ease with which he was able to take over Ivvah, in spite of the local gods, intimating that the God of Israel would be just as powerless before him (2 Ki 18:34; 19:13; Is 37:13). Possibly the same as AVA (2 Ki 17:24).

I′ YE-AB′ A·RIM, I′ JE-AB′ A·RIM (ruins of Abarim)

One of the encampments of the Israelites on the border of Moab (Nu 21:11; 33:44). It is also called Iyim (Nu 33:45), and Iim in the Authorized Version.

IYIM

A form of IJIM.

IZ′ HAR, I′ ZE·HAR

1. Son of Kohath, a Levite and head of a tribal family (Ex 6:18,21; Nu 3:19,27; 1 Ch 6:18, 38). Izhar's son, Korah, started an insurrection against Moses in the wilderness (Nu 16:1).

2. Son of Ashur of the family of Hezron (1 Ch 4:5-7). He is called Jezoar in the Authorized Version.

IZ·LI′ AH, JEZ·LI′ AH

Son of Elpaal, descended from Shaharaim (1 Ch 8:18).

IZ·RA·HI′ AH

Son of Uzzi, of the family of Tola of Issachar (1 Ch 7:3). Possibly the Jezrahiah mentioned in Nehemiah is the same person (12:42).

IZ′ RA·HITE

A resident of the town of Izrah. Shamhuth, one of David's captains, was so designated (1 Ch 27:8).

IZ′ RI

Also JIZRI. Son of Jeduthun, leader of the fourth course of the Levitical musicians for the sanctuary in the time of David (1 Ch 25:11), also called Zeri (1 Ch 25:3).

IZ·ZI′ AH, JE·ZI′ AH

A son of Parosh, one of those who gave up his foreign wife (Ez 10:25).

J

JA′ A·KAN

Grandson of Seir (1 Ch 1:38,42).

JA·A·KO′ BAH (supplanting)

A descendant of Simeon (1 Ch 4:36).

JA′ A·LA (doe)

A servant of Solomon whose family came back from the exile with Zerubbabel (Ez 2:56; Ne 7:58).

JA′ A·LAH

See JAALA.

JA·A·LAM
See JALAM.

JA·A·NAI
A chief of Gad (1 Ch 5:12).

JA·A·R
The wooded area where the ark of the covenant was kept for some years (Ps 132:6).

JA·A·RE-OR·E·GIM
See JAIR.

JA·AR·E·SHI·AH
Son of Jeroham, a Benjamite (1 Ch 8:27).

JA·A·SAI
Son of Bani. He renounced his foreign wife (Ez 10:37).

JA·A·SAU
See JAASAI.

JA·AS·I·EL
Two men of the Old Testament:
1. One of David's mighty men (1 Ch 11:47).
2. Son of Abner (1 Ch 27:21).

JA·A·SU
See JAASAI.

JA·AZ·A·NI·AH, JEZ·A·NI·AH *(Jehovah hears)*
Four Old Testament men:
1. A Rechabite and one of those successfully tested by Jeremiah (Je 35:3).
2. A Maachatite and a military commander (2 Ki 25:23; Je 40:8). After Gedaliah was slain, he was among those who asked advice of Jeremiah as to where the remaining Israelites should go next. Disregarding the prophet's advice, he went with the remnant into Egypt (Je 42:1; 43:4-5).
3. Son of Azur and a prince of Judah. He appeared in Ezekiel's vision (Ez 11:1).
4. A son of Shaphan (Ez 8:11).

JA·A·ZER
See JAZER.

JA·A·ZI·AH *(God consoles)*
A Levite of the family of Merari (1 Ch 24:26-27)

JA·A·ZI·EL, A·ZI·EL *(God consoles)*
A Levite musician (1 Ch 15:18,20).

JA·BAL *(a stream)*
Son of Lamech (Ge 4:20).

JAB·BOK *(effusion)*
One of the principal eastern tributaries of the Jordan. It was the western boundary of the Ammonites (Nu 21:24; De 2:36-37; Jos 12:2-6).

JA·BESH *(dry)*
1. A town. See JABESH-GILEAD.
2. Father of Shallum (2 Ki 15:10).

JA·BESH-GIL·E·AD *(Jabesh of Gilead)*
A town of Gilead east of the Jordan, a short distance from Beth-shean (1 Sa 31:11; 2 Sa 2:4) in the territory of the half tribe of Manasseh (Nu 32:39-40). When the warriors of this city failed to come to Mizpah to fight with other Israelites against the Benjamites, the city was destroyed and its men and married women were slain (Ju 21:8-15).

JA·BEZ *(sorrowful)*
A man and a place:
1. A man of Judah, who was considered more honorable than his brethren (1 Ch 4:9-10).
2. A place, probably in Judah where the families of scribes lived (1 Ch 2:55).

JA·BIN *(discerner)*
Two kings of Hazor:
1. A king of Hazor in Galilee, the head of a confederacy of kings defeated by Joshua at the waters of Merom. The king was slain in the battle (Jos 11:1-14).
2. Another Canaanite king of Hazor, probably a descendant of the preceding (Ju 4:2).

JAB·NEEL *(built by God)*
1. A town of Naphtali (Jos 19:33).
2. A town on the northern border of Judah (Jos 15:5,11), probably the same as Jabneh (2 Ch 26:6).

JAB·NEH
See JABNEEL.

JA·CAN
See JACHAN.

JA′ CHAN *(troublous)*

A chief of the tribe of Gad (1 Ch 5:13).

JA′ CHIN *(he establishes)*

1. A son of Simeon (Ge 46:10; Ex 6:15; Nu 26:12). In 1 Chronicles 4:24 he is called Jarib.

2. A priest, whose family in the time of David was the twenty-first course in the service of the sanctuary (1 Ch 24:17).

3. A priest who lived in Jerusalem after the captivity (1 Ch 9:10; Ne 11:10).

JA′ CHIN AND BO′ AZ

The names of the two pillars Solomon set up in front of the temple. Each pillar was approximately sixty feet tall; the pillar on the right was called Jachin and the pillar on the left was called Boaz (2 Ch 3:17; 2 Ki 25:13).

JA′ CHIN·ITES

The descendants of Simeon's son Jachin (Nu 26:12).

JA′ CINTH

A precious stone; either a reddish zircon or essonite, also called hyacinth. Jacinth was one of the twelve stones in the breastplate of the high priest (Ex 28:19) and one of the foundations of the heavenly city (Re 21:19-20).

JACK′ AL

A carrion-eating wild dog of yellowish color; it is more cowardly than the wolf. It resembles domesticated dogs except that its snout is longer and more pointed. Jackals hunt in packs and are considered dangerous (Is 34:13; 35:7; 43:20; Je 49:33). They are found in all parts of Palestine, especially among ruins. In the Authorized Version the word is rendered *dragon*.

JACKAL'S WELL

See SERPENT WELL.

JACKDAW

A bird related to the common crow. Jackdaws are smaller than crows, with black and grey plumage. They are well-known for their messy nests and their gregarious habits. They have been known to learn to imitate the human voice. Whether this is a good translation for Psalm 102:6 is questionable. Other translations have chosen "vulture," "pelican," and "desert owl."

JACKAL

JA′ COB

The twin brother of Esau and the son of Isaac and Rebekah. Jacob was the favorite of his mother; Esau of his father. In his youth Jacob tricked Esau into giving up his birthright and his father's blessing. Jacob then fled Esau's wrath to Haran where he lived in the home of Laban. He married Laban's daughters, Leah and Rachel. The latter, his favorite, gave birth to Joseph, his favored son. Later he returned, had a reconciliation with Esau, and settled in Canaan. On the return trip God changed his name to Israel. Joseph, who had been carried captive to Egypt, later brought his family there to escape a famine. Jacob died there but was buried in Canaan.

JACOB'S LIFE, INDEXED		
Recorded Events	**Place**	**Reference**
Birth of Jacob and Esau, sons of Isaac and Rebekah.	Beer-sheba	Ge 25:22-26
Jacob the favorite of his mother, Esau the favorite of his father.	Beer-sheba	Ge 25:27-28
Jacob purchases the birthright from Esau.	Beer-sheba	Ge 25:29-34
Jacob deceives Isaac by impersonating Esau and receives his blessing.	Beer-sheba	Ge 27:1-29
Jacob is sent by his father and mother to Padan-aram to secure a wife.	Beer-sheba	Ge 28:1-7
He spends the night at Bethel where he has the vision of the ladder and the angels, and the Lord renews the promise made to Abraham.	Bethel	Ge 28:10-15
Jacob builds a memorial and makes a vow to the Lord.	Bethel	Ge 28:16-22
He comes to Padan-aram, to the home of Laban, his mother's brother, and stipulates to serve Laban for seven years to make his daughter, Rachel his wife.	Padan-aram	Ge 29:1-20
Laban deceives him and requires him to marry Leah, and bargains for another seven	Padan-aram	Ge 29:21-30

Recorded Events	Place	Reference
years' service for which Jacob should obtain Rachel.		
Eleven of his sons are born to Jacob by his two wives and their maids. The sons of Leah: Reuben, Simeon, Levi, Judah, Issachar, Zebulun. Sons of Zilpah, Leah's maid: Gad, Asher. Son of Rachel: Joseph. Sons of Bilhah, Rachel's maid: Dan, Naphtali.	Padan-aram	Ge 29:31–30:24
Jacob by cunning gains an advantage and loses the favor of Laban.	Padan-aram	Ge 30:25-43; 31:1-2
The Lord directs Jacob to return to Canaan and assures him of His presence. With his family and property he steals away from Laban.	Padan-aram	Ge 31:3-21
Laban pursues and overtakes Jacob, and the Mizpah covenant is made between them.	Mt. Gilead	Ge 31:22-55
Fearing his brother Esau, he arranges a gift of cattle to be sent to him. He spends the night alone wrestling with the angel. His name is changed to Israel. This marks the great change in Jacob's life.	Peniel	Ge 32
The affectionate meeting of Jacob and Esau. Jacob settles in Shechem.	Shechem	Ge 33
The incident regarding Jacob's daughter. The slaying of Hamor and his family by Jacob's sons.	Shechem	Ge 34
Jacob is divinely directed to move to Bethel. Here he builds an altar and the Lord talks with him.	Bethel	Ge 35:1-15
Leaving Bethel, Rachel dies in giving birth to Benjamin, the twelfth son, and is buried near Bethlehem.	Ephrath	Ge 35:16-20
He comes to Beer-sheba and he and Esau bury Isaac.	Beer-sheba	Ge 35:21-29
Jacob's special love for Joseph. Joseph's dreams incur the enmity of his brothers.	Beer-sheba	Ge 37:1-11
Jacob sends Joseph to his brothers who are with their flocks. They sell him to some Midianites on their way to Egypt, and tell Jacob he has been killed by a wild beast.	Dothan	Ge 37:12-35
A famine in the land compels Jacob to send his sons to Egypt for corn. They are recognized by Joseph who treats them kindly and arranges for them to move to Egypt.	Beer-sheba	Ge 42–45
Jacob and his people, seventy souls, settle in Goshen where they become prosperous. After 17 years in Egypt, Jacob dies and is carried back to Canaan by his sons and buried beside his people in the cave of Machpelah.	Goshen	Ge 46:1–50:1-13

JACOB, TESTAMENT OF

See PSEUDEPIGRAPHA.

JACOB'S WELL

A well ostensibly dug by Jacob in the Samaritan city of Sychar. Jesus sat by this well and talked to the Samaritan woman about living water and eternal life (Jo 4:1-26). The well is not mentioned specifically in the Old Testament.

JA'DA (wise)

Son of Onam, of the tribe of Judah (1 Ch 2:28, 32).

JA'DAI

A son of Nebo who had married a foreign wife (Ez 10:43). Also called Iddo.

JAD'DU·A (knowing)

1. A high priest, the son of Jonathan, a descendant of Jeshua, the high priest who returned with Zerubbabel from Babylon (Ne 12:11,22). He was probably high priest when the Persian Empire was overthrown by Alexander the Great in 331 B.C.

2. A Levite chief of the people who sealed the covenant (Ne 10:21).

JADE

The REB translation of the Hebrew word which is rendered "diamond" in the KJV and NKJV. Other translations have chosen "emerald" and "jasper."

JA'DON (he judgeth)

A Meronothite. He labored on the wall of Jerusalem (Ne 3:7).

JA'EL (wild goat)

The wife of Heber the Kenite (Ju 4:17). When Sisera, Jabin's captain, was defeated by Barak, he (Sisera) fled to the tent of Heber. While asleep she drove a tent peg (probably a wooden pin) into his head (Ju 4:11-22).

JA'GUR (a lodging)

A town in the south of Judah (Jos 15:21).

JAH

A contraction for Jehovah (Ps 68:4).

JA·HA'LE·LEEL

See JEHALELEEL.

JA′ HATH

Four Old Testament men:

1. A descendant of Shobal, of the family of Hezron (1 Ch 4:2).

2. Son of Libni, a Levite of Gershom (1 Ch 6:20).

3. A Levite of the branch of Gershom and one of the heads of the house of Shimei (1 Ch 23:10).

4. A Levite of the family of Kohath (1 Ch 24:22).

5. A Levite of the family of Merari (2 Ch 34:12).

JA′ HAZ

The place in the plain of Moab where the Israelites defeated the Amorites (Nu 21:23; De 2:32; Ju 11:20). It was in the territory of Reuben and became a Levitical city (Jos 21:36).

JA·HA′ ZA

See JAHAZ.

JA·HA′ ZAH

See JAHAZ.

JA·HA·ZI′ AH *(the Lord sees)*

A son of Tikvah (Ez 10:15).

JA·HA′ ZI·EL *(God sees)*

Five Old Testament men:

1. Son of Hebron; a Levite of the family of Kohath (1 Ch 23:19).

2. A Benjamite, a warrior who joined David at Ziklag (1 Ch 12:4).

3. A priest who sounded the trumpet when the ark was brought to Jerusalem in David's reign (1 Ch 16:6).

4. Son of Zechariah (2 Ch 20:14).

5. Ancestor of a family which returned with Ezra from Babylon (Ez 8:5).

JAH′ DA·I

A Calebite (1 Ch 2:47).

JAH′ DI·EL

A chief of the half tribe of Manasseh (1 Ch 5:24).

JAH′ DO *(union)*

Son of Buz (1 Ch 5:14).

JAH′ LEEL

Son of Zebulun, head of a tribal family (Ge 46:14; Nu 26:26).

JAH′ LE·E·LITES

Descendants of Zebulun's son Jahleel (Nu 26:26).

JAH′ MA·I

A son of Tola (1 Ch 7:2).

JAH′ ZAH

See JAHAZ.

JAH′ ZEEL *(God distributes)*

Son of Naphtali (Ge 46:24; Nu 26:48; 1 Ch 7:13).

JAH′ ZE·E·LITES

Descendants of Naphtali's son Jazeel (Nu 26:48).

JAH·ZEI′ AH

See JAHAZIAH.

JAH′ ZE·RAH *(led back by God)*

The son of Meshullam, a priest (1 Ch 9:12). Maybe the same as Ahzai (Ne 11:13).

JAH′ ZI·EL

See JAHZEEL.

JAILER

The officer in charge of keeping a prison (Ac 16:23; 16:27-36).

JA′ IR *(he enlightens)*

Three Old Testament men:

1. A son of Segub and grandson of Hezron of Judah. His wife was of the tribe of Manasseh, of the family of Machir (1 Ch 2:21-22). He captured villages in the Argob which bordered on Gilead and named them Havoth-jair. He was probably the judge mentioned in Judges 10:3-5.

2. Father of El-hanan who killed Lahmi, the brother of Goliath (1 Ch 20:5). He is called Jaare-oregim in 2 Samuel 21:19.

3. A Benjamite, father of Mordecai (Es 2:5).

JA′ IR·ITE

A descendant of Jair (2 Sa 20:26).

JA·I′ RUS

A ruler of the synagogue, probably at Capernaum. His daughter was raised from the dead by Jesus (Mk 5:35-43; Lk 8:49-56).

JA' KAN

See JAAKAN.

JA' KEH *(pious)*

The father of Agur (Pr 30:1).

JA' KIM *(God raises up)*

Two Old Testament men:
1. A descendant of Aaron (1 Ch 24:12).
2. A Benjamite, son of Shimhi (1 Ch 8:19).

JA' LAM

A son of Esau, a chief of the Edomites (Ge 36:5,18; 1 Ch 1:35).

JA' LON

A son of Ezra (1 Ch 4:17).

JAM' BRES

See JANNES and JAMBRES

JAMES *(a form of the name Jacob-Jacobus)*

1. James the son of Zebedee and brother of John (Ma 4:21; 17:1; Mk 3:17). We know nothing of his birthplace or early life. He and John were partners of Peter and Andrew in the fishing business (Lk 5:10). They were two of the first four apostles called by Jesus (Ma 4:21; Mk 1:19). His mother, Salome, was the sister of Mary, mother of Jesus. James is always mentioned in connection with John. Because his name comes first, it is inferred he was older than John (Ma 10:2; Mk 5:37; Lk 5:10). James, John, and Peter were brought into close intimacy with Jesus as seen in their association with him on various occasions—the raising of the daughter of Jairus (Mk 5:37; Lk 8:51), the transfiguration (Ma 17:1; Mk 9:2), in Gethsemane (Mk 14:33). These brothers had mistaken views of our Lord's kingdom, and desirous of having a high place in it, they joined in the request made by their mother to Jesus that they sit on either side of Jesus in the "kingdom" (Ma 20:20-23; Mk 10:35). James was the first of the apostles to die for his Lord in the persecution by Herod (Ac 12:2).

2. James the son of Alphaeus. He was one of the apostles (Ma 10:3; Mk 3:18; Lk 6:15; Ac 1:13). He was called James the Less, either on account of his stature or because he was younger than James, the brother of John (Mk 16:1). Assuming that the James of Matthew 27:56; Mark 15:40; 16:1 and Luke 24:10 is this James, it may be assumed that his mother was called Mary, that she may be identified with the Mary, wife of Cleopas of John 19:25.

3. James, the Lord's brother. The most natural interpretation of Matthew 13:55 and Mark 6:3 is that James and his sisters were the children of Joseph and Mary the mother of Jesus. This James was not an apostle (Ma 10:2-4) and was not a believer in the messiahship of Jesus (Jo 7:5) until after the resurrection (Ac 1:13-14). He became the head of the church in Jerusalem.

4. James, the father of Judas (not Iscariot). Nothing more than this is known of him (Lk 6:16; Ac 1:13)

JAMES, E·PIS' TLE OF

1. The Book of James. Faith without works cannot be called faith. Faith without works is dead, and a dead faith is worse than no faith at all. Faith must work, it must produce, it must be visible. Verbal faith is not enough; mental faith is insufficient. Faith must be there, but it must be more. It must inspire action. Throughout his epistle to Jewish believers, James integrates true faith and everyday practical experience by stressing that true faith must manifest itself in works of faith.

Faith endures trials. Trials come and go, but a strong faith will face them head on and develop endurance. Faith understands temptations. It will not allow us to consent to our lust and slide into sin. Faith obeys the Word. It will not merely hear and not do. Faith produces doers. Faith harbors no prejudice. For James, faith and favoritism cannot co-exist. Faith displays itself in works. Faith is more than mere words; it is more than knowledge; it is demonstrated by obedience; and it overtly responds to the promises of God. Faith controls the tongue. This small but immensely powerful part of the body must be held in check. Faith can do it. Faith acts wisely. It gives us the ability to choose wisdom that is heavenly and to shun wisdom that is earthly. Faith produces separation from the world and submission to God. It provides us with the ability to resist the devil and humbly draw near to God. Finally, faith waits patiently for the coming of the Lord. Through trouble and trial it stifles complaining.

The name *Iakobos* (James) in 1:1 is the basis for the early title *Iakobou Epistole,* "Epistle of James." *Iakobos* is the Greek form of the Hebrew name Jacob.

2. The Author of James. Four men are

named James in the New Testament: (1) James, the father of Judas (not Iscariot), is mentioned twice (Lk 6:16; Ac 1:13) as the father of one of the twelve disciples, but is otherwise completely unknown. (2) James, the son of Alphaeus (Ma 10:3; Mk 3:18; Lk 6:15; Ac 1:13), elsewhere called James the Less (Mk 15:40), was one of the twelve disciples. Apart from being listed with the other twelve, this James is completely obscure, and it is doubtful that he is the authoritative figure behind this epistle. Some attempts have been made to identify James the Less with the Lord's brother (Ga 1:19), but this view is difficult to reconcile with the Gospel accounts. (3) James, the son of Zebedee and brother of John (Ma 4:21; 10:2; 17:1; Mk 3:17; 10:35; 13:3; Lk 9:54; Ac 1:13), was one of Jesus intimate disciples, but his early martyrdom by A.D. 44 (Ac 12:2) makes it very unlikely that he wrote this epistle. (4) James, the Lord's brother (Ma 13:55; Mk 6:3; Ga 1:19), was one of the "pillars" in the church in Jerusalem (Ac 12:17; 15:13-21; 21:18; Ga 2:9,12). Tradition points to this prominent figure as the author of this epistle, and this best fits the evidence of Scripture. There are several clear parallels between the language of the letter drafted under his leadership in Acts 15:23-29 and the Epistle of James (e.g., the unusual word *charein,* "greeting," is found only in Acts 15:23; 23:26; and James 1:1). The Jewish character of this epistle with its stress upon the law, along with the evident influence by the Sermon on the Mount (4:11-12; 5:12) complement what we know about James "the Just" from Scripture and early tradition.

It has been argued that the Greek form of this epistle is too sophisticated for a Galilean such as James, but this assumes that he never had the opportunity or aptitude to develop proficiency in Koine ("common") Greek. As a prominent church leader, it would have been to his advantage to become fluent in the universal language of the Roman Empire.

For various reasons, some assert that James was a stepbrother of Jesus by a previous marriage of Joseph, or that the "brothers" of Jesus mentioned in Matthew 13:55 and Mark 6:3 were really his cousins. However, the most natural understanding of the Gospel accounts is that James was the half brother of Jesus, being the offspring of Joseph and Mary after the birth of Jesus (Ma 1:24-25). He apparently did not accept the claims of Jesus until the Lord appeared

to him after His resurrection (1 Co 15:7). He and his brothers were among the believers who awaited the coming of the Holy Spirit on the day of Pentecost (Ac 1:14). It was not long before he became an acknowledged leader of the Jerusalem church (Ac 12:17; Ga 2:9,12), and he was a central figure in the Jerusalem Council in Acts 15. Even after Paul's missionary journey, James continued to observe the Mosaic law as a testimony to other Jews (Ac 21:18-25). Early tradition stresses his Jewish piety and his role in bringing others to an understanding of Jesus as the Messiah. He suffered a violent martyr's death not long before the fall of Jerusalem.

The brevity and limited doctrinal emphasis of James kept it from wide circulation, and by the time it became known in the church as a whole, there was uncertainty about the identity of James in 1:1. Growing recognition that it was written by the Lord's brother led to its acceptance as a canonical book.

3. The Time of James. James is addressed "to the twelve tribes which are scattered abroad" (1:1), and it is apparent from verses like 1:19 and 2:1,7 that this greeting refers to Hebrew Christians outside of Palestine. Their place of meeting is called a "synagogue" in the Greek text of 2:2, and the whole epistle reflects Jewish thought and expressions (2:19,21; 4:11-12; 5:4,12). There are no references to slavery or idolatry, and this also fits an originally Jewish readership.

These Jewish believers were beset with problems that were testing their faith, and James was concerned that they were succumbing to impatience, bitterness, materialism, disunity, and spiritual apathy. As a resident of Jerusalem and a leader of the church, James no doubt had frequent contact with Jewish Christians from a number of Roman provinces. He therefore felt a responsibility to exhort and encourage them in their struggles of faith.

According to Josephus, James was martyred in A.D. 62 (Hegesippus, quoted in Eusebius, fixed the date of James's death at A.D. 66). Those who accept him as the author of this epistle have proposed a date of writing ranging from A.D. 45 to the end of his life. However, several factors indicate that this letter may have been the earliest writing of the New Testament (c. A.D. 46-49): (1) There is no mention of Gentile Christians or their relationship to the Jewish Christians, as might be expected in a later epistle. (2) Apart from references to the person of Christ, there is practically no distinctive theology in James, suggesting an early date when Christianity was viewed in terms of messianic Judaism. (3) The allusions to the teachings of Christ have such little verbal agreement with the Synoptic Gospels that they probably preceded them. (4) James uses the word "synagogue" (assembly, 2:2) in addition to "church" and indicates a very simple organization of elders and masters, that is, teachers (3:1; 5:14), which was patterned after the early synagogue. (5) James does not mention the issues involved in the Acts 15 Council in Jerusalem (A.D. 49).

4. The Christ of James. In 1:1 and 2:1 James refers to the "Lord Jesus Christ," and in 5:7-8 he anticipates "the coming of the Lord." Compared to other New Testament writers, James says little about Christ, and yet his speech is virtually saturated with allusions to the teaching of Christ. The Sermon on the Mount is especially prominent in James's thinking (about fifteen indirect references; such as 1:2 and Ma 5:10-12; 1:4 and Ma 5:48; 2:13 and Ma 6:14-15; 4:11 and Ma 7:1-2; 5:2 and Ma 6:19). This epistle portrays Christ in the context of early messianic Judaism.

5. Keys to James.

Key Word: Faith That Works—Throughout his epistle, James develops the theme of the characteristics of true faith. He effectively uses these characteristics as a series of tests to help his readers evaluate the quality of their relationship with Christ. The purpose of this work is not doctrinal or apologetic but practical. James seeks to challenge these believers to examine the quality of their daily lives in terms of attitudes and actions. A genuine faith will produce real changes in a person's conduct and character, and the absence of change is a symptom of a dead faith.

Key Verses: James 1:19-22 and 2:14-17— "Therefore, my beloved brethren, let every man be swift to hear, slow to speak, slow to wrath; for the wrath of man does not produce the righteousness of God. Therefore lay aside all filthiness and overflow of wickedness, and receive with meekness the implanted word, which is able to save your souls. But be doers of the word, and not hearers only, deceiving yourselves" (1:19-22).

"What does it profit, my brethren, if someone says he has faith but does not have works? Can faith save him? If a brother or sister is naked and destitute of daily food, and one of you says to them, 'Depart in peace, be warmed and filled,' but you do not give them the things which are needed for the body, what does it profit? Thus also faith by itself, if it does not have works, is dead (2:14-17).

Key Chapter: James 1—One of the most difficult areas of the Christian life is that of testings and temptations. James reveals our correct response to both: to testings, count them all joy; to temptations, realize that God is not their source.

6. Survey of James. James could be called the "Proverbs of the New Testament" because it is written in the terse moralistic style of wisdom literature. It is evident that James was profoundly influenced by the Old Testament (especially the wisdom literature) and by the Sermon on the Mount. But James's impassioned preaching against iniquity and injustice also earns him the title of the Amos of the New Testament. Because of the many subjects in this epistle, it is difficult to outline; suggestions have ranged from no connection at all between the various topics to a unified scheme. The outline used here is: the test of faith (1:1-18); the characteristics of faith (1:19–5:6); and the triumph of faith (5:7-20).

The Test of Faith (1:1-18). The first part of this episode develops the qualities of genuine faith in regard to trials and temptations. After a one-verse salutation to geographically dispersed Hebrew Christians (1:1), James quickly introduces his first subject, outward tests of faith (1:2-12). These trials are designed to produce mature endurance and a sense of dependence upon God, to whom the believer turns for wisdom and enablement. Inward temptations (1:13-18) do not come from the One who bestows "every good gift" (1:17). These solicitations to evil must be checked at an early stage or they may result in disastrous consequences.

The Characteristics of Faith (1:19–5:6). A righteous response to testing requires that one be "swift to hear, slow to speak, slow to wrath" (1:19), and this broadly summarizes the remainder of the epistle. Quickness of hearing involves an obedient response to God's Word (1:19-27). True hearing means more than mere listening; the Word must be received and applied. After stating this principle (1:21-22), James develops it with an illustration (1:23-25) and an application (1:26-27). A genuine faith should produce a change in attitude from partiality to the rich to a love for the poor as well as the rich (2:1-13).

True faith should also result in actions (2:14-26). In Romans 4, Paul used the example of Abraham to show that justification is by faith, not by works. But James says that Abraham was justified by works (2:21). In spite of the apparent contradiction, Romans 4 and James 2 are really two sides of the same coin. In context, Paul is writing about justification before God while James writes of the evidence of justification before men. A faith that produces no change is not saving faith.

Moving from works to words, James shows how a living faith controls the tongue ("slow to speak," 1:19). The tongue is small, but it has the power to accomplish great good or equally great evil. Only the power of God applied by an active faith can tame the tongue (3:1-12). Just as there are wicked and righteous uses of the tongue, so there are demonic and divine manifestations of wisdom (3:13-18). James contrasts seven characteristics of human wisdom with seven qualities of divine wisdom.

The strong pulls of worldliness (4:1-12) and wealth (4:13–5:6) create conflicts that are harmful to the growth of faith. The world system is at enmity with God, and the pursuit of its pleasures produces covetousness, envy, fighting, and arrogance (4:1-6). The believer's only alternative is submission to God out of a humble and repentant spirit. This will produce a transformed attitude toward others as well (4:7-12). This spirit of submission and humility should be applied to any attempts to accrue wealth (4:13-17), especially because wealth can lead to pride, injustice, and selfishness (5:1-6).

The Triumph of Faith (5:7-20). James encouraged his readers to patiently endure the sufferings of the present life in view of the future prospect of the coming of the Lord (5:7-12). They may be oppressed by the rich or by other circumstances, but as the example of Job teaches, believers can be sure that God has a gracious purpose in His dealings with them. James concludes his epistle with some practical words on prayer and restoration (5:13-20). The prayers of righteous men are efficacious for the healing and restoration of believers. When sin is not dealt with, it can contribute to illness and even death.

OUTLINE OF JAMES

I. The Test of Faith (1:1-18)

A. The Purpose of Tests 1:1-12
B. The Source of Temptations......... 1:13-18

II. The Characteristics of Faith (1:19–5:6)

A. Faith Obeys the Word 1:19-27
B. Faith Removes Discrimination 2:1-13
C. Faith Proves Itself by Works 2:14-26
D. Faith Controls the Tongue 3:1-12

E. Faith Produces Wisdom 3:13-18
F. Faith Produces Humility 4:1-12
G. Faith Produces Dependence on God 4:13–5:6

III. The Triumph of Faith (5:7-20)

A. Faith Endures Awaiting Christ's Return 5:7-12
B. Faith Prays for the Afflicted 5:13-18
C. Faith Confronts the Erring Brother 5:19-20

JAMES, PROTOEVANGELIUM OF
See APOCRYPHA.

JAMES THE LESS
See JAMES No. 2.

JA´MIN *(right hand)*
Three Old Testament men:
1. A son of Ram, of the family of Jerahmeel of Judah (1 Ch 2:27)
2. A son of Simeon, the head of a tribal family (Ge 46:10; Ex 6:15; Nu 26:12).
3. A Levite who assisted Ezra (Ne 8:7-8).

JA´MIN·ITES
Descendants of Simeon's son Jamin (Nu 26:12).

JAM´LECH *(whom God makes a king)*
A chief of the tribe of Simeon (1 Ch 4:34,41).

JAMNIA
See JABNEEL.

JA´NAI
See JAANAI.

JANGLING

Idle talk, useless chatter (1 Ti 1:6).

JA′NIM

See JANUM.

JAN′NA

The father of Melchi, ancestor of Jesus (Lk 3:24).

JAN′NAI

See JANNA.

JAN′NES AND JAMBRES

Egyptian magicians who attempted to discredit the work of Moses (Ex 7:11-12,22). Their names are not mentioned in Exodus, but apparently were a well established tradition by the time of Paul (2 Ti 3:8).

JA·NO′AH, JA·NO′HAH *(quiet)*

Two Israelite towns:
1. A town on the border of Ephraim (Jos 16:6-7).
2. A town of Naphtali (2 Ki 15:29).

JA′NUM *(sleep)*

A town of Judah near Hebron (Jos 15:53).

JA′PHETH *(let him enlarge)*

One of the three sons of Noah, born when Noah was about five hundred years old (Ge 5:32; 6:10; 10:21).

JA′PHI·A *(bright)*

1. A king of Lachish. He was defeated and executed by Joshua (Jos 10:3-27).
2. A border town of Zebulun (Jos 19:12).
3. A son of David born at Jerusalem (2 Sa 5:15).

JAPH′LET *(he will deliver)*

A son of Heber and grandson of Asher (1 Ch 7:32-33).

JAPH′LE·TI

See JAPHLETITE.

JAPH′LE·TITE

An unidentified tribe (Jos 16:3). They lived near Ephraim's southern border.

JA′PHO

See JOPPA.

JAR

A vessel, usually of earthenware (Jo 2:6), used mostly for carrying water (Ec 12:6).

JAR′AH *(honey)*

A descendant of King Saul (1 Ch 9:42), called Jehoadah in 1 Chronicles 8:36.

JAR′EB *(adversary)*

A king of Assyria who has not been identified, but who was spoken of as a person in Hosea 5:13; 10:6. Possibly it is a nickname for Sargon II; the NIV and NRSV translate this word as "the great king."

JAR′ED

Son of Mahalaleel and father of Enoch (Ge 5:15-20; 1 Ch 1:2; Lk 3:37).

JAR·E·SI′AH

See JAARESHIAH.

JAR′HA

The Egyptian slave of Sheshan who married his master's daughter (1 Ch 2:34-41).

JAR′IB *(an adversary)*

Three Old Testament men:
1. A son of Simeon (1 Ch 4:24). See JACHIN.
2. A man sent by Ezra to Casiphia in search of Levites and Nethinim (Ez 8:16-17).
3. A priest who divorced his foreign wife in the time of Ezra (Ez 10:18).

JAR′MUTH *(a height)*

Two Old Testament towns:
1. A town in the lowland of Judah where the Canaanite king Piram dwelt. He was one of the confederacy of kings who combined to punish the Gibeonites because of their alliance with Joshua (Jos 10:3,5). He was defeated and put to death by Joshua (Jos 10:3-27; 12:11). The town was assigned to Judah (Jos 15:35)
2. A town of Issachar, a Levitical city of the Gershonites (Jos 21:28-29), called Ramoth (1 Ch 6:73) and Remeth (Jos 19:21).

JA·RO′AH

A man of Gad (1 Ch 5:14).

JASH'AR

See JASHER.

JASH'EN *(sleeping)*

Several of his sons belonged to David's bodyguard (2 Sa 23:32). He is called Hashem in 1 Chronicles 11:34.

JASH'ER

In Joshua 10:13 and 2 Samuel 1:18 the book of Jashar is quoted. It has been inferred that it was a collection of poems.

JA·SHOB'E·AM *(people returning to God)*

Three Old Testament men:

1. A warrior of David of the family of Hachmoni (1 Ch 11:11). He was the military captain over the course for the first month (1 Ch 27:2-3). In 2 Samuel 23:8 he is called Josheb-basshebeth.

2. A Benjamite of the Korahites. He joined David at Ziklag (1 Ch 12:1-2,6).

3. A commander of David's army (1 Ch 27:2).

JASH'UB *(he returns)*

Two Old Testament men:

1. A son of Issachar and founder of a tribal family (Nu 26:24; 1 Ch 7:1). In Genesis 46:13 he is called Job, probably the error of a copyist.

2. A son of Bani (Ez 10:29).

JA·SHU'BI-LE'HEM *(returner of bread)*

It is not certain if this is the name of a person or a place. It has to do with the descendants of Shelah (1 Ch 4:22).

JA'SHUB·ITES

The descendants of Issachar's son Jashub (Nu 26:24).

JAS'I·EL

See JAASIEL.

JA'SON *(to cure)*

A kinsman of Paul, a Christian (Ro 16:21), probably the same as the Jason who lived at Thessalonica (Ac 17:5-9).

JAS'PER

This precious stone is a variety of quartz. It is most often red, but can be various shades of yellow, green, or brown. It is one of the stones in the breastplate of the high priest (Ex 28:20), and is used several times to describe something of great beauty or splendor (Eze 28:13; Re 4:3).

JATH'NI·EL *(gifts bestowed by God)*

The son of Meshelemiah (1 Ch 26:2).

JAT'TIR *(excellence)*

A Levitical town in the mountain district of Judah (Jos 15:48; 21:14).

JA'VAN

1. A son of Japheth (Ge 10:2). The name was given to Greece by the Hebrews because the region was settled by Javan's descendants.

2. A people or town of Arabia (Eze 27:19).

JAVE'LIN

A weapon similar to a spear. It is somewhat lighter, and meant for throwing (Nu 25:7; 1 Sa 18:10-11; 19:9-10; 20:33).

JA'ZER, JA·A'ZER (helpful)

A city of Gilead east of the Jordan (2 Sa 24:5; 1 Ch 26:31) from which the Amorites were driven by the Israelites (Nu 21:32).

JA'ZIZ

A Hagerite who had charge of David's flocks (1 Ch 27:31).

JEALOUSY OFFERING. (Nu 5:11-31).

See OFFERINGS.

JE'A·RIM *(forests)*

A mountain marking the northern boundary of Judah (Jos 15:10). See CHESALON.

JE·AT'E·RAI

See ETHNI.

JE·ATH'E·RAI

See ETHNI.

JE·BER·E·CHI'AH *(Jehovah blesses)*

Father of Zechariah (not the prophet). He was a witness to Isaiah's marriage (Is 8:2).

JE'BUS

A name for Jerusalem, in use when the city was in possession of the Jebusites (Jos 15:63; Ju 19:10; 1 Ch 11:4).

JEB′U·SI

See JEBUSITE.

JEB′U·SITE

A member of the mountain tribe which was encountered by the Israelites on their conquest of Canaan (Nu 13:29). After the Jebusite king was slain by Joshua, their territory was assigned to Benjamin (Jos 10:23-26; 18:28). The tribe was small, and as it was not exterminated by the Hebrews, the Jebusites lived on among their conquerors. King Adoni-zedek and Araunah are the only two Jebusites specifically named (Jos 10:1, 23; 2 Sa 24:21-25).

JEC·A·MI′AH

See JEKAMIAH.

JECH·I·LI′AH

See JECOLIAH.

JECH·O·LI′AH

See JECOLIAH.

JECH·O·NI′AH

See JECONIAH.

JECH·O·NI′AS

See JECONIAH.

JEC·O·LI′AH

The mother of Uzziah, king of Judah (2 Ki 15:2; 2 Ch 26:3).

JEC·O·NI′AH

An altered form of Jehoiachin, son and successor of Jehoiakim, king of Judah (1 Ch 3:16-17; Je 24:1; 27:20; 28:4; 29:2).

JE·DAI′AH

Five Old Testament men:

1. The son of Shimri of the tribe of Simeon (1 Ch 4:37).

2. Ancestor of a family appointed by David as the second division of priests (1 Ch 24:1,6-7).

3. Son of Harumaph; he labored on the wall of Jerusalem (Ne 3:10).

4. Two priests who returned with Zerubbabel to Jerusalem (Ne 12:6-7).

5. One who came from Babylon with gifts (Ze 6:10,14).

JED·I·A′EL *(known of God)*

Four Old Testament men:

1. A son of Benjamin, and ancestor of a Benjamite tribe (1 Ch 7:6,10-11), usually regarded as another name of Ashbel (Nu 26:38).

2. Son of Shimri, a warrior of David (1 Ch 11:45).

3. A man of Manasseh who allied himself with David at Ziklag (1 Ch 12:20).

4. A Korahite. In the reign of David, he was a doorkeeper (1 Ch 26:1-2).

JE·DI′DAH *(beloved)*

Wife of Amon, mother of Josiah, king of Judah (2 Ki 22:1).

JED·I·DI′AH *(beloved of Jehovah)*

A name given Solomon by Nathan (2 Sa 12:25).

JE·DU′THUN *(praising)*

Two Old Testament men:

1. Father of Obed-edom, probably a Kohathite (1 Ch 16:38). Some hold that he was the singer of the family of Merari.

2. A Levite, a chief musician of the time of David and founder of a musical family (1 Ch 16:41; 25:1,6; Ne 11:17). He was known earlier as Ethan.

JE·E′ZER

See ABIEZER.

JE·E′ZER·ITE

See ABIEZRITE.

JE′GAR-SA·HA·DU′THA *(heap of testimony)*

The name Laban gave the memorial made of stones (Ge 31:47). See GALEED.

JE·HAL′E·LEEL

See JEHALELEL.

JE·HAL′E·LEL *(he praises God)*

Two Old Testament men:

1. A man of Judah whose parentage is unknown (1 Ch 4:16).

2. A Levite (2 Ch 29:12).

JE·HAL′LE·LEL

See JEHALELEL.

JEH·DEI′ AH

Two Old Testament men:
1. A Levite (1 Ch 24:20).
2. A Meronothite (1 Ch 27:30).

JE·HEZ′ EK·EL *(God strengthens)*

A descendant of Aaron (1 Ch 24:16).

JE·HEZ′ KEL

See JEHEZEKEL.

JE·HI′ AH *(Jehovah liveth)*

In David's reign he was a doorkeeper for the ark (1 Ch 15:24).

JE·HI′ EL *(God lives)*

1. A Levite who played a psaltery when the ark was brought to Jerusalem (1 Ch 15:18,20; 16:5).
2. A Levite of the family of Gershon. He lived in David's reign (1 Ch 23:8). He is also called Jehieli (1 Ch 26:21-22).
3. Son of Hachmoni in the reign of David (1 Ch 27:32).
4. Son of Jehoshaphat, placed by his father over the fortified cities of Judah. He was slain by Jehoram (2 Ch 21:2-4).
5. A Levite of Kohath and son of the singer, Heman (2 Ch 29:14).
6. One who labored under Hezekiah in aiding the latter's reforms (2 Ch 31:13).
7. A temple ruler who aided Josiah in his work of reform (2 Ch 35:8).
8. Father of Obadiah (not the prophet) in the time of Ezra (Ez 8:9).
9. Son of Elam (Ez 10:2).
10. A priest of the family of Harim (Ez 10:21).
11. One who divorced his foreign wife (Ez 10:26), possibly the same as No. 8.

JE·HI·E′ LI

See JEHIEL No. 2.

JE·HIZ·KI′ AH *(Jehovah strengthens)*

A son of Shallum, king of Israel (2 Ch 28:12).

JE·HO′ A·DAH

See JEHOADDAH.

JE·HO′ AD·DAH *(Jehovah adorns)*

Son of Ahaz and a descendant of Jonathan, the son of Saul (1 Ch 8:36). In 1 Chronicles 9:42 he is called Jarah.

JE·HO·AD′ DAN, JE·HO·AD′ DIN

Mother of Amaziah (2 Ki 14:2; 2 Ch 25:1).

JE·HO′ A·HAZ

Three Old Testament men:
1. Son of Jehu. He followed his father on the throne of Israel and reigned seventeen years (2 Ki 10:35; 13:1).
2. Son of Josiah; he followed his father on the throne of Judah. He reigned three months, was deposed by Pharaoh-necho and taken to Egypt (2 Ki 23:30-34; 2 Ch 36:1-4). He is called Shallum in Jeremiah 22:11.
3. Another name of Ahaziah (2 Ch 21:17).

JE·HO′ ASH

See JOASH.

JE·HO·HA′ NAN *(Jehovah is gracious)*

Seven Old Testament men:
1. A Levite in the time of David; a Korahite. The head of the sixth division of temple porters (1 Ch 26:3).
2. A captain of Jehoshaphat having command of 280,000 men (2 Ch 17:15).
3. Father of Ishmael who was allied with Jehoiada in removing Athaliah from the throne of Judah (2 Ch 23:1).
4. Son of Bebai. He renounced his pagan wife (Ez 10:28).
5. Son of Tobiah (Ne 6:18).
6. A priest, descendant of Amariah. He lived in the days of the high priest Joiakim (Ne 12:13).
7. A priest (Ne 12:42).

JE·HOI′ A·CHIN *(Jehovah establishes)*

The son of Jehoiakim. He followed his father on the throne of Judah and reigned only three months. The forces of Nebuchadnezzar of Babylon took Jerusalem and Jehoiachin and many of the leading people of Jerusalem, among them Ezekiel, were carried to Babylon. When Evil-merodach came to the throne of Babylon, he released Jehoiachin from prison (2 Ki 25:27-30; Je 52:31-34). He is frequently called Jeconiah and Coniah. See JECONIAH.

JE·HOI′ A·DA *(Jehovah knows)*

1. The father of Benaiah, a military officer under David and Solomon (2 Sa 23:22; 1 Ki 4:4).
2. A son of Benaiah and a counsellor of David following Ahithophel (1 Ch 27:34).

3. A high priest who organized a revolt against Queen Athaliah which resulted in her death. Joash, son of Ahaziah, was then crowned king of Judah. Under the influence of Jehoiada, Joash ruled well (2 Ki 11:1–12:16; 2 Ch 22:10–24:14), but he abandoned the worship of Jehovah for idolatry after Jehoiada's death (2 Ch 24:17-22).

4. A son of Paseah who lived at the time of Nehemiah (Ne 3:6).

5. A priest in Jeremiah's time. He was deposed and succeeded by Zephaniah (Je 29:26).

JE·HOI′ A·KIM

A son of Josiah, king of Jerusalem (2 Ki 23:34,36). His original name was Eliakim. He was placed on the throne by Pharaoh-necho who deposed his brother, Jehoahaz, and carried him to Egypt. He required the prophet, Jeremiah, to write his prophecies but after listening to a few of them, cut the roll and threw it in the fire (Je 36). In 606 B.C. Nebuchadnezzar came to Jerusalem, carried to Babylon the first deportation of captives, and made Jehoiakim a subject king (2 Ki 24:1; Je 46:2). He reigned eleven years and was succeeded by his son Jehoiachin (2 Ki 23:36; 24:6).

JE·HOI′ A·RIB *(Jehovah will contend)*

A descendant of Aaron (1 Ch 24:1,6-7). See JOIARIB.

JE·HON′ A·DAB

See JONADAB.

JE·HON′ A·THAN *(Jehovah hath given)*

Three Old Testament men:

1. Son of Uzziah, overseer of the store-houses under David (1 Ch 27:25).

2. A Levite appointed by King Jehoshaphat to teach in the cities of Judah (2 Ch 17:8).

3. A priest of the family of Shemaiah (Ne 12:18).

JE·HOR′ AM *(exalted by Jehovah)*

1. Son and successor of Jehoshaphat of Judah (2 Ki 8:16). His wife was Athaliah, daughter of Ahab and Jezebel of Israel. See JORAM.

2. Son of Ahab and king of Israel (2 Ki 3:1). See JORAM.

3. A priest appointed by Jehoshaphat to teach the people (2 Ch 17:8).

VALLEY OF JEHOSHAPHAT

JE·HO·SHAB′ E·ATH

See JEHOSHEBA.

JE·HOSH′ A·PHAT

Three Old Testament men:

1. Son and successor of Asa and one of the better kings of Judah. Conjointly with Asa, then alone, he reigned 25 years (1 Ki 22:41-42; 2 Ch 17:1). He honored Jehovah, carried forward the reforms of Asa, and commissioned the Levites to instruct the people in the law (2 Ch 17:7-9). He also brought an end to the conflicts between Israel and Judah. However, he made an alliance with Ahab and fought with him against the Syrians at Ramoth-gilead. Ahab was slain but Jehoshaphat escaped (1 Ki 22:1-38; 2 Ch 18:1-34). After his death he was succeeded by his son, Jehoram (1 Ki 22:50).

2. Son of Ahihud. He was recorder in the court of David and Solomon (2 Sa 8:16; 20:24; 1 Ki 4:3).

3. A priest who blew the trumpet when the ark was brought to Jerusalem (1 Ch 15:24).

JE·HOSH′ A·PHAT, VAL′ LEY OF

The valley between Jerusalem and Mount of Olives, also called the valley of the Kidron and the valley of Decision. Here Jehoshaphat defeated the enemies of Israel (2 Ch 20:26).

JE·HOSH′ E·BA *(Jehovah an oath)*

Daughter of Jehoram, son of Jehoshaphat, and sister of Ahaziah. She was the wife of Jehoiada, the high priest, and hid Joash, son of Ahaziah when his grandmother Athaliah planned to murder him (2 Ki 11:2; 2 Ch 22:11).

JEHOSHUA

See JOSHUA.

JEHOSHUAH

See JOSHUA.

JE·HO′ VAH *(Yaweh, I AM)*

One of the names of God (Ex 17:15). The later Hebrews and translators of the Septuagint substituted the word Lord. What it denotes is essentially different from El-shaddai and Elohim. The latter signifies God the Creator, the Sustainer and Moral Governor of the Universe, Mightiness. El-shaddai is the covenant God of the patriarchs, their strength and hope, God Almighty. Jehovah is the God of grace dwelling with his people, guiding them, manifesting his grace, the covenant-keeping God (1 Ki 8:43; Ps 9:10; 91:14; Is 52:6; Je 16:21). See GOD, NAMES OF.

JE·HO′VAH-JI′REH *(Jehovah will provide)*

The name given by Abraham to the place where he was commanded to sacrifice his son, Isaac (Ge 22:14).

JE·HO′VAH-NIS′SI *(Jehovah my banner)*

The name Moses gave the altar which he built at Rephidim (Ex 17:15-16).

JE·HO′VAH-SHA′LOM *(Jehovah is peace)*

The name given by Gideon to an altar erected by him in Ophrah (Ju 6:23-24).

JE·HO′ZA·BAD *(Jehovah endowed)*

Three Old Testament men:

1. Son of a Moabitess. He was a servant of Joash and one of his master's assassins. He was put to death (2 Ki 12:21; 2 Ch 24:26).

2. Son of Obed-edom, a Korhite Levite, a porter at a gate of the temple (1 Ch 26:4).

3. A Benjamite, one of Jehoshaphat's generals (2 Ch 17:18).

JE·HO′ZA·DAK

The great-grandson of Hilkiah the high priest; Jehozadak went into captivity with Judah when Nebuchadnezzar carried the people into Babylon (1 Ch 6:14-15).

JE′HU *(Jehovah is He)*

1. Son of Hanani, a prophet. He denounced Baasha, king of Israel, for his idolatry (1 Ki 16:1-4,7). He reproved Jehoshaphat, king of Judah, for his alliance with Ahab (2 Ch 19:2). He was the author of a book which recorded the acts of Jehoshaphat (2 Ch 20:34).

2. Son of Jehoshaphat and grandson of Nimshi (1 Ki 19:16; 2 Ki 9:2), the founder of the fifth dynasty of the Kingdom of Israel. He was in the service of Ahab (2 Ki 9:25). Elijah was divinely directed to anoint him king of Israel (1 Ki 19:16-

17); this was done later by Elisha. He was commanded to destroy the house of Ahab. The king at that time was Jehoram, son of Ahab. He executed his commission with bloody zeal. Jezebel, wife of Ahab, was slain (2 Ki 9:1-37). His acts were needlessly brutal and Hosea, the prophet, condemned the spirit of them (Ho 1:4). He then destroyed the prophets of Baal in the temple of Baal (2 Ki 10:12-28). He reigned 28 years, and in fulfillment of God's promise, this was the longest of the nine dynasties of Israel.

3. Son of Obed and father of Azariah of Judah (1 Ch 2:38).

4. Son of Josibiah, a chief Simeonite in the time of Hezekiah. He was with those who captured the valley of Gedor (1 Ch 4:35-41).

5. A Benjamite who came to David at Ziklag (1 Ch 12:3).

JEHU'S BLACK OBELISK

During the period of Old Testament history from about 900 to 700 B.C., the Assyrians were

JEHU'S BLACK OBELISK

the dominant world power. One of the powerful Assyrian kings, Shalmaneser III (reigned 859-824 B.C.), erected a large stone monument on which he recorded his military victories. This impressive archeological find, known as the Black Obelisk, contains a relief sculpture depicting the visit of King Jehu of Israel (reigned 841-814 B.C.) to pay tribute to Shalmaneser.

Placed outside the royal palace at Nimrod in Assyria, the monument is more than six feet high. Chiseled carefully in stone is a series of detailed drawings, with accompanying inscriptions that commemorate Shalmaneser's numerous military campaigns. The obelisk shows an event not mentioned in the Bible—Jehu bowing before Shalmaneser, with numerous Israelite servants and aids standing by with gifts for the Assyrian king.

Tribute, or compulsory payments to protect a weaker nation against a more powerful foe, was often levied by aggressor nations such as the Assyrians during Old Testament times.

After being anointed king of Israel by the prophet Elisha, Jehu eliminated all threats to his rule by killing all members of the family of Ahab, whom he succeeded (2 Ki 9–10). As a ruler, Jehu was a weak king who failed to eliminate Baal worship from the land.

The Black Obelisk is a valuable archeological find, because it helps establish a date for Jehu's rule, as well as an overall chronology for this period of Israel's history. It also shows us what an Israelite king from this period must have looked like. This is the only image or drawing of an Israelite king that has been discovered by archeologists.

JE·HUB′ BAH *(hidden)*

Son of Shamer of the tribe of Asher (1 Ch 7:34).

JE·HU′ CAL *(able)*

Son of Shelemiah (Je 37:3).

JE′ HUD

A town of Dan (Jos 19:45).

JE·HU′ DI *(a Jew)*

The man sent by Jehoiakim, king of Judah to Baruch for Jeremiah's roll of prophecies (Je 36:14, 21,23).

JE·HU·DI′ JAH *(Jewess)*

A wife of Mered (1 Ch 4:18).

JE′ HUSH (1 Ch 8:39)

See JEUSH.

JE·I′ EL

Several Old Testament men:

1. A Reubenite chief (1 Ch 5:7-8).

2. One of the ancestors of Saul, the first king of Israel (1 Ch 9:35).

3. One of David's mighty men, a son of Hotham the Aroerite (1 Ch 11:44).

4. A Levite porter, a harpist when the ark was brought to Jerusalem and afterwards appointed to serve regularly in the tent (1 Ch 15:18, 21; 16:5).

5. A Levite of the Merari family, a musician who participated in bringing the ark to Jerusalem (1 Ch 16:5). See JAAZIEL.

6. A Levite of the sons of Asaph (2 Ch 20:14).

7. A scribe who, with others, recorded the number of troops of Uzziah, king of Judah (2 Ch 26:11).

8. A Levite in the time of Hezekiah who assisted in the restoration of the temple service (2 Ch 29:13).

9. A Levite in the time of Josiah (2 Ch 35:9).

10. One of the company of Ezra who returned from Babylon (Ez 8:13).

11. A Hebrew in the time of Ezra (Ez 10:43); one who divorced his foreign wife.

JE·KAM′ E·AM *(the people will come together)*

A Levite of Kohath (1 Ch 23:19; 24:23).

JEK·A·MI′ AH, JE·CA·MI′ AH

Two Old Testament men:

1. A son of Shallum, descendant of Sheshan, of Judah (1 Ch 2:41)

2. A son of Jeconiah (Jehoiachin), king of Judah (1 Ch 3:18).

JE·KU′ THI·EL *(reverence for God)*

A man of Judah (1 Ch 4:18).

JE·MI′ MA

See JEMIMAH.

JE·MI′ MAH *(dove)*

One of Job's daughters (Job 42:14).

JE·MU′EL

Son of Simeon and founder of a tribal family (Ge 46:10; Ex 6:15). He is called Nemuel in Numbers 26:12 and 1 Chronicles 4:24.

JEPH′THAE

See JEPHTHAH.

JEPH′THAH *(he opens)*

A son of Gilead; he was expelled from his home by his brothers because of his illegitimate birth (Ju 11:1-2). He went to Tob where he became a famous hunter. At this time the Ammonites were holding the tribes east of the Jordan in subjection. Those who had driven Jephthah away now urged him to be their chief and deliver them from this oppression. A very religious man, Jephthah made a vow that if he were victorious he would sacrifice to God the first person who came from his house on his return. It was his daughter. Some believe that he actually did sacrifice her, for in Judges 11:39 it says that he "did with her according to his vow." Others believe that because of what God says about human sacrifice, Jephthah simply prevented his daughter from marrying, as a way of consecrating her to the Lord. He judged Israel six years (Ju 10:6–12:7; 1 Sa 12:11). He is one of the heroes of faith (He 11:32).

JE·PHUN′NEH

Two Old Testament men:
1. Father of Caleb. His son represented Judah as a spy when the Israelites were scouting the land of Canaan (Nu 13:6).
2. A son of Jether (1 Ch 7:38).

JE′RAH *(moon)*

A son of Joktan (Ge 10:26; 1 Ch 1:20).

JE·RAH′MEEL *(may God have compassion)*

Three Old Testament men:
1. A great-grandson of Judah and Tamar (descended through Perez and Hezron); the husband of two wives and the progenitor of many descendants (1 Ch 2:9,25-41).
2. The son of Kish who was a Merarite Levite, not the father of Saul (1 Ch 24:29).
3. One of the three men Jehoiakim ordered to arrest Jeremiah and Baruch (Je 36:26).

JE·RAH′MEEL·ITES

Probably the descendants of Jerahmeel, the descendant of Perez (1 Sa 27:10; 30:29; 1 Ch 2:9, 25-41).

JERBOA

JERBOA

A small rodent. All rodents were considered unclean (Le 11:29; Is 66:17).

JE′RED *(descent)*

Two Old Testament men:
1. Son of Mahalaleel of the line of Seth in the antediluvian period (1 Ch 1:2); also called Jared (Ge 5:15-20, KJV).
2. A man of Judah and the founder of Gedor (1 Ch 4:18).

JER·E·MA′I *(high)*

A son of Hashum in the time of Ezra (Ez 10:33).

JER·E·MI′AH *(Jehovah establishes)*

Eight Old Testament men:
1. The father of Hamutal, the wife of Josiah, king of Judah (2 Ki 23:31; 24:18; Je 52:1). He lived in Libnah.
2. A head of a family of east Manasseh (1 Ch 5:24).
3. A warrior of Benjamin who allied himself with David at Ziklag (1 Ch 12:4).
4. Two Gadites who joined David at Ziklag (1 Ch 12:10,13).
5. A priest who signed the covenant with Nehemiah (Ne 10:2).
6. A priest who came with Zerubbabel from Babylon (Ne 12:1).
7. The great prophet who worked at the time of the fall of Judah. He was the son of Hilkiah (Je 1:1). It is believed that the family was descended

JEREMIAH BEFORE THE KING

from Abiathar who was expelled to Anathoth by King Solomon (1 Ki 2:26-27). Jeremiah began his work in the thirteenth year of the reign of King Josiah (627 B.C.), continued through the declining years of the kingdom, and for some time after its fall (586 B.C.). The last evidences of his work come from Egypt where he was taken with a group of fugitives. Throughout his life he protested against the evils of idolatry. See JEREMIAH, BOOK OF, "The Author of Jeremiah."

8. Son of Habazaniah (Je 35:3).

JER·E·MI′AH, BOOK OF

1. The Book of Jeremiah. The Book of Jeremiah is the prophecy of a man divinely called in his youth from the priest-city of Anathoth. A heartbroken prophet with a heartbreaking message, Jeremiah labored for more than forty years proclaiming a message of doom to the stiff-necked people of Judah. Despised and persecuted by his countrymen, Jeremiah bathed his harsh prophecies in tears of compassion. His broken heart caused him to write a broken book, which is difficult to arrange chronologically or topically. But through his sermons and signs he faithfully declared that surrender to God's will is the only way to escape calamity.

Yirmeyahu or *Yirmeyah* literally means "Yahweh Throws," perhaps in the sense of laying a foundation. It may effectively mean "Yahweh establishes, appoints, or sends." The Greek form of the Hebrew name in the Septuagint is *Hieremias,* and the Latin form is *Jeremias.*

2. The Author of Jeremiah. Jeremiah was the son of Hilkiah the priest and lived just over two miles north of Jerusalem in Anathoth. As an object lesson to Judah he was not allowed to marry (16:2). Because of his radical message of God's judgment through the coming Babylonian invasion, he led a life of conflict. He was threatened in his home town of Anathoth, tried for his life by the priests and prophets of Jerusalem, put in stocks, forced to flee from King Jehoiakim, publicly humiliated by the false prophet Hananiah, and thrown into a cistern.

The book clearly states that Jeremiah is its author (1:1). Jeremiah dictated all his prophecies to his secretary Baruch from the beginning of his ministry until the fourth year of Jehoiakim. After this scroll was destroyed by the king, Jeremiah dictated a more complete edition to Baruch (see 36–38), and later sections were also composed. Only chapter 52 was evidently not written by Jeremiah. This supplement is almost identical to 2 Kings 24:18–25:30, and it may have been added by Baruch.

Daniel alludes to Jeremiah's prophecy of the seventy-year captivity (25:11-14; 29:10; Da 9:2), and Jeremiah's authorship is also confirmed by Ecclesiasticus, Josephus, and the Talmud. The New Testament makes explicit and implicit references to Jeremiah's prophecy: Matthew 2:17-18 (31:15); Matthew 21:13; Mark 11:17; Luke 19:4 (7:11); Romans 11:27 (31:33); and Hebrews 8:8-13 (31:31-34).

3. The Time of Jeremiah. Jeremiah was a contemporary of Zephaniah, Habbakuk, Daniel, and Ezekiel. His ministry stretched from 627 to a bout 580 B.C. Josiah, Judah's last good king (640-609 B.C.) instituted spiritual reforms when the Book of the Law was discovered in 622 B.C. Jeremiah was on good terms with Josiah and lamented when he was killed in 609 B.C. by Pharaoh Necho of Egypt. By this time, Babylon had already overthrown Nineveh, the capital city of Assyria (612 B.C.). Jehoahaz replaced Josiah as king of Judah, but reigned only three months before he was deposed and taken to Egypt by Necho. Jehoiakim (609-597 B.C.) was Judah's next king, but he reigned as an Egyptian vassal until 605 B.C., when Egypt was defeated by Babylon at Carchemish. Nebuchadnezzar took Palestine and deported key persons such as Daniel to Babylon. Judah's King Jehoiakim was now a Babylonian vassal, but he rejected Jeremiah's warnings in 601 B.C. and rebelled against Babylon. Jehoiachin became Judah's next king in 597 B.C., but was replaced by Zedekiah three months later when Nebuchadnezzar captured Jerusalem and deported Jehoiachin to Babylon. Zedekiah was the last king of Judah; his attempted alliance with Egypt led to Nebuchadnezzar's occupation and overthrow of Jerusalem in 586 B.C.

Thus, there were three stages in Jeremiah's ministry: (1) From 627 to 605 B.C. he prophesied while Judah was threatened by Assyria and Egypt. (2) From 605 to 586 B.C. he proclaimed God's judgment while Judah was threatened and besieged by Babylon. (3) From 586 to about 580 B.C. he ministered in Jerusalem and Egypt after Judah's downfall.

4. The Christ of Jeremiah. The Messiah is clearly seen in 23:1-8 as the coming Shepherd and righteous Branch who "shall reign and prosper, and execute judgment and righteousness in the earth. In His days Judah will be saved, and Israel will dwell safely; now this is His name by which He will be called: THE LORD OUR RIGHTEOUS-NESS" (23:5-6). He will bring in the new covenant (31:31-34), which will fulfill God's covenants with Abraham (Ge 12:1-3; 17:1-8), Moses and the people (De 28–30), and David (2 Sa 7:1-17).

The curse on Jehoiachin (Jeconiah, Coniah) in 22:28-30 meant that no physical descendant would succeed him to the throne. Matthew 1:1-17 traces the genealogy of Christ through Solomon and Jeconiah to His legal (but not His physical) father, Joseph. However, no son of Joseph could sit upon the throne of David, for he would be under the curse of Jehoiachin. Luke 3:23-38 traces Christ's lineage slightly differently; it is assumed that this is Mary's genealogy. Jesus's physical parent was descended from David's other son, Nathan, thereby avoiding the curse. The righteous Branch will indeed reign on the throne of David.

5. Keys to Jeremiah.

Key Word: Judah's Last Hour—In Jeremiah, God is seen as patient and holy: He always delays judgment and appeals to His people to repent before it is too late. As the object lesson at the potter's house demonstrates, a ruined vessel can be repaired while still wet (18:1-4); but once dried, a marred vessel is fit only for the garbage heap (19:10-11). God's warning is clear: Judah's time for repentance will soon pass. Because they defy God's words and refuse to repent, the Babylonian captivity is inevitable. Jeremiah lists the moral and spiritual causes for their coming catastrophe, but he also proclaims Gods gracious promise of hope and restoration. There will always be a remnant, and God will establish a new covenant.

Key Verses: Jeremiah 7:23-24 and 8:11-12—"But this is what I commanded them, saying, 'Obey My voice, and I will be your God, and you shall be My people. And walk in all the ways that I have commanded you, that it may be well with you.' Yet they did not obey or incline their ear, but walked in the counsels and in the imagination of their evil heart, and went backwards and not forward" (7:23-24).

"For they have healed the hurt of the daughter of My people slightly, saying, 'Peace, peace!' when there is no peace. Were they ashamed when they had committed abomination? No! They were not at all ashamed, nor did they know how to blush. Therefore they shall fall among those who fall, in the time of their punishment they shall be cast down, says the LORD" (8:11-12).

Key Chapter: Jeremiah 31—Amid all the judgment and condemnation by Jeremiah are the wonderful promises of Jeremiah 31. Even though Judah has broken the covenants of her great King, God will make a new covenant when He will "put My law in their minds, and write it on their hearts; and I will be their God, and they shall be My people" (31:33). The Messiah instituted that new covenant with His death and resurrection (Ma 26:26-29).

6. Survey of Jeremiah.

Jeremiah is a record of the ministry of one of Judah's greatest prophets during the darkest days. He was called as a prophet during the reign of Josiah, the last of Judah's good kings. But even Josiah's well-intentioned reforms could not stem the tide of apostasy. The downhill slide of the nation continued virtually unabated through a succession of four godless kings during Jeremiah's ministry. The people wallowed in apostasy and idolatry and grew even more treacherous than Israel was before its captivity (3:11). They perverted the worship of the true God and gave themselves over to spiritual and moral decay. Because they refused to repent or even listen to God's prophet, the divine cure required radical surgery. Jeremiah proclaimed an approaching avalanche of judgment. Babylon would be God's instrument of judgment, and this book refers to that nation 164 times, more references than all the rest of the Bible together.

Jeremiah faithfully proclaimed the divine condemnation of rebellious Judah for forty years and was rewarded with opposition, beatings, isolation, and imprisonment. His sympathy and sensitivity caused him to grieve over the rebelliousness and imminent doom of his nation. He often desired to resign from his prophetic office because of the harshness of his message and his reception, but he persevered to Judah's bitter end. He is the weeping prophet (9:1; 13:17)—lonely, rejected, and persecuted.

Although Jeremiah is not easily arranged chronologically or thematically, its basic message is clear: surrender to God's will is the only way to escape calamity. Judgment cannot be halted, but promises of restoration are sprinkled through the book. Its divisions are: the call of Jeremiah (1); the prophecies to Judah (2–45); the prophecies to the Gentiles (46–51); and the fall of Jerusalem (52).

The Call of Jeremiah (1). Jeremiah was called and sanctified before birth to be God's prophet. This introductory chapter surveys the identification, inauguration, and instruction of the prophet.

The Prophecies to Judah (2–45). Jeremiah's message is communicated through a variety of parables, sermons, and object lessons. The prophet's life became a daily illustration to Judah, and most of the book's object lessons are found in this section (13:1-14; 14:1-9; 16:1-9; 18:1-8; 19:1-13; 24:1-10; 27:1-11; 32:6-15; 43:8-13). In a series of twelve graphic messages, Jeremiah lists the causes of Judah's coming judgment. The Gentile nations are more faithful to their false gods than Judah is to the true God. They become a false vine by following idols and are without excuse. The people are condemned for their empty profession, disobedience to God's covenant, and spiritual harlotry. God has bound Judah to Himself; but like a rotten waistband, they have become corrupt and useless. Jeremiah offers a confession for the people, but their sin is too great; the prophet can only lament for them. As a sign of imminent judgment Jeremiah is forbidden to marry and participate in the feasts. Because the nation does not trust God or keep the Sabbath, the land will receive a Sabbath rest when they are in captivity. Jerusalem will be invaded and the rulers and people will be deported to Babylon. Restoration will only come under the new Shepherd, the Messiah, the nation's future King. Jeremiah announces the duration of the captivity as seventy years, in contrast to the messages of the false prophets who insist that it will not happen.

Because of his message (2:25), Jeremiah suffered misery and opposition (26–45). He was rejected by the prophets and priests who call for his death, but he was spared by the elders and officials. In his sign of the yoke he proclaimed the unpopular message that Judah must submit to divine discipline. But he assured the nation of restoration and hope under a new covenant (30–33). A remnant would be delivered and there would be a coming time of blessing. Jeremiah's personal experiences and sufferings are the focal point of 34–45 as opposition against the prophet mounted. Since he was no longer allowed in the temple, he sent his assistant Baruch to read his prophetic warnings. His scroll was burned by Jehoiakim, and Jeremiah was imprisoned. After the destruction of the city, Jeremiah was taken to Egypt by fleeing Jews, but he prophesied that Nebuchadnezzar would invade Egypt as well.

The Prophecies to the Gentiles (46–51). These chapters are a series of prophetic oracles against nine nations: Egypt, Philistia, Moab, Ammon, Edom, Damascus (Syria), Arabia, Elam, and Babylon. Only Egypt, Moab, Ammon, and Elam are given a promise of restoration.

The Fall of Jerusalem (52). Jeremiah's forty-year declaration of doom was finally vindicated in an event so significant that it is recorded in detail four times in the Scriptures (2 Ki 25; 2 Ch 36; Je 39; 52). In this historical supplement, Jerusalem was captured, destroyed, and plundered. The leaders were killed and the captives taken to Babylon.

OUTLINE OF JEREMIAH

Part One: The Call of Jeremiah (1:1-19)

I. Jeremiah's Call (1:1-10)

II. Jeremiah's Signs (1:11-16)

III. Jeremiah's Assurance (1:17-19)

Part Two: The Prophecies to Judah (2:1–45:5)

I. The Condemnation of Judah (2:1–25:38)

A. Jeremiah's First Sermon: Judah Sinned Willfully 2:1–3:5

B. Jeremiah's Second Sermon: Judah to Be Judged 3:6–6:30

C. Jeremiah's Third Sermon: Judah's Hypocrisy in Worship 7:1–10:25

D. Jeremiah's Fourth Sermon: Judah's Breach of the Covenant 11:1–12:17

E. Jeremiah's Fifth Sermon: Judah's Revived Relationship ... 13:1-27

F. Jeremiah's Sixth Sermon: The Drought in Judah 14:1–15:21

G. Jeremiah's Seventh Sermon: Jeremiah's Unmarried State 16:1–17:27

H. Jeremiah's Eighth Sermon:
Sign of the Potter's House 18:1–20:18
I. Jeremiah's Ninth Sermon:
Against Judah's Kings 21:1–23:8
J. Jeremiah's Tenth Sermon:
Against Judah's False
Prophets 23:9-40
K. Jeremiah's Eleventh Sermon:
The Two Baskets of Figs 24:1-10
L. Jeremiah's Twelfth Sermon:
The Seventy Year Captivity......... 25:1-38

II. The Conflicts of Jeremiah (26:1–29:32)

A. Conflict with the Nation 26:1-24
B. Conflict with the False
Prophets 27:1-22

C. Conflict with Hananiah 28:1-17
D. Conflict with Shemaiah 29:1-32

III. The Future Restoration of Jerusalem (30:1–33:26)

A. Restoration to the Land 30:1-24
B. Restoration of the Nation 31:1-40
C. Rebuilding of Jerusalem 32:1-44
D. Reconfirming the Covenant 33:1-26

IV. The Present Fall of Jerusalem (34:1–45:5)

A. Messages Before the Fall 34:1–36:32
B. Events Before the Fall 37:1–38:28
C. Events During the Fall.............. 39:1-18
D. Messages After the Fall 40:1–44:30
E. Message to Baruch 45:1-5

Part Three: The Prophecies to the Gentiles (46:1–51:64)

I. Prophecies Against Egypt (46:1-28)

II. Prophecies Against Philistia (47:1-7)

III. Prophecies Against Moab (48:1-47)

IV. Prophecies Against Ammon (49:7-22)

V. Prophecies Against Damascus (49:23-27)

VI. Prophecies Against Kedar and Hazor (49:28-33)

VII. Prophecies Against Elam (49:34-39)

VIII. Prophecies Against Babylon (50:1–51:64)

A. Babylon's Defeat 50:1-20
B. Babylon's Desolation 50:21-46
C. Babylon's Destiny 51:1-64

Part Four: The Fall of Jerusalem (52:1-34)

I. The Capture of Jerusalem (52:1-11)

II. The Destruction of Jerusalem (52:12-23)

III. The Exile to Babylon (52:24-30)

IV. The Liberation of Jehoiachin (52:31-34)

JEREMIAH, EPISTLE OF
See APOCRYPHA.

JEREMIAH, LAMENTATIONS OF
See LAMENTATIONS, BOOK OF.

JER·E·MI′ AS
The Greek form of the name Jeremiah (Ma 16:14).

JER′ E·MOTH *(heights)*
Eight Old Testament men:
1. A Benjamite of the family of Becher (1 Ch 7:8).
2. A son of the house of Beriah of Elpaal, of the tribe of Benjamin (1 Ch 8:14).

3. A Levite of the family of Merari; son of Mushi (1 Ch 23:23), called Jerimoth in 1 Chronicles 24:30.
4. Son of Heman; head of the fifteenth course of musicians in David's reign (1 Ch 25:4,22).
5. Son of Azriel of Naphtali in the reign of David (1 Ch 27:19).
6. A "son of Elam." He renounced his foreign wife (Ez 10:26).
7. A descendant of Zattu who renounced his foreign wife (Ez 10:27).
8. Also called Ramoth (Ez 10:29).

JER′ E·MY (Ma 2:17; 27:9)
The Greek form of JEREMIAH.

JE·RI′ AH

A Levite of the family of Kohath (1 Ch 23:19; 24:23; 26:31).

JER·I·BA′ I *(the Lord contends)*

Son of Elnaam; one of David's warriors (1 Ch 11:46).

JER′ I·CHO *(fragrant)*

Located near the Jordan River just north of the Dead Sea, Jericho is the site of one of the oldest continually inhabited cities in the world. Situated seventeen miles northeast of Jerusalem, Jericho has actually been positioned at three different sites within a few miles of each other. Throughout its long history the city has apparently changed location after sieges, earthquakes, and other catastrophes. Present day Jericho is a small village (er-Riha) on the main highway from Jerusalem to Amman, Jordan.

Known as the "city of palms" (Ju 3:13) because of the trees that grow in its oasis location, Jericho at 800 feet below sea level sits lower than any other city on earth. Its position at the bottom of a deep gorge contributes to its hot, tropical climate.

Old Testament Jericho was the first city captured by Joshua in his invasion of Canaan during the thirteenth century B.C. Under orders from the Lord, the Israelites marched around the massive walls at the fortified city for six days. On the seventh day the priests blew their trumpets and all the warriors let out a loud shout. The walls came tumbling down, leaving the city exposed to the invaders (Jos 6).

Excavations of Old Testament Jericho indicate that the site had been occupied for thousands of years before Joshua captured the city. Unfortunately, extensive archeological excavations there have failed to uncover conclusive evidence of Joshua's conquest, because there are few remains from this period. This lack of evidence is most often attributed to centuries of erosion on the ruin.

New Testament Jericho, located about two miles south of the Old Testament site, is associated with the ministry of Jesus. The rough hilly road from Jerusalem to Jericho was the setting for Jesus's famous parable of the Good Samaritan (Lk 10:30-37). On visits to Jericho, Jesus healed blind Bartimaeus (Mk 10:46-52) and brought salvation to Zacchaeus (Lk 19:1-10).

JER′ I·EL *(founded by God)*

A descendant of Tola of Issachar (1 Ch 7:2).

JE·RI′ JAH

See JERIAH.

JER′ I·MOTH *(heights)*

Several Old Testament men:

1. A son of Bela who was son of Benjamin (1 Ch 7:7).

2. A Benjamite who joined David at Ziklag, an archer (1 Ch 12:5).

3. A son of Becher and head of a house of Benjamin (1 Ch 7:8).

4. A son of Heman and head of the fifteenth course of musicians, also called Jeremoth (1 Ch 25:4,22).

5. A son of David. His daughter, Mahalath, was the wife of Rehoboam, grandson of David (2 Ch 11:18).

6. A Levite (2 Ch 31:13).

See JEREMOTH.

JER′ I·OTH *(curtains)*

A wife of Caleb (1 Ch 2:18).

JER·O·BO′ AM

Two kings of the Northern Kingdom:

1. Son of Nebat, of the tribe of Ephraim, the founder of the Northern Kingdom of Israel. His father was an official under Solomon (1 Ki 11:26) and Jeroboam, because of his ability, was made overseer of a part of Solomon's building operations at Jerusalem (1 Ki 11:27-28). Jeroboam represented the ten tribes in demanding that the tax burdens be lightened. Rehoboam's foolish reply brought about the disruption and, with Jeroboam as their leader, ten tribes revolted. To keep the people from going to Jerusalem to worship, Jeroboam set up two centers of worship, at Dan in the North and Beth-el in the South with a golden calf at each place, thereby violating the commandment that God must not be worshipped by means of images (1 Ki 12:26-30; 2 Ch 13:8). When the priests and Levites in this territory returned to Judah (1 Ki 12:31; 2 Ch 11:13-15; 13:9), he instituted his own priestly system. Thus idolatry became firmly rooted in Israel and continued until the fall of the kingdom (1 Ki 15:26,34; 22:52; 2 Ki 3:3; 13:2,11). He made Shechem the capital and reigned twenty-two years (1 Ki 14:20).

2. Jeroboam II, son and successor of Joash of the fifth dynasty of Israel, the dynasty of Jehu. From about the year 790 B.C., he reigned forty-one years, the longest reign of any king in Israel. He was a man of unusual executive and administrative ability. He captured Damascus and Hamath and restored to Israel the territory from Hamath to the Dead Sea, successes that were predicted by Jonah (2 Ki 14:23-28). It was during his reign that the three prophets of Israel arose: Jonah, Amos, and Hosea.

JE·RO′ HAM (compassionate)

Seven Old Testament men:

1. The father of Elkanah, the father of Samuel, a Levite (1 Sa 1:1; 1 Ch 6:27,34).

2. The father of several chiefs of Benjamin who lived at Jerusalem (1 Ch 8:27).

3. Father of Ibneiah, a Benjamite (1 Ch 9:8).

4. An inhabitant of Gedor, a Benjamite. His sons allied themselves to David at Ziklag (1 Ch 12:7).

5. A priest, father of Adaiah. The son was a priest at Jerusalem (1 Ch 9:12; Ne 11:12).

6. Father of the chief of the tribe of Dan in the reign of David (1 Ch 27:22).

7. Father of Azariah (2 Ch 23:1).

JER·UB·BA′ AL (let Baal contend)

A name given to Gideon by his father after Gideon had destroyed the altars to Baal (Ju 6:32; 9:1-2,5,16,19,24,28,57).

JE·RUB′ BE·SHETH

A name of Gideon (2 Sa 11:21), given to supplant his previous name, Jerubbaal (Ju 6:32).

JE·RU′ EL (founded of God)

A wilderness west of the Dead Sea (2 Ch 20:16).

JE·RU′ SA·LEM

When David became king of Judah, one of his first acts was to capture Jerusalem from the Jebusites and make the city the capital of his kingdom (2 Sa 5:6-10; 1 Ch 11:4-9). The city served from that point on as the religious and political capital of the Jewish nation.

Jerusalem was a good choice as a capital city site. Easy to defend because of its hilltop location, it was also centrally located between the northern and southern tribes of the nation. David's first task as king was to unite these tribes under his leadership. This is probably why he selected Jerusalem as his capital.

Jerusalem grew into a magnificent city under Solomon, David's son and successor. Solomon built the temple as the place of worship for the Israelites (1 Ki 6–7; 2 Ch 3:4). He also planted many vineyards, orchards, and gardens to beautify the city.

Several centuries after Solomon's time, in 586 B.C., the Babylonians destroyed Jerusalem and carried its inhabitants into captivity. Although the temple and the city and its surrounding walls were rebuilt by the returning Jewish exiles some time later, Jerusalem was not restored to its previous splendor. This task, ironically, fell to Herod the Great, Roman ruler of Palestine about the time of Jesus. He restored the temple to its previous state in an attempt to please the Jewish people and also built several other beautiful buildings in Jerusalem. This building program continued throughout the period of Jesus's public ministry.

The holy city played a significant role in the life and ministry of Jesus. At the age of twelve, He went to Jerusalem, where He amazed the temple leaders with His wisdom and knowledge (Lk 2:47). At the close of His public ministry, He was crucified, buried, and resurrected at Jerusalem.

As Jesus had predicted (Ma 23:37-39), the city of Jerusalem was destroyed in A.D. 70 when the Jewish people rebelled against Roman authority. Rome eventually built a city on the site, but it was considered off limits for the Jews. This situation changed in 1919, when Israel regained its status as a Jewish nation and Jerusalem was reestablished as its capital city.

After the reinstatement of Israel, many Jews from throughout the world moved back to their homeland. Most of these Jews settled in a new city west of the old city of Jerusalem. Following the Arab-Israeli War of 1948-49, the new city was allotted to the Jews, while the old city remained in Muslim hands. But Israel reunited Jerusalem during the Six-Day War of 1967 when it took control of the Muslim section of the city.

The modern visitor to the city is impressed with the stark contrast between the old city section, with its crooked, narrow streets, and the modern architecture of the new city section of Jerusalem.

One of the most popular tourist sites in Jerusalem is known as "Gordon's Calvary," a rocky knoll just outside the walls of the old city, identified by Charles Gordon in 1885 as the site of Jesus's crucifixion. This rock formation does seem to resemble a skull. The Hebrew word for Calvary is *Golgotha,* which means "Place of a Skull" (Mk 15:22). The traditional site of the crucifixion is found at the Church of the Sepulchre inside the walls of the old city, but the fact that it is inside the walls makes it a less likely choice.

Jerusalem is considered to be a holy city by three of the world's major religions: Christianity, Judaism, and Islam.

JERUSALEM COUNCIL, THE

The council was called together to discuss the question of the necessity of Gentile believers following the law (Ac 15). Did a Gentile believer have to be circumcised and keep the law of Moses in order to accept Christ? Some believers from Judea had been teaching just that, and when Paul heard it he argued strongly to the contrary. The church decided that this important issue should be discussed without delay, and Paul and Barnabas set off towards Jerusalem to meet with the elders and apostles there. Paul, Barnabas, and Simon Peter testified at the meeting of their experiences with Gentile conversions. They had all seen obvious manifestations of God's power and approval upon uncircumcised Gentiles who turned to the Lord, and Peter said, "Now therefore, why do you test God by putting a yoke on the neck of the disciples which neither our fathers nor we were able to bear? But we believe that through the grace of the Lord Jesus Christ we shall be saved in the same manner as they." After listening to the testimony of Paul and Barnabas, James joined in, pointing out that the Scriptures taught that Gentiles would be saved (Am 9:11-12). The council agreed that the Gentile believers should be taught to abstain from sexual immorality, from idols, from strangled meat, and from blood. Therefore, they wrote an encouraging letter to the believers in Antioch, telling them that they were not required to be under the burden of keeping the Mosaic law. They should abstain from the things mentioned, but were not asked to be circumcised or to follow the strict dietary rules.

JERUSALEM, NEW

The holy city that John the apostle describes in Revelation 21-22. The New Jerusalem is described as coming down from heaven "prepared as a bride adorned for her husband" (Re 21:2). The New Jerusalem is where God and the Lamb reign, *Immanuel,* "God with us" (Re 21:3). There will be no need for the sun's light because God's presence will be all its light. Sorrow, sin, and the curse will all pass away. Those who are saved by the blood of the Lamb shall walk here, but nothing defiling and no one whose name is not in the Lamb's book of life will enter the city (Re 21:24,27).

JE·RU′ SHA *(possession)*
Wife of Uzziah (2 Ki 15:33; 2 Ch 27:1).

JE·RU′ SHAH
See JERUSHA.

JE·SAI′ AH
See JESHAIAH.

JE·SHAI′ AH
1. Son of Jeduthun, a harpist at the head of the eighth division of musicians in the reign of David (1 Ch 25:3).
2. A son of Hananiah and grandson of Zerubbabel (1 Ch 3:21). Another form is Jesaiah.
3. A son of Rehabiah, a Levite, in the reign of David. He was of the Levitical branch of Eliezer (1 Ch 26:25).
4. Son of Athaliah and head of the house of Elam. With seventy males he returned from Babylon with Ezra (Ez 8:7).
5. A Levite of the Merari branch. He came to Jerusalem with Ezra (Ez 8:19).
6. The father of Ithiel, a Benjamite (Ne 11:7).

JE·SHA′ NAH *(old)*
A city of Ephraim (2 Ch 13:19).

JE·SHA′ NAH GATE
One of the gates of Jerusalem (Ne 3:6; 12:39). Also called "Old Gate" (NKJV).

JESH·A·RE′ LAH
See ASHARELAH.

JE·SHEB′ E·AB *(father's dwelling)*
A descendant of Aaron (1 Ch 24:13).

JE′ SHER *(uprightness)*
A son of Caleb, the son of Hezron (1 Ch 2:18).

JE′ SHI·AH
See JESSHIAH.

JE·SHI′MON *(a waste)*

A desolate stretch of wasteland in Judah to the West and near the middle of the Dead Sea (1 Sa 23:19,24; 26:1,3).

JE·SHISH′AI *(aged)*

Son of Jahdo, a Gadite of Gilead (1 Ch 5:14).

JESH·O·HAI′AH

A prince of Simeon. He went to Gedor (1 Ch 4:36).

JESH′U·A

Eight Old Testament men:

1. A form of Joshua, son of Nun (Ne 8:17).

2. A descendant of Aaron. In the time of David, his family was the ninth course of priests (1 Ch 24:1,6,11).

3. A Levite in the reign of Hezekiah. He was one of those in charge of the temple offerings (2 Ch 31:15).

4. A high priest who came from Babylon with Zerubbabel (Ez 2:2; Ne 7:7). He labored on the altar and urged the people to build the second temple (Ez 3:2-9). He is called Joshua in Zechariah 3:1-10; 6:11-13.

5. The head of a Levitical family who returned from Babylon with Zerubbabel (Ez 2:40; Ne 7:43; 12:8). He took an active part in stimulating the people to rebuild the temple.

6. A man of Pahath-moab. His descendants numbering 2812 returned with Zerubbabel from Babylon to Jerusalem (Ez 2:6; Ne 7:11).

7. A Levite who assisted Ezra in teaching the people the law (Ne 8:7; 9:4-5).

8. A village in the southern section of Judah (Ne 11:26).

JESH′U·AH (Ne 7:39)

JE·SHU′RUN, JES·U′RUN

A term meaning righteous nation (De 32:15; 33:5,26; Is 44:2).

JE·SI′AH

See ISSHIAH.

JE·SIM′I·EL *(God sets up)*

A Simeonite who lived in the time of Hezekiah (1 Ch 4:36).

JES′SE

Son of Obed, father of David, and grandson of Ruth and Boaz. He was descended from Nah-

shon, who in the days of Moses was chief of the tribe of Judah (Ru 4:18-22). David was the youngest of the eight sons of Jesse (1 Sa 17:12-14).

JES·SHI′AH

A Kohathite, the son of Uzziel (1 Ch 23:20); also called Isshiah (1 Ch 24:25).

JES′U·I

The third of Asher's sons (Nu 26:44); also called Isui (Ge 46:17) or Ishvi (1 Ch 7:30).

JESUITES

The descendants of Asher's son Jesui (Nu 26:44).

JES′U·RUN

See JESHURUN.

JE′SUS

Jesus is an imitation of the Greek form of Jeshua. It means "Jehovah is salvation."

1. A military leader of the Israelites (Ac 7:45; He 4:8); he is also called Joshua.

2. An ancestor of the family of Christ; also called Jose (Lk 3:29).

3. A Jewish Christian associated with Paul (Col 4:11). He was also called Justus.

4. The name given to the Messiah (Ma 1:21).

JE′SUS CHRIST

1. Name. The name Jesus, announced by the angel as that divinely selected for Mary's son (Ma 1:21; Lk 1:31-33), signifies *the Lord is salvation.* The word Christ (the Anointed One) is essentially an official title borne by Jesus as the Messiah (Jo 1:41) and as the Son of the living God (Ma 16:16).

2. Date. Jesus was born in the year 4 (some say late 5) B.C. The Roman abbot who (prior to A.D. 550) devised the Christian calendar fixed the year 1, the year intended to mark Christ's birth, too late.

3. Political situation. The political situation in Palestine in the time of Jesus was complicated and seething with discontent. The country, since the exile, had been successively under Persian, Greek, Egyptian, and Syrian domination. Foreign rule was followed by about a century of independence under the Maccabees, which ended near the middle of the first century B.C. when the country was incorporated into the Roman Empire as part of the province of Syria. Jewish reaction to Roman rule ranged from mildly critical to hostile but was usually tempered with the spirit of opportunism.

4. Religious situation. The religious life of Judaism in Jesus's time was at a low ebb. Formal religion was dominated by two powerful sects—the Pharisees and the Sadducees. The former were the more influential, but to the word of God they added much religious tradition and theological subtleties. The latter, while rejecting the traditions of the Pharisees, were more interested in politics than religion. Sadducees controlled the Sanhedrin and limited the high priests to members of their own families. Both sects were denounced by John the Baptist, and Jesus warned against them (Ma 3:7; 16:6; Lk 11:42-52). It was to the common people that the gospel of Jesus was destined to appeal (Mk 12:37; Lk 19:47-48).

5. Early life. The events and circumstances connected with the birth of Jesus (Ma 1-2; Lk 1:26-35; 2:1-39) are well-known. The genealogy of the family is traced by Matthew to Abraham and by Luke to Adam. The political situation is reflected in episodes such as the flight into Egypt and the return to Nazareth (Ma 2:13-15; 19-23). Only one of his boyhood experiences has been recorded—that of his visit to the temple at the age of twelve (Lk 2:41-52). His vocation was that of carpenter (Mk 6:3).

6. His baptism. John the Baptist, probably in the summer of A.D. 26, began to proclaim the approach of the day of the Lord. John called upon individuals and nations to repent and be baptized. Among the Galileans who came to the region of the lower Jordan to be baptized was Jesus. As an individual Jesus had no need of baptism—but in submitting to it, he identified himself with men as their Redeemer. It was at his baptism that he heard the heavenly voice declaring him to be the beloved Son in whom God was well pleased (Ma 3:1-17; Mk 1:10-11).

7. His temptation. After the baptism, Jesus was led by the Spirit into the wilderness to be tempted (Ma 4:1-11; Lk 4:1-13). The attractions of the world were presented to him in three successive visions or experiences, yet he yielded not (He 4:15; 7:26; 1 Pe 2:21-22).

8. Early Judean ministry. After certain, rather informal, opening events which included the calling of some disciples and the miracle at Cana (Jo 1:35-47; 2:1-11), Jesus began his work in Judea, making occasional visits to Galilee (Jo 4:3). Among the recorded events of this period were the cleansing of the temple, the conversations with Nicodemus, and with the woman at the well (Jo 2:13-17; 3:1-21; 4:3-26).

9. The early or main Galilean ministry. The fame which Jesus had achieved in Judea preceded him into Galilee (Jo 4:43-45). The synagogue at Nazareth rejected him at the outset (Lk 4:16-30), but the people generally gave him a tumultuous welcome. He declared that the Spirit of the Lord was upon him and that he was anointed to preach the gospel to the poor (Lk 4:18-21). He moved his residence from Nazareth to Capernaum, called additional disciples, and performed many miracles of healing (Ma 4:13; 18-22; 9:2-6,9; Jo 4:46-54). A new phase of this early work in Galilee began with a visit to Jerusalem where he incurred the opposition of the Pharisees by healing a crippled man on the Sabbath (Jo 5:1-16). This antagonism was intensified by other deeds performed on the Sabbath (Ma 12:1-14). Jesus continually proclaimed Himself to be the fulfillment of Old Testament prophecy (Ma 5:17-18; Lk 24:44-48). He chose twelve apostles and sent them forth (Ma 10; Lk 6:13-16). Doctrine was presented through the Sermon on the Mount (Ma 5:1–7:29), various discourses, and parables (Ma 13:1-53).

10. The later Galilean ministry in northern Galilee and beyond. In these northern districts (including the vicinity of Capernaum) and in Decapolis, he exercised a ministry of some six months. His purpose was primarily that of preparing his disciples for his approaching death. He elicited from Peter his great confession, he foretold his death and resurrection, and was manifested to certain disciples in the transfiguration (Ma 16:13-28; 17:1-13).

11. The Perean ministry. During this period it seems clear that He moved back and forth between Perea and Judea. The seventy disciples had been sent out to announce his coming (Lk 10:1-24). At this time he uttered many of his most famous parables (Lk 10:30-37; 15–16:1-12,19-31). He delivered discourses on prayer, on the coming of the kingdom, and against the Pharisees (Lk 11:1-13,37-54; 17:20-37).

12. Passion Week. Six days before the Passover Jesus went to Bethany where Mary anointed his head with precious ointment (Jo 12:1-8). On the next day (the beginning of Passion Week) he made his triumphal entry into Jerusalem (Ma 21:1-11; Jo 12:12-19), then returned to Bethany, probably to the house of Mary, Martha, and Lazarus. On Monday he entered Jerusalem, cleansed the temple and cursed a barren fig tree which, by the following day, had withered away (Mk 11:11-26). On Tuesday he went again to Jerusalem where his authority was challenged by the religious leaders (Ma 21:23-27). They asked him three questions, to each of which Christ gave a silencing reply (Ma 22:15-46). He pronounced woes against the scribes and Pharisees but commended the poor widow who cast two mites into the temple treasury (Ma 23; Mk 12:41-44). He delivered a lengthy discourse on the destruction of the temple, the end of the world, and the last judgment (Ma 24–25:31-46). It was on this day that Judas Iscariot conspired to betray him (Ma 26:3,14-16). On Wednesday he remained in retirement at Bethany. On Thursday he instituted the Last Supper and delivered farewell discourses (Ma 26:17-30; Jo 13:1–17:26). On Friday he underwent the agony in Gethsemane, was betrayed by Judas, and was arrested (Lk 22:39-54; Jo 18:1-28). His trial was first before the Jewish authorities, then before Pilate. Pilate found no fault in him, but in order to pacify the Jews who clamored for his death, turned him over to them for execution (Jo 18:29–19:22).

13. His death, burial and resurrection. See CRUCIFIXION. When death came to Jesus on the cross, the crowd had dispersed, but a few faithful followers remained. Joseph of Arimathaea, a secret disciple of Jesus and member of the Sanhedrin who had not consented to his death, went boldly to Pilate and asked for the body, a request which was granted. Nicodemus, another secret disciple and a member of the Sanhedrin, also came, bringing myrrh and aloes. The little group bound the body with linen cloths and spices, then placed it in a new, rock-hewn tomb (Ma 27:26-66,28; Mk 15:16-47; 16; Lk 23:32-56; 24; Jo 19:23–21:25). Despite the huge stone which had been rolled against the door of the tomb and the watch which had been placed on guard, Jesus rose on the third day (Ma 28:1-7). See RESURRECTION, ASCENSION.

Also see CHRIST, TITLES OF; GOSPELS HARMONIZED and INCARNATION.

JESUS JUSTUS (Col 4:11)

See JUSTUS.

JESUS, SON OF SIRACH

See APOCRYPHA.

JE'THER (*abundance*)

Five Old Testament men:

1. A descendant of Judah; son of Ezra (1 Ch 4:17).

2. Gideon's first son. He was commanded by Gideon to slay two kings of Midian, but he could not bring himself to do it because of youthful fears (Ju 8:20-21).

3. Son of Zophah of Asher; probably the same as Ithran (1 Ch 7:37).

4. Son of Jada and a descendant of Hezron of Judah (1 Ch 2:32).

5. Father of Amasa (1 Ki 2:5).

JE'THETH

A chief of Edom (Ge 36:40; 1 Ch 1:51).

JETH'LAH

See ITHLAH.

JETH'RO (*excellence*)

A priest of Midian who became the father-in-law of Moses (Ex 3:1). He was also called Reuel (Ex 2:18). Moses was the shepherd of the family of Jethro and married his daughter, Zipporah. Moses asked Jethro's permission to return to Egypt and find out what was happening to his fellow Hebrews (Ex 4:18). The wife and the sons of Moses apparently stayed with Jethro at least part of the time while Moses was away. (Ex 18:1-7). Jethro was also instrumental in helping Moses delegate some of the responsibilities of leadership (Ex 18:17-27).

JE'TUR

A son of Ishmael (Ge 25:15). The name also signifies his descendants, the Ituraeans (1 Ch 1:31; 5:19). See ITURAEA.

THE MEETING OF MOSES AND JETHRO

JEU´ EL

Three Old Testament men:

1. A Levite who assisted Hezekiah, king of Judah in his work of reform (2 Ch 29:13); also called Jeiel.

2. A descendant of Zerah of Judah. After the exile, he and 690 of his people lived in Jerusalem (1 Ch 9:6).

3. One of those who returned with Ezra (Ez 8:13); also called Jeiel (KJV).

JE´ USH, JE´ HUSH

Five Old Testament men:

1. A son of Esau and Aholibamah and a chief in Edom (Ge 36:5,18).

2. Son of Shimei, a Levite of the family of Gershon (1 Ch 23:10-11).

3. Son of Bilhan of Benjamin (1 Ch 7:10).

4. A descendant of Jonathan (1 Ch 8:39), also called Jehush.

5. Son of Rehoboam (2 Ch 11:19).

JE´ UZ *(counsellor)*

Son of Shaharaim and Hodesh of Benjamin (1 Ch 8:10).

JEW

A descendant of Judah, of the tribe of Judah, and later of the kingdom of Judah (2 Ki 16:6; 25:25). The word came into use after the captivity of Judah and denoted anyone returned from the captivity (Es 2:5; Ma 2:2).

JEW´ EL

The rendering of several Hebrew words for various ornaments, usually made of gold or silver (Nu 31:50-51; 1 Sa 6:8,15; Eze 16:12,17,39; Ho 2:13).

JEWELS AND PRECIOUS STONES OF THE BIBLE

Following is a list of the jewels and precious stones mentioned in the Bible. The exact definition of some of the various Hebrew words in question is not certain, but these stones are the ones which translators believed to be the best choices. More information may be found about each word in the appropriate section of the dictionary.

Adamant, Agate, Amber, Amethyst, Bdellium, Beryl, Carbuncle, Chalcedony, Chrysolite, Chrysoprase, Coral, Crystal, Diamond, Emerald, Flint, Glass, Green Feldspar,

Jacinth, Jade, Jasper, Lapis Lazuli, Ligure, Onyx, Pearl, Purple Garnet, Ruby, Sapphire, Sardius, Sardonyx, Topaz, Turquoise

JEW´ ESS

A female of the tribe of Judah (1 Ch 4:18) or of the Hebrew race (Ac 16:1; 24:24). See JEHUDIJAH.

JEWISH (Tit 1:14)

See JEW.

JEWRY (archaic, Norman French origin, Old English)

The land of Judea (Da 5:13).

JEZ·A·NI´ AH

In 2 Kings 25:23 he is called Jaazaniah, son of Hoshaiah, a Maacathite (Je 40:8; 42:1). After the fall of Jerusalem, he and his men offered allegiance to Gedaliah.

JEZ´ E·BEL *(chaste)*

1. A Phoenician princess, daughter of Ethbaal, king of Sidon (1 Ki 16:31). She became the wife of Ahab, king of Israel, and became the power behind the throne. She was a zealous worshipper of Baal and established that idolatry in Israel (1 Ki 16:32-33). She killed the prophets of Jehovah (1 Ki 18:4-13) and by false judicial action had Naboth slain (1 Ki 21:16-22). The divine judgment that she would be devoured by dogs was fulfilled when Jehu put to death the house of Ahab (2 Ki 9:7-10; 30-37).

2. The name is applied to the lewd woman of Revelation (Re 2:20,23).

JE´ ZER *(formation)*

Son of Naphtali (Ge 46:24; Nu 26:49; 1 Ch 7:13).

JE´ ZER·ITES

The descendants of Jezer, son of Naphtali (Nu 26:49).

JE·ZI´ AH

See IZZIAH.

JE´ ZI·EL *(assembly of God)*

Son of Azmaveth a Benjamite (1 Ch 12:3).

JEZ·LI´ AH

See IZLIAH.

JEZ·RA·HI′AH *(Jehovah will shine)*

One who was placed over the singers (Ne 12:42).

JEZ′REEL *(God sows)*

1. A town of the mountainous district of Judah (Jos 15:56). Probably from this place David secured his wife, Ahinoam (1 Sa 25:43; 27:3).

2. A descendant of Hur of Judah (1 Ch 4:3).

3. A son of Hosea the prophet, so called because of the slaughter predicted by Hosea 1:4-5.

4. A town in the territory of Issachar near Mount Gilboa (Jos 19:17-18; 1 Ki 21:23). It was the camping place of the forces of the Israelites in Saul's last battle with the Philistines (1 Sa 29:1). It was here that Jezebel, wife of Ahab, was destroyed by the dogs (2 Ki 9:10,30-35), and here were stacked the heads of the seventy sons of Ahab when the house of Ahab was destroyed (2 Ki 10:1-11). The name, valley of Jezreel, was afterwards extended to the whole plain of Esdraelon (Jos 17:16; Ju 6:33).

JEZ′REEL·ITE

An inhabitant of Jezreel. Naboth, who had a vineyard in the valley of Jezreel, is called a Jezreelite (1 Ki 21:1,4,6-7,15-16). Jezebel, Ahab's wicked wife, arranged to have Naboth killed in order to gratify Ahab's desire to own the vineyard.

JEZ′REEL·IT·ESS

A woman of Jezreel. Ahinoam, one of David's wives, was a Jezreelitess (1 Sa 27:3; 30:5; 2 Sa 2:2; 3:2; 1 Ch 3:1).

JIBSAM

One of the sons of Tola, a descendant of Issachar (1 Ch 7:2).

JID′LAPH *(tearful)*

Son of Nahor and Milcah (Ge 22:22) and nephew of Abraham.

JIM′NA

See IMNAH.

JIM′NAH

See IMNAH.

JIPH′TAH

See IPHTAH.

JIPH′THAH-EL

See IPHTAH-EL.

JISHUI

See ISHUI.

JISSHIAH

See ISSHIAH.

JITHLAH

See ITHLAH.

ITHLAH

See ITHRA.

JITHRAN

See ITHRAN.

JIZLIAH

See IZLIAH.

JIZRI

See IZRI.

JO′AB *(Jehovah is father)*

Three Old Testament men:

1. Son of Zeruiah, the half sister of David (2 Sa 8:16; 1 Ch 2:16). He was a companion of David in his exile and commander-in-chief of his troops throughout his reign. Joab was an efficient general who was also independent in his attitude toward King David. Occasionally he disobeyed David's instructions, as in the case of the slaying of Abner and Absalom (2 Sa 3:22-39; 18:10-15).

2. Son of Seraiah of the line of Kenaz. He was the progenitor of the inhabitants of the valley of Charashim (1 Ch 4:13-14).

3. The head of a family (Ez 2:6; Ne 7:11).

JO′AH *(Jehovah is brother)*

Four Old Testament men:

1. Son of Zimmah, a Levite of the family of Gershom (1 Ch 6:21). It may have been he who aided Hezekiah in his reformation (2 Ch 29:12).

2. Son of Obed-edom, a porter of the sanctuary in the time of David (1 Ch 26:4).

3. A son of Asaph, the recorder of Hezekiah, king of Judah (2 Ki 18:18,26; Is 36:3,11,22).

4. Son of Joahaz. He was recorder under Josiah (2 Ch 34:8).

JO′A·HAZ *(Jehovah holds)*

Father of Joah, the recorder of King Josiah (2 Ch 34:8).

JO·A′NAN

See JOANNAS.

JO·AN′NA

1. The wife of Chuza, Herod's steward (Lk 8:3; 24:10).

2. Variant of JOANNAS.

JO·AN′NAS

Son of Rhesa, an ancestor of Christ (Lk 3:27).

JO′ASH

Eight Old Testament men:

1. Father of Gideon of the family of Abiezer of the tribe of Manasseh (Ju 6:11,15). He erected an altar to Baal which Gideon destroyed (Ju 6:11-32).

2. A descendant of Shelah the son of Judah (1 Ch 4:22).

3. Son of Shemaah, a Benjamite of Gibeah. He allied himself with David at Ziklag (1 Ch 12:3).

4. One who is called a son of Ahab, but the rendering is questionable. He was ordered by that king to imprison the prophet Micaiah because Micaiah had advised against the plan to seize Ramoth-gilead (1 Ki 22:26; 2 Ch 18:25).

5. A Benjamite of the family of Becher (1 Ch 7:8).

6. One whom David appointed to have charge of his oil supplies (1 Ch 27:28).

7. Son of Ahaziah, king of Judah. His grandmother, Athaliah usurped the throne and tried to exterminate the royal heirs of Judah. Joash escaped by being hidden in the temple by his aunt, Jehosheba, wife of the high priest, Jehoiada. The latter headed a revolt with the result that Joash was crowned king, Athaliah was slain, and the house and images of Baal were destroyed (2 Ki 11:1-20; 2 Ch 23:10-21).

8. Son of Jehoahaz, king of Israel. During the sixteen years of his reign he supported the worship of calves set up at Beth-el and Dan. His son, Jeroboam II, succeeded him and his reign was the most brilliant of the Kingdom of Israel (2 Ki 14:8-16; 2 Ch 25:17-24). Also called Jehoash.

JOATHAM

See JOTHAM.

JOB

1. Son of Issachar (Ge 46:13), called Jashub (Nu 26:24; 1 Ch 7:1).

2. An Old Testament saint who lived in the land of Uz (Job 1:1). He is mentioned by Ezekiel (14:14,16,20).

JOB, BOOK OF

1. The Book of Job. Job is perhaps the earliest book of the Bible. Set in the period of the patriarchs (Abraham, Isaac, Jacob, and Joseph), it tells the story of a man who loses everything—his wealth, his family, his health—and wrestles with the question, "Why?"

The book begins with a heavenly debate between God and Satan, moves through three cycles of earthly debates between Job and his friends and concludes with a dramatic "divine diagnosis" of Job's problem. In the end, Job acknowledges the sovereignty of God in his life, and receives back more than he had before his trials.

Iyyob is the Hebrew title for this book, and the name has two possible meanings. If derived from the Hebrew word for persecution, it means "Persecuted One." It is more likely that it comes from the Arabic word meaning "To Come Back" or "Repent." If so, it may be defined "Repentant One." Both meanings apply to the book. The Greek title is *Iob,* and the Latin title is *Job.*

2. The Author of Job. The author of Job is unknown, and there are no textual hints as to his identity. Commentators, however, have been generous with suggestions: Job, Elihu, Moses, Solomon, Isaiah, Hezekiah, Jeremiah, Baruch, and Ezra have all been nominated. The non-Hebraic cultural background of this book may point to Gentile authorship. The rabbinic tradition is inconsistent, but one Talmudic tradition suggests that Moses wrote the book. The land of Uz (1:1) is adjacent to Midian, where Moses lived for forty years, and it is conceivable that Moses obtained a record of the dialogue left by Job or Elihu.

3. The Time of Job. Lamentations 4:21 locates Uz in the area of Edom, southeast of the Dead Sea. This is also in the region of northern Arabia, and Job's friends come from nearby countries.

It is important to distinguish the date of the

events of Job from the date of its writing. Accurate dating of the events is difficult because there are no references to contemporary historical occurrences. However, a number of facts indicate a patriarchal date for Job, perhaps between Genesis 11 and 12 or not long after the time of Abraham: (1) Job lived 140 years *after* the events in the book (42:16); his lifespan must have been close to 200 years. This fits the patriarchal period (Abraham lived 175 years, Ge 25:7). (2) Job's wealth is measured in terms of livestock (1:3; 42:12) rather than gold and silver. (3) Like Abraham, Isaac, and Jacob, Job is the priest of his family and offers sacrifices. (4) There are no references to Israel, the exodus, the Mosaic law, or the tabernacle. (5) Fitting Abraham's time, the social unit in Job is the patriarchal family-clan. (6) The Chaldeans who murder Job's servants (1:17) are nomads and have not yet become city-dwellers. (7) Job uses the characteristic patriarchal name for God, *Shaddai* ("the Almighty"), thirty-one times. This early term is found only seventeen times in the rest of the Old Testament. The rare use of Yahweh "the LORD" also suggests a pre-Mosaic date. Ezekiel 14:14,20 and James 5:11 show that Job was a historical person.

Several theories have been advanced for the date of writing: (1) It was written shortly after the events occurred, perhaps by Job or Elihu. (2) It was written by Moses in Midian (1485-1445 B.C.). (3) It was written in the time of Solomon (c. 950 B.C.). (Job is similar to other wisdom literature of this time; compare the praises of wisdom in Job 28 and Proverbs 8. The problem here is the great time lag of about a thousand years.) (4) It was written during or after the Babylonian captivity.

4. The Christ of Job. Job acknowledges a redeemer (see 19:25-27) and cries out for a mediator (9:33; 25:4; 33:23). The book raises problems and questions which are answered perfectly in Christ who identifies with our sufferings (He 4:15). Christ is the believer's Life, Redeemer, Mediator, and Advocate.

5. Keys to Job.

Key Word: Sovereignty—The basic question of the book is, "Why do the righteous suffer if God is loving and all-powerful?" Suffering itself is not the central theme; rather, the focus is on what Job *learns* from his suffering—the sovereignty of God over all creation. The debate in chapters 3–37 regards whether God would al-

low this suffering to happen to a person who is innocent. The oversimplified solutions offered by Job's three friends are simply inadequate. Elihu's claim that God can use suffering to purify the righteous is closer to the mark. The conclusion at the whirlwind is that God is sovereign and worthy of worship in *whatever* He chooses to do. Job must learn to trust in the goodness and power of God in adversity by enlarging his concept of God. Even this "blameless" man (1:1) needs to repent when he becomes proud and self-righteous. He has to come to the end of his own resources, humble himself, and acknowledge the greatness and majesty of the Lord. Job teaches that God is Lord "of those in heaven, and of those on earth, and of those under the earth" (Ph 2:10). He is omniscient, omnipotent, and good. As such, His ways are sometimes incomprehensible to men and women, but He can always be trusted. Without the divine perspective in chapters 1–2 and in 38–42, chapters 3–37 are a mystery. Job does not have access to chapters 1–2, but he is responsible to trust God when all appearances are contrary. Suffering is not always associated with sin; God often sovereignly uses it to test and teach.

Key Verses: Job 13:15; 37:23-24—"Though He slay me, yet will I trust Him. Even so, I will defend my own ways before Him" (13:15).

"As for the Almighty, we cannot find Him; He is excellent in power, in judgment and abundant justice; He does not oppress. Therefore men fear Him; He shows no partiality to any who are wise of heart" (37:23-24).

Key Chapter: Job 42—The last chapter of the book records the climax of the long and difficult struggle Job has with himself, his wife, his friends, and even his God. Upon Job's full recognition of the utter majesty and sovereignty of the Lord, he repents and no longer demands an answer as to the "why" of his plight.

6. Survey of Job. The Book of Job concerns the transforming crisis in the life of a great man who lived perhaps four thousand years ago. Job's trust in God (1–2) changes to complaining and growing self-righteousness (3–31; see 32:1 and 40:8), but his repentance (42:1-6) leads to his restoration (42:7-17). The trials bring about an important transformation: The man after the process is different from the man before the process. The Book of Job divides into three parts: the dilemma of Job (1–2), the debates of Job (3–37), and the deliverance of Job (38–42).

The Dilemma of Job (1–2). Job is not a logical candidate for disaster (see 1:1,8). His moral integrity and his selfless service to God heighten the dilemma. Behind the scene, Satan (the Accuser) charges that no one loves God from pure motives, but only for material blessings (1:10). To refute Satan's accusations, God allows him to strike Job with two series of assaults. In his sorrow Job laments the day of his birth but does not deny God (1:21; 2:10).

The Debates of Job (3–37). Although Job's "comforters" reach wrong conclusions, they are his friends: of all who know Job, they are the only ones who come; they mourn with him in seven days of silent sympathy; they confront Job without talking behind his back. However, after Job breaks the silence, a three-round debate follows in which his friends say that Job must be suffering because of his sin. Job's responses to their simplistic assumptions make the debate cycles increase in emotional fervor. He first accuses his friends of judging him, and later appeals to the Lord as his judge and refuge.

Job makes three basic complaints: (1) God does not hear me (13:3,24; 19:7; 23:3-5; 30:20); (2) God is punishing me (6:4; 7:20; 9:17); and (3) God allows the wicked to prosper (21:7). His defenses are much longer than his friends accusations; in the process of defending his innocence, he becomes guilty of self-righteousness.

After Job's five-chapter closing monologue (27–31), Elihu freshens the air with a more perceptive and accurate view than those offered by Eliphaz, Bildad, or Zophar (32–37). He tells Job that he needs to humble himself before God and submit to God's process of purifying his life through trials.

The Deliverance of Job (38–42). After Elihu's preparatory discourse, God Himself ends the debate by speaking to Job from the whirlwind. In His first speech God reveals His power and wisdom as Creator and Preserver of the physical and animal world. Job responds by acknowledging his own ignorance and insignificance; he can offer no rebuttal (40:3-5). In His second speech God reveals His sovereign authority and challenges Job with two illustrations of His power to control the uncontrollable. This time Job responds by acknowledging his error with a repentant heart (42:1-6). If Job cannot understand God's ways in the realm of nature, how then can he understand God's ways in the spiritual realm? God makes no reference to Job's personal sufferings and hardly touches on the real issue of the debate. However, Job catches a glimpse of the divine perspective and when he acknowledges God's sovereignty over his life, his worldly goods are restored twofold. Job prays for his three friends who have cut him so deeply, but Elihu's speech is never rebuked. Thus Satan's challenge becomes God's opportunity to build up Job's life. "Indeed we count them blessed who endure. You have heard of the perseverance of Job and seen the end *intended by* the Lord—that the Lord is very compassionate and merciful" (Jam 5:11; see also Jam 1:12).

OUTLINE OF JOB

Part One: The Dilemma of Job (1:1–2:13)

I. The Circumstances of Job
(1:1-5)

II. The First Assault of Satan
(1:6-22)

III. The Second Assault of Satan
(2:1-10)

IV. The Arrival of Job's Friends
(2:11-13)

Part Two: The Debates of Job (3:1–37:24)

I. The First Cycle of Debate (3:1–14:22)

A. Job's First Speech 3:1-26
B. Eliphaz's First Speech 4:1–5:27
C. Job's Reply to Eliphaz 6:1–7:21
D. Bildad's First Speech 8:1-22
E. Job's Response to Bildad 9:1–10:22
F. Zophar's First Speech 11:1-20
G. Job's Response to Zophar 12:1–14:22

II. The Second Cycle of Debate
(15:1–21:34)

A. Eliphaz's Second Speech 15:1-35
B. Job's Response to Eliphaz 16:1–17:16
C. Bildad's Second Speech 18:1-21
D. Job's Response to Bildad............ 19:1-29
E. Zophar's Second Speech 20:1-29
F. Job's Response to Zophar 21:1-34

III. The Third Cycle of Debate (22:1–26:14)

A. Eliphaz's Third Speech 22:1-30
B. Job's Response to Eliphaz 23:1–24:25
C. Bildad's Third Speech 25:1-6
D. Job's Response to Bildad............ 26:1-14

IV. The Final Defense of Job (27:1–31:40)

A. Job's First Monologue 27:1–28:28
B. Job's Second Monologue 29:1–31:40

V. The Solution of Elihu (32:1–37:24)

A. Elihu Intervenes in the
Debate 32:1-22
B. Elihu's First Rebuttal 33:1-33
C. Elihu's Second
Rebuttal 34:1-37
D. Elihu's Third Rebuttal............... 35:1-16
E. Elihu's Conclusion 36:1–37:24

Part Three: The Deliverance of Job (38:1–42:17)

I. The First Controversy of God with Job (38:1–40:5)

A. God's First Challenge to
Job 38:1–40:2
B. Job's First Answer to
God 40:3-5

II. The Second Controversy of God with Job (40:6–42:6)

A. God's Second Challenge to
Job 40:6–41:34
B. Job's Second Answer to God 42:1-6

III. The Deliverance of Job and His Friends (42:7-17)

JO′BAB *(howling)*

Four Old Testament men:

1. A tribe of Arabia descended from Joktan (Ge 10:29; 1 Ch 1:23).

2. Son of Zerah of Bozrah, a king of Edom (Ge 36:33; 1 Ch 1:44-45).

3. One of the kings that formed the northern confederacy against Joshua. He was defeated in the battle of Merom (Jos 11:1; 12:19).

4. A son of Shaharaim of Benjamin (1 Ch 8:9, 18).

JOCH′E·BED *(Jehovah is glorious)*

A daughter of Levi. She married Amram, her nephew, and was the mother of Miriam, Aaron, and Moses (Ex 6:20; Nu 26:59).

JO′DA

See JUDAH.

JO′ED *(Jehovah is witness)*

Son of Pedaiah (Ne 11:7).

JO′EL *(Jehovah is God)*

Thirteen or fourteen men of the Old Testament:

1. Samuel's oldest son, the father of Heman the singer (1 Sa 8:2; 1 Ch 6:33; 15:17). He is

called Vashni in 1 Chronicles 6:28, probably a clerical error.

2. A prince of Simeon, one of those who settled in the valley of Gedor (1 Ch 4:35-43).

3. A man of Reuben (1 Ch 5:4).

4. A chief of the Gadites in Bashan (1 Ch 5:12).

5. A Levite of the family of Kohath. He was an ancestor of Samuel (1 Ch 6:34,36,38).

6. A man of Issachar, son of Izrahiah, in the time of David (1 Ch 7:3).

7. Brother of Nathan and one of David's mighty men (1 Ch 11:38). See IGAL.

8. A Levite, chief of the family of Gershom. At the head of 130 of his brethren he assisted in bringing the ark from the home of Obed-edom to Jerusalem (1 Ch 15:7,11-12). He was probably the son of Laadan (1 Ch 23:8).

9. Son of Pedaiah, and chief of the half tribe of Manasseh in David's reign (1 Ch 27:20).

10. Son of Azariah, a Levite of the family of Kohath. In the reform work of Hezekiah he assisted in cleansing the temple (2 Ch 29:12).

11. Son of Nebo. He renounced his foreign wife in the time of Ezra (Ez 10:43).

12. Son of Zichri, of Benjamin, an overseer at Jerusalem under Nehemiah's governorship (Ne 11:9).

13. Son of Pethuel, a minor prophet of whose history nothing is known (Joel 1:1). See "The Author of Joel."

JO′EL, BOOK OF

1. The Book of Joel. Disaster struck the Southern Kingdom of Judah without warning. An ominous black cloud descended upon the land—the dreaded locusts. In a matter of hours, every living green thing has been stripped bare. Joel, God's spokesman during the reign of Joash (835-796 B.C.), seizes this occasion to proclaim God's message. Although the locust plague has been a terrible judgment for sin, God's future judgments during the day of the Lord will make that plague pale by comparison. In that day, God will destroy His enemies, but bring unparalleled blessing to those who faithfully obey Him.

The Hebrew name *Yo'el* means "Yahweh Is God," this name is appropriate to the theme of the book, which emphasizes God's sovereign work in history. The courses of nature and nations are in His hand. The Greek equivalent is *Ioel,* and the Latin is *Joel.*

2. The Author of Joel. Although there are several other Joels in the Bible, the prophet Joel is known only from this book. In the introductory verse, Joel identifies himself as the son of Pethuel (1:1), meaning "Persuaded of God." His frequent references to Zion and the house of the Lord (1:9,13-14; 2:15-17,23,32; 3:1,5-6,16-17,20-21) suggest that he probably lived not far from Jerusalem. Because of his statements about the priesthood in 1:13-14 and 2:17, some think Joel was a priest as well as a prophet. In any case, Joel was a clear, concise, and uncompromising preacher of repentance.

3. The Time of Joel. Since this book includes no explicit time references, it cannot be dated with certainty. Some commentators assign a late date (usually postexilic) to Joel for these reasons: (1) It does not mention the Northern Kingdom and indicates it was written after the 722 B.C. demise of Israel. (2) The references to priests but not kings fit the postexilic period. (3) Joel does not refer to Assyria, Syria, or Babylon, perhaps because these countries have already been overthrown. (4) If Joel 3:2 refers to the Babylonian captivity, this also supports the postexilic date. (5) The mention of the Greeks in 3:6 argues for a late date.

Commentators who believe Joel was written in the ninth century B.C. answer the arguments in this way: (1) Joel's failure to mention the Northern Kingdom is an argument from silence. His prophecy was directed to Judah, not Israel. (2) Other early prophets omit references to a king (Obadiah, Jonah, Nahum, and Habbakkuk). This also fits the political situation during 841-835 B.C. when Athaliah usurped the throne upon the death of her son Ahaziah. Joash, the legitimate heir to the throne, was a minor and protected by the high priest, Jehoida. When Athaliah was removed from power in 835, Joash came to the throne but ruled under the regency of Jehoida. Thus, the prominence of the priests and lack of reference to a king in Joel fit this historical context. (3) It is true that Joel does not refer to Assyria or Babylon, but the countries Joel mentions are more crucial. They include Phoenicia, Philistia, Egypt, and Edom—countries prominent in the ninth century but not later. Assyria and Babylon are not mentioned because they had not yet reached a position of power. Also, if Joel was postexilic, a reference to Persia would be expected. (4) Joel 3:2 does not refer to the Babylonian captivity but to an event that has not yet occurred. (5) Greeks are mentioned in Assyrian records from the eighth century B.C. It is just an assumption to state that the Hebrews had no knowledge of the Greeks at an early time.

Evidence also points to a sharing of material between Joel and Amos (cf. 3:16 and Am 1:2; 3:18 and Am 9:13). The context of the books suggests that Amos, an eighth-century prophet, borrowed from Joel. Also, Joel's style is more like that of Hosea and Amos than of the postexilic writers. The evidence seems to favor a date of about 835 B.C. for Joel. Since Joel does not mention idolatry, it may have been written after the purge of Baal worship and most other forms of idolatry in the early reign of Joash under Jehoida the priest. As an early prophet of Judah, Joel would have been a contemporary of Elisha in Israel.

4. The Christ of Joel. Christ promised to send the Holy Spirit after His ascension to the Father (Jo 16:7-15; Ac 1:8). When this was fulfilled on the day of Pentecost, Peter said, "This is what was spoken by the prophet Joel" (2:28-32; Ac 2:16-21). Joel also portrays Christ as the One who will judge the nations in the valley of Jehoshaphat in 3:2,12.

5. Keys to Joel.

Key Word: The Great and Terrible Day of the Lord—the key theme of Joel is the day of the Lord in retrospect and prospect. Joel uses the terrible locust plague that has recently occurred in Judah to illustrate that coming day of judgment when God will directly intervene in human history to vindicate His righteousness. This will be a time of unparalleled retribution upon Israel (2:1-11) and the whole nation (3:1-17), but this time will culminate in great blessing and salvation for all who trust in the Lord (2:18-32; 3:18-21). "And it shall come to pass that whoever calls on the name of the LORD shall be saved" (2:32).

Joel is written as a warning to the people of Judah of their need to turn humbly to the Lord with penitent hearts (2:12-17) so that God can bless rather than buffet them. If they continue to spurn God's gracious call to repentance, judgment will be inevitable. Joel stresses the sovereign power of God over nature and nations, and points out how God uses nature to get the attention of people.

Key Verses: Joel 2:11,28-29—"The LORD gives voice before His army, for His camp is very great; for strong is the One who executes His word. For the day of the LORD is great and very terrible; who can abide it?" (2:11).

"And it shall come to pass afterward that I will pour out My Spirit on all flesh; your sons and your daughters shall prophesy, your old men shall dream dreams, your young men shall see visions; and also on My menservants and My maidservants I will pour out My Spirit in those days" (2:28-29).

Key Chapter: Joel 2—The prophet calls for Judah's repentance and promises God's repentance (2:13-14) from His planned judgment upon Judah if they do indeed turn to Him. Though the offer is clearly given, Judah continues to rebel against the Lord, and judgment is to follow. In that judgment, however, is God's promise of His later outpouring, fulfilled initially on the day of Pentecost (Ac 2:16) and ultimately when Christ returns for the culmination of the day of the Lord.

6. Survey of Joel. The brief Book of Joel develops the crucial theme of the coming day of the Lord (1:15; 2:1-2,11,31; 3:14,18). It is a time of awesome judgment upon people and nations that have rebelled against God. But it is also a time of future blessing upon those who have trusted in Him. The theme of disaster runs throughout the book (locust plagues, famine, raging fires, invading armies, celestial phenomena), but promises of hope are interspersed with the pronouncements of coming judgment. The basic outline of Joel is: the day of the Lord in retrospect (1:1-20) and the day of the Lord in prospect (2:1–3:21).

The Day of the Lord in Retrospect (1:1-20). Joel begins with an account of a recent locust plague that has devastated the land. The black cloud of insects has stripped the grapevines and fruit trees and ruined the grain harvest. The economy has been brought to a further standstill by a drought and the people are in a desperate situation.

The Day of the Lord in Prospect (2:1–3:21). Joel makes effective use of this natural catastrophe as an illustration of a far greater judgment to come. Compared to the terrible day of the Lord, the destruction by the locusts will seem insignificant. The land will be invaded by a swarming army; like locusts they will be speedy and voracious. The desolation caused by this army will be dreadful: "The day of the LORD is great and very terrible; who can endure it?" (2:11).

Even so, it is not too late for the people to avert disaster. The prophetic warning is designed to bring them to the point of repentance (2:12-17). " 'Now, therefore,' says the LORD, 'turn to me with all your heart, with fasting, with weeping, and with mourning' " (2:12). But God's gracious offer falls on deaf ears.

Ultimately, the swarming, creeping, stripping and gnawing locusts (1:4; 2:25) will come again in a fiercer form. But God promises that judgment will be followed by great blessing in a material (2:18-27) and spiritual (2:28-32) sense.

These rich promises are followed by a solemn description of the judgment of all nations in the valley of decision (3:14) in the end times. The nations will give an account of themselves to the God of Israel who will judge those who have rebelled against Him. God alone controls the course of history. "So you shall know that I am the LORD your God, dwelling in Zion My holy mountain" (3:17). Joel ends with the kingdom blessings upon the remnant of faithful Judah: "But Judah shall abide forever, and Jerusalem from generation to generation" (3:20).

OUTLINE OF JOEL

I. The Day of the Lord in Retrospect (1:1-20)

A. The Past Day of the Locust............ 1:1-12
B. The Past Day of the Drought 1:13-20

II. The Day of the Lord in Prospect (2:1-3:21)

A. The Imminent Day of the Lord 2:1-27
B. The Ultimate Day of the Lord ... 2:28–3:21

JO·E′ LAH

Son of Jeroham (1 Ch 12:7).

JO·E′ ZER *(Jehovah is help)*

A Korahite who joined David at Ziklag (1 Ch 12:6).

JOG′ BE·HAH *(lofty)*

A city of the tribe of Gad (Nu 32:35).

JOG′ LI *(exiled)*

Father of Bukki (Nu 34:22).

JO′ HA

Two Old Testament men:
1. A son of Beriah of Benjamin, and a tribal chief (1 Ch 8:16).
2. Son of Shimri, a Tizite; one of David's soldiers (1 Ch 11:45).

JO·HA′ NAN *(Jehovah is gracious)*

Ten men of the Old Testament:
1. Son of Kareah, a captain (2 Ki 25:22-23; Je 40:8-9).
2. King Josiah's eldest son (1 Ch 3:15).
3. A son of Elioenai (1 Ch 3:24).
4. A man who executed the high priest's office (1 Ch 6:10).
5. A Benjamite who joined David at Ziklag (1 Ch 12:4).
6. A Gadite captain of David's forces (1 Ch 12:12,14).
7. Father of Azariah, of Ephraim; he demanded that those taken from Judah be returned (2 Ch 28:12).
8. Son of Hakkatan. He and 110 others were of the company of Ezra that returned from Babylon (Ez 8:12).
9. Son of Eliashib (Ez 10:6).
10. Son of Tobiah, enemy of Nehemiah; he married a Jewess (Ne 6:18).
11. Grandson of Eliashib, a high priest (Ne 12:22). In verse 11 he is called Jonathan.

JOHN *(Jehovah is gracious)*

1. John Mark, writer of the Second Gospel (Ac 12:12,25). See MARK, JOHN
2. A Jewish official who opposed Peter and John in association with Caiaphas, Annas, and Alexander (Ac 4:6).
3. John the Apostle.
4. John the Baptist.

JOHN THE APOSTLE

He and James were sons of Zebedee. It is believed their mother was Salome. They were fishermen on the Sea of Galilee in partnership with Peter (Lk 5:10). After Pentecost he remained in Jerusalem during the persecutions of the early Christians and was active with Peter in missionary labors (Ac 3:1; 15:6; Ga 2:9). See JOHN, GOSPEL OF, "The Author of John."

JOHN THE BAPTIST

The son of Zacharias. His mother, Elisabeth, was a descendant of Aaron (Lk 1:5) and a cousin of the Virgin Mary. His parents lived in the hill country of Judea. When the angel informed Zacharias that a son was to be born to them, he instructed him to name the baby John (Lk 1:8-17). John's early years were spent in seclusion in the wilderness, and there, near the Jordan, he began his preaching as the forerunner of Jesus (Ma 3:1-3). His preaching was designed to prepare the hearts of the people for the acceptance of the Christ about to appear. Repenting of their sins, the people obeyed John's preaching and were baptized (Ma 3:5-6). They were not baptized in any name, and this baptism should not be confused with Christian baptism instituted much later by our Lord (Ma 28:19; Ac 19:1-5). When our Lord at baptism began his public ministry, it was John who baptized him (Ma 3:13-17). John denounced Herod Antipas for taking as wife Herodias, the wife of his half brother Philip and was imprisoned by Herod (Lk 3:19-20). Later at the solicitation of Herodias he was beheaded (Ma 14:1-12).

JOHN, EPISTLES OF

FIRST JOHN.

1. The Book of 1 John. God is light; God is love; and God is life. John is enjoying a delightful fellowship with that God of light, love, and life, and he desperately desires that his spiritual children enjoy that same fellowship.

God is light. Therefore, to engage in fellowship with Him we must walk in light and not in darkness. As we walk in the light, we will regularly confess our sins, allowing the blood of Christ to continually cleanse us. Christ will act as our defense attorney before the Father. Proof of our "walk in the light" will be keeping the commandments of God and replacing any hatred we have toward our brother with love. Two major roadblocks to hinder this walk will be falling in love with the world and falling for the alluring lies of false teachers.

God is love. Since we are His children we must walk in love. In fact, John says that if we do not love, we do not know God. Additionally, our love needs to be practical. Love is more than just words; it is actions. Love is giving, not getting. Biblical love is unconditional in its nature. It is an "in spite of" love. Christ's love fulfilled those qualities and when that brand of love characterizes us, we will be free of self-condemnation and experience confidence before God.

God is life. Those who fellowship with Him must possess His quality of life. Spiritual life begins with spiritual birth. Spiritual birth occurs through faith in Jesus Christ. Faith in Jesus Christ infuses us with God's life—eternal life. Therefore, one who walks in fellowship with God will walk in light, love, and life.

Although the apostle John's name is not found in this book, it was given the title *Ioannou A,* "First of John."

2. The Author of 1 John. The external evidence for the authorship of 1 John shows that from the beginning it was universally received without dispute as authoritative. It was used by Polycarp (who knew John in his youth) and Papias in the early second century, and later in that century Irenaeus (who knew Polycarp in his youth) specifically attributed it to the apostle John. All the Greek and Latin church fathers accepted this epistle as Johannine.

The internal evidence supports this universal tradition because the "we" (apostles), "you" (readers), and "they" (false teachers) phraseology places the writer in the sphere of the apostolic eyewitnesses (cf. 1:1-3; 4:14). John's name was well-known to the readers, and it was unnecessary for him to mention it. The style and vocabulary of 1 John are so similar to the Gospel of John that most scholars acknowledge these books to be by the same hand (see "The Author of John"). Both share many distinctively Johannine phrases, and the characteristics of limited vocabulary and frequent contrast of opposites are also common to them. Even so, some critics have assailed this conclusion on various grounds, but the theological and stylistic differences are not substantial enough to overcome the abundant similarities.

The traditional view is also rejected by those who hold that the Fourth Gospel and these three epistles were written by John the "elder" or "presbyter," who is to be distinguished from John the apostle. But the only basis for this distinction is Eusebius' interpretation in his *Ecclesiastical History* (A.D. 323) of a statement by Papias. Eusebius understood the passage to refer to two distinct Johns, but the wording does not require this; the elder John and the apostle John may be one and the same. Even if they were different, there is no evidence for contradicting the consistent acknowledgment by the early church that this book was written by the apostle John.

3. The Time of 1 John. In Acts 8:14, John is associated with "the apostles who were at Jerusalem," and Paul calls him one of the "pillars" of the Jerusalem church in Galatians 2:9. Apart from Revelation 1, the New Testament is silent about his later years, but early Christian tradition uniformly tells us that he left Jerusalem (probably not long before its destruction in A.D. 70) and that he ministered in and around Ephesus. The seven churches in the Roman province of Asia, mentioned in Revelation 2 and 3, were evidently a part of this ministry. Although there is no address in 1 John, it is likely that the apostle directed this epistle to the Asian churches that were within the realm of his oversight.

The believers in these congregations were well established in Christian truth, and John wrote to them not as novices but as brethren grounded in apostolic doctrine (2:7,18-27; 3:11). The apostle does not mention his own affairs, but his use of such terms of address as "beloved" and "my little children" gives this letter a personal touch that reveals his close relationship to the original recipients. First John was probably written in

Ephesus after the Gospel of John, but the date cannot be fixed with certainty. No persecution is mentioned, suggesting a date prior to A.D. 95 when persecution broke out during the end of Domitian's reign (A.D. 81-96).

Advanced in years, John wrote this fatherly epistle out of loving concern for his "children," whose steadfastness in the truth was being threatened by the lure of worldliness and the guile of false teachers. The Gnostic heresy taught that matter is inherently evil, and a divine being therefore could not take on human flesh. This resulted in the distinction between the man Jesus and the spiritual Christ who came upon Jesus at His baptism and departed prior to His crucifixion. Another variation was Docetism (from *dokeo*, "to seem"), the doctrine that Christ only seemed to have a human body. The result in both cases was the same—a flat denial of the incarnation.

The Gnostics also believed that their understanding of the hidden knowledge *(gnosis)* made them a kind of spiritual elite, who were above the normal distinctions of right and wrong. This led in most cases to deplorable conduct and complete disregard for Christian ethics.

4. The Christ of 1 John. The present ministry of Christ is portrayed in 1:5–2:22. His blood continually cleanses the believer from all sin, and He is our righteous Advocate before the Father. This epistle places particular stress on the incarnation of God the Son and the identity of Jesus as the Christ (2:22; 4:2-3), in refutation of Gnostic doctrine. Jesus Christ "came by water and blood" (5:6). He was the same individual person from the beginning (His baptism) to the end (His crucifixion) of His public ministry.

5. Keys to 1 John.

Key Word: Fellowship with God—The major theme of 1 John is fellowship with God. John wants his readers to have assurance of the indwelling God through their abiding relationship with Him (2:28; 5:13). Belief in Christ should be manifested in the practice of righteousness and love for the brethren, which in turn produces joy and confidence before God. John writes this epistle to encourage this kind of fellowship and to emphasize the importance of holding fast to apostolic doctrine.

First John is also written to refute the destructive teachings of the Gnostics by stressing the reality of the incarnation and the emptiness of profession without practice. These antichrists fail the three tests of righteous living,

love for the brethren, and belief that Jesus is the Christ, the incarnate God-man.

Key Verses: 1 John 1:3-4 and 5:11-13— "That which we have seen and heard we declare to you, that you also may have fellowship with us; and truly our fellowship is with the Father and with His Son Jesus Christ. And these things we write to you that your joy may be full" (1:3-4).

"And this is the testimony: that God has given us eternal life, and this life is in His Son. He who has the Son has life; he who does not have the Son of God does not have life. These things I have written to you who believe in the name of the Son of God, that you may know that you have eternal life, and that you may continue to believe in the name of the Son of God" (5:11-13).

Key Chapter: 1 John 1—The two central passages for continued fellowship with God are John 15 and 1 John 1. John 15 relates the positive side of fellowship, that is, abiding in Christ. First John 1 unfolds the other side, pointing out that when Christians do not abide in Christ, they must seek forgiveness before fellowship can be restored.

6. Survey of 1 John. John writes his first epistle at a time when apostolic doctrine is being challenged by a proliferation of false teachings. Like 2 Peter and Jude, 1 John has a negative and a positive thrust: it refutes erroneous doctrine and encourages its readership to walk in the knowledge of the truth. John lists the criteria and characteristics of fellowship with God and shows that those who abide in Christ can have confidence and assurance before Him. This simply written but profound work develops the meaning of fellowship in the basis of fellowship (1:1–2:27) and the behavior of fellowship (2:28–5:21).

The Basis of Fellowship (1:1–2:27). John's prologue (1:1-4) recalls the beginning of apostolic contact with Christ. It relates his desire to transmit this apostolic witness to his readers so that they may share the same fellowship with Jesus Christ, the personification of life. This proclamation is followed by a description of the conditions of fellowship (1:5–2:14).

The readers' sins have been forgiven and they enjoy fellowship with God. As a result, they know "Him who is from the beginning" and are strengthened to overcome the temptations of the evil one (2:12-14). The cautions to fellowship are both practical (the lusts of the corrupt world system which opposes God, 2:15-17) and doctrinal (the teachings of those who differentiate between Jesus and the Christ, 2:18-23). In contrast between these antichrists, the readers have the knowledge of the truth and an anointing from the Holy One. Therefore, it would be foolish for them to turn away from the teachings of the apostles to the innovations of the antichrists. The antidote to these heretical teachings is abiding in the apostolic truths that they "heard from the beginning," which are authenticated by the anointing they have received (2:24-27).

The Behavior of Fellowship (2:28–5:21). The basic theme of 1 John is summarized in 2:28—assurance through abiding in Christ. The next verse introduces the motif of regeneration, and 2:29–3:10 argues that regeneration is manifested in the practice of righteousness. Because we are children of God through faith in Christ, we have a firm hope of being fully conformed to Him when He appears (3:1-3). Our present likeness to Christ places us in a position of incompatibility with sin, because sin is contrary to the person and work of Christ (3:4-6). The concept in 3:6 does not contradict 1:8 because it is saying that the abider, insofar as he abides, does not sin. When the believer sins, he does not reflect the regenerate new man but Satan, the original sinner (3:7-10).

Regeneration is shown in righteousness (2:29–3:10), and righteousness is manifested in love (3:10-23). The apostle uses the example of Cain to illustrate what love is not: hatred is murdering in spirit, and it arises from the worldly sphere of death. John then uses the example of Christ to illustrate what love is: love is practiced in self-sacrifice, not mere profession. This practical expression of love results in assurance before God and answered prayers because the believer is walking in obedience to God's commands to believe in Christ and love one another.

In 3:24 John introduces two important motifs, which are developed in 4:1-16: the indwelling God, and the Spirit as a mark of this indwelling. The Spirit of God confesses the incarnate Christ and confirms apostolic doctrine (4:1-16). The mutual abiding of the believer in God and God in the believer is manifested in love for others, and this love produces a divine and human fellowship that testifies to and reflects the reality of the incarnation (4:7-16). It also anticipates the perfect fellowship to come and creates a readiness to face the One from whom all love is derived (4:17-19).

John joins the concepts he has presented into a circular chain of six links that begins with love for the brethren (4:20–5:17): (1) Love for believers is the inseparable product of love for God (4:20–5:1). (2) Love for God arises out of obedience to His commandments (5:2-3). (3) Obedience to God is the result of faith in His Son (5:4-5). (4) This faith in Jesus, who was the Christ not only at His baptism (the water), but also at His death (the blood; 5:6-8). (5) The divine witness to the person of Christ is worthy of complete belief (5:9-13). (6) This belief produces confident access to God in prayer (5:14-17). Since intercessory prayer is a manifestation of love for others, the chain has come full circle.

The epilogue (5:18-21) summarizes the conclusions of the epistle in a series of three certainties: (1) Sin is a threat to fellowship, and it should be regarded as foreign to the believer's position in Christ (Ro 6). (2) The believer stands with God against the satanic world system. (3) The incarnation produces true knowledge and communion with Christ. Since He is the true God and eternal life, the one who knows Him should avoid the lure of any substitute.

OUTLINE OF 1 JOHN

Part One: The Basis of Fellowship
(1:1–2:27)

I. Introduction
(1:1-4)

II. The Conditions for Fellowship
(1:5–2:14)

A. Walk in the Light 1:5-7
B. Confessions of Sin 1:8–2:2
C. Obedience to His
Commandments............................ 2:3-6

D. Love for One
Another 2:7-14

III. The Cautions to Fellowship
(2:15-27)

A. Love of the World 2:15-17
B. Spirit of the
Antichrist 2:18-27

Part Two: The Behavior of Fellowship (2:28–5:21)

I. Characteristics of Fellowship (2:28–5:3)

A. Purity of Life 2:28–3:3
B. Practice of Righteousness 3:4-12
C. Love in Deed and Truth 3:13-24
D. Testing the Spirits....................... 4:1-6
E. Love as Christ Loved 4:7–5:3

II. Consequences of Fellowship (5:4-21)

A. Victory over the World 5:4-5
B. Assurance of Salvation.................. 5:6-13
C. Guidance in Prayer 5:14-17
D. Freedom from Habitual
Sin.. 5:18-21

SECOND JOHN

1. The Book of 2 John. "Let him who thinks he stands take heed lest he fall" (1 Co 10:12). These words of the apostle Paul could well stand as a subtitle for John's little epistle. The recipients, a chosen lady and her children, were obviously standing. They were walking in truth, remaining faithful to the commandments they had received from the Father. John is deeply pleased to be able to commend them. But he takes nothing for granted. Realizing that standing is just one step removed from falling, he hesitates not at all to issue a reminder: love one another. The apostle admits that this is not new revelation, but he views it sufficiently important to repeat. Loving one another, he stresses, is equivalent to walking according to God's commandments.

John indicates, however, that this love must be discerning. It is not a naïve, unthinking, open to anything and anyone kind of love. Biblical love is a matter of choice; it is dangerous and foolish to float through life with undiscerning love. False teachers abound who do not acknowledge Christ has having come in the flesh. It is false charity to open the door to false teaching. We must have fellowship with God. We must have fellowship with Christians. But we must not have fellowship with false teachers.

The "elder" of verse 1 has been traditionally identified with the apostle John, resulting in the Greek title *Ioannou B,* "Second of John."

2. The Author of 2 John. Because of the similarity of the contents and circumstances of 2 and 3 John, the authorship of both will be considered here. These letters were not widely circulated at the beginning because of their brevity and their specific address to a small number of people. This limited circulation, combined with the fact that they have few distinctive ideas to add that are not found in 1 John, meant that they were seldom quoted in the patristic writings of the early church. Their place in the canon of New Testament books was disputed for a time, but it is significant that there was no question in the minds of those church fathers who lived closest to the time of John that these two epistles were written by the apostle. The second-century writers Irenaeus and Clement of Alexandria entertained no other view. Only as the details of their origin were forgotten did doubts arise, but the positive evidence in their favor eventually won for them the official recognition of the whole church.

It is obvious that the recipients of 2 and 3 John well knew the author's identity, although he did not use his name. Instead, he designated himself in the first verse of both letters as "the elder." This is not an argument against the Johannine authorship of 2 and 3 John, since the context of these epistles reveals that his authority was far greater than that of an elder in a local church. The apostle Peter also referred to himself as an elder (1 Pe 5:1) and John uses the distinguishing term "the elder."

The similarity of style, vocabulary, structure and mood between 2 and 3 John makes it clear that these letters were written by the same author. In addition, both (especially 2 John) bear strong resemblances to 1 John and to the Fourth Gospel. Thus, the external and internal evidence lends clear support to the traditional view that these epistles were written by the apostle John.

3. The Time of 2 John. The identification of the original readers of this epistle is difficult because of the disagreement regarding the interpretation of "the elect lady and her children" (v. 1). Some scholars believe the address should be taken literally to refer to a specific woman and her children, while others prefer to take it as a figurative description of a local church.

The evidence is insufficient for a decisive conclusion, but in either case, the readers were well known to John and probably lived in the province of Asia, not far from Ephesus. If the figurative view is taken, "the children of your elect sister" (v. 13) refers to the members of a sister church.

In his first epistle, John wrote that a number of false teachers had split away from the church ("they went out from us, but they were not of us," 1 Jo 2:19). Some of these became traveling teachers who depended upon the hospitality of individuals while they sought to infiltrate churches with their teachings.

Judging by the content and circumstances of 2 John, it was evidently contemporaneous with 1 John, or was written slightly later. It was probably written about A.D. 90. All three of John's epistles may have been written in Ephesus (see "The Time of 1 John").

4. The Christ of 2 John. John refutes the same error regarding the person of Christ in this epistle as he did in his first epistle. Again he stresses that those "who do not confess Jesus Christ as coming in the flesh" (v. 7) are deceivers who must be avoided. One must abide "in the doctrine of Christ" (v. 9) to have a relationship with God. The doctrine of the person and work of Jesus Christ affects every other area of theology.

5. Keys to 2 John.

Key Word: Avoid Fellowship with False Teachers—The basic theme of this brief letter is steadfastness in the practice and purity of the apostolic doctrine that the readers "have heard from the beginning" (v. 6). John writes it as God's commandment to love one another (practical exhortation, vv. 4-6). His primary purpose is to deliver a warning not to associate with or assist teachers who do not acknowledge the truth about Jesus Christ (doctrinal exhortation, vv. 7-11).

It has been suggested that 2 and 3 John were written as cover letters for 1 John to provide a personal word to the church (2 Jo) and to Gaius (3 Jo) that would supplement the longer epistle. However, there is no way to be sure.

Key Verses: 2 John 9-10—"Whoever trans-

gresses and does not abide in the doctrine of Christ does not have God. He who abides in the doctrine of Christ has both the Father and the Son. If anyone comes to you and does not bring this doctrine, do not receive him into your house nor greet him" (vv. 9-10).

6. Survey of 2 John. This brief letter has much in common with 1 John, including a warning about the danger of false teachers who deny the incarnation of Jesus Christ. John encouraged the readers to continue walking in love but exhorts them to be discerning in their expression of love. Second John breaks with two parts: abide in God's commandments (vv. 1-6) and abide not with false teachers (vv. 7-13).

Abide in God's Commandments (vv. 1-6). The salutation (vv. 1-3) centers on the concept of abiding in the truth (mentioned four times in these three verses). The recipients are loved for their adherence to the truth by "all those who have known the truth." The apostle commends his readers on their walk in truth in obedience to God's commandment (v. 4), and reminds them that this commandment entails the practice of love for one another (vv. 5-6). The divine command is given in verse 5 and the human response follows in verse 6.

Abide Not with False Teachers (vv. 7-13). Moving from the basic test of Christian behavior (love for the brethren) to the basic test of Christian belief (the person of Christ), John admonishes the readers to beware of deceivers "who do not confess Jesus Christ as coming in the flesh" (vv. 7-9). In no uncertain terms, the apostle enjoins the readers to deny even the slightest assistance or encouragement to itinerant teachers who promote an erroneous view of Christ (and hence of salvation; vv. 10-11).

This letter closes with John's explanation of its brevity: he anticipates a future visit during which he will be able to "speak face to face" with his readers (v. 12). The meaning of the greeting in verse 13 relates to the interpretation of verse 1.

OUTLINE OF 2 JOHN

I. Abide in God's Commandments (1-6)

A. Salutation 1-3
B. Walk in Truth 4
C. Walk in Love 5-6

II. Abide Not with False Teachers (7-13)

A. Doctrine of the False Teachers 7-9
B. Avoid the False Teachers............... 10-11
C. Benediction................................ 12-13

THIRD JOHN

1. The Book of 3 John. In 1 John the apostle discusses fellowship with God; in 2 John he forbids fellowship with false teachers; and in 3 John he encourages fellowship with Christian brothers. Following his expression of love for Gaius, John assures him of his prayers for his health and voices his joy over Gaius's persistent walk in truth and for the manner in which he shows hospitality and support for the missionaries who have come to his church. The phrase "send them forward on their journey" means to provide help for the missionaries' endeavors. Included in this help can be food, money, arrangements for companions, and means of travel. By supporting these men who are ministering for Christ, Gaius has become a fellow worker of the truth.

But not everyone in the church feels the same way. Diotrephes' heart is one hundred and eighty degrees removed from Gaius's heart. He is no longer living in love. Pride has taken precedence in his life. He has refused a letter John has written for the church, fearing that his authority might be superseded by that of the apostle. He also has accused John of evil words and refused to accept missionaries. He forbids others to do so and even expels them from the church if they disobey him. John uses this negative example as an opportunity to encourage Gaius to continue his hospitality. Demetrius has a good testimony and may even be one of those turned away by Diotrephes. He is widely known for his good character and his loyalty to the truth. Here he is well commended by John and stands as a positive example for Gaius.

The Greek titles of First, Second and Third John are *Ioannou A, B,* and *G*. The *G* is gamma, the third letter of the Greek alphabet; *Ioannou G* means, "Third of John."

2. The Author of 3 John. The authorship of 2 and 3 John was considered together because the contents and circumstances of both books are similar (see "The Author of 2 John"). Although the external evidence for 2 John and 3 John is limited (there is even less for 3 John than for 2 John), what little there is consistently points to the apostle John as author. The internal evidence is stronger, and it, too, supports the apostolic origin of both letters.

3. The Time of 3 John. The parallels between 2 and 3 John suggest that these epistles were written at about the same time (A.D. 90).

Early Christian writers are unified in their testimony that the headquarters of John's later ministry was in Ephesus, the principal city of the Roman province of Asia (see "The Time of First John"). John evidently commissioned a number of traveling teachers to spread the gospel and to solidify the Asian churches, and these teachers were supported by believers who received them into their homes.

Third John, probably delivered by Demetrius, was occasioned by the report of some of the emissaries (called "brethren" in this letter), who returned to the apostle and informed him of the hospitality of Gaius and the hostility of Diotrephes. The arrogant Diotrephes seized the reins of an Asian church and vaunted himself as the preeminent authority. He maligned John's authority and rejected the teachers sent out by John, expelling those in his church who wanted to receive them.

Gaius was a common name in the Roman Empire, and three other men by that name are mentioned in the New Testament: (1) Gaius, one of Paul's traveling companions from Macedonia (Ac 19:29); (2) Gaius of Derbe (Ac 10:4); and (3) Gaius, Paul's host in Corinth, one of the few Corinthians Paul baptized (Ro 16:23; 1 Co 1:14). The Gaius of 3 John evidently lived in Asia, and it is best to distinguish him from these other men.

In verse 9, John alludes to a previous letter that Diotrephes had spurned. This may have been 1 or 2 John, but it is more likely a letter that has been lost or perhaps was destroyed by Diotrephes.

4. The Christ of 3 John. Unlike 1 and 2 John, 3 John makes no mention of the name of Jesus Christ. But verse 7 says "they went forth for His name's sake," an indirect reference to our Lord (cf. Ac 5:41, where the identical Greek construction is used to refer back to "the name of Jesus" in Ac 5:40). The concept of truth runs throughout this letter, and Christ is the source and incarnation of truth, as is obvious from John's other writings.

5. Keys to 3 John.

Key Word: Enjoy Fellowship with the Brethren—The basic theme of this letter is to enjoy and continue to have fellowship (hospitality) with fellow believers, especially fulltime Christian workers. This is contrasted between the truth and servanthood of Gaius and the error and selfishness of Diotrephes. Moving through 3 John, five specific purposes can be discerned from its contents: (1) to commend Gaius for his adherence to the truth and his hospitality to the emissaries sent out by John (vv. 1-6); (2) to encourage Gaius to continue his support of these brethren (vv. 6-8); (3) to rebuke Diotrephes for his pride and misconduct (vv. 9-11); (4) to provide a recommendation for Demetrius (v. 12); and (5) to inform Gaius of John's intention to visit and straighten out the difficulties (vv. 10, 13-14).

Key Verse: 3 John 11—"Beloved, do not imitate what is evil, but what is good. He who does good is of God, but he who does evil has not seen God" (v. 11).

6. Survey of 3 John. Third John is the shortest book in the Bible, but it is very personal and vivid. It offers a stark contrast between two men who respond in opposite ways to the itinerant teachers who have been sent out by the apostle. The faithful Gaius responds with generosity and hospitality, but the faithless Diotrephes responds with arrogance and opposition. Thus John writes this letter to comment Gaius for walking in the truth (vv. 1-8) and to condemn Diotrephes for walking in error (vv. 9-14).

Condemnation of Gaius (vv. 1-8). The "elder" writes to one of his beloved "children" whose godly behavior has given the apostles great joy (vv. 1-4). The "brethren," upon returning to John, have informed him of Gaius's faithfulness, love and generosity in their behalf. The apostle acknowledges these actions and urges Gaius to continue supporting traveling teachers and missionaries who go out "for the sake of the Name" (vv. 5-8).

Condemnation of Diotrephes (vv. 9-14). The epistle suddenly shifts to a negative note as John describes a man whose actions are diametrically opposed to those of Gaius (vv. 9-11). Diotrephes boldly rejects John's apostolic authority and refuses to receive the itinerant teachers sent out by the apostle. Diotrephes evidently has been orthodox in his doctrine, but his evil actions indicate a blindness to God in his practice.

By contrast, John gives his full recommendation to Demetrius, another emissary and probably the bearer of this letter to Gaius (v.12). John expresses his hope of a personal visit in the closing remarks (vv. 13-14), as he does in 2 John.

OUTLINE OF 3 JOHN

I. The Commendation of Gaius (1-8)

A. Salutation 1
B. Godliness of Gaius 2-4
C. Generosity of Gaius 5-8

II. The Condemnation of Diotrephes (9-14)

A. Pride of Diotrephes 9-11
B. Praise for Demetrius 12
C. Benediction 13-14

JOHN, GOS'PEL OF

1. The Book of John. Just as a coin has two sides, both valid, so Jesus Christ has two natures, both valid. Luke presents Christ in His humanity as the Son of Man; John portrays Him in His deity as the Son of God. John's purpose is crystal clear: to set forth Christ in His deity in order to spark believing faith in his readers. John's gospel is topical, not primarily chronological, and it revolves around seven miracles and seven "I am" statements of Christ.

Following an extended eyewitness description of the upper room meal and discourse, John records events leading up to the resurrection, the final climactic proof that Jesus is who He claims to be—the Son of God.

The title of the Fourth Gospel follows the same format as the titles of the Synoptic Gospels: *Kata Ioannen,* "According to John." As with the others, the word "Gospel" was later added. *Ioannes* is derived from the Hebrew name *Johanan,* "Yahweh Has Been Gracious."

2. The Author of John. Jesus nicknamed John and his brother James, "Sons of Thunder" (Mk 3:17). Their father was Zebedee; and their mother Salome, served Jesus in Galilee and was present at His crucifixion (Mk 15:40-41). John was evidently among the Galileans who followed John the Baptist until they were called to follow Jesus at the outset of His public ministry (1:19-51). These Galileans were later called to become full-time disciples of the Lord (Lk 5:1-11), and John was among the twelve men who were selected to be apostles (Lk 6:12-16). After

Christ's ascension, John became one of the "pillars" of the church in Jerusalem along with James and Peter (Ga 2:9). He is mentioned three times by name in Acts (3:1; 4:13; 8:14), each time in association with Peter. Tradition says that John later went to Ephesus (perhaps just before the destruction of Jerusalem). He was eventually exiled by the Romans for a time to the island of Patmos (Re 1:9).

The author of this Gospel is identified only as the disciple "whom Jesus loved" (13:23; 19:26; 20:2; 21:7,20). His knowledge of Palestinian geography and Jewish customs makes it clear that he was a Palestinian Jew, and his meticulous attention to numbers (2:6; 6:13,19; 21:8-11) and names (1:45; 3:1; 11:1; 18:10) indicates that he was an eyewitness. This fits his own claim to be a witness of the events he described (1:14; 19:35; 21:24-25). The disciple "whom Jesus loved" was part of the inner circle of disciples and was closely associated with Peter. The Synoptic Gospels name this inner circle as Peter, James, and John. Since Peter is separate from the beloved disciple, only James and John are left. James was martyred too early to be the author (Ac 12:1-2), so the apostle John was the author of this Gospel. This conclusion from internal evidence is consistent with the external testimony of the early church. Irenaeus (c. A.D. 185) was a disciple of Polycarp who was in turn a disciple of the apostle John. In his *Against Heresies,* Ireneaus bore witness to Johannine authorship of this Gospel and noted that John lived until the time of the emperor Trajan (A.D. 98-117). Clement of Alexandria, Theophilus of Antioch, Origen, and others also ascribe this book to John.

3. The Time of John. In spite of the strong internal and external testimony supporting Johannine authorship of this Gospel, theological assumptions have motivated a number of critics to deny this claim. Until recently it was popular to propose a second-century date for this book. The discovery of the John Rylands Papyrus 52 containing portions of John 18:31-33,37-38 has overthrown this conjecture. This fragment has been dated at about A.D. 135, and a considerable period of time must have been required for John's Gospel to be copied and circulated before it reached Egypt, where the papyrus was found.

On the other hand, John was written after the last of the Synoptic Gospels (c. A.D. 66-68). His familiarity with the topography of Jerusalem (e.g. 5:2; 19:13) does not necessarily require a date before A.D. 70. Since John's three epistles and Revelation were written after his Gospel, the probable range for this work is A.D. 60-90. By this time, John would have been one of the last surviving eyewitnesses of the Lord. According to tradition, John wrote this Gospel in Ephesus.

4. The Christ of John. This book presents the most powerful case in the entire Bible for the deity of the incarnate Son of God. "A Man called Jesus" (9:11) is also "Christ, the Son of the living God" (6:69). The deity of Christ can be seen in His seven "I am" statements: "I am the bread of life" (6:35,48); "I am the light of the world" (8:12; 9:5); "I am the door" (10:7,9); "I am the good shepherd" (10:11,14); "I am the resurrection and the life" (11:25); "I am the way, the truth, and the life" (14:6); "I am the true vine" (15:1-5). The seven signs (1-12) and the five witnesses (5:30-40) also point to His divine character. On certain occasions, Jesus equates Himself with the Old Testament "I AM," or Yahweh (see 4:25-26; 8:24,28,58; 13:19; 18:5-6, 8). Some of the most crucial affirmations of His deity are in 1:1; 8:58; 10:30; 14:9; 20:28.

The Word was God (1:1), but the Word also became flesh (1:14). The humanity of Jesus can be seen in His weariness (4:6), thirst (4:7), dependence (5:19), grief (11:35), troubled soul (12:27), and His anguish and death (19).

5. Keys to John.
Key Words: Believe That Jesus is the Son of God—The Fourth Gospel has the clearest statement of purpose in the Bible: "But these are written that you may believe that Jesus is the Christ, the Son of God, and that believing you may have life in His name" (20:31). John selected the signs he used for the specific purpose of creating intellectual ("that you may believe") and spiritual ("that believing you may have life") conviction about the Son of God. The key verb in John is "believe," and requires both knowledge (8:32; 10:38) and volition (1:12; 3:19; 7:17).

The predominant theme of this Gospel is the dual response of faith and unbelief to the person of Jesus Christ. Those who place their faith in the Son of God have eternal life, but those who reject Him are under the condemnation of God (3:36; 5:24-29; 10:27-29): this is the basic issue. John 1:11-12 summarizes the responses of accepting or rejecting the Son of God that are traced through the rest of the book. The rejection of Jesus by His own people can be seen over and over in chapters 2–19 ("His own did not receive Him"), but John also lists a number of men and women who believed in Him ("But as many as received Him").

Key Verses: John 1:11-13 and John 20:30-31—"He came to His own, and His own did not receive Him. But as many as received Him, to them He gave the right to become children of God, even to those who believe in His name; who were born, not of blood, nor of the will of the flesh, nor of the will of man, but of God" (1:11-13).

"And truly Jesus did many other signs in the presence of His disciples, which are not written in this book; but these are written that you may believe that Jesus is the Christ, the Son of God, and that believing you may have life in His name" (20:30-31).

Key Chapter: John 3—John 3:16 is without doubt the most quoted and preached verse in all of Scripture. Captured in it is the gospel in its clearest and simplest form: that salvation is a gift of God and is obtainable only by belief. The conversation with Nicodemus and the testimony of John the Baptist provide the setting that clearly points out that being "born again" is the only way to find the "kingdom of God."

6. Survey of John. This most unusual gospel, with its distinct content and style, serves as a supplement to the three Synoptics. It is easily the simplest and yet the most profound of the Gospels, and for many people it is the greatest and most powerful. John writes his Gospel for the specific purpose of bringing people to spiritual life through belief in the person and work of Jesus Christ. The five basic sections of this Gospel are: the incarnation of the Son of God (1:1-18); the presentation of the Son of God (1:19-4:54); the opposition to the Son of God (5:1–12:50); the preparation of the disciples by the Son of God (13:1–17:26); the crucifixion and resurrection of the Son of God (18:1–21:25).

The Incarnation of the Son of God (1:1-18). This prologue introduces the rest of the book and gives the background for the historical narrative that follows. It dates the nature of Jesus, introduces His forerunner, clarifies His mission, and notes the rejection and acceptance He will find during His ministry.

The Presentation of the Son of God (1:19-4:54). In this section Christ is under careful consideration and scrutiny by Israel. He is intro-

duced by John the Baptist who directs his own disciples to Christ. Shortly the author begins listing the seven signs, which continue through the next section. John carefully selects seven miracles out of the many that Christ accomplished (Jo 21:25) in order to build a concise case for His deity. They are called signs because they symbolize the life-changing results of belief in Jesus— (1) water to wine: the ritual of law is replaced by the reality of grace (2:1-11); (2) healing the nobleman's son: the gospel brings spiritual restoration (4:46-54); (3) healing the paralytic: weakness is replaced by strength (5:1-16); (4) feeding the multitude: Christ satisfies spiritual hunger (6:1-13); (5) walking on water: the Lord transforms fear to faith (6:16-21); (6) sight to the man born blind: Jesus overcomes darkness and brings in light (9:1-7); (7) raising of Lazarus: the gospel brings people from death to life (11:1-44). These signs combine to show that Jesus is indeed the Son of God.

The Opposition to the Son of God (5:1–12:50). John's unusual pattern in these chapters is to record the reactions of belief and disbelief after the performance of one miracle before moving to the next. In a series of growing confrontations, John portrays the intense opposition that will culminate in the Lord's final rejection on the cross. Even though many people received Him, the inevitable crucifixion is foreshadowed in several places (2:4,21-22; 7:6,39; 11:51-52; 12:16).

The Preparation of the Disciples by the Son of God (13:1–17:26). John surveys the incarnation and public ministry of Jesus in twelve chapters, but radically changes the pace in the next five chapters to give a detailed account of a few crucial hours. In this clear and vivid recollection of Jesus's last discourse to His intimate disciples John captures the Lord's words of comfort and assurance to a group of fearful and confused followers. Jesus knows that in less than twenty-four hours He will be on the cross. Therefore, His last words speak of all the resources that will be at the disciples' disposal after His departure. They will be indwelled and empowered by the Triune Godhead. The Upper Room Discourse contains the message of the epistles in capsule form as it reveals God's pattern for Christian living. In it, the key themes of servanthood, the Holy Spirit, and abiding in Christ are developed.

The Crucifixion and Resurrection of the

Son of God (18:1–21:25). After recording Christ's high priestly prayer on behalf of His disciples and all who believe in Him "through their word" (17:20), John immediately launches into a dramatic description of Jesus's arrest and trials before Annas, Caiaphas, and Pilate. In His crucifixion, Jesus willingly fulfills John the Baptist's prophetic words: "Behold! The Lamb of God who takes away the sin of the world!" (1:29). John closes his profound Gospel with a particularly detailed account of the post-resurrection appearances of the Lord. The resurrection is the ultimate sign that points to Jesus as the Son of God.

OUTLINE OF JOHN

Part One: The Incarnation of the Son of God (1:1-18)

I. The Deity of Christ (1:1-2)

II. The Preincarnate Work of Christ (1:3-5)

III. The Forerunner of Christ (1:6-8)

IV. The Rejection of Christ (1:9-11)

V. The Acceptance of Christ (1:12-13)

VI. The Incarnation of Christ (1:14-18)

Part Two: The Presentation of the Son of God (1:19–4:54)

I. The Presentation of Christ by John the Baptist (1:19-34)

A. John's Witness to the Priests and Levites 1:19-28

B. John's Witness at Christ's Baptism 1:29-34

II. The Presentation of Christ to John's Disciples (1:35-51)

A. Andrew and Peter Follow Christ 1:35-42

B. Philip and Nathanael Follow Christ 1:43-51

III. The Presentation of Christ in Galilee (2:1-12)

A. First Sign: Christ Changes Water to Wine...................................... 2:1-10

B. The Disciples Believe 2:11-12

IV. The Presentation of Christ in Judea (2:13–3:36)

A. Christ Cleanses the Temple 2:13-25

B. Christ Witnesses to Nicodemus 3:1-21

C. John the Baptist Witnesses Concerning Christ..................... 3:22-36

V. The Presentation of Christ in Samaria (4:1-42)

A. Christ Witnesses to the Woman at the Well 4:1-26

B. Christ Witnesses to the Disciples 4:27-38

C. Christ Witnesses to the Samaritans 4:39-42

VI. The Presentation of Christ in Galilee (4:43-54)

A. Christ is Received by the Galileans 4:43-45

B. Second Sign: Christ Heals the Nobleman's Son........................ 4:46-54

Part Three: The Opposition to the Son of God (5:1–12:50)

I. The Opposition at the Feast in Jerusalem (5:1-47)

A. Third Sign: Christ Heals the Paralytic Man 5:1-9

B. Jews Reject Christ..................... 5:10-47

II. The Opposition During Passover Time in Galilee (6:1-71)

A. Fourth Sign: Christ Feeds 5,000 ... 6:1-14

B. Fifth Sign: Christ Walks on the Water 6:15-21

C. Christ Announces: "I Am the Bread
of Life"................................... 6:22-71

III. The Opposition at the Feast of Tabernacles in Jerusalem (7:1–10:21)

A. Before the Feast of Tabernacles...... 7:1-13
B. In the Middle of the Feast of
Tabernacles............................. 7:14-36
C. In the Last Day of the Feast of
Tabernacles............................. 7:37-53
D. After the Feast of Tabernacles... 8:1–10:21

IV. The Opposition at the Feast of Dedication in Jerusalem (10:22-42)

V. The Opposition at Bethany (11:1–12:11)

A. Seventh Sign: Christ Raises
Lazarus 11:1-44
B. The Pharisees Plan to Kill
Christ 11:45-57
C. Mary Anoints Christ.................. 12:1-11

VI. The Opposition at Jerusalem (12:12-50)

A. The Triumphal Entry 12:12-22
B. The Messiah Teaches 12:23-50

Part Four: The Preparation of the Disciples by the Son of God (13:1–17:26)

I. The Preparation in the Upper Room (13:1–14:31)

A. Christ Washes the Disciples' Feet ... 13:1-20
B. Christ Announces Judas, the
Betrayer 13:21-30
C. Christ Gives the Upper Room
Discourse......................... 13:31–14:31

II. The Preparation on the Way to the Garden (15:1–17:26)

A. Christ Instructs the
Disciples 15:1–16:33
B. Christ Intercedes with the
Father 17:1-26

Part Five: The Crucifixion and Resurrection of the Son of God (18:1–21:25)

I. The Rejection of Christ (18:1–19:16)

A. The Arrest of Christ.................. 18:1-11
B. The Trials of Christ 18:12–19:16

II. The Crucifixion of Christ (19:17-37)

A. Christ's Crucifixion 19:17-18
B. Pilate's Inscription 19:19-22
C. Soldiers Cast Lots 19:23-24
D. Mary's Committal 19:25-27
E. Christ's Death 19:28-37

III. The Burial of Christ (19:38-42)

IV. The Resurrection of Christ (20:1-10)

V. The Appearances of Christ (20:11–21:25)

A. Christ Appears to Mary
Magdalene 20:11-18
B. Christ Appears to the Disciples
Except Thomas 20:19-25
C. Christ Appears to Thomas and the
Other Disciples 20:26-29
D. The Purpose of John's Gospel ...20:30-31
E. Christ Appears to the Seven
Disciples 21:1-14
F. Christ Speaks to Peter 21:15-23
G. The Conclusion of John's Gospel... 21:24-25

JOHN MARK
See MARK, GOSPEL OF:
The Author of Mark

JOHN, REVELATION OF
See REVELATION, BOOK OF.

JOI′A·DA
A high priest and the great-grandson of
Jeshua (Ne 12:10; 13:28).

JOI′A·KIM
A high priest, son of Jeshua and father of
Eliashib (Ne 12:10,12,21-26).

JOI′A·RIB, JE·HOI′A·RIB *(Jehovah defends)*
Five Old Testament men:
1. A chief priest of the company of Zerubbabel that returned to Jerusalem from Babylon
(Ne 12:6-7).

2. One in Ezra's company returning to Jerusalem from Babylon who was sent to secure Levites and Nethinim for temple service (Ez 8:16-17).

3. Son of Zechariah and father of Adaiah, a descendant of Judah (Ne 11:5).

4. An Aaronite (1 Ch 24:7).

5. Father of Jedaiah (Ne 11:10).

JOK′ DE·AM

A town south of Hebron in the mountain region of Judah (Jos 15:56).

JO′ KIM

A descendant of Shelah of Judah (1 Ch 4:22).

JOK′ ME·AM

A town of Ephraim given to the Levites of the Kohath family (1 Ch 6:66,68). Kibzaim of Joshua 21:22 is thought to be its other name.

JOK′ NE·AM

A city on the border of the territory of Zebulun (Jos 12:22; 19:11).

JOK′ SHAN *(a fowler)*

Second son of Abraham and Keturah (Ge 25:1-3).

JOK′ TAN *(small)*

He and Peleg were the two sons of Eber (Ge 10:25,29; 1 Ch 1:19-23).

JOK′ THEEL

1. A town in the lowlands of Judah (Jos 15:33,38).

2. A name given to the town of Sela by Amaziah (2 Ki 14:7).

JO′ NA

Variant of JONAH.

JON′ A·DAB, JE·HON′ A·DAB *(Jehovah is bounteous)*

1. Son of Shimeah, David's brother (2 Sa 13:3).

2. Son of Rechab (Je 35:6-7).

JO′ NAH

1. Father of Peter the apostle (Ma 16:17; Jo 1:42; 21:15). See BAR-JONAH.

2. A prophet of Israel, son of Amittai. He was a resident of Gath-hepher in Galilee. His prediction about the expansion of Israelite territory in 2 Kings 14:25 is all that is known of him outside the Book of Jonah. See "The Author of Jonah."

JO′ NAH, BOOK OF

1. The Book of Jonah. Nineveh is northeast; Tarshish is west. When God called Jonah to preach repentance to the wicked Ninevites, the prophet knew that God's mercy might follow. He turned down the assignment and headed for Tarshish instead. But once God dampened his spirits (by tossing him out of the boat and into the water) and demonstrated His protection (by moving him out of the water and into the fish), Jonah realized God was serious about His command. Nineveh must hear the word of the Lord; therefore Jonah went. Although the preaching was a success, the preacher came away angry and discouraged. He needed to learn firsthand of God's compassion for sinful men.

Yonah is the Hebrew word for "dove." The Septuagint Hellenized this word into *Ionas,* and the Latin Vulgate used the title *Jonas.*

2. The Author of Jonah. The first verse introduces Jonah as "the son of Amittai." Nothing more would be known about him were it not for another reference to him in 2 Kings 14:25 as a prophet in the reign of Jeroboam II of Israel. Under Jeroboam, the borders of Israel were expanded "according to the word of the LORD God of Israel, which He had spoken through His servant Jonah the son of Amittai, the prophet who was from Gath Hepher." Gath Hepher was three miles north of Nazareth in lower Galilee, making Jonah a prophet of the Northern Kingdom. The Pharisees were wrong when they said, "Search and look, for no prophet has arisen out of Galilee" (Jo 7:52), because Jonah was a Galilean. One Jewish tradition says that Jonah was the son of the widow of Zarephath whom Elijah raised from the dead (1 Ki 17:8-24).

Some critics claim that Jonah was written during the fifth to third centuries B.C. as a historical fiction to oppose the narrow nationalism of Ezra and Nehemiah by introducing universalistic ideas. They say an anonymous writer created this work to counteract the Jewish practice of excluding the Samaritans from worship and divorcing foreign wives. To support this view, it is noted that the book is written in the third person with no claim that Jonah wrote it. The use of Aramaic words and the statement that "Nineveh was an exceedingly great city" (3:3) indicate a late date after Nineveh's fall in 612 B.C.

Conservative scholars refute this claim with these arguments: (1) The idea of God's inclusion of the Gentiles in His program is found elsewhere in the Scripture (cf. Ge 9:27; 12:3; Le 19:33-34; 1 Sa 2:10; Is 2:2; Joel 2:28-32). (2) Aramaic words occur in early as well as late Old Testament books. Aramaic is found in Near Eastern texts as early as 1500 B.C. (3) The fact that the book does not explicitly say that it was written by Jonah is an argument from silence. (4) Use of the third person style was common among biblical writers. (5) The text in 3:3 literally means "had become." At the time of the story, Nineveh had already become a very large city. (6) Jonah was a historical prophet (2 Ki 14:25), and there are no hints that the book is fictional or allegorical. (7) Christ supported the historical accuracy of the book (Ma 12:39-41).

3. The Time of Jonah. Jonah was a contemporary of Jeroboam II of Israel (782-753 B.C.) who ministered after the time of Elisha and just before the time of Amos and Hosea. Israel under Jeroboam II was enjoying a period of resurgence and prosperity (see "The Time of Amos"). Conditions looked promising after many bleak years, and nationalistic fervor was probably high. During these years, Assyria was in a period of mild decline. Weak rulers had ascended the throne, but Assyria remained a threat. By the time of Jonah, Assyrian cruelty had become legendary. Graphic accounts of their cruel treatment of captives have been found in ancient Assyrian records, especially from the ninth and seventh centuries B.C. The repentance of Nineveh probably occurred in the reign of Ashurdan III (773-755 B.C.). Two plagues (765 and 759 B.C.) and a solar eclipse (763 B.C.) may have prepared the people for Jonah's message of judgment.

4. The Christ of Jonah. Jonah is the only prophet whom Jesus likened to Himself. "But He answered and said to them, 'An evil and adulterous generation seeks after a sign, and no sign will be given to it except the sign of the prophet Jonah. For as Jonah was three days and three nights in the belly of the great fish, so will the Son of Man be three days and three nights in the heart of the earth. The men of Nineveh will rise in the judgment with this generation and condemn it, because they repented at the preaching of Jonah; and indeed a greater than Jonah is

here' " (Ma 12:39-41). Jonah's experience is a type of the death, burial, and resurrection of Christ.

5. Keys to Jonah.

Key Word: The Revival in Nineveh—God's loving concern for the Gentiles is not a truth disclosed only in the New Testament. More than seven centuries before Christ, God commissioned the Hebrew prophet Jonah to proclaim a message of repentance to the Assyrians. Jewish nationalism, however, blinded both God's prophets and the covenant people to God's worldwide purposes of salvation. The story of Jonah is one of the clearest demonstrations of God's love and mercy for all mankind in the entire Scripture.

Key Verses: Jonah 2:8-9; 4:2—"Those who regard worthless idols forsake their own Mercy. But I will sacrifice to You with the voice of thanksgiving; I will pay what I have vowed. Salvation is of the LORD" (2:8-9).

"So he prayed to the LORD, and said, 'Ah LORD, was not this what I said when I was still in my country? Therefore I fled previously to Tarshish; for I know that You are a gracious and merciful God, slow to anger and abundant in lovingkindness, One who relents from doing harm' " (4:2).

Key Chapter: Jonah 3—The third chapter of Jonah records perhaps the greatest revival of all time as the entire city of Nineveh "believed God and proclaimed a fast," crying out to God for forgiveness.

6. Survey of Jonah. Jonah is an unusual book because of its message and messenger. Unlike other Old Testament books, it revolves exclusively around a Gentile nation. God was concerned for the Gentiles as well as for His covenant people Israel. But God's messenger was a reluctant prophet who did not want to proclaim his message for fear that the Assyrians would respond and be spared by the compassionate God of Israel. Of all the people and things mentioned in the book—the storm, the lots, the sailors, the fish, the Ninevites, the plant, the worm, and the east wind—only the prophet himself fails to obey God. All these were used to teach Jonah a lesson in compassion and obedience. The four chapters divide: the first commission of Jonah (1–2) and the second commission of Jonah (3–4).

The First Commission of Jonah (1–2). This chapter records the commission of Jonah (1:1-2), the disobedience of Jonah (1:3), and the judgment on Jonah (1:4-17). Jonah does not want to see God spare the notoriously cruel Assyrians. To preach a message of repentance to them would be like helping Israel's enemy. In his patriotic zeal, Jonah put his country before his God and refused to represent Him to Nineveh. Instead of going five hundred miles northeast to Nineveh, Jonah attempted to go two thousand miles west to Tarshish (Spain). But the Lord used a creative series of countermeasures to accomplish His desired results. Jonah's efforts to thwart God's plan were futile.

God prepared a "great fish" to preserve Jonah and deliver him on dry land. The fish and its divinely appointed rendezvous with the sinking prophet became a powerful reminder to Jonah of the sovereignty of God in every circumstance. While inside the fish (2), Jonah uttered a declarative praise psalm which alludes to several psalms that were racing through his mind (Ps 3:8; 31:22; 42:7; 69:1). In his unique "prayer closet," Jonah offered thanksgiving for his deliverance from drowning. When he acknowledged that "salvation is of the LORD" (2:9), he was finally willing to obey and be used by God. After he was cast up on the shore, Jonah had a long time to reflect on his experiences during his eastward trek of five hundred miles to Nineveh.

The Second Commission of Jonah (3–4). Jonah obeyed his second commission to go to Nineveh (3:1-4) where he became a "sign to the Ninevites" (Lk 11:30). The prophet was a walking object lesson from God, his skin no doubt bleached from his stay in the fish. As he proceeded through the city, his one-sentence sermon brought incredible results: it was the most responsive evangelistic effort in history. Jonah's words of coming judgment were followed by a proclamation by the king of the city to fast and repent. Because of His great mercy, God "relented from the disaster that He had said He would bring upon them" (3:10).

In the final chapter, God's love and grace are contrasted with Jonah's anger and lack of compassion. He was unhappy with the good results of his message because he knew God would now spare Nineveh. God used a plant, a worm, and a wind to teach Jonah a lesson in compassion. Jonah's emotions shifted from fierce anger (4:1), to despondency (4:3), then to great joy (4:6), and finally to despair (4:8). In a humorous but meaningful account, Jonah was forced to see that he has more concern for a plant than for hundreds of thousands of people (if 120,000 children are in mind in 4:11, the population of the area may have been 600,000). Jonah's lack of a divine perspective made his repentance a greater problem than the repentance of Nineveh.

OUTLINE OF JONAH

I. The First Commission of Jonah (1:1–2:10)

A. The Disobedience to the First Call 1:1-3
B. The Judgment on Jonah is Exacted 1:4-17
C. The Prayer of Jonah..................... 2:1-9
D. The Deliverance of Jonah 2:10

II. The Second Commission of Jonah (3:1–4:11)

A. The Obedience to the Second Call 3:1-4
B. The Judgment of Nineveh Averted 3:5-10
C. The Prayer of Jonah..................... 4:1-3
D. The Rebuke of Jonah by God 4:4-11

JO′NAM, JO′NAN

Son of Eliakim and ancestor of Joseph (Lk 3:30).

JO′NAS

Variant of JONAH.

JON′A·THAN (*God given*)

1. A Levite who acted as priest for an Ephraimite named Micah. Micah had made a shrine and images, and he hired a young Levite who was passing through to be his priest. This young Levite was happy to serve Micah, for he paid well, until a group of Danites came raiding the hill country of Ephraim. They inquired of the Lord at the house of the priest, and then when the priest gave them a positive answer they were pleased. Upon returning from a successful raid, they stopped at Micah's house a second time, to make off with his valuable silver images. The priest at first protested, but when they invited him to return with them and continue as their priest, he was happy to accompany the idols and the Danites. He and his sons served the tribe of Dan until the exile (Ju 18:30).

2. Saul's eldest son. His father gave him the command of 1000 men at Geba at which point he defeated the Philistine garrison (1 Sa 13:3). This brought on war. Accompanied by his armor bearer, Jonathan climbed the gorge of Michmash, surprised an outpost of the Philistines, slew twenty of them and created a panic. When Saul's army arrived he found the Philistines confused and demoralized (1 Sa 14:1-14). The friendship of David and Jonathan began when David slew Goliath and it continued in the face of Saul's persecution of David (1 Sa 18:1-4). He acted in behalf of David (1 Sa 20:1-42), and they entered into "a covenant before the Lord" (1 Sa 23:15-18). We hear nothing more of him until Saul's last battle at Gilboa when Jonathan and his two brothers were slain by the Philistines and Saul took his own life (1 Sa 31:1,11-13; 1 Ch 10:2,8-12). David deeply lamented his death (2 Sa 1:17-27) and cared for Jonathan's crippled son, Mephibosheth (2 Sa 4:4).

3. Son of Abiathar, the high priest. The latter was loyal to David at the time of Absalom's rebellion (2 Sa 15:27,36). Jonathan sent David information of what was occurring in Jerusalem during Absalom's rebellion (2 Sa 15:36; 17:15-22). He brought the news that Solomon had been proclaimed king to Adonijah (1 Ki 1:41-49).

4. Son of Shimeah and nephew of David. He slew a Philistine giant (2 Sa 21:21-22).

5. Son of Shage and one of David's mighty men (2 Sa 23:32; 1 Ch 11:34).

6. A son of Jada, grandson of Jerahmeel of Judah (1 Ch 2:32-33).

7. David's uncle (1 Ch 27:32), a scribe, counselor, and wise man.

8. A descendant of Adin (Ez 8:6).

9. Son of Asahel. He opposed the separation of the people from their foreign wives (Ez 10:15).

10. Son of Joiada and a high priest, also called Johanan (Ne 12:11,22).

11. A priest in the days of the high priest Joiakim (Ne 12:14).

12. Son of Shemaiah (Ne 12:35).

13. A scribe in whose house Jeremiah was imprisoned (Je 37:15,20).

14. A Son of Kareah. He placed himself under the protection of Gedaliah whom Nebuchadnezzar appointed governor of Jerusalem (Je 40:8).

JO´ NATH-E´ LEM-RE·CHO´ KIM

A term in the title to Psalm 56 which probably denotes the tune of which the psalm was to be sung.

JOP´ PA

The modern city of Jaffa, a suburb of Tel Aviv, Israel, is located on the coast of the Mediterranean Sea, about midway between the northern and southern borders of the country. In Bible times, the city was called Joppa, a name that means, "Beautiful."

This city is first mentioned in the Bible as a portion of the land allotted to the tribe of Dan (Jos 19:46). In later years, the prophet Jonah tried to escape his call to preach to the city of Nineveh by going to Joppa to catch a ship bound for Tarshish (Jon 1:3).

Joppa was the only natural harbor on the Mediterranean Sea between Egypt and Accho (or Ptolemais), north of Mount Carmel. It served as a maritime shipping center for the inland city of Jerusalem in both Old and New Testament times. Solomon's temple at Jerusalem was built in part with cedar logs from Phoenicia. These were floated on rafts from the forests of Lebanon to Joppa, where they were hauled by land to the temple site (2 Ch 2:16).

Two New Testament personalities are connected with Joppa. The city was the home of Tabitha, or Dorcas (Ac 9:36-43). After Tabitha was restored to life by Simon Peter, many people believed on the Lord.

Simon the tanner also lived at Joppa (Ac 10:32). While praying on the roof of Simon's house, Simon Peter received his famous vision of a sheet descending from heaven (Ac 10:9-22). This vision led Peter to the conviction that "God shows no partiality. But in every nation whoever fears Him and works righteousness is accepted by Him" (Ac 10:34-35). From that point on, Peter preached the gospel of Christ to Gentiles as well as to his own Jewish countrymen.

JOR´ AH

See HARIPH.

JO´ RA·I

One of seven Gadite chieftains (1 Ch 5:13).

JOR´ AM, JE·HOR´ AM

1. Son of Toi, king of Hamath. His father sent him to congratulate David on his victory over

Hadadezer (2 Sa 8:9-10). In 1 Chronicles 18:10 he is called Hadoram.

2. A Levite, the descendant of Eliezer, son of Moses (1 Ch 26:25).

3. A priest sent by Jehoshaphat to instruct the people (2 Ch 17:8).

4. Son of Jehoshaphat. He followed his father on the throne and murdered his brothers (2 Ch 21:1-4). His wife was Athaliah, daughter of Ahab and Jezebel of Israel. She introduced Phoenician idolatry as did her mother (2 Ki 8:18; 2 Ch 21:6,11). The Edomites and Libnah rebelled during his reign (2 Ki 8:20-22; 2 Ch 21:8-10). Later the palace was plundered by Philistines and Arabs who carried off the wives and children of the king with the exception of Ahaziah, also called Jehoahaz, who succeeded Joram (2 Ch 21:16-17; 22:1-4). Joram was the wicked son of a pious father.

5. Son of Ahab, king of Israel. He followed his brother, Ahaziah, on the throne and reigned for eleven years (2 Ki 3:1-27; 9:14-26).

JOR′DAN *(the descender)*

The Jordan River has such an important role in biblical history that many visitors to the Holy Land ask to be baptized in its waters, near Jericho, where Jesus was baptized by John (Ma 3:13).

This famous river begins as a small stream in the foothills of Mount Hermon near Caesarea Philippi (now called Banias). Popularly, the name *Jordan* is thought to mean "descender" or "the river that rushes down," which it does at the rate of 25 feet per mile along its twisting 100 mile journey. Its descent ranges from about 1,200 feet above sea level to about 1,286 feet below sea level. The course of the river is almost directly south. At Lake Huleh it is only a few feet above sea level. From this marshy region it continues to the Sea of Galilee where it is almost 700 feet below the level of the Mediterranean. Ninety miles farther south, where it empties into the Dead Sea, is the lowest point on earth. In its course the river receives two tributaries from the East, the Yarmuk and the Jabbok. The Jordan's tributaries from the west are unimportant. The river is small in normal times but becomes a torrent in the rainy season (Jos 3:15). It is not navigable though small craft have been known to descend it. At several points between the Sea of Galilee and the Dead Sea the river can be forded.

Through the centuries, the Jordan has served as a natural boundary between Palestine and other nations. In the period between the Old Testament and the New Testament, the Jordan River formed the main eastern boundary of the Persian and Greek province of Judea. The Decapolis, a federation of Ten Greek Cities, was formed on the eastern side of the Jordan in the Greek period.

The Old Testament speaks of the Jordan as the site of the land favored by Lot (Ge 13:10-11); the place where Israel would cross into the land of Canaan in Joshua's time (De 3:20,25,27); and the scene of events in Elijah's and Elisha's lives (1 Ki 17:2-5); 2 Ki 2:13-15).

Because the Jordan is a short and rather shallow river, it was compared unfavorably by Naaman the leper to the two larger rivers in his homeland of Syria. When the prophet Elisha directed him to dip in the Jordan to be healed of his leprosy, he replied, "Are not the Abanah and the Pharpar, the rivers of Damascus, better than all the waters of Israel? Could I not wash in them and be clean?" (2 Ki 5:12).

But his servants persuaded him to do as Elisha asked, and Naaman was healed.

JO′RIM

Son of Matthat and ancestor of Jesus (Lk 3:29).

JOR′KE•AM

See JORKOAM.

JOR′KO•AM

The name of a man of Judah (1 Ch 2:44).

JOS′A•BAD

See JOZABAD.

JOS′A•PHAT

See JEHOSHAPHAT.

JO′SE

A form of JOSES (Lk 3:29).

JOSECH

A name in the genealogy of Jesus (Lk 3:26 NIV), also Joseph (NKJV, KJV, NASB).

JOS′E•DECH

See JOZADAK.

JO′SEPH *(may he add)*

1. The eleventh son of Jacob. His mother, Rachel, was Jacob's favorite wife, and he was Jacob's favorite son. Because of jealousy, his brothers caused him to be sold as a slave and carried into Egypt (Ge 30:22-24; 37:2-36). Because he was able to interpret Pharaoh's dream, he was placed in a high position in Egypt and made responsible for preparing the country against the famine. Later, after he met his brothers, he brought his family to Egypt so that they could weather the famine. In his high position Joseph was able to preserve many Israelites from starvation (Ge 39:1–48:22). He lived in Egypt until his death at the age of one hundred and ten (Ge 50:26). See JOSEPH'S LIFE, INDEXED.

2. Father of Igal, the spy from the tribe of Issachar (Nu 13:7).

3. A son of Asaph (1 Ch 25:2,9).

4. A son of Bani. He put away his foreign wife in the time of Ezra (Ez 10:42).

5. A priest, head of the family of Shebaniah.

6. The husband of Mary, the mother of Jesus (Ma 1:16; Lk 3:23). When Augustus issued his decree that all should be enrolled, or taxed, Joseph and Mary went to Bethlehem. At that time Jesus was born (Mi 5:2; Lk 2:4,16). After the death of Herod, they returned to Nazareth from Egypt (Ma 2:22-23). He was a carpenter (Ma 13:55), as was Jesus (Mk 6:3). At the beginning of our Lord's work Joseph was evidently alive (Ma 13:55) but probably died prior to the crucifixion since, on the cross, Jesus committed his mother to the care of John (Jo 19:26-27).

7. Son of Mattathias, an ancestor of Jesus (Lk 3:24-25).

8. The father of Semei who lived after the exile; an ancestor of Jesus (Lk 3:26).

9. An ancestor of Christ (Lk 3:30).

10. Joseph of Arimathaea. He was a member of the Sanhedrin and, like Nicodemus, was a secret disciple of Jesus. He took a positive stand regarding his Lord by going boldly to Pilate and asking for the body of Jesus. His request was granted and he had the body placed in a new tomb which belonged to him (Ma 27:58-60; Mk 15:43-46).

11. A Christian called Barsabbas, i.e., son of Sabbas. He was of the company of Jesus during his labors (Ac 1:21,23).

12. The personal name of Barnabas; called Joses in the Authorized Version (Ac 4:36).

JOSEPH'S LIFE, INDEXED		
Recorded Events	Place	Reference
Jacob's eleventh son by his favorite wife, Rachel.	Padan-aram	Ge 30:22-24

Recorded Events	Place	Reference
Jacob loves Joseph more than all his children, and makes him a coat of many colors. For this his brothers hate him.	Beer-sheba	Ge 37:1-4
He relates two dreams which indicate his future superior position, and they hate him the more.	Beer-sheba	Ge 37:5-11
Sent by Jacob to his brothers at Dothan they conspire to slay him. Judah proposes that they sell him to some Midianites on their way to Egypt. Dipping his coat in the blood of a kid, they tell Jacob he was slain by a wild beast. The Midianites sell him to Potiphar, Pharaoh's officer.	Dothan	Ge 37:12-36
Joseph's efficiency wins Potiphar's favor, who makes him overseer of his house.	Egypt. House of Potiphar	Ge 39:1-6
Failing in her attempt to entice Joseph to sin, Potiphar's wife makes a false charge against him and prison. Potiphar has him confined in prison. He is placed in charge of the prisoners.	Egypt. In prison.	Ge 39:7-23
He interprets the dreams of two prisoners, the king's butler and baker. They are fulfilled.	Egypt. Prison	Ge 40
Two years afterward Pharaoh has two dreams that trouble him. Joseph interprets them. There will be seven years of plenty and seven years of famine, and he counsels Pharaoh how to deal with the situation.	Court of Pharaoh	Ge 41:1-36
Pharaoh makes Joseph his prime minister. He acts wisely and the storehouses of Egypt are filled.	Court of Pharaoh	Ge 41:37-57
The famine in Palestine compels Jacob to send his sons to Egypt to buy corn. Joseph recognizes his brothers, but does not reveal his identity. He sends them back with corn and hides their money in the bags.	Court of Pharaoh	Ge 42
He requires them to return with Benjamin. He reveals himself to his brothers, treats them with great kindness and offers them a home in Egypt.	Egypt	Ge 43–45
Jacob and his people, seventy souls, are placed by Joseph in Goshen, where they greatly prosper. Jacob blesses Ephraim and Manasseh, sons of Joseph, gives a prophetic statement of the tribes and dies. Joseph and his brothers bury him beside his people in the cave of Machpelah in Hebron.	Egypt. Israel in Goshen	Ge 46:1–50:13
After Jacob's death, Joseph deals kindly with his brethren, assures them that God will restore them to their own land and receives from them a pledge that they will carry back with them his remains. He dies at the age of 110 years.	Egypt	Ge 50:14-26

Recorded Events	Place	Reference
In some of the circumstances of his life, Joseph is peculiarly typical of Christ. He is sold by his own people into slavery. He is cast into prison, to his humiliation. According to his statement one prisoner is greatly favored, the other suffers death. On the cross, Jesus talks one malefactor into paradise; the other dies in his sins. Joseph rises from humiliation to exaltation; from His humiliation of death and the grave Jesus rises in the glory of His resurrection.	Egypt	Ge 50:14-26

JOSEPHUS, FLAVIUS

A Jewish historian whose works contain valuable information about intertestamental and New Testament times.

JO′ SES *(a Greek form of Joseph)*

1. The son of Mary and Cleopas, one of the brethren of the Lord (Ma 13:55; Mk 6:3).

2. The personal name of Barnabas, a Levite of Cyprus, and Paul's companion (Ac 4:36).

JO′ SHAH

Son of Amaziah of the tribe of Simeon (1 Ch 4:34).

JOSH′ A·PHAT *(Jehovah has judged)*

1. A Mithnite who was one of David's warriors (1 Ch 11:43).

2. A priest who served as a trumpeter at the time the ark was brought to Jerusalem (1 Ch 15:24). He is called Jehoshaphat in the Authorized Version.

JOSH·A·VI′ AH

A warrior of David, son of Elnaam (1 Ch 11:46).

JOSH·BE·KASH′ AH

Son of Heman and head of the seventeenth course of singers (1 Ch 25:4,24).

JO′ SHEB-BAS·SHE′ BETH

A Tachmonite who was chief of David's captains (2 Sa 23:8). He is called Jashobeam in 1 Chronicles 11:11.

JOSH·I·BI′ AH, JOS·I·BI′ AH

A Simeonite of the family of Asiel (1 Ch 4:35).

JOSH′ U·A

Four Old Testament men:

1. The son of Nun. His name was changed by Moses from Oshea to Joshua (Nu 13:8,16). He was the commander of the Israelites in their first battle and defeated the Amalekites at Rephidim (Ex 17:8-16). He was with Moses on Sinai (Ex 24:13; 32:17). He was the representative of Ephraim when the twelve spies were sent to Canaan and he and Caleb strove to persuade the people to go and occupy the land (Nu 13:8; 14:6-9). The Lord rewarded their loyalty, allowing them to settle in the land. At the end of the wandering, by divine direction, Moses placed Joshua before the high priest and publicly ordained him as his successor (Nu 27:18-23; De 1:38; 31:14,23). His leadership of Israel is recorded in the book that bears his name.

2. A native of Beth-ahemesh. He owned the field through which was driven the cart that carried the ark from the land of the Philistines (1 Sa 6:14).

3. The governor of Jerusalem at the time King Josiah was engaged in his reform work (2 Ki 23:8).

4. The high priest during Zerubbabel's governorship of Judah. In Ezra and Nehemiah he is called Jeshua (Ez 3:2,8-9; Ne 12:1,7,10,26; Hag 1:1,12,14; 2:2-4; Ze 3:1-9).

JOSH′ U·A, BOOK OF

1. The Book of Joshua. Joshua, the first of the twelve historical books (Joshua through Esther), forges a link between the Pentateuch and the remainder of Israel's history. Through three major military campaigns involving more than thirty enemy armies, the people of Israel learned a crucial lesson under Joshua's capable leadership: victory comes through faith in God and obedience to His word, rather than through military might or numerical superiority.

The title of this book is appropriately named after its central figure, Joshua. His original name is *Hoshea,* "Salvation" (Nu 13:8); but Moses evidently changed it to *Yehoshua* (Nu 13:16), "Yahweh is Salvation." He is also called *Yeshua,* a shortened form of *Yehoshua.* The Greek equivalent of this Hebrew name is *Iesous* (Jesus). Thus, the Greek title given to the book in the Septuagint is *Iesous Naus,* "Joshua the Son of Nun." The Latin title is *Liber Josue,* the "Book of Joshua."

His name is symbolic of the fact that although he was the leader of the Israelite nation during the conquest, the Lord is the Conqueror.

2. The Author of Joshua. Although it cannot be proven, Jewish tradition seems correct in assigning the authorship of this book to Joshua himself. Joshua 24:26 makes this clear statement: "Then Joshua wrote these words in the Book of the Law of God." This refers at least to Joshua's farewell charge, if not to the book as a whole (see also 18:9). Joshua, as Israel's leader and an eyewitness of most of the events, was the person best qualified to write the book. He even uses the first person in one place (5:6, "us"; "we" appears in some manuscripts of 5:1). The book was written soon after the events occurred: Rahab was still alive (6:25). Other evidences for early authorship are the detailed information about Israel's campaigns and use of the ancient names of Canaanite cities. The unity of style and organization suggests a single authorship for the majority of the book. Three small portions, however, must have been added after Joshua's death. These are: (1) Othniel's capture of Kirjath-sepher (15:13-19); cf. Ju 1:9-15), (2) Dan's migration to the north (19:47; cf. Ju 18:27-29), and (3) Joshua's death and burial (24:29-33). These may have been inserted early in the time of the judges by Eleazer the priest and his son Phinehas (24:33).

Joshua, born a slave in Egypt, became a conqueror in Canaan. He served as personal attendant to Moses, as one of the twelve spies (of whom only he and Caleb believed God), and as Moses's successor. His outstanding qualities were obedient faith, courage, and dedication to God and His Word.

3. The Time of Joshua. Joshua divides neatly into three geographical settings: (1) the Jordan River (1-5); (2) Canaan (6:1-13:7); and (3) the twelve tribes situated on both sides of the Jordah (13:8-24:33).

The setting of the first five chapters begins east of the Jordan as Joshua replaced Moses, crossed the Jordan on dry land, and finally prepared for war west of the Jordan.

Like a wise general, Joshua utilized the divide-and-conquer strategy; and his campaign led him to central Canaan (6-8), southern Canaan (9-10), and finally to northern Canaan (11-12).

After listing those areas yet to be conquered (13:1-7), Joshua undertook the long task of dividing the promised land to all the tribes. First, he settled those two-and-a-half tribes east of the Jordan (13:8-33) and then the nine-and-a-half tribes west of the Jordan (14:1-19:51). Completing this, he was free to assign the six Cities of Refuge and the forty-eight Cities of Levites, which are scattered among all the tribes.

The Book of Joshua cannot be dated precisely, but utilizing the same threefold division noted above, the following dates can be assigned:

A. One month, March-April 1405 B.C. (Jos 1-5)
  1. Death of Moses, March 1405 B.C. (De 34:5-9).
  2. Crossing the Jordan, April 10, 1405 B.C. (Jos 4:19)
B. Seven Years, April 1405-1398 B.C. (Jos 6:1-13:7
  1. Caleb forty years old at Kadesh (Jos 14:7)
  2. Caleb eighty-five years old at that time (Jos 14:10)
    Note: forty-five years less thirty-eight years of wandering leaves seven years.
C. Eight Years, 1398/7-1390 B.C. (Jos 13:8-24)
  1. Division begun 1398/7 B.C. (Jos 14:7-10)
  2. Joshua dies at 110, c. 1390 B.C. (Jos 24:39).

4. The Christ of Joshua. Although there are not direct messianic prophecies in the book, Joshua can be seen as type of Christ. His name *Yeshua* ("Yahweh Is Salvation") is the Hebrew equivalent of the name Jesus. In his role of triumphantly leading his people into their possessions, he foreshadows the One who will bring "many sons to glory" (He 2:10). "Now thanks be to God who always leads us in triumph in Christ" (2 Co 2:14; see Ro 8:37). Joshua succeeds Moses and wins the victory unreached by Moses. Christ will succeed the Mosaic law and win the victory unreachable by the law (Jo 1:17; Ro 8:2-4; Ga 3:23-25; He 7:18-19).

The "Commander of the army of the LORD" (5:13-15) met by Joshua is thought to be a pre-incarnate appearance of Christ (cf. Jos 5:15 with Ex 3:2).

Rahab's scarlet cord portrays safety through the blood (He 9:19-22); and amazingly, this Gentile woman is found in Christ's genealogy (Ma 1:5).

5. Keys to Joshua.

Key Word: Conquest—The entire Book of Joshua describes the entering, conquering, and occupying of the land of Canaan. The book begins with a statement of the promise of conquest. "Moses My servant is dead. Now therefore, arise, go over this Jordan . . . Every place that the sole of your foot shall tread upon I have given you" (1:2-3) and ends with the completion of conquest "that not one thing has failed of all the good things which the LORD your God spoke concerning you. All have come to pass for you, and not one word of them has failed" (23:14).

Key Verses: Joshua 1:8; 11:23—"This Book of the Law shall not depart from your mouth, but you shall meditate in it day and night, that you may observe to do according to all that is written in it. For then you will make your way prosperous, and then you will have good success" (1:8).

"So Joshua took the whole land, according to all that the LORD had said to Moses; and Joshua gave it as an inheritance to Israel according to their divisions by their tribes. Then the land rested from war" (11:23).

Key Chapter: Joshua 24—Some of the most critical periods in Israel's history are the transitions of leadership: Moses to Joshua; Joshua to the judges; the judges to the kings, and so on. Before his death and in preparation for a major transition of leadership by one man (Joshua) to many (the judges), Joshua reviewed for the people God's fulfillment of His promises and then challenged them to review their commitment to the covenant (24:24-25), which is the foundation for all successful national life.

6. Survey of Joshua.

Joshua resumes the narrative where Deuteronomy left off, and took Israel from the wilderness to the promised land. Israel had now reached its climactic point of fulfilling the centuries-old promise in Genesis of a homeland. The first half of Joshua (1:1–13:7) describes the seven-year conquest of the land, and the second half (13:8–24:33) gives the details of the division and settlement of the land.

Conquest (1:1–13:7). The first five chapters record the spiritual, moral, physical, and military preparation of Joshua and the people for the impending conquest of Canaan. Joshua is given a charge by God to complete the task begun by Moses (1:2). After being encouraged by God, Joshua sends out two spies who come back with a favorable report (in contrast to the spies of the previous generation). Obedience and faith are united in the miraculous crossing of the Jordan River (3:1–4:24).

Joshua's campaign in central Canaan (6:1–8:35) placed a strategic wedge between the northern and southern cities preventing a massive Canaanite alliance against Israel. This divide-and-conquer strategy proved effective, but God's directions for taking the first city (Jericho) sound like foolishness from a military point of view. The Lord uses this to test the people and to teach them that Israel's success in battle will always be by His power and not their own might or cleverness. Sin must be dealt with at once because it brings severe consequences and defeat at Ai (7:1-26).

The southern and northern campaigns (9:1–13:7) are also successful, but an unwise oath made to the deceptive Gibeonites forces Israel to protect them and to disobey God's command to eliminate the Canaanites.

Settlement (13:8–24:33). Joshua was growing old, and God told him to divide the land among the twelve tribes. Much remained to be won, and the tribes were to continue the conquest by faith after Joshua's death. Chapters 13:8–21:45 describe the allocation of the land to the various tribes as well as the inheritance of Caleb (14–15) and the Levites (21).

The last chapters (22:1–24:33) record the conditions for continued successful settlement in Canaan. Access to God, as well as His forgiveness, comes only through the divinely established sacrificial system; and civil war almost broke out when the eastern tribes built an altar that was misinterpreted by the western tribes.

Realizing that blessing would come from God only as Israel obeyed His covenant, Joshua preached a moving sermon, climaxed by Israel's renewal of her allegiance to the covenant.

OUTLINE OF JOSHUA

Part One: The Conquest of Canaan (1:1–13:7)

I. Israel is Prepared for the Conquest (1:1–5:15)

A. Joshua Replaces Moses 1:1-18
B. Joshua Prepares Israel Militarily 2:1–5:1
C. Joshua Prepares Israel Spiritually 5:2-12
D. The Commander of the Lord's Army Appears 5:13-15

II. The Conquest of Canaan by Israel (6:1–13:7)

A. Conquest of Central Canaan 6:1–8:35
B. Conquest of Southern Canaan.................................. 9:1–10:43
C. Conquest of Northern Canaan ... 11:1-15
D. Conquest of Canaan Is Summarized 11:16–12:24
E. Unconquered Parts of Canaan 13:1-7

Part Two: The Settlement in Canaan (13:8–24:33)

I. The Settlement East of the Jordan (13:8-33)

A. Geographical Boundaries............ 13:8-13
B. Tribal Boundaries 13:14-23

II. The Settlement West of the Jordan (14:1–19:51)

A. The First Settlement Done at Gilgal 14:1–17:18
B. The Second Settlement Done at Shiloh 18:1–19:51

III. The Settlement of the Religious Community (20:1–21:42)

A. Six Cities of Refuge 20:1-9
B. Selection of the Levitical Cities ... 21:1-42
C. The Settlement of Israel Is Completed 21:43-45

IV. The Conditions for Continued Settlement (22:1–24:33)

A. The Altar of Witness................. 22:1-34
B. Blessings of God Come Only Through Obedience 23:1–24:28
C. Joshua and Eleazar Die 24:29-33

JOSHUA, GATE OF

A gate of Jerusalem (2 Ki 23:8).

JO·SI′ AH (Jehovah heals)

Two Old Testament men:

1. Son of Amon, king of Judah, whom he succeeded as king in about 639 B.C. at the age of eight. In his youth he was doubtless under the influence of Hilkiah, the high priest. In the twelfth year of his reign he instituted a reform program (2 Ki 22:1-2; 2 Ch 34:1-7,33). Josiah was killed at Megiddo in a battle with the Egyptians (2 Ki 23:29-30).

2. A son of Zephaniah (Ze 6:10).

JO·SI′ AS

See JOSIAH.

JOS·I·BI′ AH

See JOSHIBIAH.

JOS·I·PHI′ AH (increased by Jehovah)

Head of the house of Shelomith (Ez 8:10).

JOT

Derived from *Iota,* the smallest letter of the Greek alphabet, which corresponds to the Hebrew *yod* and is its equivalent etymologically. It is used figuratively to express what is trifling. In many Hebrew words it is unimportant whether the yod is employed, and may or may not be used hence, figuratively, it signifies a matter of small moment (Ma 5:18).

JOT′ BAH (pleasantness)

The town where Haruz lived. He was the maternal grandfather of Amon, king of Judah. (2 Ki 21:19).

JOT′ BATH

One of the encampments of the Israelites (Nu 33:33-34).

JOT′ BA·THAH

Variant of JOTBATH.

JO′ A·THAM

Variant of JOTHAM.

JO′ THAM

Two Old Testament men:

1. The youngest son of Gideon, who escaped the massacre of his seventy brothers ordered by Abimelech. After Abimelech became king of Shechem, Jotham, on Mount Gerizim, spoke the parable to the Shechemites of the trees anointing a king (Ju 9:1-21).

2. King of Judah, son of Uzziah (Azariah). Jotham became king after his father contracted leprosy. He was twenty-five years old at the time (2 Ki 15:5,32-33). Near the end of his rule, Pekah of Israel and Rezin of Syria began their invasion of Judah (2 Ki 15:32-38; 2 Ch 27:1-9).

JOZ′ A·BAD

Several Old Testament men:

1. An inhabitant of Gederah. He allied himself with David at Ziklag (1 Ch 12:4).

2. Two men of Manasseh had this name. They assisted David in his conflict with the Amalekites (1 Ch 12:20).

3. A Levite, an overseer of the tithes in the reign of Hezekiah (2 Ch 31:13).

4. A Levite prince in the reign of Josiah (2 Ch 35:9).

5. Son of Jeshua (Ez 8:33).

6. A son of Pashur (Ez 10:22).

Also see JOZACHAR.

JO′ ZA·CAR

Variant of JOZACHAR.

JO′ ZA·CHAR *(remembered by Jehovah)*

One of the assassins of Joash, king of Judah, who was slain in Millo (2 Ki 12:21). He is also called Jozabad (NIV).

JO′ ZA·DAK *(Jehovah is just)*

Father of Jeshua, the high priest of Zerubbabel's time (Ez 3:2,8; Hag 1:12,14; Ze 6:11). Jozadak was carried into captivity by Nebuchadnezzar.

JU′ BAL *(stream)*

The son of Lamech. He is described as "the father of all those who play the harp and flute" (Ge 4:21).

JU′ BI·LEE *(ram's horn, trumpet)*

The Jubilee year, also known as the "year of liberty" (Eze 46:17), was proclaimed on the fiftieth year after seven cycles of seven years. This fiftieth year was a time when specific instructions about property and slavery outlined in the Jewish law took effect (Le 25:8-55).

The word *jubilee* comes from a Hebrew word meaning "ram's horn," or "trumpet." The Jubilee year was launched with a blast from a ram's horn on the Day of Atonement, signifying a call to celebration, liberation, and the beginning of a year for "doing justice" and "loving mercy."

The fiftieth year was a special year in which to "proclaim liberty throughout all the land" (Le 25:10). Individuals who had sold themselves as slaves or servants indentured because of indebtedness were released from their debts and set free. If a family's land had been taken away because of indebtedness, this land was returned to the original owners in the Jubilee year.

God apparently established the Jubilee year to prevent the Israelites from oppressing and cheating one another (Le 25:17). This law prevented a permanent system of classes from developing; it gave everyone the opportunity to start over, economically and socially.

The Jubilee year reminds us of God's concern for human liberty. God wants people to be free (Lk 4:18-19). Calling into question any social practice that leads to permanent bondage and loss of economic opportunity, it also stands as a witness to God's desire for justice on earth.

JU′ CAL

See JEHUCAL.

JU′ DA

Variant of JUDAH.

JU·DAE′ A

Variant of JUDEA.

JU′ DAH

1. The fourth son of Jacob. His mother was Leah, Jacob's first wife. His two sons, Er and Onan, by his Canaanite wife, were slain for their sinfulness by divine judgment (Ge 38:1-10). The mother of his two sons, Pharez and Zarah, was Tamar, the widow of Er (Ge 38:11-30; 46:12; Nu 26:19). Through Pharez Judah became the ancestor of David (Ru 4:18-22) and of Jesus in the Davidic line (Ma 1:3-16). In Jacob's dying prophetical vision Judah was selected as the tribe of the Messiah. It is called the "Shiloh Prophecy" (Ge 49:10).

2. Tribe of Judah. It consisted of five tribal families (Nu 26:19-21; 1 Ch 2:3-6). In the early period of the wandering Nahahon, son of Amminadab, was the prince of the tribe (Nu 1:7; 2:3; 7:12-17; 10:14). The tribe occupied the large part of southern Palestine. Its western boundary was the Mediterranean, and the eastern the Dead Sea. From north to south the length of its territory was about fifty miles.

3. A Levite (Ez 3:9).

4. A Levite who renounced his foreign wife (Ez 10:23).

5. Son of Hassenuah, a Benjamite (Ne 11:9).

6. A Levite who returned with Zerubbabel (Ne 12:8).

7. One who officiated when the wall of Nehemiah was dedicated (Ne 12:34).

JUDAH, KINGDOM OF

The division of the Kingdom of Israel occurred in 931 B.C., after the death of Solomon, son of David. Due to Rehoboam's foolish political moves, the ten northern tribes revolted under Jeroboam and formed the Kingdom of Israel. The kingdom of Judah in the south included Judah and Benjamin. David's descendants continued to sit on the throne of Judah; many of them were wicked, but every once in a while a good king rose up who tried to turn the nation back to worshipping God. The Northern Kingdom existed from 931 to 722 B.C.; Judah continued until 586 B.C. when Nebuchadnezzar carried the people into captivity.

JUDAIZERS

Those who were teaching that it is necessary to follow the Mosaic law in order to be saved (Ac 15:1). The Jerusalem Council was held to discuss and refute this way of thinking, but this did not put an end to the idea. Paul's letter to the Galatians deals extensively with the problem of the Judaizers.

JU'DAS

The Greek form of the Hebrew Judah.

1. Judah, son of Jacob (Ma 1:2-3), in the genealogy of Jesus.

2. An ancestor of Jesus, who lived prior to the exile (Lk 3:30).

3. Judas of Galilee. In the days of the enrollment he instigated a revolt, was slain, and his

followers were scattered (Ac 5:37). He gave rise to a party of zealots who had much to do with starting the war that resulted in the destruction of Jerusalem, A.D. 70.

4. Judas Iscariot. His father was Simon Iscariot. His surname distinguished him from another apostle named Judas (Lk 6:16; Jo 14:22). His motive in following Jesus appears to have been of a mercenary nature, expecting to gain a worldly advantage in the establishment of the kingdom. He had charge of the funds of the band, and John declared he was a thief (Jo 12:6). He bargained with the chief priests to betray Jesus for "thirty pieces of silver," the price of a slave. At the Last Supper he was declared by our Lord to be the traitor, and that night earned his fee in the garden of Gethsemane (Ma 26:47-50). When he awoke to the enormity of his guilt, he confessed to the chief priests the sinfulness of his act and returned the money. His last act was to hang himself (Ma 27:3-5; Ac 1:18).

5. An apostle, distinguished from Judas Iscariot (Jo 14:22). He was called Thaddaeus (Ma 10:3; Mk 3:18), as well as Lebbaeus.

6. One of the four brethren of Jesus (Ma 13:55; Mk 6:3), probably Jude the author of the Epistle of Jude.

7. A man of Damascus with whom Paul remained following his conversion (Ac 9:11).

8. Judas, surnamed Barsabas. A prominent man in the Church of Jerusalem (Ac 15:22,27,32).

JUDAS ISACARIOT

See JUDAS No. 4.

JUDAS MACCABAEUS

See MACCABEES, THE.

JUDE

An English form of Judas. He was the author of the Epistle of Jude and was a brother of James. See "The Author of Jude."

JUDE, E·PIS'TLE OF

1. The Book of Jude. Fight! Contend! Do battle! When apostasy arises, when false teachers emerge, when the truth of God is attacked, it is time to fight for the faith. Only believers who are spiritually "in shape" can answer the summons. At the beginning of his letter Jude focuses on the believer's common salvation, but then feels compelled to challenge them to contend for the faith. The danger is real. False teachers have crept into the church, turning God's grace into unbounded license to do as they please. Jude reminds such men of God's past dealings with unbelieving Israel, disobedient angels, and wicked Sodom and Gomorrah. In the face of such danger Christians should not be caught off guard. The challenge is great, but so is the God who is able to keep them from stumbling.

The Greek title *Iouda,* "Of Jude," comes from the name *Ioudas* which appears in verse 1. This name, which can be translated Jude or Judas, was popular in the first century because of Judas Maccabaeus (died 160 B.C.), a leader of the Jewish resistance against Syria during the Maccabean revolt.

2. The Author of Jude. In spite of its limited subject matter and size, Jude was accepted as authentic and quoted by early church fathers. There may be some older allusions, but undisputed references to this epistle appear in the last quarter of the second century. It was included in the Muratorian Canon (c. A.D. 170) and accepted as part of Scripture by early leaders, such as Tertullian and Origen. Nevertheless, doubts arose concerning the place of Jude in the canon because of its use in the Apocrypha. It was a disputed book in some parts of the church, but it eventually won universal recognition.

The author identifies himself as "a servant of Jesus Christ, and brother of James" (v. 1). This designation, combined with the reference in verse 17 to the apostles, makes it unlikely that this is the apostle Jude, called "Judas the son of James" in Luke 6:16 and Acts 1:13. This leaves the traditional view that Jude was one of the Lord's brothers, called Judas in Matthew 13:55 and Mark 6:3 (see "The Author of James"). His older brother James (note his position on the two lists) was the famous leader of the Jerusalem church (Ac 15:13-21) and author of the epistle that bears his name. Like his brothers, Jude did not believe in Jesus before the resurrection (Jo 7:1-9; Ac 1:14). The only other biblical allusion to him is in 1 Corinthians 9:5 where it is recorded that "the brothers of the Lord" took their wives along on their missionary journeys (the Judas of Acts 15:22,32 may be another reference to him). Extrabiblical tradition adds nothing to our limited knowledge of Jude.

3. The Time of Jude. Jude's general address does not mark out any particular circle of readers, and there are no geographical restrictions. Nevertheless, he probably had in mind a specific region that was being troubled by false teachers. There is not enough information in the epistle to settle the question of whether his readers were predominately Jewish or Gentile Christians (they were probably a mixture of both). In any case, the progress of the faith in their region was threatened by a number of apostates who rejected Christ in practice and principle. These proud libertines were especially dangerous because of their deceptive flattery (v. 16) and infiltration of Christian meetings (v. 12). They perverted the grace of God (v. 4) and caused divisions in the church (v. 19).

Jude's description of these heretics is reminiscent of that found in 2 Peter and leads to the issue of the relationship between the two epistles (see "The Author of 2 Peter"). The strong similarity between 2 Peter 2:1-3:4 and Jude 4-18 can hardly be coincidental, but the equally obvious differences rule out the possibility that one is a mere copy of the other. It is also doubtful that both authors independently drew from an unknown third source, so the two remaining options are that Peter used Jude or Jude used Peter. Both views have their advocates, and a number of arguments have been raised in support of either side. But two arguments for the priority of 2 Peter are so strong that they tip the scales in favor of this position: (1) A comparison of the two books shows that 2 Peter anticipates the future rise of apostate teachers (2 Pe 2:1-2; 3:3) while Jude records the historical fulfillment of Peter's words (Jude 4,11-12, 17-18); (2) Jude directly quotes 2 Peter 3:3 and acknowledges it as a quotation from the apostles (cf. 1 Ti 4:1; 2 Ti 3:1).

Because of the silence of the New Testament and tradition concerning Jude's later years, we cannot know where this epistle was written. Nor is there any way to be certain of its date. Assuming the priority of 2 Peter (A.D. 64-66), the probable range is A.D. 66-80. (Jude's silence concerning the destruction of Jerusalem does not prove that he wrote this letter before A.D. 70.)

4. The Christ of Jude. In contrast to those who stand condemned by their licentiousness and denial of Christ (v. 4), the believer is "preserved in Jesus Christ" (v. 1). Jude tells his readers to "keep yourselves in the love of God, looking for the mercy of our Lord Jesus Christ unto eternal life" (v. 21). But at the same time, the Lord "is able to keep you from stumbling, and to present you faultless before the presence of His glory with exceeding joy" (v. 24).

5. Keys to Jude.

Key Word: Contend for the Faith—This epistle is intensely concerned with the threat of heretical teachers in the church and the believer's proper response to that threat. The contents reveal two major purposes: first, to condemn the practices of the ungodly libertines who were infesting the churches and corrupting believers; and second, to counsel the readers to stand firm, grow in their faith, and contend for the truth. Jude says little about the actual doctrines of these "raging waves of the sea," but they may have held to an antinomian version of Gnosticism (see "The Time of 1 John"). The readers are encouraged to reach out to those who have been misled by these men.

Key Verse: Jude 3—"Beloved, while I was very diligent to write to you concerning our common salvation, I found it necessary to write to you exhorting you to contend earnestly for the faith which was once for all delivered to the saints" (v. 3).

6. Survey of Jude. A surprisingly large number of the Pauline and non-Pauline epistles confront the problem of false teachers, and almost all of them allude to it. But Jude goes beyond all other New Testament epistles in its relentless and passionate denunciation of the apostate teachers who have "crept in unnoticed." With the exception of its salutation (vv. 1-2) and doxology (vv. 24-25), the entire epistle revolves around this alarming problem. Combining the theme of 2 Peter with the style of James, Jude is potent in spite of its brevity. This urgent letter has four major sections: purpose of Jude (vv. 1-4); description of false teachers (vv. 5-16); defense against false teachers (vv. 17-23); and doxology of Jude (vv. 24-25).

Purpose of Jude (vv. 1-4). Jude addresses his letter to believers who are "called," "sanctified," and "preserved," and wishes for them the threefold blessing of mercy, peace, and love (vv. 1-2). Grim news about the encroachment of false teachers in the churches has impelled Jude to put aside his commentary on salvation to write this timely word of rebuke and warning (vv. 3-4). In view of apostates who turn "the grace of our God into licentiousness" and deny Christ, it is crucial that believers "contend earnestly for the faith."

Description of False Teachers (vv. 5-16). Jude begins his extended exposé of the apostate teachers by illustrating their ultimate doom with three examples of divine judgment from the Pentateuch (vv. 5-7).

Like unreasoning animals, these apostates are ruled by the things they revile, and they are destroyed by the things they practice (vv. 8-10). Even the archangel Michael is more careful in his dealings with superhuman posers than are these arrogant men. He compares these men to three spiritually rebellious men from Genesis (Cain) and Numbers (Balaam and Korah) who incurred the condemnation of God (v. 11). Verses 12 and 13 succinctly summarize their character with five highly descriptive metaphors taken from nature. After affirming the judgment of God upon such ungodly men with a quote from the non-canonical Book of Enoch (vv. 14-15), Jude catalogs some of their practices (v. 16).

Defense Against False Teachers (vv. 17-23). This letter has been exposing apostate teachers (vv. 8,10,12,14,16), but now Jude directly addresses his readers ("but you, beloved, remember" v. 17). He reminds them of the apostolic warning that such men would come (vv. 17-19) and encourages them to protect themselves against the onslaught of apostasy (vv. 20-21). The readers must become mature in their own faith so that they will be able to rescue those who are enticed or already ensnared by error (vv. 22-23).

Doxology of Jude (vv. 24-25). Jude closes with one of the greatest doxologies in the Bible. It emphasizes the power of Christ to keep those who trust in Him from being overthrown by error.

OUTLINE OF JUDE

I. Purpose of Jude (1-4)

II. Description of False Teachers (5-16)

A. Past Judgment of False Teachers 5-7
B. Present Characteristics of False
    Teachers 8-13

C. Future Judgment of False
    Teachers 14-16

III. Defense Against False Teachers (17-23)

IV. Doxology of Jude (24-25)

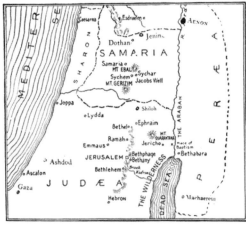

JUDEA

JU·DE′A

The Greek and Roman name for the land which was once the kingdom of Judah. Its northern boundary extended from Joppa on the Mediteranean to a point on the Jordan about ten miles north of the Dead Sea. Its southern boundary extended from about seven miles southwest of Gaza to the southern portion of the Dead Sea. The name "Judea" is first mentioned in Scripture in Ezra 5:8.

JUDGE

A civil magistrate invested with authority to hear and decide disputes. Moses originally acted as the only leader of Israel (Ex 18:13-26), and he appointed Joshua as his successor.

After the death of Joshua, the nation of Israel was ruled by judges, or heroic military deliverers, for about 300 years until the united monarchy was established under King Saul. The era of the judges was a time of instability and moral depravity, a dark period when everyone "did what was right in his own eyes" (Ju 17:6). The judges tried to rally the people against their enemies, but many of the judges were morally weak and the people often turned to idolatry. Along with the well-known judges, there were several minor judges whose battles are not recorded in the Bible: Abimelech, Tola, Jair, Ibzan, Elon, and Abdon.

When the monarchy was established, the king became the supreme judge in civil affairs (2 Sa 15:2; 1 Ki 3:9,28; 7:7). Six thousand officers and judges were appointed by David (1 Ch 23:4; 26:29).

JUDG′ES, BOOK OF

1. The Book of Judges. The Book of Judges stands in stark contrast to Joshua. In Joshua an obedient people conquered the land through trust in the power of God. In Judges, however, a disobedient and idolatrous people are defeated time and time again because of their rebellion against God.

In seven distinct cycles of sin to salvation, Judges shows how Israel had set aside God's law and in its place substituted "what was right in his own eyes" (21:25). The recurring result of abandonment of God's law is corruption from within and oppression from without. During the nearly four centuries spanned by this book, God raised up military champions to throw off the yoke of bondage and to restore the nation to pure worship. But all too soon the "sin cycle" began again as the nation's spiritual temperature grew steadily colder.

The Hebrew title is *Shophetim,* meaning "judges," "rulers," "deliverers," or "saviors." *Shophet* not only carries the idea of maintaining justice and settling disputes, but is also used to mean "liberating" and "delivering," First the judges deliver the people; then they rule and administer justice. The Septuagint used the Greek equivalent of this word, *Kritai* ("Judges"). The Latin Vulgate called it *Liber Judicum,* the "Book of Judges." This book could also appropriately be titled "The Book of Failure."

2. The Author of Judges. The author of Judges is anonymous, but Samuel or one of his prophetic students may have written it. Jewish tradition contained in the Talmud attributes Judges to Samuel, and certainly he was the crucial link between the period of the judges and the period of the kings.

It is clear from 18:31 and 20:27 that the book was written after the ark was removed from Shiloh (1 Sa 4:3-11). The repeated phrase "In those days there was no king in Israel" (17:6; 18:1; 19:1; 21:25) shows that Judges was also written after the commencement of Saul's reign but before the divided kingdom. The fact that the Jebusites were dwelling in Jerusalem "to this day" (1:21) means that it was written before 1004 B.C. when David dispossessed the Jebusites (2 Sa 5:5-9). Thus, the book was written during the time of Samuel; and it is likely that Samuel compiled this book from oral and written source material. His prophetic ministry clearly fits the moral commentary of Judges, and the consistent style and orderly scheme of Judges point to a single compiler.

Judges 18:30 contains a phrase that poses a problem to this early date of composition: "until the day of the captivity of the land." If this refers to the 722 B.C. Assyrian captivity of Israel it could have been inserted by a later editor. It is more likely a reference to the Philistine captivity of the land during the time of the judges. This event is described as "captivity" in Psalm 78:61.

3. The Time of Judges. If Judges was not written by Samuel it was at least written by one of his contemporaries between 1043 B.C. (the beginning of Saul's reign) and 1004 B.C. (David's capture of Jerusalem).

Joshua's seven-year conquest is general in nature; much of the land remained to be possessed (Jos 13:1). There were still important Canaanite strongholds to be taken by the individual tribes. Some of the nations were left to "test Israel" (Ju 3:1,4). During this time, the Egyptians maintained strong control along the coastal routes, but they were not at all interested in the hill country where Israel was primarily established.

The events covered in Judges range from about 1380 B.C. to 1045 B.C. (c. 335 years), but the period of the judges extends another thirty years since it includes the life of Samuel (1 Sa 1:1–25:1). Evidently, the rule of some of the judges overlap because not all of them ruled over the entire land. Judges describes the cycles of apostasy, oppression, and deliverance in the southern region (3:7-31), the northern region (4:1–5:31), the central region (6:1–10:5), the eastern region (10:6–12:15), and the western region (13:1–16:31). The spread of apostasy covered the whole land.

4. The Christ of Judges. Each judge is a savior and a ruler, a spiritual and political deliverer. Thus, the judges portray the role of Christ as the Savior-King of His people. The Book of Judges also illustrates the need for a righteous king.

Including 1 Samuel, seventeen judges are mentioned altogether. Some are warrior-rulers (such as Othniel and Gideon), one is a priest (Eli), and one is a prophet (Samuel). This gives a cumulative picture of the three offices of Christ, who excelled all His predecessors in that He was the ultimate Prophet, Priest, and King.

5. Keys to Judges.

Key Word: Cycles—The Book of Judges is written primarily on a thematic rather than a chronological basis (ch. 16–21 actually precede ch. 3–15). The author uses the accounts of the various judges to prove the utter failure of living out the closing verse of Judges: "Everyone did what was right in his own eyes." To accomplish this, the author uses a five-point cycle to recount the repeated spiral of disobedience, destruction, and defeat. The five parts are: (1) sin, (2) servitude, (3) supplication, (4) salvation, and (5) silence.

Key Verses: Judges 2:20-21; 21:25—"Then the anger of the LORD was hot against Israel; and He said, 'Because this nation has transgressed My covenant which I commanded their fathers, and has not heeded My voice, I also will no longer drive out before them any of the nations which Joshua left when he died' " (2:20-21).

"In those days there was no king in Israel; everyone did what was right in his own eyes" (21:25).

Key Chapter: Judges 2—The second chapter of Judges is a miniature of the whole book as it records the transition of the godly to the ungodly generation, the format of the cycles, and the purpose of God in not destroying the Canaanites.

6. Survey of Judges. Following the death of Joshua, Israel plunged into a 350 year dark age. After Joshua and the generation of the conquest passed on, "another generation arose after them who did not know the LORD nor the work which He had done for Israel" (2:10). Judges opens with a description of Israel's deterioration, continues with seven cycles of oppression and deliverance, and concludes with two illustrations of Israel's depravity.

Deterioration (1:1–3:4). Judges begins with short-lived military successes after Joshua's death, but quickly turns to the repeated failure of all the tribes to drive out their enemies. The people felt the lack of a unified central leader, but the primary reasons for their failure were a lack of faith in God and a lack of obedience to Him (2:1-3). Compromise led to conflict and chaos. Israel did not drive out the inhabitants

(1:21,27,29,30); instead of removing the moral cancer spread by the inhabitants of Canaan, they contract the disease. The Canaanite gods literally become a snare to them (2:3). Judges 1:11-23 is a microcosm of the pattern found in chapters 3–16 of Judges.

Deliverances (3:5–16:31). This section describes seven apostasies (falling away from God), seven servitudes, and seven deliverances. Each of the seven cycles has five steps: sin, servitude, supplication, salvation, and silence. These also can be described by the words *rebellion, retribution, repentance, restoration,* and *rest.* The seven cycles connect together as a descending spiral of sin (2:19). Israel vacillates between obedience and apostasy as the people continually fail to learn from their mistakes. Apostasy grows, but the rebellion is not continual. The times of rest and peace are longer than the times of bondage. The monotony of Israel's sins can be contrasted with the creativity of God's methods of deliverance.

The judges are military and civil leaders during this period of loose confederacy. Thirteen are mentioned in this book, and four more are found in 1 Samuel (Eli, Samuel, Joel, and Abijah).

Depravity (17:1–21:25). These chapters illustrate (1) religious apostasy (17–18) and (2) social and moral depravity (19–21) during the period of the judges. Chapters 19–21 contain one of the worst tales of degradation in the Bible. Judges closes with a key to understanding the period: "everyone did what was right in his own eyes" (21:25). The people are not doing what is wrong in their own eyes, but what is "evil in the sight of the LORD."

OUTLINE OF JUDGES

Part One: The Deterioration of Israel and Failure to Complete the Conquest of Canaan
(1:1–3:4)

I. The Failure of Israel to Complete the Conquest (1:1-36)

A. Failure of Judah............................ 1:1-20
B. Failure of Benjamin 1:21
C. Failure of Tribes of Joseph 1:22-29
D. Failure of Zebulun............................1:30
E. Failure of Asher........................ 1:31-32
F. Failure of Naphtali 1:33
G. Failure of Dan 1:34-36

II. The Judgment of God for Not Completing the Conquest (2:1–3:4)

A. Angel Announces Judgment 2:1-5
B. Godly Generation Dies.................. 2:6-10
C. Judgment of God Is Described................................ 2:11-19
D. Enemy Is Left as a Test 2:20–3:4

Part Two: The Deliverance of Israel During the Seven Cycles
(3:5–16:31)

I. The Southern Campaign (3:5-31)

A. The Judge Othniel 3:5-11
B. The Judge Ehud 3:12-30
C. The Judge Shamgar 3:31

II. The Northern Campaign: The Judges Deborah and Barak (4:1–5:31)

A. Deborah and Barak Are Called 4:1-11
B. Canaanites Are Defeated........... 4:12-24
C. Song of Deborah and Barak 5:1-31

III. The Central Campaign (6:1–10:5)

A. The Judge Gideon 6:1–8:32
B. The Judge Abimelech 8:33–9:57
C. The Judge Tola 10:1-2
D. The Judge Jair 10:3-5

IV. The Eastern Campaign: The Judge Jepthah (10:6–12:7)

A. Israel Sins 10:6-18
B. Salvation: Jepthah 11:1–12:7

V. The Second Northern Campaign (12:8-15)

A. The Judge Ibzan 12:8-10
B. The Judge Elon 12:11-12
C. The Judge Abdon 12:13-15

VI. The Western Campaign: The Judge Samson (13:1–16:31)

A. Miraculous Birth of Samson 13:1-25
B. Sinful Marriage of Samson 14:1-20
C. Judgeship of Samson 15:1-20
D. Failure of Samson 16:1-31

Part Three: The Depravity of Israel in Sinning Like the Canaanites (17:1–21:25)

I. The Failure of Israel Through Idolatry (17:1–18:31)

A. Example of Personal Idolatry 17:1-13
B. Example of Tribal Idolatry 18:1-31

II. The Failure of Israel Through Immorality (19:1-30)

A. Example of Personal Immorality 19:1-10

B. Example of Tribal Immorality 19:11-30

III. The Failure of Israel Through the War Between the Tribes (20:1–21:25)

A. War Between Israel and Dan 20:1-48
B. Failure of Israel After the War 21:1-25

JUDGMENT

Discerning between right and wrong; also, the punishment for wrongdoing. God is the judge of all the earth, and the only one who is able to judge perfectly. However, humans have some capacity for judging between good and evil, and God holds us accountable to use this judgment.

JU′DITH

The daughter of Beeri, the Hittite, and one of the wives of Esau (Ge 26:34). In Genesis 36:2 she is called Aholibamah.

JU′DITH, BOOK OF

One of the books of the Apocrypha, belonging to the Maccabean period, B.C. 175-135. An early example of historical fiction. See APOC-RYPHA.

JUG

An earthenware jar or pot, or a vessel made of skin for storing liquid (Ju 4:17-21)

JU′LI·A *(the feminine of Julius)*

A Christian woman at Rome (Ro 16:15).

JU′LI·US

The Centurion who took Paul as a prisoner to Rome (Ac 27:1,42-43).

JU′NI·AS, JU′NI·A

A Christian Jew at Rome, a kinsman of Paul (Ro 16:7).

JU′NI·PER

A species of shrub with scarcely any leaves (1 Ki 19:4-5; Job 30:4; Ps 120:4).

JU′PI·TER

Chief god of the Romans, corresponding to the Grecian god, Zeus (Ac 14:12-13).

JU′SHAB-HE′SED *(kindness returned)*

A son of Zerubbabel (1 Ch 3:20).

JUSTICE

The practice and maintenance of what is good and right, upholding what is just. God told His people that what He required of them was to "do justly, to love mercy, and to walk humbly with your God" (Mi 6:8). Moses taught the Israelites that it was wrong to show partiality when judging a case, and the Book of Proverbs warns against the wicked who will pervert justice by accepting bribes.

JUS′TI·FI·CA′TION

Paul's great discussion of sin and justification in Romans 5 is so crucial to Christian doctrine that it takes a great deal of time to comprehend it.

As with sanctification and faith, the doctrine of justification is made a little more difficult for users of English because roots that are the same in the original are different in English due to the dual origin of our tongue. Our words *just, justice, justify,* and *justification* are from the Latin; our words *righteous* and *righteousness* are from the Anglo-Saxon. Even though these words have different roots, they are from the same family of meaning, and they are used to translate a group of Greek words which all come from the basic root for *justice, justify, righteousness.*

Justify (dikaioo). "Justify" is used thirty-nine times in the New Testament, fifteen times in Romans and eight times in Galatians alone.

But what does "justify" mean? The popular definition "just as if I'd never sinned" is easy to remember, but not very accurate. That definition would stress forgiveness—a subtraction of sin, while justification implies something more, namely that one is just or righteous in Jesus Christ.

The big question is: Does "justify" mean "to make righteous" or "to declare righteous"? The answer of the Reformers is that *justification* means "to declare righteous." For example, in Luke 7:29, the tax collectors are said to have "justified God." Obviously, it cannot mean they made Him righteous (He already was), so it must, here at least, mean "to declare righteous." (See also 1 Timothy 3:16, where Christ is said to be "justified in the Spirit.") "Making us righteous" is properly the doctrine of sanctification (see SANCTIFICATION). In Romans 3:24, Paul writes that we are "justified freely by His grace" and in verse 28 that a person is "justified by faith." This is no contradiction—faith is the channel; grace is the source.

Not only are we justified by grace through faith, but the great apostle also tells us that "having now been justified by His blood, we shall be saved from wrath through Him" (Ro 5:9).

This declaration by God is no legal fiction. He credits Christ's perfect righteousness to our spiritual account, having put our sin on His account. This is called *imputation.*

James 2 speaks of being justified by works, and some have said that he is writing to contradict Paul. This is absurd. In the first place, nearly all scholars agree that James was written years before Romans. Actually, Paul and James are not contradictory—they simply are not talking about the same thing. Paul is writing that we cannot earn justification before God—justification comes by faith. James is writing that if our faith doesn't show in our actions, it isn't faith. Abraham and Rahab showed their faith in God by their actions. Their actions did not earn them justification, but they showed that faith was real.

Justification (dikaiosis). "Justification" is used only twice in the Greek New Testament, and both examples are in Romans. Jesus our Lord "was delivered up because of our offenses, and was raised because of our justification" (Ro 4:25). The same preposition (*dia* plus the accusative) is used in both clauses, and both are translated "because of" in the NKJV. If we take the verse as it stands, it means that Christ died for our sins (taught throughout the New Testament) and that God raised Him up because of His successful work of justifying believing sinners.

Romans 5:18 teaches that Adam's act of disobedience brought condemnation to all people and Christ's "righteous act" resulted in "justification of life."

To summarize, *to justify* in the New Testament theological sense is "to declare, to acknowledge, or to treat someone as righteous or just."

The result of justification and the One to whom credit is due for that justification are spelled out in Romans 5:1: "Therefore, having been justified by faith, we have peace with God through our Lord Jesus Christ."

JUS′ TUS *(just)*

Three New Testament men:

1. The surname of Joseph, also called Barsabas, one of two persons considered by the apostles to fill the place of Judas Iscariot (Ac 1:23).

2. A disciple at Corinth with whom Paul lodged and in whose house Paul preached (Ac 18:7).

3. A Jewish Christian, also called Jesus (Col 4:11).

JU′ TAH

Variant of JUTTAH.

JUT′ TAH

A Levitical city in the hill country of Judah (Jos 15:55; 21:16).

K

KAB

A unit of measure. Its capacity was about 1.16 quarts as a dry measure (2 Ki 6:25), or two quarts as a liquid measure. See WEIGHTS AND MEASURES.

KAB′ZEEL

A city in the south of Judah (Jos 15:21), also called Jekabzeel.

KA′DESH

See KADESH-BARNEA.

KA′DESH-BAR′NE•A *(holy, holy place of Barnea)*

An ancient town with a water supply located in the wilderness of Paran or the wilderness of Zin (Nu 13:3,26; 20:1; 27:14). It was situated on the southern border of Judah about eleven days journey north of Sinai. Abraham was here for a time (Ge 20:1). Twice the Israelites camped here. From this point Moses sent ambassadors to the king of Edom requesting permission to pass through his land (Nu 20:14,16,22; Ju 11:16-17).

KAD′MI•EL *(God's presence)*

Two Old Testament men:

1. A Levite who returned with Zerubbabel (Ez 2:40; Ne 7:43; 12:8) and was placed over the workmen in the erection of the temple (Ez 3:9).

2. A Levite who assisted in the religious instruction and devotions of the people (Ne 9:4-5; 10:9).

KAD′MO•NITES *(people of the east)*

A tribe mentioned in Genesis 15:19.

KAIN

1. The tribal name from which Kenite is derived (Nu 24:22).

2. A town in Judah. Also spelled Cain (Jos 15:57).

KA•LA′I

Variant spelling of KALLAI.

KAL•LA′I

Son of Sallai (Ne 12:20).

KA′MON

A place, the location of which is unknown. Jair, the Gileadite who judged Israel for twenty-two years, was buried here (Ju 10:5). Also spelled Camon.

KA′NAH *(place of reeds)*

1. A stream that marked, in part, the boundary between Ephraim and Manasseh (Jos 16:8; 17:9).

2. A town on the northern border of Asher (Jos 19:28).

KA•RE′AH *(bald)*

His sons, Johanan and Jonathan, came for protection to Gedaliah (2 Ki 25:23; Je 40:8). Also spelled CAREAH.

KAR′KA

Variant spelling of KARKAA.

KAR′KA•A *(ravine)*

A place in the extreme south of Judah (Jos 15:3).

KAR′KOR *(foundation)*

A place east of the Jordan (Ju 8:10).

KAR′TAH *(city)*

A town of the Levites in Zebulun (Jos 21:34).

KAR′TAN

A town of Naphtali assigned to the Gershonite Levites (Jos 21:32). In 1 Chronicles 6:76, it is called Kirjathaim.

KAT′TATH

A town of Zebulun (Jos 19:15), identified by some with Kitron (Ju 1:30).

KE′DAR

Descendants of Ishmael (Ge 25:13).

KE•DE′MAH *(eastward)*

An Ishmaelite tribe (Ge 25:15; 1 Ch 1:31).

KE′DE•MOTH *(beginnings)*

A city east of the Jordan in the territory of Reuben (De 2:26; Jos 13:18) and assigned to the Levites of the Merari branch (Jos 21:37; 1 Ch 6:79).

KE′DESH *(sanctuary)*

Three Israelite towns:

1. A town on the southern border of Judah (Jos 15:23); possibly the same as Kadesh-barnea.

2. A town of Naphtali (Jos 12:22; 19:37) and called Kedesh-naphtali (Ju 4:6). It was a city of refuge, the residence of Gershonite Levites (Jos 21:32), and the home of Barak (Ju 4:6).

3. A Levitical city of Issachar (1 Ch 6:72). In Joshua 21:28 it is called Kishon.

KEDRON
See KIDRON.

KEFR KENNA
See CANA.

KE·HE·LA′ THAH *(assembly)*
One of the encampments of the Israelites (Nu 33:22-23).

KE·I′ LAH
A town of Judah delivered from the Philistines by David (Jos 15:44; 1 Ch 4:19).

KE·I′ LAH THE GARMITE
A man of the tribe of Judah, a descendant of Hodiah (1 Ch 4:19).

KE·LAI′ AH
See KELITA.

KE·LI′ TA *(dwarf)*
A Levite who renounced his foreign wife (Ez 10:23), assisted Ezra in instructing the people (Ne 8:7), and sealed the covenant (Ne 10:10).

KE·MU′ EL *(assembly of God)*
Three Old Testament men:

1. A prince of Ephraim who assisted in the division of the land (Nu 34:24).

2. Son of Nahor and Milcah and father of Aram (Ge 22:20-21).

3. Father of Hashabiah, a Levite (1 Ch 27:17).

KE′ NAN
See CAINAN.

KE′ NATH *(possession)*
The most easterly of the ten cities of the Decapolis (Nu 32:42).

KE′ NAZ *(hunter)*
Two Old Testament men:

1. A son of Eliphaz who was the son of Esau (Ge 36:11). He was a chieftain of a tribe of Edom (Ge 36:40-43).

2. Son of Jephunneh (Jos 15:17; 1 Ch 4:15).

KE′ NEZ·ITE
See KENIZZITE.

KE′ NITE
A member of a nomadic tribe. In the time of Abraham, a branch of the tribe dwelt in Canaan (Ge 15:19); another branch in Midian (Ju 1:16; 4:11). Hobab, the brother-in-law of Moses, was a Kenite (Nu 10:29-32).

KE·NIZ′ ZITE
A member of an Edomite clan of southern Judah (Ge 15:19; Nu 32:12; Jos 14:6,14).

KENOSIS *(emptying)*
A doctrinal word used to describe one aspect of the incarnation. When Christ came down to earth to take on humanity, His pre-incarnate glory was veiled. When He became a man, He voluntarily did not use some aspects of His deity. The term "kenosis" or "emptying" comes from Philippians 2:6-7: "who, being in the form of God did not consider it robbery to be equal with God, but made Himself of no reputation (*ekenosen*, 'emptied Himself'), taking the form of a servant, and coming in the likeness of men." The concept of kenosis does not imply that Christ discarded His deity; rather He chose to be confined by the limitations of flesh in order to become a servant. He did not consider His position to be something that He needed to clutch, but was willing to humble himself. Paul urges us to imitate Christ's perfect example of loving service (Ph 2:5).

KER′ EN-HAP′ PUCH *(paint horn)*
One of Job's daughters born after his affliction (Job 42:14).

KER′ I·OTH
1. A border town in the south of Judah (Jos 15:25). It is quite possible it was the birthplace of Judas Iscariot.

2. A town of Moab (Je 48:24; Am 2:2).

KER′ I·OTH-HEZ′ RON
A place in southern Judah (Jos 15:25, Revised Version). See KERIOTH and HAZOR.

KE′ ROS *(curved)*
A Nethinim. Members of his family returned to Jerusalem (Ez 2:44; Ne 7:47).

KET′ TLE
A cooking pot (1 Sa 2:14; 2 Ch 35:13; Job 41:20).

KE·TU′ RAH *(incense)*

A wife or concubine of Abraham (Ge 25:1).

KEY

An instrument for unlatching the bolt of a lock. In biblical times a key was usually a wooden stick or bar containing a few metal pins driven in at right angles. When inserted into the lock and turned, these pins lifted a device which released the bolt (Ju 3:25). The key is used symbolically to represent authority (Is 22:22; Ma 16:19; Re 3:7; 9:1). See LOCK.

KE·ZI′ A

Variant of KEZIAH.

KE·ZI′ AH

Job's second daughter, born after his affliction (Job 42:14).

KE′ ZIZ

See EMEK-KEZIZ.

KIB′ ROTH-HAT·TA′ A·VAH *(graves of lust)*

A place between Mount Sinai and Hazeroth (Nu 11:33-35; 33:16-17; De 9:22).

KIB·ZA′ IM

One of the cities given to the Levites (Jos 21:22), called Jokmeam in 1 Chronicles 6:68.

KID

A young goat, a food considered to be a delicacy (Lk 15:29). The law forbade the cooking of the kid in the milk of its mother (Ex 23:19; Ju 13:15,19).

KI′ DRON *(dark, gloomy)*

A ravine between Jerusalem and Mount of Olives beginning a short distance northeast of the city. Passing beyond the city to the south, it follows a twisting course to the Dead Sea. During the hot season there is no water in it. It must be crossed in order to go from Jerusalem to Bethany and Jericho (2 Sa 15:23). At the south of the city, the valley was used for burying purposes (2 Ki 23:6).

KI′ NAH *(lamentation)*

A village in the extreme south of Judah (Jos 15:22).

KIDRON VALLEY

KINE (archaic)

Cattle (Ge 41:1-2).

KING

The head of a kingdom. This might include such rulers as Pharaoh (Ge 12:15), Nebuchadnezzar, and others, who exercised the chief rule over a state. There were also kings who ruled one city only (Ge 14:2; 20:2), as in the case of thirty-one kings conquered by Joshua within Palestine (Jos 12:7-24). In the time of the judges, the nations about Palestine were ruled by kings. The Israelites wanted to be more like their neighbors, and demanded that a monarchy be established. This, however, did not abolish the theocracy. The king was required to be the vicegerent of Jehovah who was the divine sovereign of Israel.

Kings came to the throne in several ways. Both Saul and David were anointed by Samuel, acting under the direction of God (1 Sa 10:1; 16:1,13). After the first kings were set up, many generations of kings came to the throne by inheritance (1 Ki 9:36). In the Northern Kingdom, the dynasties were often interrupted by usurpation (1 Ki 15:27-28). During the days of Babylonian domination, the king was chosen by Babylon (2 Ki 24:17).

The ultimate King is God (Ps 10:16); the King of kings (1 Ti 6:15). In Revelation 19:16, Christ is called the "King of kings and Lord of lords."

KINGDOM OF GOD

The kingdom of God refers to God's rule of grace in the world, a period foretold by the prophets of the Old Testament and identified by Jesus as beginning with His ministry.

A conquered and downtrodden Israel looked forward to the day when God, the King, would display His power and establish His kingdom of peace and righteousness (Ze 9:9; Is 24:23). His deliverance was often associated with the coming of a Davidic king (Is 9:7).

In many striking ways, Jesus proclaimed that He was the fulfillment of the Old Testament expectations of God's deliverance (Lk 4:17-21). One way He expressed this idea was by the phrase, "the kingdom of God." To Nicodemus He declared, "Unless one is born again, he cannot see the kingdom of God" (Jo 3:3). He made it clear to others that the kingdom was already present in His ministry (Ma 12:28). He compared Himself to a sower scattering seed in a field, with the good seed taking root and growing among "the sons of the kingdom" (Ma 13:38).

Jesus also declared that a day was coming when the kingdom of God would be manifested in a different way, not yet seen, and that its coming would be soon (Ma 16:28). He explained that the kingdom was present in an unexpected form, like a hidden treasure (Ma 13:44). Although the Gospels focus on the present aspect of the kingdom, it is also clear that the kingdom will be realized perfectly only at the second coming of Christ.

In its spiritual nature, the kingdom of God is the salvation of His people, and the kingdom is His gift. It is also a gift of forgiveness of sin. Those who are forgiven must also forgive others (Ma 18:35). Participation in the new reality of the kingdom involves the follower of Jesus in a call to the highest righteousness (Ma 5:20).

KINGS, FIRST AND SECOND BOOKS OF

1. The Books of Kings. The first half of 1 Kings traces the life of Solomon. Under his leadership, Israel rose to the peak of her size and glory. Solomon's great accomplishments, including the unsurpassed splendor of the temple which he constructed in Jerusalem, brought him worldwide fame and respect. However, Solomon's zeal for God diminished in his later years, as pagan wives turned his heart away from worship in the temple of God. As a result, the king with the divided heart left behind a divided kingdom. The Book of 1 Kings traces the twin histories over the next century of two sets of kings and two nations of disobedient people who are growing indifferent to God's prophets and precepts.

The Book of 2 Kings continues the drama begun in 1 Kings—the tragic history of two nations on a collision course with captivity. The author systematically traces the reigning monarchs of Israel and Judah, first by carrying one nation's history forward, then retracing the same period for the other nation.

Nineteen consecutive evil kings ruled in Israel, leading to the captivity by Assyria. The picture was somewhat brighter in Judah, where godly kings occasionally emerged to reform the evils of their predecessors. In the end, however, sin outweighed righteousness and Judah was marched off to Babylon.

Like the two books of Samuel, the two books of Kings were originally one in the Hebrew Bible. The original title was *Melechim,* "Kings," taken from the first word in 1:1, *Vehamelech,* "Now King..." The Septuagint artificially divided Kings into two books, right in the middle of the story of Ahaziah. It called the books of Samuel "First and Second Kingdoms" and the books of Kings "Third and Fourth Kingdoms." The Septuagint may have divided Samuel, Kings, and Chronicles into two books each because the Greek required a greater amount of scroll space than did the Hebrew. The Latin title for these books is *Liber Regum Tertius et Quartus,* "Third and Fourth Book of Kings."

2. The Author of Kings. The author of 1 and 2 Kings is unknown, but evidence supports the Talmudic tradition that Kings was written by the prophet Jeremiah. The author was clearly a prophet/historian as seen in the prophetic exposé of apostasy. Both 1 and 2 Kings emphasize God's righteous judgment on idolatry and immorality. The style of these books is also similar to that found in Jeremiah. The phrase "to this day" in 1 Kings 8:8 and 12:19 indicates a time of authorship prior to the Babylonian captivity (586 B.C.). It has been observed that the omission of Jeremiah's ministry in the account of King Josiah and his successors may indicate that Jeremiah himself was the recorder of the events. However, the last two chapters of 2 Kings were evidently written after the captivity, probably by a Jewish captive in Babylon. Jeremiah was forced to flee to Egypt (Je 43:1-8), not to Babylon. It is interesting to note that 2 Kings 24:18–25:30 is almost the same as Jeremiah 52.

Evidently, the majority of 1 and 2 Kings was written before 586 B.C. by a compiler who had access to several historical documents. Some of these are mentioned: "the book of the acts of Solomon" (11:41), "the book of the chronicles of the kings of Israel" (14:19), and "the book of the chronicles of the kings of Judah" (14:29; 15:7). These books may have been a part of the official court records (see 2 Ki 18:18). In addition, Isaiah 36–39 was probably used as a source (2 Ki 18-20).

3. The Time of Kings. The Book of Kings was written to the remaining kingdom of Judah before and after its Babylonian exile. The majority was compiled by a contemporary of Jeremiah, if not by Jeremiah himself (c. 646-570 B.C.). It is a record of disobedience, idolatry, and ungodliness which serves as an explanation for the Assyrian captivity of Israel (722 B.C.) and the Babylonian captivity of Judah (586 B.C.). First Kings covers the 120 years from the beginning of Solomon's reign in 971 B.C. through Ahaziah's reign ending in 851 B.C. The key date is 931 B.C., the year the kingdom was divided into the northern nation of Israel and the southern nation of Judah.

The last recorded event in 2 Kings is the release of Jehoiachin (25:27-30), which takes place in 560 B.C. Most of 1 and 2 Kings probably was written just prior to 586 B.C., but chapters 24 and 25 were written after Jehoiachin's release, perhaps about 550 B.C.

Chapters 1–17 cover the 131 years from 853 B.C. (King Ahaziah of Israel) to 722 B.C. (the Assyrian captivity of Israel). Chapters 18–25 cover the 155 years from the beginning of Hezekiah's reign in 715 B.C. to the release of Jehoiachin in Babylon in 560 B.C. The united kingdom lasted for 112 years (1043-931 B.C.), the Northern Kingdom of Israel existed for another 209 years (931-722 B.C.) During this 457-year kingdom period, there were great shifts of world power. Egyptian and Assyrian control over Palestine fluctuated; Assyria rose to preeminence, declined, and was finally conquered by Babylon.

The books of Kings show that judgment came to the kingdoms of Israel and Judah because of their idolatry, immorality, and disunity. Judah lasted 136 years longer than Israel (722-586 B.C.) because of the relative goodness of eight of its twenty kings. Israel never broke away from Jeroboam's idolatrous calf worship, but Judah experienced some periods of revival in the worship of Yahweh. During these years, God sent many of His prophets. Elijah, Elisha, Amos, and Hosea were in the Northern Kingdom, while in the Southern Kingdom Obadiah, Joel, Isaiah, Micah, Nahum, Zephaniah, Jeremiah and Habakkuk were prophesying.

4. The Christ of Kings. Solomon typifies Christ in a number of ways. His fabled wisdom points ahead to "Christ Jesus, who became for us wisdom from God" (1 Co 1:30). Solomon's fame, glory, wealth, and honor foreshadow Christ in His kingdom. Solomon's rulership brings knowledge, peace and worship. However, despite Solomon's splendor, the Son of Man later says of His coming, "indeed a greater than Solomon is here" (Ma 12:42).

Unlike the nine different dynasties in the Northern Kingdom, the kings of Judah reigned as one continuous dynasty. In spite of Queen Athaliah's attempt to destroy the house of David, God remained faithful to His covenant with David (2 Sa 7) by preserving his lineage. Jesus the Messiah is the direct descendant of David.

5. Keys to Kings.

1 Kings: *Key Word: Division of the Kingdom*—The theme of 1 Kings centers around the fact that the welfare of Israel and Judah depends upon the faithfulness of the people and their king to the covenant. Historically, it was written to give an account of the reigns of the kings from Solomon to Jehoshaphat (Judah) and Ahaziah (Israel). The two books of Kings as a whole trace the monarchy from the point of its greatest prosperity under Solomon to its demise and destruction in the Assyrian and Babylonian captivities.

Theologically, 1 Kings provides a prophetically oriented evaluation of the spiritual and moral causes that led to the political and economic demise of the two kingdoms. The material is too selective to be considered a biography of the kings. For example, Omri was one of Israel's most important rulers from a political point of view, but because of his moral corruption, his achievements are dismissed in a mere eight verses. The lives of these kings are used to teach that observance of God's law produces blessing, but apostasy is rewarded by judgment.

Key Verses: 1 Kings 9:4-5; 11:11—"Now if you walk before Me as your father David walked, in integrity of heart and in uprightness, to do according to all that I have commanded you, and if you keep My statutes and my judgments, then I will establish the throne of your kingdom over Israel forever, as I promised David your father, saying, 'You shall not fail to have a man on the throne of Israel'" (9:4-5).

"Therefore the LORD said to Solomon, 'Because you have done this, and have not kept My covenant and My statutes, which I have commanded you, I will surely tear the kingdom away from you and give it to your servant'" (11:11).

Key Chapter: 1 Kings 12—The critical turning point in 1 Kings occurs in chapter 12 when the united kingdom became the divided kingdom. Solomon died, and his son Rehoboam became king. Rehoboam unwisely led the nation into civil war, which tragically ripped Israel into two separate and at times conflicting nations. Instead of unity, 1 Kings records the history of the two kings, two capitals, and two religions.

2 Kings: *Key Word: Captivities of the Kingdom*—Second Kings records both the destruction and captivity of Israel by the Assyrians (2 Ki 17), and the destruction and captivity of Judah by the Babylonians (2 Ki 25).

The book was written selectively, not exhaustively, from a prophetic viewpoint to teach that the decline and collapse of the two kingdoms occurred because of failure on the part of the rulers and people to heed the warnings of God's messengers. The spiritual climate of the nation determined its political and economic conditions.

The prophets of Jehovah play a prominent role in 1 and 2 Kings as God used them to remind the kings of their covenant responsibilities as His administrators. When the king keeps the covenant, he and the nation are richly blessed. But judgment consistently falls upon those who refuse to obey God's law. God is seen in Kings as the controller of history who reveals His plan and purpose to His people. Unhappily, the people were concerned more with their own plans, and their rejection of God's rule led to exile at the hands of the Assyrians and Babylonians.

Key Verses: 2 Kings 17:22-23; 23:27—"For the children of Israel walked in all the sins of Jeroboam which he did; they did not depart from them, until the LORD removed Israel out of His sight, as He had said by all His servants the prophets. So Israel was carried away from their own land to Assyria, as it is to this day" (17:22-23).

"And the LORD said, 'I will also remove Judah from My sight, as I have removed Israel, and will cast off this city Jerusalem which I have chosen, and the house of which I said, "My name shall be there"'" (23:27).

Key Chapter: 2 Kings 25—The last chapter of 2 Kings records the utter destruction of the city of Jerusalem and its glorious temple. Only the poor of Israel are left, and even some of them flee for their lives to Egypt. Hope is still alive, however, with the remnant in the Babylonian captivity as Evil-merodach frees Jehoiachin from prison and treats him kindly.

6. Survey of 1 Kings. The first half of 1 Kings concerns the life of one of the most amazing men who ever lived. More than any man before or since, he knew how to amass and creatively use great wealth. With the sole exception of Jesus Christ, Solomon is the wisest man in human history. He brought Israel to the peak of its size and glory, and yet, the kingdom was disrupted soon after his death, torn in two by civil strife. This book divides clearly into two sections: the united kingdom (1–11) and the divided kingdom (12–22).

United Kingdom (1–11). These chapters give an account of Solomon's attainment of the throne, wisdom, architectural achievements, fame, wealth, and tragic unfaithfulness. Solomon's half brother, Adonijah, attempted to take the throne as David's death was nearing, but Nathan the prophet alerted David who quickly directed the coronation of Solomon as coregent (ch.1). Solomon still had to consolidate his power and deal with those who opposed his rule. Only when this was done was the kingdom "established in the hand of Solomon" (2:46). Solomon's ungodly marriages (3:1) eventually turned his heart from the Lord, but he began well with a genuine love for Yahweh and a desire for wisdom. This wisdom led to the expansion of Israel to the zenith of her power. Solomon's empire stretched from the border of Egypt to the border of Babylonia, and peace prevailed.

From a theocratic perspective, Solomon's greatest achievement was the building of the temple. The ark was placed in this exquisite building, which was filled with the glory of God. Solomon offered a magnificent prayer of dedication and bound the people with an oath to remain faithful to Yahweh.

Because the Lord was with him, Solomon continued to grow in fame, power and wealth. However, his wealth later became a source of trouble when he began to purchase forbidden items. He acquired many foreign wives who led him into idolatry. It is an irony of history that this wisest of men acted as a fool in his old age. God pronounced judgment and foretold that Solomon's son would rule only a fraction of the kingdom (Judah).

Divided Kingdom (12–22). Upon Solomon's death, God's words came to pass. Solomon's son Rehoboam chose the foolish course of promising more severe taxation. Jeroboam, an officer in Solomon's army, led the ten northern tribes in revolt. They made him their king, leaving only Judah and Benjamin in the South under Rehoboam. This was the beginning of a chaotic period with two nations and two sets of kings. Continual enmity and strife existed between the Northern and Southern Kingdoms. The North was plagued by apostasy (Jeroboam set up a false system of worship) and the South by idolatry. Of all the northern and southern kings listed in this book, only Asa (15:9-24) and Jehoshaphat (22:41-50) did "what was right in the eyes of the LORD" (15:11; 22:43). All of the others were idolaters, usurpers, and murderers.

Ahab brought a measure of cooperation between the Northern and Southern Kingdoms, but he reached new depths of wickedness as a king. He was the man who introduced Jezebel's Baal worship to Israel. The prophet Elijah ministered during this low period in Israel's history, providing a ray of light and witness of the word and power of God. But Ahab's encounters with Elijah never brought him to turn from his false gods to God. Ahab's treachery in the matter of Naboth's vineyard caused a prophetic rebuke from Elijah (21). Ahab repented (21:27-29) but later died in battle because of his refusal to heed the words of Micaiah, another prophet of God.

OUTLINE OF 1 KINGS

Part One: The United Kingdom (1:1–11:43)

I. The Establishment of Solomon as King (1:1–2:46)

A. Appointment of Solomon as King ... 1:1-53
B. Solidification of Solomon as King 2:1-46

II. The Rise of Solomon as King (3:1–8:66)

A. Solomon's Request for Wisdom 3:1-28
B. Solomon's Administration of Israel 4:1-34

C. The Temple and Solomon's House Are Constructed......................... 5:1–8:66

III. The Decline of Solomon as King (9:1–11:43)

A. Reiteration of the Davidic Covenant 9:1-9
B. Disobedience of Solomon to the Covenant 9:10–11:8
C. Chastening of Solomon for Breaking the Covenant 11:9-40
D. Death of Solomon 11:41-43

Part Two: The Divided Kingdom (12:1–22:53)

I. The Division of the Kingdom (12:1–14:31)

A. Cause of the Division 12:1-24
B. Reign of Jeroboam in Israel ... 12:25–14:20
C. Reign of Rehoboam in Judah 14:21-31

II. The Reigns of Two Kings in Judah (15:1-24)

A. Reign of Abijam in Judah 15:1-8
B. Reign of Asa in Judah 15:9-24

III. The Reigns of Five Kings in Israel (15:25–16:28)

A. Reign of Nadab in Israel 15:25-31
B. Reign of Baasha in Israel 15:32–16:7

C. Reign of Elah in Israel............... 16:8-14
D. Reign of Zimri in Israel 16:15-20
E. Reign of Omri in Israel 16:21-28

IV. The Reign of Ahab in Israel (16:29–22:40)

A. Sin of Ahab............................ 16:29-34
B. The Ministry of Elijah 17:1–19:21
C. Wars with Syria 20:1-43
D. Murder of Naboth 21:1-16
E. Death of Ahab 21:17–22:40

V. The Reign of Jehoshaphat in Judah (22:41-50)

VI. The Reign of Ahaziah in Israel (22:51-53)

7. Survey of 2 Kings. Without interruption 2 Kings continues the narrative of 1 Kings. The twin kingdoms of Israel and Judah pursue a collision course with captivity as the glory of the once united kingdom becomes increasingly diminished. Division has led to decline and now ends in double deportation with Israel captured by Assyria and Judah by Babylon. This book traces the history of the divided kingdom in chapters 1–17 and the history of the surviving kingdom in chapters 18–25.

Divided Kingdom (1–17). These chapters record the story of Israel's corruption in a relentless succession of bad kings from Ahaziah to Hoshea. The situation in Judah during this time (Jehoram to Ahaz) was somewhat better, but far from ideal. This dark period in the Northern Kingdom of Israel was interrupted only by the ministries of such godly prophets as Elijah and Elisha. At the end of Elijah's miraculous ministry, Elisha was installed and authenticated as his successor. He was a force for righteousness in a nation that never served the true God or worshipped at the temple in Jerusalem. Elisha's ministry was characterized by miraculous provisions of sustenance and life. Through him God demonstrated His gracious care for the nation and His concern for any person who desires to come to Him. However, like his forerunner Elijah, Elisha was basically rejected by Israel's leadership.

Elisha instructed one of his prophetic assistants to anoint Jehu king over Israel. Jehu fulfilled the prophecies concerning Ahab's descendants by putting them to death. He killed Ahab's wife Jezebel, his sons, and also the priests of Baal. But he did not depart from the calf worship originally set up by Jeroboam. The loss of the house of Ahab meant the alienation of Israel and Judah and the weakening of both. Israel's enemies began to get the upper hand. Meanwhile, in Judah, Jezebel's daughter Athaliah killed all the descendants of David, except for Joash, and usurped the throne. However, Jehoida the priest eventually removed her from the throne and placed Joash in power. Joash restored the temple and served God.

Syria gained virtual control over Israel, but there was no response to God's chastisement; the kings and people refused to repent. There was a period of restoration under Jeroboam II, but the continuing series of wicked kings in Israel led to its overthrow by Assyria.

Surviving Kingdom (18–25). Of Israel's nineteen kings, not one was righteous in God's sight. All but one of its nine dynasties were created by murdering the previous king. In Judah, where there was only one dynasty, eight of its twenty rulers did what was right before God. Nevertheless, Judah's collapse finally came, resulting in the Babylonian exile. Chapters 18–25 read more easily than chapters 1–17 because alternating the histories of the Northern and Southern Kingdoms is no longer necessary. Only Judah remained.

Six years before the overthrow of Israel's capital of Samaria, Hezekiah became king of Judah. Because of his exemplary faith and reforms, God spared Jerusalem from Assyria and brought a measure of prosperity to Judah. However, Hezekiah's son Manasseh was so idolatrous that his long reign led to the downfall of Judah. Even Josiah's later reforms could not stem the tide of evil, and the four kings who succeeded him were exceedingly wicked. Judgment came with three deportations to Babylon. The third occurred in 586 B.C. when Nebuchadnezzar destroyed Jerusalem and the temple. Still, the book ends on a note of hope with God preserving a remnant for Himself.

OUTLINE OF 2 KINGS

Part One: The Divided Kingdom (1:1–17:41)

I. The Reign of Ahaziah in Israel (1 Ki 22:51–2 Ki 1:18)

A. Spiritual Evaluation of Ahaziah .... 1 Ki 22:51-53

B. Political Situation Under Ahaziah 1:1

C. Death of Ahaziah 1:2-18

II. The Reign of Jehoram in Israel (2:1–8:15)

A. Transition from Elijah to Elisha 2:1-25

B. Spiritual Evaluation of Jehoram ... 3:1-3

C. Political Situation Under Jehoram ... 3:4-27

D. Ministry of Elisha 4:1–8:15

III. The Reign of Amon in Judah (21:19-26)

IV. The Reign of Josiah in Judah (22:1–23:30)

A. Spiritual Evaluation of Josiah 22:1-2
B. Renewal of the Covenant by Josiah 22:3–23:27
C. Political Situation under Josiah...23:28-29
D. Death of Josiah 23:30

V. The Reign of Jehoahaz in Judah (23:31-34)

VI. The Reign of Jehoiakim in Judah (23:35–24:7)

VII. The Reign of Jehoiachin in Judah (24:8-16)

VIII. The Reign of Zedekiah in Judah (24:17–25:21)

A. Spiritual Evaluation of Zedekiah 24:17-19
B. Political Situation under Zedekiah 24:20–25:21

IX. The Governorship of Gedaliah (25:22-26)

X. The Release of Jehoiachin in Babylon (25:27-30)

KIR *(fortress)*

The place is not certainly identified. Tiglath-pileser took the people of Damascus here as captives (2 Ki 16:9; Am 1:3-5; 9:7).

KIR-HAR'A·SETH

The chief city of Moab (2 Ki 3:25; Is 16:7,11; Je 48:31,36).

KIR-HAR'ESH

Variant spelling of KIR-HERES.

KIR-HE'RES

Variant spelling of KIR-HARESH.

KIR'I·ATH

Variant spelling of KIRJATH.

KIR·I·A·THA'IM *(twin cities)*

1. An ancient town east of the Jordan, a city of the Emim conquered by the Moabites (Ge 14:5).
2. A city of Naphtali (1 Ch 6:76).

KIR'I·ATH-AR'BA

Variant spelling of KIRJATH-ARBA.

KIR'I·ATH-BA'AL *(city of Baal)*

See KIRJATH-JEARIM.

KIR'I·ATH-HU'ZOTH

Variant spelling of KIRJATH-HUZOTH.

KIR'I·ATH-JE'A·RIM

Variant spelling of KIRJATH-JEARIM.

KIR'I·ATH-SAN'NAH

See DEBIR.

KIR'I·ATH-SE'PHER

See DEBIR.

KIR'I·OTH

See KERIOTH.

KIR'JATH *(city)*

A town of Benjamin (Jos 18:28). The identification of Kirjath-jearim is disputed.

KIR'JATH-AR'BA *(city of Arba)*

An ancient name for Hebron (Ge 23:2; Jos 14:15; 20:7; Ju 1:10; Ne 11:25).

KIR'JATH-HU'ZOTH *(city of streets)*

A town of Moab near Bamoth-baal (Nu 22:39).

KIR'JATH-JE'A·RIM *(city of forests)*

A town of the Gibeonites (Jos 9:17) on the boundary line between Judah and Benjamin (Jos 15:9; 18:14-15). It fell to Judah (Jos 15:48,60; Ju 18:12). It was here the ark remained twenty years after the Philistines sent it back to the Israelites (1 Sa 6:19–7:2). It was also called Kirjath-baal (Jos 15:60; 18:14) and Baalah (Jos 15:9, 11).

KIR'JATH-SAN'NAH

See DEBIR.

KIR'JATH-SE'PHER

See DEBIR.

KIR OF MO′AB

This city and Ar were the two fortified cities of Moab (Is 15:1). It is believed to be the same as Kir-hareseth (2 Ki 3:25; Is 16:7,11; Je 48:31, 36).

KISH

Five Old Testament men:

1. A son of Jeiel and Maachah. He was a Benjamite who lived in Jerusalem (1 Ch 8:30; 9:35-36).

2. Father of King Saul of Benjamin, and a descendant of Abiel (1 Sa 9:1; 10:11,21; 14:51). He sent his son, Saul, after the straying asses (1 Sa 9:3).

3. Son of Mahli, a Levite; he lived at the time of David (1 Ch 23:21-22; 24:29).

4. A Levite, son of Abdi, of the Merari family. He aided Hezekiah in his work for religious reform (2 Ch 29:12).

5. An ancestor of Mordecai; a Benjamite (Es 2:5).

KISH′I

See KUSHAIAH.

KISH′I·ON *(hardness)*

A town of Issachar, a Gershonite Levitical city (Jos 21:28). The town of Kedesh in 1 Chronicles 6:72 is probably the same place. Also called Kishon (KJV).

KI′SHON *(bending, tortuous)*

A river of Palestine, next to the Jordan in importance. It rises between Mounts Gilboa and Tabor and empties into the Mediterranean (Ju 5:19-21; 1 Ki 18:40; Ps 83:9).

KI′SON

Variant of KISHON.

KISS

In patriarchal times and later, a kiss was a common form of salutation. Children were kissed by their parents (Ge 31:28,55; 48:10), children kissed parents (Ge 27:26-27; 1 Ki 19:20), and brothers kissed each other (Ge 45:15; Ex 4:27), as did other relatives (Ge 29:11; Ru 1:9). Between friends of the same sex it was the usual form of greeting (1 Sa 20:41; Ac 20:37). When a guest entered a house, it was customary for the one receiving to kiss the guest (Lk 7:45). Paul's in-

junction was to greet each other with a holy kiss (Ro 16:16; 2 Co 13:12). There was nothing unusual about Judas kissing Jesus (Ps 2:12; Ma 26:49; Lk 22:47-48); this was a common way to greet a friend.

KITE

A bird of the falcon family (Le 11:14).

KITH′LISH

A town in the valley of Judah (Jos 15:40).

KIT′RON

A town in Zebulun (Ju 1:30).

KIT′TIM

Islands west of Palestine, particularly the island of Cyprus (Ge 10:4; 1 Ch 1:7; Is 23:1-12; Eze 27:6).

KNEAD

The working of dough into a mass with the hands. The work was done by women. The Egyptians used their feet also. (Ex 12:34).

KNEADING TROUGH

Kneading bowl. A shallow dish, probably made most often of wood or earthenware, used for kneading bread dough. At the exodus, the people left in such a hurry that there was no time to let the bread rise, and they took their bread unleavened, with the kneading troughs already packed (12:34).

KNIFE

Prior to the introduction of iron and steel the Egyptians used sharpened stone and flint to make knives. They were used for killing animals either for food or for sacrificial purposes (Ge 22:6; Le 8:20; Ju 19:29). Ancient peoples also honed their knives to a sharp edge, to use as a razor for shaving one's head or beard (Nu 6:5,9,19; Eze 5:1). Curved knives were used as pruning hooks (Is 18:5).

KITE

KNOP

A decorative knob or knot; a protuberant ornament.

1. The rendering of the Hebrew word *kaphtor* designating the ball-shaped ornaments on the branches of the golden candlesticks (Ex 25:33-36; 37:17-22).

2. The translation of another Hebrew word denoting the carvings with which the interior of the temple was decorated. The ornaments were cut in cedar (1 Ki 6:18; 7:24).

KO'A

Apparently a people from east of the Tigris River (Eze 23:23).

KO'HATH *(assembly)*

A son of Levi and head of the Kohathite family (Ge 46:11; Ex 6:16,18).

KO'HATH·ITES

Descendants of Kohath, son of Levi (Ex 6:20).

KO·LAI'AH *(voice of Jehovah)*

Two Old Testament men:
1. Father of Ahab, the false prophet (Je 29:21).
2. A Benjamite (Ne 11:7).

KOR'AH *(ice)*

Four Old Testament men:
1. A son of Esau. His mother was Aholibamah (Ge 36:5,14).
2. A son of Eliphaz and grandson of Esau (Ge 36:16).
3. A Levite of the family of Kohath, of the house of Izhar (Nu 16:1). He, with Abiram, Dathan, and On, conspired against Moses and Aaron. Moses ordered the people to leave the locality where Korah, Dathan, and Abiram had their tents. At that spot the earth opened and swallowed the conspirators (Nu 16; 26:10). Fire then destroyed those that offered incense (Nu 16:35).
4. Son of Hebron of the family of Caleb (1 Ch 2:43).

KOR'A·HITE

A descendant of the Korah. Samuel was a Korahite (1 Sa 1:1; 1 Ch 6:26), also the singer Heman (1 Ch 6:33-38; 9:31-32).

KOR'A·THITE

See KORAHITE.

KOR'E (a partridge)

Two Old Testament men:
1. A Levite (1 Ch 9:19; 26:1), father of two of the gatekeepers of the tabernacle.
2. Son of Immah, a Levite (2 Ch 31:14), who kept the East Gate of the temple.

KOR'HITE

See KORAHITE.

KOZ *(thorn)*

See HAKKOZ, (Ez 2:61; Ne 3:4).

KU·SHA'IAH

A Levite of the Merarite family of the house of Mushi (1 Ch 15:17). His son was Ethan who was appointed the assistant of Heman by David. In 1 Chronicles 6:44 he is called Kishi.

L

LA'A·DAH

Son of Shelah of Judah and founder of Mareshah (1 Ch 4:21).

LA'A·DAN *(order)*

Two Old Testament men:
1. An Ephramite, son of Tahan (1 Ch 7:26).
2. A son of Gershom (1 Ch 23:7-9; 26:21).

LA'BAN *(white)*

1. Son of Bethuel and grandson of Nahor, the brother of Abraham. He lived at Haran in Padan-aram (Ge 24:10,15; 28:5,10). Jacob stayed with him after fleeing the fury of Esau. Eventually Jacob married his two daughters, Leah and Rachel (Ge 29:16-28). On Mount Gilead Laban made a covenant with Jacob (Ge 29-31).
2. A place in the Sinaitic peninsula (De 1:1), thought by some to be the same as Libnah (Nu 33:20).

LABORERS IN THE VINEYARD, PARABLE OF

(Ma 20:1-16).

LACE

A cord used to bind something together (Ex 28:28; Nu 15:38; Ju 16:9).

LA' CHISH *(impregnable)*

A city in the lowland of Judah (Jos 15:33,39) which was taken by Joshua (Jos 10:3-35; 12:11). Amaziah, king of Judah, fled to this city and was slain by conspirators (2 Ki 14:19; 2 Ch 25:27). It was besieged by Sennacherib (2 Ki 18:14,17) and by Nebuchadnezzar (Je 34:7). Excavations have restored the wall of the ancient city and other things that belong to the period of Judah from Rehoboam to Manasseh.

LA' DAN

Variant of LAADAN.

LADE (archaic)

To burden; to load (Lk 11:46).

LADLE

Long handled spoons or dippers. The ladles Solomon had made for the temple were pure gold (1 Ki 7:50; 2 Ch 4:22). When Nebuchadnezzar took Judah captive, these articles were among the treasures taken from the temple (2 Ki 25:14; Je 52:18-19).

LA' EL *(devoted to God)*

Father of Eliasaph of the family of Gershom (Nu 3:24).

LA' HAD *(oppression)*

Son of Jahath of Judah (1 Ch 4:2).

LA' HAI-ROI

See BEER-LAHAI-ROI.

LAH·MAS

A village in the plain of Judah (Jos 15:40).

LAH' MI

The brother of Goliath who was slain by Elhanan (1 Ch 20:5).

LA' ISH *(a lion)*

1. A city in the north of Palestine, also called Leshem. When the land was divided, this city was given to the tribe of Dan, and they renamed the city after their progenitor, Dan (Jos 19:47; Ju 18:7-29).

2. The father of Paltiel, to whom Saul gave David's wife, Michal (1 Sa 25:44; 2 Sa 3:15).

3. A city of Benjamin near Anathoth (Is 10:30); sometimes called Laishah (NRSV).

LA' I·SHAH

See LAISH.

LAKE OF GENNESARET

See GALILEE, SEA OF.

LAK' KUM *(obstruction)*

A town of Naphtali (Jos 19:33).

LA' KUM

See LAKKUM.

LAMA

The Hebrew word for "why." On the cross, Jesus quoted Psalm 22:1, *"Eloi, Eloi, lama sabachthani,"* "My God, My God, why have You forsaken me?" (Ma 27:46; Mk 15:34).

LAMB

Lambs were used both as food and as sacrificial offerings. A lamb was used as a burnt offering every morning and evening. Four were used on the Sabbath (Nu 28:3-4,9). Seven lambs were offered on the first of the month and lambs were also sacrificed on the Day of Atonement and on all high feast days (Nu 28:11,19,27; 29:2,8,13). Sacrificial lambs were generally male, and without blemish (Ex 12:5). The gentleness of the lamb has caused it to become a symbol of innocence and uncomplaining submissiveness. Christ is called the Lamb of God (Jo 1:29,36), also the Lamb (Re 5:6,8).

LAME

Crippled in the limbs, unable to walk properly. A lame man was not allowed to serve as priest before the Lord (Le 21:17-21). While on earth, Jesus healed the lame on several occasions (Ma 11:5; Lk 7:22), and after His ascension Peter and John healed the lame man who sat begging at the temple gate (Ac 3:1-11).

LA' MECH *(vigorous)*

Two antediluvian men:

1. Son of Methusael of the line of Cain. His wives were Adah and Zillah. He was father of Jabal, Jubal, and Tubal-cain (Ge 4:18-24).

2. Son of Methuselah and father of Noah of the line of Seth (Ge 5:25,28-31).

LAMED

The twelfth letter of the Hebrew alphabet. It is the heading of verses 89-96 of Psalm 119. In Hebrew each of these eight verses began with the letter lamed. See ACROSTIC.

LAMENT

A song or psalm of mourning. The longest lament in the Bible is Jeremiah's book of Lamentations, where he mourns the sin and downfall of Israel.

LAMENTATIONS, BOOK OF

1. The Book of Lamentations. Lamentations describes the funeral of a city. It is a tear-stained portrait of the once proud Jerusalem, now reduced to rubble by the invading Babylonian hordes. In a five-poem dirge, Jeremiah exposes his emotions. A death has occurred; Jerusalem lies barren.

Jeremiah writes his lament in acrostic or alphabetical fashion. Beginning each chapter with the first letter *A* (aleph) he progresses verse by verse through the Hebrew alphabet. And then, in the midst of this terrible holocaust, Jeremiah triumphantly cried out, "Great is Your faithfulness" (3:23). In the face of death and destruction, with life seemingly coming apart, Jeremiah turned tragedy into a triumph of faith. God had never failed him in the past. God promised to remain faithful in the future. In the light of the God he knew and loved, Jeremiah found hope and comfort.

The Hebrew title of this book comes from the first word of chapters 1, 2, and 4: *Ekah,* "Ah, how!" Another Hebrew word *Ginoth* ("Elegies" or "Lamentations") has also been used as the title because it better represents the contents of the book. The Greek title *Threnoi* means "Dirges" or "Laments," and the Latin title *Threni* ("Tears" or "Lamentations") was derived from this word. The subtitle in Jerome's Vulgate reads: *"Id est lamentationes Jeremiae prophetae,"* and this became the basis for the English title "The Lamentations of Jeremiah."

2. The Author of Lamentations. The author of Lamentations is unnamed in the book, but internal and external evidence is consistently in favor of Jeremiah.

External Evidence. The universal consensus of early Jewish and Christian tradition attributes this book to Jeremiah. The superscription to La-

mentations in the Septuagint says: "And it came to pass, after Israel had been carried away captive, and Jerusalem had become desolate, that Jeremiah sat weeping, and lamented with this lamentation over Jerusalem, saying . . ." This is also the position of the Talmud, the Aramaic Targum of Jonathan, and early Christian writers such as Origen and Jerome. In addition, 2 Chronicles 35:25 says that "Jeremiah also lamented for Josiah." This was an earlier occasion, but Jeremiah was obviously familiar with the lament form.

Internal Evidence: The scenes in this graphic book were clearly portrayed by an eyewitness to Jerusalem's siege and fall soon after the destruction took place (1:13-15; 2:6,9; 4:1-12). Jeremiah witnessed the fall of Jerusalem and remained behind after the captives were deported (see Je 39). Although some critics claim that the style of Lamentations is different from the Book of Jeremiah, the similarities are, in fact, striking and numerous, especially in the poetic sections of Jeremiah. Compare these passages from Lamentations and Jeremiah: 1:2 (Je 30:14); 1:15 (Je 8:21); 1:16 and 2:11 (Je 9:1,18); 2:22 (Je 6:25); 4:21 (Je 49:12). The same compassion, sympathy, and grief over Judah's downfall are evident in both books.

3. The Time of Lamentations. The historical background of Lamentations can be found in "The Time of Jeremiah." The book was written soon after Jerusalem's destruction (Je 39; 52) at the beginning of the exile. Nebuchadnezzar laid siege to Jerusalem from January 588 B.C. to July 586 B.C. It fell on July 19, and the city and temple were burned on August 15. Jeremiah probably wrote these five elegies before he was taken captive to Egypt by his disobedient countrymen not long after the destruction (Je 43:1-7).

4. The Christ of Lamentations. The weeping prophet Jeremiah may be seen as a type of Christ, who wept over the same city of Jerusalem six centuries later. "O Jerusalem, Jerusalem, the one who kills the prophets and stones those who are sent to her! How often I wanted to gather your children together, as a hen gathers her chicks under her wings, but you were not willing! See! Your house is left to you desolate" (Ma 23:37-38). Like Christ, Jeremiah identified himself personally with the plight of Jerusalem and with human suffering caused by sin.

Lamentations also includes elements that typify Christ's life and ministry as the man of sorrows who was acquainted with grief. He was afflicted (1:12; 3:19), despised, and derided by His enemies (2:15-16; 3:14,30).

5. Keys to Lamentations.

Key Word: Lamentations—Three themes run through the five laments of Jeremiah. The most prominent is the theme of mourning over Jerusalem's fall. The holy city was laid waste and desolate: God's promised judgment for sin had come. In his sorrow, Jeremiah spoke for himself, for the captives, and sometimes for the personified city. The second theme is a confession of sin and an acknowledgment of God's righteous and holy judgment upon Judah. The third theme is least prominent but very important: it is a note of hope in God's future restoration of His people. Yahweh has poured out His wrath, but in His mercy He will be faithful to His covenant promises.

Key Verses: Lamentations 2:5-6 and 3:22-23—"The Lord was like an enemy. He has swallowed up Israel, He has swallowed up all her palaces; He has destroyed her strongholds, and has increased mourning and lamentation in the daughter of Judah. He has done violence to His tabernacle, as if it were a garden; He has destroyed His place of assembly; the LORD has caused the appointed feasts and Sabbaths to be forgotten in Zion. In His burning indignation He has spurned the king and the priest" (2:5-6).

"Through the LORD's mercies we are not consumed, because His compassions fail not. They are new every morning; great is Your faithfulness" (3:22-23).

Key Chapter: Lamentations 3—In the midst of five chapters of ruin, destruction, and utter hopelessness, Jeremiah rose and grasped with strong faith the promises and character of God. Lamentations 3:22-25 expresses a magnificent faith in the mercy of God—especially when placed against the dark backdrop of chapters 1, 2, 4, and 5.

6. Survey of Lamentations.

For forty years Jeremiah suffered rejection and abuse for his warnings of coming judgment. When Nebuchadnezzar finally comes and destroys Jerusalem in 586 B.C., a lesser man might say, "I told you so!" But Jeremiah compassionately identified with the tragic overthrow of Jerusalem and composed five beautiful and emotional lament poems as a requiem for the once proud city. These dirges reflect the tender heart of the man who was divinely commissioned to communicate a harsh message to a sinful and stiff-necked people. The city, the temple, the palace, and the walls were reduced to rubble and its inhabitants were deported to distant Babylon. Jeremiah's five mournful poems could be entitled: the destruction of Jerusalem (1), the anger of Yahweh (2), the prayer for mercy (3), the siege of Jerusalem (4), and the prayer for restoration (5).

The Destruction of Jerusalem (1). This poem consists of a lamentation by Jeremiah (1:11) and a lamentation by the personified Jerusalem (1:12-22). The city has been left desolate because of its grievous sins, and her enemies "mocked at her downfall" (1:7). Jerusalem pled with God to regard her misery and repay her adversaries.

The Anger of Yahweh (2). In his second elegy Jeremiah moves from Jerusalem's desolation to a description of her destruction. Babylon has destroyed the city, but only as the Lord's instrument of judgment. Jeremiah presents an eyewitness account of the thoroughness and severity of Jerusalem's devastation. Through the Babylonians, God has terminated all religious observances, removed the priests, prophets, and kings, and razed the temple and palaces. Jeremiah grieves over the suffering the people brought on themselves through rebellion against God and Jerusalem's supplications complete the lament.

The Prayer for Mercy (3). In the first eighteen verses, Jeremiah enters into the miseries and despair of his people and makes them his own. However, there is an abrupt turn in verses 19-39 as the prophet reflects on the faithfulness and loyal love of the compassionate God of Israel. These truths enable him to find comfort and hope in spite of his dismal circumstances. Jeremiah expresses his deep sorrow and petitions God for deliverance and for God to avenge Jerusalem's misery.

The Siege of Jerusalem (4). The prophet rehearses the siege of Jerusalem and remembers the suffering and starvation of rich and poor. He also reviews the causes of the siege, especially the sins of the prophets and priests and their foolish trust in human aid. This poem closes with a warning to Edom of future punishment and a glimmer of hope for Jerusalem.

The Prayer for Restoration (5). Jeremiah's last elegy is a melancholy description of his people's lamentable state. Their punishment is complete, and Jeremiah prayerfully desires the restoration of his nation.

OUTLINE OF LAMENTATIONS

I. The Lament of Jerusalem (1:1-22)

A. The Lament of the Prophet
Jeremiah 1:1-11
B. The Lament of the City of
Jerusalem 1:12-22

II. The Anger of God (2:1-22)

A. The Anger of God 2:1-9
B. The Agony of Jerusalem 2:10-17
C. The Appeal of Jerusalem............ 2:18-22

III. The Prayer for Mercy (3:1-66)

A. Jeremiah's Cry of
Despair...................................... 3:1-18

B. Jeremiah's Confession of Faith ... 3:19-39
C. Jeremiah's Condition of Need ... 3:40-54
D. Jeremiah's Confidence in God ... 3:55-66

IV. The Siege of Jerusalem (4:1-22)

A. The Conditions During the Siege ... 4:1-10
B. The Cause of the Siege.............. 4:11-20
C. The Consequences of the Siege ... 4:21-22

V. The Prayer for Restoration (5:1-22)

A. The Review of the Need for
Restoration 5:1-15
B. The Repentance of Sin.............. 5:16-18
C. The Request for Restoration 5:19-22

LAMP

For ordinary use lamps were made of clay with an inside hollow for oil; the wick protruding from one end, and at the other end a projection held by the thumb. More elaborate lamps such as the seven lamps of the candlestick of the tabernacle and temple were made of gold (Ex 37:23; 1 Ki 7:49). Fuel was generally olive oil (Ex 27:20).

LANCET

A spear (1 Ki 18:28).

LANDMARK

A boundary stone or other marker to define property lines. Tampering with such landmarks was forbidden by God (De 19:14; 27:17; Job 24:2; Ho 5:10).

LANE

A narrow street, alley (Lk 14:21). In Jesus's parable of the Great Supper, the master's command to search the streets and lanes indicates that the servants were not inviting those from the best part of town anymore.

LAN′ GUAGE

See TONGUE.

LANGUAGES OF THE BIBLE

Nearly all of the Old Testament was written in Hebrew, the language of the descendants of the twelve sons of Israel. A small amount of it (Ez 4:8–6:18; 7:12-26; Da 2:46–7:28) was written in Aramaic. The Jews brought this language back

from the Babylonian captivity, and by the time of Christ, this was the common language of the land. Aramaic phrases and words are sprinkled through the Greek of the New Testament, since this was the language that Jesus and His disciples spoke every day. Aside from these few words, the New Testament is written entirely in Koine Greek, the common spoken language of the Roman Empire. Koine Greek is somewhat different from Classical Greek, it was the ordinary language of the ordinary people of the world in the first century.

LAN′ TERN

A lamp with a translucent shade or globe fixed so that it could be carried outside or while walking without the light being blown out. The Romans used bladder or transparent horn for the sides of the lantern. When Jesus was taken by the soldiers the latter carried lanterns (Jo 18:3).

LA·OD·I·CE′ A

In New Testament times, Laodicea was the most important city in the Roman province of Phrygia in central Asia Minor. Located about ninety miles east of Ephesus and about ten miles west of Colosse, Laodicea stood on the banks of the Lycus River. It served as an important commercial center at a major crossroads in this part of the Roman Empire.

This city was known throughout the ancient world for its beautiful black wool, which was woven into fine, expensive garments. It was populated by a number of wealthy and socially prominent citizens, many of whom earned their livelihood by raising the sheep which produced this wool.

Although it had many natural advantages, Laodicea had one serious shortcoming—lack of good drinking water. Nearly all the streams in the area come from hot springs, which are filled with impurities. When the apostle John addressed the Christians at Laodicea, he referred to them as "lukewarm," and "neither cold nor hot" (Re 3:16). Many have guessed that this is a reference to Laodicea's thermal springs. John's statement "I will spew you out of My mouth" (Re 3:16) also brings to mind a mouthful of warm water, which is not a pleasant way to quench one's thirst!

Excavations at Laodicea have revealed that the city apparently tried to solve its water supply problem by bringing water in through stone pipes from an outside source. But these pipes contain limestone deposits, a sign that this water was not much better than the supply from Laodicea's hot springs.

This water problem may have led to the eventual decline of Laodicea. The site is easily recognized today from the remains of the huge city gate in the walls that surrounded the city.

The apostle Paul evidently wrote a letter to the Laodiceans (Col 4:16), but it has apparently been lost. His fellow worker Epaphras worked for a while with the Christians in this city (Col 4:12-13).

LAP

To take up liquid with the tongue, like a dog or cat. God used a curious method to choose the men for Gideon's army, taking only those who lapped water from their hands rather than kneeling down to drink directly from the stream (Ju 7:5-7).

LAP'I·DOTH (torches)

The husband of Deborah (Ju 4:4).

LAPIS LAZULI

A silicate of alumina, calcium and sodium, thought to be a more probable translation for the word usually rendered "sapphire." This stone was found on the breastplate of the high priest (Ex 28:18; 39:11), and in the foundation of the New Jerusalem (Re 21:19). See SAPPHIRE.

LAP'PI·DOTH

Variant of LAPIDOTH.

LAP'WING

A bird of the plover family. It appears in Palestine in March after spending the winter in Egypt. It is listed as an unclean bird (Le 11:19; De 14:18 KJV). Other translations call this bird a HOOPOE.

LAS·CIV'I·OUS·NESS

Wantonness, lewdness, salaciousness; stirring up lust.

LA·SE'A

A seaport of Crete (Ac 27:8).

LA'SHA (spring)

A city of Canaan, near the Dead Sea (Ge 10:19). It is listed with Sodom and Gomorrah and other Cities of the Plain.

LA·SHAR'ON

A city of unknown location, whose king Joshua defeated (Jos 12:18).

LAST DAYS

See ESCHATOLOGY.

LAST SUPPER

See LORD'S SUPPER.

LATCH'ET

The cord that bound the sandal to the foot (Is 5:27; Mk 1:7).

LAT'IN

The language used by the Romans. The inscription above the cross of Christ was in Latin as well as Greek and Hebrew (Jo 19:20).

LATIN VERSIONS

See VULGATE.

LATTER DAYS

See ESCHATOLOGY.

LAT'TICE

Crossed strips of wood which were used to cover a window (Ju 5:28; 2 Ki 1:2).

LAUNDERER

One who washes clothes, see FULLER.

LAUREL

The bay tree. This tree's green leaves were used to make the victor's crown for the games,

LAVER

and also as a seasoning (as they still are). The term "winning his laurels" goes back to this ancient custom. See BAY TREE.

LA'VER

A basin for washing. The laver of the tabernacle was made of bronze (copper alloyed with tin) and placed between the tabernacle and altar. It rested upon a metal base, the base and laver being made of the mirrors of the women (Ex 38:8). Before serving at the altar or in the sanctuary, the priests washed their hands and feet in the laver which symbolized holiness in God's service (Ex 30:17-21; Le 8:11). The Solomonic temple had ten lavers (1 Ki 7:38), as well as the enormous brazen sea (1 Ki 7:23-26).

LAW

The word *law* is the usual rendering of the Hebrew word *Torah,* instruction. The expression "the law" sometimes denotes the whole of the Old Testament (Jo 12:34; 15:25) but much more frequently is applied to the Pentateuch (Jos 1:8; Ne 8:2-3,14; Ma 5:17; Lk 16:16; Jo 1:17). The law of Moses, that which God revealed through Moses and recorded in the books of Moses (Ex 20:19-22; Ma 15:4), includes the legislation of Exodus, Leviticus, Numbers, Deuteronomy. The Ten Commandments, or the Moral Law, constitute the fundamental law of the theocracy.

LAWGIVER

One of the titles of God (Is 33:22). He gave Israel the law through Moses, but through Jesus Christ come grace and truth (Jo 1:17; 7:19).

LAW'YER

The professional interpreter of the law of Moses and not a legal practitioner in the present-day sense (Ma 22:35; Lk 10:25; 11:45-52; 14:3).

LAY'ING ON OF HANDS

The laying on of hands has great significance as a religious rite or ceremony in the Bible. This rite is associated with the bestowal of divine blessings upon a person, and it also is used as a special form of recognition for persons set apart for God's service.

On the Day of Atonement, the high priest placed his hands on the head of a goat before releasing it into the wilderness. Through this rite, he symbolically transferred the sins of the people to the scapegoat (Le 16:21).

Abraham and the other patriarchs placed hands on their descendants to confirm a birthright or to convey a special blessing, as when Jacob blessed the sons of Joseph (Ge 48:14-18). The ceremony sometimes implied the transfer of authority (Nu 27:18-20). Joshua was said to be "full of the spirit of wisdom, for Moses had laid his hands on him" (De 34:9).

The laying on of hands apparently served also as a formal declaration of identification by the church at Antioch with Paul and Barnabas, whom they were sending out as missionaries (Ac 13:2-3). This same sense of identification with sacrificial animals as a substitute for the people may be implied in the burnt offering presented by the priests in Old Testament times (Le 1:4).

Placing hands on persons in need of healing has a strong biblical precedent. The practice was used by Jesus during His healing ministry (Ma 9:18) and when He blessed the children (Ma 19:15). The apostles laid their hands on the sick (Ac 14:3) and on the newly baptized persons (Ac 8:16-17). There also appears to be a connection between the laying on of hands and the reception of the Holy Spirit (Ac 8:18).

The Levites were consecrated to service by the laying on of hands (Nu 8:10-11). In the New Testament, the practice is associated with the ordination of deacons (Ac 6:6) and ministers (1 Ti 4:14; 5:22) and the setting apart of missionaries for divine service (Ac 13:2-3).

LAZ'A·RUS *(a form of Eleazar)*

Two men mentioned in the New Testament:

1. A resident of Bethany; the brother of Mary and Martha and the subject of Jesus's greatest miracle, resurrection from the dead (Jo 11:1-46).

2. The beggar in the parable of the rich man and Lazarus (Lk 16:19-31).

LAZINESS

In spite of its initial charms, laziness produces discomfort (Ec 10:18) and, eventually, ruin (Pr 24:30-34). Paul warned that laziness and idleness would lead to gossip and strife (1 Ti 5:13-14). He urged believers to be industrious (1 Th 4:11-12), and to bear their own burdens as much as possible (Ga 6:5).

LEAD

A heavy, soft, white metal used in ancient times by the Egyptians. It was found in great quantities in the peninsula of Sinai as well as in Egypt. It was used in weights (Ze 5:8) and in inscriptions (Job 19:24).

LEAGUE

An alliance or covenant between nations (Da 11:23).

LE′AH

Laban's daughter who, by the trickery of Laban, became Jacob's first wife (Ge 29:16-35; 30:17-21).

LEAS′ING

An obsolete, old English word meaning lying; falsehood (Ps 4:2; 5:6).

LEATHER

The Hebrews knew the art of tanning and dyeing skins (Ex 25:5; Ac 9:43). Leather was used for bottles, for sandals (Eze 16:10), for clothing (Le 13:48; Nu 31:20), girdles (2 Ki 1:8; Ma 3:4), and for shields (2 Sa 1:21; Is 21:5).

LEATHER WORKER

See TANNER.

LEAV′EN

Yeast, a rising agent for bread (Ex 13:7). The Jews were required to keep it from all offerings made by fire (Le 2:11). It was allowed only when the offering was to be eaten (Le 7:13). During the Passover week no leaven was allowed in the house. Throughout Scripture yeast is used as a symbolic term for sin and corruption. False doctrine (Ma 16:11) and impure conduct (1 Co 5:6-8) are compared to yeast, because like yeast once they begin to ferment, they will grow and eventually permeate the entire being.

LEAVEN, PARABLE OF (Ma 13:33).

LEAVES

1. The first mention of leaves is in connection with Adam and Eve. When they discovered they were naked, they covered themselves with leaves (Ge 3:7). A leaf was brought by a dove to Noah's ark after the flood (Ge 8:11).

2. A column of writing on a scroll (Je 36:23).

3. Sections of the doors in Solomon's temple were called leaves (1 Ki 6:34).

LE·BA′NA

Variant of LEBANAH.

LE·BA′NAH (white, the poetic word for moon)

One of the Nethinim. His descendants returned from Babylon in the first expedition (Ez 2:45; Ne 7:48).

LEB′A·NON (white)

A mountain range along the northwestern boundary of the promised land (De 11:24; Jos 1:4; 12:7; 13:5). It consists of two ranges with hills running from it (Ho 14:5). The nation of Lebanon took its name from these mountains, which hem the beautiful valley of Lebanon (Jos 11:17). The country covers much of the territory that was once Phoenicia. The beauties of Lebanon are often mentioned in Scripture, especially its richness and fertility (Ps 72:16; 92:12; Song 4:15; 5:15). The famed cedars of Lebanon were used in the construction of the temple, as well as in construction of various kinds by many other nations. Eventually, the cedars were almost gone, and this wanton destruction is used as a figurative illustration of what would happen to Israel (Je 22:7; Eze 27:5; Ze 11:2).

LE·BA′OTH (lioness)

A town in the south of Judah (Jos 15:32). See BETH-LEBAOTH.

LEB·BAE′US (a man of heart)

See THADDAEUS.

LEB KAMAI

This word is thought to be a cryptic reference to Chaldea (Je 51:1).

LE·BO′NAH (incense)

A town north of Shiloh (Ju 21:19).

LE′CAH (a journey, or progress)

A town of Judah (1 Ch 4:21).

LEECH

A parasitic worm-like creature which attaches itself to its host and sucks its blood. Physicians

LEEK

used to use leeches to "bleed" their patients, believing that many ills were caused by bad blood, or too much of it. Proverbs 30:15 describes the "daughters of the leech" who are never satisfied.

LEEK

An onion-like plant, the flavor of which is said to be more delicate than the onion or garlic (Nu 11:5). The Hebrews in the wilderness longed for this tasty vegetable that they had enjoyed in Egypt.

LEES *(dregs)*

"Wines on the lees," were wines allowed to stand after the first fermentation for better preservation of the wine (Is 25:6). Figuratively, it means contentment with one's self and state, indifference and sloth (Je 48:11; Zep 1:12). To drink the lees, or dregs, is a picture of God's punishment (Ps 75:8). No one can escape until He is completely finished; the cup must be drained, not tasted.

LEFT

In Hebrew, "left" is sometimes used to indicate "north" (Ge 14:14; Eze 16:46), assuming that one is facing the sunrise in the east. In many cultures the left hand has a negative connotation, while the right hand has a positive connotation. Occasionally this can be seen in Scripture, as when Israel blessed Joseph's sons (Ge 48:13-19), or in the description of the final judgment (Ma 25:31-46). However, left-handedness was obviously not a drawback for a warrior. The tribe of Benjamin boasted seven hundred left-handed men who could "sling a stone at a hair's breadth and not miss" (Ju 20:16). Ehud, one of the deliverers of Israel, achieved victory over the Moabite king with an unexpected left-handed attack (Ju 3:15-21).

LEGACY

Inheritance. According to Proverbs, foolishness will reap a shameful inheritance (Pr 3:35).

LE′GION

The main subdivision of the Roman army, the number running from three to six thousand men.

In the New Testament, this word is used to indicate a large number rather than a specific military organization, as when the demons in the Gadarene man called themselves "Legion, for we are many" (Ma 26:53; Mk 5:9).

LE′HA·BIM *(flaming, fiery)*

A tribe of the Egyptians (Ge 10:13; 1 Ch 1:11). Quite possibly the Lehabim were the ancestors from which Libya and the Libyans derived their name.

LE′HI *(cheek, jawbone)*

In this place in Judah, Samson slew one thousand Philistines with the jawbone of an ass (Ju 15:9,14,16).

LEM′U·EL *(devoted to God)*

An unknown king whose mother taught him the lessons of chastity and temperance (Pr 31).

LEN′TIL

A legume, similar to beans and peas. Its seed pods are threshed when the plants are dry; the small, round, flat seeds are cooked like any other dry bean or pea, and used as a staple food. Lentils range in color from red-brown to greenish-brown. Esau sold his birthright for a stew made from red lentils (Ge 25:34). Lentils can also be used in bread (Eze 4:9).

LEOP′ARD

One of the "big cats," leopards are predatory animals, smaller than lions, with beautiful spotted coats (Je 5:6; 13:23). Leopards are swift and dangerous (Hab 1:8). Daniel and John both saw strange beasts resembling leopards in their visions of the end times (Da 7:6; Re 13:2).

LEP′ER, LEPROSY

This often mentioned disease was a dreaded skin affliction in ancient times. Modern medicine has isolated several different types of leprosy, variously characterized by the formation of nodules, ulcers, deformities, and loss of feeling in the flesh. In Old Testament times, a symptom used to diagnose the disease was the persistence of shiny white spots under the skin (Le 13:3-4).

Some medical experts believe the ancient disease was a severe type of psoriasis, or scaling of the skin, that is rarely seen today. It was probably more prevalent than Hansen's disease, which is what people think of as leprosy in our day.

The leper, considered to be ceremonially unclean, was isolated and forced to live apart from others. Detailed instructions are given in the Book of Leviticus on how to recognize leprosy, and how others were to be protected from those unfortunate enough to contract the dread disease. The leper was cast outside the camp (Le 13:46), required to wear mourning clothes, and to cry out "Unclean! Unclean!" to keep others at a safe distance (Le 13:45-46).

Several miraculous cures of leprosy are reported in the Bible. Both Moses (Ex 4:6-7) and Miriam (Nu 12:10-15) were afflicted with leprosy and cured by the Lord. God used the prophet Elisha to heal Naaman (a Syrian military officer) of his leprosy (2 Ki 5:1-14). In an expression of compassion, Jesus healed ten lepers, then told them to "show yourselves to the priests" (Lk 17:14) for specific instructions on how to re-enter society. One of the lepers returned to express his thanks to Jesus (Lk 17:15-19).

This miraculous healing of the ten lepers was a clear sign of Jesus's messiahship, since leprosy was curable only by divine intervention.

LE′ SHEM *(precious stone)*

A city in the north of Palestine (Jos 19:47), also called Laish.

LET (archaic)

To hinder or obstruct (Ro 1:13).

LE•TU′ SHIM *(hammered)*

Second son of Dedan son of Jokshan, and great-grandson of Abraham by Keturah (Ge 25:3).

LE•UM′ MIM *(nations)*

The last of the sons of Dedan (Ge 25:3).

LE′ VI *(adhesion)*

Four Old Testament men:

1. Third son of Jacob by Leah (Ge 29:34). Together with his brother, Simeon, he massacred Shechem and the males of his city to punish Shechem for violating Levi's sister, Dinah (Ge 34:25-31). Jacob, on his deathbed, referred to this act of cruelty and predicted that Levi's descendants would be scattered (Ge 34:26; 49:7). He had three sons: Gershon or Gershom, Kohath, and Merari (Ge 46:11), and he died in Egypt at the age of 137 (Ex 6:16). See LEVITES.

2. Son of Melchi and an ancestor of Christ (Lk 3:24).

3. Son of Simeon and an ancestor of Christ (Lk 3:29).

4. The first name of the apostle, Matthew (Mk 2:14-17; Lk 5:27-32).

LE•VI′ A•THAN

This word occurs only six times in the Old Testament but the term has stirred up great interest and controversy. *Leviathan* has become a word for anything of enormous size and power. The word is thought to be derived from a verb meaning "to twist." Job 41 is devoted to a detailed description of Leviathan, with God challenging Job to master him.

Some scholars believe that in Job the word poetically describes the Nile crocodile with his scaly hide, terrible teeth, and fast swimming. They feel that this fits in with the overthrow of Egypt in the Red Sea, since "Leviathan" is used for Egyptian troops in Psalm 74:13-14. But in Psalm 104:25-26, some envision a dolphin or a whale. However, the description in Job 41:33-34 seems too majestic for a crocodile or dolphin, or even for a whale: "On earth there is nothing like him, which is made without fear. He beholds every high thing; he is king over all the children of pride." Since we really do not know for certain what a Leviathan was (or is), the best we can say is "great sea animal whose identity we do not know."

LEVIRATE MARRIAGE

Leviratic marriage, a family and inheritance custom among the Jewish people, is clearly demonstrated in the Book of Ruth. A near kinsman of the widowed Ruth gave up his right to buy the family property and marry Ruth, making it possible for Boaz to take her as his wife (Ru 4).

The custom of levirate marriage specified that when an Israelite died without leaving a male heir, his nearest relative should marry the widow in order to continue the family name of the deceased brother. The term *levirate* means "husband's brother."

If brothers on the father's side of the family lived in the same area and one of them died childless, the widow was not to marry a stranger; rather, the surviving brother was to take her as his wife. The firstborn son by her took the name of the deceased brother, continuing his name in the family register.

Such marriages were not strictly required under Jewish law but were considered an act of love. If a brother-in-law did not wish to marry the widow, he was not forced to do so. Apparently the next male relative in such cases then had the right to do so. This was the situation that led to the marriage of Boaz and Ruth in the Book of Ruth.

The first mention of the concept of leviratic marriage occurs in Genesis, when Onan was called upon to marry his brother Er's widow (Ge 38:8). However, Onan refused to "give an heir to his brother" (Ge 38:9).

Leviratic marriage was the basis for the question asked of Jesus by the Sadducees (Ma 22:23-28). The Sadducees did not believe in the resurrection of the dead at all, and were posing a question which seemed to them to discredit the idea of the resurrection. How could a woman be married to seven brothers at once? Jesus answered that "in the resurrection they neither marry nor are given in marriage" (Ma 22:30). In other words, the resurrected life will be a different type of life, one that cannot be judged in earthly terms.

LE′VITES

Descendants of Levi, son of Jacob. His sons, Gershon or Gershom, Kohath, and Merari, were each the founder of a tribal family (Ge 46:11; Ex 6:16; Nu 3:17; 1 Ch 6:16-48). Moses and Aaron were of the line of Kohath of the house of Amram. The Levites at Sinai remained true to Jehovah, and were chosen for religious services (Ex 32:26-29; Nu 3:9,11-13,40-41; 8:16-18). When the census was taken the firstborn of Israel, exclusive of Levites, numbered 22,273 (Nu 3:43, 46). There were 22,000 Levites. The firstborn belonged to God, but He arranged that, instead of the firstborn from each family, He would choose one family to serve before Him. The 22,000 Levites took the place of 22,000 firstborn of Israel, and the remaining 273 firstborn of the other tribes were redeemed by paying five shekels apiece (Nu 3:46-51). At thirty years of age the Levites were eligible to full service in connection with the sanctuary (Nu 4:3; 1 Ch 23:3-5), although they began to assist in these duties at the age of twenty (1 Ch 23:24, 28-31). Luke notes that Jesus entered upon his public ministry, inaugurated by baptism, when thirty years of age (Lk 3:23).

LEVITICAL CITIES

Instead of being given a portion of the land as an inheritance, along with the other tribes, the tribe of Levi was allotted 48 cities scattered throughout the territories of the other eleven tribes (Nu 35:1-8; Jos 20-21). Among these were the six cities of refuge. See CITIES OF REFUGE.

LE·VIT′I·CUS, BOOK OF

1. The Book of Leviticus. Leviticus is God's guidebook for His newly redeemed people, showing them how to worship, serve, and obey a holy God. Fellowship with God through sacrifice and obedience show the awesome holiness of the God of Israel. Indeed, "'you shall be holy, for I the LORD your God am holy'" (19:2).

Leviticus focuses on the worship and walk of the nation of God. In Exodus, Israel was redeemed and established as a kingdom of priests and a holy nation. Leviticus shows how God's people are to fulfill their priestly calling.

The Hebrew title is *Wayyiqra,* "And He Called." The Talmud refers to Leviticus as "The Law of the Priests," and the "Law of the Offerings." The Greek title appearing in the Septuagint is *Leuitikon,* "That Which Pertains to the Levites." From this word, the Latin Vulgate derived its name *Leviticus* which was adopted as the English title. This title is slightly misleading because the book does not deal with the Levites as a whole but more with the priests, a segment of the Levites.

2. The Author of Leviticus. The kind of arguments used to confirm the Mosaic authorship of Genesis and Exodus also apply to Leviticus because the Pentateuch is a literary unit. In addition to these arguments, others include the following:

External Evidence: (1) A uniform ancient testimony supports the Mosaic authorship of Leviticus. (2) Ancient parallels to the Levitical system of trespass offerings have been found in the Ras Shamra Tablets dating from about 1400 B.C. and discovered on the coast of northern Syria. (3) Christ ascribes the Pentateuch (which includes Leviticus) to Moses (Ma 8:2-4 and Le 14:1-4; Ma 12:4 and Le 24:9; Lk 2:22).

Internal Evidence: (1) Fifty-six times in the twenty-seven chapters of Leviticus it is stated that God imparted these laws to Moses (1:1; 4:1; 6:1,24; 8:1). (2) The Levitical Code fits the time of Moses. Economic, civil, moral, and religious considerations show it to be ancient. Many of the laws are also related to a migratory lifestyle.

3. The Time of Leviticus. No geographical movement takes place in Leviticus: the children of Israel remain camped at the foot of Mount Sinai (25:1-2; 26:46; 27:34). The new calendar of Israel begins with the first Passover (Ex 12:2); and, according to Exodus 40:17, the tabernacle is completed exactly one year later.

Leviticus picks up the story at this point and takes place in the first month of the second year. Numbers 1:1 opens at the beginning of the second month. Moses probably wrote much of Leviticus during that first month and may have put it in its final form shortly before his death in Moab, about 1405 B.C.

4. The Christ of Leviticus. The Book of Leviticus is replete with types and allusions to the person and work of Jesus Christ. Some of the more important include: (1) *The five offerings:* The burnt offering typifies Christ's total offering in submission to His Father's will. The meal offering typifies Christ's sinless service. The peace offering is a type of the fellowship believers have with God through the work of the cross. The sin offering typifies Christ as our guilt-bearer. The trespass offering typifies Christ's payment for the damage of sin. (2) *The high priest:* There are several comparisons and contrasts between Aaron, the first high priest, and Christ, our eternal high priest. (3) *The seven feasts:* Passover speaks of the substitutionary death of the Lamb of God. Christ died on the day of Passover. Unleavened Bread speaks of the holy walk of the believer (1 Co 5:6-8). Firstfruits speaks of Christ's resurrection as the firstfruits of the resurrection of all believers (1 Co 15:20-23). Christ rose on the day of the Firstfruits. Pentecost speaks of the descent of the Holy Spirit after Christ's ascension. Trumpets, the Day of Atonement, and Tabernacles speak of events associated with the second advent of Christ. This may be why these three are separated by a long gap from the first four in Israel's annual cycle.

5. Keys to Leviticus.

Key Word: Holiness—Leviticus centers around the concept of the holiness of God, and how an unholy people can acceptably approach Him and then remain in continued fellowship. The way to God is only through blood sacrifice, and the walk with God is only through obedience to His laws.

Key Verses: Leviticus 17:11; 20:7-8—"For the life of the flesh is in the blood, and I have given it to you upon the altar to make atonement for your souls; for it is the blood that makes atonement for the soul" (17:11).

"Sanctify yourselves therefore, and be holy, for I am the LORD your God. And you shall keep My statutes, and perform them: I am the LORD who sanctifies you" (20:7-8).

Key Chapter: Leviticus 16—The Day of Atonement (*"Yom Kippur"*) was the most important single day in the Hebrew calendar as it was the only day the high priest entered into the holy of holies to "make atonement for you, to cleanse you, that you may be clean from all your sins before the LORD" (16:30).

6. Survey of Leviticus. It has been said that it took God only one night to get Israel out of Egypt, but it took forty years to get Egypt out of Israel. In Exodus, Israel is redeemed and established as a kingdom of priests and a holy nation; and in Leviticus, Israel is taught how to fulfill their priestly call. They have been led out from the land of bondage in Exodus and into the sanctuary of God in Leviticus. They move from redemption to service, from deliverance to dedication. This book serves as a handbook for the Levitical priesthood, giving instructions and regulations for worship. Used to guide a newly redeemed people into worship, service, and obedience to God, Leviticus falls into two major sections: (1) sacrifice (1–17), and (2) sanctification (18–27).

Sacrifice (1–17). This section teaches that God must be approached by the sacrificial offerings (1–7), by the mediation of the priesthood (8–10), by the purification of the nation from uncleanness (11–15), and by the provision for national cleansing and fellowship (16–17). The blood sacrifices remind the worshippers that because of sin the holy God requires the costly gift of life (17:11). The blood of the innocent sacrificial animal becomes the substitute for the life of the guilty offerer: "without shedding of blood there is no remission" (He 9:22).

Sanctification (18–27). The Israelites serve a holy God who requires them to be holy as well. To be holy means to be "set apart" or "separated." They are to be separated *from* other nations *unto* God. In Leviticus the idea of holiness appears eighty-seven times, sometimes indicating ceremonial holiness (ritual requirements), and at other times moral holiness (purity of life). This sanctification extends to the people of Israel (18–20), the priesthood (21–22), their worship (23–24), their life in Canaan (25–26), and their special vows (27). It is necessary to remove the defilement that separates the people from God so that they can have a walk of fellowship with their Redeemer.

OUTLINE OF LEVITICUS

Part One: The Laws of Acceptable Approach to God: Sacrifice (1:1–17:16)

Part Two: The Laws of Acceptable Walk with God: Sanctification (18:1–27:34)

LEWDNESS

Wickedness, baseness; often in the sense of sexually immoral conduct or obscene behavior. The proconsul of Achaia refused to try Paul when he saw that he was not accused of wickedness or lewdness, but only breaking some obscure Jewish law (Ac 18:14-15, KJV).

LIBANUS

See LEBANON.

LIBERALITY

A generous attitude; to give with liberality means to give abundantly (Ro 12:8; 2 Co 8:2).

LIB′ER·TINES *(freedmen)*

The word occurs in Acts 6:9. They were Jews made captive by the Romans under Pompey and later set free. They built a synagogue at Jerusalem. They joined the foes of Stephen the first martyr.

LIB′NAH *(whiteness)*

Two geographical locations:
1. A place in the wilderness where the Israelites camped (Nu 33:20).
2. A city near Lachish in the territory of Judah (Jos 10:29-31), which was taken by Joshua (Jos 10:30,39; 12:15). It revolted against Judah in the reign of Jehoram (2 Ki 8:22). Libnah was the birthplace of the father-in-law of Josiah (2 Ki 23:31; 24:18).

LIB′NI *(white)*

1. Son of Gershon, grandson of Levi and founder of the Libnites (Ex 6:17; Nu 3:18-21; 26:58).
2. A Levite (1 Ch 6:29).

LIBNITES

Descendants of Levi's grandson Libni (Nu 3:21; 26:58; Ex 6:17)

LIB′Y·A

Country of the Libyans on the Mediterranean, west of lower Egypt (Eze 27:10; 30:5); also called Put (NIV, NRSV) or Phut (KJV). One of its cities was Cyrene (Ac 2:10), and Libyans were present in Jerusalem at Pentecost. Simon, who carried Jesus's cross, was from Cyrene (Ma 27:32). Libya is mentioned in the prophets (Je 46:9; Na 3:9), called Lubim in the KJV.

LICE

Small pernicious insects with flat, grayish bodies. They are parasitic, and make their homes in the clothing or hair of people or animals, sucking the blood of their hosts. They were sent as the third plague on Egypt when Pharaoh would not let the people go (Ex 8:16-18; Ps 105:31). Other translations render this third plague as "gnats" (NIV, NRSV, NASB) or "maggots" (REB).

LICENTIOUSNESS

Undisciplined, immoral behavior, outrageously bad conduct (Mk 7:22; 2 Co 12:21). Also translated "lasciviousness" (KJV).

LIE

To state something as fact, knowing it to be false; information or action which purposely deceives. The first lie recorded in Scripture is the serpent's lie to Eve in the garden of Eden, telling her that God was deceiving her and that disobedience would not result in death (Ge 3:1-13). Lies and deceit are one of the hallmarks of the sin nature (Ro 3:13). God's law strictly commanded, "You shall not give false witness against your neighbor" (Ex 20:16), but this is exactly what happened at Jesus's trials (Ma 26:60-75). The Book of Proverbs tells us that God hates "a lying tongue" and "a false witness who speaks lies" (Pr 6:17,19). Ananias and Sapphira died because of their attempt to lie to the Holy Spirit (Ac 5:1-11).

LIEUTENANTS (Da 3:2; 6:1)

See SATRAP.

LIFE

The functioning of the physical processes of plants, animals, and humans; physically speaking, life is the space of time between conception and death. Life is a gift from God (Ge 2:7; Ps 36:9). In the spiritual sense, life does not end when the body dies. After the "breath of life" leaves the body, the spirit continues to exist. See ETERNAL LIFE.

LIFE, BOOK OF

See BOOK OF LIFE.

LIFE, TREE OF

See TREE OF LIFE.

LIGHTS, FEAST OF

See DEDICATION, FEAST OF.

LIGN ALOES

See ALOES.

LIG'URE

This gem was the first stone in the third row of the priestly breastplate (Ex 28:19). See JACINTH.

LIK'HI

Ancestor of a Manassite family (1 Ch 7:19).

LIL'Y

In the Bible the word lily refers to a number of different plants. Some believe that the term is simply a general name for all flowers, others believe that specific varieties of lily are meant. The "lily of the valley" mentioned by Solomon (Song 2:1) was probably an iris, not the western lily of the valley. The lilies of the field were probably gladioli or anemone (Ma 6:28; Lk 12:27).

LILY WORK

The artistic representations of lilies on the capitals of the two columns Solomon set up in front of the temple (1 Ki 7:19,22).

LIME

Produced from limestone and other substances (Is 33:12; Am 2:1), it was used in mortar and for whitewashing (De 27:2; Ma 23:27; Ac 23:3). See MORTAR.

LINE

A measuring tape or similar device, for marking distance (2 Sa 8:2; Am 7:17; Ze 2:1); also a cord or small rope (Jos 2:18, 21).

LINEAGE

See GENEALOGY.

LIN'EN

The Hebrew word *shesh* is rendered fine linen. It was the material in which Joseph was arrayed in Egypt (Ge 41:42); the material of the hangings and veil of the tabernacle (Ex 26:1,31,36; 27:9,16,18). The ephod and breastplate of the high priest were made of fine linen (Ex 28:6,15), also the girdle (Ex 39:29). Linen is made from the stem fibers of the flax plant. After the flax is harvested, it is kept in a damp place to soften and rot the stiff outer fibers of the stems. The softened stems are pounded thoroughly, and the flax is combed (heckled) to get rid of the hard outer stem and any other foreign matter. The heckled flax can then be spun into a fine thread, and woven into cloth. Varying qualities of fabric are made, depending upon the part of the flax used, and the method of preparing it. Rough tow sacking is made from the bits discarded after the heckling of the softened stems. Flax which has been softened in clear running water makes the whitest linen, and the fabric can be bleached to blinding whiteness by laying it out in the sun.

LIN'TEL

The horizontal beam which is part of the framework of a door (Ex 12:22).

LI'NUS

This Christian at Rome sent greetings to Timothy (2 Ti 4:21).

LI'ON

An animal common in Palestine in Bible times. In the Scriptures it is mentioned relative to its strength (2 Sa 1:23; Pr 30:30); teeth (Joel 1:6); courage (Pr 28:1); preying nature (1 Sa 17:34; Is 11:6-7); hiding to lie in wait for its prey (Je 4:7; 25:38). Christ is described as the Lion of the tribe of Judah (Re 5:5).

LIQUID MEASURES

See WEIGHTS AND MEASURES.

LISTETH (archaic)

List; to please, to choose (Jo 3:7-9).

LITTER

A stretcher or portable couch, used for transportation. A litter might have a canopy or curtains, it had shafts so that it could be carried by slaves or animals (Is 66:20).

LITTER

LITTLE OWL

See OWL.

LIVELIHOOD

One's means of support. Jesus commended the widow for giving all that she had, even though it was a small amount of money (Mk 12:44).

LIVING CREATURES

Two passages of Scripture describe four angelic beings who are described as the "four living creatures" (Eze 1:4-14; 10:15,20; Re 4:6-9). In both passages, they are described as having wings, and four different faces. Their specific duty seems to be to proclaim God's holiness.

LIZ'ARD

A reptile which abounds in Palestine. They are in the list of unclean animals (Le 11:30). Several varieties of lizards are mentioned in Leviticus, but it is a little uncertain exactly which species are meant. In the NKJV the list includes the "gecko, monitor lizard, sand reptile, sand lizard, and chameleon." The NIV chose "gecko, monitor lizard, wall lizard, skink, chameleon," while the KJV says "ferret, chameleon, lizard, snail, and mole." The NASB list is "gecko, crocodile, lizard, sand reptile, and chameleon."

LOAF

Barley and wheat were used for bread loaves (Le 23:17; 2 Ki 4:42; Jo 6:9). The loaf was round and small and could be easily carried (Ju 8:5; 1 Sa 10:3; Ma 14:17). See BREAD.

LO-AM'MI *(not my people)*

The figurative name Hosea gave his second son (Ho 1:8-9).

LOAN

The lending (especially) of money. In the early period of the Hebrews money was not loaned in the commercial sense. Crop failures were the most common cause for obtaining a loan (Ne 5:2-3). To secure a loan a debtor was often forced to pledge his children or himself (2 Ki 4:1; Am 8:6). The law regulated lending. Loans to fellow Hebrews were not to bear interest (Ex 22:25; De 23:19-20). A millstone could never be taken in pledge because this would leave the family no way to obtain its daily food (De 24:6). Every seventh year debts were to be forgiven and bondservants freed (De 15:1-2, 12). A highly developed system of commercial lending and banking existed in Palestine at the time of the Roman occupation (Ma 25:14-30; Lk 19:11-27). See BANKER and BORROW.

LOCK

Ancient doors were secured by bars of wood or iron, with the bolt fastened in the doorpost, held in place by pins set in holes. The pins were raised by a key constructed to raise them so the bolt could be turned back (Is 22:22).

LO'CUST

A word used interchangeably with grasshopper, referring to a winged insect two or more inches long. Locusts have six legs, the hindmost pair used for springing. Their sharp jaws are used to cut and consume leaves and grass, and when they appear in any great numbers, their voracious eating habits turn them from a pest to a menace (Joel 1:4,7). The eighth plague on the Egyptians came in the form of swarms of locusts which ate every green thing in their path (Ex 10:4-19). Later, the marauding Midianites were compared to locusts in their destructiveness (Ju 6:5).

Locusts also occur symbolically in prophecy; Revelation 9 describes a fearsome army of locust-like creatures with the power of death.

Locusts were considered ceremonially clean; they were roasted and eaten for food by many people (Le 11:22). Probably the most famous example of this is John the Baptist, who ate locusts and honey (Ma 3:4). In some areas of the world, locusts are still used as food.

LOD

A town of Benjamin (1 Ch 8:12). It is now called Lydda (Ez 2:33; Ne 7:37).

LO DE'BAR *(no pasture)*

Probably the same as Debir (Jos 13:26), a place in Gilead near Mahanaim (2 Sa 9:4-5; 17:27). See DEBIR.

LODGE

A shed for the watchman of the garden (Is 1:8). It is also used as a verb meaning to spend the night (Ac 10:6).

LOFT

An upstairs room (1 Ki 17:19; Ac 20:9).

LOG

A liquid measure equal to about a pint (Le 14:10,12,15,21,24). See WEIGHTS AND MEASURES.

LOGIA

Words purported to have been spoken by Christ, but not recorded in the Gospels. Paul quotes one of these sayings in his farewell to the Ephesian elders (Ac 20:35).

LOINS (archaic)

The hip area and abdominal region of the body. The KJV often speaks of someone having a girdle around the loins where other translations say "waist" (Ma 3:4). The Lord charged Job to "gird up now thy loins like a man" (Job 38:3); in other words, to belt one's robes in around the waist to shorten them in preparation for running or working hard. Peter uses the same figure of speech to encourage believers to discipline their mental processes (1 Pe 1:13).

LO'IS

The grandmother of Timothy. She was commended by Paul for her godliness and devotion (2 Ti 1:5; 3:15).

LONGSUFFERING

Patient with the sins of others. The Lord is often described as longsuffering, "keeping mercy for thousands, forgiving iniquity and transgressions and sin" (Ex 34:6-7). This longsuffering patience with our sins is designed to lead us to repentance. Love "suffers long and is kind" (1 Co 13:4-5); Christians are urged to be longsuffering, not seeking revenge (Ro 12:19; Ep 4:31-32).

LOOK'ING GLASS

See MIRROR.

LOOM

See WEAVING.

LORD

The most used name of God in the Bible. Exodus 3 records one of the greatest revelations in the Old Testament: the personal name of God. (The words translated *God* in our Bible ['El, 'Elohim, 'Eloah] are not names, but the standard vocabulary for the Deity and even for false gods.) God had told Moses His plan to use him in

delivering the Israelites from Egyptian bondage, and Moses had asked whom he should tell the people had sent him. God answered Moses: "I AM WHO I AM." He told Moses to tell them that "I AM" had sent him, "the LORD God." "I AM" and "LORD" are both probably derived from the Hebrew verb *to be (hayah)* because God is the ever-present One, "the Eternal."

Many people are puzzled that in this and many other passages (over six thousand) some Bibles read *LORD* in all capitals (KJV, NKJV, NIV), some read "Jehovah" (ASV, Darby), and some read "Yahweh" (Jerusalem Bible).

Because the name of God is so important—Jews devoutly refer to Him as "the Name" (*ha Shem*)—it is well worth exploring this revelation in some detail. It is merely a question of a Jewish tradition and how various Christian scholars handle that tradition.

In the Ten Commandments, God forbids us to take His name "in vain." We must not treat the name of God carelessly, as though it means nothing. In their great fear of violating this command, devout Hebrews went beyond the law, and when they read the Hebrew Scriptures aloud they would read the word *Lord* (*'Adonai*) whenever they saw the four letters (YHWH, or traditionally JHVH in Latin pronunciation) that spelled out God's revealed covenant name. This was the sacred name by which He had committed Himself to Israel as a nation.

The most ancient copies of the Hebrew text were written in consonants only. As the language became less and less used, scholars (called Masoretes) added little dots and dashes called "vowel points" to indicate how the text was to be pronounced. Oddly enough, they put the vowels that go with the word *'Adonai* together with the sacred four-letter name (called "tetragrammaton") to guide the readers to say *'Adonai* aloud in synagogue services.

This is the origin of the name "Jehovah." It is actually a hybrid name, combining the vowels of *'Adonai* with the consonants of YHWH into JeHoVaH or YeHoWah. The people who produced this name were medieval Christian Hebrew scholars; the Jews never acknowledged such a name. The defense of this Christian hybrid is the same as the defense of the Jewish avoidance of pronouncing the name—tradition. There are many lovely hymns and paraphrases of the Psalms that use this name, so it would be a loss to eliminate it from our Christian vocabulary. The poetical form of Jehovah is *Jah.*

It is very likely that the name was actually pronounced very much like "Yahweh." Comparisons with transliterations of the name into other alphabets from very ancient times confirm this. The best argument for this spelling is that it is probably historically accurate. However, it is less familiar than Jehovah, and it seems to many to be an unnecessary striving to try and change to the form which is probably more correct. Actually, all the names which begin with "J" in our English Bibles were pronounced in their original language with a "Y" sound, as in "hallelu-Yah."

Most recent major English Bibles, dissatisfied with both *Jehovah* and *Yahweh,* have retained the KJV's LORD. The NASB, which is an updating of the ASV, actually restored LORD (the 1901 text read *Jehovah*).

The word "Lord" also often appears with only a capital "L." In these passages, "Lord" is the translation of *'Adon* which means "Master" or "Lord." For example, if one looks closely at Psalm 8, one will notice the capitalization. "O LORD, our Lord" means "O Jehovah [Yahweh] our Lord [Master]." In Psalm 136:3, we are told to "give thanks to the Lord of lords," in other words, the One Master over all masters.

When the personal suffix for "my" in Hebrew is put on *'adon,* it is generally *'adoni* (singular) for men and *'adonai* (plural) for God. We use lowercase letters in the English Bible when the word *lord* refers to a mortal man. We have already noticed that David was called "lord." Pharaoh (Ge 40:1) and Saul (1 Sa 16:16) are referred to as "lord." Other important leaders called *'adon* include Joseph (Ge 42:10), Eli the priest (1 Sa 1:150), David's commander Joab (2 Sa 11:9), and the prophet Elijah (1 Ki 18:7). Even ordinary people were called by this title of respect: Abraham was addressed as "lord" by Sarah (Ge 18:12) and by his servant Eliezer (Ge 24). Ruth also called Boaz "my lord" in Ruth 2:13.

LORD, JESUS IS

Lord or *Master (Kyrios)* is a most important New Testament word. In secular usage, the word meant "master," "guardian," or "trustee." This ancient usage still occurs in New Testament passages, such as Ephesians 6:5 and Colossians 4:1, regarding masters and servants.

In the Septuagint, *Kyrios* was chosen as the translation of the Hebrew *Adonai* ("Lord"), as well as *Yahweh.*

Kyrios can also mean "Sir," therefore we cannot always be sure how the speaker was using the title. When Thomas, after seeing the risen Lord, exclaimed, "My Lord and my God!" (Jo 20:28), there can be no doubt he recognized Christ's Lordship. When the Samaritan woman in John 4 addressed Him as an unknown traveler from a rival ethnic group, the KJV translation "sir" is no doubt correct. There are also several doubtful passages. For example, in Matthew 8:2,6, were the leper and the centurion aware of who Jesus was, or were they just being polite?

Jesus is Lord of His church and Lord of lords (1 Ti 6:15; Re 11:15); He should receive the service and homage He deserves. We who know Him as Savior and Lord do well to address Him as "Lord Jesus."

LORD OF HOSTS

An important title of God, used frequently in the Old Testament. The Hebrew word for "hosts" is used by both Paul and James, transliterated into Greek as *Sabaoth.* Paul quotes the LXX Isaiah, which along with the LXX 1 Samuel, includes this transliterated (rather than translated) form. Even though *Sabaoth* looks like *Sabbath* in English letters, the two words are totally unrelated. *Sabbath* comes from the word meaning "to cease" or "rest," and *Sabaoth* is from the Hebrew word meaning "host" or "army."

The word "hosts" can refer to the host of heaven (singular) or hosts of soldiers, that is, armies. The term first occurs in 1 Samuel 1:3. Elkanah "went up from his city yearly to worship and sacrifice to the LORD of hosts in Shiloh." God was the head of the forces of Israel (1 Sa 17:45); and not merely of Israel's armies, but of all hosts, celestial and terrestrial—angelic and human. God can and does rule all the armies of the whole world. Also, perhaps as a warning against joining the heathen in worshipping the host of heaven (sun, moon, and stars) God stresses that He controls all the heavenly host.

One of the most familiar passages using this regal title is Psalm 24: "Who is the King of glory? The LORD of hosts, He is the King of glory" (v. 10).

The title is not always military: "Even the sparrow has found a home, and the swallow a nest for herself, where she may lay her young—even Your altars, O LORD of hosts" (Ps 84:3).

The prophets Jeremiah, Isaiah, Zechariah, and Malachi used this title of God numerous times in their books.

LORD'S DAY

The expression occurs but once in the New Testament (Re 1:10) when John says "I was in the Spirit on the Lord's day." It is believed that John was referring not to the Sabbath, but to the first day of the week. This was the day on which Christ rose from the tomb (Ma 28:1,9; Lk 24:1,15), He reappeared on the same day the following week (Jo 20:1,26).

LORD'S PRAYER

This model prayer is cherished by all Christians because of its simplicity, beautiful imagery, and instructive value. In contrast to the prayers of the heathen, Jesus emphasized that we should pray with faith and simplicity (Ma 6:7-8). Jesus drew great strength from His heavenly Father through prayer, and it was only natural that He should teach His followers about the significance and meaning of prayer.

Matthew's account of the Lord's Prayer (6:9-13) comes from a portion of Jesus's Sermon on the Mount that warned against hypocrisy in prayer. Luke's version of the prayer consists of Jesus's response to a request from the disciples to "teach us to pray" (11:1). Consequently, the popular prayer might more accurately be called the "Disciple's Prayer," since it cannot be prayed in a meaningful way except by those who are disciples of Jesus.

The invocation of the prayer, "Our Father in heaven, hallowed be Your name" (Ma 6:9), indicates the spirit of adoration and reverence in which the heavenly Father should be approached by His children.

"Your kingdom come. Your will be done on earth as it is in heaven" (6:10) expresses the longing for a society on earth where God's will is as perfectly done as it is in heaven. In our prayers, we should indicate our submission to the dominion and authority of God in our lives.

"Give us this day our daily bread" (6:11) addresses a loving Father who is concerned for our physical welfare, and it expresses our dependence on Him for our physical needs. "And forgive us our debts, as we forgive our debtors" (6:12) is a petition for pardon as we approach God in a spirit of forgiveness toward others. "And do not lead us into temptation, but deliver us from the evil one" (6:13) is a request for continual protection from the snares of Satan and all evil forces.

The prayer's closing doxology, "For Yours is the kingdom and the power and the glory forever" (6:13) appropriately attributes all power and glory to God for all eternity.

LORD'S SUPPER

The designation by Paul (1 Co 11:20) of the memorial instituted by Christ on the evening before the crucifixion. Paul's statement is the earliest record of the facts. This Epistle to the Corinthians was written about A.D. 57 or 58, about 27 years after the institution of the ordinance, and prior to the writing of any of the Gospels. Paul stated that he received from the Lord the particulars of this institution (1 Co 11:20-29); Christ directly revealed to Paul exactly what had happened. See COMMUNION and LOVE FEAST.

LO-RU·HA′MAH (not favored)

The symbolic name given to the daughter of Hosea the prophet and his wife, Gomer (Ho 1:6-8).

LOST COIN, PARABLE OF. (Lk 15:8-10).

LOST SHEEP, PARABLE OF. (Lk 15:1-7).

LOST SON, PARABLE OF. (Lk 15:11-32).

LOT (a covering)

A Shemite, who was the son of Haran and nephew of Abraham. He came with Abraham from Mesopotamia to Canaan (Ge 11:31; 12:5), went with him to Egypt, and returned to Canaan (Ge 13:1). When trouble arose over the matter of pasturage, they decided to separate. Lot was given the first selection as to district. He chose the Jordan Valley and made Sodom his residence. When Chedorlaomer invaded the land, Lot was taken prisoner, but was rescued by Abraham and his allies (Ge 13–14:1-16). When divine judgment fell upon Sodom, Lot and his family were saved from destruction (Ge 19:1-29).

LO′TAN

Son of Seir (Ge 36:20,29; 1 Ch 1:38).

LOTS, CASTING OF

See CASTING OF LOTS.

LOTS, FEAST OF

See PURIM.

LOTUS

A type of lily. See LILY.

LOVE

What is love? The early Christians faced a problem similar to the one we face today in that the surrounding society was so corrupt that "love" often equaled sheer lust.

Fortunately, the language in which the New Testament was originally penned has four "love words" to express various aspects of love. They are presented here in ascending order of Christian usage.

Physical Love (eros): The very common Greek family of words from which English derives the word *erotic* is not even used in the New Testament due to its bad connotations in pagan society. Forms of the word do occur in the Septuagint, but chiefly for "paramours" or "lovers." However, there is a valid place in Christian thinking for this love of physical attraction when it is between a married couple (see Song of Solomon).

Family Love (storge). The Judeo-Christian tradition has always been strongly family-oriented. Today, as the Christian family is under constant attack by secular and humanistic forces, the fondness people share for their relatives, especially love between parents and children, is very crucial. Paul uses the negative form of the word in Romans 1:31 and 2 Timothy 3:3.

Another interesting form of *storge* in the New Testament combines the "love-root" of this word with the next one we discuss. It forms the word *philostorgos*. Paul uses it to command us to be "kindly affectionate to one another" (Ro 12:10).

Affectionate Love (philia). Americans, especially Easterners, know this Greek root from the name of a great Pennsylvania city: Philadelphia, "the city of brotherly love." This city's name (from Re 3) speaks of warm-hearted, spontaneous affection, liking, attractive appeal, and friendship.

Fortunately for us, God never commands us to have this kind of love for everyone, because our reactions to different types of people are often beyond our control. However, if we do

LOTUS

obey the commands to choose to love, we often end up liking and becoming fond of people who originally "turned us off."

God the Father loves the Son in both this affectionate way—He pleases Him so well (Jo 5:20)—and in the love of choice (Jo 3:35).

Love of Choice (agape). Many Christians have heard of this Greek word. *Agape* was practically "born within the bosom of revealed religion," although it did occur a few times before Christians took it over and poured into it all the wonderful meanings of revelation.

Just because it is so popular a word, *agape* has also been misunderstood by many. Commonly *agape* is called "divine" love. This is misleading because it is used for love from man to God and from God to man. It is also used for love between people. It is divine in the sense that it is the love that God commands, the love of choice. Even if someone does not "appeal" to us we can still show *agape* to that person—accept him, treat him rightly, and do all we can do to help build up that person in faith (if a believer) or to win him to the faith (if not).

The word *agape* is used in 1 Corinthians 13. The King James translators, partly because the Latin Vulgate had *charitas* there, and partly, no doubt, in an effort to lift the concept above the carnal connotations of love in seventeenth century England, chose "charity" to represent it. Unfortunately that word now has a restricted meaning that is most unsuitable for Christian love of the highest order. When we are told to love our neighbors as ourselves, the verb form of *agape* is employed. John 13–17, the intimately Christian "Upper Room Discourse," is full of both *agape* and *philia*.

In John 3:16, the verb "loved" expressed this concept of *agape*. God (even in our sin) decided to love us, because it is His nature to love. In fact, while it is wrong to turn the verse around (as some do) and teach that "love is God," it is quite true that "God is love" (1 Jo 4:8).

LOVE FEAST

This feast, for the fostering of mutual affection, was held by Christians in connection with the Lord's Supper (Jude 12). Acts 6:1-3 is probably referring to this custom.

Eating meals together is a common expression of good fellowship. Since the first time Jesus gave His disciples the bread and wine at a meal they were sharing, the early Christians seem to have continued to celebrate the Lord's Supper in conjunction with common meals. The reference to "breaking bread" together in Acts 2:42 is probably a reference to such shared meals, ending with the symbolic bread and wine. Jesus chose as symbols the most common and ordinary of common, ordinary, everyday food; it seems that in the earliest days the disciples "remembered the Lord" daily—every time they had bread and wine together was a "communion service." At some point, probably due to carelessness and abuse of the symbolic meal (1 Co 11:17-34), the Lord's Supper became slightly more formal. As time went on, it appears that the purity and innocence of the feast disappeared (2 Pe 2:13), and eventually the meal and the Lord's Supper were separated. Only a few groups still celebrate the Lord's Supper with a full meal.

LOVINGKINDNESS *(hesed)*

The traditional understanding of *hesed* is that it means "lovingkindness" (KJV, NKJV), "mercy," "love," or even "grace." The ancient versions would seem to bear out this understanding. The Septuagint (LXX translates *hesed* chiefly by "mercy" and so does the Vulgate. Some scholars connect this word with the concept of loyal love, or loyalty to a covenant relationship.

The *hesed* of people: All scholars seem to agree that the traditional idea of lovingkindness is correct in Esther 2:9,17. The LXX even uses the word "grace" in this passage, and the NKJV uses the word "favor." "The king loved Esther more than all the other women, and she obtained grace and favor in his sight more than all the other virgins" (Es 2:17). The king certainly had no covenant obligations to this Jewish girl, no matter how lovely she was.

After Saul's death in battle, the men of Jabesh Gilead marched all night to provide him and his sons a decent burial (2 Sa 2:5). They acted out of "lovingkindness" (*hesed*) because he had saved them from each one having an eye gouged out.

Boaz commended Ruth as follows: "You have

shown more kindness [*hesed*] at the end than at the beginning" (Ru 3:10).

The Lord compared Israel's former attitude to that of a bride: "I remember you, the kindness [*hesed*] of your youth, the love of your betrothal" (Je 2:2). Of course, a bride does make a marriage covenant, but behind that covenant is love.

The *hesed* of the Lord: In the Ten Commandments (Ex 20; De 5), the Lord describes Himself as "a jealous God, visiting the iniquity of the fathers on the children to the third and fourth generations of those who hate Me, but showing mercy [*hesed*] to thousands, to those who love Me and keep My commandments" (Ex 20:5-6).

Even more gracious is the Lord's self-description spoken after the apostasy of the golden calf, when the Israelites had shown how disloyal they were to God's covenant. "The LORD God, merciful and gracious, longsuffering, and abounding in goodness and truth, keeping mercy [*hesed*] for thousands, forgiving iniquity . . ." (Ex 34:67).

Jonah, like many religious but harsh people, was displeased with the Lord's graciousness. Saying, "I told You so," the sulky prophet says, "I know that You are a gracious and merciful God, slow to anger and abundant in lovingkindness [*hesed*]" (Jon 4:2).

Fifteen times in the Old Testament, *hesed* is paired with a word of mercy as a close synonym. For example: "Remember, O LORD, Your tender mercies and Your lovingkindnesses, for they have been from of old" (Ps 25:6). This word occurs again and again in the Psalms.

LOW (archaic)

The sound cows make (Job 6:5).

LOWLAND

The low area between Philistia and the Mediterranean Sea, including the cities of Lachish and Beth-shemesh. These lowlands are to the east of Hebron and Debir (1 Ki 10:27).

LU'BIM

An African people mentioned in connection with the Egyptians and Ethiopians (2 Ch 12:3; 16:8). See LIBYA.

LUCAS

Another form of the name LUKE (Phile 24).

LU′ CI•FER *(brightness)*

The "bright star," or "morning star." This name often refers to Venus; though Jupiter, Mars, Mercury, and Saturn may also be seen with the naked eye if they are in the morning sky before sunrise. Isaiah likens the glory of the king of Babylon to Lucifer, whom he calls the "son of the morning" (Is 14:12). Isaiah speaks of Lucifer "fallen from heaven" because of his pride and desire to be like the Most High (Is 14:12-15). At least from the time of Jerome the name has been applied to Satan. It is assumed by many that Jesus statement, "I saw Satan fall like lightning from heaven" (Lk10:18) is a reference to Isaiah 14:12-15, and probably Ezekiel 28:12-19 as well. The prophecies of Isaiah and Ezekiel specifically refer to the kings of Babylon and Tyre, but these nations are often used as symbolic references to evil governments (as in the book of Revelation). If these passages do refer to Satan, it seems that the name "Lucifer" or "morning star" is not a name or a title, but rather a description of the original beauty of this angel. In Revelation 22:16 Jesus describes Himself as the bright, the morning star; this is clearly a description of beauty and majesty, not an identifying name.

LU′ CI•US

A Christian of Cyrene. He was a teacher in the church at Antioch (Ac 13:1).

LUCRE (archaic)

Money, gain (1 Ti 3:2-3).

LUD *(strife)*

Lud was the fourth son of Shem (Ge 10:22; 1 Ch 1:17).

LU′ DIM

The Ludim (Ge 10:13; 1 Ch 1:11) were the descendants of Mizraim.

LU′ HITH *(made of planks, floored)*

A town of Moab (Is 15:5; Je 48:5).

LUKE *(light-giving)*

A friend and traveling companion of Paul (Col 4:14; 2 Ti 4:11; Phile 24) who wrote the Third Gospel and Acts. A Greek, he was a doctor and is often referred to as the beloved physician. He joined Paul at Troas (Ac 16:10) and remained with him about nine years. See "The Author of Luke."

LUKE, GOSPEL OF

1. The Book of Luke. Luke, a physician, writes with the compassion and warmth of a family doctor as he carefully documents the perfect humanity of the Son of Man, Jesus Christ. Luke emphasizes Jesus's ancestry, birth, and early life before moving carefully and chronologically through His earthly ministry. Growing belief and growing opposition develop side by side. Those who believe are challenged to count the cost of discipleship. Those who oppose will not be satisfied until the Son of Man hangs lifeless on a cross. But the resurrection insures that His purpose will be fulfilled: "to seek and to save that which was lost" (19:10).

Kata Loukon, "According to Luke," is the ancient title that was added to this Gospel at a very early date. The Greek name *Luke* appears only three times in the New Testament (Col 4:14; 2 Ti 4:11; Phile 24).

2. The Author of Luke. It is evident from the prologues to Luke and Acts (Lk 1:1-4; Ac 1:1-5) that both books were addressed to Theophilus as a two-volume work (Luke is called "the former account"). Acts begins with a summary of Luke and continues the story from where the Gospel of Luke concludes. The style and language of both books are quite similar. The "we" portions of Acts (Ac 16:1-17; 20:5–21:18; 27:1–28:16) reveal that the author was a close associate and traveling companion of Paul. Because all but two of Paul's associates are named in the third person, the list can be narrowed to Titus and Luke. Titus has never been seriously regarded as a possible author of Acts, and Luke best fits the requirements. He was with Paul during his first Roman imprisonment, and Paul referred to him as "Luke the beloved physician" (Col 4:14; Phile 24). During his second Roman imprisonment, Paul wrote "Only Luke is with me" (2 Ti 4:11), an evidence of Luke's loyalty to the apostle in the face of profound danger.

Luke may have been a Hellenistic Jew, but it is more likely that he was a Gentile (this would make him the only Gentile contributor to the New Testament). In Colossians 4:10-14, Paul lists three fellow workers who are "of the circumcision" (vv. 10-11) and then includes Luke's name with two Gentiles (vv. 12-14). Luke's obvious skill with the Greek language and his phrase "their own language" in Acts 1:19 also imply that he was not Jewish. It has been suggested that Luke may have been a Greek physician to a Roman family who at some point was set free and given Roman citizenship. Another guess is that he was the "brother" referred to in 2 Corinthians 8:18-19. Ancient traditions (including the Muratorian Fragment, Irenaeus, Tertullian, Clement of Alexandria, Origen, Eusebius, and Jerome) strongly support Luke as the author of Luke and Acts. Tradition also says that Luke was from Syrian Antioch, remained unmarried, and died at the age of eighty-four.

3. The Time of Luke. Luke was not an eyewitness of the events in his Gospel, but he relied on the testimony of eyewitnesses and written sources (1:1-4). He carefully investigated and arranged his material and presented it to Theophilus ("Friend of God"). The title "most excellent," or "most noble" (Ac 23:26; 24:3; 26:25), indicates that Theophilus was a man of high social standing. He probably assumed responsibility for publishing Luke and Acts so that they would be available to Gentile readers. Luke translated Aramaic terms with Greek words and explained Jewish customs and geography to make his Gospel more intelligible to his original Greek readership. During Paul's two-year Caesarean imprisonment, Luke may have traveled in Palestine to gather information from eyewitnesses of Jesus's ministry. The date of this Gospel depends on that of Acts since this was the first volume (see "The Time of Acts"). If Luke was written during Paul's first imprisonment in Rome it would have been dated in the early 60s. However, it may have been given final form in Greece. In all probability, its publication preceded the destruction of Jerusalem (A.D. 70).

4. The Christ of Luke. The humanity and compassion of Jesus are repeatedly stressed in Luke's Gospel. Luke gives the most complete account of Christ's ancestry, birth, and development. He is the ideal Son of Man who identified with the sorrow and plight of sinful men in order to carry our sorrows and offer us the priceless gift of salvation. Jesus alone fulfills the Greek ideal of human perfection.

5. Keys to Luke.

Key Word: Jesus the Son of Man—Luke clearly states his purpose in the prologue of his Gospel: "to write to you an orderly account . . . that you may know that certainty of those things in which you were instructed" (1:3-4). Luke

wanted to create an accurate, chronological, and comprehensive account of the unique life of Jesus the Christ to strengthen the faith of Gentile believers and stimulate saving faith among nonbelievers. Luke also had another purpose, and that was to show that Christ was not only divine but also human. Luke portrays Christ in His fullest humanity by devoting more of his writing to Christ's feelings and humanity than any other Gospel.

Key Verses: Luke 1:3-4 and 19:10—"It seemed good to me also, having had perfect understanding of all things from the very first, to write to you an orderly account, most excellent Theophilus, that you may know the certainty of those things in which you were instructed" (1:3-4).

" 'For the Son of Man has come to seek and to save that which was lost' " (19:10).

Key Chapter: Luke 15—Captured in the three parables of the lost sheep, lost coin, and lost son is the crux of this Gospel: that God through Christ has come to seek and to save that which was lost.

5. Survey of Luke. Luke builds the Gospel narrative on the platform of historical reliability. His emphasis on chronological and historical accuracy makes this the most comprehensive of the four Gospels. This is also the longest and most literary Gospel, and it presents Jesus Christ as the Perfect Man who came to seek and to save sinful men. This book can be divided into four sections: the introduction of the Son of Man (1:1–4:13); the ministry of the Son of Man (4:14–9:50); the rejection of the Son of Man (9:51–19:27); the crucifixion and resurrection of the Son of Man (19:28–24:53).

The Introduction of the Son of Man (1:1–4:13). Luke places a strong emphasis on the ancestry, birth, and early years of the Perfect Man and of His forerunner John the Baptist. Their infancy stories are intertwined as Luke records their birth announcements, advent, and temple presentations. Jesus prepares over thirty years (summarized in one verse, 2:52) for a public ministry of only three years. The ancestry of the Son of Man is traced back to the first man, Adam, and His ministry commences after His baptism and temptation.

The Ministry of the Son of Man (4:14–9:50). The authority of the Son of Man over every realm is demonstrated in 4:14–6:49. In this section His authority over demons, disease, nature, the effects of sin, tradition, and all people is presented as a prelude to His diverse ministry of preaching, healing, and discipling (7:1–9:50).

The Rejection of the Son of Man (9:51–19:27). The dual responses of growing belief and growing rejection has already been introduced in the Gospel (4:14; 6:11), but from this time forward the intensity of opposition to the ministry of the Son of Man increased. When the religious leaders accused Him of being demonized, Jesus pronounced a series of divine woes upon them (11). Knowing that He is on His last journey to Jerusalem, Jesus instructs His disciples on a number of practical matters including prayer, covetousness, faithfulness, repentance, humil-

ity, discipleship, evangelism, the second advent, and salvation (12:1–19:27).

The Crucifixion and Resurrection of the Son of Man (19:28–24:53). After His triumphal entry into Jerusalem, Jesus encountered the opposition of the priests, Sadducees, and scribes and predicted the overthrow of Jerusalem (19:28–21:38). The Son of Man instructed His disciples for the last time before His betrayal in Gethsemane. The three religious and three civil trials culminate in His crucifixion. The glory and foundation of the Christian message is the historical resurrection of Jesus Christ. The Lord conquered the grave as He promised, and appeared on a number of occasions to His disciples before His ascension to the Father.

OUTLINE OF LUKE

Part One: The Introduction of the Son of Man (1:1–4:13)

I. The Purpose and Method of Luke's Gospel (1:1-4)

II. The Events Preceding Christ's Birth (1:5-56)

A. John the Baptist's Birth Is Foretold 1:5-25
B. Jesus the Christ's Birth Is Foretold 1:26-56

III. The Events Accompanying Christ's Birth (1:57–2:38)

A. The Birth of John the Baptist ... 1:57-80
B. The Birth of Jesus Christ 2:1-38

IV. The Events During Christ's Childhood (2:39-52)

A. Jesus Returns to Nazareth 2:39-40
B. Jesus Celebrates the Passover ... 2:41-50
C. Jesus Grows in Wisdom 2:51-52

V. The Events Preceding Christ's Presentation (3:1–4:13)

A. The Ministry of John the Baptist ... 3:1-20
B. The Baptism of Christ 3:21-22
C. The Genealogy of Christ (Through Mary) 3:23-38
D. The Temptation of Christ 4:1-13

Part Two: The Ministry of the Son of Man (4:14–9:50)

I. The Presentation of Christ (4:14-30)

A. Acceptance Throughout Galilee ... 4:14-15
B. Rejection at Nazareth 4:16-30

II. The Demonstration of Christ's Powers (4:21–5:28)

A. Demons Are Cast Out 4:31-37
B. Peter's Mother-In-Law Is Healed 4:38-39
C. Jesus Ministers Throughout Galilee 4:40-44
D. The First Disciples Are Called 5:1-11
E. A Leper Is Cleansed 5:12-15
F. A Paralytic Is Healed 5:16-26
G. Matthew Is Called 5:27-28

III. The Explanation of Christ's Program (5:29–6:49)

A. Jesus Teaches the Pharisees ... 5:29-6:11
B. Jesus Teaches the Disciples 6:12-49

IV. The Expansion of Christ's Program (7:1–9:50)

A. A Centurion's Servant Is Healed ... 7:1-10
B. A Widow's Son Is Raised 7:11-16
C. Christ Comments on John the Baptist 7:17-35
D. Christ Dines at a Pharisee's Home 7:36-50
E. Certain Women Minister to Christ ... 8:1-3
F. Parable of the Soils 8:4-15

Part Three: The Rejection of the Son of Man
(9:51–19:27)

Part Four: The Crucifixion and Resurrection of the Son of Man
(19:28–24:53)

LUKEWARM

Neither hot nor cold; tepid. The church in Laodicea was rebuked for being "lukewarm." They were complacent and self-satisfied, with none of the good and useful properties of either cold or heat (Re 3:14-22). See LAODICEA.

LU′NA·TIC

The Greek word is derived from the word for moon, as the English word *lunatic* is derived from the Latin *Luna,* moon. It was believed that the light or changes of the moon affected the reason of the mentally unstable (Ma 17:15; Mk 9:17).

LUST (De 12:15,20-21; 1 Co 10:6; Ga 5:24; Tit 2:12).

LUTE

Thought to be a small harp-like instrument with three strings, though its exact definition is not known. Not the round-back guitar-like instrument of the Renaissance era. See HARP.

LUZ *(nut tree)*

Two towns:

1. An ancient town of the Canaanites which was later called Beth-el (Ge 28:19; 35:6; 48:3; Jos 18:13).

2. A town of the Hittites, built by an inhabitant of the former Luz. This man betrayed the first town to the Israelites (Ju 1:22-26).

LXX

Abbreviation of Septuagint (LXX is the Roman numeral 70). See SEPTUAGINT.

LY·CA·O′NI·A

A district of Asia Minor, adapted to pasturage. Paul preached in three of its cities, Iconium, Derbe, Lystra (Ac 13:51–14:1-23). Timothy came from this area (Ac 16:1).

LY·CA·O′NI·AN

The language of Lycaonia. It is thought to have been a Greek dialect mingled with Syriac, or possibly a language descended from the ancient Assyrian language. When Paul and Barnabas healed a crippled man at Lystra, the people wanted to worship them as gods. At first Paul and Barnabas did not understand what was happening, because the people spoke in Lycaonian rather than common Greek (Ac 14:11).

LYC′I·A

A Roman province in the southwest of Asia Minor. On his voyage to Jerusalem Paul stopped at Patara in this district (Ac 21:1-2). He landed at Myra, another of its cities, on the way to Rome (Ac 27:5-6).

LYD′DA *(strife)*

A village near Joppa, or Jaffa (Ac 9:32,38).

LYD′I·A

1. A woman of Thyatira, a town of Asia. This city was noted for the art of dyeing and when Lydia settled in Philippi, she sold the dyed garments of Thyatira. She was a pious woman, a true worshipper of God. When she heard Paul she accepted the gospel. It was in Philippi the gospel was first preached in Europe. Paul and Silas lodged in her home (Ac 16:14-15,40).

2. *(land of Lydus).* A region on the western coast of Asia Minor. Its capital was Sardis and Philadelphia and Thyatira were within its bounds (Re 1:11).

LYDIANS

Soldiers, also referred to as "men of Lydia" (NIV) or "men of Ludim" (NRSV), who fought at

LYDIA

the Battle of Carchemish with the Egyptians (Je 46:9). They may have come from Lydia (in modern Turkey), or an African people. See LUDIM.

LYE

A strong alkaline cleaning agent, used on its own or combined with fat to make soap (Je 2:22). The word is also translated "soda" or "nitre" in other translations. Proverbs 25:20 compares "vinegar and soda" to the reaction of a miserable person to joy in others. The acid of vinegar combined with an alkaline makes a vigorous foaming.

LYRE

A small harp. See HARP.

LY·SA′NI·AS (sadness ended)

The tetrarch of Abilene during the time of John the Baptist and Jesus (Lk 3:1).

LYS′I·AS CLAUDIUS

The commander of the Roman troops in Jerusalem. He rescued Paul from an angry mob, and sent him by night to Caesarea for safekeeping (Ac 21:31-38; 22:24-30; 23:17-30; 24:7, 22). He was a tribune, the commander of a cohort (600 to 1,000 men).

LYS′TRA

A city of Lycaonia. Paul visited this city on his first missionary journey. After he healed a lame man, the people insisted that he and Barnabas be worshipped as gods. As soon as they figured out what was happening, they managed to prevent the sacrifices, but it was only with great difficulty that the crowds were restrained. Only a short time later, the same crowds were enthusiastically stoning Paul, at the instigation of the hostile Jews from the neighboring town. Paul survived this ordeal, and continued on his way the next day (Ac 14:6-21; 2 Ti 3:11). Timothy came from this town, the son of a believing Jewish woman and her Gentile husband (Ac 16:1-2).

M

MA′A·CAH, MA′A·CHAH (oppression)

Six women, three men, and a kingdom:
1. The son of Reumah, the concubine of Nahor, the brother of Abraham (Ge 22:24).

2. A wife of David, the mother of Absalom. She was the daughter of Talmai, king of Geshur (2 Sa 3:3; 1 Ch 3:2).

3. An Aramean kingdom, also called Syrian Maachah, from whose king the Ammonites hired 1,000 soldiers to fight against David (2 Sa 10:6,8; 1 Ch 19:6-7).

4. Father of Achish and king of Gath in the time of Solomon (1 Ki 2:39).

5. Granddaughter of Abishalom and wife of Rehoboam, king of Judah, and mother of Abijah (1 Ki 15:2). Because she encouraged idolatry, her grandson, Asa, removed her from the throne (1 Ki 15:10-13; 2 Ch 15:16).

6. Concubine of Caleb, mother of Sheber and Tirhanah (1 Ch 2:48).

7. Wife of Machir, the son of Manasseh (1 Ch 7:15-16).

8. Wife of Jehiel, who was the father of Gibeon. Maacah was an ancestress of King Saul (1 Ch 8:29; 9:35).

9. Father of Hanan, one of David's mighty men (1 Ch 11:43).

10. Father of Shephatiah, ruler of the Simeonites in David's reign (1 Ch 27:16).

MA·ACH′A·THITE, MA·AC′A·THITE

Inhabitants of Maacah,, probably the descendants of Maacah the son of Nahor (see MAACAH No. 1; De 3:14; Jos 12:5; 11:13; 2 Sa 23:34; 2 Ki 25:23; Je 40:8).

MA·A·DA′I

A son of Bani, one of the group who had married foreign wives (Ez 10:34).

MA·A·DI′AH (ornament of Jehovah)

A priest who returned from Babylon (Ne 12:5, 7), perhaps the same as Moadiah (Ne 12:17).

MA·A′I (compassionate)

A priest who blew a trumpet at the dedication of the rebuilt wall of Jerusalem (Ne 12:36).

MA′A·LEH-AC·RAB′BIM (ascent of scorpions) (Jos 15:3)

See AKRABBIM.

MA′A·RATH (desolation)

A town in the mountains of Judah (Jos 15:59). Its present day location is uncertain, but other towns mentioned in conjunction with it are located a few miles to the north of Hebron.

MA′ A·SAI *(work of Jehovah)*

A priest of the family of Immer (1 Ch 9:12; Maasiai, KJV).

MA·A·SEI′ AH *(work of Jehovah)*

Possibly as many as twenty-one Old Testament men:

1. A Levite who played a psaltery as the ark was brought to Jerusalem (1 Ch 15:18,20).

2. A captain of a force which assisted Jehoiada in the removal of Athaliah from the throne of Judah (2 Ch 23:1).

3. An officer in the reign of Uzziah (2 Ch 26:11).

4. A son of Ahaz, king of Judah, slain by Zichri, the mighty man of Ephraim (2 Ch 28:7).

5. Governor of Jerusalem during the days of Josiah, king of Judah (2 Ch 34:8).

6. A priest of the descendants of Jeshua (Ez 10:18).

7. A priest of the sons of Harim (Ez 10:21).

8. A priest of the house of Pashur (Ez 10:22).

9. A descendant of the house of Pahathmoab (Ez 10:30).

10. Father of Azariah (Ne 3:23).

11. One who was with Ezra when he instructed the people (Ne 8:4).

12. A priest who explained the law (Ne 8:7).

13. A chief of the people, one who sealed the covenant (Ne 10:25).

14. A man of Judah who resided in Jerusalem at the time of Nehemiah (Ne 11:5).

15. Son of Ithiel, a Benjamite (Ne 11:7).

16. A priest who participated in the dedication of the wall, one of the trumpeters (Ne 12:41).

17. Another priest who participated in the dedication of the wall, a singer (Ne 12:42).

18. Father of Zephaniah, who was a priest during the time of King Zedekiah of Judah (Je 21:1; 29:25).

19. Father of the false prophet, Zedekiah (Je 29:21).

20. Ancestor of Seraiah, quartermaster to King Zedekiah; and Baruch, Jeremiah's scribe (Je 32:12; 51:59).

21. Son of Shallum and doorkeeper of the temple during the time of Jehoiakim, king of Judah (Je 35:4).

MA·AS·I′ AI

See MAASAI.

MA′ ATH *(small)*

An ancestor of Jesus (Lk 3:26).

MA′ AZ *(anger)*

A son of Ram (1 Ch 2:27).

MA·A·ZI′ AH

Two Old Testament men:

1. A descendant of Aaron (1 Ch 24:18).

2. A priest who signed the covenant with Nehemiah (Ne 10:8). Possibly another name for Maadiah (Ne 12:5).

MAC′ BAN·NAI

See MACHBANAI.

MAC′ CA·BEES, THE *(hammer)*

A family of Jewish patriots also known as the Asmonaeans, or Hasmonaeans. The name is derived from one of the family's most prominent members, Judas, whose surname was Maccabaeus. Judas Maccabaeus led the revolt against the rule of the defiler, Antiochus Epiphanes. See INTERTESTAMENTAL PERIOD and HASMONEAN.

MAC′ CA·BEES, BOOKS OF

See APOCRYPHA.

MACE

An instrument of war; a battle ax or a club with a metal head. It is believed that the traditional king's scepter is a symbolic representation of a mace, indicating the power and authority which is invested in the royal position.

MAC·E·DO′ NI·A

A country north of Greece. It rose to worldwide power under Philip of Macedon (359-336 B.C.) and his celebrated son Alexander the Great (336-323 B.C.). Macedonia is first mentioned in Acts 16:6-10; Paul received a vision of a Macedonian man begging for someone to come and explain the gospel to them. Luke describes Paul's journey through Macedonia in chapters 16:6–17:14. Paul later returned to Macedonia to encourage the churches there (Ac 20:1). See PHILIPPI, and THESSALONICA.

MAC·E·DO′ NI·ANS

Inhabitants of Macedonia. Two of Paul's traveling companions, Gaius and Aristarchus, were Macedonians (Ac 19:29). Paul also mentions the

Macedonian believers in his letter to the Corinthian church (2 Co 9:2).

MACHAERUS

According to Josephus, the place where John the Baptist was imprisoned and beheaded.

MACH·BA′ NAI *(bond of the Lord)*

A Gadite hero who joined David at Ziklag (1 Ch 12:13).

MACH·BE′ NA

See MACHBENAH.

MACH·BE′ NAH *(bond)*

A name, probably of a town, mentioned in a genealogical list (1 Ch 2:49).

MA′ CHI *(decrease)*

Father of Geuel (Nu 13:15).

MA′ CHIR *(sold)*

Two Old Testament men:
1. The son of Manasseh, son of Joseph. He was the founder of the Machirites (Ge 50:23; Nu 26:29; Jos 17:1) who were given the district taken from the Amorites, east of the Jordan (Nu 32:39-40; De 3:15).
2. A son of Ammiel in Lodebar (2 Sa 9:4-5; 17:27-29).

MACHIRITES

Descendants of Machir, son of Manasseh, son of Joseph (Nu 26:29).

MACH·NAD′ E·BAI

A son of Bani. He renounced his foreign wife (Ez 10:40).

MACH·PE′ LAH *(double)*

A field that belonged to Ephron the Hittite. In it was a cave (Ge 23:9,17,19). Abraham purchased it for 400 shekels of silver and made it a sepulchre for his wife, Sarah. It became also the tomb of Abraham (Ge 25:9-10), of Isaac, Rebekah, Jacob, and Leah (Ge 35:29; 47:28-31; 49:29-33; 50:12-13). See HEBRON.

MA′ DA·BA

See MEDEBA.

MA′ DAI *(middle land)*

The son of Japheth, from whom the Medes probably descended (Ge 10:2; 1 Ch 1:5).

MAD′ I·AN

See MIDIAN (Ac 7:29).

MAD·MAN′ NAH *(dunghill)*

A town in the extreme south of Judah (Jos 15:31; 1 Ch 2:49).

MAD′ MEN *(dunghill)*

A town in Moab (Je 48:2).

MAD·ME′ NAH *(dunghill)*

A town north of Jerusalem near Gibeah (Is 10:31).

MADNESS

Mental imbalance; insanity. In ancient times, it was generally believed that madness was connected with demonization (Jo 10:20); many Jews, including His brothers, thought Jesus was crazy.

MA′ DON *(strife)*

A city of the Canaanites in the north of Palestine (Jos 11:1-12; 12:19).

MAG′ A·DAN *(a tower)*

A place probably on the western shore of the Sea of Galilee (Ma 15:39). A variant of MAGDALA.

MAG′ BISH

A name listed with those who returned to Jerusalem with Zerubbabel (Ez 2:30); apparently the town these families originally came from.

MAG′ DA·LA *(tower)*

A town on the west shore of the Sea of Galilee near Tiberias (Ma 15:39), where Jesus and His disciples went after the feeding of the 4,000. Mark's account of this miracle says they went to Dalmanutha (Mk 8:10). Mary Magdalene was probably born in this town, and/or lived there.

MAG′ DA·LENE

One from Magdala. See MARY.

MAG′ DI·EL *(honor of God)*

An Edomite chief descended from Esau (Ge 36:43; 1 Ch 1:54).

MAGGOT

Fly larvae. This word is used in some versions as the translation of the pests of the third plague on the Egyptians, otherwise rendered "lice" or "gnats." This may also be a good translation for some of the "worms" mentioned, such as Job 7:5, "My flesh is caked with worms and dust."

MA' GI

The plural of *magus,* designating a priestly caste, a tribe of Media, who retained an important place after the Medes were conquered by the Persians. They worshipped fire, the earth, water, air. They wore white robes. They claimed to be mediators between God and man and to have the gift of prophecy. The wise men who came from the East to worship the newly born Jesus were of this religious caste (Ma 2:1). Also called "Wise Men." See MAGIC, SORCERY, AND DIVINATION.

MAGIC, SORCERY, AND DIVINATION

In our modern culture, attitudes range from complete disbelief in any spiritual realm to a fatal fascination with the dark powers. Satan and his henchmen are very real, and God has consistently warned His people to have nothing to do with occult practices. All forms of magic, sorcery, and divination are strictly forbidden by God. Deuteronomy 18:10-11 give us a list of the kinds of things God is talking about: "When you come into the land which the LORD your God is giving you, you shall not learn to follow the abominations of those nations." The various terms overlap one another in meaning somewhat.

"passing through the fire" A particularly loathsome pagan practice, involving burning a human alive as a sacrifice to the god Molech (2 Ki 23:10), or to two of the gods of the Sepharvaim (2 Ki 17:31), or to Baal (Je 19:5). Two of the kings of Judah, Ahaz the father of Hezekiah and Manasseh the son of Hezekiah, were guilty of this sin (2 Ki 16:3; 21:6; 2 Ch 33:6).

"one who practices witchcraft" Also translated "divination." Balaam practiced witchcraft professionally, accepting a fee for cursing or blessing (Nu 22:7). The Moabites tried to hire Balaam to curse Israel, however, Balaam found that he could not do it (Nu 23:23). Because God is over everything, He frequently interferes in the business of those who practice witchcraft, and will not allow them to carry out their purposes (Is 44:25). In spite of the fact that they had access to the true God, Israel continued to fall into the sin of consulting witches or soothsayers rather than God. Because their information was not from God, it was not reliable, and Jeremiah told the people that only a prophet whose words always come true can be trusted (Je 27:9; 29:8). God said that His hand would be against all these diviners who prophesied lies. (Eze 13:9). Not a great deal is known about the practice of witchcraft or divination. Some of the methods appear to have included consulting idols, "shaking arrows" and using the liver of an animal in some way (Eze 21:21-23). Genesis speaks of a cup belonging to Joseph, which he used to "practice divination" (Ge 44:5); apparently his servants assumed that his ability to interpret dreams was through divination.

"a soothsayer" One who casts spells. Balaam is described as a "soothsayer" (Jos 13:22); apparently this is synonymous with "one who practices witchcraft" or "a diviner." All such practices were forbidden (Le 19:26); however, Ahaz and Manasseh (the father and son of Hezekiah) both were involved in the occult (2 Ki 21:6; 2 Ch 33:6). This was one of the sins of the people when they forsook God (Is 2:6; 57:3; Je 27:9; Mi 5:12).

"one who interprets omens" (KJV translates this "enchantments"). Joseph interpreted dreams through the power of God, but he apparently represented himself to his brothers as one with powers of divination to account for his uncanny knowledge of them (Ge 44:5,15). The term "enchanted" or "charmed" is used in terms of snake charming in Ecclesiastes 10:11.

"a sorcerer" The penalty for sorcery was death (Ex 22:18). Jezebel was a militant promoter of Baal worship, and apparently also practiced witchcraft or sorcery (2 Ki 9:22), as did Manasseh the son of Hezekiah, king of Judah (2 Ch 33:6).

"one who conjures spells" Also translated "charm" (Ps 58:5). Sometimes translated "enchantments" (Is 47:9,12). The effect of a charm or enchantment is to render the victim pliable to the will of the charmer.

"a medium" One who claims to communicate with spirits and act as an intermediary between the spiritual realm and the everyday world (for a fee of course). When King Saul found that God no longer answered him, he turned to a medium to try and gain some supernatural knowledge of what he ought to do (1 Sa 28:7-9). Isaiah speaks of the futility of consulting mediums, asking advice from the dead for the living (Is 8:19). Isaiah 29:4 sounds like it is saying that mediums' supposed conversations with spirits were actually elaborate deceptions.

"a spiritist" This term always appears with the word "witch;" it could be translated "wizard." It refers to one who claims to have special knowledge from the spirit world.

"one who calls up the dead" Necromancy. This word only appears in Deuteronomy 18:11, but this was apparently a part of the work of a medium (see above). King Saul went to the witch at Endor to ask her to call up the spirit of the dead Samuel so that Saul could consult him (1 Sa 28:7-20). The woman seemed to be surprised and terrified when Samuel actually appeared; most of her consultations with the dead were probably either false or with demons. Consulting the dead is probably the type of spiritism which has continued to fascinate more people than any other. Many otherwise skeptical people are attracted by the idea of being able to contact those who have died. Humans dislike the idea of ceasing to exist, and communication from the "other side" seems both exciting and comforting. However, aside from this encounter at Endor, there is no biblical evidence that the dead can be reached in any way. We do not know why God allowed Samuel to be disturbed this time, but it is clear that trying to bring back the spirits of the dead is strictly forbidden. However, we do have one who can tell us about the other side of death. Jesus Christ died and rose again, conquering death forever, and opening the way for all who believe in Him to inherit eternal life.

The passage in Deuteronomy ends: "For all who do these things are an abomination to the LORD, and because of these abominations the LORD your God drives them out before you. For these nations which you will dispossess listened to soothsayers and diviners; but as for you, the LORD your God has not appointed such for you." Instead, God had given His people the opportunity to consult the one true God. As long as they remained obedient, they could trust that He would answer them, protect them and teach them.

The Hebrew word for "magic" is only used in connection with the magicians of Pharaoh and Nebuchadnezzar (Ge 41:8,24; Ex 7:11–9:11; Da 1:20; 2:2,10,27; 4:7,9; 5:11). Magicians were men who practiced various sorts of divination, soothsaying, sorcery, enchantments, or spiritism. In the Babylonian courts, the king's advisors and wise men were magicians. This elite class was made up of the learned men in the kingdom. Daniel and his friends were categorized with the king's other wise men, even though their wisdom came from God rather than the practice of magic. The "Magi" or "Wise men" who came to worship the infant Christ were of this group (Ma 2:1-12). In the Book of Acts, both Peter and

Paul encountered men who practiced magic, performing apparent miraculous feats and gaining great influence with the people. Simon the Sorcerer was fascinated by the evident power of God that he saw in Peter, and offered to pay for a dose of the Holy Spirit for himself. Peter rebuked him severely (Ac 8:9-25). Paul encountered another sorcerer named Elymas, who opposed Paul's preaching of the gospel to the Roman proconsul. As a result, Elymas was stricken blind for a time (Ac 13:6-8).

One of the Greek words connected with magic and sorcery is *pharmakeia,* the word from which we get our modern word "pharmacy" (Re 9:21; 18:23; 21:8; 22:15). The connection between hallucinogenic drugs and occult spiritual experiences has been known since ancient times. Various primitive tribes have used hallucinogenic fungi in their search for connection with the spirit world, risking death to experience the weird, drug induced visions which they believed would bring messages from the gods. Those who have come out of the modern drug culture can testify to the spiritual bondage which accompanies drug use, and to the connection between drugs and New Age and Eastern religious experiences. The connection between the physical reaction of the body to drugs and the spiritual realm is very unclear—the lines between hallucinogenic drugs, medication, and poison are sometimes very fuzzy, but it is clear that any drug use should be approached with caution and prayer. Certain drugs appear to open the mind and spirit to demonic influences.

MA·GI´ CIAN

One who practices magic; a sorcerer. Magicians claimed to possess supernatural powers that came through connections with evil spirits. The magicians of the Bible acquired considerable knowledge (Ex 7:11) and claimed to be able to interpret dreams (Ge 41:8; Da 2:10). Paul named two magicians who opposed Moses in Egypt, Jannes and Jambres (2 Ti 3:8). See MAGIC, SORCERY, AND DIVINATION.

MAG′ IS·TRATE

See RULER.

MAGNIFICAT *(magnifies)*

Mary's song, giving honor and glory to God. She said or sang these words while she was staying with her cousin Elizabeth, after the angel had announced that she was to be the mother of the Messiah (Lk 1:46-56).

MA′ GOG

Descendants of Japheth (Ge 10:2). They are usually identified with the barbaric Scythians north of the Crimea. It was prophesied that their ruler, Gog, would fail in his expedition against the restored Israel (Ge 10:2-3; Eze 38:2; 39:6). Figuratively the expression, Gog and Magog, refers to nations which Satan will muster for the final attack on the Messiah (Re 20:8).

MA′ GOR-MIS′ SA·BIB *(fear round about)*

A name given to Pashur by Jeremiah (Je 20:3).

MAG′ PI·ASH *(moth killer)*

A chief of the people who sealed the covenant (Ne 10:20).

MA·HA′ LAB

A town of Asher (Jos 19:29; NRSV). Also translated "at the sea" (NKJV).

MAH′ A·LAH

See MAHLAH.

MA·HAL′ A·LEEL *(praise of God)*

Two Old Testament men:

1. Grandson of Seth (Ge 5:12-17; Lk 3:37).

2. A man of Judah of the family of Perez who lived in Jerusalem after the exile (Ne 11:4).

MA′ HA·LATH *(sickness)*

Two Old Testament women:

1. Wife of Esau and daughter of Ishmael also called Bashemath (Ge 28:9).

2. A wife of Rehoboam (2 Ch 11:18).

MA′ HA·LATH-LEANNOTH

A musical term of uncertain meaning, used in the titles to Psalms 53 and 88. It is conjectured to refer to the character of the psalm, or possibly to a specific instrument.

MA′ HA·LI

See MAHLI.

MA·HA·NA′ IM *(two camps)*

A place east of the Jordan where Jacob was met by angels after leaving Padan-aram (Ge 32:2). Jacob gave the place the name Mahanaim after he saw the angels. A town of this name (presumably the same place) was assigned to the Merarite branch of the Levites. It was situated between the territories of Gad and Manasseh (Jos 13:26-30; 21:38-39; 1 Ch 6:80). Saul's son Ishbosheth made Manahaim his capital after his father's death, during the time David was reigning in Hebron (2 Sa 2:8,12); David later used the same town as a base when he was fleeing from Absalom (2 Sa 17:24). One of Solomon's twelve food-purveyors was stationed in Mahanaim (1 Ki 4:14).

MA′ HA·NEH-DAN *(camp of Dan)*

An encampment of the Danites (Ju 13:25; 18:12).

MA′ HA·RAI *(hasty)*

One of David's warriors, a Netophathite (2 Sa 23:28; 1 Ch 11:30; 27:13).

MA′ HATH *(gasping)*

Two Old Testament Levites:

1. A Levite of the family of Kohath and an ancestor of Samuel (1 Ch 6:33-35).

2. A Levite who lived during the days of Hezekiah , an overseer of priests who assisted in Hezekiah's reforms (2 Ch 29:12; 31:13).

MA·HA′ VITE

The designation of Eliel, one of David's mighty men (1 Ch 11:46).

MA·HA′ ZI·OTH *(visions)*

A descendant of Heman, a Levite (1 Ch 25:4).

MA·HER-SHAL′ AL-HASH′ -BAZ *(hastens to the prey)*

These were the words Isaiah wrote upon a scroll which afterwards became the name of his second son (Is 8:1-4). This symbolic name was a prophecy of what would happen to Israel at the hands of the Assyrians.

MAH′ LAH

Two Old Testament women:

1. Daughter of Zelophehad of Manasseh (Nu 26:33; 27:1).

2. The daughter of Gilead's sister Hammoleketh (1 Ch 7:18).

MAH' LI *(weak)*

Two Old Testament men:

1. A son of Merari and brother of Mushi, a Levite. He was founder of a tribal house (Ex 6:19; Nu 3:20,33; 26:58).

2. A Levite (1 Ch 6:47; 23:23; 24:30).

MAH' LITES

The descendants of Mahli, son of Merari, a Levite (Nu 3:33; 26:58).

MAH' LON *(sickly)*

Son of Elimelech and Naomi and the first husband of Ruth (Ru 1:2; 4:10).

MA' HOL *(dance)*

Father of three men noted for wisdom—Heman, Chalcol, and Darda (1 Ki 4:31). Solomon is described as being wiser than any of these three.

MAH•SEI' AH

See MAASEIAH No. 20.

MAID

A young girl. See MAIDSERVANT.

MAIDSERVANT

A young female slave or servant (Ge 16:1; Ex 11:5; Le 25:44; 1 Sa 1:11). It was not uncommon for a maidservant to become her master's concubine, as in the case of Sarah's servant Hagar, or the maidservants of Rachel and Leah. (Also see Ju 19:9.)

MAIL, COAT OF

A shirt made of interlocking loops of metal, designed to protect the wearer in battle. See BODY ARMOR.

MAIMED

Crippled by injury, often indicating the loss of a limb. Jesus healed the maimed (Ma 15:30).

MA' KAZ *(an end)*

A town under the supervision of the son of Dekar, one of Solomon's twelve food-purveyors (1 Ki 4:9).

MAK•HE' LOTH *(assemblies)*

An encampment of the Israelites in the wilderness (Nu 33:25-26).

MAK•KE' DAH *(place of herdsmen)*

A town in the lowland taken by Joshua (Jos 15:41).

MAK' TESH *(mortar)*

A valley in Jerusalem having a peculiar shape. The Targum calls it the Kidron Valley (Zep 1:11). Also called the "Mortar" (NASB, NRSV) and the "market district" (NIV).

MAL' A•CHI, BOOK OF

1. The Book of Malachi. Malachi, a prophet in the days of Nehemiah, directed his message of judgment to a people plagued with corrupt priests, wicked practices, and a false sense of security in their privileged relationship with God. Using the question and answer method, Malachi probed deeply into their problems of hypocrisy, infidelity, mixed marriages, divorce, false worship, and arrogance. So sinful had the nation become that God's words to the people no longer had any impact. For four hundred years after Malachi's ringing condemnations, God remained silent. Only with the coming of John the Baptist (3:1) did God again communicate to His people through a prophet's voice.

The meaning of the name *Mal'aki* ("My Messenger") is probably a shortened form of *Mal'a-ya*, "Messenger of Yahweh," and it is appropriate to the book which speaks of the coming of the "messenger of the covenant" ("messenger" is mentioned three times in 2:7; 3:1). The Septuagint used the title *Malachias* even though it also translated it "by the hand of his messenger." The Latin title is *Maleachi*.

2. The Author of Malachi. The only Old Testament mention of Malachi is in 1:1. The authorship, date, and unity of Malachi have never been seriously challenged. The unity of the book can be seen in the dialectic style that binds it together. Nothing is known of Malachi (not even his father's name), but a Jewish tradition says that he was a member of the Great Synagogue (see ZECHARIAH, BOOK OF, "The Author of Zechariah").

3. The Time of Malachi. Although an exact date cannot be established for Malachi, internal evidence can be used to deduce an approximate date. The Persian term for governor, *pechah* (1:8; Ne 5:14; Hag 1:1,14; 2:21), indicates that this book was written during the Persian domination of Israel (539-333 B.C.). Sacrifices were being offered in the temple (1:7-10; 3:8), which was rebuilt in 516 B.C. Evidently many years had passed since the offerings were instituted, because the priests had grown tired of them and corruptions had crept into the system. In addition, Malachi's oracle was inspired by the same problems that Nehemiah faced: corrupt priests (1:6–2:9; Ne 13:1-9), neglect of tithes and offerings (3:7-12; Ne 13:10-13), and intermarriage with pagan wives (2:10-16; Ne 13:23-28). Nehemiah came to Jerusalem in 444 B.C. to rebuild the city walls, thirteen years after Ezra's return and reforms (457 B.C.). Nehemiah returned to Persia in 432 B.C., but came back to Palestine about 425 B.C. and dealt with the sins described in Malachi. It is therefore likely that Malachi proclaimed his message while Nehemiah was absent between 432 B.C. and 425 B.C., almost a century after Haggai and Zechariah began to prophesy (520 B.C.).

4. The Christ of Malachi. The Book of Malachi is the prelude to four hundred years of prophetic silence, broken finally by the words of the next prophet, John the Baptist: "Behold! The Lamb of God who takes away the sin of the world!" (Jo 1:29). Malachi predicted the coming of the messenger who would clear the way before the Lord (3:1; Is 40:3). John the Baptist later fulfilled this prophecy, but the next few verses (3:2-5) jump ahead to Christ in His second advent. This is also true of the prophecy of the appearance of "Elijah, the prophet" (4:5). John the Baptist was this Elijah (Ma 3:3; 11:10-14; 17:9-13; Mk 1:3; 9:10-11; Lk 1:17; 3:4; Jo 1:23), but Elijah will also appear before the second coming of Christ.

5. Keys to Malachi.

Key Word: An Appeal to Backsliders—The divine dialogue in Malachi's prophecy is designed as an appeal to break through the barrier of Israel's unbelief, disappointment, and discouragement. The promised time of prosperity had not yet come, and the prevailing attitude that it is not worth serving God became evident in their moral and religious corruption. However, God revealed His continuous love in spite of Israel's lethargy. His appeal in this oracle was for the people and priests to stop and realize that their lack of blessing was not caused by God's lack of concern, but by their disobedience of the covenant law. If they would repent and return to God with sincere hearts, the obstacles to the flow of divine blessing would be removed. Malachi also reminded the people that a day of reckoning will surely come when God will judge the righteous and the wicked.

Key Verses: Malachi 2:17–3:1; 4:5–6—"You have wearied the LORD with your words; yet you say, 'In what way have we wearied Him?' In that you say, 'Everyone who does evil is good in the sight of the LORD, and He delights in them' or 'Where is the God of justice?'"

"Behold, I send My messenger, and he will prepare the way before Me. And the Lord, whom you seek, will suddenly come to His temple, even the Messenger of the covenant, in whom you delight. Behold, He is coming,' says the LORD of hosts" (2:17–3:1).

"Behold, I will send you Elijah the prophet before the coming of the great and dreadful day of the LORD. And he will turn the hearts of the fathers to the children, and the hearts of the children to their fathers, lest I come and strike the earth with a curse" (4:5-6).

Key Chapter: Malachi 3—The last book of the Old Testament concludes with a dramatic prophecy of the coming of the Lord and John the Baptist: "I will send My messenger, and he will prepare the way before Me" (3:1). Israel flocked to the Jordan four hundred years later when "the voice of one crying in the wilderness: 'Prepare the way of the LORD'" (Ma 3:3) appeared, breaking the long silence of prophetic revelation. Malachi 3 and 4 record the coming of the Messiah and His forerunner.

6. Survey of Malachi. The great prophecies of Haggai and Zechariah were not yet fulfilled, and the people of Israel became disillusioned and doubtful. They began to question God's providence as their faith imperceptibly degenerated into cynicism. Internally, they wondered whether it was worth serving God after all. Externally, these attitudes surfaced in mechanical observances, empty ritual, cheating on tithes and offerings, and crass indifference to God's moral and ceremonial law. Their priests were corrupt and their practices wicked, but they were so spiritually insensitive that they wondered why they were not being blessed by God.

Using a probing series of questions and answers, God sought to pierce their hearts of stone. In each case the divine accusations were denied: How has God loved us? (1:2-5); How have we (priests) despised God's name? (1:6–2:9); How have we (the people) profaned the covenant? (2:10–3:6); How have we robbed God? (3:7-12);

How have we spoken against God? (3:13-15). In effect, the people sneered, "Oh, come on now: it isn't that bad!" However, their rebellion was quiet, not open. As their perception of God grew dim, the resulting materialism and externalism became settled characteristics that later gripped the religious parties of the Pharisees and Sadducees. In spite of all this, God still loved His people and once again extended His grace to any who would humbly turn to Him. Malachi explored: the privilege of the nation (1:1-5), the pollution of the nation (1:6–3:15), and the promise to the nation (3:16–4:6).

The Privilege of the Nation (1:1-5). The Israelites blinded themselves to God's love for them. Wallowing in the problems of the present, they were forgetful of God's works for them in the past. God gave them a reminder of His special love by contrasting the fates of Esau (Edom) and Jacob (Israel).

The Pollution of the Nation (1:6–3:15). The priests had lost all respect for God's name and in their greed offered only diseased and imperfect animals on the altar. They had more respect for the Persian governor than they did for the living God. Moreover, God was withholding His blessings from them because of their disobedience to God's covenant and because of their insincere teaching.

The people were indicted for their treachery in divorcing the wives of their youth in order to marry foreign women (2:10-16). In response to their questioning the justice of God, they received the promise of the Messiah's coming, but also a warning of the judgment that He will bring (2:17–3:6). The people had robbed God of the tithes and offerings due Him, but God was ready to bless them with abundance if they would put Him first (3:7-12). The final problem is the arrogant challenge to the character of God (3:13-15), and this challenge is answered in the remainder of the book.

The Promise to the Nation (3:16–4:6). The Lord assured His people that a time is coming when the wicked will be judged and those who fear Him will be blessed. The day of the Lord will reveal that it is not "vain to serve God" (3:14).

Malachi ends on the bitter word *curse.* Although the people were finally cured of idolatry, there was little spiritual progress in Israel's history. Sin abounded, and the need for the coming Messiah was greater than ever.

OUTLINE OF MALACHI

I. The Privilege of the Nation (1:1-5)

II. The Pollution of the Nation (1:6–3:15)

A. The Sin of the Priests of Israel 1:6–2:9

B. The Sin of the People of Israel 2:10–3:15

III. The Promise to the Nation (3:16–4:6)

A. The Rewards of the Book of Remembrance.......................... 3:16-18

B. The Rewards of the Coming of Christ 4:1-3

C. The Prophecy of the Coming of Elijah 4:4-6

MAL'A·CHITE

The most common copper ore; a bright green stone formed by the reaction of copper carbonate with limestone. This word is used in the REB in Esther 1:6, describing the pavement of King Ahasuerus' palace. Other translations have used "alabaster" or "porphyry."

MAL'CAM *(rule)*

1. Son of Shaharaim, a Benjamite (1 Ch 8:9).
2. A god of the Ammonites (Zep 1:5). See MOLECH.

MAL'CHAM

See MALCAM, also a form of Milcom (Ze 1:5, KJV).

MAL·CHI'AH

See MALCHIJAH.

MAL'CHI·EL *(God is king)*

Son of Beriah and grandson of Asher (Ge 46:17; Nu 26:45).

MAL·CHI′ JAH, MAL·CHI′ AH *(Jehovah is king)*

Ten Old Testament kings:

1. A Levite of Gershom (1 Ch 6:40).

2. A descendant of Aaron. His house became the fifth course of priests in the time of David (1 Ch 24:1,6,9).

3. Son of Parosh who put away his foreign wife (Ez 10:25).

4. Son of Harim. He put away his foreign wife and labored on the wall of Nehemiah (Ez 10:31; Ne 3:11).

5. A son of Rechab. He labored on the wall under Nehemiah (Ne 3:14).

6. A goldsmith who labored on Nehemiah's wall (Ne 3:31).

7. One who stood by Ezra when he explained the law (Ne 8:4).

8. A priest who signed the covenant (Ne 10:3).

9. A priest who participated in the dedication of the wall (Ne 12:42).

10. Father of Pashur (Je 38:1; 21:1), who threw Jeremiah into the cistern. Pashur's father Malchiah was evidently a prince, and the cistern was in his courtyard (Je 38:6).

MAL·CHI′ RAM *(God exalted)*

A son of Jehoiachin, born in captivity (1 Ch 3:18).

MAL′ CHI·SHU′ A

A son of King Saul (1 Sa 14:49; 31:2; 1 Ch 8:33; 9:39).

MAL′ CHUS *(king)*

Servant of the high priest. His ear was cut off by Peter at the time of Christ's arrest (Jo 18:10). According to Luke, Christ healed the severed ear (Lk 22:51).

MALEFACTOR

Criminal, evildoer. Jesus was crucified between two malefactors, specifically identified as thieves (Lk 23:32-33,39; Jo 18:30).

MAL′ E·LEEL

See MAHALALEEL.

MALICE

Evil motives, the desire or intention to harm. Believers are commanded to "put away" all malice, and instead be "kind to one another, tenderhearted, forgiving one another, just as God in Christ also forgave you" (Ep 4:31-32). Love is directly opposed to malice (1 Co 13:4-7).

MAL·KI′ JAH

See MALCHIJAH.

MAL·LO′ THI

Son of Heman, one of the musicians in the tabernacle service at the time of King David (1 Ch 25:4,26).

MAL′ LOWS

The rendering of the Hebrew word for salt plant (Job 30:4). It is only mentioned once in the Bible, also rendered "saltwort" or "salt herbs." This is probably referring to a plant which grows in the dry area surrounding the Dead Sea.

MAL′ LUCH *(reigning or counselor)*

Six Old Testament men:

1. A Levite of the house of Mushi, of the family of Merari, ancestor of Ethan (1 Ch 6:44).

2. A son of Bani. He put away his foreign wife (Ez 10:29).

3. A son of Harim who divorced his Gentile wife (Ez 10:32).

4. A priest who signed the covenant (Ne 10:4).

5. A chief of the people who signed the covenant (Ne 10:27).

6. A chief of the priests who returned from Babylon with Zerubbabel (Ne 12:2,7); also called Malluchi (Ne 12:14, NASB, NRSV), Melichu (NKJV), or Melicu (KJV).

MAL·LU′ CHI

See MALLUCH No. 6.

MALTA

An island in the Mediterranean, located between Sicily and Africa. When Paul was being transported to Rome, his ship was caught in a storm and they were shipwrecked on this island (Ac 28:1,11). He stayed there for about three months, using the time to preach the gospel and start another church. Malta is also called Melita (KJV).

MAM·MAI′ AS

See SHEMAIAH (Ez 8:16).

MAM′ MON *(wealth)*

A transliteration of an Aramaic word signifying "material possessions" or "riches" (Ma 6:24; Lk 16:9,11,13). This word has the specific connotation of wealth which is in opposition to God. The fact is that wealth has the tendency to take this place in the lives of people, even when they don't intend to let it. Believers must learn to recognize that wealth will not bring security or salvation (Ma 16:26; Mk 8:36; Lk 9:25; 12:13-21). Pursuit of wealth automatically rules out pursuit of God; there is not room in one person's life for more than one "first love."

MAM'RE *(strength, fatness)*

1. A chieftain of the Amorites who lived at Mamre. He and his brothers assisted Abraham in rescuing Lot (Ge 14:13,24).

2. The name of the district of Hebron where Abraham lived (Ge 23:19; 35:27).

MAN

Adam is the term used in the first three chapters of Genesis for "man" (both male and female) as the pinnacle of God's creation, and as having been created in God's image and likeness. The word is also the personal name of the first man, Adam. Adam was this in both senses of our English word; first human and first male. The root word is believed to suggest ruddiness, and is related to the word for "ground" (*adamah*), from which man was formed. Genesis 1:27 is very important here: "So God created man in His own image; in the image of God He created him; male and female He created them."

Adam is in the image of God in the sense that he is a reasoning, moral being with emotions and a spiritual nature. It is the moral and spiritual nature that is lacking in the rest of the creatures on earth. Animals do not build churches.

When husband and wife relationships are in view, *ish* and *ishah* are common forms (there are separate words for male and female in the sense of gender). Though the two forms may not be from the same root, at the very least Adam makes a pun when he says: "She shall be called Woman [*ishah*], because she was taken out of Man [*ish*]" (Ge 2:23).

Ish is also commonly used for any male individual and can even simply mean "each" or "whoever."

Both *adam* and *ish* stress the value of humankind. Since man is created in God's image, it is an attack on that image to destroy a fellow man or woman.

Enosh is the word for mankind that often stresses its mortality and frailty. Psalm 8:4, for example, reads, "What is man [*enosh*] that You are mindful of him, and the son of man that You visit him?" The word is also more likely to appear in poetry, as in Psalm 8. If *enosh* is derived from *anash,* "to be weak or sick," this would fit the common Hebrew usage. Some scholars prefer to derive the word from a similar root not proven to exist in Hebrew but definitely found in the related Semitic languages, Arabic and Ugarite. This root stresses sociability and companionship. Humans certainly are social creatures. If this origin is correct, the "frailty" motif would come more from the context and the Old Testament's stress on God's majesty and man's lowly position.

Geber and *gibbor* both come from the root *gabar,* to "prevail," "be strong or great." Both of these words are the opposite of the common understanding of *enosh.* If *enosh* is man in his frailty, these words stress man in his strength.

Geber occurs sixty-six times and describes a man at the height of his masculine strength. It is somewhat similar to the Hispanic term *macho,* which has become so popular in everyday English.

Gibbor is usually a military term for warriors and heroes, "mighty men of valor." It is used for Nimrod, the "mighty hunter before the LORD" (Ge 10:9), for the Philistine "champion," Goliath (1 Sa 17:51), and for David's mighty men (2 Sa 23:8).

MAN'A·EN *(Greek form of Menahem)*

A teacher in the church at Antioch (Ac 13:1), probably of a noble family because he was "brought up with Herod the Tetrarch."

MAN'A·HATH *(rest)*

1. Son of Shobal, the Horite (Ge 36:23).

2. A place where Benjamites of Geba were held captive (1 Ch 8:6).

MAN·A·HA'THITES

Variant of MANAHETHITES.

MAN·A·HE'THITES

The descendants of Manahath, or else the inhabitants of Manahath (1 Ch 2:52,54).

MA·NAS'SEH *(forgetting)*

1. The elder son of Joseph and brother of Ephraim (Ge 41:50-51; 48:8-21).

2. Tribe of Manasseh. It comprised seven tribal families, one springing from Manasseh's son, Machir, and the others from his grandson, Gilead (Nu 26:28-34; Jos 17:1-2). A half of the tribe was settled east of the Jordan and the other half west of the Jordan in the central section, north of Ephraim (Nu 32:33,42; De 3:13-15; Jos 13:29-33).

3. The grandfather of the Jonathan who acted as priest of the carved image, first for Micah the Ephraimite, and later for the tribe of Dan (Ju 18:30).

4. Son of Hezekiah. He followed his father to the throne at the age of twelve and had the longest reign of all the kings of Judah (2 Ki 21:1-16). He is also remembered as one of the most wicked kings, because he sacrificed his children to idols, engaged in occult practices, and led Israel in idolatry. He was carried to Babylon by the Assyrian king (2 Ch 33:11). At this point, in the midst of his affliction, Manasseh turned back to the Lord God, and repented of his sins. God restored him to his throne, and Manasseh removed the idols from the temple, commanding the rest of the nation to follow him in worshipping the true God.

5. Son of Pahath-moab (Ez 10:30).

6. A son of Hashum (Ez 10:33).

MANASSES

Alternate spelling of Manasseh.

1. Manasseh, king of Judah (Ma 7:10).

2. Manasseh, son of Joseph (Re 7:6).

MANASSITES, THE

The tribe of Manasseh; the descendants of Joseph's oldest son Manasseh (De 4:43; Ju 12:4; 2 Ki 10:33).

MAN′DRAKE

A beautiful, odoriferous plant supposed to act as a love potion (Ge 30:14-16; Song 7:13). Its blossoms are purple; the fruit is small and yellowish in color. It is of the same family as nightshade, tomatoes, and potatoes. The forked root was supposed to have magical qualities, and was apparently used as a narcotic.

MA′NEH

An ancient weight and monetary unit. Also called "mina," it was equal to about 50 shekels (Eze 45:12). See MONEY OF THE BIBLE.

MAN′GER

An shallow trough for feeding animals. When Mary had given birth to Jesus, she wrapped him in swaddling clothes, and laid him in the manger of the stable (Lk 2:7,12,16). A manger might have been made of wood, of stones or bricks mortared together, or carved out of rock. Crib is another word for the same object (Pr 14:4; Is 1:3).

MAN′NA

Manna was the food miraculously supplied by God to the Israelites during their years of wandering in the wilderness. The Lord told Moses, "I will rain bread from heaven for you" (Ex 16:4). The spiritual purpose of the daily provision was "that He might humble you and that He might test you, to do you good" (De 8:16).

The manna was to be gathered each day, except the Sabbath, by every household according to need (Ex 16:16-18). Manna gathered in excess of need melted in the sun or became infested with worms (Ex 16:20-21). The miracle food, which fell like dew, is described as "a small round substance, as fine as frost on the ground" (Ex 16:14). It tasted like "wafers made with honey" (Ex 16:31). The exact nature of this miracle food remains a mystery, although it is compared to "white coriander seed" (Ex 16:31). It was cooked in various different ways; boiled, ground, beaten, made into cakes (Ex 16:23; Nu 11:8). God supplied manna for forty years until the Israelites entered Canaan and the "food of the land" (Jos 5:12) became available.

During the wilderness years, God provided water for the Israelites when Moses struck a rock with his rod (Ex 17:6). Quail were also miraculously supplied when the people complained they had no meat to eat with their manna (Ex 16:13).

Throughout the Bible, references are made to God's provision in the wilderness to show the Lord's continuing concern for His people. Jesus alluded to the "bread from heaven" given through Moses (Jo 6:32), but He described Himself as the "bread of life," which permanently satisfies (Jo 6:35).

MA·NO′AH *(rest)*

The father of Samson, a Danite of the town of Zorah (Ju 13:1-25). When told of the announcement of the angel to his wife promising the birth of Samson, he prayed for the angel's return to give him instruction concerning the rearing of the child. The petition was granted.

MAN OF SIN

See ANTICHRIST.

MANSERVANT
See SLAVE.

MANSIONS
Jesus told the twelve disciples that He was preparing a place for them in heaven. The KJV uses the word "mansions," a better translation is probably "rooms" (Jo 14:2).

MAN′ SLAY·ER
See MURDER.

MAN′ TLE
A sleeveless outer garment. See CLOTHING.

MANUHOTH
Descendants of Caleb (1 Ch 2:52).

MANURE
Animal excrement. Manure has been used as fertilizer since ancient times, but it also has a decided connotation with filth and undesirable rubbish (Is 25:10).

MA′ OCH (oppressed)
Father of Achish, king of Gath (1 Sa 27:2). See ACHISH.

MA′ ON (dwelling)
1. Son of Shammai of Judah, founder of Beth-zur (1 Ch 2:45).
2. A town of Judah, south of Hebron (Jos 15:55; 1 Sa 25:2).

MA′ ON·ITES
A people mentioned in Judges 10:12 as oppressors of Israel.

MAR′ A (bitter)
The name by which Naomi asked to be called after her bitter experiences in Moab (Ru 1:20).

MAR′ AH (bitterness)
One of the encampments of the Israelites before coming to Sinai (Ex 15:23-24; Nu 33:8-9).

MAR′ A·LAH (trembling)
A place on the border of Zebulun (Jos 19:11).

MAR·AN-A′ THA
"Our Lord has come" or "Our Lord is coming." This can refer to the incarnation or the second coming. Maran atha ("Our Lord, come!") is a plea for the Lord to come back. That many Christians have chosen maranatha as the name of their church probably indicates that most people see the expression as a plea: "If anyone does not love the Lord Jesus Christ, let him be accursed [anathema]. O Lord, come [Maran atha]!" (1 Co 16:22).

MAR′ BLE
A stone composed of calcium carbonate, capable of being polished. It is used for pavements and columns and is found in different colors in Lebanon and Arabia. White marble was used in Solomon's temple (1 Ch 29:2; Es 1:6; Song 5:15).

MAR′ CUS
See MARK, GOSPEL OF.

MARE
A female horse. See HORSE.

MAREAL
See MARALAH.

MA·RE′ SHAH (summit)
1. The father of Hebron, among the descendants of Caleb (1 Ch 2:42).
2. A town of Judah in the lowland (Jos 15:44; 2 Ch 14:9-10).

MARHESHVAN
Heshvan, the eighth month of the sacred year and the second month of the civil year, corresponding roughly to October/November. See CALENDAR.

MARISHES (archaic)
Marshes; ponds (Eze 47:9,11).

MARJORAM
See HYSSOP.

MARK, GOSPEL OF
1. The Book of Mark. The message of Mark's Gospel is captured in a single verse: "For even the Son of Man did not come to be served, but to serve, and to give His life a ransom for many" (10:45). Chapter by chapter, the book unfolds the dual focus of Christ's life: service and sacrifice.

Mark portrays Jesus as a Servant on the move, instantly responsive to the will of the Father. By preaching, teaching, and healing, He ministered to the needs of others even to the point of death.

After the resurrection, He commissioned His followers to continue His work in His power—servants following in the steps of the perfect Servant.

The ancient title for this Gospel was *Kata Markon,* "According to Mark." The author is best known by his Latin name *Marcus,* but in Jewish circles he was called by his Hebrew name, John. Acts 12:12,25 and 15:37 refer to him as "John, whose surname was Mark."

2. The Author of Mark. According to Acts 12:2, Mark's mother Mary had a large house that was used as a meeting place for believers in Jerusalem. Peter apparently went to this house often because the servant girl recognized his voice at the gate (Ac 12:13-16). Barnabas was Mark's cousin (Col 4:10), but Peter may have been the person who led him to Christ (Peter called him "Mark my son," 1 Pe 5:13). It was this close association with Peter that lent apostolic authority to Mark's Gospel, since Peter was evidently Mark's primary source of information. It has been suggested that Mark was referring to himself in his account of "a certain young man" in Gethsemane (14:51-52). Since all the disciples had abandoned Jesus (14:50), this little incident may have been a firsthand account.

Barnabas and Saul took Mark along with them when they returned from Jerusalem to Antioch (Ac 12:25), and again when they left on the first missionary journey (Ac 13:5). However, Mark left early and returned to Jerusalem (Ac 13:13). When Barnabas wanted to bring Mark on the second missionary journey, Paul's refusal led to a disagreement. The result was that Barnabas took Mark to Cyprus and Paul took Silas through Syria and Cilicia (Ac 15:36-41). Nevertheless, Paul wrote that Mark was with him during his first Roman imprisonment (Col 4:10; Phile 24) about twelve years later, so there must have been a reconciliation. In fact, at the end of his life Paul sent for Mark, saying, "he is useful to me for ministry" (2 Ti 4:11).

The early church uniformly attested that Mark wrote this Gospel. Papias, Irenaeus, Clement of Alexandria, and Origen are among the church fathers who affirmed Markan authorship.

3. The Time of Mark. Many scholars believe that Mark was the first of the four Gospels, but there is uncertainty over its date. Because of the prophecy about the destruction of the temple (13:2), it should be dated before A.D. 70, but early traditions disagree as to whether it was written before or after the martyrdom of Peter (c. A.D. 64). The probable range for this book is A.D. 55-65.

The Book of Mark was evidently directed to a Roman readership and early tradition indicates that it originated in Rome. This may be why Mark omitted a number of items that would not have been meaningful to Gentiles, such as the genealogy of Christ, fulfilled prophecy, references to the law, and certain Jewish customs that are found in other Gospels. Mark interpreted Aramaic words (3:17; 5:41; 7:34; 15:22) and used a number of Latin terms in place of their Greek equivalents (4:21; 6:27; 12:14,42; 15:15-16,39).

4. The Christ of Mark. The Lord is presented as an active, compassionate, and obedient Servant who constantly ministers to the physical and spiritual needs of others. Because this is the story of a Servant, Mark omits Jesus's ancestry and birth and moves right into His busy public ministry. The distinctive word of this book is *euthus,* translated "immediately" or "straightaway," and it appears more often in this compact Gospel (forty-two times) than in all the rest of the New Testament. Christ is constantly moving toward a goal that is hidden to almost all. Mark clearly shows the power and authority of this unique Servant, identifying Him as no less than the Son of God (1:1,11; 3:11; 5:7; 9:7; 13:32; 14:61; 15:39).

5. Keys to Mark.

Key Word: Jesus the Servant—Even in the first verse it is obvious that this Gospel centers on the person and mission of the Son of God. Mark's theme is captured well in 10:45 because Jesus is portrayed in this book as a Servant and as the Redeemer of men (Ph 2:5-11). Like the other Gospels, Mark is not a biography but a topical narrative. Mark juxtaposes Christ's teachings and works to show how they authenticate each other. Miracles are predominant in this book (there are eighteen), and they are used to demonstrate not only the power of Christ but also His compassion. Mark shows his Gentile readers how the Son of God—rejected by His own people—achieved ultimate victory through apparent defeat. There was no doubt an evangelistic purpose behind this Gospel as Mark directed his words to a Gentile audience that knew little about Old Testament theology.

Key Verses: Mark 10:43-45 and 8:34-37— "Yet it shall not be so among you; but whoever desires to become great among you shall be your servant. And whoever of you desires to be first shall be slave of all. For even the Son of Man did not come to be served, but to serve, and to give His live a ransom for many" (10:43-45).

"And when He had called the people to Him, with His disciples also, He said to them, "Whoever desires to come after Me, let him deny himself, and take up his cross, and follow Me. For whoever desires to save his life will lose it, but whoever loses his life for My sake and the gospel's will save it. For what will it profit a man if he gains the whole world, and loses his own soul? Or what will a man give in exchange for his soul?" (8:34-37).

Key Chapter: Mark 8—As in Matthew, Mark's Gospel contains a pivotal chapter showing the change of emphasis in Jesus's ministry. In Matthew it is chapter 12; in Mark it is chapter 8. The pivotal event lies in Peter's confession, "You are the Christ." That faith-inspired response triggered a new phase in both the content and the course of Jesus's ministry. Until this point He had sought to validate His claims as Messiah. But now He began to fortify His men for His forthcoming suffering and death at the hands of the religious leaders. Jesus's steps began to take Him daily closer to Jerusalem—the place where the Perfect Servant would demonstrate the full extent of His servanthood.

6. Survey of Mark. Mark, the shortest and simplest of the four Gospels, gives a crisp and fast-moving look at the life of Christ. With few comments, Mark lets the narrative speak for itself as it tells the story of the Servant who constantly ministers to others through preaching, healing, teaching, and ultimately, His own death. Mark traces the steady building of hostility and opposition to Jesus as He resolutely moves toward the fulfillment of His earthly mission. Almost forty percent of this Gospel is devoted to a detailed account of the last eight days of Jesus's life, climaxing in His resurrection. The Lord is vividly portrayed in this book in two parts: to serve (1–10); to sacrifice (11–16).

To Serve (1-10). Mark passes over the birth and early years of Jesus's life, and begins with the events that immediately preceded the inauguration of His public ministry—His baptism by John and His temptation by Satan (1:1-13). The first four chapters emphasize the words of the Servant while chapters 5–7 accent His works. However, in both sections there is a frequent alternation between Christ's messages and miracles in order to reveal His person and power. Though He came to serve others, Jesus's authority prevailed over many realms

Although Jesus had already been teaching and testing His disciples (4), His ministry with them became more intense from this point on as He began to prepare them for His departure. The religious leaders were growing more antagonistic, and Christ's "hour" was only about six months away. Mark 8:31 is the pivotal point in the Gospel as the Son of Man spoke clearly to His disciples about His coming death and resurrection. The disciples struggled with this difficult revelation, but Jesus's steps headed inexorably to Jerusalem.

To Sacrifice (11-16). Mark allots a disproportionate space to the last weeks of the Servant's redemptive ministry. During the last seven days in Jerusalem, hostility from the chief priests, scribes, elders, Pharisees, Herodians, and Sadducees reached crisis proportions as Jesus publicly refuted their arguments in the temple. After His last supper with the disciples, Jesus offered no resistance to His arrest, abuse, and agonizing crucifixion. His willingness to bear countless human sins is the epitome of servanthood.

OUTLINE OF MARK

Part One: The Presentation of the Servant (1:1–2:12)

I. The Forerunner of the Servant (1:1-8)

II. The Baptism of the Servant (1:9-11)

III. The Temptation of the Servant (1:12-13)

IV. The Mission of the Servant (1:14–2:12)

A. The Work of the Servant 1:14-15
B. The First Disciples Are Called 1:16-20
C. The First Miracles Are Performed 1:21–2:12

Part Two: The Opposition to the Servant (2:13–8:26)

Part Three: The Instruction by the Servant (8:27–10:52)

Part Four: The Rejection of the Servant (11:1–15:47)

IV. The Instruction on the Future (13:1-37)

A. Question from the Disciples 13:1-4
B. The Tribulation 13:5-23
C. The Second Coming 13:24-27
D. Parable of the Fig Tree 13:28-31
E. Exhortation to Watch 13:32-37

V. The Passion of the Servant (14:1–15:47)

A. Leaders Plot to Kill Jesus 14:1-2
B. Mary Anoints Jesus 14:3-9

C. Judas Plans to Betray Jesus 14:10-11
D. The Passover Is Prepared 14:12-16
E. The Passover Is Celebrated........ 14:17-21
F. The Lord's Supper Is Instituted 14:22-25
G. Jesus Predicts Peter's Denial 14:26-31
H. Jesus Prays in Gethsemane 14:32-42
I. Judas Betrays Jesus 14:43-52
J. Jesus Is Tried.................... 14:53–15:14
K. Jesus Is Beaten 15:15-23
L. Jesus Is Crucified 15:24-41
M. Jesus Is Buried 15:42-47

Part Five: The Resurrection of the Servant (16:1-20)

I. The Resurrection of Jesus (16:1-8)

II. The Appearance of Jesus (16:9-18)

III. The Ascension of Jesus (16:19-20)

MARK, JOHN

See MARK, GOSPEL OF: The Author of Mark.

MAR′KET

The word used in Ezekiel 27:13, denoting place of trade and barter. The Greek word in the New Testament means a public place for business purposes (Mk 7:4); for conducting trials (Ac 16:19), or for meetings (Ac 17:17).

MARKET OF APPIUS

A marketplace outside of Rome, where believers came to meet Paul as he journeyed towards the city for prison and trial (Ac 28:15).

MAR′OTH *(bitterness)*

A town of Judah not far from Jerusalem (Mi 1:12).

MAR′RIAGE

A divine institution, the condition of the propagation of the race (Ge 1:27-28). Marriage is designed to be monogamous, the union of one man and one woman for life (Ge 1:18-24; Ma 19:5; 1 Co 6:16). It is a permanent relation, to be dissolved only by death (Ro 7:2-3), though there seems to be room for exceptions in the case of adultery (Ma 19:3-9) or desertion (1 Co 7:15).

Moses discouraged polygamy (Le 18:18; De 17:17) and restricted divorce (De 22:19,29; 24:1-4). Nevertheless, polygamy continued after the time of Moses. Gideon, Elkanah, Saul, David, Solomon,

Rehoboam and others had multiple wives (Ju 8:30; 1 Sa 1:2; 2 Sa 5:13; 12:8; 1 Ki 11:3). Contrasted with the destructive conditions of polygamy are the pleasing pictures of the felicity of the monogamous state (Ps 128:3; Pr 5:18; 31:10-29; Ec 9:9). When the wedding day arrived the bride appeared in white robes (Re 19:8), adorned with jewels (Is 61:10; Re 21:2) and covered with a veil (Ge 24:65). The bridegroom in company with friends, attended by musicians, went to the home of the bride (Ju 14:11; Is 61:10; Ma 9:15), possibly in the evening, by torchlight (Ma 25:7). The whole party with the bride returned to the home of the bridegroom where there were music and dancing (Song 3:6-11).

The marriage relation is used figuratively to express the spiritual relation between Jehovah and his people (Is 62:4-5; Ho 2:19; Ma 9:15; Jo 3:29; 2 Co 11:2; Re 19:7; 21:2,9; 22:17).

MARROW

The soft inner tissues of bones, the place where blood is manufactured for the body. The marrow was considered a delicacy, rich in nutrients (Job 21:24; Is 25:6).

MAR•SE′NA

One of the Persian princes in the court of Ahasuerus (Es 1:14).

MARSH

A low lying swampy area. The area where the mouth of a large river widens will often form marshy wetlands (Eze 47:11).

MARSHAL

Military title also rendered "captain" or "commander" (Je 51:27).

MARS' HILL

See AREOPAGUS.

MAR'THA *(mistress, or lady)*

Sister of Mary and Lazarus of Bethany (Jo 11:1-2). Jesus was a frequent guest at their home. Martha once complained to Jesus that Mary should do more housework, but Jesus defended Mary's interest in things of a spiritual nature (Lk 10:38-42).

MARTYR *(witness)*

The word simply means "witness," but it has come to mean specifically one who has died for the faith. Paul refers to Stephen as a "martyr". He is an example of the ultimate witness for Christ, because he was willing to stick by the truth of the gospel even to the point of death (Ac 22:20). The Book of Revelation also mentions the saints who die in the tribulation as martyrs (Re 17:6).

MA'RY

The name of six women mentioned in the New Testament.

1. The Virgin Mary, mother of Jesus. She is assumed to be the daughter of Heli (Eli) of the lineage of David, but of the line of Nathan, the royal rights of the Solomonic line being transferred through the daughter of Jeconiah and in this manner transferred from Mary to Jesus. She lived in Nazareth and was betrothed to Joseph, a carpenter, a descendant of David (Lk 1:26-27). She was informed by the angel, Gabriel, that she

MARY OF BETHANY WITH JESUS AND MARTHA

would be the mother of the promised Messiah (Lk 1:32-35). At the home of Elizabeth, her kinswoman, she spoke her hymn of praise, "The Magnificat" (Lk 1:46-55). The angel's explanation to Joseph was in fulfillment of Isaiah's prophecy (Ma 1:18-25). The "brethren of the Lord" were doubtless the children of Mary and Joseph. There were also sisters (Mk 6:3) so that Mary was the mother of a large family. When on the cross, Jesus commended her to the care of John (Jo 19:25-27).

2. Mary, the wife of Clopas or Cleophas (Jo 19:25). They were the parents of James the Less, an apostle, and of Joses (Ma 27:56; Mk 15:40; Lk 24:10). It is the view of some that this Mary was the sister of the Virgin, but it seems very improbable that there would be two daughters in one family who were both named Mary. This Mary followed the body of Jesus to the tomb (Ma 27:61) and was there on the third day with spices (Ma 28:1; Mk 15:47; 16:1; Lk 24:10).

3. Mary Magdalene. A resident, doubtless, of Magdala, on the southwestern coast of the Sea of Galilee (Ma 27:56,61; 28:1; Mk 15:40,47; Lk 8:2; 24:10; Jo 19:25; 20:11-18). She was afflicted with seven demons which Jesus expelled (Mk 16:9; Lk 8:2). The old view that she was a woman of bad character is wholly groundless. It is based on the fact that the first mention of her follows the account of the sinful woman who anointed the feet of Jesus (Lk 7:36-50) which is far from proving that the same person is referred to. She was a devoted follower of her Lord (Lk 8:1-3), was at the cross (Ma 27:56; Mk 15:40; Jo 19:25), and at the sepulchre on the third day (Mk 16:1). Mark states that Jesus, after his resurrection, appeared first to her (Mk 16:9).

4. Mary of Bethany, sister of Martha and Lazarus (Jo 11:1; 12:1). When Jesus visited their home, Mary was so interested in what He had to say that she neglected her household duties in order to hear Him. Martha wanted Jesus to rebuke her, but Jesus commended her spiritual interest (Lk 10:38-42).

5. Mary, mother of Mark. She was a Christian woman, and it was at her house the disciples met for prayer at the time of the imprisonment of Peter by Herod Agrippa I (Ac 12:12). It is believed that the early Christians of Jerusalem made her house one of their meeting places.

6. A Christian woman at Rome who was, according to Paul in Romans 16:6, an active Christian worker.

MAS′ CHIL

A word in the titles of Psalms 32;42;44;52–55; 74;78;88;89;142; an undefined literary or musical term.

MASH *(drawn out)*

A son of Aram, the son of Shem (Ge 10:23). In 1 Chronicles 1:17 he is called Meshech.

MA′ SHAL *(entreaty)*

See MISHAL (1 Ch 6:74).

MAS′ KIL

Variant spelling of MASCHIL.

MASON

A stoneworker who builds walls and buildings of dressed stone or bricks (2 Ki 22:6; 1 Ch 22:2; 2 Ch 24:12).

MAS·RE′ KAH *(vineyard)*

A city of Edom (Ge 36:36; 1 Ch 1:47).

MAS′ SA *(burden)*

A tribe of Arabia descended from Ishmael (Ge 25:14; 1 Ch 1:30).

MAS′ SAH *(trial, test)*

A name Moses gave the place where the rock yielded water because the people put Jehovah to a test (Ex 17:7; Ps 95:8-9). It is also called Meribah (De 6:16; 9:22).

MASTER

A term of respect, equivalent to the English "sir;" also a title which recognizes another's authority and right to command (Lk 5:5; 17:13). This is the same Greek word which is most often translated "Lord." See LORD.

MAS′ TICH

Resinous sap from the mastic tree, used as a varnish.

MA·THU′ SA·LA

See METHUSELAH (Lk 3:37).

MA′ TRED *(driving forward)*

Mother-in-law of Hadar, king of Edom (Ge 36:39; 1 Ch 1:50).

MA′ TRI *(rainy)*

A family of Benjamin to which Kish and Saul belonged (1 Sa 10:21).

MAT′ TAN *(a gift)*

Two Old Testament men:

1. Father of Shephatiah (Je 38:1).

2. A priest of Baal (2 Ki 11:18; 2 Ch 23:17).

MAT·TA′ NAH *(a gift)*

A station of the Israelites near Moab (Nu 21:18-19).

MAT·TA·NI′ AH *(gift of Jehovah)*

Ten Old Testament men:

1. Son of King Josiah. He was the third of Josiah's sons to be on the throne of Judah. Nebuchadnezzar changed his name to Zedekiah (2 Ki 24:17). See ZEDEKIAH.

2. Son of Heman in David's time; a singer (1 Ch 25:4,16).

3. A descendant of Asaph, a Levite, head of a branch of the family (2 Ch 20:14).

4. A descendant of Asaph, a Levite. He assisted Hezekiah in his religious reforms (2 Ch 29:13).

5. A son of Elam who put away his Gentile wife (Ez 10:26).

6-8. Three Israelites, a son of Zattu (Ez 10:27), a son of Pahath-moab (Ez 10:30), a son of Bani (Ez 10:37), who divorced their pagan wives.

9. A Levite, ancestor of Hanan who was treasurer of the storehouse in the days of Nehemiah (Ne 13:13).

10. A singer among the Levites, descended from Asaph (1 Ch 9:15; Ne 11:17; 12:25,35); he lived in Jerusalem after the captivity.

MAT′ TA·THAH *(gift)*

1. Son of Nathan (Lk 3:31, Mattatha, KJV), listed in the genealogy of Christ. See MATTATTAH.

MAT·TA·THI′ AH *(gift of Jehovah)*

Three Israelite men:

1. A priest and the founder of the Maccabee family (B.C. 168).

2. The name of two ancestors of Jesus (Lk 3:25-26; Mattathias, KJV, NASB, NIV, NRSV).

MAT·TA·THI′ AS

See MATTATHIAH.

MAT′ TAT·TAH *(gift)*

Son of Hashum (Ez 10:33), one who divorced his pagan wife (Mattathah, KJV).

MAT·TE′ NAI *(gift of Jehovah)*

1-2. Two Hebrews: son of Hashum (Ez 10:33); a son of Bani (Ez 10:37), who divorced their foreign wives.

3. A priest of the family of Joiarib in the time of Joiakim (Ne 12:19).

MAT′ THAN *(gift)*

An ancestor of Joseph, husband of Mary (Ma 1:15).

MAT′ THAT *(gift of God)*

Two ancestors of the family of Jesus (Lk 3:24,29).

MAT′ THEW *(gift of Jehovah)*

A publican or taxgatherer who, before he was called by Jesus to discipleship, was called Levi, the son of Alphaeus (Ma 9:9; Lk 5:27). Tradition says that he stayed in Jerusalem for approximately fifteen years, and then went as missionary to the Persians, Parthians and Medes. He may have died as martyr in Ethiopia. See MATTHEW, GOSPEL OF: The Author of Matthew.

MAT′ THEW, GOS′ PEL OF

1. The Book of Matthew. Mathew is the Gospel written by a Jew to Jews about a Jew. Matthew is the writer, his countrymen are the readers, and Jesus Christ is the subject. Matthew's design is to present Jesus as the King of the Jews, the long-awaited Messiah. Through a carefully selected series of Old Testament quotations, Matthew documents Jesus Christ's claim to be Messiah. His genealogy, baptism, messages, and miracles all point to the same inescapable conclusion: Christ is King. Even in His death, seeming defeat is turned to victory by the resurrection, and the message again echoes forth: the King of the Jews lives.

At an early date this Gospel was given the title *Kata Matthaion,* "According to Matthew." As this title suggests, other Gospel accounts were known at that time (the word *gospel* was added later). Matthew ("Gift of the Lord") was also surnamed Levi (Mk 2:14; Lk 5:27).

2. The Author of Matthew. The early church uniformly attributed this Gospel to Matthew, and no tradition to the contrary ever emerged. This book was known early and accepted quickly. In his Ecclesiastical History (A.D. 323), Eusebius quoted a statement by Papias (c. A.D. 140) that

Matthew wrote *logia* ("sayings") in Aramaic. No Aramaic Gospel of Matthew has been found, and it is evident that Matthew is not a Greek translation of an Aramaic original. Some believe that Matthew wrote an abbreviated version of Jesus's sayings in Aramaic before writing his Gospel in Greek for a larger circle of readers.

Matthew, the son of Alphaeus (Mk 2:14), occupied the unpopular post of tax collector in Capernaum for the Roman government. As a publican he was no doubt disliked by his Jewish countrymen. When Jesus called him to discipleship (9:9-13; Mk 2:14; Lk 5:27-28), his quick response probably meant that he had already been stirred up by Jesus's public preaching. He gave a large reception for Jesus in his house so that his associates could meet Jesus. He was chosen as one of the twelve apostles, and the last appearance of his name in the Bible is in Acts 1:13. Matthew's life from that point on is veiled in tradition.

3. The Time of Matthew. Like all the Gospels, Matthew is not easy to date; suggestions have ranged from A.D. 40-140. The two expressions "to this day" (27:8) and "until this day" (28:15) indicated that a substantial period of time had passed since the events described in the book, but they also point to a date prior to the destruction of Jerusalem in A.D. 70. The Olivet Discourse (24–25) also anticipated this event. The strong Jewish flavor of this Gospel is another argument for a date prior to A.D. 70. If Matthew depended on Mark's Gospel as a source, the date of Mark would determine the earliest date for Matthew. The likely time frame for this book is A.D. 58-68. It may have been written in Palestine or Syrian Antioch.

4. The Christ of Matthew. Matthew presents Jesus as Israel's promised messianic King (1:23; 2:2,6; 3:17; 4:15-17; 21:5,9; 22:44-45; 26:64; 27:11,27-37). The phrase "the kingdom of heaven" appears thirty-two times in Matthew but nowhere else in the New Testament. To show that Jesus fulfills the qualifications for the Messiah, Matthew used more Old Testament quotations and allusions than any other book (almost 130). Often used in this Gospel is the revealing phrase "that what was spoken through the prophet might be fulfilled," which appears nine times in Matthew and not once in the other Gospels. Jesus is the climax of the prophets (12:39-40; 13:13-15,35; 17:5-13), "the Son of Man" (24:30ff), the "Servant" of the Lord (12:17-21), and the "Son of David" (the Davidic reference occurs nine times in Matthew, but only six times in all of the other Gospels).

5. Keys to Matthew.

Key Word: Jesus the King—A Jewish tax collector named Matthew wrote to a Jewish audience to convince them that the King of Jews had come. By quoting repeatedly from the Old Testament, Matthew validates Christ's claims that He is, in fact, the prophesied Messiah (the Anointed One) of Israel. Everything about this King is unique: His miraculous birth and obscure yet carefully prophesied birthplace, His flight into Egypt, His announcement by John, His battle with Satan in the wilderness, all support the only possible conclusion—Jesus is the culmination of promises delivered by the prophets over a period of a thousand years. Thus God's redemptive plan is alive and well, even after four hundred years of prophetic silence.

Key Verses: Matthew 16:16-19 and 28:18-20—"And Simon Peter answered and said, 'You are the Christ, the Son of the living God.' Jesus answered and said to him, 'Blessed are you, Simon Bar-Jonah, for flesh and blood has not revealed this to you, but My Father who is in heaven. And I also say to you, that you are Peter, and on this rock I will build My church, and the gates of Hades shall not prevail against it. And I will give you the keys of the kingdom of heaven, and whatever you bind on earth will be bound in heaven, and whatever you loose on earth will be loosed in heaven" (16:16-19).

"Then Jesus came and spoke to them, saying, 'All authority has been given to Me in heaven and on earth. Go therefore and make disciples of all the nations, baptizing them in the name of the Father and of the Son and of the Holy Spirit, teaching them to observe all things that I have commanded you; and lo, I am with you always, even to the end of the age.' Amen" (28:18-20).

Key Chapter: Matthew 12—The turning point of Matthew comes in the twelfth chapter when the Pharisees, acting as the leadership of the nation of Israel, formally rejected Jesus Christ as the Messiah, saying that His power came not from God but from Satan. Christ's ministry changed immediately with His new teaching of parables, increased attention given to His disciples, and His repeated statement that His death is now near.

6. Survey of Matthew.

The Old Testament prophets predicted and longed for the coming of the Anointed One who would enter history to bring redemption and deliverance. The first verse of Matthew succinctly announces the fulfillment of Israel's hope in the coming of Christ: "The book of the genealogy of Jesus Christ, the Son of David, the Son of Abraham." Matthew was placed first in the canon of New Testament books by the early church because it is a natural bridge between the Testaments. This Gospel describes the person and work of Israel's messianic King. An important part of Matthew's structure is revealed in the phrase "when Jesus had ended" (7:28; 11:1; 13:53; 19:1; 26:1), which is used to conclude the five key discourses of the book: the Sermon on the Mount (5:3–7:27), Instruction of the Disciples (10:5-42), Parables of the Kingdom (13:3-52), Terms of Discipleship (18:3-35), and the Olivet Discourse 24:4–25:46). Matthew can be outlined as follows: the presentation of the King (1:1–4:11); the proclamation of the King (4:12–7:29); the power of the King (8:1–11:1); the progressive rejection of the King (11:2–16:12); the preparation of the King's disciples (16:13–20:28); the presentation and rejection of the King (20:29–27:66); the proof of the King (28:1-20).

The Presentation of the King (1:1–4:11). The promise to Abraham was that "in you all the families of the earth shall be blessed" (Ge 12:3). Jesus Christ, the Savior of the world, is "the Son of Abraham" (1:1). However, He is also "the Son of David"; and as David's direct descendant, He is qualified to be Israel's King. The magi knew that the "King of the Jews" (2:2) had been born and came to worship Him. John the Baptist, the messianic forerunner who broke the four hundred years of prophetic silence, also bore witness of Him (Mal 3:1). The sinlessness of the King was proved when He overcame the satanic temptation to disobey the will of the Father.

The Proclamation of the King (4:12–7:29). In this section, Matthew uses a topical rather than a chronological arrangement of his material in order to develop a crucial pattern in Christ's ministry. The words of the Lord are found in the Sermon on the Mount (5–7). This discourse requires less than fifteen minutes to read, but its brevity has not diminished its profound influence on the world. The Sermon on the Mount presents new laws and standards for God's people.

The Power of the King (8:1–11:1). The works of the Lord are presented in a series of ten miracles (8–9) that reveal His authority over every realm (disease, demons, death, and nature). Thus, the words of the Lord are supported by His works; His claims are verified by His credentials.

The Progressive Rejection of the King (11:2–16:12). Here we note a series of reactions to Christ's words and works. Because of increasing opposition, Jesus began to spend proportionately more time with His disciples as He prepared them for His coming death and departure.

The Preparation of the King's Disciples (16:13–20:28). In a series of discourses, Jesus communicated the significance of accepting or rejecting His offer of righteousness. His teaching in 16:13–21:11 is primarily directed to those who accept Him.

The Presentation and Rejection of the King (20:29–27:66). The majority of Christ's words in this section are aimed at those who reject their King. The Lord predicted the terrible judgment that would fall on Jerusalem, resulting in the dispersion of the Jewish people. Looking beyond these events (fulfilled in A.D. 70), He also described His second coming as the Judge and Lord of the earth.

The Proof of the King (28). Authenticating His words and works are the empty tomb, resurrection, and appearances, all proving that Jesus Christ is indeed the prophesied Messiah, the very Son of God.

Christ's final ministry in Judea (beginning in 19:1) reached a climax at the cross as the King willingly gave up His life to redeem sinful persons. Jesus endured awesome human hatred in this great demonstration of divine love (Ro 5:7-8). His perfect sacrifice was acceptable, and this Gospel concludes with His glorious resurrection.

OUTLINE OF MATTHEW

Part One: The Presentation of the King (1:1-4:11)

I. The Advent of the King (1:1-2:23)

A. Genealogy of Christ 1:1-17
B. Birth of Christ 1:18-25
C. Visit of Wise Men 2:1-12
D. Flight into Egypt 2:13-15
E. Herod Kills the Children 2:16-18
F. Jesus Returns to Nazareth 2:19-23

II. The Announcer of the King (3:1-12)

A. The Person of John the Baptist 3:1-6
B. The Preaching of John the
Baptist 3:7-12

III. The Approval of the King (3:13–4:11)

A. Baptism of Jesus 3:13-17
B. Temptation of Jesus 4:1-11

Part Two: The Proclamation of the King (4:12–7:29)

I. The Background for the Sermon (4:12-25)

A. Jesus Begins His Ministry 4:12-17
B. Jesus Calls His First
Disciples 4:18-22
C. Jesus Ministers in
Galilee 4:23-25

II. The Sermon on the Mount (5:1–7:29)

A. The Subjects of the Kingdom 5:1-16
B. The Relationship of Jesus to the
Law 5:17–7:6
C. Jesus Instructs on Entering the
Kingdom 7:7-27
D. Response to the Sermon 7:28-29

Part Three: The Power of the King (8:1–11:1)

I. The Demonstration of the King's Power (8:1-9:34)

A. Miracles of Healing 8:1-17
B. Demands of Discipleship 8:18-22
C. Miracles of Power 8:23–9:8
D. Distinctions of Disciples 9:9-17
E. Miracles of Restoration 9:18-34

II. The Delegation of the King's Power (9:35–11:1)

A. The Need for Delegation of
Power 9:35-38
B. The Twelve Apostles Are Sent 10:1-4
C. The Twelve Apostles Are
Instructed 10:5–11:1

Part Four: The Progressive Rejection of the King (11:2–16:12)

I. The Commencement of Rejection (11:2-30)

A. John the Baptist's Questions 11:2-15
B. Rejection by Jesus's Generation 11:16-19
C. Rejection of Chorazin, Bethsaida, and Capernaum 11:20-24
D. Invitation to Come to Jesus 11:25-30

II. The Rejection of Christ by the Pharisees (12:1-50)

A. Controversy over Sabbath-Labor 12:1-8
B. Controversy over Sabbath-Healing 12:9-13
C. Pharisees Plan to Destroy Christ 12:14-21
D. Pharisees Blaspheme the Holy Spirit 12:22-30

E. Pharisees Commit the Unpardonable Sin 12:31-37
F. Pharisees Demand a Sign 12:38-45
G. Jesus and the True Brethren 12:46-50

III. The Consequences of the Rejection (13:1-53)

A. Parables Spoken to the Multitude............................... 13:1-35
B. Parables Spoken to the Disciples 13:36-53

IV. The Continuing Rejection of the King (13:54–16:12)

A. Rejection at Nazareth 13:54-58
B. Rejection by Herod 14:1-36
C. Rejection by Scribes and Pharisees................................ 15:1-39
D. Rejection by Pharisees and Sadducees 16:1-12

Part Five: The Preparation of the King's Disciples (16:13–20:28)

I. The Revelation in View of Rejection (16:13-17:13)

A. Revelation of the Person of the King 16:13-17
B. Revelation of the Program of the King 16:18–17:13

II. The Instruction in View of Rejection (17:14–20:28)

A. Instruction About Faith 17:14-21
B. Instruction About Jesus's Death ... 17:22-23

C. Instruction About Taxes 17:24-27
D. Instruction About Humility 18:1-5
E. Instruction About Causing Offense.................................. 18:6-20
F. Instruction About Forgiveness 18:21-35
G. Instruction About Divorce 19:1-15
H. Instruction About Wealth ... 19:16–20:16
I. Instruction About Jesus's Death 20:17-19
J. Instruction About Ambition 20:20-28

Part Six: The Presentation and Rejection of the King (20:29–27:66)

I. The Blind Men Recognize the King (20:29-34)

II. The Public Presentation of the King (21:1-17)

A. The Triumphal Entry 21:1-11
B. The Cleansing of the Temple 21:12-17

III. The Nation Rejects the King (21:18–22:46)

A. Cursing of the Fig Tree 21:18-22
B. Conflict with Priests and Elders 21:23–22:14
C. Conflict with Pharisees and Herodians 22:15-22

D. Conflict with Sadducees 22:23-33
E. Conflict with Pharisees 22:34-46

IV. The King Rejects the Nation (23:1-39)

A. Jesus Characterizes the Pharisees............................... 23:1-12
B. Jesus Condemns the Pharisees............................... 23:13-36
C. Jesus Laments over Jerusalem ... 23:37-39

V. The Predictions of the King's Second Coming (24:1-25:46)

A. The Temple to Be Destroyed 24:1-2

B. The Disciples Two Questions: "When?" and "What?" 24:3
C. Jesus Answers the "What?" 24:4-31
D. Jesus Answers the "When?" 24:32-51
E. Jesus Predicts Judgment at His Coming............................ 25:1-46

VI. The Passion of the King (26:1–27:66)

A. The Religious Leaders Plot to Kill Jesus.. 26:1-5

B. Mary Anoints Jesus for Burial 26:6-13
C. Judas Agrees to Betray Jesus......26:14-16
D. The Disciples Celebrate the Passover 26:17-35
E. Jesus Is Arrested in Gethsemane 26:36-56
F. Jesus Is Tried..................... 26:57–27:25
G. Jesus Is Crucified 27:26-56
H. Jesus Is Buried 27:57-66

Part Seven: The Proof of the King (28:1-20)

I. The Empty Tomb (28:1-8)

II. The Appearance of Jesus to the Women (28:9-10)

III. The Bribery of the Soldiers (28:11-15)

IV. The Appearance of Jesus to the Disciples (28:16-17)

V. The Great Commission (28:18-20)

MATTH·I′ AS *(gift of God)*

A follower of Christ closely associated with the apostles. While the apostles were waiting for the advent of the Holy Spirit, the question arose regarding the filling of the place of Judas. Lots were cast and the lot fell to Matthias (Ac 1:21-26). Peter's qualification list tells us that he was one who had followed Jesus from the beginning, and had seen His ministry, death, and resurrection. He may well have been one of "the seventy" Jesus sent out in Luke 10:1,17. After this passage in Acts where he is chosen to replace Judas, Matthias is not mentioned again in Scripture. Nothing more is known of

MATTHIAS

him, but tradition says that he died as a martyr, either at the hands of the Jews or as a missionary in Ethiopia. There is no way of knowing whether this is true or not, but it is not unlikely that he did die as a martyr, along with many other first-century Christians.

MAT·TI·THI′ AH *(gift of Jehovah)*

Four Old Testament men:

1. A son of Shallum of the branch of Korah, a Levite. He had charge of baked offerings (1 Ch 9:31).

2. Son of Jeduthun, a Levite and harpist (1 Ch 15:18,21; 25:3,21).

3. A son of Nebo who put away his foreign wife (Ez 10:43).

4. One who stood by Ezra when he read the law (Ne 8:4).

MAT′ TOCK

An instrument having two blades, used especially for extricating the roots of trees and breaking clods (1 Sa 13:20-21; Is 7:25).

MAUL

A heavy club used as a weapon of war, often equipped with a metal or spiked metal head (Pr 25:18). See MACE.

MAW (archaic)

Stomach or crop. The stomach of cud chewing animals was considered a great delicacy (De 18:3).

MAZZ' A·ROTH

A word in Job 38:32, believed to denote the twelve signs of the zodiac. Also translated "constellations" (NIV).

MEAD' OW

The rendering of an Egyptian word in Genesis 41:2,18 denoting reed-grass or flags; hence, pastureland (Job 8:11).

ME' AH *(a hundred)*

A tower of Jerusalem near the sheep gate (Ne 3:1; 12:39), also called the Tower of the Hundred.

MEAL

Grain ground into flour.

MEAL OF' FER·ING

See OFFERINGS.

MEALS

The two regular meals of the Hebrews were those of the morning and evening (Ex 16:12; 1 Ki 17:6; Jo 21:4,12), the latter being the chief meal (Ru 3:7). On the Sabbath the first meal was about noon following the synagogue service. They sat on mats on the floor, the present custom of the Arabs (Ge 27:19). It was during a later period that reclining on couches became the custom (Eze 23:41; Jo 21:20), the body lying diagonally on the couch (Jo 13:23-25).

ME·AR' AH *(a cave)*

A place near Sidon (Jos 13:4).

MEAS' URE

See WEIGHTS AND MEASURES.

MEASURING LINE

See LINE.

MEAT (archaic)

In the English of the King James Bible, the word meat is not used in the modern sense, to refer exclusively to the flesh of an animal, but to refer to food in general. The word "flesh" is used to describe what today would be called "meat;" "meat" describes what today would be simply referred to as "food."

MEAT OF' FER·ING

In today's language, more properly "Grain Offering." See OFFERING.

MEAT SACRIFICED TO IDOLS

Christians living in pagan societies in the first century faced an interesting dilemma. Most of the meat that was available in the marketplaces was meat which had been offered as sacrifices in the temples of the various pagan gods. The early believers wondered whether it was wrong to eat such meat, or whether it mattered. Paul addressed the subject in his letter to the Corinthians, teaching that the meat had no inherent evil—food is food, and something to thank God for. On the other hand, if eating such meat proved to be a stumbling block for a believer, it should certainly be avoided (1 Co 8:13).

ME·BUN' NAI *(built)*

A warrior of David; a Hushathite (2 Sa 23:27). In 1 Chronicles 11:29; 27:11 he is called Sibbecai.

ME·CHE' RA·THITE

A native or inhabitant of Mecherah (1 Ch 11:36).

ME·CO' NAH

A town of Judah (Ne 11:28; Mekonah, KJV).

ME' DAD *(love)*

An elder who received the gift of prophecy (Nu 11:26-29).

ME' DAN

A son of Abraham and Keturah (Ge 25:2; 1 Ch 1:32).

MEDE, ME' DI·AN

A native or inhabitant of Media (2 Ki 17:6; Es 1:19; Da 5:28,31). Darius, son of Ahasuerus (Da 5:31) is referred to as "the Median," and also "the Mede" (11:1).

ME' DE·BA *(water of quiet)*

A town of Moab (Nu 21:30), assigned to Reuben (Jos 13:9,16). This town apparently went back and forth between Moabite and Israelite domination (2 Ki 14:25; 1 Ch 19:7). By the time of Isaiah, the town was in Moabite control (Is 15:2).

ME' DI·A

A country of Asia bounded on the North by the Caspian Sea, on the east by Parthia, and on the South by Elam; it was about six hundred miles in length and about two hundred and fifty miles broad. The area which was once Media is now parts of Iran, Iraq and Turkey. A Median kingdom was established by the ninth and eighth centuries B.C., and Assyria battled with it, demanding tribute. Media was conquered by Tiglath-pileser of Assyria between 745 and 727 B.C. The first mention of Media is in 2 Kings 17:6; 18:11, when Shalmanesar of Assyria deported the conquered Israelites there.

Media was dominated by Assyria until 614-612 B.C., when the Babylonians and Medians formed an alliance and overthrew the Assyrian Empire. Intermarriage between the ruling families increased the strength of this bond. Some years later, the Babylonian Empire under Belshazzar was overthrown by the Medes and the Persians (Da 5:28). The laws of the Medes and Persians were considered unbreakable, even by the king (Es 1:19). See DANIEL, BOOK OF, and ESTHER, BOOK OF. The religion of Media and Persia was Zoroastrianism.

MEDIATOR

One who intercedes between two opposing people or groups to resolve a disagreement; a go-between, or arbitrator. In the Old Testament, Moses acted as mediator between God and the Israelites, offering sacrifices for the sins of the people, and interceding for them to beg God not to destroy them (Ex 20:19-22; 32:31-35). In the New Testament, we see only one mediator between God and man, and that is Jesus Christ (1 Ti 2:5). Moses as the mediator of the Old Covenant is compared with Christ the mediator of the New Covenant in Hebrews 3:1-6; much of the rest of Hebrews discusses the differences between the New and Old Covenants. Jesus is the only one who can effectively mediate between God and man, because He is the one who paid the price and covered our sins, making it possible for us to meet God (Ro 8:34).

MED′I·CINE

A curative substance; also the field which deals with the healing of disease. Egyptian physicians had an extensive knowledge of medicine (Je 46:11). Early medical allusions in the Bible are in connection with difficult cases of midwifery (Ge 25:24-26; 35:16-19; 38:27-30). Embalming is also mentioned, as are antidotes for poison and the use of a fig poultice for boils (2 Ki 2:21; 4:39-41; Is 38:21).

MEDITATION

Reflection, dwelling upon a certain theme of thought, thinking deeply and long about something. Mediation on God's law helps us to internalize and remember what He has said (Ps 1:2; 19:14; Jos 1:8). The New Testament also speaks of meditating on God's word as a safeguard and growth tool (1 Ti 4:15; Ph 4:8; Col 3:2).

MED′I·TER·RA′NE·AN SEA

A large body of water in the Middle East bordered by many important nations, including Israel, Greece, Lebanon, and Italy. Its southern coastline stretches 2,200 miles from the coast of Palestine to the Straits of Gibraltar off the coast of Spain. The sea is 80 miles wide at its narrowest point between Sicily and North Africa. Many ancient civilizations grew up around this sea, using it for transportation and commerce.

While the Israelites were wandering in the wilderness, they received instructions from God about the future boundaries of the land that God had promised to Abraham and his descendants. The Mediterranean Sea was established as the western boundary of their territory (Nu 34:6).

In the Bible, the Mediterranean is also referred to as "the Great Sea" (Jos 1:4), "the Western Sea" (De 11:24), and simply "the sea" (Jos 16:8). The Romans called it *Mare Nostrum,* or "Our Sea," because of its importance to their empire in trade and commerce. In the time of Jesus and Paul, the Mediterranean was controlled by the Romans, who also used it to transport soldiers to the East to keep order in the provinces.

Perhaps the first people to exploit the trading advantages offered by the Mediterranean Sea were the Phoenicians. Through their fine port cities of Tyre and Sidon, they imported and exported goods from many nations of the ancient world. But the Israelites were never a seafaring people. Even Solomon, with all his wealth, formed an alliance with the Phoenicians under which they conducted import and export services for the Israelites (1 Ki 9:27).

The Philistines also loved the sea. Some scholars believe they migrated to Palestine from their original home on the island of Crete, or Caphtor, in the Mediterranean. The Mediterranean is called "the Sea of the Philistines" in Exodus 23:31.

The Mediterranean also played a key role in the early expansion of Christianity. Paul crossed the Mediterranean during his missionary journeys and set sail from many of its ports, including Caesarea (Ac 9:30), Seleucia (Ac 13:4), and Cenchrea (Ac 18:18). He was shipwrecked in the Mediterranean while sailing to Rome in late autumn (Ac 27).

MEDIUM

See MAGIC, SORCERY AND DIVINATION.

MEEKNESS

Humility, gentleness. Our culture often tends to associate meekness with weakness, but this is an erroneous view. It has been said, "Meekness is strength under control." Believers are to use meekness and gentleness when dealing with one another, rather than force or anger (Ga 6:1). Jesus taught that the meek would be blessed (Ma 5:5), or "happy," and described Himself as "meek [or gentle] and lowly in heart" with an easy yoke for His followers to bear (Ma 11:29). Ephesians 4:1-2 couples meekness with longsuffering, and "bearing with one another in love."

MEET (archaic)

Agreeable; fit; proper (Mk 7:26-27).

ME·GID′DO (place of troops)

A walled city in the Carmel Mountains, the most strategic city in Palestine. All major traffic through the nation traveled past the city, making it an important military stronghold where many major battles were fought.

Megiddo is first mentioned in the Old Testament as a site where Joshua conquered one of thirty-one Canaanite kings (Jos 12:21). During the period of the judges, the forces of Deborah and Barak defeated the army of Sisera "in Taanach, by the waters of Megiddo" (Ju 5:19).

In spite of these minor victories, Megiddo did not become firmly occupied by the Israelites until the time of Solomon, who reconstructed the city as one of his storage cities (1 Ki 9:15-19). The original walls of the city were about thirteen feet thick, and they were apparently enlarged and reinforced at selected points to twice this thickness.

Zechariah prophesied that great mourning would take place "in the plain of Megiddo" (Ze 12:11). The fulfillment of this prophecy is to be at the end of time, the Battle of Armageddon. The word *Armageddon* means "mountain of Megiddo" in Hebrew. At the end of time God will destroy the armies of the beast and the false prophet (Re 16:13-16), and the King of kings

and Lord of lords will reign forever and ever (Re 11:15; 19:16).

ME·GID′DON

See MEGIDDO.

ME·HET′A·BEEL

Father of Delaiah (Ne 6:10). Also see MEHETABEL.

ME·HET′A·BEL (God blesses)

Wife of Hadar, king of Edom (Ge 36:39; 1 Ch 1:50). Also see MEHETABEEL.

ME·HI′DA (union)

Founder of a family of Nethinim (Ez 2:43, 52).

ME′HIR (price)

Son of Chelub of Judah, and the brother of Shuah (1 Ch 4:11).

ME·HO′LA·THITE

A native perhaps of Abel-meholah (1 Sa 18:19; 2 Sa 21:8).

ME·HU′JA EL (smitten of God)

Son of Irad, the fourth in descent from Cain (Ge 4:18).

ME·HU′MAN (faithful)

A chamberlain in the service of Ahasuerus, one of the seven eunuchs who served as his personal servants. (Es 1:10).

ME·HU′NIM

See MEUNIM.

ME-JAR′KON (yellow waters)

A place in Dan near Joppa (Jos 19:46).

ME·KO′NAH

See MECONAH.

MEL·A·TI′AH (Jehovah delivers)

A Gibeonite (Ne 3:7).

MEL′CHI (my king)

Two ancestors of Christ, one of whom was the father of Levi (Lk 3:24); the other the son of Addi (Lk 3:28).

MEL·CHI′AH

See MALCHIJAH.

MEL·CHIS′E·DEC

See MELCHIZEDEK.

MELCHISHUA

A son of Saul (1 Sa 14:49; 31:2). See MALCHISHUA.

MEL·CHIZ′E·DEK *(king of righteousness)*

The king-priest of Salem (doubtless Jerusalem) (Ge 14:18). His genealogy is not recorded; when he appears in Genesis it is without the usual "son of" added to let people know his background. He simply appears in the story, obviously an important character, but with no credentials. He is described as being without parents in Hebrews (He 7:1-3). When he met Abraham, he refreshed him with bread and wine, received tithes from him, and blessed him (Ge 14:17-20). The endless priesthood of the Messiah, the Lord Jesus Christ is declared to be after the order of Melchizedek (Ps 110:4; He 7:15-17).

MEL′E·A

An ancestor of Christ. He lived shortly after the time of David (Lk 3:31).

ME′LECH *(king)*

Son of Micah, son of Mephibosheth (1 Ch 8:35; 9:41).

MELCHIZEDEK

MEL′I·CHU, MEL′I·CU

Forms of MALLUCH.

MEL′I·TA *(honey)*

An island now called Malta on which Paul was shipwrecked (Ac 28:1). See MALTA.

MEL′ON

A fruit eaten by the Israelites in Egypt and Palestine (Nu 11:5). During their wilderness wanderings, they longed for the melons of Egypt.

MEL′ZAR *(steward)*

The chief of the eunuchs who was given charge of Daniel and his companions (Da 1:11,16).

MEM

The thirteenth letter of the Hebrew alphabet. It is the heading of verses 97-104 of Psalm 119. In Hebrew each of these eight verses began with the letter mem. See ACROSTIC.

MEMBER

This word is used both in a physical sense and in a spiritual sense. Physically speaking, "member" refers to a part of the physical body (Job 17:7; Ma 5:29-30). Spiritually speaking, every believer is a "member" of the church, the body of Christ (Ro 12:5; Ep 4:25). All believers belong to one another, and must learn to work together as different parts of the same body.

MEM′PHIS *(haven of the good)*

The capital of Egypt. According to Herodotus it was built by Menes, the first king of Egyptian history. It was an important city. The Hebrews knew Memphis as Noph (Is 19:13). Some of the remnant, after the fall of Judah, settled in Memphis (Je 44:1). The prophets pronounced judgments against the city (Je 46:19; Eze 30:13,16; Ho 9:6).

ME·MU′CAN

A prince of Persia who advised Ahasuerus concerning Vashti (Es 1:14-15,21).

MEN′A·HEM *(comforter)*

Son of Gadi and king of the last period of Israel. He came to the throne by murdering Shallum (2 Ki 15:14).

MEN′AN

See MENNA.

ME′ NE, ME′ NE, TEK′ EL U•PHAR′ SIN

The words of the handwriting which appeared on the wall of the palace at the time of Belshazzar's feast (Da 5:25). The words may be translated as "numbered, numbered, weighed, divided." It was a warning that Belshazzar had been counted, weighed and found wanting, and therefore his kingdom would be divided and given to the Medes and Persians.

MENI *(fate, fortune)*

A pagan god (Is 65:11).

MEN′ NA

An ancestor of Christ after the time of David (Lk 3:31).

MEN•U′ HOTH

See MANUHOTH.

ME•O′ NE•NIM *(enchanters)*

The name of the diviners' terebinth tree (Ju 9:37). Micah 5:12 renders this word "soothsayers."

ME•O′ NO•THAI *(my dwellings)*

Father of Ophrah of Judah (1 Ch 4:14), and one of the sons of Caleb's younger brother Othniel (Ju 1:13).

MEPH′ A•ATH

A town of Reuben assigned to the Merarite Levites (Jos 13:18; 21:37; 1 Ch 6:79).

ME•PHIB′ O•SHETH *(destroyer of shame)*

Two men of the house of Saul:

1. Son of King Saul and Rizpah. He was slain by the Gibeonites during the harvest (2 Sa 21:8-9).

2. Son of Jonathan. When Saul was defeated at Gilboa and Jonathan fell in battle, Mephibosheth's nurse fled with the child who was five years old. She let him fall and he was crippled in both feet (2 Sa 4:4). He is called Merib-baal in 1 Chronicles 8:34; 9:40. The story of Mephibosheth's later dealings with David is told in 2 Samuel 16:1-4 and 19:24-30.

ME′ RAB *(increase)*

Eldest daughter of Saul (1 Sa 14:49). She was promised to David as the reward for slaying the giant, but Saul gave her to Adriel instead (1 Sa 18:17-19).

Later, he gave his younger daughter Michal to David.

ME•RAI′ AH *(rebellion)*

A priest in the days of Joiakim (Ne 12:12).

ME•RAI′ OTH *(rebellious)*

Three priests of the Old Testament:

1. A priest, son of Ahitub and father of Zadok (1 Ch 9:11; Ne 11:11).

2. A priest, son of Zerahiah (1 Ch 6:6-7,52). He lived during the time of Eli.

3. A priestly family in the time of Joiakim (Ne 12:15).

ME•RAR′ I *(bitter)*

Son of Levi (Ge 46:11; Ex 6:16; Nu 26:57).

ME•RAR′ ITES

One of the three families of the tribe of Levi, descended from Merari. They had charge of portions of the tabernacle (Nu 3:36; 4:29-33; 7:8). The two divisions of the family were the Mahlites and Mushites (Nu 3:20,33).

MER•A•THA′ IM *(double rebellion)*

A symbolic name given to Babylon (Je 50:21).

MERCHANT

A buyer and seller of goods. Merchants have been plying their trade since ancient times (Ge 37:28; Pr 31:14; Eze 17:4; Ne 3:22; 13:16; Ma 22:5).

MER•CU′ RI•US

See MERCURY.

MER′ CU•RY

A Roman and Grecian deity (Ac 14:12). The Latin Mercury corresponds with the Greek HERMES.

MERCY

Mercy is closely related to grace. Man needs both mercy and grace in order to be saved. Logically, mercy precedes grace. The devout German scholar Bengel distinguished *grace* and *mercy* precisely in six Latin words: "Gratia tollit culpam, misericordia miseriam" ("Grace takes away the guilt; mercy [takes away] the misery").

From the human viewpoint, grace precedes mercy. We must accept God's grace through faith before we can have our misery removed. It is not surprising that this is the biblical order (Ze

12:10; 1 Ti 1:2; 2 Ti 1:2; Tit 1:4; 2 Jo 3). Likewise, grace always precedes peace. We cannot have peace until we have experienced the forgiveness of our sins through God's unmerited favor to us—His *charis,* His grace. SEE SATISFACTION and RECONCILIATION.

MERCY SEAT

The lid of the ark of the covenant, made of pure gold. Upon it were the two cherubim facing each other with their outstretched wings extending over the mercy seat. Between the cherubim the glory of God was exhibited (Ex 25:17-22; 30:6; Nu 7:89). Once a year the high priest of Israel sprinkled the blood of atonement on this cover. The New Testament equivalent (from the LXX) is *hilasterion,* "place of propitiation." The traditional rendering "mercy seat" is not very literal. For one thing it was not a seat (unless the metaphorical usage, such as "seat of authority," is meant) and the stress is not so much on mercy as it is on satisfaction. Christ Himself is called our mercy seat, our propitiation in Romans 3:25 (KJV, NKJV). The mercy seat signified atonement (Ex 26:34; He 9:5).

ME′ RED *(rebellion)*

Son of Ezrah. His wife was a daughter of Pharaoh (1 Ch 4:17-18).

MER′ E•MOTH *(heights)*

Three Old Testament men:

1. Son of Uriah (Ez 8:33; Ne 3:4,21).

2. Son of Bani. He divorced his foreign wife (Ez 10:36).

3. A chief priest who returned from Babylon with the first expedition (Ne 12:3,7).

ME′ RES *(lofty)*

One of the princes of Persia in the reign of Ahasuerus (Es 1:14).

MER′ I•BAH

Two places where water came from a rock to satisfy the thirsty Israelites: the first time was at the beginning of the wilderness journey, near Mount Horeb (Ex 17:1-7). The second time, the Israelites were camped near Kadesh, close to the end of their forty years of wandering (Nu 20:1-13; De 32:51). See MERIBAH-KADESH.

MER′ I•BAH-KA′ DESH *(contention, strife)*

A place near Kadesh where the Israelites became angry at Moses because of the lack of water. Moses then struck a rock and water gushed forth (Nu 20:1-13; 27:14; De 32:51).

MER′ IB-BA′ AL *(contender against Baal)*
(2 Sa 9:6; 1 Ch 8:34; 9:40)
See MEPHIBOSHETH.

MER′ O•DACH *(death)*

The god, Marduk, the patron deity of Babylon (Je 50:2); also known as Bel.

MER′ O•DACH-BAL′ A•DAN

Son of Baladan and king of Babylon. He seized the throne of Babylon in 722 B.C. when Israel, the Northern Kingdom, was overthrown by Assyria. He reigned eleven years (2 Ki 20:12-19; 2 Ch 32:31; Is 39:1-8). He was driven from the throne by the son of Sargon. Also called BERODACH-BALADAN.

ME′ ROM, WATERS OF *(a height)*

A lake on the Jordan, about ten miles north of the Sea of Galilee. It was here that Joshua defeated the northern chiefs united under Jabin (Jos 11:1-7).

ME•RO′ NO-THITE

The native of a place called Meronoth which has not been identified. The Bible names two Meronothites; Jehdeiah (1 Ch 27:30); and Jadon (Ne 3:7).

ME′ ROZ *(refuge)*

In the conflict with Sisera this town failed to render assistance (Ju 5:23).

ME′ SECH

See MESHECH.

ME′ SHA *(freedom)*

Four Old Testament men:

1. The region inhabited by the descendants of Joktan (Ge 10:30) in Arabia.

2. Son of Shaharaim of Benjamin. His mother was Hodesh (1 Ch 8:8-9).

3. Son of Caleb of the family of Hezron and founder of Ziph (1 Ch 2:42).

4. A king of Moab. He paid tribute to Ahab, king of Israel (2 Ki 3:4). When Israel was defeated in the attempt to recover Ramoth-gilead and Ahab was slain, Mesha refused to pay that year's tribute (2 Ki 1:1). The Moabites, Ammonites, and Edomites invaded Judah and were defeated by Jehoshaphat (2 Ch 20:1).

ME'SHACH *(guest of a king)*

The name given one of the companions of Daniel (Da 1:7; 2:49; 3:13-30).

ME'SHECH

A people of the line of Japheth (Ge 10:2; 1 Ch 1:5; Eze 38:2-3; 39:1; 27:13; Ps 120:5).

ME·SHEL·E·MI'AH *(Jehovah awards)*

A Levite of the branch of Kohath (1 Ch 9:21; 26:1). He is called Shelemiah in 1 Chronicles 26:14. A porter or gatekeeper of the house of the Lord during the reign of David.

ME·SHEZ'A·BEEL *(God delivers)*

Three Old Testament men:
1. A man of Judah (Ne 11:24).
2. One who sealed the covenant (Ne 10:21).
3. Father of Berechiah (Ne 3:4).

ME·SHEZ'A·BEL

See MESHEZABEEL.

ME·SHIL'LE·MITH

See MESHILLEMOTH.

ME·SHIL'LE·MOTH *(recompense)*

Two Old Testament men:
1. Father of Berechiah, an Ephraimite who opposed the slavery of those brought from Judah by Pekah, king of Israel (2 Ch 28:12).
2. A priest, the son of Immer (Ne 11:13). In 1 Chronicles 9:12 he is called Meshillemith.

ME·SHO'BAB *(restored)*

A prince of Simeon (1 Ch 4:34-41).

ME·SHUL'LAM *(ally, friend)*

1. Grandfather of Shaphan. He was appointed by Josiah to take charge of the funds to be used for temple repairs (2 Ki 22:3).
2. Son of Zerubbabel (1 Ch 3:19).
3. A chief of Gad in Bashan (1 Ch 5:13).
4. A descendant of Elpaal, a Benjamite (1 Ch 8:17).
5. Son of Hodaviah (1 Ch 9:7) or Joed (Ne 11:7) father of Sallu.

6. Son of Shephatiah, a Benjamite (1 Ch 9:8).
7. A priest whose descendants lived in Jerusalem. He was son of Zadok and father of high priest, Hilkiah, in the reign of Josiah (1 Ch 9:11; Ne 11:11).
8. Son of Meshillemith, a priest of the house of Immer (1 Ch 9:12).
9. A Kohathite, an overseer of the temple repairs in the reign of Josiah (2 Ch 34:12).
10. A chief sent by Ezra to Iddo to secure Levites to return to Jerusalem (Ez 8:16).
11. One who opposed Ezra (Ez 10:15).
12. A son of Bani who put away his foreign wife (Ez 10:29).
13. Son of Berechiah; he labored on the wall of Nehemiah (Ne 3:4,30). His daughter married the son of Tobiah, the Ammonite (Ne 6:18).
14. Son of Besodeiah. He repaired the old gate of the wall (Ne 3:6).
15. One who stood by Ezra when he read the law (Ne 8:4).
16. A priest who signed the covenant (Ne 10:7).
17. One of the leaders of the people who sealed the covenant (Ne 10:20).
18. A priest in the days of Joiakim, head of the house of Ezra (Ne 12:13).
19. A priest, a son of Ginnethon (Ne 12:16).
20. A gatekeeper in the days of Nehemiah (Ne 12:25).
21. A leader of the people who took part in the dedication of the rebuilt wall (Ne 12:33). Quite possibly the same person as No. 17.

ME·SHUL'LE-METH *(friend)*

Wife of Manasseh (2 Ki 21:19).

ME·SOB'A·ITE

See MEZOBAITE.

MES·O·PO·TA'MI·A *(a land between rivers)*

The Greek name for the country located between the Euphrates and Tigris rivers (Ge 24:7-10).

MESS (archaic)

A course of food served at a meal (Ge 43:33-34).

MESSENGER

See ANGEL.

MES·SI'AH *(anointed one)*

The Hebrew word *Messiah,* meaning "Anointed One," is translated, "the Christ" in the Greek language. In the Old Testament, the word is often associated with the anointing of a prophet, a priest, king, or other ruler. God's promise to Abraham that in him and his descendants all the world would be blessed (Ge 12:1-3) created the expectancy of a kingdom of God on earth among the Hebrew people. The reign of David as king of Judah further shaped popular messianic expectations that the coming kingdom would be one like King David's (2 Sa 7).

As the Hebrew kingdom divided after Solomon's time, the idea of a messianic deliverer became popular. The people of Israel looked for a political ruler to deliver them from their enemies. The "salvation" spoken of in the Psalms and some prophecies of Isaiah and Jeremiah was interpreted as referring to deliverance from Israel's enemies, especially threatening world powers (Ps 69:35; Is 25:9; Je 42:11). The Hebrew people tended to overlook or ignore such prophecies as the Suffering Servant message of Isaiah 53, which foretold that the Messiah would suffer and die.

Major Old Testament passages indicated that the Messiah would be born of a virgin (Is 7:14), in Bethlehem (Mi 5:2), and that He would be a descendant of the house of David (2 Sa 7:12). He would be "a Man of sorrows" (Is 53:3) who would suffer rejection by His own people (Ps 69:8), followed by betrayal by a friend (Ps 41:9), and crucifixion between two thieves (Is 53:12). As the Messiah died, His spirit would be commended to His Father (Ps 31:5). He would be raised from the dead (Ps 16:10) to take His place at God's right hand (Ps 110:1).

Jesus fulfilled these prophecies as Prophet, Priest, and King, but He came to deliver humankind from the reign of sin and bind us into God's family (Lk 4:18-19; Ac 2:36-42). "My kingdom is not of this world" (Jo 18:36), He told Pilate. He ruled by serving (Ma 20:25-28). As a priest, He offered not the blood of animals, but Himself, as a full and final sacrifice for sins (Jo 10:11-18; He 9:12).

MES·SI·AN′IC LINE

The concept of the Messiah shows up first in Genesis, where mention is made of the promised Redeemer (Ge 3:15). Seth was chosen to be head of the messianic line and in the Antediluvian Age it passed from Seth through Enos, Cainan, Mahalaleel, Jared, Enoch, Methuselah, Lamech, and Noah (Ge 5:3-32). Following the flood, Shem, son of Noah, was chosen, "Blessed be the Lord God of Shem" (Ge 9:26). Of his sons, Elam, Asshur, Arphaxad, Lud, and Aram (Ge 10:22), Arphaxad was chosen as the line of the Messiah and the genealogy of that branch is designed to introduce Abraham—Salah, Eber, Peleg, Reu, Serug, Nahor, Terah, and Abraham (Ge 11:10-26). The messianic idea takes on a national significance with Abraham, the head of the messianic nation, and Jacob, the father of Israel. There are twelve tribes and Judah is chosen (Ge 49:10). The family of the tribe must be selected and in Ruth 4:18-22, we see how it passes from Judah to David: Pharez, Hezron, Ram, Amminadab, Nahahon, Salmon, Boaz, Obed, Jesse, and David. The Davidic line proceeds through Solomon to Rehoboam, and from him to Jeconiah (Jehoiachin); and through Neri of the line of Nathan it appears again in Salathiel and Zerubbabel and through the latter to Mary (Lk 3:24-38).

MES·SI′AS

See MESSIAH.

METALSMITH

One who works with metal, including smelting ore, refining, casting or forging and shaping metal. Solomon imported a skilled bronze worker from Tyre to supervise the work on the temple (1 Ki 7:13-14). The first metalworker mentioned in Scripture is Tubal-cain, the son of Lamech and a descendant of Cain. He was "an instructor of every craftsman in bronze and iron" (Ge 4:22). Metalsmiths are called by several different terms in Scripture, including "artificer," "artisan," "blacksmith" (one who works with iron), "bronze worker," "craftsman," "engraver," "finer" (refiner), "forger," "founder," "refiner," and "smelter."

METALS OF THE BIBLE

Gold, silver, copper, and bronze are the metals most often mentioned in the Bible. The first mention of gold occurs in Genesis 2:11-12, in the description of the garden of Eden. Gold, silver (Ge 13:2), copper (De 8:9; Job 28:2), and bronze (Ge 4:22; Ex 25:2) were all used by ancient civilizations, along with iron (Ge 4:22; Le 26:19), tin (Nu 31:22), and lead (Eze 22:18). Because they are so soft, gold and silver are not useful for making tools or weapons, instead, they were used to make jewelry, decorations, and utensils. Copper is also soft, but it is more useful than gold

THE MESSIANIC LINE

ANTEDILUVIAN AGE

FROM SHEM TO DAVID

The Edenic Era—The Fall.
The Germ—Ge 3:15—Seed of the Woman.

Sethite Line

Cainite Line

Seth—Head of Line
Enos
Cainan
Mahalaleel
Jared
Enoch—Translated
Methuselah
Lamech
Noah—Sons of Noah
—Ham, Shem, Japheth

Abel Slain by Cain
Enoch
Irad
Mehujael
Methusael
Lamech
Jabal
Jubal

LINE OF MESSIAH

FLOOD

Mingling of the two lines led to great wickedness and the flood

Shem
Arphaxad—Shemitic Branch of the Line
Salah—Eber—Peleg—Reu
Serug—Nahor—Terah

Patriarchal Era

Abraham—Head of Messianic Nation
Isaac—Heir to Covenant Promises
Jacob—Father of Israel—Twelve Sons

From Judah to David

Judah—Messianic Tribe
Pharez
Hezron
Ram
Amminadab
Nashon
Salmon
Boaz—Obed—Jesse—David

MESSIANIC FAMILY—DAVIDIC LINE

THE MONARCHY

FROM THE EXILE TO CHRIST

David—Head of Messianic Family
Solomon

The Divided Kingdom

Rehoboam
Abijam
Asa
Jehoshaphat
Jehoram
Ahaziah
Joash
Amaziah

Uzziah
Jotham
Ahaz
Hezekiah
Manasseh
Amon
Josiah
Jehoiakim

Jehoiachin

Jehoiachin
Salathiel
Zerubbabel
Abiud
Eliakim
Azor
Sadoc
Achim
Eliud
Eleasar
Matthan
Jacob
Joseph—Husband of Mary

Matthew's Genealogy

JESUS CHRIST

and silver. When alloyed with tin to form bronze, it is much harder, and was used to make tools and weapons (Ex 38:3; Nu 16:39; Je 52:18), as well as ornamental castings (1 Ki 7:15-26) and even wheels (1 Ki 7:33).

The Hebrews apparently did not use iron until the after the days of King Saul, even though its use was known. The Philistines used iron, and as a part of their subjugation of the Israelites, they suppressed the blacksmith's trade and the use of iron tools and weapons. The few iron implements had to be taken to the Philistines for repairs, and swords and spears were almost unknown (1 Sa 13:19-22). Goliath and the Philistines were battling a basically weaponless people, and the sword that Saul offered to David was the only one in the army.

When God showed Moses the promised land, He told him not only about the milk and honey, but also that the land was rich in iron and copper ore (De 8:7,9). In later years, copper-smelting was established as an important industry by Solomon (1 Ki 9:26; 22:48; 2 Ch 8:17; 20:36). See MINING.

METE (archaic)

To measure; to deal out (Mk 4:24).

METEYARD (archaic)

A measuring rod (Le 19:35).

METH′ EG-AM′ MAH *(bridle of the mother city)*

A town of the Philistines (2 Sa 8:1).

ME·THU′ SA·EL

See METHUSHAEL.

ME·THU′ SE·LAH *(man of the dart)*

The son of Enoch of the line of Seth and an ancestor of Jesus (Ge 5:21-27). The oldest man in the Scriptures, he lived to be 969 years old.

ME·THU′ SHA·EL *(man of God)*

Son of Mehujael, father of Lamech, fourth in descent from Cain (Ge 4:18).

ME·U′ NIM

One of the Nethinim, whose descendants served in the temple after the captivity (Ez 2:50; Ne 7:52).

ME·U′ NITES *(habitations)*

An Arabian tribe of tent dwellers. A group of them living in the valley of Gedor were attacked

and wiped out by the Simeonites during the reign of Hezekiah (1 Ch 4:24,39-41). The Meunites were a Hamitic people. Previously, Uzziah had also battled with this group (2 Ch 26:7).

ME′ ZA·HAB *(golden waters)*

Grandfather of Mehetabel (Ge 36:39; 1 Ch 1:50).

ME·ZOB′ A·ITE

A term of unknown meaning (1 Ch 11:47).

MI′ A·MIN *(of the right hand)*

See MIJAMIN.

MIB′ HAR *(choice)*

Son of Haggeri and one of David's warriors (1 Ch 11:38).

MIB′ SAM *(sweet odor)*

Two Old Testament men:

1. A son of Ishmael, and a founder of a tribe (Ge 25:13; 1 Ch 1:29).

2. Son of Shallum of Simeon (1 Ch 4:25).

MIB′ ZAR *(fortress)*

A chieftain of Edom (Ge 36:42; 1 Ch 1:53).

MI′ CAH *(who is like God?)*

Six Old Testament men:

1. An Ephraimite who stole his mother's money but returned it. Part of it then was used to make an image. Micah appointed a Levite, Jonathan, to act as his personal priest. Through Micah's idolatry, the Danites were also led into idolatry (Ju 17–18).

2. A Reubenite who lived before the exile (1 Ch 5:5).

3. Son of Merib-baal, son of Jonathan, son of Saul (1 Ch 8:34-35; 9:40-41). Merib-baal is also called Mephibosheth, and Micah is also called Micha (2 Sa 9:12).

4. A descendant of Asaph (1 Ch 9:15; Ne 11:17, 22; 12:35), also called Michaiah.

5. Father of Abdon, prior to the reign of Josiah (2 Ch 34:20); called Michaiah in 2 Kings 22:12.

6. A Morasthite who was one of the Minor Prophets. A contemporary of Isaiah, he prophesied during the reigns of Jotham, Ahaz, and Hezekiah (Mi 1:1;3:1-4,11). See MICAH, BOOK OF: The Author of Micah.

MI' CAH, BOOK OF

1. The Book of Micah. Micah, called from his rustic home to be a prophet, left his familiar surroundings to deliver a stern message of judgment to the princes and people of Jerusalem. Burdened by the abusive treatment of the poor by the rich and influential, the prophet turned his verbal rebukes upon any who would use their social or political power for personal gain. One-third of Micah's book exposes the sins of his countrymen; another third pictures the punishment God was about to send; the final third holds out the hope of restoration once that discipline has ended. Through it all, God's righteous demands upon His people are clear: "to do justly, to love mercy, and to walk humbly with your God" (6:8).

The name *Michayahu* ("Who Is Like Yahweh?") is shortened to *Michaia.* In 7:18, Micah hints at his own name with the phrase "Who is a God like You?" The Greek and Latin titles of this book are *Michaias* and *Micha.*

2. The Author of Micah. Micah's hometown of Moresheth-gath (1:14) was located about twenty-five miles southwest of Jerusalem on the border of Judah and Philistia, near Gath. Like Amos, Micah was from the country. His family and occupation are unknown, but Moresheth was in a productive agricultural belt. Micah was not as aware of the political situation as Isaiah or Daniel, but he showed a profound concern for the sufferings of the people. His clear sense of prophetic calling is seen in 3:8; "But truly I am full of power by the Spirit of the LORD, and of justice and might, to declare to Jacob his transgression and to Israel his sin."

3. The Time of Micah. The first verse indicates that Micah prophesied in the days of Jotham (739-731 B.C.), Ahaz (731-715 B.C.), and Hezekiah (715-686 B.C.), kings of Judah. Although Micah dealt primarily with Judah, he also addressed the Northern Kingdom of Israel and predicted the fall of Samaria (1:6). Much of his ministry, therefore, took place before the Assyrian captivity of Israel in 722 B.C. His strong denunciations of idolatry and immorality largely preceded the sweeping religious reforms of Hezekiah. Thus, Micah's prophecies ranged from about 735-710 B.C. He was a contemporary of Hosea in the Northern Kingdom and of Isaiah in the court of Jerusalem.

After the prosperous reign of Uzziah in Judah (767-739 B.C.), his son, Jotham, came to power and followed the same policies (739-731 B.C.). He was a good king, although he failed to remove the idolatrous high places. Under the wicked King Ahaz (731-715 B.C.), Judah was threatened by the forces of Assyria and Syria. Hezekiah (715-686 B.C.) opposed the Assyrians and successfully withstood an Assyrian siege with the help of God. He was an unusually good king who guided the people of Judah back to a proper course in their walk with God.

During the ministry of Micah, the Kingdom of Israel continued to crumble inwardly and outwardly until its collapse in 722 B.C. The Assyrian Empire under Tiglath-pileser III (745-727 B.C.), Shalmanesar V (727-722 B.C.), Sargon II (722-705 B.C.), and Sennacharib (705-681 B.C.) reached the zenith of its power and became a constant threat to Judah. Babylon was still under Assyrian domination, and Micah's prediction of future Babylonian captivity for Judah (4:10) must have seemed unlikely.

4. The Christ of Micah. Micah 5:2 is one of the clearest and most important of all Old Testament prophecies: "But you, Bethlehem Ephrathah, though you are little among the thousands of Judah, yet out of you shall come forth to Me the One to be ruler in Israel, whose goings forth have been from of old, from everlasting." This prophecy about the birthplace and eternity of the Messiah was made seven hundred years before His birth. The chief priests and scribes paraphrased this verse in Matthew 2:5-6 when questioned about the birthplace of the Messiah. Micah 2:12-13; 4:1-8; and 5:4-5 offer some of the best Old Testament descriptions of the righteous reign of Christ over the whole world.

5. Keys to Micah.

Key Word: The Judgment and Restoration of Judah—Micah exposes the injustice of Judah and the righteousness and justice of Yahweh. About one-third of the book indicts Israel and Judah for specific sins, including oppression; bribery among judges, prophets, and priests; exploitation of the powerless; covetousness; cheating; violence; and pride. Another third of Micah predicts the judgment that would come as a result of those sins. The remaining third of the book is a message of hope and consolation. God's justice will triumph and the divine Deliverer will come. True peace and justice will prevail only when the Messiah reigns. The "goodness and severity of God" (Ro 11:22) are illustrated in Micah's presentation of divine judgment and pardon. This book emphasizes the integral relationship between true spirituality and social ethics. Micah 6:8 summarizes what God wants to see in His people: justice and equity tempered with mercy and compassion, as the result of a humble and obedient relationship with Him.

Key Verses: Micah 6:8; 7:18—"He has shown you, O man, what is good; and what does the LORD require of you but to do justly, to love mercy, and to walk humbly with your God?" (6:8).

"Who is a God like You, pardoning iniquity and passing over the transgressions of the remnant of His heritage? He does not retain His anger forever, because He delights in mercy" (7:18).

Key Chapters: Micah 6–7—The closing section of Micah describes a courtroom scene. God has a controversy against His people, and He calls the mountains and the hills together to form the jury as He sets forth His case. The people have replaced heartfelt worship with empty ritual, thinking that this is all God demands. They have divorced God's standards of justice from their daily dealings in order to cover their unscrupulous practices. They have failed to realize what the Lord requires of man. There can only be one verdict: guilty.

Nevertheless, the book closes on a note of hope. The same God who executes judgment also delights to extend mercy. No wonder the prophet exclaims, "Therefore I will look to the LORD; I will wait for the God of my salvation; my God will hear me" (7:7).

6. Survey of Micah. Micah is the prophet of the downtrodden and exploited people of Judean Society. He prophesied during a time of great social injustice and boldly opposed those who imposed their power upon the poor and weak for selfish ends. Corrupt rulers, false prophets, and ungodly priests all became targets for Micah's prophetic barbs. Micah exposed judges who were bought by bribes and merchants who used deceptive weights. The pollution of sin had permeated every level of society in Judah and Is-

rael. The whole earth was called to witness God's indictment against His people (1:2; 6:1-2), and the guilty verdict led to a sentence of destruction and captivity. However, while the three major sections begin with condemnation (1:2–2:11; 3:6) they all end on a clear note of consolation (2:12-13; 4; 5; 7). After sin is punished and justice established, "He will again have compassion on us, and will subdue our iniquities. You will cast all our sins into the depths of the sea" (7:19). The three sections of Micah are: the prediction of judgment (1–3), the prediction of restoration (4–5), and the plea for repentance (6–7).

The Prediction of Judgment (1–3). Micah begins by launching into a general declaration of the condemnation of Israel (Samaria) and Judah (Jerusalem). Both kingdoms would be overthrown because of their rampant treachery. Micah used a series of wordplays on the names of several cities of Judah in his lamentation over Judah's coming destruction (1:10-16). This is followed by some of the specific causes for judgment: premeditated schemes, covetousness, and cruelty. Nevertheless, God will re-gather a remnant of His people (2:12-13). The prophet then systematically condemns the princes (3:1-4) and the prophets (3:5-8), and concludes with a warning of coming judgment (3:9-12).

The Prediction of Restoration (4–5). Micah then moves into a two-chapter message of hope, which describes the reinstitution of the kingdom (4:1-5) and the intervening captivity of the kingdom (4:6–5:1), concluding with the coming Ruler of the Kingdom (5:2-15). The prophetic focus gradually narrows from the nations to the remnant to the King.

The Plea for Repentance (6–7). In His two controversies with His people, God called them into court and presented an unanswerable case against them. The people have spurned God's grace, choosing instead to revel in wickedness. Micah concludes with a sublime series of promises that the Lord will pardon their iniquity and renew their nation in accordance with His covenant.

OUTLINE OF MICAH

I. The Prediction of Judgment (1:1–3:12)

A. Introduction to the Book of Micah ... 1:1
B. The Judgment on the People 1:2–2:13
C. The Judgment on the Leadership ... 3:1-12

II. The Prediction of Restoration (4:1–5:15)

A. The Promise of the Coming Kingdom 4:1-5

B. The Promise of the Coming
Captivities 4:6–5:1
C. The Promise of the Coming
King 5:2-15

III. The Plea for Repentance (6:1–7:20)
A. The First Plea of God 6:1-9
B. The Second Plea of God 6:10–7:6
C. The Promise of Final Salvation 7:7-20

MI·CAI′ AH *(who is like God?)*

Son of Imlah, a prophet in Israel during the time of King Ahab. Ahab hated this prophet because he claimed that Micaiah never prophesied anything good about him. Because Micaiah was a true prophet of God, and Ahab was a wicked, disobedient king, this was probably quite true. When Ahab called Micaiah to inquire of the Lord for him as he was preparing to go out into battle with Jehoshaphat, king of Judah, Micaiah at first gave him a sarcastic answer. However, his true prophecy that Ahab would die came to pass (1 Ki 22:8-28; 2 Ch 18:6-27).

MICE

Small rodents. Many varieties of small rodents were found in Israel, including field mice, hamsters, and rats. All rodents were considered unclean (Le 11:29; Is 66:17), and God sent a plague of them on the Philistines when they stole the ark of God (1 Sa 6:4-5,11,18). Mice and rats are small, but they are capable of great destruction. Because of their rapid reproduction rates, mice can multiply into a plague which will completely destroy crops or stored grain.

MI′ CHA·EL *(who is like God?)*

1. Father of the Asherite spy sent to Canaan (Nu 13:13).
2. A descendant of Buz of Gad, head of a house in Gilead (1 Ch 5:11-13).
3. Another Gadite (1 Ch 5:14).
4. Son of Baaseiah and father of Shimea, a Levite of the family of Gershom (1 Ch 6:40).
5. A chief of Issachar, of the family of Tola and house of Uzzi (1 Ch 7:3).
6. A son of Beriah (1 Ch 8:16).
7. A captain of Manasseh. He allied himself with David at Ziklag (1 Ch 12:20).
8. Father of Omri, appointed by David as ruler of Issachar (1 Ch 27:18).
9. A son of Jehoshaphat, king of Judah. He and his brothers were slain by Jehoram, their brother, when he became king (2 Ch 21:2-4).

10. Father of Zebadiah. He returned to Jerusalem with Ezra (Ez 8:8).
11. An archangel who was called the prince of Israel (Da 10:13,21) and the great prince (Da 12:1). He is mentioned twice in the New Testament, once in Jude's puzzling reference to the dispute over Moses's body (Jude 9), and once in Revelation 12:7. "Michael and his angels" are described as struggling with Satan and his angels and throwing them out of heaven.

MI′ CHAH

A Levite, a Kohathite of the house of Uzziel, who served during the time of David (1 Ch 23:20; 24:24-25).

MI·CHAI′ AH

1. Father of Achbor (2 Ki 22:12; 2 Ch 34:20).
2. Daughter of Uriel; wife of Rehoboam, king of Judah, and mother of Abijah (2 Ch 13:2). She is also called Maacah.
3. A prince in the reign of Jehoshaphat (2 Ch 17:7).
4. A descendant of Asaph (Ne 12:35), also called Micah (1 Ch 9:15), and Micha (Ne 11:17, 22).
5. A priest and trumpeter (Ne 12:41).
6. Son of Gemariah (Je 36:11-13).

MI′ CHAL *(brook)*

Daughter of Saul, given to David on condition that he kill a hundred Philistines. Saul was hoping that David would be killed in the attempt, but instead David killed two hundred Philistines and came off unscathed. Saul saw that Michal was in love with David, and had to stand by his word and give her to him, but he became even more afraid of David's influence (1 Sa 18:27-28). Michal helped David to escape from her father, but she did not accompany him on his flight. After a time David took two other wives; in the meantime Saul had given his daughter Michal to another man (1 Sa 19:11-17; 25:44). After David became king, he demanded that Michal be returned to him. Her brother Ishbosheth complied, taking her from

Paltiel, her second husband, and sending her back to David. Paltiel apparently loved Michal very much; he followed after her weeping until he was finally turned back by Abner (2 Sa 3:13-16). Michal's relationship with David had obviously soured; when David danced before the Lord as the ark was brought into Jerusalem, Michal ridiculed his enthusiasm. Because of her attitude, she was barren until she died (2 Sa 6:20-23). Second Samuel 21:8 should probably read Merab, not Michal (1 Sa 18:19). Her five sons were slain to avenge Saul's wrongful killing of the Gibeonites.

MICH′ MASH *(something hidden)*

A town of Benjamin southeast of Beth-el (1 Sa 13:2). Two hundred men from this town returned from the captivity (Ez 2:27).

MICHME′ THATH *(hiding-place)*

A town on the border of Ephraim and Manasseh (Jos 16:6; 17:7).

MICH′ RI *(worthy of price)*

A Benjamite (1 Ch 9:8).

MICH′ TAM

A word in the titles of Psalms 16; 56-60. Its meaning is uncertain.

MIDDAY

Noon, or the time close to it (Ne 8:3; Ac 26:13). Also see CALENDAR.

MID′ DIN *(measures)*

A village west of the Dead Sea in the wilderness of Judah (Jos 15:61).

MIDDLE GATE

A gate of Jerusalem. When Babylon conquered Judah and penetrated the city, the king of Babylon came and sat in this gate, along with the princes of Babylon (Je 39:3).

MIDDLE WALL

The dividing wall between the inner court of the temple and court of the Gentiles. No Gentile was allowed to pass beyond this wall, on pain of death. This wall was a physical picture of the real hostility between Jew and Gentile. When Gentiles began to be born again, and to receive the Holy Spirit, it became clear that this wall of separation must be at an end.

Christ had received both Jews and Gentiles as believers, and both Jews and Gentiles must learn to receive one another as brothers. Jesus Christ is "our peace, who has made both one, and has broken down the middle wall of division between us" (Ep 2:14).

MID′ I·AN *(strife)*

1. A son of Abraham and Keturah (Ge 25:1-6).

2. A region in Arabia occupied by Midianites (Ju 6:3).

MID′ I·A·NITES

A nomadic people of northwestern Arabia. They are represented as descendants of Abraham and Keturah. Joseph was carried to Egypt by Midianite merchants (Ge 37:28). Jethro, the father-in-law of Moses, was a Midianite (Ex 3:1).

MIDNIGHT

The middle of the night, around 12:00 A.M. Samson waited until midnight, a time when everyone would be asleep, to make his escape from Gaza (Ju 16:3). Paul and Silas were set free by an earthquake at midnight, when they were in the Philippian jail (Ac 16:25). The angel of death passed over Egypt at midnight, as the last plague (Ex 11:4; 12:29). In each of these instances, midnight is a time when most people are not on the alert, but the psalmist also speaks of midnight as a time to remember God's word and power (Ps 119:62).

MIDWIFE

A woman who helps other women to give birth. When the Hebrews were living in Egypt, there were two midwives who served the Hebrew women, named Shiphrah and Puah. They disobeyed the order to kill all boy babies, because they feared the Lord. The Lord blessed them for their actions, and the Hebrew people continued to flourish in Egypt.

MIG′ DAL-EL *(tower of God)*

A fortified city of Naphtali (Jos 19:38).

MIG′ DAL-GAD *(tower of fortune)*

A town of Judah (Jos 15:37).

MIG′ DOL *(tower)*

An encampment of the Israelites near the Red Sea (Ex 14:2; Nu 33:7).

MIGHTY MEN

David's special group of skilled warriors. Many of these men had joined him while he was in hiding, and they had many brave exploits to their credit (2 Sa 23:8-39; 1 Ch 11:10-47). See MAN.

MIG′ RON *(precipice)*

A town of Benjamin north of Michmash (Is 10:28).

MI′ JA·MIN *(from the right hand)*

Three Old Testament men:
1. A descendant of Aaron. In the time of David the family was the sixth course of the priests (1 Ch 24:1,6,9).
2. A chief priest who returned from Babylon with the first expedition (Ne 12:5,7).
3. Son of Parosh (Ez 10:25).

MIKHTAM

See MICHTAM.

MIK′ LOTH *(rods)*

Two Old Testament men:
1. Son of Jeiel of Gideon, father of Shimeah (1 Ch 8:32; 9:37-38).
2. A captain of the army (1 Ch 27:4).

MIK·NEI′ AH *(possession of Jehovah)*

A Levite (1 Ch 15:18,21).

MIKTAM

See MICHTAM.

MIL′ A·LAI *(eloquent)*

A Levite (Ne 12:36).

MIL′ CAH *(counsel)*

Two Old Testament women:
1. A daughter of Zelophehad (Nu 26:33).
2. Daughter of Haran and wife of Nahor (Ge 11:29; 22:20-23; 24:15,24).

MILCH (archaic)

Milk. A "milch camel" (or cow or goat or sheep) is an animal which is kept specifically for the purpose of milking it (Ge 32:13-15).

MIL′ COM *(great king)*

See MOLECH.

MILDEW

A parasitic fungus which grows in damp places, and can spoil anything from crops to clothing. Because of its destructive properties, mildew is often used as a symbol of judgment. Mildew would be one of the consequences of disobedience (De 28:22; 2 Ch 6:28).

MILE *(thousand paces)*

The Roman mile of a thousand paces was over 100 yards shorter than an English or American mile—only about 4854 feet (Ma 5:41).

MI·LE′ TUS, MI·LE′ TUM

A city on the coast of Ionia, 36 miles south of Ephesus (Ac 20:15,17-38; 2 Ti 4:20).

MILK

In the East the milk of cows (Is 7:22), of sheep (De 32:14), of camels, and of goats (Pr 27:27) was used. It was also made into a substance which is often translated "cheese" or "curds" (Ju 5:25; 2 Sa 17:29), or sometimes "butter" (KJV). It is probable that this was not cheese, but rather a cultured milk, something like yogurt. Such a product would keep longer without refrigeration than sweet milk.

MILL

A tool for grinding grain into flour, usually between two stones. Mills were in use at an early period (Ge 18:6). One type of mill consisted of two circular stones about eighteen inches in diameter and three or four inches thick. The surface of the lower stone was slightly convex, while the upper was concave so that the one fitted into the other. The upper revolved about a peg in the center and into this hole the grain was dropped. An upright piece was placed near the edge by which the upper stone was turned. The work was usually done by women (Ec 12:3; Ma 24:41), by slave women (Ex 11:5; Is 47:2) and by prisoners (Ju 16:21).

MILLENNIUM *(thousand)*

The thousand-year reign of Christ in connection with His return to earth. Some Christians believe the millennium will be an age of blessedness on earth. Some believe the millennium is the present church age—a period of indefinite length. Still others regard the millennium as a way of referring to the ages of eternity.

The Bible's only specific mention of the millennium is in the twentieth chapter of Revelation, a book of vision and prophecies written by the apostle John while in exile on the Isle of Patmos off the coast of Asia Minor. Many Old Testament passages also seem to point to a millennial reign (Is 11:4; Je 3:17; Ze 14:9). See ESCHATOLOGY.

MIL′LET

This cereal is greatly in use in southern Asia, southern Europe, and northern Africa (Eze 4:9). Its grains are smaller than wheat or rice. It was exported from Israel as trade goods (Eze 27:17, "pannag," KJV).

MIL′LO (a rampart, mound)

1. A house or citadel at Shechem (Ju 9:6,20).
2. The place where Joash was killed; possibly the same as the preceding (2 Ki 12:20). A Jebusite city captured by David (2 Sa 5:9; 1 Ki 9:15; 11:27; 2 Ch 32:5).

MINA

An ancient weight and monetary unit, equal to about 50 shekels (Eze 45:12). See MONEY OF THE BIBLE.

MINAS, PARABLE OF (Lk 19:11-28)

MINERALS OF THE BIBLE

Many specific mineral (inorganic) substances are mentioned in the Bible, including gemstones and metals. These substances were put to many different uses. Following is a list of minerals mentioned in the Bible. More information can be found under the specific word in the appropriate section of the dictionary: *Alabaster, Antimony, Ash, Asphalt, Bitumen, Brass, Brimstone, Bronze, Chalkstone, Chrysolite, Clay, Coal, Copper, Crystal, Flint, Glass, Gold, Hyacinth, Iron, Jacinth, Jasper, Lead, Ligure, Lime, Lye, Malachite, Marble, Mortar, Oil, Pearl, Pitch, Plaster, Porphyry, Quartz, Salt, Sand, Sapphire, Silver, Steel, Tin, Turquoise, Vermilion.*

MINING

Digging mineral ore out of the ground. Mining has been known since ancient times. Job speaks of cutting into rock, seeking precious substances (Job 28:9-10). Most valuable minerals are not found in a pure state; metal ores are rich in the metal sought, but also contain dirt and other impurities. In order for the mined ore to be of any use, it must be refined. This is done by heating the metal, and either burning out any impurities, or else skimming the dross off the top of the molten metal. The Psalmist compares God's words to the purity of "silver tried in the furnace of earth, purified seven times" (Ps 12:6). God's judgment is compared to the heat of a refiner's furnace (Jer 6:28-30; Eze 22:18-22).

MIN·I′A·MIN (from the right hand)

Three Old Testament Levites:
1. A Levite who had charge of the freewill offerings in the reign of Hezekiah (2 Ch 31:15).
2. A priest in the days of the high priest, Joiakim (Ne 12:17).
3. A priest who blew the trumpet when the wall was dedicated (Ne 12:41).

MIN′ISH (archaic)

Diminish (Ps 107:39-40).

MIN′IS·TER

One who gives service—either secular or ecclesiastical. In the Old Testament mention is made of Joshua as a minister or personal attendant of Moses (Ex 24:13; Jos 1:1). Mention is also made of secular ministers at Solomon's court (1 Ki 10:5), angelic ministers (Ps 103:20-21; 104:4), of priests, Levites, and Nethinim as ministers in the tabernacle and temple (Ex 28:35; 1 Ki 8:11; Ez 8:17). In the New Testament the word implies humility together with the thought of service. Paul considered himself a minister of Christ (Ro 15:16).

MINJAMIN

See MINIAMIN.

MIN′NI (division)

A kingdom of Armenia referred to by Jeremiah (Je 51:27).

MIN′NITH (distribution)

A town of the Ammonites (Ju 11:33).

MIN′STREL

One who plays a stringed instrument, the harp (2 Ki 3:15) or flute (Ma 9:23).

MINT

A sweet-smelling herb. Jesus accused the scribes and Pharisees of paying so much attention to the tithes of mint, anise, etc., that they neglected more important matters (Ma 23:23; Lk 11:42).

MIPH' KAD GATE (appointed place)

The name of a gate at Jerusalem (Ne 3:31).

MIR' A-CLE

A sign, a special manifestation of God. Miracles set forth God's character, and are used to accredit his messengers. They are used only on specific and necessary occasions, for instance during such periods as the time of Moses and Joshua, of the divided kingdom, and of the exile. Our Lord performed miracles in support of His divine claims, consequently more belong to this period than to all the others combined. The miracles of the Bible cannot be explained away. To accept the Scriptures, and to accept Christ and His claims, is to accept the miraculous.

MIRACULOUS DELIVERANCES

See DELIVERANCES, MIRACULOUS.

MIR' I•AM (rebellion)

A Hebrew name whose Greek form is "Mary." Two Old Testament women:

1. Sister of Aaron and Moses (Ex 15:20; Nu 26:59). When the Israelites passed through the Red Sea, she took a timbrel and sang a song of triumph (Ex 15:20-21). In a spirit of jealousy, she and Aaron took a seditious attitude relative to the leadership of Moses, making the occasion of their murmuring Moses's marriage with a Cushite woman. Miriam was smitten with leprosy. Moses interceded for her and she was healed (Nu 12:1-16; De 24:9). She was buried in Kadesh (Nu 20:1).

2. A man or woman named in the genealogy of Judah (1 Ch 4:17).

MIR' MA

See MIRMAH.

MIR' MAH (deceit)

Son of Shaharaim and Hodesh, a Benjamite (1 Ch 8:10, Mirma, KJV).

MIR' ROR

Ancient mirrors were made of highly polished metal, such as silver, bronze, or copper (Job

MIRIAM, SISTER OF MOSES

37:18). The Hebrew women brought bronze mirrors out of Egypt, which they donated to the tabernacle project. They were made into the bronze laver (Ex 38:8).

MIS' GAB (high fort)

A city of Moab (Je 48:1).

MI' SHA•EL (who is God?)

Three Old Testament men:

1. A Kohathite Levite of the house of Uzziel (Ex 6:22; Le 10:4).

2. One of the companions of Daniel whose name was changed to Meshach (Da 1:6-7,11,19; 2:17).

3. One who was with Ezra when he instructed the people (Ne 8:4).

MI' SHAL (entreaty)

A village of Asher, given to the Gershonite Levites (Jos 19:26; 21:30, Misheal KJV).

MI' SHAM (purification)

Son of Elpaal, a Benjamite (1 Ch 8:12).

MI' SHE•AL

See MISHAL.

MISH′MA *(hearing)*

Two Old Testament men:

1. A son of Ishmael and head of a tribe (Ge 25:14; 1 Ch 1:30).

2. Son of Mibsam, a Simeonite (1 Ch 4:25).

MISH·MAN′NAH *(fatness)*

A Gadite warrior who allied himself with David (1 Ch 12:10).

MISH′RA·ITES

One of the four families of Kirjath-jearim (1 Ch 2:53).

MIS′PAR

One who returned to Jerusalem in the first expedition (Ez 2:2). The feminine form, Mispereth, is used in Nehemiah 7:7.

MIS′PE·RETH

See MISPAR.

MIS′RE·PHOTH-MA′IM *(burning of waters)*

When Joshua defeated the kings at Merom he pursued them to this place on the border of Zidon (Jos 11:8; 13:6).

MIST

Fine droplets of water suspended in the air near the earth; fog. According to Genesis 2:6, before the flood the earth was watered by mist rather than rain.

MITE

Translation of the word "lepton," a coin worth only about 25 cents (Mk 12:42). See MONEY OF THE BIBLE.

MI′TER

See MITRE

MITH′CAH

See MITHKAH.

MITH′KAH *(sweetness)*

An encampment of the Israelites (Nu 33:28-29).

MITH′NITE

The designation of Joshaphat, one of David's men (1 Ch 11:43).

MITH′RE·DATH *(given by Mithra)*

1. A Persian treasurer who, by the order of Cyrus, restored the sacred vessels to the Jews (Ez 1:8).

2. One who wrote Artaxerxes, king of Persia, from Samaria in opposition to the Jews (Ez 4:7).

MITRE

A turban made of linen and worn on the head of the high priest. On it was a golden plate with the words *Holiness to the Lord* (Ex 28:4,36-39; Le 16:4; Eze 21:26).

MIT·Y·LE′NE

The capital of Lesbos, an island situated in the Aegean Sea (Ac 20:13-15).

MIXED MULTITUDE

A crowd of mixed ethnicity. When the Hebrews left Egypt, many non-Hebrews went with them so they were a mixed multitude (Ex 12:38; Nu 11:4). After the captivity, the Jews separated all the Moabites and Ammonites from their midst, because of the law (Ne 13:3).

MI′ZAR *(small)*

A proper name for a hill east of the Jordan (Ps 42:6).

MIZ′PAH *(watch tower)*

Six or seven Old Testament towns:

1. A heap of stones at which Jacob and Laban made a compact (Ge 31:44-49).

2. Land of Mizpah, the territory inhabited by Hivites, a nation affiliated with the northern confederacy which was defeated by Joshua at the waters of Merom (Jos 11:3). It was located southwest of Mount Hermon in the territory of Manasseh.

3. A valley to which Joshua pursued the Canaanites after their defeat (Jos 11:8); possibly the same as the preceding.

4. A village of Judah (Jos 15:38).

5. A place in Benjamin to which Samuel summoned the Israelites to gather for prayer and repentance (Jos 18:26; 1 Sa 7:5-12). See also 1 Samuel 7:16-17; 10:17; 1 Kings 15:22; 2 Kings 25:23,25; Nehemiah 3:7,15,19).

6. A town in Gilead east of the Jordan which was the residence of Jephthah (Ju 11:11,29,34).

7. A town in Moab (1 Sa 22:3).

MIZ' PAR

See MISPAR.

MIZ' PEH

See MIZPAH.

MIZ' RA·IM

The Hebrew word for Egypt, particularly upper Egypt (Ge 10:6).

MIZ' ZAH *(fear)*

A duke of Edom (Ge 36:13,17; 1 Ch 1:37).

MNA' SON *(remembering)*

A native of Cyprus, in whose house Paul lodged in Jerusalem (Ac 21:16).

MO' AB

Son of Lot by his elder daughter (Ge 19:37).

MO' AB·ITES

Descendants of Lot's son, Moab. They were closely related to the Ammonites who were the descendants of Lot's son, Ammon (Ge 19:37-38). By the time of the exodus they had become numerous and were in possession of the district from the plain of Heshbon to the wady Kurahi, east of the Jordan. Moses was forbidden to attack them because the Lord gave the land to the children of Lot (De 2:9). It was on the plain of Moab the Israelites had their last encampment (Nu 22:1). Eglon, king of Moab, invaded Israel and oppressed the people until they were delivered by Ehud (Ju 3:12-30; 1 Sa 12:9). Ruth, the Moabitess, married Boaz of Bethlehem and became an ancestress of Jesus.

MO' AB·ITE STONE

A slab of black basalt, two feet broad and a foot and three inches thick, found in the territory of Moab in 1868. It bears an inscription of thirty-four lines of Moabite history. It records Mesha's recovery of Moab from Israel and facts of his reign, some of which are mentioned in the Scriptures (2 Ki 1:1; 3:5).

MO·A·DI' AH

See MAADIAH.

MODERATION (Ma 23:24; 1 Co 9:25)

MODIN

The hometown of the Maccabean family, made famous in the intertestamental period.

MODIUS

A dry measure of about 7.68 quarts. See WEIGHTS AND MEASURES.

MO·LA' DAH *(birth)*

A town in the extreme south of Judah (Jos 15:26).

MOLE

A small burrowing rodent which spends most of its time in darkness. Idol worshippers are compared to moles and bats, because of their spiritual blindness (Is 2:20).

MO' LECH *(king)*

An Ammonite deity (1 Ki 11:7) who was also called Milcom (1 Ki 11:5,33) and Malcam (Je 49:1-3; Zep 1:5). This god was worshipped with human sacrifices (2 Ki 23:10).

MO' LID *(begetter)*

A man of Judah of the family of Hezron (1 Ch 2:29).

MO' LOCH

See MOLECH.

MOL' TEN SEA

A great basin made of brass which stood in the court of Solomon's temple (1 Ch 18:8). It was decorated with flower-like ornaments. It was placed on the backs of twelve bronze oxen, had an estimated capacity of 16,000 gallons, and served the priests as a place for washing (1 Ki 7:23-26,39; 2 Ch 4:2-6).

MOLTEN SEA

MOMENT

A very short space of time, the "twinkling of an eye" (Ex 33:5; Job 7:18). When Christ returns, we will all be changed in an instant (1 Co 15:52).

MON' EY CHANG' ER

One who exchanged foreign for native money or who changed money into different denominations. Jesus rebuked them and cast them from the temple (Ma 21:12-13; Mk 11:15-17; Lk 19:45-46; Jo 2:13-16).

MONEYLENDER

One who makes a living by lending out money and charging interest for it. God commanded His people not to charge one another interest, especially the poor (Ex 22:25; Le 25:35-38). Proverbs teaches that money which is made by extortion and usury will end up being given to someone who will return it to the poor (Pr 28:8). See BANKER and BORROW.

MONEY OF THE BIBLE

The Hebrews probably first used coins in the Persian period (500-350 B.C.). However, minting began around 700 B.C. in other nations. Prior to this, precious metals were weighed, not counted as money.

Some units appear as both measures of money and measures of weights. This comes from naming the coins after their weight. For example, the shekel was a weight long before it became the name of a coin.

It is helpful to relate biblical monies to current values, but we cannot make exact equivalents. The fluctuating value of money's purchasing power is difficult to determine in our own day. It is even harder to evaluate currencies used two to three thousand years ago. Therefore, it is best to choose a value meaningful over time, such as a common laborer's daily wage. One day's wage corresponds to the ancient Jewish system (a silver shekel is four days' wages), as well as to the Greek and Roman systems (the drachman and the denarius were each coins representing a day's wage).

The money chart below takes a current day's wage as thirty-two dollars. Though there are differences of economies and standards of living, this measure will help us apply meaningful values to the monetary units in the chart and in the biblical text.

Unit	Monetary Value	Equivalents	Translations
Jewish Weights			
Talent	Gold—$5,760,000[1] Silver—$384,000	3,000 Shekels; 6,000 bekas	talent
Shekel	Gold—$1,920 Silver—$128	4 days' wages; 2 bekas; 20 gerahs	shekel
Beka	Gold—$960 Silver—$64	½ shekel; 10 geras	bekah
Gerah	Gold—$96 Silver—$6.40	1/20 shekel	gerah
Persian Coins			
Daric	Gold—$1,280[2] Silver—$64	2 days' wages; ½ silver shekel	Drachma
Greek Coins			
Tetradrachma (Stater)	$128	4 drachmas	piece of money
Greek Coins			
Didrachma	$64	2 drachmas	tribute
Drachma	$32	1 day's wage	piece of silver
Lepton	$0.25	½ a Roman kodrantes	mite
Roman Coins			
Aureus	$800	25 denarii	
Denarius	$32	1 day's wage	denarius
Assarius	$2	1/16 of a denarius	copper coin
Kodrantes	$0.50	¼ of an assarius	cent, quadrans

[1]Value of gold is fifteen times the value of silver.
[2]Value of gold is twenty times the value of silver.

MONITOR LIZARD

See LIZARD.

MONKEY

Solomon had these exotic animals imported, along with other strange animals and valuable goods (1 Ki 10:22; 2 Ch 9:21). This word is also translated "peacock." See APE.

MONOTHEISM

The concept that there is only one God. In order for God to be God, there must be only one. Godhead is not a position which can be shared.

MONTH

See CALENDAR.

MOON

One of the celestial bodies. It was worshipped as a god by many ancient peoples including the Egyptians, Assyrians, and Babylonians. Some Hebrews worshipped the moon (Je 19:13; Zep

1:5) despite the fact that it was forbidden (De 17:3-5). The most famous temple to the moon god was in the city of Ur of the Chaldees. The moon served as a measure for marking off months and in regulating feasts (Ge 1:14; Ps 104:19).

MOON, NEW

The special sacrifices made on the first day of the new month. The tabernacle was set up for the first time on the first day of the first month of the year (Ex 40:2,17). After this, the first day of every month had a special ceremony. Trumpets were blown over the offerings (Nu 10:10) and two young bulls, one ram, and seven yearling lambs were sacrificed, along with several grain offerings (28:11-15).

MO·RASH′TITE

See MORASTHITE.

MO·RAS′THITE

One who lived in Moresheth (Je 26:18; Mi 1:1).

MOR·DE·CA′I *(little man)*

1. The son of Jair, a descendant of Kish, a Benjamite (Es 2:5). His people were carried to Babylonia in the second stage of the captivity. He was a close relative of Esther whom he reared as his foster-daughter (Es 2:7). See ESTHER, BOOK OF

2. A Jew who returned to Jerusalem (Ez 2:2; Ne 7:7).

MO′REH *(teacher)*

1. The place where the sacred terebinth grew, near Shechem, where Abraham built an altar and the Lord appeared to him (Ge 12:6; De 11:30).

2. The hill of Moreh was in the valley of Jezreel (Ju 7:1).

MO′RESH·ETH-GATH *(possession of Gath)*

Apparently the city of Micah, the prophet (Mi 1:14) who was called a Morasthite (Mi 1:1).

MO·RI′AH *(chosen by Jehovah)*

A mountainous region near Jerusalem. To one of its mountains Abraham took his son, Isaac, to offer him as a sacrifice (Ge 22:2).

MORNING

The beginning of the day, dawn (Ma 16:3). The days of creation are described in terms of "evening and morning" (Ge 1:5).

MORNING STAR

See LUCIFER.

MORTAL

Subject to death. Human mortality divides us sharply from the immortal God (Job 4:17; 10:5; Is 13:12), but Christ came to abolish death, and bring "life and immortality to light through the gospel (2 Ti 1:10).

MOR′TAR

1. A vessel used to pulverize grain or spices. The earliest notice of it is in connection with the preparation of the manna by the Israelites (Nu 11:8). A mortar is a bowl made of stone or wood; it is used in conjunction with a blunt utensil called a pestle, which is used to pound or crush the material placed in the mortar.

2. A substance containing lime used in holding together bricks or stones. Clay or mud without lime was used by the poorer classes but for the better class of houses, sand and lime mixed with water were employed (Eze 13:10; Na 3:14).

MORTIFY *(archaic)*

To put to death (Ro 8:13).

MOSAIC COVENANT

The covenant with Moses is the second of the theocratic covenants (covenants pertaining to the rule of God) and is conditional. It is introduced by the conditional formula, "if you will indeed obey My voice . . . then you shall be a special treasure." This covenant was given to the nation of Israel so that those who believed God's promise given to Abraham in the Abrahamic Covenant (Ge 12:1-3) would know how they should conduct themselves. The Mosaic Covenant in its entirety governs three areas of their lives: (1) the commandments governed their personal lives particularly as they related to God (Ex 20:1-26); (2) the judgments governed their social lives particularly as they related to one another (Ex 21:1–24:11); and (3) the ordinances governed their religious lives so that the people would know how to approach God on the terms that He dictates (Ex 24:12–

31:18). The Mosaic Covenant in no way replaced or set aside the Abrahamic Covenant. Its function is clearly set forth by Paul (Ga 3:17-19), who points out that the law, the Mosaic Covenant, came 430 years after the Abrahamic Covenant. The Mosaic Covenant was added alongside the Abrahamic Covenant so that the people of Israel would know how to conduct their lives until "the seed," the Christ, comes and makes the complete and perfect sacrifice, toward which the sacrifices of the Mosaic Covenant only point. The Mosaic Covenant was never given so that by keeping it people could be saved, but so that they might realize that they cannot do what God wants them to do even when God writes it down on tablets of stone. The law was given that man might realize that he is helpless and hopeless when left to himself, and realize that his only hope is to receive the righteousness of God by faith in Jesus (Ga 3:22-24).

MO′SE·RAH (bond)

One of the places where the Israelites camped in the wilderness (De 10:6). Moseroth, the plural form, is used in Numbers 33:30.

MO′SE· ROTH

See MOSERAH.

MO′SES (drawn out)

This great leader and lawgiver of the covenant people was a Levite of the family of Kohath, of the house of Amram (Ex 6:18,20). He was the brother of Aaron, the head of the priestly family, and also the brother of Miriam. It was probably she who watched over the infant Moses on the Nile, when his mother placed him there to hide him from the Egyptians. He was found by Pharaoh's daughter (Ex 2:10), and the watching sister offered her own mother as a nurse for the baby. Moses was brought up as the son of Pharaoh's daughter, but he did not forget who his people really were. At the age of 40 he killed an Egyptian and as a result fled to the region of Horeb. There he lived with Jethro, priest of Midian, and later married his daughter, Zipporah, who bore him two sons (Ex 2:11-22; 18:1-4; Ac 7:23-29). After forty years, the Lord bid him to liberate his people from Egypt (Ex 3:1-10; Ac 7:30-36). He obeyed and henceforth, from the plagues of Egypt through the difficulties of the exodus and forty years

of wandering, to his death and burial on the mountains of Moab (De 34:1-7), his influence continually increased.

MOSES' LIFE, INDEXED		
Recorded Events	Place	Reference
The Egyptians are slaying the Hebrew male children so as to weaken that race. The Hebrews are the slaves of the Egyptians. A new line of kings that knew not Joseph and are hostile to the Jews come to the throne. They adopt various inhuman measures for repression of the Israelites.	Egypt	Ex 1
Moses is born, and in the ark of bulrushes is found by the king's daughter, adopted by her, cared for by his own mother and grows up in the court of Egypt.	Egypt	Ex 2:1-10
He sympathizes with his people and slays an Egyptian who is smiting one of the Hebrews.	Egypt	Ex 2:11-14
Pharaoh seeking to slay him, he flees to Midian, where he is employed by Jethro, a Midian priest, whose daughter he marries, and tends the flocks.	Midian	Ex 2:15-25
God talks with Moses at the burning bush and commissions him to lead his people out of Egypt. Moses expresses his doubts, is told how to proceed and is assured of God's presence. His rod is turned into a serpent. His brother, Aaron, is to be his mouthpiece.	Midian	Ex 3:1-22; 4:1-17
Moses assembles the elders of Israel. He appeals to Pharaoh, who refuses to let Israel go, and ten plagues are sent upon the Egyptians. The Passover is instituted and the people leave Egypt.	Egypt	Ex 4:18–13:22
Israel, pursued by the Egyptians, cross the Red Sea on dry land. The song of Moses.	Red Sea	Ex 14:1–15:19
Moses brings Israel to Sinai. Manna is provided.	Sinai	Ex 15:20–18:27
They remain at Sinai about one year, where Moses receives from God the Ten Commandments, and many other laws and institutions for the people.	Sinai	Ex 19–40 Book of Leviticus Nu 1:1–10:10
Leaving Sinai, they come to Kadesh. Spies are sent to Canaan. The people are afraid to go in and take the land and are doomed to wander for 40 years.	Kadesh	Nu 10:11–14:45
Moses leads Israel through the wilderness, and at the end of the 40 years brings them to the plains of Moab. With the exception of Joshua and Caleb, all the people who left Egypt died by the way. These two men, at Ka-	Wilderness	Nu 15–36

Recorded Events	Place	Reference
desh, had urged the people to take possession of the land and not to be influenced by the adverse report of the other spies, hence they are permitted to enter the land.	Wilderness	Nu 15–36
Israel's last encampment in the plains of Moab. During these last weeks, Moses delivers his last addresses set forth in Deuteronomy.	Plains of Moab	De 1:1–30:20
The last acts of Moses. His charge to Joshua, his successor, his last instructions, his last song.	Plains of Moab	De 31–33
On Nebo, Moses has a view of the land of promise.	Plains of Moab	De 34
At Meribah, Moses and Aaron fail to give God the glory in striking the rock for water, and for this sin are not allowed to enter the land. He dies at the age of 120 and is buried in the land of Moab. "And there arose not a prophet since in Israel like unto Moses, whom the Lord knew face to face."	Nebo	

MOST HIGH

A title of God, indicating His superiority to any other being (Ps 92:1; Is 14:14; Da 4:17). See GOD, NAMES OF.

MOTE

A speck of dust.

MOTH

A cocoon forming insect (Job 27:18). Moths are well-known for their destructiveness to clothing. The larva feed on wool fibers, leaving garments and fabric full of holes (Job 13:28; Ma 6:19; Jam 5:2).

MOTHER

Eve was the first mother, and is described as the "mother of all living" because from her children all the people of the earth would be descended (Ge 3:20). In ancient Hebrew culture, the position of the mother was a position of honor. For a woman to be without children was to be without significance, and barrenness was considered a disgrace and sorrow (Ge 30:1; 1 Sa 1). The mother of a household had a good deal of authority and responsibility. She must feed and clothe her husband and children, and often had opportunity to add to the family income (Pr 31). The love and tenderness of a mother's care is a picture we all relate to; Paul describes his care for the new believers in these terms (1 Co 3:1; 1 Th 2:7).

MOTHER-IN-LAW

The mother of one's spouse. One of the most tender stories of love and loyalty is found in the relationship between Ruth the Moabitess and her mother-in-law, Naomi (Ru 1:1-4).

MOUNTAIN OF THE VALLEY

A mountain in the territory of Reuben, east of the Jordan (Jos 13:19).

MOUN'TAINS

Several important mountains are mentioned in the Bible. The two highest mountains in or near Palestine are Hermon and Lebanon. **Hermon** marked the northern limit of the conquest of Canaan (Jos 11:3,17). **Lebanon** was the source of the cedar wood for Solomon's temple in Jerusalem (1 Ki 5:14,18). On **Mount Carmel,** Elijah was victorious over the prophets of Baal (1 Ki 18:9-42). Saul and his sons were killed in a battle with the Philistines on Mount Gilboa (1 Ch 10:1,8). Moses commanded an altar to be built on **Mt. Gerazim** after the Hebrews entered the promised land (De 27:4-8). Opposite Mt. Gerazim is **Mt. Ebal,** where Jesus talked with the Samaritan woman at the well (Jo 4:20). Further south is **Mt. Pigsah,** or **Nebo,** where Moses viewed the promised land (De 34:1). Near Jerusalem is the **"Mount of Olives"** where Jesus gave the discourse on His second coming (Ma 24:3). Two other important mountains are **Ararat** (in modern Turkey), where Noah's ark came to rest (Ge 8:4); and **Sinai,** or **Horeb** (near Egypt), where the law was given to Moses (Ex 19:2-25).

Mountains are used figuratively to denote things of a difficult or dangerous nature (Je 13:16), perpetuity and stability (Is 54:10; Hab 3:6), or obstacles (Ze 4:7; Ma 21:21).

MOUNTAIN SHEEP

See SHEEP.

MOUNTAINS OF THE AMALEKITES

A place in the territory of Ephraim (Ju 12:15).

MOUNTAINS OF THE AMORITES

Near Kadesh-barnea, one of the places the twelve spies explored in the first venture into the promised land (De 1:7,20).

MOUNT BAAL HERMON

A mountain where the Hivites continued to live after the Hebrews took over the promised land (Ju 3:3); also called "Baal-gad below Mount Hermon" (Jos 13:5; 1 Ch 5:23).

MOUNT EPHRAIM

See EPHRAIM, MOUNTAINS OF.

MOUNT HERES

A mountain on the border between the territories of Judah and Dan (Ju 1:35).

MOUNT OF BEATITUDES

The mountain where Jesus delivered the "Sermon on the Mount" (Ma 5:1–7:29). It is believed to be northwest of the Sea of Galilee.

MOUNT OF CON'GRE·GA'TION

A mythical mountain in the far north which the Babylonians believed to be the home of the gods (Is 14:13).

MOUNT OF CORRUPTION

A slope of the Mount of Olives where Solomon had set up high places for his foreign wives to worship their pagan gods (2 Ki 23:13). These high places were destroyed when Josiah restored true worship to Judah.

MOUNT OF OLIVES

See OLIVES, MOUNT OF.

MOURN'ING

The ancient peoples expressed grief in a very noticeable manner, by tearing their garments (2 Sa 13:31; Joel 2:13), putting on sackcloth, and sprinkling dust or ashes on their heads (2 Sa 15:32; Joel 1:8), and by removing from their persons anything of an ornamental nature (2 Sa 14:2; 19:24; Ma 6:16-18). Professional mourners, mainly women, were sometimes employed (Je 9:17-18; Ma 9:23; Ac 9:39). There was an extended period of mourning. They mourned for Aaron and Moses thirty days (Nu 20:29; De 34:8) and for Saul seven days (1 Sa 31:13).

MOUSE *(the corn eater)*

Ceremonially an unclean animal (Le 11:29). The field mouse fed on grains and was very destructive (1 Sa 6:5). See MICE.

MOWING

Cutting of grass or grain (Am 7:1). In ancient times, mowing was done with a sickle.

MO'ZA *(going forth)*

1. Son of Caleb of the family of Hezron (1 Ch 2:46).

2. Son of Zimri, a descendant of Jonathan (1 Ch 8:36-37).

MO'ZAH

A town of Benjamin (Jos 18:26).

MUFFLER

A scarf or veil (Is 3:18-19).

MUL'BER·RY TREE

A tree of uncertain identity (2 Sa 5:23-24; 1 Ch 14:14-15).

MULE

A hybrid between the horse and the ass (2 Sa 13:29; 2 Ki 5:17; 1 Ch 12:40). See ASS.

MUP'PIM *(serpent)*

A Benjamite (Ge 46:21), a descendant of Rachel. He is also called Shupham and Shuppim (Nu 26:39; 1 Ch 7:12,15). See SHEPHUPHAN.

MUR'DER

After the flood a law was announced that "Whoever sheds man's blood, by man shall his blood be shed" (Ge 9:6). An unintentional murderer could be put to death by the avenger of blood (Nu 35:19) unless he reached a city of refuge. Intentional murder required the death penalty (Nu 35:20-25,30-32).

MUR'RAIN

A pestilence, the fifth plague of Egypt (Ex 9:1-6).

MU'SHI

Son of Merari, a Levite (Ex 6:19; Nu 3:20; 26:58; 1 Ch 24:26,30).

MUSHITES

Descendants of Mushi the Levite (Nu 3:20, 33).

MU'SIC

Music has been known to humans since ancient pre-flood days (Ge 4:21), and probably since the beginning. Music affects humans deeply; it is used to express both joy and sorrow, to soothe and to excite. David played his harp to sooth King Saul's torment (1 Sa 16:16-23). David obviously loved music, and fostered its use in the worship services at the tabernacle (2 Sa 6:5); he also wrote many of the Psalms. Solomon continued this tradition (1 Ki 10:12), and Hezekiah and Josiah both reinstituted worship music with their other reforms (2 Ch 29:25; 35:15). Descriptions of the temple musicians and choirs can be found in 1 Chronicles 15–16; 23; 25.

The Book of Psalms contains many musical notations, whose meaning is not precisely known today. It is assumed that these words give indications of what tunes were used, what sort of mood is intended, or what instruments to play it on.

In New Testament days, music continued to play an important part in religious activity. Jesus and His disciples sang hymns together (Ma 26:30). Mary and Zacharias sang songs of praise and blessing to God concerning the miraculous events which were taking place in their lives (Lk 1:46-55,68-79). The Church continued to sing for worship, probably from the Psalms (Ac 16:25; Ep 5:19; 1 Ti 3:16). Believers are urged to encourage one another with the singing of "psalms and hymns and spiritual songs" (Ep 5:19; Col 3:19).

MUSICAL INSTRUMENTS OF THE BIBLE

Following is a list of the musical instruments mentioned in the Bible. The exact identity of all of these is not clear, but these are the words translators have chosen for the various Hebrew words. More information about the different instruments may be found under each word in the appropriate section of the dictionary. *Bagpipe, Bell, Cornet, Cymbal, Dulcimer, Fife, Flute, Gong, Harp, Horn, Lute, Lyre, Organ, Pipe, Psaltery, Ram's Horn, Sackbut, Tabret, Timbrel, Triangle, Trigon, Trumpet, Viol, Zither.*

MUS' TARD

A common herb of Palestine, proverbial for the smallness of its seeds (Ma 17:20; Lk 17:6).

MUSTARD SEED, PARABLE OF (Ma 13:31-32; Mk 4:30-32)

MUSTER GATE, MUSTERING GATE

A gate of Jerusalem (Ne 3:31), also called Miphkad Gate.

MUTENESS

Inability to speak, dumbness.

MUTE SPIRIT

An evil spirit which prevents the one it is oppressing from speaking. See DEMONIACS.

MUTH-LAB' BEN

An expression in the title of Psalm 9, the meaning of which is uncertain.

MUZZLE

A device which prevents an animal from biting or from eating. God told the Israelites not to muzzle the animals which were used for threshing grain, but rather to allow them to eat as they worked (De 25:4).

MY' RA

A city of Lycia; Paul transferred ships here on his way to Rome (Ac 27:5-6).

MYRIAD

Numerous, many; an indefinite large number, almost uncountable (Ac 21:20).

MYRRH

An aromatic gum resin of brownish color obtained from certain trees of Arabia and East Africa. It was used to perfume beds and clothing (Ps 45:8; Pr 7:17; Song 3:6). The anointing oil of the priests contained myrrh (Ex 30:23). Myrrh was valuable, and was included in the gifts brought to Jesus by the Magi (Ma 2:11). Mixed with wine it was offered to Jesus when he was on the cross (Mk 15:23) and later was used to anoint his body (Jo 19:39).

MYR' TLE

A common tree, found in the hills near Jerusalem. Myrtle is an evergreen, with white flowers and dark foliage. At the feast of tabernacles, when the people lived in booths during those

MYRRH

seven days, branches of this tree were used (Ne 8:15). See also Isaiah 41:19; 55:13; Zechariah 1:8,10-11.

MY′SI-A

A northwestern province of Asia Minor. One of its cities was Troas, and in coming to this point Paul and Silas passed through the province (Ac 16:7-8). Another city was Assos (Ac 20:13), and another was Pergamos, one of the seven churches of Revelation (Re 1:11; 2:12-17).

MYS′TER-Y

The use of the word in the New Testament denotes the secret or hidden purpose of God in the salvation of Christ to be fully revealed in due time (Ro 16:25; 1 Co 2:7; Ep 1:9; 3:9; Col 1:26). The "mysteries of the kingdom of heaven" (Ma 13:11; Mk 4:11; Lk 8:10) are God's secret purpose relative to his kingdom. It is no longer a secret to those who have become citizens of the kingdom of grace, by the Spirit of God.

N

NA′AM *(pleasantness)*

Son of Caleb (1 Ch 4:15).

NA′A·MAH *(pleasant)*

1. Daughter of Lamech and sister of Tubal-cain (Ge 4:22).
2. Wife of Solomon (1 Ki 14:21,31; 2 Ch 12:13).
3. A town of Judah (Jos 15:41).

NA′A·MAN *(pleasantness)*

1. A son of Benjamin (Ge 46:21).
2. Son of Bela (Nu 26:40).
3. A Syrian, commander of the army of Ben-hadad, king of Damascus. He had leprosy (2 Ki 5:1-27). Naaman's wife had a Hebrew servant girl, who had been captured in a Syrian raid. This girl told her mistress that in Israel there was a prophet who could heal Naaman. Naaman made his way to see this prophet, Elisha, and at first he objected to the cure set out for him. He was to wash seven times in the Jordan River, and this would cleanse him of his leprosy. Eventually, he decided to follow Elisha's instructions, and He was healed.
4. A Benjamite, son of Ehud (1 Ch 8:7).

NA·AM′A·THITE

An inhabitant of Naamah (Job 2:11; 11:1; 20:1; 42:9).

NA′A·MITE

The descendents of Benjamin's son Naaman (Nu 26:40).

NA′A·RAH

1. A town east of Beth-el on the border of Ephraim (Jos 16:7; Naarath, KJV), probably the same as Naaran (1 Ch 7:28).
2. Wife of Ashur of Judah (1 Ch 4:5-6).

NA′A·RAI

One of David's mighty men, son of Ezbai (1 Ch 11:37), also called Paarai (2 Sa 23:35).

NA′A·RAN

See NAARAH.

NA′A·RATH

See NAARAH.

NA·ASH′ON

See NAHSHON.

NA·AS′SON (Ma 1:4; Lk 3:32)

See NAHSHON.

NA·BA·JOTH′

Ishmael's firstborn son (1 Ch 1:29), also called Nebajoth.

NA′BAL *(foolish)*

A resident of Maon. He had large flocks of sheep and goats. David had protected his property and that of others from thieves. When persecuted by Saul, he sent ten of his band to Nabal asking for help. Nabal refused rudely, and only escaped being annihilated by David because of the clever intervention of his intelligent wife Abigail (1 Sa 25:1-42). Nabal died of a stroke shortly thereafter, and Abigail became the wife of David.

NA·BA·TE′A

A land between the Dead Sea and the Gulf of Aqaba. It is thought that Ishmael's eldest son Nabajoth was probably the ancestor of the Nabateans. The unique city of Petra was the capital of the Nabateans. When Paul was in Damascus, the "governor, under Aretas the king" was trying to apprehend Paul, and Paul's friends let him out of a window in the wall in a basket. This Aretas was Aretas IV (9 B.C.–A.D. 40), a Nabatean king. Rome did not annex Nabatea until A.D. 106, under the emperor Trajan.

NA·BO·PO·LASS′AR (2 Ki 25:1-7)

Father of Nebuchadnezzar; reigned (626-605 B.C.).

NA′BOTH *(fruits)*

A man of Jezreel, owner of a vineyard that Ahab, king of Israel, wanted to buy. He refused to sell, because the vineyard was part of the family inheritance, and in a sense it was not his to sell. Jezebel, wife of Ahab, had Naboth and his sons put to death and Ahab seized the vineyard. The judgment of God was pronounced against them (1 Ki 21:1-24; 22:34-38; 2 Ki 9:26,30-37).

NA·BU·CHO·DON′OS·OR

See NEBUCHADNEZZAR.

NA′CHON *(prepared)*

Nachon's Threshing Floor: the place where Uzzah was struck dead when he placed his hand on the ark in an attempt to steady it as it was being brought to Jerusalem (2 Sa 6:6). Also called Nacon. The place was later called Perez-Uzzah. See PEREZ-UZZAH.

NA′CHOR

See NAHOR.

NA′CON

See NACHON.

NA′DAB *(liberal)*

1. Eldest son of Aaron (Ex 6:23; Nu 3:2; 26:60; 1 Ch 24:1). He and his brother, Abihu, were priests (Ex 28:1). They offered strange fire to God and were instantly destroyed (Le 10:1-7; Nu 26:61).

2. Son and successor of Jeroboam, king of Israel. (1 Ki 14:10-11,20; 15:25-30).

3. Son of Shammai (1 Ch 2:28,30).

4. A son of Jehiel and Maachah of Benjamin (1 Ch 8:29-30; 9:35-36).

NAG′GAI

Son of Maath and an ancestor of Jesus (Lk 3:25; Nagge, KJV).

NAG′GE

See NAGGAI.

NA′HA·LAL *(pasture)*

A village of Zebulun (Jos 21:35), also called Nahallal or Nahalol.

NA·HAL′I·EL *(valley of God)*

An encampment of the Israelites near Pisgah (Nu 21:19).

NA·HAL′LAL

See NAHALAL.

NA′HA·LOL

See NAHALAL.

NA′HAM *(solace)*

A Calebite (1 Ch 4:19).

NA·HA·MA′NI *(compassionate)*

One who returned to Jerusalem (Ne 7:7).

NA′HA·RAI *(snoring)*

Joab's armorbearer, a Berothite (2 Sa 23:37; 1 Ch 11:39).

NA′HA·RI

See NAHARAI.

NA′HASH *(serpent)*

1. A king of the Ammonites. When he besieged Jabesh-gilead, he demanded as the price of peace that every man lose his right eye as a reproach to Israel (1 Sa 11:1-11).

2. The probable father of David's sisters, Abigail and Zeruiah (2 Sa 17:25). Scholars have guessed that Jesse was the second husband of David's mother.

3. A man of Rabbah, an Ammonite (2 Sa 17:27).

NA′HATH *(rest)*

1. Son of Reuel, grandson of Esau and a chieftain of Moab (Ge 36:3-4,13,17; 1 Ch 1:37).

2. A Levite of the family of Kohath (1 Ch 6:26), probably the same as Tohu (1 Sa 1:1), and Toah (1 Ch 6:34).

3. A Levite in charge of the offerings in the reign of Hezekiah (2 Ch 31:13).

NAH′BI *(hidden)*

The scout who represented Naphtali when the twelve went into Canaan to spy out the land preliminary to entering it (Nu 13:14).

NA' HOR *(snoring)*

1. Son of Serug and grandfather of Abraham (Ge 11:22-26).

2. Son of Terah and brother of Abraham (Ge 11:27). He married Milcah, his niece and sister of Lot (Ge 11:29).

3. The city in which Nahor's family continued to dwell after Abraham and Sarah had gone to Canaan. Abraham sent his servant here to find a bride for Isaac from among Abraham's extended family (Ge 24:10).

NAH' SHON *(enchanter)*

A prince of Judah (Nu 1:7; 2:3; 7:12,17; 10:14). His sister was the wife of Aaron. He was the ancestor of Boaz, husband of Ruth (Ru 4:20-22; 1 Ch 2:10-12) and ancestor of Jesus (Ma 1:4; Lk 3:32-33, Naason, KJV).

NA' HUM *(compassionate)*

1. One of the Minor Prophets, called the Elkoshite (Na 1:1). See NAHUM, BOOK OF: The Author of Nahum.

2. One mentioned in the genealogy of Jesus (Lk 3:25).

NA' HUM, BOOK OF

1. The Book of Nahum. "For everyone to whom much is given, from him much will be required' (Lk 12:48). Nineveh had been given the privilege of knowing the one true God. Under Jonah's preaching this great Gentile city had repented, and God had graciously stayed His judgment. However, a hundred years later, Nahum proclaimed the downfall of this same city. The Assyrians had forgotten their revival and had returned to their habits of violence, idolatry, and arrogance. As a result, Babylon would so destroy the city that no trace of it would remain. This prophecy was fulfilled in painful detail.

The Hebrew word *nahum* ("comfort, consolation") is a shortened form of Nehemiah ("Comfort of Yahweh"). The destruction of the capital city of Assyria was a message of comfort and consolation to Judah and all who lived in fear of the cruelty of the Assyrians. The title of this book in the Greek and Latin Bibles is *Naoum* and *Nahum*.

2. The Author of Nahum. The only mention of Nahum in the Old Testament is found in 1:1 where he is called an Elkoshite. At least four locations have been proposed for Elkosh:

(1) a sixteenth-century tradition identifies Elkosh with Al-Qush in Iraq, north of the site of Nineveh on the Tigris River. (2) Jerome believed that Elkesi, a city near Ramah in Galilee, was Elkosh because of the similarity of the consonants. (3) Capernaum means "City of Nahum" (*Kephar-Nahum*), and many believe that the name Elkosh was changed to Capernaum in Nahum's honor. (4) Most conservative scholars believe that Elkosh was a city of southern Judah (later called Elcesei) between Jerusalem and Gaza. This would make Nahum a prophet of the Southern Kingdom and may explain his interest in the triumph of Judah (1:15; 2:2).

3. The Time of Nahum. The fall of Nineveh to the Babylonians in 612 B.C. is seen by Nahum as a future event. Critics who deny predictive prophecy naturally date Nahum after 612 B.C., but this is not based upon exegetical or historical considerations. Nahum 3:8-10 refers to the fall of Thebes as a recent event, so this book must be dated after 664 B.C., the year when this took place. Thus, Nahum can safely be placed between 663 and 612 B.C. Thebes was restored a decade after its defeat, and Nahum's failure to mention this restoration has led several scholars to the conclusion that Nahum was written before 654 B.C. The fact that Nahum mentions no king in the introduction to his book (1:1) may point to the reign of the wicked King Manasseh (686-642 B.C.).

The conversion of the Ninevites in response to Jonah's message of judgment was evidently short-lived, because the Assyrians soon returned to their ruthless practices. In 722 B.C., Sargon II of Assyria destroyed Samaria, the capital of the Northern Kingdom of Israel, and scattered the ten tribes. Led by Sennacherib, the Assyrians also came close to capturing Jerusalem in the reign of King Hezekiah in 701 B.C. By the time of Nahum (c. 660 B.C.), Assyria reached the peak of its prosperity and power under Ashurbanipal (669-633 B.C.). This king extended Assyria's influence farther than had any of his predecessors. Nineveh became the mightiest city on earth with walls 100 feet high and wide enough to accommodate three chariots riding abreast. Dotted around the walls were huge towers that stretched an additional 100 feet above the top of the walls. In addition, the walls were surrounded by a moat 150 feet wide and 69 feet deep. Nineveh appeared impregnable and could withstand a twenty-year siege. Thus, Nahum's prophecy of Nineveh's overthrow seemed unlikely indeed.

Assyrian power faded under Ashurbanipal's sons, Ashuretililani (633-629 B.C.) and Sinsharishkun (629-612 B.C.). Nahum predicted that Nineveh would end "with an overflowing flood" (1:8), and this is precisely what occurred. The Tigris River overflowed its banks and the flood destroyed part of Nineveh's wall. The Babylonians invaded through this breach in the wall, plundered the city, and set it on fire. Nahum also predicted that Nineveh would "be hidden" (3:11). After its destruction in 612 B.C. the site was not discovered until A.D. 1842.

4. The Christ of Nahum. While there are no direct messianic prophecies in Nahum, the divine attributes in 1:2-8 are consistent with Christ's work as the Judge of the nations in His second advent.

5. Keys to Nahum.

Key Word: The Judgment of Nineveh—If ever a city deserved the title "Here to Stay," Nineveh was that city. Its great walls appeared invincible. But into the scene stepped Nahum—a prophet of God's judgment—to declare that Nineveh would fall. Less than half a century later the prediction of God's spokesman came true as the great city toppled before the Babylonian onslaught, never again to be rebuilt.

Key Verses: Nahum 1:7-8; 3:5-7—"The LORD is good, a stronghold in the day of trouble; and He knows those who trust in Him. But with an overflowing flood He will make an utter end of its place, and darkness will pursue His enemies" (1:7-8).

"Behold, I am against you," says the LORD of hosts; "I will lift your skirts over your face, I will show the nations your nakedness, and the kingdoms your shame. I will cast abominable filth upon you, make you vile, and make you a spectacle. It shall come to pass that all who look upon you will flee from you, and say, 'Nineveh is laid waste! Who will bemoan her?' Where shall I seek comforters for you?" (3:5-7).

Key Chapter Nahum 1—The first chapter of Nahum records the principles of divine judgment resulting in the decree of the destruction of Nineveh and the deliverance and celebration of Judah. Beginning with 1:9, the single thrust of Nahum's prophecy is the retribution of God upon the wickedness of Nineveh. Nine-

veh's judgment is irreversibly decreed by the righteous God who will no longer delay His wrath. Assyria's arrogance and cruelty to other nations will come to a sudden end: her power will be useless against the mighty hand of Yahweh.

Nahum 1:2-8 portrays the patience, power, holiness, and justice of the living God. He is slow to wrath, but God settles His accounts in full. This book concerns the downfall of Assyria, but it is written for the benefit of the surviving kingdom of Judah. (Israel had already been swallowed up by Assyria.) The people in Judah who trusted in the Lord would be comforted to hear of God's judgment upon the proud and brutal Assyrians (1:15–2:2).

6. Survey of Nahum. When God finally convinced His prophet Jonah to preach to the people of Nineveh, the whole city responded with repentance and Nineveh escaped destruction. The people humbled themselves before the one true God, but their humility soon changed to arrogance as Assyria reached its zenith as the most powerful empire in the world. About a century after the preaching of Jonah, God called Nahum to proclaim the coming destruction of Nineveh. This time there would be no escape, because their measure of wickedness was full. Unlike Jonah, Nahum did not go to the city but declared his oracle from afar. There is no hope of repentance. Nineveh's destruction is decreed (1), described (2), and deserved (3).

The Destruction of Nineveh Is Decreed (1). Nahum begins with a very clear description of the character of Yahweh. Because of His righteousness, He is a God of vengeance (1:2). God is also characterized by patience (1:3) and power (1:3-6). He is gracious to all who respond to Him, but those who rebel against Him will be overthrown (1:7-8). God is holy and Nineveh stands condemned because of her sins (1:9-14). Nothing can stand in the way of judgment, and this is a message to comfort the people of Judah (1:15). The threat of Assyrian invasion will soon be over.

The Destruction of Nineveh Is Described (2). Assyria will be conquered, but Judah will be restored (2:1-2). Nahum's description of the siege of Nineveh (2:3-7) and the sack of Nineveh (2:8-13) is one of the most vivid portraits of battle in Scripture. The storming warriors and chariots can almost be seen as they enter the city through a breach in the wall. As the

Ninevites flee in terror, the invading army plunders the treasure of the city. Nineveh is burned and cut off forever.

The Destruction of Nineveh is Deserved (3). Nahum closes his brief book of judgment with God's reasons for Nineveh's coming overthrow. The city is characterized by cruelty and corruption (3:1-7). Just as Assyria crushed the Egyptian capital city of Thebes (No Amon), Assyria's capital city will also be destroyed (3:8-10). Nineveh is fortified so well that defeat seems impossible, but God proclaims that its destruction is inevitable (3:11-19). None of its resources can deter divine judgment.

OUTLINE OF NAHUM

I. The Destruction of Nineveh Is Decreed (1:1-15)

A. The General Principles of Divine Judgment 1:1-8
B. The Destruction of Nineveh and Deliverance of Judah 1:9-15

II. The Destruction of Nineveh Is Described (2:1-13)

A. The Call to Battle 2:1-2

B. The Destruction of Nineveh 2:3-13

III. The Destruction of Nineveh Is Deserved (3:1-19)

A. The Reasons for the Destruction of Nineveh 3:1-11
B. The Destruction of Nineveh Is Inevitable 3:12-19

NAIL

A peg or pin used to hold wood or other material together. Nails were usually made of metal (1 Ch 22:3; 2 Ch 3:9) although some, as in the case of the tent pin, were made of wood (Ju 4:21).

NA' IN *(beauty)*

A city of Galilee (Lk 7:11-17). Jesus raised a widow's son to life here.

NAI' OTH *(dwellings)*

A community of prophets in Ramah who labored under the guidance of Samuel (1 Sa 19:18–20:1).

NAKED

Without clothing. In the beginning, Adam and Eve were naked without shame (Ge 2:25). After they sampled the fruit from the tree of the knowledge of good and evil, however, they realized that they were naked, and tried instinctively to cover themselves. When they heard God walking in the garden, they were even more ashamed of their nakedness and tried to hide from Him (Ge 3:7-10). Nakedness became a shame; when Noah became drunk and lay uncovered in his tent, his son Ham was cursed for laughing at him (Ge 9:21-27). Nakedness is a symbol of vulnerability (Ge 42:9), and need (Ma 25:36-44). Before God all things are "naked;" in other words, nothing is hidden from Him, there is no way to protect oneself from God (He 4:13). Jesus uses nakedness as a symbol of spiritual poverty (Re 3:17).

NAMES

In biblical times names had a definite and significant meaning. Instead of being chosen for the euphonious sound of the syllables, as so often happens today, names were chosen because of their meanings. Some names were simply descriptive, some names were chosen because of events surrounding the birth of the child, such as Eli's grandson Ichabod. His mother went into labor at the news that her husband was dead, and the ark of the Lord had been captured by the Philistines. Because of the tragedy of the day, she named her son "the glory has departed" (1 Sa 4:14-22). Some names given at birth had prophetic significance, such as the children of Isaiah the prophet, or of Hosea and his wife Gomer. The name Jesus (God Saves) was given to the Lord before He was born because of who He is and what He would do on earth (Ma 1:21). Sometimes names were changed later in life to describe something important about the character or life of a person. God changed Jacob's name from "deceiver" to Israel, "prince with God," or "he strives with God" (Ge 32:28). See also GOD, NAMES OF.

NA′O•MI *(pleasant)*

The wife of Elimelech and mother of Mahlon and Chilion (Ru 1–4). After the death of her husband and two sons, Naomi returned to Bethlehem with her daughter-in-law Ruth.

NA′PHATH DOR

See DOR.

NA′PHISH *(inspiration)*

Son of Ishmael (Ge 25:15; 1 Ch 1:31; Nephish, KJV).

NAPH′TA•LI *(my wrestling)*

1. Son of Jacob by Bilhah, Rachel's maid. Rachel wrestled in prayer for a son, hence the name (Ge 30:8).

2. The tribe descended from the four sons of Naphtali (Ge 46:24; Nu 26:48-49).

NAPH•TU′HIM *(border people)*

Descendants of Ham through Mizraim (Ge 10:13; 1 Ch 1:11); an Egyptian tribe.

NAP′KIN

See HANDKERCHIEF.

NAR•CIS′SUS

A Christian Roman family mentioned in Paul's greetings (Ro 16:11).

NARD

See SPIKENARD.

NARRATIVE

The orderly chronological recounting of a story or history. Luke describes his Gospel as "a narrative of those things which are most surely believed among us" (Lk 1:1).

NA′THAN *(he has given)*

Several Old Testament men:

1. A son of David born in Jerusalem (2 Sa 5:14). He was the father of Azariah and Zabud (1 Ki 4:5) and an ancestor of the family of Jesus (Lk 3:31).

2. An eminent prophet in the reign of David and Solomon. He was divinely used to tell David that, not he, but his son would build the temple (2 Sa 7:1-17; 1 Ch 17:1-15) and to rebuke him for his sin with Bath-sheba (2 Sa 12:1-15). He wrote a history of the reigns of Solomon and David (1 Ch 29:29; 2 Ch 9:29).

NATHANAEL AND PHILIP

3. Father of Igal, a warrior of David (2 Sa 23:36). He lived in Zobah in Syria.

4. Son of Attai of the house of Jerahmeel, family of Hezron of Judah (1 Ch 2:36).

5. The brother of Joel who was one of David's mighty men (1 Ch 11:38).

6. One sent by Ezra at the river Ahava to secure Levites for the sanctuary in Jerusalem (Ez 8:16).

7. A son of Bani; he renounced his foreign wife (Ez 10:39). He could be the same person as No. 5.

NA•THAN′A•EL *(given of God)*

One of the twelve apostles (Jo 21:2). When Jesus called Philip, the first thing Philip did was to go and find Nathanael. Nathanael was skeptical at first, ridiculing the idea that anything good could come out of Nazareth, but when he met Jesus, he changed his mind (Jo 1:45-51). He is probably the same person as Bartholomew (Ma 10:3).

NA′THAN-ME′LECH *(given of the king)*

An officer of the court. Josiah removed the horses dedicated to the sun from the entrance of the temple, near the chamber of Nathan-melech (2 Ki 23:11).

NATIONS

This term is often used for Gentile nations, or all non-Jews. It is also a translation of the poetic word *le'om,* used as a parallel of *goy* (Gentiles) or *am* (the People). The word comes from a root meaning "to assemble;" its origin stresses togetherness.

In predicting the future of Rebekah's twins, the Lord told her:

> "Two nations [*goyim*] are in your womb,
> Two people [*le'ummim*] shall be
> separated from your body;
> One people [*le'om*] shall be stronger
> than the other,
> And the older shall serve the younger"
> (Ge 25:23).

Here the Israelites and the Edomites are called by the same two words, the plurals of both *goy* and *le'om.*

All three Hebrew words for "people" occur in Psalm 67 where God is petitioned to bless:

> "That your way may be known on earth,
> Your salvation among all nations
> [*goyim*].
> Let the peoples [*ammim*] praise You,
> O God; . . . .
> Oh, let the nations [*le'ummim*] be glad
> and sing for joy!" (vv. 2-4).

See also GENTILES.

NATIVES

Those born in and belonging to a certain place, often used by a foreigner when speaking of people who have a different language and customs. When Paul shook the viper off into the fire, and suffered no ill effects, the natives of Malta were very impressed (Ac 28:3-6).

NATIVITY

Birth, specifically the birth of Christ. Jesus was born in a stable in Bethlehem because there was no room in the inn. His birth was heralded by angels (Lk 2:1-20).

NATURE

Inborn or instinctive characteristics. While all humans have a sinful and fallen nature, all are still equipped with a certain rudimentary

knowledge of right and wrong. Unnatural behavior is easily recognized, such as homosexual relations (Ro 1:26-27). Many unbelievers recognize instinctively certain "good things" and "bad things," and try to follow these natural laws (Ro 2:14). See NEW NATURE.

NA′ UM *(consolation)*

Father of Amos in the maternal ancestry of Jesus (Lk 3:25). See NAHUM.

NAVE

The center of a wheel, the hub (1 Ki 7:33).

NAVEL

The depression in the center of the abdomen where the umbilical cord was attached to the unborn infant (Eze 16:4). The lover in Song of Solomon waxed poetic over the beauty of his beloved's navel (Song 7:2).

NAVY

The word used to describe Solomon's ships (1 Ki 9:26). This was not a navy in the military sense, but a merchant fleet. Solomon sent his fleet out with the fleet of Hiram of Tyre (1 Ki 10:22). The Hebrews were generally not a seafaring people, and this fleet was partially manned by Phoenician sailors provided by Hiram, the king of Tyre (1 Ki 9:27).

NAZ′ A·RENE

A native or inhabitant of Nazareth (Ma 2:23; 26:71; Mk 16:6). Jesus was born in Bethlehem, but He was brought up in Nazareth and was called a "Nazarene." The town and its people were held in low esteem (Jo 1:46).

NAZ′ A·RETH

A town of lower Galilee where Jesus spent His boyhood years (Ma 2:23), Nazareth is located about thirty miles from the Mediterranean Sea. Its mild climate and sheltered location in the hills of Galilee made Nazareth an ideal place to live.

Nazareth is not mentioned in the Old Testament, although artifacts discovered on the site indicate that Nazareth was a settled community at least 1,500 years before the New Testament era. In Jesus's time, the town apparently had a bad reputation in morals and religion. This may have prompted Nathanael, when he first learned of Jesus of Nazareth, to ask, "Can anything good come out of Nazareth?" (Jo 1:46).

The angel appeared to Mary at Nazareth and informed her of the coming birth of Jesus (Lk 1:26-38). After their sojourn in Egypt (Ma 2:19-22), Joseph and Mary brought Jesus back to Nazareth where they had lived before His birth (Ma 2:23). Here Jesus spent the greater part of His life (Lk 3:23). Apparently He was well received as a young man (Lk 2:42; 4:16), but His townspeople later rejected Him (Mk 6:1-6).

Because of His close association with the city, He became known as "Jesus of Nazareth" (Jo 1:45). There was also prophetic significance to His being known as a "Nazarene"—"that it might be fulfilled which was spoken by the prophets, 'He shall be called a Nazarene' " (Ma 2:23).

Modern Nazareth, known as En-Nasira, is a city of about 30,000 people. Its location on the site of old Nazareth makes it impossible to conduct extensive archeological excavations. The Church of the Annunciation, the major tourist attraction, has a special significance for all Bible students. This church consists of a cave where, according to legend, the angel Gabriel appeared to Mary (Lk 1:26-31). Rebuilding and excavation work on this site has turned up evidence that a Christian church existed at this location as early as the fourth century A.D.

NAZ′ A·RITE

See NAZIRITE.

NAZ′ I·RITE *(separated)*

The Nazirite vow was an oath to abstain from certain worldly influences and to consecrate oneself to God. Among the Jews, the vow was an option for all persons, and it could be taken for a short period or for life. When the specified period was completed, the Nazirite could appear before the priest for the ceremony of release. Nazirites who broke their vows could be restored only by observing specific restoration rites (Nu 6:9-20).

Nazirites expressed their dedication to God by (1) abstaining from all intoxicating drinks and grape products, (2) refusing to cut their hair, (3) avoiding contact with the dead, and (4) refusing to eat food regarded as unclean (Nu 6:3-7).

Persons associated with this Nazirite vow in the Bible include Samson, Samuel, and John the Baptist. Samson's parents were told by the angel of the Lord that their son would be a Nazirite until his death (Ju 13:7). Hannah dedicated Samuel to the Nazirite way of life even before

his birth (1 Sa 1:11,28), although it is not clear from the Bible accounts whether Samuel ever actually became a Nazirite.

The self-denying lifestyle of John the Baptist indicates that he may have been a Nazirite (Lk 1:15). John was so outspoken in his condemnation of sin in high places that he was executed by Herod, Roman governor of Palestine (Mk 6:17-28), at Herod's fortress palace in Machaerus.

NE′ AH *(shaking)*

A place on the southern border of Zebulun (Jos 19:13).

NE·A′ PO·LIS *(new city)*

The seaport of the city of Philippi (Ac 16:11).

NE·A·RI′ AH *(servant of Jehovah)*

1. A son of Shemaiah of the royal line of Judah (1 Ch 3:22-23).

2. A son of Ishi and a Simeonite captain (1 Ch 4:42).

NE·BA′ I

One of the leaders of the people who signed the covenant (Ne 10:19).

NE·BAI′ OTH

The Arabian tribe descended from Ishmael's son Nebajoth (Is 60:7).

NE·BA′ JOTH *(heights)*

A son of Ishmael and the founder of a tribe (Ge 25:13; 28:9; 36:3; 1 Ch 1:29), also called Nebaioth.

NE·BAL′ LAT *(hidden folly)*

A town of Benjamin occupied after the return from Babylon (Ne 11:34).

NE′ BAT *(aspect)*

Father of Jeroboam (1 Ki 11:26; 12:2).

NE′ BO

A town, a mountain, two men and a pagan god:

1. A town of the Moabites on or near Mount Nebo (Nu 32:3). It was assigned to the Reubenites and was rebuilt by them (Nu 32:37-38; 33:47).

2. The mountain, the highest point of Pisgah, from which Moses viewed the land of promise (De 32:49; 34:1) and near which he was buried

(De 32:50; 34:6). It is a peak of the Abarim mountains.

3. A man some of whose descendants returned from Babylon with Zerubbabel (Ez 2:29; Ne 7:33).

4. The ancestor of several Jews who married foreign women (Ez 10:43).

5. A god of the Babylonians (Is 46:1).

NEB·U·CHAD·NEZ′ZAR *(may Nebo protect the crown)*

Son of Nabopolassar and most famous of the Babylonian kings. In 625 B.C., his father founded the New Babylonian Empire which became one of the first of the world empires. In the battle of Carchemish the forces of Nabopolassar were under the command of his son and the Egyptians were defeated. This was in 605 B.C. (2 Ki 24:7; Je 46:2). In that year, upon the death of his father, Nebuchadnezzar ascended the throne. In biblical history he is linked with three great prophets: Jeremiah, Ezekiel, and Daniel. In 606 B.C., in the reign of Jehoiakim, he invaded Palestine, placed it under tribute (2 Ki 24:1), and carried away some of the people, one of whom was Daniel. In 597 B.C., he returned and carried to Babylon the king, Jehoiachin, and many of the people, one of them Ezekiel. He placed Zedekiah on the throne (2 Ch 36:6-10). Nebuchadnezzar received several prophetic dreams from God, which Daniel interpreted (Da 2; 4). His second dream foretold that unless he humbled himself before God, he would be humiliated before man. For a time, Nebuchadnezzar heeded this warning, but when he began to take glory for himself that belongs to God, he was stricken with insanity, and spent seven years living like an animal. At the end of this time, his reason was restored. He repented, gave glory to God and was restored to his kingdom (Da 4:34-37).

NEB·U·CHAD-REZ′ZAR

See NEBUCHADNEZZAR.

NEB·U·SHAS′BAN *(Nebo saves me)*

An officer of Nebuchadnezzar (Je 39:11-14).

NEB·U·SHAZ′BAN

See NEBUSHASBAN.

NEB·U′ZAR-A′DAN *(chief whom Nebo favors)*

The chief commander of the troops of Nebuchadnezzar (2 Ki 25:8-11; 18-21; Je 39:9-10; 52:12-30).

NE′CHO (2 Ch 35:20,22; 36:4)

See PHARAOH.

NE′CHOH, NE′CO, NE′COH

Variants of NECHO.

NECKLACE

Jewelry to be worn around the neck. Chains of gold or silver were typical ornaments (Song 1:10; Eze 16:11). A chain of gold was also used as a symbol of authority (Ge 41:42; Da 5:17,29).

NEC′RO·MAN′CY

A type of magic. The practice of inquiring of the dead. Necromancers were declared an abomination to the Lord (De 18:11-12). See MAGIC, SORCERY AND DIVINATION.

NED·A·BI′AH *(abundance of Jehovah)*

Son of Jeconiah (1 Ch 3:18).

NEE′DLE

An instrument for sewing and embroidering (Ec 3:7; Mk 2:21). The hole in it is called an eye. Jesus said it was easier for a camel to go through the eye of a needle than for those who put their faith in riches to get into heaven (Mk 10:24-26). See EYE OF A NEEDLE.

NEEDLEWORK

See EMBROIDERER and EMBROIDERY.

NEESINGS (archaic)

Sneezing (Job 41:18).

NEG′EV

A dry pastoral region, south of Hebron, which is called "the south" (Nu 13:22).

NEG′I·NAH

See NEGINOTH.

NEG′I·NOTH

A musical term in the title of many Psalms. It is often translated "stringed instrument," but it may simply mean "a song" (Ps 4; 6; 54–55; 61; 67; 76).

NE·HEL′A·MITE

A designation of uncertain meaning for Shemaiah (Je 29:24,31-32).

NE·HEM·I′AH *(Jehovah consoles)*

1. One who returned with Zerubbabel from Babylon (Ez 2:2; Ne 7:7).

2. Son of Azbuk. He ruled part of the district of Bethzur and labored on the wall under Nehemiah (Ne 3:16).

3. Son of Hachaliah (Ne 1:1), a Jewish statesman, patriot, and reformer of the period of the exile. While at the Persian capital, Nehemiah requested permission of Artaxerxes, the king, to go to Jerusalem because of reports reaching him concerning the poor state of affairs there. The permission was granted. His first task was to rebuild the wall of the city. This was completed in two months by the inhabitants (Ne 2:10–6:15). He then turned his attention to religious reform. He had the Book of the Law read publicly, the Feast of the Tabernacles observed, the new walls dedicated, and a covenant to observe all obligations signed (Ne 8–10). See NEHEMIAH, BOOK OF: The Author of Nehemiah.

NE·HEM·I′AH, BOOK OF

1. The Book of Nehemiah. Nehemiah, contemporary of Ezra and cupbearer to the king in the Persian palace, led the third and last return to Jerusalem after the Babylonian exile. His concern for the welfare of Jerusalem and its inhabitants prompted him to take bold action. Granted permission to return to his homeland, Nehemiah challenged his countrymen to arise and rebuild the shattered wall of Jerusalem. In spite of opposition from without and abuse from within, the task was completed in only fifty-two days, a feat even the enemies of Israel must attribute to God's enabling. By contrast, the task of reviving and reforming the people of God within the rebuilt wall demands years of Nehemiah's godly life and leadership.

The Hebrew for Nehemiah is *Nehemyah*, "Comfort of Yahweh." The book is named after its chief character, whose name appears in the opening verse. The combined book of Ezra-Nehemiah is given the Greek title *Esdras Deuteron,* "Second Esdras" (see EZRA, BOOK OF) in the Septuagint. The Latin title of Nehemiah is *Liber Secundus Esdrae,* "Second Book of Ezra" (Ezra was the first). At this point, it was considered a separate book from Ezra, and was later called *Liber Nehemiae,* "Book of Nehemiah."

2. The Author of Nehemiah. Clearly, much of this book came from Nehemiah's personal memoirs. The reporting is remarkably candid and vivid. Certainly 1:1–7:5; 12:27-43; and 13:4-31 are the "words of Nehemiah" (1:1). Some scholars think that Nehemiah composed those portions and compiled the rest. Others think that Ezra wrote 7:6–12:26 and 12:44–13:3, and that he compiled the rest making use of Nehemiah's diary. A third view that neither wrote it seems least likely from the evidence. Nehemiah 7:5-73 is almost the same as Ezra 2:1-70, and both lists may have been taken from another record of the same period.

As cupbearer to Artaxerxes I, Nehemiah held a position of great responsibility. His role of tasting the king's wine to prevent him from being poisoned placed Nehemiah in a position of trust and confidence as one of the king's advisers. As governor of Jerusalem from 444 to 432 B.C. (5:14; 8:9; 10:1; 13:6), Nehemiah demonstrated courage, compassion for the oppressed, integrity, godliness, and selflessness. He was willing to give up the luxury and ease of the palace to help his people. He was a dedicated layman who had the right priorities and was concerned for God's work, who was able to encourage and rebuke at the right times, who was strong in prayer, and who gave all glory and credit to God.

3. The Time of Nehemiah. See "The Time of Ezra," because both Ezra and Nehemiah share the same historical background. The Book of Nehemiah fits within the reign of Artaxerxes I of Persia (464-423 B.C.). Esther was Artaxerxes' stepmother, and it is possible that she was instrumental in Nehemiah's appointment as the king's cupbearer. Nehemiah left Persia in the twentieth year of Artaxerxes (2:1), returned to Persia in the thirty-second year of Artaxerxes (13:6), and left again for Jerusalem "after certain days" (13:6), perhaps about 425 B.C. This book could not have been completed until after his second visit to Jerusalem.

The historical reliability of this book is supported by the Elephantine papyri. These ancient documents mention Sanballat (2:19) and Jehohanan (6:18; 12:23) and indicate that Bigvai replaced Nehemiah as governor of Judah by 410 B.C.

Malachi lived and ministered during Nehemiah's time, and a comparison of the books shows that many of the evils encountered by Nehemiah were specifically denounced by Malachi. The coldhearted indifference toward God described in both books remained a problem in Israel during the four hundred years before Christ, during which time there was no revelation from God.

4. The Christ of Nehemiah. Like Ezra, Nehemiah portrays Christ in His ministry of restoration. Nehemiah illustrates Christ in that he gave up a high position in order to identify with the plight of his people; he came with a specific mission and fulfilled it; and his life was characterized by prayerful dependence upon God.

In this book, everything was restored except the king. The temple was rebuilt, Jerusalem was reconstructed, the covenant was renewed, and the people were reformed. The messianic line was intact, but the King was yet to come. The decree of Artaxerxes in his twentieth year (2:2) marked the beginning of Daniel's prophecy of the seventy weeks (see Da 9:25-27). "Know therefore and understand, that from the going forth of the command to restore and build Jerusalem until Messiah the Prince, there shall be seven weeks and sixty-two weeks; the street shall be built again, and the wall, even in troublesome times" (Da 9:25). The Messiah would come at the end of the sixty-nine weeks, and this was exactly fulfilled at the triumphal entry into Jerusalem (see "The Christ of Daniel").

5. Keys to Nehemiah.

Key Word: Jerusalem Walls—While Ezra deals with the religious restoration of Judah, Nehemiah is primarily concerned with Judah's political and geographical restoration. The first seven chapters are devoted to the rebuilding of Jerusalem's walls because Jerusalem was the spiritual and political center of Judah. Without walls, Jerusalem could hardly be considered a city at all. As governor, Nehemiah also established firm civil authority. Ezra and Nehemiah worked together to build the people spiritually and morally so that the restoration would be complete.

Key Verses: Nehemiah 6:15-16; 8:8—"So the wall was finished on the twenty-fifth day of the month of Elul, in fifty-two days. And it happened, when all our enemies heard of it, and all the nations around us saw these things, that they were very disheartened in their own eyes; for they perceived that this work was done by our God" (6:15-16).

"So they read distinctly from the book, in the Law of God; and they gave the sense, and helped them to understand the reading" (8:8).

Key Chapter: Nehemiah 9—The key to the Old Testament is the covenant, which is its theme and unifying factor. Israel's history can be divided according to the nation's obedience or disobedience. Nehemiah 9 records that upon completion of the Jerusalem wall the nation reaffirmed its loyalty to the covenant.

6. Survey of Nehemiah. Nehemiah was closely associated with the ministry of his contemporary, Ezra. Ezra was a priest who brought spiritual revival; Nehemiah was a governor who brought physical and political reconstruction and led the people in moral reform. They combined to make an effective team in rebuilding the postexilic remnant. Malachi, the last Old Testament prophet, also ministered during this time to provide additional moral and spiritual direction. The Book of Nehemiah takes us to the end of the historical account in the Old Testament, about four hundred years before the birth of the promised Messiah. Its two divisions are: the reconstruction of the wall (1–7), and the restoration of the people (8–13).

The Reconstruction of the Wall (1–7). Nehemiah's great concern for his people and the welfare of Jerusalem led him to take bold action. The walls of Jerusalem, destroyed by Nebuchadnezzar in 586 B.C., evidently had been almost rebuilt after 464 B.C. when Artaxerxes I took the throne of Persia (see Ez 4:6-23). When he heard that opposition led to their second destruction, Nehemiah prayed on behalf of his people and then secured Artaxerxes' permission, provision, and protection for the massive project of rebuilding the walls.

The return under Nehemiah in 444 B.C. took place thirteen years after the return led by Ezra, and ninety-four years after the return led by Zerubbabel. Nehemiah inspected the walls and challenged the people to "rise up and build" (2:18). Work began immediately on the wall and its gates, with people building portions corresponding to where they were living.

However, opposition quickly arose, first in the form of mockery, then in the form of conspiracy when the work was progressing at an alarming rate. Nehemiah overcame threats of force by setting half of the people on military watch and half on construction. While the external opposition continued to mount, internal opposition also surfaced. The wealthier Jews were abusing and oppressing the people, forcing them to mortgage their property and sell their children into slavery. Nehemiah again dealt with the problem by the twin means of prayer and action. He also led by example when he sacrificed his governor's salary. In spite of deceit, slander, and treachery, Nehemiah continued to trust in God and to press on with singleness of mind until the work was completed. The task was accomplished in an incredible fifty-two days, and even the enemies recognized that it could only have been accomplished with the help of God (6:16).

The Restoration of the People (8–13). The construction of the walls was followed by consecration and consolidation of the people. Ezra the priest was the leader of the spiritual revival (8–10), reminiscent of the reforms he had led thirteen years earlier (Ezra 9–10). Ezra stood on a special wooden podium after the completion of the walls and gave the people a marathon reading of the law, translating from the Hebrew into Aramaic so that they could understand. They responded with weeping, confession, obedience, and rejoicing. The Levites and priests led them in a great prayer that surveyed God's past work of deliverance and

loyalty on behalf of His people, and magnified God's attributes of holiness, justice, mercy, and love. The covenant was then renewed with God as the people committed themselves to separate from the Gentiles in marriage and to obey God's commandments.

Lots were drawn to determine who would remain in Jerusalem and who would return to the cities of their inheritance. One-tenth were required to stay in Jerusalem, and the rest of the land was resettled by the people and priests. The walls of Jerusalem were dedicated to the Lord in a joyful ceremony accompanied by instrumental and vocal music.

Unfortunately, Ezra's revival was short-lived; and Nehemiah, who returned to Persia in 432 B.C. (13:6), made a second trip to Jerusalem about 425 B.C. to reform the people. He cleansed the temple, enforced the Sabbath, and required the people to put away all foreign wives.

OUTLINE OF NEHEMIAH

Part One: The Reconstruction of the Wall (1:1–7:73)

I. The Preparation to Reconstruct the Wall (1:1–2:20)

A. Discovery of the Broken Wall 1:1-3
B. Intercession of Nehemiah 1:4–2:8
C. Arrival of Nehemiah in Jerusalem 2:9-11
D. Preparation to Reconstruct the Wall 2:12-20

II. The Reconstruction of the Wall (3:1–7:73)

A. Record of the Builders 3:1-32
B. Opposition to the Reconstruction 4:1–6:14
C. Completion of the Reconstruction 6:15-19
D. Organization of Jerusalem 7:1-4
E. Registration of Jerusalem 7:5-73

Part Two: The Restoration of the People (8:1–13:31)

I. The Renewal of the Covenant (8:1–10:39)

A. Interpretation of the Law 8:1-18
B. Reaffirmation of the Covenant 9:1–10:39

II. The Obedience to the Covenant (11:1–13:31)

A. Resettlement of the People 11:1-36
B. Register of the Priests and the Levites 12:1-26
C. Dedication of the Jerusalem Wall... 12:27-47
D. Restoration of the People 13:1-31

NE′ HIL·OTH

A musical term, possibly denoting a wind instrument (Ps 5, title).

NE′ HUM *(consolation)*

One who returned from Babylon with Zerubbabel (Ne 7:7).

NE·HUSH′ TA *(bronze)*

Daughter of Elnathan. She was the wife of Jehoiakim (2 Ki 24:8).

NE·HUSH′ TAN *(made of brass)*

See BRAZEN SERPENT.

NEI′ EL *(moved by God)*

A village of Asher (Jos 19:27).

NEIGHBOR

One who lives nearby. The Ten Commandments give instructions concerning the proper treatment of neighbors. They are to be treated with honesty, and no one is to covet his neighbor's goods (Ex 20:16-17; De 5:20-21). Neighbors are not to be cheated; if a person injures his neighbor, retribution must not exceed the extent of the original injury (Le 19:13; 24:19-20). It is a sin to despise one's neighbor (Pr 14:21; Ze 8:17); and a mistake to trick him and then claim that it was only a joke (Pr 26:19). The Israelites regarded these patterns of neighborly conduct as applying only to one's fellow Jews, but Jesus expanded this view in His parable of the good Samaritan. He made it clear that our neighbors include even people we dislike or don't agree with (Lk 10:25-37). Anyone we encounter may be considered our neighbor. Paul taught that all the "horizontal commandments" (those pertaining to our relationship with others) can be summed up in one, namely " 'You shall love your neighbor as yourself.' Love does no harm to a neighbor, therefore love is the fulfillment of the law" (Ro 13:9-10).

NE′ KEB *(a cavern)*

A border town of Naphtali (Jos 19:33).

NE·KO′ DA *(distinguished)*

1. One of the Nethinim, descendants of whom returned from Babylon (Ez 2:48; Ne 7:50).

2. Sons of Nekoda (Ez 2:60; Ne 7:62); this family could not prove its ancestry after the captivity.

NEM′ U·EL *(day of God)*

Two Old Testament men:

1. Son of Eliab, and brother of Dathan and Abiram, of the tribe of Reuben (Nu 26:9).

2. Son of Simeon (Nu 26:12). Also called Jemuel (Ge 46:10).

NEMUELITES

The descendants of Nemuel, son of Simeon (Nu 26:12).

NEPH′ EG *(sprout)*

Two Old Testament men:

1. Son of Izhar, family of Kohath (Ex 6:21).

2. A son of David born in Jerusalem (2 Sa 5:15; 1 Ch 3:7; 14:6).

NEPHEW

The son of one's sister or brother. In the Bible this term seems to be used for several family connections. The word translated "nephews" in the KJV is translated "grandsons" in the NKJV (Ju 12:14); in Job 18:10 is translated "posterity"; other passages use "offspring" (Is 14:22) and "grandchildren" (1 Ti 5:4).

NEPH′ I·LIM

Giants. The Nephilim are something of a mystery. They are described in Genesis as the offspring of "the sons of God" and "the daughters of men." They were the "mighty men who were of old" and "men of renown" (Ge 6:4). Exactly who the "sons of God" were remains unknown, but apparently the Nephilim did not die out with the flood because the Israelites encountered them in the promised land. They were clearly giants, so tall that they made the Hebrews feel like grasshoppers (Nu 13:33).

NE′ PHISH

See NAPHISH.

NE·PHISH′ E·SIM

A family of Nethinim (Ez 2:50; Ne 7:52).

NE·PHI′ SIM, NE·PHU′ SIM, NE·PHUSH′ E·SIM

Variants of NEPHISHESIM

NEPHTHALIM

A form of Naphtali (Ma 4:13,15; Re 7:6).

NEPH-TO′ AH *(an opening)*

A town or small stream on the border between Judah and Benjamin (Jos 15:9; 18:15).

NER *(light)*

A Benjamite who was probably either the uncle or grandfather of Saul (1 Sa 14:50; 1 Ch 8:33).

NE′ REUS *(lamp)*

A Christian at Rome (Ro 16:15).

NER′ GAL *(hero)*

A god of the Babylonians (2 Ki 17:30), a god of war and pestilence.

NER′ GAL-SHA•RE′ ZER *(prince of fire)*

A prince of Nebuchadnezzar (Je 39:3,13).

NE′ RI

Son-in-law of Jeconiah and father of Sala-thiel (Lk 3:27).

NE•RI′ AH *(lamp of Jehovah)*

Son of Maaseiah (Je 32:12; 36:4; 51:59).

NE′ RO

The fifth Roman Emperor (A.D. 54-68). Nero became emperor while still in his teens, suc-ceeding his stepfather, Claudius I. His mother was a ruthless woman, commonly supposed to have murdered her husband and engineered the crowning of her son. Although in his youth, Nero seems to have had some human impulses, and a desire to encourage the arts and improve society, he became a corrupt ruler, extravagant and with little management capability. His two deputies, Burrus and Seneca, did much of the actual administration of the government, while Nero gratified his pleasures with ever wilder and more riotous living. He crossed the line of proper decorum in the eyes of Rome, fulfilling his interest in the arts by acting on stage, and giving musical performances. He was as ruth-less as his mother, and arranged to have her murdered when she became too interfering. He later had his wife killed as well, in order to marry the woman he had been having an affair with. He was a persecutor of the church, and is particularly remembered for the atrocious cruelties to Christians which he perpetrated af-ter the fires in Rome in A.D. 64. Nero blamed the Christians for the fire, but it was widely believed that he started the fires himself in or-der to be able to direct the rebuilding of Rome on more artistic lines. He became more and

NERO

more suspicious and distrustful of those around him, and continued to have inconvenient and threatening people murdered. In A.D. 68, his misrule finally sparked a revolt, and Nero cut his throat. He was 30 years old.

NEST

The receptacle birds make in which they lay their eggs and raise their young. Job uses the term probably as a description of the close fam-ily circle in which he hoped to end his days (Job 29:18).

NET

A meshed fabric used in hunting and fishing. Dragnets, or seines, and casting nets were used in fishing. The cords of the dragnet were made of flax and the lower edge was weighted with lead, causing it to sink to the bottom while the upper edge made of wood floated on the surface (Ma 13:47-48; Jo 21:6). Bird nets were traps con-structed of netting thrown about light wooden frames. Pecking at the baited trigger caused the structure to collapse and enclose the bird.

NET, PARABLE OF (Ma 13:47-50)

NE•TA′ IM

A place where potters dwelled, in the terri-tory of Judah (1 Ch 4:23).

NETH′ A•NE•AL

See NETHANEEL.

NETH′ A•NEEL *(God hath given)*

Also Nethanael and Nethanel.

1. A prince of Issachar (Nu 1:8; 2:5; 7:18, 23; 10:15).

2. David's brother, son of Jesse (1 Ch 2:14).

3. A priest, one of the musicians at the time the ark was brought to Jerusalem (1 Ch 15:24).

4. Father of Shemaiah, a Levite (1 Ch 24:6).

5. Son of Obed-edom in the time of David (1 Ch 26:4).

6. A prince commissioned by Jehoshaphat to teach the people of Judah (2 Ch 17:7).

7. A Levite in the time of Josiah (2 Ch 35:9).

8. A son of Pashur. He renounced his for-eign wife (Ez 10:22).

9. A priest in the time of Joiakim, the high priest (Ne 12:21).

10. A Levite musician (Ne 12:36).

NETH′A·NEL

See NETHANEEL.

NETH·A·NI′AH *(given of Jehovah)*

Four Old Testament men:

1. Father of Ishmael who slew Gedaliah, Babylonian governor of Judah (2 Ki 25:23,25).

2. An Asaphite Levite who was head of the fifth course of singers (1 Ch 25:2,12).

3. A Levite (2 Ch 17:8).

4. Father of Jehudi (Je 36:14).

NETH′I·NIM

The name given those doing the more menial work of the sanctuary. They were temple servants or slaves. At an earlier time their ancestors, the Gibeonites, were hewers of wood and drawers of water for the tabernacle (Jos 9:23). The office was founded by David but the word Nethinim occurs only in Ezra and Nehemiah. One other reference is in 1 Chronicles 9:2. A few hundred of these slaves returned from Babylon with Zerubbabel (Ez 2:58; Ne 7:60), and 220 more with Ezra 78 years later (Ez 8:17-20).

NE·TO′PHAH *(distillation)*

A town of Judah near Bethlehem (1 Ch 27:13,15). One hundred eighty-eight people from Netophah and Bethlehem returned from Babylon with Zerubbabel (Ez 2:22; Ne 7:26).

NE·TOPH′A·THITE

One who lived in Netophah (2 Sa 23:28).

NET′TLE

An unpleasant weed, whose leaves give a painful sting if they come into contact with the skin. The edges of the leaves are equipped with tiny hairlike projections which secrete an acid. These tiny hairs easily penetrate the skin and the acid produces an instant irritating, stinging sensation (Job 30:7; Pr 24:41; Ho 9:6; Is 34:13). The word in Zephaniah 2:9 refers to weeds which spring up in uncultivated land (such weeds would probably include nettles).

NETWORK

The grate of the altar (Ex 27:4; 38:4) and the decorative bronze work on the capitals of the two pillars, Jachin and Boaz, which Solomon had made for the temple (1 Ki 7:18; 2 Ch 4:12; Je 52:22-23).

NEW AGE

The days when the New Covenant is fulfilled (Je 31:31); the time of Christ's return and rule (Ma 19:28).

NEW BIRTH

See REGENERATION.

NEW COVENANT

The New Covenant is the fifth and last of the theocratic covenants (pertaining to the rule of God). Four provisions are made in this covenant: (1) regeneration—God will put His law in their inward parts and write it in their hearts (Je 31:33); (2) a national restoration—Yahweh will be their God and the nation will be His people (Je 31:33); (3) personal ministry of the Holy Spirit—they will all be taught individually by God (Je 31:34); and (4) full justification—their sins will be forgiven and completely removed (Je 31:34). The New Covenant is made sure by the blood that Jesus shed on Calvary's cross. That blood which guarantees to Israel its New Covenant also provides for the forgiveness of sins for the believers who comprise the church. Jesus's payment for sins is more than adequate to pay for the sins of all who will believe in Him. The New Covenant is called "new" in contrast to the covenant with Moses which is called "old" (Je 31:32; He 8:6-13) because it actually accomplishes what the Mosaic Covenant could only point to, that is, the child of God living in a manner that is consistent with the character of God.

NEW GATE

A gate of the temple. Baruch read the words of Jeremiah's prophecy aloud to the people near this gate (Je 36:10).

NEW HEAVENS

See EARTH, NEW.

NEW JERUSALEM

See JERUSALEM, NEW.

NEW MOON

See MOON, NEW.

NEW NATURE

The term *new nature* refers to the spiritual transformation that occurs within the inner man when a person believes in Christ as Savior. The Christian is now a *new man* as opposed to the *old man* that he was before he became a Christian (Ro 6:5; Ep 2:15; 4:22-24; Col 3:9-10). This concept of *newness* may be traced to an important choice between two Greek words, both meaning "new." One word means "new" in the sense of renovation (to repair), the other in the sense of fresh existence. The latter term is used to describe the Christian. He is not the old man renovated or refreshed; he is a brand-new man with a new family, a new set of values, new motivations, and new possessions.

The old man is still present in the new life, and expresses himself in corrupting deeds such as lying (Ep 4:22; Col 3:10). In other words, the new nature must be cultivated or nurtured by spiritual decisiveness to grow in Christ. We must not revert to putting on the *old suit* of this former life; rather we must continue to change to match the new life (Ep 5:8).

The message of the new nature is a message of supreme hope: the Spirit of God can accomplish a life-changing transformation for all who will only believe in Christ.

NEW TES′ TA·MENT

The book which is the foundation of the Christian religion. The New Testament is made up of the last twenty-seven books of the Bible. It deals with the New Covenant (2 Co 3:14) of which Christ is the Mediator (He 9:15). See BIBLE.

NEW YEAR

See TRUMPETS, FEAST OF.

NE·ZI′ AH *(illustrious)*

One of the Nethinim, descendants of whom returned from Babylon with Zerubbabel (Ez 2:54; Ne 7:56).

NEZ′ IB *(idol, statue)*

A town of the lowland district of Judah (Jos 15:43).

NIB′ HAZ

An idol worshipped by the Avvites (2 Ki 17:31).

NIB′ SHAN

A town of Judah (Jos 15:62).

NI·CA′ NOR *(victor)*

One of the seven deacons of the church of Jerusalem (Ac 6:5).

NICENE CREED

This creed was adopted in A.D. 325 by the first council of Nicea; this council was brought together by Constantine to discuss doctrinal issues. Its particular action was to deny Arianism (the rejection of Christ's divinity). The creed was revised a few years later at the Council of Constantinople (A.D. 381). It affirms the deity of Christ and the doctrine of the Trinity.

I believe in one God the Father Almighty, Maker of heaven and earth, and all things visible and invisible. And I believe in one Lord, Jesus Christ, the only-begotten Son of God, born of the father before all ages, God of God, Light of Light, true God of true God; begotten, not made, of one substance with the father, by whom all things were made, who for us and for our salvation came down from heaven. And he became flesh by the Holy Spirit of the Virgin Mary and was made man. He was also crucified for us, suffered under Pontius Pilate, and was buried. And on the third day He rose again, according to the Scriptures. He ascended into heaven and sits at the right hand of the Father. He will come again in glory to judge the living and the dead. And of His kingdom there will be no end. And I believe in the Holy Spirit, the Lord and Giver of life, who proceeds from the Father and the Son, who together with the Father and the Son is adored and glorified, and who spoke through the prophets, and one holy, catholic, and apostolic church. I confess one baptism for the forgiveness of sins. And I await the resurrection of the dead. And the life of the world to come. AMEN.

NIC·O·DE′ MUS *(victorious)*

A secret follower of Christ. Nothing is known of his family. He was a Pharisee and member of the Sanhedrin who became intensely interested in Jesus's message, and came secretly by night to find out more. In this midnight visit, Jesus explains the necessity of the New Birth, and tells of God's love, the mission of the Son, and the response of the world (Jo 3:1-21). Nicodemus later defended Jesus when the other Pharisees were trying to find a way to get rid of him (Jo 7:50-52). When Jesus was crucified, Nicodemus assisted Joseph of Arimathea to bury His body (Jo 19:39).

NIC·O·LA′ I·TANS

It is probable that this sect or party followed the teachings of one called Nicolaus. In John's vision, Jesus commended the church in Ephesus for hating the teaching of the Nicolaitans (Re 2:6). The church at Pergamos was rebuked for allowing this doctrine to creep in. It appears that this teaching was associated with a kind of libertarianism, behaving exactly like Balaam and leading God's people into sexual immorality and idol worship (Re 2:14-15). This was contrary to and in defiance of the action of the Council at Jerusalem in A.D. 50 (Ac 15:29).

NIC′O·LAS

One of the seven deacons of the church of Jerusalem (Ac 6:5). Some have suggested that he started the Nicolaitan sect, but there is nothing to support this idea except the possible similarity of names.

NIC′O·LA·US

See NICOLAS.

NI·COP′O·LIS *(city of victory)*

There were several cities having this name, but the one where Paul expected to spend the winter and where he wrote the Epistle to Titus was most likely the Nicopolis of Epirus, about four miles from Actium (Tit 3:12).

NI′GER *(black)*

The Latin surname of Simeon who taught in the church at Antioch (Ac 13:1). There is no evidence to support the theory, but some scholars have thought that this may be the same person as Simon of Cyrene, who carried Jesus's cross (Ma 27:32).

NIGHT

Paul uses this term symbolically for evil, contrasting the "sons of day" with the "sons of night" (1 Th 5:5).

NIGHT CREATURE

Probably an owl.

NIGHT HAWK

A ceremonially unclean bird (Le 11:16; De 14:15). Night hawks are not predators, as are the other unclean birds. Some translations render this word as a type of owl.

NIGHT JAR

See NIGHT HAWK.

NIGHT MONSTER

The rendering in the Revised Version of the Hebrew word *lilith*. It is translated screech owl in the Authorized Version (Is 34:14). See OWL.

NIGHT WATCH

The periods of time into which the night was divided (Ps 63:6; La 2:19; Lk 12:38). See CALENDAR and WATCHES OF NIGHT.

NILE

The one great river of Egypt (Is 23:3). It has its source in two rivers, the White Nile flowing out of Lake Victoria, and the Blue Nile flowing out of Ethiopia. It flows northward, and empties into the Mediterranean Sea. This river had an enormous impact on the Egyptian civilization and culture. Its yearly flood deposited a layer of rich silt on the arable farmland along its banks; thus the river provided moisture and fertility for the crops of the coming year. Because of the Nile's importance to farming, and thus to the well-being of the people, it was worshipped as a god by the Egyptians. Several of the plagues of the exodus affected the Nile, clearly showing the superiority of the God of the Hebrews over the Egyptian god of the Nile (Ex 7:20).

The land promised to Abraham for his posterity was measured from the river of Egypt (the Nile) to the river Euphrates (Ge 15:18).

NIM′RAH *(limpid)*

An abbreviation of Beth-nimrah (Nu 32:3,36). See BETH-NIMRAH.

NIM′RIM

A fertile district in Moab noted for its waters, southeast of the Dead Sea (Is 15:6; Je 48:34).

NIM′ROD *(rebellion or the valiant)*

The son of Cush (Ge 10:8-10; Mi 5:6) and a mighty hunter. He was the founder of the Assyrian empire and several Babylonian cities.

NIM′SHI *(active)*

Grandfather of Jehu (1 Ki 19:16; 2 Ki 9:21), also called his father (2 Ki 9:20).

NIN′E·VEH *(abode of Ninus)*

Founded by Nimrod, great-grandson of Noah (Ge 10:6-12), Nineveh was for many years the capital city of the mighty Assyrian Empire.

NINEVEH

At the height of its prosperity, Nineveh was a "great city" (Jon 1:2; 3:2) with a population of 120,000 (Jon 4:11). It would have taken a traveler three days to go around greater Nineveh, with its numerous outlying suburbs, and a day's journey to reach the center of the city (Jon 3:4).

The most famous biblical personality connected with ancient Nineveh was the prophet Jonah. Assyrian kings were cruel and ruthless. This pagan nation had invaded and pillaged the homeland of the Israelites on numerous occasions by the time Jonah visited Nineveh about 760 B.C. The prophet wanted the city destroyed—not saved—because of its wickedness. But the people repented and were spared by a compassionate God (Jon 3:10). God's love for a pagan people was deeper than His messenger could understand or accept.

Nineveh was eventually destroyed about 150 years after Jonah's visit—in 612 B.C. It fell after a long siege by an alliance of Medes, Babylonians, and Scythians. The attackers entered the city through walls made weak by a flooding of the Khosr and Tigris rivers. The sun-dried bricks of its buildings were also dissolved. This was a remarkable fulfillment of the prophecy of Nahum: "The gates of the rivers are opened, and the palace is dissolved" (Na 2:6).

Significant archeological discoveries at Nineveh include the temples of Nabu and Ishtar, Assyrian gods, and the palaces of three Assyrian kings—Ashurbanipal, Ashurnasirpal, and Sennacherib. One of the most important discoveries was the royal library of Ashurbanipal, which contained over sixteen thousand cuneiform tablets. These include Mesopotamian stories of creation and the flood, as well as many other religious and historical texts. It was to Nineveh that Sennacherib brought the tribute he exacted from King Hezekiah of Judah (2 Ki 18:13-15).

Nineveh was one of the oldest cities of the ancient Near East. Excavations down to the virgin soil indicate the site was first occupied about 4500 B.C.

NINEVITES

Those who dwelled in Nineveh (Lk 11:30).

NI′ SAN

The first month of the Hebrew sacred year (Ne 2:1; Es 3:7).

NIS′ ROCH *(the great eagle)*

The god worshipped by Sennacherib (2 Ki 19:37; Is 37:38).

NI′ TER

See LYE.

NITRE

See LYE.

NO

See NO-AMON.

NO·A·DI′ AH *(Jehovah convenes)*

A man and a woman of the Old Testament:

1. A Levite, son of Binnui; he had charge of the vessels of the temple brought back from Babylon (Ez 8:33).

2. A prophetess (Ne 6:14).

NO′ AH *(rest)*

A man and woman in the Old Testament:

1. Son of Lamech in the line of Seth; an ancestor of Jesus (Ge 5:28-29). The pre-flood world had become increasingly wicked, and God determined to send a flood to destroy the earth. Noah was a righteous man, one who walked with God as his ancestor Enoch had done (Ge 5:21-24; 6:9). God told him to build an ark on which he, his family, and two of each kind of animal were to survive the flood (Ge 6:14–8:19).

Because he believed God and built the ark, Noah is remembered as a hero of the faith (He 11:7), and a model of confidence in God's word in spite of the ridicule of others (1 Pe 3:20).

2. *(motion)* A daughter of Zelophehad of the tribe of Manasseh (Nu 26:33; 27:1; 36:11; Jos 17:3).

NOAHIC COVENANT

The covenant with Noah is the third general or universal covenant. Noah has just passed through the universal flood in which all the world's population had been wiped out. Only Noah, his wife, his three sons, and their wives—eight persons—constituted the world's population. Noah might have thought that the things provided by the covenant with Adam had now been changed. However, God gives the Noahic Covenant so that Noah and all the human race to follow might know that the provisions made in the Adamic Covenant remain in effect with one notable addition: the principle of human government which includes the responsibility of suppressing the outbreak of sin and violence, so that it will not be necessary to destroy the earth again by a flood. The provisions of the covenant are:

a. The responsibility to populate the earth is reaffirmed (v. 1).
b. The subjection of the animal kingdom to man is reaffirmed (v. 2).
c. Man is permitted to eat the flesh of animals. However, he is to refrain from eating blood (vv. 3-4).
d. The sacredness of human life is established. Whatever sheds man's blood, whether the murderer is man or beast, must be put to death (vv. 5-6).
e. This covenant is confirmed to Noah, all mankind, and every living creature on the face of the earth (vv. 9-10).
f. The promised is given never to destroy the earth again by a universal flood (v. 11). The next time God destroys the earth, the means will be fire (2 Pe 3:10).
g. The rainbow is designated as a testimony of the existence of this covenant and the promise never to destroy the earth by flood. As long as we can see the rainbow, we will know that the Noahic Covenant is in existence (vv. 12-17).

NO-A′ MON (temple of Amon)

The name of the ancient Thebes, an Egyptian city. Its tutelary god was Amon, the worship of whom was denounced by Jeremiah (Je 46:25). It was on both sides of the Nile and was the capital of upper Egypt. (Eze 30:14-16).

NOB (high place)

A Levitical city in Benjamin (1 Sa 22:19; Ne 11:32) near Jerusalem (Is 10:32). The tabernacle was here for a time; in the days when Ahimelech was the priest, David came to the tabernacle as he was fleeing from Saul. Without knowing that he was running from Saul, Ahimelech gave him the showbread to eat and the sword of Goliath. David was betrayed by a loiterer named Doeg, and when Saul heard of how they had helped David, he had the priests and inhabitants slain. One priest, Abiathar, escaped and came to David (1 Sa 21-22).

NO′ BAH (barking)

A man and a town:
1. A man of Manasseh (Nu 32:42).
2. A town of Gad (Ju 8:11).

NO·BA′ I

A chief of the people who sealed the covenant (Ne 10:19), also called Nebai.

NOBLE

One who has authority and leadership. A noble may be one of a royal family, but the concept of leadership is dominant. See PRINCE.

NOD (exile)

A place to which Cain went after being banished. It was east of Eden (Ge 4:16).

NO′ DAB (nobility)

An Arab tribe (1 Ch 5:19).

NO′ E

See NOAH.

NO′ GAH (shining)

A son of David born in Jerusalem (1 Ch 3:7; 14:6).

NO′ HAH (rest)

The fourth son of Benjamin, probably born in Egypt (1 Ch 8:2).

NON

See NUN.

NOON

Midday, the time when the sun is highest in the sky (2 Ki 4:20; Ps 91:5-6; Je 6:4).

NOOSE

A loop of rope, made with a slipknot so that it can be tightened. A noose is used to trap or capture (Job 18:10).

NOPH (Is 19:13)

See MEMPHIS.

NO´ PHAH (*windy*)

A town of Moab (Nu 21:30).

NORTH EASTER

See EUROCLYDON.

NOSE JEWEL

See NOSE RING.

NOSE RING

A ring or jewel inserted in the nose (Is 3:21; Eze 16:12).

NOSTRILS

The respiration holes in air breathing creatures. When God created man, he "breathed into his nostrils the breath of life; and the man became a living being" (Ge 2:7). This term is afterwards used as a way of speaking about life (Ge 7:22).

NOVICE

A new believer (1 Ti 3:6).

NUM´ BER

It is evident from Maccabean coins after the exile that the Hebrews used letters for figures. There is no evidence that they used figures before that time. The letters of the alphabet were employed for coinage purposes, aleph, the first letter of the alphabet, being used for one, beth the second letter for two, and so on.

The numbers seven (Ge 2:2; 4:24; 21:28), ten (Ex 20:3-17; 34:28), and forty (Ex 24:18; 1 Ki 19:8; Jon 3:4; Ma 4:2) are often used as significant numbers.

NUM´ BERS, BOOK OF

1. The Book of Numbers. Numbers is the book of wanderings. It takes its name from the two numberings of the Israelites—the first at Mount Sinai and the second on the plains of Moab. Most of the book, however, describes Israel's experiences as they wander in the wilderness. The lesson of Numbers is clear. While it may be necessary to pass through wilderness experiences, one does not have to live there. For Israel, an eleven-day journey became a forty-year agony.

The title of Numbers comes from the first word in the Hebrew text, *Wayyedabber,* "And He Said." Jewish writings, however, usually refer to it by the fifth Hebrew word in 1:1, *Bemidbar,* "In the

Wilderness," which more nearly indicates the content of the book. The Greek title in the Septuagint is *Arithmoi,* "Numbers." The Latin Vulgate followed this title and translated it *Liber Numeri,* "Book of Numbers." These titles are based on the two numberings: the generation of Exodus (Nu 1) and the generation that grew up in the wilderness and conquered Canaan (Nu 26). Numbers has also been called the "Book of the Journeyings," the "Book of the Murmurings," and the "Fourth Book of Moses."

2. The Author of Numbers. The evidence that points to Moses as the author of Numbers is similar to that for the previous books of the Pentateuch. These five books form such a literary unit that they rise or fall together on the matter of authorship.

External Evidences: The Jews, the Samaritans, and the early church give testimony to the Mosaic authorship of Numbers. Also a number of New Testament passages cite events from Numbers and associate them with Moses. These include John 3:14; Acts 7; 13; 1 Corinthians 10:1-11; Hebrews 3–4; and Jude 11.

Internal Evidence: There are more than eighty claims that "the LORD spoke to Moses" (the first is 1:1). In addition, Numbers 33:2 makes this clear statement: "Now Moses wrote down the starting points of their journeys at the command of the LORD." Moses kept detailed records as an eyewitness of the events in this book. As the central character in Exodus through Deuteronomy, he was better qualified than any other man to write these books.

Some scholars have claimed that the third-person references to Moses point to a different author. However, use of the third person was a common practice in the ancient world. Caesar, for example, did the same in his writings.

3. The Time of Numbers. Leviticus covers only one month, but Numbers stretches over almost thirty-nine years (c. 1444-1405 B.C.). It records Israel's movement from the last twenty days at Mount Sinai (1:1; 10:11), the wandering around Kadesh-barnea, and finally the arrival in the plains of Moab in the fortieth year (22:1; 26:3; 33:50; De 1:3). Their tents occupy several square miles whenever they camp since there are probably over two-and-a-half million people (based on the census figures in Numbers 1; 26). God miraculously fed and sustained them in the desert—He preserved their clothing and gave them manna, meat, water, leaders, and a promise (14:34).

4. The Christ of Numbers. Perhaps the clearest portrait of Christ in Numbers is the bronze serpent on the stake, a picture of the crucifixion (21:4-9): "And as Moses lifted up the serpent in the wilderness, even so must the Son of Man be lifted up" (John 3:14). The rock that quenches the thirst of the multitudes is also a type of Christ: "they drank of that spiritual Rock that followed them, and that Rock was Christ" (1 Co 10:4). The daily manna pictures the Bread of Life who later comes down from heaven (Jo 6:31-33).

Balaam foresaw the rulership of Christ: "I see Him, but not now; I behold Him, but not near; a Star shall come out of Jacob; a Sceptor shall rise out of Israel" (24:17). The guidance and presence of Christ is seen in the pillar of cloud and fire, and the sinner's refuge in Christ may be seen in the six cities of refuge. The red heifer sacrifice (Nu 19) is also considered a type of Christ.

5. Keys to Numbers.

Key Word: Wanderings—Numbers records the failure of Israel to believe in the promise of God and the resulting judgment of wanderings in the wilderness for forty years.

Key Verses: Numbers 14:22-23; 20:12— "Because all these men who have seen My glory and the signs which I did in Egypt and in the wilderness, and have put Me to the test now these ten times, and have not heeded My voice, they certainly shall not see the land of which I swore to their fathers, nor shall any of those who rejected Me see it" (14:22-23).

"Then the LORD spoke to Moses and Aaron, 'Because you did not believe Me, to hallow Me in the eyes of the children of Israel, therefore you shall not bring this congregation into the land which I have given them' "(20:12).

Key Chapter: Numbers 14—The crucial turning point of Numbers may be seen in Numbers 14 when Israel rejected God by refusing to go up and conquer the promised land. God judged Israel "according to the number of the days in which you spied out the land, forty days, for each day you shall bear your guilt one year, namely forty years, and you shall know My rejection" (14:34).

6. Survey of Numbers. Israel as a nation is in its infancy at the outset of this book, only thirteen months after the exodus from Egypt. In Numbers, the book of divine discipline, it becomes necessary for the nation to go through the painful process of testing and maturation. God must teach His people the consequences of irresponsible decisions. The forty years of wilderness experience transforms them from a rabble of ex-slaves into a nation ready to take the promised land. Numbers begins with the old generation (1:1–10:10), moves through a tragic transitional period (10:11–25:18), and ends with the new generation (26–36) at the doorway to the land of Canaan.

The Old Generation (1:1–10:10). The generation that witnessed God's miraculous acts of deliverance and preservation receives further direction from God while they are still at the foot of Mount Sinai (1:1–10:10). God's instructions are very explicit, reaching every aspect of their lives. He is the Author of order, not confusion; and this is seen in the way He organizes the people around the tabernacle. Turning from the outward conditions of the camp (1–4) to the inward conditions (5–10), Numbers describes the spiritual preparation of the people.

The Tragic Transition (10:11–25:18). Israel followed God step-by-step until Canaan was in sight. Then in the crucial moment at Kadesh they drew back in unbelief. Their murmurings had already become incessant, "Now when the people complained, it displeased the LORD; for the LORD heard it" (11:1). But their unbelief after sending out the twelve spies at Kadesh-barnea was something God refused to tolerate. Their rebellion at Kadesh marks the pivotal point of the book. The generation of the exodus would not be the generation of the conquest.

Unbelief brought discipline and hindered God's blessing. The old generation was doomed to kill time for forty years of wilderness wandering—one year for every day spent by the twelve spies in inspecting the land. They were judged by disinheritance and death as their journey changed from one of anticipation to one of aimlessness. Only Joshua and Caleb, the two spies who believed God, entered Canaan. Almost nothing is recorded about these transitional years.

The New Generation (26–36)—When the transition to the new generation was complete, the people moved to the plains of Moab, directly east of the promised land (22:1). Before they can enter the land they must wait until all is ready. Here they receive new instructions, a new census is taken, Joshua is appointed as Moses's successor, and some of the people settled in the Transjordan.

Numbers records two generations (1–14 and 21–36), two numberings (1; 26), two journeys

(10–14 and 21–27), and two sets of instructions (5–9 and 28–36). It illustrates both the kindness and severity of God (Ro 11:22) and teaches that God's people can move forward only as they trust and depend on Him.

OUTLINE OF NUMBERS

Part One: The Preparation of the Old Generation to Inherit the Promised Land (1:1–10:10)

I. The Organization of Israel (1:1–4:49)

A. Organization of the People 1:1–2:34
B. Organization of the Priests......... 3:1–4:49

II. Sanctification of Israel (5:1–10:10)

A. Sanctification Through
Separation 5:1-31

B. Sanctification Through the Nazirite
Vow 6:1-27
C. Sanctification Through
Worship 7:1–9:14
D. Sanctification Through Divine
Guidance 9:15–10:10

Part Two: The Failure of the Old Generation to Inherit the Promised Land (10:11–25:18)

I. The Failure of Israel En Route to Kadesh (10:11–12:16)

A. Israel Departs Mount Sinai......... 10:11-36
B. Failure of the People.................... 11:1-9
C. Failure of Moses....................... 11:10-15
D. God Provides for Moses 11:16-30
E. God Provides for the
People 11:31-35
F. Failure of Miriam and
Aaron 12:1-16

II. The Climactic Failure of Israel at Kadesh (13:1–14:45)

A. Investigation of the Promised
Land 13:1-33
B. Israel Rebels Against God 14:1-10
C. Moses Intercedes 14:11-19
D. God Judges Israel 14:20-38
E. Israel Rebels Against the Judgment
of God 14:39-45

III. The Failure of Israel in the Wilderness (15:1–19:22)

A. Review of the Offerings 15:1-41
B. Rebellion of Korah 16:1-40
C. Rebellion of Israel Against Moses
and Aaron 16:41-50
D. Role of the Priesthood 17:1–19:22

IV. The Failure of Israel En Route to Moab (20:1–25:18)

A. Miriam Dies 20:1
B. Moses and Aaron Fail 20:2-13
C. Edom Refuses Passage.............. 20:14-21
D. Aaron Dies 20:22-29
E. Israel's Victory over the
Canaanites 21:1-3
F. The Failure of Israel.................... 21:4-9
G. Journey to Moab 21:10-20
H. Israel's Victory over Ammon 21:21-32
I. Israel's Victory over Bashan 21:33-35
J. Failure with the Moabites 22:1–25:18

Part Three: The Preparation of the New Generation to Inherit the Promised Land (26:1–36:13)

I. The Reorganization of Israel (26:1–27:33)

A. The Second Census 26:1-51
B. Method for Dividing the Land ...26:52-56
C. Exceptions for Dividing the
Land 26:57–27:11

D. Appointment of Israel's New
Leader 27:12-23

II. The Regulations of Offerings and Vows (28:1–30:16)

A. The Regulations of
Sacrifices 28:1–29:40

B. The Regulations of Vows	30:1-16	**C.** The Summary of Israel's Journeys		33:1-49

III. The Conquest and Division of Israel (31:1–36:13)

A. Victory over Midian 31:1-54

B. Division of the Land East of Jordan 32:1-42

D. Division of the Land West of Jordan 33:50–34:29

E. Special Cities in Canaan.................................. 35:1-34

F. Special Problems of Inheritance in Canaan 36:1-13

NUN *(fish)*

Father of Joshua of the tribe of Ephraim (Ex 33:11; Jos 1:1).

NURSE

1. A wet nurse, a woman who suckles the child of another. Pharaoh's daughter hired Moses's own mother to nurse and feed him (Ex 2:7-9). The infant Joash was cared for by such a nurse (2 Ki 11:2).

2. Any female in charge of children. Naomi helped Ruth to care for her first son (Ru 4:16). Mephibosheth was injured when his nurse dropped him as she fled in terror at the news of Jonathan's death (2 Sa 4:4). A nurse might stay with her charge as a servant for the rest of her life. Rebekah's nurse Deborah accompanied her to Isaac's home, and remained with her until her death. She was obviously a valued companion, because they named the place of her burial "tree of weeping" (Ge 24:59; 35:8).

3. A man who acted as constant companion to a child (Nu 11:12, also guardian; Is 49:23, also foster father).

NUTS

Nuts have long been an important food source, containing both fat and protein (Song 6:11). See ALMOND and PISTACHIO NUT.

NYM′ PHAS *(sacred to the muses)*

A Christian in Laodicea (Col 4:15; also called Nympha).

O

OAK

A hardwood tree, nine species of which flourish in Palestine. Its wood is used for fuel, tanning, and shipbuilding. It is thought that the Hebrew words often rendered "oak" may refer to any large spreading tree, such as the terebinth or elm. The word *elah,* usually rendered "oak," is also rendered "terebinth," "teil tree" and "elm" (Is 6:13; Ho 4:13). It was in the branches of an *elah* that Absalom's hair was entangled (2 Sa 18:9-10,14). The *elim* in Isaiah 57:5 is rendered "idols" in the KJV but "oaks" in the RV. The oak under which Saul and his sons were buried (1 Ch 10:12) is also called "tamarisk" in 1 Samuel 31:13 (RV). In the KJV the word *plain* frequently appears where other translations use the word "oak" or "terebinth tree," such as the plain (oak, terebinth tree) of Moreh, of Mamre, of Zaanannim, of Tabor (Ge 12:6; 13:18; Ju 4:11; 1 Sa 10:3). Large trees such as oaks and terebinths were often used as important landmarks (Is 2:13; Ze 11:2; Ge 35:8), and the terebinth tree seems to have had some pagan religious significance. See DIVINER'S TEREBINTH TREE.

OAR

A wooden paddle for propelling a ship (Is 33:21; Eze 27:6,29). An oar could be used as a rudder as well.

OARSMEN

Men who handled the oars to propel a ship; also translated: sailors, marines, rowers (Eze 27:8-9,26). See SHIP.

OATH

An oath was taken declaring a statement to be true, or to assure the keeping of a promise (Ge 21:23; 31:53; Ga 1:20; He 6:16). When God made his promise, He confirmed it by an oath (He 6:13-20). When made, the hand was lifted upward, calling upon God to witness (Ge 14:22; Re 10:5). Again, the hand at times was placed under the thigh of the person to whom the promise was made denoting, likely, that the oath be kept by his posterity (Ge 24:2; 47:29). Walking between the parts of a slain animal signified that the fate of the animal was to fall upon the one who broke the covenant (Ge 15:8-18). Swearing by a false god was prohibited (Jos 23:7). The judicial oath was divinely enjoined (Ex 22:11).

Jesus taught his disciples to live by such a high standard of honesty that people would be able to trust their simple given word as one would trust a solemn oath (Ma 5:33-37). See COVENANT.

O·BA·DI′ AH *(worshipper of Jehovah)*

1. An officer in the court of Ahab who hid a hundred prophets in a cave when Jezebel was persecuting the prophets of God (1 Ki 18:3-4). During the drought he met Elijah, who had him inform Ahab of Elijah's presence. This led to the contest at Carmel (1 Ki 18:5-16).

2. A descendant of David (1 Ch 3:21).

3. A descendant of Issachar of the house of Uzzi (1 Ch 7:3).

4. A son of Azel, a descendant of Jonathan (1 Ch 8:38; 9:44).

5. Son of Shemaiah (1 Ch 9:16).

6. A Gadite who came to David at Ziklag (1 Ch 12:9).

7. Father of Ishmaiah, chief of Zebulun in the reign of David (1 Ch 27:19).

8. A prince commissioned by Jehoshaphat to teach the law in the cities of Judah (2 Ch 17:7).

9. A Levite of the family of Merari, an overseer of the work of repairing the temple in the reign of Josiah (2 Ch 34:12).

10. The son of Jehiel. He came with Ezra from Babylon (Ez 8:9).

11. A priest who signed the covenant with Nehemiah (Ne 10:5).

12. One of the porters of the temple after the return from captivity (Ne 12:25).

13. A prophet of Judah and author of the book which bears his name (Ob 1). See OBADIAH, BOOK OF: The Author of Obadiah.

O·BA·DI′ AH, BOOK OF

1. The Book of Obadiah. A struggle that began in the womb between twin brothers, Esau and Jacob, eventuates in a struggle between their respective descendants, the Edomites and the Israelites. For the Edomites' stubborn refusal to aid Israel, first during the time of wilderness wandering (Nu 20:14-21) and later during a time of invasion, they were roundly condemned by Obadiah. This little-known prophet described their crimes, tried their case, and pronounced their judgment: total destruction.

The Hebrew name *Obadyah* means "Worshipper of Yahweh" or "Servant of Yahweh." The Greek title in the Septuagint is *Obadiou,* and the Latin title in the Vulgate is *Abdias.*

2. The Author of Obadiah. Obadiah was an obscure prophet who probably lived in the Southern Kingdom of Judah. Nothing is known of his hometown or family, but it is not likely that he came out of the kingly or priestly line, because his father is not mentioned (1:1). There are thirteen Obadiahs in the Old Testament, and some scholars have attempted to identify the author of this book with one of the other twelve. Four of the better prospects are: (1) the officer in Ahab's palace who hid God's prophets in a cave (1 Ki 18:3); (2) one of the officials sent out by Jehoshaphat to teach the law in the cities of Judah (2 Ch 17:7); (3) one of the overseers who took part in repairing the temple under Josiah (2 Ch 34:12); or (4) a priest at the time of Nehemiah (Ne 10:5).

3. The Time of Obadiah. Obadiah mentions no kings, so verses 10-14 provide the only historical reference point to aid in determining the book's time and setting. However, scholars disagree about which invasion of Jerusalem Obadiah had in mind. There are four possibilities: (1) In 926 B.C., Shishak of Egypt plundered the temple and palace of Jerusalem in the reign of Rehoboam (1 Ki 14:25-26). At this time, Edom was still subject to Judah. This does not fit Obadiah 10-14, which indicates that Edom was independent of Judah. (2) During the reign of Jehoram (848-841 B.C.), the Philistines and Arabians invaded Judah and looted the palace (2 Ch 21:16-17). Edom revolted during the reign of Jehoram and became a bitter antagonist (2 Ki 8:20-22; 2 Ch 21:8-20). This fits the description of Obadiah. (3) In 790 B.C., King Jehoash of Israel invaded Judah (2 Ki 14; 2 Ch 25). However, Obadiah in verse 11 calls the invaders "strangers." This would be an inappropriate term for describing the army of the Northern Kingdom. (4) In 586 B.C., Nebuchadnezzar of Babylon defeated and destroyed Jerusalem (2 Ki 24–25).

The two best candidates are (2) and (4). Obadiah 10-14 seems to fit (2) better than (4) because it does not indicate the total destruction of the city, which took place when Nebuchadnezzar burned the palace and temple and razed the walls. Nebuchadnezzar certainly would not have "cast lots for Jerusalem" (11) with anyone. Also, all of the other prophets who speak of the destruction of 586 B.C. identify Nebuchadnezzar and the Babylonians as the agents; but Obadiah leaves the enemy unidentified. For these and other reasons, it appears likely that the plundering of Jerusalem written of in Obadiah was by the Philistines between 848 and 841 B.C. This would make the prophet a contemporary of Elisha, and Obadiah would be the earliest of the writing prophets, predating Joel by a few years.

The history of Edom began with Esau who was given the name Edom ("Red") because of the red stew for which he traded his birthright. Esau moved to the mountainous area of Seir and absorbed the Horites, the original inhabitants. Edom refused to allow Israel to pass through their land on the way to Canaan. The Edomites opposed Saul and were subdued under David and Solomon. They fought against Jehoshaphat and successfully rebelled against Jehoram. They were again conquered by Judah under Amaziah, but they regained their freedom during the reign of Ahaz. Edom was later controlled by Assyria and Babylon; and in the fifth century B.C. the Edomites were forced by the Nabateans to leave their territory. They moved to the area of southern Palestine and became known as Idumeans. Herod the Great, an Idumean, became king of Judea under Rome in 37 B.C. In a sense, the enmity between Esau and Jacob was continued in Herod's attempt to murder Jesus. The Idumeans participated in the rebellion of Jerusalem against Rome and were defeated along with the Jews by Titus in A.D. 70. Ironically, the Edomites applauded the destruction of Jerusalem in 586 B.C. (See Ps 137:7) but died trying to defend it in A.D. 70. After that time they were never heard of again. As Obadiah predicted, they would be "cut off forever" (10); "and no survivor shall remain of the house of Esau" (18).

4. The Christ of Obadiah. Christ is seen in Obadiah as the judge of the nations (15-16), the Savior of Israel (17-20), and the Possessor of the kingdom (21).

5. Keys to Obadiah.

Key Word: The Judgment of Edom—The major theme of Obadiah is a declaration of Edom's coming doom because of its arrogance and cruelty to Judah: "I will make you small among the nations" (2); "the pride of your heart has deceived you" (3); "how you will be cut off!" (5);

"how Esau shall be searched out!" (6); "your mighty men, O Teman, shall be dismayed" (9); "shame shall cover you" (10); "you shall be cut off forever" (10); "as you have done, it shall be done to you" (15). Even the last few verses, which primarily deal with Israel, speak of Edom's downfall (17-21). The secondary theme of Obadiah is the future restoration of Israel and faithfulness of Yahweh to His covenant promises. God's justice will ultimately prevail.

Key Verses: Obadiah 10,21—"For your violence against your brother Jacob, shame shall cover you, and you shall be cut off forever" (10).

"Then saviors shall come to Mount Zion to judge the mountains of Esau, and the kingdom shall be the LORD's" (21).

6. Survey of Obadiah. Obadiah is the shortest book in the Old Testament (twenty-one verses), but it carries one of the strongest messages of judgment in the Old Testament. For Edom there are no pleas to return, no words of consolation or hope. Edom's fate is sealed, and there are no conditions for possible deliverance. God will bring total destruction upon Edom, and there will be no remnant. Obadiah is Edom's day in court, complete with Edom's arraignment, indictment, and sentence. This prophet of poetic justice describes how the Judge of the earth will overthrow the pride of Edom and restore the house of Jacob. The two sections of Obadiah are: the judgment of Edom (1-18) and the restoration of Israel (19-21).

The Judgment of Edom (1-18). The first section of Obadiah makes it clear that the coming overthrow of Edom is a certainty, not a condition. Edom is arrogant (3) because of its secure position in Mount Seir, a mountainous region south of the Dead Sea. Its capital city of Sela (Petra) is protected by a narrow canyon that prevents invasion by an army. But God says this will make no difference. Even a thief does not take everything, but when God destroys Edom it will be totally ransacked. Nothing will avert God's complete judgment. Verses 10-14 describe Edom's major crime of gloating over the invasion of Jerusalem. Edom rejoiced when foreigners plundered Jerusalem, and became as one of them. On the day when she should have been allies with Judah, she instead became an aggressor against Judah. Edom will eventually be judged during the coming day of the Lord when Israel "shall be a fire . . . but the house of Esau shall be stubble" (18).

The Restoration of Israel (19-21). The closing verses give hope to God's people that they will possess not only their own land, but also that of Edom and Philistia.

OUTLINE OF OBADIAH

I. The Predictions of Judgment on Edom (1-9)

II. The Reasons for the Judgment on Edom (10-14)

III. The Results of the Judgment on Edom (15-18)

IV. The Possession of Edom by Israel (19-21)

O'BAL

Son of Joktan (Ge 10:28).

O'BED *(serving)*

1. Son of Boaz and Ruth and grandfather of David (Ru 4:17,21-22).

2. Son of Ephlal of Judah (1 Ch 2:37).

3. One of David's mighty men (1 Ch 11:47).

4. Son of Shemaiah, a Levite of the house of Obed-edom and gatekeeper in David's time (1 Ch 26:7).

5. Father of Azariah (2 Ch 23:1).

O'BED-E'DOM *(serving Edom)*

1. A Gittite or Gathite, a native of the Levitical city of Gath-rimmon in Dan. The ark, when sent back by the Philistines, was placed in his house, which was situated between Kirjath-jearim and Jerusalem. It remained here three months (2 Sa 6:10-12; 1 Ch 13:13-14; 15:25), and he and his family were blessed during the time the ark stayed with them.

2. A Levite gatekeeper who was part of the procession bringing the ark into Jerusalem (1 Ch 15:18-24; 26:4,8)

3. A Levite musician who ministered before the Lord in the tabernacle in Jerusalem (1 Ch 16:5).

3. Son of Jeduthun, a doorkeeper of the temple (1 Ch 16:38).

OBEDIENCE

Submitting to the will of and carrying out the commandments of another person. God promised the Israelites that if they would obey Him they would be blessed (Ex 19:5). True worship of God includes obedience. When Saul disobeyed God, he thought that he could get away with it by offering sacrifices afterwards to appease God. But God is not like the pagan gods, to be hated and feared, manipulated and ap-

peased. He is not interested in offerings, He is interested in obedient hearts (1 Sa 15:22). Part of the New Covenant with Israel promised that God's law would be written on their hearts, changing them from the inside out (Je 31:33). Our perfect example of obedience is Jesus Christ. Sin entered the world through the disobedience of one man (Adam); through the obedience of one man (Jesus Christ) the way of salvation has been opened (Ro 5:12-21).

OBEISANCE

To bow down, to show honor and submission by the position of the body; to prostrate, to do homage (Ge 37:7; Ex 18:7; 2 Sa 1:2; 1 Ki 1:16).

OBELISK

A pillar or monument of stone. Such a pillar may have had some religious connotation (Je 43:13) or be a monument to a certain person (Ge 35:20; 2 Sa 18:18). Stone monuments also were used to record information. See PILLAR and SENNACHARIB'S PRISM.

O'BIL

An Ishmaelite who was appointed as royal camel keeper in David's stables (1 Ch 27:30).

OB·LA'TION

A religious offering or sacrifice. See OFFERINGS.

O'BOTH

An encampment of the Israelites near Moab (Nu 21:10-11; 33:43-44).

OBSCENE

Offensive, abhorrent, immoral, grotesque, filthy. This word is associated with idolatry in the Old Testament; Asa, king of Judah, removed his mother from her position as queen mother because of her obscene idolatry (1 Ki 15:13; 2 Ch 15:16).

OBSERVING TIMES

Deuteronomy 18:10 (KJV), also translated "interpreting omens." See MAGIC, SORCERY AND DIVINATION and OMEN.

OCCUPATIONS AND TRADES

Following is a list of occupations and trades of Bible times. For more information about each subject, look under its name in the appropriate section of the dictionary.

Ambassador, Apothecary, Archery, Armor Bearer, Armorer, Artificers, Astrologers, Baker, Banker, Barber, Basketmaker, Beggar, Brewer, Brickmaker, Brickworker, Builder, Carpenter, Centurion, Chamberlain, Charioteer, City Clerk, Comptroller, Confectioner, Coppersmith, Counselor, Courtier, Cupbearer, Deputy, Disciple, Diviner, Doorkeeper, Duke, Embalmer, Embroiderer, Engraver, Envoy, Eunuch, Executioner, Exorcist, Farmer, Finer, Fisherman, Footman, Fowler, Fuller, Gardener, Gleaners, Goldsmith, Government Official, Guard, Harvester, Herald, Horsemen, Hunter, Husbandmen, Judge, Launderer, Lawyer, Maid/maidservant, Mason, Merchant, Metalsmith, Midwife, Noble, Nurse, Officer, Orator, Overseer, Perfumer, Plowman, Porter, Potter, President, Prince, Princess, Procurator, Prognasticator, Quartermaster, Recorder, Refiner, Ruler, Sage, Sailor, Scribe, Secretary, Serpent Charmer, Sheepshearer, Shepherd, Shipmaster, Silversmith, Singer, Slave, Smelter, Soldier, Steward, Stonecutter, Stonemason, Stoneworker, Tanner, Taskmaster, Tentmaker, Thief, Town clerk, Trader, Treasurer, Viceroy, Vine-dresser, Well digger, Woodcutter, Woodworker.

OCH′ RAN

See OCRAN.

OC′ RAN *(troubled)*

Father of Pagiel of Asher (Nu 1:13).

O′ DED *(restoration)*

1. A prophet of Israel in the reign of Pekah (2 Ch 28:9-15).

2. Father of the prophet Azariah (2 Ch 15:1).

ODOLLAM

See ADULLAM.

ODOR

Scent, smell. See INCENSE.

OFFAL

The unused parts of a butchered animal; refuse. The Israelites were instructed to take the offal outside of the camp and burn it (Ex 29:14; Le 4:11-12; Nu 19:5).

OFFENSE

An affront, an outrage to the physical or moral senses. The teaching of the cross was an offense to the Jews (Ga 5:11). The word also has the older meaning of stumbling or tripping; God said that He was "a stone of stumbling and a rock of offense to both the houses of Israel" (Is 8:14). In this sense, a temptation to sin is an "offense" (Ma 5:29; 17:23; 18:6-9; Ro 14:13; 1 Co 8:13).

OF′ FER·INGS

The patriarchs of the Old Testament—Abraham, Isaac, and Jacob—built altars and made sacrifices to God wherever they settled (Ge 12:8; 26:25; 28:18). Cain and Abel made the first offerings recorded in the Bible (Ge 4:3-5). Noah offered sacrifices of thanksgiving after the great flood (Ge 8:20). Most of these sacrifices involved the shedding of blood, a method God instituted to prepare His people for the Messiah's ultimate sacrifice for sins.

Several different types of offerings are specified by God throughout the Old Testament. These demonstrate human need and God's merciful provision.

The burnt offering involved a male animal wholly consumed by fire. The animal was killed and the priest collected the blood and sprinkled it about the altar (Nu 28:1-8). The burning symbolized the worshipper's desire to be purged of sinful acts. The meal offering, or grain offering, described in Leviticus 2 was similar in purpose to the burnt offering. The grain was brought to the priest, who threw a portion on the fire, accompanied by the burning of incense.

The peace offering was a ritual meal shared with God, the priests, and often other worshippers (Le 3). A voluntary animal offering, the sacrifice expressed praise to God and fellowship with others. Jacob and Laban offered this sacrifice when they made a treaty (Ge 31:43-55). The sin offering, also known as the guilt offering, was offered to make atonement for sins for which restitution was not possible (Le 4:5-12). The trespass offering was made for lesser or unintentional offenses for which restitution was possible (Le 5:14-19).

The author of the Book of Hebrews identified Jesus as the great High Priest (He 9:11) who replaced the system of animal sacrifices with a once-for-all sacrifice of Himself (He 9:12-28). In the light of Christ's full and final offering for sin, Paul urged Christians to "present your bodies a living sacrifice" (Ro 12:1).

OFFICER

A government official of some kind—the exact position is not certain.

OFF·SCOUR′ING (archaic)

Scum; filth (La 3:45; 1 Co 4:11-13).

OFFSPRING

Progeny, both one's own children, and one's descendants (Ge 3:15; Ru 4:12).

OG

An Amorite king of Bashan (Nu 21:33; 32:33; De 3:1-8). He was a man of great physical build, having an iron bedstead nine cubits long (De 3:11).

O′HAD

Son of Simeon (Ge 46:10; Ex 6:15).

O′HEL (tent)

Son of Zerubbabel (1 Ch 3:20).

O·HO′LAH (her tent)

A harlot, made the symbol of the idolatry and unfaithfulness of Israel (Eze 23:1-49).

O·HO′LI·AB (father's tent)

A Danite who aided Bezaleel in making the furniture for the tabernacle (Ex 31:6; 35:34-35).

O·HOL′I·BAH

Like Oholah, she was a harlot used to symbolize the unfaithfulness of the Israelites (Eze 23:1-49).

O·HOL·I·BA′MAH (my tent in a high place)

Daughter of Anah, the Hivite, and wife of Esau (Ge 36:2), also called Judith (Ge 26:34).

OIL

Except for the once-mentioned oil of myrrh (Es 2:12), all scriptural references to oil are to olive oil. Olive oil is produced by crushing and pressing the fruit of the olive tree. This product was put to a variety of uses by the Hebrews. It was a staple food (1 Ki 17:12,14), and therefore a valuable commercial item (Eze 27:17; Ho 12:1). Solomon paid the king of Tyre in olive oil (1 Ki 5:11). It was used as a cosmetic (Is 61:3), a fuel for lamps (Ex 25:6; 27:20), and a healing agent (Is 1:6; Mk 6:13). It was also an ingredient of the meal offering (Le 2:1,4-7). See OLIVE.

OIL TREE

Possibly a kind of pine, or possibly a reference to the olive tree (Is 41:19). The oleaster, or wild olive, was used for producing lower grades of olive oil, and this could be the tree in question. See OLIVE and OINTMENT.

OINT′MENT

A salve, usually a preparation of perfumed oil, used chiefly for anointing. It was used on the skin and hair (Es 2:12), as a cosmetic (Ru 3:3; Ec 9:8), and in connection with burial (Mk 14:3, 8; Lk 23:56; Jo 12:3,7). On several occasions Jesus was anointed with ointment (Ma 26:6-13; Lk 7:36-50). The fragrant oil of the holy ointment used in the tabernacle was prepared by special formula (Ex 30:25-28,34-36). See PERFUME.

OLD GATE

A gate of Jerusalem (Ne 3:6; 12:36).

OLD TES′TA·MENT

The first 39 books of the 66 books of the Bible, beginning with the creation of the world, and detailing God's dealing with His covenant people. It is divided into four sections: The Pentateuch (the first five books), twelve historical books (from Joshua to Esther), five poetical books (Job to Song of Solomon), and seventeen prophetical books (from Isaiah to Malachi). It was originally written in Hebrew excepting a few portions which are in Aramaic (Ez 4:7–6:18; 7:12-26; Da 2:4–

7:28). Its name comes from 2 Corinthians 3:14. The first 39 books talk about the Old Covenant (or Testament) God made with His people; Jesus established the New Covenant, or New Testament prophesied by Jeremiah (Je 31:31-34). See BIBLE.

OLD TESTAMENT CHRONOLOGY

Not all the books of the Old Testament are in chronological order. Genesis through 2 Kings essentially follow a consecutive timeline. The two books of Chronicles repeat 1 and 2 Samuel and 1 and 2 Kings, ending with the nation of Judah being carried into captivity, while Ezra and Nehemiah take up the story of the captives returning seventy years later. Esther is set in Babylon during the time of the captivity between the end of Chronicles and the return to Jerusalem. Job probably belongs to the time of Abraham and the Book of Psalms covers a longer span of years, including psalms written by Moses, David, and the sons of Asaph. Proverbs, Ecclesiastes, and the Song of Solomon fit into the time of Solomon, son of David (1 Ki 1-11; 2 Ch 1-9). The seventeen prophetical books are grouped together because of their content, but chronologically they fit into the times of the historical books. For more information about the time of each book, see "The Time of _____" in the entry for each book in the appropriate section of the dictionary.

OL'IVE

A slow growing evergreen tree with hard wood, grown extensively in Israel and many other Mediterranean countries (Jos 24:13; Ju 15:5; 1 Sa 8:14). Its oval fruits are used for food and also pressed to extract their oil. Olive trees have very twisted, furrowed trunks and many branches. The silvery green leaves are rather narrow and long; the fruits are classified as drupes, in the same category with peaches, plums, and almonds. Olive trees can live and continue to bear fruit for many hundreds of years, and even when the top of an old tree dies, its roots will often put out new shoots to replace the old trunk. Some of the oldest olive trees today are over one thousand years old. Olive harvest begins in the fall. Since there are people who like olives in almost every stage of ripeness, olive harvests last for some time. Green olives are pickled for eating; olives meant for oil are allowed to stay on the trees until they turn black, and have reached their highest oil content. The Bible mentions olives being harvested by being beaten or shaken from the trees (De 24:20; Is 17:6; 24:13). The olives to be used for oil were crushed in a stone press, and the oil was drained off. The oil produced by the first crushing is the finest, after this, the olives are pressed again and a mixture of water, oil and sediment is drained off. The lesser quality oil is skimmed off the top of this second squeezing, and is perfectly adequate for many applications. See OIL and OINTMENT.

OL'IVES, MOUNT OF

A hill consisting of a series of four peaks located east of Jerusalem, overlooking the temple. This area was once thickly wooded with olive trees (Ne 8:15). It is separated from Jerusalem by the Kidron Valley and it is a Sabbath day's journey from its summit to Jerusalem (Ac 1:12). When David fled from Absalom, he "went up by the ascent of the Mount of Olives" weeping, and barefoot (2 Sa 15:11). Jesus often spent time here during his time on earth. It was the scene of the Olivet discourse (Ma 24:3; Lk 21:37; 22:39; Jo 8:1), and after the last supper, Jesus and His disciples walked out to the Mount and the garden of Gethsemane on its western slope. The disciples stood on this hill to watch Him ascend to heaven (Ac 1:11-12), and when He returns again, it will be to this same place (Ze 14:4; Ac 1:11-12).

OL'I·VET *(place of olives)*

See OLIVES, MOUNT OF.

OLIVET DISCOURSE

Jesus's teaching on the end of the age (Ma 24:1–25:46; Mk 13:1-37; Lk 21:5-36). Jesus and

OLIVES, MOUNT OF

His disciples had left the temple and were sitting on the Mount of Olives overlooking Jerusalem when Peter, James, John, and Andrew asked Him to explain to them the signs of the end of the age.

O·LYM′ PAS

A Christian in Rome to whom Paul sent greetings (Ro 16:15).

O′ MAR (eloquent, talkative)

Son of Eliphaz (Ge 36:11,15).

O·ME′ GA

The last letter of the Greek alphabet. It is used figuratively in Jesus's description of Himself as the "Alpha and Omega, the Beginning and the End . . . the First and the Last" (Re 1:8,11; 21:6; 22:13).

OMEN

A sign or portent by which a magician is supposed to be able to tell the future (De 18:10). God's people were forbidden to read omens. See also MAGIC, SORCERY, AND DIVINATION.

O′ MER

A dry measure, a tenth of an ephah (Ex 16:36), equal to almost six pints. See WEIGHTS AND MEASURES.

OM′ NI·PO′ TENCE

The quality of being all powerful. Omnipotence is one of the attributes of God. He is the Almighty One. He not only knows all things, He is fully able to control all things, past, present, and future (Ge 1:1-3; He 1:3; Is 40:15; Re 19:6).

OMNIPRESENCE

The quality of being present everywhere at the same time. Omnipresence is an attribute of God. It is impossible to hide from God. It is also impossible to get into any situation in which He is not close beside us. While God is ever-present, we do not always have a strong sense of His nearness. Occasionally He will reveal His presence to us in a special way (Ps 139:7-12; Ma 6:1-18).

OMNISCIENCE

The quality of knowing everything, past, present, and future; real and potential. Omni-science is an attribute of God. In all the infinite possibilities, God always chooses the best plan. He is not confused with details but is able to keep all nuances perfectly in mind. God knows the answer to the "what ifs" (Ps 139:1-6,13-16; Is 40:13-14; 53; Ro 8:18-39; 1 Co 15:51-57; 2 Co 3:17).

OM′ RI

Four Old Testament men:

1. A son of Becher of Benjamin (1 Ch 7:8).

2. A descendant of Judah of the family of Perez (1 Ch 9:4).

3. Son of Michael and prince of Issachar in the reign of David (1 Ch 27:18).

4. The sixth king of Israel and founder of the fourth dynasty (1 Ki 16:15-20).

ON

A city and a man of the Old Testament:

1. A city of lower Egypt on the east side of the Nile, about twenty miles north of Memphis. Being the seat of the worship of the sun, the Greeks called it Heliopolis. In Jeremiah it is called Beth-shemish (Je 43:13).

2. Son of Peleth of Reuben (Nu 16:1).

ONAGER

See ASS.

O′ NAM (strong)

Two Old Testament men:

1. A descendant of Seir, a Horite (Ge 36:23; 1 Ch 1:40).

2. Son of Jerahmeel of Judah (1 Ch 2:26,28).

O′ NAN (strong)

A son of Judah. His mother was Shush, a Canaanite (Ge 38:4-10; 46:12). He refused to become the husband of the widow of his brother, Er, and was killed by the Lord.

O·NES′ I·MUS (profitable)

A slave of the Christian, Philemon of Colossae, who ran away from his master to Rome. There he met Paul who converted him to Christianity. The Epistle to Philemon was written on behalf of the slave. See PHILEMON, BOOK OF.

O·NES·IPH′ O·RUS (profit bearing)

A Christian who showed Paul great kindness when he was a prisoner at Rome (2 Ti 1:16,18; 4:19).

ONI'AS

During the period between the Old and New Testaments, five high priests bore this name.

ON'ION

A hardy, well-known plant belonging to the lily family with a strongly flavored edible bulb. Onions have been cultivated since prehistoric times, and are popular worldwide. The Hebrews longed for the onions of Egypt as they wandered in the wilderness (Nu 11:5). Onions go far back in Egypt's history; there are even pictures of onions in some of the ancient tombs.

ONLY BEGOTTEN

See BEGOTTEN, ONLY.

O'NO (strong)

A town of Benjamin (Ne 11:35). It was rebuilt by Shamed (1 Ch 8:12), and some of its inhabitants returned from Babylon with Zerubbabel (Ez 2:33; Ne 7:37).

ON'Y·CHA

An ingredient in the perfume used in the tabernacle service (Ex 30:34). Onycha is believed to be the resin of the ladanum or rockrose. Ladanum is a waist-high bush with large white flowers almost as broad as a man's hand. The myrrh referred to in Genesis 37:25 and 43:11 is believed by some scholars to actually be onycha.

ON'YX

A precious stone (Job 28:16; Eze 28:13), a form of chalcedony. It is formed of layers of different colors, black or brown and white. One was used on the breastplate of the high priest (Ex 28:9,12,20). David gathered onyx for the building of the temple (1 Ch 29:2).

O'PHEL

The site of the original city of the Jebusites. This triangular hill is located south of the temple area, and since it is surrounded by deep valleys on three sides, it was considered impregnable. David, however, was able to capture it, and Jerusalem became the religious and political center of Israel (2 Sa 5:6-9). Jotham, one of the righteous kings of Judah, did extensive building on the wall of Ophel, the fortification on its eastern ridge, overlooking the Kidron

Valley (2 Ch 27:3). Later, Manasseh extended the city walls to completely enclose Ophel and the city of David (2 Ch 33:14). After the captivity the Nethinim lived in this quarter (Ne 3:26; 11:21).

O'PHIR

A man and a region of the Old Testament:

1. A son of Joktan and great-grandson of Shem (Ge 10:29; 1 Ch 1:23).

2. A celebrated gold region (Job 22:24; 28:16; Is 13:12). Its exact location is a mystery; some have guessed that it may have been somewhere in India or Africa. Solomon and David both obtained gold from Ophir for use in the building of the temple and to augment Solomon's treasury (1 Ki 9:28; 1 Ch 29:4; 2 Ch 8:17-18; 2 Ch 9:10). Many years later, Jehoshaphat, king of Judah attempted to send a fleet of ships to Ophir for gold as his ancestors had done, but the ships were wrecked and the venture came to nothing (1 Ki 22:48). The gold of Ophir is frequently used as a metaphor for beauty and value (Job 28:16; Ps 45:9).

OPH'NI (moldy)

A town of Benjamin, the identity of which is uncertain (Jos 18:24).

OPH'RAH

Two cities and a man of the Old Testament:

1. A town of Benjamin, the location of which is uncertain, perhaps north of Michmash (Jos 18:23; 1 Sa 13:17).

2. A town of Manasseh east of the Jordan (Ju 6:11,13), the home of Gideon (Ju 6-8).

3. A son of Menothai of Judah (1 Ch 4:14).

OR'A·CLE

A divine utterance given man for his guidance. Balaam's prophecies concerning the blessing of Israel are referred to as oracles (Nu 23–24; translated "parable" in the KJV). This word is also used in the KJV to refer to the inner sanctuary of the temple, apparently as the place where words from God were received (1 Ki 6:5,16,19-23; 8:6,8; Ps 28:2). The wisdom of David's advisor, Ahithophel, is compared to the counsel that one might receive if he "inquired at the oracle of God," presumably at the temple (2 Sa 16:23). The Book of Jeremiah mentions oracles (Je 23:33-38 also translated "burden," KJV) as messages from God for the people. The New Testament uses the term in the sense of God's revealed Word, His message to His people (Ac 7:38; Ro 3:2; He 5:12; 1 Pe 4:11).

OR′A·TOR

An advocate or pleader; a skilled speaker. Tertullus, who argued against Paul before Felix (Ac 24:1-8) was called an orator (or "lawyer," NIV). Paul was also a skilled orator, as can be seen by his speech on Mars' Hill (Ac 17:22-31).

ORCHARD

A grove of trees planted for their fruit (Ec 2:5; Song 4:13). An orchard might be made up of fruit or nut trees, such as almonds, pomegranates, olives, figs, or spices.

ORDAIN, ORDINATION

The official recognition of or appointing of an authority figure. The priests were ordained in a special ceremony before they took up their duties at the tabernacle (Ex 29). Jesus's appointing of the twelve apostles could be seen as an ordination (Mk 3:13-19; Lk 6:12-16). These same twelve ordained deacons to take up some of the serving work of the leadership of the church (Ac 6:6). Paul and Barnabas were commended to special service as missionaries (Ac 13:3).

OR′EB (raven)

A prince of the Midianites put to death by Gideon (Ju 7:25; 8:3; Ps 83:11). THE ROCK OREB is where the Oreb and the Midianite army were defeated by Ephraim. It probably derived its name from the event (Is 10:26).

O′REN (ash tree)

Son of Jerahmeel of Judah (1 Ch 2:25).

OR′GAN

A musical wind instrument (Ge 4:21), also translated "flute." Flute is probably a better word choice.

O·RI′ON (the giant)

A constellation east of Taurus on the celestial equator, made up of 80 significant stars— 17 of which are large and bright. The name comes from Greek mythology concerning Orion, the hunter; the constellation was also called "The Giant," named after Nimrod, the mighty hunter of the early postflood world (Job

9:9; 38:31; Am 5:8). Betelgeuse, Rigel, and Bellatrix are its brightest stars. The row of three stars making the Hunter's belt is the most recognizable feature of this constellation.

OR′NA·MENTS

In ancient times both men and women adorned themselves with jewelry (Ex 3:22; 11:2; Nu 31:50). Women customarily wore their dowries. Pearls, beads, jewels and coins were all used as ornaments (Song 1:10-11; 1 Ti 2:9), also chains, necklaces, armlets, and rings (Ge 24:22,47; Ex 35:22; Is 3:18-23). Men wore finger rings as well as rings on the arms.

OR′NAN

See ARAUNAH.

ORONTES

This river is not mentioned in the Bible, but the cities of Riblah (2 Ki 23:33-35), Hamath (1 Ki 8:65), and Kadesh were located on it.

OR′PAH (mane)

A Moabitess, the wife of Chilion, and the daughter-in-law of Naomi. Along with Ruth, Orpah was prepared to accompany her widowed mother-in-law back to the land of Israel, but she allowed Naomi to persuade her to stay in her own homeland (Ru 1:4,11,15).

ORPHAN

A child with no parents, particularly no father. God promised to be the advocate of the helpless, including widows, orphans, and strangers (De 18:10). He is described as the helper of the fatherless (Ps 10:14), and the father of the fatherless (Ps 68:5). Before His crucifixion, when Jesus was preparing His disciples for what would happen, He promised them to not leave them orphans but to send the Holy Spirit to comfort and guide them (Jo 14:18). The "Father of the fatherless" would never abandon them. Part of believing is learning to be like Him; James teaches that "pure religion" is caring for those who are orphaned and helpless (Jam 1:26-27).

ORYX

See ANTELOPE.

O′SEE

Variant form of Hosea (Ro 9:25).

OSSIFRAGE

O'SHE·A

See HOSHEA, JOSHUA.

OS·NAP'PER

See ASNAPPER.

OS'PREY

A ceremonially unclean fish-eating eagle (Le 11:13; De 14:12).

OS'SI·FRAGE *(bone breaker)*

The bearded vulture, about three feet high with a wingspread of about nine feet (Le 11:13,18; De 14:12,17). Also called "lammergeier" and "gier eagle."

OSTIA

An ancient city located about 15 miles from Rome, at the mouth of the Tiber River. It was a principle seaport for the city of Rome.

OSTRACA

Broken potsherds. Pottery fragments were used as an inexpensive writing surface in ancient times, and large quantities of such scraps have been unearthed. They were used for such purposes as receipts and memoranda, things which did not merit the expense of parchment or papyrus. Potsherds are not mentioned in the Bible as writing material, but Job used broken potsherds to scrape himself when he was afflicted with painful boils, and they are mentioned a few other times (Job 2:8; Ps 22:15; Is 45:9).

OS'TRICH

Earth's largest living bird. Ostriches can be as high as eight feet tall, and even though they cannot fly, they are remarkable for the speed with which their long legs can cover the ground. They are remarkably careless with their nests, and during the day they typically leave the eggs to the tender mercies of the sun-warmed sand and passing wild beasts (Job 39:13-18). They are remarkably well fitted for desert life, and can live for as long as seventy years. Because of their size and speed, they need fear few predators, and they are able to survive with very little water. Ostriches were considered ceremonially unclean (Le 11:16; De 14:15), and unsuitable for food. The ostrich utters a mournful roaring sound (Mi 1:8).

OTH'NI

The son of Shemaiah, a Levite. In the days of David, Othni was a gatekeeper for the tabernacle (1 Ch 26:7).

OTH'NI·EL *(powerful one of God)*

1. Son of Kenaz (Jos 15:17; 1 Ch 4:13). He won his wife Achsah, the daughter of Caleb, by capturing the town of Debir (Jos 15:15-17; Ju 1:12-13).

2. Ancestor of Heldai (1 Ch 27:15).

OUCH'ES (archaic)

Settings for gems; sockets (Ex 28:11).

OUTCASTS

Those who were exiled from Israel (Ps 147:2; Is 11:12; 56:8).

OUTWENT (archaic)

To go before in advance (Mk 6:32-33).

OV'EN

The exact nature of all the cooking devices used in Old Testament times is not really known. The "oven" mentioned in Genesis 15:17 is also translated "furnace" (KJV), "brazier" (REB), and "fire pot" (NIV and NRSV). Hive-shaped ovens of brick or clay were used to bake bread. A fire was built inside of the oven, and once the oven was hot, the fire could either be raked aside and the bread put inside, or flat loaves could be baked on the hot outside of the oven. By New Testament times, pottery stoves were used; the fire was built inside, and the flat top was used for cooking. Dried animal dung, straw, and small chips and pieces of wood were used to make quick hot fires for cooking.

OVENS, TOWER OF THE

Also called tower of the furnaces, a part of the wall of Jerusalem, restored in the days of

Nehemiah by Malchijah and Hashub (Ne 3:11; 12:38). It may have been a place where bread was baked commercially, or even more likely, it may have been a place where potters' or brickmakers' kilns were fired, or possibly metalwork was done.

OVERSEER

1. A taskmaster, foreman, driver or slave master; one who is responsible for directing a group of slaves or workmen (Ex 1:11-14; 2 Ch 2:18).

2. One who helps rule a household or people; a governor. Joseph was made overseer over Potiphar's household (Ge 39:4-5). Nehemiah mentions various men who were given governing authority over Jerusalem (Ne 11:9).

3. One who holds a place of responsibility and leadership in the church. Some believe that the term "overseer" is synonymous with "elder," some think that there is a distinction (Ac 20:28; Ph 1:1; 1 Ti 3:2; Tit 1:7). Jesus is the Overseer of our souls (1 Pe 2:25).

OWL

A ceremonially unclean, night-feeding bird of prey with a large head and eyes, a short bill, and strong talons. Owls appear in the Bible numerous times (Le 11:16-17; Ps 102:6; Je 50:39; Mi 1:8). Owls of various sizes are native to the land of Israel, from the large eagle owl to the small screech owl. Several Hebrew words are translated as several types of owls, but the exact definitions are not sure. These translations include "short eared owl" (Le 11:16; NKJV, REB); "long eared owl" (Le 11:16; NIV); "little owl" (Le 11:17; KJV, NIV, NASB); "tawny owl" (Le 11:17; REB); "fisher owl" (Le 11:17; NKJV); "desert owl" (Le 11:18; NIV); "white owl" (Le 11:18; NKJV, NIV, NASB). The KJV translates Isaiah 34:14 as "screech owl" ("night creature" NKJV, NIV, "night monster" RV), "great owl" appears in Isaiah 34:15 ("arrow snake" NKJV; "owl" NIV; "dart snake" RV). Some scholars believe that the "satyr" (KJV) of Isaiah 34:14 is some type of owl.

OX

A castrated adult male bovine animal. Oxen were used for plowing (1 Ki 19:19), for drawing wagons (Nu 7:3; 2 Sa 6:6), and for tramping out grain (De 25:4). They were also used for food (1 Ki 1:25) and for sacrificial purposes (Nu 7:87-88; 2 Sa 24:22; 2 Ch 5:6).

OX' GOAD

See GOAD.

O' ZEM

Two Old Testament men:

1. David's older brother, the sixth son of Jesse (1 Ch 2:15).

2. Son of Jerahmeel (1 Ch 2:25).

O·ZI' AS

See UZZIAH.

OZ' NI *(attentive)*

Son of Gad and founder of the tribal family of Oznites (Nu 26:16), also called Ezbon (Ge 46:16).

OZNITES

Descendants of Ozni (Nu 26:16).

P

PA' A·RAI

One of David's mighty men (2 Sa 23:35). A variant reading in 1 Chronicles 11:37 is Naarai.

PA' DAN, PAD' DAN

Variants of Padan-aram.

PA' DAN-A' ·RAM *(plain of Aram)*

The country lying to the northeast of Palestine. It embraced both Syria and Upper Mesopotamia. Haran, the home of Abram after he moved from Ur of the Chaldeans (Ge 11:31), was located in Padan-aram. When Abraham decided that it was time to find a bride for Isaac, he sent his servant back to Padan-aram, to the city where his brother Nahor had raised his family (Ge 24:10; 25:20). Isaac did the same by his son, sending Jacob to his mother's family in Padan-aram to look for a wife (Ge 28:2,5). The area is also called Padan (Ge 48:7, NKJV), Paddan (Ge 48:7, NIV), Paddan Aram (Ge 25:20, NIV) and Paddan-aram (Ge 25:20, NRSV).

PA' DON *(freedom)*

Head of a family of Nethinim who returned to Jerusalem with Zerubbabel (Ez 2:44; Ne 7:47).

PAGAN

Those who do not follow God. Nehemiah and Ezra both strenuously opposed the intermarriage of the Israelites with pagan women after the captivity (Ez 10:2,10-18,44; Ne 13:26-27,30).

PAGAN GODS

The Israelites were God's special people who followed the one true God, but they were surrounded by nations and cultures that worshipped heathen gods. The people of the covenant often gave in to the temptation to worship these pagan deities. Especially tempting in Old Testament times was the Canaanite fertility god known as Baal, who was thought to produce abundant crops and livestock. Diana, or Artemis, of Ephesus (Ac 19:24-28), was the goddess with many breasts, which were thought to provide succor for those who were born through her gift of fertility. Other prominent pagan gods mentioned in the Old and New Testaments are Ashtaroth, Baal's wife or female counterpart; Bel, a god identified with Merodach (Marduk), who was a chief Babylonian god connected with war; Chemosh, god of the Moabites and Ammonites; Chiun, a star-god, identified with Saturn; Dagon, the chief Philistine god; Molech, Ammonite god connected with child sacrifice; Nebo, a Babylonian god of wisdom and the arts; Rimmon, the Syrian god of rain; Tammuz, a Babylonian fertility god; Castor and Pollux, twin sons of Zeus who was the chief Greek god; and Hermes, the Greek god of commerce and speed.

These gods and goddesses are the fruits of misguided human minds, which searched for meaning in the elementary forces of life. But real meaning and purpose are found only in the one true God and His Son Jesus Christ. See GODS, PAGAN.

PA′ GI·EL (meeting with God)

Son of Ocran of Asher (Nu 1:13; 2:27; 7:72, 77; 10:26), a leader who helped take the first census.

PA′ HATH-MO′ AB

1. Head of a family, members of which returned to Jerusalem with Zerubbabel (Ez 2:6; 8:4; Ne 7:11).

2. One who signed the covenant in the days of Nehemiah (Ne 10:14).

PA′ I

An Edomite city, dwelling place of Hadad, king of Edom (1 Ch 1:50). Also called Pau (Ge 36:39).

PAINT

A powder made from almond shells, resin, or possibly antimony, which was used by women to decorate the eyes. The eyebrows were also blackened with various dye stuffs. The Hebrews seem to have looked upon the practice with disfavor (2 Ki 9:30; Je 4:30; Eze 23:40). See ANTIMONY.

PAL′ ACE

A large house which is the official residence of a sovereign. David built a royal palace in Jerusalem (2 Sa 5:9; 7:1-2). Solomon also constructed a residence of great magnificence which took thirteen years to build. It contained a great hall, 150 feet long, called "the house of the forest of Lebanon" (1 Ki 7:2). Solomon's throne was in the "porch of judgment," the room in which he acted as judge.

PA′ LAL (judge)

Son of Uzai. He labored on the wall of Jerusalem (Ne 3:25).

PALANQUIN

A sedan chair; a canopied seat carried on two poles on the shoulders of slaves (Song 3:9-10), also translated chariot (KJV), carriage (NIV), sedan chair (NASB).

PAL·ES·TI′ NA

See PALESTINE.

PAL′ ES·TINE

The land of the Israelites, only once called Palestine (Joel 3:4, KJV; "Philistia" NKJV). In the Old Testament the name signifies the "land of the Philistines." It was called Canaan by the Hebrews in distinction from Gilead, east of the Jordan. When taken by Joshua, it became known as the land of Israel (1 Sa 13:19; Ma 2:20). It is called the land of promise (He 11:9) and the Holy Land (Ze 2:12). During the Middle Ages, the name "Holy Land" was the most popular. In those days, Palestine was considered to be the center of the earth, and in a sense this is perfectly true. It is strategically located on a tiny strip of land on the eastern coast of the Mediterranean Sea which unites three continents

(Africa, Asia, and Europe). It was situated between the most dominant ancient kingdoms of the world (Egypt, Babylon, Assyria, and Persia). As occupied by the Israelites, the land extended from Mount Hermon on the north to Kadesh-barnea on the south and from the sea on the west to the Jordan and the region east of the river occupied by Reuben, Gad, and half-tribe of Manasseh. The Israelites never expanded their kingdom to include all the area promised to them in Numbers 34.

PALESTINIAN COVENANT

The covenant concerning the land of Palestine is the third of the theocratic covenants (pertaining to the rule of God). The Palestinian Covenant has two aspects: (1) the legal aspects which are immediate and conditional (De 27–29); and (2) the grace aspects which are future and unconditional (De 30:1-9). The enjoyment of the immediate blessings is introduced by the conditional formula: "if you diligently obey the voice of the LORD your God . . . the LORD your God will set you high above all nations of the earth" (De 28:1). Sadly, Israel did not meet the condition of obedience, and is still experiencing God's curses and punishment for their disobedience (De 28:15-68). The unconditional grace aspects of the Palestinian Covenant have yet to be realized. God will regather the scattered people of Israel and establish them in the land He has promised unconditionally to give them. Deuteronomy concludes the Palestinian Covenant with a final warning and challenge for obedience (De 30:1-20).

PALLET

A mattress (Jo 5:8-11; Ac 5:15), also translated "bed" (NKJV) or "mat" (NIV).

PAL′LU *(distinguished)*

A son of Reuben and head of a tribal family (Ex 6:14; Nu 26:5), also called Phallu (Ge 46:9, KJV).

PAL′LU·ITES

The descendants of Reuben's son Pallu (Nu 26:5).

PALM

A tall, straight tree (Song 7:7-8; Je 10:5). Palm trees were carved on panels of the temple walls and on the olive wood doors of the inner sanctu-ary (1 Ki 6:29,32,35). The long feathery leaves of the palm were emblematic of peace, also of victory (Jo 12:13; Re 7:9). The Israelites found palm trees at Elim (Ex 15:27). The woman's name Tamar means "palm" (Ge 38:6; 2 Sa 13:1).

PALM′ER·WORM

An destructive creature which eats trees, vines, vegetables, and cereals (Joel 1:4; 2:25; Am 4:9). It may have been the plant eating larvae of any one of various insects.

PAL′SY

See PARALYTIC.

PAL′TI *(deliverance)*

1. The spy who represented Benjamin (Nu 13:9).
2. Same as Paltiel (2 Sa 3:15).

PAL′TI·EL *(deliverance of God)*

1. Prince of Issachar (Nu 34:26).
2. The man to whom Saul gave his daughter, Michal, the wife of David (1 Sa 25:44; 2 Sa 3:3, 15), after David went into hiding. He is also called Phaltiel (KJV).

PAL′TITE

A native of Bethpelet (Jos 15:27). One of David's mighty men was a Paltite (2 Sa 23:26; also called a Pelonite, 1 Ch 27:10).

PAM·PHYL′I·A

A coast region in the south of Asia Minor (modern Turkey). Perga was its capital, and its largest city. People from Pamphylia were present in Jerusalem at Pentecost (Ac 2:10). Paul and Barnabas traveled through Pamphylia on their way into Asia Minor on the first missionary journey, and John Mark left them in Perga to return to Jerusalem. Later, Paul and Barnabas passed through Pamphylia again on their way home (Ac 13:13; 14:24-25; 15:38).

PAN

A cooking dish or other bowl or basin (Ex 25:29; Nu 7:14-86; 2 Sa 13:9; 2 Ch 35:13), also translated "spoon," "dish," and "saucer."

PAN′NAG

Perhaps a kind of confection or sweetmeat (Eze 27:17). Pannag was exported to Tyre. It is also translated "millet" (NKJV, NRSV), "cakes" (NASB), "confections" (NIV), "meal" (REB).

PANTHER

The REB translation for Hosea 5:14, otherwise translated "lion." See LION.

PA´PER

See PAPYRUS.

PA´PER REEDS

The rendering of a word of uncertain meaning in Isaiah 19:7, translated *meadow* in the RV, *papyrus reeds* in the NKJV, *bulrushes* in the NASB and *plants* in the NIV.

PA´PHOS

Capital of Cyprus and residence of the Roman proconsul. When Paul was talking to the Roman proconsul in Paphos, the magician Elymas (Bar-Jesus) did his best to turn Sergius Paulus against the gospel message. Paul told him that because of this sin, the Lord would blind him, and immediately Paul's words came true. Sergius Paulus was astonished at what he saw, and believed Paul's teaching (Ac 13:6-13).

PAPS (archaic)

Breasts; bosom (Lk 11:27-28); chest (Re 1:13).

PA·PY´RUS

A variety of sedge, or solidstemmed grass, native to the region around the Nile. The word also refers to the ancient writing paper prepared from this plant. The tough stems of this plant were split and flattened, and then arranged in interlocking layers and pounded or pressed into a thin, tough sheet. It is probably the plant referred to as *bulrush* in Exodus 2:3 and Isaiah 18:2, and *rush* in Job 8:11. See PAPER REEDS.

PAR´A·BLE

A story or fable for the illustration of moral or religious truth. It is not to be confused with simile, metaphor, or figure of speech. John's Gospel makes use of the latter but not of parables in the proper use of the word. In the discourse on the Good Shepherd the word parable is used (Jo 10:6), but it is not the word for parable commonly used by the Synoptic Gospels. Jesus clothed the truths of the kingdom in images and narrative form. Sometimes this was in order to illustrate and make clear His meaning as in the parable of the good Samaritan (Lk 10:25-37); other times He used parables to cloak His meaning from all but the spiritually discerning (Ma 13:10-17).

PARABLES IN CHRONOLOGICAL ORDER			
GALILEAN MINISTRY			
	Ma	Mk	Lk
Second Period			
1. The Two Debtors			7:41-50
2. The Sower	13:1-23	4:1-20	8:4-15
3. The Seed		4:26-29	
4. The Tares	13:24-30, 36-43		
5. The Mustard Seed	13:31-32	4:30-32	
6. The Leaven	13:33		
7. The Hidden Treasure	13:44		
8. The Costly Pearl	13:45-46		
9. The Drag-net	13:47-50		
Third Period			
10. The Wicked Servant	18:21-35		
THE PEREAN MINISTRY			
11. The Good Samaritan			10:25-37
12. The Rich Fool			12:16-21
13. The Barren Fig Tree			13:6-9
14. The Wedding Guest			14:7-11
15. The Great Supper			14:15-24
16. Counting the Cost			14:25-35
17. The Lost Sheep			15:1-7
18. The Lost Coin			15:8-10
19. The Prodigal Son			15:11-32
20. The Unjust Steward			16:1-13
21. The Rich Man and Lazarus			16:19-31
22. The Unprofitable Servant			17:1-10
23. The Unjust Judge			18:1-8
24. The Pharisee and Publican			18:9-14
25. The Labourers in the Vineyard	20:1-16		
26. The Pounds			19:11-28
THE PASSION WEEK			
Tuesday			
27. The Two Sons	21:28-32		
28. The Vineyard	21:33-46	12:1-12	20:9-19
29. The Wedding Feast	22:1-14		
30. The Ten Virgins	25:1-13		
31. The Talents	25:14-30		

PAR´A·CLETE

One of the Greek verbs in the New Testament that is richly freighted with meaning is *parakaleo* (from *para* "along side" as in parallel lines, and *kaleo*, "call"). Its many occurrences are variously translated *exhort, comfort, console, encourage, entreat, beg,* and *beseech,* for no single English word covers its range of meanings. Three typical translations for the related noun *paraklesis* are *comfort, encouragement,* and *exhortation.*

Parakletos occurs five times in the Greek New

Testament, four times in the Upper Room Discourse (Jo 13-17), and once in 1 John.

Many Christians know that the Holy Spirit is called "the Paraclete." What is perhaps less known is that Jesus Himself is called a Paraclete and that the Holy Spirit is "another Paraclete."

Christ the Paraclete: In 1 John 2:1, the apostle urges his readers not to sin. Yet being a realist, he knows that the most devout believers are subject to failure and do sin. So he adds a word of encouragement. "And if anyone sins, we have an Advocate [*Parakletos*] with the Father, Jesus Christ the righteous. And He Himself is the propitiation [sacrifice that satisfies God] for our sins, and not for ours only but also for the whole world." (1 Jo 2:1-2).

The translation "Advocate" in the KJV/NKJV comes from a Latin word *advocatus.* It is very similar to the Greek word in origin and meaning. The main part of the word (*-vocatus*) means "called," just like the *–kletos* part of *Paraclete.* Instead of *para* ("alongside"), however, the Latin calls someone "to" (*ad*) his side to help. The meanings are nearly the same. An advocate is someone who takes up your cause. For example, on a professional level he may be a lawyer.

Moulton and Milligan's valuable *The Vocabulary of the Greek Testament* gives the original idea as "one called in" to support, hence "advocate," "pleader," "a friend of the accused person called to speak to his character, or otherwise enlist the sympathy of the judges." The word must have been popular because both the Hebrew and Aramaic languages borrowed the word.

Since we Christians cannot very well plead the merits of our "character" before God's throne (we have none), Christ steps in with His own merits—the merits of His sacrifice on Calvary, which we appropriate by faith.

Another Paraclete (John 14:16): While the Savior was here on earth the disciples could call Him aside at any time to answer a question or solve a problem. But in the Upper Room Discourse He was preparing them for the time when He would not be personally present with them. Yes, He would be at God's right hand pleading their case and their needs, but He was going to leave someone else on earth for them (and for us) to turn to. This is His "Vicar," or personal representative on earth, the Holy Spirit.

In John 14:16-17 our Lord made this promise: "And I will pray the Father and He will give you another Helper [*Parakletos*], that He may abide with you forever, even the Spirit of truth, whom the world cannot receive, because it neither sees Him nor knows Him; but you know Him, for He dwells with you and will be in you." He was predicting Pentecost, when the Spirit would come in a unique and new way that the Old Testament saints could not enjoy.

Precisely how to translate *Parakletos* in this passage is difficult. No English word is a close match. The KJV has "Comforter." In 1611, this was a better rendering than it is today because then all educated Englishmen knew Latin and recognized the root *–fort* in "Comforter" as meaning "strong."

The NIV uses "Counselor" in John 14. The Living Bible retains the KJV "Comforter," but with "Helper" in a footnote. Twentieth Century, Moffatt, Basic English, Good News, and NKJV all use "Helper."

It is noteworthy that Jesus calls the Holy Spirit *another* Paraclete (*allos,* "another of the same kind"). He is like Jesus.

PAR′ A·DISE *(a park)*

A blessed, happy place, devoid of the cares of the world; a word used to denote heaven. It is the place of the justified and the righteous. When the dying thief asked Jesus to remember him, Jesus promised that the thief would that day join Him in paradise (Lk 23:43). Paul speaks of "a man" (possibly himself) who was taken to paradise for a short time (2 Co 12:4), and the book of Revelation says that the tree of life is in the "midst of the paradise of God" (Re 2:7). In His parable of the rich man and Lazarus, Jesus says that Lazarus was in "Abraham's bosom." It is obvious that this is the good place to be, though whether this is the same as paradise is not certain (Lk 16:22-23).

PA′ RAH *(heifer)*

A village of Benjamin (Jos 18:23).

PARALLELISM

See POETRY, HEBREW.

PARALYTIC

One who suffers from a nerve dysfunction, disease, or injury, which damages muscle function; particularly one who cannot walk. Jesus healed the paralyzed man who was let down through the roof because there was no room in the house (Mk 2:1-12). The apostles also healed paralytics by the power of God (Ac 8:7; 9:33-34, *palsy* KJV).

PAR′ AMOUR (archaic)

A male or female lover (Eze 23:19-20).

PAR′ AN

A wilderness between Sinai and Canaan (Nu 10:12; 12:16) east of the wilderness of Shur (Ge 21:21). In it the Israelites wandered 38 years.

PARAPET

A low wall around the edge of the flat roof of a house. In ancient times, the roof was used as an extra room, and the law instructed people to build walls around them so that the danger of anyone falling off would be minimized (De 22:8; "battlement," KJV).

PAR′ BAR

A section on the western side of the court of the temple (2 Ki 23:11; 1 Ch 26:18).

PARCHED CORN

Roasted grain. This was one of the first foods that the Israelites ate upon entering the land of Canaan (Jos 5:11). Roasted grain continued to be a staple food (Ru 2:14; 2 Sa 17:28).

PARCH′ MENT

A thin piece of animal skin, scraped smooth to make a clean writing surface (2 Ti 4:13). Parchment was made from sheep or goat skin, or sometimes deer skin.

PARDON

To forgive, to excuse an offense without requiring payment (Mi 7:18).

PAR′ ENTS

While the Fifth Commandment sets forth the duty of children to parents, the obligations parents sustain to their children are clearly taught. The child should be trained to fear the Lord, and the parent to refrain provoking their children unnecessarily (De 6:7; Ep 6:4).

PAR′ LOR

A cool airy room built upon the roof of a house, as in the case of the parlor of Eglon (Ju 3:20-25). A parlor was also a room in the house used to receive guests (1 Sa 9:22). The word is also

used to refer to the inner rooms of the temple (1 Ch 28:11).

PAR·MASH′ TA

A son of Haman (Es 9:9).

PAR′ ME·NAS

One of the seven deacons selected to care for the temporal interests of the widows and financial matters of the early church (Ac 6:5).

PAR′ NACH

A man of Zebulun, father of Elizaphan (Nu 34:25).

PAR′ OSH *(a flea)*

1. The ancestor of 2172 captives who returned with Zerubbabel (Ez 2:3; Ne 7:8, also called Pharosh). Another group of people descended from this man also returned with Ezra (Ez 8:3).

2. A man who signed the covenant with Nehemiah (Ne 10:14, also called Pharosh).

PAROUSIA

The transliteration of the Greek word used to speak of the second coming of Christ (Tit 2:13), it could be translated "appearance," "arrival," or "presence."

PAR·SHAN·DA′ THA

The eldest of Haman's ten sons (Es 9:7).

PAR′ SIN

See MENE, MENE, TEKEL, UPHARSIN.

PAR′ THI·ANS

Inhabitants of Parthia, a region which, in the fifth century B.C., corresponded closely to the modern Persian province of Khorasan. People from this area were present in Jerusalem at Pentecost (Ac 2:9). Parthia was one of the provinces of Persia which Darius set up (Da 6:1).

PARTIALITY

Favoritism. God commanded His people to judge justly, and not to show partiality to the rich or mighty or to those who offer bribes (Le 19:15; De 16:19). God is completely impartial, He is not influenced by wealth or position, and He never takes bribes (2 Ch 19:7). The Christian church is supposed to operate on these same

PARTRIDGE

principles, for in Christ, all have equal value (Ga 3:28).

PAR·TI′ TION, MID′ DLE WALL OF
See MIDDLE WALL.

PAR′ TRIDGE
A game bird hunted on the mountains of Palestine (Is 34:15). Partridges were considered clean and suitable for food. A startled partridge flees with a great racket of whirring wings; David compared his flight from Saul with the flight of a partridge (1 Sa 26:20).

PA′ RU·AH *(increase)*
The father of a purveyor of Solomon in Issachar (1 Ki 4:17).

PAR·VA′ IM
The name of a place where gold was found, probably a locality in Ophir (2 Ch 3:6).

PARZITES
The descendants of Perez, son of Judah (Nu 26:20; Perezite, NASB, NIV, NRSV; Pharzites, KJV).

PA′ SACH *(to divide)*
A son of Japhlet of Asher (1 Ch 7:33).

PAS·DAM′ MIM
A place where David's mighty men defeated the Philistines (1 Ch 11:13-14).

PA·SE′ AH *(lame)*
1. A son of Eshton of Judah (1 Ch 4:12).
2. The head of a family of Nethinim (Ez 2:49; Ne 3:6; Phaseah, KJV).

PASH′ HUR
Several Old Testament men:
1. Head of a priestly family (Ez 2:38; Ne 7:41). Some of this family had married foreign women, whom they later divorced (Ez 10:22). Probably the same as Pashur (1 Ch 9:12).
2. A priest who sealed the covenant with Nehemiah (Ne 10:3).

3. Son of Immer, a priest. He persecuted Jeremiah because of his predictions (Je 20:1-6).
4. Son of Melchiah and a bitter foe of Jeremiah (Je 21:1; 38:1,4).
5. Father of Gedaliah and an opponent of Jeremiah (Je 38:1). He may be the same person as number 3 or 4.

PASHUR
Head of a priestly family who returned to Israel from Babylon (1 Ch 9:12), probably the same as PASHHUR No. 1.

PAS′ SAGES
1. The right to pass through. The Edomites refused to allow the Israelites to travel through their land on their way to Canaan (Nu 20:21).
2. A place where one can cross a river, a ford (Je 51:32).

PASSION OF CHRIST
The KJV word used to speak of the suffering and death of the Lord Jesus Christ (Ac 1:3).

PASS′ O·VER *(passing over)*
The first of the three annual Hebrew festivals at which all the men must appear at the sanctuary (Ex 12:43; 13:3-10; De 16:1). The Passover commemorated the sparing of the Hebrew firstborn in the tenth plague of Egypt, and the exodus. Moses warned the people that if they would save their firstborn sons from the angel of death, they must kill a lamb and spread its blood upon their doorposts. When the angel saw the blood, it would pass over them. They were to prepare the lambs at twilight, and eat the roasted meat with bitter herbs and unleavened bread. They must be dressed for travel, and eat in haste. Every year following, they were to repeat the Passover meal: roasted lamb, bitter herbs, and unleavened bread (Ex 12:1–13:10).

The Passover meal is a clear type of Christ. Christ Himself is our "Passover Lamb," whose blood rescues us from death (1 Co 5:7). He is without blemish, pure and sinless (Ex 12:5; 1 Pe 1:18-19); that a bone should not be broken (Ex 12:46; Jo 19:36). The present day Jewish Seder meal has many traditions added to the exodus account, and these also point to the Messiah.

PASTOR
Shepherd. This word is a descriptive term for a believer who has been given the gift of leading,

serving, and caring for other believers (Ep 4:11). Jesus is the true Shepherd of our souls; the Good Shepherd who knows His sheep, and cares for them to the point of giving His life for them (Jo 10). Those who are given the work of spiritual shepherds have a great responsibility. The prophet Jeremiah spoke very strongly against the false shepherds who destroyed and scattered rather than building up and serving (Je 23:1-2).

PASTORAL EPISTLES

The last three letters written by the apostle Paul are known as the Pastoral Epistles—so named because they deal with matters pertaining to pastors, or shepherds of God's people. The Epistles of 1 Timothy and Titus are our earliest guides to church organization; they are noted for their lists of qualifications for elders and deacons in the early church. All three of these epistles emphasize sound doctrine, challenging believers to good works.

First Timothy was written from Macedonia to remind Paul's young preacher friend and colleague, who was ministering in Ephesus, to preach sound doctrine (1:3-11) and to avoid false teaching (6:20-21). The Epistles emphasized the conduct of public worship (2:8-15) and gave instructions to both servants and the wealthy. Paul also urged Timothy to be diligent and faithful (4:11-16).

Second Timothy was written several years later during Paul's final Roman imprisonment. The apostle encouraged Timothy to be trustworthy in carrying out his responsibilities (2:1-13), even in times of hardship, and to preach the Word faithfully in the future when additional testings were sure to come (3:1-9). Even as he praised Timothy, Paul warned him of pitfalls that could be hindrances to his ministry (4:1-5).

The Letter to Titus, a Greek who had become a believer under Paul's ministry (Gal 2:3), was written at about the same time as 1 Timothy. Paul had left Titus on the island of Crete in the Mediterranean Sea to supervise a large ministry. He encouraged Titus to organize the church carefully—to ordain qualified persons (1:5-16), rebuke false teachers (3:9-11), preach sound doctrine, and encourage good works (3:1-8).

These letters contained important messages for early Christian churches, and they also serve as a model for effective church life today.

PAT'A·RA

A city southwest of Lycia (Ac 21:1).

PATE (archaic)

Forehead; crown of the head (Ps 7:16).

PATH'ROS

The name of upper (southern) Egypt (Is 11:11). Some Jews moved to Pathros after the fall of Judah (Je 44:1-2,15-16). Ezekiel prophesied the judgment of the Egyptians, but also promised that God would one day return them to Pathros, their own land (Eze 29:14; 30:13-18).

PATH·RU'SIM

A people descended from Mizraim (Ge 10:14; 1 Ch 1:12).

PATIENCE

One of the fruits of the Spirit (Ga 5:22). The ability to wait peacefully and hopefully. The heroes of faith inherited the promises after much patient waiting, and their patience under suffering is an example to us (He 6:12; Jam 5:10). Jesus illustrated the patience and forbearance of God in His parable of the unmerciful servant (Ma 18:26,29). God does not quickly bring us to the judgment we deserve, rather He is patient and longsuffering, leading us to repentance by His goodness (Ro 2:4; 2 Pe 3:9).

We often equate patience with passiveness, but this is far from a true definition of the word. Paul urged the believers in Rome to bear tribulation patiently, and in the same verses, he also urged them to be "not lacking in diligence, fervent in spirit, serving the Lord, rejoicing in hope . . . continuing steadfastly in prayer, distributing to the needs of the saints, given to hospitality" (Ro 12:12). In the midst of all this activity, there is no room for passive waiting. Patience is active. After describing the faith and patience of those who have gone before us, the author of Hebrews urges all believers "since we are surrounded by so great a cloud of witnesses," to throw off every encumbrance, and "run with patience" (KJV) the race set before us. One cannot run a race passively and expect to win. This kind of patience is not sitting back and waiting. It is running with endurance, running to win and not giving up when the end looks small and far away.

PAT′MOS

A rocky island in the Grecian Archipelago, one of the Sporades, off the southwestern coast of Asia Minor. It is a barren land about thirty miles in circumference. The apostle John was banished here in the reign of Domitian, and it was here he received the visions related in the Book of Revelation (Re 1:9). See REVELATION, BOOK OF.

PA′TRI·ARCH

The founder of a family or a race. In the New Testament this term is applied to Abraham, the head of the messianic nation (He 7:4); also to the sons of Jacob (Ac 7:8-9), Jacob, the father of Israel, and to David (Ac 2:29). It applies to the heads of families of the age prior to the time of Moses so that the Patriarchal Era was the period prior to the institutions of Sinai.

PATRIMONY

The inheritance passed down from a father to his descendants (De 18:8).

PAT′RO·BAS

A Christian of the Roman church to whom Paul sent greetings (Ro 16:14).

PATTERN

See TYPE.

PA′U *(bleating)*

A town of Edom (Ge 36:39); in 1 Chronicles 1:50 it is called Pai.

PAUL *(little)*

The great Apostle to the Gentiles. Though he was responsible for the persecution of Christians before his conversion (Ac 9:1-9), he became a faithful follower of Christ, a dedicated missionary, and a respected leader in the early church. His Hebrew name was Saul; at some point, for unknown reasons, he took the name Paul, and this is the name he is best remembered by. It is used for the first time in the account of his visit to Paphos, where Sergius Paulus was converted (Ac 12:9). He was of the tribe of Benjamin, a native of Tarsus, the chief city of Cilicia (Ac 9:11; 21:39; 22:3; Ph 3:5). In this intellectual center, the seat of a famous school of philosophy, he was reared under Grecian influences. Like other Jewish boys he was

taught a trade, and learned to make tents (Ac 18:3). In Jerusalem he was trained in the Scriptures by one of the most learned and distinguished rabbis of the day, Gamaliel, grandson of the famous Hillel. He was a Pharisee, an able student, and well versed in the Scriptures. He was an eager and enthusiastic persecutor of the followers of the new Way (Ac 9:1-2); he was one who stood by giving his approval of Stephen's murder (Ac 8:1), and "made havoc of the church," dragging men and women alike to prison (Ac 8:3). This persecution was undoubtedly hard to bear, but it had unlooked-for results. As the believers scattered from the "hot spot" in Jerusalem, they carried the good news with them, and Christianity was spreading like wildfire. In an attempt to once more bring this strange sect to an end, Paul determined to travel to Damascus and hunt out the believers there to drag them into Jerusalem to stand trial before the religious authorities. While on the road to carry out his plans, Paul was stunned by a bright light, and the voice of Jesus spoke to him, calling him by name, and demanding, "why are you persecuting Me?" Paul was both terrified and astonished, but when he realized that the same Jesus he had been persecuting was the one who had spoken to him, he completely changed his mind. Struck blind by the light, he was taken into Damascus, where he was healed and baptized by a believer named Ananias (Ac 9:1-25). After his conversion, Paul spent several years in his home city of Tarsus until Barnabas asked him to join him in teaching the newly formed church at Antioch (Ac 11:19-26). Later Paul participated in three great missionary journeys extending from Jerusalem and Antioch westward through Cyprus and Asia Minor, and even into Europe. Among his traveling companions at various times were Barnabas, John Mark, Silas, and Luke. One of his journeys took him back to Jerusalem where he was taken prisoner, and then sent to Rome to await trial. He is believed to have been released and then imprisoned again, suffering martyrdom in Rome late in the reign of Nero (about A.D. 67). Thirteen letters written by Paul during his lifetime, under the inspiration of the Spirit, are preserved in the New Testament: Romans, 1 and 2 Corinthians, Galatians, Ephesians, Philippians, Colossians, 1 and 2 Thessalonians, 1 and 2 Timothy, Titus, and Philemon.

PAUL'S LIFE, INDEXED

Recorded Events	Place	A.D.	Reference
Born at Tarsus, the capital of Cilicia	Tarsus	1-5	Ac 22:3
Learns the trade of tent making	Tarsus		Ac 18:3
Taught according to "the perfect manner of the law of the fathers" by Gamaliel	Jerusalem		Ac 22:3
While a "young man" he participated vigorously in the persecution of Christians			Ac 7:58; 8:1-3
Still breathing out murderous threats, he obtained a commission from the high priest to go into Damascus on his cruel errand of persecution	Damascus		Ac 9:1-2; 22:4-5; 26:9-12
Near Damascus a vivid, miraculous light shone from heaven and blinded him, both Saul and his company fell to the earth	Near Damascus	36	Ac 9:3-4, 8
Jesus spoke to him, directing him to go into the city to learn what he should do next	Near Damascus		Ac 9:4-6, 22; 1 Co 15:8
He arose and was led into Damascus, where he remained blind for three days	Damascus		Ac 9:7-9
Ananias, being sent by the Lord, came to Paul, restored his sight and baptized him	Damascus		Ac 9:10-18
He immediately began preaching Christ in the synagogue, amazing those who had known him as a persecutor of the church	Arabia and Damascus		Ac 9:20-22; Ga 1:17
The Jews of Damascus lay in wait day and night to kill him, but he escaped by being let down out of a window in the wall in a basket at night		36	Ac 9:23-25; 2 Co 11:33
He proceeded to Jerusalem, where the disciples were at first afraid of him, but being convinced of the change in his character, received him into their fellowship	Jerusalem		Ac 9:26-28
He preached boldly; the Jews again sought his life and he escaped to his native city	Tarsus		Ac 9:29-30
Some time later, Barnabas went to Tarsus after him, to ask him to assist in teaching in Antioch	Antioch	43	Ac 11:25-26
Barnabas and Paul carried relief to the poor brethren in Judea	Judea	44	Ac 11:29-30
Having fulfilled their charge, they returned to Antioch, accompanied by John Mark	Antioch		Ac 12:25

Recorded Events	Place	A.D.	Reference
Paul and Barnabas were set apart by the church at Antioch, as commanded by the Holy Ghost, for missionary work among the Gentiles; they started on their first tour, taking Mark with them; at Salamis they preached in the synagogue	Salamis	46	Ac 13:1-5
At Paphos, Elymas (Bar-jesus), the sorcerer, was struck blind; Sergius Paulus, the proconsul, was converted	Paphos		Ac 13:6-12
They traveled to Perga, in Pamphylia, where Mark left them	Perga		Ac 13:13
Thence they went to Antioch, in Pisidia, where Paul preached a powerful sermon to the Jews	Antioch		Ac 13:14-48
From there they traveled to Iconium, where many were converted	Iconium		Ac 13:51; 14:1
They went to Lystra and Derbe; at the former, Paul cured the man lame from his birth and people regarded the apostles as gods	Lystra and Derbe; Derbe		Ac 14:2-10; Ac 14:11-18
Not long after some Jews from Antioch (in Pisidia) and Iconium induced the fickle people of Lystra to stone Paul; they left him for dead but he recovered and he and Barnabas went to Derbe	Derbe		Ac 14:19-20
Thence they went again via Lystra to Perga, in Pampylia, and into Attalia, and then returned to Syrian-Antioch, ending Paul's first missionary tour	Antioch		Ac 14:21-28
Paul attended the church council	Jerusalem	52	Ac 15:1-21
Paul went back to Antioch, bearing the decision to the Gentile churches in Syria	Antioch		Ac 15:22-35
His second missionary tour commenced		53	Ac 15:36-40
He passed through Syria and Cilicia to Derbe and Lystra, where he met with Timothy	Derbe and Lystra		Ac 16:1-3
He traveled from city to city, doing much good			Ac 16:4-7
At Troas, Luke joined the company, and in response to a vision, Paul went into Macedonia; at Philippi, Lydia was converted	Troas and Philippi		Ac 16:8-15
Paul exorcised a spirit of divination from a young girl, whose masters brought him and Silas before the magistrates; they were cast into prison			Ac 16:16-24

Recorded Events	Place	A.D.	Reference
At midnight the prison doors were miraculously opened and their bonds loosed; the jailer was converted			Ac 16:25-34
In the morning they were released and departed from Philippi, going to Thessalonica, where many people were converted	Thessalonica		Ac 16:35; 17:1-4
Paul and his company went to Berea, where they were very successful	Berea		Ac 17:5-12
Thence to Athens, where Paul delivered a powerful sermon, and converted but few people	Athens	54	Ac 17:13-34
He soon went to Corinth; here he preached on the Sabbaths; he remained in this city a year and a half	Corinth	55	Ac 18:1-17
He went to Ephesus; touching at Caesarea, to Jerusalem, and returned to Antioch	Ephesus, etc.		Ac 18:18-22
After a brief rest, he made a rapid tour (the third) through Galatia and Phrygia		56	Ac 18:23
He went again to Ephesus, where he baptized twelve of John the Baptist's disciples in Jesus's name and they received the Holy Spirit; he preached almost two years in the school of Tyrannus	Ephesus	58	Ac 19:1-20
Paul left Ephesus and visited Macedonia and Greece; then returned to Philippi	Philippi	59	Ac 19:21–20:5
He went to Troas, where Eutychus was killed by a fall from an upstairs window and was restored to life; he sailed to Miletus	Troas		Ac 20:6-12
Thence they sailed to Caesarea, where Agabus foretold what awaited Paul in Jerusalem; he went to Jerusalem	Caesarea		Ac 21:1-26
Paul was seized and cast out of the temple, but was rescued by a Roman officer; he was granted permission to speak to the multitude, and made his defense	Jerusalem		Ac 21:27–22:29
Being arraigned before the Sanhedrin, Paul skillfully set his judges at variance, and was again taken in charge by the Roman authorities; the Lord appeared to him and encouraged him, telling him that he was to bear witness in Rome			Ac 22:30–23:11
He was arraigned before Felix; Tertullus made a plausible speech of accusation, which Paul effectually answered	Caesarea		Ac 24

Recorded Events	Place	A.D.	Reference
Paul was arraigned successfully before Festus and Agrippa; though guilty of no crime, he appealed to Caesar and they could not release him		62	Ac 25–26
Paul was sent a prisoner on board a ship bound for Rome; they were wrecked on Melita.	Malta		Ac 27
Here Paul was bitten by a viper without injury; he cured the father of Publius of a fever			Ac 28:1-10
They sailed after three months' delay for Rome	Rome	63	Ac 28:11-16
Paul preached to the chief of the Jews; he dwelled two years in his own hired house, "preaching the Kingdom of God and teaching those things which concern the Lord Jesus Christ, with all confidence, no man forbidding him"			Ac 28:17-31

PAUL'S MAJOR TEACHINGS

Next to the Master Teacher Himself, the apostle Paul is probably the most eloquent and persuasive teacher in the Bible. Many of the doctrines he expounded are considered the hallmarks of the Christian faith.

Here are a few of his major teachings.

1. *Justification by faith.* According to Paul, God ushered in a new era through the death of His Son. Under the Old Covenant, people, such as Abraham, were justified by believing God, looking forward to the promise of the coming Messiah (see Ge 15:6; Ro 4:22). Now we are justified, or declared righteous before God through faith in the Messiah, Jesus Christ, and His atoning death on our behalf. Our justification is based on the work of Christ, accomplished through His blood (Ro 5:9), and is brought to His people through His resurrection (Ro 4:25).

2. *Jesus Christ as the risen and living Son of God.* From the moment Jesus appeared to Paul at his dramatic conversion, Paul never hesitated to proclaim Him as the mystery of the ages and the great Redeemer of sinful humanity (1 Co 15:1-20). To Paul, Jesus was the Messiah, God's Son, the center of the gospel, and the One through whom "all things were created" (Col 1:16).

3. *The Church as the body of Christ.* The only New Testament writer who speaks of the church as a body, Paul emphasized this fact in such passages as Ephesians 1:22-23; 4:7-16; and 1 Corinthians 12. He also reminded Christians that their various gifts were to be used in building up the body of Christ and that they should work together for the common good of the Christian cause (Ro 12: 4-5).

4. *The power and influence of the Holy Spirit in the Christian's life.* Paul taught that the Holy Spirit was a more effective power for holy living in the Christian's life than the old Jewish law had ever been. The law told people what to do, but it could not provide the will or the power to do it. God's Spirit could provide the necessary power and motivation (Ro 8:9-17; Ga 5:16-25).

5. *The second coming of Christ and the consummation of the kingdom of God as the redeemed are received into God's presence.* Paul taught that Christ will return to earth at the end of this age and that all Christians will share in His glory in the age to come (1 Th 4:13-18; 1 Co 15:20-28).

PAULOS
See PAUL.

PAULUS, SERGIUS
See SERGIUS PAULUS.

PAVE′ MENT
The place where Pilate sat in the judgment seat to listen to the evidence against Jesus (Jo 19:13). See GABBATHA.

PAVILION
Tent, tabernacle, a moveable shelter (2 Ki 16:18; Je 43:10). Psalms 27:5 and 31:20 refer to God's "pavilion" as a place of shelter and safety for the righteous.

PE
The seventeenth letter of the Hebrew alphabet. It is the heading of verses 129-136 of Psalm 119. In Hebrew each of these eight verses began with the letter pe. See ACROSTIC.

PEACE
A sense of well-being and tranquility; freedom from fear and strife. Peace has a connotation of security (Ps 4:8); prosperity (Ps 122:6-7); and the ending of hostilities between warring parties (1 Sa 7:14). The path to peace is submission to God's rule over us (Ps 119:165) and the centering of our minds on Him (Is 26:3). Jesus Christ is the Prince of Peace (Is 9:6-7). At His advent the angels proclaimed "Peace on earth," and when He was preparing for His death, He promised His disciples that He would give this peace to them. This peace belongs to every believer who has faith in God (Ro 5:1).

PEACE OF′ FER·ING
See OFFERINGS.

PEA′ COCK
A bird which is native to India. It is about the size of a turkey, and the male of the species has a spectacular, brilliantly colored tail. Solomon imported peacocks along with other valuable and exotic items (1 Ki 10:22; 2 Ch 9:21; some translations say *baboon* or *monkey*).

PEARL
A precious jewel created by certain mollusks. When an irritant such as a bit of sand or a small stone becomes lodged in its shell, the creature coats it with a white, slightly translucent and slightly iridescent coating, similar to the coating on the inside of its shell. The beautiful white pearls thus made have long been considered valuable as jewels, though they are not gemstones. Jesus used pearls as an example of something of great value (Ma 7:6; 13:45-46). Paul lists pearls among other common adornments for women (1 Ti 2:9). The heavenly city of Revelation is described as having twelve gates made of pearl (Re 18:12,16; 21:21).

PEARL OF GREAT PRICE, PARABLE OF (Ma 13:45-46)

PECULIAR (archaic)
Belonging particularly to someone. Both Israel and the church are described as God's "peculiar people," His special treasure, the people belonging particularly to Him (Ex 19:5; De 14:2; 1 Pe 2:9).

PE·DAH′ EL *(God saves)*
Son of Ammihud and prince of Naphtali (Nu 34:28).

PE·DAH′ZUR (*a rock saves*)

Father of Gamaliel, prince of Manasseh. He assisted Moses in numbering the people (Nu 1:10; 2:20; 7:54,59; 10:23).

PE·DAI′ AH (*Jehovah hath saved*)

1. Maternal grandfather of Jehoiakim, king of Judah (2 Ki 23:36).

2. Brother of Shealtiel (Salathiel), possibly, but not probably, his son (1 Ch 3:18-19); also held to be the father of Zerubbabel by the widow of Salathiel. A descendant of Jeconiah. See ZE-RUBBABEL.

3. Father of Joel, prince of Manasseh (1 Ch 27:20).

4. A son of Parosh who labored on the wall of Jerusalem (Ne 3:25).

5. One who stood by Ezra as he taught the people (Ne 8:4).

6. A Benjamite of the family of Jeshaiah (Ne 11:7).

7. A Levite, one of the treasurers in the time of Nehemiah (Ne 13:13).

PEG

Tent peg; the nail or pin used to anchor a tent to the ground. The pegs for the tabernacle were made of bronze (Ex 27:19; Nu 3:37; 4:32). Sisera was killed by the woman Jael who pounded a tent peg through his head with a hammer (Ju 4:21-22; 5:26). Tent pegs could be made of wood or metal.

PE′ KAH (*opening of the eyes*)

The son of Remaliah and king of the eighth dynasty of Israel. He was a captain of King Pekahiah until he killed the king and assumed the throne (2 Ki 15:25-28).

PEK·A·HI′ AH (*Jehovah hath given sight*)

Son of Menahem and second king of the seventh dynasty of Israel (2 Ki 15:23-26).

PE′ KOD

A name applied to Babylonia, under divine judgment (Je 50:21; Eze 23:23).

PE·LAI′ AH (*distinguished by Jehovah*)

1. Son of Elioenai of Judah (1 Ch 3:24).

2. One who helped explain the law to the people as Ezra read it aloud (Ne 8:7).

3. A Levite who sealed the covenant (Ne 10:10).

PEL·A·LI′ AH (*Jehovah has judged*)

A priest, a descendant of Malchijah (Ne 11:12).

PEL·A·TI′ AH (*Jehovah has freed*)

1. Son of Hananiah, descendant of Salathiel (1 Ch 3:21).

2. A Simeonite captain who participated in the war with the Amalekites, son of Ishi (1 Ch 4:42).

3. A chief of the people who signed the covenant (Ne 10:22).

4. Son of Benaiah. In a vision Ezekiel saw Pelatiah die as the prophet prophesied (Eze 11:1-13).

PE′ LEG (*division*)

Son of Eber, a descendant of Noah through Shem (Ge 10:25; 11:16). His name means divided, and Scripture records that he received this name because "in his days the earth was divided" (Ge 10:25; 1 Ch 1:19). Some believe that this is a reference to the scattering of the people of the earth after their languages were confused at Babel. Others surmise that it is a reference to a physical/geographical change on the earth's surface which possibly caused natural land bridges between continents to be flooded, thus dividing the earth. No one knows for sure exactly why Peleg received his name.

PE′ LET (*liberation*)

1. Son of Jahdai (1 Ch 2:47).

2. Son of Azmaveth (1 Ch 12:3).

PE′ LETH (*swiftness*)

1. A Reubenite, father of On (Nu 16:1).

2. Son of Jonathan (1 Ch 2:33).

PEL′ E·THITES

Faithful soldiers who belonged to David's bodyguard (2 Sa 15:18-22; 20:7).

PEL′ I·CAN

A bird which inhabits waste places such as marshes and ruins (Is 34:11; Zep 2:14). Pelicans are among the largest of the web-footed birds with a potential wing span of up to 10 feet. They feed on fish, which they scoop up in their beaks. They are remarkable for the unique pouch of skin under the lower half of the beak; this serves as a handy carrying pocket and serving bowl as they collect fish to feed their youngsters. Pelicans were considered ceremonially unclean (Le 11:18; De 14:17). Whether the bird in the Scripture references is really the pelican is not certain. The underlying Hebrew word is also rendered *jackdaw, cormorant, vulture,* and *desert owl* in various different translations.

PELLA

One of the ten cities of the Decapolis. This city is not mentioned by name in the Bible, but the Decapolis is mentioned (Ma 4:25; Mk 5:20; 7:31).

PE'LO·NITE

Designations for Helez and Ahijah, two of David's mighty men (1 Ch 11:27,36). Helez was said to be of the tribe of Ephraim (1 Ch 27:10). He is also called the Paltite in 2 Samuel 23:26.

PEN

1. An instrument made of a reed for writing on papyrus with ink (2 Jo 12; 3 Jo 13).

2. An engraving tool used to cut letters in stone (Job 19:24; Ps 45:1; Je 8:8; 17:1).

PENDANT

An article of jewelry; a jewel or gold ornament suspended from an earring or necklace (Ju 8:26; "collars," KJV).

PEN'I·EL

See PENUEL.

PE·NIN'NAH *(coral)*

The second wife of Elkanah, Samuel's father (1 Sa 1:2-6). Peninnah ridiculed Elkanah's other wife, Hannah, because she was barren.

PENKNIFE

A scribe's knife, the knife used for making pens or cutting papyrus or parchment sheets. When Jehudi read to Jehoiakim, king of Judah, from the scroll of Jeremiah's prophecy, the king only listened to a few columns before he took the scroll and cut it up with his pen knife and burned it (Je 36:23, KJV).

PEN'NY

The KJV rendering of the Greek *denarion*. This Roman silver coin was worth a day's wage (Ma 18:28; 20:2; 22:19-21; Mk 6:37; 12:15; Lk 20:24; Jo 6:7; Re 6:6). See MONEY OF THE BIBLE.

PEN'TA·TEUCH

A Greek word meaning "five volumes," refers to the first five books of the Old Testament—Genesis, Exodus, Leviticus, Numbers, and Deuteronomy. The Jews traditionally refer to this collection as "the Book of the Law," or simply "the Law." Another word for this collection of sacred writings is *Torah,* which means "instruction," "teaching," or "doctrine."

The Pentateuch was also called "the Law of the LORD" (2 Ch 31:3) and "the Book of the Law of God" (Ne 8:18). The word *book* should not be understood in the modern sense, however, for many different writing materials were used in Old Testament times, including papyrus or leather scrolls and clay tablets.

The five books of the Pentateuch present a history of humanity from creation to the death of Moses, with particular attention to the development of the Hebrew people. The God revealed in these books is not only the Judge of the earth but also the loving Father of all humankind. In the last book of the Pentateuch, Moses pleaded with the people to observe God's laws and commandments after they settled in their permanent home in the land of Canaan (De 4).

The Pentateuch is generally divided into six major sections: (1) the creation of the world (Ge 1–11); (2) the period from Abraham to Joseph (Ge 12–50); (3) Moses and the departure of the Israelites from Egypt (Ex 1–18); (4) God's revelation at Mount Sinai (Ex 19–Nu 10); (5) the wilderness wanderings (Nu 11–16); and (6) the addresses of Moses in the Book of Deuteronomy.)

From the time it was written, the Pentateuch has been accepted as the work of Moses. His specific writing or compiling activity is mentioned in Exodus (17:14; 24:4; 34:27). This tradition was supported by Jesus in New Testament times (Mk 12:26; Jo 7:23).

PENTATEUCH, SAMARITAN

See SAMARITAN PENTATEUCH.

PEN'TE·COST

A Jewish feast also known as the Feast of Weeks, which marked the completion of the barley harvest. On this annual holiday about 50 days after the resurrection of Jesus, Jewish people from throughout the Roman Empire were gathered in the city of Jerusalem to observe this great religious festival. When the Holy Spirit was poured out on the apostles, they began to speak with "other tongues," and all the people from other nations understood them perfectly (Ac 2:5-13). The different regions of the Roman Empire represented in Jerusalem on the Day of Pentecost included Judea, Lybia, Cyrene, Crete, Asia, Phrygia, Pamphylaia, Pontus, Cappadocia, Parthia, Media, Elam, Mesopotamia, Arabia, Egypt, and Rome herself.

PEN′U·EL *(face of God)*

1. A place east of the Jordan, the site unknown, where Jacob wrestled with the angel and saw God face-to-face on his way back to Canaan from Padan-aram (Ge 32:30-31). Later a city was built near this site; when Gideon was pursuing the Midianites, the people of this town refused to assist them and Gideon later killed the men of the city as revenge (Ju 8:17).

2. Son of Hur of the tribe of Judah (1 Ch 4:4).

3. Son of Shashak of Benjamin (1 Ch 8:25).

PEOPLE

See NATIONS.

PE′OR *(a cleft)*

1. A god of the Moabites worshipped in Mount Peor, frequently called Baal-peor. See BAAL-PEOR.

2. A mountain in Moab (Nu 23:28; 24:2).

PER′AD′VEN·TURE (archaic)

Perhaps (2 Ti 2:24-25).

PE·RAE′A

See PEREA.

PE·RA′ZIM

See BAAL-PERAZIM.

PERDITION

Destruction or ruin, particularly the eternal destruction which God will bring upon the wicked (He 10:39; 2 Pe 3:7; Ma 7:13; Ph 1:28; 1 Ti 6:9; 2 Pe 3:7). Judas Iscariot is described as a "son of perdition." The same word is used to describe the "man of sin" or "man of lawlessness" (Jo 17:12; 2 Th 2:3). The word also refers to the place of eternal punishment (Re 17:8,11).

PE·RE′A

The name given by Josephus to the region east of the Jordan.

PEREA

PERES *(divided)*

The singular form of *parsin,* one of the words which appeared in the mysterious handwriting on the wall at Belshazzar's feast. *Upharsin* means *"and parsin."* (Da 5:25,28). See MENE, MENE, TEKEL, UPHARSIN.

PE′RESH

Son of Machir (1 Ch 7:16).

PER′EZ *(a breach)*

A twin son of Judah and Tamar (Ge 38:24-30), also called Pharez (KJV).

PEREZITES

See PARZITES.

PE′REZ-UZ′ZA, PE′REZ-UZ′ZAH
(breach of Uzza)

The place where Uzza died when he placed his hand upon the ark (2 Sa 6:8; 1 Ch 13:11).

PERFECT

Without fault, flawless; complete or fulfilled. God is the only one who is truly perfect (Job 36:4; Ps 18:20; 19:7; Ma 5:48).

The word *perfect* is also used in Scripture in a less exact sense, to describe one who leads a righteous lifestyle; not indicating sinlessness, but position before God (Ge 6:9; Job 1:1; Jam 3:2). Maturity is referred to as "perfection" (Ph 3:15;

Jam 1:4); even though a mature person will continue to deal with sin (Ph 3:12,15; 1 Jo 1:8). However, in the next life, perfection will be actual (Ep 5:27; Col 1:28; 1 Th 5:23).

PER′ FUME

A sweet-smelling substance which consisted of various spices such as cassia, aloes, myrrh, spikenard, frankincense, and cinnamon. In the sanctuary it was used as incense (Ex 30:22-38).

PERFUMER

One who compounds perfumes. Professional perfumers were employed in the service of the tabernacle, to make fine perfumes and incense for the worship services (Ex 30:25,35; 1 Ch 9:30). Apparently this was work which was commonly done by women (1 Sa 8:13), as well as men (Ne 3:8). The KJV uses the terms *apothecary* and *confectioner* to speak of perfumers.

PER′ GA *(citadel)*

The capital of Pamphylia (Ac 13:13-14; 14:25). See PAMPHYLIA.

PER′ GA·MOS *(citadel)*

A city in northwest Asia Minor where one of the seven churches addressed by the apostle John in the Book of Revelation (Re 2:12-17) was located. The city was a center of Greek culture for many years; its magnificent library contained more than 200,000 volumes. Parchment, a superior writing material, was developed and manufactured at Pergamos.

John issued the church at Pergamos a stern warning against compromise with evil (Re 2:13). As capital of the Roman province of Asia, the city became the first site where the cult of emperor worship was practiced, beginning in 29 B.C. This shameful distinction may have caused John to identify Pergamos as the site "where Satan's throne is" (Re 2:13). Refusal to burn incense before the Roman emperor's statue brought charges of disloyalty and possibly death. Antipas, a Christian leader, was martyred, perhaps for his refusal to worship the emperor (Re 2:13).

Pergamos was also a center of other types of idolatry and pagan worship. The city featured temples dedicated to worship of the chief pagan god Zeus and to Aesculapius, the Greco–Roman God of healing.

The Christian community in Pergamos was too tolerant of evil. Some church teachers apparently advised Christians to participate in immoral sexual practices, as well as pagan worship (Re 2:14-15). John commanded, on behalf of the Lord, "Repent, or else I will come to you quickly and will fight against them with the sword of My mouth" (Re 2:16). Choice spiritual blessings were promised to those Christians who were faithful witnesses (Re 2:17).

The Pergamos of New Testament times has disappeared, although the site is occupied today by the town of Bergama in modern Turkey. Excavation of the old city has uncovered the ruins of the temple where the Roman emperor was worshipped and a huge temple of Zeus.

PER′ GA·MUM

A variant of Pergamos.

PE·RI′ DA

See PERUDA.

PERISH

To die, to be destroyed, to come to an untimely end. Without the intervention of Christ, this is the fate of sinful humans (Jo 3:16).

PE·RIZ′ ZITES

A tribe of Palestine (Ge 15:20; Ex 3:8; Jos 9:1). They were in the land settled by Abraham and Lot (Ge 13:7).

PERJURY

To violate a sworn promise. See OATH.

PERSECUTION

Unjust attack by hostile opponents. Jesus warned His disciples that because the world is hostile to the light of God's truth, they could expect it to be hostile to them in the same way (Jo 15:18-22). The prophets of God have always faced persecution (Ma 5:12; He 11:35-38). While persecution for the sake of Christ may be very hard to bear, Jesus said that those who are persecuted are blessed, or happy (Ma 5:10). The early church had ample opportunity to discover the truth of this, as they were persecuted heavily by the Jewish religious leaders (Ac 5:14,34; 23:6). Later, the Roman government joined the ranks of persecutors. Many Christians met terrible deaths at the hands of sinful men, even as has happened to the prophets of God's truth since Cain murdered Abel.

PERSEVERANCE

Not giving up; determined pursuit of a goal. God has called believers to persevere in the struggle against sin, looking ahead to eternity (Ga 6:9).

PER'SIA

A territory bounded on the north by Media, on the south by the Persian Gulf, on the west by Elam, on the east by Carmania. Persia became the second world empire and was brought into direct relation with the Jews.

The Persians apparently sprang from a people from the hills of Russia who began to settle in upper Mesopotamia and along the Black Sea as early as 2000 B.C. Ancient Media was located in what is now northwestern Iran, west of the Caspian Sea. Cyrus the Great, first ruler of the Persian Empire, united the Medes and Persians to conquer Babylonia and Assyria, thus becoming the dominant power of the ancient world.

After his conquest of Babylonia about 539 B.C., Cyrus authorized the rebuilding of the temple at Jerusalem and the resettlement of the Jewish community in their homeland (2 Ch 36:22-23). Many of the Israelites had been carried to Babylonia as captives after the fall of Jerusalem about 586 B.C. (2 Ch 36:17-21).

Of all the ancient peoples who lived in the upper reaches of the Tigris and Euphrates Rivers, the Medes and Persians probably had the greatest influence on the Israelites. The prophet Isaiah wrote that Cyrus, although he did not know God, was anointed by God for the special mission of returning God's people to Jerusalem (Is 45:1,4).

Daniel 6:8-9 refers to "the law of the Medes and Persians." Once a Persian law was handed down by the king, it could not be changed or revoked. While he was a captive in the royal court of the Babylonians, Daniel predicted that Babylonia would fall to the Medes and Persians (Da 5).

The Book of Esther records events that occurred during the reign of King Ahasuerus, or Xerxes, of Persia in the fifth century B.C. By faithfully recording the manners and customs of the Persian Empire, the book serves as a reliable historical record of the period.

Among the nations of the ancient world, Persia is noted for its beautiful cities. Persepolis, the nation's ceremonial capital, was a showplace of Persian culture. Ecbatana, capital of the Median Empire, became a resort city for the Persians.

Susa, called Shushan in the Book of Esther, was the capital of the Elamites before it became the administrative capital of the Persian Empire.

The Book of Esther records events during the reign of King Ahasuerus (Xerxes) in the fifth century B.C. at Shushan (Susa), administrative capital of the Persian Empire. After the death of Darius I (the Persian king who had allowed any Jews who desired to return to their homeland to do so), his son Ahasuerus became king. Ahasuerus was the king who became dissatisfied with his queen Vashti and banished her, marrying Esther.

Royal Persian feasts were noted for their splendor and opulence. Esther describes the Persian custom of eating while reclining on beds or couches. All eating utensils were made of gold, "each vessel being different from the other" (Es 1:7).

Special laws protected the Persian king. Esther 1:14 refers to the seven princes who "had access to the king's presence." These were the chief nobles who were his advisors. Only a person summoned by the king could visit him, a custom which signified his royalty, as well as protected him from would-be assassins. Esther feared going to Ahasuerus without being called, because the punishment for such a visit was death (Es 4:11).

The Persian Empire boasted a well-organized postal system (Es 3:13). The king's ring (Es 8:8) was the signet ring with which official documents were signed. In ancient Persia, documents were sealed in two ways: with a signet ring if they were written on papyrus, or with a cylinder seal if written on clay tablets. Among the objects excavated at the royal city of Persepolis was a cylinder seal, which belonged to King Xerxes.

The Book of Esther refers to "the laws of the Persians and Medes" (1:19). This phrase, also used in Daniel 6, again refers to the ironclad nature of the laws that governed the Persian Empire. Once a law was issued, it could not be changed or revoked—not even by the king himself, not even at the request of his beloved queen, not even if it was shown to have been made out of spite and injustice. That was why King Darius had to allow Daniel, who he knew was a faithful servant, to be put into the lion's den, and later King Ahasuerus found himself with the same situation in the case of Haman requesting a "law" to set a day to kill all the Jews. The king could not change the law, but he could provide a way for the Jews to protect themselves with his sanction, which effectively countered the earlier decree.

PER′SIS

A Christian of the Roman church (Ro 16:12).

PERSISTENT WIDOW, PARABLE OF
(Lk 18:1-8)

PE·RU′DA *(a kernel)*

A servant of Solomon (Ez 2:55; also called Perida, Ne 7:57).

PESTILENCE (archaic)

Plague, disease.

PES′TLE

A short, blunt instrument used for crushing grain in a mortar (Pr 27:22).

PE′TER *(rock)*

His name was formerly Simon, the son of Jonas (Jo 1:42; 21:15-16). He was a native of Bethsaida (Jo 1:44) but later dwelt at Capernaum (Ma 8:14; Lk 4:38). His brother Andrew, a disciple of John the Baptist, brought him to Jesus, whose disciple he became (Jo 1:40). He became associated with Jesus (Ma 4:19; Mk 1:17; Lk 5:10) and then became an apostle (Ma 10:2; Lk 6:13-14). He was a man of great earnestness, was self-assertive and impulsive, and had the qualities of leadership. In the lists of the apostles his name is always first (Ma 17:1; Mk 5:37; 9:2; 13:3; Lk 8:51; 9:28). In the fishing industry he was in partnership with Zebedee and his two sons on the Sea of Galilee (Ma 4:18; Mk 1:16; Lk 5:3) but, with James and John, he responded without hesitation to the call of Christ. He, with James and John, beheld the marvelous transfiguration of Christ (Ma 17:1-2), and they were again his companions in the scene of Jesus's agony in Gethsemane (Ma 26:36-37). Peter played an important role in the early church, and in the spread of the gospel to the Samaritans and Gentiles (Ac 2-10). After the Jerusalem Council of Acts 15, little is recorded of Peter's activities. He evidently traveled extensively with his wife (1 Co 9:5) and ministered in various Roman provinces. According to tradition, Peter spent his last years in Rome and was eventually martyred there, being crucified upside down sometime before Nero's death in A.D. 68.

The Catholic teaching that Peter was the first Pope in Rome is based upon their interpretation of Matthew 16:18. However one interprets this passage, papal succession is neither mentioned or implied.

PE′TER, E·PIS′TLES OF

1. The Book of 1 Peter. Persecution can cause either growth or bitterness in the Christian life. Response determines the result. In writing to Jewish believers struggling in the midst of persecution, Peter encourages them to conduct themselves courageously for the Person and program of Christ. Both their character and conduct must be above reproach. Having been born again to a living hope, they are to imitate the Holy One who has called them. The fruit of that character will be conduct rooted in submission: citizens to government, servants to masters, wives to husbands, and Christians to one another. Only after submission is fully understood does Peter deal with the difficult area of suffering. The Christians are not to think it "strange concerning the fiery trial which is to try you, as though some strange thing happened to you" (4:12), but are to rejoice as partakers of the sufferings of Christ. That response to life is truly the climax of one's submission to the good hand of God.

This epistle begins with the phrase *Petros apostolos Iesou Christou,* "Peter, an apostle of Jesus Christ." This is the basis of the early title *Petrou A,* the "First of Peter."

2. The Author of 1 Peter. The early church universally acknowledged the authenticity and authority of 1 Peter. The internal evidence supports this consistent external testimony in several ways. The apostle Peter's name is given in 1:1, and there are definite similarities between certain phrases in this letter and Peter's sermons as recorded in the Book of Acts (1 Pe 1:20 and Ac 2:23; 1 Pe 4:5 and Ac 10:43). Twice in Acts Peter used the Greek word *xylon,* "wood, tree," to speak of the cross, and this distinctive use is also found in 1 Peter (see 2:24; Ac 5:30; 10:39). The epistle contains a number of allusions to events in the life of Christ that held special significance for Peter (2:23; 3:18; 4:1; 5:1,5; Jo 13:4).

Nevertheless, critics since the nineteenth century have challenged the authenticity of 1 Peter on several grounds. Some claim that 1:1-2 and 4:12–5:14 were later additions that turned an anonymous address or a baptismal sermon into a Petrine epistle. Others argue that the sufferings experienced by readers of this letter must refer to the persecution of Christians that took place after the time of Peter in the reigns of the emperors Domitian (A.D. 81-96) and Trajan (A.D. 98-117). There is no basis for the first argument, and the second argument falsely assumes that Christians were not being reviled for their faith during the life of Peter. Another challenge asserts that the quality of the Greek of this epistle is too high for a Galilean like Peter. But Galileans were bilingual (Aramaic and Greek), and writers such as Matthew and James were skillful in their use of Greek. It is also likely that Peter used Silvanus as his scribe (5:12; Paul calls him Silvanus in 2 Co 1:19; 1 Th 1:1; 2 Th 1:1; Luke calls him Silas in Ac 15:40–18:5), and Silvanus may have smoothed out Peter's speech in the process.

3. The Time of 1 Peter. This letter is addressed "to the strangers scattered," or more literally, "pilgrims of the Dispersion" (1:1). This, coupled with the injunction to keep their behavior "honorable among the Gentiles" (2:12), gives the initial appearance that the bulk of the readers are Hebrew Christians. A closer look, however, forms the opposite view that most of these believers were Gentiles. They were called "out of darkness" (2:9), and they "once were not a people but are now the people of God" (2:10). Their former "aimless conduct received by tradition from their fathers" was characterized by ignorance and futility (1:14,18; Ep 4:17). Because they no longer engage in debauchery and idolatry, they are maligned by their countrymen (4:3-4). These descriptions do not fit a predominantly Hebrew Christian readership. Though Peter was an apostle "to the circumcised" (Ga 2:9), he also ministered to Gentiles (Ac 10:34-48; Ga 2:12), and a letter like this would not be beyond the scope of his ministry.

This epistle was addressed to Christians throughout Asia Minor, indicating the spread of the gospel in regions not evangelized when Acts was written (Pontus, Cappadocia, Bithynia; 1:1). It is possible that Peter visited and ministered in some of these areas, but there is no evidence. He wrote this letter in response to the news of growing opposition to the believers in Asia Minor (1:6; 3:13-17; 4:12-19; 5:9-10). Hostility and suspicion were mounting against Christians in the empire, and they were being reviled and abused for their lifestyles and subversive talk about another kingdom. Christianity had not yet received the official Roman ban, but the stage was being set for the persecution and martyrdom of the near future.

Peter's life was dramatically changed after the resurrection, and he occupied a central role in the early church and in the spread of the gospel to the Samaritans and Gentiles (Ac 2-10). After the Jerusalem Council in Acts 15, little is recorded of Peter's activities. He evidently traveled extensively with his wife (1 Co 9:5) and ministered in various Roman provinces. According to tradition, Peter was crucified upside down in Rome prior to Nero's death in A.D. 68.

This epistle was written from Babylon (5:13), but scholars are divided as to whether this refers literally to Babylon in Mesopotamia or symbolically to Rome. There is no tradition that Peter went to Babylon, and in his day it had few inhabitants. On the other hand, tradition consistently indicates that Peter spent the last years of his life in Rome. As a center of idolatry, the term "Babylon" was an appropriate figurative designation for Rome (the later use of Babylon in Re 17-18). Peter used other figurative expressions in this epistle, and it is not surprising that he would do the same with Rome. His mention of Mark (5:13) also fits this view because Mark was in Rome during Paul's first imprisonment (Col 4:10). This epistle was probably written shortly before the outbreak of persecution under Nero in A.D. 64.

4. The Christ of 1 Peter. This epistle presents Christ as the believer's example and hope in times of suffering in a spiritually hostile world. He is the basis for the Christian's "living hope" and "inheritance" (1:3-4), and the love relationship available with Him by faith is a source of inexpressible joy (1:8). His suffering and death provide redemption for all who trust in Him: "who Himself bore our sins in His own body on the tree, that we, having died to sins, might live for righteousness—by whose stripes you were healed" (2:24; 1:18-19; 3:18). Christ is the Chief Shepherd and Overseer of believers (2:25; 5:4), and when He appears, those who know Him will be glorified.

5. Keys to 1 Peter.
Key Word: Suffering for the Cause of Christ—The basic theme of 1 Peter is the proper response to Christian suffering. Knowing that his readers will be facing more persecution than ever before, Peter wrote this letter to give them a divine perspective on these trials so that they will be able to endure them without wavering

in their faith. They should not be surprised at their ordeal because the One they follow also suffered and died (2:21; 3:18; 4:1,12-14). Rather, they should count it a privilege to share the sufferings of Christ. Peter therefore exhorts them to be sure that their hardships are not being caused by their own wrongdoings, but for their Christian testimony. They are not the only believers who are suffering (5:9), and they must recognize that God brings these things into the lives of His children, not as a punishment but as a stimulus to "perfect you" in Christ (5:10). Peter wanted to overcome the attitudes of bitterness and anxiety, replacing them with dependence on and confidence in God.

Another theme is stated in 5:12: "I have written to you briefly, exhorting and testifying that this is the true grace of God." In this epistle, Peter frequently speaks of the believer's position in Christ and future hope, and he does so to remind his readers that they are merely sojourners on this planet: their true destiny is eternal glory "when His glory is revealed" (4:13). The grace of God in their salvation (1:1–2:10) shall give them an attitude of submission (2:11–3:12) in the context of suffering for the name of Christ (3:13–5:14).

Key Verses: 1 Peter 1:10-12 and 4:12-13— "Of this salvation the prophets have inquired and searched diligently, who prophesied of the grace that would come to you, searching what, or what manner of time, the Spirit of Christ who was in them was indicating when He testified beforehand the sufferings of Christ and the glories that would follow. To them it was revealed that, not to themselves, but to us they were ministering the things which now have been reported to you through those who have preached the gospel to you by the Holy Spirit sent from heaven— things which angels desire to look into" (1:10-12).

"Beloved, do not think it strange concerning the fiery trial which is to try you, as though some strange thing happened to you; but rejoice to the extent that you partake of Christ's sufferings, that when His glory is revealed, you may also be glad with exceeding joy" (4:12-13).

Key Chapter: 1 Peter 4—Central in the New Testament revelation concerning how to handle persecution and suffering caused by one's Christian testimony is 1 Peter 4. Not only is Christ's suffering to be our model (4:12), but also we are to rejoice in that we can share in His suffering (4:12-14).

6. Survey of 1 Peter. Peter addresses this epistle to "pilgrims" in a world that is growing increasingly hostile to Christians. These believers are beginning to suffer because of their stand for Christ, and Peter uses this letter to give them counsel and comfort by stressing the reality of their living hope in the Lord. By standing firm in the grace of God (5:12) they will be able to endure their "fiery trial" (4:12), knowing that there is a divine purpose behind their pain. This letter logically proceeds through the themes of the salvation of the believer (1:1–2:12); the submission of the believer (2:13–3:12); and the suffering of the believer (3:13–5:14).

Salvation of the Believer (1:1–2:12). Addressing his letter to believers in several Roman provinces, Peter briefly describes the saving work of the triune Godhead in his salutation (1:1-2). He then extols God for the riches of this salvation by looking in three temporal directions (1:3-12). First, Peter anticipates the future realization of the Christian's manifold inheritance (1:3-5). Second, he looks at the present joy that this living hope produces in spite of various trials (1:6-9). Third, he reflects upon the prophets of the past who predicted the gospel of God's grace in Christ (1:10-12).

The proper response to this salvation is the pursuit of sanctification or holiness (1:13–2:10). This involves a purifying departure from conformity with the world to godliness in behavior and love. With this in mind, Peter exhorts his readers to "desire the pure milk of the word, that they may grow" (2:2) by applying "the word of God which lives and abides forever" (1:23) and acting as a holy priesthood of believers.

The Submission of the Believer (2:13–3:12). Peter turns to the believer's relationships in the world and appeals for an attitude of submission as the Christlike way to harmony and true freedom. Submission for the Lord's sake to those in governmental (2:13-17) and social (2:18-20) authority will foster a good testimony to outsiders. Before moving on to submission in marital relationships (3:1-7), Peter again picks up the theme of Christian suffering (mentioned in 1:6-7 and 2:12,18-20) and uses Christ as the supreme model: He suffered sinlessly, silently, and as a substitute for others (2:21-25; Is 51:13–53:12). Peter summarizes his appeal for Christlike submission and humility in 3:8-12.

The Suffering of the Believer (3:13–5:14). Anticipating that growing opposition to Christianity will require a number of his readers to defend their faith and conduct, Peter encourages them to be ready to do so in an intelligent and gracious way (3:13-16). Three times he tells them that if they must suffer, it should be for righteousness sake and not as a result of sinful behavior (3:17; see 2:20; 4:15-16). The end of this chapter (3:18-22) is an extremely difficult passage to interpret, and several options have been offered. Verses 19-20 may mean that Christ, during this period between His death and resurrection, addressed demonic spirits or the spirits of those who were alive before the flood. Another interpretation is that Christ preached through Noah to his pre-flood contemporaries.

As believers in Christ, the readers are no longer to pursue the lusts of the flesh as they did formerly, but rather the will of God (4:1-6). In view of the hardships that they may suffer, Peter exhorts them to be strong in their mutual love and to exercise their spiritual gifts in the power of God so that they will be built up (4:7-11). They should not be surprised when they are slandered and reviled for their faith because the sovereign God has a purpose in all things, and the time of judgment will come when His name and all who trust in Him will be vindicated (4:12-19). They must therefore "commit their souls to Him in doing good" (4:19).

In a special word to the elders of the churches in these Roman provinces, Peter urges them to be diligent but gentle shepherds over the flocks that have been divinely placed under their care (5:1-4). The readers as a whole are told to clothe themselves with humility toward one another and toward God who will exalt them at the proper time (5:5-7). They are to resist the adversary in the sure knowledge that their calling to God's eternal glory in Christ will be realized (5:8-11). Peter ends his epistle by stating his theme ("the true grace of God") and conveying greetings and a benediction (5:12-14).

OUTLINE OF 1 PETER

Part One: The Salvation of the Believer (1:1–2:12)

I. Salutation (1:1-2)

II. Salvation of the Believer (1:3-12)

A. Hope for the
Future 1:3-4
B. Trials for the
Present..................................... 1:5-9
C. Anticipation in the
Past 1:10-12

III. Sanctification of the Believer (1:13–2:12)

A. "Be Holy" 1:13-21
B. "Love One Another" 1:22-25
C. "Desire the Pure Milk of the
Word" 2:1-3
D. "Offer Up Spiritual
Sacrifices" 2:4-10
E. "Abstain from Fleshly Lusts" ... 2:11-12

Part Two: The Submission of the Believer (2:13–3:12)

I. Submission to the Government (2:13-17)

II. Submission in Business (2:18-25)

III. Submission in Marriage (3:1-8)

IV. Submission in All of Life (3:9-12)

Part Three: The Suffering of the Believer (3:13–5:14)

I. Conduct in Suffering (3:13-17)

II. Christ's Example of Suffering (3:18–4:6)

III. Commands in Suffering (4:7-19)

IV. Minister in Suffering (5:1-9)

A. Elders, Shepherd the Flock............ 5:1-4
B. Saints, Humble Yourselves 5:5-9

V. Benediction (5:10-14)

7. The Book of 2 Peter. First Peter deals with problems from the outside; Second Peter deals with problems from the inside. Peter writes to warn the believers about the false teachers who are peddling damaging doctrine. He begins by urging them to keep close watch on their personal lives. The Christian life demands diligence in pursuing moral excellence, knowledge, self-control, perseverance, godliness, brotherly kindness, and selfless love. By contrast, the false teachers are sensual, arrogant, greedy, and covetous. They scoff at the thought of future judgment and live their lives as if the present would be the pattern for the future. Peter reminds them that although God may be longsuffering in sending judgment, ultimately it will come. In view of that fact, believers should live lives of godliness, blamelessness, and steadfastness.

The statement of authorship in 1:1 is very clear: "Simon Peter, a servant and apostle of Jesus Christ." To distinguish this epistle from the first by Peter it was given the Greek title *Petrou B,* "Second of Peter."

8. The Author of 2 Peter. No other book in the New Testament poses as many problems of authenticity as does 2 Peter. Unlike 1 Peter, this letter has very weak external testimony, and its genuineness is hurt by internal difficulties as well. Because of these obstacles, many scholars reject the Petrine authorship of this epistle, but this does not mean that there is no case for the opposite position.

External Evidence. The external testimony for the Petrine authorship of 2 Peter is weaker than that for any other New Testament book, but by the fourth century it became generally recognized as an authentic work of the apostle Peter. There is no undisputed second century quotations from 2 Peter, but in the third century it is quoted in the writings of several church fathers, notably Origen and Clement of Alexandria. Third century writers were generally aware of 2 Peter and respected its contents, but it was still catalogued as a disputed book. The fourth century saw the official acknowledgement of the authority of 2 Peter in spite of some lingering doubts. For several reasons 2 Peter was not quickly accepted as a canonical book: (1) Slow circulation kept it from being widely known. (2) Its brevity and contents greatly limited the number of quotations from it in the writings of the early church leaders. (3) The delay in recognition meant that 2 Peter had to compete with several later works which falsely claimed to be Petrine (such as the Apocalypse of Peter). (4) Stylistic differences between 1 and 2 Peter also raised doubts.

Internal Evidence. On the positive side, 2 Peter bears abundant testimony to its apostolic origin. It claims to be by "Simon Peter" (1:1), and 3:1 says "Beloved, I now write to you this second epistle." The writer refers to the Lord's prediction about the apostle's death in 1:14 (Jo 21:18-19) and says he was an eyewitness of the transfiguration (1:16-18). As an apostle (1:1), he places himself on an equal level with Paul (3:15). Here are also distinctive words that are found in 2 Peter and in Peter's sermons in Acts, as well as unusual words and phrases shared by 1 and 2 Peter.

On the negative side, a number of troublesome areas challenge the traditional position: (1) There are differences between the style and vocabulary of 1 and 2 Peter. The Greek of 2 Peter is rough and awkward compared to that of 1 Peter, and there are also differences in informality and in the use of the Old Testament. But these differences are often exaggerated, and they can be explained by Peter's use of Silvanus as his secretary for 1 Peter and his own hand for 2 Peter. (2) It is argued that 2 Peter used a passage from Jude to describe false teachers, and that Jude was written after Peter's death. However, this is a debated issue, and it is possible that Jude quoted from Peter or that both used a common source (see JUDE, EPISTLE OF: The Author of Jude). (3) The reference to a collection of Paul's letters (3:15-16) implies a late date for this epistle. But it is not necessary to conclude that all of Paul's letters were in mind here. Peter's contact with Paul and his associates no doubt made him familiar with several Pauline Epistles. (4) Some scholars claim that the false teaching mentioned in 2 Peter was a form of Gnosticism that emerged after Peter's day, but there is insufficient evidence to support this stand.

The alternative to Petrine authorship is a later forgery done in the name of Peter. Even the claim that 2 Peter was written by a disciple of Peter cannot overcome the problem of misinterpretation. In addition, 2 Peter is clearly superior to any pseudonymous writings. In spite of the external and internal problems, the traditional position of Petrine authorship overcomes more difficulties than any other option.

9. The Time of 2 Peter. Most scholars regard 3:1 ("Beloved, I now write to you this second epistle") as a reference to 1 Peter. If this is so, Peter had the same readers of Asia Minor in mind (see "The Time of 1 Peter"), although the more general salutation in 1:1 would also allow for a wider audience. Peter wrote this epistle in response to the spread of heretical teachings which were all the more insidious because they emerged from within the churches. These false teachers perverted the doctrine of justification and promoted a rebellious and immoral way of life.

This epistle was written just before the apostle's death (1:14), probably from Rome. His martyrdom took place between A.D. 64 and 66 (if Peter were alive in 67 when Paul wrote 2 Timothy during his second Roman imprisonment, it is likely that Paul would have mentioned him).

10. The Christ of 2 Peter. Apart from the first verse of his epistle, Peter employs the title *Lord* every time he names the Savior. The Lord Jesus Christ is the source of full knowledge and power for the attainment of spiritual maturity (1:2-3,8; 3:18). Peter recalls the glory of His transfiguration on the holy mountain and anticipates His *parousia,* "coming," when the whole world, not just three men on a mountain, will behold His glory.

11. Keys to 2 Peter.

Key Word: Guard Against False Teachers—The basic theme that runs through 2 Peter is the contrast between the knowledge and practice of truth versus falsehood. This epistle is written to expose the dangerous and seductive work of false teachers, and to warn believers to be on their guard so that they will not be "led away with the error of the wicked" (3:17). It is also written to exhort the readers to "grow in Jesus Christ" (3:18), because this growth into Christian maturity is the best defense against spiritual counterfeits. This letter serves to remind its readers of the foundational elements in the Christian life from which they must not waver (1:12-13; 3:1-2). This includes the certainty of the Lord's return in power and judgment.

Key Verses: 2 Peter 1:20-21 and 3:9-11— "Knowing this first, that no prophecy of Scripture is of any private interpretation, for prophecy never came by the will of man, but holy men of God spoke as they were moved by the Holy Spirit" (1:20-21).

"The Lord is not slack concerning His promise, as some count slackness, but is longsuffer-

ing toward us, not willing that any should perish but that all should come to repentance. But the day of the Lord will come as a thief in the night, in which the heavens will pass away with a great noise, and the elements will melt with fervent heat; both the earth and the works that are in it will be burned up. Therefore, since all these things will be dissolved, what manner of persons ought you to be in holy conduct and godliness" (3:9-11).

Key Chapter: 2 Peter 1—The Scripture clearest in defining the relationship between God and man on the issue of inspiration is contained in 1:19-21. Three distinct principles surface: (1) that the interpretation of Scriptures is not limited to a favored elect but is open for all who "rightly divide the word of truth" (2 Ti 2:15); (2) that the divinely inspired prophet did not initiate the Scripture himself, and (3) that the Holy Spirit (not the emotion or circumstances of the moment) moved holy men.

12. Survey of 2 Peter. Peter wrote his first epistle to encourage his readers to respond properly to external opposition. His second epistle focuses on internal opposition caused by false teachers whose "destructive heresies" (2:1) can seduce believers into error and immorality. While 1 Peter speaks of the new birth through the living Word, 2 Peter stresses the need for growth in the grace and knowledge of Christ. The best antidote for error is a mature understanding of the truth. Second Peter divides into three parts: cultivation of Christian character (1); condemnation of false teachers (2); and confidence of Christ's return (3).

Cultivation of Christian Character (1). Peter's salutation (1:1-2) is an introduction to the major theme of chapter 1, that is, the true knowledge of "great and precious promises" that are theirs because of their calling to faith in Christ (1:3-4). They have been called away from the corruption of the world to conformity with Christ, and Peter uges them to progress by forging a chain of eight Christian virtues from faith to love (1:5-7). If a believer does not transform profession into practice, he becomes spiritually useless, perverting the purpose for which he was called (1:8-11).

This letter was written not long before Peter's death (1:14) to remind believers of the riches of their position in Christ and their responsibility to hold fast to the truth (1:12-21). Peter knew that his departure from this earth was imminent and he left this letter as a written legacy. As an eyewitness of the life of Christ (he illustrates this with a portrait of the transfiguration in 1:16-18), Peter affirms the authority and reliability of the prophetic word. The clearest biblical description of the divine-human process of inspiration is found in 1:21; "but holy men of God spoke as they were moved by the Spirit."

Condemnation of False Teachers (2). Peter's discussion of true prophecy leads him to an extended denunciation of false prophecy in the churches. These false teachers were especially dangerous because they arose within the church and undermined the confidence of believers (2:1-3). Peter's extended description of the characteristics of these false teachers (2:10-22) exposes the futility and corruption of their strategies. Their teachings and lifestyles reek of arrogance and selfishness, but their crafty words are capable of enticing immature believers.

Confidence of Christ's Return (3). Again Peter states that this letter is designed to stir up the minds of his readers "by way of reminder" (1:13; 3:1). This very timely chapter is designed to remind them of the certain truth of the imminent *parousia* (this Greek word, used in 3:4,

12, refers to the second coming or advent of Christ) and to refute those mockers who will deny this doctrine in the last days. These scoffers will claim that God does not powerfully intervene in world affairs, but Peter calls attention to two past events and one future event showing the tremendous power of God at work on earth: the creation, the flood, and the dissolution of the present heavens and earth (3:1-7). It may appear that the promise of Christ's return will not be fulfilled, but this is untrue for two reasons: God's perspective on the passing of time is quite unlike that of men, and the apparent delay in the *parousia* is due to His patience in waiting for more individuals to come to a knowledge of Christ (3:8-9). Nevertheless, the day of consummation will come, this present world will be burned up, and God will fashion a new cosmos (3:10-13).

In light of this coming day of the Lord, Peter exhorts his readers to live lives of holiness, steadfastness, and growth (3:14-18). He mentions the letters of "our beloved brother Paul" and significantly places them on a level with the Old Testament Scriptures (3:15-16). After a final warning about the danger of false teachers, the epistle closes with an appeal to growth, and a doxology.

OUTLINE OF 2 PETER

I. Cultivation of Christian Character (1:1-21)

A. Salutation 1:1-2
B. Growth in Christ 1:3-14
C. Grounds of Belief 1:15-21

II. Condemnation of False Teachers (2:1-22)

A. Danger of False
Teachers 2:1-3

B. Destruction of False
Teachers 2:4-9
C. Description of False Teachers...... 2:10-22

III. Confidence of Christ's Return (3:1-18)

A. Mockery in the Last Days 3:1-7
B. Manifestation of the Day of
the Lord 3:8-10
C. Maturity in View of the Day of
the Lord 3:11-18

PETER, GOSPEL OF

See APOCRYPHA.

PETH·A·HI' AH *(freed by Jehovah)*

1. A priest whose family in the time of David became the nineteenth course of priests (1 Ch 24:16).

2. A man of the family of Zerah of Judah, in the service of Artaxerxes. His work was relative to Jewish interests (Ne 11:24).

3. A Levite (Ez 10:23), probably the same as in Nehemiah 9:5.

PE' THOR

A town in Mesopotamia (Nu 22:5; 23:7; De 23:4).

PE·THU' EL *(enlarged of God)*

Father of the prophet, Joel (Joel 1:1).

PETITION

Request, prayer. See PRAYER.

PETRA

The unique red rock city south of the Dead Sea. Many of the buildings of this ruined city are carved directly into the face of the huge rock cliffs. It was the capital of Nabatea, and is believed by some scholars to be the Sela mentioned in Judges 1:36 and 2 Kings 14:7. Most of the monuments, temples, and buildings date from approximately 50 B.C. to A.D. 150. The beautiful pagan temple to the goddess Isis was commissioned by the Emporer Hadrian in A.D. 131. The city is located in a basin only about one mile long and 3,000 feet wide, surrounded by high red rock cliffs. The only entrance to this secluded basin is a narrow gorge almost a mile long; this geographical arrangement made the city easy to defend against invasion.

PE·UL′LE·THAI

Ssee PEULTHAI.

PE·UL′THAI

Son of Obed-edom, a Levite and porter of the tabernacle (1 Ch 26:5).

PETRA

PHA′LEC (Lk 3:35)

See PELEG.

PHAL′LU

See PALLU.

PHAL′TI

See PALTI.

PHAL′TI·EL

See PALTIEL.

PHA·NU′EL *(face of God)*

Father of Anna, the prophetess (Lk 2:36).

PHA′RAOH

The title of the kings of Egypt. The word means "great house." Used originally to describe the king's palace, the term came to mean something like "his honor" or "his majesty."

The Egyptians believed their ruler was a god and the key to the nation's relationship to the cosmic gods of the universe. His word was law, and he owned everything in the land. When Pharaoh died, he became the ruler of the underworld and those who live after death. The Egyptians took great pains to prepare their dead for the afterlife. They perfected the intricate process of mummification. In lavish interiors of the great pyramids of Egypt the mummified bodies of royalty were buried, along with many of their earthly treasures.

In all, there were thirty dynasties of Pharaohs during Egypt's long history. Several different accounts in the Old Testament refer to a Pharaoh. Abraham's wife Sarah was summoned to Pharaoh's palace (Ge 12:14-20). Solomon married the daughter of a Pharaoh, who became a firm ally of the Hebrew monarch (1 Ki 3:11). This Pharaoh later conquered the city of Gezer and gave it to his daughter as a dowry (1 Ki 9:16). Jeroboam sought refuge in the court of the Pharaoh Shishak (1 Ki 11:40).

The most famous Pharaoh in the Bible is the ruler of whom Moses asked permission to lead the Israelites out of Egypt. Scholars debate whether this was Amenhotep II (ruled 1450-1423 B.C.) or Raameses II (ruled 1301-1234 B.C.). This Egyptian ruler repeatedly refused to release the people, in spite of the plagues God sent to break his will. Only when the Pharaoh's son was killed in the last plague did he submit to God's power and let the people go (Ex 12:29-33).

During his ministry as a refugee in Egypt, the prophet Jeremiah predicted that Pharaoh Hophra, king of Egypt, would be overthrown by his enemies, just as the nation of Judah had been defeated by the Babylonians (Je 44:30).

Following is a list of the Pharaohs mentioned in the Bible:

Name	Scripture Reference
Pharaoh (probably a ruler of the 12th Dynasty)	Ge 12:14-20
Pharaoh (probably a Hyksos king of the 15th Dynasty)	Ge 37–50
King of Egypt; Pharaoh (Thutmos III (?) 1504-1450 B.C.)	Ex 1–2
Pharaoh (Amenhotep II (?) 1450-1425 B.C.)	Ex 5–12
Pharaoh (probably Siamun; 978-959 B.C.)	1 Ki 3:1; 7:8; 9:16,24; 11:1
Pharaoh, king of Egypt (Amenemope; 993-984 B.C.; or Siamun)	1 Ki 11:18-22
Shishak (Sheshonq I; 945-924 B.C.)	1 Ki 11:40; 14:25-26; 2 Ch 12:1-12
So, king of Egypt (Osokorn IV (?) 727-716 B.C.)	2 Ki 17:4
Tirhakah (Tarharqa; 690-664 B.C.)	2 Ki 19:9; Is 37:9
Pharaoh Neco (Neco II; 610-595 B.C.)	2 Ki 23:29; 2 Ch 35:20-24
Pharaoh Hophra (Waibre; 589-570 B.C.)	Je 44:30; Eze 17:11-21; 29:1-16

PHA′RAOH'S DAUGHTER

Three Egyptian princesses are named in Scripture:

1. The daughter of Pharaoh who rescued the infant Moses and raised him as her own son (Ex 2:5-10).

2. The bride of Solomon, king of all Israel. He built her a splendid house in Jerusalem (1 Ki 3:1; 7:8; 9:24).

3. The wife of Mered, a descendant of Judah (1 Ch 4:18).

PHA′RAOH, WIFE OF (1 Ki 11:18-20)

See TAHPENES.

PHAR′ES

See PEREZ.

PHARISEE AND PUBLICAN (or TAX COLLECTOR), PARABLE OF (Lk 18:9-14)

PHAR′I·SEES (separated)

The Pharisees were one of the two major sects or special-interest groups among the Jews in New Testament times. These groups (the Pharisees and Sadducees) stood for different principles, but Jesus clashed with both parties at different times during his ministry.

The word *Pharisee* means "separated." Their burning desire was to separate themselves from those people who did not observe the laws of tithing and ritual purity—matters they considered very important. The sect arose prior to the period of the Maccabees when there was a tendency on the part of the Jews to adopt Grecian customs. In opposition to this, the Pharisees conformed in the strictest manner to the Mosaic institutions. The name "Pharisee" was first used in the time of John Hyrcanus.

The Pharisees exerted strong influence in Jesus's time. The essential characteristic of their religion was conformity to the law. In addition to the Mosaic law they adhered strongly to traditions of the elders. They supported the scribes and rabbis in their interpretation of the Jewish law as handed down from the time of Moses. In Jesus's day, this interpretation of the law had become more authoritative and binding than the law itself. Jesus often challenged these traditional interpretations and the minute rules that had been issued to guide the people in every area of their behavior.

Jesus was also sensitive to the needs and hurts of individuals—an attitude that brought Him into conflict with the Pharisees. Matthew's Gospel (23:1-36) contains Jesus's harsh words against the Pharisees. He accused them of placing too much emphasis on minor details, while ignoring "the weightier matters of the law," such as "justice and mercy and faith" (Ma 23:23).

PHARISEE

The Pharisees often tried to trick Jesus into making statements that would be considered heretical or disloyal to Rome. On one occasion, Jesus used a denarius, a common coin of the day, to show that citizens of His country had responsibilities to ruling authorities, as well as to God.

Not all Pharisees were legalistic and hypocritical, however. Three Pharisees favorably recognized in the New Testament are Joseph of Arimathea (Lk 23:50-53), Nicodemas (Jo 3:1-21), and Gamaliel (Ac 5:34-39).

The apostle Paul emphasized his own heritage as a Pharisee (Acts 22:3), but he also recognized the importance of abandoning this emphasis for the way of Christ (Ph 3:1-14).

The Pharisees were distinguished from the Sadducees in their doctrinal beliefs concerning belief in the resurrection and the immortality of the soul, and in angelic beings (Ac 23:8). See also SADDUCEES.

PHAR′ OSH

See PAROSH.

PHAR′ PAR *(swift)*

A river of Damascus mentioned by Naaman (2 Ki 5:12).

PHARZITES

Those descended from Perez, the son of Judah and Tamar (Nu 26:20).

PHA·SE′ AH

See PASEAH.

PHE′ BE

See PHOEBE.

PHE·NI′ CE

See PHOENICIA and PHOENIX.

PHE·NI′ CI·A

See PHOENICIA.

PHI′ CHOL *(mouth of all)*

A captain of Abimelech (Ge 21:22; 26:26).

PHI′ COL

See PHICHOL.

PHIL·A·DEL′ PHI·A *(brotherly love)*

A city of Lydia in Asia Minor, one of the seven churches addressed by Jesus in the beginning of John's vision (Re 1:11; 3:7-13).

PHI·LE′ MON *(affectionate)*

A Christian of Colosse, to whom the Paul's Epistle to Philemon is addressed. He was the owner of the runaway slave, Onesimus, for whom Paul pleads. See also PHILEMON, EPISTLE TO: The Time of Philemon.

PHI·LE′ MON, E·PIS′ TLE TO

1. The Book of Philemon. Does Christian brotherly love really work, even in situations of extraordinary tension and difficulty? Will it work, for example, between a prominent slave owner, and one of his runaway slaves? Paul had no doubt that it would. He wrote a "postcard" to Philemon, his beloved brother and fellow worker, on behalf of Onesimus—a deserter, thief, and formerly worthless slave, but now Philemon's brother in Christ. With much tact and tenderness, Paul asked Philemon to receive Onesimus back with the same gentleness with which he would receive Paul himself. Any debt Onesimus owed, Paul promised to make good. Knowing Philemon, Paul was confident that brotherly love and forgiveness would carry the day.

Since this letter is addressed to Philemon in verse 1, it became known as *Pros Philemona,* "To Philemon." Like 1 and 2 Timothy and Titus, it is addressed to an individual, but unlike the Pastoral Epistles, Philemon is also addressed to a family and a church (v. 2).

2. The Author of Philemon. The authenticity of Philemon was not called into question until the fourth century, when certain theologians concluded that its lack of doctrinal content made it unworthy of the apostle Paul. But men like Jerome and Chrysostom soon vindicated this epistle, and it was not challenged again until the nineteenth century. Some radical critics who denied the authenticity of Colossians also turned against the Pauline authorship of Philemon because of the close connection between the two epistles (the same people are associated with Paul in both letters; compare vv. 10,23-24; with Colossians 4:9-10,12,14). The general consensus of scholarship, however, recognized Philemon as Paul's work. There could have been no doctrinal motive for its forgery, and it is supported externally by consistent tradition and internally by no less than three references to Paul (vv. 1,9,19).

3. The Time of Philemon. Reconstructing the background of this letter, it appears that a slave named Onesimus had robbed or in some other way wronged his master Philemon and had escaped. He had made his way from Colosse to Rome where he had found relative safety among the masses in the Imperial City. Somehow Onesimus had come into contact with Paul: it is possible that he had even sought out the apostle for help. (Onesimus had no doubt heard Philemon speak of Paul.) Paul had led him to Christ (v. 10), and although Onesimus had become a real asset to Paul, both knew that as a Christian, Onesimus had a responsibility to return to Philemon. That day came when Paul wrote his Epistle to the Colossians. Tychicus was the bearer of that letter, and Paul decided to send Onesimus along with Tychicus to Colosse (v. 12; Col 4:7-9).

Philemon is one of the four Prison Epistles (see Ephesians, Philippians, and especially "The Time of Colossians" for background). It was written in A.D. 60 or 61 and dispatched at the same time as Colossians during Paul's first Roman imprisonment (1,9-10,13,23). Philemon 22 reflects Paul's confident hope of release: "prepare a guest room for me, for I trust that through your prayers I shall be granted to you."

Philemon was a resident of Colosse (vv. 1-2; Col 4:9,17) and a convert of Paul (v. 19), perhaps through an encounter with Paul in Ephesus during Paul's third missionary journey. Philemon's house was large enough to serve as the meeting place for the church there (v. 2). He was benevolent to other believers (vv. 5-7), and his son Archippus evidently held a position of leadership in the church (v. 2; Col 4:17). Philemon may have had other slaves in addition to Onesimus, and he was not alone as a slave owner among the Colossian believers (Col 4:1). Thus this letter and his responses would provide guidelines for other master-slave relationships.

According to Roman law, runaway slaves such as Onesimus could be severely punished or condemned to a violent death. It is doubtful that Onesimus would have returned to Philemon even with this letter if he had not become a believer in Christ.

4. The Christ of Philemon. The forgiveness that the believer finds in Christ is beautifully portrayed by analogy in Philemon. Although Onesimus was guilty of a great offense (vv. 11,18), Paul was moved to intercede on his behalf (vv. 10-17). Paul laid aside his rights (v. 8) and became Onesimus's substitute by assuming his debt (vv. 18-19). By Philemon's gracious act, Onesimus was restored and placed in a new relation-

ship (vv. 15-16). In this analogy, we are as Onesimus. Paul's advocacy before Philemon is parallel to Christ's work of mediation before the Father. Onesimus was condemned by law but saved by grace.

5. Keys to Philemon.

Key Word: Forgiveness—Philemon develops the transition from bondage to brotherhood that is brought about by Christian love and forgiveness. Just as Philemon was shown mercy through the grace of Christ, so he must graciously forgive his repentant runaway who has returned as a brother in Christ. Paul wrote this letter as his personal appeal that Philemon receive Onesimus even as he would receive Paul. This letter is also addressed to other Christians in Philemon's circle, because Paul wanted it to have an impact on the Colossian church as a whole.

Key Verses: Philemon 16-17—"No longer as a slave but more than a slave, as a beloved brother, especially to me but how much more to you, both in the flesh and in the Lord. If then you count me as a partner, receive him as you would me" (vv. 16-17).

6. Survey of Philemon. This briefest of Paul's Epistles (only 334 words in the Greek text) is a model of courtesy, discretion, and loving concern for the forgiveness of one who would otherwise face the sentence of death. This tactful and highly personal letter can be divided into three components: prayer of thanksgiving for Philemon (vv. 1-7); petition of Paul for Onesimus (vv. 8-16); promise of Paul to Philemon (vv. 17-25).

Prayer of Thanksgiving for Philemon (vv. 1-7). Writing this letter as a "prisoner of Christ Jesus," Paul addressed it personally to Philemon (a Christian leader in Colosse), to Apphia and Archippus (evidently Philemon's wife and son), as well as to the church that meets in Philemon's house. The main body of this compact letter begins with a prayer of thanksgiving for Philemon's faith and love.

Petition of Paul for Onesimus (vv. 8-16). Basing his appeal on Philemon's character, Paul refused to command Philemon to pardon and receive Onesimus. Instead, Paul sought to persuade his friend of his Christian responsibility to forgive even as he was forgiven by Christ. Paul urged Philemon not to punish Onesimus but to receive him "no longer as a slave" but as "a beloved brother" (v. 16).

Promise of Paul to Philemon (vv. 17-25). Paul placed Onesimus's debt on his account, but then reminded Philemon of the greater spiritual debt which Philemon himself owed as a convert to Christ (vv. 17-19).

Paul closed this effective epistle with a hopeful request (v. 22), greetings from his companions (vv. 23-24), and a benediction (v. 25). The fact that it was preserved indicates Philemon's favorable response to Paul's pleas.

OUTLINE OF PHILEMON

I. The Prayer of Thanksgiving for Philemon (1-7)

II. The Petition of Paul for Onesimus (8-16)

III. The Promise of Paul to Philemon (17-25)

PHILIPPI

PHI·LE′TUS *(beloved)*

A teacher condemned by Paul for false teaching concerning the resurrection (2 Ti 2:17-18).

PHIL′IP *(lover of horses)*

1. One of the twelve apostles. He lived in Bethsaida on the Sea of Galilee. He met Jesus beyond the Jordan and was called to be his disciple. Later, he brought Nathanael to Jesus (Jo 1:43-48). It was to him certain Greeks expressed their desire to see Jesus (Jo 12:20-21).

2. Philip the Evangelist. He was one of the seven deacons of the early church (Ac 6:5). When the disciples were dispersed by persecution, he preached in Samaria (Ac 8:4-8; 21:8). He was then divinely directed to go to Gaza where he met, taught, and baptized the eunuch (Ac 8:26-39) and went on to Caesarea (Ac 8:40). His four daughters had the gift of prophecy (Ac 21:8-9).

3. Son of Herod the Great and half brother of Herod Antipas (Ma 14:3; Lk 3:1).

4. Philip, the tetrarch. See HEROD.

PHI′LIP·PI

Philippi, known originally as Krenides (meaning "wells" or "springs"), was named after Philip II, father of the Greek conqueror Alexander the Great. This city of the Roman province of Macedonia was strategically located on the Egnatian Way, the main overland route between Asia and the West, making it an important bridge in the early spread of the gospel.

The ruins of the city bear the marks of a rich Roman history, including an agora, or marketplace, where trade took place, and the western arch, or "gate," of the city, described in Acts 16:13. The agora was an important archeological discovery, with its seat of judgment, library, and adjacent jail site, possibly the very place where Paul and Silas were imprisoned (Ac 16:23-40).

Paul founded the church at Philippi in the early fifties as the first church on European soil. Soon after he and Silas entered the city, they met with a group of women for prayer outside the city gate. This indicates that the city did not have a large Jewish population, since they generally preached at the local synagogue if one was available. When Paul and Silas cast the spirit out of the slave girl, her angry owners took them to court. Beaten and jailed, they prayed and sang until an earthquake shook the jail during the night. The next day the magistrates were alarmed to discover that Paul and Silas were Roman citizens and should not have been beaten or jailed without a fair trial.

Lydia, a businesswoman, became the first Christian convert in all of Europe through the witness of Paul and Silas at Philippi (Ac 16:12-15,40). Because of the influence of the church in this city, the way was opened for the gospel to spread to the rest of Europe.

PHILIPPIANS, EPISTLE TO THE

1. The Book of Philippians. Paul wrote a thank-you note to the believers at Philippi for their help in his hour of need, and he used the occasion to send along some instruction of Christian unity. His central thought is simple: Only in Christ are real unity and joy possible. With Christ as your model of humility and service, you can enjoy a oneness of purpose, attitude, goal, and labor—a truth which Paul illustrated from his own life, and one the Philippians desperately needed to hear. Within their own ranks, fellow workers in the Philippian church were at odds, hindering the work in proclaiming the new life in Christ. Because of this, Paul exhorts the church to "stand fast . . . be of the same mind . . . rejoice in the Lord always . . . but in everything by prayer and supplication, with thanksgiving, let your requests be made known . . . and the peace of God, which surpasses all understanding, will guard your hearts and minds through Christ Jesus" (4:1-2,4,6-7).

This epistle is called *Pros Philippesious,* "To the Philippians." The church at Philippi was the first church founded in Macedonia.

2. The Author of Philippians. The external and internal evidence for the Pauline authorship of Philippians is very strong, and there is scarcely any doubt that anyone but Paul wrote it.

3. The Time of Philippians. In 356 B.C., King Philip of Macedonia (the father of Alexander the Great) took this town and expanded it, renaming it Philippi. The Romans captured it in 168 B.C.; and in 42 B.C., the defeat of the forces of Brutus and Cassius by those of Anthony and Octavian (later Augustus) took place outside the city. Octavian turned Philippi into a Roman colony (Ac 16:12) and a military outpost. The citizens of this colony were regarded as citizens of Rome and given a number of special privileges. Because Philippi was a military city and not a commercial center, there were not enough Jews for a synagogue when Paul came (Ac 16:13).

Paul's "Macedonian Call" in Troas during his second missionary journey led to his ministry in Philippi with the conversion of Lydia and others. Paul and Silas were beaten and imprisoned, but this resulted in the conversion of the Philippian jailer. The magistrates were placed in a dangerous position by beating Roman citizens without a trial (Ac 16:37-40), and that embarrassment may have prevented future reprisals against the new Christians in Philippi. Paul visited the Philippians again on his third missionary journey (Ac 20:1,6). When they heard of his Roman im-

prisonment, the Philippian church sent Epaphroditus with financial help (4:18); they had helped Paul in this way on at least two other occasions (4:16). Epaphroditus almost died of an illness, yet remained with Paul long enough for the Philippians to receive word of his malady. Upon his recovery, Paul sent this letter back with him to Philippi (2:25-30).

Silas, Timothy, Luke, and Paul first came to Philippi in A.D. 51, eleven years before Paul wrote this letter. Philippians 1:13 and 4:22 suggest that it was written from Rome, although some commentators argue for Caesarea or Ephesus. Paul's life was at stake, and he was evidently awaiting the verdict of the Imperial Court (2:20-26).

4. The Christ of Philippians. The great *kenosis* passage is one of several portraits of Christ in this epistle. In chapter 1, Paul sees Christ as his life ("For me, to live is Christ," 1:21). In chapter 2, Christ is the model of true humility ("Let this mind be in you which was also in Christ Jesus," 2:5). Chapter 3 presents Him as the One "who will transform our lowly body that it may be conformed to his glorious body" (3:21). In chapter 4, He is the source of Paul's power over circumstances ("I can do all things through Christ who strengthens me," 4:13).

5. Keys to Philippians.

Key Word: To Live Is Christ—Central to Philippians is the concept of "For to me, to live is Christ, and to die is gain" (1:21). Every chapter resounds with the theme of centrality of Jesus in the Christian's life. High points include the following: "Let this mind be in you which was also in Christ Jesus" (2:5); "I also count all things loss for the excellence of the knowledge of Jesus Christ" (3:8); and "I can do all things through Christ who strengthens me" (4:13).

Key Verses: Philippians 1:21 and 4:12— "For to me, to live is Christ, and to die is gain" (1:21). "I know how to be abased, and I know how to abound. Everywhere and in all things I have learned both to be full and to be hungry, both to abound and to suffer need" (4:12).

Key Chapter: Philippians 2—The grandeur of the truth of the New Testament seldom exceeds the revelation of the humility of Jesus Christ when He left heaven to become a servant of man. Christ is clearly the Christian's example, and Paul encourages "Let this mind be in you which was also in Christ Jesus" (2:5).

6. Survey of Philippians. Philippians is the epistle of joy and encouragement in the midst of adverse circumstances. Paul freely expressed his fond affection for the Philippians, appreciated their consistent testimony and support, and lovingly urged them to center their actions and thoughts on the pursuit of the person and power of Christ. Paul also sought to correct the problems of disunity and rivalry (2:2-4) and to prevent the problems of legalism and antinomianism (3:1-19). Philippians focuses on: Paul's account of his present circumstances (1); Paul's appeal to have the mind of Christ (2); Paul's appeal to have the knowledge of Christ (3); Paul's appeal to have the peace of Christ (4).

Paul's Account of His Present Circumstances (1): Paul's usual salutation (1:1-2) is followed by his thanksgiving, warm regard, and prayer on behalf of the Philippians (1:3-11). For years, they have participated in the apostle's ministry, and he prays for their continued growth in the real knowledge of Christ. Paul shares the circumstances of his imprisonment and rejoices in the spread of the gospel in spite of and because of his situation (1:12-26). As he considers the outcome of his approaching trial, he expresses his willingness to "depart and be with Christ" (1:23) or to continue in ministry. Paul encourages the Philippians to remain steadfast in the face of opposition and coming persecution (1:27-30).

Paul's Appeal to Have the Mind of Christ (2): Paul exhorts the Philippians to have a spirit of unity and mutual concern by embracing the attitude of humility (2:1-4), the greatest exam-

ple of which is the incarnation and crucifixion of Christ (2:5-11). The *kenosis,* or "emptying," of Christ does not mean that He divested Himself of His deity, but that He withheld His preincarnate glory and voluntarily restricted His use of certain attributes (omnipresence and omniscience). Paul asks the Philippians to apply this attitude to their lives (2:12-18), and he gives two more examples of sacrifice, the ministries of Timothy and Epaphroditus (2:19-30).

Paul's Appeal to Have the Knowledge of Christ (3): It appears that Paul is about to close his letter ("Finally, my brethren," 3:1) when he launches into a warning about the continuing problem of legalism (3:1-9). Paul refutes this teaching with revealing autobiographical details about his previous attainments in Judaism. Compared to the goal of knowing Christ, those pursuits are as nothing. True righteousness is received through faith, not by mechanical obedience to any law. Paul yearns for the promised attainment of the resurrected body.

Paul's Appeal to Have the Peace of Christ (4): In a series of exhortations, Paul urges the Philippians to have peace with the brethren by living a lifestyle of unity, prayerful dependence, and holiness (4:13). In 4:4-9, Paul describes the secrets of having the peace of God as well as peace with God. He then rejoices over their gift, but explains that the power of Christ enables him to live above his circumstances (4:10-20). This joyous letter from prison closes with greetings and benediction (4:21-23).

OUTLINE OF PHILIPPIANS

I. Paul's Account of His Present Circumstances (1:1-30)

A. Paul's Prayer of Thanksgiving 1:1-11
B. Paul's Afflictions Promote the
Gospel 1:12-18
C. Paul's Afflictions Exalt the
Lord 1:19-26
D. Paul's Exhortations to the
Afflicted 1:27-30

II. Paul's Appeal to Have the Mind of Christ (2:1-30)

A. Paul's Exhortation to
Humility 2:1-4
B. Christ's Example of
Humility 2:5-16

C. Paul's Example of
Humility 2:17-18
D. Timothy's Example of
Humility 2:19-24
E. Epaphroditus's Example of
Humility 2:25-30

III. Paul's Appeal to Have the Knowledge of Christ (3:1-21)

A. Warnings Against Confidence
in the Flesh.............................. 3:1-9
B. Exhortation to Know
Christ 3:10-16
C. Warnings Against Living for the
Flesh...................................... 3:17-21

IV. Paul's Appeal to Have the Peace of Christ (4:1-23)

A. Peace with the Brethren 4:1-3

B. Peace with the Lord 4:4-9
C. Peace in All Circumstances 4:10-19
D. Conclusion 4:20-23

PHIL·IS′TI·A

The land of the Philistines (Ps 60:8; 87:4; Is 14:29). It was the maritime district of Canaan that extends from Joppa to Gaza.

PHIL′IS·TINES

A fierce tribal people who lived in southwest Palestine. Also referred to as "the sea people." The Philistines probably migrated to central Palestine from the island of Crete or Caphtor, in the Mediterranean Sea (Ge 10:14; Am 9:7), in the twelfth century. They displaced the Avim and occupied their territory—the maritime plain of the land that became Israel (De 2:23; Je 47:4; Am 9:7). Their presence in their new home was so prominent in Bible times that the entire land of Palestine was named for the coastal territory, Philistia, which they occupied along the Mediterranean.

The Philistines are mentioned prominently in the Bible during two distinct periods of biblical history—in Abraham's time about 1900 B.C. and during the period of the judges and Kings Saul and David from about 1200 to 1000 B.C.

The Philistines of Abraham's time were peace-ful, in contrast to those who are mentioned later. The earlier Philistines were governed in a single city-state by one king, Abimelech (Ge 26:1,8). But the later Philistines were ruled by five lords, who united the Philistines into a confederation of five city-states—Ashkelon, Ashdod, Ekron, Gath, and Gaza (Jos 13:3; Ju 3:3).

Archaeologists have discovered weapons of iron used by the Philistines against the Israelites. So strong was their threat that the tribe of Dan retreated to the north away from their territory. In Samuel's time, the Philistines destroyed the city of Shiloh, which served as the center of worship for the Israelites.

The threat of the Philistines was one factor that led the Israelites to ask for a king and a united kingdom. The first Hebrew ruler, King Saul, and his sons were killed in a battle with the Philistines (1 Sa 31:1-4). But Saul's successor, David, was able to defeat the Philistines and break their power (1 Ch 18:1).

PHI·LOL′O·GUS *(lover of words)*

A Christian of the Roman church (Ro 16:15).

PHI·LOS′O·PHY *(love of wisdom)*

Any of many schools of thought regarding the facts and principles of ultimate reality. The Greek philosophy with which the early Christians came in contact (Ac 17:18; Col 2:8) was concerned with problems such as man's chief duty and the dualism between mind and matter (Col 2:8).

PHIN′E·HAS *(mouth of brass)*

Three Old Testament men:

1. Son of Eleazar and grandson of Aaron (Ex 6:25). When the Israelites were at Shittim at the close of the wandering, they were punished by a plague because of the idolatry and impurity into which they had fallen through the women of the Midianites. When an Israelite brought a Midianite woman into the camp, Phineas ran a spear through both, for which he was commended and an extended priesthood promised his descendants. This was fulfilled in the history of the priestly office (Nu 25:1-18; Ps 106:30). He was

PHILISTINES

sent to inquire regarding the altar set up east of the Jordan (Jos 22:13).

2. A son of Eli the high priest. He was slain in the battle with the Philistines. On the same day, the ark was captured, and his father fell, broke his neck, and died when he heard what had happened. All this news caused his wife to go into premature labor; she died shortly after her child was born (1 Sa 1:3; 2:34; 4:11,19-22).

3. Father of a certain Eleazar, probably a priest (Ez 8:33).

PHLEG' ON *(burning)*

A Christian of the Roman church (Ro 16:14).

PHOE' BE *(radiant)*

A deaconess of the church at Cenchreae, the eastern part of Corinth. She took up her residence at Rome and Paul recommended her to the Christians of Rome (Ro 16:1-2).

PHOE·NI' CI·A

A narrow strip of land on the eastern shore of the Mediterranean, north of Israel in the area which is modern day Lebanon and coastal Syria. The lush vegetation of this area is mentioned by the prophets (Ho 14:5-7), and the cedars of Lebanon were highly prized for building material. The Phoenician cities of Tyre and Sidon are mentioned often in the New Testament. Jesus healed a demon-possessed girl in this area (Ma 15:21-28). Early Christian believers witnessed in Phoenicia after leaving Jerusalem (Ac 11:19). Paul often traveled through the area (Ac 15:3).

PHOENICIANS

These people lived on a narrow strip of land northwest of Palestine on the eastern shore of the Mediterranean Sea in the area now known as Lebanon and coastal Syria. A group which once occupied the land of Canaan, the Phoenicians were driven out by Israel around 1380 B.C. and crowded onto this narrow strip of coastline.

Hemmed in by the ocean and the mountains of Lebanon, the Phoenicians took to the sea to expand their empire. This led them to become distinguished seafaring merchants who founded many colonies along the Mediterranean. The nation was at the pinnacle of its power and prosperity from 1050 to 850 B.C.

With excellent ports such as Tyre and Sidon and a good supply of timber (cypress, pine, and cedar), the Phoenicians became noted shipbuild-

ers and sea merchants (Eze 27:8-9). Since the Israelites were generally not seafarers, the Phoenicians generally enjoyed good working relations with Israel. Hiram of Tyre, a friend of David and Solomon, helped Israel equip its merchant fleet (1 Ki 9:26-28).

Phoenician religion was largely a carryover from the Canaanite worship system, which included child sacrifice. The gods were mainly male and female nature deities with Baal as the primary god. The marriage of King Ahab to Jezebel, a Phoenician woman, was a corrupting influence on Israel. Ahab allowed Jezebel to place the prophets of Baal in influential positions (1 Ki 18:19). Years before, King Solomon had lapsed into idolatry by worshiping Ashtoreth, the supreme goddess of the Sidonians (1 Ki 11:5).

PHOE' NIX *(date palm)*

The name of a harbor in Crete (Ac 27:12,14; Phenice, KJV).

PHRYG' I·A

A province of Asia Minor, in the mountainous region of modern Turkey (Ac 2:10; 16:6; 18:23). The apostle Paul visited this province on his first two missionary journeys (Ac 13:14–14:5,21; 16:6). He also passed through the area on his third journey (Ac 18:22-24).

PHU' RAH

See PURAH.

PHU' RIM

See PURIM.

PHUT

See PUT.

PHU' VAH

See PUAH.

PHY·GEL' LUS, PHY·GEL' US

A Christian of Asia who deserted Paul when he was imprisoned (2 Ti 1:15).

PHY·LAC' TE·RY, FRONT' LET

A small case made of leather worn by Jewish men on the forehead and the left arm. The forehead case contained four strips of parchment inscribed with scriptural quotations from the Pentateuch (Ex 13:1-10; 13:11-17; De 6:4-9; 11:13-21). The arm case held the same passages. Phylac-

PHYLACTERY

teries were made from the skin of clean animals. The wearing of phylacteries comes from Deuteronomy 6:8, "You shall bind them as a sign on your hand, and they shall be as frontlets between your eyes." Jesus rebuked the Pharisees for their ostentatious display in wearing unnecessarily large phylacteries (Ma 23:5).

PHY·SI′CIAN

One who is skilled in treating disease and injury; one who practices medicine. Not much is known about the medical practices of the Bible times. In ancient Egypt, the physicians did the work of embalming (Ex 50:1-2). The prophet Isaiah speaks of "wounds and bruises and putrefying sores" which had not been "closed or bound up, or soothed with ointment" (Is 1:6). In Jesus's parable of the Good Samaritan, the wounded traveler's wounds were treated with oil and wine (Lk 10:34). Luke, Paul's traveling companion, and the author of the Book of Acts, is described as "the beloved physician" (Col 4:14).

PI-BE′SETH

A city of lower Egypt about 45 miles northeast of Cairo (Eze 30:17).

PIECES OF GOLD

Gold used as money (2 Ki 5:5), more properly rendered "shekels of gold." These were not coins—coins were not common in Israel until the Persian era. Some of the earliest coins minted were made by King Croesus of Lydia about the middle of the sixth century B.C. The number of shekels of gold or silver was an enumeration of the weight of the pile—a statement of value rather than number of pieces.

PIECES OF SILVER

In the Old Testament, this means silver used as money (2 Ki 6:25), more properly rendered "shekels of silver." See PIECES OF GOLD. In the New Testament, "piece of silver" is a translation for the drachma (Lk 15:8-9), a Greek silver coin about the same value as Roman denarius.

PIETY

Devoutness, reverence, religious devotion (1 Ti 5:4).

PIG

An unclean animal (Le 11:7). Eating pork was considered an abomination (Is 65:3-5). In the intertestamental period, Antiochus Ephiphanes enraged the Jews by sacrificing a pig on the altar of the temple. When Jesus drove the demons out of the Gadarene man, they begged to be allowed to enter a nearby herd of pigs. They were given permission to do so, and drove the maddened herd over a cliff into the sea (Ma 8:28-34).

PI′GEON

See DOVE.

PI-HA·HI′ROTH

The last point in Egypt where the Israelites stopped before passing through the Red Sea (Ex 14:2,9; Nu 33:7-8).

PI′LATE, PON′TIUS

He was appointed by the Emperor Tiberius to be procurator of Judea in 26 A.D. (Lk 3:1). Pilate was obstinate and merciless—a hard, cruel man. When duty conflicted with personal interests, the claims of duty were disregarded, as in the case of Jesus. Because his liberation would have increased Pilate's unpopularity (Ma 27; Lk 23), he gave Jesus over to be crucified, even though he fully believed that he was innocent and had power and authority to set him free. For his unbridled cruelty he was finally summoned to Rome, banished, and at last took his own life.

PIL′DASH

The son of Nahor (Ge 22:22).

PI′LE·HA

See PILHA.

PILGRIMAGE

A journey. This word is used in two slightly different senses in Scripture. In a purely physical sense, a journey to a special religious location is called a pilgrimage. Every year, many Israelites traveled to Jerusalem to celebrate the Passover, or other feasts. On the journey they sang a special group of psalms, called the Psalms of Ascents (see ASCENTS).

The word is also used somewhat figuratively to describe the course of a human life. Jacob described his 130 years of life as a pilgrimage on earth (Ge 47:9; Ex 6:4). The author of Hebrews calls the heroes of faith "strangers and pilgrims" on earth (He 11:13). Since the permanent home of a believer is in heaven, we are on earth only as travelers, strangers who don't really belong.

PIL'HA

One who sealed the covenant with Nehemiah (Ne 10:24).

PILL (archaic)

A verb meaning to peel, or to strip off rind or bark (Ge 30:38).

PIL'LAR

1. The support for roofs and the upper structure of buildings. The word is also used figuratively, as pillar of cloud and pillar of fire (Ex 13:21; 26:32; Ju 16:26).

2. A stone set up in memory of some event, such as the memorial at Gilgal (Jos 4:5-9), the Ebenezer of Samuel (1 Sa 7:12), and Absalom's pillar (2 Sa 18:18).

PILLAR OF FIRE AND CLOUD

The visible symbol of God's presence with the Israelites during the exodus. While they were escaping from the Egyptians, and wandering in the wilderness, they were led by a pillar of cloud by day, and a pillar of fire by night (Ex 14:24; Nu 12:5; De 31:15).

PILLAR OF SALT

When Lot's wife disobeyed God, and looked back longingly at Sodom and Gomorrah, she was turned into a pillar of salt (Ge 19:26). Near the Dead Sea, there are numerous natural rock-salt formations, some of which are pillars about the size of a human.

PIL'LOW

The rendering in the Authorized Version for something placed at the head. It might be a stone (Ge 28:18,22); a quilt or netting of goat's hair (1 Sa 19:13,16); or an oarsman's cushion (Mk 4:38). See BOLSTER.

PIL·TA'I (my deliverance)

A priest of the house of Moadiah (Ne 12:17).

PIM

A weight, about two thirds of a shekel. This was what the Philistine blacksmiths charged for sharpening plowshares for the Hebrews (1 Sa 13:21). See WEIGHTS AND MEASURES.

PIN

Peg; a tent peg (Ex 27:19; 39:40; Nu 4:32), or a peg fixed in a wall for hanging things on (Eze 15:3).

PINE TREE

An evergreen; it is not known exactly what tree is meant (Is 41:19; 60:13). More than one variety of pine grows in Israel and Lebanon. This tree is also rendered *ash, fir, cypress, cedar,* and *juniper.*

PIN'NA·CLE

The point of the temple from which Satan tempted Jesus to fling Himself (Ma 4:5).

PI'NON

An Edomite chief (Ge 36:41; 1 Ch 1:52).

PIPE

A wind instrument which might be a single reed blown by the mouth or a double pipe of two tubes played with two hands, having several holes like a flute (1 Sa 10:5; 1 Ki 1:40). The pipes mentioned in some versions of Daniel 3:5 may have been a type of bagpipe, or a flutelike instrument.

PI'RAM (wild, swift)

A Canaanite king of Jarmuth who was defeated by Joshua (Jos 10:3).

PI·RA'THON

A town of Ephraim where Abdon the judge lived (Ju 12:13-15).

PI·RA'THON·ITE

An inhabitant or native of Pirathon (Ju 12:13-15; 1 Ch 27:14).

PIS'GAH (division)

A part of the Abarim range of mountains overlooking the northeastern end of the Dead Sea (De 3:17,27; 32:49; 34:1).

PI'SHON

See PISON.

PI·SID'I·A

A district of Asia Minor. Paul and Barnabas passed through this area on their first missionary journey, and again on their return (Ac 13:14; 14:24).

PI' SON

One of the rivers of Eden (Ge 2:11).

PIS' PAH

Son of Jether of Asher (1 Ch 7:38).

PISTACHIO NUT

The fruit of the pistachio tree is nearly an inch in diameter and inside the shell is a sweet oily kernel. It is a tree of western Asia and is common in Palestine. Jacob sent pistachio nuts as a gift to the overseer of Egypt, not realizing that this man was his own son, Joseph (Ge 43:11).

PIT

See HELL.

PITCH

The substance used as a covering for Noah's ark. It was probably mineral pitch, that is, asphalt or bitumen (Ge 6:14).

PITCH' ER

A jar of earthenware with one and sometimes two handles (Ju 7:16,19). Women carried such vessels on their heads or shoulders when they went to the well for water (Ge 24:15-20). When the disciples went to prepare the upper room for the last supper, they were told to look for a man carrying water this way (Mk 14:13; Lk 22:10).

PI' THOM

A store city built by the enslaved Israelites for Pharaoh (Ex 1:11). Its identity was established by the excavations of Naville at Tell el-Maskhuta.

PI' THON

A descendant of Jonathan, the son of Saul (1 Ch 8:35; 9:41).

PLACENTA

The afterbirth. When a baby is in the womb, the placenta is the organ which transfers nourishment from the mother's bloodstream to the baby's through the umbilical cord (De 28:57).

PLAGUE

A punitive affliction brought about because of sin. It was a judgment that might take any one of several forms. The first of these was the affliction of Pharaoh in connection with Abraham and Sarah (Ge 12:17).

PLAGUES, THE TEN

The ten plagues which God sent upon the Egyptians because of Pharaoh's refusal to let the Hebrews go (Ex 7:8–12:31).

1. The water of the Nile was turned to blood (Ex 7:14–12:30).

2. Frogs covered the land (Ex 8:1-15).

3. Lice throughout the land (Ex 8:16-19).

4. Swarms of flies (Ex 8:20-32).

5. Pestilence of livestock (Ex 9:1-7).

6. Boils on man and beast (Ex 9:8-12).

7. Heavy hail, with thunder and lightning (Ex 9:13-35).

8. Swarms of locusts (Ex 10:1-20).

9. Three days of darkness (Ex 10:21-29).

10. Death of Egyptian firstborn (Ex 11:1–12:30).

After the terrible tenth plague, Pharaoh finally gave up and allowed the Israelites to leave. Their Egyptian neighbors by this time were eager to be rid of them, and speeded them on their way with many gifts.

PLAIN

A valley or low, level surface of land. See ARABAH.

PLAISTER

Old spelling of PLASTER.

PLANE

A tool used for shaping wood (Is 44:13). A plane is a knife fixed at an angle in a holder with a perfectly flat bottom surface. It is used to smooth and flatten pieces of wood, to make a *plane* (flat) surface. It is not known whether this is the most accurate translation for this passage. Other versions use the word *chisel*.

PLANE TREE

A tree of uncertain identity (Ge 30:37; Eze 31:8). It is rendered *chestnut* in the KJV and NKJV.

PLANK

A board or beam. The word is used figuratively in Matthew 7:3-5, contrasted with a speck of dust to show the foolishness of picking at the small faults of others when we have much worse sins in our own lives.

PLANTS OF THE BIBLE

Many varieties of vegetation are mentioned in the pages of Scripture. Translators are not certain of the exact meanings of many of these terms, and different versions have chosen different translations. Following is a list of plants of the Bible. More information can be found about each plant in the appropriate section of the dictionary.

Acacia, Algum, Almug, Almond, Aloes, Amaranth, Anise, Apple, Apricot, Ash, Aspen, Asphodel, Balm, Balsam, Barley, Bay Tree, Beans, Bitterweed, Box Tree, Bramble, Brier, Broom, Bulrush, Calamus, Camphire, Cane, Caperberry, Cassia, Cedar, Cinnamon, Citron, Coriander, Corn, Cucumber, Cummin, Cypress, Darnel, Dill, Ebony, Elm, Fig, Fir Tree, Fitches, Flag, Flax, Frankincense, Galbanum, Gall, Garlic, Gopher Wood, Gourd, Hazel, Heath, Hemlock, Henna, Hyssop, Juniper, Laurel, Leek, Lentil, Lily, Lotus, Mallows, Mandrake, Melon, Mint, Mulberry Tree, Mustard, Myrrh, Myrtle, Nettle, Oak, Oil Tree, Olive, Onion, Onycha, Palm, Pannag, Papyrus, Pine Tree, Pistachio Nut, Plane Tree, Pomegranate, Poplar, Raisin, Reed, Rose, Rue, Rye, Saffron, Salt Herb, Saltwort, Shittah, Spelt, Spikenard, Stacte, Straw, Sycamine Tree, Sycamore, Tamarisk Tree, Tares, Teil Tree, Terebinth, Thorns/Thistles, Thyine Wood, Vine, Wheat, Wormwood

PLAS′TER

1. A kind of cement, used to make walls, floors, or roofs of houses smooth (Le 14:42; Da 5:5). Sometimes houses were plastered in mud or clay; plaster was also made of a mixture of lime, clay, and water.

2. A poultice (Is 38:21). Hezekiah was healed when he put a poultice of figs on his boil.

PLATTER

A large, shallow dish, used for serving food. The twelve tribes presented twelve silver platters at the dedication of the altar of the tabernacle (Nu 7:13-85). In the New Testament, a large platter served a very gruesome purpose. Herod's stepdaughter, at the instigation of his wife, demanded that the head of John the Baptist be brought to her on a platter, and she received her wish (Ma 14:11; Mk 6:28).

PLATTED (archaic)

Braided; intertwined (Ma 27:28-29).

PLEDGE

See LOAN.

PLEI′A·DES (cluster)

A brilliant constellation of seven visible stars (Job 9:9; 38:31; Am 5:8). It is located on the shoulder of Taurus.

PLEROMA

The Greek word translated "fullness" or "completeness." In Matthew 9:16, it means "patch," something which fills up a hole. Paul uses the word in several slightly different senses. He wrote that love is the fulfillment, the completion of the law (Ro 13:10). He also wrote of the time when the "fullness of the Gentiles" should be added to the church (Ro 11:25); in other words, when all those who will believe, have believed. This word also is used in relation to time: in the "fullness of time," that is, at exactly the right time, or when the appointed time had come, Jesus came to earth (Ga 4:4), and in the "fullness of time" He will return again and gather us all to Himself (Ep 1:10). The "fullness of Christ" is a way of speaking about Christian maturity (Ep 4:13).

PLOUGH

English spelling, or archaic American. See PLOW.

PLOW

A farm implement used to break up the ground for planting. Ancient plows were made of wood (1 Ki 19:19-21), with either a wood or iron plowshare (1 Sa 13:19-21). Of course an iron plowshare is far more effective since it can be sharpened to cut through the earth, and it is less likely to break. Plows were drawn by oxen and directed by the hand (Job 1:14; Lk 9:62).

PLOWMAN

One who plows; a farmer (Is 28:24).

PLOWSHARE

The part of the plow which digs into the ground and turns over the earth (1 Sa 13:19-21).

PLUMB LINE

A tool used by builders to make sure their walls were plumb (straight up and down). A plumb line is one of the simplest tools in existence, taking advantage of the gravity of the earth with a weight tied to the end of a string. If the string is held up and the weight allowed to freely hang, the pull of the earth's gravity on the weight will bring the string into a perfectly straight vertical line. The English word comes from the Latin *plumbus* (lead) because the weight was often made of lead.

God used a plumb line as an illustration of His standard of measurement for His people. In a vision, the prophet Amos saw God measuring Israel with a plumb line, and finding that they did not stand straight and true beside God's law. They had abandoned true worship and were serving false gods (Am 7:7-8).

PLUMMET

See PLUMBLINE.

PO´ CHE·RETH-HAZ·ZE·BA´ IM

A member of Solomon's body of servants, whose descendants returned from captivity with Zerubbabel (Ez 2:57; Ne 7:59). Possibly a reference to the town of Zeboim (Ne 11:34).

PODS

The seeds of the carob tree, or locust tree. These pods were used as animal feed. When the prodigal son had spent all he had, and was reduced to feeding pigs, he was so hungry he wanted to eat the pig fodder (Lk 15:16; *husks* KJV).

PO´ ET·RY, HEBREW

The Bible is filled with poetic writings. In addition to entire books such as Psalms and Lamentations which are written almost totally in poetic style, small sections of poetry are found in almost all the remaining books of the Bible.

As applied to the Bible, however, the word *poetry* means something different than the typical English-language structure to which we are accustomed. The main characteristic of Hebrew poetry is parallelism. This is a construction in which the content of one line is repeated, contrasted, or advanced by the content of the next—a type of sense rhythm characterized by thought arrangement rather than by word arrangement or rhyme.

There are three main types of parallelism in the Old Testament. Each is found in abundance in the Book of Psalms.

In **synonymous parallelism,** the second line of a poetic construction expresses essentially the same idea as the first: "The LORD of hosts *is* with us; / The God of Jacob *is* our refuge" (Ps 46:11).

In **antithetic parallelism,** the second line introduces a thought that is the direct opposite of the first idea: "For the LORD knows the way of the righteous / But the way of the ungodly shall perish" (Ps 1:6).

In **progressive parallelism,** part of the first line of the poetic expression is repeated in the second line, but something more is added: "The floods have lifted up, O LORD, / The floods have lifted up their voice" (Ps 93:3).

Another literary device the biblical writers used to give their psalms a peculiar style was the alphabetic acrostic. The best example of this technique is Psalm 119, which contains twenty-two different sections of eight verses each. Each major section of this psalm is headed by a different letter of the Hebrew alphabet. In the original language, each verse in these major divisions of the psalm begins with the Hebrew letter that appears as the heading for that section. Many modern translations of the Bible, including the New King James Version, print these Hebrew letters as headings throughout Psalm 119. See ACROSTIC.

POI´ SON

A substance which produces a harmful or deadly effect when swallowed or introduced into the bloodstream (Job 6:4). Poisonous snakes were well-known and feared (De 32:24,33; Job 20:16; Ps 140:3; Ro 3:13). When Paul was on the island of Malta, he was bitten by a poisonous snake but suffered no harm (Ac 28:1-6). Poisonous plants are also mentioned; hemlock (De 29:18) and "poisonous gourds" (2 Ki 4:38-41).

POLE

When the Israelites were struck by the plague of poisonous snakes, God instructed Moses to make a bronze serpent, and erect it upon a pole or staff so that all could see it. Everyone who looked upon it would be healed (Nu 21:4-9). This event was a type of Christ, who would have to be "lifted up" on the cross in order for humans to be healed of the disease of sin (Jo 3:14-15).

POLITARCH

Ruler of a city (Ac 17:6,8).

POLL (archaic)

To cut hair from the head (Eze 44:20).

POLLUTE

To defile, to make unclean or corrupt. Allowing murderers to go free and practicing human sacrifice are both marked as actions which would pollute the land of Israel (Nu 35:33; Ps 106:38; Je 7:30).

POL'LUX

See CASTOR AND POLLUX.

POLYGAMY

The practice of being married to two or more women at the same time. See MARRIAGE.

POME' GRAN' ATE

A tree about twelve feet high. Its fruit is about the size of an apple, having a red rind and a red pulp enclosing many seeds (Nu 13:23; 20:5; De 8:8; Song 4:3,13; 6:7; Joel 1:12). The leaves of the pomegranate are lance-shaped, and the blossoms are red. Pomegranates were a popular motif for decorative borders and carvings; both the priestly robes and Solomon's temple carried representations of pomegranates (Ex 28:33-34; 39:24-26; 1 Ki 7:18,20).

POM' MEL

The KJV word for the round ornaments of the chapter of a column (2 Ch 4:12-13). First Kings 7:41-42 says bowl; the NKJV says "bowl shaped capitals."

POND

See POOL.

PON' TIUS PILATE

See PILATE, PONTIUS.

PON' TUS (the sea)

A large district of Asia Minor extending along the coast of the Black Sea. Six of its kings had the name Mithridates, the last of whom was in bitter conflict with the Romans until 63 B.C. There were many Jews in this district (Ac 2:9-10; 18:2; 1 Pe 1:1).

POMEGRANATE

POOL

A small body of water fed by springs or rain. Gihon, Bethesda, and Siloam were noted pools in Jerusalem (2 Ch 33:14; Jo 5:2; 9:7). There were also pools at Samaria, Heshbon, Hebron, and Gibeon (2 Sa 2:13; 4:12; 1 Ki 22:38; Song 7:4).

POOL OF GIBEON

See GIBEON, POOL OF.

POOR

The impoverished, for whom the Mosaic law made ample provision. The poor laws were very explicit. Cancellation of considerable indebtedness was required in years of Jubilee (Le 25; 27:14-25). A hungry person was permitted to satisfy his immediate needs in the field or vineyard of another (De 23:24-25). The poor were expected to glean after the reapers, and the reapers were ordered to leave a reasonable amount standing in the fields. Also, the last of the fruit left on the branches was the property of the poor (Le 19:9-10; 23:22; De 24:19-21). The poor should be remembered on joyous occasions and at the time of sacrificial feasts (De 16:11,14). Injustice toward the poor was denounced by the prophets (Is 1:23; 10:2; Eze 22:7,29; Mal 3:5).

POOR IN SPIRIT

Those who realize the fact that their own righteousness is inadequate, and recognize their need for God's mercy (Lk 18:9-14). The poor in spirit will be blessed by inheriting the kingdom of heaven (Ma 5:3).

POP' LAR

A tree of uncertain identity, possibly the white poplar (Ge 30:37; Ho 4:13).

POR·A' THA

One of Haman's ten sons, slain in the conflict with the Jews (Es 9:8).

PORCH

A colonnade with a roof supported by columns running around the building (Ju 3:23; 1 Ki 7:6-21).

POR′CI·US FESTUS

See FESTUS, PORCIUS.

POR′CU·PINE

A wild creature mentioned by the prophets Isaiah and Zephaniah as inhabiting ruins and dreary, desolate places (Is 14:23; 34:11). The porcupine, or hedgehog, is a small rodent covered with sharp quills. Porcupines do live in Israel, but it is uncertain whether this word is the best translation for this verse. The NIV uses "owl," the KJV is "bittern," the REB is "bustard."

PORPHYRY

A dark red or purple rock, imbedded with feldspar crystals. See MARBLE.

PORPOISE

One of the marine mammals. A possible translation for Exodus 26:14 and Numbers 4:6-25. The tent of the tabernacle was covered with some kind of skins, but no one knows what they were. Guesses have included goatskins, porpoise hides, hides of sea cows, and badger skins.

POR′TER

Doorkeeper. One stationed at a city gate (2 Sa 18:26; 2 Ki 7:10) or at the door of a private house (Mk 13:34).

PORTION

A part or piece, an allotted amount, including:
1. A ration of food or other necessity (Ge 14:24; Da 1:8-16).
2. Inheritance, both temporal (Ge 31:14; Lk 15:12) and eternal (2 Ch 10:16; Ps 119:57). The inheritance of the wicked is eternal punishment (Ma 24:51).
3. A piece of real estate (2 Ki 9:10)
4. One's lot in life (Job 3:22).

POSSESSION BY DEMONS

See DEMONIACS.

POST

1. An upright timber at the side of a door (Ex 21:6; De 11:20).

2. A courier or messenger (Je 51:31-32; 2 Ch 30:6,10; Es 3:13,15).

POT

A vessel of various sizes and materials, the most common of which were earthenware and metal (Ex 38:30). Its chief purpose was for cooking food (2 Ch 35:13; Job 41:31); also called fleshpots (Ex 16:3), caldrons (Eze 11:3,7), kettles, and pans.

POTENTATE

A ruler, one in authority. Jesus is the highest ruler of all (1 Ti 6:15).

POT′I·PHAR

A Egyptian in whose home Joseph was a slave (Ge 39:1-20). Potiphar was an officer of Pharaoh, a captain of the guard, and a well-to-do man. He was so impressed with Joseph's abilities that he made him overseer over all his estates.

PO′TI·PHE·RA

Variant of Potipherah.

PO′TI·PHE·RAH

A priest of On, the father of Joseph's wife Asenath, and grandfather of Ephraim and Manasseh (Ge 41:45-50; 46:20).

POT′SHERD (archaic)

A piece of broken pottery (Ps 22:14-15). See OSTRACA.

POTSHERD GATE

The gate of Jerusalem looking out over the Valley of the Son of Hinnom (Je 19:2).

POTTAGE

Stew or porridge. Esau sold his birthright to his twin in exchange for a meal of lentil stew (Ge 25:29-34).

POT′TER

One who makes earthenware. Clay was worked over and made soft and pliable, apparently by treading on it with the feet (Is 41:25). Clay is seldom usable just as it is found in nature. It must be cleaned, and worked over. Large bits of stone are filtered out, and sometimes fine sand is mixed with the clay. Kneading the clay is very important: it removes air bubbles and ensures an even consistency. Many items were made on a potter's wheel. The lump of clay was placed in the center of the wheel and as the wheel revolved, the potter shaped the clay with his hand (Je 18:1-4). It was then dried and baked in a furnace to harden it permanently. This molding of the clay is used to illustrate the power of God in human affairs (Is 45:9; Je 18:5-12; Ro 9:20-25).

POT′TER'S FIELD

See AKELDAMA.

POTTERY

Earthenware: pots, jars, tiles, and other such things. See POTTER.

POUND

1. A unit of weight, also called a *mina;* it weighed about 1.25 pounds, and was equal to fifty shekels (1 Ki 10:17; Ez 2:69; Ne 7:71-72). See WEIGHTS AND MEASURES.
2. A monetary unit called a *mina* (Lk 19:13-25). See MONEY OF THE BIBLE.

POUNDS (or MINAS), PARABLE OF

(Lk 19:11-28)

POVERTY

See POOR.

POWDERS

Ground spices, used as perfume or incense (Song 3:6).

POWER

In the English New Testament, this word is often used almost interchangeably with "authority," as the translation of the Greek word *exousia.* The term "power" often has the connotation of strength or ability, while the word "authority" indicates the right to exercise power. While it may be difficult sometimes to decide which word should translate *exousia,* there is no doubt that Jesus Christ has both power and authority (Lk 4:36; 10:19).

PRAE′TOR

A chief magistrate of a Roman colony (Ac 16:20,35,38).

PRAE·TO′RI·UM

The official residence of a Roman governor. The palace of Pilate at Jerusalem where Jesus

was taken after his capture was called the Praetorium (Ma 27:27; Mk 15:16).

PRAISE

Giving glory, acknowledging greatness or specific actions, extolling, giving honor to. On a certain level, humans can apply praise to one another, and thus offer encouragement and kindness (1 Co 11:2; 1 Pe 2:14), but false praise or flattery is extremely destructive (Pr 27:21). Jesus warns us not to seek praise for the good deeds we do. When we do good things for the sake of human praise, that is all the reward we will get. When we do good things quietly, God notices and He will provide a reward that is far nicer than praise we have jockeyed to obtain (Ma 6:1-5; 25:21; 1 Co 4:5; Ep 1:3-14).

The most important expression of praise is praise toward God. Praising God is an act of worship, an expression of devotion to His person. Thanksgiving and adoration are both forms of praising God: for who He is and for what He does (Ps 150:2; 71:6,14).

PRATING (archaic)

Babbling; chattering (Pr 10:8-10).

PRAYER

The most direct expression of the religious nature in its communion with God. From earliest times man has prayed and the race has never outgrown it. The Bible cites many examples of prayer (Ge 4:26; 20:17; 25:21; Ex 32:11). Prayer expresses the innate conviction of the soul of the personality of God. It is instinctive with man, but rationally grounded in the Word of God. It is a remarkable fact that the great prayers of the Bible are in the Old Testament—the intercessory prayers of Abraham and Moses (Ge 18:23-32; Ex 32:11-14; Nu 14:13-19); the great penitential prayer of David (Ps 51); the prayer of Solomon for wisdom (1 Ki 3:5-9); Solomon's prayer of dedication of the temple (1 Ki 8:23-53); the prayer of Daniel (Da 9:3-19). Jesus was often in prayer but there is record of only one extended prayer (Jo 17).

PRAYER, LORD'S

(See the LORD'S PRAYER).

PRAYER OF AZARIAH, PRAYER OF MANASSEH

See APOCRYPHA.

PRAYERS OF THE OLD TESTAMENT	
THE PENTATEUCH	
Prayers of Abraham	
1. For a son. The aged Sarah was childless	Ge 15:1-2
2. For God's acceptance of Ishmael—not granted	Ge 17:17-18
3. For Sodom. His stipulations	Ge 18:23-32
Prayer of Abraham's Servant. Eliezer's prayer for the success of his mission in procuring a wife for Isaac	Ge 24:12
Prayer of Jacob. At Peniel. The wrestling and the prevailing prayer. His name changed to Israel	Ge 32:9-12,24-30
Prayers of Moses	
1. Intercession for Israel. Idolatry at Sinai	Ex 32:11-14
2. For the Divine Presence and Glory	Ex 33:12-23
3. For Divine help for the performance of his duties	Nu 11:11-15
4. On behalf of Miriam, to be cured of leprosy	Nu 12:13
5. At Kadesh. On behalf of faithless Israel	Nu 14:13-19
6. For a successor—that the people have a shepherd	Nu 27:15-17
7. To enter Canaan—not granted	De 3:24-25
PERIOD OF JOSHUA AND THE JUDGES	
Prayer of Joshua. Why the defeat at Ai? How it will be interpreted and Jehovah be discredited	Jos 7:7-9
Prayer of Manoah. For divine guidance in training his unborn son	Ju 13:8-9
Prayer of Samson. For divine help in his last act in destroying the temple of the Philistines	Ju 16:28
Prayer of Hannah. For a son to be dedicated to God—Samuel	1 Sa 1:10-11
THE MONARCHY	
Prayers of David	
1. The Penitential Prayer. Forgiveness for his great sin	Ps 51
2. After numbering the people. Intercedes for the people	2 Sa 24:17
3. For the offerings for the temple, and for Solomon	1 Ch 29:10-19
Prayers of Solomon	
1. Prayer for wisdom. Need of Divine guidance	1 Ki 3:5-9
2. Dedication of the temple—one of the greatest prayers	1 Ki 8:23-53
THE DIVIDED KINGDOM	
I. ISRAEL	
Prayers of Elijah	
1. For the restoration of the widow's son	1 Ki 17:20-21
2. On Mount Carmel—for the miraculous power of God	1 Ki 18:36-37
Prayer of Elisha. That his servant's eyes be opened; that the Syrians be blinded	2 Ki 6:15-18
Prayer of Jonah. For deliverance. Will keep his vows	Jon 2
II. JUDAH	
Prayer of Asa. In the conflict with Zerah	2 Ch 14:11
Prayer of Jehoshaphat. For deliverance from foes	2 Ch 20:6-13

Prayers of Hezekiah	
1. In the midst of great danger. Threatened by the Assyrian host. Faith in God's supremacy	2 Ki 19:14-19
2. In the midst of serious illness	2 Ki 20:1-6
3. For the unsanctified. Those who had eaten the Passover unprepared	2 Ch 30:17-20
Prayer of Jeremiah. In a time of persecution	Je 15:15-18
Prayer of Habakkuk. For the revival of God's work. In the midst of the years	Hab 3:1-16
PERIOD OF THE EXILE	
Prayer of Ezekiel. Intercession for the people	Eze 9:8
Prayer of Daniel. A prayer for his people	Da 9:3-19
POSTEXILIC PERIOD	
Prayer of Ezra. His sense of shame for the iniquity of his people allied with the heathen	Ez 9:5-15
Prayers of Nehemiah	
1. Prayer for the remnant. The state of things in Jerusalem	Ne 1:5-11
2. God's dealings with their enemies	Ne 4:4-5
Prayer of the Levites. Their repentance and covenant	Ne 9:5-38

PRAYERS OF THE NEW TESTAMENT	
Prayers of Jesus Christ	
1. The Lord's Prayer—the Model Prayer	Ma 6:9-15
2. Thanksgiving for things hidden and revealed	Ma 11:25-26
3. At the grave of Lazarus. That His Father heard Him	Jo 11:41-42
4. For Peter—that his faith fail not	Lk 22:31-32
5. The great intercessory prayer, on the way to Gethsemane	Jo 17
6. The prayer in Gethsemane—surrendered to the Father's will	Lk 22:41-44
7. The prayer on the cross—for His murderers	Lk 23:34
Prayer of the Pharisee. Thankfulness for what he is not and what he does	Lk 18:11-12
Prayer of the Publican. For divine mercy	Lk 18:13-14
Prayer of the Malefactor. On Calvary with Jesus. To be remembered	Lk 23:42-43
Prayer of Stephen. The intercessory prayer of the first Christian martyr	Ac 7:59-60
Last Prayer of the Bible. For the return of the Lord	Re 22:20

PREACHER, PREACHING

A preacher is one who proclaims wisdom from God, or the good news of God's saving grace; one who teaches the way to God. Several Old Testament men are called preachers. The first is Noah (2 Pe 2:5), who preached to his fellow humans during the hundred years he was building the ark, telling them of God's coming judgment and urging them to repent. Solomon, in the beginning of Ecclesiastes, is called a preacher; his special purpose was the teaching of wisdom (Ec 1:2; 12:9-10). Jonah preached repentance to the wicked city of Nineveh (Jon 3:2). In the

New Testament, John the Baptist, Jesus, and His disciples all preached concerning the kingdom of heaven (Ma 3:11-12; 10:7; Mk 16:20; Lk 4:18-19). After Jesus returned to heaven, the apostles continued to preach the good news (Ac 2–28). Jesus commanded all His disciples to go out and preach the gospel to all nations (Mk 16:15), for "How shall they hear without a preacher?" (Ro 10:14).

PRECIOUS STONES
See JEWELS AND PRECIOUS STONES OF THE BIBLE.

PRE·DES'TI·NA'TION
See ELECTION.

PREFECT
See GOVERNMENT OFFICIAL

PREP·A·RA'TION DAY
The day preceding the Sabbath, the Passover, and other sacred festivals (Mk 15:42; Jo 19:14, 31). Since no work was done on the Sabbath, extra work must be done the day before to prepare for it.

PRESBYTER *(elder)*
If overseers and elders are the same office in the New Testament, why the double terms, one might ask? It is matter of emphasis: *Bishop* or *overseer* stresses the office and what it entails; *presbyter* or *elder* stresses the maturity of the man holding that office.

English *elder* is an excellent translation of the Greek *presbyteros,* because it has the same double meaning: "older man" and "a church official." The KJV translates 1 Timothy 5:1 with the word *elder* ("rebuke not an elder") although the context of different age groups suggests "older man" as the meaning. Of the many references that include this word, more than half do not refer to church elders. In the Gospels, elders of the Jews are usually meant for elders of the synagogue. The first churches were organized much like the synagogues, which had a plurality of elders (Ac 14:23). The Book of Revelation speaks of *presbyteroi* who appear to be angelic beings (Re 4:10).

In 1 Peter 5:1-2, the apostle Peter nicely weaves all the church concepts together in one passage: "The elders [*presbyteroi*] who are among you, I exhort, I who am a fellow elder [*sympresbyteros*]

and a witness of the suffering of Christ, . . . Shepherd [*poimaino*] the flock of God which is among you, serving as overseers [*epispoko*]." See BISHOP, ELDER.

PRES'BY·TER·Y
The *presbuteroi,* the body of elders in a church (1 Ti 4:14).

PRES'ENTS
See GIFTS.

PRESIDENT
Satrap, the governor of a Persian province (Da 6:1).

PRESS
See WINE PRESS.

PRICKS
The sharp pointed sticks used for prodding recalcitrant animals along (Ac 9:5, KJV).

PRIDE
Thinking of oneself more highly than one ought to think (Ro 12:3). Pride is a sin which has many destructive results. Sin separates us from God (Ps 138:6). Sin causes us to treat others wrongly (Ps 10:2,4). Pride causes us to forget God, and believe that we are entirely self-sufficient (De 8:10,14-18). We must purpose to thank God for His goodness.

Not all forms of what we call "pride" are wrong. It is right and good to feel "proud" of someone, to feel an unselfish pleasure in their accomplishments or blessings (2 Co 7:4).

PRIEST
Prior to the Mosaic institution of priesthood, the functions of priest were exercised by individuals, as in the case of Abel and Cain. The natural head of a body of people stood in this relation, as in the case of the patriarchs. At Sinai the office was instituted in the most solemn manner. The tribe of Levi was set apart for religious service, and the priesthood was made hereditary in the family of Aaron (Ex 28:1; 40:12-15; De 10:6; 1 Ki 8:4; Ez 2:36). When Aaron died, his oldest living son, Eleazar, succeeded him in the high priesthood (Nu 20:25-28; De 10:6), and he was succeeded by his son Phinehas (Ju 20:28; 1 Ch 6:4,50). See HIGH PRIEST.

PRINCE

One who had chief authority, such as a king (1 Ki 14:7), the head of a province (Da 3:2), the head of a tribe, or of a tribal family (Nu 1:16; 25:14).

PRINCESS

This term is seldom used in Scripture. Most often a princess is simply referred to as "the daughter of the king."

PRINCIPALITY

The province ruled by a prince. Paul speaks of the "principalities" of the spiritual realm (Ep 6:12), using the term to illustrate the strength and organization of the evil powers.

PRIS'CA

A variant of Priscilla.

PRIS·CIL'LA

The wife of Aquila (Ac 18:1-3,18,26; Ro 16:3; 2 Ti 4:19). See AQUILA.

PRIS'ON

A place for the confinement of criminals. Prisons appear to have had no place in the penal system of the ancient Hebrews. Joseph's imprisonment was in Egypt and Samson's was in Philistia (Ge 39:20,23; 40:3,5; Ju 16:21,25). From the time of Jeremiah, mention is made of dungeons and pits in the sense of prisons (Je 37:16; 38:6; Ze 9:11). In New Testament times, the prisons were patterned after Greek and Roman models. There were prison rooms in the palace of Herod, and the palace at Caesarea (Ac 12:6, 10; 26:10).

PRISON, GATE OF THE

A gate in the reconstructed wall of Jerusalem (Ne 12:39).

PRI'VY (archaic)

"to be privy to"—to be aware of, or knowledgeable of (Ac 5:1-2).

PRIZE

A reward, such as the reward for the winner of an athletic competition. Paul compares the Christian life with a race, and urges us to run in such a way as to get the prize (1 Co 9:24).

PROCH'O·RUS

One of the seven deacons of the early church (Ac 6:5).

PROCLAIM

See PREACHER, PREACHING.

PRO·CON'SUL

The governor of a Roman province (Ac 13:7; 18:12; 19:38).

PROC'U·RA'TOR

The administrator of a province under the Roman emperor; also called chief magistrate and governor (Ac 24:27).

PRODIGAL SON, PARABLE OF

(Lk 15:11-32)

PROFANE

To treat a holy thing as common, to defile or pollute. The Israelites were warned not to violate or defile the Sabbath (Is 56:6) or the covenant (Mal 2:10) by ignoring them. The author of Hebrews called Esau a "profane" person, because he despised his birthright instead of valuing his position as heir to the promise (He 12:16).

PROG'NAS·TI'CA'TOR (archaic)

One who foretells the future (Is 47:12-13).

PROMISE

A pledge or covenant. God promised a beautiful land, flowing with milk and honey, to the Israelites (Ex 12:2; He has also promised us a "new land," eternal life (He 9:15).

PROMISED LAND

The land of Canaan, which God gave to the Hebrews as their own. See PALESTINE.

PROPHECIES FULFILLED CONCERNING CHRIST		
Nature	Prophecy	Fulfillment
Seed of the woman	Ge 3:15	Ga 4:4; Re 12:5
Generation, human	Ge 12:3; 18:18; 49:10; Is 11:1	Jo 1:45; Ac 3:25; 13:23; Ga 3:8
Time of His advent	Da 9:24-25	Jo 1:41; 4:25-26
Born of a virgin	Is 7:14; Mi 5:3	Ma 1:23; Lk 1:26-35
Descendant of Shem Of Abraham	Ge 9:27 Ge 12:3; 18:18	Lk 3:36 Ma 1:1-2; Lk 3:34; Ac 3:25

Nature	Prophecy	Fulfillment
Descendant of Shem— Cont'd		
Of Isaac	Ge 17:19; 21:12	Ma 1:2; Lk 3:34; Ro 9:7
Of Jacob	Ge 28:14; Nu 24:17	Ma 1:2; Lk 3:34
Of the Tribe of Judah	Ge 49:10; Mi 5:2	Ma 1:2; 2:6; Re 5:5
Of the House of David	Is 9:7; Je 23:5	Ma 1:1,6; Lk 3:31; Jo 7:42
Birthplace	Mi 5:2	Ma 2:1-6; Lk 2:4; Jo 7:42
Massacre of Innocents	Je 31:15	Ma 2:17-18
Flight into Egypt	Ho 11:1	Ma 2:15
Ministry in Galilee	Is 9:1-2	Ma 4:15-16
A Prophet	De 18:15	Jo 1:45; 6:14; Ac 3:22; 7:37
Priest like Melchisedek	Ps 110:4	He 5:6; 6:20; 7:17,21
Purification of the Temple	Ps 69:9	Jo 2:17
Rejected by Jews and Gentiles	Ps 2:1	Jo 6:66; Ac 4:25-26
Spiritual graces	Ps 45:7; Is 11:2	Lk 4:18
Triumphal entry into Jerusalem	Is 62:11; Ze 9:9	Ma 21:1-10; Jo 12:14-16
Betrayal by a friend	Ps 41:9	Ma 26:15; Mk 14:10,21
For thirty pieces of silver	Ze 11:12-13	Ma 26:15; Mk 14:10,21
Trial and Crucifixion Silence against accusation	Ps 38:13; Is 53:7	Ma 26:63; 27:12-14
Vicarious suffering	Is 53:4-6,12; Da 9:26	Ma 8:17; Ro 4:25; 1 Co 15:3; He 9:28; 1 Pe 3:18
Death with malefactors	Is 53:9-12	Ma 27:38; Lk 23:40-43
Piercing of hands and feet	Ps 22:16; Ze 12:10	Jo 20:27
Insult, mocking	Ps 109:25; 22:6-7	Ma 27:39; Mk 15:29
Offered gall and vinegar	Ps 69:21	Ma 27:34,48; Jo 19:29
Lots cast for vesture	Ps 22:18	Mk 15:24; Jo 19:24
Not a bone to be broken	Ex 12:46; Ps 34:20	Jo 19:36
Burial with the rich	Ps 16:9; Is 53:9	Ma 27:57-60
Resurrection	Ps 16:10; Ho 6:2	Ma 27:63; 28:6; Ac 2:27-31
Ascension	Ps 68:18; 110:1	Lk 24:51; Ac 1:9; Ep 4:8-10; He 1:3

PROPHECY

Prophecy can be the foretelling of future events, or it can be a special message from God for the time in which it is received. Both kinds of prophecy are seen in the books of the Prophets. Sometimes the prophet recounts strange visions of the future, and sometimes he is preaching a special inspired message to the people of his time.

PROPH′ET

A divinely inspired minister of Jehovah; originally called a seer (1 Sa 9:9). Abraham, Aaron, and others were considered prophets but it was not until Samuel that prophecy came into its own. In the period from Samuel to Elisha the so-called schools of the prophets were established in important commercial centers. Until the period of the exile the prophets were advisers to kings. In this capacity they never hesitated to administer a deserved rebuke to the monarch. In their writings the prophets consistently attacked unrighteousness, self-indulgence, and greed. They stood for monothesism and sometimes they predicted future events. Prophecy reached its peak with the messianic prophecy. Prophets and prophecy are mentioned in the New Testament, and Jesus is described as a Prophet (Ma 13:57; 21:11; Lk 13:33).

PROPHET, FALSE

See FALSE PROPHET, THE.

PROPH′ET·ESS

A woman divinely called to prophesy, such as Miriam (Ex 15:20-21; Nu 12:2; Mi 6:4), Deborah (Ju 4:4-6,14), Huldah (2 Ki 22:14-20), and the daughters of Philip, the evangelist (Ac 21:9).

PRO·PHET′I·CAL COM·MU′NI·TIES

Schools of prophets located in various communities. At Ramah there was a company of prophets of which Samuel was the head (1 Sa 7:17; 19:18-20; 28:3). At a later time similar communities gathered about Elijah and Elisha (2 Ki 4:38).

PRO·PI·TI·A′TION

See ATONEMENT.

PROS′E·LYTE

A New Testament term designating a convert to Judaism (Ac 6:5; 8:27).

PROSTITUTION

Promiscuous extramarital sexual relations, usually in exchange for money. Prostitution was often connected with pagan worship; many gods and goddesses had temple prostitutes who resided at the temples and engaged in their trade as a part of heathen worship (Ho 4:12-14; 2 Ki 23:4-14). This was a practice which God detested. When Israel turned away to other gods, God compared the people to spiritual harlots (Eze 16:15-59; Ju 2:17).

PROVERB

A wise saying, often short and pithily expressed. Solomon spoke three thousand proverbs, but only a selected few have been preserved (1 Ki 4:32; 9:7).

PROVERBS, THE

1. The Book of Proverbs. The key word in Proverbs is *wisdom,* "the ability to live life skillfully." A godly life in an ungodly world, however, is no simple assignment. Proverbs provides God's detailed instructions for His people to deal successfully with the practical affairs of everyday life: how to relate to God, parents, children, neighbors, and government. Solomon, the principle author, uses a combination of poetry, parables, pithy questions, short stories, and wise maxims to give, in strikingly memorable form, the common sense and divine perspective necessary to handle life's issues.

Because Solomon, the pinnacle of Israel's wise men, was the principle contributor, the Hebrew title of this book is *Mishle Shelomah,* "Proverbs of Solomon" (1:1). The Greek title is *Paroimiai Salomontos,* "Proverbs of Solomon." The Latin title *Liber Proverbiorum,* "Book of Proverbs," combines the words *pro* "for" and *verba* "words" to describe the way the proverbs concentrate many words into a few. The Rabbinical writings called Proverbs *Sepher Hokhmah,* "Book of Wisdom."

2. The Author of Proverbs. Solomon's name appears at the beginning of the three sections he wrote: 1:1 for chapters 1–9; 10:1 for chapters 10:1–22:16; and 25:1 for chapters 25–29. According to 1 Kings 4:32, he spoke 3,000 proverbs and 1,005 songs. Only about 800 of his 3,000 proverbs are included in the two Solomonic collections in this book. No man was better qualified than Solomon to be the principal contributor. He asked for wisdom (1 Ki 3:5-9) and God granted it to him (1 Ki 4:29-31) to such a degree that people from foreign lands came to hear him speak (1 Ki 4:34; 10:1-13,24). His breadth of knowledge, aptitude, skill, and perception were extraordinary. In every area Solomon brought

prosperity and glory to Israel until his latter years (1 Ki 11:4).

It is likely that Solomon collected and edited proverbs other than his own. According to Ecclesiates 12:9, "he pondered and sought out and set in order many proverbs." The second collection of Solomonic proverbs in 25–29 was assembled by the scribes of King Hezekiah because of his interest in spiritually benefiting his subjects with the Word of God. The prophets Isaiah and Micah ministered during Hezekiah's time, and it has been suggested that they also might have been involved in this collection.

Proverbs 22:17–24:34 consists of "the words of the wise" (22:17; 24:23). Some of these sayings are quite similar to those found in The Wisdom of Amememope, a document of teachings on civil service by an Egyptian who probably lived between 1000 B.C. and 600 B.C. Wise men of this period went to hear one another, and it is probable that Amenemope borrowed certain aphorisms from Hebrew literature. If the *hakhamim* ("wise men") lived before Solomon's time, he may have been the collector and editor of this series of wise sayings.

There is no biblical information about Agur (30) or Lemuel (31). Agur ben Jakeh (30:1) is simply called an oracle, and Lemuel is called a king and an oracle (31:1). Both have been identified with Solomon, but there is no basis for this suggestion.

3. The Time of Proverbs. Proverbs is a collection of topical maxims and is not a historical book. It is a product of the wisdom school in Israel. According to Jeremiah 18:18 and Ezekiel 7:26, three groups communicated to the people on behalf of God: the priests imparted the law; the prophets communicated the divine word and visions; and the sages, or elders, gave counsel to the people. The sages provided the practical application of godly wisdom to specific problems and decisions. The "Preacher" of Ecclesiastes is a good example of the wisdom school (Ec 1:1, 12; 7:27; 12:8-10). *Qoheleth,* or "Preacher," meant "one who addresses an assembly": he presided over a "school" of wise men and "taught the people knowledge" (Ec 12:9). "My son" in Proverbs and Ecclesiastes evidently refers to the pupil. This was parallel to Samuel's role of heading Israel's school of prophets.

Wisdom literature is also found in other countries of the ancient Near East. In Egypt, written examples can be found as early as 2700 B.C. Although the style was similar to Israel's wisdom literature, the proverbs and sayings of these countries differed from those of Israel in content because they lacked the character of the righteous standards of the Lord.

Solomon's proverbs were written by 931 B.C., and his proverbs in chapters 25–29 were collected by Hezekiah about 230 years later (Hezekiah reigned from 715 to 686 B.C.). Under Solomon, Israel was at its spiritual, political, and economic summit. Solomon probably wrote his proverbs in his middle years, before his character began to decline into carnality, materialism and idolatry.

4. The Christ of Proverbs. In Proverbs 8, wisdom is personified and seen in its perfection. It is divine (8:22-31), it is the source of biological and spiritual life (8:35-36; 3:18), it is righteous and moral (8:8-9), and it is available to all who will receive it (8:1-6,32-35). This wisdom became incarnate in Christ "in whom are hidden all the treasures of wisdom and knowledge" (Col 2:3). "But of Him you are in Christ Jesus, who became for us wisdom from God—and righteousness and sanctification and redemption" (1 Co 1:22–24,30).

5. Keys to Proverbs.

Key Word: Wisdom—Proverbs is one of the few biblical books that clearly spells out its purpose. The purpose statement in 1:2-6 is twofold: (1) to impart moral discernment and discretion (1:3-5), and (2) to develop mental clarity and perception (1:2,6). The words "wisdom and instruction" in 1:2 complement each other because *wisdom (hokhmah)* means "skill" and *instruction (musar)* means "discipline." No skill is perfected without discipline, and when a person has skill he has freedom to create something beautiful. Proverbs deals with the most fundamental skill of all: practical righteousness before God in every area of life. This requires knowledge, experience, and a willingness to put God first (see 3:5-7). Chapters 1–9 are designed to create a felt need for wisdom, and Proverbs as a whole is designed both to prevent and to remedy ungodly lifestyles. The book served as a manual to impart the legacy of wisdom, prudence, understanding, discretion, knowledge, guidance, competence, correction, counsel, and truth—from generation to generation.

Key Verses: Proverbs 1:5-7 and 3:5-6—"A wise man will hear and increase learning, and a man of understanding will attain wise counsel, to understand a proverb and an enigma, the words of the wise and their riddles. The fear of the LORD is the beginning of knowledge, but fools despise wisdom and instruction" (1:5-7).

"Trust in the LORD with all your heart, and lean not on your own understanding; in all your ways acknowledge Him, and He shall direct your paths" (3:5-6).

Key Chapter: Proverbs 31—The last chapter of Proverbs is unique in ancient literature, as it reveals a very high and noble view of women. The woman in these verses is: (1) a good woman (31:13,15-16,19,25), (2) a good wife (31:11-12, 23-24), (3) a good mother (31:14-15,18,21,27) and (4) a good neighbor (31:20-26). Her conduct, concern, speech, and life stand in sharp contrast to the woman pictured in Proverbs 7.

6. Survey of Proverbs. Proverbs is the most intensely practical book in the Old Testament because it teaches skillful living in the multiple aspects of everyday life. Its specific precepts include instruction on wisdom and folly, the righteous and the wicked, the tongue, pride and humility, justice and vengeance, the family, laziness and work, poverty and wealth, friends and neighbors, love and lust, anger and strife, masters and servants, life and death. Proverbs touches upon every facet of human relationships, and its principles transcend the bounds of time and culture.

The Hebrew word for "proverb" (*mashal*) means "comparison, similar, parallel." A proverb uses a comparison or figure of speech to make a pithy but poignant observation. Proverbs have been defined as simple illustrations that expose fundamental realities of life. These maxims are not theoretical but practical; they are easily memorized, based on real-life experience, and designed for use in the mainstream of life. The proverbs are general statements and illustration of timeless truth, which allow for, but do not condone, exceptions to the rule. The key word is *hokhmah* "wisdom": it literally means "skill" (in living). Wisdom is more than shrewdness or intelligence. Instead, it relates to practical righteousness and moral acumen. The Book of Proverbs may be divided into six segments: the purpose of Proverbs (1:1-7), the proverbs to the youth (1:8–9:18), the proverbs of Solomon (10:1–24:34), the proverbs of Solomon copied by Hezekiah's men (25:1–29:27), the words of Agur (30:1-33), and the words of King Lemuel (31:1-31)

The Purpose of Proverbs (1:1-7). The brief prologue states the author, theme, and purpose of the book.

The Proverbs to the Youth (1:8–9:18). Following the introduction, there is a series of ten exhortations, each beginning with "My son" (1:8–9:18). These messages introduce the concept of wisdom in the format of a father's efforts to persuade his son to pursue the path of wisdom in order to achieve godly success in life. Wisdom rejects the invitation of crime and foolishness, rewards seekers of wisdom on every level, and wisdom's discipline provides freedom and safety (1–4). Wisdom protects one from illicit sensuality and its consequences, from foolish practices and laziness, and from adultery and the lure of the harlot (5–7). Wisdom is to be preferred to folly because of its divine origin and rich benefits (8–9). There are four kinds of fools, ranging from those who are naïve and uncommitted to scoffers who arrogantly despise the way of God. The fool is not mentally deficient; he is self-sufficient, ordering his life as if there were no God.

The Proverbs of Solomon (10:1–24:34). There is a minimal amount of topical arrangement in these chapters. There are some thematic clusters (26:1-16,20-22), but the usual units are one-verse maxims. It is helpful to assemble and organize these proverbs according to such specific themes as money and speech. This collection consists of 375 proverbs of Solomon. Chapters 10–15 contrast right and wrong in practice, and all but nineteen proverbs use antithetic parallelism, that is, parallels of paired opposite principles. Chapters 16:1–22:16 offer a series of self-evident moral truths, and all but eighteen proverbs use synonymous parallelism, that is, parallels of paired identical or similar principles. The words of wise men (22:17–24:34) are given in two groups. The first group includes thirty distinct sayings (22:17–24:22), and six more are found in the second group (24:23-34).

The Proverbs of Solomon Copied by Hezekiah's Men (25:1–29:27). This second Solomonic collection was copied and arranged by "the men of Hezekiah" (25:1). These proverbs in chapters 25–29 further develop the themes in the first Solomonic collection.

The Words of Agur (30:1-33). The last two chapters of Proverbs form an appendix of sayings by two otherwise unknown sages, Agur and Lemuel. Most of Agur's material is given in clusters of numerical proverbs.

The Words of King Lemuel (31:1-31). The last chapter includes an acrostic of twenty-two verses (the first letter of each verse consecutively follows the complete Hebrew alphabet) portraying a virtuous wife (31:10-31).

OUTLINE OF PROVERBS

I. The Purpose of Proverbs (1:1-7)

II. Proverbs to the Youth (1:8–9:18)

A. Obey Parents 1:8-9
B. Avoid Bad Company 1:10-19
C. Seek Wisdom 1:20–2:22
D. Benefits of Wisdom 3:1-26
E. Be Kind to Others 3:27-35
F. Father Says Get Wisdom 4:1-13
G. Avoid the Wicked 4:14-22
H. Keep Your Heart 4:23-27
I. Do Not Commit Adultery 5:1-14
J. Be Faithful to Your Spouse 5:15-23
K. Avoid Surety 6:1-5
L. Do Not Be Lazy 6:6-19
M. Do Not Commit
    Adultery 6:20–7:27
N. Praise of Wisdom 8:1–9:12
O. Foolish Woman 9:13-18

III. Proverbs of Solomon (10:1–24:34)

A. Proverbs Contrasting the Godly
    and the Wicked 10:1–15:33
B. Proverbs Encouraging Godly
    Lives 16:1–22:16
C. Proverbs Concerning Various
    Situations 22:17–24:34

IV. Proverbs of Solomon Copied by Hezekiah's Men (25:1–29:27)

A. Proverbs Regulating Relationships
    with Others........................... 25:1–26:28
B. Proverbs Regulating Various
    Activities 27:1–29:27

V. The Words of Agur (30:1-33)

VI. The Words of King Lemuel (31:1-31)

A. Wisdom for Leaders 31:1-9
B. Wise Woman 31:10-31

PROVIDENCE

God's guiding and governing care for the universe (Ps 103:19).

PROV' INCE

An administrative district either within or without the confines of the controlling nation. The provinces of the Bible were usually subject to Babylonia, Persia, or Rome. The word also denotes the divisions of the Babylonian and Persian empires (Ez 2:1; Ne 7:6; Es 1:1; 2:3; Da 2:49; 3:1,30).

PROVOCATION

That which provokes. God is specifically provoked by rebellion (He 3:8,15).

PROW

The bow or front of a ship (Ac 27:30,41).

PRUDENCE

Good sense; calm and careful judgment. David is described as being "prudent in speech" (1 Sa 15:18); his son Solomon was also endowed with prudence (2 Ch 2:12). Solomon wrote a number of proverbs dealing with the subject of prudence (Pr 1:4; 12:16,23; 18:15).

PRUNING HOOK

A sharp knife in the shape of a sickle, designed for pruning trees and vines. The prophets contrast spears and pruning hooks as symbols of war and peace (Joel 3:10; Is 2:4; Mi 4:3).

PSALMS, Categorized

The Book of Psalms is a collection of prayers, poems, and hymns that focus the worshiper's thoughts on God in praise and adoration. Parts of the book were used as a hymnal in worship services of ancient Israel. The book contains 150 individual psalms, which may be grouped into the following types or categories.

1. **Individual and communal lament psalms,** or prayers for God's deliverance. Psalms of this type are 3–7; 12–13; 22; 25–28; 35; 38–40; 42–44; 51; 54–57; 59–61; 63–64; 69–71; 74; 79–80; 83; 85–86; 88; 90; 102; 109; 120; 123; 130; and 140–143. These psalms speak to believers in moments of desperation and despair, when our need is for God's deliverance.

2. **Thanksgiving psalms,** consisting of praise to God for His gracious acts. This theme occurs in Psalms 8; 18–19; 29–30; 32–34; 36; 40–41; 66; 103–106; 111; 113; 116–117; 124; 129; 135–136; 138–139; 146–148; and 150. Every prayer we utter should include the element of thanksgiving. These psalms make us aware of God's blessings and lead us to express our thanks with feeling and conviction.

3. **Enthronement psalms,** which describe God's sovereign rule. Psalms of this type are 47; 93; and 96–99. Through these psalms we acknowledge God as powerful Creator and sovereign Lord over all His creation.

4. **Pilgrimage psalms,** which were sung by worshipers as they traveled to Jerusalem to celebrate the Jewish festivals. Pilgrimage psalms are 43; 46; 76; 84; 87; and 120–134. These psalms can help us establish a mood of reverent worship.

5. **Royal psalms,** which portray the reign of the earthly king, as well as of the heavenly king of Israel. This theme is evident in Psalms 2; 18; 20; 21; 45; 72; 89; 101; 110; 132; and 144. These psalms can make us aware of our daily need to make Christ the sovereign ruler of our lives.

6. **Wisdom psalms,** which instruct the worshiper in the way of wisdom and righteousness. Individual wisdom psalms are 1; 37; and 119. These psalms are especially appropriate in times of decision when we are searching for God's will and direction in our lives.

7. **Imprecatory psalms,** in which the worshiper invokes God's wrath and judgment against his enemies. This theme occurs in Psalms 7; 35; 40; 55; 58; 59; 69; 79; 109; 137; 139; and 144. These psalms can help us be honest about our feelings toward people who have done us wrong and work our way through these feelings to a point of forgiveness.

PSALMS, BOOK OF

1. The Book of Psalms. The Book of Psalms is the largest and perhaps the most widely used book in the Bible. It explores the full range of human experience in a very personal and practical way. Its 150 "songs" run from creation through the patriarchal, theocratic, monarchical, exilic and postexilic periods. The tremendous breadth of subject matter in the Psalms includes diverse topics, such as jubilation, war, peace, worship, judgment, messianic prophecy, praise, and lament. The Psalms were set to the accompaniment of stringed instruments and served as the temple hymnbook and devotional guide for the Jewish people.

The Book of Psalms was gradually collected and originally unnamed, perhaps due to the great variety of material. It came to be known as *Sepher Tehillim*—"Book of Praises"—because almost every psalm contains some note of praise to God. The Septuagint uses the Greek word *Psalmoi* as its title for this book, meaning poems sung to the accompaniment of musical instruments. It also calls it the *Psalterium* ("a collection of songs"), and this word is the basis for the term *Psalter*. The Latin title is *Liber Psalmorum*, "Book of Psalms."

2. The Author of Psalms. Although critics have challenged the historical accuracy of the superscriptions regarding authorship, the evidence is strongly in their favor. Almost half (seventy-three) of the psalms are designated as Davidic: 3-9; 11-32; 34-41; 51-65; 68-70; 86; 101; 103; 108-110; 122; 124; 131; 133; and 138-145. David's wide experience as shepherd, musician, warrior, and king (1011-971 B.C.) is reflected in these psalms. The New Testament reveals that the anonymous Psalms 2 and 95 were also written by this king whose name means "Beloved of Yahweh" (Ac 4:25; He 4:7). In addition to the seventy-five by David, twelve were by Asaph, "Collector," a priest who headed the service of music (50; 73-84; Ez 2:41); ten were by the sons of Korah, "Bald," a guild of singers and composers (42; 44-49; 84-85; 87; Nu 26:9-11); two were by Solomon, "Peaceful," Israel's most powerful king (72; 127); one was by Moses, "Son of the Water," a prince, herdsman, and deliverer (90); one was by Heman, "Faithful," a wise man (88; 1 Ki 4:31; 1 Ch 15:19); and one was by Ethan, "Enduring," a wise man (89; 1 Ki 4:31; 1 Ch 15:19). The remaining fifty psalms are anonymous; 1-2; 10; 33; 43; 66-67; 71; 91-100; 102; 104-107; 111-121; 123; 125-126; 128-130; 132; 134-137; and 146-150. Some of the anonymous psalms are traditionally attributed to Ezra.

3. The Time of Psalms. The psalms cover a wide time span from Moses (c. 1410 B.C.) to the postexilic community under Ezra and Nehemiah (c. 430 B.C.). Because of their broad chro-

nological and thematic range, the psalms were written to different audiences under many conditions. They therefore reflect a multitude of moods and as such are relevant to every reader.

The five books were compiled over several centuries. As individual psalms were written, some were used in Israel's worship. A number of small collections were independently made, like the pilgrimage songs and groups of Davidic psalms (1-41, 51-70, 138-145). These smaller anthologies were gradually collected into the five books. The last stage was the uniting and editing of the five books themselves. David (1 Ch 15:16), Hezekiah (2 Ch 29:30; Pr 25:1), and Ezra (Ne 8) were involved in various stages of collecting the psalms. David was the originator of the temple liturgy of which his psalms were a part. The superscription of thirteen psalms specify key events in his life: 1 Samuel 19:11 (Ps 59); 21:11 (Ps 56); 21:13 (Ps 34); 22:1 (Ps 142); 22:9 (Ps 52); 23:19 (Ps 54); 24:3 (Ps 57); 2 Samuel 8:13 (Ps 60); 12:13 (Ps 51); 15:16 (Ps 3); 15:23 (Ps 63); 16:5 (Ps 7); 22:2-51 (Ps 18).

When interpreting the psalms, we must remember four things: (1) When the superscription gives the historical event, the psalm should be interpreted in that light. When it is not given, there is little hope in reconstructing the historical occasion. Assuming occasions will probably hurt more than help the interpretive process. (2) Some of the psalms are associated with definite aspects of Israel's worship (5:7; 66:13; 68:24-25), and this can help in understanding those psalms. (3) Many of the psalms anticipate Israel's Messiah and are fulfilled in Christ. However, care must be taken not to allegorize them and forget the grammatical-historical method of interpretation.

4. The Christ of Psalms. Many of the psalms specifically anticipated the life and ministry of Jesus Christ, the One who came centuries later as the promised Messiah ("Anointed One").

There are five different kinds of messianic psalms: (1) *Typical Messianic.* The subject of the psalm is in some respects a type of Christ (see 34:20; 69:4, 9), (2) *Typical Prophetic.* The psalmist uses language to describe his present experience, which points beyond his own life and become historically true only in Christ (see 22). (3) *Indirectly Messianic.* At the time of composition the psalm refers to a king or the house of David in general, but awaits final fulfillment in Christ (see 2; 45; 72). (4) *Purely Prophetic.*

Refers solely to Christ without reference to any other son of David (see 110). (5) *Enthronement.* Anticipates the coming of Yahweh and the consummation of His kingdom, which will be fulfilled in the person of Christ.

Some of the specific messianic prophecies in the Book of Psalms include:

Prophecy		Fulfillment
2:7	God will declare Him to be His son.	Ma 3:17
8:6	All things will be put under His feet.	He 2:8
16:10	He will be resurrected from the dead.	Mk 16:6-7
22:1	God will forsake Him in His hour of need.	Ma 27:46
22:7-8	He will be scorned and mocked.	Lk 23:35
22:16	His hands and feet will be pierced.	Jo 20:25,27
22:18	Others will gamble for His clothes.	Ma 27:35-36
34:20	Not one of His bones will be broken.	Jo 19:32-33,36
35:11	He will be accused by false witnesses.	Mk 14:57
35:19	He will be hated without a cause.	Jo 15:25
40:7-8	He will come to do God's will.	He 10:7
41:9	He will be betrayed by a friend.	Lk 22:47
45:6	His throne will be forever.	He 1:8
68:18	He will ascend to God's right hand.	Mk 16:19
69:9	Zeal for God's house will consume Him.	Jo 2:17
69:21	He will be given vinegar and gall to drink.	Ma 27:34
109:4	He will pray for His enemies.	Lk 23:34
109:8	His betrayer's office will be fulfilled by another.	Ac 1:20
110:1	His enemies will be made subject to Him.	Ma 22:44
110:4	He will be a priest like Melchizedek.	He 5:6
118:22	He will be the chief cornerstone.	Ma 21:42
118:26	He will come in the name of the Lord	Ma 21:9

5. Keys to Psalms.

Key Word: Worship—The central theme of the Book of Psalms is worship—God is worthy of all praise because of who He is, what He has done, and what He will do. His goodness extends through all time and eternity. The psalms present personal responses to God as they reflect on His program for His people. There is a keen desire to see His program fulfilled and His name extolled. Many of the psalms survey the Word of God and the attributes of God, especially during difficult times. This kind of faith produces confidence in His power in spite of circumstances.

The psalms were used in the two temples and some were part of the liturgical service. They also served as an individual and communal devotional guide.

Key Verses: Psalm 19:14; 145:21—"Let the words of my mouth and the meditation of my heart be acceptable in Your sight, O LORD, my strength and my redeemer" (19:14).

"My mouth shall speak the praise of the LORD, and all flesh shall bless His holy name forever and ever" (145:21).

Key Chapter: Psalm 100—So many of the favorite chapters of the Bible are contained in the Book of Psalms that it is difficult to select the key chapter among such psalms as Psalms 1; 22–24; 37; 72; 100–101; 119; 121; and 150. The two central themes of worship and praise are beautifully wed in Psalm 100.

6. Survey of Psalms. The Psalter is really five books in one, and each book ends with a doxology. The last psalm is the closing doxology for Book 5 and for the Psalter as a whole. After the psalms were written, editorial superscriptions or instructions were added to 116 of them. These superscriptions are historically accurate and are even numbered as the first verses in the Hebrew text. They designate fifty-seven psalms as *mizmor,* "psalm"—a song accompanied by a stringed instrument. Another twenty-nine are called *shir,* "song," and thirteen are called *maskil,* "contemplative poem." Six are called *miktam,* perhaps meaning "epigram" or "inscription poem." Five are termed *tepillah,* "prayer" (see Hab 3), and only one is called *tehillah,* "praise" (145). In addition to these technical terms, the psalms can be classified according to certain themes: creation psalms (8; 19), exodus psalm (78), penitence psalm (6), pilgrimage psalms (120–134), and messianic psalms (see "The Christ of Psalms"). There are even nine acrostic psalms in which the first verse or line begins with the first letter of the Hebrew alphabet, the next begins with the second, and so on (9–10; 25; 34; 37; 111–112; 119; 145).

First Chronicles 16:4 supports another approach to classification: "to invoke, to thank, and to praise the LORD, the God of Israel" (RSV). This leads to three basic types—lament, thanksgiving, and praise psalms. The following classification further divides the psalms into ten types: (1) *Individual Lament Psalms:* Directly addressed to God, these psalms petition Him to rescue and defend an individual. They have these elements: (a) and introduction (usually a cry to God), (b) the lament, (c) a confession of trust in God, (d) the petition, (e) a declaration or vow of praise. Most psalms are of this type (3–7; 12–13; 22; 25–28; 35; 38–40; 42–43; 51; 54–57; 59; 61; 63–64; 69-71; 86; 88; 102; 109; 120; 130; 140-143). (2) *Communal Lament Psalms:* The only difference is that the nation rather than an individual makes the lament (44; 60; 74; 79; 80; 83; 85; 90; and 123). (3) *Individual Thanksgiving Psalms:* The psalmist publicly acknowledges God's activity on his behalf. These psalms thank God for something He has already done or express confidence in what He will yet do. They have these elements: (a) a proclamation to praise God, (b) a summary statement, (c) a report of deliverance, and (d) a renewed vow of praise (18; 30; 32; 34; 40–41; 66; 106; 116; and 138). (4) *Communal Thanksgiving Psalms:* In these psalms the acknowledgement is made by the nation rather than by an individual (124 and 129). (5) *General Praise Psalms:* These psalms are more general than the thanksgiving psalms. The psalmist attempts to magnify the name of God and boast about His greatness (8; 19; 29; 103–104; 139; 148; 150). The joyous exclamation "hallelujah" ("praise the LORD!") is found in several of these psalms. (6) *Descriptive Praise Psalms:* These psalms praise God for His attributes and acts (33; 36; 105; 111; 113; 117; 135–136; 146–147). (7) *Enthronement Psalms:* These psalms describe Yahweh's sovereign reign over all (47; 93; 96–99). Some anticipate the kingdom rule of Christ. (8) *Pilgrimage Songs:* Also known as Songs of Zion, these psalms were sung by pilgrims traveling up to Jerusalem for the three annual religious feasts of Passover, Pentecost, and Tabernacles

(43; 46; 48; 76; 84; 87; 120–134). (9) *Royal Psalms:* The reigns of the earthly king and the heavenly King are portrayed in most of these psalms (2; 18; 20–21; 45; 72; 89; 101; 110; 132; and 144). (10) *Wisdom and Didactic Psalms:* The reader is exhorted and instructed in the way of righteousness (1; 37; 119).

There is a problem with the so-called imprecatory ("to call down a curse") psalms. These psalms invoke divine judgment on one's enemies (7; 35; 40; 55; 58–59; 69; 79; 109; 137; 139; 144). Although some of them seem unreasonably harsh, a few things should be kept in mind: (1) they call for divine justice rather than human vengeance; (2) they ask for God to punish the wicked and thus vindicate His righteousness; (3) they condemn sin (in Hebrew thinking no sharp distinction exists between a sinner and his sin); and (4) even Jesus called down a curse on several cities and told His disciples to curse cities that do not receive the gospel (Ma 10:14-15).

A number of special musical terms (some obscure) are used in the superscriptions of the psalms. "To the Chief Musician" appears in fifty-five psalms indicating that there is a collection of psalms used by the conductor of music in the temple, perhaps for special occasions. "Selah" is used seventy-one times in the psalms and three times in Habakkuk 3. This word may mark a pause, a musical interlude, or a crescendo.

OUTLINE OF PSALMS

I. Book One: Psalms 1–41

1. Two Ways of Life Contrasted
2. Coronation of the Lord's Anointed
3. Victory in the Face of Defeat
4. Evening Prayer for Deliverance
5. Morning Prayer for Guidance
6. Prayer for God's Mercy
7. Wickedness Justly Rewarded
8. God's Glory and Man's Dominion
9. Praise for Victory over Enemies
10. Petition for God's Judgment
11. God Tests the Sons of Men
12. The Pure Words of the Lord
13. The Prayer for God's Answer—Now
14. The Characteristics of the Godless
15. The Characteristics of the Godly
16. Eternal Life for One Who Trusts
17. "Hide Me Under the Shadow of Your Wings"
18. Thanksgiving for Deliverance by God
19. The Works and Words of God
20. Trust Not in Chariots and Horses but in God
21. Triumph of the King
22. Psalm of the Cross
23. Psalm of the Divine Shepherd
24. Psalm of the King of Glory
25. Acrostic Prayer for Instruction
26. "Examine Me, O LORD, and Prove Me"
27. Trust in the Lord and Be Not Afraid
28. Rejoice Because of Answered Prayer
29. The Powerful Voice of God
30. Praise for Dramatic Deliverance
31. "Be of Good Courage"
32. The Blessedness of Forgiveness
33. God Considers All Man's Works
34. Seek the Lord
35. Petition for God's Intervention

126. "Sow in Tears . . . Reap in Joy"
127. Children Are God's Heritage
128. Blessing on the House of the God-Fearing
129. Plea of the Persecuted
130. "My Soul Waits for the Lord"
131. A Childlike Faith
132. Trust in the God of David
133. Beauty of the Unity of the Brethren
134. Praise the Lord in the Evening
135. God Has Done Great Things!
136. God's Mercy Endures Forever
137. Tears in Exile
138. God Answered My Prayer

139. "Search Me, O God"
140. Preserve Me from Violence
141. "Set a Guard, O LORD, over My Mouth"
142. "No One Cares for My Soul"
143. "Teach Me to Do Your Will"
144. "What Is Man?"
145. Testify to God's Great Acts
146. "Do Not Put Your Trust in Princes"
147. God Heals the Brokenhearted
148. All Creation Praises the Lord
149. "The LORD Takes Pleasure in His People"
150. "Praise the LORD"

PSAL′TER·Y

A stringed instrument used to accompany the voice.

PSEUDEPIGRAPHA

A collection of Jewish writings of unknown authorship. They include folk tales, legends, and wise sayings. Several of them were written in the first century A.D.

The Book of Jubilees
The Martyrdom of Isaiah
The Assumption of Moses
The Book of Adam and Eve
The Testament of the Twelve Patriarchs
The Sayings of the Fathers (included in the Talmud).

PTOL·E·MA′IS

See ACCO.

PSALTERY

PTOL′E·MY

The name of the dynasty of Macedonian kings who ruled over Egypt from 305 to 31 B.C.

PU′A

See PUAH.

PU′AH

Two men and one woman of the Old Testament:

1. Son of Issachar and founder of the family of Punites (Ge 46:13; Nu 26:23; 1 Ch 7:1).
2. Father of Tola (Ju 10:1).
3. A Hebrew midwife (Ex 1:15).

PUB′LI·CAN

A member of a company to which the Romans auctioned off the right to collect taxes. They were required to give security for the amount the government should receive. They sold to others certain portions of the revenue. Publicans were engaged to do the actual collecting of the customs. The system afforded opportunity for extortion, and tax collectors had the reputation for taking advantage of it (Lk 3:12-13; 19:8). A Jewish publican was a social outcast, looked upon with contempt as a traitor who had sold himself to the enemy by raising taxes for a foreign and heathen government. At least two disciples of Christ were tax-collectors. Zacchaeus, a Jew, had charge of the revenues of Jericho (Lk 19:1-2) and Matthew had charge of the customs of Capernaum (Ma 9:9; Mk 2:14; Lk 5:27).

PUBLICAN AND PHARISEE, PARABLE
OF (Lk 18:9-14)

PUB′ LI·US

A man of importance who lived on the island of Melita (Ac 28:7-8).

PU′ DENS (modest)

A Christian at Rome who sent greetings to Timothy (2 Ti 4:21).

PU′ HITES

See PUTHITES.

PUL

1. An African country that, according to the best evidence, should be identified with Phut or Put (Is 66:19).

2. A king of Assyria. See TIGLATH-PILESER.

PULSE

Seeds of a leguminous plants like beans or peas. It was nourishing food for Daniel and his three companions in Babylon (Da 1:12,16).

PUN′ ISH·MENT

It is inflicted to maintain the majesty of the law that has been violated, and should be proportionate to the crime committed. This is the basic purpose of punishment. Under the Hebrew theocratic system, capital punishment was inflicted for certain offenses, such as the breaking of the Sabbath (Ex 31:14-15; 35:2), blasphemy (Le 24:10-16), sacrificing to idols (Ex 22:20; Le 20:2; De 13:6-17; 17:2-7). Under the theocracy such offenders were guilty of treason. The same penalty was inflicted for various forms of immorality (Ex 22:19; Le 20:10; De 22:21-27). Conjugal relations of a less heinous nature were punished by cutting off the offenders from their people, or being deprived of children (Le 20:17-21). Death was by stoning and in some cases the body was hanged and then burned. In the case of chastisement, the stripes could not exceed forty (De 25:3). One who testified fasely must suffer the penalty of the crime of the one accused (De 19:16,19). The Hebrew laws were severe, but not cruel. See REWARDS AND PUNISHMENTS.

PUNITES

The descendants of Puah, the son of Issachar (Nu 26:23).

PU′ NON (darkness)

A place where the Israelites camped shortly before they entered Moab (Nu 33:42-43).

PU′ RAH (bough)

A servant of Gideon (Ju 7:10-11).

PURE

See CHASTE.

PURGE

To cleanse; to remove all defiling influences, to refine (Da 11:35). Christians are urged to purge the "old leaven," the old sin nature (1 Co 5:7).

PU′ RI·FI-CA′ TION

The process by which a ceremonially unclean person was made clean again. Contact with a dead body, for example, rendered one unclean under the Mosaic law and purification by the ashes of a heifer was necessary (Nu 19). Purification for certain bodily disorders was required in the form of cleansing and offering of a burnt offering (Le 15; Nu 5:2-3). If one came in contact with a person in that condition, a bath was required and he remained ceremonially unclean until evening (Le 15:5-11). Following childbirth, the mother was placed under rigid requirements not to touch a hallowed thing or to enter the sanctuary (Le 12:8; Lk 2:21-24). The cleansed leper was sprinkled with the blood of a bird by the priest, and after washing and cutting the hair he appeared at the sanctuary with his offering of lambs, and was sprinkled with the blood of the offering (Le 14).

PU′ RIM (lots)

An annual Jewish festival celebrating the deliverance of the Jews in Persia from the destruction planned by Haman. The event is narrated in the Book of Esther.

PURITY

The state or quality of being pure, untouched, unblemished, unmixed. Pure gold (Ex 25:17) and pure oil (Le 24:2) are the most valuable forms. Christians strive for spiritual purity (Ma 5:8; Jam 1:27).

PUR′ LOIN (archaic)

To steal; to pilfer (Tit 2:9-10).

PUR′ PLE

A dye obtained from murex shellfish. Huge quantities of these mollusks were required to make just a small amount of dye. Because of its costliness it was worn only by the rich, and

PUTEOLI

those in high official positions (Es 8:15). It was considered a royal color (Ju 8:26). In mockery of his kingly claims, it was placed upon Jesus. Lydia, one of the converts of Philippi, was a dealer in purple dye (Ac 16:14).

PURPLE GARNET

One of the translations for an uncertain Hebrew word. Ezekiel 28:13 has also been translated "emerald" or "turquoise."

PURSE

A bag, pouch, or girdle in which money was carried (Ma 10:9; Lk 10:4; 12:33; 22:35).

PUT

1. A son of Ham (Ge 10:6; 1 Ch 1:8).
2. The race descended from Ham which furnished mercenaries to Nineveh (Na 3:9).

PU·TE′ O·LI *(wells)*

The seaport in Italy where Paul was kindly treated by Christians (Ac 28:13).

PU′ THITES

A family of Kirjath-jearim, descended from Shobal (1 Ch 2:53; also called Puhites, KJV).

PU′ TI·EL *(afflicted of God)*

Father-in-law of Eleazar, Aaron's son and successor (Ex 6:25).

PU′ VAH

See PUAH.

PY′ GARG *(leaper)*

A ceremonially clean animal (De 14:5), probably the white-rumped antelope. Also translated *ibex, mountain goat, addax.*

PYRAMID

The Egyptian pyramids are not mentioned in Scripture, but some scholars believe that the tower of Babel was built like a pyramid (Ge 11:1-9); others believe that it was styled more like a ziggurat.

PYR′ RHUS

Father of Sopater of Berea (Ac 20:4). Because not all ancient Greek manuscripts contain Pyrrhus, some translations do not include his name.

Q

Q

A hypothetical document which some scholars believe that Luke and Matthew consulted when writing the Gospels. It is supposed to contain the sayings of Jesus, in narrative form, and to be the basis for certain sections of the Gospels. The initial Q stands for the German word *quelle,* which means "source."

QUAIL

A small species of brown partridge. It was sent to the Israelites in the desert first to satisfy hunger (Ex 16:12-13), and later as a judgment (Nu 11:31-34).

QUARRY

An excavation, often a wide, open pit, from which stone is extracted and shaped into blocks for building (1 Ki 6:7). The final dressing of stones may be done either at the quarry or on the jobsite to ensure a perfect fit.

QUARRYMAN

See STONEWORKER.

QUARTERMASTER

Master of quarters, in other words, the servant or official in charge of arranging food and lodging for the king or nobles he attended. In the military, the quartermaster is in charge of collecting and distributing food and clothing to the soldiers and arranging for adequate lodging.

QUAR′ TUS *(fourth)*

A Christian, probably of the Corinthian church (Ro 16:23). Early church tradition taught that Quartus was one of the 70 sent out by Jesus in Luke 10:1-24, and later became a bishop.

QUARTZ

Silicon dioxide, one of the most common minerals. Quartz is hard enough that it cannot be scratched with a knife (7 on Mohs' scale). In very pure crystalline form, it can be as clear as water. Quartz appears in many different colors and forms, including agate, amethyst, rose quartz, tiger eye, onyx, carnelian, chrysoprase, bloodstone, jasper, and flint. Job 28:18 says that the value of wisdom is above rubies, and coral and quartz are not even worth mentioning beside it.

QUA·TER′NI·ON

A squad of four Roman soldiers (Ac 12:4).

QUEEN

The wife of a king or a woman reigning in her own right. If a son followed the father on the throne, the widow continued to hold an influential position (2 Ki 10:13). Athaliah usurped the throne of Judah and reigned for six years (2 Ki 11:1-13).

QUEEN OF HEAVEN

One of the false gods the Israelites worshipped in their days of rebellion. This fertility goddess particularly commanded the worship of women (Je 7:18; 44:17-19,25). "Queen of heaven" may have been a name for the goddess Ashteroth, also mentioned many times in the books of Kings and Chronicles.

QUEEN OF SHEBA

See SHEBA.

QUENCH

Dampen, put out (a fire). The prophet Isaiah spoke of the Messiah, saying "smoking flax He will not quench, till he sends forth justice to victory (Ma 12:20). Paul enjoined believers to take up the shield of faith with which they could quench the fiery darts of the evil one (Ep 6:16). When met by faith, the "arrows" of doubt and fear lose their power and sting. Christians are also urged not to quench the Holy Spirit or despise prophecies (1 Th 5:19-20), in other words, not to ignore the leading of the Holy Spirit.

QUICK, QUICKEN (archaic)

Living, alive; to give life to, or revive. The Greek and Hebrew words translated as "quick" in the KJV are rendered "alive," (Ps 55:15), "revive" (Ps 119:25), or "living" (Ac 10:42) by more modern translations.

QUICKSANDS (Ac 27:17)

See SYRTIS SANDS.

QUI·RI′NI·US, CY·RE′NI·US

A Roman who was governor of Syria (A.D. 6). He was in charge of the enrollment and the taxing that caused Joseph and Mary to go to Bethlehem just prior to the birth of Christ (Lk 2:1-5).

QUIT (archaic)

Conduct, acquit, behave (1 Co 16:13-14).

QUIV′ER

A receptacle for arrows; a deep narrow basket made to be slung over the archer's shoulder, within easy reach for reloading (Ge 27:3; Ps 127:3-5; Is 49:2; La 3:13).

QUMRAN, KHIRBET

The ruins of a community of Essene Jews from about 130 B.C.-135 A.D. This community collected and saved the famous Dead Sea Scrolls discovered in 1947 in caves near the ruins of Khirbet Qumran. See DEAD SEA SCROLLS and ESSENES.

QUOPH

The nineteenth letter of the Hebrew alphabet. This letter is used as a heading for verses 145-152 of Psalm 119; each of these verses begins with the letter *quoph* in Hebrew.

R

RA′A·MAH, RA′A·MA *(trembling)*

1. A son of Cush (Ge 10:7; 1 Ch 1:9).
2. A region of southwestern Arabia whose merchants traded with Tyre (Eze 27:22).

RA·A·MI′AH

See REELAIAH.

RA·AM′SES

See RAMESES.

RAB′BAH

Two ancient cites:
1. A strong city east of the Jordan, chief city of the Ammonites. In David's conflict with them, Aramaeans were used by the Ammonites to attack the Israelites in the rear. Joab divided his

RABBAH

army and defeated both forces (2 Sa 10:8-9,13-14; 1 Ch 19:9). Joab later besieged Rabbah and the city was captured (2 Sa 11:1; 12:26-31; 1 Ch 20:1-3). The city was denounced by the prophets (Je 49:2-6; Eze 21:20).

2. A city of Judah (Jos 15:60).

RAB′BI, RAB′BO·NI

A title of respect given by the Jews to their teachers (Ma 23:7; Jo 1:38). It was also applied to doctors and other learned persons. This name was often used for Jesus (Jo 1:38,49; 3:2; 6:25; 20:16) and once for John the Baptist (Jo 3:26).

RABBIT

An medium-sized rodent, considered an unclean animal (Le 11:6; De 14:7). They appear to chew the cud because of their constant nibbling and gnawing habits, but they do not regurgitate their food for continued chewing as true cud-chewing animals do. Also, they certainly do not have cloven hooves.

RAB′BITH *(multitude)*

A village of Issachar (Jos 19:20).

RAB′BO·NI

A form of RABBI.

RAB′MAG

The title of one of Nebuchadnezzar's chief princes, an official position rather than a proper name (Je 39:3,13).

RAB′SA·RIS

A title signifying a chief official, not a proper name:

1. One of the officers sent by Sennacharib to lead the attack against King Hezekiah of Judah (2 Ki 18:17).

2. One of Nebuchadnezzar's chief princes (Je 39:3,13); one of those who arranged for Jeremiah's release.

RAB′SHA·KEH

The title of one of the Assyrian officials sent by Sennacherib to demand the surrender of Jerusalem (2 Ki 18:17; Is 36-37).

RA′CA

A word used in the time of Christ to express contempt. It carried the meaning of "ignorant," "senseless," "emptyheaded," "fool" (Ma 5:22).

RA′CAL

See RACHAL.

RACE

A contest in which two or more entries compete for speed and endurance. Scripture often uses racing as an illustration of spiritual truth (Ac 20:24; 1 Co 9:24; 2 Ti 4:7; He 12:1).

RA′CHAB

See RAHAB.

RA′CHAL *(traffic)*

A town of Judah (1 Sa 30:29).

RA′CHEL *(ewe)*

Laban's younger daughter whom Jacob loved when he first met her in Mesopotamia. To secure her as his wife he served Laban seven years. He was tricked by Laban into marrying Leah, the older daughter. Jacob still loved Rachel, and served another seven years in order to marry her (Ge 29:30). She had two sons, Joseph and Benjamin, but died giving birth to the latter in Canaan. Benjamin was the only one of the twelve sons born in the land of promise. Her burial place is near Bethlehem (Ge 30:22-25; 35:16-18).

RAD′DA·I *(subjugating)*

David's brother, son of Jesse (1 Ch 2:14).

RA′GAU

See REU.

RA·GU′EL

See REUEL.

RA' HAB

A harlot who lived in Jericho, whose house was on the wall. When Joshua sent spies to the city, she concealed them and enabled them to escape by lowering them by a cord on the outside of the wall (Jos 2:1-24). She and her family were spared when the city fell and became part of the chosen people (Jos 6:22-25). She is part of the genealogy of Jesus (Ma 1:5) and is listed as a heroine of faith (He 11:31; Jam 2:25).

RA' HAB-HEM-SHE' BETH *(Rahab sits idle)*

A symbolic name given to Egypt (Ps 87:4; Is 30:7). See RAHAB THE DRAGON.

RAHAB THE DRAGON

A symbolic creature representing the forces of evil (Job 9:13; 26:12; Ps 87:4; 89:10; Is 30:7; 51:9). The image of Rahab the dragon came to be used as a symbolic name—particularly for Egypt, the land which had held the Hebrews captive for so many years. The Book of Revelation carries out the theme of the dragon representing evil (Re 20:2).

RA' HAM *(pity)*

A man of the family of Hebron, a descendant of Caleb (1 Ch 2:44).

RA' HEL

Variant of RACHEL.

RAIL

To revile, to scold with harsh language, to speak abusively or vituperatively (2 Ch 32:17; 1 Sa 25:14). Also translated "blasphemed" (Mk 15:29; Lk 23:39) or "reviling" (1 Ti 6:4; 1 Pe 3:9; 2 Pe 2:11; Jude 9).

RAIMENT

Clothing.

RAIN

Precipitation in liquid form. God promised His people that he would send rain at the proper times as long as they were obedient (Le 26:4; De 11:14). When Ahab and Jezebel were promoting Baal worship and other wickedness throughout Israel, God withheld the rains for three long years (1 Ki 17:1; 18:42-45). Rain is a symbol of favor (Pr 16:15), and of the grace and mercy of God who sends rain to both "the just and the unjust" (Ma 5:45). The rainy season (or winter) in Israel begins between mid-October and January, ending in April or early May; there is no rain from May to October (Song 2:11). Sometimes in January and February it snows. The Old Testament frequently mentions the "former and latter" rains (Joel 2:23); they were seen as a blessing from God.

RAIN' BOW

A beautiful arc exhibiting the colors of the spectrum, formed opposite the sun by the refraction and reflection of the sun's rays on rain drops or mist. In Genesis, God tells Noah that the rainbow is the symbol of the covenant between God, Noah, and every living creature (Ge 9:12-17; Re 4:3).

RAI' SIN

A dried grape. They were preserved in clusters or as pressed cakes (1 Sa 25:18; 30:12). Because of their high sugar content, they do not spoil easily. They were highly practical for travelers or soldiers to carry with them.

RA' KEM

A descendant of Manasseh and grandson of Machir and his wife Maacah (1 Ch 7:16).

RAK' KATH *(shore)*

A city of Naphtali (Jos 19:35).

RAK' KON

A town of Dan (Jos 19:46).

RAM

See BATTERING RAM.

RAM *(high)*

1. Son of Hezron and brother of Jerahmeel, descendant of Pharez, of the tribe of Judah (Ru 4:19; 1 Ch 2:9; Ma 1:3; Lk 3:33; Aram, KJV). He was an ancestor of Jesus.

2. Son of Jerahmeel and nephew of the preceding (1 Ch 2:25-27).

3. Member of the family to which Elihu belonged (Job 32:2).

RAM, SHEEP

A male sheep. One of the clean animals the Jews were permitted to eat (Ge 31:38). They were used as burnt or peace offerings (Ge 22:13; Le 1:10; 8:18) and also as a sin offering (Le 5:15;

6:6). The skin of the ram was used for covering the tabernacle (Ex 26:14).

RA'MA
See RAMAH.

RA'MAH *(heights)*
Six different Old Testament towns:

1. A town of Benjamin (Jos 18:25). It was near here that Deborah lived, between Ramah and Beth-el (Ju 4:5). It lay between Israel and Judah and was strengthened by Baasha to guard against an invasion by Judah (1 Ki 15:17,21-22). The descendants of former inhabitants occupied it after the exile (Ez 2:26; Ne 11:33).

2. A town of Asher, mentioned but once in connection with the limits of Asher (Jos 19:29).

3. A city of Naphtali (Jos 19:36) about seventeen miles east of Acre.

4. Ramah of Samuel. The town of Samuel's parents, his birthplace and residence (1 Sa 1:9; 2:11; 7:17; 8:4; 16:13; 20:1). Here he was buried (1 Sa 25:1; 28:3). It has been located near Gibeah of Saul (1 Sa 10:26; 14:16; 26:1) but it cannot be located with certainty.

5. Ramah of Gilead (2 Ki 8:28-29; 2 Ch 22:5-6). It was also called Ramoth-gilead.

6. A town in Simeon, also called Ramath (Jos 19:8). Probably the same as Ramoth of the South (1 Sa 30:27).

RA'MATH
See RAMAH.

RA·MA·THA'IM-ZO'PHIM *(twin heights)*
The town of Ephraim where Samuel's father Elkanah lived with his two wives (1 Sa 1:1). See RAMAH number 4.

RA'MATH·ITE
A native of Ramah. Shimei, the overseer of David's vineyards was a Ramathite (1 Ch 27:27).

RA'MATH-LE'HI *(hill of the jawbone)*
The place where Samson fought the Philistines, and killed a thousand of them with the jawbone of a donkey (Ju 15:17).

RA'MATH-MIZ'PAH *(hill of the watchtower)*
A town on the border of the territory of Dan (Jos 13:26).

RA'MATH-MIZ'PEH
Variant of RAMATH MIZPAH.

RA'MATH-NE'GEB
See RAMAH.

RA'MATH OF THE SOUTH
See RAMAH No. 6.

RAM'E·SES (RAMSES)
1. A town in the land of Goshen in Egypt, a section of great fertility, where Joseph settled his people (Ge 47:11). It was located on the Nile Delta. Since Joseph was well before the time of Rameses II, it has been suggested that the author of Genesis was using the "present day" name for the area, rather than the name used in Joseph's time. One of the supply cities the enslaved Israelites were forced to build was called Raamses (Ex 1:11). Since the date for the exodus has been set for 1446 B.C., before the time of Rameses II, some think that this is another instance of a "modern" name being applied to the story. At the time of the exodus, the Israelites left from Rameses and marched to Succoth (Ex 12:37).

2. Rameses, an Egyptian king. See PHARAOH.

RA·MI'AH *(Jehovah exalted)*
Son of Parosh. He renounced his foreign wife (Ez 10:25).

RA'MOTH *(heights)*
1. Son of Bani. He divorced his foreign wife (Ez 10:29).

2. A Levitical city of Issachar, assigned to the Gershonites (1 Ch 6:73). See JARMUTH.

3. A town of Gilead.

4. A town of Simeon (1 Sa 30:27).

RA'MOTH-GIL'E·AD *(heights of Gilead)*
A town in the territory of Gad, one of the cities assigned by Moses as a City of Refuge (De 4:43; Jos 20:8). One of Solomon's twelve officials in charge of provisions lived in Ramoth-gilead (1 Ki 4:13). Because of its location, Ramoth-gilead was captured by the Syrians several times. Ahab, king of Israel was killed while trying to retake the city (2 Ch 28–34); his son Joram was wounded in a similar attempt (2 Ki 8:28).

RA'MOTH-MIZ'PAH
See RAMATH MIZPAH.

RA'MOTH-NE'GEB
See RAMAH.

RAMPART

A fortification such as a trench, wall, or bulwark (La 2:8).

RAM'SES

See PHARAOH and RAMESES.

RAM'S HORN

A trumpet made from the long curving horn of a ram; in Hebrew it is called a *shofar*. It was used to give signals, to call people together, and to celebrate (Ju 3:27; 1 Sa 13:3; Job 39:24-25; Je 6:1; Am 3:6).

RAMS SKINS

See RAM.

RANK

Luxuriant, heavily productive; vegetation which experiences vigorous growth, such as "rank weeds," or the "rank" heads of grain in Pharaoh's vision (Ge 41:5-7).

RANSOM

See REDEMPTION.

RAPE

Forcing sexual intimacy upon another person. God gave strict rules for the way sexual sins were to be handled by His people. If a man enticed or raped a virgin, he was required to marry her. If her father refused to give the girl to him, he was still required to give the bride-price (Ex 22:16-17). Since she was no longer a virgin, it was unlikely that another man would wish to marry her. If the guilty man married her, then her shame would be lessened. No divorce was permitted in such a case (De 22:28-29). If a man raped a girl who was betrothed, the penalty was much more stiff. A betrothed woman was regarded as already belonging to another man, and thus the sin was essentially adultery; a sin against the woman's husband and against marriage. The penalty for adultery was death for both parties, but the law made provision for the protection of innocent women. If she was in a place where she could have cried out for help and did not do it, she was considered guilty of adultery, and bore the same punishment as the man. If, however, she was in a situation where there was no help to be had, she was considered innocent, and the man was stoned for rape (De 22:25-27).

RA'PHA

Two men mentioned in the Old Testament:
1. Also called "the giant," the father of four Philistines from Gath who were killed by David's warriors (2 Sa 21:15-22).
2. Fifth son of Benjamin (1 Ch 8:2).

RAPHAEL *(God heals)*

Traditionally, one of the four angels around God's throne, along with Gabriel, Michael, and Uriel.

RA'PHAH

A man of the tribe of Benjamin (1 Ch 8:37; also called Rephaiah, 9:43).

RA'PHU *(healed)*

Father of Palti (Nu 13:9).

RAT

A medium-sized rodent (larger than a mouse, and smaller than a rabbit) with gnawing, nibbling habits like mice. When the Philistines captured the ark of God, God sent a plague of rats which ravaged the land (2 Sa 5:6; 6:4-5).

RA'VEN

A black bird related to the common crow, but much larger. Their wingspan is about three feet, and their feathers are a glossy black (Song 5:11). Ravens were considered ceremonially unclean (Le 11:15), and fed on carrion (Pr 30:17). Noah sent a raven out from the ark to see whether the waters had receded (Ge 8:7). Elijah was fed by the ravens as he rested by the brook Cherioth (1 Ki 17:4-6).

RA'VISH

To seize, to carry away by force, to plunder or rape (Is 13:15-16).

RA'ZOR

A sharp knife for removing hair.

RE·A'IA

See REAIAH.

RE·A'IAH *(Jehovah has seen)*

1. Son of Shobal (1 Ch 4:2). He is called Haroeh in 1 Chronicles 2:52.
2. A Reubenite, son of Micah (1 Ch 5:5); also called Reaia (KJV).

3. Founder of a family of Nethinim, some of whom returned from Babylon (Ez 2:47; Ne 7:50).

REAPING

Harvesting grain. The standing stalks were cut down with a sharp sickle and bound into sheaves, which could then be easily carried onto the threshing floor. The harvesters were followed by poor people who gleaned the dropped stalks or bits of uncut grain (De 24:19; Ru 2:23).

RE′BA *(fourth part)*

A Midianite king who was slain by the Israelites (Nu 31:8; Jos 13:21).

RE·BEC′CA

Greek variant of REBEKAH (Ro 9:10).

RE·BEK′AH *(a noose, or figuratively speaking, a maiden who ensnares men by her beauty)*

Daughter of Bethuel and sister of Laban. The servant of Abraham was sent to Mesopotamia to secure a wife for Isaac. He met Rebekah at a well and was not only impressed by her beauty, but by her willingness to water his camels, thus fulfilling the sign he had asked for from God. In her home he explained his mission and she agreed to return with him to Canaan. She became the wife of Isaac and the mother of Esau and Jacob (Ge 24:1-67). Jacob was her favorite. With him she contrived to deceive Isaac and secured for Jacob the blessing (Ge 25:28; 27:1–28:5). Jacob fled for his life from Esau, and Rebekah never saw him again. She was buried in the cave of Machpelah, the same place where Abraham, Isaac, Jacob, Sarah, and Leah were also buried.

RE′CAB

See RECHAB.

RE′CAH

See RECHAH.

RE′CHAB *(a horseman)*

1. A son of Rimmon, a Beerothite. He was one of the assassins of Ishbosheth (2 Sa 4:2,6).

2. Father of Jehonadab who witnessed Jehu's zeal in destroying the worshippers of Baal (2 Ki 10:15,23), and ancestor of the RECHABITES.

3. Father of Malchijah, who helped rebuild the wall (Ne 3:14).

RE′CHAB·ITES

Descendants of Jehonadab, son of Rechab (Je 35:1-19).

RE′CHAH

An unidentified place of Judah (1 Ch 4:12).

RECONCILIATION

To establish a state of peace between two persons; in the biblical sense it specifically means reconciliation between God and man by the atoning work of Christ. It embraces two ideas, the first of which is that of God being reconciled to man. It denotes that necessary attitude of opposition to sin on the part of God, and that in order to pardon and receive the sinner, the demands of justice and holiness must be met. God made this possible by sending his Son that sinners might be reconciled to God (Jo 3:16; Ro 5:6-21). Reconciliation is made possible because of the death of Christ on the cross. Christ in heaven intercedes on behalf of man (He 7:25). The second fact is that of man being reconciled to God. This is accomplished when man accepts the provision God has made for his salvation; at that moment there is a cessation of his enmity to God. It is to be noted that there are some who feel that reconciliation *in* the New Testament refers *only to* the latter idea (2 Co 5:18-21).

Reconcile (katallasso) comes from the verb *allasso,* "to change completely." By faith in Christ, a person's spiritual relationship with God is thoroughly changed *(katallasso).* He or she is reconciled to God.

The verb occurs six times and the noun four, all but one in Romans 5 and 2 Corinthians 5. For a good understanding of reconciliation, read 2 Corinthians 5:18-20, thinking in terms of a complete change of relationship.

RECORDER

One who recorded important events and acted in the capacity of the king's adviser (2 Sa 8:16; 1 Ki 4:3; 2 Ki 18:18,37; 2 Ch 34:8).

REDEEM

Make good a lapsed claim. *Gaal* occurs 118 times in the Old Testament, counting words derived from this verb. The main idea is to redeem one's relatives from difficulty or danger, such as by buying back some family property or purchasing an Israelite out of slavery.

REDEEMER

As in redeeming relative. *Goel* is the masculine participle of *gaal*. God Himself is presented in the Psalms as Israel's Redeemer, and Job's famous passage "I know *that* my Redeemer lives" (Job 19:25) is generally taken to refer to Christ and His redemption.

The most famous and most attractive illustration of redemption is the case of Ruth and Boaz. Boaz fulfilled two different functions here. First was *levirate* (from Latin *levir*, "husband's brother") marriage, in that he married the widow Ruth as a near relative ("kinsman redeemer" is the KJV rendering). Second, he also bought back (redeemed) the field that Naomi had sold in her poverty.

The requirements of a *goel* were fulfilled by Boaz and later on a larger scale by Christ: Boaz was a close relative (Le 25:48-49; Ru 2:20) and he was willing to fulfill his duty (Ru 4:4). As a man of wealth Boaz was able to meet his obligation to Ruth. Christ was born of a woman, yet was infinite, as God the Son. He was perfect God and perfect man. Because Christ could "sympathize with our weaknesses" and "was in all *points* tempted as *we are, yet* without sin" (He 4:15), He could fulfill His role as the perfect sacrifice for our sins, (He was in a position to redeem us) and like Boaz, He was willing to redeem us. (He 10:4-10).

REDEMPTION

There are several Greek words that mean "to purchase or redeem." The orthodox theological teaching is that at the cross God paid a ransom price (the blood of Christ) to buy sinners from the slave market of sin.

Agorazo comes from the Greek word for market (*agora*) and is used thirty times in the New Testament, usually of simple buying. Three times in the KJV and NKJV, the word has the theological "redeem," including the well-known text, "You [the Lamb] . . . have redeemed us to God by Your blood" (Re 5:9).

Exagorazo is a strengthened form of the above, occurring four times, always translated "redeem." Twice it has the idea of Christ's redeeming us "from the curse of the law" (Ga 4:5).

Lutroo is a verb occurring three times in the New Testament and also translated "redeem." More specifically, it means "to set at liberty"

upon receipt of a ransom (*lutron*). Peter tells us that the price was the precious blood of Christ (1 Pe 1:18-19). Paul says that the purpose of the ransom was to "redeem us from every lawless deed" to be "*His* own special people" (Tit 2:14).

Lutron is the noun for "ransom." In two parallel passages Christ says the reason He came was "to give His life a ransom for many" (Ma 20:28; Mk 10:45).

Antilutron is a strengthened form of *lutron*. The prefix *anti-* emphasizes Christ's taking our place (1 Ti 2:6).

Lutrosis occurs three times and is yet another word for "redemption." Hebrews 9:12 uses it to express redemption of transgressions under the Old Covenant to make way for the New.

Redemption denotes release, freedom, by the payment of a price. All firstborn belonged to God: when the Levites were set apart for the service of the sanctuary, they took the place of the firstborn, redeeming them from service. Ever afterwards, a redemption price was paid for each firstborn. See LEVITES.

The concept of redemption implies bondage, whether physical bondage as a literal slave, or bondage to the curse and dominion of sin (Ga 3:13) and to death as the penalty of sin (Ac 26:18; He 2:14-15). We cannot set ourselves free, only a redeemer who is outside of bondage can do this. Jesus Christ came as our Redeemer. He paid the redemption price in His own blood on the cross. By this we are made free, redeemed from the curse of the law upon sin. When we accept him, Satan's power and dominion are broken. We have the power to lead a new, a holy, a free life, and death has lost its sting and terror. This redemption embraces not only the soul, but the redemption of the body (Ro 8:15-23; 1 Co 15:55-57; Ep 1:7; 2 Ti 2:26; He 2:9). See ATONEMENT.

RED HEIFER

A perfect red heifer without a defect, which had never been under a yoke, was completely burned by the priest, along with "cedar wood, hyssop and scarlet" (probably wool or thread), and its ashes gathered up and stored in a clean place. These ashes were used for special ceremonies of cleansing (Nu 19:2-17).

RED JASPER

See RUBY.

RE′ DOUND *(archaic)*

To abound; to exceed; to be over and above (2 Co 4:14-15).

RED SEA

A long narrow body of water which separates Arabia and Yemen from Egypt, the Sudan, and Ethiopia. It is approximately 1,300 miles long, and considered one of the hottest and saltiest bodies of water on earth. It has very little circulation of waters, and it is also situated over a volcanic area. It is called the Red Sea because of a form of algae which sometimes lends a reddish cast to the waters. Its northern end branches into two channels, the Gulf of Suez and the Gulf of Aqaba. Today, the Red Sea is used heavily for shipping since the Suez Canal has opened access to the Mediterranean.

The Red Sea appears in the Bible in the account of the Hebrew exodus from Egypt (Ex 14:16; Nu 33:8; De 11:4; Ac 7:36). The word translated "Red Sea" in most translations is the Hebrew *yam suph*, which actually means "sea of reeds." Many scholars agree that the translation "Red Sea" is not accurate. Papyrus reeds and other vegetation do not grow on the Red Sea, and thus it seems that the crossing could not have been here but rather some unidentified body of water bordered with marshy flats and reeds.

It is true however, that later in Scripture the term *yam suph* is certainly applied to the Red Sea, reeds or no. Solomon had a seaport called Ezion Geber on the shore of the *yam suph* in the territory of Edom, clearly the Gulf of Aqaba, the eastern arm of the northern Red Sea (1 Ki 9:26). Jeremiah also mentions the *yam suph* in connection with Edom. This is not to say that the *yam suph* which the Israelites crossed was the Gulf of Aqaba—this would be highly unlikely, to say the least. It does tell us, however, that at least part of the Red Sea was called the *yam suph*. If the eastern arm was called by this name, it is reasonable to suppose that the western arm (the Gulf of Suez) could have been called *yam suph* also.

The exact place of the famous crossing is not known, speculation has included an unknown marshy lake, possibly in the area which was drained when the Suez canal was built. This area is directly opposite the wilderness of Shur

RED SEA

where the Israelites made their first camp (Ex 15:22).

REED

A tall grass having broad leaves growing out of water (Is 42:3).

REED PIPE

See FLUTE.

REED, VESSELS OF

Boats made of bundles of reeds bound together and coated with pitch. Such vessels were used on the Nile and on the Tigris and Euphrates Rivers (Is 18:2).

RE·EL·AI′ AH *(made to tremble)*

One who came from Babylon with Zerubbabel (Ez 2:2). In Nehemiah 7:7 he is called Raamiah.

REFINER

One who refines metal, melting it and removing the impurities. God's work of purifying sinful humans is often spoken of in terms of refining metal (Is 1:25; Je 6:29; Mal 3:3).

REFINING POT

The vessel in which metal was melted for refining. Such pots were made of clay so that they could withstand the great heat of the refining process (Pr 17:3; 27:21).

REFORMATION

Remaking, changing character and improving behavior. Hebrews 9:10 speaks of the New Covenant as a reformation of the old way of relating to God.

REFUGE, CITIES OF

See CITIES OF REFUGE.

REFUSE

See DUNG.

REFUSE GATE

See DUNG GATE.

RE' GEM *(friend)*

A son of Jahdai (1 Ch 2:47).

RE' GEM-MEL' ECH *(friend of the king)*

One sent from Beth-el to inquire of the priests concerning the continuation of weeping and fasting (Ze 7:1-3).

RE·GEN' ER·A' TION

The theological term describing what happens when a person believes in Jesus and repents of his sin. The word comes from Jesus's conversation with Nicodemus where He tells him that unless a person is born again (Jo 3:1-16), he cannot enter the kingdom of God. The term "born again" is used again in 1 Peter 1:23; "born of God" (1 Jo 5:1,4), and "born of the Spirit" (Jo 3:6) also express the idea of regeneration. When a person believes in Jesus and confesses and repents of sin, that person is actually made into a new person (2 Co 5:17). He is declared righteous, he receives the indwelling Holy Spirit, the promise of eternal life, new power (Ac 1:8), and spiritual attitudes (Ga 5:18-25; Ep 4:22-32; Col 3:8-24; 1 Pe 3:8-18; 2 Pe 1:5-8; 1 Jo 3:9-17; 4:7,20-21; 5:1-8). We are justified by or through faith, but we are not regenerated by faith, or by any external act, such as baptism. Regeneration comes by the agency of the Holy Spirit by which our nature is renewed, i.e., made new (1 Pe 1:23; 1 Jo 3:9;

4:7; 5:1). Furthermore, regeneration is not to be confused with sanctification. The new nature originated and effected by the Holy Spirit (regeneration) is now, by the operations of the Spirit, developed in its growth in grace in which the spiritual life is brought to perfection (sanctification). The one is the beginning of the new life, the other the development and consummation of it. See SALVATION and HOLY SPIRIT.

REGIMENT

A tenth of a Roman legion, a cohort. A legion was made up of 6,000 men, each cohort or regiment had 600 men, commanded by a tribune. Under the tribune were the Centurions, each in charge of 100 men. Two regiments, the Italian and the Augustan, are mentioned in Acts (Ac 10:1; 27:1).

REGISTER

See CENSUS.

RE·HA·BI' AH *(Jehovah enlarges)*

Son of Eliezer (1 Ch 23:17; 24:21; 26:25).

RE' HOB *(width)*

Two men and three cities of the Old Testament.

1. When the first spies explored the promised land, they penetrated as far north as Rehob (Nu 13:21). Also called Beth-rehob (Ju 18:28; 2 Sa 10:6).

2. A town on the border of Asher (Jos 19:28). It may be the same as the Rehob of Joshua 19:30 which was assigned to the Levites of the Gerahom family (Jos 21:31; 1 Ch 6:75).

3. Father of Hadadezer, king of Zobah. The latter was defeated by David (2 Sa 8:3,12).

4. A Levite who sealed the covenant with Nehemiah (Ne 10:11).

RE·HO·BO' AM *(the people enlarged)*

Son and successor of Solomon. His mother was Naamah, an Ammonitess. The Ammonites were the descendants of Lot, and therefore of the line of Arphaxad, of Shem, the line that through Abraham brought forth the Messiah (1 Ki 14:31). When Rehoboam assumed the throne, the representatives of the tribes asked him to lessen their tax burdens. The king countered with a plan to tax them even more. As a result ten tribes withdrew from the nation. Rehoboam later prepared an army in order to subjugate them but he was forbidden to do it by the prophet, Shemiah. Rehoboam reigned for seventeen years, during which time his country was invaded by Shishak of Egypt who seized Jerusalem and other cities. Rehoboam and his nation reverted to idolatry (1 Ki 11:43–15:6; 2 Ch 9:31–13:7).

RE′ HO·BOTH (broad places)

1. A city built by Nimrod; apparently a suburb of Nineveh (Ge 10:11). It was also called Rehoboth-Ir.

2. The name of one of the three wells dug by Isaac in the valley of Gerar. The first two were claimed by Philistine herdsmen. Since no claims were made on the third one, Isaac named it Rehoboth denoting room, or freedom (Ge 26:22).

3. A town which was the residence of Saul, king of Edom (Ge 36:37; 1 Ch 1:48). Also called Rehoboth by the River.

RE′ HO·BOTH BY THE RIVER

See REHOBOTH No. 1.

RE′ HO·BOTH-IR

See REHOBOTH No 3.

RE′ HUM (beloved)

1. One who returned with Zerubbabel from Babylon (Ez 2:2); called Nehum in Nehemiah 7:7.

2. A Persian officer who was perhaps an official in Samaria. He wrote Artaxerxes, king of Persia, denouncing the building of the temple by the Jews (Ez 4:8-9).

3. Son of Bani, a Levite. He labored on the wall (Ne 3:17).

4. A chief of the people who signed the covenant with Nehemiah (Ne 10:25).

5. A priest who returned with Zerubbabel from Babylon (Ne 12:3,7).

RE′ I (friendly)

One who refused to support Adonijah (1 Ki 1:8).

REINS

A name for the kidneys, used in a symbolic sense as the seat of emotions (Ps 7:9; 16:7; 26:2; 73:21; Je 11:20; 12:2; 17:10).

RE′ KEM (variegation)

Three men and a town of the Old Testament:

1. One of the five kings of Midian. He and Balaam were slain in the conflict with Moses (Nu 31:8; Jos 13:21).

2. A town of Benjamin (Jos 18:27).

3. A son of Hebron of Judah (1 Ch 2:43).

4. A descendant of Machir, son of Manasseh (1 Ch 7:16). He was also called Rakem.

RELEASE, YEAR OF

See JUBILEEE.

REM·A·LI′ AH (Jehovah adorns)

Father of Pekah, king of Israel (2 Ki 15:25; 16:1,5).

REM′ ETH (high place)

A town of Issachar (Jos 19:21).

RE′ MIS·SION

Release, as in the remission of sins (Ac 2:38; He 9:22). See also FORGIVENESS and REPENT.

REM′ MON, REM′ MON-ME·THO′ AR

See RIMMON.

REMNANT

A small nucleus of God's people preserved by His unmerited grace, which form a foundation for a new community devoted to His redemptive work. Long before the prophets, a type of remnant theology may be seen in God's preservation of Noah and his family from the great flood (Ge 7:1). In the same way, God used Joseph in Egypt to sustain a remnant during the worldwide famine (Ge 45:7).

Remnant theology is also evident in the Book of Deuteronomy where Moses warned Israel that they would be scattered, but the obedient remnant would eventually be restored to their homeland (De 4:27-31). This concept was picked up by the prophets and applied to the Hebrew people when they were carried into captivity by the Assyrians and Babylonians.

In the eighth century B.C., the prophet Amos proclaimed Israel's doom (Am 5:15). In Isaiah's vision of Judah's judgment, the prophet warned, "Unless the LORD of Hosts had left to us a very small remnant, we would have become like Sodom" (Is 1:9). Isaiah even named one of his sons Shear-jashub, meaning "a remnant shall return" (Is 7:3). He predicted that the nation of Judah would be overthrown by a foreign power but that a remnant would survive to serve as a witness to God's continuing work of world redemption (Is 10:20-23). The prophet Micah, a contemporary of Isaiah, tied the restoration remnant to God's future reign in Zion (Mi 2:12-13).

In the New Testament, the apostle Paul applied remnant theology to the church, indicating that God's new people would include both believing Jews and Gentiles (Ro 9:22-27). Alluding to the seven thousand who had not worshiped Baal in Elijah's time (1 Ki 19:18), Paul declared, "Even so then, at this present time there is a remnant according to the election of grace" (Ro 11:5).

Throughout history God has always preserved a remnant from among His people to serve as a lighthouse in the midst of a dark and sinful world.

REMORSE

To have remorse (*metamelomai*) is similar in both Greek and English to repenting. It is used only five times in the New Testament, once of God (He 7:21) in an Old Testament quotation. The word "relent" (NKJV) is an improvement over the "repent" (KJV), since God only appears to change; it is really His invariable reaction to our change of mind. Jesus used this verb twice in His parable of the two sons. The son who said he would not work in his father's vineyard later changed his mind and "regretted [*metamelomai*] it and went" (Ma 21:29). Jesus applied this to the chief priests and elders for not relenting (NKJV) and believing when they saw tax collectors and harlots accepting John the Baptist's message. Judas is a clear example of the difference between repentance and remorse: "His betrayer, seeing that He had been condemned, was remorseful [*metamelomai*] and brought back the thirty pieces of silver to the chief priests and elders, saying, 'I have sinned by betraying innocent blood'" (Ma 27:3-4). Judas was sorry for his mistake, but he did not repent and seek forgiveness. Paul uses both concepts: "For godly sorrow produces repentance [*metanoia*] to salvation, not to be regretted [*ametamelotos*]" (2 Co 7:10). No one who truly repents will ever regret it.

REM'PHAN

See REPHAN.

REND

Rip or tear. Rending one's garments was a symbolic action, representing rage, grief or sorrow. The Bible also speaks of "rending the heart," a figurative way of speaking of repentance and sorrow for sin (Joel 2:13; Ps 51:17).

REPENT

The word *repent* literally means "to change the mind," "to have second thoughts," or "to regret." The basic meaning of "a change of mind" still exists in New Testament usage, but in a context of accepting Christ by faith. For example: "Testifying to Jews, and also to Greeks, repentance [*metanoia*] toward God and faith toward our Lord Jesus Christ" (Ac 20:21). Repentance is so closely related to believing that many view it as the reverse side of "the coin of faith." That is, one cannot truly believe in Christ as Savior without changing one's mind about one's relationship with Him.

The Christian era started when John the Baptist, the Messiah's forerunner, called on Israel, saying, "Repent, for the kingdom of heaven is at hand" (Ma 3:2). He added, "Therefore bear fruits worthy of repentance" (v.8). The change should be visible to others. After being tempted by Satan in the wilderness, our Lord repeats the same message: "Repent, for the kingdom of heaven is at hand" (Ma 4:17).

At Pentecost Peter opened the Christian era with a call to Israel to repent of crucifying the Messiah and to express that change by being baptized with water (Ac 2:38). God is good to us in order to lead us to repentance (Ro 2:4). God's desire is "that all should come to repentance" (2 Pe 3:9).

Repentance is prominent in Revelation, especially in the letters to the churches. People in churches often desperately need to repent. Hardened latter-day sinners undergoing God's wrath against a Christ-rejecting world are four times said not to repent (Re 9:20-21; 16:6,11).

REPH'A•EL *(God heals)*

Son of Shemaiah, a Levite (1 Ch 26:7).

RE'PHAH *(riches)*

Son of Beriah (1 Ch 7:25).

RE·PHAI′ AH *(healed by Jehovah)*

1. The founder of a family registered with descendants of David (1 Ch 3:21).

2. A captain of Simeon. He helped destroy a colony of Amalekites and then seized their land (1 Ch 4:42-43).

3. Son of Tola of Issachar, head of a family (1 Ch 7:2).

4. Son of Binea, a descendant of Jonathan, Saul's son (1 Ch 9:43). In 1 Chronicles 8:37 he is called Rapha.

5. Son of Hur (Ne 3:9).

REPH′ A·IM *(strong)*

1. A race in Palestine before the time of Abraham (Ge 14:5; De 2:11,20; 3:11; Jos 17:15). When the Israelites entered Canaan, a remnant of this giant race seems to have been living among the Philistines (2 Sa 21:16,18,20).

2. The Valley of Rephaim, called valley of the giants in Jos 15:8; 18:16. Its fertility was famous (Is 17:5). It was here that David twice defeated the Philistines (2 Sa 5:18-22; 23:13; 1 Ch 11:15; 14:9).

RE′ PHAN, REM′ PHAN

A god worshipped by the Israelites in the wilderness (Ac 7:43).

REPH′ I·DIM

A camping place of the Israelites between the wilderness of Sin and Sinai (Ex 17:1; 19:2; Nu 33:12,15).

REPROACH

Shame, scorn, or rebuke. Elders are to live an irreproachable lifestyle (1 Ti 3:7) in the sense that no just rebuke can be brought against him. At the same time, Christians are supposed to expect reproach and persecution from unbelievers because of their faith (2 Co 12:10; 1 Pe 4:14).

REPROBATE

Condemned, rejected because of evil conduct (Ro 1:28; Je 6:30).

REPUTATION

The estimation of one's character by others. A good reputation is a valuable asset to be guarded (Pr 25:8-10), but Jesus "made Himself of no reputation" in order to redeem us (Ph

2:7). He was willing to bear a shameful death for the sake of lost sinners.

RE′ SEN

A suburb of Nineveh, built by Nimrod (Ge 10:12).

RESH

Letter of Hebrew alphabet.

RE′ SHEPH *(a flame)*

1. An Ephraimite, son of Beriah (1 Ch 7:25).

2. A pagan god of the Canaanites, supposed to be lord of the underworld.

RESIN

See BDELLIUM.

RESPECT OF PERSONS

Giving preferential treatment to some because of their position or wealth (Ac 10:34; Jam 2:1,9).

RESTITUTION

Making reparation for sin. The law taught that when a person sins against his neighbor, he is supposed to do all he can to make it right. A thief must return what he stole, a liar must confess his falsehood (Le 6:1-7). If a thief stole an animal, and it was found alive, he had to return it as well as paying the value of the animal over again (Ex 22:4). If the animal was dead or sold, the thief had to pay four or five times the value of the animal (Ex 22:1; 2 Sa 12:6). When Zacchaeus believed in Jesus and turned his life around, he began by restoring fourfold what he had stolen from people (Lk 19:8).

RES′ UR·REC′ TION

Being raised to life from the dead. The doctrine of the reunion of body and soul which have been separated by death. This doctrine is not explicitly dealt with in the earlier portions of the Old Testament. There are allusions to it in Psalm 49:14-15; Isaiah 26:19-20; Ezekiel 37, while Daniel 12:2 states it directly. In the time of Christ the resurrection was denied by the Sadducees and upheld by the Pharisees (Ma 22:30; Lk 20:39; Jo 11:24; Ac 23:6,8). It was specifically taught by the apostles (1 Co 15; Ph 3:20-21; 1 Th 4:14; Re 20:6-14). The Scriptures clearly teach the body shall rise again having its identity preserved; that it will be a glorious body, like the glorified body of Christ, and will endure with the soul through all eternity; that the resurrection of Christ is the first fruits of the resurrection, the guarantee of our resurrection in the likeness of his body. The Bible distinctly teaches the doctrine of two resurrections. The first is to occur at the first stage of Christ's second coming (1 Th 4:13-17). Those rising in this resurrection are designated "the dead in Christ" and immediately following that will be the translation of living saints. There is nothing ambiguous about this language. This is supported by our Lord's statement that the reward of the righteous will occur at "the resurrection of the just" (Lk 14:14), which clearly implies there will be another resurrection, that of the unjust. It is the Book of Revelation that speaks distinctly of the two resurrections. The first is as stated by Paul, and that the second, that of the lost, will not occur until the thousand years have expired, and then states, "Blessed and holy is he that hath part in the first resurrection" (Re 20:4-6). This period of a thousand years is mentioned, in different connections, six times in this chapter. However that may be interpreted, two resurrections are distinctly taught.

RETRIBUTION

Giving a person the punishment he deserves. See REWARDS AND PUNISHMENTS.

RETURN OF CHRIST

When the disciples were staring at the sky after Jesus ascended into heaven, an angel appeared to them, telling them, "This same Jesus, who was taken up from you into heaven, will so come in like manner as you saw Him go into heaven" (Ac 1:11). We do not know the exact time (Ma 24:36), but ever since that day on the Mount of Olives believers have been expecting and looking for the return of Christ. Paul urges to be alert, ready, and waiting for the coming of the Lord (1 Th 5:6-8). When he does come, it will be with a shout and the sound of trumpets (1 Th 4:16).

RETURN OF THE EXILES

After the city of Jerusalem was destroyed by the Babylonians about 586 B.C., the leading citizens of Judah were carried away as captives and resettled in the pagan city of Babylon. When the Babylonians were overthrown by the

Persians about seventy years later, the stage was set for God's people to return to their beloved homeland.

There were actually three separate groups of Jewish citizens who made the return from Babylon and Persia to Jerusalem. Each of these groups had a specific task to accomplish.

1. The first group under Zerubbabel returned about 525 B.C. to rebuild the temple. Completed about 515 B.C., the temple was dedicated with great celebration and rejoicing by the Jewish people (Ez 6:15-22).

2. The second group of Jewish exiles, under the leadership of Ezra the priest, returned to Jerusalem about 458 B.C. Ezra's task was to reestablish the law as the basis of Jewish life. In a special assembly in the city of Jerusalem, Ezra read from the Law and challenged the people to follow the Lord's teachings (Ne 8:1-12).

3. The third group under Nehemiah returned about 444 B.C. Nehemiah led the people to rebuild the wall around Jerusalem. In spite of opposition from their enemies, Nehemiah rallied and encouraged the people so effectively that the entire project was completed in fifty-two days (Ne 6:15).

Three prophets of the Old Testament—Haggai, Zechariah, and Malachi—lived and ministered in Jerusalem during this time known as the postexilic period. Haggai and Zechariah encouraged the people to complete the task of building the temple, and Malachi rebuked the returned captives for their sin, idolatry, and shallow worship practices.

RE'U (friend)

The son of Peleg in the line of Arphaxad (Ge 11:18-26).

REU'BEN (behold a son)

1. The eldest son of Jacob by Leah, Jacob's first wife (Ge 29:31-32; 35:23; 46:8). It was Reuben who saved the life of his brother, Joseph, when the other brothers wished to kill him. Reuben suggested putting him in a pit, and planned to return Joseph to his father when the other brothers left the scene. However, before Reuben was able to rescue him, Joseph was sold to the Midianites (Ge 37:21-29). He had four sons: Hanoch, Phallu, Hezron, and Carmi (Ge 46:8-9; Ex 6:14; 1 Ch 5:3). Because of his conduct with Bilhah, his father's

concubine, he forfeited his birthright (Ge 35:22; 49:3-4).

2. The tribe of Reuben had an inconspicuous place in Israelite history. The request of the Reubenites and Gadites that they be assigned the district east of the Jordan was granted on condition that they would do their part in the taking of the land. This they did (Nu 32:1-42; Jos 4:12; 18:7).

REUBENITES

Descendants of Reuben, son of Israel (Nu 26:7; 1 Ch 5:6,26).

REU'EL *(friend of God)*

Four Old Testament men:

1. Son of Esau and Bashemath (Ge 36:2-4,13,17).

2. Father-in-law of Moses (Ex 2:18). See JETHRO.

3. Father of Eliasaph of Gad (Nu 2:14). See DEUEL.

4. Son of Ibnijah (1 Ch 9:8).

REU'MAH *(honored)*

The concubine of Nahor, brother of Abraham (Ge 22:24).

REV·E·LA'TION, BOOK OF

1. The Book of Revelation. Just as Genesis is the book of beginnings, Revelation is the book of consummation. In it, the divine program of redemption is brought to fruition, and the holy name of God is vindicated before all creation. Although there are numerous prophecies in the Gospels and Epistles, Revelation is the only New Testament book that focuses primarily on the prophetic events. Its title means "unveiling" or "disclosure." Thus, the book is an unveiling of the character and programs of God. Penned by John during his exile on the island of Patmos, Revelation centers around visions and symbols of the resurrected Christ, who alone has authority to judge the earth, to remake it, and to rule it in righteousness.

The title of this book in the Greek text is *Apokalypsis Ioannou*, "Revelation of John." It is also known as the Apocalypse, a transliteration of the word *apokalypsis*, meaning "unveiling," "disclosure," or "revelation." Thus, the book is an unveiling of that which otherwise could not be known. A better title comes from the first verse: *Apokalypsis Iesou Christou*,

"Revelation of Jesus Christ." This could be taken as a revelation which came from Christ or as a revelation which is about Christ—both are appropriate. Because of the unified contents of this book, it should not be called Revelations.

2. The Author of Revelation. The style, symmetry, and plan of Revelation show that it was written by one author, four times named "John" (1:1,4,9; 22:8; see "The Author of John"). Because of its contents and its address to seven churches, Revelation quickly circulated and became widely known and accepted in the early church. It was frequently mentioned and quoted by second and third century Christian writers and was received as part of the canon of New Testament books. From the beginning, Revelation was considered an authentic work of the apostle John, the same John who wrote the Gospel and three Epistles. This was held to be true by Justin Martyr, the Shepherd of Hermas, Melito, Irenaeus, the Muratorian Canon, Tertullian, Clement of Alexandria, Origen, and others.

This view was seldom questioned until the middle of the third century when Dionysius presented several arguments against the apostolic authorship of Revelation. He observed a clear difference in style and thought between Revelation and the books that he accepted as Johannine, and he concluded that the Apocalypse must have been penned by a different John. Indeed, the internal evidence does pose some problems for the traditional view: (1) The Greek grammar of Revelation is not on par with the Fourth Gospel or the Johannine Epistles. (2) There are also differences in vocabulary and expressions used. (3) The theological content of this book differs from John's other writings in emphasis and presentations. (4) John's other writings avoid the use of his name, but it is found four times in this book. While these difficulties exist, two things should be kept in mind: (1) There are a number of remarkable similarities between the Apocalypse and the other books traditionally associated with the apostle John (the distinctive use of terms, such as *word, lamb,* and *true,* and the careful development of conflicting themes, such as light and darkness, love and hatred, good and evil). (2) Many of the differences can be explained by the unusual circumstances surrounding this book. The apocalyptic subject matter demands a different treatment, and John received the contents not by reflection but by a series of startling and ecstatic visions. It is also possible that John used a secretary who smoothed out the Greek style of his other writings, and that his exile on Patmos prevented the use of such a scribe when he wrote Revelation.

Thus, the internal evidence, while problematic, need not overrule the early and strong external testimony to the apostolic origin of this important book. The author was obviously well-known to the recipients in the seven Asian churches, and this fits the unqualified use of the name John and the uniform tradition about his ministry in Asia. Alternate suggestions, such as John the elder or a prophet named John, create more problems than they solve.

3. The Time of Revelation. John directed this prophetic word to seven selected churches in the Roman province of Asia (1:3-4). The messages to these churches in chapters 2 and 3 begin with Ephesus, the most prominent, and continue in a clockwise direction until Laodicea is reached. It is likely that this book was initially carried along this circular route. While each of these messages had particular significance for these churches, they were also relevant for the church as a whole ("He who has an ear, let him hear what the Spirit says to the churches").

John's effective testimony for Christ led the Roman authorities to exile him to the small desolate island of Patmos in the Aegean Sea (1:9). This island of volcanic rock was one of several places to which the Romans banished criminals and political offenders.

Revelation was written at a time when Roman hostility to Christianity was erupting into overt persecution (1:9; 2:10-13). Some scholars believe that it should be given an early date during the persecution of Christians under Nero after the A.D. 64 burning of Rome. The Hebrew letters for Nero Caesar (*Neron Kesar*) add up to 666, the legend that Nero would reappear in the East after his apparent death (Re 13:3,12,14). This kind of evidence is weak, and a later date near the end of the reign of the emperor Domitian (A.D. 81-96) is preferable for several reasons: (1) This was the testimony of Irenaeus (disciple of Polycarp who was a disciple of John) and other early Christian writers. (2) John probably did not move from Jerusalem

to Ephesus until about A.D. 67, shortly before the Roman destruction of Jerusalem in A.D. 70. The early dating would not give him enough time to have established an ongoing ministry in Asia by the time he wrote this book. (3) The churches of Asia appear to have been in existence for a number of years, long enough for some to reach a point of complacency and decline (2:4; 3:1,15-18). (4) The deeds of Domitian are more relevant than those of Nero to the themes of the Apocalypse. Worship of deceased emperors had been practiced for years, but Domitian was the first emperor to demand worship while he was alive. This led to a greater clash between the state and the church, especially in Asia, where the worship of Caesar was widely practiced. The persecution under Domitian presaged the more severe persecutions to follow.

Thus, it is likely that John wrote this book in A.D. 95-96. The date of his release from Patmos is unknown, but he was probably allowed to return to Ephesus after the reign of Domitian. Passages such as 1:11; 22:7,9-10,18-19 suggest that the book was completed before John's release.

4. The Christ of Revelation. Revelation has much to say about all three persons of the Godhead, but it is especially clear in its presentation of the awesome resurrected Christ who has received all authority to judge the earth. He is called Jesus Christ (1:1), the faithful witness, the firstborn from the dead, the ruler over the kings of the earth (1:5), the First and the Last (1:17), He who lives (1:18), the Son of God (2:18), holy and true (3:7), the Amen, the Faithful and True Witness, the Beginning of the creation of God (3:14), the Lion of the tribe of Judah, the Root of David (5:5), a Lamb (5:6), Faithful and True (19:11), The Word of God (19:13), KING OF KINGS AND LORD OF LORDS (19:16), Alpha and Omega (22:13), the Bright and Morning Star (22:16), and the Lord Jesus Christ (22:21).

This book is indeed "The Revelation of Jesus Christ" (1:1) since it comes from Him and centers on Him. It begins with a vision of His glory, wisdom, and power (1), and portrays His authority over the entire church (2–3). He is the Lamb who was slain and declared worthy to open the book of judgment (5). His righteous wrath is poured out upon the whole earth (6–18), and he returns in power to judge His enemies and to reign as the Lord over all (19–20). He will rule forever over the heavenly city in the presence of all who know Him (21–22).

The Scriptures close with His great promise "Behold, I am coming quickly" (22:7,12). " 'Surely I am coming quickly,' Amen. Even so, come, Lord Jesus" (22:20).

5. Keys to Revelation.

Key Word: The Revelation of the Coming of Christ—The purposes for which Revelation was written depend to some extent on how the book as a whole is interpreted. Because of its complex imagery and symbolism, Revelation is the most difficult biblical book to interpret, and there are four major alternatives: (1) The symbolic or idealist view maintains that Revelation is not a predictive prophecy, but a symbolic portrait of the cosmic conflict of spiritual principles. (2) The preterist view (the Latin word *praeter* means "past") maintains that it is a symbolic description of the Roman persecution of the church, emperor worship, and the divine judgment of Rome. (3) The historicist view approaches Revelation as an allegorical panorama of the history of the (Western) church from the first century to the second advent. (4) The futurist view acknowledges the obvious influence that the first century conflict between Roman power and the church had upon the themes of this book. It also accepts the bulk of Revelation (4–22) as an inspired look into the time immediately preceding the second advent (the "Tribulation"), usually seen as seven years; (6–18), and extending from the return of Christ to the creation of the new cosmos (19–22).

Advocates of all four interpretive approaches to Revelation agree that it was written to assure the recipients of the ultimate triumph of Christ over all who rise up against Him and His saints. The readers were facing dark times of persecution, and even worse times would follow. Therefore they needed to be encouraged to persevere by standing firm in Christ in view of God's plan for the righteous and the wicked. This plan is especially clear in the stirring words of the epilogue (22:6-21). The book was also written to challenge complacent Christians to stop compromising with the world. According to futurists, Revelation serves the additional purpose of providing a perspective on end-time events that would have meaning and relevance to the spiritual lives of all succeeding generations of Christians.

Key Verses: Revelation 1:19 and 19:11-15—" 'Write the things which you have seen, and the things which are, and the things which will take place after this' " (1:19).

"Then I saw heaven opened, and behold, a white horse. And he who sat on him was called Faithful and True, and in righteousness He judges and makes war. His eyes were like a flame of fire, and on His head were many crowns. He had a name written that no one knew except Himself. He was clothed with a robe dipped in blood, and His name is called The Word of God. And the armies in heaven, clothed in fine linen, white and clean, followed Him upon white horses. Now out of His mouth goes a sharp sword, that with it He should strike the nations. And He Himself will rule them with a rod of iron. He Himself treads the winepress of the fierceness and wrath of Almighty God" (19:11-15).

Key Chapters: Revelation 19–22—When the end of history is fully understood, its impact radically affects the present. In Revelation 19–22 the plans of God for the last days and for all of eternity are recorded in explicit terms. Careful study of and obedience to them will bring the blessings that are promised (1:3). Uppermost in the mind and deep in the heart should be guarded the words of Jesus, "Behold, I am coming quickly."

6. Survey of Revelation. Revelation is written in the form of apocalyptic literature (Daniel and Zechariah) by a prophet (10:11; 22:9) and refers to itself as a prophetic book (1:3; 22:7,10,18-19). The three major movements in this profound unveiling are captured in 1:19: "the things which you have seen" (1); "the things which are" (2–3); and "the things which will take place after this" (4–22).

"The Things Which You Have Seen" (1): Revelation contains a prologue (1:1-3) before the usual salutation (1:4-8). The Revelation was received by Christ from the Father and communicated by an angel to John. This is the only biblical book that specifically promises a blessing to those who read it (1:3), but it also promises a curse to those who add to or detract from it (22:18-19). The salutation and closing benediction show that it was originally written as an epistle to seven Asian churches.

A rich theological portrait of the triune God (1:4-8) is followed by an overwhelming theophany (visible manifestation of God) in 1:9-20.

The omnipotent and omniscient Christ who will subjugate all things under His authority is the central figure in this book.

"The Things Which Are" (2–3). The messages to the seven churches (2–3) refer back to an aspect of John's vision of Christ and contain a command, a commendation and or condemnation, a correction, and a challenge.

"The Things Which Will Take Place After This" (4–22). John is translated into heaven where he is given a vision of the divine majesty. In it, the Father ("One sat on the throne") and the Son (The Lion/Lamb) are worshipped by the twenty-four elders, the four living creatures, and the angelic host because of who they are and what they have done (creation and redemption; 4–5).

Three cycles of seven judgments in chapters 6–16 consist of seven seals, seven trumpets, and seven bowls. There is a prophetic insert between the sixth and seventh seal and trumpet judgments and an extended insert between the trumpet and bowl judgments. Because of the similarity of the seventh judgment in each series, it is possible that the three sets of judgments take place concurrently or with some overlap so that they all terminate with the return of Christ. An alternate approach views them as three consecutive series of judgments, so that the seventh seal is the seven trumpets, and the seventh trumpet is the seven bowls.

The seven seals (6:1–8:5) include war, the famine and death that are associated with war, and persecution. The prophetic insert between the sixth and seventh seals (7) describes the protective sealing of 144,000 "children of Israel," 12,000 from every tribe. It also looks ahead to the multitudes from every part of the earth who come "out of the great tribulation." The catastrophic events in most of the trumpet judgments are called "woes" (8:2–11:19). The prophetic interlude between the sixth and seventh trumpets (10:1–11:14) adds more details about the nature of the tribulation period and mentions a fourth set of seven judgments (the "seven thunders"), which would have extended it if they had not been withdrawn. Two unnamed witnesses minister during three-and-a-half years of the tribulation (forty-two months or 1,260 days). At the end of their ministry they are overcome by the beast, but their resurrection and ascension confound their enemies.

Chapters 12–14 contain a number of miscellaneous prophecies that are inserted between the trumpet and bowl judgments to give further background on the time of tribulation. In chapter 12 a woman gives birth to a male child, who is caught up to God. The woman flees into the wilderness and is pursued by a dragon, who is cast down to earth. Chapter 13 gives a graphic description of the beast and his false prophet, both empowered by the dragon. The first beast is given political, economic, and religious authority; and because of his power and the lying miracles performed by the second beast, he is worshipped as the ruler of the earth. Chapter 14 contains a series of visions including the 144,000 at the end of the tribulation, the fate of those who follow the beast, and the outpouring of the wrath of God.

The seven bowl judgments of chapter 16 are prefaced by a heavenly vision of the power, holiness, and glory of God in chapter 15.

Chapters 17–18 anticipate the final downfall of Babylon, the great harlot sitting upon a scarlet-colored beast.

The marriage banquet of the Lamb is ready and the King of kings, Lord of lords leads the armies of heaven into battle against the beast and his false prophet. They are cast into a lake of fire (19).

In chapter 20 the dragon—Satan—is bound for a thousand years. He is cast into a bottomless pit. During this one thousand year period Christ reigns over the earth with His resurrected saints, but by the end of this millennium, many have been born who refuse to submit their hearts to Christ. At the end of the thousand years, Satan is released and a final battle ensues. This is followed by the judgment at the great white throne.

A new universe is created, this time unspoiled by sin, death, pain, or sorrow. The New Jerusalem, described in 21:9–22:5, is shaped like a gigantic cube, 1,500 miles in length, width, and height (the most holy place in the Old Testament tabernacle and the temple was also a perfect cube). Its multicolored stones will reflect the glory of God, and it will continually be filled with light. But the greatest thing of all is that believers will be in the presence of God and "they shall see His face."

Revelation concludes with an epilogue (22:6-21), which reassures the readers that Christ is coming quickly (22:7,12,20) and invites all who wish to "take the water of life freely" (22:17) to come to the Alpha and Omega, the Bright and Morning Star.

OUTLINE OF REVELATION

Part One: "The Things Which You Have Seen" (1:1-20)

I. Introduction (1:1-8)

II. Revelation of Christ (1:9-20)

Part Two: "The Things Which Are" (2:1–3:22)

I. Message to Ephesus (2:1-7)

II. Message to Smyrna (2:8-11)

III. Message to Pergamos (2:12-17)

IV. Message to Thyatira (2:18-29)

V. Message to Sardis (3:1-6)

VI. Message to Philadelphia (3:7-13)

VII. Message to Laodicea (3:14-22)

Part Three: "The Things Which Will Take Place After This" (4:1–22:21)

I. Person of the Judge (4:1–5:14)

A. The Throne of God 4:1-11
B. The Sealed Book 5:1-14

II. Prophecies of Tribulation (6:1–19:6)

A. Seven Seals of Judgment............ 6:1–8:5
B. Seven Trumpets of Judgment 8:6–11:19
C. Explanatory Prophecies 12:1–14:20
D. Seven Bowls of Judgment 15:1–19:6

III. Prophecies of the Second Coming (19:7-21)

A. Marriage Supper of the Lamb ... 19:7-10
B. Second Coming of Christ............19:11-21

IV. Prophecies of the Millennium (20:1-15)

A. Satan Is Bound 1,000 Years 20:1-3
B. Saints Reign 1,000 Years 20:4-6
C. Satan Is Released and Leads Rebellion 20:7-9
D. Satan Is Tormented Forever 20:10
E. Great White Throne Judgment ...20:11-15

V. Prophecies of the Eternal State (21:1–22:5)

A. New Heaven and Earth Are Created 21:1
B. New Jerusalem Descends 21:2-8
C. New Jerusalem Is Described ... 21:9–22:5

VI. Conclusion (22:6-21)

REVELRY

Wild partying, boisterous behavior, carousing. This was often associated with the worship of pagan gods, and also sexual misconduct (Ro 13:13; 1 Pe 4:3).

RE·VEN′GER

See AVENGER OF BLOOD.

REVERENCE

An attitude of respect and awe for God (He 12:28-29).

REVILE

See SCORN.

REWARDS AND PUNISHMENTS

God is "a rewarder of those who diligently seek Him" (He 11:6). He also negatively "rewards" or recompenses those who run away from or reject Him and live sinful, selfish lives.

Reward (misthos) is used in thirteen of the New Testament books. Significantly, Christ the rewarder uses the word first (Ma 5:12) in promising great reward in heaven to those who are persecuted for His sake. At the very end of the Bible, He mentions that "My reward is with Me" (Re 22:12) to repay His people for their works.

Paul makes it clear that salvation is not a reward, but is reckoned to us by grace (Ro 4:4).

However, the apostle does promise that each one will be rewarded according to individual labor for the Lord (1 Co 3:8). This text has to do with rewards for Christians. The "fire" here (v.13) tests the works to see if they are genuine. These are not fires to burn the Christian, but to burn away the dross of works done for the wrong reason (e.g. praise of men). The remaining works will receive a reward (v.14).

The following words are used for both reward and punishment. Since they can be translated either in a negative or positive way, depending on context, they are only translated in discussion.

Misthapodosia occurs three times in the Greek New Testament (all in Hebrews), twice for rewards, and once for punishment.

Reward (He 10:35): "Therefore do not cast away your confidence, which has great reward." The author is encouraging his readers to remain steadfast in light of eternal reward. The context (v.34) is largely one of temporal loss through persecution.

In the famous "faith chapter," Moses is praised for giving up the glamour and pleasure of the Egyptian court because he counted the reproach of Christ greater riches than the treasures in Egypt; for he "looked to the reward" (He 11:26). He had his eye on eternity, not Egypt.

Punishment (He 2:2-4): The author warns Christians not to think they will escape punishment when Old Testament law breakers "receive a just reward."

Antapodoma occurs twice, once positively and once negatively.

Reward (Lk 14:12-14): Christ warns of inviting only people who can invite you back so that you will "be repaid" (lit. "get a reward," *antapodoma*). He tells His people to show charity to the really unfortunate; then they will "be repaid" (verb forming this noun) "at the resurrection of the just." When Christians serve the poor, they serve Christ and will receive an eternal *apodoma*.

Punishment (Ro 11:9): Paul quotes David from Psalm 69:22: "Let their table become a snare and a trap, a stumbling block and recompense to them." He uses this verse to show that *unbelieving* Israelites, in contrast to the godly remnant, will be recompensed for their hardheartedness.

Antimisthia is also used twice, positively and negatively:

Reward (2 Co 6:13): The derivation of this word suggests give-and-take, and that is what Paul requests of the Corinthians: "Now in return [*antimisthia*] for the same (I speak as to children), you also be open." This speaks of everyday rewards between people.

Punishment (Ro 1:26): The context is a detailed "sin catalog" of the Roman world. Now Paul writes that those that perverted God's natural order will receive "in themselves a penalty [*antimisthia*] of their error which was due" (v.27). This probably refers chiefly to the psychological and physical problems that perversion fosters. If they repent, of course, the penalty need not stretch into eternity.

The subject of rewards and punishments is both solemn and encouraging: solemn to those who are either rejecting God or frittering away their time, and encouraging to those who are working for the Kingdom.

RE′ZEPH

A city near Haran mentioned by Sennacherib (2 Ki 19:12; Is 37:12).

RE′ZI·A

See RIZIA.

RE′ZIN

Two men mentioned in the Old Testament:

1. A king of Damascus in the time of Jotham and Ahaz of Judah and Pekah of Israel. He was allied with Pekah, their purpose being to dethrone Ahaz and place their own king upon the throne of Judah. Isaiah encouraged Ahaz not to fear these pagan kings (Is 7:1–9:12). Ahaz, however, did not listen to Isaiah, and secured the cooperation of Tiglath-pileser of Assyria who beseiged Damascus and killed Rezin (2 Ki 15:37; 16:6-9).

2. Head of a family of Nethinim (Ez 2:48; Ne 7:50).

RE′ZON

Son of Eliadah of Zobah (1 Ki 11:23-25).

RHE′GI·UM

A city opposite Messina in Sicily on the coast of Italy (Ac 28:13).

RHE´ SA

A descendant of Zerubbabel and ancestor of Christ (Lk 3:27).

RHO´ DA *(rose)*

A servant of the mother of Mark (Ac 12:13-16).

RHODES *(a rose)*

An island southwest of Asia Minor (Ac 21:1).

RI·BA´ I *(contentious)*

Father of Ittai, a Benjamite (2 Sa 23:29; 1 Ch 11:31).

RIB´ LAH *(fertility)*

A town of Hamath to which Jehoahaz, son of Josiah and king of Judah, was brought when taken from the throne by Pharaoh-necho (2 Ki 23:33).

RICH FOOL, PARABLE OF (Lk 12:16-21)

RICH MAN AND LAZARUS, PARABLE OF (Lk 16:19-31)

RID´ DLE

A saying, the meaning of which is concealed and can only be understood by shrewd thinking. Samson asked the Philistines a riddle (Ju 14:12-19).

RIE Archaic spelling of rye

See SPELT.

RIGHTEOUSNESS

One of the most awesome requirements of God made upon men and women is that they be righteous, that is, conform to His ethical and moral standards (Ps 15:2; Mi 6:8). Since God is holy, He cannot allow sinners into His presence (Is 6:3-5). Since all persons are sinners, they could not be saved apart from the supernatural intervention of God (Ro 3:10,23). The righteous demands of God coupled with the inability of man might present an insoluble dilemma. God Himself, however, has graciously solved the problem. He sent Christ, who never sinned, to die for our sins and thus satisfy His own wrath toward us. Simply put, it means that God, at the cross, treated Christ as though He had committed our sins even though He was righteous. On the other hand, when we believe in Christ,

He treats us as though we were as righteous as Christ (2 Co 5:21). The Bible calls this type of righteousness "imputed righteousness" (Ro 4:6). That simply means that God puts to our spiritual account the very worth of Christ, much as though He were a banker adding an inexhaustible deposit to our bank account. There are, sadly, many people who still refuse to believe that such an abundant blessing can be theirs as a free gift (Ep 2:8-9). Nevertheless, the Bible clearly urges all men to trust in Jesus Christ as Savior and thus be reckoned as righteous by God (Ro 4:24).

RIM´ MON *(pomegranate)*

Two towns, a rock, a man, and a pagan god:

1. A town in the south of Judah (Jos 15:32; 1 Ch 4:32; Ze 14:10). It was afterwards assigned to Simeon (Jos 19:7).

2. A town of Zebulun assigned to the Levites (Jos 19:13; 1 Ch 6:77), also called Rimmon-methoar (KJV).

3. The rock of Rimmon. A rock near Gibeah where the defeated Benjamites remained for four months (Ju 20:45-47; 21:13). Ravines and caves afforded them safe shelter.

4. A Benjamite whose sons assassinated Ish-bosheth, king of Israel (2 Sa 4:2).

5. A god of the Syrians (2 Ki 5:18).

RIM´ MON-ME·THO´ AR

See RIMMON No. 2.

RIM´ MON-PAR´ EZ

See RIMMON PEREZ.

RIM´ MON-PER´ EZ *(pomegranate of the cleft)*

A place where the Israelites camped in the wilderness (Nu 33:19-20).

RIM´ MON, ROCK OF

See RIMMON No. 3

RING

An article of jewelry, a circlet of precious metal worn on the finger, ornamented with jewels or with a signet. A king's signet ring was a symbol of authority (Ge 41:42; Es 3:10). See SEAL.

RINGLEADER

The leader of a group, usually a group of troublemakers. Paul was derisively called the "ringleader" of the obnoxious new followers of Jesus (Ac 24:5).

RIN′ NAH *(a shout)*

A son of Shimon of Judah (1 Ch 4:20).

RI′ PHATH

Son of Gomer and grandson of Japheth (Ge 10:3). Also called Diphath (1 Ch 1:6; RV).

RIS′ SAH *(a ruin)*

A campsite of the Israelites in their wanderings (Nu 33:21-22).

RITHMAH

A campsite of the Israelites in the wilderness (Nu 33:18-19).

RIV′ ER OF E′ GYPT

1. The Nile (Ge 15:18). This and the Euphrates are designated as the bounds of the land of promise, the inheritance of the chosen people.

2. The desert stream, called the river of Egypt (Nu 34:5; 1 Ki 8:65; 2 Ki 24:7). See EGYPT, BROOK OF.

RIVERS OF THE BIBLE

Fourteen of the great rivers of the Bible are as follows:

Abanah and Pharpar are two rivers of Damascus regarded by Naaman the Syrian leper as superior to the Jordan River (2 Ki 5:12).

Arnon is a river in southern Canaan mentioned in Joshua's invasion of the land (Jo 12:1).

Chebar is a river or canal in Babylon, beside which some of the Jewish people, including the prophet Ezekiel lived as captives (Eze 1:3).

The Habor (the River at Gozan) is an Assyrian River beside which citizens of the Northern Kingdom were settled as captives (2 Ki 17:6).

Jabbock is a tributary of the Jordan where Jacob struggled with an angel (Ge 32:22-32).

Jordan is the major river of Palestine; the stream where Jesus was baptized (Ma 3:6,13) and the river boundary that the Israelites crossed into the promised land (Jo 3).

Kishon is a river in northern Canaan where Deborah and Barak were victorious over their enemies.

Nile (or Sihor) is the greatest river of Egypt and the world's longest (Je 2:18).

Pishon, Gihon, Hiddekel (Tigris), and Euphra-

tes are four rivers that flowed out of the garden of Eden (Ge 2:11-14).

Ulai, the river or canal near Shushan in Persia is mentioned in Daniel's vision (Da 8:2,16).

(See also EUPHRATES, JORDAN, NILE, TIGRIS,).

RI′ ZI•A *(delight)*

Son of Ulla of Asher (1 Ch 7:39).

RIZ′ PAH *(a hot coal)*

A concubine of Saul and daughter of Aiah, a Hivite. Her sons were hanged by the Gibeonites during the reign of David (2 Sa 21:8-11).

ROADS, PALESTINIAN

The prophet Isaiah spoke symbolically of a "Highway of Holiness" over which "the unclean shall not pass" (Is 35:8). But the Bible makes few references to the actual physical roads that connected the cities of Palestine and surrounding regions in Bible times. Scholars do know that two major north-to-south trade routes passed through the nation. The first, called "The Way of the Sea," connected the ancient Phoenician seaports of Tyre and Sidon with other cities along the Mediterranean. This road may have stretched as far south as the northern reaches of Egypt.

The second major north-south route across Palestine was the King's Highway, which connected Ezion Geber, or Elath, in the South with the city of Damascus, Syria, in the North.

While Israel was a relatively small nation, other nations often passed through it because of its strategic location as a land bridge between Egypt in the South and the nations of Syria, Assyria, Persia, and Babylon to the North and Northeast.

ROADS, ROMAN

The Romans were enthusiastic road builders. Across a period of about five centuries they completed roads that extended to every corner of their empire. This road system opened up areas to trade and allowed Rome to deploy troops to all regions they controlled in the ancient world.

The Romans built their roads in straight lines as much as possible, often cutting tunnels through mountains. Trenches were dug the width of the road and four or five feet deep. Successive layers of large and small stones were added to the roadbed until it was even with the surrounding terrain. Then the roads were surfaced with a layer of gravel, although in high traffic areas they were often paved with volcanic sand or large stones carefully fitted together.

Mile markers along these routes helped travelers keep track of the distances they traveled on their journeys and navigate from city to city.

One of the most famous Roman roads, the Appian Way, was named for the Roman censor Appius Claudius, who began its construction in 312 B.C. This road ran from just south of Rome along the coast of western Italy to the southernmost tip of Italy on the Adriatic Sea. The apostle Paul probably traveled this road to meet friends at Appii Forum, about forty miles south of Rome (Ac 28:15). It is one of the roads that continues to be used today.

Another road probably traveled by Paul on his missionary journeys was the route which ran from Antioch of Syria to Antioch of Pisidia. This road served Tarsus, Derbe, Lystra, and Iconium (Ac 14). On his travels still further west, Paul probably used another major Roman road, linking the cities of Berea, Thessalonica, Amphipolis, Philippi, and Neapolis (Ac 17:1-13).

Since nearly all important roads led to the city of Rome in Paul's time, this advanced transportation network helped Christianity to spread to the far reaches of the Roman world.

ROB′BER

See THIEF.

ROBBERY

Apart from the normal meaning of robbery, the word appears in an unusual sense in some translations of Philippians 2:6. Jesus "who being in the form of God, did not consider it robbery to be equal with God . . ." (KJV and NKJV). This makes a curious statement. How is equality with God robbery? Other translations have said that He "did not consider equality with God something to be grasped" (NIV and NASB). The difficulty in translation comes from the fact that the Greek word *harpagmos* occurs only once in the New Testament (Ph 2:6), and nowhere else in extant Greek writings. Many people believe that this was a term coined by Paul himself. It comes from the word *harpōzō*, which means "to carry away by force," or "snatch up." In 1 Thessalonians 4:17, this word is translated "caught up." The Latin translation of this verse gave us the English word "rapture." It is also

used to mean the actions of a thief (Ma 12:29). It appears that Paul took this verb meaning "snatch" or "grab," and made it into a noun: "a thing to be grabbed or clutched." Jesus did not consider equality with God something that He had to take by force. He did not need to grab or snatch at it, He didn't need to commit robbery in order to gain equality. It was already His, simply because of who He is. He was "in the very form of God," and yet willingly gave up this position in order to become a servant.

ROBE

An article of clothing, an outer garment.

RO·BO′AM

See REHOBOAM.

ROCK

The translation of several Greek and Hebrew words meaning both a solid piece of stone and a cliff or crag. It might serve as a dwelling or a place of refuge (Job 30:6; Je 4:29). Many rocks were given names; for example, the rocks of Oreb, Etam, and Rimmon (Ju 7:25; 15:8; 20:45; 21:13). The word was often used figuratively to denote the strength of God, the church, and of faith (De 32:4,31,37; 2 Sa 22:2-3; Ps 18:1-2; 62:7; Is 17:10; Ma 16:18). Christ was called the Rock (1 Co 10:4).

ROCK BADGER

A small animal found among rocks. It is also called the coney or rock hyrax (Ps 104:18; Pr 30:26). It has long whiskers, a short tail and ears, and appears to chew its cud because of its habit of constant nibbling.

ROCK GOAT

Wild sheep which lived in the mountains of Canaan (De 14:5); also referred to as "mountain sheep," or "chamois."

ROCK HYRAX

See ROCK BADGER.

ROD

A staff, particularly a shepherd's staff. People carried rods as walking sticks (Ge 32:10; Ex 4:2), used them as weapons (Ex 21:20; 1 Sa 14:27), and to inflict punishments (2 Sa 7:14; 1 Co 4:21). The rods of Aaron and Moses were used to perform miraculous signs (Ex 4:20; Nu 17:2-10). A shepherd's rod is a good example of the multiple uses of such a staff. A shepherd used his rod to protect the sheep against enemies, as a tool to rescue the sheep from awkward situations, and to discipline unruly animals. Thus the shepherd's rod was a symbol of security and protection (Ps 23:4). The reference to the rod in Proverbs 13:24 is not only speaking of the rod in the sense of punishment or discipline, but in the full sense of the shepherd's rod. A parent who does not protect, rescue and train his children does not love them.

RO'DA·NIM

See DODANIM.

ROE, ROE'BUCK

A small deer or gazelle which was regarded as ceremonially clean (De 12:15,22; 14:5; 15:22; 1 Ki 4:23). It changes color in winter from dark brown to yellowish gray. The roebuck roams about Carmel and Lebanon in Palestine.

RO'GE·LIM *(fullers)*

A town in Gilead which was the residence of Barzillai (2 Sa 17:27; 19:31).

ROH'GAH *(clamor)*

Son of Shamer of Asher (1 Ch 7:34).

ROLL

A sheet of parchment or papyrus rolled around a stick. It was used by the ancients as writing paper (Je 36:2). It was also called a volume (Ps 40:7).

RO·MAM'TI-E'ZER *(I have raised a help)*

A son of Heman, a singer (1 Ch 25:4,31).

ROMAN

One who lived in Rome (Ac 2:10) or a representative of the Roman government (Ac 25:16; 28:17); anyone who had the rights of citizenship in the empire, irrespective of nationality. See ROMAN CITIZENSHIP.

ROMAN CITIZENSHIP

The apostle Paul was born at Tarsus, the chief city of the Roman province of Cilicia in southeast Asia Minor. While he was thoroughly Jewish by nationality, he was also born a Roman citizen (Ac 22:28), a privilege which worked to his advantage on several occasions during his ministry.

As the ruling world power of Paul's time, the Romans consolidated their empire by granting Roman citizenship to certain non-Romans. Paul's parents must have enjoyed this right before him, and he automatically became a Roman citizen at birth.

A Roman citizen could not be bound or imprisoned without a trial. Neither could he be beaten or scourged—the common form of torture used by the Romans to extract a confession from a prisoner. Finally, if a Roman citizen felt he was not receiving a fair trial under local authorities, he could appeal his cause to Rome.

Paul and his partner Silas were bound, beaten, and imprisoned by Roman authorities at Philippi. When Paul made it clear that he at least was a Roman citizen, the authorities quickly released them and begged them to leave town (Ac 16:12-40).

Later, in Jerusalem, Paul was taken into protective custody by Roman soldiers as a group of Jewish zealots threatened his life. He was spared a scourging by the soldiers and granted a hearing before their commander when he revealed his Roman citizenship (Ac 22:24-29). The soldiers also gave him safe passage out of Jerusalem when the zealots persisted in their threats against Paul (Ac 23: 23-24).

Imprisoned by Roman officials at Caesarea for two years, Paul finally appealed to Rome (Ac 25:11-12). He was sent on a merchant ship to Rome (Ac 27), where he spent two years under house arrest. Here he was allowed to preach and make converts (Ac 28:30-31).

Even the tradition that Paul was beheaded in Rome shows the influence of his Roman citizenship. Non-Roman criminals were generally crucified; beheading was a more honorable and merciful form of capital punishment reserved for Roman citizens.

ROMAN EMPIRE

Modern Israel still bears many signs of the Roman occupation of that country. Ruins of the aqueduct and theater at Caesarea, the Roman encampment at Masada, and the Roman road at Emmaus bring to mind many mental pictures of what life under the Romans must have been like during New Testament times.

Rome was founded about 750 B.C., but it did not reach the status of a world power until several centuries later through victories over the Carthaginians and the Greeks. By New Testament times, the Romans were thoroughly entrenched as the ruling power of the ancient world.

Throughout the entire New Testament period various emperors ruled over the Roman Empire. During the reign of Augustus, Christ was born (Lk 2:1). His crucifixion occurred during the reign of the succeeding emperor, Tiberius (Lk 3:1). The martyrdom of James, the brother of John, took place in the reign of the emperor Claudius (Ac 11:28; 12:1-2). Paul appealed his case to the emperor Nero (Ac 25:11). The destruction of Jerusalem prophesied by Jesus (Lk 19:41-44) was accomplished in A.D. 70 by the Roman general Titus, who later became emperor. Thus, all of the New Testament story unfolded under the reign of Roman emperors.

The entire territory around the Mediterranean Sea ruled by the Romans enjoyed a time of peace and prosperity during New Testament times. The great Roman roads were built mainly as military routes from the capital city of Rome into the provinces and territories Rome controlled. A stable money system and improved methods of banking and credit encouraged economic expansion. Rome sent its merchant ships throughout the ancient world, trading in wine, olive oil, and grain.

The general stability of these times contributed to the spread of Christianity throughout the Roman world. Paul could travel easily from one Roman province to another over the great Roman roads and sea routes to spread the gospel. While the Romans themselves worshiped pagan gods, they were generally tolerant of all religions among the peoples and nations whom they controlled.

The Book of Acts shows how Christianity spread throughout the Roman Empire. Under Paul, the great missionary to the Gentiles, the gospel was preached as far west as the city of Rome and perhaps even into Spain (Ro 15:28). By the time Paul wrote his Epistle to the Romans, a large Christian community existed in the capital city of Rome (Ro 1:7).

In its early stages, Christianity was ignored by the Romans because they thought it was a harmless sect of Judaism. But this apparently changed when Nero became emperor of Rome. Many Christians were arrested, tortured, crucified, and burned during his administration, seemingly in an attempt to blame them for the widespread rebellion and unrest that marked his years

of rule. This persecution continued under the emperor Domitian.

The Romans worshiped many pagan gods: Jupiter, who was believed to control the universe; Mars, god of war; Juno, patron goddess of women; and Minerva, goddess of war, wisdom, and skill. The capital city of Rome was filled with shrines and temples devoted to worship of these pagan gods. Eventually, of course, the clash between dead idolatry and the living Christ broke down the original "Roman tolerance." But as Paul said, even that served to further the gospel. (Ph 1:12-18).

ROMAN ROADS
(See ROADS, ROMAN).

RO′MANS, E·PIS′TLE TO THE

1. The Book of Romans. Romans, Paul's greatest work, is placed first among his thirteen epistles in the New Testament. While the four Gospels present the words and works of Jesus Christ, Romans explores the significance of His sacrificial death. Using a question-and-answer format, Paul records the most systematic presentation of doctrine in the Bible. Romans is more than a book of theology; it is also a book of practical exhortation. The good news of Jesus Christ is more than facts to be believed; it is also a life to be lived—a life of righteousness befitting the person "justified freely by God's grace through the redemption that is in Christ Jesus" (3:24).

Although some manuscripts omit "in Rome" in 1:7,15, the title *Pros Romaious,* "To the Romans," has been associated with the epistle almost from the beginning.

2. The Author of Romans. All critical schools agree on the Pauline authorship (1:1) of this foundational book. The vocabulary, style, logic, and theological development are consistent with Paul's other epistles. Paul dictated this letter to a secretary named Tertius (16:22), who was allowed to add his own greeting.

The problem arises not with the authorship but with the disunity of the epistle. Some Latin (but no Greek) manuscripts omit 15:1–16:24, and the closing doxology (16:25-27) is placed at the end of chapter 14 in some manuscripts. These variations have led some scholars to conclude that the last two chapters were not originally part of the epistle, or that Paul issued it in two editions. However, most scholars believe that chapter 15 fits in logically with the rest of the epistle. There is more debate over chapter 16, because Paul greets by name twenty-six persons in a church he has never visited. Some scholars contend that it was a separate letter, perhaps written to Ephesus, which was appended to this epistle. Such a letter would be surprising, to say the least (nothing but greetings), especially in the ancient world. It is simpler to understand the list of greetings as Paul's effort as a stranger to the Roman church to list his mutual friends. Paul met these people in the cities of his missionary journeys. Significantly, the only other Pauline Epistle that lists individual greetings was addressed to the believers at Colosse, another church Paul had never visited. It may be that this portion was omitted from some copies of Romans because it did not seem relevant.

3. The Time of Romans. Paul did not found the church at Rome, and the tradition that Peter was its founder is contrary to the evidence. It is possible that it began when some of the Jews and proselytes to Judaism who became followers of Christ on the day of Pentecost (Ac 2:10) returned to Rome, but it is more likely that Christians from churches established by Paul in Asia, Macedonia, and Greece settled in Rome and led others to Christ. According to this epistle, Gentiles were predominant in the church at Rome (1:13; 11:13,28-31; 15:15-16), but there were also Jewish believers (2:17–3:8; 3:21–4:1; 7:1-14; 14:1–15:12).

Rome was founded in 753 B.C., and by the time of Paul it was the greatest city in the world with over one million inhabitants (one inscription says four million). It was full of magnificent buildings, but the majority of people were slaves; opulence and squalor coexisted in the Imperial City. The church in Rome was well-known (1:8), and it had been established for several years by the time of this letter (see 14:14; 15:23). The believers there were probably numerous, and evidently they met in several places (16:1-16). The historian Tacitus referred to the Christians who were persecuted under Nero in A.D. 64 as "an immense multitude." The gospel filled the gap left by the practically defunct polytheism of Roman religion.

Paul wrote Romans in A.D. 57, near the end of his third missionary journey (Ac 18:23–21:14; Ro 15:19). It was evidently written during his three-month stay in Greece (Ac 20:3-6), more specifically, in Corinth. Paul was staying with Gaius of Corinth (16:23; 1 Co 1:14), and he also mentioned "Erastus, the treasurer of the city" (16:23). A first-century inscription in Corinth mentions him: "Erastus, the commissioner of public works, laid this pavement at his own expense." Paul's collection from the churches of Macedonia and Achaia for the needy Christians in Jerusalem was complete (15:26), and he was ready to deliver it (15:25). Instead of sailing directly to Jerusalem, Paul avoided a plot by the Jews by first going north to Philippi. He evidently gave this letter to Phoebe from the church at Cenchrea, near Corinth, and she carried it to Rome (16:1-2).

4. The Christ of Romans. Paul presents Jesus Christ as the second Adam whose righteousness and substitutionary death have provided justification for all who place their faith in Him. He offers His righteousness as a gracious gift to sinful men, having borne God's condemnation and wrath for their sinfulness. His death and resurrection are the basis for the believer's redemption, justification, reconciliation, salvation, and glorification.

5. Keys to Romans.

Key Word: The Righteousness of God— The theme of Romans is found in 1:16-17: God offers the gift of His righteousness to everyone who comes to Christ by faith. Paul writes Romans to reveal God's sovereign plan of salvation (1–8), to show how Jews and Gentiles fit into that plan (9–11), and to exhort them to live righteous and harmonious lives (12–16). In his sweeping presentation of God's plan of salvation, Paul moves from condemnation to glorification and from positional truth to practical truth. Key words, such as *righteousness, faith, law, all,* and *sin* each appear at least sixty times in this epistle.

Key Verses: Romans 1:16-17 and 3:21-25— "For I am not ashamed of the gospel of Christ, for it is the power of God to salvation for everyone who believes, for the Jew first and also for the Greek. For in it the righteousness of God is revealed from faith to faith; as it is written, 'The just shall live by faith'" (1:16-17).

"But now the righteousness of God apart from the law is revealed, being witnessed by the Law and the Prophets, even the righteousness of God which is through faith in Jesus Christ to all and on all who believe. For there is no difference; for all have sinned and fall short of the glory of God, being justified freely by His grace through the redemption that is in Christ Jesus, who God set forth to be a propitiation by His blood, through faith, to demonstrate His righteousness, because in His forbearance God had passed over the sins that were previously committed" (3:21-25).

Key Chapters: Romans 6–8—Foundational to all teaching on the spiritual life is the central passage of Romans 6–8. The answers to the questions of how to be delivered from sin, how to live a balanced life under grace, and how to live the victorious Christian life through the power of the Holy Spirit are all contained here. Many consider this to be the principle passage on conforming to the image of Jesus Christ.

6. Survey of Romans. The poet Samuel Taylor Coleridge regarded Romans as "the most profound book in existence," and the commentator Godet called it "the cathedral of the Christian faith." Because of its majestic declaration of the divine plan of salvation, Martin Luther wrote: "This epistle is the chief part of the New Testament and the very purest gospel. . . . It can never be read or pondered too much, and the more it is dealt with the more precious it becomes, and the better it tastes." The four Gospels present the words and works of the Lord Jesus, but Romans, "the Gospel According to Paul," delves more into the significance of His death and resurrection. The theology of Romans is balanced by practical exhortation, because Paul sees the believer's position as the basis for his practice. The theme of righteousness that runs through the book is reflected in the following outline: the revelation of the righteousness of God (1–8); the vindication of the righteousness of God (9–11); the application of the righteousness of God (12–16).

The Revelation of the Righteousness of God (1–8). The prologue (1:1-17) consists of a salutation (1:1-7), a statement of Paul's desire to minister in Rome (1:8-15), and the theme of the book (1:16-17). This two-verse theme is the basic text of Romans because it combines the three crucial concepts of salvation, righteousness, and faith.

In 1:18–3:20, Paul builds a solid case for the condemnation of all people under the holy God. The Gentiles are without excuse because they have suppressed the knowledge of God they received from nature and their conscience (1:18-32; their seven-step regression is traced in 1:21-

31). The Jews are also under the condemnation of God, and Paul overcomes every objection they could raise to this conclusion (2:1–3:8). God judges according to the truth (2:2-5), works (2:6-10), and impartiality (2:11-16), and both the moral and religious Jews fail to meet His standard. Paul concludes his discussion of the reasons for the guilt of the Jews by reminding them they do not obey the law (2:17-29) nor believe the Oracles of God (3:1-8). The divine verdict (3:9-20) is universal: "all have sinned and fall short of the glory of God" (3:23).

The section on justification (3:21–5:21) centers on and develops the theme of God's provision for man's need. The first eleven verses are the core of the book (3:21-31), revealing that in Christ, God is both Judge and Savior. Justification is by grace (the source of salvation; 3:21-24), by blood (the basis of salvation; 3:25-26), by faith (the condition of salvation; 3:27-31).

Chapter 4 illustrates the principles of justification by faith apart from works in the life of Abraham. Justification issues in reconciliation between God and man (5:1-11). It is brought about by the love of God which is causeless (5:6), measureless (5:7-8), and ceaseless (5:9-11). In 5:12-21 Paul contrasts the two Adams and the opposite results of their two acts. The righteousness of the second Adam is imputed to all who trust in Him, leading to reconciliation.

Chapter 6 describes the believer's relationship to sin: in his position he is dead to the principle of sin (6:1-14) and the practice of sin (6:15-23). The reality of identification with Christ is the basis for the sanctified Christian life. After describing the Christian's emancipation from the law (7), Paul looks at the work of the Holy Spirit who indwells and empowers every believer (8:1-17). The next major topic after condemnation, justification, and sanctification is glorification (8:18-39). All Christians can anticipate a time when they will be perfectly conformed to Jesus Christ not only in their position (present) but also in their practice (the future resurrection).

The Vindication of the Righteousness of God (9–11). It appears that God has rejected His people, Israel, but it is really Israel who has rejected her Messiah. God's rejection of Israel is only partial (there is a spiritual remnant that has trusted in Christ) and temporary (they will be grafted back; 11:23-27). Paul appropriately quotes frequently from the Old Testament in this section, and he emphasizes that God will be faithful to His covenant promises and restore Israel.

The Application of the Righteousness of God (12–16). Paul recognizes that behavior must be built upon belief, and this is why the practical exhortations of this epistle appear after his teaching on the believers position in Christ. The salvation described in the first eleven chapters should transform a Christian's life in relation to God (12:1-2), society (12:3-21), higher powers (13:1-7), and one's neighbors (13:8-14). In chapters 14–15 the apostle discusses the whole concept of Christian liberty, noting its principles (14) and its practice (15:1-13). A changed life is not a condition for salvation, but it should be the natural outcome of saving faith. The epistle closes with Paul's statement of his plans (15:14-33), a long series of personal greetings (16:1-16), and an admonition followed by a doxology (16:17-27).

OUTLINE OF ROMANS

Part One: The Revelation of the Righteousness of God (1:1–8:39)

I. Introduction (1:1-17)

II. Condemnation: The Need for God's Righteousness (1:18–3:20)

A. Guilt of the Gentile 1:18-32
B. Guilt of the Jew........................ 2:1–3:8
C. Conclusion: All Are Guilty Before God 3:9-20

III. Justification: The Imputation of God's Righteousness (3:21–5:21)

A. Description of Righteousness 3:21-31

B. Illustration of Righteousness 4:1-25
C. Benefits of Righteousness 5:1-11
D. Contrast of Righteousness and Condemnation 5:12-21

IV. Sanctification: The Demonstration of God's Righteousness (6:1–8:39)

A. Sanctification and Sin 6:1-23
B. Sanctification and the Law 7:1-25
C. Sanctification and the Spirit 8:1-39

Part Two: The Vindication of the Righteousness of God (9:1–11:36)

I. Israel's Past: The Election of God (9:1-29)

A. Paul's Sorrow.............................. 9:1-5
B. God's Sovereignty 9:6-29

II. Israel's Present: The Rejection of God (9:30–10:21)

A. Israel Seeks Righteousness by Works 9:30-33

B. Israel Rejects Christ.................. 10:1-15
C. Israel Rejects the Prophets......... 10:16-21

III. Israel's Future: The Restoration by God (11:1-36)

A. Israel's Rejection Is Not Total ... 11:1-10
B. Israel's Rejection Is Not Final ...11:11-32
C. Israel's Restoration: The Occasion for Glorifying God.................... 11:33-36

Part Three: The Application of the Righteousness of God (12:1–16:27)

I. Righteousness of God Demonstrated in Christian Duties (12:1–13:14)

A. Responsibilities Toward God 12:1-2
B. Responsibilities Toward Society 12:3-21
C. Responsibilities Toward Higher Powers 13:1-7
D. Responsibilities Toward Neighbors 13:8-14

II. Righteousness of God Demonstrated in Christian Liberties (14:1–15:13)

A. Principles of Christian Liberty ... 14:1-23
B. Practices of Christian Liberty ... 15:1-13

III. Conclusion (15:14–16:27)

A. Paul's Purpose for Writing 15:14-21
B. Paul's Plans for Traveling 15:22-33
C. Paul's Praise and Greetings 16:1-27

ROME, CITY OF

Seat of the mighty Roman Empire. Rome was the largest and most magnificent city of its day, with a population of more than 1,000,000 people in New Testament times. Situated near where the Tiber River meets the Mediterranean Sea, it was called *Urbis Septicollis* ("City of the Seven Hills") because of the seven hills upon which it is built.

When the apostle Paul entered Rome as a prisoner about A.D. 58, the city boasted of a history extending back more than 800 years. According to the legends of the Romans, the city was founded in 753 B.C. by Romulus, the son of the Roman god Mars. The city grew across the years as the Roman Empire expanded its power and influence throughout the ancient world.

Rome reached the height of its splendor under the emperor Augustus. Especially notable was the Forum, the center of the city with roads leading off in all directions, and the great outdoor theater known as the Colosseum, where Roman games and public events were held. The city featured more than 400 temples dedicated to worship of pagan gods. It was also noted for its public buildings, baths, aqueducts, arches, temples, and roads.

To keep from being killed by hostile Jews at Jerusalem, and because he was a Roman citizen (Ac 22:27), Paul appealed to Caesar, an act that ultimately brought him to Rome as a prisoner to await trial. Paul must have seen many of Rome's pagan temples and spectacular public buildings when he entered the city on the famous road known as the Via Appia (Appian Way). He was kept at first under house arrest, and later, according to tradition, as a condemned prisoner in a dungeon near the Forum.

The Great Missionary to the Gentiles proclaimed the gospel to all classes of people while in Rome, especially to Greek-speaking easterners (called "Greeks" in Romans 1:16) and Jews. According to tradition, he was executed outside the city at a spot on the Via Ostia about A.D. 68.

Paul's first known connection with Rome had occurred several years before he actually visited the city. During his ministry at Corinth, he worked with Priscilla and Aquila, who had left Rome when the emperor Claudius expelled all Jews from the city (Ac 18:2). An active Christian church also existed at Rome several years before Paul arrived in the city; these were the Christians to whom Paul addressed his letter known as the Epistle to the Romans.

In Paul's time the houses of the wealthy people of Rome were elaborately constructed and situated on the various hills of the city. But the common people lived in tenements, much like the crowded inner city of a modern metropolis. Thousands of people were crowded into these tenements, which were surrounded by narrow, noisy streets with a constant flow of traffic.

The citizens of Rome received food and entertainment from the government. Wine was cheap and plentiful. Admission to the Roman games was free. Thousands of people attended these games, which included contests among the gladiators, chariot races, and theatrical performances.

Like Babylon, the city of Rome became a symbol of idolatry and paganism in the New Testament. The Christians, with their steadfast loyalty to the one true God known through Jesus Christ, and who seemed such a threat to the Emperors Nero and Domitian, left an indelible mark on Rome through their martyrdom. Many scholars believe that the eventual fall of Rome was linked to the kind of character that was willing to see "sport" in the death of the enemies of the state.

ROOF

Houses in ancient Israel were often built with flat roofs, and the roof was used as an extra room (2 Sa 11:2). The people were instructed to build low walls around their roofs to prevent people from accidentally falling off (De 22:8).

ROOM

A compartment or a chamber of a house. The word is also used to denote a place at the banquet table. The "highest" or "uppermost rooms" were considered places of distinction at the table. Jesus rebuked the scribes and Pharisees for seeking this kind of honor (Ma 23:6; Lk 14:7-8; 20:46).

ROOSTER

Adult male common domesticated chicken. Jesus predicted that Peter would deny him three times before the roosters began to crow in the early morning (Mk 14:30; Ma 26:34; Lk 22:34; Jo 13:38).

ROSE

A flowering plant mentioned in Isaiah 35:1 and in the expression "rose of Sharon" (Song

ROSETTA STONE

2:1). The flower of Isaiah 35:1 is most probably not the flower which we call a rose, but rather a bulb. Some translations use the word "crocus" or "asphodel." The modern Rose of Sharon is a plant native to China, and probably not the flower mentioned by Solomon.

ROSETTA STONE

A stone tablet, discovered in 1799, the archeological find which unlocked the secrets of the ancient Egyptian hieroglyphs. The same text was inscribed on the stone in three different languages: Koine Greek, hieroglyphic, and another Egyptian writing.

ROSH *(the head)*

1. Son of Benjamin mentioned only in Genesis 46:21. He probably died childless as a tribal family did not arise from him.

2. A word in Ezekiel 38:2-3; 39:1, translated *chief prince* in the KJV; possibly a northern tribal people.

ROYAL CITY

A capital city, where the king lived and ruled (2 Sa 12:26).

RUBBISH

That which is worthless, and worthy only to be discarded. See DUNG.

RU'BY

A precious stone having a ruddy, or red, color (Job 28:18; Pr 3:15; 8:11; 31:10; La 4:7). This precious stone is very rare and valuable; the Bible often uses it as a comparison for precious quali-

ties such as wisdom or virtue. Some scholars believe that the Hebrew word translated "ruby" was actually a red coral or pink pearl. It is also translated "agate," "rubies," "red jasper" and "coral." See ADAMANT.

RUDDY

The tint of healthy skin, a reddish color (Song 5:10; La 4:7). The youthful David is described as being "ruddy and handsome" (1 Sa 16:12; 17:42). It is generally considered to be a reference to his complexion, though some have interpreted it to mean that he had red hair.

RUDIMENTS

See ELEMENTS.

RUE

A shrub which grew to a height of two or three feet, having a strong odor. Its leaves are grayish green, and the flowers are small and yellow, growing in clusters. It was used medicinally. Mention is made of it in connection with the paying of tithes (Lk 11:42).

RU'FUS *(red)*

Son of Simon of Cyrene who was compelled to carry the cross of Jesus (Mk 15:21; Lk 23:26). It is supposed that he is the same Rufus to whom Paul sent greetings (Ro 16:13).

RU·HA'MAH *(mercy obtained)*

The name given to the daughter of Hosea (Ho 2:1), a symbolic reference to the people of Israel.

RUINS

The remains of a place once inhabited by man, which has been destroyed or allowed to fall into decay. The worship of idols or failure to act on our spiritual knowledge will bring us into spiritual decay and ruin (2 Ch 28:23; Lk 6:46-49).

RUE

RU' LER

The translation of a number of Greek and Hebrew words which for the most part mean one in authority. The word is used for a member of the Sanhedrin (Jo 3:1), for a king (1 Sa 25:30), a prime minister (Ge 41:43), a city magistrate (Ac 16:19; 17:6,8), a chief treasurer (1 Ch 26:24), and one who directed a feast (Jo 2:9).

RU' MAH *(high place)*

The residence of the grandfather of Jehoiakim, king of Judah, probably the same as Arumah (2 Ki 23:36).

RUN' NERS

The king's bodyguard (1 Sa 22:17). They were stationed at the door of the palace (1 Ki 14:27; 2 Ki 11:19) and accompanied the king to the temple (1 Ki 14:28).

RUSH

See REED.

RUST

Corrosion of metals by oxidation (Ma 6:19-20; Jam 5:3). Today, the word specifically means iron oxide, but here it refers to tarnish and corrosion of other metals. Ezekiel 24:6-13 compares sinful Israel with a disgustingly corroded cooking pot of copper or bronze.

RUTH, BOOK OF

1. The Book of Ruth. Ruth is a cameo story of love, devotion, and redemption set in the black context of the days of the judges. It is the story of a Moabite woman who forsook her pagan heritage in order to cling to the people of Israel and to the God of Israel. Because of her faithfulness in a time of national faithlessness, God rewarded her by giving her a new husband (Boaz), a son (Obed), and privileged position in the lineage of David and Christ (she was the great-grandmother of David).

Ruth is the Hebrew title of this book. This name may be a Moabite modification of the Hebrew word *reuit,* meaning "friendship or association." The Septuagint entitles the book *Routh,* the Greek equivalent of the Hebrew name. The Latin title is *Ruth,* a transliteration of *Routh.*

2. The Author of Ruth. The author of Ruth is not given anywhere in the book, nor is he known from any other biblical passage. Talmudic tradition attributes it to Samuel, but this is unlikely

since David appears in Ruth 4:17,22, and Samuel died before David's coronation (1 Sa 25:1). Ruth was probably written during David's reign since Solomon's name is not included in the genealogy. The anonymity of the book, however, should not detract from its spiritual value or literary beauty.

3. The Time of Ruth. Ruth divides neatly into four distinct settings: (1) the country of Moab (1:1-18); (2) a field in Bethlehem (1:19–2:23); (3) a threshing floor in Bethlehem (3:1-18); and (4) the city of Bethlehem (4:1-22).

The setting of the first eighteen verses is Moab, a region northeast of the Dead Sea. The Moabites, descendants of Lot, worshipped Chemosh and other pagan gods. Scripture records two times when they fought against Israel (Ju 3:12-30 and 1 Sa 14:47). Ruth took place about two centuries after the first war and about eighty years before the second.

Ruth 1:1 gives the setting for the remainder of the book: "Now it came to pass, in the days when the judges ruled." This was a time of apostasy, warfare, decline, violence, moral decay, and anarchy. Ruth provides a cameo of the other side of the story—the godly remnant who remained true to the laws of God.

Because Ruth is written more to tell a beautiful story than to give all the historical facts of that period, the assignment of time is somewhat difficult. Utilizing the same fourfold divisions noted above, the following can be assigned:

A. Ruth 1:1-18 (note 1:4): The country of Moab (c. ten years).
B. Ruth 1:19–2:23 (note 1:22; 2:23): A field in Bethlehem (months).
C. Ruth 3:1-18 (note 3:2,8,14,18,): A threshing floor in Bethlehem (one day).
D. Ruth 4:1-22 (note 4:13-16): The city of Bethlehem (c. one year).

4. The Christ of Ruth. The concept of the kinsman-redeemer or *goel* (3:9, "close relative") is an important portrayal of the work of Christ. The *goel* must (1) be related by blood to those he redeems (De 25:5,7-10; Jo 1:14; Ro 1:3; Ph 2:5-8; He 2:14-15); (2) be able to pay the price of redemption (2:1; 1 Pe 1:18-19); (3) be willing to redeem (3:11; Ma 20:28; Jo 10:15,18; He 10:7); (4) be free himself (Christ was free from the curse of sin). The word *goel,* used thirteen times in this short book, presents a clear picture of the mediating work of Christ.

5. Keys to Ruth.

Key Word: Kinsman-Redeemer—The Hebrew word for kinsman (*goel*) appears thirteen times in Ruth and basically means "one who redeems." By buying back the land of Naomi, as well as marrying Ruth and fathering a son to keep the family line alive, Boaz acted as a redeemer.

Key Verses: Ruth 1:16; 3:11—"But Ruth said: 'Entreat me not to leave you, or to turn back from following after you; for wherever you go, I will go; and wherever you lodge, I will lodge; your people *shall be* my people, and your God my God' " (1:16).

"And now, my daughter, do not fear. I will do for you all that you request, for all the people of my town know that you are a virtuous woman" (3:11).

Key Chapter: Ruth 4—In twenty-two short verses, Ruth moves from widowhood and poverty to marriage and wealth (2:1). In exercising the law regulating the redemption of property (Le 25:25-34) and the law concerning a brother's duty to raise up seed (children) in the name of the deceased (De 25:5-10), Boaz brought a Moabite woman into the family line of David and eventually of Jesus Christ.

6. Survey of Ruth. Ruth is the story of a virtuous woman who lived above the norm of her day. Although it was probably written during the time of David, the events take place during the time of the judges. This period in Israel's history was generally a desert of rebellion and immorality, but the story of Ruth stands in contrast as an oasis of integrity and righteousness.

Ruth was "a virtuous woman" (3:11) who showed loyal love to her mother-in-law Naomi and her near-kinsman Boaz. In both relationships, goodness and love are clearly manifested. Her love is demonstrated in chapters 1–2 and rewarded in chapters 3–4.

Ruth's Love Is Demonstrated (1–2). The story begins with a famine in Israel, a sign of disobedience and apostasy (De 28–30). An Israelite named Elimelech ("My God Is King") in a desperate act moved from Bethlehem ("House of Bread"—note the irony) to Moab. Although he sought life in that land, he and his two sons Mahlon ("Sick") and Chilion ("Pining") found only death. The deceased sons left two Moabite widows, Orpah ("Stubbornness") and Ruth ("Friendship"). Elimelech's widow, Naomi heard that the famine in Israel was over and decided to return, no longer as Naomi ("Pleasant") but as Mara ("Bitter"). She told her daughters-in-law to remain in Moab and remarry since there was no security for an unmarried woman in those days. Orpah chose to leave Naomi, and is never mentioned again. Ruth, on the other hand, resolved to cling to Naomi and follow Yahweh, the God of Israel. She therefore gave up her culture, people, and language because of her love.

Naomi's misfortune led her to think that God was her enemy, but He had plans she did not yet realize. In her plight, she must let Ruth glean at the edge of the fields. This was a humiliating and dangerous task because of the character of many of the laborers. However, God's providential care brought her to the field of Boaz, Naomi's kinsman. Boaz ("In Him Is Strength") began to love, protect, and provide for Ruth.

Ruth's Love Is Rewarded (3–4). Boaz took no further steps toward marriage, so Naomi followed the accepted customs of the day and requested that Boaz exercise his right as kinsman-redeemer. In 3:10-13, Boaz revealed why he had taken no action: he was older than Ruth (perhaps twenty years her senior), and he was not the nearest kinsman. Nevertheless, God rewarded Ruth's devotion by giving her Boaz as a husband and by providing her with a son, Obed, the grandfather of David.

OUTLINE OF RUTH

Part One: Ruth's Love Is Demonstrated (1:1–2:23)

I. Ruth's Decision to Remain with Naomi (1:1-18)

A. Ruth's Need to Remain with Naomi 1:1-5

B. Ruth's Opportunity to Leave Naomi 1:6-15

C. Ruth's Choice to Remain with Naomi 1:16-18

II. Ruth's Devotion and Care for Naomi (1:19–2:23)

A. Ruth and Naomi Return to Bethlehem 1:19-22

B. Ruth Gleans for Food 2:1-23

Part Two: Ruth's Love Is Rewarded (3:1-4:22)

I. Ruth's Request for Redemption by Boaz (3:1-18)

A. Naomi Seeks Redemption for Ruth 3:1-5
B. Ruth Obeys Naomi 3:6-9
C. Boaz Desires to Redeem Ruth 3:10-18

II. Ruth's Reward of Redemption by Boaz (4:1-22)

A. Boaz Marries Ruth 4:1-12
B. Ruth Bears a Son, Obed 4:13-15
C. Naomi Receives a New Family 4:16
D. Ruth Is the Great-Grandmother of David 4:17-22

RYE

A grain. In the KJV, Exodus 9:32 and Isaiah 28:25 are translated as "rye;" Ezekiel 4:9 is translated "fitches." Other translations use the word "spelt," which is a variety of wheat.

S

SA·BACH′ THA·NI

One of the words said by Jesus on the cross. It was part of a phrase "Eloi, Eloi, lama sabachthani," which means "My God, my God, why have you forsaken me?" (Ps 22:1; Ma 27:46; Mk 15:34). See also SEVEN WORDS FROM THE CROSS.

SA·BA′ OTH *(hosts)*

A word used as part of a name of God, literally "hosts" (Ro 9:29; Jam 5:4). This is the word translated "hosts" in Ps 44:9. "Lord Sabaoth" means "Lord of Hosts," signifying His control over all the powers of the universe.

SAB′ BATH *(rest)*

The day on which labor ceases and attention is given to worshipping God. It occurs on the seventh day of the week because according to Genesis that was the day on which the Lord rested after creating the world (Ge 2:1-3). Other sacred days and periods were also called "sabbaths," such as the Day of Atonement, the sabbatical year and the year of Jubilee. From the flood to the exodus the Sabbath is not definitely mentioned, but before reaching Sinai and before the giving of the Decalogue containing legislation regarding the Sabbath, it appears in the record in connection with the manna in the wilderness of Sin (Ex 16:23-26). It was at Sinai that the law was first announced relative to maintaining the sanctity of the Sabbath. It was the fourth commandment (Ex 20:8-11; 31:16-18; De 5:15). The Sabbath was to be a day for a holy convocation for divine worship (Le 23:3), a sign indicating they were sanctified by Jehovah (Ex 31:13). When the Jews were restored to their land after the exile and their Mosaic institutions were re-established by Ezra and Nehemiah, they covenanted to keep the Sabbath. When traders brought their wares from Tyre to be sold in Jerusalem on the Sabbath, Nehemiah put a stop to it (Ne 10:31; 13:15-22). In the time of Christ the Pharisees applied the law regarding Sabbath observance in the most scrupulous manner with the result that they missed the whole spirit and purpose of the Sabbath. In opposition to them, in the performance of works of necessity and mercy, our Lord stated that the Sabbath was made for man, that the Son of man is not the slave but the lord of the Sabbath.

SABBATH DAY'S JOURNEY

The distance that it was considered permissible to walk on the Sabbath day without breaking the command to "rest" and not do any work. The Mount of Olives is described as being "a Sabbath day's journey" from Jerusalem (Ac 1:12). The Israelites were not supposed to travel on the Sabbath day (Ex 16:29, except to go to the tent of meeting, which was separated from the rest of the camp by a space of "two thousand cubits" (Jos 3:4). For this reason, a Sabbath day's journey was fixed at a distance of no further than about a thousand yards.

SAB·BAT′ I·CAL YEAR

A year-long Sabbath in which no farming was done. The land was not cultivated during this year and all debts were canceled. It was designed to be a year of quiet religious contemplation, as well as a rest for the land (Le 25:4-5; Ex

23:11; De 15:1-18). From the time of Solomon onward, the Israelites failed to observe the Sabbatical year; as punishment, they were sent into captivity for seventy years—one year for each Sabbatical they had ignored (Je 34:14-22).

SA·BE′ANS

Inhabitants of the kingdom of Sheba in southwestern Arabia (Job 1:15; Joel 3:8).

SAB′TAH, SAB′TA

The third son of Cush, grandson of Ham (Ge 10:7; 1 Ch 1:9).

SAB·TE′CA

See SABTECHA.

SAB·TE′CHA

Son of Cush and grandson of Ham (Ge 10:7; 1 Ch 1:9), also called Sabteca or Sabetchah.

SA′CAR

Two Old Testament men:
1. Father of Ahiam and one of David's men, a Hararite (1 Ch 11:35). He was called Sharar in 2 Samuel 23:33.
2. Son of Obed-edom (1 Ch 26:4).

SA′CHAR

See SACAR.

SA·CHI′A

See SACHIAH.

SA·CHI′AH

A Benjamite, son of Hodesh (1 Ch 8:10), also called Sachia, Sakia, Shachia.

SACK′BUT

The English word refers to a medieval wind instrument, a form of trombone having a slide to regulate the pitch. It can also mean a trigon (a small triangular harp). It is believed that this is a better description of the instrument spoken of in Daniel 3:5.

SACK′CLOTH

A coarse dark cloth made of goat's hair (Is 50:3; Re 6:12), the garment of mourners (2 Sa 3:31; 2 Ki 19:1-2), often of prophets (Is 20:2). It had the appearance of a sack and was usually worn over the other garments (Jon 3:6), sometimes underneath (1 Ki 21:27; Job 16:15; Is 32:11).

SACRAMENT

An religious action or ritual which sanctifies. A sacrament is something which is supposed to be a means of transmitting God's grace to the individual who performs the action, whether symbolically or actually.

The Catholic and Orthodox churches teach that there are seven sacraments:

1. Eucharist
2. Baptism
3. Confirmation
4. Penance (Confession)
5. Matrimony
6. Holy Orders
7. Extreme Unction (Holy Unction)

These seven rituals are regarded as the means by which God imparts grace to believers.

Protestants generally only accept two sacraments—baptism and the Lord's Supper. Many object to the word "sacraments," preferring the term "ordinances," since they do not believe that the outward symbols of the bread and wine, or the waters of baptism, or even the action of the person partaking of the rituals can be means of grace. Rather, they are symbols of God's grace already bestowed.

Some sects have carried this idea even further, also rejecting the outward symbols of baptism and communion as superfluous.

SACRIFICE, HUMAN

See HUMAN SACRIFICE

SACRIFICIAL SYSTEM

Sacrifice was a ritual through which the Hebrew people offered the blood or flesh of an animal to God in payment for their sins. Sacrifice originated in the garden of Eden, when God killed animals and made garments for Adam and Eve (Ge 3:21). God's provision of this covering symbolized that sinful man could come before God without fear of death.

When Noah left the ark, his first act was to build an altar and sacrifice animals to God (Ge 8:20). Abraham regularly worshiped God by offering sacrifices to Him (Ge 12:7).

In the Mosaic law, sacrifice had three central ideas: consecration, expiation (covering of sin), and propitiation (satisfaction of divine anger). Sacrifice as worship required man to give back to God what God had given to him.

Some specific sacrificial offerings called for in the Mosaic law included the burnt offering, which pointed to Christ's atoning death for sinners (2 Co 5:21) and His total consecration to God (Lk 2:49); the meal offering, which symbolically presented the best fruits of human living to God (He 10:5-10); the peace offering, which celebrated the covering of sin, forgiveness by God, and the restoration of a right relationship with God (Ju 20:26); and the sin offering, in which guilt for the worshiper's sin was transferred symbolically to the animal through the laying on of the offerer's hands (Le 16:8-10).

Both Old and New Testaments confirm that sacrifices were symbolic. Because of their sins, the Hebrews presented offerings by which they gave another life in place of their own. These substitutes pointed forward to the ultimate sacrifice, Jesus Christ (He 10:1-8), who laid down His life for the sins of the people.

Paul says "I beseech you therefore, brethren, by the mercies of God, that you present your bodies a living sacrifice, holy, acceptable to God, which is your reasonable service" (Ro 12:1). This, for Christians, is the summary of the Christian understanding of Christ's sacrifice. The Israelites gave the various sacrifices as a sign of their understanding that they needed consecration, expiation, and propitiation. So the Christian, who has been born again by the blood of Christ, offers back to God his very life which has been made new in Christ. This is the symbol of his understanding of his need for and acceptance of the atonement—and this is only reasonable, considering the price Christ paid.

SACRILEGE

The violation of something sacred.

SAD′DU•CEES *(followers of Zadok)*

The Sadducees were one of the two major sects or special-interest groups among the Jews in New Testament times. These groups (the Pharisees and Sadducees) stood for different principles, but Jesus clashed with both parties at different times during his ministry.

The Sadducees took their name from Zadok, a high priest in the reign of David. They were the party of the priesthood for about two hundred years, ending with the fall of Jerusalem in A.D. 70. Most of the high priests of this time were Sadducees. They were the elite of Jewish society in the time of Jesus. As priests, merchants, and aristocrats, they supported the Roman authorities because they enjoyed a privileged status under Roman rule. In contrast to the Pharisees, they advocated loyalty to the original law of Moses, insisting that interpretation of the law could not be trusted. Also, unlike the Pharisees, they did not believe in the resurrection of the dead, the future state of the soul, or the theory of rewards or punishment after death—beliefs which Jesus challenged (Mk 12:18-27).

SA′DOC *(righteous)*

An ancestor of Jesus who lived after the time of the exile (Ma 1:14). See ZADOK.

SAF′FRON

A variety of sweet-smelling crocus (Song 4:14). Saffron particularly refers to the dried stigmas of the flowers, which are used as a seasoning for food, and in ancient times as a medicine and a dyestuff.

SAGE

A wise person. In Scripture, this term is used to refer to a "wise man" or astrologer who was respected for his ability to interpret dreams or tell the future. See ASTROLOGY.

SAILOR

Those who man a ship. The Hebrews were not a seafaring people, and it appears that they generally relied upon the Phoenicians for marine transport and shipping. The Phoenicians have the reputation for having been skilled and intrepid sailors. The ship Jonah boarded to go to Tarshish was doubtless manned by Phoenician sailors (Jo 1:3,5).

SAINTS

Literally "holy ones." This is the New Testament term for those who believe in Jesus Christ and have been reborn, justified and reconciled with God. They are "holy," set apart to belong to God. See SANCTIFICATION.

SAKIA

See SACHIAH.

SA′LA

See SHELAH.

SA′LAH

The son of Arphaxad, grandson of Shem, and father of Eber (Ge 10:24). Also called Shelah (1 Ch

1:18,24; Lk 3:35) and Sala (Lk 3:35, KJV). He is in the genealogy of Christ.

SAL′A·MIS

A city at the eastern end of the island of Cyprus (Ac 13:4-5). Tradition teaches that this was the hometown of Barnabas, and that he was eventually stoned to death here by a mob.

SA·LA′THI·EL

See SHEALTIEL.

SAL′CAH

A town of Bashan (De 3:10; Jos 12:5; 13:11; 1 Ch 5:11).

SAL′CHAH, SAL′E·CAH

See SALCAH

SA′LEM *(peaceful)*

1. The city or area over which Melchizedek was king (Ge 14:18; He 7:1-2). Its location is uncertain, but many believe that the Salem of Melchizedek was the original Jebusite city of Jerusalem.

2. An abbreviation of Jerusalem (Ps 76:2). See JERUSALEM and MELCHIZEDEK.

SA′LIM

A place near Aenon where John the Baptist baptized (Jo 3:23).

SAL·LA′I

Two Old Testament men:

1. Head of a priestly house after the exile (Ne 12:20). He is called Sallu in Nehemiah 12:7.

2. A chief of the Benjamites (Ne 11:8).

SAL′LU

Two Old Testament men:

1. Son of Meshullam, a Benjamite. He lived in Jerusalem after the exile (1 Ch 9:7; Ne 11:7).

2. Head of a priestly house after the exile (Ne 12:7). He is called Sallai in Nehemiah 12:20.

SAL′MA

See SALMON.

SAL′MAI

Head of a family of Nethinim (Ez 2:46; Ne 7:48), also called Shalmai, and Shamlai (Ez 2:46).

SAL′MON

A man and a hill of the Old Testament:

1. Father of Boaz, the husband of Ruth. Descended from Perez and Hezron, he was an ancestor of the family of Jesus (Ru 4:18-21; Ma 1:4; Lk 3:32), also called Salmah and Salma.

2. A wooded hill near Shechem where Abimelech cut timber to burn down the tower of Shechem (Ps 68:14). It is called Zalmon in Judges 9:48.

SAL·MO′NE

A point at the eastern extremity of Crete (Ac 27:7). Today it is called Cape Sidero.

SA·LO′ME *(peace)*

Two New Testament women:

1. Daughter of Herodias and Philip. Her mother left Philip for his half brother, Herod Antipas, the man who imprisoned John the Baptist. Salome so delighted Antipas with her dancing that he offered to gratify any wish. Her mother instructed her to ask for the head of John the Baptist. Her request was granted (Ma 14:6). Later Salome married Philip, tetrarch of Iturea and Trachonitis, her uncle; her cousin Aristobulus was her second husband.

2. Wife of Zebedee and mother of James and John (Ma 20:20; 27:56; Mk 15:40; 16:1). Probably Mary's sister (Jo 19:25).

SALT

Sodium chloride. Used since ancient times as a seasoning and a preservative (Job 6:6) and in certain offerings (Le 2:13; Eze 43:24). It was used to make a land unfruitful. To doom completely the defeated city of Shechem, Abimelech ordered its surrounding land to be covered with salt (Ju 9:45). Newborn babies were rubbed with salt (Eze 16:4).

Salt in ancient times was a valuable commodity, even used as currency in some cases. Roman soldiers were paid in salt. Jesus told His disciples that they were the salt of the earth (Ma 5:13), and Paul urged Christians to let their speech always be with grace, "seasoned with salt" (Col 4:6).

SALT, CITY OF

A town allotted to Judah, near the Dead Sea (Jos 15:62). It is believed by some scholars to be Khirbet Qumran, the city whose ruins are near the caves where the famous Dead Sea Scrolls were found.

SALT, COVENANT OF

An everlasting covenant (Nu 18:19). When a covenant of salt is made, the two parties each take a little salt, and mix it together. After the two portions of salt are mixed it is impossible to separate them. This is a symbol of the permanence of the covenant.

SALT HERB

See MALLOWS.

SALT, PILLAR OF

See PILLAR OF SALT.

SALT PITS

Either pits where salt was mined, or more probably, shallow depressions which were allowed to fill with sea water and then evaporate in the hot sun. The salt which was left behind could be collected for use (Zep 2:9).

SALT SEA

The Old Testament name for the Dead Sea (Ge 14:3; Nu 34:3,12; De 3:17; Jos 15:2,5). See DEAD SEA.

SALT, VALLEY OF

A valley at the southern end of the Dead Sea. Several battles were fought here by David (2 Sa 8:13), Amaziah of Judah (2 Ki 14:7; 2 Ch 25:11), and Abishai (1 Ch 18:12).

SALT' WORT

See MALLOWS.

SA' LU (exalted)

Father of Zimri. The son was slain for bringing a woman of the Midianites into the camp of Israel (Nu 25:14). See PHINEHAS.

SAL' U·TA' TION

The Hebrews saluted each other with such expressions as "God be gracious unto thee" (Ge 43:29), "Blessed be thou of the Lord" (Ru 3:10; 1 Sa 15:13), "The Lord bless thee" (Ru 2:4). At parting, such expressions as "Go in peace," or "Farewell" (1 Sa 1:17; 20:42; Mk 5:34; Ac 15:36) were in use. Paul's letters began with salutations of an extended nature as in Romans 1:1-7; and in a briefer form as "Grace unto you and peace." Letters were also closed with salutations

from himself in which others would join (1 Th 1:1; 5:26-28).

SAL·VA' TION

Save from eternal death: Of the numerous New Testament passages using *sozo,* Matthew 1:21 gives a perfect illustration of salvation, God in Christ freely granting believers eternal life: "You shall call His name JESUS, for He will save His people from their sins." The name *Jesus (Yeshua)* comes from the Hebrew verb for "save." Among the typical verses presenting this most important meaning are "Believe on the Lord Jesus Christ, and you will be saved," (Ac 16:31) and "that the world through Him might be saved" (Jo 3:17).

Save from Danger or Death: Examples from the New Testament are Peter's plea to be saved from drowning (Ma 14:30) and Paul and his fellow passengers being saved from shipwreck (Ac 27:31).

Save from Disease, Heal: Jesus told the woman with the hemorrhage, "Daughter, your faith has made you well" (lit. "saved you," Mk 5:34). Here and elsewhere the physical healing and spiritual salvation may have taken place at the same time.

Save One's Life from Being Wasted: Because many people have a fixation on the word *saved* as only referring to escaping from hell, and of the word *soul* as only referring to the immortal part of man, this last usage has not been recognized by everyone. As we have seen, *sozo* definitely has meanings other than "rescue from eternal destruction." So does *psyche* have meanings other than "soul" in the popular sense (see entries on SOUL and SPIRIT, SOUL, AND BODY). The word *psyche* can just as easily mean "life" as "soul," and sometimes must mean that. The popular Christian expression "save a soul" has come to always equal meaning salvation from death, but it is virtually never so used in the Scriptures.

In Luke 9:24 and its parallel passages, our Lord appears to use *sozo* and *psyche* to mean "save your Christian life from being wasted." There are other passages, such as in James and Philippians 2:12 that in context would be better taken as referring to good works for rewards, or escaping sinful patterns rather than to escaping from hell.

SALVE

A soothing balm or ointment. Laodicea was famed for its production of an eye medication;

Jesus makes a reference to this when He talks about the poor spiritual condition of the church in that city (Re 3:18).

SA·MAR'I·A

Samaria is probably best known as the setting for Jesus's visit with the woman at the well (Jo 4:5-42); but Samaria's importance as both a city and a region was well-established long before the time of Jesus. This ancient city is second only to Jerusalem and Babylon in the number of times it is mentioned in the Bible.

One of the most striking features of Samaria was its hilltop location. Built by King Omri about 880 B.C. on a hill he purchased from Shemer (1 Ki 16:24) as the capital of the Northern Kingdom of Israel, it contributed significantly to the history and culture of ancient Israel.

Samaria was one of the few major Jewish cities actually founded and built from the ground up by the Israelites. They took most of their cities from other nations and then either rebuilt or renovated them into distinctively Jewish population centers.

After succeeding Omri as king, Ahab (reigned 874-853 B.C.) remodeled and expanded Omri's beautiful palace in the city of Samaria. Some of Ahab's decorations, especially the expensive ivory with which he adorned his furniture and palace walls, have been discovered by archaeologists. But in spite of its wealth and splendor, the city fell to the Assyrians in 722 B.C., fulfilling Amos's prophecy of its destruction (Am 3:11-15). The citizens of Samaria were carried away to Assyria as captives.

After its fall to the Assyrians, Samaria continued to be inhabited by several different groups under the successive authority of Assyria, Babylonia, Persia, Greece, and Rome. Herod the Great, Roman governor of Palestine (ruled 37 B.C.-A.D. 4), made many improvements to the city and renamed it Sebaste—the Greek term for Augustus—in honor of the emperor of Rome. This Herodian city is probably the "city of Samaria" mentioned in the Book of Acts (Ac 8:5).

The name is also used occasionally to refer to the entire Northern Kingdom (1 Ki 21:1; 2 Ki 17:24; Je 31:5). It was also one of the subdivisions of a Persian province (Ne 4:2).

SAMARIA, REGION OF

By the time of Jesus, the land of Israel east of the Jordan was divided into three provinces:

SAMARIA

Galilee, Samaria, and Judea. Samaria was sandwiched between Galilee to the north and Judea to the south, but the animosity between Jews and Samaritans was so strong that Jews traveling from Galilee to Judea would cross the Jordan and travel through Decapolis and Perea rather than set foot in Samaritan territory.

SAMARITAN

The inhabitants of the district of Samaria, between the districts of Judea and Galilee on the east side of the Jordan River. In the days of the divided kingdom, this was the territory of Ephraim and the half-tribe of Manasseh. When the Northern Kingdom fell into the hands of the Assyrians in 722 B.C., most of the inhabitants were deported and scattered through Assyria and Mesopotamia. The Assyrian king repopulated the land with foreigners (2 Ki 17:24) who intermarried with the remaining Israelites. These settlers were troubled by lions, and assumed that they were offending the god of the land, so they asked to have a priest of Israel come and teach them how to worship God (2 Ki 17:25-29). What developed was a strange mixture of Judaism and paganism. The Samaritans were neither pure religiously nor ethnicly, and relationships with the rest of the Jews were strained. When the remnant returned under Zerubbabel, the Samaritans offered to help with the temple project. Zerubbabel and the others refused this offer because the Samaritans were not Hebrews, and those who were had disobeyed God by marrying foreigners and participating in pagan worship. The Samaritans were offended and set about to hinder the work (Ez 4:1-10). Later, when Nehemiah came back to work on the wall, the Samaritans continued to cause trouble. No doubt the divorcing of the pagan wives did not make the relationship any easier. Later, the Samaritans built a temple of their own on Mount Gerizim, rejecting the temple in Jerusalem and the religion of the returned captives. At some point, the pagan elements of 2 Kings 17:29 were weeded out of the Samaritan practice of religion. Today, Samaritans accept only the five books of Moses as authoritative, and reject the rest of the Old Testament and the Talmud. Very few Samaritans survived the upheaval and religious persecution of the Holy Roman Empire, but they still retain many of their ancient beliefs and continue to sacrifice a Passover lamb on Mount Gerizim every year.

SAMARITAN PENTATEUCH

The ancient version of the five books of Moses which the Samaritans accept as the only authoritative Scripture. It seems probable that the priest who returned to Samaria to teach the new inhabitants about the God of Israel had a copy of the law of Moses with which to teach the people. These manuscripts are written in a particular Hebrew script, a style which was common in the era before the captivity of Judah. They are nearly the same as the Jewish Pentateuch, with a few scribal additions and variations in spelling. A few places have been altered slightly to favor Mount Gerizim as the proper place of worship (the Samaritans believe that the Jewish books were altered by Ezra to favor his opinion). Fragments of the Samaritan Pentateuch were found among the Dead Sea Scrolls.

SA′MECH, SA′MEKH

See SAMEK.

SA′MEK

The 15th letter of the Hebrew alphabet. It is the heading of verses 113-120 of Psalm 119. In Hebrew each of these eight verses began with the letter samek. See ACROSTIC.

SAM′GAR-NE′BO

An officer of Nebuchadnezzar who participated in the siege on Jerusalem (Je 39:3).

SAM′LAH (a garment)

An Edomite king of the city of Masrekah (Ge 36:36-37).

SA′MOS

An island in the Aegean Sea, near the coast of Lydia in Asia Minor (Ac 20:15).

SAM·O·THRA′CE

An island off the coast of Thrace in the Aegean Sea (Ac 16:11).

SAM′SON (sunlike)

An extraordinary man and judge of Israel. His father was Manoah of the tribe of Dan. Samson's birth was heralded by an angel, and God told his parents that he was to be set apart as a Nazirite from birth (Ju 13:1-24). He was destined to deliver his people from the oppression of the Philistines which was felt especially by Judah and Dan. Samson possessed marvelous physical strength, which he used against the Philistines, but sadly he was not correspondingly morally strong. After Samson set the foxes loose in the fields of the Philistines, the Philistines demanded that Samson be surrendered to them (Ju 14:1–15:5). He allowed himself to be bound by his cowardly countrymen who failed to realize that he was their deliverer, but breaking the bands, he slew a thousand of his foes. Samson courted a Philistine woman, Delilah, and at length told her that the source of his strength was his hair, uncut because of his Nazirite vows. While he was asleep, she cut his hair. Unable any longer to resist his Philistine enemies, he was taken prisoner and blinded (Ju 16:16-30). In the end, Samson did fulfill his role as the deliverer of Israel. His captors brought him into the temple of their god Dagon, in order to be entertained by the sight of their vanquished foe. A festival was going on to celebrate their victory over Israel and about three thousand people were in the building and on the roof. Samson prayed for God to give him his great strength just once more, that he might be revenged on the Philistines, and with a mighty push, he knocked the supporting pillars down and the whole temple fell with a crash, killing thousands of people. Samson is mentioned in Hebrews 11:32-34 as a hero of the faith, one who was made strong out of his weakness by the power of the Lord.

SAM′U·EL (heard of God)

The son of Elkanah and Hannah, a Levite family of Kohath, house of Ishar (1 Sa 1:1; 1 Ch 6:26, 35). He lived in the hill country of Ephraim, at

Ramah. Samuel's mother, Hannah, was the second wife of her husband, and she had a great sorrow for she was barren. The other wife had both sons and daughters, and mocked Hannah because she was childless. In spite of the fact that she knew that her husband loved her very much, Hannah longed for children. Each year, Elkanah took his family to Shiloh to make sacrifices to the Lord, and one year Hannah went into the tabernacle and wept and prayed before the Lord. She vowed that if the Lord would give her a son, she would give that son back to the Lord. God granted her prayer, and a year later, Samuel was born. Hannah stayed at home until Samuel was old enough to be weaned, and then she brought him to Shiloh, and left him in the care of the high priest. True to her vow, she was giving him back to the Lord. Every year, she returned with a new little robe for Samuel, and the Lord blessed her with five more children. Samuel grew up under the care of Eli, the high priest, and it was clear very early in his life that he had a special call from God. The first prophetic message he received was when he was still a child, concerning the wickedness of Eli's sons. Following the death of Eli, Samuel, the prophet, became the chief religious authority in the land. In his administration the moral and religious state of things greatly improved. He anointed Saul as the first king of Israel, and he anointed David as his successor.

SAM'U·EL, BOOKS OF

1. The Books of Samuel. The Book of 1 Samuel describes the transition of leadership in Israel from judges to kings. Three characters are prominent in the book: Samuel, the last judge and first prophet; Saul, the first king of Israel; and David, the king-elect, anointed but not yet recognized as Saul's successor.

The Book of 2 Samuel records the highlights of David's reign, first over the territory of Judah, and finally over the entire nation of Israel. It traces the ascension of David to the throne, his climactic sins of adultery and murder, and the shattering consequences of those sins upon his family and the nation.

The books of 1 and 2 Samuel were originally one book in the Hebrew Bible, known as the "Book of Samuel" or simply "Samuel." This name has been variously translated "The Name of God," "His Name Is God," "Heard of God," and "Asked of God." The Septuagint divides Sam-

uel into two books even though it is one continuous account. This division artificially breaks up the history of David. The Greek (Septuagint) title is *Bibloi Basileion,* "Books of Kingdoms," referring to the later kingdoms of Israel and Judah. First Samuel is called *Basileion Alpha,* "First Kingdoms." Second Samuel and 1 and 2 Kings are called "Second, Third, and Fourth Kingdoms," respectively. The Latin Vulgate originally called the books of Samuel and Kings *Libri Regum,* "Books of the Kings." Later the Latin Bible combined the Hebrew and Greek titles for the first of these books, calling it *Liber I Samuelis,* the "First Book of Samuel," or simply "First Samuel," and *Liber II Samuelis,* the "Second Book of Samuel," or simply "Second Samuel."

2. The Author of Samuel. The author of 1 and 2 Samuel is anonymous, but Jewish Talmudic tradition says that it was written by Samuel. Samuel may have written the first portion of the book, but his death recorded in 1 Samuel 25:1 makes it clear that he did not write all of 1 and 2 Samuel. Samuel did write a book (10:25), and written records were available. As the head of a company of prophets (10:5; 19:20), Samuel would be a logical candidate for biblical authorship.

First Chronicles 29:29 refers to "the book of Samuel the Seer," "the book of Nathan the Prophet," and "the book of Gad the Seer." All three men evidently contributed to these two books; and it is very possible that a single compiler, perhaps a member of the prophetic school, used these chronicles to put together the Book of Samuel. This is also suggested by the unity of plan and purpose and by the smooth transitions between sections.

3. The Time of Samuel. If Samuel wrote the material in the first twenty-four chapters, he did so soon before his death (c. 1015 B.C.). He was born around 1105 B.C., and ministered as a judge and prophet in Israel between about 1067 and 1015 B.C. The books of Samuel end in the last days of David; so they must have been compiled after 971 B.C. The reference in 1 Samuel 27:6 to the divided monarchy in which Judah is separate from Israel indicates a compilation date after Solomon's death in 931 B.C. However, the silence regarding the Assyrian captivity of Israel in 722 B.C. probably means that 1 Samuel was written before the key event.

First Samuel covers the ninety-four-year period from the birth of Samuel to the death of

Saul (c. 1105-1011 B.C.). The Philistines strongly oppressed Israel from 1087 B.C. until the battle of Ebenezer in 1047 B.C. (7:10-14). However, even after this time the Philistines exercised military and economic control. They lived in the coastal plains; and the hill country in which the Israelites dwelled protected them from total conquest by the Philistines.

4. The Christ of Samuel. Samuel is a type of Christ in that he was a prophet, priest, and judge. Highly revered by the people, he brought in a new age.

David is one of the primary Old Testament portrayals of the person of Christ. He was born in Bethlehem, worked as a shepherd, and ruled as a king of Israel. He was the anointed king who became the forerunner of the messianic King. His typical messianic psalms are born of his years of rejection and danger (see Ps 22). God enabled David, a man "after His own heart" (13:14), to become Israel's greatest king. The New Testament specifically calls Christ the "seed of David according to the flesh" (Ro 1:3) and "the Root and the Offspring of David" (Re 22:16).

In spite of his sins, he remained a man after God's own heart because of his responsive and faithful attitude toward God. He sometimes failed in his personal life, but he never flagged in his relationship to the Lord. Unlike most of the kings who succeeded him, he never allowed idolatry to become a problem during his reign. He was a true servant to Yahweh, obedient to His law, and an ideal king. His rule was usually characterized by justice, wisdom, integrity, courage, and compassion. Having conquered Jerusalem, he sat upon the throne of Melchizedek, the "righteous king" (Ge 14:18). David was the standard by which all subsequent kings were measured.

Of course, David's life as recorded in chapters 1–10 of 2 Samuel is a far better portrayal of the future Messiah than is his life as it is seen in 11–24. Sin mars potential. The closest way in which he foreshadows the coming King can be seen in the important covenant God made with him (7:4-17). David wanted to build a house for God; but instead, God made a house for David. The same three promises of an eternal kingdom, throne, and seed are later given to Christ (Lk 1:32-33). There are nine different dynasties in the Northern Kingdom of Israel, but there is only one dynasty in Judah. The promise of a permanent dynasty is fulfilled in Christ, the "Son of David" (Ma 21:9; 22:45), who will sit upon the throne of David (Is 9:7; Lk 1:32).

5. Keys to 1 Samuel.

Key Word: Transition—First Samuel records the critical transition in Israel from the rule of God through the judges to His rule through the kings.

The transition goes through three stages: Eli to Samuel, Samuel to Saul, and Saul to David.

Key Verses: 1 Samuel 13:14; 15:22—"But now your kingdom shall not continue. The LORD has sought for Himself a man after His own heart, and the LORD has commanded him to be commander over His people, because you have not kept what the LORD commanded you" (13:14). "Then Samuel said, 'Has the LORD as great delight in burnt offerings and sacrifices, as in obeying the voice of the LORD? Behold, to obey is better than sacrifice, and to heed than the fat of rams'" (15:22).

Key Chapter: 1 Samuel 15—First Samuel 15 records the tragic transition of kingship from Saul to David. As in all three changes recorded in 1 Samuel, God removed His blessing from one and gave it to another because of sin. "Because you have rejected the word of the LORD, He also has rejected you from being king" (15:23).

6. Survey of 1 Samuel. First Samuel records the crucial transition from the theocracy under the judges to the monarchy under the kings. The book is built around three key men: Samuel (1–7), Saul (8–31), and David (16–31).

Samuel (1–7). Samuel's story begins late in the turbulent time of the judges when Eli was the judge-priest of Israel. The birth of Samuel and his early call by Yahweh are found in chapters 1–3. Because of his responsiveness to God (3:19), he was confirmed as a prophet (3:20-21) at a time when the "word of the LORD was rare . . . there was no widespread revelation" (3:1).

Corruption at Shiloh by Eli's notoriously wicked sons leads to Israel's defeat in the crucial battle with the Philistines (4:1-11). The ark of the covenant, God's "throne" among the people, is lost to the Philistines; the priesthood is disrupted by the deaths of Eli and his sons; and the glory of God departed from the tabernacle (Ichabod, "No Glory," 4:21). Samuel begins to function as the last of the judges and the first in the order of the prophets (Ac 3:24). His prophetic ministry (7:3-17) leads to a revival in Israel, the return of the ark, and the defeat of the Philistines. When Samuel is old and his sons prove to be unjust judges, the people wrongly cried out for a king. They wanted a visible military and judicial ruler so they could be "like all the nations" (8:5-20).

Saul (8–15). In their impatient demand for a king, Israel chose less than God's best. Their motive (8:5) and criteria (9:2) are wrong. Saul began well (9–11), but his good characteristics soon degenerated. In spite of Samuel's solemn prophetic warning (12), Saul and the people began to act wickedly. Saul presumptuously assumed the role of a priest (2 Ch 26:18) and offered up sacrifices (13). He made a foolish vow (14) and disobeyed God's command to destroy the Amalekites (15). Samuel's powerful words in 15:22-23 evoked a pathetic response in 15:24-31.

Saul and David (16–31). When God rejected Saul, He commissioned Samuel to anoint David as Israel's next king. God's king-elect served in Saul's court (16:14–23:29) and defeated the Philistine Goliath (17). Jonathan's devotion to David led him to sacrifice the throne (20:30-31) in acknowledgment of David's divine

right to it (18). David became a growing threat to the insanely jealous Saul; but he was protected from Saul's wrath by Jonathan, Michal, and Samuel (19).

Saul's open rebellion against God was manifested in his refusal to give up what God had said could not be his. David was protected again by Jonathan from Saul's murderous intent (20), but Saul became more active in his pursuit of David. The future king fled to a Philistine city where he feigned insanity (21), and flees again to Adullam where a band of men formed around him (22).

David continued to escape from the hand of Saul, and on two occasions spared Saul's life when he had the opportunity to take it (24–26). David again sought refuge among the Philistines, but was not allowed to fight on their side against Israel. Saul, afraid of impending battle against the Philistines, foolishly consulted a medium at Endor to hear the deceased Samuel's advice (28). The Lord rebuked Saul and pronounced his doom; he and his sons were killed by the Philistines on Mount Gilboa (31).

OUTLINE OF 1 SAMUEL

Part One: Samuel, the Last Judge (1:1–7:17)

I. The First Transition of National Leadership: Eli—Samuel (1:1–3:21)

A. The Birth of the New Leader 1:1–2:11
B. The Need of the New
    Leader 2:12–3:36
C. The Transition from Eli to
    Samuel 3:1-18

D. Samuel Is Recognized as the New
    Leader of Israel 3:19-21

II. The Judgeship of Samuel (4:1–7:17)

A. The Need for Samuel's
    Leadership 4:1–6:21
B. The Victories Under Samuel's
    Leadership 7:1-17

Part Two: Saul, the First King (8:1–31:13)

I. The Second Transition of National Leadership: Samuel—Saul (8:1–12:25)

A. The Causes of the Transition 8:1-9
B. The Transition from Samuel
    to Saul 8:10–12:25

II. The Reign of King Saul (13:1–15:9)

A. The Early Success of King Saul 13:1-4
B. The Failures of King Saul 13:5–15:9

III. The Third Transition of National Leadership: Saul—David (15:10–31:13)

A. The Transition of Kingship from
    Saul to David 15:10–18:9
B. The Attempts of Saul to Slay
    David 18:10–20:42
C. The Rise of David in
    Exile 21:1–28:2
D. The Final Decline of
    Saul 28:3–31:13

7. Keys to 2 Samuel.

Key Word: David—The central character of 2 Samuel is David, around whom the entire book is written. The key truth illustrated is the same as the theme of Deuteronomy: obedience brings blessing and disobedience brings judgment.

Key Verses: 2 Samuel 7:12-13; 22:21—"When your days are fulfilled and you rest with your fathers, I will set up your seed after you, who will come from your body, and I will establish his kingdom. He shall build a house for My name, and I will establish the throne of his kingdom forever" (7:12-13).

"The LORD rewarded me according to my righteousness; according to the cleanness of my hands He has recompensed me" (22:21).

Key Chapter: 2 Samuel 11—The eleventh chapter of 2 Samuel is pivotal for the entire book. This chapter records the tragic sins of David regarding Bath-sheba and her husband Uriah. All of the widespread blessings on David's family and his kingdom were quickly removed as God chastised His anointed one.

8. Survey of 2 Samuel. Second Samuel continues the account of the life of David at the point where 1 Samuel concludes. Soon after the death of Saul, the king-elect became the king enthroned, first over Judah when he reigned in Hebron for seven-and-a-half years and finally over all Israel when he reigned in Jerusalem for thirty-three years. This book reviews the key events in the forty-year reign of the man who was the halfway point between Abraham and Christ. It can be surveyed in the three divisions: the triumphs of David (1–10), the transgressions of David (11), and the troubles of David (12–24).

The Triumphs of David (1–10). Chapters 1–4 record the seven-year reign of David over the territory of Judah. Even though Saul was David's murderous pursuer, David did not rejoice in his death, because he recognized that Saul had been divinely anointed as king. Saul's son Ishbosheth was installed by Abner as a puppet king over the northern tribes of Israel. David's allies led by Joab defeated Abner and Israel (2:17; 3:1). Abner defected and arranged to unite Israel and Judah under David, but Joab killed Abner in revenge. The powerless Ishbosheth was murdered by his own men, and David was made king of Israel (5:3). David soon captured and fortified Jerusalem and made it the civil and religious center of the now united kingdom. Under David's rule the nation prospered politically, spiritually, and militarily. David brought the ark to Jerusalem and sought to build a house for God (7). His obedience in placing the Lord at the center of his rule led to great national blessing (8–10). "And the LORD preserved David wherever he went" (8:14).

The Transgressions of David (11). David's crimes of adultery and murder mark the pivotal point of the book. Because of these transgressions, David's victories and successes were changed to the personal, family, and national troubles which are recorded throughout the rest of 2 Samuel.

The Troubles of David (12–24). The disobedience of the king produced chastisement and confusion at every level. David's glory and fame faded, never to be the same again. Nevertheless, David confessed his guilt when confronted by Nathan the prophet and was restored by God. A sword remained in David's house as a consequence of the sin; the baby born to David and Bath-sheba died, his son Amnon committed incest, and his son Absalom murdered Amnon.

The consequences continued with Absalom's rebellion against his father. He shrewdly "stole the hearts of the men of Israel" (15:6). David was forced to flee from Jerusalem, and Absalom set himself up as king. David would have been ruined, but God kept Absalom from pursuing him until David had time to regroup his forces. Absalom's army was defeated by David's, and Joab killed Absalom in disobedience of David's orders to have him spared.

David sought to amalgamate the kingdom, but conflict broke out between the ten northern tribes of Israel and the two southern tribes of Judah and Benjamin. Israel decided to follow a man named Sheba in a revolt against David, but Judah remained faithful to him. This led to war, and Joab defeated the rebels.

The closing chapters are actually an appendix to the book because they summarize David's words and deeds. They show how intimately the affairs of the people as a whole are tied to the spiritual and moral condition of the king. The nation enjoyed God's blessing when David was obedient to the Lord, and suffered hardship when David disobeyed God.

OUTLINE OF 2 SAMUEL

Part One: The Triumphs of David (1:1–10:19)

I. The Political Triumphs of David (1:1–5:25)

A. The Reign of David in Hebron over Judah 1:1–4:12
B. The Reign of David in Jerusalem ... 5:1-25

II. The Spiritual Triumphs of David (6:1–7:29)

A. The Transportation of the Ark 6:1-23

B. The Institution of the Davidic Covenant 7:1-29

III. The Military Triumphs of David (8:1–10:19)

A. Over His Enemies 8:1-12
B. His Righteous Rule 8:13–9:13
C. Over Ammon and Syria 10:1-19

Part Two: The Transgressions of David (11:1-27)

I. The Sin of Adultery (11:1-5)

II. The Sin of Murder (11:6-27)

A. Uriah Does Not Sleep with Bath-sheba 11:6-13

B. David Commands Uriah's Murder 11:14-25
C. David and Bath-sheba Marry 11:26-27

Part Three: The Troubles of David (12:1–24:25)

I. The Troubles in David's House (12:1–13:36)

A. Prophecy by Nathan 12:1-14
B. David's Son Dies 12:15-25
C. Joab's Loyalty to David 12:26-31
D. Incest in David's House 13:1-20
E. Amnon Is Murdered 13:21-36

II. The Troubles in David's Kingdom (13:37–24:25)

A. Rebellion of Absalom 13:37–17:29
B. Absalom's murder 18:1-33
C. David Is Restored As King 19:1–20:26
D. The Commentary on the Reign of David 21:1–24:25

SAN·BAL′LAT

A Horonite, probably a man of Beth-horon or of Horonaim in Moab. He had considerable influence in Samaria and served Artaxerxes (Ne 2:10,19; 4:2).

SANCTIFICATION

Being set apart, made holy. Bible sanctification is a very basic and through-going work of grace. In the Old Testament, especially Leviticus, the Holy Spirit stresses the importance of holiness in everyday life. Peter quotes Leviticus 11:44, "Be holy, for I am holy," as crucial to a true Christian walk (1 Pe 1:16).

Holy, Saint (hagios) was a very rare word in classical Greek, but is an important part of the New Testament vocabulary. The main idea behind the word is one of separation, a setting apart for a special purpose, particularly connected with consecration and service to God.

The word is first used in the New Testament for the Holy Spirit (Ma 1:18), and also many times after. We find "Holy Father" in John 17:11 and "Your holy servant Jesus" in Acts 4:27. Because God is thrice holy Himself (Is 6:3), He wants His people to be holy too.

Sometimes the word *hagios* is used as a noun, and then it is translated "saint." In the New Testament, it is always plural (*hagioi*, "saints") in this sense. "Saint John," and "Saint Mary" are postbiblical expressions. For example, 2 Corinthians is addressed to "all the saints who are in all Achaia" (1:1). In New Testament times, all Christians were called saints. How can this be when we know of the very unsaintly goings-on at the Corinthian congregation? The answer is that sanctification has a positional, as well as a practical aspect. All believers are set apart by the Holy Spirit as soon as they believe. They become saints. That is *positional sanctification.*

But these saints should also be constantly growing more holy in actual lifestyle. That is *practical* or *progressive sanctification.* There is also a *future, final sanctification* when we will be delivered from the very presence of sin.

When set apart for God's use, even things can be holy, such as "the holy city" (Ma 4:5), "the holy place" (Ma 24:15), "His holy covenant" (Lk 1:72), "a holy kiss" (1 Th 5:26), and "holy faith" (Jude 20).

Sanctify, hallow (hagiazo) is used twenty-eight times, always translated "sanctify," except in the Lord's Prayer (Ma 6:9; Lk 11:2), where it is rendered "hallowed." The meaning "set apart" is especially prominent in the verb form. For example, when Paul wrote that "the unbelieving husband is sanctified by the wife, and the unbelieving wife is sanctified by the husband" (1 Co 7:14), he did not mean that the non-Christian spouse of a believer will definitely come to experience the sanctification that accompanies salvation. Rather, he or she is set apart by God with special privileges for the sake of the family. Often, of course, this does lead to salvation.

Holiness (hagiosyne) is the abstract noun form of *hagios* and occurs three times, all in Paul's Epistles. Christ is "declared *to be* the Son of God with power, according to the Spirit of holiness" (Ro 1:4), probably referring to the Holy Spirit. The Corinthians were urged to join Paul in practical sanctification, "perfecting holiness in the fear of God" (2 Co 7:1). Paul prayed that God would establish the Thessalonians' "hearts blameless in holiness" (1 Th 3:13).

Sanctification, holiness (hagiasmos) is a similar word but stresses the "process, or more often, its result (the state of being made holy)" (Arndt, Gingrich, Danker, *A Greek-English Lexicon of the New Testament,* p. 9). It is a word unique to Christianity and is used ten times in the New Testament: eight times by Paul, once in Hebrews, and once by Peter.

Christ Himself is our sanctification (1 Co 1:30), and sanctification is God's will for us (1 Th 4:3). The great importance of being sanctified is clearly stated in Hebrews 12:14: "Pursue peace with all *men,* and holiness without which no one will see the Lord."

SANCTUARY

A holy place, a place set apart. God commanded the Israelites to build Him a sanctuary, a place that would be set apart as holy and where His spirit would rest (Ex 25:8; 36:1). After the Hebrews entered the land of Canaan, they set up the sanctuary at Shiloh (Jos 18:1). Many years later, David prepared the materials for a permanent sanctuary, the temple which his son Solomon would build (1 Ch 22:19). The Psalmist also describes heaven as God's sanctuary (Ps 102:119), and in the New Jerusalem there will be no temple or sanctuary because the "the Lord God Almighty and the Lamb are its temple" (Re 21:22).

SAND

Tiny particles of rock and various minerals which is often found along the shores of large bodies of water, and in large deposits in desert regions. Sand is often used symbolically in Scripture to represent an innumerable quantity (Ge 22:17; Is 10:22; Re 20:8). Because of its shifting qualities and its vulnerability to wind and rain, sand is a poor foundation for a building. Jesus compared a building with a sand foundation to a person whose life is centered around worldly concerns rather than on Jesus Christ (Ma 7:26).

SAN'DAL

An open shoe, strapped to the foot with a leather thong. John the Baptist described the superiority of the Messiah, saying that he was unworthy to fasten His sandals. In ancient times, exchanging sandals was a formal legalization of a transaction (Ru 4:7). Sandals were removed in the house, as a symbol of courtesy. God told Moses to remove his sandals when he stood before the burning bush, for he was "standing on holy ground" (Ex 3:5). The word shoe is also used occasionally in some translations (Ps 60:8; 108:9; NKJV), but the "sandal" is probably a more accurate description of the footwear of the day.

SAND FLY
See FLY.

SAND LIZARD
See LIZARD.

SAND PARTRIDGE
See PARTRIDGE.

SAND VIPER
See SNAKE.

SANHEDRIN

SAN' HE·DRIN

The Jewish Sanhedrin, also referred to as the Council, was the highest ruling body among the Jews in New Testament times. This group probably evolved from the council of advisors to the high priest during the years when the Jewish people lived under the domination of the Persians and the Greeks from about 500 to 150 B.C. The Council originally was composed of leading priests and distinguished aristocrats among the Jewish people, but later scribes and Pharisees and Sadducees were added to the group.

With an assembly of seventy-one members, the Council was headed by the high priest. The body was granted limited authority over certain religious, civil, and criminal matters by the Romans during their years of dominance in Palestine. Most of the day-to-day business was left to the Sanhedrin, which was permitted to have its own police force. However, the Council was denied the right to exercise the death penalty (Jo 18:31). In spite of these restrictions, the Sanhedrin exercised considerable influence in religious matters.

The Council played a prominent role in the arrest and trial of Jesus, although it is not clear whether He was formally tried by the Council or given preliminary hearings. Christ was arrested by the temple police in the garden of Gethsemane (Mk 14:43) and subjected to false accusations before the high priest (Ma 26:59). Several of the apostles, including Peter, John, and Paul, were charged before the Sanhedrin (Ac 4:1-23; 5:17-41; 22–24) in later years.

Prominent members of the Sanhedrin mentioned in a favorable light in the New Testament were Joseph of Arimathea (Mk 15:43); Gamaliel (Ac 5:34); and Nicodemus (Jo 3:1; 7:50).

During most of its history, the Council met at Jerusalem. But after A.D. 150, it convened at Tiberias, a Roman city on the shores of the Sea of Galilee.

SAN·SAN' NAH (palm leaf)

A town in the south of Judah (Jos 15:31). It was probably the same as Hazar-susah in Joshua 19:5.

SAPH (a basin or threshold)

A giant of the Philistines. In a conflict at Gob he was slain by Sibbechai the Hushathite (2 Sa 21:18). In 1 Chronicles 20:4 he is called Sippai.

SAPH' IR

See SHAPHIR.

SAPPH·I' RA (beautiful)

The wife of Ananias. Together this couple sold a piece of real estate and donated part of the money to the apostles. Trying to give an appearance of sacrificial generosity, they pretended that the money they donated was the whole sum. Peter rebuked them for their dishonesty, and God struck both of them dead. This remarkable example of God's omniscience, and His intolerance of sin was a frightening lesson to the early church (Ac 5:1-10).

SAP' PHIRE

A precious stone, a transparent bluish variety of corundum. It was found in Ethiopia and India. It was one of the stones of the breastplate of the high priest, and in John's vision of the New Jerusalem, it was in the foundation (Ex 28:18; Song 5:14; Is 54:11; Re 21:19). The sapphires mentioned in the Bible may be lapis lazuli. See ADAMANT and LAPIS LAZULI.

SAR' AH (a princess)

The wife of Abraham; also his half sister (Ge 20:12). She was ten years younger than her husband. She came with him from Ur of the Chaldees (Ge 11:28-31; 17:17). Sarah apparently had great beauty, even in her old age. When they were in Egypt, Abraham introduced her as his sister rather than as his wife (though both were true), because he was afraid men would slay him in order to marry her (Ge 12:10-20). Sarah was taken into Pharaoh's harem, but God rescued both Abraham and Sarah from Abraham's folly. Nevertheless, Abraham did not seem to learn his lesson, because he tried the same trick in Gerar (Ge 20:1-18). This time, Sarah was about ninety years old, and she was still automatically placed in the king's harem because of her beauty.

When God made the covenant with Abraham, He promised him an heir, a son who would carry the promise and the covenant, and from whom the great nation would be descended. When Sarah was about 75 years old, she came to the conclusion that she would never have any children, and she could not imagine how the covenant was to be fulfilled. She urged Abraham to take Hagar, Sarah's Egyptian maid, and have a son by her. Sarah planned to adopt this child, and thus have a son for Abraham. Abraham complied with this plan, and Hagar conceived. Not surprisingly, after this happened Hagar began to despise her mistress and Sarah grew jealous of Hagar. She treated the maid harshly, and Hagar tried to run away. However, God spoke to her as she fled from Sarah, and told her to return to Sarah and Abraham, promising that her son would also be blessed by God (Ge 16:1-16). Thirteen years later, the Angel of the Lord told Sarah and Abraham that within a year, Sarah would have a son (Ge 17:1-19; He 11:11-12). Sarah laughed at the idea at first, but just one year later Isaac was born—the child of promise. At this point her name was changed from Sarai to Sarah (Ge 17:15-22; 18:9-15; 21:1-5).

Sarah is mentioned among the heroes of the faith in Hebrews 11:11-12, and also commended for her submission to her husband in 1 Peter 3:6.

SAR′ A·I *(my princess)*

Sarah, Abraham's wife, was originally called Sarai (Ge 11:28-31). See SARAH.

SAR′ APH *(burning)*

A descendant of Shelah, the son of Judah (1 Ch 4:22).

SAR′ DIN

See SARDIUS.

SAR′ DIS

A city of Asia Minor at the foot of Mount Tmolus, on the east bank of the Pactolus River (Re

1:11; 3:1,4). It was the capital of Lydia, in western Asia (modern Turkey). The church in this city is one of the seven addressed in the beginning of Revelation. See SEVEN CHURCHES OF REVELATION.

SARDITES

Those descended from Zebulon's son Sered (Nu 26:26).

SAR′ DI·US

A precious stone which garnished the sixth foundation of the wall about the New Jerusalem of John's vision (Re 21:20) and was one of the stones of the breastplate of the high priest (Ex 28:17). It is also mentioned in the description of the king of Tyre (Eze 28:12-13). It is believed by many to be a variety of reddish-brown chalcedony which is called carnelian. See CHALCEDONY.

SAR′ DO·NYX

A variety of chalcedony, mentioned as the stone adorning the fifth foundation of the New Jerusalem (Re 21:20). This word is also translated "onyx."

SA·REP′ TA

See ZAREPHATH.

SAR′ GON

Three kings of ancient Mesopotamia had this name, but only one is mentioned in the Bible. Sargon II was one of the greatest of Assyrian kings. His immediate predecessor was Shalmaneser IV, who had besieged Samaria for three years (2 Ki 17:3-6; 18:9-12). Sargon had apparently succeeded him by the time the city actually fell in 722 B.C., and according to an inscription found in his palace, he claimed the glory of victory for himself. The people of Samaria were carried away into captivity, and foreigners imported to take their place in the land (2 Ki 17:6,24).

Sargon is only mentioned by name once in the Bible, in the Book of Isaiah. The city of Ashdod had rebelled against Assyria, and Sargon retook the city. When this happened, God instructed Isaiah to walk around naked and barefoot as a sign of what would happen to Egypt and Ethiopia as they fought against Assyria. This may have been a warning to Judah to avoid entering the conflict.

SAR′ID *(survivor)*

A village or landmark in the southern district of Zebulun (Jos 19:10,12).

SA′RON (Ac 9:35)

See SHARON.

SAR′SE·CHIM

A prince of Nebuchadnezzar (Je 39:3).

SA′RUCH

See SERUG.

SASH

See BELT.

SATAN *(adversary)*

Satan, or Adversary, is the most frequently used name for the devil in the New Testament, appearing over fifty times. Devil, or Slanderer is used over thirty times. Satan, the personification of evil in this world, is the great superhuman enemy of God, His people, and all that is good. His character is vile and evil, and he is portrayed as the great deceiver. So sly is Satan in his deception that he sometimes transforms himself into an angel of light (2 Co 11:14).

Satan is mentioned first by name in Job 1:6-12; 2:1. His first appearance in the history of mankind was in Eden as the seducer of Adam and Eve (Ge 3:1-6; 2 Co 11:3; Re 12:9).

Regarded by many scholars as a fallen angel, Satan has a continuing ambition to replace God and have others worship him (Ma 4:8-9). He constantly tempts people to try to entice them into sin (1 Th 3:5). In falling from God's favor, Satan persuaded other angels to join him in his rebellion (Re 12:9). When Christ returns, Satan will be defeated and ultimately cast into the lake of fire (Re 20:1-10).

The following names or titles for Satan in the New Testament throw further light on the devil's character: Beelzebub, ruler (or prince) of demons (Ma 12:24); the wicked one (Ma 13:19); the enemy (Ma 13:39); murderer (Jo 8:44); a liar (Jo 8:44); ruler of this world (Jo 12:31; 14:30); god of this age (2 Co 4:4); Belial (which means wickedness, or ungodliness; found in the Old Testament: De 15:9; Ps 41:8; Pr 19:28; as well as 2 Co 6:15); prince of the power of the air (Ep 2:2); ruler of darkness (Ep 6:12); the tempter (1 Th 3:5); the king of death (He 2:14); a roaring lion

and adversary (1 Pe 5:8); angel of the bottomless pit, Abaddon (Destruction), and Apollyon (Destroyer), (Re 9:11); the dragon (Re 12:7); accuser of our brethren (Re 12:10); serpent of old (Re 20:2); and the deceiver (Re 20:10).

Satan's character is one of cunning (Ge 3:1 and 2 Co 11:3); he is slanderous (Job 1:9); fierce (Lk 8:29); deceitful (2 Co 11:14); powerful (Ep 2:2); proud (1 Ti 3:6); cowardly (Jam 4:7) and wicked (1 Jo 2:13). He has power over the wicked. They are his children (Ac 13:10; 1 Jo 3:10); they do his will (Jo 8:44), they are punished with him (Ma 25:41). He possesses (Lk 22:3); blinds (2 Co 4:4); deceives (Re 20:7-8); and ensnares (1 Ti 3:7).

Satan also has power over God's people to tempt (1 Ch 21:1); afflict (Job 2:7); oppose (Ze 3:1); sift (Lk 22:31); deceive (2 Co 11:3); and to disguise himself (2 Co 11:14-15). But the believers are not powerless; they can watch against Satan (2 Co 2:10-11); fight against him (Ep 6:11-16); resist him (Jam 4:7; 1 Pe 5:9) and overcome him (1 Jo 2:13; Re 12:10-11).

Best of all, Christ has triumphed over Satan. This was predicted (Ge 3:15); portrayed (Ma 4:1-11); proclaimed (Lk 10:18) and perfected (Mk 3:22-28). What this means to believers in Christ is thoroughly explained in the eighth chapter of Paul's Epistle to the Romans. "There is now no condemnation to those who are in Christ Jesus [no falling into Satan's ways] who do not walk according to the flesh, but according to the Spirit" (Ro 8:1). The last part of the chapter particularly talks about the believer's ability to live the Christian life, of Christ's intercession on the believer's behalf, and the fact that nothing can separate the believer from the love of God. This is a life lived with the knowledge of Satan and his enmity to the people of God, but it is not a life of fear.

SATAN, SYNAGOGUE OF

A gathering of Satan's followers; the term used by Jesus to describe those who claimed to be Jews, but were not. Presumably, this refers to those who claimed the national heritage while rejecting God, specifically those who opposed the church (Re 2:9; 3:9).

SATISFACTION

One of the blessings that a person who accepts Jesus Christ as Savior receives is the understanding that God is *satisfied*. There are three related Greek words in the New Testament that concern this concept; the main teaching of these three words is that not only is God satisfied with the Person and work of His Son, but through faith in Him, we can be reconciled to God.

This cluster of theologically important and related Greek words each occur twice in the New Testament, and all three start with the same root, *hilas-*.

Make propitiation (hilaskomai) occurs first in Luke 18:13 in a very famous passage. Our Lord tells the story of two men who went up to the temple to pray. The Pharisee praised himself and his own record in his "prayer." The tax collector dared not lift his eyes, but beat his breast and said, "God be merciful [a form of this verb] to me, a sinner!" He, not the self-righteous religionist, went away justified. A more literal rendering of his prayer would be, "God be propitiated with me, the sinner!" *To propitiate* means "to satisfy the demands of," in this case, an offended Deity. Sacrifice for sins is the method God chose to make satisfaction for sins. In the Old Testament, animal sacrifices were pictures looking forward to the once-for-all infinite sacrifice of the Lamb of God. *God is satisfied with the sacrifice of His Son.* We do not have to plead with Him to accept us. He loves us and desires that we put our faith in His Son.

The other use of *hilaskomai* is in Hebrews 2:17: "Therefore, in all things He had to be made like *His* brethren, that He might be a merciful and faithful High Priest in things *pertaining* to God, to make propitiation for the sins of the people." The Lord Jesus became Man to meet the needs of mankind and died on the cross to satisfy God's righteous demands against sinners. He propitiated, or made satisfaction for, the sins of His people.

Propitiation (hilasmos), a noun form, occurs twice, both in 1 John. In 1 John 2:2, an important doctrinal verse, we read: "And He Himself is the propitiation for our sins, and not for ours only but also for the sins of the whole world." Christ Himself is the satisfaction or satisfying sacrifice for sins. The New Testament concept of propitiation is not at all like the pagan idea of appeasing a cruel deity. Propitiation in the New Testament is a result of God's love (I Jo 4:10).

Mercy seat (hilasterion) occurs twice, once meaning the cover of the ark of the covenant

(He 9:5) and once translated the same as *hilasmos*. The mercy seat is "the place where propitiation is made," the place where the blood of propitiation had been sprinkled with the blood of atonement. Like so much of the Tabernacle, it pictured Christ and His work on the cross. The ark was the place where God revealed His will to the priests—Christ is the place where God meets with man. Christ is not only the propitiation, but the place where propitiation is made. He is the satisfier and the satisfaction and the one with whom our Heavenly Father is satisfied. See RECONCILIATION.

SATON

A unit of dry measure, thought to be equal to about ⅜ of a bushel (Ma 13:33; Lk 13:21); also translated "measure," "bushel," "peck," and "large amount."

SA'TRAP

The governor of a province of ancient Persia (Ez 8:36; Es 3:12). The Persian satraps were vassals of the emperor, but they had great power in their own provinces, and essentially reigned as kings. Also called "lieutenants" (KJV).

SA'TYR

A god of the ancient Greeks, a sylvan creature having the appearance of a goat and possessed of a lustful nature. In English, probably through its use in the King James Version of Isaiah 13:21 and 34:14, the word has also come to refer to a wild and hairy demon or creature which inhabits wastelands and ruins. The Hebrew word in these passages is now considered by most translators to refer to some type of owl.

SAUL

Three men of the Bible:

1. A king of Edom (Ge 36:37-38). He was called Shaul in 1 Ch 1:48.

2. The son of Kish, a Benjamite and the first king of Israel. Initially he was a faithful worshipper of Jehovah, as well as a man of considerable military ability. When Israel demanded a king, Samuel anointed Saul as the first king of Israel. He was fully accepted by Israel after his victory over the Ammonites at Jabesh-gilead (1 Sa 11:1-15). Sadly, in spite of his good start and his first enthusiasm for following God, Saul fell into spiritual decay. He disobeyed

God and insulted Him by treating God as the pagans treated their deities. Instead of consulting the Lord and submitting fully to His leadership, Saul chose to disobey God, trusting that he could appease Him later by sacrifices and devotion. Because of Saul's disobedience and lack of sincere repentance, God rejected Saul as king and instructed Samuel to anoint the young man David instead. The Spirit of God left Saul, and an evil spirit was sent to torment him. Only the music from David's harp soothed his fits of tormented madness (1 Sa 16:14-23). After David killed the Philistine giant, Saul began to see him as a serious threat to his position and tried to kill him. He spent his last years driven by jealousy and hatred in futile pursuit of the fleeing David. Time and again, David showed Saul that he wished him no harm and would not kill him to gain the kingdom, but Saul could not let go of his fear. Eventually, in a losing battle with the Philistines, Saul was wounded and took his own life rather than fall into the hands of the Philistines (1 Sa 31:1-10).

3. The name of the apostle Paul before his conversion (Ac 7:58). See PAUL.

SAV' IOR

One who saves; a deliverer from danger or evil. In the Old Testament God is the Savior, deliverer of the covenant people (Ps 106:21; Is 43:3,11; 45:15,21; 63:8; Je 14:8; Ho 13:4). The word applies especially to Jesus Christ who was called Savior by the angel announcing his birth (Lk 2:11), by some Samaritans (Jo 4:42), by Paul (Ph 3:20), and by others (Ac 5:31; 2 Pe 2:20; 1 Jo 4:14). See SALVATION.

SAVOR

A pleasing odor or flavor. See INCENSE.

SAW

Ancient saws were long flint knives with jagged edges or bits of flint fitted into wooden frames. Later saws were made of thin bronze strips with one edge equipped with teeth and the other set in a wooden frame. In addition to their use on wood, saws were also used to cut stone (1 Ki 7:9).

SCABBARD

The sheath of a sword; the protective case in which a sword (or similar weapon) rests while

it is being carried, both to protect the keen edge of the blade, and to protect the wearer from injury. Scabbards or sheaths are mentioned along with swords in several passages (1 Sa 17:51; 2 Sa 20:8; 1 Ch 21:27; Eze 21:3-5,30; Jo 18:11).

SCABS

The hard covering of dried blood and pus which forms over an open wound and protects it from contamination and contusion. This word is used in some translations instead of the word "boils." See BOILS.

SCALE

1. The scales of fish. Only fish with scales and fins were considered clean and suitable for food (Le 11:9-12). The mighty sea creature Leviathan is described as possessing scales (Job 41:15).

2. A balance for weighing (Is 40:12).

3. When Paul was healed of his blindness after he saw the vision on the road to Damascus, "something like scales" fell from his eyes (Ac 9:18).

4. To climb up (Pr 21:22).

SCALL *(archaic)*

A scaly skin eruption (Le 14:54-57).

SCAPE' GOAT

See AZAZEL, and ATONEMENT, DAY OF.

SCAR' LET

A rich crimson color taken from an insect which the Arabs called *Kermez* and which was frequently found on the oak of Palestine. The insect is about the size of a pea, is without wings, and clings to leaves. The female insect furnishes the substance for coloring, which comes from the red matter contained in the eggs (Ge 38:28). This color was used in the garments of the high priest, and also the hangings of the tabernacle, and for ceremonial purposes (Le 14:4; Nu 19:6; He 9:19).

SCENT

An odor, smell. See INCENSE.

SCEP' TER

A staff or rod which served as an emblem of authority, especially for royalty (Ps 45:6; Am 1:5; He 1:8). Among such ancients as the Egyptians and Persians it was a rod, probably about five feet long bearing at one end an ornamental ball or other figure. The word "scepter" is used as a reference to the coming Messiah, who would have power and authority as a ruler (Ge 49:10).

SCE′VA

A Jewish chief priest in Ephesus at the time of Paul (Ac 19:14-16). His seven sons attempted to cast out demons in the name of "Jesus whom Paul preaches." The demons recognized their lack of authority, and the demon-possessed man attacked them, wounding them and forcing them to flee naked and bleeding.

SCHIN

See SHIN.

SCHISM

A division between religious factions, also called "dissension" or "division" (1 Co 12:25). The church at Corinth was suffering from such strife, jealousy, and lack of love and trust (1 Co 1:10; 11:18).

SCHOOL

In ancient Israel children were instructed in religion by their parents (Ge 18:19; De 6:7; 2 Ti 3:15). The people were instructed in the law at the Feast of Tabernacles during the Sabbatic year (De 31:10-13). Religious knowledge was disseminated and religious life stimulated by the work of the prophets. At a later period there were schools in connection with the synagogues. Children were taught to read the Scriptures and to write. The law was taught by the scribes in the court of the temple (Lk 2:46). Samuel was the earliest of the prophets. He dwelt at Ramah where he was the head of a community of prophets (1 Sa 19:18-20) who devoted their time to religious study (1 Sa 10:10; 19:20-23). Two hundred years later there were prophetical communities or schools of the prophets, probably established by Elijah. The members were called sons of the prophets (1 Ki 20:35,38; 2 Ki 2:3,5; 9:1).

SCHOOL′MAS′TER

This is the rendering of the Greek *paidagogos,* a boy leader, pedagogue (Ga 3:24-25), or a tutor (1 Co 4:15). In a Greek home a trusted slave had the care of children, to watch over them, keep them from danger and conduct them to and from school. In the same way, the law was a pedagogue to lead us to Christ. That is, it prepared us to see in him the Redeemer by declaring our unrighteousness, the inability of the works of the law to bring us salvation, and in types and symbols revealed the plan of redemption (Ro 3:19-21; 4:15; 7:7-25).

SCI′ENCE

The Hebrew and Greek words so rendered (Da 1:4; 1 Ti 6:20) mean simply knowledge and do not convey the modern sense of systematized knowledge pertaining specifically to the physical world and its function.

SCOFFER

One who is contemptuous of what is good and right; one who ridicules truth, a scornful, sneering person (Ge 21:9; Ps 73:8). Scoffing is clearly linked with wickedness.

SCORN

As a noun: something which is mocked or ridiculed (Ps 44:13; 79:4). One who is scornful is one who mocks and ridicules others, despising them, holding them in contempt. Scornfulness is associated with arrogance and wickedness. The final end of the scornful will be judgment (Ps 1).

SCOR′PI′ON

A creature of the spider class with a sting in its tail. Scorpions look a little like a tiny lobster or crawdad at first glance. They are common in Israel, and were a terror to the Hebrews in the wilderness (De 8:15). The sting of a scorpion is not usually fatal, but it is very painful. In John's vision of the last days, he saw an army of terrible creatures which could sting like scorpions, and which were given the power to kill one third of the earth's population (Re 9:5,10).

SCOUNDREL

An evil person, one who behaves disgracefully. Nabal was described as a scoundrel (1 Sa 25:17,25), also a "son of Belial" (KJV).

SCOURGE

To punish or torture, particularly by lashing. Mosaic law permitted no more than forty lashes as punishment (De 25:2-3). As a safeguard against breaking the law, the general practice was 39. Paul said that he received from the Jews 39 stripes five different times (2 Co 11:24). Under Roman law Roman citizens could not be beaten without a trial. Once Paul saved himself from a scourging by revealing his Roman citizenship (Ac 22:24-30).

SCREECH OWL

See OWL.

SCRIBE

A public writer. He may have been simply an amanuensis, as Baruch (Je 36:4,18,32). He may have acted in a secretarial capacity or as a governmental clerk (2 Ki 12:10; Ez 4:8). As one who copied the Scriptures, Ezra was the most distinctive of Old Testament scribes (Ez 7:6,10). He also taught the statutes of the law. In New Testament times scribes were the interpreters and teachers of the law. They held the highest place among the people and many members of the Sanhedrin were of this class (Ma 16:21; 26:3). They had the respect and reverence of the people. They bitterly opposed Jesus (Ma 21:15), and He denounced them for their hypocrisy and false religion (Lk 11:44).

SCRIBE'S KNIFE

See PENKNIFE.

SCRIP

A bag or wallet used for carrying food and money when traveling (Ma 10:10). It was made of leather and carried on the shoulder. A shepherd who spent most of his time far from his dwelling would carry food and necessities in such a bag (1 Sa 17:40).

SCRIPT

Writing, style of forming the letters of different languages (Ez 4:7; Es 1:22).

SCRIP'TURE

In an archaic sense: that which is written—book, letter (Ma 28:56). Most commonly, this is a term denoting the Bible as a whole or some portion of it. When regarded collectively the word is used in the plural (Ma 21:42; Lk 24:27; Jo 5:39; Ro 1:2; 2 Ti 3:15). Specific portions are indicated by the singular (Mk 12:10; Lk 4:21; Jo 19:37). See BIBLE.

SCROLL

A roll of papyrus or parchment used for writing. Jeremiah wrote out his prophecy on a scroll, so that it could be read to the king (Je 36:1-32). The king, however, was angry with what Jeremiah wrote, and destroyed the document.

SCRUPLES

Ethical considerations or convictions of conscience which cause a person to decide against certain behaviors. Paul urged believers to be respectful of one another's scruples, because it is important for each person to follow his own conscience (Ro 15:1).

SCUM

Translation of a word which probably means corrosion or rust. It is used figuratively to describe the sin of Jerusalem (Eze 24:6-13).

SCURF

See LEPER, LEPROSY.

SCURVY

Scurvy is a disease which is caused by a severe lack of ascorbic acid (vitamin C). It is characterized by spongy gums, a loosening of the teeth, and skin problems. In Scripture, this word probably refers to eczema (Le 21:20; 22:22, KJV).

SCYTH'I·AN

A native of Scythia, the region north of the Black Sea (Col 3:11).

SCYTHOPOLIS

See BETH-SHEAN.

SEA

The word has various designations:

1. The waters in general, the ocean (1 Ki 10:22; Ps 8:8; 24:2; Re 7:1-3; 21:1).

2. A particular body of water. The Israelites were acquainted particularly with four seas—Red Sea, Mediterranean Sea, Sea of Galilee, and Dead Sea. The Mediterranean was also called the Great Sea. The enormous lake in Galilee was also called a sea.

3. The word sea is also applied to large rivers, as the Nile (Is 19:5; Na 3:8) and Euphrates (Je 51:36,42).

4. The Brazen Sea, the great laver for priestly washings before they entered the sanctuary in Solomon's temple, also called the Molten Sea (1 Ki 7:39; Je 52:17).

5. The sea is used figuratively to express the roaring of hostile armies (Is 5:30), unsteadiness (Jam 1:6), diffusing of spiritual truth (Is 11:9; Hab 2:14).

SEA, BRAZEN
See BRAZEN SEA.

SEA, CHINNERETH
See GALILEE, SEA OF.

SEA COW
See BADGER.

SEA, DEAD
See DEAD SEA.

SEA, SALT
See DEAD SEA.

SEA, THE GREAT
See MEDITERRANEAN SEA.

SEA, TIBERIUS
See TIBERIAS.

SEAH
A unit of dry measure equal to about seven quarts, or one third of a bushel. See WEIGHTS & MEASURES.

SEAL
A small engraving of a design or the name of the owner, designed for stamping an impression into wax or clay (Job 38:14). Seals were made of precious stone, metal, or clay; they were typically engraved on a signet ring, or made so that they could be strung on a cord and worn about the neck (Ex 28:11; Es 8:8). Seals were used to give authority to a document, or to certify a signature (Ne 9:38; Es 8:8; Jo 3:33).

The word seal also refers to the blob of wax used to hold a scroll or document closed. This blob of wax bore the imprint of the signet, and served as a safeguard of privacy. If the seal was unbroken it was certain the letter or document had not been opened. A seal was also an easily recognizable signature to persons who could not write or read.

Pilate complied with the requests of the Jewish leaders, and authorized the setting of a guard around the tomb. The Jewish leaders went one step further and sealed the tomb so that there could be no question of someone creeping in at night and removing the body without being seen.

The word "seal" is also used in a figurative sense, as divine approval and authorization (Jo 6:27; 1 Co 9:2; 2 Ti 2:19).

SEA MEW
A ceremonially unclean bird (Le 11:16; De 14:15) which is called the cuckow in the Authorized Version.

SEA, MOLTEN
See BRAZEN SEA.

SEA MON' STER
The biblical term for unknown large sea creatures. Psalm 148:7 refers to "sea monsters," or "great sea creatures." Whales, large eels, sharks, and giant squid could all bear such a title. The most carefully described unidentifiable "sea monster" of the Bible is the LEVIATHAN.

SEAMSTER
See WEAVING.

SÉANCE
An occult ritual in which people attempt to contact the dead. Saul went to the witch of Endor to try and communicate with Samuel (1 Sa 28:8-11). See MAGIC, SORCERY, AND DIVINATION.

SEA OF GALILEE
See GALILEE, SEA OF.

SEA OF GLASS
The sea before the throne of God in the throne room of heaven (Re 4:6; 15:2). When Moses and the elders of Israel went up on the mountain at Sinai, they saw God standing on a "paved work of sapphire stone, and it was like the very heavens in its clarity" (Ex 24:10). Ezekiel's vision of God describes the firmament of heaven as a clear crystal (Eze 1:22-28).

SEA OF JAZER
A sea mentioned in Jeremiah's prophecy against Moab (Je 48:32). See JAZER.

SEAR
To burn with hot coals or other hot object. The writer of Proverbs warns that trifling with

adultery is like walking barefoot on hot coals—no one can do it without being burned (Pr 6:28). A person who has become comfortable with wickedness is described as having a seared conscience (1 Ti 4:2).

SEASON

The natural divisions of the year, marked by annual predictable weather changes (Le 26:4; De 11:14).

SEAT

See MERCY SEAT.

SE′ BA

The oldest son of Cush and ancestor of a Cushite tribe (Is 43:3; 45:14).

SEBAM

See SHEBAM.

SE′ BAT

See SHEBAT.

SE•CA′ CAH *(inclosure)*

A town in the wilderness of Judah (Jos 15:61).

SE′ CHU *(watchtower)*

A place near Ramah (1 Sa 19:22).

SECOND COMING

See RETURN OF CHRIST.

SECOND DEATH

Another name for the lake of fire, or hell (Re 20:14).

SECOND QUARTER, THE

The section of Jerusalem where Huldah the prophetess lived (2 Ki 22:14).

SECRET

See MYSTERY.

SECRETARY

A scribe or amanuensis. The apostle Paul apparently dictated his letters to a secretary (Ro 16:22; Ga 6:11; 2 Th 3:17).

SECT

A group or division; a party. Particularly an offshoot or denomination of a certain religion (Ac 26:4-5).

SECU

See SECHU.

SE•CUN′ DUS *(second)*

A Christian of Thessalonica; one of Paul's party when Paul went from Macedonia into Asia Minor (Ac 20:4).

SEDITION

The attempt to start a rebellion against the governing authority (Ez 4:15).

SEDUCTRESS

A woman who seeks to seduce men and lead them into sexual sin (Pr 2:16; 7:5; 27:13).

SEED

Seed was supposed to be ceremonially clean and mixed seed was not to be sown in the same field (Le 11:37-38; 19:19; De 22:9).

SEED, PARABLE OF (Mk 4:26-29)

SEEDTIME

The season of the year which is best for planting. God promised that as long as the earth lasted the four seasons (summer, winter, seedtime, and harvest) would continue (Ge 8:22).

SEER

See PROPHET.

SEETHE (archaic)

To cook by boiling (Ez 24:3-5).

SE′ GUB *(exalted)*

Two Old Testament men:

1. Son of Hezron and father of Jair. His mother was the daughter of Machir (1 Ch 2:21-22).

2. Son of Hiel. Joshua declared that anyone attempting to rebuild Jericho would be cursed. When Hiel set up the gates of the city, Segub, his son, died (Jos 6:26; 1 Ki 16:34).

SE′ IR

The mountain range of Edom running south from the Dead Sea (Ge 36:21; Nu 24:18; Eze 35:15). This district was once settled by Horites (Ge 14:6). The land was taken from them by the descendants of Esau (Ge 32:3; De 2:12; Jos 24:4). Another Seir was on the north of Judah, west of Kirjath-jearim (Jos 15:10).

SE·I′ RAH *(shaggy)*

A place in Ephraim to which Ehud fled after slaying Eglon at Jericho (Ju 3:26-27).

SE·I′ RATH

See SEIRAH.

SE′ LA

1. The capital of Edom. It was later the site of Petra, the great Nabatean city. It was captured by Amaziah of Judah who changed the name from Sela to Joktheel (2 Ki 14:7; 2 Ch 25:12).

2. A place on the border between the territory of Judah and the territory of the Amorites (Ju 1:36). Also called "the rock" (KJV).

3. A place in Moab (Is 16:1).

SE′ LAH

A word which occurs in the Psalms seventy-one times, as well as three times in the Book of Habakkuk. It is probably a musical direction. Any guesses as to its meaning can only be conjecture.

SE·LA-HAM·MAH′ LE·KOTH *(rock of division)*

A cliff in the wilderness of Maon where David escaped from Saul (1 Sa 23:28).

SE′ LED *(exultation)*

A descendant of Jerahmeel (1 Ch 2:30).

SE·LEU′ CI·A

A city not far from the mouth of the Orontes on the coast of Syria. Built by Seleucus Nicator, founder of Syria, it was the seaport of Antioch. Nicator built other cities and called them by the same name. From this point Paul and Barnabas sailed for Cyprus on the first missionary journey (Ac 13:4).

SELF-CONTROL

The practice and ability of using the will to control one's emotions and desires. Self-control is one of the fruits of the Spirit (Ga 5:22-23).

SELF-DENIAL

Refusing to allow oneself to enjoy certain pleasures or comforts, particularly anything that is not strictly necessary. Christians are supposed to practice self-denial, not indulging themselves unnecessarily, but it is also wrong to move into asceticism.

SELF-INDULGENCE

Never saying no to one's appetites and pleasures. Jesus accused the Pharisees of being full of self-indulgence, in spite of their appearance of godliness (Ma 23:25).

SELF-SUFFICIENCY

Denying the need for help from any source. Self-sufficiency is a trait of sinners, who believe that they do not need God (Job 20:22).

SELVAGE

The nonraveling edge of woven fabric, often woven more tightly, or with heavier threads. The curtains of the tabernacle had loops attached to the selvage edge to fasten the separate curtains together (Ex 26:4; 36:11).

SEM

See SHEM.

SEM·A·CHI′ AH *(sustained by Jehovah)*

Son of Shemaiah, son of Obed-edom, a Levite and porter (1 Ch 26:7).

SEM′ E·I

Father of Mattathias, ancestor of Christ (Lk 3:26).

SEM′ E·IN

See SEMEI.

SEMITIC LANGUAGES

See HEBREW.

SEN′ A·AH

The head of a family—3,680 of whom returned to Israel with Zerubbabel (Ez 2:35), possibly the same person as HASENNAH.

SEN′ EH *(bramble)*

One of the two rocks in the mountain pass of Michmash. It was climbed by Jonathan and his armorbearer when they surprised the garrison of the Philistines (1 Sa 14:4-5).

SE′ NIR

Possibly the Ammonite name for Mount Hermon (De 3:9) or a peak near Mount Hermon (1 Ch 5:23; Song 4:8). The fir trees from this area were used for shipbuilding (Eze 27:5).

SEN·NACH′ER·IB

Son of Sargon. He ascended the throne of Assyria when his father was assassinated (705 B.C.). He put down the revolt of Merodach-baladan of Babylon and placed Belibni on the throne. About twenty years after the capture of Samaria by his father, he invaded Judah and, according to his account, he captured 46 towns and carried away over 200,000 captives. He attacked the city of Jerusalem, boasting against the Lord and saying that the God of Israel was not powerful enough to save Jerusalem from his hand. The prophet Isaiah told the righteous king Hezekiah that in fact God would deliver them, and a short time later the angel of the Lord went through the Assyrian camp and killed 185,000 soldiers. Sennecherib abandoned the siege and returned to Nineveh (2 Ki 18:17–19:37). Later he again captured Babylon, massacred the people, and ruined the city. He built a great palace in Nineveh, 1,500 feet long and 700 broad and brought water into the city by a system of canals. In 680 B.C. he was assassinated by two of his sons which brought another son, Esar-haddon, to the throne (2 Ki 19:37; 2 Ch 32:21). See SENNACHERIB'S PRISM.

SENNACHERIB'S PRISM

The monument known as Sennacherib's Prism is a fascinating artifact from Assyria's past. It gives a different account than the Bible about an important event in Israel's history—a siege against Jerusalem conducted by King Sennacherib of Assyria (ruled 705-681 B.C.) about 690 B.C. (Is 36:37).

The fifteen-inch high clay prism contains well-preserved Assyrian script that verifies the attack on Jerusalem and King Hezekiah of Judah by Assyrian forces. "As to Hezekiah, the Jew, he did not submit to my yoke," the prism reads. "I laid siege to 46 of his strong cities, walled forts and to countless small cities in their vicinity, and conquered them, [Hezekiah] I made a prisoner in Jerusalem, his royal residence, like a bird in a cage."

While Sennacherib's siege against Jerusalem is a verified historical fact, it is interesting that Sennacherib's account does not mention how the siege ended. This leads to suspicion among historians that the siege failed, since the Assyrians never mentioned their defeats in their official records—only their victories.

The biblical account records that Sennacherib suffered a crushing defeat in his siege of Jerusalem because of divine intervention. During the night, thousands of soldiers in the Assyrian army died through the action of the angel of the Lord (2 Ki 19:35).

Rulers of the ancient world used monuments such as this prism on which to record their exploits. These documents of stone and clay have survived for centuries in the rubble and ruin of ancient cities. They provide valuable insight into life in Bible times, confirming and, in many cases, adding valuable information about biblical events.

SENSUAL

Pertaining to the senses; specifically, a lifestyle of gratifying physical pleasures, often that which is immoral or lewd (Jam 3:15; Jude 19).

SEN′U·AH

See HASSENUAH.

SE·OR′IM

A descendant of Aaron. In the time of David his family constituted the fourth course of the priests (1 Ch 24:1,6,8).

SE′PHAR *(numbering)*

A place, probably in southern Arabia, located on the boundary of the territory of the descendants of Joktan (Ge 10:30).

SE·PHAR′AD

A place, believed by some to be Sardis in Asia Minor. The captives of Judah were taken here (Ob 20).

SE·PHAR·VA′IM

A city under the rule of Assyria. Inhabitants of this city were brought to settle Samaria after the Israelites were taken away (2 Ki 17:24,31). It has been identified with the city of Sippar, ruins of which were found at Abu Habbah, southwest of Baghdad, near the Euphrates.

SE·PHAR′VITES

Inhabitants of Sepharvaim. They sacrificed their children by fire to their gods Adrammalech and Anammalech (2 Ki 17:31).

SEPTUAGINT *(the seventy)*

The Septuagint is a translation of the Old Testament from Hebrew into Greek (284-247 B.C.).

The name itself means "seventy," and it is often referred to in abbreviation as LXX, the Roman numerals for seventy. According to tradition, the work was done by 70 Jewish elders brought from Palestine to Alexandria for the express purpose of translating the Old Testament from Hebrew into Greek. Many of the Jews, scattered throughout the Mediterranean world, had lost their working knowledge of Hebrew, and this translation (considered to be the oldest Bible translation in the world) enabled them to read their Scriptures in Greek, the language that had become their common language.

The widespread acceptance and use of the Septuagint in the Roman world paved the way for the spread of the gospel, because the Christian missionaries could build the explanation of the gospel on the foundation of the Old Testament histories and prophecies, which were available, and often familiar to their Greek speaking audience. Indeed, many of the Old Testament references found in the New Testament are quotes from the LXX, which shows that the apostles certainly considered it not only foundational to New Testament teaching, but a reliable translation.

The Septuagint has also been useful to scholars in finding the meanings to certain unfamiliar Hebrew words as they work with old Hebrew manuscripts. It is generally considered that the LXX translation of the Pentateuch is more literal than some of the other Old Testament books, perhaps reflecting the extreme importance the Jews place on the writings of Moses.

SEP′UL·CHRE

Tomb. Caverns, both natural and artificial, were used by the Hebrews for the burial of their dead (Ge 23:9; Is 22:16; Jo 11:38). Jerusalem is the center of a great cemetery as the cliffs about the city have numerous tombs. To protect the tomb, a stone was placed against the entrance (Ma 27:60). Sepulchres were generally outside the city, and often on the face of a cliff some distance from the ground. It was often whitewashed so it could be clearly seen and not touched, as contact with it would render one ceremonially unclean. In many instances it was a shaft in the side of the cavern. There were also family burial places (Ge 49:29-31; 2 Sa 2:32; 1 Ki 13:22) and public places for the poor and strangers (2 Ki 23:6; Je 26:23; Ma 27:7).

SE′RAH *(abundance)*

A daughter of Asher, son of Jacob and Leah's handmaid, Zilpah (Ge 46:17; 1 Ch 7:30).

SE·RAI′AH

1. A scribe who lived in the reign of David (2 Sa 8:17). See SHAVSHA.

2. The chief priest, son of Azariah. When Jerusalem was taken by Nebuchadnezzar, Seraiah was sent to him at Riblah and was put to death (2 Ki 25:18-21; 1 Ch 6:14; Je 52:24-27).

3. The son of Tanhumeth, a Netophathite. He was one of those Gedaliah advised to yield to the Chaldeans (2 Ki 25:23; Je 40:8).

4. Son of Kenaz (1 Ch 4:13).

5. Son of Asiel and father of Josibiah of the tribe of Simeon; ancestor of Jehu (1 Ch 4:35).

6. One who returned with Zerubbabel (Ez 2:2).

7. An ancestor of Ezra (Ez 7:1).

8. A son of Hilkiah, a priest (Ne 11:11).

9. A priest who returned from Babylon with Zerubbabel (Ne 12:1,7).

10. Son of Azriel. He was ordered by Jehoiakim to arrest Baruch and Jeremiah (Je 36:26).

11. Son of Neriah. He was taken to Babylon with Zedekiah, Judah's last king. He is described as "a quiet prince." Jeremiah the prophet gave him a book which contained the prophecy of doom for Babylon (Je 51:59-64).

SER′A·PHIM *(burning)*

Seraphim are mentioned in Isaiah 6 when Isaiah received his commission from God. The word *seraphim* comes from the verb *seraph* ("to burn") and appears in the context of holiness. Isaiah sensed his own lack of holiness in the light of the seraphim's ascription of praise to God: "Holy, holy, holy!" Seraphim are seen as burning with holiness. Some scholars believe cherubim and seraphim are not really that different. In fact, the living creatures in Revelation seem to have some characteristics of both.

It should be underscored that the study of angels is not theoretical; it should be practical and encouraging. Hebrews 1:14 gives believers a wonderful assurance: "Are they not all ministering spirits sent forth to minister for those who will inherit salvation?" (See ANGEL).

SE′RED *(fear)*

A son of Zebulun and head of a tribal family (Ge 46:14; Nu 26:26).

SEREDITES

See SARDITES.

SER′GI·US PAU′LUS

The Roman proconsul of Cyprus (Ac 13:7-12).

SERMON ON THE MOUNT

Jesus's long discourse known as the Sermon on the Mount (Ma 5–7) is so named because He taught His disciples and the crowds that followed Him from a mountainside at the beginning of His public ministry (Ma 5:1). The traditional site of the Sermon is marked today by a beautiful little church, the Chapel on the Mount of Beatitudes, one of the major stopping points for tourists who visit the Holy Land.

The central theme of the Sermon is summarized in Matthew 5:48, "You shall be perfect, just as your Father in heaven is perfect." The word *perfect* does not refer to sinless or moral perfection. It indicates completeness, wholeness, maturity—being all that God wants a person to be. This goal, although we never attain it in this life, should continually challenge us to greater service for the Lord.

The ten major sections of the Sermon on the Mount are as follows:

1. The Beatitudes (5:3-12): The blessed rewards of living as citizens of Christ's Kingdom.
2. The lessons of salt and light (5:13-16): The effects of Christian living on the world.
3. True righteousness (5:17-48): The deeper meaning of the law of God.
4. Practice without hypocrisy (6:1-18): The right motives for giving, praying, and fasting.
5. The Christian's concerns (6:19-34): Serving God with singleness of purpose and putting the concerns of His Kingdom first are actions that free us from anxiety over lesser things.
6. Warning against judgment (7:1-6): The dangers of judging others harshly and carelessly.
7. Invitation to prayer (7:7-12): The blessings and privileges of prayer.
8. The two ways (7:13-14): Choose the narrow way, not the broad way that leads to destruction.
9. A tree and its fruit (7:15-20): "By their fruit you will know them."
10. The importance of deeds (7:21-29): To obey God is far better than talking about your obedience.

SERMONS IN ACTS

One of the most eloquent sermons in the Book of Acts is Paul's speech to the Athenian philosophers from the Areopagus, or Mars' Hill, a stony point named for the Greek god of war Ares (Roman god Mars). This hill overlooked the city of Athens. In his speech Paul declared that God will hold all people accountable for their response to His Son (Ac 17).

Several other important sermons and speeches, including the following, occur in the Book of Acts.

Speech	Theme	Reference
Peter to crowds at Pentecost	Peter's explanation of the meaning of Pentecost.	Ac 2:14-40
Peter to crowds at the temple	The Jewish people should repent for crucifying the Messiah.	Ac 3:12-26
Peter to the Sanhedrin	Testimony that a helpless man was healed by the power of Jesus	Ac 4:5-12
Stephen to the Sanhedrin	Stephen's rehearsal of Jewish history, accusing the Jews of killing the Messiah	Ac 7
Peter to Gentiles	Gentiles can be saved in the same manner as Jews	Ac 10:28-47
Peter to church at Jerusalem	Peter's testimony of his experiences at Joppa and a defense of his ministry to the Gentiles	Ac 11:4-18
Paul to synagogue at Antioch	Jesus was the Messiah in fulfillment of Old Testament Prophesies	Ac 13:16-41
Peter to Jerusalem council	Salvation by grace available to all	Ac 15:7-11
James to Jerusalem council	Gentile converts do not require circumcision	Ac 15:13-21
Paul to Ephesian elders	Remain faithful in spite of false teachers and persecution	Ac 20:17-35
Paul to crowd at Jerusalem	Paul's statement of his conversion and his mission to the Gentiles	Ac 22:1-21
Paul to Sanhedrin	Paul's defense, declaring himself a Pharisee and a Roman citizen	Ac 23:1-6
Paul to King Agrippa	Paul's statement of his conversion and his zeal for the gospel	Ac 26
Paul to Jewish leaders at Rome	Paul's statement about his Jewish heritage	Ac 28:17-20

SER′PENT

See SNAKE.

SERPENT, BRONZE
See BRAZEN SERPENT.

SERPENT CHARMER
One who hypnotized snakes. The prophets speak of the danger of poisonous snakes which have not been subdued in this way (Ec 10:11; Je 8:17). The practice was probably associated with the practice of magic. Apparently, the charmers used their voices to subdue the snakes (Ps 58:4).

SERPENT WELL
A well outside of Jerusalem between the Valley Gate and the Refuse Gate (Ne 2:13), also called "dragon well" and "Dragon's Spring."

SE′RUG (branch, shoot)
The son of Reu and great-grandfather of Abraham, in the line of Arphaxad, son of Shem, and ancestor of Jesus (Ge 11:20,23; 1 Ch 1:26; Lk 3:35; Saruch, KJV).

SERV′ANT
See SLAVE.

SERV′ANT OF JE·HO′VAH
One who acknowledges God and performs his will. Moses was called the servant of God (Ps 105:26), as were David (Ps 132:10), and Abraham (Ps 105:6). Specifically, "The Servant of Jehovah" is the Messiah as depicted in Isaiah 52:13–53:12; the one who would suffer affliction and death, thereby atoning for the sins of man.

SERVING
God intended that the Christian life should be dynamic, not static. We should sit under the teaching of the Word of God, understand and apply its meaning and implications, and serve God and our fellow believers. The Spirit of God has given us spiritual gifts, but those gifts are worthless unless they are put to use in the service of God and His church. Paul uses the figure of the human body to show the dependence of the members of the body upon one another and the importance of each member serving the other (Ro 12:4-5; 1 Co 12:12-31). While some members of the body have more prominent places of service than others, all are equally important. The worst thing that can happen to the human body is for one of its members to become nonfunctioning. Paralysis, sickness, deterioration, and sometimes death occur when a body member ceases to serve the other members of the body in the particular way that God intended. To maintain strength, health, and vitality, every member of the body must function and serve all the other members of the body. This is also true of the spiritual or new life. We will grow in the new life, become strong, and maintain good spiritual health as we use the talents and abilities that God has given us to meet the needs of the other members of the body.

SER′VI·TOR (archaic)
Attendant; he who performs as a servant (2 Ki 4:42-43).

SETH, SHETH (appointed, substituted)
Third son of Adam. He was born after the murder of Abel by Cain. Seth was the head of the genealogical line which produced Jesus (Lk 3:38). He died at the age of 912 (Ge 5:6-8).

SE′THUR (hidden)
Son of Michael. He was a spy, the representative of Asher, sent to Canaan by Moses from Kadesh-barnea (Nu 13:13).

SEVEN
The number seven has symbolic significance in Scripture. It was often used to represent completion, perfection, or rest. The first indication of the significance of this number occurs in the first chapter of Genesis in the creation account. The Lord created the world in six days and rested on the seventh, thereby establishing the seven day week. Many ancient cultures considered seven to be an important number. Some have suggested that this was because of the seven easily visible "heavenly bodies" (moon, sun, and the five visible planets: Jupiter, Mars, Mercury, Saturn, and Venus), but it is just as likely that the reverence for the number was left over from original knowledge of the creation.

Jacob worked for seven years for each of his wives (Ge 29:15-30), and Pharaoh's dreams prophesied seven years each of plenty and famine (Ge 41:1-7). Throughout the Books of the Law, the number seven is used several times in rituals and ceremonies (Le 4:6). The Hebrews were commanded to remember the seventh day of the week as a Sabbath (rest) day and keep it holy, because God had rested on the seventh day of creation (Ex 20:8). Namaan the leper was required to dip in the Jordan seven times in order to be healed (2 Ki 5:10). The number seven appears frequently in the prophetic books of Daniel and Revelation.

SEVEN CHURCHES OF REVELATION

The Book of Revelation contains special messages directed to churches in seven specific cities throughout the Roman province of Asia. These cities were important trade and communication centers, which were connected by major roads in New Testament times. Interestingly, John addressed the churches in exactly the order they would be if he had traveled the road, from Ephesus north to Pergamos, then south all the way to Laodicea. Some scholars believe that Revelation was a circular letter that would have been read first by the Ephesian church, then passed on the next church on the route. John received his vision and wrote the Revelation while he was in exile on Patmos, an island in the Aegean Sea. The message themes that he delivered to each church are as follows, each in their order:

1. Message to Ephesus: "You have left your first love" (2:4).
2. Message to Smyrna: "Be faithful until death, and I will give you the crown of life" (2:10).
3. Message to Pergamos: "I have a few things against you" (2:14).
4. Message to Thyatira: "Hold fast what you have until I come" (2:25).
5. Message to Sardis: "You have a name that you are alive, but you are dead" (3:1).
6. Message to Philadelphia: "I have set before you an open door" (3:8).
7. Message to Laodicea: "You are neither cold nor hot" (3:15).

SEVEN DEADLY SINS

Also called the Seven Mortal Sins. This list is not found in the Bible as such, but was compiled by theologians in the Middle Ages. These sins are sins of the heart which are regarded as having a particularly deadening effect on spiritual life. They are as follows: *Pride, Anger, Envy, Slothfulness, Lust, Gluttony, Greed.*

SE·VE′ NEH

See SYENE.

SEVENTH MONTH FESTIVAL

See TRUMPETS, FEAST OF.

SEVENTY, THE

The group of seventy disciples whom Jesus sent out to heal the sick and preach the good news of the kingdom throughout Israel (Lk 10:1-17). Also refers to the Septuagint, LXX. SEE SEPTUAGINT.

SEV′ EN·TY WEEKS

The prophecy of Daniel states that "seventy weeks are determined . . . to finish the transgression, to make an end of sins . . . to seal up vision and prophecy, and to anoint the Most Holy" (Da 9:24). The word translated weeks is simply "sevens." Here it is thought to refer to a period of seven years, rather than the seven days of the common week.

SEVENTY YEARS

See CAPTIVITY and SABBATICAL YEAR.

SEVEN WORDS FROM THE CROSS

According to the Gospel accounts of the crucifixion, Jesus spoke seven times as He hung on the cross.

1. "Father forgive them, for they do not know what they do" (Lk 23:34).
2. To the thief: "Assuredly, I say to you, today you will be with Me in Paradise" (Lk 23:43).
3. To Mary: "Woman, behold your son!" To John: "Behold your mother!" (Jo 19:26-27).
4. "Eli, Eli, lama sabachthani?" that is, "My God, My God, why have You forsaken me?" (Ma 27:46; Mk 15:34; Ps 22:1).
5. "I thirst" (Jo 19:28).
6. "It is finished" (Jo 19:30).
7. In a loud voice: "Father, into Your hands I commit my spirit" (Lk 23:46; Ps 31:5; Ma 27:50; Mk 15:37).

SHA·AL′ AB·BIN *(foxes)*

A city of the Amorites in the territory of Dan (Ju 1:35; 1 Ki 4:9).

SHA·AL′ BIM

See SHAALABBIN.

SHA·AL·BO′ NITE

A native of a place called Shaalbon or Shaalbim. Eliahba, one of David's mighty men, was a Shaalbonite (2 Sa 23:32; 1 Ch 11:33).

SHA′A·LIM, SHA′LIM *(foxes)*

A district in Ephraim or Benjamin in which Saul searched for his father's asses (1 Sa 9:4).

SHA′APH

Two Old Testament men:

1. A son of Jahdai of Judah, in the registry of Caleb (1 Ch 2:47).

2. Son of Caleb (1 Ch 2:49).

SHA·A·RA′IM *(two gates)*

Two Old Testament towns:

1. A town of Simeon (1 Ch 4:31).

2. A town of Judah in the lowland west of Socoh (1 Sa 17:52), also called Sharaim (Jos 15:36).

SHA·ASH′GAZ

A eunuch or chamberlain in the court of Ahasuerus, king of Persia (Es 2:14).

SHAB′BE·THAI

A chief Levite of Jerusalem after the exile. He was an overseer of the temple and helped interpret the law. However, he opposed Ezra in the matter of the Israelites divorcing the foreign women (Ez 10:15; Ne 8:7; 11:16).

SHA·CHI′A

Son of Shaharaim of Benjamin (1 Ch 8:10).

SHACKLE

Fetters; iron bands with chains attached, locked around the wrists or ankles to restrain a prisoner (Mk 5:4; Lk 8:29).

SHAD′DAI

A name of God, denoting Almighty (Ge 48:3; 49:25; Ex 6:3).

SHA′DRACH *(command of Aku [a Babylonian god])*

The name given by the Babylonian eunuch to Hananiah, one of Daniel's three companions (Da 1:7; 3:12-30).

SHA′GEE, SHA′GE

See SHAGEH.

SHAGEH

A Hararite, the father of Jonathan who was one of David's mighty men (1 Ch 11:34; also see SHAMMAH, 2 Sa 23:11).

SHA·HA·RA′IM *(double dawn)*

A man of Benjamin, father of nine tribal leaders (1 Ch 8:8-11).

SHA·HA·ZI′MAH *(heights)*

A town of Issachar (Jos 19:22-23).

SHA·HA·ZU′MAH

See SHAHAZIMAH.

SHA′LEM

A town near Shechem (Ge 33:18, KJV). Modern translations render this word as "peace" or "safely" rather than as the name of a town.

SHA′LIM

See SHAALIM.

SHAL′I·SHA

A district mentioned in connection with Saul's search for his father's asses, probably in Ephraim (1 Sa 9:4).

SHAL′I·SHAH

See SHALISHA.

SHAL′LE·CHETH *(casting out)*

A western gate of Solomon's temple (1 Ch 26:16).

SHAL′LUM *(retribution)*

Thirteen or fourteen Old Testament men:

1. King of Israel, son of Jabesh. He slew Zechariah, son of Jeroboam II and the last king of the fifth dynasty (2 Ki 15:10).

2. A son of Tikvah. He was the husband of the prophetess Huldah in the reign of Josiah and an official of the temple (2 Ki 22:14; 2 Ch 34:22).

3. Son of Josiah, king of Judah. His other name was Jehoahaz. He followed Josiah on the throne (2 Ki 23:30-34; 1 Ch 3:15). See JEHOAHAZ.

4. Son of Sisamai and descendant of Judah (1 Ch 2:40-41).

5. Son of Shaul, grandson of Simeon (1 Ch 4:25).

6. Son of Zadok, high priest and father of Hilkiah and ancestor of Ezra (1 Ch 6:12-13; Ez 7:2). In 1 Chronicles 9:11 he is called Meshullam.

7. Son of Naphtali (1 Ch 7:13). In Genesis 46:24 he is called Shillem.

8. A descendant of Kore and a porter of the sanctuary in the time of David (1 Ch 9:17-18). He may be the same as Meshelemiah or Shelemiah (1 Ch 26:1,14).

9. Father of Jehizkiah (2 Ch 28:12).

10. A Levite, gatekeeper of the temple, who divorced his foreign wife in the time of Ezra (Ez 10:24).

11. A son of Bani. He renounced his Gentile wife (Ez 10:42).

12. A son of Hallohesh, ruler of the half of Jerusalem. He labored with his daughters on the wall of Jerusalem (Ne 3:12).

13. Uncle of Jeremiah, father of Hanameel (Je 32:7-8), possibly the same as No. 2.

14. Father of Maaseiah (Je 35:4).

SHAL′LUN

Son of Colhozeh (Ne 3:15).

SHAL′MAI

See SALMAI.

SHAL′MAN

An abbreviation of Shalmaneser, king of Assyria (Ho 10:14).

SHAL·MAN·E′SER

There were four kings by this name in Assyrian history, only one of whom is mentioned by name in the Old Testament—Shalmaneser V. He succeeded Tiglath-pileser III in 727 B.C. He demanded tribute from Hoshea, king of Israel, and when Hoshea attempted to rebel, he laid a siege on Samaria which lasted for three years. Samaria fell in 722 B.C., but apparently Shalmaneser died shortly before the victory, and his successor, Sargon, arranged the deportation of the inhabitants and claimed the victory as his own. See SARGON.

SHA′MA

A son of Hotham, one of David's mighty men (1 Ch 11:44).

SHAM·A·RI′AH

See SHEMARIAH.

SHAM·BLES (archaic)

Meat market (1 Co 10:25).

SHA′MED

See SHEMED.

SHA′MER

See SHEMER.

SHAM′GAR

Son of Anath (Ju 5:6). He killed six hundred Philistines with an ox goad, or sharp stick (Ju 3:31).

SHAM′HUTH *(desolation)*

A captain of David's army (1 Ch 27:8).

SHA′MIR *(a thorn)*

Two towns and a man of the Old Testament:

1. A town of Ephraim, the residence and burial place of Tola, a judge of Israel (Ju 10:1-2).

2. A town in the mountain region of Judah (Jos 15:48), possibly thirteen miles southwest of Hebron.

3. Son of Micah, a Levite (1 Ch 24:24).

SHAM′LAI

See SALMAI.

SHAM′MA *(desolation)*

Son of Zophah (1 Ch 7:37).

SHAM′MAH *(desolation)*

Four Old Testament men:

1. A son of Reuel, son of Esau. He became a duke of Edom (Ge 36:3-4,13,17).

2. A son of Jesse, brother of David (1 Sa 16:9; 17:13). He is called Shimea in 1 Chronicles 20:7.

3. A son of Agee, a Hararite (2 Sa 23:11), a captain of David. Perhaps he is the same as Shage (1 Ch 11:34).

4. A warrior of David, a Harodite (2 Sa 23:25). He is also called Shammoth (1 Ch 11:27), and Shamhuth (1 Ch 27:8).

SHAM′MA·I *(waste)*

Three Old Testament men:

1. Son of Onam of Judah (1 Ch 2:28).

2. Son of Rekem of Judah (1 Ch 2:44).

3. Son of Ezra of Judah (1 Ch 4:17).

SHAM′MOTH

See SHAMMAH.

SHAM′MU·A, SHAM′MU·AH *(fame)*

1. Son of Zaccur, the representative of Reuben sent to spy the land of Canaan (Nu 13:4).

2. David's son by Bath-sheba (2 Sa 5:14; 1 Ch 3:5). In the latter passage he is called Shimea.

3. The father of Abda (Ne 11:17), also called Shemaiah (1 Ch 9:16).

4. A priest of the family of Bilgah in the time of the high priest, Joiakim (Ne 12:18).

SHAM' SHE·RAI

A son of Jeroham, a Benjamite (1 Ch 8:26).

SHA' PHAM

A chief of the Gadites in the days of Jotham (1 Ch 5:12).

SHA' PHAN

1. The scribe and secretary of King Josiah of Judah (2 Ki 22:8-14; Je 26:24; 39:14).

2. The father of Ahikam, who stood by Jeremiah to prevent him from being killed (Je 26:24). Akikam went with Shaphan the scribe (No. 1) to inquire of Huldah the prophetess concerning the books of the Law which had been found. It is quite likely that Shaphan No. 2 is the same as Shaphan No. 1. Ithikam's son Gedaliah, the grandson of Shaphan, took Jeremiah from prison and took him home (Je 39:14).

3. The father of Elasah who carried Jeremiah's letter to the captives (Je 29:3). Probably the same as Shaphan No. 1.

4. A scribe and the father of Gemariah, in whose chamber Baruch stood to read the words of Jeremiah's scroll to the people (Je 36:10-12). Probably the same as Shaphan No. 1.

5. The father of Jaazaniah, an elder who took part in "wicked abominations" in the Lord's house (Eze 8:9,11).

SHA' PHAT *(hath judged)*

Five Old Testament men:

1. Son of Hori. He represented Simeon in the group of spies sent to scout in the land of Canaan (Nu 13:5).

2. Father of Elisha, the prophet (1 Ki 19:16; 2 Ki 3:11).

3. A son of Shemaiah of Judah (1 Ch 3:22).

4. A chief of the Gadites in Bashan (1 Ch 5:12).

5. Son of Adlai, the herdsman in charge of David's herds in the valleys (1 Ch 27:29).

SHA' PHER

See SHEPHER.

SHA' PHIR, SA' PHIR *(beautiful)*

An unidentified town of Judah (Mi 1:11).

SHAR·A' I

A son of Bani who divorced his foreign wife (Ez 10:40).

SHA·RA' IM

See SHAARAIM.

SHAR' AR

A Hararite and father of Ahiam (2 Sa 23:33). He is called Sacar in 1 Chronicles 11:35.

SHA·RE' ZER

1. Son of Sennacherib. He and another son murdered their father and then fled, leaving their brother to ascend to the throne (2 Ki 19:37; Is 37:38).

2. A man of Beth-el (Ze 7:2).

SHAR' ON *(a plain)*

1. A pasture east of the Jordan (1 Ch 5:16).

2. The plain on the seacoast between Carmel and Joppa. It was a pasture area (1 Ch 27:29; Is 35:2; 65:10).

SHARONITE

One who dwells in Sharon. The herdsman in charge of David's herds which fed in Sharon was called a Sharonite (1 Ch 27:29).

SHA·RU' HEN

A village of Simeon (Jos 19:6). Also called Shilhim (Jos 15:32) and Shaaraim (1 Ch 4:31).

SHA' SHAI *(pale)*

A son of Bani who divorced his foreign wife (Ez 10:40).

SHA' SHAK

Son of Beriah, in the family tree of King Saul (1 Ch 8:14).

SHA' UL *(asked)*

1. Son of Simeon. His mother was a Canaanite woman (Ge 46:10; Ex 6:15; 1 Ch 4:24). He was the head of a tribal family (Nu 26:13).

2. A king of Edom from Rehoboth (Ge 36:37). He is also called Saul.

3. A Levite descended from Korah (1 Ch 6:24).

SHAUL' ITES

The descendants of Simeon's son Shaul (Nu 26:13).

SHA′ VEH *(a plain)*

A valley, called also the "king's dale," near Jerusalem (Ge 14:17-18; 2 Sa 18:18).

SHA′ VEH KIR·I·A·THA′ IM *(plain of Kiriathaim)*

A plain of Moab near the city of Kiriathaim (Ge 14:5; Jos 13:19).

SHAVING

The removal of hair with a sharp knife. The ancient Egyptians and Greeks both preferred to shave all facial hair. Shaving was a part of the consecration of the priests (Nu 8:7), and also a part of some rituals of ceremonial cleansing (Le 13:33; 14:8). Those who took the Nazirite vows did not shave any part of their hair as long as they were bound by the vows, unless they accidentally came into contact with a dead body (Nu 6:9,18; Ac 18:18). Shaving was also used as a symbol of mourning, though priests were forbidden to do this (De 14:1; Job 1:10; Le 21:5).

SHAV′ SHA

A scribe of David and Solomon (1 Ch 18:16; 1 Ki 4:3). He was probably the same as Seraiah (2 Sa 8:17) and Sheva (2 Sa 20:25).

SHAWM (archaic)

Prayer-book rendering of Psalm 98:6; translated 'cornet' in the KJV.

SHEAF

A bundle of cut grain. The first sheaves were offered to the Lord (Le 23:10). At harvest time, several people cut the grain with sharp sickles while others followed behind to bind up the sheaves, stack the sheaves, and carry them to the threshing floor (Je 9:22; Ex 22:6; Am 2:13). God instructed the harvesters not to be too careful in their cutting and binding of the grain, but rather to leave some in the field for the poor to glean (De 24:9; Ru 2:7).

SHE′ AL *(asking)*

A son of Bani who divorced his pagan wife (Ez 10:29).

SHE·AL′ TI·EL

Son of Jeconiah and father of Zerubbabel (1 Ch 3:17; Ez 3:2,8; 5:2; Ne 12:1). He was an ancestor of the family of Christ (Ma 1:12; Lk 3:27; Salathiel, KJV).

SHE·A·RI′ AH

A son of Azel, a descendant of Saul (1 Ch 8:38).

SHEAR′ ING HOUSE

A place between Jezreel and Samaria where Jehu put to death 42 men of the royal house of Judah (2 Ki 10:12-14).

SHE′ AR-JASH′ UB *(a remnant shall return)*

A son of Isaiah, born in the time of Ahaz, king of Judah (Is 7:3). This symbolic name was connected to the prophecy of the future return of a remnant after the seventy years of captivity (Is 10:21-22).

SHEATH

See SCABBARD.

SHE′ BA

1. A son of Raamah, son of Cush (Ge 10:7; 1 Ch 1:9).

2. A son of Joktan and grandson of Eber, of the family of Shem (Ge 10:28; 1 Ch 1:22). His descendants settled in southern Arabia, and founded the kingdom of Sheba.

3. A son of Jokshan and grandson of Keturah and Abraham (Ge 25:3; 1 Ch 1:32).

4. A town assigned to Simeon (Jos 19:2), possibly the same as Beer-sheba.

5. A son of Bichri, a Benjamite. He supported Absalom in his rebellion. After it was crushed, he blew a horn to assemble the ten tribes to induce them to renounce their allegiance to David. He entered the fortress of Abel of Beth-maacah but was besieged and beheaded by the inhabitants. His head was tossed over the wall (2 Sa 20:1-22).

6. A kingdom in southwestern Arabia whose queen heard of the fame of Solomon and came to Jerusalem to see and hear for herself. Sheba exported perfumes and incense, and sent out trading caravans to the nations of the Middle East. See SHEBA, QUEEN OF.

7. A Gadite chief who lived in Gilead in Bashan during the time of Jeroboam II of Israel (1 Ch 5:13,16).

SHEBA, QUEEN OF

The queen of a kingdom in southwestern Arabia, called the "land of the queen of the South" in Luke 11:31. She was so impressed with the tales she had heard of Solomon's great wealth

THE QUEEN OF SHEBA AND SOLOMON

and wisdom that she decided to come and see for herself whether the stories were true. She asked Solomon many questions, but none of them were too hard for his great wisdom and intelligence (1 Ki 10:1-13; 2 Ch 9:1-12). The queen left Jerusalem dazzled with the wealth and wisdom of Israel's king. Jesus mentioned the queen of Sheba in His teaching, rebuking the Jews for not following her example of eagerly traveling a very long distance in order to listen to a wise preacher.

SHE′ BAH *(seven, oath)*

The well dug by Isaac's servants at Beer-sheba, after he had sworn an oath of friendship with Abimelech (Ge 26:33).

SHE′ BAM

A city assigned to Reuben and Gad, east of the Jordan near Heshbon (Nu 32:3). Probably the same place as Shibmah (Nu 32:38) and Sibmah (Jos 13:19).

SHEB·A·NI′ AH *(reared by Jehovah)*

Four Levites of the Old Testament:

1. A Levite who blew the trumpet when the ark was brought by David to Jerusalem (1 Ch 15:24).

2. A Levite who sealed the covenant and offered the prayer at the Feast of Tabernacles (Ne 9:4-5; 10:10).

3. A priest who sealed the covenant (Ne 10:4; 12:14).

4. Another Levite who sealed the covenant (Ne 10:12).

SHEB′ A·RIM *(ruins)*

Possibly stone quarries near Ai (Jos 7:5).

SHE′ BAT

Eleventh month of the sacred year and the fifth month of the civil year, corresponding roughly to January/February (Ze 1:7). Also called Sebat (KJV).

SHE′ BER *(fracture)*

Son of Caleb; his mother was Maacah, Caleb's concubine (1 Ch 2:48).

SHEB′ NA

An official in the court of Hezekiah of Judah in whom was vested considerable authority as minister of the household (Is 22:15). Later he was given a secretarial position, while his former position was taken by Eliakim (2 Ki 18:18,26, 37; 19:2; Is 36:3; 37:2).

SHE·BU′ EL

Two Old Testament men:

1. Son of Gershom and grandson of Moses (1 Ch 23:16; 26:24). In 1 Chronicles 24:20 he is called Shubael.

2. A son of Heman, a musician in the time of David (1 Ch 25:4). In 1 Chronicles 25:20 he is called Shubael.

SHEC·A·NI′ AH, SHECH·A·NI′ AH *(Jehovah has dwelt)*

Eight Old Testament men:

1. A descendant of David (1 Ch 3:21-22).

2. A descendant of Aaron. In the time of David his family was the tenth course of priests (1 Ch 24:1,6,11).

3. A priest and a distributor of tithes in the reign of Hezekiah (2 Ch 31:15).

4. The head of a family who returned with Ezra (Ez 8:3).

4. A son of Jahaziel who returned with Ezra from Babylon (Ez 8:5).

5. A son of Jehiel, of the sons of Elam. He proposed to Ezra that foreign wives be renounced (Ez 10:2-3).

6. The father of Shemaiah (Ne 3:29).

7. The father-in-law of Tobiah, the Ammonite, and son of Arah (Ne 6:17-18).

8. A priest who returned to Jerusalem with Zerubbabel (Ne 12:3).

SHE′ CHEM *(shoulder)*

1. Son of Hamor, the Hivite, a prince of Shechem. He seduced Dinah, daughter of Jacob an act which was avenged by Simeon and Levi, her brothers (Ge 34:1-31; Ac 7:16).

2. Son of Gilead and head of a tribal family (Nu 26:31; Jo 17:2).

3. Son of Shemidah of Manasseh (1 Ch 7:19).

4. A fortified city on the edge of a fertile plain in central Palestine where main highways and trade routes converged. Associated particularly with Abraham, Jacob, and Joseph, Shechem was a place where several altars for worship of the one true God were erected, and was also one of the six cities of refuge designated when Joshua divided the land among the tribes.

When Abraham entered Canaan about 2000 B.C., he stopped in Shechem. God appeared to him at Shechem and promised to give the land of Canaan to his descendants (Ge 12:6-7). In response, Abraham built an altar to the Lord.

Upon his return to Shechem many years later, Abraham's grandson Jacob also built an altar (Ge 33:18-20). John 4:12 says he dug a deep well there. Joseph visited his brothers when they were tending their father's herds at Shechem (Ge 37:12). Joseph's body was taken from Egypt during the exodus and buried at Shechem (Jos 24:32).

After Joshua led the Israelites to victory in Canaan, an altar was built at Shechem. Its construction was accompanied by a covenant-renewal ceremony in which offerings were given and the law was read (Jos 8:30-35). Shechem's location between barren Mount Ebal and fertile Mount Gerizim gave the ceremony symbolic meaning— the advantages of keeping the covenant were pro-

SHECHEM

claimed from Gerizim, while the curses for breaking it were proclaimed from Ebal.

For a short time after the Northern Kingdom of Israel was founded, Shechem served as the capital city of this nation before Samaria was built and designated as the capital city (1 Ki 12:25).

Some scholars identify the New Testament town Sychar (Jo 4:5) with Shechem. If this is correct, then this is where Jesus spoke with the Samaritan woman at Jacob's well. He promised her living water that would become "a fountain of water springing up into everlasting life" (4:14).

SHECHEMITES

Family and descendents of Shechem, son of Gilead (Nu 26:31).

SHECHINAH

See SHEKINAH

SHED′ E•UR *(sending of light)*

Father of Elizur (Nu 1:5; 2:10).

SHEEP

An animal extensively raised in Palestine for its wool, skin, meat, and milk. They are mentioned about 750 times, more often than any other animal in the Bible. They were considered ceremonially clean, and were much used in sacrifice (Le 1:10; 4:32; 5:15; 22:21). The Hebrews in the patriarchal age were shepherds (Ge 12:16) as were their descendants who settled in Canaan after the exodus (1 Ch 27:31), and the images of shepherds and sheep are used again and again in Scripture. Isaiah 53:6 describes sinners as sheep who have gone astray, and Jesus is compared to a lamb being led to slaughter (Is 53:7; Jo 1:29-36). Sheep are herd animals, helpless in the face of danger, and in need of constant shepherding. Sheep will learn to know the voice of the one who cares for them, and they will only come to their own shepherd's call (Jo 10:3-5).

Wild sheep which lived in the mountains are mentioned (De 14:5); they are also called "mountain sheep," "chamois," or "rock goats."

SHEEP′ COTE

An old word for SHEEPFOLD.

SHEEPFOLD

An enclosure within which sheep were herded for the night (Nu 32:16; Eze 34:14). The enclosing wall which was pierced by a gateway or door

(Jo 10:1-2) might also be surmounted with thorns to provide additional protection. A watchtower often stood close by (2 Ki 17:9; 2 Ch 26:10; Mi 4:8).

SHEEP GATE

A gate of Jerusalem, at which point Nehemiah began the building of the wall (Ne 3:1).

SHEEP MAR′ KET

Also translated Sheep Gate (Jo 5:2). It is generally agreed that a gate, not a market, is intended.

SHEEP SHEARER

One who clips the fleece off of a sheep (Is 53:7).

SHE′ E·RAH, SHE′ RAH *(kinswoman)*

A daughter of Ephraim (1 Ch 7:24).

SHE·HA·RI′ AH

A son of Jeroham of Benjamin (1 Ch 8:26).

SHEK′ EL

An ancient weight and money unit introduced into Palestine from Babylonia. See MONEY OF THE BIBLE.

SHEKINAH

The "glory" which was the visible presence of God (Ex 24:9-18). This word does not actually occur in the Bible; it is a transliteration of a Hebrew word which is found in many later Jewish writings, used to describe the visible glory which indicated the presence of God. The "Shekinah" rested between the wings of the cherubim on the cover of the ark of the covenant. When Solomon brought the ark into the newly completed temple, the Shekinah filled the whole place. It is described as a cloud which filled the temple so that the priests could not continue ministering (1 Ki 8:10-11). After the destruction of Jerusalem by the Babylonians, the ark was lost, and the Shekinah was not seen again. It did not fill the temple which the captives rebuilt, nor the temple of Herod.

SHE′ LAH *(prayer)*

1. Son or grandson of Arphaxad (Ge 10:24; 11:12-15; 1 Ch 1:18). He was an ancestor of Abraham and the family of Christ (Lk 3:35-36, also called Sala, KJV).

2. The third son of Judah by the daughter of Shush. He was head of a tribal family (Ge 38:2, 5,11,14,26; Nu 26:20).

3. A pool by the King's Garden (Ne 3:15), also translated Siloah (KJV) and Siloam (NIV). See SILOAM.

SHELANITES

Descendents of Shelah, the youngest son of Judah (Nu 26:20).

SHEL·E·MI′ AH *(Jehovah rewards)*

Nine Old Testament men:

1. A porter of the tabernacle in David's time (1 Ch 26:14). In 1 Chronicles 9:21 he is called Meshelemiah.

2-3. Two descendants of Bani. They divorced their foreign wives (Ez 10:39,41).

4. Father of the Hananiah who labored on the wall of Jerusalem (Ne 3:30).

5. A priest appointed by Nehemiah to take charge of and distribute the tithes (Ne 13:13).

6. Grandfather of Jehudi. He was sent by the princes to ask Baruch to read to them the roll of Jeremiah (Je 36:14).

7. Son of Abdeel. He was ordered by Jehoiakim to arrest Baruch and Jeremiah (Je 36:26).

8. Father of Jucal, or Jehucal (Je 37:3; 38:1).

9. Son of Hananiah and father of Irijah (Je 37:13).

SHE′ LEPH *(a drawing forth)*

A son of Joktan (Ge 10:26; 1 Ch 1:20).

SHE′ LESH *(triplet)*

Son of Helem and a descendant of Asher (1 Ch 7:35).

SHE·LO′ MI *(peaceful)*

Father of Ahihud, a prince of Asher (Nu 34:27).

SHE·LO′ MITH, SHE·LO′ MOTH

Seven Old Testament men and women:

1. The daughter of Dibri, or Dan. She was mother of the man put to death for blasphemy at the time of the exodus (Le 24:11).

2. Daughter of Zerubbabel (1 Ch 3:19).

3. A son of Shimei, a Levite of the family of Gershon (1 Ch 23:9).

4. A descendant of Eliezer, son of Moses. In the reign of David he was a temple treasurer (1 Ch 26:25-26).

5. A Levite of the family of Kohath, of the house of Izhar in the time of David (1 Ch 23:18). In 1 Chronicles 24:22 he is called Shelomoth.

6. The son or daughter of Rehoboam (2 Ch 11:20).

7. Son of Josiphiah (Ez 8:10).

SHE·LU′MI·EL *(peace of God)*

A prince of Simeon in the wilderness. He was the son of Zurishaddai (Nu 1:6; 2:12; 7:36,41; 10:19).

SHEM *(name)*

A son of Noah, probably the firstborn of the three sons (Ge 5:32). At the time of his birth his father was five hundred years old. At the age of one hundred, Shem entered the ark (Ge 7:7; 1 Pe 3:20). Because they respectfully covered their father's nakedness, Shem and Japheth received Noah's blessing (Ge 9:23-37). Shem lived to be six hundred years old (Ge 11:11), and he was the father of Arphaxad and the ancestor of Abraham and of the family of Jesus (Lk 3:36).

SHE′MA *(rumor)*

Four men and a town of the Old Testament:

1. A town in the south of Judah (Jos 15:26), also called Sheba (Jos 19:3).

2. Son of Hebron of Judah (1 Ch 2:43-44). See MARESHAH.

3. A son of Joel of Reuben (1 Ch 5:8).

4. A son of Elpaal, a Benjamite and head of the house in Aijalon (1 Ch 8:13).

5. One who assisted Ezra when he read the law (Ne 8:4).

SHE·MA′, THE *(hear thou)*

The confession of faith found in Deuteronomy 6:4: "Hear, O Israel: The Lord our God, the LORD is one!" The complete shema includes Deuteronomy 6:4-9; 11:13-21 and Numbers 15:37-41.

SHEM′A·AH *(rumor)*

A man of Gibeah who allied himself with David at Ziklag (1 Ch 12:3).

SHEM·AI′AH *(Jehovah heard)*

The name of a number of Old Testament men:

1. A prophet in the reign of Rehoboam who told the king he should not attack the Kingdom of Israel (1 Ki 12:22-24; 2 Ch 11:2-4). He also explained the invasion of Shishak of Egypt as divine punishment for the sins of Judah (2 Ch 12:5-8). He wrote a history of this reign (2 Ch 12:15).

2. The son of Shechaniah, of the tribe of Judah (1 Ch 3:22).

3. Father of Shimri, a Simeonite (1 Ch 4:37).

4. The son of Joel and father of Gog (1 Ch 5:4), possibly the same as Shema No. 3.

5. Son of Hasshub. He was a Levite of the Merari family (1 Ch 9:14) and overseer of the business of the house of God in the time of Nehemiah (Ne 11:15).

6. Father of Obadiah, a Levite (1 Ch 9:16), also called Shammua (Ne 11:17).

7. Son of Elizaphan, a Levite. He participated in the removal of the ark to Jerusalem (1 Ch 15:8-11).

8. A Levite, son of Nethaneel and a scribe in the time of David (1 Ch 24:6).

9. Son of Obed-edom (1 Ch 26:4-8) and a doorkeeper of the sanctuary in the time of David.

10. A Levite commissioned by Jehoshaphat to teach the people (2 Ch 17:8).

11. A descendant of Jeduthun. In the reign of Hezekiah he assisted in purifying the temple (2 Ch 29:14-15). Possibly the same person as No. 6.

12. A Levite. In the reign of Hezekiah he had charge of the freewill offerings (2 Ch 31:15).

13. A Levite in the reign of Josiah. He and others contributed generously to the offerings of the Passover (2 Ch 35:9).

14. A son of Adonikam. He and his two brothers came with Ezra to Jerusalem from Babylon (Ez 8:13).

15. One sent by Ezra to Iddo to secure Levites to accompany the Israelites to Jerusalem (Ez 8:16).

16. A priest descended from Harim. He renounced his foreign wife (Ez 10:21).

17. Son of another Harim, a layman, who divorced his foreign wife (Ez 10:31).

18. A son of Shechaniah, a Levite who assisted Nehemiah in building the wall of Jerusalem (Ne 3:29).

19. A false prophet. He was the son of Delaiah and grandson of Mehetabeel. Tobiah and Sanballat of Samaria bribed him to get Nehemiah to seek safety in the temple to escape assassination (Ne 6:10-13).

20. One of the priests who sealed the covenant with Nehemiah (Ne 10:8).

21. A chief priest who returned from Babylon with Zerubbabel (Ne 12:6-7,18).

22. A prince of Judah who had a part in the dedication of the wall of Jerusalem (Ne 12:34).

23. A Levite of the line of Asaph (Ne 12:35).

24. A Levite musician who assisted in the dedication of the wall of Jerusalem (Ne 12:36).

25. A priest who blew the trumpet when the wall of Jerusalem was dedicated (Ne 12:42).

26. Father of Urijah, the prophet of Kirjath-jearim whom Jehoiakim put to death because of his true prophecies (Je 26:20-23).

27. A Nehelamite, a false prophet among the captives in Babylon, who declared they would return in a short time to Jerusalem. Jeremiah predicted Shemaiah would not live to the end of the exile (Je 29:24-32).

28. Father of Delaiah, a prince in the reign of Jehoiakim who heard Baruch read the roll of Jeremiah (Je 36:12).

SHEM·A·RI′ AH *(Jehovah hath kept)*

Four Old Testament men:

1. A man of Benjamin who joined David at Ziklag (1 Ch 12:5).

2. A son of Rehoboam. His mother was Abihail (2 Ch 11:19; also called Shamariah).

3. A son of Harim in the time of Ezra. He renounced his Gentile wife (Ez 10:32).

4. A son of Bani (Ez 10:41).

SHEM·E′ BER

The king of Zeboiim in the days of Abraham. He was defeated by Chedorlaomer (Ge 14:2,8, 10).

SHE′ MED

A descendant of Shaharaim through Elpaal, a Benjamite (1 Ch 8:12; Shamed, KJV).

SHE′ MER

Three Old Testament men:

1. A Levite of the family of Merari and son of Mahli, also called Shamer (1 Ch 6:46).

2. A man of Asher, also called Shomer or Shamer (1 Ch 7:32,34).

3. The man who sold Omri the hill of Samaria (1 Ki 16:24).

SHE·MI′ DA *(fame of wisdom)*

A descendant of Manasseh (Nu 26:32; Jos 17:2; 1 Ch 7:19).

SHE·MI′ DAH

See SHEMIDA.

SHE·MI′ DA·ITES

Descendants of Shemida of the tribe of Manasseh (Nu 26:32).

SHEM′ IN·ITH

A musical term of uncertain meaning, used in the titles of two psalms and mentioned in the description of the worship service David organized when the ark was brought into Jerusalem (1 Ch 15:21; titles of Ps 6;12).

SHE·MI′ RA·MOTH *(an exalted name)*

Two Levites of the Old Testament:

1. A Levite singer who lived in the time of David (1 Ch 15:18,20).

2. A Levite appointed by Jehoshaphat of Judah to teach the people (2 Ch 17:8)

SHE·MU′ EL *(name of God)*

1. Son of Ammihud. He represented the tribe of Simeon at the time of the division of the land of Canaan (Nu 34:20).

2. A form of the name Samuel, used once for Samuel the prophet (1 Ch 6:33, KJV).

3. A descendant of Tola of Issachar (1 Ch 7:2).

SHEN *(a tooth)*

A place near the spot where Samuel set up the memorial stone called Ebenezer (1 Sa 7:12).

SHEN·A′ ZAR

See SHENAZZAR.

SHEN·AZ′ ZAR

A son of Jeconiah (Jehoiachin) and brother of Salathiel (1 Ch 3:18; Shanazzar, KJV).

SHE′ NIR

See SENIR.

SHE′ OL

Everyone who reads the Old Testament is agreed that *Sheol* has to do with a place or state to which one (or one's body) goes after death. Because of differing theological views however, there is agreement on little else regarding this word.

The Hebrew word is apparently related to *shaal* "to ask," but exactly how is unknown. It occurs sixty-four times in the Old Testament. The KJV translates about half of them by "grave" nearly half by "hell," and three by "pit." Most modern versions, such as NKJV, also sometimes transliterate the Hebrew word, and frequently do so in footnotes.

Sheol as the Grave. Jacob uses the term four times in Genesis in reference to his being brought down in sorrow "to the grave" (Ge 42:38). This meaning is undoubted. It frequently occurs in a parallel construction with *qeber,* "grave."

Job's description of *Sheol* as a place of darkness, dust, worms, and decay certainly describe the physical grave (Job 17:13-16; 21:13; 24:19-20).

Peter quoted Psalm 16:10 in Acts 2:27 to prove that Christ arose from the grave, and Paul quoted Hosea 13:14 in 1 Corinthians 15:55 to teach the resurrection of Christians from the grave.

Sheol as Hell. When the context suggests a negative, fearful future, the translation "hell" is called for. For example, using "grave," or "Sheol" rather than "hell" in Psalm 9:17 would weaken that text considerably: "The wicked shall be turned into hell *and* all the nations that forget God." Righteous people also go to the grave and the unseen world, so punishment for disobedience must inspire a more fearful response. Proverbs 7:27 describes the harlot's temptations as "the way to hell." "Grave" could be used here, but would not provide as forceful a warning to a young man.

Sheol is paired with *abaddon* ("destruction") in both Proverbs 15:11 and 27:20. This is capitalized as "Hell and Destruction" in the NKJV to indicate personification. Since even the wise go to the grave, it is likely that avoiding eternal punishment in hell is meant here: "The way of life *winds* upward for the wise, that he may turn away from hell below" (Pr 15:24).

Several of the occurrences of *Sheol* translated "hell" in the KJV probably refer to the grave. Unfortunately, when these are changed, some people insist that the translators do not believe in the doctrine of hell. This is certainly not true for the translators of the NASB, NIV, and NKJV, all of whose translators held orthodox views on eternal punishment (however unpopular that doctrine may be to modern man).

Sheol as Pit. In Numbers 16:30,33, Korah and his fellow rebels went "down alive into the pit." KJV and NKJV translators believed this should be taken in quite a physical sense, as the ground opened up to swallow the rebels.

The KJV's third occurrence of *Sheol* as "pit" (Job 17:16) in the NKJV is translated to allow

other interpretations, since the second line of the parallelism uses "dust," which would suggest "grave" to many Bible readers. See GEHENNA.

SHE′PHAM

An unidentified place on the eastern boundary of Canaan (Nu 34:10-11).

SHEPH·A·TI′AH *(Jehovah judges)*

Nine Old Testament men:

1. A son of David born at Hebron. His mother was Abital (2 Sa 3:4; 1 Ch 3:3).

2. Son of Reuel, a Benjamite. After the exile he lived at Jerusalem (1 Ch 9:8; Shephathiah, KJV).

3. A Benjamite, a Haruphite, who joined David at Ziklag (1 Ch 12:5).

4. Son of Maacah. In the time of David he was the head of the tribe of Simeon (1 Ch 27:16).

5. A son of Jehoshaphat of Judah (2 Ch 21:2).

6. Head of a family, a large number of whose members returned to Jerusalem with Zerubbabel and in the second expedition with Ezra (Ez 2:4; 8:8; Ne 7:9).

7. A servant of Solomon. His descendants returned with Zerubbabel from Babylon (Ez 2:57; Ne 7:59).

8. A descendant of Judah (Ne 11:4).

9. Son of Mattan. He was a prince of Judah who advised Zedekiah, the king, to imprison Jeremiah because of his prophecies (Je 38:1).

SHE′PHER *(beauty)*

A station of the Israelites in the wilderness (Nu 33:23-24; Shapher, KJV, REB).

SHEP′HERD

A herder of sheep. In biblical times he led them to pasture, to watering places, and at night to the fold. He was responsible for driving away attacking wild beasts (1 Sa 17:34-36). The patriarchs of Genesis were shepherds in the literal sense, keeping large flocks of sheep for meat, milk, wool, and hides (Ge 13:6). The term is also used in a more spiritual sense, as an illustration. Many times God is called a shepherd; the beautiful words of the most beloved Psalm begin with this image: "The Lord is my shepherd . . ." (Ps 23:1). Jesus called Himself the good shepherd, who would lay down His life for the sheep (Jo 10:1-30). The leaders of God's people are called "shepherds" in both the Old and New Testaments (Nu 27:17; 1 Ki 22:17; Je 23:1-4; Ac 20:28-30).

SHE´PHI, SHE´PHO

A son of Shobal and grandson of Seir (Ge 36:23; 1 Ch 1:40).

SHE·PHU´PHAM

See SHEPHUPHAN.

SHE·PHU´PHAN

Head of a Benjamite family (Nu 26:39; 1 Ch 8:5). The name also appears as Muppim and Shuppim (Ge 46:21; 1 Ch 7:12,15; 26:16).

SHE´RAH

See SHEERAH.

SHERD

See POTSHERD.

SHER·E·BI´AH

Three Old Testament Levites:
1. Head of a Levitical family who returned with Ezra (Ez 8:18).
2. A Levite who aided Ezra when he read the law to the people (Ne 8:7; 9:4).
3. A Levite who returned from Babylon with Zerubbabel. He was the head of a family of musicians (Ne 10:12; 12:8,24).

SHE´RESH *(root)*

Son of Machir of Manasseh (1 Ch 7:16).

SHE·RE´ZER

See SHAREZER.

SHE´RIFF *(archaic)*

One knowledgeable in the law (Da 3:3).

SHE´SHACH

The symbolic name for Babylon (Je 25:26; 51:41).

SHE´SHAI *(whitish)*

A son of Anak who lived in Hebron (Nu 13:22).

SHE´SHAN

A son of Ishi of the family of Hezron of Judah (1 Ch 2:31).

SHESH·BAZ´ZAR

The "prince of Judah," who brought the golden vessels from Babylon and who helped to lay the foundation of the second temple (Ez 1:8,11; 5:14-

16). The name may be the Babylonian equivalent of Zerubbabel. Some regard him as the latter's uncle.

SHETH

1. One of the sons of Adam and head of the messianic line (1 Ch 1:1). See SETH.
2. A chief of the Moabites (Nu 24:17).

SHE´THAR

One of the princes of Persia attached to the court of Ahasuerus (Es 1:14).

SHE´THAR-BOZ´E·NAI

See SHETHAR-BOZNAI.

SHE´THAR-BOZ´·NAI

A Persian officer of high rank who, in the reign of Darius, joined others to prevent the Jews from rebuilding the temple (Ez 5:3,6; 6:6).

SHE´VA

Two Old Testament men:
1. David's secretary (2 Sa 20:25), also called Seraiah (2 Sa 8:17) and Shavsha (1 Ch 18:16).
2. A man of Judah of the house of Caleb, son of Maacah (1 Ch 2:49).

SHEW´BREAD *(archaic)*

See SHOWBREAD.

SHI´BAH

See SHEBAH.

SHIB´BO·LETH *(a stream)*

When the Ephraimites were defeated by Jephthah and the men of Gilead, the fords of the river Jordan were seized by the victors to prevent the Ephraimites from returning to their own territory. Anyone seeking to cross was required to say the word *Shibboleth*. The Ephraimites were unable to pronounce the sound of *sh* at the beginning of a word, so this password was a dead giveaway. All those who said *Sibboleth* were put to death (Ju 12:5-6).

SHIB´MAH

See SHEBAM.

SHIC´RON *(drunkenness)*

A town on the northern border of Judah (Jos 15:11), also written Shikkeron.

SHIELD

An important piece of armor, used to protect the body of a warrior in battle. Shields were made of thick, hardened leather, wood, or metal. A shield was carried in one hand or strapped to the arm and used as a defense against wounds in hand-to-hand combat. Ephesians 6 speaks of the shield of faith with which we can protect ourselves from the attacks of Satan.

SHIG·GAI' ON, SHIG·I·O' NOTH

A musical term (Ps 7, title; Hab 3:1). It probably denotes a wild, enthusiastic song.

SHI' HON

See SHION.

SHI' HOR (black, turbid)

The eastern boundary of the promised land, described as being "east of Egypt" (Jo 13:3) and also "in Egypt" (1 Ch 13:5). It is uncertain whether this is referring to a branch of the Nile or to the Wadi el-'arish, the Brook of Egypt (Is 23:3; Je 2:18).

SHI' HOR-LIB' NATH (turbid)

A small river near Carmel (Jos 19:26).

SHIK' KE·RON

See SHICRON.

SHIL' HI (missive)

The father of Azubah, the mother of Jehoshaphat of Judah (1 Ki 22:42).

SHIL' HIM

A town in the south of Judah (Jos 15:32), possibly the place to which David pursued the Philistines (1 Sa 17:52; 1 Ch 4:31).

SHIL' LEM (retribution)

Son of Naphtali (Ge 46:24; Nu 26:49). In 1 Chronicles 7:13 he is called Shallum.

SHIL' LE·MITES

The descendants of Naphtali's youngest son, Shillem (Nu 26:49).

SHI·LO' AH

See SILOAM.

SHI' LOH (rest)

1. Shiloh was a small Old Testament village about twenty miles north of Jerusalem in the land designated for the tribe of Ephraim. It was important because it served as the religious center for the Hebrew people during the period of the judges before the kingdom was united under the leadership of David.

Numerous references are made to Shiloh during this period as the city where the "house of God" was located (Ju 18:31). These references are probably to the tabernacle with its ark of the testimony.

Hannah prayed for a son at Shiloh. God granted this request by sending Samuel. During his boyhood, Samuel worked with the high priest Eli at Shiloh. One of the most beautiful stories of the Old Testament is the account of Samuel's response to the voice of the Lord. Thinking his master Eli was calling him, he awakened the high priest to find out what the high priest wanted. Finally Eli realized that it was God calling Samuel, and Samuel's response to God's next call was as Eli had directed: "Speak, LORD, for your servant hears" (1 Sa 3:1-10).

Samuel eventually succeeded Eli as the judge over Israel. The tabernacle was located in Shiloh during Samuel's early years as Israel's prophet and judge (1 Sa 1:9; 4:3-4). However, during a battle with the Philistines, while Eli was still priest, the ark of the testimony was captured by Israel's enemies, when God forsook Shiloh as the center of worship because of Israel's idolatry and unfaithfulness (Ps 78:60). When the ark was returned to Israel by the Philistines, it was not placed at Shiloh (2 Sa 6:2-17). It was lodged instead at Kirjath-jearim (1 Ch 13:3-14).

After the ark was moved to another city, Shiloh gradually lost its importance. This loss was made complete when Jerusalem was established as capital of the kingdom in David's time. In the days of the prophet Jeremiah, Shiloh was in ruins (Je 7:12,14). It became an inhabited town again in the days of the Greeks and Romans several centuries later.

2. A word in Jacob's blessing of Judah (Ge 49:10). Most commentators agree that the passage is a great messianic prophecy.

SHI·LO' NI

The father of Zechariah, a man of the tribe of Judah who lived in Jerusalem after the captivity (Ne 11:5), also translated "the Shilonite."

SHI′ LO•NITE

1. A native or resident of Shiloh, such as Ahijah the prophet (1 Ki 11:29).

2. A member of the house of Shelah (1 Ch 9:5; Ne 11:5; Ge 38:5; Nu 26:20).

SHIL′ SHAH *(triad)*

Son of Zophah of Asher (1 Ch 7:37).

SHIM′ E•A, SHIM′ E•AH *(fame)*

1. David's brother, the third son of Jesse (2 Sa 13:3), father of Jonadab and Jonathan (2 Sa 13:3, 32; 21:21). Also called Shammah (1 Sa 16:9) and Shimma (1 Ch 2:13).

2. Son of David by Bath-sheba (1 Ch 3:5), also called Shammua (2 Sa 5:14; 1 Ch 14:4).

3. Son of Uzza, a Levite of the family of Merari (1 Ch 6:30).

4. A Levite of the family of Gershom (1 Ch 6:39,43).

5. A descendant of Jeiel, a Benjamite (1 Ch 9:38), also called Shimeah (1 Ch 8:32).

SHIM′ E•AM

Son of Mikloth of Benjamin (1 Ch 9:38). In 1 Chronicles 8:32 he is called Shimeah.

SHIM′ E•ATH

A woman of Ammon; mother of one of those who killed Joash (2 Ki 12:21).

SHIM′ E•A-THITES

A family of scribes who lived at Jabez in Judah (1 Ch 2:55).

SHIM′ E•I *(famous)*

A number of Old Testament men:

1. Son of Gershon and grandson of Levi (Ex 6:17; Nu 3:18,21).

2. Son of Gera of Benjamin, of the house of Saul. He lived on the eastern side of the Mount of Olives. When David was passing down the mount leaving Jerusalem in the time of Absalom's rebellion, Shimei hurled insults at him. David forgave him but he was put to death later by Solomon for disobeying a royal order (2 Sa 16:5-13; 1 Ki 2:8-9,36-46).

3. The son of Elah. He remained loyal to Solomon when Adonijah attempted to seize the throne (1 Ki 1:8).

4. Solomon's purveyor in the territory of Benjamin (1 Ki 4:18).

5. A brother of Zerubbabel, of the royal line of Judah (1 Ch 3:19).

6. Son of Zacchur of Simeon. He had 22 children (1 Ch 4:24-27).

7. Son of Gog and father of Micah of Reuben (1 Ch 5:4).

8. A Levite family of Merari (1 Ch 6:29).

9. Son of Jahath, a Levite of the family of Gershon (1 Ch 6:42).

10. A Benjamite (1 Ch 8:21; Shimha, KJV; or Shema, 1 Ch 8:13).

11. A family of Gershom (1 Ch 23:6-9).

12. Son of Jeduthun. He was head of the tenth division of singers in the reign of David (1 Ch 25:3-17).

13. A Ramathite. He had charge of David's vineyards (1 Ch 27:27).

14. A son of Heman, a Levite. In the reign of Hezekiah he assisted in the cleansing of the temple (2 Ch 29:14-16).

15. The brother of Conaniah, a Levite. He had charge of the offerings in the reign of Hezekiah (2 Ch 31:12-13). He may be the same as the preceding.

16. A Levite in the time of Ezra who divorced his foreign wife (Ez 10:23).

17. A son of Hashum who divorced his foreign wife (Ez 10:33).

18. A son of Bani who divorced his foreign wife (Ez 10:38).

19. Son of Kish of Benjamin, an ancestor of Mordecai (Es 2:5).

SHIM′ E•ITES

See SHIMITES.

SHIM′ E•ON *(a hearing)*

A son of Harim who divorced his foreign wife (Ez 10:31).

SHIM′ HI

See SHIMEI.

SHIMI

See SHIMEI.

SHIMITES

Descendants of Shimei, grandson of Levi (Nu 3:21).

SHIM′ MA

See SHIMEA.

SHI′MON

A man of Judah. His genealogy is obscure (1 Ch 4:20).

SHIM′RATH (guarding)

Son of Shimei of Aijalon (1 Ch 8:21), a Benjamite.

SHIM′RI (watchful)

Four Old Testament men:

1. Son of Shemaiah of Simeon (1 Ch 4:37).

2. Father of Jediael, one of David's warriors (1 Ch 11:45).

3. Son of Hosah, a Levite of Merari; gatekeeper in the time of David (1 Ch 26:10; Simri, KJV).

4. Son of Elizaphan, a Levite who assisted in Hezekiah's reforms (2 Ch 29:13).

SHIM′RITH

Mother of one of the murderers of Joash; a Moabitess (2 Ch 24:26). Also called Shomer (2 Ki 12:21).

SHIM′ROM

See SHIMRON No. 1.

SHIM′RON (a guard)

1. Son of Issachar and head of a tribal family (Ge 46:13; Nu 26:24).

2. A town on the border of Zebulun (Jos 11:1; 19:15).

SHIM′RON·ITES

Descendants of Issachar's son Shimron (Nu 26:24).

SHIM′RON-ME′RON

A town of the Canaanites conquered by Joshua (Jos 12:20), possibly the same as SHIMRON No. 2.

SHIM′SHAI (sunny)

A scribe who, with others, made a complaint to Artaxerxes protesting against the rebuilding of the wall (Ez 4:8).

SHIN

The twenty-first letter of the Hebrew alphabet. It is the heading of verses 161-168 of Psalm 119. In Hebrew each of these eight verses began with the letter shin. See ACROSTIC.

SHI′NAB

The king of Admah (Ge 14:2,8,10).

SHI′NAR

The plain of Babylon (Ge 10:10; 11:2; Da 1:2).

SHI′ON (ruin)

A town of Isaachar (Jos 19:19; Shihon, KJV).

SHIP

A craft used in water transportation, propelled in ancient times by oars or sails. The Hebrews had little to do with ships as the Mediterranean coast during ancient times was occupied by Phoenicians and Philistines. However, Solomon possessed a navy manned by Phoenician sailors, by means of which he carried on trade with Ophir. His port was Ezion-geber on Gulf of Aqaba, the eastern arm of the northern Red Sea (1 Ki 9:26-28).

SHI′PHI (abundant)

Son of Allon and father of Ziza of Simeon. He lived in the time of Hezekiah (1 Ch 4:37).

SHIPH′MITE

Probably a native of Shepham or Siphmoth (1 Ch 27:27).

SHIPH′RAH (splendor)

A Hebrew midwife who refused to obey the order of Pharaoh to kill the male infants (Ex 1:15).

SHIPH′TAN (judicial)

Father of Kemuel of Ephraim (Nu 34:24).

SHIPMASTER

The ship captain, the one who is responsible for the ship (Re 18:17).

SHIPWRECK

This word is used in the New Testament both literally and figuratively. Paul was literally shipwrecked three times (2 Co 11:25); he also uses the word as a descriptive term for a person who is having serious spiritual difficulties (1 Ti 1:19).

SHI′SHA

See SHAVSHA.

SHI′SHAK

See PHARAOH.

SHIT·RA′I

The Sharonite who had charge of David's herds (1 Ch 27:29).

SHIT´ TAH

A tree which was a species of acacia. Its wood, called shittim wood, was used in the construction of the ark and various articles of tabernacle furniture (Ex 25:5,10,13,23,28; De 10:3). See ACACIA.

SHIT´ TIM *(acacia)*

1. The last encampment of the Israelites in the plains of Moab, east of the Jordan (Nu 25:1). It was while the Israelites were here that the Moabite king Balak tried to hire Balaam to curse them (Nu 22–24) and here the people sinned and were punished (Nu 25). The second census was taken at this point and laws were given regarding the inheritance of daughters. From this point Joshua sent the spies to Jericho (Jos 2:1).

2. A barren valley near Jerusalem and the Dead Sea, probably the lower Kidron Valley (Joel 3:18).

See ABEL ACACIA GROVE.

SHI´ ZA

A Reubenite and father of Adina who was one of David's warriors (1 Ch 11:42).

SHO´ A

A country and its people mentioned by Ezekiel as future enemies of Judah (Eze 23:23).

SHO´ BAB

Two Old Testament men:

1. The son of Caleb and grandson of Hezron of Judah. His mother was Azubah (1 Ch 2:18).

2. A son of David (2 Sa 5:14).

SHO´ BACH *(pouring out)*

The general of Hadarezer, king of Zobah (2 Sa 10:16). Also called Shophach (1 Ch 19:16,18).

SHO·BA´ I *(taking captive)*

A Levite (Ez 2:42; Ne 7:45).

SHO´ BAL *(flowing)*

Two Old Testament men:

1. The second son of Seir and one of the Horite princes (Ge 36:20,29).

2. A son of Caleb of Judah (1 Ch 2:50; 4:1).

SHO´ BEK *(forsaking)*

One of the peoples' leaders who sealed the covenant with Nehemiah (Ne 10:24).

SHO´ BI

An Ammonite, son of Nahash of Rabbah (2 Sa 17:27).

SHO´ CHO, SHO´ CHOH, SO´ COH

See SOCHOH.

SHOE

See SANDAL.

SHOFAR

See RAM'S HORN.

SHO´ HAM

Son of Jaaziah (1 Ch 24:27).

SHO´ MER *(keeper)*

1. Son of Heber of Asher (1 Ch 7:32). See SHEMER.

2. The mother of one of the murderers of King Joash, a Moabitess (2 Ki 12:21). See SHIMRITH.

SHO´ PHACH

See SHOBACH.

SHO´ PHAN

See ATROTH-SHOPHAN.

SHOPHAR

See RAM'S HORN.

SHO-SHANN´ IM,
SHO-SHANN´ IM-E´ -DUTH,
SHU´ SHAN-E´ DUTH *(lilies)*

A word in the titles of Psalms 45;60;69;80 probably signifying the air to which the psalm was to be sung.

SHOULDER PIECE

The shoulder straps of the ephod, presumably bands which went over the shoulders to hold the front and back of the ephod together (Ex 28:5-14).

SHOVELS

Some of the bronze utensils of the tabernacle (Ex 27:3). These shovels were used for handling the coals and ashes of the sacrificial fires. All of these utensils were taken when Babylon captured Jerusalem and took its people captive (Je 52:18).

SHOW´ BREAD

The word denotes literally "bread of the presence." It was placed on the table in the holy place of the sanctuary in two rows, six loaves in each row. It was changed on the Sabbath and eaten by the priests (Ex 25:30; Le 24:5-9; Ma 12:4). According to Josephus it was unleavened. The number represented the tribes of Israel (Le 24:7).

SHREWD MANAGER, PARABLE OF

(Lk 16:1-13)

SHRINE

A place which is regarded as holy, set apart for worship. This word in the Bible is always used to refer to places devoted to the worship of pagan gods (Ju 17:1-5; Eze 16:24,31).

SHU´ A

A man and a woman of the Old Testament:

1. A Canaanite. His daughter was the wife of Judah and the mother of Er, Onan, and Shelah (Ge 38:2,12).

2. A daughter of Heber of Asher (1 Ch 7:32).

SHU´ AH *(pit)*

A son of Abraham and Keturah (Ge 25:2; 1 Ch 1:32). Also see SHUHAH.

SHU´ AL *(fox)*

1. A district near Beth-el invaded by the Philistines (1 Sa 13:17).

2. Son of Zophah of Asher (1 Ch 7:36).

SHU´ BA·EL

See SHEBUEL.

SHU´ HAH *(pit)*

A man of Judah (1 Ch 4:11; also called Shuah).

SHU´ HAM *(depression)*

Son of Dan and head of a tribal family (Nu 26:42). In Genesis 46:23 he is called Hushim.

SHU´ HAM·ITES

Descendants of Dan's son Shuham (Nu 26:42).

SHU´ HITE

The surname of Bildad, one of Job's friends (Job 2:11; 8:1; 18:1; 25:1; 42:9).

SHU´ LA·MITE

The young woman who was the shepherd's beloved in the Song of Solomon is called a Shu-lamite (Song 6:13). Some believe that she was a resident of Shunem (1 Sa 28:4), possibly Abishag, the Shunammite girl who was brought in to be a nurse to David in his old age (1 Ki 1:1-4, 15).

SHU´ LAM·MITE

See SHULAMITE.

SHU´ MA·THITES

One of the families of Kirjath-jearim (1 Ch 2:53).

SHU·NAM´ MITE

A native of Shunem. Two Shunammite women are mentioned in the Bible. The first is Abishag, the beautiful young woman brought in to care for David in his last days (1 Ki 1:3; 2:17,21). The second is the woman whose child Elisha restored to life (2 Ki 4:8,12; 8:1).

SHU´ NEM

A border town of Issachar, some sixteen miles southwest of the Sea of Galilee (Jos 19:18). It was the place where the Philistines camped before their victory over Saul (1 Sa 28:4).

SHU´ NI *(quiet)*

A son of Gad and head of a tribal family (Ge 46:16; Nu 26:15).

SHU´ NITES

The family descended from Gad's son Shuni (Nu 26:15).

SHU´ PHAM

See SHEPHUPHAM.

SHU´ PHAMITE

The family descended from Shuphim or Shephupham (Nu 26:39).

SHUP´ PIM

1. A man of Benjamin (1 Ch 7:12,15). See SHEPHUPHAM.

2. A Levite doorkeeper of the temple (1 Ch 26:16).

SHUR

A place or district on the border of Egypt mentioned in connection with Abraham, Hagar, and the sons of Ishmael (Ge 16:7; 20:1; 25:18).

SHUSHAN

SHU' SHAN *(lily)*

The Persian capital (Ne 1:1; Es 1:2; Da 8:2). It was also called Susa.

SHU·SHAN' CHITES

Inhabitants of Susa (Ez 4:9).

SHU' SHAN-E' DUTH

See SHOSHANNIM.

SHU·THAL' HITES

See SHUTHELAH.

SHU·THE' LAH

1. Son of Ephraim and head of a tribal family (Nu 26:35-36; 1 Ch 7:20).

2. A descendant of Ephraim (1 Ch 7:21).

SHUTTLE

A weaving tool: an elongated spool or bobbin which is filled with thread (weft). It is thrown back and forth through the shed (the separated threads of the warp), carrying the weft thread. A skillful weaver can throw the shuttle back and forth very quickly, and Job compares the shortness of life to the swiftness of a weaver's shuttle (Job 7:6).

SI' A, SI' A·HA *(assembly)*

A Nethinim family (Siaha, Ez 2:44; Sia, Ne 7:47).

SIB' BE·CAI

See SIBBECHAI.

SIB' BE·CHAI

A Hushathite and one of David's mighty men (1 Ch 11:29).

SHUTTLE

SIB' BO·LETH

See SHIBBOLETH.

SIB' MAH *(coolness)*

A town of Reuben east of the Jordan (Jos 13:19). See SHEBAM.

SIB' RA·IM

An unidentified place on the northern boundary of Palestine (Eze 47:16).

SI' CHEM

See SHECHEM.

SICKLE

A knife with a crescent shaped blade used for harvesting grain. Sickles were made with flint teeth set in wood, or later out of metal.

SID' DIM

A valley in the region of the Dead Sea (Ge 14:3, 8).

SI' DON

A city of Phoenicia, north of Tyre. It is called Sidon in the New Testament and Zidon in the Old Testament. It was the northern limit of Zebulun and Asher (Ge 49:13; Jos 19:28; Ju 1:31). In the course of time the city was subject to Tyre, to Sennacherib in 701 B.C., to Alexander the Great in 333 B.C., and to Rome in 64 B.C. The city supplied cedar for the building of the second temple (Ez 3:7). It was repeatedly denounced by the prophets (Is 23:12; Eze 28:21-22). Persons from Sidon heard Jesus preach in Galilee and once Jesus visited this vicinity (Ma 15:21; Mk 3:8). Paul landed at Sidon on his voyage to Rome as a prisoner (Ac 27:3). See TYRE AND SIDON.

SIDONIANS

Inhabitants of Sidon (De 3:9). The Israelites were supposed to drive the Sidonians out of the land, but they failed to do so (Jos 13:4,6; Ju 3:3). The Sidonians were skillful lumbermen (1 Ki 5:6).

SIEGE

See WAR.

SEIVE

A tool used for sifting (Is 30:20; Am 9:9).

SIGN

A symbol or recognizable detail to ensure authenticity (such as the sign to the shepherds: they would find the baby wrapped in swaddling clothes and lying in a manger; Lk 2:12). Miracles are often called "signs" because they are sent to point people toward God (Ex 7:3; Is 8:18). Jesus's miracles were a sign that He was actually the Messiah (Lk 7:22), and yet the crowds were rebuked for looking for miracles rather than believing simple preaching (Lk 11:29).

SIG′ NET

See SEAL.

SI′ HON

The Amorite king who refused the Israelites passage through his territory (Nu 21:21-32).

SI′ HOR

See SHIHOR.

SI′ LAS

The contracted form of Silvanus. Silas was a member of the church at Jerusalem (Ac 15:22), probably a Hellenistic Jew. He was commissioned by the Council at Jerusalem to report its decision about circumcision to the church of Antioch (Ac 15:22,27,32). When Paul and Barnabas disagreed regarding Mark, Silas became Paul's companion on the second journey (Ac 15:40). At Philippi they were imprisoned (Ac 16:19,25). He remained with Timothy at Berea and both joined Paul at Corinth (Ac 18:5). In the Epistles he is called Silvanus.

SILK

A fabric made from strong, fine fibers secured from the cocoons of silk worms. The word is used frequently in the Bible, but in Proverbs 31:22 and in Ezekiel 16:10,13 it is believed that fine linen is intended.

SIL′ LA (twig, basket)

A place near the house of Millo (2 Ki 12:20).

SI·LO′ AM (sent, conducted)

A famous pool of Jerusalem, also called the upper pool to distinguish it from the nearby old or lower pool (Is 7:3; 22:9), and probably identical with king's pool (Ne 2:14). It was south of the temple area and just west of the Kidron Valley (Jo 9:6-7). See also HEZEKIAH'S WATER TUNNEL.

SI·LO′ AM, TOW′ ER OF

A tower mentioned by Jesus. It had recently collapsed, and eighteen people were killed (Lk 13:4). It was probably near the pool of Siloam, but its exact location is unsure. It may have been on the site of the modern village of Siloam, across the valley from the Gihon spring.

SIL·VA′ NUS

See SILAS.

SIL′ VER

A precious metal. Its ore is mined (Job 28:1) and refined from the dross by means of a furnace (Ps 12:6; Pr 17:3; 25:4; Eze 22:22). Silver was found in Tarshish (Je 10:9; Eze 27:12) and Arabia (2 Ch 9:14), and it was used as money at an early period (Ge 23:16; 37:28). Minted coins were not yet in use, so value was determined by weight (Is 46:6). It was not until some time after the exile that it was coined among the Jews. It was used for various purposes—cups (Ge 44:2), musical instruments (Nu 10:2), ornaments (Ex 3:22), crowns (Ze 6:11), parts of the tabernacle and temple (Ex 27:10; 38:19; 1 Ch 28:17; Ez 1:9-10), shrines (Ac 19:24).

SILVERING (archaic)

Silver, money (Is 7:23).

SILVERSMITH

One who works with silver. See METALSMITH.

SIM′ E·ON (hearing)

Five Old Testament men and a tribe of Israel:

1. The second son of Jacob. His mother was Leah (Ge 29:33). After Shechem defiled Simeon's sister, Dinah, Levi and Simeon massacred the inhabitants of the city of Shechem. Later Jacob deplored this deed (Ge 34:24-31; 49:5-7). See DINAH.

2. The tribe descended from the sons of Simeon. The six sons were Jemuel, Janim, Jachin, Zohar, Shaul, and Ohad, and all but the latter founded a tribal family (Ge 46:10; Nu 26:12-14; 1 Ch 4:24). The tribe was located in the extreme south of Judah and eventually was absorbed by the tribe of Judah (Jos 19:1,2,9).

3. The son of Judah and an ancestor of Jesus (Lk 3:30).

4. A devout man who had been divinely assured that he would not die until he had seen Jesus. When Mary and Joseph brought Jesus to the temple to be presented to the Lord and make the proper sacrifices for a firstborn son, Simeon was at the temple, and immediately recognized the baby as the Messiah he had been waiting for (Lk 2:25-35).

5. A prophet or teacher of Antioch, surnamed Niger (Ac 13:1).

6. A variant of Simon Peter (Ac 15:14). See PETER.

SIMEONITES

Descendants of Jacob's son, Simeon (Ge 29:33; Nu 25:14; 1 Ch 27:16).

SIMILITUDE

Likeness. James speaks of humans being made in the "similitude" of God (Jam 3:9) just as Genesis speaks of being made in the image of God (Ge 1:26-27).

SI'MON *(hearing)*

Eight New Testament men:
1. Simon Peter. See PETER.
2. Father of Judas Iscariot (Jo 6:71).
3. Simon the Zealot, called "Simon the Canaanite," one of the apostles (Lk 6:15; Ac 1:13).

4. A brother of Jesus, along with James and Jude (Ma 13:55; Mk 6:3). See BRETHREN OF THE LORD.

5. Simon the Leper. He lived at Bethany and it is probable Christ cured him of leprosy. It was in his house, after Lazarus had been raised to life, that Mary anointed Jesus with the spikenard. It is possible he was the husband of Martha (Ma 26:6-13; Mk 14:3-9; Jo 12:1-8).

6. A Pharisee in whose house Christ was a guest at the time a sinful woman anointed his feet (Lk 7:36-50).

7. Simon of Cyrene, father of Alexander and Rufus (Mk 15:21). When Jesus fell under the weight of his cross on the way to Calvary, Simon was dragged from the crowd and forced to carry it for Him (Ma 27:32).

8. Simon the sorcerer, usually called Simon Magnus. A magician of Samaria, he was converted to Christianity by the preaching of Philip. He was severely rebuked by Peter when he of-

fered to purchase the wonder-working power of the Holy Spirit (Ac 8:9-24).

9. Simon the tanner, a Christian who lived at Joppa. Peter was staying at his house when he had the vision of the clean and unclean animals and received the summons from Cornelius (Ac 9:43; 10:6,17,32).

SIMON PETER

See PETER.

SIMPLICITY

In a negative sense: mental simplicity or foolishness (Pr 1:22). In a positive sense: simplicity of heart; lack of manipulation, hypocrisy, or selfish motives (Ac 2:46; 2 Co 1:12; 11:3).

SIM'RI

See SHIMRI.

SIN

In Romans 3, Paul proves that all humankind—Jew and Gentile, religious and pagan—have sinned. Both testaments have large and interesting vocabularies for the various forms of sin, showing how important a fact of human life sin really is.

The following paragraphs treat several of these words in the order of frequency of usage. Sin is seen as the following things:

Falling Short *(hamartia, hamartema, hamartano,* etc.). This word-group is the broadest and most frequently used in the New Testament, occurring over 250 times. The root idea is failing, missing the mark, "[falling] short of the glory of God" (Ro 3:23). The most general word is *hamartia,* which can be sin in general or a specific act of sin. The similar word *hamartema* stresses individual acts. The heretic Pelagius misquoted the golden-tongued preacher Chrysostom as saying that infants are without sin. He should have checked the original Greek of that great preacher. What he really said was "that infants are innocent of *hamartemata,* individual acts of sin, and were not free from *hamartia,* which was sin in general" (Nigel Turner, *Christian Words,* p.413).

Unrighteousness, Iniquity *(adikia, adikos,* etc.). The basic meaning of these words is "injustice" or "dishonesty" in classical Greek, and the common translations of the verb *(adikeo)* are "to do wrong," "to be unjust," "to hurt." *Adikia* is the opposite of *uprightness.* A famous passage using this word is 1 John 1:9: "If we confess our sins, he is faithful and just to forgive us our sins and to cleanse us from all unrighteousness."

Trespass (*paraptoma*), occurring twenty-one times in the New Testament, is used in one popular rendition of the Lord's Prayer: "Forgive us our trespasses." It means to fall (*pipto*) when one should have resisted a temptation or maintained a spiritual walk. James tells us, "Confess your trespasses one to another and pray for one another" (5:16).

Iniquity (*anomia*), occurs fifteen times and literally means "lawlessness," though the word is generally translated "iniquity" in the KJV tradition. First John 3:4 uses *anomia* as a definition of sin.

Transgression (*parabasis*), occurring only seven times, means "violating a specific law." *To transgress* is to cross a line that God has drawn: it is a specific disobedience of a command.

Ungodliness (*asebeia*, etc.) The noun for *ungodliness* occurs six times, the verb twice, and the adjective ten times. Just as *eusebeia* (*eu*=good and *sebia*=worship) means "piety," "godliness," or "religion," so this is the same root with a negative prefix *a-* (as in *atheist*—"no God"). *Asebia* is the impious irreverence of the village atheist, living in rebellion against God and godly standards. It is irreligion in general. Jude, quoting an ancient prophecy of Enoch preserved by the Holy Spirit, uses all three forms of this word in a trenchant way (vv.15-18).

Debt (*opheilema*) occurs in the sense of a sin in Matthew's version of the Lord's Prayer: "Forgive us our debts, as we forgive our debtors" (Ma 6:12). Debts that we owe to God are sins that we need restitution for.

Disobedience (*parakoe*) occurs three times, including the very central passage on how sin entered our world: by one man's disobedience (Ro 5:19). The root idea is to neglect to hear and heed God's commands.

Ignorance (*agnoema*), sins committed inadvertently (He 9:7 only), nevertheless need atonement by blood. Ignorance is no excuse.

Each individual man, woman, and child who composes mankind is a sinner. Paul points out in Romans 3:13-16 that "their throat is an open tomb . . . the poison of asps [a small, deadly poisonous snake] *is* under their lips; whose mouth *is* full of cursing and bitterness. Their feet *are* swift to shed blood [consider the high incidence of violent crime, murder, and abortion that in-

fects our society, how easy it is to lash out in anger]; destruction and misery *are* in their ways [whatever man touches he corrupts]." All of this shows that there is no person who seeks after God and no person who does right (Ro 3:10-11). Each individual man, woman, and child needs the righteousness of God. Without God's righteousness no one can ever enter or stand in God's presence. Plainly every man, woman, and child needs to have a new life because each is a sinner.

Sin, regardless of its degree, always has an effect—separation. Sin separates one from God. This separation from God is death. Adam was told that if he ate of the tree of the knowledge of good and evil that he would die (Ge 3:3). Adam ate of the tree and immediately died spiritually—his soul was separated from God—and he began to die physically. The entrance of sin into the human race brought with it death (Ro 5:12; 6:23). That man is a sinner is proven by the fact that he dies—where there is death, there is sin. Sin's penalty, death, can be remedied by life—union with God. This is achieved by belief in Jesus, who died to pay the penalty of man's sin (Ro 5:21). For the one who believes in Jesus, the penalty of sin is broken. He has been born again (Jo 3), and through the work of the Holy Spirit in his life, and can live a new life that is pleasing to God. Yes, he will die physically (unless he is alive when Jesus returns to take all believers to heaven with Himself, 1 Th 4:14-18), but physical death for him is only the doorway into the presence of God.

Even though the believer has been freed from the penalty of sin, he still must deal with the presence of sin. First John 1:8 says that if we say we have no sin, we are liars. Believers still sin, but they have the power through the Holy Spirit to deal with this sin. The believer should never condone or attempt to excuse his sin. There are only two things that should be done about sin: confess it and forsake it. The Old and New Testaments are agreed on this. David confessed his sin and experienced the Lord's forgiveness. John agrees as he points out: "If we confess our sins, He is faithful and just to forgive us our sins and to cleanse us from all unrighteousness" (1 Jo 1:9). To "confess" means *to acknowledge,* or to agree with God that this is indeed sin. When the believer confesses his sin he has the assurance that God "is faithful" (He can be counted upon to keep His word) and "just" (He is just in dealing with our sins because He paid the price for them) "to forgive us *our* sins and to cleanse us from all unrighteousness." There is no sin too great and no sin too small—God is able to cleanse us completely from anything that is inconsistent with His own moral character. Having received forgiveness and cleansing, the believer is to forsake his sin and yield himself completely to God. In doing this the believer is restored to full fellowship with God.

In the face of all these words about sin, it is comforting to remember that "You [those who have been redeemed, bought back from the ways of sin by the precious blood of Jesus] are a chosen generation, a royal priesthood, a holy nation, His own special people, that you may proclaim the praises of Him who called you out of darkness into His marvelous light" (1 Pe 2:9). Through Jesus Christ, there is a very good answer to the problem of sin.

SIN

A fortified city on the border of Egypt (Eze 30:15-16).

SIN, MAN OF
See ANTICHRIST.

SIN, UNFORGIVABLE
See BLASPHEMY.

SIN, WILDERNESS OF
A wilderness through which the Israelites passed on their way to Mount Sinai (Ex 16:1; 17:1; Nu 33:12). God first sent the manna while they were in this area, and also the quail.

SIN OFFERING
See SACRIFICIAL SYSTEM.

SI′NA
Sinai in the Greek form (Ac 7:30,38).

SI′NAI
The Peninsula: A large triangular peninsula forming a natural bridge between Africa and the Middle East. The base of the triangle is on the eastern edge of the south shore of the Mediterranean, the point juts out into the Red Sea. The two upper arms of the Red Sea (the Gulf of Suez and the Gulf of Aqaba) form the other two sides of the triangle. The base of the peninsula is about 150 miles across, it is about 250 miles down to the tip.

The Wilderness: After the Hebrews left the land of Egypt, they came to the wilderness of Sinai (Ex 19:1). The whole of the peninsula is a desert area, it is not known whether this term includes all the wildernesses of Sinai, or whether it refers only to the area around the mountain.

The Mountain: The mountain on which God met Moses and gave him the law (Ex 19); it is also called Horeb (Ex 3:1). It is believed that this mountain is either Jebel Musa (Mount Moses) in the south of the peninsula, or Jebel Serbal in the central area.

SINGER
In the Bible, this term is used specifically for those who sang for worship services. When David organized the music for worship, he had 4,000 Levites as musicians. Some of these probably included a choir (1 Ch 25). Two hundred men and women who were singers returned to Jerusalem after the captivity (Ez 2:65).

SIN′GLE (archaic)
Clear; sound, healthy (Lk 11:34-35).

SINGLENESS OF HEART
Undivided, with one purpose; unwavering commitment (2 Ch 30:12).

SI′NIM
A distant land from which exiles shall return (Is 49:12).

SI′NITE
A Canaanite tribe (Ge 10:17).

SINNER
One who sins. Because of the fall of all mankind, there is no one who does not fall into this category (Ro 3:23). See SIN.

SI′ON
1. An ancient name for Mount Hermon (De 4:48).
2. The Greek form of Zion. This term is used to specifically apply to the temple mount, and more generally to the city of Jerusalem (Ro 9:33).

SIPH′MOTH
A place where David took refuge when persecuted by Saul (1 Sa 30:28).

SIP′PA·I
See SAPH.

SIR

See LORD.

SI′ RAH *(retreat)*

A well near Hebron where Joab and his brother murdered Abner (2 Sa 3:26).

SI′ RI·ON *(coat of mail)*

The name by which Hermon was known to the Sidonians (De 3:9; Ps 29:6).

SIS′ A·MAI

See SISMAI.

SIS′ E·RA

Two Old Testament men:

1. Commander of a Canaanite army. He fled after his defeat by Deborah and Barak. He hid in the home of Heber, the Kenite, whose wife, Jael, killed him as he slept (Ju 4:2-22; 5:20-30; 1 Sa 12:9; Ps 83:9).

2. Ancestor of Nethinim (Ez 2:53; Ne 7:55).

SIS′ MAI

Son of Eleasah of the line of Jerahmeel of Judah (1 Ch 2:40; Sisamai, KJV).

SIS′ TER

Among the Hebrews this name was used with considerable latitude, as was the word *brother.* It may denote a full or half sister (Ge 20:12; De 27:22) or a woman of the same tribe or religion (Nu 25:18; Ro 16:1; Jam 2:15).

SITH′ RI *(a hiding place)*

A Levite of the family of Kohath (Ex 6:22).

SIT′ NAH *(enmity)*

A well in the Philistine country near Gerar (Ge 26:21).

SI′ VAN

The third month of the sacred year and ninth of the civil year, corresponding roughly to May/June (Es 8:9).

SIYON

See ZION.

SKINK

See LIZARD.

SKIRT

An article of clothing, the exact nature of which is not known.

SKULL, PLACE OF THE

See CALVARY.

SLANDER

Malicious talk, falsely charging with wrongdoing, which is designed to damage a person's reputation or destroy the person (Ps 31:13; 50:20; Eze 22:9). Slander is forbidden in the Ten Commandments (Ex 20:16; De 5:20). Satan, the accuser, is the ultimate slanderer (Job 1:9-11; Re 12:10). When people slander others, they are following in Satan's footsteps.

SLAUGHTER, VALLEY OF

See TOPHET.

SLAUGHTER OF THE INNOCENTS

See INNOCENTS, SLAUGHTER OF.

SLAVE

Slavery is an ancient institution, involving the buying and selling of human beings as property. Slaves were sometimes purchased (Ge 37:28,36; Eze 27:13). Sometimes people became slaves because of inability to pay a debt, but to enslave a debtor or his children was against the Mosaic law (Ex 22:3; 2 Ki 4:1; Am 2:6). Many slaves were the captives of war (Nu 31:9; 2 Ki 5:2). One might sell himself or a child into slavery (Ex 21:2,7; Le 25:39,47). The brothers of Joseph sold him for twenty pieces of silver (Ge 37:28). The Jewish laws safeguarded the treatment of Hebrew slaves, and after six years of service slaves were given their freedom unless they chose to remain with a loved master. If this was the case, the slave had an awl driven through his ear into the door of his master's house, and he was then a slave forever (Ex 21:6; De 15:17). In the year of Jubilee all Hebrew slaves were liberated (Le 25:40). Foreign slaves had the rights of the people in regard to the Sabbath, religious festivals and sacrifices (Ex 12:44; De 12:12,18; 16:11,14).

Christian slaves were urged to be obedient to their masters, not only when they were being watched, but at all times, "as unto the Lord" (Ep 6:5-8; Col 3:22-25). Masters were required to treat their slaves kindly (Ep 6:9; Col 4:1). When Paul sent Onesimus, the runaway slave, back to his Christian master, Philemon, Paul urged Philemon to give the slave his freedom, and treat him like the brother he now was.

SLEEP

Often used as a metaphor for death (1 Ki 2:10; 11:43; 1 Th 4:14), slothfulness (Pr 6:9-11; 1 Th 5:6), and peace (Eze 34:25; Ps 4:8; Ec 5:12).

SLIME (Ge 11:3; 14:10; Ex 2:3)

See BITUMEN.

SLING

An offensive weapon. It consisted of a leather thong wider in the middle than at the ends. After placing a stone in the broad middle portion, the slinger grasped its two ends with one hand and swung it in a circle around his head. Upon releasing one end of the thong, the stone was sent toward its mark (Ju 20:16).

SLINGSTONES

The stones flung by a sling, ranging from pebbles to fist sized chunks of flint (Job 41:28; Ze 9:15).

SLOTHFUL

Lazy, sluggish (Pr 6:9-11; 15:19; 26:13-15). According to the Book of Proverbs, slothfulness leads to folly and poverty. Diligence and hard work is the opposite of slothfulness.

SMART (archaic)

To experience sharp uncomfortable pain (Pr 11:15).

SMELTER

The crucible for heating metal ores for smelting. Jeremiah prophesied against Jerusalem, say-

SLING

ing that it was so corrupt that there was more dross than good metal.

SMITH

See METALSMITH.

SMYR′ NA *(myrrh)*

A city of Ionia. Smyrna was a center for emperor worship. They had built a temple dedicated to Tiberius Caesar in 23 B.C., and under such emperors as Nero and Domitian, persecution of Christians was severe. (Re 1:11; 2:8-11). See SEVEN CHURCHES OF REVELATION.

SNAIL

1. Probably a variety of lizard (Le 11:30).

2. A creature with a spiral shell which leaves a trail of slime (Ps 58:8).

SNAKE

The first snake mentioned in the Bible is the Satanic serpent who tempted Eve to disobey God (Ge 3; Re 20:2). After this, many different snakes are mentioned. Not all of these are identifiable, so various translations have chosen different words. Asps and adders are two common snakes of the area. Asps are a variety of cobra; adders (or vipers) are also poisonous. The horned viper hides in the sand which it resembles in color and thus escapes detection. It has a venomous, deadly bite (Ge 49:17; Ps 58:4-5; 91:13). Israel also has many varieties of nonpoisonous snakes, but all snakes were ceremonially unclean. Because of the serpent in the garden of Eden, snakes are often used as metaphors of evil (Ps 140:3; Je 8:17; Ro 3:13).

SNARE

A trap (Ps 91:3; Am 3:5).

SNOW

In January or February there may be snow in Palestine in the hill country. It is unusual that even a considerable fall of snow remains longer than a day, although on the summit of Hermon it lasts throughout the year. In the Scriptures snow denotes purity (Ps 51:7; Is 1:18; Ma 28:3).

SNUFFDISHES, SNUFFERS

Utensils for caring for the tabernacle lamps. These snuffers or wick-trimmers were tongs made of purest gold, used for snuffing the lights and trimming of the charred wicks so the lamps would burn cleanly (Ex 25:38; 2 Ch 4:21).

SO

A king of Egypt to whom Hoshea of Israel sent letters (2 Ki 17:4).

SOAP

A cleansing agent, made usually by the action of alkali on oil or fatty acid, a crude form of which is mentioned in Jeremiah 2:22 and Malachi 3:2. See LYE and FULLER.

SOBER

Self-controlled; maintaining an attitude of watchful alertness (Tit 2:12; 1 Pe 1:13; 5:8).

SO'CHOH, SO'COH, SO'CO *(hedge)*

1. A town in the lowland of Judah (Jos 15:35), also spelled Shochoh or Shoco.

2. A town in the hill country of Judah (Jos 15:48).

3. A city under the jurisdiction of Ben-hesed, one of Solomon's twelve food purveyors (1 Ki 4:10).

4. A man of Judah, son of Heber (1 Ch 4:18; Shocho, KJV), or possibly the same as No. 1, and not a person.

SOD (archaic)

Past tense of *seethe* "to cook by boiling" (Ge 25:29-30).

SODA

See LYE.

SO'DI *(intimate)*

Father of the spy who represented Zebulun (Nu 13:10).

SOD'OM

One of the five cities of the plain of the Jordan (Sodom, Gomorrah, Admah, Zeboiim, Zoar; Ge 13:10). It was famous for its wickedness, particularly its extremely promiscuous homosexuality (Ge 13:13; 18:20; Is 3:9; La 4:6). It was the home of Lot and his family. However, before the Lord destroyed the city because of its evil, Lot was allowed to escape with his family. As fire and brimstone rained down from heaven on the city, Lot's wife disobeyed the word of the two angels who had been sent to rescue them and gazed back at the city. She

was immediately turned into a pillar of salt (Ge 19:1-26).

Many scholars believe that the ruins of the five cities of the plain are probably located under the shallow southern end of the Dead Sea. Five streams flow into the Dead Sea in this area; if the Sea was smaller in Abraham's day, this area might have been a well-watered plain. This theory is further substantiated by the Jewish historian, Josephus, who recorded the interesting fact that Zoar, one of the five cities, was visible in this area during his time.

SODOM, VINE OF

See VINE OF SODOM.

SOD'OM·ITE

An inhabitant of the city of Sodom (Ge 19:5). The word has come to mean anyone who engages in homosexual acts.

SOJOURNER

A foreigner residing temporarily in a land not his own. As specified by the Mosaic law, one living among the Hebrew people but not of that nationality. He might also be a visitor in the land (Le 16:29; 17:8; 2 Sa 1:13). While in the land he had claims upon the kind treatment of the Hebrews (De 10:18-19) and his rights were safeguarded (Ex 22:21; 23:9). He was required to refrain from the things prohibited to the Israelites (Le 17:10; 20:2; 24:16). While he must observe the laws regarding the sanctity of the Sabbath, he was not required to perform religious duties peculiar to the Hebrews (Ex 12:43-46). The law taught that no outsiders or sojourners were allowed to eat the Passover, unless a sojourner wanted to celebrate it and was willing to have all the males in his household circumcised, in which case the family would be allowed to join in the feast (Ex 12:43-49). Further regulations regarding strangers and foreigners are found in Deuteronomy 14:21; 15:3; and 23:20.

Christians are to consider themselves as strangers and sojourners on earth, their real home is in heaven and the trials and struggles of this time will only last a short while (He 11:13; 1 Pe 2:11).

SOLDIER

A man who is a part of the military forces. See ARMY.

SOL′O·MON

The son of David and Bath-sheba; born in Jerusalem. He became the third king of a united Israel after the death of his father David, and reigned from 970 to 931 B.C. At the beginning of his reign, "Solomon loved the Lord, walking in the statutes of his father David" (1 Ki 3:3). Once when he was offering sacrifices to God, the Lord appeared to him in a vision, and said, "Ask! What shall I give you?" Solomon asked for one thing: an understanding heart so that he could judge the people well. The Lord was pleased with his request, and said that he would give him not only wisdom but wealth and honor as well. As long as Solomon walked in God's ways, God would lengthen his days and Solomon would be like no other king, before or since (1 Ki 3:5-15).

As king Solomon strengthened the fortifications of Jerusalem, he embellished it with royal buildings and the famous temple (1 Ki 9:15,24; 11:27) which his father had collected materials for. He had a large army with many chariots and horsemen (1 Ki 4:26; 10:26), and he also controlled a navy and a lucrative sea trade. His wisdom and wealth became known far and wide (1 Ki 3:16-28; 4:20-34). He was the author of 3,000 proverbs and 1,005 songs. He wrote the biblical books of Ecclesiastes and Song of Solomon.

Sadly, even though he started out so well, Solomon lost his first love for the Lord. His downfall was the love of foreign women. According to the Scriptures he had 700 wives and 300 concubines (1 Ki 11:3). He began by allowing his foreign wives to worship their own gods, and later he joined with them, abandoning his devotion to the one true God. His reign was characterized by luxury and extravagance. His lavishness caused much popular discontent and laid the groundwork for the later disruption of the kingdom. Solomon died after a forty-year rule and was succeeded by his son, Rehoboam (1 Ki 11:42-43).

SOL′O·MON'S PORCH

The outer corridor on the east side of Herod's temple (Jo 10:23; Ac 3:11). It was so named because of a supposed connection with Solomon's temple.

SOL′O·MON'S SERV′ANTS

The remnants of the old Canaanite tribes which had not been wiped out were forced to labor for Solomon (1 Ki 9:20-22). Apparently they were taken into captivity along with the Jews, for a number of them returned with Zerubabbel (Ez 2:55,58-59; Ne 7:57,60-61; 11:3), along with the Nethinim.

SOL′O·MON'S SONG

See SONG OF SOLOMON.

SON

A term denoting a male child (Ge 17:16,19; Ma 1:21,23), but also a grandson (Ge 29:5), or a more distant descendant (Ez 8:15; Ma 1:1). It is also used to denote a foster son (Ex 2:10; He 11:24) and a subject or disciple (1 Ki 20:35; 2 Ki 16:7). It can indicate a member of a tribe; for example, the Israelites were called the sons of Jacob (Lk 1:16). Believers in the Lord Jesus are called sons of God (Jo 1:12-13; Ro 8:14-17; Ga 3:26; 1 Jo 3:1-2).

SON OF GOD

One of the titles of the Messiah. In the New Testament it occurs nearly fifty times and is expressive of the relation that exists between the Father and the eternal Son (Ma 16:16; 27:43; Mk 1:1; Jo 3:18). He has all the perfections of God and is equal with God (Jo 1:1-14; 5:17-25; Ph 2:6). In receiving the commission of the Father, in His mode of operation He is subordinate, but not inferior (Jo 3:1,17; 8:42; Ga 4:4; He 1:2). It was because He claimed he was the Son of God that He was charged with blasphemy by the Sanhedrin (Ma 26:63-66; Mk 14:61). At His baptism and transfiguration He was divinely acknowledged as the Son of God (Ma 3:16-17; 17:5).

SON OF MAN

This title was applied by Christ to Himself. This title does not mean that He was merely human and not divine. He identified Himself with man in His human nature and in His sufferings for mankind (Ma 20:28; Jo 1:14).

SONG OF DEGREES

See ASCENTS, SONG OF.

SONG OF SOL′O·MON

1. The Book of Song of Solomon. The Song of Solomon is a love song written by Solomon and abounding in metaphors and oriental imagery. Historically, it depicts the wooing

and wedding of a shepherdess by King Solomon, and the joys and heartaches of wedded love.

Allegorically, it could be seen as picturing Israel as God's espoused bride (Ho 2:19-20), and the Church as the bride of Christ. As human life finds its highest fulfillment in the love of man and woman, so spiritual life finds its highest fulfillment in the love of God for His people and Christ for His Church.

The book is arranged like scenes in a drama with three main speakers: the bride (Shulamite), the king (Solomon), and a chorus (daughters of Jerusalem).

The Hebrew title *Shir Hashirim* comes from 1:1, "The song of songs." This is in the superlative and speaks of Solomon's most exquisite song. The Greek title *Asma Asmaton* and the Latin *Canticum Canticorum* also mean "Song of Songs" or "The Best Song." The name *Canticles* ("Songs") is derived from the Latin title. Because Solomon is mentioned in 1:1, the book is also known as the Song of Solomon.

2. The Author of Song of Solomon. Solomonic authorship is rejected by critics who claim it is a later collection of songs. Many take 1:1 to mean "which is about or concerning Solomon." But the internal evidence of the book strongly favors the traditional position that Solomon is its author. Solomon is specifically mentioned seven times (1:1,5; 3:7,9,11; 8:11-12), and he is identified as the groom. There is evidence of royal luxury and rich imported goods (3:6-11). The king by this time also had sixty queens and eighty concubines (6:8). Solomon's harem at its fullest extent reached seven hundred queens and three hundred concubines (1 Ki 11:3).

First Kings 4:32-33 says that Solomon composed 1,005 songs and had intimate knowledge of the plant and animal world. This greatest of his songs alludes to twenty-one species of plants and fifteen species of animals. It cites geographical locations in the north and in the south, indicating that they were still one kingdom. For example, 6:4 mentions both Tirzah and Jerusalem, the northern and southern capitals (after Solomon's time, Samaria became the northern capital). Because of the poetic imagery, the Song of Solomon uses forty-nine words that occur nowhere else in Scripture.

3. The Time of Song of Solomon. This song was written primarily from the point of view of the Shulamite, but Solomon was its author, probably early in his reign, about 965 B.C. There is a problem regarding how a man with a harem of 140 women (6:8) could extol the love of the Shulamite as though she were his only bride. It may be that Solomon's relationship with the Shulamite was the only pure romance he ever experienced. The bulk of his marriages were political arrangements. It is significant that the Shulamite was a vineyard keeper of no great means. This book was also written before Solomon plunged into gross immorality and idolatry. "For it was so, when Solomon was old, that his wives turned his heart after other gods; and his heart was not loyal to the LORD his God" (1 Ki 11:4).

The Shulamite addresses the king as "my beloved" and the king addresses his bride as "my love." The daughters of Jerusalem were probably attendants to the Shulamite. The term *Shulamite* appears only in 6:13, and it may be derived from the town of Shunem which was southwest of the Sea of Galilee in the tribal area of Issachar. The song refers to fifteen geographical locations from Lebanon in the north to Egypt in the south: Kedar (1:5), Egypt (1:9), En Gedi (1:14), Sharon (2:1), Jerusalem (2:7), Lebanon (3:9), Mount Gilead (4:1), Amana (4:8), Senir (4:8), Hermon (4:8), Tirzah (6:4), Heshbon (7:4), Damascus (7:4), Carmel (7:5), and Baal-hamon (8:11).

4. The Christ of Song of Solomon. In the Old Testament, Israel is regarded as the bride of Yahweh (see Is 54:5-6; Je 2:2; Ez 16:8-14; Ho 2:16-20). In the New Testament, the Church is seen as the bride of Christ (2 Co 11:2; Ep 5:23-25; Re 19:7-9; 21:9). The Song of Solomon illustrates the former and anticipates the latter.

5. Keys to Song of Solomon.

Key Word: Love in Marriage—The purpose of this book depends upon the viewpoint taken as to its primary thrust. Is it fictional, allegorical, or historical?

(1) *Fictional:* Some hold that this song is a fictional drama that portrays Solomon's attraction and marriage to a poor but beautiful girl from the country. However, the book gives every indication that the story really happened.

(2) *Allegorical:* In this view, the primary purpose of the Song is to illustrate the truth of God's love for His people whether the events are fictional or not. Some commentators insist

that the book is indeed historical, but its primary purpose is typical, that is, to present God's love for His bride Israel or Christ's love for His Church. However, this interpretation is subjective and lacking in evidence. In other Scriptures the husband and wife relationship is used symbolically (cf. Eze 16; 23; Ho 1–3), but these are always indicated as symbols. This may be an application of the book, but it should not be the primary interpretation.

(3) *Historical:* The Song of Songs is a poetic record of Solomon's actual romance with a Shulamite woman. The various scenes in the book exalt the joys of love in courtship and marriage and teach that physical beauty and sexuality in marriage should not be despised as base or unspiritual. It offers a proper perspective of human love and avoids the extremes of lust and asceticism. Only when sexuality is viewed in the wrong way, as something akin to evil, is an attempt made to allegorize this book. But this is part of God's creation with its related desires and pleasures, and it is reasonable that He would provide us with a guide to a pure sexual relationship between a husband and wife. In fact, the union of the two sexes was originally intended to illustrate the oneness of the Godhead (Ge 1:27; 2:24; 1 Co 6:16-20). Thus, the Song is a bold and positive endorsement by God of marital love in all its physical and emotional beauty. This interpretation does not mean that the book has no spiritual illustrations and applications. It certainly illustrates God's love for His covenant people Israel, and anticipates Christ's love for His bride, the Church.

Key Verses: Song of Solomon 7:10–8:7— "I am my beloved's, and his desire is toward me" (7:10).

"Many waters cannot quench love, nor can the floods drown it. If a man would give for love all the wealth of his house, it would be utterly despised" (8:7).

Key Chapter: Song of Solomon—Since the whole book is a unity, there is no key chapter; rather, all eight chapters beautifully depict the love of a married couple.

6. Survey of Song of Solomon. Solomon wrote 1,005 songs (1 Ki 4:32), but this beautiful eulogy of love stood out among them as the "song of songs" (1:1). The great literary value of this song can be seen in its rich use of metaphor and oriental imagery as it extols the purity, beauty, and satisfaction of love. It is never crass, but

often intimate, as it explores the dimensions of the relationship between two lovers: attraction, desire, companionship, pleasure, union, separation, faithfulness, and praise. Like Ecclesiastes, this little book is not easily outlined, and various schemes can be used. It abounds with sudden changes of speakers, and they are not identified. The beginning of love is seen in 1:1–5:1, and the broadening of love is found in 5:2–8:14.

The Beginning of Love (1:1–5:1). King Solomon has a vineyard in the country of the Shulamite (6:13; 8:11). The Shulamite must work in the vineyard with her brothers (1:6; 8:11-12) and when Solomon visits the area, he wins her heart and eventually takes her to the palace in Jerusalem as his bride. She is tanned from hours of work outside in the vineyard, but she is "fairest among women" (1:6,8).

This song is arranged like scenes in a one-act drama with three main speakers—the bride (the Shulamite), the king (Solomon), and a chorus (the daughters of Jerusalem). It is not always clear who is speaking, but this is a likely arrangement:

The Bride: 1:2-4,5-7,12-14,16-17; 2:1,3-6,8-17; 3:1-4; 4:16; 5:2-8,10-16; 6:2-3,11-12; 7:9-13; 8:1-3, 6-7,10-12,14.

The Lover: 1:8-10,15; 2:2,7; 3:5; 4:1-15; 5:1; 6:4-10,13; 7:1-9; 8:4-5,13.

The Chorus: 1:4,11; 3:6-11; 5:9; 6:1,13; 8:5, 8-9.

Chapters 1–3 give a series of recollections of the courtship: (1) the bride's longing for affection at the palace before the wedding (1:2-8), (2) expressions of mutual love in the banquet hall (1:9–2:7), (3) a springtime visit of the king to the bride's home in the country (2:8-17), (4) the Shulamite's dream of separation from her beloved (3:1-5), and (5) the ornate wedding procession from the bride's home to Jerusalem (3:6-11).

In 4:1–5:1, Solomon praised his bride from head to foot with a superb chain of similes and metaphors. Her virginity is compared to "a garden enclosed" (4:12), and the garden is entered when the marriage is consummated (4:16–5:1). The union is commended, possibly by God, in 5:1.

The Broadening of Love (5:2–8:14). Some time after the wedding, the Shulamite had a troubled dream (5:2) in the palace while Solomon was away. In her dream Solomon comes to her door, but she answers too late—he is gone. She panics and searches for him late at night in Jerusalem. Upon his return, Solomon assures her of his love and praises her beauty (6:4–7:10). The Shulamite begins to think of her country home and tries to persuade her beloved to return there with her (7:11–8:4). The journey takes place in 8:5-7 and their relationship continues to deepen. Their love will not be overthrown by jealousy or circumstances. At her homecoming (8:8-14) the Shulamite reflects on her brothers' care for her when she was young (8:8-9). She remains virtuous ("I am a wall," 8:10) and is now in a position to look out for her brothers' welfare (8:11-12). The song concludes with a dual invitation of lover and beloved (8:13-14).

OUTLINE OF SONG OF SOLOMON

I. The Beginning of Love (1:1–5:1)

A. Falling in Love 1:1–3:5
B. United in Love 3:6–5:1

II. Broadening of Love (5:2–8:14)

A. Struggling in Love..................... 5:2–7:10
B. Growing in Love 7:11–8:14

SONG OF SONGS

See SONG OF SOLOMON.

SONG OF THE THREE YOUNG MEN

See APOCRYPHA.

SONS OF GOD

A designation for certain godlike beings or angels (Ge 6:2-4; Job 1:6; 2:1).

SOOTH′ SAY·ER (*speaker, sayer of truth*)

One who claimed the power to foresee future events; a diviner (Jos 13:22; Je 27:9), one who professed to have the power to interpret dreams and mysterious utterances (Da 4:7,9; 5:11-12). They were employed to bring to light secrets (Da 2:27). See MAGIC, SORCERY, AND DIVINATION.

SOP

A piece of bread used as an eating utensil (Jo 13:26-30). It is typical in eastern countries to eat with the fingers and with pieces of bread for scooping up softer foods.

SO′ PA·TER

A Christian of Berea. On Paul's return from his third missionary journey he accompanied the apostle from Philippi to Asia. His father's name was Pyrrhus (Ac 20:4).

SO′ PHE·RETH (*scribe*)

A family among the descendants of Solomon's servants, members of which came with Zerubbabel from Babylon (Ez 2:55; Ne 7:57, also called Hassophereth).

SOR′ CER·ER

One who practices sorcery. His power is allegedly gained from the aid or control of evil spirits, particularly for purposes of gaining hidden knowledge (Ex 7:11; Da 2:2; Re 21:8; 22:15). He does not foretell the future but rather compels it or determines fate by means of his incantations, potions, or magical charms. Sorcerers were common in Egypt, Assyria, and Babylon (Is 47:9,12; Da 2:2), but they were banned from Israel (De 18:10-12). They were also called witches. The practice of such occultism was punishable by death (Ex 22:18). Simon Magnus and Bar-jesus were prominent sorcerers in New Testament times (Ac 8:9-24; 13:6-12). See MAGIC, SORCERY, AND DIVINATION.

SO′ REK (*vine*)

A valley about twelve miles west of Jerusalem which follows a northerly twisting course to the Mediterranean. It was through this valley the ark was taken to Beth-shemesh (1 Sa 6:7-13; Ju 16:4).

SORES

See BOIL.

SORREL

A reddish brown, or an animal of this color (Ze 1:8).

SO·SIP′ A·TER (*a saviour of a father*)

A Christian who sent greetings to the church at Rome (Ro 16:21).

SOS′ THE·NES *(of full strength)*

Ruler of the synagogue of Corinth. In the riot caused by Paul's preaching, Sosthenes was seized and beaten by the Greeks (Ac 18:17).

SO·TA′ I *(one who deviates)*

A servant of Solomon. His descendants returned from exile with Zerubbabel (Ez 2:55; Ne 7:57).

SOUL

The Hebrew word for soul (*nephesh*) has many meanings and seldom equals what English-speaking Christians mean by the term. *Nephesh* probably comes from the concept of breathing. Genesis 2:7 tells us that God "breathed into his [man's] nostrils the breath of life; and man became a living being [*nephesh*]." This shows that man's *nephesh* is from God. The KJV has over twenty different translations of this word, including "fish." (Is 19:10).

Nephesh as Soul: The closest to our English concept of *soul* that is, the inner, immaterial part of humankind (Greek *psyche*) as distinguished from the body, occurs in several passages. For example, in Genesis 35:18, we read of Rachel that "her soul was departing (for she died)." Job 14:22 presents body and soul as parts of one person: "But his flesh will be in pain over it, and his soul will mourn over it."

Nephesh as Life: *Nephesh* relating to life is used for both people and animals. This life is in the blood (Le 17:11). Therefore, Israel was not to drink blood, blood had sacrificial value, and purposeful bloodshed of another human being had to be punished by death.

Nephesh as the Person: *Nephesh* as the person is the closest to the meaning of "SOS—save our souls," the international distress signal. This does not mean "save our immortal souls from perdition," but "Save our whole persons (or lives; see above)." When the newspapers talked about how many "souls" were rescued in the shipwreck of the *Titanic,* they were talking about how many people's lives were saved. God told Abraham that if a male was not circumcised "that person [*nephesh*] shall be cut off from his people" (Ge 17:14). Sometimes *nephesh* is used like a reflexive pronoun: *myself* or *yourself,* for example. The elders in Jeremiah 26:19 complained, " But we are doing great evil against ourselves."

Nephesh as a Personal Pronoun: This usage occurs especially in poetry. In Psalms, "my soul" (*naphshi*) is a very common expression, not always meaning much more than "I" or "me."

Nephesh as the Seat of Appetite: The hunger in Psalm 107:9 is not spiritual, but physical: "For He satisfies the longing soul, and fills the hungry soul with goodness."

In Proverbs 16:24, "soul" probably indicates physical taste ("the bones" suggests the body), although it may be referring to "spiritual" appreciation: "Pleasant words *are like* a honeycomb, sweetness to the soul and health to the bones."

Nephesh as the Seat of Feelings: Love, the strongest emotion, is understandably prominent in the Song of Songs. The Shulamite says, "my soul loveth" (KJV) in 1:7; 3:1-4. Since in English the soul is not seen as the source of love, the NKJV updated this to simply "I love" (see *nephesh* as the person, above). The opposite emotion also occurs: "Has Your [God's] soul loathed Zion?" (Je 14:19). A soul may be troubled (Is 19:10) or refreshed (Pr 25:13).

Of course the most famous poem in all literature includes the words, "He restores my soul [*nephesh*]." No matter which nuance of *nephesh* we may prefer here, the marvelous thing is that for the believer, the Lord restores every aspect we have discussed—plus several more. See SPIRIT, SOUL, AND BODY.

SOUTH, THE

See NEGEV.

SOUTH GATE

A gate of the temple, assigned to Obed-edom, one of the gatekeepers in the time of David (1 Ch 26:15).

SOUTH RAMOTH

See RAMAH NO. 6.

SOVEREIGNTY OF GOD

The doctrine that God has unlimited power and authority over the entire creation, including all history, past, present, and future (Is 45:9-19; Ro 8:18-39). The doctrine of the sovereignty of God is taught in Romans 8–11. See also OMNISCIENCE, OMNIPOTENCE, OMNIPRESENCE.

SOW

A female pig. See SWINE.

SOWER

One who scatters seeds. Before the advent of modern farming machinery, grain was broadcast over the plowed fields. The sower walked up and down the field, tossing out handfuls of seeds with a smooth circular motion, scattering them evenly over the earth. Jesus's parable of the sower describes what happens to the seeds which fall outside of the good plowed ground, illustrating the different spiritual responses that different people have (Ma 13:4).

SOWER, PARABLE OF (Ma 13:1-23; Mk 4:1-20; Lk 8:4-15)

SPAIN

The territory now called Spain and Portugal. In his Epistle to the Romans Paul expressed his desire to visit Spain (Ro 15:24,28).

SPAN

A measure of length, the distance between the tip of the thumb and the tip of the little finger when the hand is stretched out (1 Sa 17:4). The average span was considered to be half a cubit (about 9 inches). See WEIGHTS AND MEASURES.

SPAR′ROW

The word is used to refer to any small bird of the sparrow order. Sparrows are social birds, who like to gather in flocks. The Psalmist compared his loneliness to a solitary sparrow (Ps 102:7). Another psalm speaks of the sparrows who built their nests in the temple courts, and the security they enjoyed with their homes so close to God's altar. Sparrows were sold for very little, they are small and insignificant, but God keeps track even of the lives of sparrows (Ma 10:29; Lk 12:6-7).

SPEAR

A weapon of war, consisting of a wooden shaft with a pointed metal head (1 Sa 13:19; 17:7). It was used both for thrusting and throwing (1 Sa 26:7-8; 2 Sa 2:23).

SPECK

A tiny crumb or piece of dust (Ma 7:3-5; Lk 6:41-42).

SPECKLED

Spotted with more then one color. Laban paid Jacob for his work by giving him all the speckled or spotted sheep in the flock; the Lord blessed Jacob and the flock continued to bear more spotted or speckled lambs than plain ones (Ge 30:32-39; 31:8,12).

SPECTACLE

Something to stare at, a strange sight, something which is being made a show of. This often means something which is held up for ridicule or contempt (Na 3:6; He 10:33). Because the gospel seems like foolishness to the world, believers must expect to be considered a spectacle some of the time (1 Co 4:9).

SPELT

A low order of wheat (Ex 9:32; Is 28:25). It was raised in Egypt and used to make bread. Also translated "fitches" and "rye."

SPHERE

The area of life which is a person's particular responsibility (2 Co 10:13-16).

SPICE

Plants with aromatic qualities, used to flavor food and as sweet smelling incense or perfume. Spices were used to prepare people for burial (2 Ch 16:14; Jo 19:39). Spices came from southern Arabia (1 Ki 10:2; Eze 27:22). Myrrh, sweet cinnamon, sweet calamus, cassia, galbanum, onycha, and atacte are the varieties specifically named (Ex 30:23-24,34). Myrrh and aloes were the spices used on the body of Jesus (Jo 19:39-40). At Herod's funeral there were five hundred spice-bearers.

SPI′DER

A web-weaving animal (Job 8:14; Is 59:5). There are over six hundred species of spiders in Palestine.

SPIKE′NARD

A plant from which a fragrant ointment was made (Song 4:13-14). The Greek word is *nardos* (Mk 14:3). The plant grows in the Himalaya Mountains at a great elevation.

SPINDLE

A tool used for spinning thread. A spindle is a long stick with a tapered end. Twirling the spindle as the thread is being drawn out twists the thread and makes it possible to make it smooth and even (Pr 31:19).

SPIN´NING

The process of converting fibrous material into thread. The spindle and distaff were used (Pr 31:19). The material, usually goat's hair, wool, or flax, was wound on the distaff which was stuck in the ground. The thread was drawn out and fastened to the spindle. When the spindle was turned it twisted the material into thread. The work was done by women (Ex 35:25).

SPIR´IT

When the Bible says we were created in God's image, it does not mean God looks like us—a most carnal theory—for God in essence is Spirit (Jo 4:24). We are like God in creative personality, having intellect, sensibility, and will. In addition God has given us marvelously working bodies to work and live in the world he created for mankind. Body, soul, and spirit are meant to work in harmony for the glory of God. We can only imagine what Adam and Eve were like before the fall. On this side of the garden of Eden, we struggle with our will, our emotions, and our bodies, and especially with our relationship to God as we deal with sin.

In 1 Thessalonians 5:23, the apostle Paul differentiates among three components: ". . . . may your whole spirit, soul, and body be preserved blameless as the coming of our Lord Jesus Christ." As we think of these three parts "being preserved" it helps to think of the things one might do to keep them "blameless" before Christ. It is very hard for a believer to separate "soul" and "spirit" but if one thinks of the soul as the thinking, feeling part of a living being, and the spirit as the part that relates to God, it helps some. One can have wrong thinking, wrong actions (things done in the body) and a wrong or neglected relationship with God. In all of these areas we need the help of the Holy Spirit to live blamelessly.

Spirit (pneuma) has the same double meaning in both Testaments: Hebrew *ruah* and Greek *pneuma* both mean "wind" or "spirit." This explains Jesus's play on words in John 3 in His discussion on being born from above by the Spirit, and the wind blowing where it wills.

The spirit is that part of humans that differentiates us from animals; it is the part that seeks a relationship with God. Animals obviously have bodies, and they also have "souls" in the sense of sentient life, but what animal has ever built a church or even prayed to God?

The spiritual aspect of human beings is the most important. Our spiritual growth and knowledge will last for all eternity.

Soul (psyche) is the Greek word that has spawned many an English derivative beginning with *psycho*. The main usages of *psyche* are "soul" (in its many meanings, including "person" and "life." There are passages where it is hard to know which of these is the better translation. For example, when Jesus asked "What shall a man give in exchange for his [*psyche*]?" He could have referred to man's soul or to his life here on earth and the rewards that come from living for God.

We are so used to using "soul" for the personality that will last forever that we miss another meaning. We say, "Make the most of your life [*psyche*] for the Lord." The best and "most" we can make of our life is to believe in the Lord Jesus Christ so that we can live eternally with Him. If we are not believers we cannot serve God acceptably. However, since *psyche* also refers to our personality and our "aliveness" on earth, we must also make the most of our lives so that we can give glory to God, teach others about Him, and have a reward for our labors in the Day of Christ.

Body (soma): There is far too much stress on the body in today's culture. We work out, we diet, we struggle for the perfect shape and color, we use cosmetics and surgery in our search for perfection. This is all supported by gigantic industries. But in reacting to this, we must not fail to take good care of our bodies. They are tools that God has designed for his good purposes on earth, for us to use and use well. Anyone who has struggled with health problems has a deep appreciation for a body that works well without pain. The human body is a masterpiece of divine engineering and should be properly maintained for health to serve God and our fellow man. Not only that, we are very familiar with the faces, the hands, the characteristics of the walk or smile of our friends and families. It is the body which identifies us in this physical world. And when someone dies and the body is left, we look at the shell and know how much it was the soul and spirit that made that person lovable to us. The body is not really the person, and yet, it was through the body that we related to one another. It is in this body, and this body only that we have the chance to secure eternal life and live the life of faith in Jesus Christ, and it was His body that bore our sins on the cross. In the resurrection, believers will receive perfect bodies with none of the weaknesses of mortality. We know that these immortal bodies will not be just like our earthly bodies, yet they will clearly be "ours," just as the body we wear now is "ours."

In the end, we can do no better than repeat Paul's prayer: "Now may the God of peace Himself sanctify you completely; and may your whole spirit, soul, and body be preserved blameless at the coming of our Lord Jesus Christ (1 Th 5:23).

See SOUL, HOLY SPIRIT, SPIRIT, SOUL and BODY.

SPIRIT, HOLY

See HOLY SPIRIT.

SPIRITS, FAMILIAR

See MAGIC, SORCERY, AND DIVINATION; and FAMILIAR SPIRIT.

SPIRITS IN PRISON

First Peter 3:19 says that Jesus "went and preached to the spirits in prison," describing them as "those who formerly were disobedient." This passage is somewhat puzzling, and several suggestions have been made for interpretations. One of these ideas is that Jesus went down to the grave (Sheol), and preached to the Old Testament saints who were awaiting the coming of the Messiah. However, the word for "spirit" in this passage is not the word typically used to refer to a human spirit. It seems that these "spirits in prison" are supernatural beings, probably the rebellious angels (see 2 Pe 2:4 and Jude 6).

SPIRITUAL

That which pertains to the nonmaterial realm.

SPIRITUAL BLESSINGS

See BLESS, BLESSINGS.

SPIRITUAL BODY

See BODY, GLORIFIED.

SPIRITUAL GIFTS

Special gifts given to all believers for the building up and edification of the church. Not every believer has all the gifts, but every believer has some gifts. The list includes wisdom, knowledge, faith, healing, miracles, prophecy, discerning of spirits, speaking in tongues, and interpretation of tongues (1 Co 12:8-10; Ep 4:7-13; Ro 12:3-8). All these gifts are valuable, and all should be respected and used to honor and glorify God. All gifts must be controlled by love (1 Co 13).

SPIT, SPITTLE

Saliva. The saliva of an unhealthy person was unclean (Le 15:8).

SPITE (archaic)

Vexation; anger; grief (Ps 10:12-14).

SPOIL

Booty, prey (Isaiah 8:4).

SPOKESMAN

One who speaks on behalf of another. Moses was afraid to speak, so God appointed Aaron to be his spokesman (Ex 4:14,16).

SPONGE

A peculiar sea animal with a very porous body. When harvested, the "skeleton" of the creature is a very soft, absorbent object. Sponges have been used since ancient times; when Jesus was on the cross someone offered him a sponge soaked in vinegar (Ma 27:48; Mk 15:36; Jo 19:29).

SPOONS

See PAN.

SPOT

Blemish, defect (1 Pe 1:19).

SPOUSE

A husband or wife. See MARRIAGE.

SPREAD OF THE GOSPEL

Philip and Peter, two of the original apostles of Jesus, were the first to preach the gospel throughout Palestine in the cities around Jerusalem in response to the command of Jesus, "You shall be witnesses to Me in Jerusalem, and in Judea and Samaria, and to the end of the earth" (Ac 1:8).

Phillip fled from persecution in Jerusalem to the city of Samaria, where many received Christ (Ac 8:4-13). Phillip also witnessed in the desert area south of Jerusalem to an official from Ethiopia, a Gentile, who believed and was baptized (Ac 8:26-39), and he preached in several cities along the Mediterranean coast—from Gaza to Caesarea—spreading the gospel south to north throughout Palestine (Ac 8:26,40). Peter worked miracles and preached the gospel in the cities of Lydda and Joppa (Ac 9:32-43). He also traveled from Joppa to Caesarea where Cornelius the Roman soldier and other Gentiles believed and were baptized (Ac 10:1-48). In later years, the apostle Paul became the Great Missionary to the Gentiles, proclaiming Christ in other nations throughout the Roman Empire.

SPRING
See FOUNTAIN.

SPRINKLING
A part of the ritual of consecration. Unclean objects were sprinkled with water, olive oil, or blood (Le 14:48-52; Nu 19:18-20; Le 3:7-8). The sprinkling of sacrificial blood for cleansing was a picture of the coming sacrifice of Christ (Is 52:15; He 9:13-14).

SPRINKLING BOWLS
Large bronze, gold, or silver bowls used in the temple service (2 Ki 12:6-14).

SQUAD
A group of four Roman soldiers (Ac 12:4,6).

STABLE
A building in which animals were kept. See STALL.

STACH′YS (ear of grain)
A Christian at Rome (Ro 16:9).

STAC′TE (drop)
A sweet spice, probably a fragrant gum used in making incense (Ex 30:34), perhaps from the storax tree.

STADION
One eighth of a Roman mile, or 606 feet. See WEIGHTS & MEASURES.

STAFF
See ROD.

STAG
A male deer. See DEER.

STAKES
See PEG.

STALL
The place where animals were kept. King Solomon had stalls for thousands of horses in his stables and all kinds of livestock (2 Ch 9:25; 32:28). In the New Testament, the word only occurs once, in Luke 2, and is usually translated "manger" rather than "stall."

STAN′DARD (archaic)
Flag; banner (Je 50:1-2).

STAR
It is not strange that the stars, on account of their number, and constellations, should have attracted the attention of the ancients (Ge 22:17; Is 13:10). In Job there is reference to Orion, Pleiades, the Bear, Mazzaroth-the Zodiac (Job 9:9; 38:31-32). With the exception of the sun and moon all heavenly bodies were designated stars by the Hebrews. They recognized the stars as the handiwork of God (Ps 8:3) and under his power (Is 13:10; Je 31:35). But apart from the ordinary observations of the heavens there is nothing in the Scriptures to show that the ancient Hebrews had any real knowledge of astronomy. Following the heathen nations, Israelites who left the pure worship of Jehovah, made the stars objects of worship (De 4:19; 2 Ki 17:16; 23:5). It was the belief of the heathen that the stars directly influenced human affairs, and it may be that Deborah in her song had something of this in mind when she spoke of the stars fighting against Sisera (Ju 5:20). The star in the East, of the wise men, the star of Bethlehem, guided the Magi to the Christ child (Ma 2:1-12). Jesus is spoken of as "the bright and morning star" (Re 22:16).

STARGAZER
See ASTROLOGY and MAGIC, SORCERY, AND DIVINATION.

STAR OF BETHLEHEM

The special star which led the wise men from the East to Bethlehem to find the King of the Jews (Ma 2:2,7,9-10). This may be the star of Balaam's prophecy in Nu 24:17.

STA'TER

A silver coin (also called the tetradrachma), worth four drachmas (Ma 17:27). See MONEY OF THE BIBLE.

STATURE

Height. The phrase "grew in stature" simply means growing taller (1 Sa 2:26; Lk 2:52). Zacchaeus, the little tax collector is described as being "short in stature" (Lk 19:3).

STATUTE

A law or commandment (Ge 26:5; Ps 18:22; Eze 5:6).

STAVE

See ROD.

STEADFASTNESS

Stability; unshakeable commitment (Col 2:5). Steadfastness is formed by "growing in grace and knowledge of our Lord and Savior" (2 Pe 3:1).

STEALTH

Secret, sly, undercover action. Paul told the Galatian believers that legalizers were infiltrating the body, trying to bring believers into bondage to the old law (Ga 2:4).

STEEL

Iron carbonized to give it hardness and elasticity. The melting point of iron is very high, so adequately smelting iron ore requires great heat. Iron oxide heated in a simple furnace does not get hot enough to completely melt both the metal and the slag, so the resulting mass is still very impure. Through working on an anvil, it can be improved, but it is still much softer than hardened bronze, and inadequate for weapons or edge tools. At some point it was discovered that by heating the iron mass to a red heat in a bed of charcoal, and keeping it at this temperature for a long period of time, the iron absorbed enough carbon to be much harder. This carbonized iron is known as "steel." Steel has a great advantage over iron because it can be significantly hardened by heating it to a red heat and then quenching it by plunging it into water or other coolant. The maximum degree of hardness is directly related to the amount of carbon alloyed with the iron. It is difficult to pinpoint dates for the discovery and perfection of steelmaking, but it is certain that it was known to the ancient Greeks at the time of the writing of the Odyssey. The blinding of Polyphemus is compared to the quenching of a red-hot steel blade. It is known that the Hittites were involved in the development of the iron and steel industry as far back as 1400 B.C. A letter exists from the Hittite king Hattusilis III (1275-1250 B.C.) mentioning an "iron dagger blade" which he was sending to a contemporary ruler. This was most probably a form of carbonized iron, since soft iron is not a very desirable material for edge tools. The Philistines began smelting iron about 1200 B.C.; they probably also made products of hardened steel. Steel is mentioned only a few times in the Old Testament, and while it is perfectly plausible to think that steel was available in some form, most translators believe that the words are better translated "bronze" (2 Sa 22:35; Job 20:24; Ps 18:34; Je 15:12).

STEPH'A·NAS (crowned)

A man of Corinth who was converted. He and his household were baptized by Paul, thus becoming the first of Paul's converts in Achaia. He was with Paul when he wrote the First Epistle to the Corinthians in Ephesus (1 Co 1:16; 16:15,17).

STE'PHEN (a crown)

His Greek name would indicate that he was a Hellenist but his birthplace is unknown. He is first mentioned in connection with his appointment as one of seven deacons of the church of Jerusalem (Ac 6:5). He was a man of great faith (Ac 6:8). The activities of Stephen aroused the opposition of foreign Jews who had synagogues in Jerusalem, beginning with the synagogue of the Libertines (freed men), the Cyrenians and Alexandrians. They charged Stephen with blasphemy. They claimed to have heard him say that Jesus would set aside the Mosaic institutions (Ac 6:11-14), and they arranged for false witnesses to testify against him (Ac 6:13). In his defense (Ac 7:2-60), he set forth God's selection of Israel for divine ends but he pointed out that the Israelites were often in opposition to God and his purpose. When he said that he saw Christ, they rushed upon him to kill him; with Saul of Tarsus holding the clothes of the mob, he was stoned to death. Stephen was the first Christian martyr.

STEWARD

The manager of a household or estate, a head servant (Ge 43:19; Ma 20:8; Ga 4:2).

STEWARDSHIP

The responsibility we have as believers to obey the Lord, and manage the work and resources of the church, with the goal of spreading the gospel (1 Co 9:17). Jesus's parable of the talents shows us that we will be held responsible for the way we manage the resources He gives us (Ma 25:14-30). We are expected to preach the gospel (Col 1:24-28) and care for the needy (Ma 25:31-46).

STIFF-NECKED

Stubborn, recalcitrant, arrogant, unyielding. This vividly descriptive phrase is used many times to describe the stubborn rebellion of the Israelites (De 31:27; Ne 9:16-17,29; Je 17:23).

STOCKS

A wooden frame in which the hands, feet and neck were firmly held, forcing the body into a bent and painful position (Job 13:27; 33:11; Ac 16:24).

STO'ICS (Greek *stoikos, of a porch*)

An adherent to a school of philosophy which believed that the best life is one lived in harmony with nature. They desired to be free of human passions, unaffected by either joy or grief, able to submit peacefully to everything that happened. People cannot change the natural order. They must instead learn to cooperate with it, and become identified with the "world-soul" which is "God," and which is in every-

STOCKS

thing. Stoicism emphasized self-sufficiency, lack of emotional involvement, and virtuous living. There were Stoics in Paul's audience at Athens (Ac 17:18).

STOM'A·CHER

An article of female clothing worn over the stomach or breast. It was apparently a wide girdle (Is 3:24).

STONE

A piece of detached rock. Palestine is a stony country—limestone, sandstone, marble, and flint can be found. Stone was particularly useful in ancient times as a building material. The Phoenicians were well-known for their ability to cut stone for building purposes (2 Sa 5:11). Stones were used in memorial pillars (Ge 28:18; 31:45; 35:14; Jos 4:9; 1 Sa 7:12). They were used to close the entrances to tombs (Ma 27:60; Jo 11:38) and caves (Jos 10:18; Da 6:17). The abundance of stones cleared from the fields provided an endless supply of ammunition. They could be thrown by hand, or hurled by means of catapults and slings with deadly accuracy (1 Sa 17:40,49; 2 Ch 26:14-15). Boundary marks and scale weights were normally made of stone (De 19:14; 25:13).

STONECUTTER

One who quarries stone, cutting it into manageable blocks (1 Ki 5:17; 6:7). The word of God is compared to a quarryman's hammer, capable of breaking stones into pieces (Je 23:29).

STONEMASON

One who dressed blocks of stone for building, shaping them, fitting them together, and making them into walls.

STONES, PRECIOUS

See PRECIOUS STONES.

STONEWORKER

Anyone who works with stone, as quarryman, mason, or sculptor. The Phoenicians were the skilled stoneworkers of the ancient world (2 Sa 5:11; 1 Ch 14:1). Stoneworkers, or "hewers of stone" also cut tombs, water tunnels, cisterns, and wine presses out of enormous chunks of stone. See STONECUTTER and STONEMASON.

STON'ING

This was the usual mode of inflicting capital punishment provided by the Mosaic law. The witnesses placed their hands on the head of the criminal to indicate he was the bearer of his guilt (Le 24:14), and the first stones were hurled by the witnesses (De 13:9; Jo 8:7). The law required death by stoning for eighteen different crimes including idolatry, wizardry, blasphemy, adultery, bestiality, and Sabbath breaking (Le 20:27; 24:16; Nu 15:32-36; De 17:2-5). The death penalty could not be enacted on the testimony of only one witness. If it was discovered that a person had lied in his testimony against his neighbor, he had to bear the same punishment he had thought to have done to the accused (De 17:6; 19:15-19).

STORAGE CITY, STOREHOUSE

A place where a government stores military supplies, food, and treasure (1 Ch 26:15; 27:25; 2 Ch 11:11).

When the Hebrews were slaves in Egypt, they were forced to build the supply cities of Pithom and Raamses (Ex 1:11). Solomon, Baasha, and Hezekiah all built storehouses or cities to accommodate their wealth (1 Ki 9:19; 2 Ch 8:4,6; 16:5-6; 17:12; 32:27-29).

The storage of food as advance preparation for bad times is an old practice. Joseph engineered the collection and storage of the abundant Egyptian harvests for seven years, in preparation for the seven lean years to follow (Ge 41).

STORK

A common bird of Palestine which was considered ceremonially unclean (Le 11:19; De 14:18). Its nesting places were in trees (Ps 104:17), chimneys, and ruins.

STOVE

See OVEN.

STRAIGHT STREET

The street of Damascus where Paul stayed after his blinding vision on the road leading to the city (Ac 9:11). Ananias visited him there, and laid hands on him, healing his blindness.

STRAN' GER

See SOJOURNER.

STRANGLED

Choked to death, asphyxiated. The Jews were forbidden to eat meat from strangled animals because the blood had not been shed, and blood was forbidden (Ge 9:4).

STRAW

The stalks of threshed grain (Ge 24:25; Ex 5:7; 1 Ki 4:28; Is 11:7). It was used as fodder for horses and cattle, and the Egyptians used it for brick making, mixing the chopped straw and clay (Ex 5:7,16).

STREAM

See BROOK.

STREET

A village or city thoroughfare. In the villages the streets were usually narrow, dirty, and crooked, and it was with difficulty that two packed camels passed each other. In some instances they were wide enough for a chariot to pass through (Je 17:25; Na 2:4). Men of the same trade usually lived along the same street, such as bakers' street (Je 37:21).

STRINGED INSTRUMENTS

A number of stringed instruments are mentioned in Scripture, such as the harp, lyre, lute, psaltery, viol and zither.

STRIPES

See SCOURGE.

STRONG DRINK

See DRINK, STRONG.

STUBBLE

The remnants of the grain stalks left in the field after the harvest. Because stubble is very dry, it burns quickly; a fire racing through a stubble field is used as an illustration of God's judgment upon the unrighteous (Ex 15:7; Joel 2:5; Job 41:29; 1 Co 3:12).

STUMBLING BLOCK

Something which causes another person to stumble. This word is used completely literally as God commanded the Israelites to treat the blind and deaf with gentleness (Le 19:14); it is also used in the sense of something which causes someone to stumble in a spiritual sense (Je 6:21; Zep 1:3). The cross is an offense and a stumbling block to the Jews; it is hard for them to believe because it seems offensive (1 Co 1:23). Christians are taught strongly to make sure that their own liberty does not become a stumbling block to anyone else. It is more important to protect your brother's conscience than to exercise your own freedom (1 Co 8:9).

SU' AH *(sweepings)*

A son of Zophah and head of the tribe of Asher (1 Ch 7:36).

SU' CA·THITE

See SUCHATHITE.

SUC' COTH *(booths)*

Two geographical locations:

1. The place of the first encampment of the Israelites after leaving Rameses in Egypt (Ex 12:37; 13:20; Nu 33:5-6). It is believed that this is the Hebrew name of the Egyptian Thuku, the chief city of the district.

2. A place east of the Jordan where Jacob, returning from Padan-aram, built a house with booths for his cattle (Ge 32:22; 33:17).

SUC' COTH-BE' NOTH

An idol set up in Samaria and worshipped by settlers from Babylon (2 Ki 17:30-31).

SU' CHA·THITE

A family of scribes at Jabez (1 Ch 2:55).

SUFFERING

In the Word of God there are four great examples of believers suffering for the sake of righteousness. These are Joseph, Job, Jeremiah, and Paul.

The sufferings of Joseph: He was hated by his brothers (Ge 37:4-5,8): he was sold into slavery (Ge 37:28); he was severely tempted (Ge 39:7); and he was imprisoned (Ge 39:20).

The sufferings of Job: His oxen and donkeys were stolen and his farmhands killed (Job 1:14-15); his sheep and herdsmen were burned by a fire (Job 1:16); his camels were stolen and his servants killed (Job 1:17); his sons and daughters died in a windstorm (Job 1:18-19); and he was struck with boils (Job 2:7).

The sufferings of Jeremiah: He was persecuted by his own family (Je 12:6); he was plotted against by his own hometown (Je 11:18-23); he was rejected and ridiculed by his religious peers (Je 20:1-3,7-9); and he was arrested, beaten, and accused of treason (Je 37:11-16).

The sufferings of Paul: He was plotted against

(Ac 9:23,29; 20:3; 21:30; 23:10,12; 25:3); he was stoned and left for dead (Ac 14:19); he was subjected to satanic pressure (1 Th 2:18); he was beaten and jailed at Philippi (Ac 16:19-24); he was ridiculed (Ac 17:16-18; 26:24); he was falsely accused (Ac 21:21,28; 24:5-9); he endured a number of violent storms at sea (2 Co 11:25; Ac 27:14-20); he was bitten by a serpent (Ac 28:3-4) and he was forsaken by all (2 Ti 4:10,16).

Each of these men would say with Joseph "You [men] meant evil against me, but God meant it for good" (Ge 50:20). God can take the most difficult circumstance and use it for His glory and to work out His likeness in the lives of believers.

SUFFERING SERVANT

See SERVANT OF JEHOVAH.

SUICIDE

A person putting an end to his or her own life. While this word does not occur in Scripture, several suicides are recorded (1 Sa 31:4-5; 1 Ki 16:18; Ma 27:5). There are no laws relating to suicide, because there is no civil punishment which could possibly apply. Since murder is clearly against God's law (Ex 20:13), and murderers will not be in heaven (Re 22:15), it is safe to assume that God does not look favorably upon suicide.

SUK' KI·IM

An African tribe which fought with the army of the Pharaoh, Shishak when he attacked Jerusalem during the reign of Rehoboam, king of Judah (2 Ch 12:3).

SUK' KITES

See SUKKIM.

SULPHUR

See BRIMSTONE.

SUMER

The fertile area between the Tigris and Euphrates Rivers; southern Babylonia. Today this area is the southern portion of Iraq. In the time of Abraham, this area was called Shinar (Ge 10:10; Is 11:11) or Chaldea (Je 50:10; Eze 16:29). The tower of Babel was built in the land of Shinar, or Sumer (Ge 11:2). One of its main cities was Ur of the Chaldees (Ge 11:28,31) where Abraham and his family lived before setting out for the promised land.

SUN

A radiant heavenly body around which the earth and other planets revolve. In the account of its creation it is described as "the greater light to rule the day" (Ge 1:16). It was referred to as the vital power bringing forth vegetation (De 33:14; 2 Sa 23:4) and it is represented in the same "language of apparency" that we use today. The Bible speaks of the sun rising and setting and moving across the sky (2 Ki 20:11; Ps 19:4-6; Hab 3:11). Joshua's request that the sun stay up until the Israelites defeated the Amorites was granted (Jos 10:12-13). Many of the peoples with whom the Israelites came in contact worshipped the sun. The Egyptian sun god was called Ra; the Phoenician, Baal; and the Assyrian, Shamash. In the time of the divided kingdom some of the Israelites built altars and burned incense to the sun (2 Ki 23:5). They also dedicated horses to it (2 Ki 23:11). In Malachi 4:2 the promised Messiah was called the "Sun of righteousness."

SUNDAY

See LORD'S DAY.

SUNDIAL OF AHAZ

See DIAL OF AHAZ.

SUPERSTITIOUS

Also translated "religious" (Ac 17:22), Paul's description of the Athenians who had an altar to every imaginable god, including an unknown one.

SUPH (reeds)

A place in the wilderness where Moses delivered his farewell address (De 1:1).

SU'PHAH

A place somewhere east of the Jordan, near Moab (Nu 21:14).

SUP'PER, Lord'S

See LORD'S SUPPER.

SUR

A gate of Solomon's temple, called "the gate of the foundation" (2 Ki 11:6; 2 Ch 23:5).

SUR'E·TY

One who assumes liability for the financial obligations of another. When Paul wrote his intercessory letter to Philemon on behalf of Onesimus, he declared he would protect Philemon against any loss he might sustain at the hands of his slave. He would go his security, he said (Phile 18). In being surety for the debt of another the hand was given the creditor in the presence of others with the promise that the debt would be paid if the debtor failed to meet his obligation (Pr 6:1-2; 17:18). Security was offered to assure a service would be rendered (Ge 44:32) and also in commercial matters to protect the credit granted. Jesus is our surety of a better covenant (He 7:22).

SURNAME

An additional name given because of a significant event or characteristic in the life of the person, a descriptive "nickname" (Mk 3:16-17).

SU'SA

See SHUSHAN.

SU·SAN'CHITES

See SHUSHANCHITES.

SU·SAN'NA (lily)

A woman who followed and ministered to Jesus (Lk 8:3).

SU'SI (a horseman)

Father of Gaddi, who represented the tribe of Manasseh when Moses appointed the twelve spies (Nu 13:11).

SWAD'DLING BAND, SWAD'DLING CLOTHES

The cloths with which newborn babies were wrapped. Very new infants like the secure feeling of being tightly wrapped. The proper treatment for newborn babies described in Ezekiel 16:4 included washing in water, rubbing with salt, and wrapping in swaddling clothes. Mary wrapped Jesus in this way, and the shepherds were told to look for a very new baby in swaddling clothes, lying in a manger (Lk 2:7,12).

SWAL'LOW

One of a family of birds including swifts and martins noted for their long wings, graceful flight, twittering note, and regular migrations (Ps 84:3; Pr 26:2; Is 38:14). The Hebrew word is also rendered "thrush" or "wryneck" (Je 8:7).

SWAN

A ceremonially unclean bird (Le 11:18; De 14:16); the Hebrew word is also translated "owl," "ibis," "stork," "water hen," and "white owl."

SWEARING

See OATH.

SWEAT

Perspiration, the system for cooling the body by evaporation. Humans sweat in excessive heat, due to hard work, and sometimes with emotion. Part of the curse included the change in the nature of work, making it a hard sweaty business to gain a living (Ge 3:19). The priests were supposed to wear lightweight linen garments which would not cause them to sweat (Eze 44:18).

In the garden of Gethsemane, as Jesus wrestled with the knowledge of His coming torture and agony, He prayed earnestly and "His sweat became like great drops of blood falling down to the ground" (Lk 22:44). It is not known for sure whether this description is meant to be taken figuratively or literally. A rare medical condition does exist, called *diapedesis*, in which blood actually passes through the intact walls of the capillaries, or through the mucous membranes without visible wounds.

SWELLING

One of the possible signs of leprosy which the priests were trained to diagnose (Le 13:2-43; 14:56).

SWIFT

A small bird, similar in appearance to a swallow. They are well named because they can fly extremely fast, even up to 100 mph (for a short distance). They migrate in season, and feed on flying insects (Je 8:7).

SWINE

A word used collectively, usually in regard to domestic hogs. Swine were ceremonially unclean (Le 11:7; De 14:8). Phoenicians, Ethiopians, and Egyptians regarded them as unclean as well, but the Egyptians did eat pigs at the time of their festival of the moongod. A swine-

herd was debarred from a temple, and his wife had to be from a family of swineherds. The Jews regarded pigs as the symbol of filth (Ma 7:6; 2 Pe 2:22). Christ's picture of the prodigal son clearly portrayed him in the lowest state to which a Jew could be reduced as he tended swine and wanted to eat their food (Lk 15:15). See also PIGS.

SWORD

A weapon with an iron or bronze blade, which was sometimes two-edged. It was worn in a scabbard on the left side (2 Sa 20:8; Eze 32:27). It was the symbol of war (Is 2:4).

SYC′A·MINE TREE

The black mulberry tree which grows to a height of twenty to thirty feet (Lk 17:6).

SYC′A·MORE

A genus of fig tree known as the sycamore fig, valued for its fruit, shade and timber (Ps 78:47; Is 9:10). Although scarce today, its former abundance in Palestine was proverbial (1 Ki 10:27; 2 Ch 1:15; 9:27). It may attain a height of fifty feet. Zacchaeus climbed an overhanging branch of a wayside sycamore in order to glimpse Jesus as he passed with the throng (Lk 19:4). Its fruit is edible. The farmer-prophet Amos tended the sycamore trees (Am 7:14).

SY′CHAR

A town in Samaria near Jacob's well (Jo 4:5).

SY′CHEM

See SHECHEM.

SYC′O·MORE

See SYCAMORE.

SY·E′NE

A town of Egypt, far in the south, near the border of Ethiopia (Eze 29:10; 30:6).

SYMEON

See SIMON.

SYN′A·GOGUE *(gathering together)*

A local assembly of Jews organized chiefly for worship; also its building or place of meeting. The word appears only once in the Old Testament (Ps 74:8) but repeatedly in the New Testament. The synagogue as a Jewish religious institution probably arose after the Israelites returned from exile in Babylon. The public readings of the law by Ezra the priest after the exiles resettled in Jerusalem (Ne 8) may have signaled the beginning of the movement that led to the development of the synagogue system.

The synagogue, as distinguished from the tabernacle and temple with their sacrifices, was a local gathering place where Jews of all ages met for prayer and study of the law of Moses. Scores of these synagogues sprang up in Jerusalem and surrounding cities during the two hundred years or so before the New Testament era. They were organized wherever ten or more men showed interest in preserving their Jewish customs and learning and obeying the law.

Synagogue worship included readings from the Law, prayers, and a commentary or sermon on the Bible passage. Any competent member of the congregation might be asked to read the Scriptures or bring the sermon. This privilege was apparently extended to Jesus in the synagogue at Nazareth early in His ministry. He read from the prophet Isaiah, identifying Himself as the Messiah whom Isaiah had prophesied hundreds of years before (Lk 4:16-30).

Several synagogue buildings, including one at the city of Capernaum, have been uncovered by archaeologists. These were generally rectangular structures with a large central seating area, much like a modern church building. The congregation sat on stone benches along the walls, or cross-legged on the floor. The main piece of furniture in a synagogue was the ark, where the sacred scrolls with the law were kept. The ark was placed along the wall nearest to the city of Jerusalem—the direction which the people faced during a synagogue service.

Synagogue life, as influenced by the rabbis who attached themselves to these local Jewish centers, came to dominate the religious thinking of the Jewish people during New Testament times. Each local synagogue had its own ruling group, which governed religious behavior among the Jews in that community.

The apostle Paul regularly proclaimed Christ at synagogues on his missionary journeys (Ac 13:5; 14:1). The emphasis of the synagogue on Scripture, prayer, and a sermon in worship has influenced the order of service used in most Christian churches today.

SYN′TY·CHE

A Christian woman of Philippi who seemed to be at variance with another woman named Euodia. Paul exhorted them to come to a state of harmony (Ph 4:2).

SYR′A·CUSE

A city of importance on the east coast of Sicily. On his voyage to Rome Paul touched at this port (Ac 28:12).

SYR′I·A

A somewhat indefinite region bounded in general by the Taurus Mountains, the Euphrates River, the Syrian and Arabian deserts, northern Palestine, and the Mediterranean (2 Sa 8:6; 15:8; Lk 2:2; Ac 15:23,41). Its political history is interwoven with the Assyrian, Babylonian, Persian, Greek, Roman, and Mohammedan empires.

SYR′I·AN

An inhabitant of Syria (Ge 28:5).

SY′RO·PHOE·NIC′I·AN

The racial designation in Mark 7:26 of a woman whose daughter was cured by Jesus. The name comes from the Roman combining of the nation of Phoenicia with the land of Syria, making its inhabitants Syro-Phoenicians. She was called a woman of Canaan in Matthew 15:22.

SYRTIS SANDS, THE

Syrtis Major, a dangerously shallow area off the African coast. A smaller area of shallows is further west. The ship which carried Paul to Rome was caught in a terrible storm, and the sailors feared they would run aground on these treacherous sandbars (Ac 27:17).

T

TA′A·NACH

A city of the Canaanites. Its king was one of those conquered by Joshua (Jos 12:21).

TA′A·NATH-SHI′LOH *(approach to Shiloh)*

A border town on the northern boundary of Ephraim (Jos 16:6).

TAB·BA′ OTH *(rings)*

A Nethinim. His descendants returned from Babylon with Zerubbabel (Ez 2:43; Ne 7:46).

TAB′ BATH

A place mentioned in connection with the defeat of the Midianites by Gideon (Ju 7:22).

TAB′ E·EL

1. Father of the man whom Pekah, king of Israel, and Rezin, king of Syria, intended to place on the throne of Judah in the place of Ahaz (Is 7:6). It was in this connection that Isaiah spoke the prophecy of the one to be born of a virgin.

2. A Persian official in Samaria (Ez 4:7).

TAB′ E·RAH *(burning)*

A place in the wilderness of Paran (Nu 11:1-3; De 9:22).

TA′ BER·ING

An obsolete word for beating a taber or small drum. In Nahum 2:7 it means the beating of the breast in anguish.

TABERNACLE

The tabernacle was a portable tent or sanctuary used by the Israelites as a place for worship during their early history. In the Old Testament, it is frequently called "the tent of meeting," indicating that it was the primary place of encounter between God and His people. The structure was built in accordance with God's instructions to Moses on Mount Sinai during their years of wandering in the Wilderness (Ex 26; 35). With the people contributing materials and labor, the tabernacle was completed to God's specifications. God blessed their handiwork by covering the tent with a cloud and filling the sanctuary with His glory (Ex 40:34).

The outer courtyard of the tabernacle was a fenced rectangle about 150 feet long by 75 feet wide (Ex 27:9-19). The courtyard contained a bronze altar for animal sacrifices (Ex 27:1-8) and a laver where the priests washed before entering the tent (Ex 30:17-21).

The tabernacle itself, measuring 15 by 45 feet, had two main sections: the outer room known as the holy place, and the inner room called the holy of holies, or most holy place (Ex 26:33).

The outer room contained an altar where an incense offering was burned (Ex 30:1-10), the seven-branched gold candlestick (Ex 25:31-40), and a table for showbread, signifying God's presence (Ex 25:23-30).

The inner room, or holy of holies, was separated from the outer area by a veil or curtain (Ex 26:31-37). This sacred part of the tabernacle was entered only once a year by the high priest on the Day of Atonement. In a special ceremony on this day, he made atonement for his own sins and then offered a sacrifice to atone for the sins of the people. This most sacred enclosure had only one item of furniture, the ark of the covenant.

The lid of the ark was called the mercy seat. Upon it were two gold cherubim that faced each other. The ark contained the stone tablets with the Ten Commandments (De 10:4-5), a gold pot filled with manna (Ex 16:33-34), and Aaron's rod that budded (Nu 17:10).

During the years when the people of Israel were wandering in the wilderness, the tabernacle was moved with them from place to place (Ex 40:36-38). When the Israelites pitched camp in the wilderness, the tabernacle was to be placed in the center, with the Levites, who were charged with its care (Nu 4), camping next to it (Nu 1:53). Then the tribes were to be arrayed in specific order on the four sides of the tabernacle (Nu 2). This shows what an important role the tabernacle played in the religious life of God's people.

After the conquest of Canaan, the tabernacle was moved to Shiloh, where it remained through the period of the judges (Jos 18:1). Later the tabernacle was also stationed at Nob (1 Sa 21:1-6) and Gibeon (1 Ki 3:4). When the temple was completed, Solomon had the tabernacle moved to Jerusalem (1 Ki 8:4). Apparently there was no further need for the tabernacle after the completion of the temple, which became the permanent place of worship for the nation and the center of its religious life.

The many references to the tabernacle in the New Testament should be understood in light of the incarnation, when God's Son became a human being. Because the tabernacle was the place where God and His people met, John declared that the Word had become flesh and "tabernacled" among us" (Jo 1:14; the Greek word is translated "dwelt" in the KJV). Paul spoke of Christ as the "propitiation" for sin in Romans 3:25. He used the same Greek word that referred to the mercy seat of the ark where the high priest made annual atonement. The laver where priests washed before serving in the tabernacle may be reflected in Titus 3:5 ". . . according to His mercy He has saved us, through the washing of regeneration and renewing of the Holy Spirit."

Revelation 8:3-5 speaks of the golden incense altar. Practically every feature of the tabernacle is found in the Epistle to the Hebrews, a book that describes Jesus as the great High Priest and the ultimate and eternal sacrifice for our sins.

TABERNACLE OF MEETING

The tent which Moses set up outside the camp to serve as a sanctuary until the tabernacle could be completed to God's specifications (Ex 33:7). The finished tabernacle was also called by this name; it indicated the fact that this tent was the place where God met with His people (Ex 27:21; 38:8).

TABERNACLE OF THE CONGREGATION

See TABERNACLE OF MEETING.

TABERNACLES, FEAST OF

One of the three great annual festivals at which the men of Israel were required to appear (De 16:16; 2 Ch 8:12-13; Ze 14:16). During this time, the celebrants lived in tents (tabernacles) in commemoration of the period of wandering in the wilderness (Le 23:40-42).

TABITHA

See DORCAS.

TABLE

An article of furniture. Part of the furnishing of the tabernacle included a table made of acacia wood, covered in gold. The showbread was placed on this table inside the tent (Ex 25:23-30; Nu 3:31; He 9:2). A similar golden table was made for the temple in Jerusalem (1 Ki 7:48). The Scripture also refers to the altar as the Lord's table (Mal 1:7,12).

Tables have been used for serving food for thousands of years (Ju 1:7; Is 28:8). The word "table" is often used as a blanket term for meals, food, or provisions (2 Sa 9:7-13; 1 Ki 2:7; 4:27). One step further from the literal meaning "table" is used figuratively for God's provision and care for His people (Ps 23:5).

TABLET

A flat piece of stone, soft clay, or wood coated with wax which was used as a writing surface

(Eze 4:1; Lk 1:63). The Ten Commandments were carved onto tablets of stone (Ex 24:12; De 10:1-5). The Bible also speaks figuratively of the "tablets of the heart," a metaphor which pictures the way both sin and relationship with God will leave an indelible mark on our lives (Pr 3:3; Je 17:1; 2 Co 3:3).

TA' BOR

1. A mountain in the plain of Esdraelon and on the boundary of Issachar, conical in shape, about thirteen hundred feet high. It is about twelve miles north of Mount Gilboa and six miles southeast of Nazareth. While a notable mountain (Ps 89:12), it is greatly inferior in size to Hermon. Here the forces of Barak gathered for the conflict with Sisera (Ju 4:6,12,14), and here the Midianite kings killed Gideon's brothers (Ju 8:18-19). Mount Tabor is on the adjoining borders of Issachar, Zebulun, and Naphtali. Hosea the prophet speaks of judgment to fall upon Israel and Judah because they had been "a net spread on Tabor" (Ho 5:1). From this it may be construed that a sanctuary for pagan worship may have been situated on this mountain.

2. The terebinth or plain of Tabor (1 Sa 10:3), a place located in the territory of Benjamin, and mentioned in connection with Saul's journey homeward after Samuel met him and anointed him as the first king of Israel.

3. A town of Zebulun assigned to the Levites of the Merari family (1 Ch 6:77).

TAB' RET

A musical instrument (1 Sa 10:5). See TIMBREL.

TAB·RIM' MON

Father of Ben-hadad, king of Syria (1 Ki 15:18; Tabrimon, KJV).

TACHE

A clasp for holding together the curtains of the tabernacle (Ex 26:6,11).

TACH' MO·NITE

Josheb-basshebeth, one of David's mighty men, is called "the Tachmonite (2 Sa 23:8; also Tachemonite or Tahkemonite). Some believe that this should read "Hachmonite," because the corresponding list of David's mighty men in 1 Chronicles lists a man with a very similar name: "Jashobeam the son of a Hachmonite." See HACHMONI.

TACKLE, TACKLING

The rigging and gear of a sailing ship (Is 32:23; Ac 27:19).

TAD′ MOR *(palm)*

A city built by Solomon in the wilderness (1 Ki 9:18; 2 Ch 8:4). It was a part of the northeastern border of his empire, about 120 miles northeast of Damascus and strategically situated on both the north-south and east-west trade routes of Canaan and Mesopotamia. After Solomon's death, and the shrinking of the kingdom, Tadmor passed into the hands of other rulers. The Greeks and Romans called the city Palmyra; it was eventually destroyed by Rome in the third century A.D. and remains an impressive ruin.

TA′ HAN

The head of a tribal family of Ephraim (Nu 26:35), and ancestor of Joshua son of Nun (1 Ch 7:25-27).

TA′ HAN·ITES

The descendants of Ephraim's son Tahan (Nu 26:35).

TA·HAP·AN′ ES

See TAHPANHES.

TA′ HASH

See THAHASH.

TA′ HATH

Three men and a geographical location of the Old Testament:

1. A place where the Israelites encamped in the wilderness (Nu 33:26-27).

2. A Levite of the family of Kohath. He was the son of Assir and the father of Uriel (1 Ch 6:22,24).

3. Son of Bered of Ephraim (1 Ch 7:20).

4. Son of Eladah and probably grandson of the preceding (1 Ch 7:20).

TAH′ CHE·MON·ITE

See TACHMONITE.

TAH′ KE·MON·ITE

See TACHMONITE.

BLOCK AND TACKLE

TAH′ PAN·HES

A city of Egypt on the Nile. After the assassination of Gedaliah, many of the Jewish remnant fled from the Chaldeans. In spite of Jeremiah's advice, they went to Tahpanhes in Egypt, and they forced Jeremiah to come with them (Je 2:16; 43:7-9; 44:1; 46:14; Eze 30:18). Some seem to have settled there permanently.

TAH′ PE·NES

A queen of Egypt whose sister became the wife of Hadad, a descendant of the king of Edom and the adversary of Solomon (1 Ki 11:18-25).

TAH′ RE·A

See TAREA.

TAH′ TIM-HOD′ SHI

A region between Gilead and Dan-jaan (2 Sa 24:6), mentioned in the description of King David's census of the fighting men of Israel.

TALEBEARER

A gossip is one who tells damaging stories about others (Pr 18:8). Such talk is enjoyable at the time, but creates harm which is unseen at first. See WHISPERERS.

TAL′ ENT

An ancient weight and money unit, equivalent to 3,000 shekels. The common shekel was equal to about 75 lbs., the royal shekel was about 150 lbs. See WEIGHTS AND MEASURES.

TALENTS, PARABLE OF (Ma 25:14-30)

TAL′ I·THA CU′ MI

An Aramaic expression which means, "Little girl, arise" (Mk 5:41).

TAL′ MAI *(furrowed)*

Two men of the Old Testament:

1. Descendant of Anak (Nu 13:22; Jos 15:14; Ju 1:10).

2. A king of Geshur, whose daughter Maacah was a wife of David and the mother of Absalom (2 Sa 3:3; 13:37). His kingdom was in Bashan.

TAL´MON *(oppressed)*

The head of a family of porters (1 Ch 9:17).

TALMUD

The interpretation and commentary on the Jewish law, compiled by Jewish rabbis between 250 and 500 B.C. The word means, "study" or "learning."

After the captivity and return to Jerusalem, it seems that some Jews at least, had learned their lesson about following pagan gods and ignoring God's laws. During the intertestamental period, two sects of Judaism were developed: the Pharisees and the Sadducees. The Pharisees were particularly interested in the study and interpretation of the Mosaic law. By the time of Christ, oral tradition included numerous regulations which are not in the Mosaic law. It seems that these regulations had come to be regarded as equal to Scripture, and Jesus rebuked the Pharisees for their devotion to petty laws while ignoring the heart issues (Ma 15:3-20).

All of these additional regulations were collected in a book called the Mishna. The Talmud is essentially an exhaustive response and detailed clarification of the Mishna. It fills many volumes and deals with everything, including agriculture, feasts and festivals, rules concerning food, purity, marriage, temple sacrifices, and much more.

TA´MAH

See TEMAH.

TA´MAR *(a palm tree)*

Three Old Testament women and a place:

1. The wife of Er, son of Judah. After the death of Er she became the mother of Perez and Zarah by Judah (Ge 38:6-30). From them several tribal families sprang (Nu 26:20-21). She is an ancestress of the family of Jesus (Ma 1:3).

2. The sister of Absalom who was violated by her half brother, Amnon (2 Sa 13).

3. A daughter of Absalom, probably named after Absalom's sister (2 Sa 14:27).

4. A place on the southern border of the land promised Ezekiel by the Lord (Eze 47:19).

TAM´A·RISK TREE

A small tree, having small leaves which it sheds at maturity. There are several species in Palestine, the largest of which attains a height of from twenty to thirty feet. One was planted by Abraham in Beer-sheba (Ge 21:33). Tamarisk trees or groves provided shady resting places for travelers (1 Sa 22:6).

TAMBOURINE

See TIMBREL.

TAM´MUZ

1. A deity worshipped by Babylonians, Assyrians, and Phoenicians. Ezekiel speaks of the women "weeping for Tammuz" (Eze 8:14). In his vision they were at the gate of the temple in Jerusalem. The wife of this deity was the goddess Ishtar. Tammuz was the god of flocks and of shepherds.

2. The fourth month of the Jewish sacred year, tenth month of the civil year. It corresponded roughly with June/July.

TA´NACH

See TAANACH.

TAN·HU´METH *(consolation)*

The father of Seraiah, a Netophathite (2 Ki 25:23; Je 40:8).

TAN´NER

One who prepared animal skins for use as clothing or other purposes. Peter lodged with a tanner in Joffa (Ac 9:43; 10:6,32). See LEATHER.

TAPESTRY MAKER

See WEAVING.

TA´PHATH

A daughter of Solomon. Her husband was Ben-abinadab (1 Ki 4:11).

TAP´PU·AH *(an apple)*

A man and two towns of the Old Testament:

1. A son of Hebron of the line of Caleb (1 Ch 2:43).

2. A town on the border of Manasseh and Ephraim (Jos 16:8; 17:7-8).

3. A town in the Shephelah (lowland) of Judah (Jos 15:34.)

TAR

See ASPHALT and BITUMEN.

TA′RAH

See TERAH.

TAR′A·LAH

A town of Benjamin (Jos 18:27).

TAR′E·A

A descendant of Saul through Jonathan (1 Ch 8:35; also called Tahrea, 1 Ch 9:41).

TARES

A weed, or bearded darnel, that in the blade state looked very similar to wheat. However, when the wheat was in the ear, the weeds looked quite dissimilar and could be easily separated during harvest. Since the grain was being cut down, the tares could be uprooted and discarded without being in danger of also pulling up the surrounding wheat (Ma 13:25-30). Jesus used the picture of tares among the wheat to illustrate the evil which is mixed into this world, and which will not be separated until the end of the age.

TARES AMONG THE WHEAT, PARABLE OF (Ma 13:24-30,36-43)

TAR′PE·LITES

A people which Shalmaneser of Assyria settled in Samaria after the Israelites were taken captive (Ez 4:9), also called "men from Tripolis" (NIV).

TAR′SHISH

1. Son of Javan, grandson of Japheth, and great-grandson of Noah (Ge 10:4; 1 Ch 1:7; also called Tarshishah).

2. Son of Bilhan of Benjamin (1 Ch 7:10).

3. A prince of Persia in the time of Xerxes I (Es 1:14).

4. The city of Tarshish, often mentioned in the Old Testament. It was on the Mediterranean, and a considerable distance from Palestine (Is 66:19; Jon 1:3). From this city the Phoenicians imported silver, iron, tin, and lead (Eze 27:12).

TARSHISHA

See TARSHISH No.1.

TAR′SUS

The capital of Cilicia, on the river Cydnus in Asia Minor (Ac 9:30; 11:25; 21:39; 22:3). This city was the birthplace of Paul the apostle (Ac 21:39; 22:3; Ac 9:11).

Located in a strategic area, protected by the Taurus Mountains, with easy access to the Mediterranean, and close to a good trade route, Tarsus was an important city. During its history it was under the control of numerous empires, but in the second century B.C. it became a free city. It was a center for culture, art, and education in the Roman world (Ac 21:39).

TAR′TAK

An idol worshipped by the Avvites in Samaria (2 Ki 17:31).

TAR′TAN

A title of the commander-in-chief of the Assyrian army (2 Ki 18:17; Is 20:1).

TASKMASTER

A slave driver or overseer. See OVERSEER.

TASSEL

The Mosaic law required that a tassel be attached to each of the four corners of a robe (De 22:12). Presumably, these tassels were a symbol of their "differentness," to remind them that they were a people set apart to do the will of God.

TAT′TE·NAI

A Persian governor who opposed the plan of Zerubbabel and others to build the second temple (Ez 5:3,6; 6:6,13).

TATTOO

A permanent mark on the skin, made by injecting tiny amounts of indelible dye just under the skin's surface. Apparently, pagans tattooed themselves as mark of mourning or respect for the dead. God commanded the Hebrews not to indulge in any such practices (Le 19:28).

TAU

The twenty-second letter of the Hebrew alphabet. It is the heading of verses 169-176 of Psalm 119. In Hebrew each of these eight verses begins with the letter tau. See ACROSTIC.

TAUNT SONG

A by-word of mockery and contempt; the target of scorn (Job 30:9).

TAVERNS, THREE

See THREE INNS.

TAWNY OWL
See OWL.

TAX COLLECTOR

A man who was employed by the Roman government to collect taxes. The Jews who worked in this capacity were universally despised. They had a reputation for cheating their brothers by demanding more than the law required and pocketing the excess. Besides this, the more zealous Jews considered them traitorous for assisting a foreign government in the oppression of their own people.

Jesus broke the traditional social stigma, and not only associated with tax-collectors, but also chose one of them for a close friend (Ma 9:9). He ate with them, showed love to them, and many believed in Him (Mk 2:16; Lk 19:9).

TAX COLLECTOR AND PHARISEE, PARABLE OF (Lk 18:9-14)

TAXES

When the Israelites became settled in Palestine, taxation took on an organized form. In the time of the judges, the Jews were obliged to pay tithes and the redemption money of the firstborn. The tabernacle and priesthood were thus provided for and also the Levites. Under the monarchy, to meet the greater expenditure, heavier taxes were imposed by Solomon on livestock and products of the field (1 Ki 4:7-28). Other peoples under the domination of the Israel were required to pay tribute (2 Sa 8:6,14; 1 Ki 10:15; 2 Ki 3:4). These measures became oppressive and contributed largely to the division of the kingdom under Rehoboam (1 Ki 12:4). Under the Persians, the Jews were heavily taxed in addition to taxes levied for their own national interests (Ne 5:4; 9:37). The same was true of the taxes levied by the Egyptians and Syrian kings. At this time, and during the Roman period, taxes were collected by a member of a company which purchased the right from the government to collect taxes in a certain region. Called publicans in the Roman period, these men were hated by the people because of their harsh methods. During the reign of Julius Caesar (about 45 B.C.) the system of tax collection was reformed. Taxes were lowered, and no taxes were required during the sabbatical years. However, the Herods reinstituted a heavier tax. It has been estimated that the Jews of the New Testament era were pay-

ing something on the order of 30 to 40 percent of their incomes in taxes, including their tithes and religious taxes.

The KJV translation of Luke 2:1 says that Caesar Augustus had decreed that the whole world should be taxed. Other translations have rendered this more correctly as "registered," but it is very likely that the purpose of this registration was to compile information for levying taxes. Whatever the reason, and however little Caesar Augustus may have realized it, this census was God's means for bringing Mary and Joseph into Bethlehem at the right time so that the prophecies concerning the birth of Christ might be fulfilled (Mi 5:2; Ma 2:5-6; Lk 2:1-20).

TEACHERS OF THE LAW
See SCRIBES.

TE′ BAH (slaughter)

The son of Nahor and his concubine Reumah (Ge 22:24).

TEB·A·LI′ AH (Jehovah has purified)
The son of Hosah (1 Ch 26:11).

TE′ BETH

The tenth month of the Hebrew sacred year (Es 2:16), and fourth month of the civil year. It corresponds roughly with December/January.

TEETH
See TOOTH.

TE·HAPH′ NE·HES
See TAHPANHES.

TE·HIN′ NAH (grace)

A descendant of Chelub and founder of the city of Ir-nahash (1 Ch 4:12).

TEIL TREE

The rendering in the Authorized Version of terebinth (Is 6:13). See OAK and TEREBINTH.

TE′ KEL
See MENE, MENE, TEKEL, UPHARSIN.

TE·KO′ A

A town of Judah about six miles south of Bethlehem (2 Ch 20:20). In the period of the divided kingdom it was fortified by Rehoboam (2 Ch 11:6).

The prophet Amos lived here until he was called to Beth-el to prophesy for Israel (Am 1:1).

TE·KO′ AH

See TEKOA.

TE′ KO·ITE

A native of Tekoa (2 Sa 23:26; 1 Ch 11:28; 27:9).

TEL-A′ BIB *(hill of grain)*

A place in Babylon on the river Chebar. Ezekiel and some of the captives were settled there (Eze 3:15).

TE′ LAH *(breach)*

A descendant of Ephraim (1 Ch 7:25).

TE·LA′ IM *(young lambs)*

A place where Saul mustered his troops before his fight with the Amalekites (1 Sa 15:4).

TEL′ AS·SAR *(hill of Asshur)*

A city in the northwestern part of Mesopotamia (2 Ki 19:12; Thelasar, KJV).

TE′ LEM *(oppression)*

1. A town on the southern border of Judah (Jos 15:24), possibly the same as Telaim.

2. A porter of the temple who renounced his foreign wife (Ez 10:24).

TEL-HAR′ ·ESH·A

See TEL-HARSHA.

TEL-HAR′ SA

See TEL HARSHA.

TEL-HAR′ SHA

A town of Babylonia from which some Jews returned to Palestine (Ez 2:59; Ne 7:61; Tel Harsa, KJV).

TELL

The mound of an ancient ruined city. In the ancient Middle East, when a city was destroyed or fell into decay, it was common to build another city directly on top of it. These mounds grew as successive settlements built on the ruins of their predecessors, and the tells of many ancient cities have been excavated by archaeologists. The prophet Jeremiah foretold that the Ammonite's chief city would become a "desolate mound," that is, a permanent ruin, because of their sins.

TELL EL AMARNA

See AMARNA.

TEL-ME′ LAH *(hill of salt)*

A place in Babylonia (Ez 2:59; Ne 7:61).

TE′ MA

1. A son of Ishmael (Ge 25:15; 1 Ch 1:30).

2. A town or district about 200 miles north of Medina (Job 6:19; Is 21:14; Je 25:23).

TE′ MAH

Head of a family of Nethinim (Ez 2:53; Ne 7:55; Thamah, KJV).

TE′ MAN *(the south)*

1. Son of Eliphaz, grandson of Esau (Ge 36:11), and a chief of Edom (Ge 36:15; 1 Ch 1:36).

2. A tribe and their district in northeast Edom (Ge 36:34). The members of the tribe were noted for their wisdom (Je 49:7,20) and were mentioned by several prophets (Eze 25:13; Am 1:12; Ob 9; Hab 3:3).

3. Another chief of Edom (Ge 36:42; 1 Ch 1:53).

TE′ MAN·I

See TEMANITE.

TE′ MAN·ITE

A member of the tribe of Teman or inhabitant of the land (Ge 36:34; Temani, KJV). Eliphaz, one of the friends with whom Job debated, was a Temanite (Job 2:11).

TE′ ME·NI

A son of Ashur and Naarah and founder of the town of Tekoa (1 Ch 4:5-6).

TEMPERANCE

Refraining from excess; self-control over physical or sensual desires. One who is running a race must be temperate in all things in order to run well (1 Co 9:24-27). This term has come to be particularly associated with the consumption of alcoholic beverages, but it should be understood to also apply to food, physical comfort, sexual pleasures, or any other physical or sensual desires.

TEMPLE

The temple, located in Jerusalem, was the center of the religious life of the Jewish people. In this sanctuary devoted to worship of the one true

God, priests offered sacrifices to God to atone for the sins of the nation of Israel. Through temple services, the Jewish people pledged their lives to follow the laws and teachings of their creator.

Before the temple was built, the tabernacle was used as a place of worship by the Hebrew people. During much of their history, the tabernacle was moved from place to place to accompany the nation of Israel in their wanderings (Ex 40). But after they settled in their permanent home in the land of promise, God commanded through His servant David that the temple be constructed. This more ornate structure, devoted to worship, would be a permanent fixture in their capital city (1 Ch 28).

Three separate temples were actually built in Jerusalem across a period of about a thousand years in Jewish history. All three were built on the same site—on a hill known as Mount Moriah in the eastern section of the holy city (2 Ch 3:1).

The first temple, built by King Solomon about 960 B.C., stood on a platform about ten feet high with ten steps leading to an entrance flanked by two stone pillars. Thousands of common laborers and skilled craftsmen were involved in its construction (1 Ki 6–7; 2 Ch 3–4). This building was destroyed by the Babylonians when they captured Jerusalem in 586 B.C. But Cyrus, king of Persia, authorized reconstruction of this building on the same site when he allowed the Jewish people to return to Jerusalem (Ez 1). This structure, known as Zerubbabel's temple, was completed about 515 B.C. at the urging of the prophets Haggai and Zechariah (Ez 6:13-15).

Several centuries later, Herod the Great, Roman ruler of Palestine, ordered construction of the third temple—an ornate, cream-colored building of stone and gold—to appease the Jewish people. This temple was the structure to which Jesus referred in speaking of His resurrection (Jo 2:19-20). As He predicted, this temple was destroyed by the Romans about 40 years after His resurrection and ascension—in A.D. 70.

The accounts of Solomon's temple in the Old Testament suggest it had an inner courtyard, as well as an outer courtyard. The three main objects in the inner courtyard were (1) the bronze altar used for burnt offerings (1 Ki 8:22,64; 9:25); (2) the sea of cast bronze, which held water for ritual washings by the priests (1 Ki 7:23-26); and (3) twelve oxen, apparently also cast bronze, which held the sea of bronze on their backs (1 Ki 7:25).

In the inner courtyard was an area known as the holy place, which contained the golden incense altar, the table with showbread, five pairs of lampstands, and utensils used for offering sacrifices (1 Ki 7:48-50). Beyond this area was a room known as the most holy place, or the holy of holies, a restricted place which only the high priest could enter. Even he could go into this area only once a year—on the Day of Atonement when he went inside to make atonement for his own sins and then for the sins of the people (Le 16). In this room was the ark of the covenant, containing the stone tablets on which the Ten Commandments were written. God's presence was manifested in the most holy place as a cloud (1 Ki 8:5-11).

Jesus related to the temple in several ways. He showed respect for the temple and referred to it as "My Father's House" (Jo 2:16). His zeal led Him to purge the temple of merchants who were selling sacrificial animals, thus defiling the "house of prayer" (Mk 11:15-17). But as much as He respected the house of God, Jesus also taught that He was greater than the temple (Ma 12:6).

His superiority to the temple was clearly shown when the veil of the temple was split from top to bottom at His death (Ma 27:51). The veil hung before the most sacred place in the temple to keep out all persons except the Jewish high priest. The tearing of the veil symbolized that every believer has unhindered access to God through His Son Jesus Christ because of His sacrificial death on our behalf.

TEMPLE SHEKEL

Equal to 20 gerahs (about 0.4 oz), the same as the common shekel (Ex 30:13; Eze 45:12). It is thought that the term "temple shekel" came into use because the standard of weight was kept in the sanctuary.

TEMPTATION

Temptation by the flesh: *Flesh* in the Bible often means something other than the substance of the human body. It is used constantly to refer to the carnal, sinful principle within man that is opposed to God (Ro 8:7). The actions produced by the flesh are given in detail in Galatians 5:19-21. Among these are all types of sexual immorality, impurity, hatred, anger, false religions, envy, and drunkenness. A person whose life is characterized by these sins cannot be a true Christian and is under the wrath of God (Ep 2:3).

Though the flesh is not eradicated for the Christian, he does not have to obey it (Ro 7:15-25). He possesses a new nature empowered by the Holy Spirit. Since the flesh and the Spirit are totally opposed to each other, the one whom the believer allows to dominate him will take charge in his life and produce its own fruit. The solution to the urges of the flesh lies in acknowledging that the power of sin was nullified by Jesus's death (Ro 6:11) and in living under the control of the Spirit's power (Ga 5:16). The believer must choose by an act of his will to benefit from the Spirit's enablement.

Temptation by Satan: The role of Satan against the Christian is well summed up by the meaning of the name Satan—"adversary." He is also called "the devil," meaning "accuser." He can appear as a hideous dragon (Re 12:3-4,9) or as a beautifully deceptive "angel of light" (2 Co 11:4). He stands hatefully opposed to all the work of God and resourcefully promotes defiance among men (Mk 4:15; Job 2:4,5).

When Satan sinned he was expelled from heaven (Lk 10:18), although apparently he still had some access to God (Job 1:6). A multitude of angels cast in their lot with him in his fall and subsequently became the demons mentioned often in the Bible (Ma 12:24; Re 12:7). Although Satan's doom was secured by Jesus's death on the cross (Jo 16:11), he will continue to hinder God's program until he and his angels are cast into the lake of fire (Ma 25:41; Re 20:10).

The terrifying work of Satan in the unbeliever is described in Scripture as follows: he blinds their minds (2 Co 4:4), he takes the Word of God from their hearts (Lk 8:12), and he controls them (Ac 13:8). In regard to Christians, Satan may accuse them (Re 12:10), devour their testimony for Christ (1 Pe 5:8), deceive them (2 Co 11:14), hinder their work (1 Th 2:18), tempt them to immorality (1 Co 7:5), and even be used by God to discipline Christians (1 Co 5:5; 2 Co 12:7).

TEMPTATION OF CHRIST

After His baptism, Jesus went into the wilderness and fasted forty days and forty nights. At the end of this time, Satan came to tempt Him (Ma 4:1-13; Mk 1:12-13). Satan's temptation came in three parts:

1. The temptation to prove divine power and satisfy physical hunger by a miracle: "If you are the Son of God, make these stones bread."
2. The temptation to prove His divine Sonship, and gain a following by flinging Himself from the temple and being miraculously saved by angels: "If you are the Son of God, throw Yourself down."
3. The temptation to gain possession of the kingdoms of the world without the suffering, by worshipping Satan: "All these things I will give You if You will fall down and worship me."

Hebrews 4:15 says, "For we do not have a High Priest who cannot sympathize with our weaknesses, but was in all points tempted as we are, yet without sin." Jesus's temptation was a part of His humanness.

Many have wondered how Jesus, as God, could be tempted, or if He was tempted, how He could still be Holy God. If, on the other hand, the temptation was effortlessly turned aside, because of His Deity, how can He genuinely sympathize with temptable humanity?

It is important for us to remember that temptation is not sin. Giving in to temptation is sin. Perfect man is temptable. God cannot be tempted with evil. Jesus Christ is fully God and fully man, therefore He could be tempted without falling into sin.

Two views express this truth: *Pase non picar* (able not to sin); and *non pase picar* (not able to sin). These two ideas have slightly different implications, but the point is the same: Jesus withstood the temptation and did not sin. It is doubtless best to state this truth with the second statement: Jesus was not able to sin. It is also true that the other applies in a way to His humanity. Being God, He could not sin; being man, His humanity could be tempted. One could also say that because He was God He was able to withstand temptation.

The account of the temptation of Jesus gives us some important insight into resisting temptation. When Satan tempted, Jesus responded with Scripture which was perfectly applicable to the temptation. Ephesians tells us to take up the "sword of the Spirit, which is the word of God" (Ep 6:17). The psalmist wrote, "Your word I have hidden in my heart, that I might not sin against You" (Ps 119:11). A thorough working knowledge of God's word is our best defensive weapon against the onslaught of Satan's temptation. With this powerful aid, we are not battling an enemy too strong for us. James 4:7 promises that if we submit to God, and resist the devil, the devil will flee from us.

TEN COMMANDMENTS

The Ten Commandments (Ex 20:1-17; De 5:6-21) were laws given by God as guidelines for daily living. Although God gave the commandments to His people through Moses at Mt. Sinai more than three thousand years ago, they are still relevant today. These laws are also known as the Decalogue, from the Greek word meaning "ten words."

The Ten Commandments are divided into two sections. The first four Commandments govern our relationship to God, while Commandments five through ten speak of our relationship to other people. The Ten Commandments are summarized below:

1. You shall have no other gods before Me. [There is only one God].
2. You shall not make for yourself any carved image or bow down to them or serve them. [No idol worship].
3. You shall not take the name of the LORD your God in vain. [No cursing or using His name as an expletive.]
4. Remember the Sabbath Day to keep it holy. [God rested on the seventh day after creation, and God's people should rest and honor the Lord once a week also].
5. Honor your father and mother. [This is the commandment with the promise, "so that it will go well with you".]
6. You shall not murder. [This addresses vengeance as well as the sacredness of human life.]
7. You shall not commit adultery. [God is faithful in His relationships and his people must be also.]
8. You shall not steal. [Where there is stealing there can be no trust.]
9. You shall not bear false witness against your neighbor. [No lying.]
10. You shall not covet. [Be satisfied with what you have.]

About 1,300 years after God gave these Commandments, Jesus upheld them (Ma 5-7). He actually placed these laws on a higher plane, explaining that the spirit, as well as the legal aspect of the laws must be obeyed. Hating someone is linked with murder; God intended marriage to be for life, even if you have a "legal" right to divorce. Lust is linked with adultery. He goes on to say, "Love your enemies, bless those who curse you, do good to those who hate you, and pray for those who spitefully use you and persecute you. . . . you shall be perfect, just as your Father in heaven is perfect" (Ma 5:44,48).

TENDER HEARTED

An attitude of love, kindness, forgiveness, and humility in regard to others; the direct opposite of malice, envy, strife and bitterness (Ep 4:32; also see Ge 43:30; Ph 1:8).

TEN PLAGUES

Pharaoh, the ruler of Egypt, refused to release the Hebrew people from slavery and allow them to leave his country. So the Lord sent ten plagues upon the Egyptians to break Pharaoh's stubborn will, not only to demonstrate His power and superiority over the pagan gods of the Egyptians, but also to establish His ability and His right to take his chosen people from bondage. The Hebrews needed to see this as well as the Egyptians.

These plagues occurred within a period of about nine months, in the following order:

1. The water of the Nile River turned into blood (Ex 7:14-25).
2. Frogs overran the countryside (Ex 8:1-15).
3. People and animals were infested with lice (Ex 8:16-19).
4. Swarms of flies covered the land (Ex 8:20-32).
5. Disease killed the livestock of Egypt (Ex 9:1-7).
6. Boils and sores infected the Egyptians and their animals (Ex 9:8-12).
7. Hail destroyed crops and vegetation (Ex 9:13-35).
8. Swarms of locusts covered the land (Ex 10:1-20).
9. Thick darkness covered Egypt for three days (Ex 10:21-29).
10. The Egyptian firstborn, both of the people and their animals, were destroyed by God's death angel (Ex 11:1-12:30).

In all of theses plagues, the Israelites were protected, while the Egyptians and their property were destroyed. The Hebrews were delivered from the final plague when they marked their houses, at God's command, by sprinkling the blood of a lamb on their doorposts. The death angel "passed over" the Hebrew houses.

At this final demonstration of God's power, the Pharaoh gave in and allowed Moses and the Israelites to leave Egypt. This deliverance became one of the most memorable occasions in Hebrew history. The Passover is celebrated annually even today to commemorate God's deliverance of the Hebrew people from slavery.

TENT

The moveable habitation used by shepherds and soldiers (Ge 25:27; Ju 8:11). Tent material was often made from the coarse, black hair of goats (Song 1:5). They were made in various shapes—round and oblong—and they were fastened to the ground by stakes (Ex 35:18; Is 54:2).

TENTMAKER

One who makes tents. Paul, the apostle, was trained as a tentmaker; when he was in Corinth he earned his living working with Aquila and Priscilla, who were also tentmakers (Ac 18:3).

TENT OF MEETING

See TABERNACLE OF MEETING.

TEN VIRGINS, PARABLE OF (Ma 25:1-13)

TE' RAH

1. The father of Abraham. During the greater part of his life he lived in Ur of the Chaldees. He was an idolater (Jos 24:2), and like the people among whom he dwelt, he was probably a worshipper of the moon-god. His family migrated to Haran where he died at the age of 205 (Ge 11:25-32).

2. An encampment of the Israelites (Nu 33:27-28).

TER' A·PHIM

A household image, greatly venerated because it was regarded as a guardian through which came prosperity and comfort. They were of different sizes, some small enough to be carried or concealed easily (Ge 31:19,30,34). When Jacob left Padan-aram, his wife, Rachel, stole Laban's teraphim (Ge 31:19-35). Micah, who lived

TEREBINTH TREE

in Mount Ephraim, set up a sanctuary for himself having ephod and teraphim (Ju 17:5).

TER' E·BINTH

The turpentine tree from which the ancients extracted turpentine and resin. It ranges in height from about fifteen feet to thirty feet, its leaves are reddish green and it produces a red berry. The underlying Hebrew word is also translated oak, terebinth, and teil tree. See OAK and DIVINER'S TEREBINTH TREE.

TE' RESH (severe)

One of the eunuchs who planned to assassinate Ahasuerus (Es 2:21-23; 6:2). Mordecai learned of the plot and warned the king in time to avert the danger.

TER' TIUS (third)

The secretary or scribe who took Paul's dictation of the book of Romans (Ro 16:22).

TER·TUL' LUS (diminutive form of Tertius)

A lawyer employed by the Jews to make the accusation against Paul (Ac 24:1-8).

TESTAMENT

A covenant, a will (He 7:6-10,13; 9:1,4,16-17). The word is used to designate the two portions of the Bible. See OLD TESTAMENT; NEW TESTAMENT; BIBLE.

TESTIMONY, ARK OF THE

The ark of the covenant. See ARK.

TETH

The ninth letter of the Hebrew alphabet. It is the heading of verses 65-72 of Psalm 119; in Hebrew each of these eight verses begins with the letter teth. See ACROSTIC.

TETRAGRAMMATON

(See LORD.)

TE′ TRARCH

Originally the ruler of the fourth part of a country. The term also applied to subordinate princes or petty kings. The title was applied to Herod Antipas, ruler of Galilee and Perea (Ma 14:1; Lk 3:1,19; 9:7; Ac 13:1).

THAD·DAE′ US

One of the twelve apostles (Mk 3:18). Matthew calls him "Lebbaeus, whose surname was Thaddaeus" (Ma 10:3), and also "Judas, son of James" (Lk 6:16; Ac 1:13), as distinguished from Judas Iscariot (Jo 14:22). See JUDAS.

THA′ HASH

Son of Nahor. His mother was Reumah (Ge 22:24).

THA′ MAH

See TEMAH.

THA′ MAR

See TAMAR.

THANK OFFERING

A variety of peace offering (2 Ch 29:31). See OFFERINGS.

THANKSGIVING

The importance and spiritual benefits of thanksgiving in our prayer life cannot be overemphasized. The Bible tells us God resists the proud but gives grace to the humble (Jam 4:6). But the question is, "How do you become humble?" It is done by being thankful. A good rule is to be careful (worried) for nothing (Ph 4:6), be prayerful in all things (1 Th 5:18), and be thankful for anything. It was the sin of not glorifying God and thanklessness that caused the ancient world to plunge into the terrible depths of sexual depravity (Ro 1:21). In the Old Testament, a special group of priests was appointed to do nothing else but praise and thank the Lord (2 Ch 31:2).

There are two main things we are to thank God for:

a. We are to thank Him for His work in creation. David reminds us concerning this area of thanksgiving in Psalm 100. Later, John the apostle tells us we will thank God for His work in creation throughout all eter-

nity. Note the words of this song of praise: "You are worthy, O Lord, to receive glory and honor and power; for You created all things, and by Your will they exist and were created" (Re 4:11).

b. We are to thank Him for His work in redemption. John also informs us that our second song in heaven will feature thanksgiving for God's work in redemption: "And they sang a new song, saying, 'You are worthy to take the scroll, and to open its seals; for You were slain, and have redeemed us to God by Your blood'" (Re 5:9).

THARA

See TERAH.

THAR′ SHISH

See TARSHISH.

THE′ A·TER

A place used for dramatic performances, for games, and for public assemblies. It was also used as a place to transact public business (Ac 19:29, 31).

THEBES

See NO-AMON.

THE′ BEZ (*splendor*)

A fortified city of Ephraim near Shechem (Ju 9:50-55; 2 Sa 11:21).

THEL·A′ SAR

See TELASSAR.

THEOCRACY (*rule of God*)

A form of government in which God is regarded as the head of the state and the one responsible for the institution of the laws. This was the form of government of the ancient Hebrews. To them, God was king and the law was the constitution. The basis of the government was the Ten Commandments, or Decalogue (Ex 20:1-22; De 4:12, 33).

THEOPHANY

This is a Greek word meaning a physical manifestation or personal presentation of (deity) God. This is a theological term, but not a Bible term. Some scholars consider the fourth man in the fiery furnace with Shadrach, Meshach, and Abednego (Da 3:24-25) was a pre-incarnate manifestation of Christ (a theophany) but the Bible does not actually say so.

THE·OPH′ I·LUS *(loved of God)*

The person to whom Luke addressed the Acts of the Apostles and the Gospel according to St. Luke (Lk 1:3; Ac 1:1). Nothing more is known of his identity, he is mentioned only in Luke's introductions to his books.

THESSALONIANS, EPISTLES TO THE

1. The Book of 1 Thessalonians. Paul had many pleasant memories of the days he spent with the infant Thessalonian church. Their faith, hope, love, and perseverance in the face of persecution were exemplary. Paul's labors as a spiritual parent to the fledgling church have been richly rewarded, and his affection is visible in every line of his letter.

Paul encouraged them to excel in their new-found faith, to increase in their love for one another, and to rejoice, pray, and give thanks always. He closes his letter with instruction regarding the return of the Lord, whose advent signifies hope and comfort for believers both living and dead.

Because this is the first of Paul's two canonical letters to the church at Thessalonica, it received the title *Pros Thessalonikeis A,* the "First to the Thessalonians."

2. The Author of 1 Thessalonians. First Thessalonians went unchallenged as a Pauline Epistle until the nineteenth century, when radical critics claimed that its dearth of doctrinal content made its authenticity suspect. But this is a weak objection on two counts: (1) the proportion of doctrinal teaching in Paul's epistles varies widely, and (2) 4:13–5:11 is a foundational passage for New Testament eschatology (future events). Paul had quickly grounded the Thessalonians in Christian doctrine, and the only problematic issue when this Epistle was written concerned the matter of Christ's return. The external and internal evidence points clearly to Paul.

3. The Time of 1 Thessalonians. In Paul's time, Thessalonica was the prominent seaport and the capital of the Roman province of Macedonia. This prosperous city was located on the Via Egnatia, the main road from Rome to the East, within sight of Mount Olympus, legendary home of the Greek pantheon. Cassander expanded and strengthened this site around 315 B.C. and renamed it after his wife, the half sister of Alexander the Great. The Romans conquered Macedonia in 168 B.C. and organized it into a single province twenty-two years later with Thessalonica as the capital city. It became a "free city" under Augustus with its own authority to appoint a governing board of magistrates who were called "politarchs." The strategic location assured Thessalonica of commercial success, and it boasted a population of perhaps 200,000 in the first century. Thessalonica survives under the shortened name Salonika.

Thessalonica had a sizable Jewish population, and the ethical monotheism of Judaism attracted many Gentiles who had become disenchanted with Greek paganism. These God-fearers quickly responded to Paul's reasoning in the synagogue when he ministered there on his second missionary journey (Ac 17:10). The Jews became jealous of Paul's success and organized a mob to oppose the Christian missionaries. Not finding Paul and Silas, they dragged Jason, Paul and Silas's host, before the politarchs and accused him of harboring traitors of Rome. The politarchs extracted a pledge guaranteeing the departure of Paul and Silas, who left that night for Berea. After a time, the Thessalonian Jews raised an uproar in Berea so that Paul departed for Athens, leaving orders for Silas and Timothy to join him there (Ac 17:11-16). Because of Luke's account in Acts some scholars have reasoned that Paul was in Thessalonica for less than a month ("three Sabbaths," Ac 17:2), but other evidence suggests a longer stay: (1) Paul received two separate offerings from Philippi, 100 miles away, while he was in Thessalonica (Ph 4:15-16). (2) According to 1:9 and 2:14-16, most of the Thessalonian converts were Gentiles who came out of idolatry. This would imply an extensive ministry directed to the Gentiles after Paul's initial work with the Jews and Gentile God-fearers. (3) Paul worked "night and day" (2:9; 2 Th 3:7-9) during his time there. He may have begun to work immediately, but Paul supported himself by tentmaking, which took many hours away from his ministry, requiring a longer stay to accomplish the extensive ministry of evangelism and teaching that took place in that city. After Silas and Timothy met Paul in Athens (3:1-2), he sent Timothy to Thessalonica (Silas also went back to Macedonia, probably Philippi), and his assistants later rejoined him in Corinth (Ac 18:5; 1 Th 1:1 where Silas is called Silvanus). There he wrote this epistle in A.D. 51 as his response to Timothy's good report.

3. The Christ of 1 Thessalonians. Christ is seen as the believer's hope of salvation both now and at His coming. When He returns, He will deliver (1:10; 5:4-11), reward (1:19), perfect (3:13), resurrect (4:13-18), and sanctify (5:23) all who trust Him.

4. Keys to 1 Thessalonians.

Key Word: Holiness in Light of Christ's Return—Throughout this letter is an unmistakable emphasis upon steadfastness in the Lord (3:8) and a continuing growth in faith and love in view of the return of Christ (1:3-10; 2:12-20; 3:10-13; 4:1–5:28). The theme is not only the returning of Christ, but also the life of the believer in every practical relationship, each aspect of which can be transformed and illuminated by the glorious prospect of His eventual return.

Key Verses: 1 Thessalonians 3:12-13 and 4:16-18—"And may the Lord make you increase and abound in love to one another and to all, just as we do to you, so that He may establish your hearts blameless in holiness before our God and Father at the coming of our Lord Jesus Christ with all His saints" (3:12-13).

"For the Lord Himself will descend from heaven with a shout, with the voice of an archangel, and with the trumpet of God. And the dead in Christ will rise first. Then we who are alive and remain shall be caught up together with them in the clouds to meet the Lord in the air. And thus we shall always be with the Lord. Therefore comfort one another with these words" (4:16-18).

Key Chapter: 1 Thessalonians 4—Chapter 4 includes the central passage of the epistles on the coming of the Lord when the dead in Christ shall rise first, and those who remain are caught up together with them in the clouds.

6. Survey of 1 Thessalonians. After Paul's forced separation from the Thessalonians, he grew increasingly concerned about the progress of their faith. His great relief upon hearing Timothy's positive report prompts him to write this warm epistle of commendation, exhortation, and consolation. They are commended for remaining steadfast under afflictions, exhorted to excel still more in their Christian walk, and consoled concerning their loved ones who have died in Christ. The theme of the coming of the

Lord recurs throughout this epistle and 4:13–5:11 is one of the fullest New Testament developments of this crucial truth. The two major sections of 1 Thessalonians are: Paul's personal reflections of the Thessalonians (1–3), and Paul's instructions for the Thessalonians (4–5).

Paul's Personal Reflections on the Thessalonians (1–3). Paul's typical salutation in the first verse combines the customary Greek ("grace") and Hebrew ("peace") greetings of his day and enriches them with Christian content. The opening chapter is a declaration of thanksgiving for the Thessalonians' metamorphosis from heathenism to Christian hope. Faith, love, and hope (1:3) properly characterize the new lives of these believers. In 2:1-16, Paul reviews his brief ministry in Thessalonica and defends his conduct and motives, apparently to answer enemies who are trying to impugn his character and message. He sends Timothy to minister to them and is greatly relieved when Timothy reports the stability of their faith and love (2:17–3:10). Paul therefore closes this historical section with a prayer that their faith may continue to deepen (3:11-13).

Paul's Instructions to the Thessalonians (4–5). The apostle deftly moves into a series of exhortations and instructions by encouraging the Thessalonians to continue progressing. He reminds them of his previous teaching on sexual and social matters (4:1-12), since these Gentile believers lack the moral upbringing in the Mosaic law provided in the Jewish community. Now rooted in the Word of God (2:13), the readers must resist the constant pressures of a pagan society.

Paul has taught them about the return of Christ, and they have become distressed over the deaths of some among them. In 4:13-18, Paul comforts them with the assurance that all who die in Christ will be resurrected at His *parousia* ("presence," "coming," or "advent"). The apostle continues his discourse on eschatology by describing the coming day of the Lord (5:1-11). In anticipation of this day, believers are to "watch and be sober" (5:6) as "sons of light" (5:5) who are destined for salvation, not wrath. Paul requests the readers to deal with integrity toward one another and to continue growing spiritually (5:12-22). The epistle closes with a wish for their sanctification, three requests, and a benediction (5:23-28).

OUTLINE OF 1 THESSALONIANS

I. Paul's Personal Reflections on the Thessalonians (1:1–3:13)

A. Paul's Commendation for Their Growth...................................... 1:1-10

B. Paul's Founding of the Church 2:1-16

C. Timothy's Strengthening of the Church 2:17–3:13

II. Paul's Instructions to the Thessalonians (4:1–5:28)

A. Directions for Growth 4:1-12

B. Revelation Concerning the Dead in Christ 4:13-18

C. Description of the Day of the Lord 5:1-11

D. Instruction for Holy Living......... 5:12-22

E. Conclusion 5:23-28

---

7. The Book of 2 Thessalonians. Since Paul's first letter, the seeds of false doctrine had been sown among the Thessalonians, causing them to waver in their faith. Paul removed these destructive seeds and again planted the seeds of truth. He began by commending the believers on their faithfulness in the midst of persecution and encouraging them that present suffering will be repaid with future glory. Therefore, in the midst of persecution, expectation can be high.

Paul then dealt with the central matter of his letter: a misunderstanding spawned by false teachers regarding the coming day of the Lord. Despite reports to the contrary, that day has not yet come, and Paul recounted the events that must first take place. Laboring for the gospel, rather than lazy resignation, is the proper response.

As the second letter in Paul's Thessalonian correspondence, this was entitled *Pros Thessalonikeis B,* the "Second to the Thessalonians."

8. The Author of 2 Thessalonians. The external attestation to the authenticity of 2 Thessalonians as a Pauline epistle is even stronger than that for 1 Thessalonians. Internally, the vocabulary, style, and doctrinal content support the claims in 1:1 and 3:17 that it was written by Paul.

9. The Time of 2 Thessalonians. See "The Time of 1 Thessalonians" for the background to the Thessalonian correspondence. This letter was probably written a few months after 1 Thessalonians, while Paul was still in Corinth with Silas and Timothy (1:1; Ac 18:5). The bearer of the first epistle may have brought Paul an update on the new developments, prompting him to write this letter. They were still undergoing persecution, and the false teaching about the day of the Lord led some of them to overreact by

giving up their hopes. The problem of idleness recorded in 1 Thessalonians 4:11-12 had become more serious (3:6-15). By this time, Paul was beginning to see the opposition he would face in his ministry in Corinth (3:2; see Ac 18:5-10).

10. The Christ of 2 Thessalonians. The return of Christ is mentioned more times (318) in the New Testament than any other doctrine, and this is certainly the major concept in chapters 1–2 of this episode. The return of the Lord Jesus is a reassuring and joyful hope for believers, but His revelation from heaven holds awesome and terrifying implications for those who have not trusted in Him (1:6-10; 2:8-12).

11. Keys to 2 Thessalonians.

Key Word: Understanding the Day of the Lord—The theme of this epistle is an understanding of the day of the Lord and the resulting lifestyle changes. The doctrinal error of chapter 2 has been causing the practical error that Paul seeks to overcome in chapter 3. Some of the believers have abandoned their work and have begun to live off others, apparently assuming that the end is at hand. Paul commands them to follow his example by supporting themselves and instructs the rest of the church to discipline them if they fail to do so.

Key Verses: 2 Thessalonians 2:2-3 and 3:5-6—"Not to be soon shaken in mind or troubled, either by spirit or by word or by letter, as if from us, as though the day of Christ had come. Let no one deceive you by any means; for that Day will not come unless the falling away comes first, and the man of sin is revealed, the son of perdition" (2:2-3).

"Now may the Lord direct your hearts into the love of God and into the patience of Christ. But we command you, brethren, in the name of our Lord Jesus Christ, that you withdraw from every brother who walks disorderly and not according to the tradition which he received from us" (3:5-6).

Key Chapter: 2 Thessalonians 2—The second chapter is written to correct the fallacious teaching that the day of the Lord has already come upon the Thessalonian church. This teaching, coupled with the afflictions they have been suffering, is causing a great disturbance among the believers who wonder when their "gathering together to Him" (2:1; 1 Th 4:13-18) will take place. Paul makes it clear that certain identifiable events will precede that day and that those events have not yet occurred.

12. Survey of 2 Thessalonians. This epistle is the theological sequel to 1 Thessalonians, which developed the theme of the coming day of the Lord (1 Th 5:1-11). However, not long after the Thessalonians receive that letter, they fall prey to false teaching or outright deception, thinking the day of the Lord has already begun. Paul writes this brief letter to correct the error and also to encourage those believers whose faith is being tested by the difficulties presented by persecution. He also reproves those who have decided to cease working because they believe the coming of Christ is near. Second Thessalonians deals with Paul's encouragement in persecution (1); Paul's explanation of the day of the Lord (2); and Paul's exhortation to the church (3).

Paul's Encouragement in Persecution (1). After his two-verse salutation, Paul gives thanks for the growing faith and love of the Thessalonians and assures them of their ultimate deliverance from those who are persecuting them (1:3-10). They are encouraged to patiently endure their afflictions, knowing that the Lord Jesus will judge their persecutors when He is "revealed from heaven with His mighty angels, in flaming fire" (1:7-8). Before Paul moves to the next topic, he concludes this section with a prayer for the spiritual welfare of his readers (1:11-12).

Paul's Explanation of the Day of the Lord (2). Because of the severity of their afflictions, the Thessalonians have become susceptible to false teaching (and possibly a fraudulent letter in the name of Paul), claiming that they are already in the day of the Lord (2:1-2). This was particularly disturbing because Paul's previous letter had given them the comforting hope that they were not destined for the wrath of that day (1 Th 5:9). Paul therefore assures them that the day of the Lord is yet in the future and will not arrive unannounced (2:3-12). Paul then concludes with a word of encouragement and a benedictory prayer of comfort before moving to his next topic (2:13-17).

Paul's Exhortation to the Church (3:1-18). Paul requests the Thessalonian church to pray on his behalf and to wait patiently for the Lord (3:1-5). Having thus commended, corrected, and comforted his readers, the tactful apostle closes his letter with a sharp word of command to those who have been using the truth of Christ's return as an excuse for disorderly conduct (3:6-15; 1 Th 4:11-12). The doctrine of the Lord's return requires a balance between waiting and working. It is a perspective that should encourage holiness, not idleness. This final section, like the first two, closes on a benedictory note (3:16-18).

OUTLINE OF 2 THESSALONIANS

I. Paul's Encouragement in Persecution (1:1-12)

A. Thanksgiving for Their Growth...... 1:1-4
B. Encouragement in Their
 Persecution 1:5-10
C. Prayer for God's Blessing 1:11-12

II. Paul's Explanation of the Day of the Lord (2:1-17)

A. The Events Preceding the Day of
 the Lord 2:1-12

B. The Comfort of the Believer
 on the Day of the Lord.............. 2:13-17

**III. Paul's Exhortation
to the Church
(3:1-18)**

A. Wait Patiently for
 Christ 3:1-5
B. Withdraw from the
 Disorderly 3:6-15
C. Conclusion 3:16-18

THESSALONICA

THESS·A·LO'NI·CA

Thessalonica was founded in 315 B.C. by the Macedonian king Cassander. He named the city after his wife Thessalonica, sister of the Greek military conqueror, Alexander the Great. The apostle Paul worked for several months in Thessalonica and later addressed two letters (1 and 2 Thessalonians) to the church in this city.

Paul visited Thessalonica in the early fifties during his second missionary journey through the Roman province of Macedonia (Ac 17:1-9). The church that he worked with here consisted of former members of the Jewish synagogue, as well as non-Jews from pagan backgrounds. The tender words with which Paul addressed the Thessalonians make it clear that he developed strong affection for the Thessalonian church (1 Th 2:1-12).

Thessalonica's natural harbor made it a vital trading center, which brought in people from many places. This may have been why it was selected as the site for a church. At the time of his visit, Thessalonica was the most populous city in the entire Roman province of Macedonia.

Roman influence on Thessalonica is evident in the city's physical structure. Vital to the city's prosperity was the Egnatian Way, a Roman military highway which provided a route to the empire's eastern provinces. This route still serves as one of the main streets for modern Thessalonica (known as Salonika). Roman arches stood at Thessalonica's two entrances to the Egnatian Way. The one built in A.D. 297 to honor the Roman emperor Galerius remains intact.

Thessalonica's importance is also demonstrated by the great wall that surrounded the city, portions of which are still standing. The modern wall was built after Paul's time, but it was constructed on the foundations of the old city wall from the New Testament era.

THEU'DAS

The leader of about 400 men in an unsuccessful Jewish revolt against Rome (Ac 5:36).

THIEF

Anyone who takes what does not belong to him. He may be a petty thief or highwayman (Ma 6:20; Lk 10:30; Jo 12:6). The penalty for stealing under the Mosaic law was that twice the amount of what was stolen must be returned, or the thief could be made to serve as a slave until the amount was earned. Jesus was crucified between two thieves (Ma 27:38), thus fulfilling the prophecy of Isaiah: "And He was numbered with the transgressors, and He bore the sin of many" (Is 53:12).

THIM'NA·THAH

See TIMNAH.

THIRD PART OF A SHEKEL

The amount which Nehemiah's covenant required to be brought each year for the service of God's house.

THISTLE

See THORNS.

THOM'AS *(twin)*

An apostle who was also called Didymus, the Greek form of his name (Ma 10:3). It was he who expressed concern for the safety of Jesus when the latter went to Bethany at the time of the death of Lazarus. Thomas proposed that all the apostles go with Jesus and die with him if necessary (Jo 11:16). Thomas refused to believe the testimony of the others regarding the

THOMAS

resurrection of Jesus. He preferred to trust only his own senses, saying that he would not believe unless he could actually touch Jesus's wounds (Jo 20:24-29). When he saw Jesus, he did believe, but his initial skepticism earned him the traditional title "Doubting Thomas."

THOMAS, GOSPEL OF

See APOCRYPHA.

THORN IN THE FLESH

An unknown malady which tormented the apostle Paul. He asked three times for God to remove it, but the answer was "no." God said, "My grace is sufficient for you, for My strength is made perfect in weakness" (2 Co 12:7-10). Therefore, Paul rejoiced in his difficulties, knowing that God loves to show His mercy and power to the weak, and to work through those who seem inadequate.

Speculation has abounded concerning Paul's "thorn." Most assume that it was some kind of chronic illness. Some have suggested that Paul was afflicted with a disease of the eyes, because of his comments to the Galatians, reminding them that they were aware of his "physical infirmity," and "if possible, you would have plucked out your own eyes and given them to me"(Ga 4:13-15). At the end of this same epistle, he says, "See with what large letters I have written to you with my own hand!" (Ga 6:11).

Other suggestions have included recurring medical problems such as epilepsy or malaria, or possibly a non-physical interpretation of the word "flesh," meaning a painful emotional experience or a struggle with temptation.

Whatever the nature of the "thorn in the flesh," the real point is Paul's response. Instead of becoming depressed or angry, he used the opportunity to give glory to God.

THORNS, THISTLES

Prickly plants, such as the thorn, bramble, thistle, brier, and nettle, flourish in Palestine. To torture and insult Jesus, the Roman soldiers placed a crown of thorns on his head as he was being led to the cross (Ma 27:29). Thorns and thistles growing in the midst of crops are a direct result of the fall (Ge 3:18). This struggle against encroaching weeds is a part of the curse on work, making it hard and painful.

THREE CHILDREN, SONG OF THE

See APOCRYPHA.

THREE INNS

A station on the Appian Way (Ac 28:15).

THREE TAVERNS

See THREE INNS.

THRESHING

The process by which the grain is separated from its stalks and chaff. For many centuries, until the invention of modern threshing machines and combines, threshing was done by spreading the grain on a smooth tight floor and beating it with a stick or flail (Ju 6:11; Is 28:27). The ripe grain is easily loosened from the heads, and since it is heavier than the straw, it sifts down to the floor. The straw is forked off the top, and the remaining grain can easily be swept from the clean threshing floor. Grain has also often been threshed by treading on it. The unthreshed grain was placed in a circular pathway on the threshing floor and oxen were driven over it, dragging a threshing sledge or cart, their feet doing the same work as threshing flails. Oxen doing this work were not to be muzzled; they were allowed to eat as they worked (De 25:4). The threshing sledge and oxen were apparently only used for sturdier grains, delicate seeds such as cumin were threshed by hand. See FLOOR, THRESHING.

THRESHING SLEDGE

An ox-drawn implement used for threshing grain. A threshing sledge was probably made of wood, apparently with iron or flint teeth in the bottom side, and designed to be dragged over the unthreshed grain (Is 28:27). Threshing sledges are used as symbols of destruction (Am 1:3; Is 41:15).

THRONE

An elevated seat occupied by a person of authority. He may be a king, a governor, a military officer, a high priest, or a judge (1 Sa 1:9; 2 Sa 3:10; Ps 122:5; Je 1:15; Ma 19:28). Solomon's throne, overlaid with gold and inlaid with ivory, was six steps from the ground and a stone lion stood at each end of the steps (1 Ki 10:18-20; 2 Ch 9:17-19). When administering justice, issuing royal orders, or granting an audience, the king occupied the throne (1 Ki 2:19; 7:7; 10:18-20; 22:10). The throne of God is in heaven (Ps 11:4; 103:19; Is 66:1; Ma 5:35), and he set up the throne of David (2 Sa 3:10) to be established forever (2 Sa 7:13; 1 Ki 2:45; Ps 89:35-37). This prophecy (Is 9:6-7; Je 33:15-17) was fulfilled in Christ (Lk 1:31-33).

THROWING STICK

See JAVELIN and SPEAR.

THRUSH

Any of several small songbirds of the thrush family, including robins, hermit thrushes, redwings, song thrushes, and blackbirds. This word is used in the NASB to translate Jeremiah 8:7; NKJV uses the word "swallow" in this verse.

THUM'MIM

See URIM AND THUMMIM.

THUNDER

The sound following a flash of lightning, sometimes spoken of as the voice of God (Job 37:2-5; 40:9; Ps 29:3-9; Re 6:1; 14:2). It accompanied divine action in moments of vast significance, such as the giving of the law on Mount Sinai (Ex 19:16; 20:18), the affliction by hail of the Egyptians (Ex 9:23), and John's vision of the throne (Re 4:5).

THUNDER, SONS OF

The nickname Jesus gave to the sons of Zebedee, James and John (Mk 3:17).

THY·A·TI'RA

A city of Asia Minor, located on the banks of the Lycus River, between Pergamum and Sardis. Lydia, the first convert in Philippi, was from Thyatira (Ac 16:14). The Book of Revelation also mentions this city; one of the letters to the seven churches was addressed to Thyatira (Re 1:11; 2:18-24).

THY'INE WOOD

The sweet scented wood from the sandarac tree (Re 18:12), also called citron wood.

TI·BE'RI·AS

A city on the Sea of Galilee built by Herod Antipas, and named after Tiberius who was then emperor. It was the capital of Galilee until the reign of Herod Agrippa II. The Sea of Galilee is also called the Sea of Tiberias (Jo 6:1; 21:1).

TI·BE'RI·AS, SEA OF

See TIBERIAS and GALILEE, SEA OF.

TI·BE'RI·US CAE'SAR

See CAESAR.

TIB'HATH *(slaughter)*

A city of Aramzobah (1 Ch 18:8). In 2 Samuel 8:8 it is called Betah.

TIB'NI

The son of Ginath (1 Ki 16:21-22).

TI'DAL

One of the kings who joined with Chedorlaomer, the ancient king of Elam, in a raid into Palestine (Ge 14:1-10).

TIG'LATH-PI·LE'SER

An Assyrian king who reigned from 745 to 727 B.C. Under the name of Pul, he also reigned as king of Babylonia from 729-727 B.C. (2 Ki 15:19). He is also called Tilgath-pilneser (1 Ch 5:6,26; 2 Ch 28:20).

Tiglath-pileser led Assyria in a period of expansion and military greatness. In the last period of the Northern Kingdom of Israel, Assyria came against the nation and its king, Menahem. In order to deal with the threat of Assyrian invasion, Menahem paid an exorbitant tribute of 1,000 talents of silver in tribute to Tiglath-pileser. He exacted this money from all the wealthy of the land (2 Ki 15:17-20).

During the reign of Pekah, the assassin who murdered Menahem's son and took over the throne, Tiglath-pileser came against Israel again and captured many of its towns. The entire tribe of Naphtali was carried off into captivity at this time (2 Ki 15:29). Pekah later made an alliance with Syria and came against Judah. Ahaz, king of Judah, appealed to Tiglath-pileser for help, offering him the silver and gold from the house of the Lord. This relationship with Assyria proved to be a means of introducing more pagan worship to Judah. On a visit of state to Damascus, Ahaz was impressed by a heathen altar he saw there, had a copy made and proceeded to offer sacrifices on it. He also rearranged many of the articles of the temple in order to make it more like the things he had seen in Assyria (2 Ki 16:7-20).

TI′ GRIS

One of the great rivers of Asia, the Tigris rises in the Taurus Mountains of eastern Turkey, flows through Syria and Iraq, and empties into the Persian Gulf. It is about 1,150 miles long. For hundreds of miles, the Tigris flows roughly parallel to the Euphrates. North of Basra, about 90 miles above the mouth, the two rivers become one. It is considered by many to be the same as the Hiddekel, one of the four rivers flowing out of the garden of Eden (Ge 2:14).

TIK′ VAH *(hope)*

1. Son of Harhas and father of Shallum whose wife was Huldah, the prophetess (2 Ki 22:14). He is called Tikvath in 2 Chronicles 34:22.

2. The father of Jahaziah (Ez 10:15).

TIK′ VATH

See TIKVAH.

TILE

A brick of clay which served as the writing material of the Babylonians. Characters were inscribed upon it while it was soft and it was then baked. Tiles of fired clay were also used for roofing purposes (Lk 5:19).

TIL′ GATH-PIL•NE′ SER

See TIGLATH-PILESER.

TILLER

See FARMER.

TI′ LON

A son of Shimon of Judah (1 Ch 4:20).

TI•MAE′ US

Father of Bartimaeus, the blind man Jesus healed (Mk 10:46).

TIM′ BREL

A musical instrument played with the fingers (Ex 15:20; 1 Sa 10:5; Ps 81:2; Is 5:12). The underlying Hebrew word is also translated "tambourine," and "tabret." The timbrel was a small percussion instrument played by women (Ps 68:25). It was probably very much like a modern tambourine. They were used in joyous celebrations (Ge 31:27).

TIMES, LAST

See ESCHATOLOGY.

TIMES, OBSERVING

One who engages in some kind of occult practices (De 18:10, KJV). Other translations use "soothsayer" in this passage. See MAGIC, SORCERY, AND DIVINATION.

TIMEUS

See TIMAEUS.

TIM′ NA

1. A chief of Edom (Ge 36:40; 1 Ch 1:51).

2. The daughter of Seir and concubine of Eliphaz (Ge 36:12,22; 1 Ch 1:39). Also called Timnah (1 Ch 1:51; Ge 36:40).

TIM′ NAH

1. See Timna No.2.

2. A town in the hill district of Judah (Jos 15:57). It was near this place that Tamar met Judah (Ge 38:12-14). The town was captured by the Philistines (2 Ch 28:18).

2. A town of Dan, later held by the Philistines (Jos 15:10). Samson's wife lived in this town (Ju 14:1,2,5; 15:6). Also called Thimnathah (Jos 19:43).

TIM′ NATH-HE′ RES

See TIMNATH-SERAH.

TIM′ NATH-SE′ RAH

A city of Ephraim in the mountains; the inheritance of Joshua son of Nun, and his burial place (Jos 19:50; 24:30). In Judges 2:9 it is called Timnath-heres. It is thought to be the modern town of Khirbet Tibneh.

TIM′ NITE

A native of Timnah (Ju 15:6).

TI′ MON *(worthy)*

One of the seven deacons appointed to serve in the church in Jerusalem (Ac 6:5).

TI•MOTH′ E•US

A variant of TIMOTHY.

TIM′ O•THY *(worshipping God)*

Paul's companion and assistant. A native of Lystra, Timothy was the child of a mixed mar-

TIMBREL

riage. His mother was Jewish, his father was Greek (Ac 16:1). He was given religious instruction at an early age by his mother, Eunice, and his grandmother, Lois (2 Ti 1:5; 3:15). To forestall criticism of Timothy on the part of the Jews, Paul caused him to be circumcised (Ac 16:3). He was the recipient of two of Paul's epistles, and his name appears with Paul's in the greetings of six of Paul's other epistles (2 Corinthians; Philippians; Colossians; 1 and 2 Thessalonians; and Philemon).

TIMOTHY, EPISTLES TO

1. The Book of 1 Timothy. Paul, the aged and experienced apostle, writes to the young pastor Timothy who is facing a heavy burden of responsibility in the church at Ephesus. The task is challenging: false doctrine must be erased, public worship safeguarded, and mature leadership developed. In addition to the conduct of the church, Paul talks pointedly about the conduct of the minister. Timothy must be on his guard lest his youthfulness become a liability, rather than an asset, to the gospel. He must be careful to avoid false teachers and greedy motives, pursuing instead righteousness, godliness, faith, love, perseverance, and the gentleness that befits a man of God.

The Greek title for this letter is *Pros Timotheon A,* the "First to Timothy." *Timothy* means "honoring God" or "honored by God," and probably was given to him by his mother Eunice.

2. The Author of 1 Timothy. Since the early nineteenth century, the Pastoral Epistles have been attacked more than any other Pauline Epistles on the issue of authenticity. The similarity of these epistles requires that they be treated as a unit in terms of authorship because they stand or fall together.

The external evidence solidly supports the conservative position that Paul wrote the letters to Timothy and Titus. Post-apostolic church fathers, such as Polycarp and Clement of Rome, allude to them as Paul's writing. In addition, these epistles are identified as Pauline by Irenaeus, Tertullian, Clement of Alexandria, and the Muratorian Canon. Only Romans and 1 Corinthians have better attestation among the Pauline Epistles.

Suggestions of an author other than Paul are supported wholly on the basis of internal evidence. Even though these letters claim to be written by Paul (1:1; 2 Ti 1:1; Tit 1:1), critics assert that they are "pious forgeries" that appeared in the second century. There are several problems with this: (1) Pseudonymous writing was unacceptable to Paul (see 2 Th 2:2; 3:17) and to the early church, which was very sensitive to the problem of forgeries. (2) The adjective *pious* should deceive no one: a forgery was as deliberately deceptive then as it is now. (3) The many personal facts and names that appear in the Pastoral Epistles would have been avoided by a forger who would have taken refuge in vagueness. Nor would a forger have used expressions like those in 1:13,15 if he had been an admirer of Paul. The doctrinal teaching and autobiographical details (1:12-17; 2:7; 2 Ti 1:8-12; 4:9-22; Tit 1:5; 3:12-13) fit very well with "Paul, the aged" (Phile 9). (4) What purpose or advantage would these epistles serve as forgeries written years later? There are too many personal elements, and the doctrinal refutations do not refer to second-century Gnosticism. (5) The style and content of the post-apostolic writings or apocryphal books differ greatly with these three letters.

3. The Time of 1 Timothy. Pauline authorship of the Pastoral Epistles requires Paul's release from his Roman imprisonment (Ac 28), the continuation of his missionary endeavors, and his imprisonment for a second time in Rome. Unfortunately, the order of events can only be reconstructed from hints, because there is no concurrent history paralleling Acts to chronicle the last years of the apostle. The following reconstruction, therefore, is only tentative:

As he anticipated in Philippians (1:19,25-26; 2:24), Paul was released from his first Roman imprisonment. It is possible that his Jewish accusers decided not to appear at his trial before Caesar. In fulfillment of his promise to the Philippians (Ph 2:19-23), he sends Timothy to Philippi to relate the good news. Paul himself went to Ephesus (in spite of his earlier expectations in Ac 20:38) and to other Asian churches like Colosse (see Phile 22). When Timothy rejoined him in Ephesus, Paul instructed his assistant to "remain in Ephesus" (1:3) while he journeyed to Macedonia. When he saw that he might be delayed in Macedonia, Paul wrote 1 Timothy, perhaps from Philippi (3:14-15). After he saw Timothy in Ephesus, the apostle journeyed on to the island of Crete (Tit 3:13). He instructed Titus to join him in Nicopolis after the arrival of his replacement in Crete; Artemus or Tychicus (Tit 3:12).

If he went to Spain as he had planned (Ro 15:24,28), Paul probably departed with Titus for that western province after his winter in Nicopolis. Early church tradition holds that Paul did go to Spain. Before the end of the first century, Clement of Rome said that Paul "reached the limits of the West" (1 Clement 5:7). Since he was writing from Rome, he evidently had Spain in mind. Paul may have been in Spain from A.D. 64-66. He returned to Greece and Asia—to Corinth, Miletus, and Troas (2 Ti 4:13-20)—and may have been arrested in Troas where he left his valuable books and parchments (2 Ti 4:13-15).

Now that Christianity had become an illegal religion in the Empire (the burning of Rome took place in A.D. 64), Paul's enemies were able to successfully accuse him. He was imprisoned in A.D. 67 and wrote 2 Timothy from his Roman cell after his first defense before the Imperial Court (2 Ti 1:8,17; 2:9; 4:16-17). He was delivered from condemnation, but he held no hope of release and expected to be executed (2 Ti 4:6-8, 18). He urged Timothy to come before that happened (2 Ti 4:9,21); and, according to tradition, the apostle was beheaded west of Rome on the Ostian Way.

Paul wrote 1 Timothy from Macedonia in A.D. 62 or 63 while Timothy was serving as his representative in Ephesus and perhaps in other churches in the province of Asia. Timothy was to appoint elders, combat false doctrine, and supervise church life as an apostolic representative.

4. The Christ of 1 Timothy. Christ is the "one Mediator between God and men" (2:5), and "God was manifested in the flesh, justified in the Spirit, seen by angels, preached among the Gentiles, believed on in the world, received up in glory" (3:16). He is the source of spiritual strength, faith, and love (1:12,14). He "came into the world to save sinners" (1:15) and "gave Himself a ransom for all" (2:6) as "the Savior of all men, especially of those who believe" (4:10).

5. Keys to 1 Timothy.

Key Word: Leadership Manual for Church Organization—The theme of this epistle is Timothy's organization and oversight of the Asian churches as a faithful minister of God. Paul writes this letter as a reference manual for leadership so that Timothy will have effective guidance for his work during Paul's absence in Macedonia (3:14-15). Paul wants to encourage and exhort his younger assistant to become an example to others, exercise his spiritual gifts, and

"fight the good fight of faith" (6:12; cf. 1:18; 4:12-16; 6:20). Timothy's personal and public life must be above reproach; and he must be ready to deal with matters of false teaching, organization, discipline, proclamation of the Scriptures, poverty and wealth, and the roles of various groups. Negatively, he is to refute error (1:7-11; 6:3-5); positively, he is to teach the truth (4:13-16; 6:2,17-18).

Key Verses: 1 Timothy 3:15-16 and 6:11-12—"But if I am delayed, I write so that you may know how you ought to conduct yourself in the house of God, which is the church of the living God, the pillar and ground of the truth. And without controversy great is the mystery of godliness: God was manifested in the flesh, justified in the Spirit, seen by angels, preached among the Gentiles, believed on in the world, received up in glory" (3:15-16).

"But you, O man of God, flee these things and pursue righteousness, godliness, faith, love, patience, gentleness. Fight the good fight of faith, lay hold on eternal life, to which you were also called and have confessed the good confession in the presence of many witnesses" (6:11-12).

Key Chapter: 1 Timothy 3—Listed in chapter 3 are the qualifications for the leaders of God's church, the elders and deacons. Notably absent are qualities of worldly success or position. Instead, Paul enumerates character qualities demonstrating that true leadership emanates from our walk with God rather than from achievements or vocational success.

6. Survey of 1 Timothy. Paul's last three recorded letters, written near the end of his full and fruitful life, were addressed to his authorized representatives Timothy and Titus. These were the only letters Paul wrote exclusively to individuals (Philemon was addressed primarily to its namesake, but also to others), and they were designed to exhort and encourage Timothy and Titus in their ministry of solidifying the churches in Ephesus and Crete. In the eighteenth century, these epistles came to be known as the Pastoral Epistles even though they do not use any terms such as shepherd, pastor, flock, or sheep. Still, this title is appropriate for 1 Timothy and Titus, since they focus on the oversight of church life. It is less appropriated in the case of 2 Timothy, which is a more personal than church-oriented letter. The Pastoral Epistles abound with principles for leadership and righteous living.

In his first letter to Timothy, Paul sought to guide his younger and less experienced assistant in his weighty responsibility as the overseer of the work at Ephesus and other Asian cities. He writes, in effect, a challenge to Timothy to fulfill the task before him: combating false teaching with sound doctrine, developing qualified leadership, teaching God's Word, and encouraging Christian conduct. Because of the personal and conversational character of this letter, it is loosely structured around five clear charges that end each section. (1:18-20; 3:14-16; 4:11-20; 5:21-25; 6:20-21): Paul's charge concerning doctrine (1); Paul's charge concerning public worship (2–3); Paul's charge concerning false teachers (4); Paul's charge concerning church discipline (5); and Paul's charge concerning pastoral motives (6).

Paul's Charge Concerning Doctrine (1). After his greetings (1:1-2), Paul warns Timothy about the growing problem of false doctrines, particularly as they relate to the misuse of the Mosaic law (1:3-11). The aging apostle then recounts his radical conversion to Christ and subsequent calling to the ministry (1:12-17). Timothy, too, has received a divine calling, and Paul charges him to fulfill it without wavering in doctrine or conduct (1:18-20).

Paul's Charge Concerning Public Worship (2–3). Turning his attention to the church at large, Paul addresses the issues of church worship and leadership. Efficacious public prayer should be a part of worship, and Paul associates this with the role of men in the church (2:1-8). He then turns to the role of women (2:9-15), wherein he emphasizes the importance of the inner quality of godliness. In 3:1-7, Paul lists several qualifications for overseers or bishops. The word for "overseer" (*episkopos*) is used synonymously with the word for "elder" (*presbuteros*) in the New Testament, because both originally referred to the same office (see Ac 20:17,28; Tit 1:5-7). The qualifications for the office of deacon (*diakonos*, "servant") are listed in 3:8-13.

Paul's Charge Concerning False Teachers (4). Timothy obviously had difficulties with some of the older men (5:1) who had left the faith. Paul carefully advises on the issues of marriage, food, and exercise. The closing charge exhorts Timothy not to neglect the spiritual gift given to him.

Paul's Charge Concerning Church Discipline (5). One of the most difficult pastoral duties for the young minister is to lead in the exercise of church discipline. Commencing with the general advice of treating all members of the church as family (5:1-2), Paul concentrates on the two special areas of widows and elders, focusing on Timothy's responsibility and providing practical instruction.

Paul's Charge Concerning Pastoral Duties (6). In addition, the insidious doctrine was being taught that godliness will eventually result in material blessing. Paul, in no uncertain terms, states "from such withdraw yourself" (6:5). The book closes with an extended charge (6:11-21), which is supplemented by an additional charge that Timothy is to give to the wealthy of this age (6:17-19).

OUTLINE OF 1 TIMOTHY

I. Paul's Charge Concerning Doctrine (1:1-20)

A. Paul's Past Charge to Timothy 1:1-11
B. Christ's Past Charge to Paul 1:12-17
C. First Charge: "Wage the Good Warfare" 1:18-20

II. Paul's Charge Concerning Public Worship (2:1–3:16)

A. Prayer in Public Worship 2:1-8
B. Women in Public Worship 2:9-15
C. Qualifications of Bishops 3:1-7
D. Qualifications of Deacons 3:8-13
E. Second Charge: "Conduct Yourself in the House of God" 3:14-16

III. Paul's Charge Concerning False Teachers (4:1-16)

A. Description of False Teachers 4:1-5
B. Instruction for the True Teacher 4:6-10
C. Third Charge: "Do Not Neglect the Gift" 4:11-16

IV. Paul's Charge Concerning Church Discipline (5:1-25)

A. How to Treat All People 5:1-2
B. How to Treat Widows 5:3-16
C. How to Treat Elders 5:17-20

D. Fourth Charge: "Observe These Things Without Prejudice" 5:21-25

V. Paul's Charge Concerning Pastoral Motives (6:1-21)

A. Exhortation to Servants 6:1-2

B. Exhortation to Godliness with Contentment 6:3-16

C. Exhortation to the Rich 6:17-19

D. Fifth Charge: "Guard What Was Committed" 6:20-21

---

7. The Book of 2 Timothy. Prison is the last place from which to expect a letter of encouragement, but that is where Paul's second letter to Timothy originates. He begins by assuring Timothy of his continuing love and prayers, and reminds him of his spiritual heritage and responsibilities. Only the one who perseveres, whether as a soldier, athlete, farmer, or minister of Jesus Christ, will reap the reward. Paul warns Timothy that his teaching will come under attack as men desert the truth for ear "itching" words (4:3). But Timothy has Paul's example to guide him and God's Word to fortify him as he faces growing opposition and glowing opportunities in the last days.

Paul's last epistle received the title *Pros Timotheon B*, the "Second to Timothy." When Paul's epistles were collected together the *B* was probably added to distinguish this letter from the first letter he wrote to Timothy.

8. The Author of 2 Timothy. Since the Pastoral Epistles have to be treated as a unit on the matter of authorship, see "The Author of 1 Timothy" for comments on the origin of 2 Timothy.

Timothy's name is found more often in the salutations of the Pauline Epistles than any other (2 Co; Ph; Col; 1 and 2 Th; 1 and 2 Ti; Phile). His father was a Greek (Ac 16:1), but his Jewish mother Eunice and grandmother Lois reared him in the knowledge of the Hebrew Scriptures (1:5; 3:15). Timothy evidently became a convert of Paul (1 Co 4:17; 1 Ti 1:2; 2 Ti 1:2) when the apostle was in Lystra on his first missionary journey (Ac 14:8-20). When he visited Lystra on his second missionary journey, Paul decided to take Timothy along with him and circumcised him because of the Jews (Ac 16:1-3). Timothy was ordained to the ministry (1 Ti 4:14; 2 Ti 1:6) and served as a devoted companion and assistant to Paul in Troas, Berea, Thessalonica, and Corinth (Ac 16–18; 1 Th 3:1-2). During the third missionary journey, Timothy labored with Paul and ministered for him as his representative in

Ephesus, Macedonia, and Corinth. He was with Paul during his first Roman imprisonment and evidently went to Philippi (2:19-23) after Paul's release. Paul left him in Ephesus to supervise the work there (1 Ti 1:3) and years later summoned him to Rome (4:9,21). According to Hebrews 13:23, Timothy was imprisoned and released, but the passage does not say where. Timothy was sickly (1 Ti 5:23), timid (2 Ti 1:7), and youthful (1 Ti 4:12), but he was a gifted teacher who was trustworthy and diligent.

9. The Time of 2 Timothy. For a tentative reconstruction of the events following Paul's first Roman imprisonment, see "The Time of 1 Timothy." The cruel and unbalanced Nero, emperor of Rome from A.D. 54-68, was responsible for the beginning of the Roman persecution of Christians. Half of Rome was destroyed in July A.D. 64 by a fire, and mounting suspicion that Nero was responsible for the conflagration caused him to use the unpopular Christians as his scapegoat. Christianity thus became a *religio illicito,* and persecution of those who professed Christ became severe. By the time of Paul's return from Spain to Asia in A.D. 66, his enemies were able to use the official Roman position against Christianity to their advantage. Fearing for their own lives, the Asian believers failed to support Paul after his arrest (1:15), and no one supported him at his first defense before the Imperial Court (4:16). Abandoned by almost everyone (4:10-11), the apostle found himself in circumstances very different from those of his first Roman imprisonment (Ac 28:16-31). At that time he was merely under house arrest, people could freely visit him, and he had the hope of release. Now he was in a cold Roman cell (4:13), regarded "as an evildoer" (2:9), and without hope of acquittal in spite of the success of his initial defense (4:6-8,17-18). Under these conditions, Paul wrote this epistle in the fall of A.D. 67, hoping that Timothy would be able to visit him before the approaching winter (4:21). Timothy evidently was in Ephesus at the time of this letter (see 1:18; 4:19), and on his way to Rome he would go through Troas (4:13) and Macedonia. Priscilla and Aquila (4:19) probably returned from Rome (Ro 16:3) to Ephesus after the burning of Rome and the beginning of the persecution. Tychicus may have been the bearer of this letter (4:12).

10. The Christ of 2 Timothy. Christ Jesus appeared on earth, "abolished death and brought life and immortality to light through the gospel" (1:10). He rose from the dead (2:8) and provides salvation and "eternal glory" (2:10); for if believers "died with Him" they will "also live with Him" (2:11). All who love His appearing will receive "the crown of righteousness" (4:8) and "reign with Him" (2:12).

11. Keys to 2 Timothy.

Key Word: Endurance in the Pastoral Ministry—In this letter, Paul commissions Timothy to faithfully endure and carry on the work that the condemned apostle must now relinquish. This set of instructions exhorts Timothy to use the Word of God constantly in order to overcome growing obstacles to the spread of the gospel. Timothy is in great need of encouragement because of the hardships he is facing, and Paul uses this letter to instruct him about handling persecution from the secular authorities and dissension and deception from within the church. As a spiritual father, Paul urged his young helper to overcome his natural timidity and boldly proclaim the gospel, even if it means that he will suffer for doing so.

Key Verses: 2 Timothy 2:3-4 and 3:14-17—"You therefore must endure hardship as a good soldier of Jesus Christ. No one engaged in warfare entangles himself with the affairs of this life, that he may please him who enlisted him as a soldier" (2:3-4).

"But as for you, continue in the things which you have learned and have been assured of, knowing from whom you have learned them, and that from childhood you have known the Holy Scriptures, which are able to make you wise for salvation through faith which is in Christ Jesus. All Scripture is given by inspiration of God, and is profitable for doctrine, for reproof, for correction, for instruction in righteousness, that the man of God may be complete, thoroughly equipped for every good work" (3:14-17).

Key Chapter: 2 Timothy 2—The second chapter of 2 Timothy ought to be required daily reading for every pastor and full-time Christian worker. Paul lists the keys to an enduring suc-

cessful ministry: (1) a reproducing ministry (1–2), an enduring ministry (3–13), a studying ministry (14–18), and a holy ministry (19–26).

12. Survey of 2 Timothy. Paul knows as he writes this final epistle that his days on earth are quickly drawing to a close. About to relinquish his heavy burdens, the godly apostle seeks to challenge and strengthen his somewhat timid but faithful associate, Timothy, in his difficult ministry in Ephesus. In spite of Paul's bleak circumstances, this is a letter of encouragement that urges Timothy on to steadfastness in the fulfillment of his divinely appointed task. Paul calls Timothy a "good soldier of Jesus Christ" (2:3), and it is clear from the sharp imperatives that this letter is really a combat manual for use in the spiritual warfare: "stir up" (1:6); "do not be ashamed" (1:8,12-13); "share with me in the sufferings" (1:8); "Hold fast . . . sound words" (1:13); "That good thing . . . keep" (1:14); "be strong" (2:1); "endure hardship" (2:3); "Be diligent to present yourself approved" (2:15); "Flee . . . pursue" (2:22); "avoid" (2:23); "You . . . must beware" (4:15). Central to everything in 2 Timothy is the sure foundation of the Word of God. Paul focuses on the need to persevere in present testing (1–2), and to endure in future testing (3–4).

Persevere in Present Testing (1–2). After his salutàtion to his "beloved son" (1–2), Paul expresses his thanksgiving for Timothy's "genuine faith" (1:5). He then encourages Timothy to stand firm in the power of the gospel and to overcome any fear in the face of opposition. At personal risk, Onesiphorus boldly sought out Paul in Rome, but most of the Asian Christians failed to stand behind Paul at the time of his arrest. Timothy must remain faithful and not fear possible persecution. Paul then exhorts his spiritual son to reproduce in the lives of others what he has received in Christ (four generations are mentioned in 2:2). He is responsible to work hard and discipline himself like a teacher, a soldier, a farmer, a workman, a vessel, and a servant, following the example of Paul's perseverance (2:1-13). In his dealings with others, Timothy must not become entangled in false speculation, foolish quarrels, or youthful lusts, which would hamper his effectiveness. As he pursues "righteousness, faith, love, peace" (2:22), he must know how to graciously overcome error.

Endure in Future Testing (3–4). Paul anticipates a time of growing apostasy and wickedness when men and women will be increasingly susceptible to empty religiosity and false teaching (3:1-9). Arrogance and godlessness will breed further deception and persecution, but Timothy must not waver in using the Scripture to combat doctrinal error and moral evil (3:10-17). The Scriptures are inspired ("God-breathed") and with them Timothy is equipped to carry out the ministry to which he was called. Paul's final

exhortation to Timothy (4:1-5) is a classic summary of the task of the man of God to proclaim the gospel in spite of opposing circumstances. This very personal letter closes with an update of Paul's situation in Rome along with certain requests (4:6-22). Paul longs to see Timothy before the end, and he also needs certain articles, especially "the parchments" (probably portions of the Old Testament Scriptures).

OUTLINE OF 2 TIMOTHY

I. Persevere in Present Testings (1:1–2:26)

A. Thanksgiving for Timothy's Faith 1:1-5

B. Reminder of Timothy's Responsibility 1:6-18

C. Characteristics of a Faithful Minister 2:1-26

II. Endure in Future Testings (3:1–4:22)

A. Approaching Day of Apostasy 3:1-17

B. Charge to Preach the Word 4:1-5

C. Approaching Death of Paul 4:6-22

TIN

A soft, silvery white metal with a fairly low melting point and the useful property of being very workable when cold. It has a long history of use by mankind. Most commonly it was alloyed with copper to form bronze, a much harder metal than either copper or tin alone, and much used in the ancient world. Examples of bronze work dating back to 3500 B.C. have been found in the vicinity of Ur. Articles of tin were among the spoils the Israelites took from the Midianites (Nu 31:22). It is thought that the Phoenicians were instrumental in marketing tin in the ancient world, which they took from Spain, and some believe, from Cornwall, England. Tyre imported tin from Tarshish (Eze 27:12).

TINDER

A substance which catches fire quickly, used for starting a fire with only a spark (Is 1:31). See TOW.

TIPH′ SAH *(fording place)*

1. A town at the extreme eastern limit of Solomon's dominions (1 Ki 4:24). It has been identified with the city of Thapsacus on the Euphrates. The ford was used by Cyrus and Alexander.

2. A place probably not far from Tirzah (2 Ki 15:16).

TI′ RAS

A son of Japheth (Ge 10:2; 1 Ch 1:5).

TI′ RA·THITES

The designation of a family of scribes who lived at Jabez (1 Ch 2:55).

TIRE (archaic)

Attire:

1. A headdress, probably an ornate turban worn by high priests, bridegrooms, and ladies (Ex 39:28; Is 3:20; 61:10; Eze 24:17).

2. An object of jewelry or clothing worn by women (Is 3:18). The KJV "round tires like the moon" is elsewhere translated "crescents" (NKJV), "crescent ornaments" (NASB), or "crescent necklaces" (NIV).

TIR′ HA·KAH

See PHARAOH.

TIR·HA′ NAH

Son of Caleb by his concubine Maachah (1 Ch 2:48).

TI′ RI·A

A son of Jehaleleel, of the tribe of Judah (1 Ch 4:16).

TIR′ SHA·THA

A Persian title given to Zerubbabel and Nehemiah at the time they governed Judah (Ez 2:63; Ne 7:65,70; 8:9; 10:1).

TIR' ZAH *(delight)*

A woman and a city of the Old Testament:
1. The youngest daughter of Zelophehad (Nu 26:33; 27:1; 36:11; Jos 17:3).
2. A city of the Canaanites (Jos 12:24).

TISH' BITE

The designation of Elijah, the prophet (1 Ki 17:1; 21:17,28; 2 Ki 1:3,8; 9:36).

TISH' RI

First month of the Jewish civil year, seventh month of the sacred year, roughly corresponding to September/October. Also called Ethanim (1 Ki 8:2). See CALENDAR.

TITHE

A tenth part of one's income to be devoted to the Lord. Tithing has very ancient roots. While tithing is most familiar as a part of the Mosaic law, the very first tithe mentioned in the Bible is in Genesis. After he had rescued Lot, and defeated Chedorlaomer and his confederates, Abraham met Melchizedek, king of Salem and priest of the Most High in the valley of Shaveh. The Scripture records that Abraham gave a tenth of the spoils of his victory to Melchizedek (Ge 14:20). No information is given concerning the reason for this, or whether it was a known and expected practice. In the book of Hebrews, the fact that Abraham gave this tithe to Melchizedek is presented as proof of Melchizedek's greatness (He 7:1-10). According to this passage, the Levites also paid the tithe to Melchizedek, through their father Abraham, thus proving the superiority of the priesthood of Melchizedek over the Levitical priesthood.

The tithe was not unique to Abraham. Jacob also promised a tenth of all he had to the Lord (Ge 28:22).

When God gave the law to Moses at Mt. Sinai, He instituted a mandatory tithe which was designed to support the Levites and to be used to help widows, orphans, and strangers who had inadequate means. The Jews were required to give a tenth of the products of the soil and of cattle "to the Lord" (Le 27:30-33). Every tenth animal of the herd and flock was set apart. The tithe offered as a heave offering was given to the Levites (Nu 18:21,24) because of their service at the sanctuary and the fact that they did not receive a portion of the land. All the tithes and offerings were taken to the

place set apart by God, where a portion was eaten by the giver and the Levites in a feast of thanksgiving (De 12:5-7, 11-12, 17-18). The balance went to the Levites. Every third year the tithe was stored in the town of the givers, and the widow, the stranger, the fatherless, and Levite could partake of it (De 14:28-29; 26:12-15).

After the people returned from the captivity, they were careless and did not tithe regularly. The prophet Malachi rebuked the people for robbing God of what they were commanded to give him. (Mal 3:8-12).

Tithing is mentioned only a few times in the New Testament, and except for the references in Hebrews to Abraham's tithe to Melchizedek, all are references to the tithing of the Mosaic law (Ma 23:23; Lk 11:42; 18:12; He 7:5-6,8-9). Nowhere are Christians commanded to give a tenth of their income. Instead, Christians are urged to give generously and sacrificially, not grudgingly, but with a cheerful heart. Paul taught the Corinthian Christians to make an orderly collection of money to be given to relieve those who were suffering, setting aside something each week, so that the money would be ready to give (1 Co 16:1-3). Paul gave further teaching on giving in 2 Corinthians 8–9, clearly teaching that there is no commandment concerning the exact amount, but rather that we should give as Christ gave, who willingly became poor so that we might gain eternal wealth. This does not mean that one person is supposed to impoverish himself so that others may live at ease, but rather that believers are to share their abundance with one another as each has a need. Generous giving has generous results.

TIT' I·US JUSTUS

A man of Corinth who lived next door to the synagogue and with whom Paul stayed (Ac 18:7; NRSV, NIV, REB, NASB). He is also called Justus (KJV, NKJV).

TITLE

The sign or placard that Pilate made to post on Jesus' cross, saying "Jesus of Nazareth, King of the Jews." This title was written in three languages: Latin, Greek, and Hebrew (Jo 19:19-20).

TIT' TLE

The smallest stroke of some of the Hebrew letters, the tiny "horn" made to distinguish one letter from another similar one (Jo 19:19-20). Also see JOT.

TI′TUS

A companion and fellow-laborer of Paul. A Christian convert of Greek parentage, he is first mentioned in the Bible when he accompanied Paul to Jerusalem where a church council considered the question of circumcision as it related to Gentile Christians. Titus was not required by the council to be circumcised (Ga 2:1-3). Titus is also mentioned several times in connection with the believers at Corinth. Paul sent Titus to Corinth after the writing of his first Epistle to the Corinthians, and he was much encouraged at the news Titus brought back to him of the Corinthians repentance. Titus became very attached to the believers in Corinth during his time there, and rejoiced with Paul over their obedience (2 Co 7:5-16). Titus was also entrusted with the collection for the saints in Judea, and Paul gives him the highest recommendations. He is described as diligent, earnest, and honorable (2 Co 8:16-17, 22); Paul freely endorses him as "my partner and fellow worker" (2 Co 8:23). Paul's personal epistle to him is addressed to "my true son in our common faith" (Tit 1:4). Paul had left Titus on Crete to strengthen the Cretan church, and this letter was written to guide his activities there (Tit 1:5–3:11). Later, Titus was a companion to Paul in his final imprisonment (2 Ti 4:10), until he left for Dalmatia, possibly on an evangelistic mission.

TITUS, EPISTLE TO

1. The Book of Titus. Titus, a young pastor, faced the unenviable assignment of setting in order the church at Crete. Paul wrote advising him to appoint elders, men of proven spiritual character in their homes and businesses, to oversee the work of the church. But elders are not the only members of the church who are required to excel spiritually. Men and women, young and old, each have their vital functions to fulfill in the church if they are to be living examples of the doctrine they profess. Throughout his letter to Titus, Paul stresses the necessary, practical working out of salvation in the daily lives of both the elders and the congregation. Good works are desirable and profitable for all believers.

This third Pastoral Epistle is simply titled *Pros* *Titon,* "To Titus." Ironically, this was also the name of the Roman general who destroyed Jerusalem in A.D. 70 and succeeded his father Vespasian as emperor.

2. The Author of Titus. Since the Pastoral Epistles have to be treated as a unit on the matter of authorship, see "The Author of 1 Timothy" for the authorship of Titus.

Titus is not mentioned in Acts, but the thirteen references to him in the Pauline Epistles make it clear that he was one of Paul's closest and most trusted companions. This convert of Paul ("my true son in our common faith," 1:4) was probably from Syrian Antioch, if he was one of the disciples of Acts 11:26. Paul brought this uncircumcised Greek believer to Jerusalem (Ga 2:3) where he became a test case on the matter of Gentiles and liberty from the law. Years later when Paul set out from Antioch on his third missionary journey (Ac 18:22), Titus must have accompanied him because he was sent by the apostle to Corinth on three occasions during that time (2 Co 2:12-13; 7:5-7,13-15; 8:6,16-24). He is not mentioned again until Paul leaves him in Crete to carry on the work (Tit 1:5). He was with Paul during his second Roman imprisonment but left to go to Dalmatia (2 Ti 4:10), possibly on an evangelistic mission. Paul spoke of this reliable and gifted associate as his "brother" (2 Co 2:13), his "partner and fellow worker" (2 Co 8:23), and his "son" (1:4). He lauded Titus's character and conduct in 2 Corinthians 7:13-15 and 8:16-17.

3. The Time of Titus. For a tentative reconstruction of the events following Paul's first Roman imprisonment, see "The Time of 1 Timothy."

The Mediterranean island of Crete is 156 miles long and up to 30 miles wide, and its first-century inhabitants were notorious for untruthfulness and immorality (1:12-13). "To act the Cretan" became an idiom meaning "to play the liar." A number of Jews from Crete were present in Jerusalem at the time of Peter's sermon on the day of Pentecost (Ac 2:11), and some of them may have believed in Christ and introduced the gospel to their countrymen. Certainly Paul would not have had opportunity to do evangelistic work during his brief sojourn in Crete while he was en route to Rome (Ac 27:7-13). The apostle spread the gospel in the cities of Crete after his release from Roman imprisonment and left Titus there to finish organizing the churches (1:5). Because of the problem of immorality among the Cretans, it was important for Titus to stress the need for righteousness in Christian living. False teachers, especially "those of the circumcision" (1:10), were also misleading and divisive. Paul wrote this letter about A.D. 63, perhaps from Corinth, taking advantage of the journey of Zenas and Apollos (3:13), whose destination would take them by way of Crete. Paul was planning to spend the winter in Nicopolis (western Greece), and he urged Titus in this letter to join him there upon his replacement by Artemas or Tychicus (3:12). Paul may have been planning to leave Nicopolis for Spain in the spring, and he wanted his useful companion Titus to accompany him.

4. The Christ of Titus. The deity and redemptive work of Christ are beautifully stated in 2:13-14: "Looking for the blessed hope and glorious reappearing of our great God and Savior Jesus Christ, who gave Himself for us, that He might redeem us from every lawless deed and purify for Himself His own special people, zealous of good works."

5. Keys to Titus.

Key Word: Conduct Manual for Church Living—This brief letter focuses on Titus's role and responsibility in the organization and supervision of the churches in Crete. It is written to strengthen and exhort Titus to firmly exercise his authority as an apostolic representative to churches that need to be put in order, refuting false teachers and dissenters and replacing immoral behavior with good deeds. Paul used this letter to remind Titus of some of the details related to his task, including the qualifications for elders and the behavior expected of various groups in the churches. Paul includes three doctrinal sections in this letter to stress that proper belief (orthodoxy) gives the basis for proper behavior (orthopraxy).

Key Verses: Titus 1:5 and 3:8—"For this reason I left you in Crete, that you should set in order the things that are lacking, and appoint elders in every city as I commanded you—" (1:5).

"This is a faithful saying, and these things I want you to affirm constantly, that those who have believed in God should be careful to maintain good works. These things are good and profitable to men" (3:8).

Key Chapter: Titus 2—Summarized in Titus 2 are the key commands to be obeyed which insure godly relationships within the church. Paul includes all categories of people instructing them to show "all good fidelity, that they may adorn the doctrine of God our Savior in all things" (2:10).

6. Survey of Titus. Titus, like 1 Timothy, was written by Paul after his release from Roman imprisonment and was also written to an associate who was given the task of organizing and supervising a large work as an apostolic representative. Paul left Titus on the island of Crete to "set in order the things that are lacking, and appoint elders in every city" (1:5). Not long after Paul's departure from Crete, he wrote this letter to encourage and assist Titus in his task. It stresses sound doctrine and warns against those who distort the truth, but it also is a conduct manual that emphasizes good deeds and proper conduct of various groups within the churches. This epistle falls into two major sections: appoint elders (1); set things in order (2–3).

Appoint Elders (1): The salutation to Titus is actually a compact doctrinal statement, which lifts up "His word" as the source of the truth that reveals the way to eternal life (1:1-4). Paul reminds Titus of his responsibility to organize the churches of Crete by appointing elders (also called overseers; see 1:5,7) and rehearses the qualifications these spiritual leaders must meet (1:5-9). This is especially important in view of the disturbances that are being caused by false teachers who are upsetting a number of the believers with their Judaic myths and commandments (1:10-16). The natural tendency toward moral laxity among the Cretans coupled with that kind of deception is a dangerous force that must be overcome by godly leadership and sound doctrine.

Set Things in Order (2–3): Titus is given the charge to "speak the things which are proper and sound doctrine" (2:1), and Paul delineates Titus's role with regard to various groups in the church, including older men, older women, young women, young men, and servants (2:2-10). The knowledge of Christ must effect a transformation in each of these groups so that their testimony will "adorn the doctrine of God" (2:10). The second doctrinal statement of Titus (2:11-14) gives the basis for the appeals that Paul has just made for righteous living. God in His grace redeems believers from being slaves of sin, assuring them the "blessed hope" of the coming of Christ that will eventually be realized. Paul urges Titus to authoritatively proclaim these truths (2:15).

In chapter 3, Paul moves from conduct in groups (2:1-10) to conduct in general (3:1-11). The behavior of believers as citizens must be different than the behavior of unbelievers because of their regeneration and renewal by the Holy Spirit. The third doctrinal statement in this book (3:4-7) emphasizes the kindness, love, and mercy of God who saves us "not by works of righteousness which we have done" (3:5). Nevertheless, the need for good deeds as a result of salvation is stressed six times in the three chapters of Titus (1:16; 2:7,14; 3:1,8,14). Paul exhorts Titus to deal firmly with dissenters who would cause factions and controversies (3:9-11) and closes the letter with three instructions, a greeting, and a benediction (3:12-15).

OUTLINE OF TITUS

I. Appoint Elders (1:1-16)

A. Introduction 1:1-4
B. Ordain Qualified Elders 1:5-9
C. Rebuke False Teachers............... 1:10-16

II. Set Things in Order (2:1–3:15)

A. Speak Sound Doctrine 2:1-15
B. Maintain Good Works 3:1-11
C. Conclusion 3:12-15

TI′ TUS JUS′ TUS

See TITIUS JUSTUS.

TI′ ZITE

The designation of Joha, son of Shimri, and one of David's mighty men (1 Ch 11:45).

TO′ AH (low, lowly)

Son of Zuph and ancestor of Samuel and Heman. He was a Levite of the family of Kohath (1 Ch 6:34). He is also called Tohu (1 Sa 1:1) and Nahath (1 Ch 6:26).

TOB (good)

A region beyond the borders of Israel, east of the Jordan (Ju 11:3,5).

TOB-AD·O·NI′ JAH (pleading to Jehovah)

A Levite (2 Ch 17:8).

TO·BI′ AH (Jehovah is good)

Two men mentioned in the Old Testament:
1. Head of a family, some of whom returned from Babylon with Zerubbabel. They were unable to establish their descent as true Israelites (Ez 2:60; Ne 7:62).
2. An Ammonite who opposed Nehemiah in building the wall of Jerusalem (Ne 2:10; 4:3,7).

TO·BI′ JAH (Jehovah is good)

Two Old Testament men:
1. A Levite appointed by Jehoshaphat to teach the people of Judah (2 Ch 17:8).

2. A Jew from whom the prophet Zechariah secured the silver and gold for the crowns to place on the head of Joshua the high priest (Ze 6:10,14).

TOBIT, BOOK OF

See APOCRYPHA.

TO′ CHEN (a measure)

A city of Simeon (1 Ch 4:32).

TO·GAR′ MAH

A son of Gomer, the son of Japheth who survived the flood (Ge 10:3). His descendants are mentioned by Ezekiel as traders in horses and mules (Eze 27:14).

TO′ HU

A son of Zuph and an ancestor of Samuel (1 Sa 1:1). See TOHU.

TO′ I (error)

King of Hamath (2 Sa 8:9-12; also called Tou, 1 Ch 18:9-11).

TO′ KHATH

See TIKVAH.

TO′ LA (worm)

Two Old Testament men:
1. Son of Issachar. He was the head of a tribal family (Ge 46:13; Nu 26:23; 1 Ch 7:1-2). In the

time of David, the Tolaites numbered 22,600 fighting men.

2. A judge of Israel (Ju 10:1-2).

TO´LAD

See ELTOLAD.

TOLAITES

The descendants of Issachar's son, Tola (Nu 26:23).

TOLL

See TAXES.

TOMB

See SEPULCHRE.

TONGUE

The organ of speech (Job 29:10; Ps 39:3; 71:24; Jam 3:6). The word is also used to denote the language or dialect of a people (Es 1:22; Da 1:4; Ac 1:19; 2:4,8,11).

TONGUES, CONFUSION OF

After the flood, all the people on earth spoke one common language. They were all of one family, and instead of obeying God and scattering over the earth to fill it again, they lived together in one area. In pride at their own accomplishments, they decided to build a tower reaching to heaven, but God frustrated their efforts by confusing their language. Suddenly, instead of speaking one common language, the group was divided into several languages. The construction of the tower ceased, and the people finally scattered (Ge 11:1-9). See BABEL, TOWER OF.

TONGUES, GIFT OF

Speaking in tongues first occurred at Pentecost (Ac 2) when the apostles were gathered in an upper room, waiting for the promised Holy Spirit. Suddenly there was a rushing wind, and tongues of fire appeared above their heads. They were filled with the Holy Spirit, and began to speak in foreign languages (other tongues). At that time Jerusalem was full of pilgrims from all over the world, and these strangers were amazed to hear the Galileans speaking in their home language. Peter used this miracle as an opportunity to preach the gospel, and about three thousand souls were added to the believers that day.

Speaking in tongues is also addressed in Paul's first letter to the Corinthians. He lists it as one of the spiritual gifts (1 Co 12:8-10,28-31), where he also teaches that all do not have the all of the gifts, but they are distributed by the Holy Spirit to do a job. Just as the different parts of the human body serve different purposes, so do believers, as members of the body of Christ, have different jobs that serve the whole.

In chapter 13 of 1 Corinthians Paul very eloquently shows that no matter how interesting or impressive spiritual gifts may be, the way of love is the more excellent way, and that all gifts without love are virtually empty. This is a serious exhortation to remember that gifts come from the Holy Spirit, and we don't decide how He disperses them, but the way of love is open to all and must be practiced by all.

Paul then goes on to say that those who speak in tongues speak to God, but those who prophesy speak edification to men. He says that he wishes everyone spoke in tongues, but he wishes even more that all prophesied. He goes on to address the problem of tongues not being understood (14:7-25). He thanks God that he speaks in tongues more than the Corinthians, but asks for maturity in using this gift so that the church is edified. He also refers to praying in tongues, as praying with his spirit but not with his understanding, and says that he chooses to pray with understanding as well. Some scholars understand these passages to refer to the concept of tongues not necessarily being a known language, but a spiritual language. Paul addresses the concept of interpretation of tongues in the rest of the chapter, (26-40), urging order in the church, and especially directing that if anyone speaks in tongues, there should also be an interpretation, and that not more than two or three take turns in this. If there is not an interpreter, then the speaker should be silent in church and speak to himself and God.

TOOLS OF THE BIBLE

Anvil, awl, ax, bellows, brazier, chisel, compass, fan, file, fire pot, forge, fork, furnace, goad, hammer, harrow, hatchet, hoe, knife, level, mallet, marking tool, mattock, maul, measuring line or rod, mill, mirror, mortar and pestle, nail, needle, oven, peg, pestle, pick, plans, plow, plowshare, plumb ling/plummet, press, pruning hook, razor,

*rule, saw, shovel, sickle, sieve, sledge, thresh-
ing sledge, wheel, winnowing fork, yoke.*

TO′PAZ

A golden yellow aluminum silicate. Topaz is
mentioned in the Bible as a precious stone found
in Ethiopia (Job 28:19). It was in the first row
of the breastplate of the high priest (Ex 28:17;
also called chrysolite), and the ninth foundation of the New Jerusalem (Re 21:20).

TO′PHEL *(mortar)*

A station of the Israelites in the wilderness.
It is associated with the last words of Moses to
the nation (De 1:1).

TO′PHET *(spitting out)*

A place in the valley of Hinnom where high
places were built and the people offered their
sons and daughters to the god Molech (2 Ki
23:10).

TO′PHETH

See TOPHET.

TO′RAH *(instruction, guidance)*

This Hebrew word is used in several ways.
It is often translated "Law" in English, and is
used to refer to the Mosaic code given at Sinai.
In a more comprehensive sense, *torah* means
more than just the moral code or the legal details of the law. It refers to the whole spectrum
of God's teaching, and thus includes the entire
Old Testament. In more recent times, the word
Torah has come to mean the first five books
of the Old Testament, also called the Law, the
Pentateuch, and the Books of Moses.

TORCH

An illuminator. Probably a stick of burning
resinous wood as distinguished from an oil
lamp or a candle (Na 2:3; Ze 12:6; Jo 18:3).

TORMENTOR

An inquisitor who used harsh means to secure a confession (Ac 22:24).

TORTOISE

A creature mentioned in the list of unclean
animals in Leviticus 11:29 (KJV), also translated "great lizard." It is not known for sure
what kind of reptile this passage is referring to.

TO′U

See TOI.

TOW

The refuse short fuzzy fibers left over from
combing flax. Tow was used for tinder, a light
dry substance which catches fire easily, useful
for starting a fire with a small spark (Ju 16:9;
Is 1:31). Historically, tow has also been used to
make a rough fabric used for sacking and such
utilitarian purposes. See FLAX.

TOW′ER

A fortified structure for the defense of a city.
In the tower a watchman could see in every
direction (2 Ki 9:17). Towers were built at the
corners of the walls and at the city gates (2 Ch
26:9-10; Ne 3:1). They contained machines for
shooting stones and arrows (2 Ch 26:15), and
provided a safe retreat (Ju 9:51-52; Ps 61:3).
Towers were also built for watchmen to guard
a vineyard (Is 1:8; 5:2; Ma 21:33).

TOWER OF BABEL

See BABEL, TOWER OF.

TOWER OF THE FURNACES

See OVENS, TOWER OF THE.

TOWN CLERK

The recorder or scribe of a city who wrote the
laws and statutes and read them in public gath-
erings (Ac 19:35).

TRACH·O·NI′TIS *(rough)*

A lava region south of Damascus; Herod's
brother Philip was tetrarch over this area (Lk
3:1).

TRADER

A merchant, one whose business is to buy or
trade goods in order to sell or trade again at a
profit. Joseph's brothers sold him to a traveling
group of Midianite traders for twenty shekels
of silver (Ge 37:28).

TRA·DI′TION

Precepts and rules, not in the written law but
believed to have been given by God to Moses.
Orally transmitted from generation to generation, they were to be obeyed with the same reverence as the law (Ma 15:2-3,6; Mk 7:3,5,9,13;
Col 2:8). See TALMUD.

TRANCE

An abnormal state in which the mind is abstracted from physical objects and sees visions— as sort of waking dream-state. Peter and Paul both experienced falling into a trance while praying, and being shown a vision from God. In both cases, the trance was not self-induced, but came from God in order to reveal an important message (Ac 10:10; 11:5; 22:17).

TRANSFIGURATION

A moment in the life of Jesus in which, while on a high mountain with Peter, James, and John, He suddenly was visited by Moses and Elijah who spoke of His coming death (Lk 9:28-31). Jesus was transfigured in appearance; His face shone brightly and His clothes appeared white as light (Ma 17:2), giving the disciples a glimpse of His heavenly glory. Just as had happened at Jesus's baptism, a voice from heaven proclaimed the Father's approval of the Son.

The transfiguration occurred at night (Lk 9:32), about six or eight days after Peter's confession to Jesus that He (Jesus) was the Messiah and the Son of God (Ma 16:13-17). After this event Jesus told the disciples to tell no one of the transfiguration until after the "Son of man be risen again from the dead" (Ma 17:9; Mk 9:9).

TRANSFORM

To change into a different form. Paul urges believers not to conform to the world, but rather to "be transformed" by the renewing of the mind (Ro 12:2). We have the assurance that God is already at work in believers, transforming them into the image of Christ (2 Co 3:18). When we reach heaven, not only our natures but our bodies will be transformed (Ph 3:21).

TRANSGRESSION

Sin, rebellion; the violation of law or duty (Ps 32:1; Ro 4:15; 1 Ti 2:14; He 2:2). See SIN.

TRANSJORDAN

The area on the east side of the Jordan. The word Transjordan is not actually used in the Bible, the area is usually referred to as "beyond the Jordan" (Ge 50:10-11). The tribes of Reuben, Gad, and the half tribe of Manasseh settled in this area (De 3:12-20; Jos 1:12-16). In the New Testament era, this area was known as the Decapolis and Perea (Ma 4:15; Mk 3:8).

The King's Highway was a road which passed through the transjordan from north to south (Nu 20:17; 21:22).

TRANSLATE

To take a person directly from one state of being to another, without transition. Enoch, an ancestor of Noah, was "translated," that is, he did not die, God simply took him away (Ge 5:24; He 11:5). Only one other person in the Bible had this interesting experience; Elijah the Tishbite was met by a chariot of fire and taken up to heaven in a whirlwind (2 Ki 2:11). This is exactly what happens when a person believes in Jesus Christ: he is translated immediately from the kingdom of darkness to the kingdom of light. There is no waiting period or gradual change over, instead the new believer instantly becomes part of another realm (Co 1:13). Those believers who are still alive when Christ returns will experience real bodily translation, like Enoch and Elijah, as they are caught up into heaven without dying (1 Co 15:51-57; 1 Th 4:13-18).

TRANSLITERATION

Writing a word in the characters of a different language so that the readers can give the foreign word its correct pronunciation. Transliteration takes only the sound into a different language, as opposed to translation which carries the meaning. Several Aramaic or Hebrew words are transliterated (not translated) in the Greek New Testament. One example is the word "Amen" (see AMEN).

TRAVAIL

Hard labor, pain, sorrow. Often used of childbirth (Ge 35:16-19); also a spiritual struggle (Is 53:11).

TREASURE

A precious substance, something of great value. The Magi brought treasures to the infant Jesus as an indication of His station (Ma 2:11). Jesus compared the truths of God's kingdom to a precious treasure, worth giving up everything to own (Ma 13:44-46). He also taught that the traditional earthly definition of treasure will not last into eternity. Treasure in heaven is based upon relationship with God which brings about a changed life (Ma 6:19-21). All the treasures of wisdom and knowledge are hidden in Christ (Col 2:3).

TREASURE CITIES

See STORAGE CITY.

TREATY

See ALLIANCE; COVENANT.

TREE OF KNOWLEDGE

A tree in the center of the garden of Eden, the one tree from which God had forbidden Adam and Eve to eat, or they would die (Ge 2:9,17). Satan, in the form of a serpent, tempted Eve to eat the fruit, encouraging her first to doubt God, and then to disobey. He told her that by knowing good and evil, she would be like God, and this seemed desirable to Eve (Ge 3:5-6). She took the fruit and ate it, Adam followed her example, and both God's warning and the serpent's promise came true—in a way. Adam and Eve now had experiential knowledge of the difference between good and evil, the great gulf between innocence and sin. They knew more, but the serpent lied when he said it would make them more like God. God's warning came true just as He had said: Adam and Eve experienced spiritual death on the day they ate the fruit. They also lost the right to eat from the tree of life, and were banished from the garden, to work hard until they finally died physically.

TREE OF LIFE

The second tree in the center of the garden of Eden, along with the tree of knowledge (Ge 2:9,16). Adam and Eve were free to eat from this tree until they disobeyed God. Then they were cast from the garden and denied the fruit of the tree.

Happily, this is not the end of the story. God loved the world, and made a way of redemption (Jo 3:16). At the end of time, when the new heavens and earth are made, and all that is old is passed away, the tree of life will once again be free for all to eat from. The curse will be ended (Re 22:2-3).

TRESPASS

See SIN.

TRESPASS OFFERING

See OFFERINGS.

TRIAL

A difficult experience, something which tests the faith or stretches the strength to withstand temptation. James exhorts believers to rejoice in trials because testing produces patience (Jam 1:2). Peter says that when we partake of Christ's sufferings we will be blessed (1 Pe 4:13-14).

TRIANGLE

A musical instrument, thought to be a type of triangular harp (Da 3:5; REB). See HARP.

TRIBE

A community of people who are all descended from a common ancestor, as well as the outsiders who have become attached to the group, such as slaves, or those who marry into the clan. Most ancient societies were tribal societies, with great importance placed on family relationships. The nation of Israel was composed of twelve tribes, descended from the twelve sons of Israel, the grandson of Abraham.

TRIBAL RIVALS

The twelve tribes of Israel encountered many tribal enemies, particularly during the Old Testament period before and after the conquest of Canaan. Important tribal rivals mentioned in the Bible are the Amalekites, Ammonites, Amorites, Edomites, Gibeonites, Horites, Hivites, Jebusites, Kenites, Midianites, and Moabites.

These tribal adversaries of Israel were nomadic people, although most of them lived in Canaan at one time or another. The Amorites, Hivites, and Jebusites were among the seven groups God commanded Israel to cast out of Canaan (De 7:1-2). Several tribes, such as the Kenites, Midianites, and Moabites, were desert wanderers, migrating throughout the desert regions of the Dead Sea or Sinai with their flocks and herds.

Many of these tribal groups were distant relatives of the Israelites. The Midianites traced their ancestry to Midian, the son of Abraham by his second wife Keturah (Ge 25:2). Three tribes—the Amorites, the Hivites, and the Jebusites—were descendants of Canaan, a son of Ham (Ge 10:6,15-18). The Moabites and Ammonites were descendants of Lot (Ge 19:36-38).

Most of these tribes were warlike and often cruel and barbaric, constantly attacking Israel and other nations. Except for those retained as slave laborers, they were eventually destroyed or expelled from Canaan. The Gibeonites became woodcutters and water carriers for Israel (Jos 9:18-21). Solomon used the Hivites and other

Canaanites who remained in the land as construction laborers (1 Ki 9:20-21).

Israel's tribal rivals were generally idol worshipers. For this reason, God commanded His people not to intermarry or make political alliances with these groups (De 7:1-4). The Moabites and Ammonites were especially rebuked by God because they refused to help the Israelites during their journey from Egypt to the promised land (De 23:3-4).

TRIBULATION

A great trouble. (Ma 13:21; Jo 16:33; Ro 5:3; Ac 14:22). See TRIAL.

TRIBULATION, THE GREAT

A terrible time of unprecedented trouble on earth when the wrath of God will be poured out on sinful humans (Mk 13:14-23). Some believers will live through this time (Re 7:14). Afterwards, the sun and moon will be darkened, and Christ will return in power and great glory (Mk 13:24). According to the prophet Daniel, this time will last for one "seven," or a period of seven years. It is divided into two parts: a time of apparent peace, and then a time of abomination, wrath, and destruction (Da 9:27). The book of Revelation speaks of a similar period of seven years. See ANTICHRIST; ESCHATOLOGY; MILLENNIUM.

TRIB′UTE

For the support of the temple worship the Hebrews were required to pay a half shekel as tribute (Ma 17:24). It was an annual tax required of every male Jew of twenty years of age and upward. In the time of Nehemiah the amount was the third of a shekel (Ne 10:32-33). Tribute, consisting of money, goods, or service, was exacted from foreign subjects (Ju 1:28; Ez 4:13; Ne 5:4; Es 10:1). In New Testament times the Hebrews paid tribute to Rome. Neither Paul nor Jesus was opposed to this (Ma 17:25; Lk 20:22-25; 13:6-7).

TRIFLES

A delicious morsel of food (most probably not the present sense of a cake soaked in wine and topped with fruit and cream). The words of a talebearer or gossip are compared to a "tasty trifle" (Pr 18:8; 26:22; NKJV), the KJV translates this word as "wounds."

TRIGON

A musical instrument, thought to be a type of triangular harp (Da 3:5; NASB, NRSV). See HARP.

TRIMMERS

See SNUFFDISHES, SNUFFERS.

TRINITY

The theological term describing the unique three-in-one God of the universe, a unified being made up of three persons: Father, Son, and Holy Spirit. The three persons are eternal, coexistent, and equal. The three persons are the same substance but different in subsistence. All parts of the Godhead possess deity, but all have different functions. This is not a doctrine of three gods, but one God in three persons.

The word "trinity" never appears in the Bible, but the doctrine is nevertheless clearly set forth. The deity of God the Father is undoubted (Jo 6:27; 1 Pe 1:2). The deity of the Son is shown as He portrays the attributes of God (Ma 9:4; 28:8,20); as He is addressed as God (Jo 20:28; Jo 8:58; Jo 1:1); and as He is doing things only God can do (Jo 1:3; Col 1:17; Jo 12:9). The deity of the Holy Spirit is taught as He is called God (Ac 5), and seen with the attributes of God (1 Co 6:19).

TRIPOLIS, MEN OF THE

See TARPELITES.

TRO′AS

A seaport of Mysia, some distance south of the Troy of Homer. Paul visited Troas several times (Ac 16:8-11; 20:6; 2 Ti 4:13). Paul was in this city when he had the vision of the man from Macedonia, asking him to come and help them. Troas was also the location of the miraculous healing of Eutychus, who fell out of an upstairs window and was picked up dead (Ac 20:5-12).

TRO·GYL′LI·UM

A city on the western coast of Asia Minor, south of Ephesus. Paul stayed in this city on his return from his third missionary journey (Ac 20:15).

TROPH′I·MUS *(nourishing)*

A native of Ephesus who was a Gentile Christian and a companion of Paul on his third journey (Ac 20:4). He inadvertently caused a riot in Jerusalem, as the Jews assumed that Paul had brought him into the temple, defiling the holy place with a Gentile presence. They seized Paul and would have killed him if it had not been for the timely intervention of the Romans. Trophimus accompanied Paul again as he traveled to Rome as a prisoner, but fell sick and had to stay in Miletus (2 Ti 4:20).

TRUMPET

A musical instrument made of metal or of a ram's horn which could be heard at a great distance (Ex 19:16,19; 2 Sa 6:15). Militarily it was used in mobilizing an army (Ju 6:34), signaling an attack, and calling off pursuit (2 Sa 2:28). It was used for celebrations such as the crowning of a king (1 Ki 1:34; 2 Ki 9:13); the bringing of the ark into the new temple (2 Ch 5:12-13); and the ushering in of the year of Jubilee (Le 25:9). The trumpet will sound at the resurrection of the dead (1 Co 15:52).

TRUMPETS, FEAST OF

On the first day of the seventh month, a Sabbath rest was taken, and the trumpets were blown as a memorial. Offerings of fire were made, and no work was done (Le 23:24-32). The offering was to consist of one young bull, one ram, seven yearling lambs, a grain offering, and a goat kid as a sin offering. In addition, the ordinary New Moon offerings were to be made (Nu 29:1-6).

TRUTH

Truth is one of the fundamental attributes of God's character (Ex 34:6; De 32:4; Ps 57:3; 89:14; 115:1). Inconsistency is impossible with God; He is, in fact, the definition of truth, and thus it impossible for Him to lie (He 6:18; Jam 1:17).

Jesus, who is God in the flesh, called Himself "the way, the truth, and the life" (Jo 14:6). Jesus not only spoke the truth, He actually is truth. The Holy Spirit is called "the Spirit of truth" (Jo 14:17), and part of His role is to guide Christians into all truth (Jo 16:13).

TRY·PHAE′NA

See TRYPHENA.

TRY·PHE′NA *(luxurious)*

A Christian woman at Rome (Ro 16:12). See TRYPHOSA.

TRY·PHO′SA *(delicate)*

A Christian woman at Rome to whom Paul sent greetings. She and Tryphena may have been sisters, or they may have labored together as deaconesses (Ro 16:12).

TSADDE

The eighteenth letter of the Hebrew alphabet. It is the heading of verses 137-144 of Psalm 119; in Hebrew each of these eight verses begins with the letter tsadde. See ACROSTIC.

TU′BAL

1. Son of Japheth (Ge 10:2; 1 Ch 1:5).
2. A tribe probably descended from the preceding. It is believed to have spread into Russia and perhaps into Spain (Is 66:19; Eze 32:26).

TU′BAL-CAIN

Son of Lamech, the descendant of Cain (Ge 4:22). He is described as "an instructor of every craftsman in bronze and iron."

TUMOR

The exact nature of this disease is not known. When the Philistines stole the ark, they were afflicted with tumors (1 Sa 6:11; "emerods," KJV). Some scholars believe this is a reference to hemorrhoids or ulcers. Tumors were also the promised punishment for disobeying God's law (De 28:27).

TUNIC

A single undergarment of simple construction, worn under a robe or mantle. Jesus's tunic was woven in one piece, without a seam (Jo 19:23). English translations have also used the term "shirt" or "coat."

TUNNEL

See HEZEKIAH'S WATER TUNNEL.

TURBAN

A headdress made from a long piece of cloth wrapped around the head (Job 29:14; Ex 28:39). This word has also been translated, "tire," "bonnet," and "mitre."

TURQUOISE

An opaque sky blue mineral, used as a gemstone for many centuries. It was found extensively in Turkey (this is the root of the English

TURBAN

word "turquoise"). Turquoise is an aluminum copper phosphate. It is thought that the scriptural references to turquoise would be better rendered "emerald" (Eze 28:13). See EMERALD.

TURTLE

This word is used several times as an abbreviation for "turtledove," rather than a reference to the hard-shelled reptile (Song 2:12; Je 8:7).

TURTLE-DOVE

A migratory bird of the pigeon family (Song 2:12; Je 8:7). It could be used as a burnt and sin offering under the law (Le 1:14). This provision of the law was favorable to the poor who could easily afford it.

TUTOR

See SCHOOLMASTER.

TWELVE, THE

Jesus chose twelve apostles to serve with Him during His ministry and to provide leadership for the church after His ascension. Twelve may have been selected because this number corresponds to the twelve tribes of Old Testament Israel.

Chosen by Jesus after he prayed all night (Lk 6:12-16), the twelve included two sets of fishermen brothers, a tax collector, and a traitor. Among the twelve, Peter, James, and John were particularly close to the Master.

The terms *disciple* and *apostle* are often used interchangeably in referring to these men. But a disciple is a learner or follower, while an apostle generally refers to a person who is sent with a special message or commission (Jo 13:16). The twelve were definitely called to be apostles, although they were still "learners" when He called them. He had a specific mission in mind for them—to carry on His work after He ended His earthly ministry.

The original twelve were chosen from among the men who had followed Jesus from the beginning (Ac 1:21-22). Like the rest of the Jewish nation, they had an incomplete understanding of Jesus's mission and the necessity for His death (Ma 15:16). During the latter part of His ministry Jesus spent a great deal of time alone with the twelve, preparing them for the events that were to come. Even so, they were astounded at His resurrection. After they were empowered by the Holy Spirit at Pentecost, the apostles were filled with boldness and understanding. They became powerful witnesses in Jerusalem and surrounding regions, in spite of harsh persecution. Many were martyred for their faith.

As listed in Matthew 10:1-4 (also see Mk 3:13-19; Lk 6:12-16; Ac 1:13), the twelve were: 1) Simon Peter (Cephas), leader of the apostles; 2) Andrew, brother of Simon; 3) James, son of Zebedee and 4) his brother John, the beloved apostle; 5) Philip, from Bethsaida; 6) Bartholomew (probably Nathaniel), from Cana of Galilee; 7) Matthew (Levi), tax collector, 8) Thomas (Didymus, which means "Twin"), from Galilee; 9) Simon the Canaanite, probably Simon the Zealot, from Galilee; 10) James, the son of Alphaeus; 11) Lebbaeus, or Thaddeaeus; and 12) Judas Iscariot, who betrayed Jesus.

Matthias was chosen by the apostles to replace Judas after the ascension of Jesus (Ac 1:26).

TWIN BROTH'ERS (Ac 28:11)

See CASTOR AND POLLUX.

TWO DEBTORS, PARABLE OF (Lk 7:41-50)

TWO SONS, PARABLE OF (Ma 21:28-32)

TYCH'I·CUS (fateful)

A fellow-laborer of the apostle Paul who went to Troas to await Paul's coming to that city at the close of the third journey (Ac 20:4). He carried Paul's epistles to the churches at Ephesus and Colosse (Ep 6:21; Col 4:7).

TYPE

A picture or representation of a future person or event. Most of the "types" of Scripture refer to Christ. Melchizedek of Salem (Ge 14:18-20) is described in Hebrews 6:20 as a type or picture of Christ's perfect priesthood. The bronze serpent which Moses made in the wilderness was a type of Christ who would be "lifted up" in order to provide salvation for the people (Nu 21:4-9; Jo 3:14-15). The tabernacle is also a detailed type or illustration of Jesus Christ; both who He is and what He does for us (He 9–10). Romans 5:14 shows Adam as a type of Christ, the first man and the perfect man.

TY·RAN´NUS (sovereign)

A man who had a school in Ephesus which he permitted Paul to use for his teaching during his two years in that city (Ac 19:9).

TYRE (a rock)

A very ancient city of Phoenicia on a strongly protected island about half a mile from the shore of the Mediterranean Sea. Tyre was about twenty-five miles from Sidon, another important Phoenician seaport city; the two cities are often mentioned together. In the fifteenth century B.C. it was under the dominion of Egypt, and it was a strong city when the Israelites came into Canaan under Joshua (Jos 19:29). At no time did it come into the hands of the Israelites.

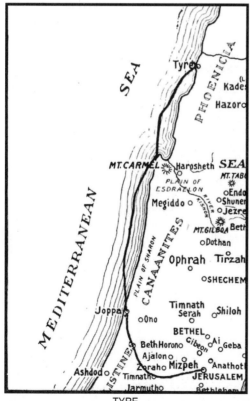

TYRE

In the time of David and Solomon very friendly relations existed between Israel and Tyre. Hiram, king of Tyre, furnished David with materials and craftsmen for his palace (2 Sa 5:11). He also provided materials for Solomon's temple and other building enterprises (1 Ki 5:1; 9:10-14; 2 Ch 2:3, 11). Sometime after the kingdom was divided in 921 B.C., Ahab, the second king of the fourth dynasty of Israel, married the daughter of Ethbaal, king of the Sidonians (1 Ki 16:31). The Tyrians were not a warlike people; like all Phoenicians they were dominantly interested in commerce, colonization, and manufacture. They traded with the remotest peoples, their productions consisting of glassware, dyes, and metalwork. In the ninth century B.C. Carthage was founded by Tyrians and became one of Rome's strongest rivals.

Throughout the history of Israel, the two Phoenician cities of Tyre and Sidon had a generally good relationship with God's people. Why, then, did the prophet Ezekial utter such bitter words against Tyre (Ez 26)? It was probably because of the taunting attitude Tyre demonstrated when the nation of Judah was overrun by the Babylonians in 586 B.C. (Ez 26:2). Judah's collapse meant that Phoenicia was a region with little competition in central Palestine. Their trade monopoly complete, Tyre and Sidon rejoiced. Their insatiable greed and prideful attitude led Ezekiel to issue his bitter condemnation.

When Ezekiel spoke these words, the cities of Tyre and Sidon had no peers on the Mediterranean shores. As early as 1000 B.C. the two cities had emerged as important population centers. As the leader of a group of small city-states, Sidon first grew to prominence in trade. After a time, it was eclipsed by Tyre, which established an empire based on maritime trade. The ships of Tyre sailed as far away as Great Britian and North Africa on trading ventures.

As predicted by Ezekiel, the cities of Tyre and Sidon were eventually judged by God. Tyre was thought to be invincible because part of the city was located offshore, completely surrounded by the sea. But the Greek conqueror, Alexander the Great, built a causeway to the city and destroyed it in 332 B.C. After the Romans became the dominant world power, they rebuilt Tyre. The ruins of this city are visible today.

Both Tyre and Sidon are mentioned in the New Testament. Jesus visited both cities during His ministry (Ma 15:21-28). Paul also visited a Christian community in Tyre, staying with believers there for a week during his third missionary journey (Ac 21:1-6).

Also see SIDON.

U

U′ CAL

One of the two unknown persons to whom Agur addressed a proverb (Pr 30:1).

U′ EL *(will of God)*

A son of Bani who put away his foreign wife (Ez 10:34).

U′ LAI

A river of Persia. Daniel was standing by this river in his second prophetic vision from God when he saw the ram and the male goat (Da 8:2,16).

U′ LAM

Two Old Testament men:
1. Son of Sheresh of the tribe of Manasseh (1 Ch 7:16-17).
2. Son of Eshek and a descendant of Saul (1 Ch 8:39-40).

ULCER

A painful sore. See TUMOR.

UL′ LA *(a yoke)*

A man of the tribe of Asher (1 Ch 7:39).

UM′ MAH

A city which was part of the inheritance of Asher (Jos 19:30).

UNCHASTITY

Sexual impurity. See FORNICATION and ADULTERY.

UNCIRCUMCISED

One who is not circumcised; used as a term for non-Jews (Ex 12:48). Stephen also called the Pharisees "uncircumcised in heart and ears," meaning that though they had the physical symbol of God's people, their hearts were not turned toward God and they did not listen to His voice (Ac 7:51).

UN′ CLE

The brother of one's father or mother. A Hebrew who was forced to sell himself as a slave to a stranger could legally be redeemed at any time by his brother, uncle, or cousin (Le 25:49). Several uncles are mentioned in Scripture, including Uzziel, the uncle of Aaron (Le 10:4); Shallum, the uncle of Jeremiah the prophet (Je 32:8,9,12); Laban, the uncle of Jacob (Ge 24:29); and Abraham, the uncle of Lot (Ge 11:27,31).

UNCLEAN ANIMALS

According to Mosaic law, unclean animals—those unfit for food or sacrifice—included:
1. Those who do not have cloven hooves and do not chew the cud (Le 11:3-8); hence all carnivorous and most other animals except oxen, sheep, goats, and certain deer and gazelles (De 14:4-8).
2. Carnivorous birds, including the owl, eagle, vulture, kite, swan, pelican, stork, bat, and several others (Le 11:13-19; De 14:12-18).
3. Water animals which lack either fins or scales, notably eels and shellfish (Le 11:9-12).
4. Insects not provided with leaping legs similar to those of a locust (Le 11:20-23).
5. All creeping things, including certain small quadrupeds (Le 11:29-31,41-43).

UNCLEANNESS

The Mosaic law distinguishes between the ceremonially clean and unclean, as well as between holy and unholy (Le 10:10). This distinction is not always easy to discern. Animals may be clean or unclean but never holy. Ceremonially unclean persons may become clean through the rites of purification. But ceremonial cleanness is by no means identical with holiness. See HOLY. Mosaic rules pertaining to uncleanness fall roughly into five groups: those having to do with sexual impurity (Le 15:16-18); with blood (Le 15:19-30; 1 Sa 14:33); with food (De 14:7-21); with death (Nu 19:11-22); and with leprosy (Le 13-14).

UNCLEAN SPIRIT

See DEMONIACS.

UNC′ TION (archaic)

An anointing (1 Jo 2:20); the translation of the Greek word "Chrism" (*charisma*). The word *charisma* is not an active noun, but means "the result of being anointed." It is used only three times and all by John in his first epistle. After mentioning the deceiving Antichrist and the many antichrists in 2:18, John gives as an antidote to antichrist delusions the anointing that Christians have "from the Holy One" (v.20). This unction abiding in us teaches us all the truth that we need to know to withstand error (vv. 26-27).

UNDEFILED

Without blemish or sin. Jesus is our High Priest who is holy and undefiled (He 7:26). Sexual relations in marriage are undefiled (pure, without sin), but sexual relations outside of marriage bring the judgment of God (He 13:4). Religion which is undefiled is characterized by care for widows and orphans and keeping oneself from joining in on the sins of the world (Jam 1:27). The inheritance of the righteous in heaven is not subject to decay or blemish, it is undefiled (1 Pe 1:4).

UNDERSETTERS

Supports (1 Ki 7:30,34; KJV).

UNICORN

In mythology, the unicorn is an animal which looks like a horse, but has a single horn growing from the center of its forehead. In the Bible, the word is used to speak of an animal of great strength, impossible to bring under a yoke (Nu 23:22; Job 39:9-10; Is 34:7). In the Middle Ages, people believed that such an animal as the unicorn really existed. No hard evidence for its reality has ever been found, and most scholars believe that the biblical term probably denotes the aurochs or wild ox.

UNITY

Oneness, harmony. After Jesus ascended into heaven, the disciples waited in one accord for the coming of the Holy Spirit (Ac 2:1). Because of the ongoing problem of being humans and subject to sin, unity in the body of Christ is something which requires constant attention. Paul wrote to the Ephesian Christians, outlining the keys to unity: lowliness, gentleness, longsuffering, bearing with one another in love, endeavoring to keep the unity of the Spirit (Ep 4:3,13). Three key concepts are shown here. First, unity is kept through love and longsuffering, not through force and authority. Second, unity is something which has to be worked on. Third, the only unity worth working for is

unity of the Spirit. It is easy to confuse unity with uniformity (everyone looking and acting identically), or with lack of conflict (thus avoiding the confrontation of sin). The unity which pleases God is unity around the truth, characterized by bearing with one another in love.

UNJUST JUDGE, PARABLE OF
(Lk 18:1-8)

UNJUST STEWARD, PARABLE OF
(Lk 16:1-13)

UNKNOWN GOD
See GOD, UNKNOWN.

UN'LADE (archaic)
To unload (Ac 21:2-3).

UNLEAVENED BREAD

Bread made without yeast or other rising agent. When the angels visited Abraham, he served the unleavened bread. Since it requires no rising time, this is the quickest form of bread to make for an unexpected visitor (Ge 19:3; 1 Sa 28:24). The Passover was celebrated with unleavened bread as a commemoration of the haste with which the Israelites left Egypt (Ex 12:8; 13:6-7). No yeast was used in the showbread of the tabernacle, or in the priestly rituals. By New Testament times, yeast had become a metaphor for sin and impurity.

UNLEAVENED BREAD, FEAST OF
See PASSOVER.

UNMERCIFUL SERVANT, PARABLE OF
(Ma 18:21-35)

UN'NI (afflicted)
Two Old Testament Levites:

1. A Levite musician who lived in the time of David (1 Ch 15:18,20).

2. A Levite who returned to Jerusalem with Zerubbabel (Ne 12:9). He is called Unno in the Revised Version.

UN'NO
See UNNI.

UNPARDONABLE SIN
See BLASPHEMY.

UNPROFITABLE (or UNWORTHY) SERVANT, PARABLE OF (Lk 17:7-10)

UNTOWARD (archaic)

Perverse; bent (Ac 2:38-40).

U·PHAR′SIN

See MENE, MENE, TEKEL, UPHARSIN.

U′PHAZ

A region from which gold was exported (Je 10:9; Da 10:5), thought by some to be the same as Ophir.

UPPER GATE

A gate of the temple which was rebuilt by Jotham, king of Judah (2 Ki 15:38).

UR

A city and a man of the Old Testament:

1. A city in northern Mesopotamia slightly west of the Euphrates, halfway between the Persian Gulf and modern day Baghdad. It was the place in which Abraham lived before moving to Canaan (Ge 11:28,31; 15:7; Ne 9:7). After the Chaldeans came into Babylonia, Ur was called "Ur of the Chaldeans." This did not happen until after the days of Abraham, so it seems clear that this was a "modern term" used by Moses when writing the account of Abraham's life. Ur was a bustling metropolis in Abraham's day; archeological finds among its ruins show that its culture was highly developed.

2. The father of Eliphal (1 Ch 11:35).

UR′BANE

See URBANUS.

UR·BA′NUS *(polite, of the city)*

A Christian of the Roman church (Ro 16:9).

U′RI *(fiery)*

1. The father of Bezalel of Judah. Bezalel was one of the men who worked on the tabernacle (Ex 31:2).

2. The father of Geber, Solomon's tax-gatherer in Gilead (1 Ki 4:19).

3. A temple porter who divorced his foreign wife (Ez 10:24).

U·RI′AH *(light of Jehovah)*

Three Old Testament men:

1. One of David's mighty men; a Hittite

(2 Sa 23:39; 1 Ch 11:41). He was the husband of Bath-sheba with whom David committed adultery. In order to cover his sin when he discovered that Bath-sheba was pregnant, David had Uriah placed in a dangerous position in the line of battle and he was killed. David then married Bath-sheba (2 Sa 11:1-27; Ma 1:6), but the child died.

2. A priest in the time of Ezra and father of Meremoth (Ez 8:33). In Nehemiah 3:4,21, he is called Urijah.

3. A priest who was a witness to a written prophecy of Isaiah concerning Maher-shalal-hashbaz (Is 8:2).

U′RI·EL *(light of God)*

Two Old Testament men:

1. A Levite of the Kohath family and house of Izhar (1 Ch 6:24).

2. The father of Micaiah, the mother of Abijah and wife of Rehoboam (2 Ch 13:2).

U·RI′JAH *(light of Jehovah)*

1. A priest in Jerusalem who built an altar for King Ahaz, a copy of an altar Ahaz saw in Damascus on a visit of state to Tiglath-pileser (2 Ki 16:10-16). Urijah apparently made no protest at the placing of this copy of a pagan altar in the temple courts, and making all sacrificial offerings on the new altar.

2. Son of Shemaiah and a prophet of Kirjath-jearim. Jehoiakim sought to kill him for the judgment he predicted would fall upon Judah. He fled to Egypt but was brought back and put to death (Je 26:20-23).

U′RIM AND THUM′MIN

Small sacred objects in the breastplate of the high priest (Ex 28:30; Le 8:8) and which were used to ascertain the Lord's will (Nu 27:21; De 33:8; 1 Sa 14:37-42; 28:6). It has been suggested that the Urim and Thummin were two small stones which were cast as lots to determine guilt or innocence. Other guesses have been put forth regarding the method in which these were used, but since the Bible does not say how they worked, it is all pure speculation. See CASTING OF LOTS.

USURP (archaic)

To seize and take hold of (1 Ti 2:12).

USURY

Interest charged on a loan. See BANKER and BORROW.

U' THAI *(helpful)*

Two Old Testament men:

1. Son of Ammihud of the family of Pharez, son of Judah (1 Ch 9:4).

2. A son of Bigvai. He returned to Jerusalem with Ezra (Ez 8:14).

UZ

Three men and a geographical area:

1. A son of Aram (Ge 10:23; 1 Ch 1:17) and grandson of Shem.

2. A son of Nahor and Milcah (Ge 22:21), also called Huz (KJV).

3. A son of Dishan and grandson of Seir (Ge 36:28).

4. The land of Uz, the home of Job (Job 1:1). The exact location is not known, but it has been suggested that Uz was east of the Jordan River, either between Edom and northern Arabia, or the area south of Damascus.

U' ZAI

The father of Palal, one who worked on repairing the wall of Jerusalem (Ne 3:25).

U' ZAL

A son of Joktan (Ge 10:27; 1 Ch 1:21).

UZ' ZA *(strength)*

1. The owner of a garden near the palace of Manasseh, king of Judah in which Manasseh and his son, Amon, were buried (2 Ki 21:18,26).

2. A descendant of Ehud (1 Ch 8:7).

3. The head of a family of Nethinim, some of whom returned from Babylon with Zerubbabel (Ez 2:49; Ne 7:51).

UZ' ZA, GARDEN OF

A garden near the palace of Manasseh, king of Judah in which Manasseh and his son, Amon, were buried (2 Ki 21:18,26).

UZ' ZAH *(strength)*

1. A son of Abinadab of Kirjath-jearim. When the ark was on its way to Jerusalem in the reign of David, it was jolted by the stumbling of the oxen. Uzzah put forth his hand to steady it and was struck dead. The place was called Perez-uzzah, meaning the breaking out against Uzzah (2 Sa 6:3-8; 1 Ch 13:7-14).

2. A Levite of the family of Merari (1 Ch 6:29).

UZ' ZEN-SHE' E·RAH

A town built by Sheerah, the daughter of Ephraim (1 Ch 7:24). Its exact location is not known.

UZ' ZI

1. Son of Bukki and father of Zerahiah; a descendant of Aaron and an ancestor of Ezra (1 Ch 6:5-6,51; Ez 7:4).

2. Son of Tola of Issachar (1 Ch 7:2-3).

3. Son of Bela (1 Ch 7:7).

4. Son of Michri, a Benjamite and father of Elah (1 Ch 9:8).

5. Son of Bani, a Levite, and overseer of the Levites in the time of Nehemiah (Ne 11:22).

6. A priest of the house of Jedaiah who lived in the time of Joiakim, the high priest (Ne 12:19). He may have been the same as the following.

7. A priest who had a part in the dedication of the wall of Jerusalem (Ne 12:42); possibly the same as No. 6.

UZ·ZI' A

One of David's mighty men, of the town of Ashtaroth (1 Ch 11:44).

UZ·ZI' AH

1. A king of Judah (2 Ch 26:1-23; Ma 1:9), also called Azariah (2 Ki 14:21; 15:1-8,23,27, 32). He was the son of Amaziah whom he succeeded at the age of sixteen (2 Ki 14:21). Uzziah was one of Judah's few righteous kings, and his reign of fifty-two years was longer than any other king of Judah or Israel. He is also unique in that both his father and his son were also righteous kings. However, in spite of his devotion to the Lord, and the many good things he did in Judah, Uzziah's success went to his head. He became proud, and decided that he did not need a priest to act as an intermediary between him and God. The high priests and eighty other priests valiantly withstood Uzziah's foolishness. As Uzziah stood there with the censer in his hand, furiously angry with the priests of God, leprosy broke out on his forehead. He rushed from the sanctuary, knowing that God had struck him for his pride and ended his days as a leper, his son Jotham taking the place of regent until his death.

2. A Levite of the line of Kohath (1 Ch 6:24).

3. Father of David's overseer, Jehonathan (1 Ch 27:25).

4. Son of Harim, a priest. He renounced his foreign wife (Ez 10:21).

5. A man of Judah who lived in Jerusalem after the captivity (Ne 11:4).

UZ′ ZI•EL *(might of God)*

1. A son of Kohath (Ex 6:18,22; Nu 3:19, 27,30). He was a kinsman of Aaron (Le 10:4).

2. Son of Ishi. He was a captain of the tribe of Simeon. In the reign of Hezekiah he helped defeat the Amalekites (1 Ch 4:41-43).

3. A Benjamite of the family of Bela (1 Ch 7:7).

4. A musician in David's reign (1 Ch 25:4). Also called Azarel.

5. A son of Jeduthun, a Levite. He labored with Hezekiah in his religious reforms (2 Ch 29:14).

6. Son of Harhaiah. He was a goldsmith and labored on the wall of Jerusalem with Nehemiah (Ne 3:8).

UZ′ ZI•EL•ITES

The descendants of the Uzziel, son of Aaron's son Kohath (Nu 3:27; 1 Ch 26:23).

V

VAGABOND

A homeless wanderer (Ps 109:10).

VA′ HEB

A place in the region of the Arnon, mentioned only in the Revised Version (Nu 21:14-15).

VAIN (archaic)

Empty; foolish; useless (Ma 6:7). See also VANITY.

VAINGLORY

See PRIDE.

VA•JEZ′ A•THA

One of the ten sons of Haman (Es 9:9).

VALE

An old word for valley.

VALLEY

Low-lying land between mountains or along rivers. Several different words are translated "valley" in our English Bibles, with varying nuances of meaning. The word used to describe the valley of Shaveh (Ge 14:17) indicates a broad, low place. The valley of Gerar, where Isaac dug wells for his flocks, is described with the word which means a narrow river valley through which a stream flows only in rainy season. The valley of Mizpeh (Jo 11:8) is a wide plain between mountains, and the valley of Hinnom (Ne 11:30) is a narrow gorge. In Joshua 11:16, the word translated "lowland" (NKJV) or "valley" (KJV) indicates the maritime slope of the land west of the Jordan.

VALLEY GATE

A gate of Jerusalem. Uzziah, king of Judah, built a fortified tower at this gate (2 Ch 26:9; Ne 2:13).

VALLEY OF SLAUGHTER

See TOPHET.

VA•NI′ AH

A son of Bani who put away his foreign wife (Ez 10:36).

VANITY

" 'Vanity of vanities,' says the Preacher; 'vanity of vanities, all *is* vanity.' " Twice the author of Ecclesiastes employs this now famous saying (1:2; 12:8). But what did he mean by *vanity?* The NKJV note gives "futility" as an alternative rendering.

Breath, vapor (hebel) is the literal meaning of the word translated "vanity." *Hebel* occurs seventy-one times in the Hebrew Bible, mostly with metaphorical meanings. Speaking of idols, Isaiah 57:13 uses the word literally: "A breath [*hebel*] will take *them.*"

In the New Testament, James wrote that our life is "a vapor that appears for a little time and then vanishes away" (Jam 4:14).

The second person born into the world was named Abel, which in the Hebrew is the same spelling as *Hebel.* This may be coincidental, but if his name was "Vapor" or "Breath" in Hebrew, it does fit with his life being cut short by murder.

Hebel occurs thirty-six times in Ecclesiastes; only chapter 10 does not use the word. The apparent futility of life "under the sun" is certainly one of the main themes of "The Preacher," if not his main idea.

Solomon was a great builder, skillful, creative, and wise. Yet he was frustrated by the emptiness of it all—including his gardens and building projects: "Then I looked on all the works that my hands had done and on the labor in which I had toiled; and indeed all *was* vanity and grasping for the wind (Ec 2:11; see also vv. 19, 21,23; 4:4,8; 6:2).

King Solomon also found the apparent unfairness of life to be vanity. Actually, we might wonder what he had to complain about. God had granted him wisdom and wealth; his life was filled with plenty of "wine, women, and song," and yet he could see the trouble and disappointment in life. He commented: " Consider the work of God; For who can make straight what He has made crooked? In the day of prosperity be joyful, But in the day of adversity consider: Surely God has appointed the one as well as the other, so that man can find nothing that will happen after him" (Ec 7:13-14). He goes on to say, "There is a vanity which occurs on earth, that there are just *men* to whom it happens according to the work of the wicked; again, there are wicked *men* to whom it happens according to the work of the righteous. I said that this also *is* vanity" (Ec 8:14; see also vv. 10-13; 2:15; 6:7-9).

These seeming contradictions, these "vanities" caused Solomon to come to the conclusion that God is bigger in the end than the things he puzzled about. Man must do what he has to do, and he should enjoy it. The last chapter in this book that looks at "vanities" is a solemn reminder to remember the Creator in the days of our youth. When you get old it is often too late to start walking with God (Ec 12).

Hebel as Idols: Since the Old Testament spares no energy in unmasking the absurdity of worshiping lifeless idols, we should not be surprised that they are called foolish idols in the Song of Moses (De 32:21). Jeremiah concurs; he calls images "futile works of errors" (Je 10:15).

Many people would not think of worshiping literal images, yet have idols that are equally vain. The most common is "mammon" or money. To get really rich in a corrupt society nearly always involves some questionable dealings or "cutting corners." But Proverbs 13:11 warns us the "wealth *gained* by dishonesty [*hebel*]" rather than by hard work "will be diminished."

Hebel as an Adverbial Accusative: Sometimes the word *hebel* is used adverbially with the idea of "no purpose" or "no result": "For the Egyptians shall help in vain and to no purpose" (Is 30:7).

Job laments, "*If* I am condemned, why then do I labor in vain [for no good purpose]?" (Job 9:29).

Elihu sums up Job's many speeches in a damping style: "Therefore Job opens his mouth in vain; he multiplies words without knowledge" (Job 35:16).

Paul uses the word in a most encouraging statement: "Therefore, my brethren, be steadfast, immovable, always abounding in the work of the Lord, knowing that your labor is not in vain in the Lord" (1 Co 15:58).

VASH′NI

The eldest son of Samuel (1 Ch 6:28; probably the same as Joel in 1 Sa 8:2; 1 Ch 6:33).

VASH′TI

The queen of Ahasuerus, the king of Persia (Es 1:9–2:17). She was deposed because she flouted the king's command and refused to come and appear before his guests.

VASSAL

A subject or slave. Shalmaneser made Hoshea, king of Israel, his vassal, and forced him to pay tribute (2 Ki 17:3). Later, Nebuchadnezzar did the same to Jehoiakim of Judah (2 Ki 24:1).

VE′DAN

A place which traded with Tyre (Eze 27:19). It is rendered "Dan also" in the KJV.

VEHEMENTLY

Violently; intensely. This word is used to describe the flood which destroyed the house built on the sand (Lk 6:48).

VEIL

A woman's headcovering (Ge 24:65; 38:14; Song 4:1,3; 6:7; Is 3:23; 1 Co 11:1-16), or a curtain, such as the curtain which separated the holy of holies from the sanctuary. See VEIL OF THE TABERNACLE.

VEIL OF THE TABERNACLE

The heavy curtain separating the most holy place from the sanctuary (Ex 26:31-37). When Jesus died, this veil was rent in two from top to bottom (Ma 27:51). See CURTAIN and TABER-NACLE.

VENGEANCE

Judgment, revenge. God commanded his people not to take revenge on one another, but rather to love their brothers (Le 19:18). Vengeance belongs exclusively to the Lord, it is not the job of humans to bring judgment on those who injure them (De 32:35; Ro 12:19).

VENISON

The meat of animals of the deer family. Jacob liked the taste of wild venison. He was pleased with his son Esau, who was a hunter (Ge 25:28; 27:3). This word is translated "game" in the KJV and NKJV; it may refer to any wild meat, not just venison.

VENOM

The poison which a snake injects into its victim through its fangs, or the poison of a spider or scorpion's sting (De 32:33; Job 20:14).

VERBAL

As a doctrinal term applied to the inspiration of Scripture, this means that every word of the original manuscripts is inspired by God—not just the sense or meaning, but the actual word choice. See INSPIRATION.

VERILY

Truly. See AMEN.

VERITY (archaic)

Truth (1 Ti 2:7).

VERMILION

A bright red, durable pigment derived from cinnabar, the mineral ore which is the most common source of mercury. It was used for painting walls and idols (Je 22:14; Eze 23:14).

VESSEL

Any kind of container, from a jar or pot (Je 40:10) to a ship (Is 18:2). Christians are described as "earthen vessels," a metaphoric way of speaking of the mortality and frailty of humans, who nevertheless have the treasure of the knowledge of God hidden inside them (2 Co 4:6-7).

VESTIBULE

A portico or covered archway, part of the temple in Jerusalem (1 Ki 6:3; 1 Ch 28:11).

VESTMENTS (archaic)

Garments; clothing (2 Ki 10:21-22).

VESTURE (archaic)

Garment; cloak; clothing (Re 19:12-13).

VIA DOLOROSA *(way of sorrow)*

The road traveled by Jesus as he carried the cross from Pilate's judgment hall to Golgotha. Many years of tradition have marked out the way, and also fourteen "stations of the cross," or events which happened during the short journey. However, the exact route the soldiers took is not recorded in the Gospels, nor are the fourteen "stations." Since Jerusalem was destroyed in 70 A.D., it is a little unlikely that the real "via dolorosa" could be found.

VIAL (archaic)

Bowl; goblet (Re 16:1-2).

VICE

Wickedness, evil conduct (1 Pe 2:16).

VICEROY

A government official.

VIGIL

To "keep a vigil" is to keep watch at night, often associated with prayer and devotion; also

VIA DOLAROSA

often associated with watching a coffin or a new grave as a mark of respect for the dead (Job 21:32).

VILLAGE

A group of dwellings and businesses, smaller than a city, and without walls or fortifications (Eze 38:11). Villages were sprinkled throughout agricultural lands; in case of danger, the inhabitants of the villages and farms would flee to the fortified cities.

VILLANY

Wickedness, disgraceful actions (Je 29:23).

VINE

In Scripture, this word nearly always refers to the grapevine. The first mention of grapevines in the Bible is in Genesis chapter 9. After the flood waters went down, the first thing that Noah did was plant a vineyard. From that time forward, grapes were extensively cultivated by the people of the East as an important means of livelihood (Ge 40:9-11; Ps 78:47). Palestine is very favorable to the growth of vineyards, especially in the hill country (Nu 13:23; Ju 9:27; 21:20; Je 31:5). When the spies first went into Canaan, they brought back grapes from Eshcol; one cluster was so large they carried it between two men on a pole (Nu 13:23).

Vineyards were protected by stone walls or hedges in order to keep out thieves and wild animals (Nu 22:24; Pr 24:31; Song 2:15; Is 5:1,5).

Grapes were eaten, both fresh and dried (raisins). The raisins were often pressed into cakes. Because of their high sugar content, they keep for a long time without spoiling as long as they are kept relatively cool and dry. Grapes were also made into wine, one of the staple foods of the ancients. The vintage, or time of harvest and winemaking, was a festive season and was attended with singing and shouting as the grapes were trodden in the press (Is 16:10; Je 25:30; 48:33).

Vines and vineyards are mentioned in a symbolic or figurative sense in numerous passages of Scripture. The prophet Isaiah describes Israel as a vineyard which would not yield good fruit (Is 5:1-7). Jesus told a parable in which Israel is pictured as the wicked vinedressers of God's vineyard. Later, Jesus uses the metaphor of the vine and its branches describe the relationship of believers with the Lord (Jo 15:1-8).

VINE-DRESSER

A farmer who specializes in grapes; cultivating vineyards and pruning the vines each year (Ma 21:33-44).

VINEGAR

A sour, acidic fermentation of any kind of alcoholic liquid (Nu 6:3; Pr 10:26). Vinegar is very similar to wine and is produced with a very similar method. Essentially, the difference is in the culture which produces the fermentation. When wine does not ferment properly, it often turns to vinegar, but vinegar is also made on purpose. Vinegar is not alcoholic, but like wine, it will keep for long periods of time without spoiling. People in the East mixed it with oil and drank it. At meal times they used it on bread (Ru 2:14). Vinegar was offered to Jesus on the cross to quench his burning thirst (Mk 15:36; Jo 19:29-30).

VINE OF SODOM

A metaphorical way of speaking of the bitter results of sin, comparing Sodom to a vine which bore only poison fruit (De 32:32-33).

VINEYARD

A field which is planted with grapevines. Grapes require a good deal of attention; they must be cultivated and pruned, kept free of pests and disease, and all this must be done to the young vines for two or three years before they begin to bear a full crop of grapes. Once the vines reach maturity, if they have proper care they will continue to bear grapes for many years. A mature vineyard was a valuable piece of property which could be counted on to bring in good returns for the farmer's labor. King Ahab's plan to buy Naboth's beautiful vineyard for any price, and then uproot it and plant a vegetable garden in its place, shows his arrogance and extravagance (1 Ki 21:1-3). See VINE.

VINEYARD, PARABLE OF (Ma 21:33-46; Mk 12:1-2; Lk 20:9-19)

VINEYARDS, PLAIN OF

See ABEL-KERAMIM.

VIOL

A musical instrument (Is 5:12; KJV), also translated "harp." The meaning of the underlying Hebrew word is not certain.

VIPER

A reptile, with a poisonous bite. Paul was attacked by a viper when on the island of Melita, but coolly shook it off, remaining unhurt (Ac 28:3-6). See SNAKE.

VIRGIN

A person who has never had sexual intercourse. Virginity was a symbol of purity. Because they served before the Lord, the priests were not to marry widows, divorced women, or ex-prostitutes (Le 21:7,14). The most important use of the word virgin is in Isaiah's prophecy of Immanuel (Is 7:14). "Therefore the Lord Himself will give you a sign: Behold, the virgin shall conceive and bear a Son, and shall call His name Immanuel." The Hebrew word for "virgin" in this passage is different than the word generally used to denote a young unmarried woman. Sometimes this fact has been construed as a proof against the virgin birth, saying that what is meant in this verse is not "virgin," but simply "young woman." However, Matthew's Gospel quotes this verse in the account of Christ's birth, and both Matthew and Luke take pains to show that the literal meaning of "virgin" is the correct translation (Ma 1:18-25; Lk 1:26-38). Mary was a virgin when Jesus was conceived in her; she did not know her husband sexually (or any other man) until after the baby was born.

VIRGIN BIRTH

The Christian doctrine which teaches that the mother of Jesus Christ was a virgin when He was conceived, and therefore He had no biological father. He was truly the son of God. Some have inferred that this means that Mary was "God's wife," or that Jesus was the product of sexual relations between mortal and immortal, in the order of the Greek myths of the gods. Such ideas are clearly repulsive and untrue. In fact, God simply produced a miraculous conception in the womb of a virgin by the power of the Holy Spirit, something which the creator of life and of the human reproductive system could easily arrange. See VIRGIN.

VIRTUE

Goodness, moral excellence. Second Peter 1:5-7 lists virtue in the "chain of growth" as the first thing to add to faith.

VI'SIONS

An order of mental phenomena in which God communicated to the mind in accordance with the mind's constitution. In the case of the prophets these visions were given to men committed to the will and service of God, and were of such a nature as to establish the fact of their divine source (Je 23:16,21-22,27). The genuineness of visions containing predictions was established by the fulfillment of the predictions. Those who falsely declared they had received visions from God were denounced (Je 14:14; 23:16; Eze 13:7).

In Old Testament times, God often used dreams (which occur when a person is asleep) and visions (which are given when awake) to make His will known. The Egyptian Pharaoh's dream could not be interpreted by his magicians. But Joseph told him that it referred to a forthcoming period of famine in the land (Ge 41). Does God still speak through dreams and visions today? Interpreters and scholars are divided on this question. Some believe God has no need to speak through dreams, since His Holy Spirit is now available to instruct us in God's will. But others believe just as strongly that dreams are still a means of God's revelation.

Joel, one of the Minor Prophets, foresaw the outpouring of the Spirit of God on believers as a time when "your old men shall dream dreams, your young men shall see visions" (Joel 2:28). This prophecy was fulfilled with the outpouring of God's Spirit at Pentecost (Ac 2:14-21). Other significant dreams and visions in the Old Testament include the following:

DREAMS		
Jacob	Assurance of God's Covenant	Ge 28:10-15
Joseph	Joseph's Future Prominence Over His Brothers	Ge 37:1-11
Solomon	Assurance of God's Wisdom	1 Ki 3:5-10
VISIONS		
Jacob	Instructed to go to Egypt	Ge 46:2-4
Isaiah	A Revelation of God's Holiness	Is 6:1-8
Ezekiel	God's promise to restore His people Israel	Eze 37
Daniel	The Great World Powers to Come and the Glories of Christ	Da 7–8 Da 10:5-9

VOCATION

A calling, invitation, summons; the task to which one has been called by God (Ep 4:1-3).

VOID

Empty, desolate. The earth at the beginning of the creation is described as being void and formless (Ge 1:2). Jeremiah prophesied of the end of the nation of Israel as a great desolation, leaving the earth "without form and void" (Je 4:23). Some Bible translations have used the word "chaos" in these passages; it is important to remember that this should not be taken in the modern sense of hopeless confusion. The word comes from a Greek word meaning an "empty chasm" or "abyss. "

VOPH′ SI

The father of Nahbi (Nu 13:14).

VOW

A promise to God to perform some service for him on condition that He, in return grant a specific favor, such as a safe journey (Ge 28:20-22), victory (Ju 11:30-31), or offspring (1 Sa 1:11). A more disinterested vow was made by the Nazirite who sought God's good will, in return for which he promised to give up strong drink, never cut his hair, and dedicate himself wholly to the Lord (Nu 6:1-21).

VULGATE *(common)*

The Latin version of the Bible, produced near the end of the fourth century A.D. It was chiefly the work of a man named Jerome, the secretary of Damasus, the bishop of Rome. It was Damasus who assigned this task to Jerome, realizing the need for a standardized, quality translation of the whole Bible into Latin, from the original languages. Previous to this time, the Latin versions of the Old Testament were translations of the Greek Septuagint rather than the Hebrew manuscripts. Jerome finished his work in A.D. 405. The Latin Vulgate was the Bible used by the missionaries to Western Europe, and later was the basis of the first English translations.

VULTURE

Large, carrion-eating members of the hawk family. Vultures can reach a wingspan of 9 or 10 feet; the heads and necks of most varieties are bald, giving them an unpleasant aspect. Because vultures regularly feed on dead bodies, they were considered ceremonially unclean (Le 11:13-14; De 14:12-13). Various large birds of the same family as hawks and vultures are mentioned in the Bible, including the lammergeier, buzzard, falcon, and bustard. The exact identification of all these species is uncertain.

W

WA′ GES

Payment for labor or service. The Mosaic law required that wages be paid at the end of each day (Le 19:13; De 24:14-15). To withhold what was due a hired man was severely denounced by the prophets (Je 22:13; Mal 3:5). In the time of Jesus the wage for a day's labor was a denarius, or penny, equivalent to about seventeen cents (Ma 20:2).

WAG′ ON

See CART.

WAL′ LET

See SCRIP.

WALLS

See METALSMITH.

WAN′ TON (archaic)

Excessive; rebellious (1 Ti 5:11-12).

WAR

An armed conflict. Among the early Hebrews war was little more than a skirmish between opposing sides, usually of a few men each. However, from the time of Saul, the menace of the Philistines and other foes necessitated a standing army. War was regarded by the Hebrews as essentially religious. Their God was the God of hosts, their battles were the Lord's battles (1 Sa 18:17; 25:28; Ps 80:7,19). Before going to war it was customary for primitive nations to use divination to determine favorable conditions and a propitious time. The Hebrews inquired of God (Ju 20:23,27; 1 Sa 14:37; 23:2). Spies were sent into a country before invading it to ascertain what would be needed in making an attack (Jos 2:1; Ju 7:10; 1 Sa 26:4). The signal for an attack was the blowing of a trumpet (Jos 6:5; Ju 7:20), and the advance was accompanied with shouting (1 Sa 17:52; Am 1:14). When a city was captured, it was common to destroy it and massacre the inhabitants (Jos 8:24-29; 10:22-27; 2 Ki 15:16).

WARD (archaic)

Prison; custody (Ge 41:9-10).

WARFARE IN BIBLE TIMES

In Old Testament times, the nation of Israel often waged war against its enemies. One notable example is the war of conquest led by Joshua to drive the Canaanites from the land of promise. To the Israelites, this was a "holy war" undertaken at God's command and carried out under His guidance and protection. Just before they attacked the city of Jericho, for example, Joshua issued this order to the priests and soldiers who were marching around the city walls: "Shout, for the LORD has given you the city!" (Jos 6:16).

The weapons used by Joshua and his warriors were the simple arms of the time: the bow and arrow, the sling, the sword, the spear or lance, the battle ax, and various pieces of protective armor. His warfare techniques included threats, intimidation, ambush and surprise attack, siege warfare against walled cities, and hand-to-hand combat.

But there is a noticeable progression throughout Old Testament history in the types of weapons used and how warfare was carried out. By the time of Solomon, mounted warriors with more sophisticated weapons were a part of Israel's armed forces. Solomon also had a fleet of chariots at his command for swift attacks against enemy forces (1 Ki 10:26).

As the nation of Israel increased its weaponry, it came to rely more on military might and less on God's guidance and protection as the key to victory in battle. Many of the prophets of the Old Testament condemned the kings of Israel and Judah for leading the people to place their trust in the sword rather than in the Word of God.

Some of the most striking warfare imagery in the Old Testament is found in the Book of Ezekiel. In a vision, the prophet saw the attack of Jerusalem by the Babylonians. He described how a besieging army gained entrance to a walled city. The king of Babylon gave orders for his army "to set battering rams against the gates, to heap up a mound, and to build a wall" (Ez 21:22).

WASH'ING

See BATHING.

WASHING, CEREMONIAL

See ABLUTION.

WATCHES OF NIGHT (La 2:19; Ju 7:19)

WA'TER OF BIT'TER·NESS

Water containing dust swept from the tabernacle floor. It was used to determine the guilt or innocence of a wife suspected of adultery by her husband when there were no witnesses to sustain the suspicion (Nu 5:12-28).

WA'TER-POT

See POT.

WAVE OF'FER·ING

A portion of the peace offering dedicated to the priest. See OFFERINGS. During the wave offering the breast of the sacrificed animal was waved to and fro as it was carried toward the altar by the priest. This symbolized its presentation to the Lord and the Lord's return of it to the priests (Ex 29:19-28; Le 7:28-36; 10:12,15). Waving was a horizontal motion made in line with the altar while the heave offering was up and down. At harvest time a sheaf of first fruits was waved on the second day of the Passover, thereby dedicating the harvest to the Lord (Le 23:10-11).

WAX (archaic)

To grow; become; advance (Lk 12:33).

WEAPONS

See ARMS.

WEA'SEL

A mole-like rodent which was ceremonially unclean (Le 11:29).

WEAV'ING

The process of turning threads into fabric. Where and by whom weaving was invented we do not know but the art may be traced back to very early times. It was practiced by the Egyptians before the Israelites settled in their land (Ge 41:42) and doubtless from them the Israelites learned the art which enabled them to make the hangings of the tabernacle (Ex 35:35). The hair of goats and camels was used for weaving coarser materials (Ma 3:4) while flax and wool were

WEASEL

used for **finer** goods (Pr 31:13). The Egyptian loom was an upright structure and the weaver stood as he did the work.

WED′DING

See MARRIAGE.

WEDDING FEAST, PARABLE OF

(Ma 22:1-14)

WEDGE

A bar of gold (Jos 7:21,24).

WEEDS, PARABLE OF (Ma 13:24-30,36-43)

WEEK

A period of seven days. From the earliest institution of the Sabbath after the creation of the world, the Bible refers to seven-day periods (Ge 2:1-3). Although the word *week* is not used, the implication is the same. The term is implied at the time of the flood (Ge 7:4,10; 8:10,12) and the use of the seven-day division of time is also used in Babylonian accounts of this event. The only day of the seven named by the Hebrews was the Sabbath. They numbered the days of the week (Ma 28:1; Ac 20:7).

WEEKS, FEAST OF

One of the three annual feasts at which time all the men of Israel were required to present themselves at the sanctuary (Ex 34:22-23). It fell seven weeks after the waving of the sheaf and is also called Pentecost (Ac 2:1) or the feast of harvest because the first fruits of the wheat harvest were presented (Ex 23:16; 34:22; Nu 28:26). All labor was avoided and the day was observed as a Sabbath (Le 23:21). Sacrifices attended the offering of the loaves (Le 23:17-19).

WEIGHTS AND MEASURES

WEIGHTS			
Unit	Weight	Equivalents	Translations
Jewish Weights Talent	c. 75 pounds for common talent, c. 150 pounds for royal talent	60 minas; 3,000 shekels	Talent
Mina	1.25 pounds	50 shekels	Mina
Shekel	c. .4 ounce (11.4 grams) for common shekel c. .8 ounce for royal shekel	2 bekas; 20 gerahs	Shekel

Unit	Weight	Equivalents	Translations
Pim	$\frac{3}{8}$ shekel		
Beka	c. .2 ounce (5.7 grams)	$\frac{1}{2}$ shekel; 10 gerahs	Half a shekel
Gerah	c. .02 ounce (.57 grams)	$\frac{1}{20}$ shekel	Gerah
Roman Weight Litra	12 ounces		Pound

MEASURES OF LENGTH			
Unit	Length	Equivalents	Translations
Day's journey	c. 20 miles		Day's journey
Roman mile	4,854 feet	8 stadia	Mile
Sabbath day's journey	3,637 feet	6 stadia	Sabbath day's journey
Stadion	606 feet	$\frac{1}{8}$ Roman mile	Furlong
Rod	9 feet 10.5 feet in Ezekiel	3 paces; 6 cubits	Measuring reed, reed
Fathom	6 feet	4 cubits	Fathom
Pace	3 feet	$\frac{1}{3}$ rod; 2 cubits	Pace
Cubit	18 inches	$\frac{1}{2}$ pace; 2 spans	Cubit
Span	9 inches	$\frac{1}{2}$ cubit; 3 handbreadths	Span
Handbreadth	3 inches	$\frac{1}{3}$ span; 4 fingers	Handbreadth
Finger	.75 inches	$\frac{1}{4}$ handbreadth	Finger

DRY MEASURES			
Unit	Measure	Equivalents	Translations
Homer	6.52 bushels	10 ephahs	Homer
Kor	6.52 bushels	1 homer; 10 ephahs	Kor, measure
Lethech	3.26 bushels	$\frac{1}{2}$ kor	Half homer
Ephah	.65 bushel, 20.8 quarts	$\frac{1}{10}$ homer	Ephah
Modius	7.68 quarts		Basket
Seah	7 quarts	$\frac{1}{3}$ ephah	Measure
Omer	2.08 quarts	$\frac{1}{10}$ ephah; 1$\frac{4}{5}$ kab	Omer
Kab	1.16 quarts	4 logs	Kab
Choenix	1 quart		Measure
Xestes	1$\frac{1}{16}$ pints		Pot
Log	.58 pint	$\frac{1}{4}$ kab	Log

LIQUID MEASURES			
Unit	Measure	Equivalents	Translations
Kor	60 gallons	10 baths	Kor
Metretes	10.2 gallons		Gallons
Bath	6 gallons	6 hins	Measure, bath
Hin	1 gallon	2 kabs	Hin
Kab	2 quarts	4 logs	Kab
Log	1 pint	$\frac{1}{4}$ kab	Log

WELL

A shaft dug into the ground to reach water. In contrast to the cistern, which is a reservoir that has to be filled with rain water or water brought from springs in aqueducts, a well is supplied by nature and as a result has fresher water (2 Sa 23:15). To avoid accidents, the top of a well was usually covered by a stone slab or surrounded by a low stone wall (Ge 29:2-3; Jo 4:6). Shallow wells were fitted with steps leading down to the water which could be dipped directly with a pitcher (Ge 24:16). Deeper wells required the use of a rope to which was attached a bucket, pitcher, or water skin (Jo 4:11). Wells are used figuratively of salvation (Is 12:3; Jo 4:10).

WEN (archaic)

A running sore (Le 22:22).

WERT (archaic)

Were (Re 3:15).

WHALE

In the Authorized Version of the Old Testament the word rendered *whale* signifies any large sea animal. In Eze 32:2 the word should be rendered *monster.* The same is true of the Greek word of Matthew 12:40 which, translated *whale* by the Revised Version, denotes any great fish or sea animal of great size.

WHEAT

This grain was cultivated from early times throughout the Orient, especially in Egypt. This country served as the granary of the Mediterranean area, notably in the Roman period when it shipped much of its wheat to Rome (Ac 27:6, 38).

WHERE' FORE (archaic)

Why? For what reason? For what cause? (Ro 9:31-32).

WHISPERERS

Whisperers (psithyristes) sounds like what it describes. The Greeks pronounced both the *p* and the *s* sounds in words beginning with their letter *psi.* Whispering is not wrong, unless one whispers gossip, evil or other unsavory things— the meaning here. Paul uses it in Romans 1:30 in his catalog of the sins of the Greco-Roman world. He uses the related word *psithyrismos* in 2 Corinthians 12:20 (both times next to the previous root *katalal-).* Here he fears to find the dreadful sins of "backbitings and whisperings" among the not-so-saintly saints at Corinth. The difference between these last two words (*katalalos* and *psithyristes*) is that the whisperers are secret slanderers and backbiters are more public in their evil speaking.

WHORE

See HARLOT.

WHORE' MONGER (archaic)

Sexually immoral person (Ep 5:5).

WICKED SERVANT, PARABLE OF *(Ma 18:21-35)*

WICKED VINEDRESSERS, PARABLE OF (Ma 21:33-46; Mk 12:1-12; Lk 20:9-19)

WID' OW

Because of the helpless position of widows, the Mosaic law required that they be kindly treated. Those who disregarded this law were to be punished (De 10:18; 24:17,19; 27:19; Ze 7:10-12; Mal 3:5; Mk 12:40). Some Hebrew widows were cared for by their children or their relatives (Ge 38:11) or had the means to support themselves (Ju 17:1-6). In addition, a brother-in-law or close relative could be required to marry a young and childless widow (De 25:5-10; Ru 4:1-13). However, those widows who had no family, or whose relatives were poor, were in a very difficult position. Ruth, for example, gleaned the field after the reapers to support herself and Naomi (Ru 2:2,17-18). In the early church, care for the widows was a duty of the congregation and provisions were made to cover their needs (Ac 6:1; 1 Ti 5:3-16; Jam 1:27).

WIFE, ROLE OF

See MARRIAGE. The woman was created by God for Adam to be "a helper and companion to him" (Ge 2:18-20). This is still the best description of a good wife. Proverbs 12:4 calls a wife "the crown to her husband," and Proverbs 18:22 says that "he who finds a wife finds a good thing, and obtains favor from the LORD." This special relationship is created to be a blessing to both the husband and the wife. First Peter

3:7 reminds the husband that the wife is the "weaker vessel." This is not a statement of lesser value, but points out the special care that the husband needs to give because of his greater physical strength. Indeed, he is reminded to "honor her . . . as *being* heirs together of the grace of life, that his prayers may not be hindered." Malachi 2:14-15 refers to the "wife of your youth" and "your companion," both of which refer to the special bond that comes from living long and closely together. A wife is to submit to her husband (1 Pe 3:5-6); reverence her husband (Ep 5:33); love her husband (Tit 2:4); learn from her husband (1 Co 14:34-35); be trustworthy (Pr 31:11-12); love her children, be chaste, and a homemaker (Tit 2:4-5). Her relationship with her husband is to be exclusive and satisfying (Pr 5:15-20); it is to be mutually agreeable (1 Co 7:1-5) and undefiled (He 13:4). In turn, her husband is to love her (Ep 5:25,28); honor her (1 Pe 3:7); provide for her (1 Ti 5:8); instruct her (1 Co 14:35); protect her (1 Sa 30:1-19); and not divorce her (1 Co 7:11). Marriage is a picture of the relationship of Christ and his church, and if the wife or husband thinks her or his role is hard, it helps to remember that this is a special role that God has chosen to display to the world what the love of Christ for the church looks like, and how the submission, trust, and companionship of the church to Christ creates a beautiful and quiet spirit. In directing women to be submissive to their husband, Peter reminds them that if their husbands are unbelievers, they may be won by the conduct of the believing wife, "without a word." This is a powerful reminder of the value of good conduct and the beauty of a woman—not her apparel and hair-do and jewelry—but her "incorruptible ornament" of a gentle and quiet heart, which is "very precious in the sight of God." Peter reminds women of the holy women of former times who trusted God, and of Sarah, who obeyed Abraham, calling him lord, and "whose daughters you are if you do good and are not afraid with any terror" (1 Pe 3:1-6). It is not hard to think of things to "do good," but in today's culture it is a lot harder to obey husbands and not give way to fear. Back in Genesis after the fall, God said to Eve that he would greatly multiply her sorrow and conception, there would be pain in childbearing, and that "your desire will be for your husband, and he shall rule over you" (Ge 3:16). This seems to refer to a woman's desire to take things into

her own hands, instead of trusting her husband to do his job. Apparently Sarah was aware of this, and made it her business not to "give way to fear." She did, at one point, take things into her own hands with disastrous results when she gave her servant to Abraham to bring forth a child because she did not see how else this promise of children would be fulfilled (Ge 16). But she must have had the right attitude in general, because she is held up as an example of a woman who did keep the role that God had for her, and that it was precious to Him. The next verse (1 Pe 3:8) finishes with the reminder that "all of you" are to be of one mind, compassionate, loving and tenderhearted, courteous, not reviling but blessing. This then, is also a clear role for a wife, and for all Christians.

WIL′DER·NESS OF THE WAN′DER·ING

The land in which the Israelites wandered for forty years before entering Canaan. It was in the peninsula of Sinai formed by the Gulf of Suez and the Gulf of Akabah, the two branches of the Red Sea. About Mount Sinai was the granite region, while along the shore of the Mediterranean was the sandy region. The northern and central districts consisted of limestone (Ex 16:1-35; Nu 14:25,33-45; 20:2-13).

WIL′LOW

A tree that grows beside rivers and streams (Is 44:4). From it were taken the branches with which the Hebrews made booths during the Feast of Tabernacles (Le 23:40; Ps 137:2; Is 44:4).

WIL′LOWS, BROOK OF THE

A brook in Moab lined with willows (Is 15:7).

WILLS (2 Sa 17:23; 2 Ki 20:1; Is 38:1)

WIM′PLE

A garment worn by women about the face and neck (Is 3:22).

WIND

The Bible often speaks of the four winds (Je 49:36; Eze 37:9; Da 8:8; Re 7:1). The cold north wind dispersed rain clouds (Job 37:22). The south wind was a sign of hot weather (Lk 12:55). The west wind brought rain (1 Ki 18:44-45; Lk 12:54). The tempestuous east northeast gale was called the Euroclydon (Ac 27:14).

WIN′DOW

The opening in the wall of a building to admit light and air. Instead of glass the Eastern houses contained lattice work or wooden shutters that could be opened and closed at will. They usually faced the court but one or more generally looked out on the street (Ju 5:28; 2 Sa 6:16; Pr 7:6; Song 2:9).

WINE

The Hebrew word *Yayim* is used to denote wine or fermented grape juice, and its intoxicating character is obvious from the scriptural use of the word. Palestine was a wine-producing country, and wine was commonly used. Lot drank wine and became intoxicated (Ge 19:32). It was used as a drink offering in connection with the daily sacrifice (Ex 29:40) and other offerings (Le 23:13; Nu 15:5). The priests were forbidden to use wine during their sacred ministrations (Le 10:9) and the Nazirite, during the period of his vow, had to abstain from wine as well as from eating of grapes (Nu 6:3-4). Mixed wine was wine mixed with water (Is 1:22), with spices and strong drink (Ps 75:8; Is 5:22). The Scriptures set forth in striking forms the effects of the intemperate use of wine. Some of these effects are the enslavement of the drinker to wine (Ho 4:11), the redness of the eye (Ge 49:12), improper speech (Pr 20:1; 23:29-32; Is 28:7), distorted judgment (Pr 31:5). What was used by Jesus in the institution of the Lord's Supper is called the "fruit of the vine" (Ma 26:29).

WINE FAT (archaic)

A collection trough beneath a winepress (Mk 12:1).

WINE PRESS

A device used to press the juice from grapes. In ancient Palestine it consisted of an upper vat in which the grapes were trodden and a lower vat into which the juice flowed (Ju 6:11; Ne 13:15). Both were usually cut out of rock (Is 5:2). It is used figuratively in Isaiah 63:3 and Revelation 19:15.

WIS′DOM

The ability to judge fairly and to understand and make wise use of facts. The Hebrew conception was that wisdom is an attribute of God (Job 28; Is 40:12-14; Ro 11:33-35) and that he

WINEPRESS

shared it with certain men (Pr 2:1-22; Ec 2:26; 1 Co 2:4-12; 12:7-8; Ep 1:17; Col 1:9). Wisdom is personified in Proverbs 8. The portion of the Bible, known as Wisdom literature, consists of Job, Proverbs, Ecclesiastes, Song of Solomon. Paul condemned worldly wisdom (1 Co 1:19-31; Col 2:8; 1 Ti 6:20. Wisdom is more than shrewdness or intelligence. Instead it relates to practical righteousness and moral acumen. Proverbs is one of the few biblical books that clearly spells out its purpose. The purpose statement in 1:2-6 is twofold: 1) to impart moral discernment and discretion (1:3-5), and 2) to develop mental clarity and perception (1:2,6). The words "wisdom and instruction" in 1:2 complement each other because *wisdom* (*hokhmah*) means "skill" and *instruction* (musar) means "discipline." No skill is perfected without discipline, and when a person has skill he has freedom to create something beautiful. Proverbs deals with the most fundamental skill of all: practical righteousness before God in every area of life. This requires knowledge, experience, and a willingness to put God first (see 3:5-7). Chapters 1–9 are designed to create a felt need for wisdom, and Proverbs as a whole is designed both to prevent and to remedy ungodly lifestyles. The book served as a manual to impart the legacy of wisdom, prudence, understanding, discretion, knowledge, guidance, competence, correction, counsel, and truth—from generation to generation.

In Proverbs 8, wisdom is personified and seen in its perfection. It is divine (8:22-31), it is the source of biological and spiritual life (8:35-36; 3:18), it is righteous and moral (8:8-9), and it is available to all who will receive it (8:1-6,32-35). This wisdom became incarnate in Christ "in whom are hidden all the treasures of wisdom and knowledge" (Col 2:3). "But of Him you are in Christ Jesus, who became for us wisdom from God—and righteousness and sanctification and redemption" (1 Co 1:30).

Key wisdom verses in Proverbs are 1:5-7 and 3:5-6—"A wise *man* will hear and increase learning, and a man of understanding will attain wise counsel, to understand a proverb and an enigma, the words of the wise and their riddles. The fear of the LORD is the beginning of knowledge, *but* fools despise wisdom and instruction (1:5-7).

"Trust in the LORD with all your heart, and lean not on your own understanding; in all your ways acknowledge Him, and He shall direct your paths (3:5-6).

Wisdom (*hokmah*). The noun *hokmah* is derived from the verb *hakam,* "to be wise," or "to act wisely." All of the ancient Near East was interested in being wise; hence, a large body of "wisdom literature" was built up in that part of the world. God gave great wisdom to King Solomon (1 Ki 4:29-30), and he is the author of much of the Old Testament's Wisdom literature.

***Hokmah* as Skill.** What we might call artistic talent or skill, the Hebrews called *hokmah:* God filled Bezaleel and Aholiab "with skill [*hokmah*] to do all manner of work of the engraver and the designer and the tapestry maker" (Ex 35:35). God also filled Bezaleel "with the spirit of God in wisdom, understanding and knowledge" (Ex 31:3). Then "artistic works" in metal, wood, and jewel cutting are listed. "The spirit of wisdom" was needed to design and sew the priestly vestments for Aaron and his sons (Ex 28:3). Military skill was also called *hokmah* in Hebrew (Is 10:13).

Wisdom Personified Hebrew, along with Greek, Latin, French, German, and many other languages, expresses gender in its nouns. That is, in learning the language a student has to memorize each noun as to whether it is masculine or feminine. Hebrew has no neuter; hence,

there is no word for "it" or "its." Thus, a masculine or feminine pronoun is used to express things or concepts depending on the gender of the noun to which it refers. *Hokmah,* like many Hebrew nouns expressing such concepts as love, truth, justice, and wickedness, is a feminine noun. For this reason, wisdom is frequently referred to in Proverbs as "she" and "her." In poetry, when an abstract quality is presented as a person, the technique is called personification. Personification, while common in some languages, is rare in Hebrew.

Lady Wisdom is pictured as building a house, preparing a banquet, teaching in public, and crowning the wise. This personification of Wisdom in Proverbs 8, often seen as a foreshadowing of Christ, reflects His attributes, but the gender refers to the noun, not to Christ.

WISDOM LITERATURE

The wisdom literature of the Old Testament consists of the Books of Job, Proverbs, and Ecclesiastes, as well as some of the Psalms. The Hebrew word for wisdom is translated "skill for living," because the Jews regarded wisdom in very practical terms. This literature provided guidance for moral behavior and everyday living.

Hebrew wisdom literature, as distinguished from the wisdom writings of other cultures, was centered on God: "The fear of the LORD *is* the beginning of knowledge, *but* fools despise wisdom and instruction" (Pr 1:7). In contrast, Egyptian wisdom, for example, focused on the wisdom of the sages and on disciplining oneself to accept the trials of life.

The three broad categories of wisdom literature in the Old Testament are 1) popular proverbs that express practical truths; 2) riddles or parables with a spiritual meaning; and 3) discussions of the problems of life.

The Book of Proverbs provides wise sayings and observations designed to develop proper attitudes and godly behavior. Ecclesiastes offers a philosophical discussion of the emptiness of life without God (Ec 1:2,14). Job is a classical examination of the problems of evil and human suffering. Its conclusion is that people can understand only what God chooses to reveal to them (Job 28:20-28).

Many of the Psalms, including 1;4;10;14;18-19; 37;49;73;90; and 112, are regarded as wisdom literature. A recurring theme in these Psalms is the problem of the prosperity of the wicked while the godly suffer. But the wise psalmist often returns to this refrain: "For evildoers shall be cut off; but those who wait on the LORD, they shall inherit the earth" (Ps 37:9).

Solomon, David's son and successor as king of Israel, was well-known for his wisdom. God appeared to Solomon in a dream at the beginning of his reign and asked him what gift he wished above all else (1 Ki 3:3-5). Solomon chose wisdom. Solomon wrote many of the sayings in the Book of Proverbs.

WISE MEN
See MAGI.

WIT (archaic)
To know; to become aware of (Ge 24:19-21).

WITCH, WITCH' CRAFT
See SORCERER.

WITH' AL (archaic)
With (Job 2:7-8).

WITHS (archaic)
Cords; ropes (Ju 6:9).

WIT' NESS
1. A memorial to an event. One such witness was the heap of stones set up by Jacob and Laban in witness of their covenant (Ge 31:46-52). Joshua set up a stone in witness of his covenant with the people of Israel (Jos 24:27). 2. A person who gave testimony, especially in legal matters. Witnesses were needed to attest a property transaction or a betrothal (Ru 4:9; Je 32:10). Under Mosaic law, in criminal cases, it was necessary to have two witnesses (De 17:6; Ma 18:16). If it were discovered that a witness had given false testimony, then he was punished with the same penalty the accused would have drawn (De 19:16-19). In carrying out a death sentence the witnesses were the first to cast the stones (De 17:6-7; 1 Ki 21:10). 3. One who testifies to his faith in Christ (Lk 24:48; He 12:1). The Greek word for witness is martyr, a word that came to denote one who had suffered death rather than abandon his faith (Ac 22:20; Re 2:13). 4. Witness of God for Christ (Ma 3:16-17; Lk 9:28-35; 1 Jo 5:7-12). 5. Witness of the Spirit in man (Ro 8:14-16).

WIZ' ARD
One who claimed to have supernatural powers and was able to speak with departed spirits (Is 8:19). See SORCERER.

WOLF
In Palestine, instead of running in packs the wolf prowls about alone. Its ferocity is noted (Eze 22:27; Ma 7:15).

WOM' AN
In her creation she was the helpmeet and equal of man (Ge 2:21-24). See EVE. For the principle of monogamy see MARRIAGE. In early times, women labored in the fields and took care of sheep (Ge 29:6; Ex 2:16; Ru 2:3,8) but their main duties were of a household nature such as grinding grain (Ma 24:41), caring for the physical needs of the family (1 Sa 2:19; 2 Sa 13:8; Pr 31:13,19; Ac 9:36-39), supervising the home (1 Ti 5:14), and instructing the children (Pr 1:8; 31:1; 2 Ti 3:15). Under the Mosaic law the wife and mother was respected and honored (Ex 20:12; Pr 1:8; 18:22; Ec 9:9). In the New Testament she was further ennobled by Jesus through his teachings on adultery, marriage, and divorce (Ma 5:27-32) and through his attitude toward his mother, the sisters at Bethany, and the woman at the well (Lk 10:38-42; Jo 4:7-30; 19:25-27). Paul said that women should not talk in church but should question their husbands at home if they wished to learn anything (1 Co 14:35).

WOMEN OF THE NEW TESTAMENT
Mary, the virgin mother of Jesus, has a place of honor among the women of the New Testament. She is an enduring example of faith, humility, and service (Lk 1:26-56).

Name	Description	Biblical Reference
Anna	Recognized Jesus as the long-awaited Messiah	Lk 2:36-38
Bernice	Sister of Agrippa before whom Paul made his defense	Ac 25:13
Candace	A queen of Ethiopia	Ac 8:27
Chloe	Woman who knew of divisions in the church at Corinth	1 Co 1:11
Claudia	Christian of Rome	2 Ti 4:21
Damaris	Woman of Athens converted under Paul's ministry	Ac 17:34
Dorcas (Tabitha)	Christian in Joppa who was raised from the dead by Peter	Ac 9:36-41

Name	Description	Biblical Reference
Drusilla	Wife of Felix, governor of Judea	Ac 24:24
Elizabeth	Mother of John the Baptist	Lk 1:5,13
Eunice	Mother of Timothy	2 Ti 1:5
Herodius	Queen who demanded the execution of John the Baptist	Ma 14:3-10
Joanna	Provided for the material needs of Jesus	Lk 8:3
Lois	Grandmother of Timothy	2 Ti 1:5
Lydia	Convert under Paul's ministry in Philippi	Ac 16:14
Martha and Mary	Sisters of Lazarus; friends of Jesus	Lk 10:38-42
Mary Magdalene	Woman from whom Jesus cast out demons	Ma 27:56-61; Mk 16:9
Phoebe	A servant, perhaps a deaconess, in the church at Chechrea	Ro 16:1-2
Priscilla	Wife of Aquila; laborer with Paul at Corinth and Ephesus	Ac 18:2,18-19
Salome	Mother of Jesus's disciples, James and John	Ma 20:20-24
Sapphira	Lied about the nature of a gift of money in the early Christian community	Ac 5:1
Susanna	Provided for the material needs of Jesus	Lk 8:3

WOMEN OF THE OLD TESTMENT

One of the outstanding women of the Old Testament was Hannah, who prayed for a son and then dedicated him to the Lord, even before he was born. Hannah's faithfulness was rewarded in the person of Samuel, who served his nation as a prophet, priest, and judge during a crucial time in its history (1 Sa 1–7). Other outstanding women of the Old Testament include the following:

Name	Description	Biblical Reference
Bath-sheba	Wife of David; mother of Solomon	2 Sa 11:3,27
Deborah	A judge who defeated the Canaanites under Sisera	Ju 4:4
Delilah	Philistine woman who tricked Samson	Ju 16:4-5
Dinah	Only daughter of Jacob	Ge 30:21
Esther	Jewish captive in Persia; saved her people from destruction by the schemer Haman	Es 2:16-17
Eve	First woman	Ge 3:20
Gomer	The prophet Hosea's unfaithful wife	Ho 1:2-3
Hagar	Sarah's maid; mother of Ishmael	Ge 16:3-16
Jezebel	Wicked wife of King Ahab of the Northern Kingdom	1Ki 16:30-31
Jochebed	Mother of Moses	Ex 6:20

Name	Description	Biblical Reference
Miriam	Sister of Moses	Ex 15:20
Naomi	Ruth's mother-in-law; great-great-grandmother of David	Ru 1:2,4
Orpah	Ruth's sister-in-law; Naomi's daughter-in-law	Ru 1:4
Rachel	Wife of Jacob	Ge 29:28
Rahab	Harlot who harbored Israel's spies; ancestor of Jesus	Jo 2:1-3; Ma 1:5
Ruth	Wife of Boaz, mother of Obed; great-grandmother of David; ancestor of Jesus	Ru 4:13,17 Ma 1:5
Sarah	Wife of Abraham; mother of Isaac	Ge 11:29; 21:2-3
Tamar	A daughter of David	2 Sa 13:1
Zipporah	Wife of Moses	Ex 2:21

WONT (archaic)

To be accustomed to (Lk 22:39-41).

WORD OF THE LORD

In nearly every verse of Psalm 119, the author magnifies God's word. Following is a study of seven of the words he uses to represent God's word, in their order of appearance.

Law (torah) occurs about 220 times in the Old Testament. It is perhaps unfortunate that "law" was chosen as the main translation of *torah*. The word is much broader than the legal implications that our word *law* might imply. The Jews refer to the first five books of the Old Testament as "the Torah." There is much more than legislation in these books, even in Exodus and Leviticus.

The basic meaning of *torah* is "teaching" or "instruction." Because God loves humankind, He has given a body of teaching and laws so that we can know what He expects from us and how we should live. "The [*torah*] of the Lord is perfect" (Ps 19:7).

Testimony (edut, v.2) comes from the verb *ud,* "to bear witness," and is used nine times in Psalm 119. The word suggests not only corroboration by testimony but sometimes includes a warning as well. It is used in the Old Testament only with reference to God. His Word is His own testimony to Himself and, as such, should be accepted and acted upon.

Precepts (piqqudim, v. 4) always appears in plural; and its twenty-four occurrences are all in Psalms, twenty-one in Psalm 119 alone. The noun is derived from the verb *paqad* ("number," "reckon," "visit," "appoint," or "punish"). The precepts of God are those responsibilities that He has appointed for His people.

Statute (*hoq* v.5) occurs 128 times and comes from the verb *haqaq*, "engrave" or "write." In ancient times, statutes were engraved on metal or stone so that people could read and keep them. *Hoq* is a general term for laws imposed by God or man. The most common Hebrew word to be used with *hoq* is *shamar* ("keep"). God's statutes are meant to be kept.

Another meaning of this word is "custom," such as in the custom of ancient Israel of women commemorating Jephthah's daughter (Ju 11:39-40).

Commandment (*mitzwah*, v. 6) is used to describe "The Ten Commandments" (Ex 24:12). The noun is derived from the verb *tsawah,* to "command" or "charge." God's commands are an expression of His Person and nature. Psalm 119 teaches that these revelations of God's will are "faithful" or reliable (v. 86), "truth" (v. 151), and "righteousness" (v. 172). Psalm 19:8 says they are also "pure." If we really love our Lord, we will keep His Commandments, and they will not be burdensome.

Judgment (*mishpat* v. 7, is derived from the verb *shaphat,* "judge" or "govern," and occurs about four hundred times in the Old Testament, sixteen times in Psalm 119 alone. The general idea is one of justice, or specific ordinances to promote justice. There are many distinct usages of the noun in both secular and religious law. Each specific ordinance of the Pentateuch is called a *mishpat* (Le 9:16; De 33:21).

"The LORD is a God of justice" (Is 30:18) and "loves justice" (Ps 37:28). His "judgments *are* a great deep" (Ps 36:6). Because God is just in His judgments, so should we His people be.

Word (*dabar,* v. 9) is one of the great words of the Bible. It is such an idiomatic word in the Old Testament that the King James translators needed eighty-five different English words to translate it. The noun comes from the verb "to say" or "speak." The main idea is that whatever God says is His word.

WORKERS IN THE VINEYARD, PARABLE OF (Ma 20:1-16)

WORLD, FLESH, DEVIL

Three powerful enemies are constantly trying to defeat the Christian's testimony and spiritual success: the world, the flesh, and the devil.

The key to conquering the world is the love of the Father. Victory over the flesh is through the Holy Spirit. Power over the devil is in the Son of God who came to "destroy the works of the devil" (1 Jo 3:8).

The World (*kosmos*) The root meaning of *kosmos* is "order" or "arrangement," hence beauty (*cosmetics* and the *cosmos* flower). The main meaning of *kosmos* is the organized system that is under the devil's control and leaves out God and Christ. *Kosmos* is a major New Testament word, with over half of its occurrences in John's Gospel, where it is one of the evangelist's key terms. His verdict: "the whole world lies *under the sway of* the wicked one" (1 Jo 5:19).

Kosmos does not always have a negative connotation. John 3:16 uses the word for the people that "God so Loved." This meaning also occurs in the expression "Savior of the world" (Jo 4:42). Paul uses *kosmos* for the created planet in his sermon on Mars' Hill (Ac 17:24).

Two related words are *kosmikos* (English *cosmic*), "worldy" or "pertaining to this earth," and *kosmoskrator.* "Worldly" in an evil sense are the "lusts" or strong desires that Paul teaches us to deny (Tit 2:12). The morally neutral sense merely describes "the earthly sanctuary" (He 9:1). The "rulers" (*kosmoskrator,* "cosmocrats," used only in Ep 6:12) are evil forces the believer has to contend with. Though they are demonic, they work through flesh-and-blood enemies.

The Flesh (*sarx*). The literal meaning of *flesh* is found in expressions like "flesh and blood" and "flesh and bones." Christianity does not teach that the human body is evil, but that it can be used for evil. The expression "vile body" (Ph 3:21, KJV) is misleading because today it suggests moral evil. The meaning is "lowly" (NKJV).

As a destructive influence, the flesh can be our most insidious enemy because it is inside the believer and ever present with its depraved cravings. Even sincere and devout Christians (including the apostle Paul) can have terrific struggles with the flesh. One should not think that he or she is not a true believer because of such temptations. Unfortunately, in a certain sense, as long as we live in the body we will have to contend with the flesh. The whole terrible catalog of the works of the flesh is recounted in Galatians 5:19-21.

The secret of victory over the flesh is to be led by the Holy Spirit. "Walk ["live your life"] in the Spirit, and you shall not fulfill the lust of the flesh" (Ga 5:16).

The Devil (*diablos*). *Devil* is simply an anglicized form of the Greek word that suggests hurling (slander) back and forth. He is an accuser of the brethren (Ze 3:1; Re 12:10). The devil is a personal enemy who is opposed to God, His people, and His plans.

An ancient secular usage of this word is "slanderer," and Paul uses it just so in warning older women not to become *diabolos* (1 Ti 3:11). Our Lord calls Judas a *diabolos* in John 6:70. He was not a misunderstood follower who had good intentions as some writers like to paint him.

The vast majority of New Testament examples of *diabolos* refer to Satan (Hebrew for "adversary"). In the Septuagint, the Greek translation of the Old Testament, *diabolos* is the translation of this word over a dozen times. Jesus was not tempted by an evil influence, but by a personal fallen angel who can cite Scripture to his purpose. The Christian's defense against the devil is "the whole armor of God" (Ep 6:10-17). The devil is a defeated foe—Christ bested him at Calvary. Nevertheless, he will remain active in the world until he is locked up for one thousand years (Re 20). The devil's ultimate doom is the lake of fire (Re 20:10). While Christians should not fear the devil, they should treat him with respect. "Michael, the archangel, in contending with the devil when he disputed about the body of Moses, dared not bring against him a reviling accusation, but said, "The Lord rebuke you!" (Jude 9).

WORM

The references to worms in the Bible denoted maggots and other insect larvae. These exist chiefly in dead bodies, open sores, and spoiled food (Ex 16:20; Job 7:5; Is 14:11). They also destroy plants (De 28:39; Jon 4:7). The term is also used to indicate man's lowly state (Ps 22:6; Is 41:14).

WORM'WOOD

A plant from which the juice is bitter and very disagreeable to the taste (De 29:18; Re 8:11).

WOR'SHIP

Religious reverence and homage, especially the act of paying divine honours to God (Ex 34:14; Ma 4:10). In the Bible four stages of public wor-

ship are discernible. In the patriarchal age and the time of the judges, it was meagerly described and scarcely distinguishable from private worship (Jos 24:14-31). Temple worship, besides featuring sacrifice, was highly ritualistic as evidenced by its use of the Psalms. Synagogue worship after the exile and through New Testament times made of prime importance the reading of the Law and the Prophets (Lk 4:14-21). Early Christian worship included preaching, prayer, reading of Scripture, singing, administration of the Lord's Supper, and almsgiving. Worship refers to the supreme honor or veneration given either in thought or deed to a person or thing. The Bible teaches that God alone is worthy of worship (Ps 29:2), but it also sadly records accounts of those who worshipped other objects. Among those were people (Da 2:46), false gods (2 Ki 10:19), images and idols (Is 2:8; Da 3:5), heavenly bodies (2 Ki 21:3), Satan (Re 13:4), and demons (Re 9:20). It is indeed tragic that many worshiped gods they could carry and not the God who could carry them. God Almighty alone is worthy of worship (Re 4:11).

True worship involves at least three important elements:

a. Worship requires *reverence*. This includes the honor and respect directed toward the Lord in thought and feeling. It is one thing to obey a superior unwillingly; it is quite another to commit one's thoughts and emotions in that obedience. Jesus said that those who worship God must do so "in spirit and in truth" (Jo 4:24). The term *spirit* speaks of the personal nature of worship: it is from my person to God's person and involves the intellect, emotions, and will. The word *truth* speaks of the content of worship: God is pleased when we worship Him, understanding His true character.

b. Worship includes public expression. This was particularly prevalent in the Old Testament because of the sacrificial system. For example, when a believer received a particular blessing for which he wanted to thank God, it was not sufficient to say it privately; he expressed his thanks publicly with a thank offering.

c. Worship means service. These two concepts are often linked together in Scripture (De 8:19). Furthermore, the words for worship in both Testaments originally referred to the labor of slaves for the master. Worship especially includes the joyful service which Christians render to Christ their Master. The concept of worship must not be restricted to church attendance, but should embrace an entire life of obedience to God.

The first reason for worship is simply that God commands it (1 Ch 16:20; Ma 4:10). The first four of the Ten Commandments, which are also the longest, clearly charge men to worship the one true God and Him alone (Ex 20:3-10). To allow any person or thing to usurp the position of lordship over us constitutes gross disobedience to the will of God and incurs His terrible wrath (Ex 20:5; De 27:15). All people are destined to pay homage to God anyway, even if it is unwillingly (Ph 2:10).

An equally important reason for worship is that God deserves our worship. He alone possesses the attributes that merit our worship and service. Among these are goodness (Ps 100:4-5), mercy (Ex 4:31), holiness (Ps 99:5,9), and creative power (Re 4:11). When men of biblical times clearly saw the unveiled glory of God, they could not help but fall prostrate in worship. Examples of this response can be seen in the actions of Moses (Ex 34:5-8), Paul (Ac 9:3-6), and John (Re 1:9-17).

A final reason for worship is that men need to give it. People cannot find personal fulfillment apart from the glad submission of themselves in worshipful obedience to God. He is the Creator and they are the creatures (Re 4:11). People who adopt as their master anything less than God are building their lives on quicksand. They will be no stronger than the object they worship (Ps 115:4-8). One who worships God, however, not only participates in the activity of the occupants of heaven (Re 7:9-12), but finds joyful satisfaction for the present (Ro 12:2; Col 3:24).

Since worship encompasses thought, feeling, and deed, there are many expressions of it. Worship especially includes praise and thanksgiving which may be expressed privately or publicly, either by grateful declarations (He 13:15) or by joyful singing (Ps 100:2; Ep 5:19; Col 3:16). Portions of early Christian hymns of worship actually may be preserved in the New Testament (1 Ti 3:16; 2 Ti 2:11-13).

WOT (archaic)

To know (Ro 11:2-3).

WRIT′ING

The art of writing dates back to an early time in the history of the race. It is quite evident that the Hebrews understood the art of writing (Ex 17:14; 24:4; Nu 33:2) and that at the time of the exodus documents were written (De 31:24). The law was inscribed (Ex 39:14,30; De 27:4,8; Jos 8:32). Clay tablets were used for the letters sent from Canaan to the king of Egypt, and the oldest Shemitic documents bearing Assyrian inscriptions were written on the same material. The Egyptians used papyrus and it is most likely that prepared skins were commonly used by the Hebrews, See BOOK, PAPYRUS, PARCHMENT.

WROTH (archaic)

To be provoked; angered (Ma 2:16).

X

XER′XES

See AHASUERUS.

Y

YAH

An abbreviation of Yahweh (Ps 68:4; Jah, KJV).

YAHWEH

See LORD and GOD, NAMES OF.

YARN (1 Ki 10:28; 2 Ch 1:16; Ex 35:25-26)

YEA (archaic)

Yes; certainly (Ma 5:37). Used poetically as an intensifier, with the sense of "even more" (Ps 19:10; 23:4; 137:1).

YEAR

The time it takes for the earth to make a complete orbit around the sun. The Hebrew calendar was arranged with twelve months (1 Ki 4:7; 1 Ch 27:1-15). The months followed the lunar cycle, producing a year with only 354 days. Every so often, a thirteenth month would be added to make up the discrepancy. See CALENDAR.

YEAR, SABBATICAL

See SABBATICAL YEAR.

YOKE

YEAR OF JUBILEE
See JUBILEE.

YEAST, PARABLE OF (Ma 13:33)

YHWH
The Hebrew name of God, probably pronounced "Yahweh." See LORD and GOD, NAMES OF.

YIRON
See IRON.

YOD
The tenth letter of the Hebrew alphabet. It is the heading of verses 73-80 of Psalm 119. In Hebrew each of these eight verses began with the letter yod. This word is the root of the English "jot" (Ma 5:18). See ACROSTIC.

YOKE
A transverse wooden bar fashioned to fit the necks of two draft animals, usually oxen. Attached to it is the pole of the plow or vehicle to be drawn (Nu 19:2; 1 Ki 19:19). The word is used figuratively of bondage and servitude (De 28:48; Ac 15:10; Ga 5:1; 1 Ti 6:1).

YOKEFELLOW
A fellow worker, companion, co-worker, teammate. In Philippians 4:3, Paul refers to an unidentified Christian as his "yokefellow." Clearly this person had worked as a teammate with Paul in the spread of the gospel.

Z

ZA·A·NA′ IM
See ZAANANNIM.

ZA′ A·NAN (place of flocks)
A city of Judah (Mi 1:11). See ZENAN.

ZA·A·NAN′ NIM
A place in Naphtali near Kedesh (Jos 19:33).

ZA′ A·VAN (disquiet)
A son of Ezer and a Horite chief (Ge 36:27). In 1 Chronicles 1:42 he is called Zavan.

ZA′ BAD (has endowed)
Six Old Testament men:
1. A descendant of Sheshan of the family of Hezron. He was one of David's warriors (1 Ch 2:31,34-37; 11:41).
2. Son of Tahath of Ephraim (1 Ch 7:21).
3. Son of Shimeath and one of the two assassins of Joash, king of Judah (2 Ch 24:26). When Amaziah came to the throne, the two were executed. His mother was a woman of Ammon. The name is more correctly written Jozachar in 2 Kings 12:21.
4, 5, 6. Three Hebrews who, in the time of Ezra, divorced their foreign wives (Ez 10:27, 33,43).

ZAB·BA′ I
A son of Bebai and the father of Baruch (Ne 3:20).

ZAB′ BUD (given)
A son of Bigvai. He returned with Ezra (Ez 8:14).

ZAB′ DI (gift of Jehovah)
Four Old Testament men:
1. Son of Zerah, of Judah (Jos 7:1,17). He is called Zimri in 1 Chronicles 2:6.
2. A son of Shimhi of the tribe of Benjamin (1 Ch 8:19).
3. An inhabitant of Shepham (a Shiphmite), who had charge of David's wine cellars (1 Ch 27:27).
4. A son of Asaph, a Levite. He lived in the time of Nehemiah (Ne 11:17).

ZAB′ DI·EL (gift of God)
Two Old Testament men:
1. The father of Jashobeam, the latter an officer of David's army (1 Ch 27:2).
2. Son of Haggedolim. He was overseer of 128 warriors in the time of Nehemiah (Ne 11:14).

ZA′ BUD (given)
Son of Nathan (1 Ki 4:5), a principle officer and the king's (Solomon) friend.

ZA·BU′ LON
See ZEBULUN.

ZAC·CA′ I *(pure)*

The head of a family, a large number of whom returned to Palestine with Zerubbabel (Ez 2:9; Ne 7:14).

ZAC·CHAE′ US *(pure)*

A chief publican who had charge of the revenues of the district of Jericho (Lk 19:1-10).

ZAC′ CHUR

See ZACCUR.

ZAC′ CUR *(mindful)*

Seven Old Testament men:

1. Father of Shammua, the spy of the tribe of Reuben (Nu 13:4).

2. Son of Hamuel of the tribe of Simeon (1 Ch 4:26). He is also called Zacchur.

3. A son of Jaaziah of the family of Merari, a Levite (1 Ch 24:27).

4. A son of Asaph, family of Gershom, a Levite and leader of the third course of musicians in the time of David (1 Ch 25:2,10; Ne 12:35).

5. A son of Imri. He labored on the wall of Jerusalem under Nehemiah (Ne 3:2).

6. A Levite who sealed the covenant (Ne 10:12).

7. A Levite, son of Mattaniah (Ne 13:13).

ZACHARIAH

See ZECHARIAH.

ZACH·A·RI′ AS

Two righteous men, one of the Old Testament, one of the New.

1. Greek spelling of Zechariah, son of Barachias, the prophet who wrote the book of Zechariah. He was referred to by Jesus as a righteous man who was put to death by the Jews at the temple (Ma 23:35; Lk 11:51). Some scholars think this could also refer to Zechariah, a priest who was the son of Jehoida, at the time of Joash, king of Judah (2 Ch 24:20-22)

2. Father of John the Baptist. He was a priest of the course of Abia (Lk 1:5). His wife, Elisabeth, was related to the mother of Jesus. They lived in the hill country of Judea, probably at Juttah (Lk 1:39-40). While he was engaged in burning incense at the hour of prayer, an angel assured him that his prayer for a son was answered. On account of the age of Elisabeth he was doubtful and asked for a sign. As a result he became dumb until John was born. When he spoke, he praised God (Lk 1:18-22,62-64).

ZA′ CHER

See ZECHARIAH.

ZA′ DOK *(righteous)*

Five men of the Old Testament:

1. The son of Ahitub, a descendant of Eleazar, son of Aaron (2 Sa 8:17; 1 Ch 24:3). After the death of Saul, he and others of his father's house went to David at Hebron (1 Ch 12:27-28). When David became king of all Israel, Zadok and Abiathar held the high priest's office (2 Sa 8:17).

2. The father of Jerusha, the wife of Uzziah, king of Judah (2 Ki 15:33).

3. A priest of the high priestly line and father of Shallum (1 Ch 6:12).

4. Son of Baana. He labored on the wall of Jerusalem under Nehemiah (Ne 3:4).

5. Son of Immer. He was a priest and labored on the wall of Jerusalem (Ne 3:29). He was probably the same as the scribe whom Nehemiah appointed as one of the treasurers of the temple (Ne 13:13).

ZA′ HAM *(loathing)*

A son of Rehoboam and Abihail (2 Ch 11:19).

ZA′ IR *(little)*

A place in Edom, east of the Dead Sea (2 Ki 8:21).

ZA′ LAPH *(fracture)*

The father of Hanun. The son labored on the wall (Ne 3:30).

ZAL′ MON *(shady)*

An Old Testament man; a forest.

1. One of David's warriors; an Ahohite (2 Sa 23:28). In 1 Chronicles 11:29 he is called Ilai.

2. A forest near Shechem (Ju 9:48). In Psalm 68:14 it is called Salmon.

ZAL′ MON, MOUNT

The place where Abimelech and his warriors each cut a bough from a tree to use in their siege against the tower of Shechem (Ju 9:48).

ZAL·MO′ NAH *(shady)*

A place southeast of Edom, one of the stopping places on the wilderness journey (Nu 33:41-42).

ZAL·MUN′ NA *(shade denied)*

A king of Midian (Ju 8:4-28; Ps 83:11). See ZEBAH.

ZAM·ZUM′ MIM

A tribe of Rephaim that occupied a region east of the Jordan, which afterwards was held by the Ammonites (De 2:20).

ZA·NO′ AH *(bog)*

Two towns of Judah.

1. A town in the hill country of Judah about ten miles southwest of Hebron (Jos 15:56).

2. A town in the lowland of Judah (Jos 15:34).

ZAPH′ E·NATH-PA·NE′ AH

Variant spelling of ZAPHNATH-PAANEAH.

ZAPH′ NATH-PA·A·NE′ AH

The name given Joseph by Pharaoh (Ge 41:45).

ZA′ PHON *(north)*

A town in the territory of Gad, east of the Jordan (Jos 13:27).

ZAR′ A, ZAR′ AH

See ZERAH.

ZA·RE′ A·THITE

See ZORATHITE.

ZAR′ ED

See ZERED.

ZAR′ E·PHATH *(refinement)*

A town of Phoenicia near Sidon where the widow who sheltered and sustained Elijah lived. Her jar of oil and bin of meal did not run out until the Lord sent rain, "according to the word of the Lord which he spoke by Elijah" (1 Ki 17:9-16). This town is also mentioned in Obadiah, verse 20, as one of the border towns that the "captives of the host of the children of Israel shall possess as far as;" Jesus refers to this widow and this incident when he talks of a prophet not receiving honor in his own country. (Lk 4:26; Sarepta, KJV)

ZAR′ E·TAN

A village near Adam and Beth-shean close to the place where the Israelites under Joshua crossed the Jordan (Jos 3:16; 1 Ki 4:12). The metal ornaments for Solomon's temple were cast near here (1 Ki 7:46; 2 Ch 4:17). The Midianites fled toward this town when Gideon and his three hundred warriors routed them (Ju 7:22).

Also called Zartanah and Zarethan (KJV).

ZAR′ E·THAN

See ZARETAN.

ZAR′ ETH·SHA′ HAR

See ZERETH-SHAHAR.

ZAR′ HITE

Two families of the Old Testament:

1. One belonging to the family of Zerah, a son of Simeon (Nu 26:13,20).

2. One belonging to the family of Zerah, a son of Judah. Achan, the man who took plunder for himself at Jericho was of this family (Jos 7:17).

3. One of the twelve captains of Israel was a Zarhite, but it does not say which family he was from (1 Ch 27:11,13).

ZAR·TA′ NAH

See ZARETAN.

ZAR′ THAN

See ZARETAN.

ZAT′ TU

The head of a family, a large number of whom returned from Babylon with Zerubbabel (Ez 2:8; 10:27; Ne 7:13; 10:14).

ZA′ VAN

See ZAAVAN.

ZAYIN

The seventh letter of the Hebrew alphabet. It is the heading of verses 49-56 of Psalm 119; in Hebrew each of these eight verses began with the letter zayin. See ACROSTIC.

ZA′ ZA

A son of Jonathan (1 Ch 2:33).

ZEAL, ZEALOUS

Ardent desire to do or have something; impassioned eagerness, especially in favor of a person or a cause. Both Greek and Hebrew also have the connotations of jealousy in this word. When one thinks of God's zeal for righteousness, and His mandate that His people be zealous for Him alone (He will not share worship and honor with another; Ex 20:1-6), the connection between desire and jealousy becomes clear. Isaiah 9:7 talks about the zeal of the Lord of hosts to establish the reign of the Messiah. But zeal does not belong only to God. Saul sought to slay the Gibeonites in his zeal (2 Sa 21:2), and [Jehu] said, "Come with me, and see my zeal for the Lord (2 Ki 10:16). The psalmist writes, "zeal for your house has eaten me up;" this is also quoted about Jesus when he cleansed the temple (Ps 69:9 and Jo 2:17). Zeal is illustrated in Paul's life in his desire to reach the Jews (Ro 9:1-3; 10:1); his determination to evangelize all (1 Co 9:19-23), and his willingness to lose all things for Christ (Ph 3:4-16).

ZEAL' OT (zealous one)

Nickname of the other Simon of the twelve (Lk 6:15; Ac 1:13), which may refer to his interest in a patriotic party originated by Judas the Galilean. Like the Pharisees, the Zealots were devoted to the law, but they were also violently opposed to submission to Rome. In their fanatical dedication to overthrowing Rome, they took over Jerusalem in A.D. 66, which resulted in the last siege and fall of Jerusalem to Rome in A.D. 70. Masada, the last Zealot fortress, was taken over by Rome in A.D. 73.

ZEB·A·DI' AH (endowed by Jehovah)

Nine Old Testament men:
1. A Benjamite of the house of Beriah (1 Ch 8:15).
2. A Benjamite, a descendant of Elpaal (1 Ch 8:17-18).
3. A son of Jeroham of Gedor. He allied himself with David at Ziklag (1 Ch 12:7).
4. A Levite appointed by Jehoshaphat to teach the law to the people of Judah (2 Ch 17:8).
5. A prince who held a high judicial position under Jehoshaphat (2 Ch 19:11), the son of Ishmael.
6. A son of Meshelemiah, a Korhite Levite who lived in the time of David (1 Ch 26:1-2).
7. The son of Asahel. The latter was also the brother of Joab (1 Ch 27:7).
8. Son of Michael, a descendant of Shephatiah. He returned from Babylon with Ezra (Ez 8:8).
9. A priest (Ez 10:20).

ZE' BAH and ZALMUNNA (sacrifice)

These were the kings of Midian who Gideon was fighting with his three hundred selected warriors. The warriors were weary, but they crossed the Jordan, took the two kings, and routed the whole army. The men of Succoth had refused to give Gideon's warriors bread, so when Gideon returned to Succoth with the captured kings, he punished the men of Succoth for ridiculing him and his men. He then questioned the kings of Midian and when he discovered that they had killed his own brothers, Gideon killed them (Ju 8:4-28). This battle is also referred to in Psalm 83:11 and Isaiah 9:4; 10:6.

ZEBAIM (gazelles)

One of Solomon's servants. Descendants of Zebaim are named as those who came back from the Babylonian captivity with Zerubbabel (Ez 2:57; Ne 7:59).

ZEB' E·DEE

The father of the apostles James and John, and probably husband of Salome. He and his sons were fishermen on the Sea of Galilee (Ma 4:21-22; 27:56).

ZE·BI' DAH

See ZEBUDAH.

ZE·BI' NA (acquired, bought)

A descendant of Nebo, one of those who put away the pagan wife he had taken during the Babylonian captivity (Ez 10:43).

ZE·BOI' IM

One of the cities of the plain destroyed by fire along with Sodom and Gomorrah (Ge 10:19; 19:17-29; De 29:23; Ho 11:8). Its king, Shemeber, was defeated by Chedorlaomer (Ge 14:2,8, 10). See SODOM and DEAD SEA.

ZE·BO' IM (gazelles)

A valley and a town:
1. A valley of Benjamin, east of Michmash (1 Sa 13:16-18).
2. A town occupied by Benjamites after the exile (Ne 11:34).

ZE·BU' DAH (bestowed)

A daughter of Pedaiah of Rumah, mother of King Jehoiakim of Judah (2 Ki 23:36).

ZE' BUL

A lieutenant of Abimelech, who was a son of Gideon by his concubine (Ju 9:28-41).

ZE·BU′ LUN (habitation)

A man, a tribe (his descendants), and a place:

1. The youngest of the sons of Jacob by Leah (Ge 30:19-20). Zebulun had three sons who were heads of the families of the tribe (Nu 26:26-27).

2. Tribe of Zebulun. In the arrangement of the tribes it was in the camp of Judah. Its territory was in the northern section between the Mediterranean and the Sea of Galilee. Within its bounds were Nazareth and Cana. Many of Christ's works were done along its eastern boundary at the sea (Ma 4:12-16), as prophesied by Isaiah (Is 9:1-2). Also within the territory was Gath-hepher, home of the prophet Jonah.

3. A place on the eastern border of Asher (Jos 19:27).

ZE·BU′ LUN·ITE

A member of the tribe of Zebulun (Nu 26:27; Ju 12:11-12).

ZECH·A·RI′ AH (remembered of Jehovah)

A number of men in the Old Testament:

1. The last king of the Jehu dynasty of Israel. He was the son of Jeroboam II, reigned six months, and was slain by Shallum who seized the throne (2 Ki 14:29; 15:10).

2. The father of Hezekiah's mother, Abi (2 Ki 18:2).

3. A chief of the tribe of Reuben when Tiglath-pileser invaded Israel (1 Ch 5:7).

4. Brother of Kish and uncle of Saul (1 Ch 9:37). He is also called Zacher or Zecher in 1 Chronicles 8:31.

5. The son of Meshelemiah, a Levite of the family of Kohath and a porter of the tabernacle in the time of David (1 Ch 9:21-22). His wisdom as a counselor is mentioned in 1 Chronicles 26:14.

6. A Levite who played a psaltery when the ark was brought to Jerusalem by David and who, afterwards, was in the service of the tabernacle (1 Ch 15:18,20; 16:5).

7. A priest and trumpeter when the ark was brought from the house of Obed-edom (1 Ch 15:24).

8. A son of Isshiah, a Levite of the family of Kohath; a descendant of Uzziel who lived in the time of David (1 Ch 24:25).

9. A son of Hosah, a Levite of the family of Merari. He lived in the reign of David (1 Ch 26:11).

10. The father of Iddo of Manasseh in Gilead. The son lived in the reign of David (1 Ch 27:21).

11. A prince appointed by Jehoshaphat to instruct the people in the law (2 Ch 17:7).

12. The son of Benaiah, a Levite of the family of Gershom (2 Ch 20:14).

13. A son of Jehoshaphat, king of Judah (2 Ch 21:2).

14. Son of Jehoiada, the high priest. He lived in the time of the reign of Athaliah, wife of Jehoram, who headed the revolt that brought Joash to the throne. Zechariah, like his father, was a righteous man. When his father died, the people forgot Jehovah and when Zechariah reproved them the king had him killed (2 Ch 24:20-22).

15. A prophet who counseled Uzziah, king of Judah. The king followed his wise counsels for a time (2 Ch 26:5).

16. A Levite who assisted Hezekiah in his reform work by cleansing the temple (2 Ch 29:13). He was descended from Asaph.

17. A Levite of the family of Kohath. He helped to repair the temple in the reign of Josiah (2 Ch 34:12).

18. A ruler of the temple in the reign of Josiah (2 Ch 35:8).

19. A descendant of Parosh, who with one hundred and fifty males, returned to Palestine with the expedition under Ezra (Ez 8:3).

20. One of the men sent by Ezra to secure Levites and Nethinim (Ez 8:16).

21. A son of Elam. He divorced his foreign wife (Ez 10:26).

22. A son of Bebai who was the chief of 28 men who returned with Ezra from Babylon (Ez 8:11).

23. A man, probably a priest (Ne 8:4).

24. A man of the family of Perez of Judah (Ne 11:4).

25. The son of Shiloni of Judah (Ne 11:5).

26. A priest and an ancestor of Adaiah who lived in Jerusalem after the captivity (Ne 11:12).

27. A son of Jonathan, a Levite (Ne 12:35-36).

28. A priest who blew a trumpet at the dedication of the wall of Nehemiah (Ne 12:41).

29. A prophet, described as the son or grandson of Iddo (Ez 5:1; Ne 12:16; Ze 1:1).

30. Son of Jeberechiah. Certain words written by Isaiah, afterwards prophetically explained, were witnessed by him (Is 8:2).

ZECH·A·RI′ AH, BOOK OF

1. The Book of Zechariah. For a dozen years or more, the task of rebuilding the temple had been half completed. Zechariah was commissioned by God to encourage the people in their unfinished responsibility. Rather than exhorting them to action with strong words of rebuke, Zechariah seeks to encourage them to action by reminding them of the future importance of the temple. The temple must be built, for one day the Messiah's glory will inhabit it. But future blessing is contingent upon present obedience. The people are not merely building a building; they are building the future. With that as their motivation, they can enter into the building project with wholehearted zeal, for their Messiah is coming.

Zekar-yah means "Yahweh Remembers" or "Yahweh Has Remembered." This theme dominates the whole book; Israel will be blessed because Yahweh remembers the covenant He made with the fathers. The Greek and Latin version of his name is *Zacharias.*

2. The Author of Zechariah. Zechariah ("Yahweh Remembers") was a popular name shared by no fewer than twenty-nine Old Testament characters. It may have been given out of gratitude for God's gift of a baby boy. Like his predecessors, Jeremiah and Ezekiel, Zechariah was of priestly lineage as the son of Berechiah and grandson of Iddo (1:1,7; Ez 5:1; 6:14; Ne 12:4,16). He was born in Babylon and was brought by his grandfather to Palestine when the Jewish exiles returned under Zerubbabel and Joshua the high priest. If he was the "young man" of 2:4, he was called to prophesy at an early age in 520 B.C. According to Jewish tradition, Zechariah was a member of the Great Synagogue that collected and preserved the canon of revealed Scripture. Matthew 23:35 indicates he was "murdered between the temple and the altar" in the same way that an earlier Zechariah was martyred (2 Ch 24:20-21). The universal testimony of Jewish and Christian tradition affirms Zechariah as the author of the entire book.

3. The Time of Zechariah. Zechariah was a younger contemporary of Haggai the prophet, Zerubbabel the governor, and Joshua the high priest. The historical setting for chapters 1–8 (520-518 B.C.) is identical to that of Haggai (see "The Time of Haggai"). Work was resumed on the temple in 520 B.C., and the project was completed in 516 B.C. Chapters 9–14 are undated, but stylistic differences and references to Greece indicate a date of between 480 and 470 B.C. This

would mean that Darius I (521-486 B.C.) had passed from the scene and had been succeeded by Xerxes (486-464 B.C.), the king who deposed Queen Vashti and made Esther queen of Persia.

4. The Christ of Zechariah. Very clear messianic passages abound in this book. Christ is portrayed in His two advents as both Servant and King, Man and God. The following are a few of Zechariah's explicit anticipations of Christ: the angel of the Lord (3:1-2); the righteous Branch (3:8; 6:12-13), the stone with seven eyes (3:9); the King-Priest (6:13); the humble King (9:9-10); the cornerstone, tent peg, and battle bow (10:4); the good Shepherd who is rejected and sold for thirty shekels of silver, the price of a slave (11:4-13); the pierced One (12:10); the cleansing fountain (13:1); the smitten Shepherd who is abandoned (13:7); the coming Judge and righteous King (14).

5. Keys to Zechariah.

Key Word: Prepare for the Messiah—The first eight chapters frequently allude to the temple and encourage the people to complete their great work on the new sanctuary. As they build the temple, they are building their future, because that very structure will be used by the Messiah when He comes to bring salvation. Zechariah eloquently attests to Yahweh's covenant faithfulness toward Israel through the work of the Messiah, especially in chapters 9–14. This book outlines God's program for His people during the times of the Gentiles until the Messiah comes to deliver them and reign upon the earth. This hope of glory provides a source of reassurance to the Jewish remnant at a time when circumstances are trying. Zechariah also seeks to promote spiritual revival so that the people will call upon the Lord with humble hearts and commit their ways to Him.

Key Verses: Zechariah 8:3; 9:9—"Thus says the LORD: 'I will return to Zion, and dwell in the midst of Jerusalem. Jerusalem shall be called the City of Truth; the Mountain of the LORD of hosts, the Holy Mountain'" (8:3).

"Rejoice greatly, O daughter of Zion! Shout, O daughter of Jerusalem! Behold, your king is coming to you; He is just and having salvation, lowly and riding on a donkey, a colt, the foal of a donkey" (9:9).

Key Chapter: Zechariah 14—Zechariah builds to a tremendous climax in the fourteenth chapter where he discloses the last siege of Jerusalem, the initial victory of the enemies of Israel, the cleaving of the Mount of Olives, the Lord's defense of Jerusalem with His visible appearance on Olivet, judgment on the confederated nations, the topographical changes in the land of Israel, the Feast of Tabernacles, and the ultimate holiness of Jerusalem and her people.

6. Survey of Zechariah. Zechariah uses a series of eight visions, four messages, and two burdens to portray God's future plans for His covenant people. The first eight chapters were written to encourage the remnant while they were rebuilding the temple; the last six chapters were written after the completion of the temple to anticipate Israel's coming Messiah. Zechariah moves from gentile domination to messianic rule, from persecution to peace, and from uncleanness to holiness. The book divides into: the eight visions (1–6), the four messages (7–8), and the two burdens (9–14).

The Eight Visions (1–6). The book opens with an introductory appeal to the people to repent and return to God, unlike their fathers who rejected the warnings of the prophets (1:1-6). A few months later, Zechariah had a series of eight night visions, evidently in one troubled night (February 15, 519 B.C.; 1:7). The angel who spoke with him interpreted the visions, but some of the symbols are not explained. The visions mix the work of the Messiah in both advents, and like the other prophets, Zechariah saw only the peaks of God's program without the intervening valleys. The first five are visions of comfort, and the last three are visions of judgment: (1) The horsemen among the myrtle trees—God will rebuild Zion and His people (1:7-17). (2) The four horns and craftsmen—Israel's oppressors will be judged (1:18-21). (3) The man with a measuring line—God will pro-

tect and glorify Jerusalem (2:1-13). (4) The cleansing of Joshua the high priest—Israel will be cleansed and restored by the coming Branch (3:1-10). (5) The golden lampstand—God's Spirit is empowering Zerubbabel and Joshua (4:1-14). (6) The flying scroll—individual sin will be judged (5:1-4). (7) The woman in the basket—national sin will be removed (5:5-11). (8) The four chariots—God's judgment will descend on the nations (6:1-8). The crowning of Joshua (6:9-15) anticipates the coming of the Branch who will be King and Priest (the composite crown).

The Four Messages (7– 8). In response to a question about the continuation of the fasts (7:1-3). God gives Zechariah a series of four messages: (1) a rebuke of empty ritualism (7:4-7); (2) a reminder of past disobedience (7:8-14); (3) the restoration and consolation of Israel (8:1-17); and (4) the recovery of joy in the kingdom (8:18-23).

The Two Burdens (9–14). The first burden (9–11) concerns the first advent and rejection of Israel's coming King. Alexander the Great will conquer Israel's neighbors, but will spare Jerusalem (9:1-8) which will be preserved for her King (the Messiah; 9:9-10). Israel will succeed against Greece (the Maccabean revolt; 9:11-17), and although they will later be scattered, the Messiah will bless them and bring them back (10:1–11:3); Israel will reject her Shepherd-King and be led astray by false shepherds (11:4-17). The second burden (12–14) concerns the second advent of Christ and the acceptance of Israel's King. The nations will attack Jerusalem, but the Messiah will come and deliver His people (12). They will be cleansed of impurity and falsehood (13), and the Messiah will come in power to judge the nations and reign in Jerusalem over the whole earth (14).

OUTLINE OF ZECHARIAH

I. The Call to Repentance (1:1-6)

II. The Eight Visions of Zechariah (1:7–6:8)

A. The Horses Among the Myrtle Trees 1:7-17
B. The Four Horns and Four Craftsmen 1:18-21
C. The Man with the Measuring Line 2:1-13

D. The Cleansing of Joshua the High Priest 3:1-10
E. The Golden Lampstand and Olive Trees 4:1-14
F. The Flying Scroll 5:1-4
G. The Woman in the Basket 5:5-11
H. The Four Chariots....................... 6:1-8

III. The Crowning of Joshua (6:9-15)

IV. The Question of Fasting (7:1-3)

V. The Four Messages of Zechariah (7:4–8:23)

A. Rebuke of Hypocrisy...................... 7:4-7
B. Repent of Disobedience 7:8-14
C. Restoration of Israel..................... 8:1-17
D. Rejoice in Israel's Future 8:18-23

VI. The Two Burdens of Zechariah (9:1–14:21)

A. The First Burden: The Rejection of the Messiah 9:1–11:17
B. The Second Burden: The Reign of the Messiah 12:1–14:21

ZE′ CHER

See ZECHARIAH.

ZE′ DAD

A place on the northern border of Palestine (Nu 34:8; Eze 47:15).

ZED·E·KI′ AH (righteousness of Jehovah)

Six men of the Old Testament:

1. Son of Chenaanah, one of the false prophets who advised Ahab to capture Ramoth-gilead from the Syrians. When Micaiah, the prophet of Jehovah, advised the king against this, saying that he would fail in his attempt, he was struck by the false prophet. Ahab followed the advice of Zedekiah, was defeated and slain (1 Ki 22:11-25; 2 Ch 18:10).

2. The last king of Judah. He was the third of Josiah's sons to succeed to the throne. His original name, Mattaniah, was changed to Zedekiah by Nebuchadnezzar when the latter placed him on the throne in 597 B.C. to be vassal-king in place of the rebellious Jehoiachin (2 Ki 24:15, 17). He reigned eleven years during which time he was urged to revolt against Babylon (Je 27:12-22).

3. A son of Jeconiah and grandson of Jehoiakim, king of Judah (1 Ch 3:16). It is the view of some that he was son in the sense of successor; others hold he was his actual son who died prior to the exile.

4. Son of Maaseiah. He was an immoral and false prophet whom Nebuchadnezzar destroyed by fire (Je 29:21-23).

5. Son of Hananiah. He was a prince of Judah in the reign of Jehoiakim (Je 36:12). He was one of several who learned through Michaiah the contents of the roll which had been read by Baruch.

6. One who signed the covenant with Nehemiah (Ne 10:1).

ZEEB (wolf)

A prince of Midian, one of those killed by the men of Ephraim during Gideon's campaign against the Midianites with his three hundred specially chosen warriors (Ju 7:25).

ZE′ LAH (side)

A town of Benjamin where the bones of Saul and Jonathan in the tomb of Kish, Saul's father (2 Sa 21:14).

ZE′ LEK (a cleft)

One of David's mighty warriors, an Ammonite (2 Sa 23:37; 1 Ch 11:39).

ZE·LOPH′ E·HAD

Son of Hepher of Manasseh. He had five daughters and no sons which, at his death, brought up the question of the inheritance of daughters when there was no son (Nu 26:33; 27:1-8).

ZE·LO′ TES (full of zeal) (Lk 6:15; Ac 1:13, KJV)

See ZEALOT.

ZEL′ ZAH (shade)

A town of Benjamin and the location of Rachel's sepulchre (1 Sa 10:2).

ZEM·A·RA′ IM (double fleece)

A town and a mountain:

1. An ancient town of Benjamin, west of the Jordan and a few miles north of Jericho; to be identified probably with es-Sumrah (Jos 18:22).

2. A mountain of Ephraim from which Abijah, king of Judah, addressed his troops before battling the forces of Israel (2 Ch 13:4).

ZEM′ A·RITE

A tribe from the sons of Canaan, son of Ham, son of Noah (Ge 10:18; 1 Ch 1:16).

ZE·MI′ RAH (music)

A son of Becher of Benjamin (1 Ch 7:8) Zemira, KJV.

ZE′ NAN

A town of Judah (Jos 15:37).

ZE′ NAS *(gift of Zeus)*

A lawyer who traveled with Apollos in Crete. Paul asks for these two men to be sent to him. (Tit 3:13).

ZEPH·A·NI′ AH *(Jehovah has hidden)*

Four Old Testament Men:

1. A Levite of the family of Kohath. He was an ancestor of Samuel (1 Ch 6:36-38).

2. Son of Maaseiah and a priest in the reign of King Zedekiah (Je 21:1). He was one of Jeremiah's loyal friends and frequently served as a messenger between the prophet and King Zedekiah. After the capture of Jerusalem he was killed by the Babylonians at Riblah (Je 21:1; 29:25,29; 37:3; 52:24-27).

3. A prophet living at the time of King Josiah (639-608 B.C.). He described himself as the son of Cushi and the great-great-grandson of Hezekiah (Hizkiah) who is believed to be the same as King Hezekiah. It is believed that he began prophesying at about the age of 25 years (Zep 1:1).

4. The father of a Josiah who lived at the time of Zerubbabel and Zechariah, the prophet (Ze 6:10,14).

ZEPH·A·NI′ AH, BOOK OF

1. The Book of Zephaniah. During Judah's hectic political and religious history, reform comes from time to time. Zephaniah's forceful prophecy may be a factor in the reform that occurs during Josiah's reign—a "revival" that produces outward change, but does not fully remove the inward heart of corruption which characterizes the nation. Zephaniah hammers home his message repeatedly that the day of the Lord, judgment day, is coming when the malignancy of sin will be dealt with. Israel and her Gentile neighbors will soon experience the crushing hand of God's wrath. But after the chastening process is complete, blessing will come in the person of the Messiah, who will be the cause for praise and singing.

Tsephan-yah means "Yahweh Hides" or "Yahweh Has Hidden" Zephaniah was evidently born during the latter part of the reign of King Manasseh. His name may mean that he was "hidden" from Manasseh's atrocities. The Greek and Latin title is *Sophonias*.

2. The Author of Zephaniah. The first verse is very unusual in that Zephaniah traces his lineage back four generations to Hezekiah. This is probably Hezekiah the king of Judah, since this would best explain the genealogy. If Zephaniah was the great-great-grandson of the godly King Hezekiah, he was the only prophet of royal descent. This may have given the prophet freer access to the court of King Josiah in whose reign he ministered. Because Zephaniah used the phrase "this place" (1:4) to refer to Jerusalem and was quite familiar with its features (1:9-10; 3:1-7), he was probably an inhabitant of Judah's royal city.

3. The Time of Zephaniah. Zephaniah solves the dating problem by fixing his prophecy "in the days of Josiah the son of Amon, king of Judah" (1:1). Josiah reigned from 640 to 609 B.C., and 2:13 indicates that the destruction of Nineveh (612 B.C.) was still a future event. Thus Zephaniah's prophecy can be dated between 640 and 612 B.C.

However, the sins catalogued in 1:3-13 and 3:1-7 indicate a date prior to Josiah's reforms when the sins from the reigns of Manasseh and Amon still predominated. It is therefore likely that Zephaniah's ministry played a significant role in preparing Judah for the revivals that took place in the reign of the nation's last righteous king. Josiah became king of Judah at the age of eight, and by the age of sixteen his heart had already begun to turn toward God. His first reform took place in the twelfth year of his reign (628 B.C.; 2 Ch 34:3-7) when he tore down all the altars of Baal, destroyed the foreign incense altars, buried the bones of the false prophets on their altars, and broke the Asherim (carved images) and molten images in pieces. Six years later (622 B.C.), Josiah's second reform was kindled when Hilkiah the priest found the book of the law in the temple (2 Ch 34:8–35:19). Thus, Zephaniah's prophecy can be dated more precisely as occurring between 630 and 625 B.C.

The evil reigns of Manasseh and Amon (a total of fifty-five years) had such a profound effect upon Judah that it never recovered. Josiah's reforms were too little and too late, and the people reverted to their crass idolatry and teaching soon after Josiah was gone. As a contemporary of Jeremiah and Habakkuk, Zephaniah was one of the eleventh-hour prophets to Judah.

4. The Christ of Zephaniah. Jesus alluded to Zephaniah on two occasions (compare 1:3 with Ma 13:41, and 1:15 with Ma 24:29). Both of these passages about the day of the Lord are associated with Christ's second advent. Although the Messiah is not specifically mentioned in Zephaniah, it is clear that He is the One who will fulfill the great promises of 3:9-20. He will gather His people and reign in victory: "The LORD has taken away your judgments, He has cast out your enemy. The King of Israel, the LORD, is in your midst; you shall see disaster no more" (3:15).

5. Keys to Zephaniah.

Key Word: The Day of the Lord—Zephaniah discusses the day of the Lord and describes the coming day of judgment upon Judah and the nations. God is holy and must vindicate His righteousness by calling all the nations of the world into account before Him. The sovereign God will judge not only His own people but also the whole world: no one escapes from His authority and dominion. The day of the Lord will have universal impact. To some degree, the day has already come for Judah and all the nations mentioned in 2:4-15, but there is also a future aspect, when all the earth will be judged. Zephaniah 3:9-20 speaks of another side of the day of the Lord: it will be a day of blessing after the judgment is complete. A righteous remnant will survive and all who call upon Him, Jew or Gentile, will be blessed. God will regather and restore His people, and there will be worldwide rejoicing.

Zephaniah is also written as a warning to Judah and as a call to repentance (2:1-3). God wants to spare the people, but they ultimately reject Him. His judgment will be great; but God promises His people a future day of hope and joy. Wrath and mercy, severity and kindness, cannot be separated in the character of God.

Key Verses: Zephaniah 1:14-15; 2:3—"The great day of the LORD is near; it is near and hastens quickly. The noise of the day of the LORD is bitter; there the mighty men shall cry out. That day is a day of devastation and desolation, a day of darkness and gloominess, a day of clouds and thick darkness" (1:14-15).

"Seek the LORD, all you meek of the earth, who have upheld His justice. Seek righteousness, seek humility. It may be that you will be hidden in the day of the LORD's anger" (2:3).

Key Chapter: Zephaniah 3—The last chapter of Zephaniah records the two distinct parts of the day of the LORD: judgment and restoration. Following the conversion of the nation, Israel finally is fully restored. Under the righteous rule of God, Israel fully inherits the blessings contained in the biblical covenant.

6. Survey of Zephaniah.

On the whole, Zephaniah is a fierce and grim book of warning about the coming day of the Lord. Desolation, darkness, and ruin will strike Judah and the nations because of the wrath of God upon sin. Zephaniah looks beyond judgment, however, to a time of joy when God will cleanse the nations and restore the fortunes of His people Israel. The book begins with God's declaration, "I will utterly consume all things from the face of the land" (1:2); but it ends with this promise, "At that time I will bring you back" and "return your captives before your eyes" (3:20). Zephaniah moves three times from the general to the specific: (1) from universal judgment (1:1-3) to judgment upon Judah (1:4–2:3); (2) from judgment upon surrounding nations (2:4-15) to judgment upon Jerusalem (3:1-7); (3) from judgment and cleansing of all nations (3:8-10) to restoration of Israel (3:11-20). The two broad divisions of the book are: the judgment in the day of the Lord (1:1–3:8), and the salvation in the day of the Lord (3:9-20).

The Judgment in the Day of the Lord (1:1–3:8). The prophetic oracle begins with an awesome statement of God's coming judgment upon the entire earth because of the sins of men (1:2-3). Zephaniah then concentrates on the judgment of Judah (1:4-18), listing some of the offenses that will cause it to come. Judah is polluted with idolatrous priests who promote the worship of Baal and nature, and her officials and princes are completely corrupt. Therefore, the day of the Lord is imminent; and it will be characterized by terror, desolation, and distress. However, by His grace, Yahweh appeals to His people to repent and humble themselves to avert the coming disaster before it is too late (2:1-3).

Zephaniah pronounces God's coming judgment upon the nations that surround Judah (2:4-15). He looks in all four directions: Philistia (west), Moab and Ammon (east), Ethiopia (south), and Assyria (north). Then he focuses on Jerusalem, the center of God's dealings (3:1-7). Jerusalem is characterized by spiritual rebellion and moral treachery. "She has not obeyed His voice, she has not received correction; she has not trusted in the LORD; she has not drawn near to her God" (3:2).

The Salvation in the Day of the LORD (3:9-20). After a broad statement of the judgment of all nations (3:8), Zephaniah changes the tone of the remainder of his book to blessing; for this, too, is an aspect of the day of the LORD. The nation will be cleansed and will call on the name of the Lord (3:9-10). The remnant of Israel will be regathered, redeemed, and re-stored (3:11-20). They will rejoice in their Redeemer, and He will be in their midst. Zephaniah opens with idolatry, wrath, and judgment, but closes with true worship, rejoicing and blessing.

OUTLINE OF ZEPHANIAH

I. The Judgment in the Day of the Lord (1:1–3:8)

A. The Judgment on the Whole Earth 1:1-3
B. The Judgment on the Nation of Judah 1:4–2:3
C. The Judgment on the Nations Surrounding Judah 2:4-15

D. The Judgment on Jerusalem 3:1-7
E. The Judgment on the Whole Earth 3:8

II. The Salvation in the Day of the Lord (3:9-20)

A. The Promise of Conversion............ 3:9-13
B. The Promise of Restoration 4:14-20

ZE′ PHATH *(watchtower)*

A town of the Canaanites near the border of Edom. The men of Judah and Simeon attacked the Canaanites who inhabited Zephath and destroyed it; the city was then called Hormah, which means *destruction* (Ju 1:17).

ZEPH′ A·THAH *(watchtower)*

A valley near Mareshah in which Asa, king of Judah, fought Zerah the Ethiopian (2 Ch 14:10).

ZE′ PHI, ZE′ PHO *(watch)*

A son of Eliphaz and grandson of Esau. He was a duke of Edom (Ge 36:11,15; 1 Ch 1:36).

ZE′ PHON *(watching)*

The eldest son of Gad and the head of a tribal family (Nu 26:15).

ZER *(rock, flint)*

A fortified town of Naphtali, not otherwise identified (Jos 19:35).

ZE′ RAH *(dawn)*

Six men of the Old Testament:
1. Son of Reuel, grandson of Esau, and a duke of Edom (Ge 36:3-4,13,17; 1 Ch 1:37).
2. The twin brother of Pharez and son of Judah and Tamar (Ge 38:30; 46:12; Nu 26:20; Jos 7:1,17). His descendants were called Zarhites. Also called Zarah and Zara (KJV).
3. Son of Simeon (Nu 26:13). In Genesis 46:10 and Exodus 6:15 he is called Zohar.
4-5. Two Levites (1 Ch 6:21,41).
6. The king of Ethiopia who in the time of

King Asa invaded Judah with a great army. Asa's forces met him in the valley of Zephathah and defeated the Ethiopians with great loss (2 Ch 14:8-15).

ZER·A·HI′ AH *(Jehovah has risen)*

Two Old Testament men:
1. Son of Uzzi. He was a descendant of Aaron and ancestor of Ezra (1 Ch 6:6,51; Ez 7:4).
2. Father of Elihoenai. His descendants returned from exile with Ezra (Ez 8:4).

ZER′ ED *(luxuriance)*

A valley crossed by the Israelites at the close of their wandering (Nu 21:12; De 2:13-14). Also called Zared (KJV).

ZER′ E·DA

An Ephramite town. Jeroboam, who became king of the Northern Kingdom of Israel, was from this town (1 Ki 11:26).

ZER′ E·DAH

A town in the plain of Jordan. The bronze castings for the temple were made in clay molds in the plain between the towns of Zeredah and Succoth (1 Ki 7:46; 2 Ch 4:17; Zeredathah, KJV).

ZER′ E·DA·THAN

See ZEREDAH.

ZER′ E·RAH

The town toward which the Midanites fled when routed by Gideon and his three hundred picked warriors. (Ju 7:22; Zererath KJV).

ZER′ E·RATH

See ZERERAH.

ZE′ RESH *(gold)*

The wife of Haman, who encouraged him in his wicked plans (Es 5:10; 6:13).

ZE′ RETH *(brightness)*

Son of Ashur of Judah (1 Ch 4:5-7).

ZER′ ETH-SHA′ HAR *(splendor of dawn)*

A town of Reuben situated on a mountain (Jos 13:19).

ZE′ RI

A son of Jeduthun (1 Ch 25:3), a Levite and harpist. In 1 Chronicles 25:11 he is called Izri.

ZE′ ROR

An ancestor of King Saul (1 Sa 9:1).

ZE·RU′ AH *(leprous)*

The mother of Jeroboam, first king of the Northern Kingdom of Israel (1 Ki 11:26).

ZE·RUB′ BA·BEL *(born in Babylon)*

One who with the high priest, Jeshua, and possibly Sheshbazzar, led a group of Jewish exiles from captivity in Babylon to Jerusalem. He later became governor of Judah (Ez 2:1-2; Ne 7:6-7; Hag 2:21). All accounts describe him as descended from David. In some passages he is called the son of Pedaiah, and in others he is called the son of Shealtiel, or Salathiel (1 Ch 3:17-19; Ez 3:2; Ma 1:12; Lk 3:27). A messianic significance is accorded Zerubbabel by Zechariah (Ze 3–4).

ZER·U·I′ AH

David's sister or half sister and the mother of Joab, Abishai, and Asahel (1 Sa 26:6; 2 Sa 2:13, 18; 8:16; 1 Ch 2:16).

ZE′ THAM

Son of Laadan; a Levite of the family of Gershom (1 Ch 23:8).

ZE′ THAN *(olive)*

A Benjamite of the family of Jediael (1 Ch 7:10).

ZE′ THAR

A chamberlain who was one of the seven eunuchs in the court of King Ahasuerus of Persia (Es 1:10).

ZEUS

A principle deity of the Greeks, the father of other gods. Zeus is typically portrayed as the sky god with a thunderbolt. A statue of Zeus in Olympia was one of the seven wonders of the ancient world. Zeus is equated with the Roman god Jupiter, and is so translated in Acts (KJV). The people of Lystra, impressed with the miracle done through Paul, called Barnabas Zeus and Paul Hermes. Paul and Barnabas were appalled, and quickly set the crowd straight, but even so they could barely keep them from offering sacrifices to them. (Ac 14:12-13; 19:35)

ZI′ A *(motion)*

A Gadite of Bashan (1 Ch 5:13).

ZI′ BA

A servant of King Saul. He had a large family (2 Sa 9:10). After the death of Jonathan, David's friend, David inquired of Ziba if there was any of the house of Saul to whom he could show kindness. Ziba brought Mephibosheth, Jonathan's crippled son, and Ziba was appointed steward of Saul's land for Mephibosheth. (2 Sa 9:9-12).

ZIB′ E·ON *(dyed)*

Father of Anah. He is called a Hivite and a Horite (Ge 36:20,24,29). He was the grandfather of Aholibamah, the wife of Esau (Ge 36:2).

ZI′ BI·A

The son of Shaharaim, a Benjamite. His mother was Hodesh (1 Ch 8:9).

ZI′ BI·AH *(roe)*

The wife of Ahaziah and mother of Jehoash, king of Judah. She was a native of Beer-sheba (2 Ki 12:1; 2 Ch 24:1).

ZICH′ RI *(famous)*

Twelve men of the Old Testament:

1. Son of Izhar, a Levite of the family of Kohath (Ex 6:21).

2. Son of Shimhi of Benjamin (1 Ch 8:19).

3. Son of Shashak of Benjamin (1 Ch 8:23).

4. Son of Jeroham of Benjamin (1 Ch 8:27).

5. Son of Asaph (1 Ch 9:15). In Nehemiah 11:17 he is called Zabdi, and in Nehemiah 12:35 he is called Zaccur.

6. A Levite and a descendant of Moses (1 Ch 26:25).

7. A member of the tribe of Reuben in the time of David (1 Ch 27:16).

8. The father of Amasiah of Judah. The son was a captain in the army of Jehoshaphat (2 Ch 17:16).

9. The father of Elishaphat, who with the aid of Jehoiada, overthrew Queen Athaliah and placed Joash on the throne (2 Ch 23:1). He was possibly the same as the preceding.

10. A man of Ephraim in the army of Pekah, king of Israel. He slew Maaseiah, the son of Ahaz, king of Judah, and two of the king's officers (2 Ch 28:7).

11. The father of Joel, the latter a chief man of the Benjamites when they returned from Babylon (Ne 11:9).

12. A priest of the family of Abijah when Joiakim was high priest (Ne 12:17).

ZID′DIM *(sides)*

A city of Naphtali (Jos 19:35), a few miles west of the Sea of Galilee.

ZID·KI′JAH

See ZEDEKIAH.

ZI′DON

See SIDON.

ZIDONIANS

Those who lived in Sidon. See SIDONIANS.

ZIF

See ZIV.

ZIGGURAT

An ancient Babylonian temple built like a pyramid. But unlike the Egyptian pyramids with their sides, the ziggurat was built like building blocks, in stepped back stages, each consecutive level smaller than the previous, with stairs up the outside and a shrine at the top. The tower of Babel (Ge 11:1-9) may have been ziggurat.

ZI′HA *(drought)*

Two Old Testament men:

1. One of the Nethinim, descendants of whom returned from Babylon after the exile (Ez 2:43; Ne 7:46).

2. A chief of the Nethinim after the return to Palestine from Babylon (Ne 11:21).

ZIK′LAG

A town in the southernmost part of Judah (Jos 15:31), first assigned to Judah, then given to Simeon (Jos 19:5; 1 Ch 4:30). It belonged to the Philistines during Saul's reign and to it David fled when he was a fugitive from Saul. Achish of Gath gave him the town as his residence. When the Amalekites plundered and burnt Ziklag, David pursued them, routed them, and recovered all the booty and prisoners. The booty he distributed among a number of Hebrew cities. Eventually the town was brought under the jurisdiction of the kings of Judah (1 Sa 27:6; 30:1-31).

ZIL′LAH *(a shadow)*

A wife of Lamech of the line of Cain and mother of Tubal-cain (Ge 4:19,22-23).

ZIL′LE·THAL, ZIL′THAI

Two Old Testament men:

1. Son of Shimhi (Shimei) of Benjamin (1 Ch 8:20).

2. A captain of a contingent of warriors who allied themselves with David at Ziklag (1 Ch 12:20).

ZIL′PAH *(a drop)*

A maidservant given Leah by her father, Laban, at the time of her marriage to Jacob (Ge 29:24). With Leah's consent, Zilpah later became Jacob's concubine and the mother of Gad and Asher (Ge 30:9-13).

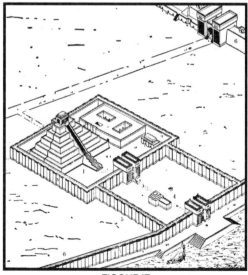

ZIGGURAT

ZIL'THAI

See ZILLETHAL

ZIM'MAH (counsel)

Two Old Testament men:
1. Son of Shimei and grandson of Jahath of the family of Gerahom (1 Ch 6:20,42-43).
2. A Gershonite Levite (2 Ch 29:12).

ZIM'RAN

A son of Abraham and Keturah (Ge 25:2; 1 Ch 1:32).

ZIM'RI

Four men and an area in the Old Testament
1. Son of Salu of Simeon. He was a chieftain of his tribe. When the Israelites were at Shittim, Zimri brought Cozbi, a woman of Midian, into the camp. Both Zimri and the woman were killed by Phinehas because contact with foreigners had been forbidden the Israelites (Nu 25:14).
2. The fifth king of Israel whose reign lasted only a week. He was commander of half of the chariots of Elah, the king. Zimri killed Elah and seized the throne. He put to death the members of the house of Baasha. But the army proclaimed Omri king. He besieged Zimri in Tirzah, his capital. When Zimri saw that the city was in the hands of Omri, he set fire to the palace and perished in the flames (1 Ki 16:8-18).
3. Son of Zerah and grandson of Judah. He was the eldest of five sons (1 Ch 2:6).
4. Son of Jehoadah and descendant of Jonathan, son of Saul (1 Ch 8:36; 9:42).
5. Unknown area, listed in Jeremiah as "all the kings of Zimri" along with the kings of Elam, the Medes, etc. as one of the nations who would drink of the cup of God's fury. (Je 25:25).

ZIN

A wilderness through which the Israelites passed in their wandering. It was near the southern boundary of Canaan (Nu 13:21; 27:14; 33:36; De 32:51). In it was Kadesh-barnea.

ZINA

One of the sons of Shimei, a Gershonite (1 Ch 23:10).

ZI'ON (possibly citadel or sunny mount)

One of the hills of Jerusalem, always rendered Sion in the Authorized Version of New Testament. It was west of the Kidron Valley and south of the temple area. Upon it was the ancient stronghold of the Jebusites, renamed the city of David (2 Sa 5:7; 1 Ch 11:5). It was here that David brought the ark (2 Sa 6:12). After Solomon had transferred the ark to the temple on a nearby hill (1 Ki 8:1; 2 Ch 5:2), the name Zion was extended to include the temple area and sometimes the whole of Jerusalem (Ps 48; 65:1; 102:21; Is 2:3; 8:18). Heaven is called Zion (He 12:22; Re 14:1), symbol of the spiritual Zion, the city of God.

ZI'OR (smallness)

A town of Judah near Hebron (Jos 15:54).

ZIPH

Two towns and an Old Testament man:
1. A town at the most southerly point of Judah (Jos 15:24).
2. A town near a wilderness to which David fled from Saul (1 Sa 23:14). It was later fortified by Rehoboam, king of Judah (2 Ch 11:8).
3. A son of Jehaleleel of Judah (1 Ch 4:16).

ZI'PHAH

Son of Jehaleleel and brother of Ziph (1 Ch 4:16).

ZIPH'IMS

See ZIPHITES.

ZIPHION

A son of Gad, also called Zephon (Ge 46:16).

ZIPH'ITES

The inhabitants of Ziph (1 Sa 23:19; 26:1). The inhabitants of Ziph went to Saul and told him that David was hiding in their area. This is referred to in the title of Psalm 54, which is David's cry to God in this circumstance.

ZIPH'RON (fragrance)

A place on the northern boundary of Palestine (Nu 34:9).

ZIP'POR (a sparrow)

Father of Balak, king of Moab (Nu 22:4,10).

ZIP'PO·RAH (sparrow)

The wife of Moses and daughter of Jethro, priest of Midian (Ex 2:21-22). When on his way to Egypt, Moses was threatened with death be-

ZITHER

cause he had failed to maintain the covenant relative to the circumcision of their son. However, he was saved when Zipporah performed the rite (Ex 4:18-26). After the escape from Egypt, Zipporah, with her two sons, Gershom and Eliezer, went ahead to inform Jethro about the exodus and to bring him to the camp at Rephidim (Ex 18:1-6).

ZITHER

A musical instrument which consists of a shallow sound box with a fretted fingerboard on one side and some 30-40 strings—some of which pass over the fingerboard—and the rest continue horizontally across the top of the sound box. The player stops the strings against the frets with his left hand and plays the melody with a plectrum on his right thumb. The melody strings (those which do not pass over the fingerboard) are tuned in fourths (Da 3:5 NIV).

ZITH'RI

See SITHRI.

ZIV (bloom)

The second month of the Jewish sacred year, and eighth month of the civil year. Also called Iyon. See CALENDAR.

ZIZ (a flower)

An ascent leading up from the Dead Sea to Tekoa (2 Ch 20:16). It was by this way the Moabites and Ammonites made their attack upon Jehoshaphat.

ZI'ZA (abundance)

Two Old Testament men:
1. Son of Shiphi, a Simeonite. He lived in the reign of Hezekiah (1 Ch 4:37).
2. Son of Rehoboam. His mother was Maacah (2 Ch 11:20).

ZI'ZAH (abundance)

Son of Shimei, a Levite of the family of Gershom (1 Ch 23:11). In 1 Chronicles 23:10 he is called Zina.

ZO'AN

An ancient city of lower Egypt. It was situated on the Tanitic branch of the Nile in the delta region. It is nearly as old as Hebron (Nu 13:22) and was the capital of Egypt in the early days of the twelfth dynasty. It was also the capital of the Hyksos kings. Following the end of that dynasty, it lost its importance for several centuries but regained its distinction under the kings of the nineteenth dynasty. It was in Zoan that Moses met Pharaoh (Ps 78:12,43). It was a city of importance in the time of Isaiah and Ezekiel (Is 19:11,13; 30:4; Eze 30:14). It was called Tanis by the Greeks. Excavations there have brought to light a large statue of Rameses II, the last great Egyptian pharaoh (1292-1225 B.C.).

ZO'AR (smallness)

One of the five cities of the plain (Ge 19:20-22). It was originally called Bela (Ge 14:2,8). When judgment was about to fall upon these cities, Lot prayed that this city be spared and that he might find refuge in it (Ge 19:20-23). As a result, the city was spared. It existed in the time of Isaiah and Jeremiah. Since they refer to it as part of Moab, it probably lay on the eastern side of the Dead Sea (Is 15:5; Je 48:34).

ZO'BA, ZO'BAH

A region of Syria between Hamath and Damascus. The inhabitants of this area fought bitterly against the Jewish nation (1 Sa 14:47; 2 Sa 8:3,5,12; 10:6,8; 1 Ki 11:23; 1 Ch 18:3,5,9). It is called Hamath-zobah in 2 Chronicles 8:3 and Aram-zobah in the title of Psalm 60.

ZO·BE'BAH (slow movement)

The second child of Hakkos (Coz) of Judah (1 Ch 4:8).

ZO'HAR (whiteness)

Two Old Testament men:
1. Father of Ephron, a Hittite (Ge 23:8). It was from Ephron that Abraham purchased the cave of Machpelah.
2. Son of Simeon (Ge 46:10). In Numbers 26:13 he is called Zerah.

ZO'HE·LETH (serpent)

A rock by En-rogel where Adonijah killed oxen and sheep (1 Ki 1:9).

ZO′ HETH

A son of Ishi (1 Ch 4:20).

ZO′ PHAH *(a cruse)*

Son of Helem of Asher (1 Ch 7:35-36).

ZOPHAI

Son of Elkanah in the Levitical line (1 Ch 6:26).

ZO′ PHAR *(sparrow)*

One of the friends who debated with Job; he was a Naamathite (Job 2:11; 11:1; 20:1; 42:9) In the end the Lord rebuked Zophar and his two companions because, "you have not spoken of Me what is right, as My servant Job has" (Job 42:9).

ZO′ PHIM *(watchers)*

A field on the top of the mountain peak, Pisgah (Nu 23:14).

ZOR′ AH

A town of Judah which was inhabited by people of Dan (Jos 15:33; 19:41; Zoreah, KJV). Here Samson was born and buried (Ju 13:2,25; 16:31). It overlooked Sorek. Rehoboam, king of Judah, fortified it, and exiles who returned from Babylon lived there (Ne 11:29).

ZOR′ A·THITE

A native of Zorah (1 Ch 2:53; 4:2).

ZOR′ E·AH

See ZORAH.

ZORITES

A member of the clans of Caleb, a descendant of Salma (1 Ch 2:54).

ZO·RO′ BA·BEL

See ZERUBBABEL.

ZU′ AR *(smallness)*

The father of Nethaneel and chief of the tribe of Issachar when the Israelites were in the wilderness (Nu 1:8; 2:5; 7:18,23; 10:15).

ZUPH *(honeycomb)*

An Old Testament man and a region:

1. A Levite of the family of Kohath and ancestor of Samuel (1 Sa 1:1; 1 Ch 6:35).

2. A district probably south of the border of Benjamin where Saul searched for his father's asses (1 Sa 9:4-6).

ZUR *(a rock)*

Two Old Testament men:

1. Son of Jehiel who founded Gibeon (1 Ch 8:30; 9:36).

2. A king of Midian and father of Cozbi, the woman who was brought into the camp of Israel and slain by Phinehas (Nu 25:15). Zur was slain in the conflict with the Israelites (Nu 31:8; Jos 13:21).

ZU′ RI·EL *(God is a rock)*

Son of Abihail, a Levite. He was chief of the Levites of Merari when Israel was in the wilderness (Nu 3:35).

ZU·RI·SHAD′ DAI *(my rock is the Almighty)*

Father of Shelumiel, the chief of the Simeonites in the wilderness (Nu 1:6; 2:12; 7:36,41; 10:19).

ZU′ ZIM, THE

An ancient people who dwelt in Ham, east of the Jordan. They were conquered by Chedorlaomer (Ge 14:5).